INTRODUCTION
TO THE OLD TESTAMENT

INTRODUCTION
TO THE
OLD TESTAMENT

by

ROBERT H. PFEIFFER

Harvard University
and Boston University

HARPER & BROTHERS PUBLISHERS
New York

INTRODUCTION TO THE OLD TESTAMENT

To my wife

To my wife.

CONTENTS

PART II: THE PENTATEUCH

PART III: THE FORMER PROPHETS

PART V: THE WRITINGS, OR HAGIOGRAPHA

APPENDICES

FOREWORD

Sicut enim a perfecta scientia procul sumus, levioris culpae
arbitramur saltem parum, quam omnino nihil dicere.

Jerome

For more than two millennia authors have been wont to say a few
intimate words to the readers who were on the point of perusing their
books. Like many others, I am filled with misgivings upon the completion
of my task, and I hereby appeal to the reader's indulgence.

The text for my *apologia* is the remark of Jerome copied at the top of
this page: "Remote as we are from perfect knowledge, we deem it less
blameworthy to say too little rather nothing at all." After a quarter of a
century of Biblical study, I am painfully aware of my inadequte information. And yet it seemed better to me "to say too little rather than
nothing at all." Yes, *too little!* For the present volume—in spite of its
bulk—is merely a brief summary of a vast field of research. One or more
large volumes could be written on the topic of each chapter of this book
indeed, such volumes are available.

My original plan had comprised a discussion of the Apocrypha and
Pseudepigrapha of the Old Testament. But as this volume grew in size
it seemed preferable to devote another book to those writings and merely
include here a bibliography of the most important works on the subject.
[The preparation of my Introduction to the Apocrypha and Pseudepigrapha is almost finished, so that the book should appear in 1948
or the following year.]

The present volume is accordingly a study of the Hebrew Bible—the
Old Testament of the Protestant Church. My method was dictated by the
invisible audience that I was addressing at my typewriter. Throughout
the book I imagined myself speaking to a class including college under-
graduates, divinity and other graduate students, ministers, and even
interested laymen. I have endeavored to convey something of the historical background, style, purpose, thought, and faith of the Biblical
writers to a group unfamiliar with ancient languages. The reader will
decide whether I have succeeded in being thorough and accurate without being technical and pedantic.

Scholars will at once recognize my indebtedness to the publications of
my predecessors—which, alas!, could not be acknowledged in every instance. More pervasive and intangible is the contribution to this book on

the part of my great teachers, particularly George Foot Moore (d. 1931) and William R. Arnold (d. 1929) of Harvard University. In spite of my limitations, I have been guided by their strict discipline in historical and literary research.

Some colleagues have generously read in manuscript some parts of this book: Professors Robert P. Blake, Henry J. Cadbury, William Thomson, and Harry A. Wolfson, of Harvard University; and William H. P. Hatch, of the Episcopal Theological School. My gratitude is also due to some of my former students, whose dissertations helped me materially: Dr. Beatrice L. Goff (who also read the whole manuscript of the book), Dr. Otis R. Fischer, Professor [now Dean] Charles L. Taylor, Jr., and Professor Rolland E. Wolfe. Dr. Milton V. Anastos has earned my cordial thanks by his labors in preparing the indices.

In closing, I subscribe to the words of Jean Astruc (d. 1766), the founder of Pentateuchal criticism: «Jamais la prévention pour mes idées ne prévaudra chez moi à l'amour de la vérité et de la Religion!» (Never will predilection for my own ideas prevail in me over the love for truth and religion!)

May, 1941   R. H. P.

PREFACE TO THE REVISED EDITION

In the present reprinting of this book, almost seven years after its first appearance, numerous regrettable errors (typographical and even more reprehensible ones) have been corrected and the *Selected Bibliography* has been brought up to date. Only the bibliography of the general works on the Apocrypha and Pseudepigrapha is given in this reprint; the publications on the individual Apocrypha and Pseudepigrapha will be listed more fully in the forthcoming volume on the subject.

February, 1948   R. H. P.

PART I

THE OLD TESTAMENT AS A WHOLE

~~~~~~

INTRODUCTION

~~~~~~

No book, or collection of books, in the history of mankind has had a more attentive reading, a wider circulation, or more diligent investigation than the Old Testament. Its influence on the thought, religion, political institutions, literature, and art of the medieval and modern worlds is immeasurable (cf. E. von Dobschütz, *The Influence of the Bible on Civilization*. New York, 1913). Certain historical periods in Europe and America seem saturated with its thought; others seem, at least superficially, to be immune to it. But in reality, its influence makes itself felt wherever Christianity or Judaism has penetrated. The great Latin Version of St. Jerome (called the Vulgate) has left its impress on medieval thought; the classical translation of Luther has been a factor in forming the German language; and the superb English translation called the Authorized, or King James, Version remains the unsurpassed masterpiece of English prose.

Only the three most obvious factors of the Old Testament's preeminence in the literature of mankind can be mentioned here: the religious, the literary, and the historical interest. Appearing in this order, singly and in conjunction, through ebb and flow, they have attracted readers without number to the Hebrew Scriptures.

After this cursory examination of the interest in the Old Testament, the history of its canonization and textual transmission must be briefly sketched before investigating the origin of the individual books, written in the course of a millennium, which constitute the Hebrew Bible.

CHAPTER I

RELIGIOUS INTEREST IN THE OLD TESTAMENT

~~~~~~

The Old Testament owes its origin primarily to the religious aspirations of the Jews. Although its contents include more purely mundane material than other sacred books, such as the New Testament and the Koran, the canonization of the Pentateuch (*ca.* 400 B.C.), Prophets (*ca.* 200 B.C.), and Writings (*ca.* A.D. 90) was dictated by the religious needs of the Jewish community. The inconsistencies of Judaism are reflected in the eclectic character of what was to be regarded as inspired Scripture. Developing from a purely national worship of a tribal god into a monotheistic religion with universal appeal,[1] Judaism never lost its nationalistic character and canonized writings whose appeal was primarily patriotic or literary, besides genuinely devotional literature. In regarding all parts of the Old Testament as written by inspired prophets and therefore divinely revealed, Judaism imparted to many pages of the Old Testament a profoundly religious character originally quite alien. Probably the most conspicuous instance of this trend is the devotional use of the Song of Songs.

"God, who at sundry times and in divers manners spake in time past unto the fathers by the prophets" (Hebr. 1:1), has revealed his character and his requirements in the pages of the Old Testament: by subtly ingenious interpretation and by allegorizing the literal meaning of the text, the deepest religious truths can be detected in the most secular words of the Scriptures, the ultimate norm of faith and morals.[2]

The authority of the Old Testament for orthodox Christianity is scarcely less sweeping than for Judaism. Jesus did not come to abrogate the Law and the Prophets but to fulfill them (Matt. 5:17-19). To a scribe inquiring after the way to eternal life he enjoined obedience to the summary of the Law (Deut. 6:5 and Lev. 19:18), saying, "This do and thou shalt live" (Luke 10:25-28). However, Jesus did not regard the Scrip-

[1] G. F. Moore, *Judaism*, Vol. I, pp. 219-234. Cambridge, Mass., 1927.

[2] On the inspiration and authority of the Scriptures in Judaism see especially: G. F. Moore, *Judaism*, Vol. I, pp. 235-250; H. L. Strack and P. Billerbeck, *Kommentar zum Neuen Testament aus Talmud und Midrasch*, Vol. IV, pp. 415-451. Munich, 1928. For Philo, see C. Siegfried, *Philo von Alexandria als Ausleger des Alten Testaments*. Jena, 1875.

tures as the complete and final revelation of God's will. In some instances, God adapted his requirements to the hardness of the human heart, and thus it happens that the Law of Moses which permits divorce is contrary to the Law of God forbidding it (Mark 10:2-12; Matt. 19:3-9). In general, mechanical obedience to the letter of the Law, without understanding of God's real purposes or keeping in mind the higher demands of the Kingdom of God (perfect love, free from selfish motives), has no place in the gospel of Jesus (Matt. 5:20-48). The twofold attitude of Jesus toward the Law of Moses is well illustrated in an incident recorded only in one manuscript (*Codex Bezae*) in Luke 6:4: "On the same day, seeing a man laboring on the sabbath he [Jesus] said to him, 'Man, if thou knowest what thou doest, blessed art thou; but if thou knowest not, accursed art thou and a transgressor of the Law.' "[3]

The Apostle Paul, however, took a step that Jesus had not taken: he forsook Judaism and definitely founded a new religion, based on the doctrine that Christ, through his death and resurrection, had brought salvation to those who have faith. The mystical and sacramental conception of the person of Christ advocated by Paul was bound to be anathema to Palestinian Jews and should logically have led to the complete rejection of the Hebrew Scriptures. But Paul never took this step; and the Old Testament (in the Greek version called the Septuagint [LXX]) remained the Bible of the early Christian Church.

Paul's attitude was inconsistent. On the one hand, the Law of Moses was permanent (Rom. 3:31), holy (7:12), given for life (7:10) so that he who fulfilled it would live (Gal. 3:12; Rom. 10:5), for it contained the embodiment of knowledge and truth (Rom. 2:20). On the other hand, Paul asserted that the Law was merely an intermezzo between the promises to Abraham and their fulfillment in Christ (Gal. 3:16-19), merely a guide leading men to Christ in the manner of a servant taking children to school (3:24), an "old testament" (II Cor. 3:14) to be supplemented by a "new testament" (3:6). The Law was incapable of producing life and righteousness (Gal. 3:21), being made weak through the flesh (Rom. 8:3), and actually produced sin and death (7:7-11; cf. 5:20-21), so that to be under the Law meant to be under the flesh and under sin (6:14; cf. 3:20).

Paul is neither the first nor the last theologian who has held irreconcilable views; paradoxically, moreover, he drew his arguments to prove the transitoriness of the Law from the Law itself (Gal. 3-4), and derived his

---

[3] Much has been written on the attitude of Jesus toward the Hebrew Scriptures, with special reference to the Pentateuch; convenient summaries, with bibliographies, will be found in J. Hastings, *Dictionary of the Bible*, Extra Vol., pp. 22-25, and in Hastings, *Dictionary of Christ and the Gospels* II, 11-17, 264-276. See in particular J. Hempel, "Der synoptische Jesus und das Alte Testament," ZAW N.F. 15 (1938) 1-34. B. H. Branscomb, *Jesus and the Law of Moses*. New York, 1930.

great anti-Jewish motto, "The just shall live by faith," (Rom. 1:17; Gal. 3:11) from the Hebrew Scriptures (Hab. 2:4)—after giving to it a new meaning. He retained the Old Testament as the Christian Bible not only because of his Jewish upbringing "at the feet of Gamaliel," but because, through rabbinical and allegorical interpretations of the Hebrew Scriptures, he obtained arguments for his polemic against the Jews and proof texts for his theological doctrines. It was nevertheless fortunate that in rejecting Judaism Paul did not reject also its Scriptures, as logical consistency would have demanded.[4]

This ambiguous attitude toward the Law was the inevitable result of Paul's doctrine of salvation. He held that the Law had been given, not to allow man to reach justification through an exact fulfillment of all its prescriptions, but to convince him of his sinfulness by realizing his inability to fulfill those prescriptions. In other words, its function was to prove that man cannot save himself through his own efforts and needs divine grace through Christ. Thus Paul emancipated the Christian from the Law, although he never doubted its divine origin. He could even assert that God had promulgated the Mosaic law about the threshing ox (Deut. 25:4) not for the benefit of oxen but for the Christian ministers (I Cor. 9:9).

For the early Christians, however, the Prophets and Psalms were of far greater importance than the Law. To justify their own faith in Jesus the Messiah, and to convert the Jews to this faith, the first Christians had only one argument at their disposal (aside from the miracles of Jesus); namely, the promises of the Old Testament fulfilled in the life, death, and resurrection of Jesus. Such a line of reasoning, out of which the first Christian theology was developed, unquestionably antedated Paul's conversion (cf. I Cor. 15:3) and may be traced back to the risen Jesus (Luke 24:25-27, 44).

This search of the Scriptures for testimonies about Jesus (cf. John 5:39; Acts 17:11) is well described in the *Preaching of Peter* (a Christian writing of the early part of the second century), as quoted by Clement of Alexandria (*Stromata* 6:15, 128):

But we turned to the books of the prophets which we had, which partly through parables, partly through riddles, partly reliably and literally, name Christ Jesus, and we found his coming as well as the death and the cross and all other tortures inflicted upon him by the Jews, and the resurrection and the ascension into heaven before the judgment of Jerusalem. (We found) that what

---

[4] On Paul's use of the Old Testament and on his relation to Judaism see: C. G. Montefiore, *Judaism and Saint Paul*. London, 1914. H. St. John Thackeray, *The Relation of Saint Paul to Contemporary Jewish Thought*. London, 1900. O. Michel, *Paulus und seine Bibel*. Beiträge zur Förderung Christlicher Theologie. Gütersloh, 1929. For the textual problems, cf. TSK (1915) 399 ff.

he was to suffer and what was to be after him was all written down. . . . For we have recognized that God has really ordained it and we affirm nothing without (the evidence of) the Scriptures.

Our earliest evidence is probably contained in the three speeches of Peter, reported in the Book of Acts. In the first (Acts 2:22-36) Peter strives to prove the resurrection and ascension of Jesus by quoting Pss. 16:8-11 (cf. Acts 13:35-37); 89:4-5; 132:11; 110:1 (cf. Mark 12:35-37, etc.). In the second (Acts 3:12-26) he asserts that Jesus is the prophet whose coming was predicted by Moses (Deut. 18:15, 19), sent by God to fulfill the promise made unto Abraham (Gen. 12:3). In the third (Acts 4:8-12) he justifies the death of Jesus on the cross by quoting Ps. 118:22 (cf. Matt. 21:42; Mark 12:10-11; Luke 20:17; I Pet. 2:7; Eph. 2:20).

The death of Jesus, "the stumbling-block of the cross" (Gal. 5:11), proved from the beginning to be the greatest obstacle to the conversion of the Jews (I Cor. 1:23). The Old Testament was searched diligently for references to the suffering and death of the Messiah. Besides Ps. 118, the following passages were regarded as prophecies of the passion of Jesus: Pss. 2, 22, 69; Is. 53. In the Book of Acts, Pss. 16, 41, 89 are quoted to prove the resurrection of Jesus; evidence for the resurrection on the third day (or after three days) was discovered in Jonah 2:1 f. and Hos. 6:2 (cf. II Kings 20:5, 8). The prediction of the second coming of Jesus was found in Dan. 7:13 f.

After proving that the passion and glorification of Jesus were predicted in the Old Testament, the early Christians undertook to show that, in many incidents of Jesus' birth and earthly career, the Scriptures were fulfilled. The Gospels of Matthew and John particularly emphasize the fulfillment of prophecy in the life of the Master (Matt. 1:23; 2:6, 15, 18, 23; 3:3 [Mark 1:3; Luke 3:4-6; John 1:23]; 4:15 f.; 8:17; 12:17; 13:35; 21:5 [John 12:5]; 26:31 [Mark 14:27]; 27:9 f., 35 [John 19:24], etc.; John 2:17; 3:14; 6:31; 7:42; 12:14 f., 37-41; 13:18; 15:25; 17:12; 19:36, 37, etc.). Mark and Luke, if only occasionally and without emphasis, see in the life of Jesus the fulfillment of prophecy (Mark 1:2 f.; 4:12; 14:27; 15:24, 29; 15:28 is an interpolated quotation of Luke 22:37; Luke 3:4; 4:21; 7:27; 20:17; 23:35; cf. 24:25). Thus it cannot be gainsaid that the Old Testament contributed something to the biographical accounts of Jesus.

It was not long before the Christians regarded themselves as the true Israel to whom the divine promises of the Old Testament were addressed. Consequently, they not only denied that the unconverted Jews had any part in the salvation through Jesus Christ, but went so far as to appropriate the Old Testament Scriptures, even forgetting that they belonged to the Synagogue. In Rom. 9-11, Paul denies that "the word of God has come to naught" because Israel according to the flesh has refused to see that the promises of God were realized in Jesus and therefore has no part in the promised salvation: "For they are not all Israel that are Israel." And the promises were made not to Israel according to the flesh but to the children of Abraham according to the spirit, whether Jews or Gentiles. In Israel, blinded and pursuing the phantom of self-righteousness through the Law, only a remnant is reckoned among the elect. A few branches of the good olive tree (Israel) have been broken off in order that branches of a wild tree (the Gentiles) may be grafted to it. Abraham became the father of all believers, including the uncircumcised (Rom. 4:11); not solely for Abraham's sake was it written (Gen. 15:6) that his faith was reckoned for righteousness, "but for us also" (Rom. 4:23 f.). The Church is "the Israel of God" (Gal. 6:16), the true circumcision (Phil. 3:3); Abraham is the father of the Gentiles (Rom. 4:17 f.; Gen. 17:5), and his "seed," to whom the promises were made, is Christ (Gal. 3:16). In this instance, Paul uses rabbinical exegesis, insisting that "seed" is in the singular, although he knows well (see Rom. 9:7) that the word has a plural sense.

Just as Paul had claimed for the Christians the Old Testament prophecies, so the author of the Epistle to the Hebrews claimed for them the Levitical Law. Thus the Church appropriated all of the Old Testament, while forgetting that it was the sacred book of Judaism. The tone of Hebrews is serenely academic, but its spirit is subtly polemic. Although the divine inspiration of the Old Testament is beyond question (1:1, etc.), the Law is said to have been "spoken by angels" rather than by Jehovah (2:2; cf. Gal. 3:19; Acts 7:53; and Deut. 33:2 in the LXX), and to consist in a "carnal commandment" (7:16) incapable of making anything perfect (7:19; 9:9), disannulled on account of its weakness and unprofitableness (7:18). The law is merely "a shadow of good things to come, and not the very image [i.e., the reality] of the things" (10:1). Moses was a servant, but Christ "a son over his own house" (3:5 f.). The great religious institutions of Judaism founded on the Old Testament revelation become mere shadows of a dream: the Sabbath (4:1-11), the priesthood (5-8), the sanctuary (9:1-5), the holy sacrifices (9:6-14; 10:1-13), the covenant or testament (9:15-24) of the Scriptures are but imperfect terrestrial images of spiritual realities. They are "the example and shadow of heavenly things" (8:5) which are "not made with hands" (9:11) and are really true (9:24). The allegorical exegesis of the author, and the contrast between shadow and reality, earthly and heavenly, ephemeral and eternal, created and uncreated, are in harmony with the teachings of Philo of Alexandria (d. *ca.* A.D. 50); but for the author of Hebrews the ultimate reality is "Jesus Christ, the same yesterday, and today, and forever" (13:8).

The Gospel of John shows even closer resemblance to the thought of

Philo, as appears by its doctrine of the *lógos* (word, reason) in 1:1-3, but the animosity against the Jews is even stronger than in the Epistle to the Hebrews. In Paul and Revelation, the term "Jew" is an honorable one; in John, it indicates an enemy of the truth and of the light manifested in Jesus. The break between Church and Synagogue is final: no reconciliation is possible between the Law of Moses and "grace and truth" that came by Jesus (1:17). The Law is something alien to the Christians; it belongs to the world, although it bears witness to Jesus (5:39). The Jews do not believe in Moses (5:46 f.) and therefore do not believe in Jesus; since they know not the Son, they know not God (7:28; 15:23 f.; 8:19). By hating the Son they hate the Father (15:22-25). Needless to say, the Jewish religious institutions ordained in the Old Testament, such as the Sabbath (5:17; 7:23), circumcision (7:23 f.), and the Temple (4:20 f.), are deemed insignificant and futile.

The Gospel of John is the most anti-Jewish book in the New Testament. Conversely, the Book of Revelation, notwithstanding its denunciation of the non-Christian Jews as the "Synagogue of Satan" (2:9; 3:9), is the most friendly to Judaism of all the writings in the New Testament. Its language is saturated with allusions to the pages of the Old Testament, which the author, departing from the usual practice in the New Testament, has read in the Hebrew rather than in the Greek text.[5] Besides the Old Testament, the author makes extensive use of Jewish apocalypses that were clearly written in Aramaic. Disregarding the slight Christian touches, certain parts of the book (notably 19:11-21:8) present the apocalyptic hopes and dreams of the Jews of the first century A.D. As in IV Esdras, the great enemy of God is the Roman Empire, which is soon to be destroyed through the agency of the Messiah.

As we have seen, the attitude of the authors of the New Testament toward the Old Testament is not uniform. But they all agree in regarding the Old Testament as divinely inspired; moreover, they firmly believe that in its pages salvation through Jesus Christ had been foretold long in advance. The New Testament is filled with quotations from the Old Testament, and its language saturated with expressions derived from the Septuagint Greek versions.[6] The same is true of the early Church Fathers.[7]

The early Church was not to be deprived of the Old Testament be-

[5] See J. A. Montgomery, "The Education of the Seer of the Apocalypse," JBL 45 (1926) 70-80; R. H. Charles, *The Revelation of St. John* (ICC) I, lxv-lxxxvi.

[6] For Old Testament quotations and allusions in the New Testament see: W. Dittmar, *Vetus Testamentum in Novo*. Göttingen, 1903. Hastings, *Dictionary of the Bible* IV, 184-188. H. B. Swete, *An Introduction to the Old Testament in Greek*. Cambridge, 1900 (rev. ed., 1914). C. H. Toy, *Quotations in the New Testament*. New York, 1884.

[7] Swete, *op. cit.*, pp. 406-432. On the use of the Apocrypha in the New Testament and in the Church see, W. O. E. Oesterley, *An Introduction to the Books of the Apocrypha*, pp. 111-130. New York. 1935.

cause of Christian hostility to the Synagogue. On the contrary, the conviction that the Hebrew Scriptures were Christian rather than Jewish
prevailed increasingly. Ignatius wrote (Epistle to the Magnesians 8:2):
"The prophets lived according to Christ Jesus." Even the Epistle of
Barnabas, which suggested that Jews observing the letter of the Old
Testament were victims of demonic deception, discovered the tenets of
Christianity in the Old Testament through allegorical and spiritual interpretations. Just as the Synagogue had made law of the entire Old Testament, so the Church found prophecy on every one of its pages.[8] The dissenting views of the Gnostics and of Marcion in the second century only
strengthened the orthodox attitude. By rejecting the Old Testament and
substituting either theosophical speculations or a misinterpretation of the
teachings of St. Paul, these heretics would have severed the organic connection of Christianity with history and destroyed some of its deepest
roots. In the ancient Church the religious significance of the Old Testament cannot be overestimated.[9] *Mirabile dictu!* Pagan philosophers were
converted to Christianity by the reading of the Old Testament (Justin,
Dialogue with Tryphon 7-8; Tatian, *Oration* 29). Tatian, for instance, confesses that the Old Testament brought about his conversion because of
its simplicity of style, its clear presentation of the creation of the world,
its knowledge of the future, the excellency of its ordinances, and its teaching of monotheism. Moreover, the influence of the Old Testament on the
Church is not confined to the five important points enumerated by Tatian:
it contributed toward molding the doctrines and institutions of the
Church; it nourished its piety both in public worship, when parts of the
Old Testament were read or chanted in the liturgies, and in the private
reading of Psalms, Prophets, and other parts of the Scriptures, attested by
Origen, Tertullian, and others.[10] It furnished the Christians with several
norms of ethical conduct (cf. II Tim. 3:16 f.) and opened before them
vistas of a glorious, divinely ordained future.[11]

[8] For the interpretation of the Old Testament as a prophecy of the Christian truths
see especially: K. Fullerton, *Prophecy and Authority*. New York, 1919.

[9] See especially: A. Harnack, *Mission und Ausbreitung des Christentums*, pp. 30-52
and 204-210. Leipzig, 1902 (English translation, 2nd ed., London, 1908). L. Diestei,
Geschichte des Alten Testaments in der Christlichen Kirche. Jena, 1869. J. M. Thomas,
The Christian Faith and the Old Testament. New York, 1908. F. Wilke, *Das Alte
Testament und der Christliche Glaube*. Leipzig, 1911. L. I. Newman, *Jewish Influence
on Christian Reform Movements*. New York, 1925. N. Isaacs, *The Influence of Judaism
on Western Law* (in Abraham, Bevan, Singer: *The Legacy of Israel*), pp. 377 ff.
Oxford, 1927.

[10] A. Harnack, *Über den privaten Gebrauch der heiligen Schriften in der alten
Kirche*. Leipzig, 1912.

[11] It should not be forgotten that the Old Testament influenced the Church, except
during the apostolic period and in the last four centuries (when some Christians could
read it in Hebrew), only in translation. The Greek Version (LXX) influenced profoundly the language and thought of the Christian Church before Jerome (cf. H.
B. Swete, *An Introduction to the Old Testament in Greek*, pp. 406-432, 462-477. See
also the books of A. Deissmann).

Indeed, this brief survey of the religious interest in the Old Testament should not entirely omit Islam, even though the Hebrew Scriptures were known only indirectly to the Moslem. Mohammed, in his Koran, recognizes the divine origin of the Bible: "For He had sent down the Law and the Gospel aforetime, as man's guidance; and now hath He sent down the 'Illumination'" (3:2). Mohammed had never read the Old Testament, but some of its contents were familiar to him through contacts with Jews and Christians. The Koran contains numerous echoes of Old Testament doctrines and stories; the latter, taken principally from Genesis, Exodus, Samuel, Kings, Job, and Jonah, are often told with legendary embellishments and occasional errors.[12]

For us moderns the Old Testament is religiously significant in three ways. First of all, as inspired scripture in Church and in Synagogue, it continues to be a norm of faith and conduct, a guide for the perplexed, and a source of edification for both congregations and individuals. Secondly, the religious teaching of the Old Testament is the ultimate source of the basic doctrines of Christianity as well as of Judaism. The Christian Church is indebted to the Old Testament for its faith in a unique God— the Creator of the world and the Father in heaven; for the assurance that this God has revealed himself in chosen men (prophecy) and in sacred books (canonicity); for the conviction that the moral law originates in the divine mind and will; for the hope in a Kingdom of God on this earth and in the invisible world; and for the assurance that in his mercy God has provided atonement for human sin, that true repentance brings forgiveness, and that salvation is offered to all human beings. In the third place, the Old Testament is a unique record of religious progress from a religion of observance national in scope to a religion in spirit and in truth whose temple "shall be called a house of prayer for all peoples" (Is. 56:7).

[12] A. Geiger, *Was hat Mohammed aus dem Judentume aufgenommen?* Bonn, 1834. Cf., for a brief summary, *Jewish Encyclopedia* VII, 557-560. See also B. Heiler, "La légende biblique dans l'Islam," REJ 98 (1934) 1-18. D. Sidersky, *Les origines des légendes musulmanes dans le Coran et dans les vies des Prophètes.* Paris, 1933.

CHAPTER II

THE LITERARY INTEREST IN THE
OLD TESTAMENT

For many centuries the religious interest in the Old Testament has over-shadowed its purely literary appeal. The Scriptures were searched for divine verities, not for literary masterpieces. Nevertheless, a few scattered bits of evidence bear explicit witness to a literary appreciation which, in the case of its finest writings, must have had its inception at the time of their publication—whether the readers realized it fully or not.

Although no direct evidence for a purely literary enjoyment of the Biblical writings before their canonization has survived, the preservation of some parts of these writings leaves no doubt about the matter. The survival of J and E after their amalgamation into JE, of JE after the publication of Deuteronomy, of JED after P became the fundamental law of the Jews; the addition of Judg. 5; 9; 17-21 and II Sam. 9-20 to the Deuteronomistic editions of Judges and Samuel, which had been published about 550 B.C. without these superb pages; the survival and canonization of books having literary rather than religious value—this and other indirect evidence proves conclusively that the early readers of the Old Testament generally had a real appreciation of belles-lettres, irrespective of their devotional appeal.

But after the canonization of the Pentateuch in 400 B.C. and the subsequent rise of the Synagogue, reading and writing among pious Jews became subservient to religion. They were dominated by desire to fulfill the divinely revealed Law, pride in Israel's past achievements, and assurance of the triumph of Israel in the Messianic age. Great literature which did not nourish the legal, historical, and Messianic interests of the congregation no longer attracted Jewish readers. The Chronicler about 250 B.C. is a typical example of this trend: in reading the Books of Samuel he characteristically ignores II Sam. 9-20—the unrivaled masterpiece of Hebrew prose which demonstrably stood in his copy of Samuel—being entirely absorbed in legal observances, national glory, and future triumphs. Sirach (Ecclus. 44-49) and the author of the Epistle to the Hebrews (Hebr. 11) read the Old Testament as an inspiring record of the lives of saints whose piety was rewarded by God. Josephus is substantially right in saying that "it is natural to all Jews, immediately from their very birth, to esteem

11

them [the Books of the Old Testament] as (containing) divine doctrines and to persist in them and to die for them, if necessary, gladly" (*Against Apion* 1:8 [§42]; cf. II Tim. 3:16 f.). But nothing indicates that they appreciated the magic of great style, the charm of fine verse and of noble prose, the fascinating portrayal of human passions, aspirations, and ideals. A literary enjoyment of the Scriptures would have seemed to them the height of irreverence, as indeed it seemed to Rabbi Akiba (d. *ca.* A.D. 132). While he and other rabbis of his day were solemnly proclaiming the sacrosanct character of Canticles, some irreverent young men were singing its love ditties in cabarets, regarding it "as a kind of secular song" (*Tosefta Sanhedrin* 12). Perversely these young rascals not only appreciated the true character of Canticles better than Akiba did, but they seem to be the only known ancient Jewish readers who saw in a portion of Scripture nothing but great literature, without recondite allegorical meanings.

Before modern times, the evidence for an interest in the form of the Scripture (poetic meter and style) is extremely scanty. The apologist Tatian relates in his *Oratio ad Graecos* (written between A.D. 152 and 173) that he was converted to Christianity by a reading of the Old Testament Scriptures. Characteristically, being a Greek rhetor, he mentions "the plain expression and the unstudied simplicity of their authors" (*Orat.* 29) before the other excellencies of the Scriptures which captivated his mind. Only men with a Greek training could appreciate intelligently the form of the Bible; nevertheless, even Greek-writing Jews like Philo, Josephus, and Paul, betray scant interest in it.

Jerome probably was more concerned with meter and style than any Biblical student until modern times. He observed that the Wisdom of Solomon was not translated from the Hebrew because its "very style gives forth the aroma of Greek eloquence" (Preface to the Books of Solomon), as likewise II Maccabees (*Prologus Galeatus*). He noted that each of the Twelve (Minor) Prophets had an individual style (Preface to the XII Prophets) and that Isaiah was a man "of urban eloquence, in whose speech there was no admixture of rusticity" (preface to Isaiah), whereas Jeremiah was "more rustic" in speech than Isaiah, Hosea, and others (Preface to Jeremiah). In asserting (Preface to Job) that Job 3:2-42:6, Psalms, and Lamentations are written in verse (hexameters, in his opinion) he referred doubters to the authority of Philo, Josephus [cf. *Antiquities* 2:16, 4; 4:18, 44; 7:12, 3], Origen, and Eusebius of Caesarea. He even dared to compare David, the author of the Psalms, to such secular poets as Pindar, Alcaeus, Horace, and Catullus (*Letter to Paulinus*).

From Jerome (*ca.* 400) we must come down to the romantic awakening in the eighteenth century before discovering a purely literary appreciation of Hebrew poetry. Only then was it discovered that the writings of the Old Testament are the remnants of a national literature and that the poems contained therein, being examples of various types of Hebrew poetry, were to be read as such rather than as sacred scripture. In this respect the book of Bishop Robert Lowth, *De sacra poesi Hebraeorum praelectiones academicae* (Oxford, 1753; English translation by G. Gregory, 1847; edited by E. F. K. Rosenmüller with learned notes of J. D. Michaelis, Leipzig, 1815), was epoch making, although his aesthetic criticism was soon surpassed by the work of J. G. von Herder (*Vom Geist der Ebräischen Poesie*. 2 vols. Dessau, 1782-1783; later editions by K. W. Justi [Leipzig, 1825] and F. Hoffmann [Gotha, 1891]). In turn Herder's brilliant intuition that a nation's literature springs from the people's soul and reflects its culture, was expounded with great learning by J. G. Eichhorn (*Einleitung in das Alte Testament*. 3 vols. Leipzig, 1780-1783; 4th ed. in 5 vols. Göttingen 1823-1824), who emphasized the importance of the Oriental setting for an understanding of the Old Testament. In our own time D. B. Macdonald (*The Hebrew Literary Genius*. Princeton, 1933) has revived this aesthetic appreciation of the Bible: rejecting the methods of higher criticism, he searches beyond the literature for "the philosophy of the mind and the races that produced it" (p. xxiv), and comes to the conclusion that the thought and literature of the Hebrews are virtually the same as those of the Arabs.

The literary excellence of the greatest pages of the Old Testament is beyond dispute, either in the original or in its classical translations such as the King James (or Authorized) Version. Since our concern here is the appreciation and literary history of the original Hebrew (and Aramaic) writings and not with a masterpiece of English literature, we shall refer the reader to the brilliant analysis of "The Noblest Monument of English Prose" penned by John Livingston Lowes (*Essays in Appreciation*, pp. 1-31. Boston, 1936) and to a few of the numerous works on the King James Version.[1]

---

[1] J. H. Lupton (Hastings, *Dictionary of the Bible*. Extra Vol. [1904], pp. 236-271) has given an account of the various English versions and a bibliography of the nineteenth century literature on the subject. Among recent works on the English Bible the following may be named: W. H. Hoare, *Our English Bible* (rev. ed., New York, 1902; reprinted in 1925). B. F. Westcott (*A General View of the History of the English Bible*. 3rd ed., revised by W. A. Wright. London, 1905). A. S. Cook (in the Cambridge *History of English Literature*; cf. his *Biblical Quotations in Old English Prose Writers*. First Series, London, 1898; Second Series, New York, 1903). J. H. Gardiner (*The Bible as English Literature*. New York, 1914). G. P. Krapp (*The Rise of English Literary Prose*, pp. 218-270. New York, 1915). J. S. Penniman (*A Book about the English Bible*. New York, 1920). C. A. Dinsmore (*The English Bible as Literature*. New York, 1931). Margaret B. Crook, Editor (*The Bible and its Literary Associations*. New York, 1937). W. O. Sypherd (*The Literature of the English Bible*. New York, 1938). D. Daiches (*The King James Version of the English Bible*. Chicago, 1941). For a brief general survey of the translations of the Old Testament, both ancient and modern, in many languages, see M. L. Margolis, *The Story of Bible Translations*. Philadelphia, 1917. A fuller, more recent, treatment is given by H. W. Robinson (editor) in *The Bible in its Ancient and English Translations* (Oxford University Press, 1940).

Great literature is the expression of arresting thoughts in brilliant diction. In the best pages of the Hebrew Old Testament the significance of the contents is matched by the beauty of the style. Reserving for parts II-V a fuller analysis of the contents and style of the individual writings, we may here consider succinctly and broadly the qualities of form and substance exhibited by the Hebrew Scriptures.

1. Style

Biblical style is conditioned by the resources of Hebrew speech and syntax. Hebrew is one of the Semitic languages,[2] which are divided into the following groups: 1. Eastern (Akkadian or Assyro-Babylonian); 2. Western: *a*. Northwestern, comprising two groups, the Aramaic (pagan, Jewish, and Christian [or Syriac]) and Amoritic or Canaanitic (Hebrew, Phoenician, Punic, Moabitic); Amoritic includes the Ugaritic of the Ras Shamra texts (unless it be regarded, with H. Bauer, J. Friedrich, and others, as a separate branch of Northwest Semitic). *b*. Southwestern (Arabic and Ethiopic). Some of the features of Hebrew style result from certain peculiarities of Semitic languages in general or of Hebrew in particular.[3]

A word should be said of the sound of Hebrew speech, even though it has no direct bearing on literary style. The Hebrew alphabet, comprising twenty-two letters representing consonants (no vowels were written before the seventh century A.D.), fails to do justice to the sounds of the language. Some letters represent two quite distinct sounds: the *ḥeth* stands for Arabic *ḥ* and *ḫ*; the *'ain* was reproduced by the Greek translators inadequately, but in two entirely different ways, at the beginning of Omri and Gomorrah (corresponding to the two sounds in the Arabic); the letter *tsade* (*ṣ*) likewise, as shown in its transcription in Greek as *t* and *s* in Tyre and Sidon, represented two radically different sounds; the *s* stands for both *ś* and *sh* (distinguished by a dot in modern Hebrew); the six letters b, g, d, k, p, t have an explosive pronunciation (as in English) following a consonant, but a fricative pronunciation (v, gh, dh, kh, f, th) following a vowel. In contrast with English, in which sounds are

---

[2] Th. Nöldeke has given a brilliant summary of the characteristics of Semitic languages in the *Encyclopaedia Britannica*, 11th ed., 1911 (xxiv, 617-630). For details see C. Brockelman, *Grundriss der vergleichenden Grammatik der semitischen Sprachen.* 2 vols. Berlin, 1908, 1913. The term "Semitic" is derived from Gen. 10:22, where the list of the sons of Shem includes Elam, Assur, Arpachshad, Lud, and Aram (Elamitic and Lydian [Lud] are, however, not Semitic), and was first used by A. L. Schlözer in 1781.

[3] Non-Hebraists, for whom the present book is particularly intended, may consult for further details on these points: W. H. Saulez, *The Romance of the Hebrew Language*, London, 1913 (not always reliable); and D. W. Thomas, *The Language of the Old Testament* (in *Record and Revelation*, edited by H. W. Robinson, pp. 374-402. Oxford, 1938).

articulated between the tongue and the lips, often scarcely opening the lips, Hebrew was rich in sounds articulated within the throat, and the *h* required a flow of breath from the very depth of the lungs. Less beautiful than Greek, ancient Hebrew retained the harshness of the desert, a Bedouin virility marked by sharp staccato tones, vigorous doubled consonants (such as persist in Italian but are lost in English), and deep-throated, rasping, guttural sounds. In a general way, Hebrew sounds more like German than like English or French.

The vocabulary of Hebrew, although very limited and only partially known, is concrete and vivid. Words still paint a picture and seldom reach the stage of pale abstractions. Ideas are often expressed by objects. Thus "my horn" (Ps. 92:10 [H. 92:11], etc.) means "my power"; "lip of Canaan" (Is. 19:18) means the Hebrew language; "hip and thigh" (literally "leg over thigh") seems to mean utterly and completely (Judg. 15:8); religion is called "the fear of God" and morality "turning away from evil" (Job 1:1, and often elsewhere); "house" may be used for family or dynasty. The most common actions are often described visually: "he opened his mouth and spoke"; "he lifted his eyes and looked"; "he put forth his hand and took." Adjectives are rare and qualities are indicated by concrete nouns: "a man of God" means "a holy man"; "Noah was a son of five hundred years" (i.e., 500 years old); "a hill son of oil" (Is. 5:1) is a fertile hill.

The English speech has been enriched by concrete expressions borrowed from the Hebrew: "to lick the dust" (Mic. 7:17; Ps. 72:9); "the sweat of thy face" (Gen. 3:19); "gall and wormwood" (Deut. 29:18 [H. 29:17]; "to heap coals of fire" (Prov. 25:22); "a land flowing with milk and honey" (Deut. 6:3; 11:9, etc.); "the stars in their courses" (Judg. 5:20); "a broken reed" (Is. 36:6, etc.); "bone of my bone and flesh of my flesh" (Gen. 2:23); "an eye for an eye" (Ex. 21:24, etc.); "the flesh pots" (Ex. 16:3); "with the skin of my teeth" (Job 19:20); "a little cloud . . . , like a man's hand" (I Kings 18:44); "hewers of wood and drawers of water" (Josh. 9:21); "the wife of thy bosom" (Deut. 13:6 [H. 13:7]); and many more.

A few general observations about the Hebrew verb may be useful for an understanding of the characteristics of Biblical style. In the Old Testament an objective aspect system, distinguishing between a completed action or state (perfect tense) and an incompleted action or state (imperfect tense), has replaced a subjective aspect system, in which past (preterit tense) and present or future (present tense) time were clearly distinguished as in Indo-European languages.[4] The Hebrew imperfect

---

[4] Cf. Z. S. Harris, *Development of the Canaanite Dialects*, pp. 83-85. American Oriental Series, Vol. 10, New Haven, Conn., 1939. On the syntax of the Hebrew verb, in addition to the standard Hebrew grammars (W. Gesenius, E. König, H.

with the *waw* consecutive, employed commonly in narration of past events (like the perfect), is an ·isolated survival of the discarded subjective verbal system. On the contrary, the perfect with *waw* conversive represents a much later linguistic development, and is used as the equivalent of the imperfect tense.

The perfect tense usually expresses actions completed in the past in general ("we *have dreamed* a dream," Gen. 40:8) or specifically before another event ("And [Jehovah] smote seventy men among the men of Beth-shemesh because they *had looked* inside the ark of Jehovah," I Sam. 6:19), but also actions or states continuing in the present ("I *hate*, I *despise* your feasts," Am. 5:21) or conceived as completed in the future ("Until cities *will have become a devastation* without inhabitants," Is. 6:11).

The imperfect tense, on the contrary, expresses incipient action in the past ("And behold, your sheaves *began to come* around [my sheaf]," Gen. 37:7), in the present ("The day has [already] turned [perfect] and the shadows of dusk *are beginning to lengthen*," Jer. 6:4), or in the future ("Then [Mesha] took his eldest son who [eventually] *would have begun to reign* in his stead and offered him as a burnt offering," II Kings 3:27). But more frequently the imperfect denotes a single action or state while still incomplete, whether in the past ("A word *was being stealthily conveyed* to me," Job 4:12), present ("Now that it *is overtaking you*, you have lost heart," Job 4:5), or future ("He [Ishmael] *will be* a wild ass of a man," Gen. 16:12), or even (like the perfect) a completed action or state in the present ("Why *does* my lord *speak* . . . ," Gen. 44:7), or future ("Until . . . the land *will have been* utterly *devastated*," Is. 6:11). The imperfect also indicates repeated, regular, or habitual actions or states as distinguished from single ones: in the past ("A single man among you *has* [*often*] *pursued* a thousand," Josh. 23:10), in the present, either for constantly repeated actions ("Lo, he [*frequently*] *passes by me*, but I see him not," Job 9:11) or for general truths ("[a tree] which [*invariably*] *produces* its fruit in its season," Ps. 1:3), and in the future ("And my people *will never be ashamed*," Joel 2:27).

The imperfect is used for the subjunctive, which has lost its ending *a* and cannot be distinguished in form from the imperfect ("What is my strength, *that I should wait?*" Job 6:11; "*That ye may live*," Deut. 4:1), and also for wishes, commands, and prohibitions ("*May I find favor* . . . !" Gen. 33:15; the Ten Commandments; "*Let* the dry land *appear*," Gen. 1:9), although for such expressions Hebrew has a cohortative in the first person, an imperative in the second, and a jussive in the third.

Bauer and P. Leander, G. Bergsträsser, P. Joüon, etc.), see: S. R. Driver, *A Treatise on the Use of the Tenses in Hebrew.* 2nd ed., Oxford, 1881. G. R. Driver, *Problems of the Hebrew Verbal System*, 1936. M. Buttenwieser, in Hebrew Union College Jubilee Volume (Cincinnati, 1925), pp. 89-111.

The following examples illustrate the basic difference between the imperfect and the perfect. "Behold, he *struck* [perfect] the rock . . . so that the brooks *were overflowing* [imperfect]" (Ps. 78:20). "There the wicked *have ceased* [perfect] from troubling and the weary are (*always*) *at rest* [imperfect]" (Job 3:17). Cf. Jer. 6:4, quoted above.

The participle and the "construct" infinitive are verbal nouns denoting respectively the agent and the action. They are used either as nouns or as verbs (cf. in English, "the winning of the West" and "he was winning the battle"), or even occasionally at the same time as nouns (with the article) and verbs (with the accusative): "Where is *he who placed* [participle with the article] his holy spirit within him [i.e., Moses]" (Is. 63:11); "The tree of *the knowing* [infinitive with article] good and evil" (Gen. 2:9). Both the participle and the infinitive are inherently timeless and may refer to the past, present, or future, according to the context. For instance, *meth* (participle) may mean dead (Judg. 3:25), dying (Gen. 48:21), and facing death in the near future (Gen. 20:3; II Kings 20:1). The participle refers to the same period of time as the main verb in the sentence (Gen. 37:15 f.). However, the participle is often used for our present (even more in Aramaic than in Hebrew) particularly in general statements (Eccl. 1:4-7) and denoting lasting conditions (Gen. 3:5; 4:10; 16:8); it is then the equivalent of an imperfect and may be followed by it ("Woe to *joiners* [participle] of house to house, *they add* [imperfect] field to field," Is. 5:4). The infinitive is also used, occasionally, for a finite verb ("For *their delivering up* the captivity . . . and they remembered not . . ." Am. 1:9).

The so-called infinitive absolute does not occur in any Semitic language except Hebrew. It is used occasionally in place of the infinitive construct (Is. 7:15) and adverbially ("she sat down *afar off*," Gen. 21:16); more frequently to emphasize a finite verb of the same root ("You will *surely* die," Gen. 2:17; "Oh that you would remain *entirely* silent!" Job 13:5), or in place of a perfect (Is. 21:5), an imperfect (II Kings 4:43), or an imperative (in military commands: Nah. 2:1 [H. 2:2]; in English such orders as "Squads right!" are the exact equivalent).

The Hebrew verb has seven voices expressing different shades of meaning of the basic root (cf. in English, fall and fell; lie and lay). The verb *yd̃*, one of the few verbs used in all the voices, may serve to illustrate their general meaning, which varies somewhat in individual verbs: 1. to know (*qal* or simple voice); 2. to make oneself known, cf. Ruth 3:3 (reflexive-passive); 3. to make known, cf. Job 38:12 (transitive-intensive); 4. to be made known, cf. Is. 12:5 (passive of the preceding voice); 5. to cause to know, cf. Ex. 18:16 (causative); 6. to be caused to know, cf. Lev. 4:23 (passive of the preceding voice); 7. to make oneself known, to reveal oneself, cf. Num. 12:6 (reflexive).

In comparison with Greek or Latin the sentence structure of Hebrew seems rudimentary. With few exceptions, such as conditional sentences, co-ordination of clauses prevails over subordination. Consequently, classical Hebrew is often atomic in structure, sentence following sentence with impressive uniformity: "My beloved had a vineyard on a very fruitful hill; and he digged it, and cleared it of stones, and planted it with the choicest vine; and he built a tower in the midst of it, and also hewed a vat therein" (Is. 5:1 f.). Even political oratory, perhaps the most verbose literary genre, is direct and simple in ancient Israel (cf. Judg. 9:28 f.; II Sam. 17:7-13). Elaborate self-conscious eloquence appears first in Deuteronomy (Deut. 8 is a good example of oratory in the grand manner); but the prolixity and majesty of the flowing sentences in Deuteronomy lack the logical clarity and well-rounded complexity of Demosthenes or Cicero. How unsuited Hebrew was for long complicated sentences, which may be perfectly lucid in Greek, Latin, or German, may be seen in the ambitious but deplorable attempt of the author of Prov. 2 to construct a colossal sentence in the Greek manner: he has only succeeded in hiding the forest by means of the trees! Even the brilliant author of Ecclesiastes strained the resources of Hebrew syntax when he described allegorically, in one long sentence (Eccles. 12:1-7), the miseries of senility. However, his picturesque imagery and vivid diction, so superior to the pedantic and moralizing dullness of Prov. 2, lend to this allegory (in spite of some obscurities) the qualities of superb literature.

For metaphors are indeed a characteristic concomitant of Hebrew literature at its best, which is poetic rather than rational, lyric rather than oratorical, vividly realistic and concrete rather than abstract and general. Hebrew writers found "tongues in trees, books in the running brooks, sermons in stones" (Shakespeare, *As You Like It*). From the stars of the heavens and the sand on the seashore (Gen. 22:17) to a spider's web (Job 8:14) and a flower of the field (Ps. 103:15 f.), nature in its manifold aspects furnishes the substance of images and metaphors, as also human life. While a Greek after Aristotle would have said, "Every cause has an effect; every effect has a cause," Amos, lacking abstract terminology, conveys these axioms through a series of vignettes (Am. 3:3-6). To Western readers, the Oriental fancy displayed in Biblical imagery is at times delightfully bewildering. In the Song of Songs, the youth compared his beloved to a mare in Pharaoh's chariots (1:9), her hair to a flock of goats (4:1), and her neck to the tower of David (4:4), while the maiden retaliated by comparing his legs to pillars of marble set upon sockets of fine gold (5:15)!

Natural objects and phenomena are poetically endowed with soul and mind, and are rhetorically personified. Job (3:9) speaks of the "eyelids of the morning" as Homer of the "rosy-fingered dawn." Deborah saw "the stars in their courses" fighting against Sisera (Judg. 5:20) and the poet of Job declares that "the morning stars sang together" (Job 38:7) when God laid the foundations of the earth; he also beheld the dawn taking hold of the ends of the earth and shaking off the wicked (Job 38:13), like a woman shaking the crumbs off a tablecloth after a meal. An inspired poet heard "the heavens declare the glory of God" and listened to the voice of day and night (Ps. 19:1 f. [H. 19:2 f.]), but a prosaic literal reader, in a gloss, denied that such words or voice could be heard (19:3 [H. 19:4]). The same poet sees the sun as a bridegroom or as a champion runner (19:5 [H. 19:6]). Likewise in Job the sea, at the beginning, is visualized as an infant at birth (Job 38:8 f.). Death appears as the "grim reaper" in Jer. 9:21 (H. 9:20) and as the "king of terrors" in Job 8:14. Shelley's following verses (from *Queen Mab*) could have been written by Jeremiah or the author of Job; "How wonderful is death, Death and his brother sleep!" Even abstractions, like Wisdom and Dame Folly are personified (Prov. 8-9). Personification of cities (Nineveh: Nah. 3:4-6; Babylon: Is. 47:1-3, 5, 8 f.; Jerusalem: II Kings 19:21 = Is. 37:22; Is. 52:1 f.) and of nations (Am. 5:2) are not uncommon, as also allegories of the same (particularly in Ezekiel).

In contrast with such imaginative and colorful style,[5] the Hebrew Scriptures do not lack classical examples of unadorned straightforward prose, lapidary in their conciseness, sublime in their simplicity. " 'Let there be light!' And there was light," or better in Latin, *Fiat lux!* (Gen. 1:3). "Ye shall be as gods, knowing good and evil" (3:5). "For dust thou art, and unto the dust thou shalt return" (3:19). "Eye for eye, tooth for tooth" (Ex. 21:24). "Thou art the man!" (II Sam. 12:7).

The superb literary qualities of such simple words may be appreciated by contrasting the lucid directness of "Thou shalt love thy neighbor as thyself" (Lev. 19:18) with A. P. Herbert's rendition into what he calls "Jungle English" (in his book *What a Word!* London, 1936): "In connection with my co-citizens, a general standard of mutual goodwill and reciprocal non-aggression is obviously incumbent upon me."

Some Biblical writers have made excellent use of irony (I Sam. 26:15; Am. 4:4 f.; Job 26:2-4) and sarcasm, as in two fables (Judg. 9:7-21 and II Kings 14:9) and in Elijah's words on Carmel (I Kings 18:27). Proverbs (particularly chs. 25-27) is the wittiest book in the Bible: with refreshing humor the sages recognize that the most vexing type of wife is a garrulous shrew (Prov. 21:9, 19; 25:24; 27:15), while the most irritating type of husband is the indolent sluggard spending his time in bed or at home

---

[5] For further details on Hebrew figures of speech, the reader may be referred to E. König, "Style of Scripture" (in Hastings, *Dictionary of the Bible*. Extra Vol. 1904, pp. 156-169) and to his more technical treatise in German (*Stilistik, Rhetorik, Poetik in Bezug auf die biblische Litteratur*. Leipzig, 1900). Numerous examples of metaphors will be given later in the analysis of the style of individual authors, particularly the Second Isaiah (Is. 40-55) and the author of Job.

in idleness (6:9 f.; 19:24; 22:13; 24:33; 26:13-16). The picture of the ideal wife, whose manifold labors support the husband in idle luxury (Prov. 31:10-31, the finest alphabetic acrostic poem in the Old Testament), may seem humorous to a Western reader, although the Oriental author was utterly unconscious of its amusing features.

In addition to the concreteness, vividness, fancifulness, sublimity, sarcasm, and humor which have been illustrated briefly, many other moods or qualities of Hebrew style could be mentioned: pathos (Am. 5:2), exultation (Ex. 15:21), dejection (Job 3), indignation (Hos. 2:2-12 [H. 2:4-14]), invective (Am. 4:1), grief (II Sam. 18:33 [H. 19:1]), tenderness (Jer. 2:2), faith (Ps. 23).

2. Contents

The Old Testament is a library, a selection from the works of many authors who were regarded as divinely inspired, written during the course of more than a millennium (ca. 1200-100 B.C.)—a span of time corresponding in length and permutations to that from Beowulf to Tennyson in English literature, and from Homer to the New Testament in Greek literature.

The Old Testament is the surviving portion of the national literature of the ancient Israelites. We shall see that the extant records explicitly or implicitly assume the existence of codes of law, poems, histories, and other works now lost beyond all hope of recovery. Although the selection was made for religious purposes, the ancient connection between nationalism and religion as well as the allegorical interpretation of secular writings has fortunately saved from oblivion some literary masterpieces, which we would scarcely regard as religious.

Hebrew literature reflects national history in an exceptional degree. Its appreciation presupposes some knowledge of the political vicissitudes of the Israelites and of their cultural and religious development.[6] The periods in the literary history correspond more or less to those in the political history. For the period preceding Moses, when the ancestors of Israel roamed in the desert or (in the case of the Joseph group) were enslaved

[6] Concise outlines of the history of Israel have been prepared by the writer for the *New Standard Bible Dictionary* (New York, 1926) and W. L. Langer's *Encyclopaedia of World History* (Boston, 1940). In English the best histories of Israel are those of J. Wellhausen ("Israel" in the 9th ed. of the *Encyclopaedia Britannica*; later editions in German), C. Noyes (*The Genius of Israel*. Boston, 1924), S. A. Cook (in the *Cambridge Ancient History*), A. T. Olmstead (*History of Palestine and Syria*, 1931), W. O. E. Oesterley and Th. H. Robinson (*History of Israel*, 2 vols. Oxford, 1934), A. Lods (*Israel*, 1932; *The Prophets*, 1937). In German the most detailed is R. Kittel's *Geschichte des Volkes Israel*, 3 vols., 1922-1929). The history of particular periods is given in the present volume in connection with certain books, and a list of the kings of Israel and Judah, with dates and references, is given in the summary of the Book of Kings.

in Egypt, we have neither historical information nor literature (except perhaps a few poems). The golden age of the literature corresponds to the period from the Exodus from Egypt under the leadership of Moses to the end of the monarchy (1225-586 B.C.). The silver age corresponds to the Neo-Babylonian (586-538), the Persian (538-332), and Hellenistic (Alexander, 332-323; the Ptolemies, 323-198; the Seleucids, 198-142) domination of the Jews in Palestine, and their brief period of independence under the Hasmoneans (142-63 B.C.).

The Old Testament contains non-Israelitic writings, re-edited by Jews. Isaiah 16-17 is based on a Moabitic elegy, Ps. 104 is an echo of the Egyptian Hymn to Aton giving expression to the solar monotheism of Ihnaton (1375-1358), Prov. 22:17-23:14 is a revised selection of some of the Egyptian maxims of Amen-em-ope. Some of Israel's oldest legislation the "J decalogue" in Ex. 22-23 and 34, and the civil legislation in Ex. 21-2 and in parts of Deut.) is Canaanitic in origin. Foreign sources were utilized in the Priestly Code, in the Joseph stories, and elsewhere. Final the present writer has reached the conclusion that the S source in G.esis, Pss. 88 and 89, Prov. 30:1-31:9, and the Book of Job, in their orinal form, were written by Edomitic sages (cf. ZAW N.F. 3 [1926] 13.; 7 [1930] 66 ff.).

For general orientation, without attempting exhaustiveness (or a selection of writings later than 600 will be listed), and referringhe reader to later parts of the book for details, we may tabulate chro-logically the poetry and prose of the Old Testament as follows:

I. Before 1200 B.C. (?)

1. Poems: Gen. 4:23 f.; Ex. 15:21; 17:16 (?); Num. 10:35 f. (?); 21:1. (?); 21:17 f.; 21:27-30 (?).
2. Laws: the "J decalogue," the Canaanitic Civil Code, the nomadi Participial Code.

II. 1200-1000 B.C.

1. Poems: Gen. 9:25-27; Josh. 10:12b-13a; Judg. 5; 14:14, 18; 15:16; I Sam. 18:7 = 21:11b (H. 21:12b) = 29:5; II Sam. 1:18-27; 3:33 f.
2. The sources of S, J, E, and of the ancient parts of Judges.

III. 1000-900 B.C.

1. Poems: Gen. 49 (and perhaps other patriarchal blessings in Gen.); Num. 24:3-9, 15-19; II Sam. 20:1; I Kings 8:12 f. [LXX] (?); Ps. 24:7-10. Anthologies: The Book of Song (Jashar or the Upright in the received text); The Book of the Wars of Jehovah.
2. Prose: S, parts of Judges, the early source of Samuel (written by Ahimaaz?), parts of the annals of Solomon and of the Jerusalem Temple chronicle.

IV. 900-722 B.C. Ephraimitic (Northern Kingdom).

  1. Poetry: Num. 23:7-10, 18-24; Deut. 33; Ps. 45.
  2. Narratives: The History of the Kings of Israel, the stories of Elijah and Elisha, the E document.
  3. Laws: Deut. 27:16-25.
  4. Prophetic oracles: Amos and Hosea.

V. 900-700 B.C. Judean (Southern Kingdom).

  1. Narratives: the J document, parts of the History of the Kings of Judah and of the Temple chronicle.
  2. Prophetic oracles: Isaiah (738-700) and Micah (*ca.* 722).

VI. 700-600 B.C.

  1. Poems: Nahum's ode (Nah. 1:10 ff.); Num. 12:6-8.
  2. Narratives: JE, parts of the late sources in Samuel; parts of the History of the Kings of Judah and of the Temple chronicle; the first edition of Kings (*ca.* 600).
  3. Prophetic oracles: Jeremiah (626-585), Zephaniah, Habakkuk. The Deuteronomic Code found in 621.
  4. Philanthropic legislation in Ex. 22-23. The Ten Commandments.
  5. Wisdom: Earliest parts of Proverbs (chs. 25-27, etc.), some psalms (104, etc.), Job (*ca.* 600).

VII. 600-500 B.C.

  1. Poetry: Lamentations. Some psalms, and parts of Proverbs.
  2. Narrative: the Deuteronomistic edition of the books from Genesis to Kings (R^D).
  3. Laws: the Holiness Code (Lev. 17-26).
  4. Prophetic oracles: Ezekiel, the Second Isaiah (Is. 40-55), Haggai, Zechar. 1-8, Mic. 6:1-7:6.

VIII. 500-400 B.C.

  1. Poetry: Deut. 32; Ex. 15:1-18. Some psalms and parts of Proverbs.
  2. Narrative: the Memoirs of Nehemiah; Ruth.
  3. The Priestly Code (P). Final edition of the Covenant Code. Canonization of the Pentateuch about 400 B.C.
  4. Prophetic oracles: Is. 56-66, Obadiah, Malachi. Parts of the books of Isaiah and Jeremiah.

IX. 400-300 B.C.

  1. Poetry: a large part of Psalms and Proverbs; Job 32-37; Nah. 1:1-9; Hab. 3; I Sam. 2:1-10.
  2. Narrative: Jonah; some sources of the Chronicler in Ezra-Nehemiah (?).
  3. Prophetic and apocalyptic oracles: Joel; parts of Isaiah, Jeremiah, and of the book of the Minor Prophets.

X. 300-200 B.C.

1. Poetry: Song of Songs; parts of Psalms and Prov.
2. Narrative: Chronicles and parts of Ezra-Nehemiah. Additions to Joshua-Kings.
3. Apocalyptic oracles: Is. 24-27; Zech. 9-14; and other parts of the four prophetic books (Is., Jer., Ez., the Twelve), canonized (with Josh.-Kings) about 200 B.C.

XI. 200-100 B.C.

1. Poetry: Maccabean (44; 74; 79; 83, etc.) and Hasmonean (2; 110, etc.) Psalms, and final edition of the Psalter.
2. Wisdom: Ben Sira's Ecclesiasticus (180 B.C.), Ecclesiastes (*ca.* 150 B.C.), and perhaps Wisdom of Solomon (*ca.* 100 ?).
3. Narrative: Dan. 1-6, Judith, Esther, and perhaps Tobit. The Greek Ezra (I Esdras). I Maccabees.
4. Apocalyptic: Daniel 7-12.

It appears from this table that the several literary genres (*Gattungen*) reach their highest level of perfection at the very beginning, in the first surviving specimens of their category: the earliest code of civil legislation, the martial odes of Miriam (Ex. 15:21) and Deborah (Judg. 5), the earliest psalms and wisdom literature, David's lament over Saul and Jonathan (II Sam. 1:18-27), the biography of David written perhaps by Ahimaaz (notably II Sam. 9-20). The oracles of Amos are supreme among those of the reforming prophets, the Second Isaiah is the greatest among the dreamers of the restoration of Israel, Daniel's visions of the end of the world were never surpassed. The J document towers over E, as the Priestly author over the Chronicler, the Deuteronomist (D) over his imitators, and the story of Elijah over those of Elisha and Jonah. One would say that in each category, the greatest masterpieces sprung perfect, at the very beginning, like Athena from the head of Zeus, without a period of laborious gestation.

That there was such a preparatory period we may take for granted, but we are no less in the dark about it than about the antecedents of the magnificent sculpture and painting of the Old Kingdom in Egypt. The origin of all living institutions is inevitably hidden from us by the mists of time. Although the birth of Hebrew literature lies beyond the scope of historical research, some scholars in recent years have searched for roots of the various literary forms represented in the Old Testament in the activity of the people, investigating their connections with practical life (*Sitz im Leben*) and their development from preliterary oral expressions.[7]

---

[7] The four best summaries of the study of the Old Testament from this point of view are: H. Gunkel, in Die Kultur der Gegenwart I, VII: *Die Orientalischen Literaturen*, pp. 51-102. Berlin and Leipzig, 1906. O. Eissfeldt, *Einleitung in das Alte Testament*, pp. 8-168. Tübingen, 1934. J. Hempel, "The Forms of Oral Tradition"

Since this study must rely entirely on inferences from the extant writings preserved in the Old Testament and on parallels in other literatures, its results remain conjectural, except for some rather obvious generalities. The preceding table, embodying the results of literary criticism, may, however, be supplemented with a classification of the Hebrew literary genres, with a few hints about their birth and growth, illustrated with typical examples. We may group the Old Testament writings under the following headings: songs, narratives, laws, oracles and prayers, wisdom.

I. Songs

1. Private songs. From the earliest times, the events heightening the emotions of an individual were celebrated in songs. We may assume that lovers expressed their emotions in verse from time immemorial. The Song of Songs, albeit a sophisticated and late anthology prepared by very able literary men, retains echoes of genuine folk love poetry, partly intense erotic effusions during the courtship (1:2-4; 2:8-14; 4:8-11), partly songs for the wedding festivities (3:6-11; 6:13-7:5 [H. 7:1-6]). A pre-exilic wedding song in honor of a king has accidentally been preserved in the Psalter (Ps. 45). At banquets for weddings or other occasions, one of the guests might propose riddles in verse (Judg. 14:14, 18), instrumental music was provided (Am. 6:4-6; Is. 5:12), and songs were sung on the theme familiar in Egyptian, Greek, and Roman banquet songs, "Let us eat and drink, for to-morrow we die!" (Is. 22:13; cf. Wisd. of Sol. 2:6-9). A member of the family departing on a journey was sped on his way "with mirth, and with songs, with tabret, and with harp" (Gen. 31:27).

Good wishes accompanied the bride leaving her father's house (Gen. 24:60), and she was received jubilantly by the bridegroom with appropriate words (cf. Gen. 2:23); friends invoked blessings on the newlyweds (Ruth 4:11 f.). The birth of a son was acclaimed by the attending women (Gen. 35:17; I Sam. 4:20); the mother's words at that time often served to name the child (Gen. 4:1; 29:32-35; 30:18-20, 23 f.; 35:18; I Sam. 4:21a, 22; cf. Gen. 30:5-13). Out of the blessings which fathers bestowed on their sons (Gen. 27:27-29, 39 f., in verse) there arose the literary blessings of whole nations, predicting their fortunes—after the event. They are either in the form of divine oracles (Gen. 16:11 f.; 25:23, and the oracles of Balaam in Num. 23-24) or in the form of a father blessing his offspring (Noah: Gen. 9:25-27; Jacob: Gen. 49; cf. the blessing of Moses in Deut. 33).

The opposite of the love song, the taunt song, originated in the mockeries of street urchins (such as in II Kings 2:23) and is exemplified but

---

and "The Contents of the Literature" in *Record and Revelation*, edited by H. W. Robinson, pp. 28-73. A. Weiser, *Einleitung in das Alte Testament*, pp. 9-59. Stuttgart, 1939. Monographs on special topics will be mentioned in later parts of this book.

once (Is. 23:16). From such personal poetic invective developed the political taunt song, in which a nation is personified as a woman of ill repute: the classical example is Is. 47 (see also Nah. 3:4 f.; Is. 37:22-29; Ez. 16 and 23).

Similarly the funeral lament, originating in the desperate cry of one bereaved (as in II Sam. 18:33 [Hebr. 19:1]), became an elegy (II Sam. 1:18-27); eventually the personal dirge was applied to a whole nation (Am. 5:2 and Lam. 1-4), sometimes with a sarcastic import (Is. 14:4-21; 23:2-4; Ez. 27).

2. *Communal songs.* A. Joyful tribal songs celebrated the two basic events in the life of nomadic clans: the provision of the means of sustenance and success in warlike undertakings. Two ancient Bedouin poems commemorated respectively the digging of a well (Num. 21:17 f., perhaps a work song) and the slaying of a foe in an avenging raid (Gen. 4:23 f.). The first type, the work song, apparently remained in its popular preliterary stage, for no other examples are preserved in Hebrew literature; but the second developed into an important literary genre. The spontaneous, enthusiastic song of triumph extolled either the deity (Ex. 15:21) or the leader (I Sam. 18:7 = 21:11b [H. 21:12b] = 29:5): both these little poems were sung antiphonally by women immediately after the victory (cf. Judg. 11:34 and I Sam. 18:6). A Philistine poem of the first type, with five rhymes in *-enu*, is preserved in Judg. 16:23 f.:

Our god has given into our hand / Samson our enemy;
And the devastator of our land / And the man who multiplied our slain.

The battle song of Joshua (Josh. 10:12b-13a), which may be incomplete, belongs perhaps to the first type.

Both the praise of the deity and the eulogy of the leader became standard compositions and tended to be dissociated more and more from the battlefield in less warlike and more civilized times. The Song of Miriam (Ex. 15:21) is the earliest example of a hymn to God in the Old Testament; and the only one which may be regarded as a folk song. The triumphal ode of Deborah (Judg. 5) is the classical example of a paean of victory in praise of Jehovah; that of Nahum (Nah. 1:10-3:19), equally classic, is less concerned with divine intervention in the battle (cf. 2:13 [H. 2:14]) than with the exultation over the fall of Nineveh, and is not a hymn. Both of them are masterpieces composed by inspired poets, exhibiting consummate literary art; neither can be classed as folk poetry.

With few exceptions, such as a late imitation of Miriam's ringing paean (Ex. 15:1-18; cf. Deut. 32; 33:1-5, 26-29), it is only in the Maccabean period that God is again praised for his military triumphs in the past (Pss. 44:1-3 [H. 44:2-4]; 80:8 f. [H. 80:9 f.]) or in the present (Pss. 47; 48; 68; 118; 124; 144). In general, however, the postexilic hymns develop the theme so majestically expressed by the seraphim in Isaiah's vision, "Holy, holy, holy is Jehovah Militant; his glory is the fullness of the whole earth" (Is. 6:3). God is praised for the creation of the world (Ps. 104; cf. Pss. 19:1-6 [H. 19:1-7]; 24:1 f.; 95), for his majestic appearance in the storm (Ps. 18 [= II Sam. 22]; cf. Pss. 97; 135), for covering the earth with vegetation (65; 147), for creating (33) and giving dominion to man (8), and for ruling over all that exists (47; 93; 96-99) in justice and mercy (103; 111; 117). In more nationalistic hymns, Jehovah is praised for his past deeds in Israel's behalf (105; 135; 136). Hymns in a similar vein appear already in the Second Isaiah (Is. 42:10-13; 44:23) and much later in I Sam. 2:1-10; Hab. 3; Nah. 1:1-9; Ecclus. 42:15-43:33; Jth. 16; Tob. 13; Luke 1:46-55, 68-79.

It has been noted that the eulogy of a leader originated, like the hymn to God, in victory songs; it similarly lost eventually its original connection with war. Incidentally, as late an author as Ben Sira (*ca.* 180 B.C.) seems to be conscious of the common ancestry of the hymn and the panegyric, for there is in his mind a close relation between his hymn to God (Ecclus. 42:15-43:33) and his panegyric of the fathers of old (44-50) which follows immediately.

The only folk song in praise of a victorious leader, as we have seen, is that in honor of David (I Sam. 18:7, etc.) and no poetic encomium appears in classical Hebrew literature, although traces of this literary type may be detected in David's elegy over Saul and Jonathan (II Sam. 1:18-27) and in a pre-exilic epithalamium in honor of a king (Ps. 45); perhaps also in II Sam. 14:17, 20. In later Hebrew literature, however, we have a number of pious eulogies in honor of kings (Pss. 20 and 21; cf. 72; 89:19-52 [H. 89:20-53]; 132 [prayers for the king]; 101 [a confession of a king]). In two cases the name of the king is concealed in acrostics: Simon Maccabeus (Ps. 110, commemorating his installation as high priest in 141 B.C.) and Alexander Janneus (Ps. 2, composed presumably on the occasion of his accession and his marriage to Alexandra in 103 B.C.). Another poetic panegyric of Simon, found in I Macc. 14:4-15, was obviously composed later in his lifetime if not after his death. A poetic eulogy of Judas Maccabeus is found in I Macc. 3:1-9. Some of the "royal psalms" just enumerated were interpreted by the Jews with reference to the coming scion of David, the Messiah; Pss. 2, 45 and 110 are referred to the Christ in the Epistle to the Hebrews and elsewhere in the New Testament, and G. Dahl (JBL 57 [1938] 10-12) regards Pss. 2, 45, and many others as unquestionably intended by their writers as Messianic prophecies. Although these songs may have been composed in honor of earthly kings (as the present writer believes), such royal panegyrics inspired the beautiful poetic eulogies composed unmistakably in praise of the coming Davidic Messiah (Jer. 23:5 f.; Is. 9:2-7 [H. 9:1-6]; 11:1-9; Mic. 4:14-5:2 [H. 5:1-3]; Zech. 9:9).

In addition to such Messianic prophecies, the eulogy of a leader inspired the panegyrics in honor of long-dead heroes, usually consisting of a series of individual eulogies: the most famous of such compositions is the long poem of Ben Sira (Ecclus. 44-49) praising "the fathers of old" from Adam to Nehemiah, and concluding with the eulogy of Simon, the contemporary high priest (Ecclus. 50). This poem probably inspired similar compositions in verse (Wisd. of Sol. 10) and prose, both Jewish (I Macc. 2:49-64; III Macc. 6:4-8) and Christian (Hebr. 11, Clement of Rome's Epistle to the Corinthians 5 [Christian heroes]). In contrast with such laudatory reminiscences of Israel's history, the other compendiums in prose (Ez. 20; cf. Clement to the Cor. 4) or poetry (Pss. 78; 106; 107) are bitter denunciations of Israel's repeated apostasies, or, as we have seen, hymns to God for his mighty deeds in behalf of the nation (Pss. 105; 135; 136).

B. Not only glad occasions, such as the digging of a well or a victory, were celebrated in song, but also national tragedies. Corresponding to the elegy for the death of an individual (which, as we have seen, became also national in scope), the national dirge bewails serious military reverses or national ruin. Such a lament, which is not technically an elegy, was composed by a Moabite when the Arabs drove his people out of their land (Is. 15-16, where the original poem has been changed into a denunciation of Moab). While this pathetic dirge is purely secular, the laments over the plight of the Jews during the persecutions of Antiochus Epiphanes in 168-165 b.c. are intensely religious (Pss. 44; 74; 78; 83; cf. 12; 28; 36; 60 [= 108]; 80; 85; 102 [in part]; 108; 123), as also the complaints of persons sick unto death (Pss. 6; 13; 22; 31; 38; 42; 55; 69; 88; 102; 144; Is. 38:10-20); see also the Book of Lamentations.

II. Narratives

Our sharp distinction between story and history, fancy and fact, seems meaningless when applied to the body of Old Testament narratives which present all the gradations between pure fiction (as in the stories about Adam, Noah, and Samson) and genuine history (as in the ancient biography of David and in the Memoirs of Nehemiah). Only in the recital of events on the part of an eyewitness (unless he be lying as in I Sam. 22:10a and II Sam. 1:7-10) may exact historicity be expected in the Old Testament narratives. Their credibility decreases in the ratio of their distance in time from the narrator.[8]

[8] Since we are concerned here primarily with folk narratives, the historical literature will not be considered in detail. The reader may be referred to the analysis of the historical books in parts II, III, and V of this volume and to the excellent summary of G. F. Moore in *Encycl. Bibl.* (1901) II, 2075-2094.

With the exception of the histories (the biography of David, the histories of the kings of Judah and Israel, and the Memoirs of Nehemiah), pseudo histories (the Priestly Code and the Chronicler), and short stories (Ruth, Jonah, Daniel, Esther), which are the work of writers relying chiefly on personal observation, eyewitness accounts, written sources, or merely their own imagination, the bulk of the narratives in the Old Testament (Gen.-I Sam.) is a rewriting of popular traditions and tales long transmitted orally. And this explains the obliteration of the line between reality and imagination in these stories. What holds a simple audience of Bedouins, shepherds, or peasants spellbound in listening to a tale is interest in the plot, curiosity as to the denouement, romantic atmosphere, conscious or unconscious art (as in the Andersen and Grimm fairy tales, respectively), but not in the least the historical accuracy. Under the spell of a good reciter, whether professional or amateur, the listeners forget the dismal familiar world of reality and live in the imaginary world of make-believe, like the audience in a theater or cinema witnessing the action of a powerful drama.

The themes of the tales span the innumerable situations in real or imaginary life. But those which have survived because they attained a great popularity have in common their power to kindle the imagination, to transfer the hearers into a romantic world, into a remote past brought to life by fancy—either out of some scanty memories of actual events or out of the storehouse of a vivid Oriental imagination.

The tribal memory of Israel does not go beyond Moses (except for Simeon and Levi's attack on Shechem, Gen. 34), but even the most historical stories from Moses to David (preserved in J and in the old source of Judg. and I Sam.) are not accurate in all details, as can be seen by comparing the two accounts of the killing of Sisera: the contemporary one (Judg. 5:24-27) and the later one (4:17-21). Moses, Joshua, Gideon, Samuel, David, Solomon, Elijah, Elisha, and other great personalities of Israel's heroic past tend to become legendary characters in popular tales even before the Jewish Church transformed them into saints, high ecclesiastics or, on the contrary (as in the cases of Eli and Saul), into reprobates. The early legends tend to be charming idyls (like the stories of the birth of Moses in Ex. 2:1-10, of Samuel in I Sam. 1, and of Saul's meeting with Samuel in I Sam. 9), tales of warlike exploits (David and Goliath, I Sam. 17), or accounts of miracles (the stories of Elijah and particularly of Elisha). The later Biblical ones have a much more pronounced ethical and religious flavor.[9]

The stories lacking all historical basis fall into two groups: stories giving

[9] The rabbinical legends about Biblical characters, collected by L. Ginzberg in his monumental work, *The Legends of the Jews* (7 vols., Philadelphia, 1913-1938), not seldom contain secular folklore, like the early Biblical legends.

a popular explanation of certain natural (myths) or historic phenomena (sagas and legends) or having the purpose to teach a moral (fables and parables); and stories told for their own sake (fairy tales and novels). Since the first group of stories has a didactic purpose, it may well be considered later within the category of wisdom literature.

Like the authors of the *Arabian Nights*, Hebrew storytellers have derived anecdotes and plots from the vast reservoir of Oriental folklore not only for fictitious tales but also for legends. The motif of the infant threatened or abandoned at birth, rescued, and eventually becoming a great leader, utilized in the birth legend of Moses (Ex. 2:1-10), [10] appears in the birth stories of Sargon of Akkad, Krishna, Romulus and Remus, Perseus, Cyrus the Great (Herodotus 1:108-113), Augustus (Suetonius, *Augustus* 94), and others. Other common folkloristic motifs appear in the story of Potiphar's wife (Gen. 39:7-20; cf. the Egyptian Tale of the Two Brothers [A. Erman, *The Literature of the Ancient Egyptians,* pp. 150 ff. London, 1927]), in the Indian tale of the Judgment of Solomon (I Kings 3:16-27), in the "fish stories" in Jonah and Tobit, and in other tales in which animals (Num. 22:22-34; I Kings 17:6), plants (Jonah 4:6), or inanimate objects (I Kings 17:13-16; II Kings 4:1-7) miraculously save a man's life. It appears from these examples that the supernatural is frequently, but not always, the *pièce de résistance* in Oriental fiction.

Out of single stories utilizing such materials, the Hebrew storytellers created cycles of tales or novels. Some, like the Joseph stories (Gen. 37; 39-48; 50), were intended for a cultivated audience. Others, like the Samson stories (Judg. 13-16), were recited originally to rustic listeners entranced by the superhuman deeds of the hero, whose coarse practical jokes remind us of the pranks of Till Eulenspiegel and Peer Gynt.

Eventually outstanding literary men wove the folk tales, sagas, and legends into the great national epics recounting the heroic age of ancient Israel—the J and E documents in Genesis-Judges. Later the short story, with or without a moral, flowered into a literary art: some tales are pseudo-historical (Ruth, Esther, Judith, Susanna, Bel and the Dragon, Achikar, The Three Pages at the Court of Darius [I Esd. 3:1-5:6]), and others frankly supernatural (Job 1-2 + 42.10b-17, Jonah, Dan., Tob., III Macc.).

III. Laws

The notion of law (i.e., right and wrong as determined by the community) is as early as organized human societies. No group (family, clan, tribe, or nation) can survive unless the rights of the members are mutually respected—at least when they do not conflict with the welfare of the

---

[10] Cf. E. Meyer, *Die Israeliten und ihre Nachbarstämme,* pp. 46 f. (Halle, 1906); S. Smith, *Early History of Assyria,* p. 82 (London, 1928).

group, which is always paramount. *Salus populi suprema lex esto* (Cicero, *De legibus* 3:3, 8), is a universal principle well illustrated in the story of Achan (Josh. 7). Law enforcement is essential to the self-preservation of the group.

Among the nomadic ancestors of the tribes of Israel, as among the Arabian and Syrian Bedouins in general, the sense of tribal solidarity was far more intense than among rural or urban populations. While for us the nation is an ideal, an abstraction, for them the tribe was the abiding reality. The individuals are like the leaves, the group is the tree without which they cannot live. Until God placed a sign on him, Cain, driven out from his group to become a fugitive and a wanderer, expected to be assassinated on sight (Gen. 4:13-15).

The integrity of the clan or tribe was safeguarded by a set of ancestral customs and institutions which, no matter how irrational, could not be violated with impunity. They were no more controversial than the dictates of fashion for modern ladies. Even after the Israelites attained a higher stage of civilization in Canaan, the strongest condemnation for an action was still, "It is not so done in Israel" (II Sam. 13:12; cf. Gen. 29:26 and 34:7). Exactly so, a breach of etiquette is unanswerably stigmatized with the words, "It is not so done in polite society."

Custom ruled inflexibly the whole of human conduct, embracing norms which we distinguish as social, legal, ethical, and religious. The reason is obvious. The clan or tribe is an organism, nay, it is a corporate personality. As the members of a body, so the tribal god and the human members of the group must act in harmony, working together in their several capacities to further the common good. Innumerable evil actions may harm the community and innumerable good ones may benefit it, but a single objective is dominant—the welfare of the group. Actions impairing the group's means of subsistence, its social cohesion, and its military strength, are just as detrimental as offenses against the tribal god, upon whose full collaboration the very existence of the group was thought to depend. This may explain the fact that not only in Israel, but in Egypt, Babylonia, and elsewhere codes of law were regarded as divinely promulgated; but it hardly justifies the statement often made that custom has a religious origin. Religion is but one of the elements in early custom.

Three immemorial Bedouin customs, which survived among the Israelites after their settlement in Canaan, illustrate the failure to discriminate between religious, ethical, and legal obligations. Blood revenge is at the same time a sacrifice to placate an angry deity one of whose worshipers has been slain (cf. II Sam. 21:1-9), a moral obligation of the kinsmen to appease the deceased, whose blood cries from the ground until he is revenged (Gen. 4:10), and a primitive notion of punitive justice. The duty of hospitality has social, ethical, and religious implications. Likewise circumcision, which, being originally a rite of initiation by which adolescents became full-fledged members of the clan, was a sacrifice to the tribal deity (cf. Ex. 4:24-26) as well as the mark of a youth's assumption of the moral and social obligations involved in membership within the clan.

Nothing could illustrate better the iron rule of custom and its embracing scope than war. It is then that the solidarity between the members of the tribe, and between the tribe and its god, is most in evidence: it becomes a sacred bond. The fighters must be in a state of ritual purity lest the god be irritated, must be no less devoted to fellow tribesmen than those Benjamites who fought to the last ditch in defense of some rascals in their midst (Judg. 19-21), and must induce their god to join them in battle, as Jehovah did at Megiddo (Judg. 5). Since the outcome of a battle was often determined by a panic (which sometimes resulted from fear of the god of the enemy; cf. I Sam. 4:7 and II Kings 3:27), it was natural, in critical situations, to attribute the victory to the tribal god.

Eventually separate civil, ritual, and ethical codes of law emerged out of tribal customs. But the Israelites, who long retained their Bedouin background after settling in Canaan, continued to join these distinct categories in their legislation (as can be seen in the Covenant Code [Ex. 20:22-23:19], in Deut., and elsewhere), although the Canaanites, from whom they derived some of their laws, separated sharply religious and civil legislation (as the Babylonians before them).

Whether the Israelites in the desert continued to be ruled by ancestral custom only or whether Moses introduced among them the rudiments of court procedure (Ex. 18:13-26) and legislation must remain uncertain. The only code of law which could conceivably be nomadic in origin is the code with a participial formulation (Ex. 21:12, 15-17; 22:19 [H. 22:18]; Lev. 20:10-13; the other laws with this formulation are late). If Moses codified these laws, he merely formulated immemorial tribal customs which decreed the death penalty for criminal actions which in various ways seriously impaired the social cohesion of family and tribe.

Except for such laws as these and perhaps a few others, the Old Testament codes have little connection with tribal customs in the desert. The early codes were adopted, with little change, from the Canaanites; the later ones are dominated by religious and ethical ideals (for details, see Part II, Chap. VII).

The *torah*, or instruction of the priest (cf. J. Begrich in Beih. ZAW 66, pp. 63-88. Berlin, 1936), though usually derived from immemorial custom and eventually codified (as in Lev. 17-26), should not be identified with law as such. It is true that the Jews, beginning with Deuteronomy, did not keep the categories of civil and ritual prescriptions sharply distinct; but the reforming prophets were fully aware of the line of demarcation between them. A good example of priestly torah is given by Haggai in 2:13 f.

IV. Oracles and Prayers

In its earliest stages, religious literature is only of two types: communications of the deity to man (oracles), and human discourse with the deity (prayers). Both evolved from oral communications into written compositions. From the prophetic oracle eventually developed the written sermon and apocalyptic vision (and inspired scripture in general); from prayer, the devotional psalms.

1. Oracles. The three methods by which the deity could communicate with mortals, according to I Sam. 28:6, are dreams, urim (the priestly oracle), and the prophetic utterance. A fourth method, omens interpreted by professional diviners, played an insignificant role in Israel. Divination, as also the legendary stories of the visible appearance of the deity or its angel to ancient personages, may be disregarded here. Since dreams and visions belong to prophetic inspiration, we may say that God's words reached men only through the priestly and the prophetic oracle.

In literary history the primitive oracular response to an inquiry, given by a priest after drawing and interpreting the sacred lots in an ark or box (see W. R. Arnold, *Ephod and Ark,* Cambridge, Mass., 1917; cf. his summary in JBL 42 [1923] 10-14), has no importance whatsoever. A purely mechanical method for deciding between two alternatives (like "flipping a coin") it became obsolete in the official circles of North Israel before the middle of the ninth century, surviving only among superstitious peasants (Jer. 3:16). The Israelites seem to have realized that no machine can be a substitute for the human mind in a difficult choice between two alternatives. The living word of an inspired man superseded the clumsy chance decision by lots and eventually the prophetic revelation achieved religious nobility and literary brilliance.

The earliest record of a prophetic oracle (at Byblos in Phoenicia) is contained in the Egyptian story of Wen-Amon, dating from about 1100 B.C. (A. Erman, *The Literature of the Ancient Egyptians,* p. 177): "the god seized one of his [Zakar-Baal's] pages and made him frenzied, and he said, 'Bring the god hither!' . . ." In the ecstatic trance the prophet believed that the deity or its spirit entered physically into him. In Israel, the prophets were at first mere religious enthusiasts given to emotional paroxysms (I Sam. 10:5 f., 10; 19:20-24), like the modern dervishes. Except for sporadic references to prophetic oracles in the time of Saul (I Sam. 28:6, 15) and David (II Sam. 12), it is only in North Israel, about the middle of the ninth century during the reign of Ahab, that the prophets became articulate either as givers of oracular responses to kings

(I Kings 22:5-28) or, in the case of Elijah and Elisha, as champions and agents of Jehovah.

With Amos (*ca.* 750), the first of the reforming prophets, the word of Jehovah uttered through the lips of inspired men (cf. Am. 3:8) attained such literary distinction and abiding significance that it was preserved in written form. Possibly already Isaiah, and certainly Jeremiah, edited their utterances in a book, and eventually, beginning with Ezekiel and particularly the Second Isaiah, prophecy in the sixth century ceased to be oral and became a written composition, eventually consisting merely of apocalyptic dreams issued anonymously or under a famous nom de plume. Before prophecy had descended to the level of predictions and visions of Messianic and eschatological triumphs of the Jews over the pagans, the books recording the superb fulminations of the eighth century prophets had inspired the composition of the prophetic oracle of Moses —the Deuteronomic Code found in the Temple in 621—destined to be received as the first divine book and consequently the nucleus of the Scriptures constituting the Hebrew Bible. Thus the notion that the word of a prophet was divinely inspired, was eventually extended to poems, national epics, histories, myths, legends, and tales; and every word of the Old Testament was regarded as divinely revealed.

In conclusion, the conception of the word of God evolved through the centuries. At first it was conceived naïvely as the utterance of the deity appearing visibly to a mortal (in the myths and legends of S and J) or conveyed to them through dreams and angels (in E); exceptionally God spoke through the lips of a man like Balaam, or revealed the "ten words," which either Moses (Ex. 34:28, J) or God's own finger (Ex. 31:18, E) wrote on two tables of stone. In the priestly oracle obtained by means of the drawing of lots and in the prophetic oracle, given through inspiration, the word of God was still oral. But with the end of prophecy soon after 400 B.C., the word of God ceased to be spoken and was fixed for all time in the canonical Scriptures, of which the first was the Book of Moses found in the Temple in 621.

2. *Prayers.* We may surmise that at first the words addressed to the deity were personal petitions for deliverance from present (cf. I Sam. 1:10) or future (cf. II Sam. 15:31) misfortune, for divine help in some undertaking (cf. Judg. 16:28), or for the welfare of another (cf. II Sam. 12:16). Presumably national petitions, offered by an individual (cf. Am. 7:2, 5; Jer. 14) or exceptionally by the community (rare in early writings: cf. perhaps Judg. 20:26), also originated in remote antiquity. The two other types of prayer, confessions of sin following repentance (cf. II Sam. 24:10) and expressions of gratitude for divine help (cf. Gen. 32:9 f. [H. 32:10 f.], introducing a petition), are clearly later. It is conceivable that the confession of sins originated in laments of individuals stricken

with serious illness (cf. Is. 38:10-20 and particularly Ps. 51), and that the expression of gratitude is merely a form of a hymn of praise such as Ex. 15:21 and Judg. 5.

Before 600 B.C., in the golden period of Hebrew literature, prayers did not attain the literary brilliance of laments and hymns (for which see above, I). The earliest example of a literary prayer, noble in diction and thought, is that of Solomon (I Kings 8:23-53, omitting the later additions in 8:23 f., 40-52), dating from about 600 B.C. The Confessions of Jeremiah gave to postexilic prayers, notably those included in the Psalter, an inwardness, a depth, a sense of communion with God previously unknown. But these devout addresses to God seldom, if ever, attain the rank of great literature.

V. Wisdom

Ordinarily Biblical scholars understand by "wisdom" (Hebrew *hokh-mâh*) the art of living: "Wisdom is a property of the soul or . . . a skill shaping the very thought which yields the right result" (J. Pedersen, *Israel, Its Life and Culture*, p. 127. London, 1926). In reality it would seem that, like our word "philosophy," wisdom had not only a practical, but also a theoretical connotation. It is mental skill in solving the problems of the universe as well as those of daily life. Essentially intellectual in the early stages, it is the prerogative of scholars as well as of a father giving sound counsel to his son. Solomon's wisdom ranges from clever diplomacy (I Kings 5:12 [H. 5:26]) and judicial brilliance (3:28) to the solution of riddles (10:1-4) and encyclopedic knowledge, including exhaustive information in botany and zoology (4:29-34 [H. 5:9-14]). And in the Old Testament wisdom denotes the innate shrewdness of intelligent women (Judg. 5:29; II Sam. 14:2; 20:16) or royal ministers (Gen. 41:33); the professional skill of craftsmen (Ex. 28:3; Is. 40:20), pilots (Ez. 27:8), wailers (Jer. 9:17 [H. 9:16]), and snake charmers (Ps. 58:5 [H. 58:6]); the amazing instincts of small animals (Prov. 30:24-28); religion (Prov. 9:10; Job 28:28), morality (Prov. 4:11; 8:13; 14:16; 29:3), and the Law of Moses (Deut. 4:6; Ezra 7:25); the mysterious plan of the cosmos (Job. 28:1-27; cf. Prov. 3:19 f.; 30:2-4). The theoretical and the practical aspects appear in personified Wisdom: she was present at the creation of the world (Prov. 8:22-31) and now teaches men how to be upright and successful (8:11-21).

1. Theoretical wisdom. The intellectual curiosity which gave rise to speculations about nature, man, and God is not characteristic of primitive man. Such problems and their solutions are not essential to human existence, nor even to human happiness, and the great majority of persons living today, lacking the inclination and the leisure for philosophical re-

flection, are not in the least aware of being deprived of an essential element for a useful and happy life.

Before the end of the monarchy in 586 B.C. the Israelites and Judeans,
to judge from available evidence, disclosed no interest in theoretical
questions universal in scope. Their intellectual curiosity was confined to
the origins of their nation and its institutions. The preceding summary
survey indicates that before 586 "wisdom" among the Israelites was conceived as the art of living and had no philosophical connotation, as in
Job. When the Deuteronomic Code was written (a few years before 621),
the speculations of the sages about the origin of the world were still
beyond the mental horizon of the authors. But about 450 B.C. the authors
of the Priestly Code not only incorporated the tenets of theoretical wisdom
in their work, but gave them such prominence that the creation of heaven
and earth (Gen. 1) became the overture of the work.

Theoretical wisdom has two aspects: it answers questions universal in
scope, at first through myths and then through speculation, or it explains
the origin of Israelitic customs and institutions, through sagas and
legends.[11]

A. Philosophical myths and speculation. The solutions of philosophical
problems presented in pre-exilic Old Testament writings originated among
the Egyptians (Ps. 104) or the Edomites (the early myths in Gen. 2-11,
collected in the S document; Pss. 88 and 89; Prov. 30:1-31:9; Job; all supplied with Jewish annotations). Characteristically these two nations were
regarded by the Israelites as those in which wisdom flourished particularly (I Kings 4:30 f. [H. 5:10 f.]; for the Edomites, cf. Obad. 8 and Jer.
49:7).

The Edomitic sages, from the ancient reciters of the folk myths in Gen.
2-11 to the philosophical editor of the S document and the brilliant author
of the Book of Job, were pessimistic and agnostic. The myths explain the
miserable condition of man on this earth as the result of the curses of an
unfriendly deity, jealous of its own prerogatives. The author of the Book
of Job regards the Creator as utterly indifferent to man's struggles and
pains and as too mysteriously transcendent to be understood by mortals.
Finally Ecclesiastes, the first unorthodox Jewish philosopher, after losing
all his illusions, drew the ultimate conclusions from the premises of Job
and, under the influence of Greek thought, became a skeptic. The under-

---

[11] I am of course aware of the usual classification of myths, sagas, and legends as
folk tales. H. Gunkel, for instance, defines a myth as a narrative in which the characters are gods, while in a saga they are human beings. This distinction is not only
superficial and often elusive (for divine beings may play a secondary role in myths
and a primary role in sagas and legends), but it ignores the essential difference between tales told merely for entertainment (which have been considered under II,
above) and tales that explain puzzling natural or historical facts (which are primitive
philosophy).

lying doctrine of this Edomitic philosophy, the conviction that God is the creator and upholder of all that exists, seems to be Egyptian in origin (cf. Ps. 104, based on Ikhnaton's Hymn to Aton): before 2000 B.C. the author of the Admonitions for King Merikere had said, "He [God] made heaven and earth. . . ." It was not until about 540 B.C. that the Second Isaiah, under the influence of Job, gave currency to this doctrine among the Jews.

The Babylonian myth of creation, according to which the god Marduk slew the dragon Tiâmat and out of the two halves of her body formed heaven and earth, is occasionally referred to in Job, Ps. 104, and later poetical writings. Tiâmat is called Rahab (Job. 9:13; 26:12; Ps. 89:10 [H. 89:11]; Is. 51:9 f.; Ecclus. 43:23), Leviathan (Ps. 74:13 f.; Is. 27:1; cf. Job 3:8; 41:1 ff. [H. 40:25 ff.]; Ps. 104:26), or the dragon (Job 7:12; Is. 27:1; 51:9; Ez. 29:3 ff.; 32:2 ff.). Needless to say, such mythological allusions were mere figures of speech, like our conversational references to Mars, Venus, and the Elysian Fields.

B. Sagas and legends. Among the sagas of the Book of Genesis (collected in the S, J, E, and P documents) some have the purpose of explaining certain facts in the later history of Israel which were obscure or disconcerting. In technical language such sagas are called etiological. The following types have been distinguished. *Ethnic sagas,* explaining the later vicissitudes or characteristics of a people, as the subjection of Canaan to Israelites and Philistines (Gen. 9:20-27), the Bedouin traits of the Ishmaelites (16:11 f.; 21:8-21) and of the Kenites (4:1-15). *Historical sagas,* depicting actual tribal events as adventures of ancient heroes, as the ill-fated attack of Simeon and Levi on Shechem (34; cf. 49:5-7) and the triumph of the Israelites over the Edomites in the time of David (25:21-34; 27). *Juridical sagas,* tracing Israel's right to certain wells (21:22-32; 26:15-22) back to the patriarchs, and Israel's title to the land of Canaan to Abraham's legal purchase of the cave of Machpelah (23). *Geological sagas,* explaining the strange volcanic features of the country around the Dead Sea (19:24-28). *Ritual sagas,* explaining some features of the Passover celebration (Ex. 12:21-39), and the abstention from eating the ischial nerve (Gen. 32:24-32 [H. 32:25-33]). *Etymological explanations* occur in most of these sagas (e.g., Gen. 4:1; 16:11; 21:31; 25:26, 30; 32:28 [H. 32:29]) and in many others.

Legends differ from sagas in having a historical character as the hero of a fictitious story. They usually have religious significance and are connected with a definite time and place. Thus Jephthah's vow, resulting in the slaying of his daughter, explains the annual mourning rite observed by the women in Gilead (Judg. 11:34-40), and the tale of Jehovah's sudden attack on Moses explains the origin of infant circumcision (Ex. 4:24-26). The story of Moses rescued in infancy from the ark of bulrushes serves to give a fanciful explanation of his name (Ex. 2:10). In general, however, legends have no ulterior motive except to enhance the character and achievements of the hero (so notably in the stories about Moses, Samuel, David, Solomon, Elisha, etc.).

2. *Practical wisdom.* The problems in the daily life of the individual arise from either extraordinary or ordinary circumstances. Since practical wisdom consists of sound counsel intended for every individual, whatever his nationality, it cannot deal with problems which are unparalleled or even extremely uncommon, but only with matters affecting the life of the average person. Only seldom, in surviving literature, are national affairs taken into account. Although frequently this wisdom is based on im- memorial custom and even on actual legislation, it differs from legislation in being suggestive rather than mandatory and in being frequently metaphorical rather than literal. Not seldom the wise saying is not direct advice, but an observation of life, a vignette, a miniature drama, in which a practical lesson is implied rather than expressed.

As in the other literary categories considered above, practical wisdom arose on the lips of the people and eventually became the professional concern of literary men. The earliest reference to a class of wise men (by the side of priests and prophets) is in Jer. 18:18, at the end of the golden period of Hebrew literature.

A. Folk wisdom. The popular proverb is the standard form of folk wisdom. Such proverbs, characterized by their pithy, epigrammatic form, are occasionally quoted in the Old Testament:

Is even Saul among the prophets?
              (I Sam. 10:12)
Even as Nimrod, the mighty hunter before Jehovah.
                        (Gen. 10:9)
What has straw in common with wheat?
              (Jer. 23:28)
Let us eat and drink, for tomorrow we die.
                  (Is. 22:13)
Out of the wicked comes wickedness.
              (I Sam. 24:13)
Let not the one putting on his armour
boast like the one taking it off.
                  (I Kings 20:11)
As the mother, so her daughter.
              (Ez. 16:44)
The fathers have eaten sour grapes,
And the children's teeth are set on edge.
              (Ez. 18:2; Jer. 31:29 f.)

In most of these cases the text itself identifies these sayings as folk proverbs (cf. also Ez. 12:22). But in addition to these, the books of Proverbs, Ecclesiastes, and Ecclesiasticus, though written by professional sages, unquestionably contain ancient folk sayings or echoes thereof; we lack, however, a criterion for positive identification. We may surmise that certain pithy questions in the prophetic books also were inspired by folk proverbs. These, for instance:

Do horses run upon the rock,
Or does one plow the sea with oxen?
                    (Am. 6:12, emended)
Will a lion roar in the forest,
When he has no prey?
                    (Am. 3:4)
Shall the ax boast itself against him
that heweth therewith?
                    (Is. 10:15)

In addition to proverbs, other types of practical wisdom seem to have originated on the lips of the common people: the riddle, the fable, and the parable. One metrical riddle and its solution is recorded in the stories of Samson; it was propounded during wedding festivities:

Out of the eater came something to eat
And out of the strong came something sweet.
                    (Judg. 14:14)
What is sweeter than honey
And what is stronger than a lion?
                    (Judg. 14:18)

It is probable that numerical proverbs (Prov. 6:16-19; 30:15-31; Ecclus. 25:1 f.), beginning with a formula such as this, "There are three things that are too wonderful for me, and four which I know not" (Prov. 30:18), and perhaps the oracles against foreign nations in Am. 1-2 ("For three transgressions of Damascus, nay for four . . .," Am. 1:3) were developed from riddles. In later literature the motif of a king propounding riddles served as the framework for moralizing disquisitions (I [III] Esd. 3:1-5:6; Letter of Aristeas §§187-300); but genuine riddles remained popular among the Jews, as shown by the twenty-two curious riddles which the Queen of Sheba is said to have propounded to Solomon (L. Ginzberg, *The Legends of the Jews,* Vol. IV, pp. 145-149).

Only two fables are preserved in the Old Testament, both of them dealing not with animals (like most of those of Aesop and La Fontaine) but with plants: the fable of Jotham (Judg. 9:7-21) and that of King Jehoash (II Kings 14:9). Bitterly sarcastic, both of them ridicule a ruler by comparing him to a worthless little plant afflicted with megalomania.

The parable, which attained such classical perfection on the lips of

Jesus, is represented in the Old Testament by two excellent examples: the parable of Nathan (II Sam. 12:1-4) and Isaiah's song of the vineyard (Is. 5:1-6). We should perhaps also class as a parable the fictitious story told to David by the wise woman from Tekoa (II Sam. 14:4-7).

B. Literary wisdom. Popular wisdom developed into a literary genre in Egypt (and, later, in Babylonia) long before Jewish professional sages began to compile collections of maxims and reflections. Just as Edomitic speculations about universal problems inspired the theoretical wisdom of the Old Testament, so Egyptian "instruction" (*sb'yt*) books (most of which are translated in A. Erman, *The Literature of the Ancient Egyptians,* pp. 54-85, 234-242) were the ultimate source of the Hebrew practical wisdom, and one of the Egyptian books, the *Teaching of Amen-em-ope,* was actually excerpted and revised in Prov. 22:17-23:14 (cf. H. Gressmann, ZAW N.F. 1 [1924] 272-296; W. O. E. Oesterley, *The Wisdom of Egypt and the Old Testament.* London, 1927). Both in Egypt and in Israel the counsel of wisdom was at first purely secular but became increasingly religious (contrast Ptah-hotep in the Old Kingdom with Amen-em-ope, about 900 B.C.).

In its first phase, wisdom in Egypt and in Israel was purely utilitarian. It was an aggregate of information and rules of conduct which should enable a young man to achieve success in his profession. The pecuniary returns of wisdom were no less emphasized by the ancient teachers of Egypt and Israel than by those educators in our time who, unmindful of the nobler ideals of Plato and Aristotle, regard a college education as primarily a sound financial investment.

The earliest Egyptian wisdom book, *Ptah-hotep's Instructions,* leaves ethics and religion out of account. Out of his own experience and success, Ptah-hotep's advice is concerned with correct manners, tact, respect for superiors, fidelity in carrying out commissions, and the like. He is convinced that the man whose conduct is right will win wealth, and concludes with the wish that the reader may attain Ptah-hotep's high office and please the king.

In Egypt the counsel was addressed to youths hoping to rise in public office, for public administration offered the greatest opportunities to able and ambitious young men.

Although in Israel, after the end of the monarchy, this career could not attract many, there are still in Proverbs words of advice for public servants (Prov. 10:26; 12:24; 13:17; 22:29; 25:6 f., 13). In general, however, the sages of Israel educated their middle-class pupils for careers in commerce and farming. To the future businessman they stress the value of wealth (10:15; 13:8; 15:15; 17:8; 19:4, 6 f.; 22:7; 25:15, etc.), the diligence and the industry needed for its acquisition (13:4; 14:23; 18:19), and the facility by which wealth is lost in riotous living (5:9 f.;

6:26; 21:17; 23:20 f., etc.) or in becoming surety for another (6:1-5, etc.). No less pointed is the advice given to the future landowner or farmer: the slothful cultivator is held up to ridicule (24:30-34; cf. 6:6-11); care of flocks (27:23-27) and work in the fields (12:11 = 28:19; 24:27; cf. 10:5; 14:4; 13:23) are enjoined categorically.

Besides work and wealth, Egyptian and Hebrew admonitions, in their secular stage, deal with relaxation and amusements; asceticism is totally foreign to them. "Ointment and perfume rejoice the heart" (27:9). Wine makes the unhappy forget their trouble (31:6 f.), but in excess it brings bitter woes (23:29-35). The joys of marriage, of the family life, and of friendship are those most prominently mentioned.

In a later stage the wisdom of Israel became more ethical and pious, without, however, losing its utilitarian character and its bourgeois outlook. In Proverbs the cult was not generally regarded as essential; morality and religion were identified (3:7, 22; 8:13, 20; 11:20; 14:3; 15:9; 16:6, 11, 17; 20:23; 21:10, 29; 28:5) and considered the essence of wisdom. Ben Sira, going one step further, identified religion with the observance of the Law of Moses: "All wisdom is fear of the Lord [i.e., religion], and in all wisdom there is the fulfilment of the Law" (Ecclus. 19:20; cf. 10:19; 15:1; 19:24; 21:11, etc.).

In conclusion, Hebrew wisdom developed along two divergent lines, the Edomitic and the Egyptian. The first reached its abrupt end in the skepticism of Ecclesiastes; the second, with Ecclesiasticus, lost itself in the orthodox piety of normative Judaism.

CHAPTER III

HISTORICAL AND CRITICAL INTEREST
IN THE OLD TESTAMENT

The study of the Old Testament as distinguished from its perusal for devotional and aesthetic purposes, reaches back in a sense to the scribes. For they were not only jurists and lawyers, but also Biblical scholars and teachers. In the time of the Chronicler (*ca.* 250 B.C.), they constituted a distinct profession with a number of organized guilds (I Chron. 2:55). Ezra was regarded by the Chronicler as the first of the scribes (Neh. 8:1 ff.; 12:26, 36; Ezra 7:6, 11), and Zadok (Neh. 13:13) as the second. The Chronicler himself may be regarded as a Biblical scholar. He not only rewrote the books of Samuel and Kings, but he was the first writer known to have expressed opinions in regard to the authorship of Biblical books, attributing the Pentateuch to Moses (II Chron. 23:18; 30:16; 35:12) and the books of Samuel to Samuel, Nathan, and Gad (I Chron. 29:29).

Jesus, son of Sira, who wrote the Book of Ecclesiasticus about 180 B.C., is the first Biblical scholar whose name is recorded (Ecclus. 50:27). The head of a school in Jerusalem (51:19, 23), he is the best-known representative of the professional scribes, and left us in Ecclus. 38:24-39:11 a picture of the ideal scholar of his time. The first duty of the scribe was the investigation of the Scriptures in all their parts: Law, Wisdom, and Prophecies are specifically named (39:1). The results of the author's own studies are summarized in his eulogy of the Old Testament heroes, from Adam to Nehemiah (44:1-49:16). In this panegyric, except for books not yet written (Dan., Eccl., Esth.), he fails to refer to two books only, Ruth and Song of Songs. The Pentateuch, "the Law which Moses commanded," is of course in a class by itself; but with refreshing candor the author does not hesitate to commend his own book as divinely inspired and therefore not inferior to the non-Mosaic parts of the Old Testament (24:23-24).

The authorship of the books of the Old Testament was investigated by the scholars of the Talmud. In *Baba Bathra* 14b-15a, after the books are enumerated in their proper order, comes the question, "And who wrote them?" The answer is, "Moses wrote his own book [the Law] and the section concerning Balaam [Num. 22:2-25:9], and Job. Joshua wrote his own book and eight verses of the Law [Deut. 34:5-12]. Samuel wrote his own book, and Judges, and Ruth. David wrote the book of Psalms together with ten elders, namely Adam [Pss. 92; 139 ?], Melchizedek [110], Abraham [89, according to the Targum], Moses [90], Heman [88], Jeduthun [39; 62; 77], Asaph [50; 73-83], and the three sons of Korah [42; 44-49; 84; 85; 87; 88]. Jeremiah wrote his own book, and the book of Kings, and Lamentations. Hezekiah and his college wrote[1] Isaiah, Proverbs [cf. Prov. 25:1], the Song of Songs, and Ecclesiastes. The Men of the Great Synagogue wrote Ezekiel, the Twelve [Minor Prophets], Daniel, and Esther. Ezra wrote his own book and the genealogies of the book of Chronicles as far as himself."

Although this celebrated deliverance of the rabbis living *ca.* A.D. 500 was motivated by a certain intellectual curiosity about the origin of the Biblical books, it was reached on the basis of doctrinal premises rather than objective research. The rabbis believed that the individual books, whose ultimate and real author is God, attained their final form through three stages: first, the divine revelation; second, the inspired utterance of a prophet; and finally, the exact transcript through a scribe. Through his Spirit, God first *spoke* his revelations, then dictated them. In the case of Moses (except for the oracles of Balaam), Joshua, Ezra, and in part of Samuel, David, and Jeremiah, the prophet and scribe were one and the same person; but Hezekiah and his "college" and the Men of the Great Synagogue merely transcribed the words divinely revealed to earlier or contemporary prophets. According to the rabbis, the oracles of forty-eight prophets and seven prophetesses have a place in the Scriptures, but the utterances of many others were never written. The last prophets were Haggai, Zechariah, and Malachi: after their death the Holy Spirit departed from Israel. This theory, according to which no books of the Old Testament were written after Ezra, is clearly formulated *ca.* A.D. 90 in Josephus, *Against Apion* 1:8 (§41) and in IV Esd. 14:44-46.

The gratuitous assumption that the entire Old Testament was completed in the time of Ezra has enjoyed long and undeserved popularity. The early Church Fathers, for example, Tertullian (*De cultu feminarum* 1:3), Irenaeus (*Adversus haeres.* [ed. Stieren] 3:21. 2), and Clement of Alexandria (*Stromata* 1:21), accepted it without question and firmly believed that the Scriptures, lost when Nebuchadnezzar destroyed Jerusalem, were rewritten seventy years later by Ezra. This conjecture was restated by Elias Levita in his book on the Masorah (Venice, 1536). Lacking all historical foundation, it acquired through the reputation of Levita general

---

[1] I.e., "put into writing" (L. Ginzberg, *The Legends of the Jews,* Vol. IV, pp. 276 f.; Vol. VI, p. 368, n. 89). On Biblical studies in Judaism see A. J. Baumgartner, *Les études isagogiques chez les Juifs.* Geneva, 1886. Cf. the article "Bible Exegesis" in the *Jewish Encyclopedia.*

currency among the Protestant Biblical scholars of the seventeenth and eighteenth centuries. Not until 1877 did A. Kuenen finally dispose of the myth of the "Great Synagogue."

It is hardly through such fanciful guesses, which by mere antiquity have attained the dignity of traditions, but by a critical study of the evidence furnished by the Old Testament itself that the authorship and date of the books of the Old Testament can, if possible, be determined. The crude beginnings of a critical and historical investigation of the Old Testament reach back at least to the second century of our era,[2] when Celsus maintained that the Pentateuch could not have been written by a single author, and Ptolemy (a disciple of the Gnostic teacher Valentinus), in his epistle to Flora, distinguished in the Pentateuchal law parts inspired by God, parts written by Moses, and parts written by the elders.

Far more brilliant and significant were the contributions of Porphyry, Jerome, and Theodore of Mopsuestia to real historical criticism of the Bible. Porphyry, a Syrian Neoplatonist philosopher who lived in Alexandria (*ca.* 233-304), attacked the historicity of the Book of Daniel, proving conclusively that it was written in the Maccabean period, and that ch. 11 was not a prophecy but a veiled history of Syria from Alexander to Antiochus IV Epiphanes (see Jerome's commentary on Daniel). Jerome (d. 420) refused to commit himself to the view either that Moses wrote the Pentateuch or that Ezra published it, but by identifying Deuteronomy with the lawbook discovered in the Temple during the reign of Josiah (*Commentary on Ezekiel, ad* 1:1)[3] he unwittingly found the key to Pentateuchal criticism. The significance of this discovery was not recognized until De Wette reached the same conclusion in 1806. Finally, Theodore of Mopsuestia, a theologian belonging to the school of Antioch (d. *ca.* 428), not only perceived that the titles and superscriptions of the Psalms were added to the original compositions, but also that a number of psalms (seventeen, in his opinion) were Maccabean in date.[4]

Thus the Jewish dogma, according to which the entire Old Testament was written not later than Ezra (or, at most, not later than Alexander the Great), was attacked from two sides and proved to be debatable, if not erroneous, in the cases of Daniel and some of the psalms. Among Jews, however, only a few isolated scholars in the Middle Ages expressed doubts about the Mosaic authorship of certain verses in the Pentateuch. The traditional views were not repudiated on critical grounds until the researches of Spinoza—and he was excommunicated by the Synagogue.

[2] Cf. E. Stein, *Alttestamentliche Bibel Kritik in der späthellenistischen Literatur.* Collectanea Theologica XVI. Lwow, 1935. He discusses Philo, Celsus, Porphyry, and Julian the Apostate.

[3] Athanasius and Chrysostom also know that the book found in the Temple contained Deuteronomy.

[4] H. Kihn, *Theodor von Mopsuestia und Junilius Africanus als Exegeten.* 1880.

Of the three great centers of Biblical studies in the ancient Christian Church, only the schools of Antioch and Nisibis advocated an objective, historical viewpoint and a critical method of interpretation.[5] The school of Alexandria, whose greatest master was Origen (d. *ca.* 254), continued to interpret the Scriptures allegorically, according to the method that Philo of Alexandria (d. *ca.* A.D. 50) had learned from the Stoics.[6] The school of Nisibis in Syria,[7] reorganized by Narsai in the fifth century, is important in the field of textual studies: it vocalized the Syriac Bible, and thus had a decisive influence on the Jewish Masorah.[8] Cassiodorus[9] reports (between 551 and 562) that Pope Agapetus requested him to organize a school in Rome similar to those in Alexandria and Nisibis. At that time the school of Antioch had ceased to exist.

Before the seventeenth century there are few other attempts to investigate the Old Testament critically for the purpose of determining the origin of its component parts. The books on the Bible written during the fourth, fifth, and sixth centuries deal primarily with the rules for interpreting the Scriptures, and with the style, authorship, canon, and text of the Bible, but in general the traditional views are not questioned.

Among the Biblical interpreters of these centuries Jerome (d. 420) was the greatest. He not only learned Hebrew and translated the Old Testament from the original languages into Latin (his "Vulgate" is the Bible of the Roman Catholic Church), but also treated problems of Biblical introduction in his prefaces to the several books of the Bible, in his commentaries, and in other writings. Augustine's *De doctrina Christiana* (426) deals primarily with the methods of Biblical interpretation, as also Tychonius's *Seven Rules for investigating and discovering the meaning of the Scriptures* (*ca.* 380), Adrian's *Introduction to the Divine Scriptures*

[5] The most eminent Biblical scholars of the school of Antioch were: Lucian (d. 311), who edited the Old and New Testaments in Greek; Diodorus (d. 394) who became Bishop of Tarsus after he had had among his pupils at Antioch John Chrysostom (d. 407), Theodore of Mopsuestia (d. 428), the latter's brother Polychronius (d. 430), and Isidore of Pelusium (d. 434). Nestorius (d. 440) and Theodoret (d. 457) were pupils of Theodore.

[6] On Philo's exegesis see particularly C. Siegfried, *Philo von Alexandrien als Ausleger des Alten Testaments.* A bibliography on Philo has been published by H. L. Goodhart and E. R. Goodenough (*The Politics of Philo Judaeus with a General Bibliography.* New Haven, 1938). Two useful books have appeared later: S. Belkin, *Philo and the Oral Law* (Cambridge, Mass., 1940); E. R. Goodenough, *An Introduction to Philo Judaeus* (New Haven, Conn., 1940).

[7] G. F. Moore, "The Theological School at Nisibis" in *Studies in the History of Religion Presented to C. H. Toy.* New York, 1912. Th. Hermann, "Die Schule von Nisibis vom 5. bis. 7. Jahrhundert," *Zeitschr. f. d. Neutestam. Wiss.* 25 (1926) 89-122.

[8] P. Kahle, *Masoreten des Westens.* Beitr. z. Wissensch. vom A. T., Neue Folge 8, pp. 52-55. Stuttgart, 1927.

[9] Preface to his "De institutione divinarum literarum" (Migne, *Patrologia Latina* LXX, 1105). Cassiodorus founded a school at Viviers and died *ca.* 585.

(in Greek; *ca.* 430), and Eucherius's *Formulae spiritualis intelligentiae* (*ca.* 440 ?). More comprehensive are the works of Junilius Africanus (*Instituta regularia divinae legis, ca.* 550), influenced by the school of Antioch, and of Cassiodorus (*De inst. div. lit.* [cf. n. 9], published between 551 and 562), who names the volumes just mentioned. In his book, Junilius has preserved for us the course of lectures on the Bible of a certain Paul the Persian, who had studied at Nisibis. Thus, through Junilius (and Cassiodorus, who is greatly indebted to him) the teaching of the school of Antioch, after being filtered through the school of Nisibis, survived in the Catholic Church. The rational exegesis of Antioch and Nisibis was, however, condemned as unorthodox, and the allegorical exegesis of Alexandria, through Augustine, prevailed over the critical methods of Jerome.

These works the Christians utilized during the Middle Ages. The only new treatments worthy of mention are found in Book VI of Isidore of Seville (d. 636), *Etymologiarum libri XX;* in Books IV-VI of Hugo of St. Victor (d. 1141), *Eruditio didascalica;* and especially in the *Postillae perpetuae in universa biblia* of Nicholas of Lyra (d. 1340), which had considerable influence on the Biblical studies of Martin Luther, and in turn owed not a little to the work of the great Jewish scholar Rashi (d. 1105). Even more important than Rashi in the history of Biblical research is Ibn Ezra (d. 1167). He recognized serious difficulties in the traditional dating of parts of the Pentateuch and Isaiah, but, remaining an orthodox Jew, refrained from voicing his misgivings in clear language. The commentaries of Rashi and Ibn Ezra, as well as those of David Kimchi (d. *ca.* 1230), enjoyed great popularity among the Jews and were printed in the Rabbinical Bibles.

A fresh impulse to Biblical studies in the sixteenth century was given by the invention of printing (*ca.* 1440), the Protestant Reformation (1517), and the humanistic revival of scholarship during the Renaissance. Although Luther, Calvin, and Carlstadt occasionally attacked the traditional views, a critical study of the Old Testament did not begin until the middle of the seventeenth century. The Catholic introductions to the Bible written by Santes Pagninus (*Isagogae ad sacras literas Liber unicus,* 1536) and by Sixtus Senensis (*Bibliotheca sancta,* 1566) are dogmatic and polemic in character, as are the Protestant works by A. Rivet (*Isagoge seu introductio generalis ad scripturam sacram,* 1627), M. Walter (*Officina biblica,* 1636) and others.

The historical and critical investigation of the Old Testament books, after the fragmentary work of such pioneers as have been mentioned, had its real beginnings in the seventeenth century. Two French scholars, L. Cappellus (Protestant; d. 1658) and J. Morinus (Catholic; d. 1659), inaugurated the criticism of the Hebrew and Greek texts of the Old

Testament, proving that they had not been preserved intact and that, as Elias Levita had proved, the vocalization of the Hebrew text was relatively recent. The English philosopher Th. Hobbes in his *Leviathan* (3:33; 1651) outlined the aims and methods of the critical study of the Old Testament: the date of the Biblical writings must be determined through exegetical study of traditional opinions. Hobbes came to the conclusion that Moses wrote only parts of Deuteronomy and that much of the Old Testament was written after the Exile. Similar conclusions were reached independently by Isaak de la Peyrère, or Peyrerius (*Systema theologicum,* 1655).

The two founders of modern Biblical criticism are the Jewish philosopher Baruch Spinoza (d. 1677) and Richard Simon, a French priest (d. 1712). Spinoza, in chapters 7-10 of his *Tractatus theologico-politicus* (Hamburg, 1670), after examining the Scriptures "in a spirit of entire freedom and without prejudice," came to the conclusion that the series of books from Genesis to II Kings constituted a single work, presumably compiled by Ezra from documents of various dates which contradicted one another. He dated the Books of Chronicles in the Maccabean period, the Psalter in postexilic times, and Proverbs not earlier than the reign of Josiah. The canon of Scriptures was not earlier than Maccabean times. R. Simon's *Histoire critique du Vieux Testament* (Paris, 1678; Rotterdam, 1685) is divided into three parts, dealing successively with the Hebrew text, the versions, and the history of Biblical interpretation. According to Simon, the Old Testament was compiled in the time of Ezra or later from the writings of a long series of inspired scribes.

The conclusions of Spinoza and Simon found little favor in the eighteenth century. Even Jean Astruc (d. 1766), who discovered in Genesis two main sources (distinguished by their use of the divine names "God" and "Jehovah"), believed that Moses was the author of the book. The traditional and doctrinal views were presented with immense erudition by J. G. Carpzov (d. 1757) in his *Introductio* (1714-1721), dealing with the individual books of the Old Testament, and in his still valuable *Critica sacra* (1728), dealing with the text and versions. A new note, however, was struck by Bishop Robert Lowth (d. 1787) with his *De sacra poësi Hebraeorum* (1753) and by J. G. von Herder (d. 1803) in his *Vom Geiste der Ebräischen Poesie* (1782): in the spirit of the romantic movement they saw in the Old Testament the literature of a people and brought out its aesthetic value.

The freedom of research with no dogmatic preconceptions was advocated by J. S. Semler (d. 1791) in his *Abhandlung von freier Untersuchung des Kanons* (4 vols., 1771-1775) and his *Apparatus ad liberalem Vet. Test. interpretationem* (1773). The way has thus been opened for the first great modern introduction to the Old Testament, the *Einleitung in das Alte Testament* (3 vols., 1780-1783) of J. G. Eichhorn (d. 1827). Although Eichhorn investigated it without regard to traditional and dogmatic opinion, his results do not differ substantially from those of J. D. Michaelis (d. 1791) who, in his *Einleitung* (only part I, on the Pentateuch and Job, 1787) defended the viewpoint of the Church against Eichhorn. On the contrary, G. L. Bauer (d. 1806) in his *Entwurf einer Einleitung* (1794) followed Eichhorn.

The literary and historical investigation of the Old Testament came to fruition in the nineteenth century, particularly in its second half. At the beginning of the century, the most important introduction was that of W. M. L. De Wette (d. 1849) (*Lehrbuch der hist.-krit. Einleitung,* 1817); his *Beiträge zur Einleitung* (I. On the Pentateuch and Chronicles, 1806; II. A critique of the history of Israel, 1807) were epoch-making. At this time, the critical investigation of the Old Testament was fertilized by the results of other fields of research: Hebrew and Semitic philology, beginning with the Hebrew dictionary and grammar of W. Gesenius, which appeared in their first editions in 1810-1812 and 1813, respectively (his great *Thesaurus linguae hebraicae* was published in 1829-1858); the theology of the Old Testament (W. Vatke, *Die biblische Theologie* I, 1835); the history of Israel (H. Ewald, *Geschichte des Volkes Israel,* 3 vols. 1843-1852; English translation of the 3rd ed. in 7 vols., 1864-1868); and the exegetical commentaries on the Old Testament (*Kurzgefasste exegetische Handbuch zum Alten Testament,* 1st ed., 1838-1862).

Numberless monographs on particular parts of the Old Testament carried forward the critical investigation. A few scholars combined sound criticism with a reverent attitude toward the Old Testament, which they regarded as divinely revealed wholly or in part; others studied the Old Testament as they would the Homeric poems, i.e., as ancient literature. However, these two mental attitudes, represented by J. D. Michaelis and J. G. Eichhorn in the preceding century, did not always lead to radically different conclusions.

Catholic introductions to the Old Testament, such as those of J. Jahn (1793; 2nd ed. 1802-1803), J. G. Herbst (1840-1844), J. M. A. Scholz (1844-1848), D. B. Haneberg (1850), F. H. Reusch (1859), H. Zschokke (4th ed., 1895), F. Kaulen (1876-1881), R. Cornely (1885-1887), are cautious, conservative, and pious. The traditional position was defended as far as possible by such Protestant conservatives as E. W. Hengstenberg (1831-1839), H. A. C. Hävernick (1836-1849), and C. F. Keil (1853). Moderately critical views were presented by F. Bleek (edited by A. Kamphausen, 1860; the 4th ed. [1878] is important for the contributions of J. Wellhausen), J. J. Stähelin (1862), Samuel Davidson (3 vols., London, 1862-1863), Th. Nöldeke (1868), H. L. Strack (1883; 6th ed. 1906), and E. Riehm-A. Brandt (1889-1890).

To the radical school of literary criticism belong the introductions of E. Reuss (1881), K. H. Graf (on the Pentateuch and the historical books only, 1866), A. Kuenen (in Dutch, 1861-1865; German translation of the 2nd ed., 1887-1894), J. Wellhausen (on the Pentateuch and the historical books: 1875, 1876; later editions), and W. Robertson Smith (*The Old Testament in the Jewish Church*, 1881; 2nd ed., 1892). During this period three Jewish scholars deserve mention: J. Fürst (1867-1870), D. Cassel (1871), and A. Geiger (*Urschrift und Übersetzungen der Bibel,* 1857; *Einleitung*, 1877); Z. Frankel (d. 1875) studied the LXX.

Considerable progress has been made during the past fifty years and, in spite of the persistence of the conflicting attitudes mentioned above, certain broad results of the critical analysis are now generally accepted. The most widely read introductions of the time are those of C. H. Cornill (1891; 7th ed., 1913; English translation, 1907), S. R. Driver (*Introduction to the Literature of the Old Testament*, 1891; 9th ed., 1913; German translation, 1896), G. Wildeboer (in Dutch, 1893; 3rd ed., 1903; German translation, 1895 and 1905), E. König (1893), W. W. Baudissin (1901), J. E. McFadyen (1905; new ed., 1932), L. Gautier (2 vols., in French, 1906; 2nd ed., 1914), C. Steuernagel (1912), O. Eissfeldt (1934), W. O. E. Oesterley and Th. H. Robinson (1934), A. Weiser (1939).

The following are concise, nontechnical treatments: M. Löhr (1912), W. Staerk (1912), G. F. Moore (1913), G. B. Gray (1913), P. Thomsen (1918), J. Meinhold (1919), G. Beer (1926; 2nd ed., 1932). The most important Catholic introductions are those of W. Fell (1906), F. Kaulen-G. Hoberg (5th ed., 1911), K. Holzhey (1912), F. Vigoroux (14th ed., 3 vols., 1917-1920), H. Höpfl (2 vols., 1920-1921; 3rd ed., 1932), J. Nikel (1924), R. Cornely (2nd ed., 1894; re-edited by A. Merk, 1927), and J. Göttsberger (1928).

Other scholars, instead of writing an introduction to the Old Testament and examining the Biblical books separately and in their canonical order, have prepared histories of the ancient Hebrew literature in which the writings contained in the Old Testament are considered chronologically. The most important of these literary histories were written by G. Wildeboer (in Dutch, 1893; 2nd ed., 1896; in German, 1894), E. Kautzsch (1894; 3rd ed., 1897; English translation, 1899), K. Budde and A. Bertholet (1906; 2nd ed., 1909), H. Creelman (1917), J. A. Bewer (1924; 2nd ed., 1933), and J. Hempel (1930-1934).

The preceding works, whether in the form of an introduction or as literary history, are based on literary criticism of the writings of the Old Testament (*Quellenkritik*). A different method of approach is that of "form criticism" (*Formgeschichte*).[10] After determining and classifying all the literary types (*Gattungen*), such as love poems, workers' songs, elegies.

---

[10] See H. Gressmann, ZAW N.F. 1 (1924) 25-30.

paeans of victory, and so on, the history of each type is traced back, before its written stage, to its origin on the lips of the people (*Stoffgeschichte*). This method was first used by the Germanists while investigating the fairy tales of German folklore and was applied to the Old Testament by H. Gunkel, particularly in his sketch of the Israelitic literature in *Die Kultur der Gegenwart* I, VII: *Die Orientalischen Literaturen*. Berlin and Leipzig, 1906; 2nd ed., 1925. Several monographs of H. Gressmann, the introduction to the Old Testament of E. Sellin (1910; 3rd ed., 1920 [English translation, 1923]; 7th ed., 1935), and the first part of O. Eissfeldt's introduction (1934) use the method of the *Formgeschichte*. D. B. Macdonald (*The Hebrew Literary Genius*. Princeton, 1933) adopts a psychological and aesthetic method and distrusts the conclusions of both literary and form criticism.[11]

[11] For additional details on the current phase of Old Testament criticism see: G. A. Barton, in *The Haverford Symposium on Archaeology and the Bible* (New Haven, 1938); H. W. Robinson (editor), *Record and Revelation*. (Ch. II, 3 by O. Eissfeldt; cf. the German text in *Theologische Rundschau* N.F. 10 [1938] 255-291). See also: W. A. Irwin, "The Study of the Old Testament: An Introspective Interval" (*AJSL* 55 [1938] 166-182); R. H. Pfeiffer, "Present Tasks for Old Testament Scholars" (*The Crozer Quarterly* 19 [1942] 223-31); H. R. Willoughby (editor), *The Study of the Bible Today and Tomorrow*. The University of Chicago Press, 1947.

CHAPTER IV

HISTORY OF THE CANON

It is axiomatic in all ancient religions that the gods could—and did—communicate intelligibly with human beings, either spontaneously or in answer to questions. The divine communication could be articulate or inarticulate. In the first case, the oracle would usually be spoken, either directly ("face to face," Ex. 33:11; cf. Num. 12:6-8; or often in visions or dreams such as those of Is. 6 and Job 4:12-17), or else indirectly through a prophet (Am. 3:8; Deut. 18:18, etc.), more seldom written ("tables of stone written with the finger of God," Ex. 31:18). In the second case, the deity manifested itself obscurely, through signs or omens that required interpretation by professional diviners. I Samuel 28:6 lists three methods by which the deity can answer a human question: by dreams, by urim (priestly oracle), by prophets.

The numerous stories about ancient heroes (from Adam to Samuel) who heard with their own ears Jehovah's words spoken in person or by his "angel" are pious legends that need not detain us here. Like similar stories in the *Iliad*, they are told of men long dead, never of contemporaries. Saul, in the passage last quoted, never expected a visible appearance of the deity but hoped for an oracle through a dream, a priest, or a prophet. Ancient Israel knew only two forms of divine revelation (since dreams belong to prophetic experience), priestly and prophetic oracles. The supernatural knowledge gained by the seer through telepathy, by the gazer through interpretation of omens, or by magical practitioners denounced in Deut. 18:9-12 was never regarded as a communication of Jehovah.

The priestly oracle (fully discussed by W. R. Arnold, *Ephod and Ark*) consisted in the manipulation and interpretation of sacred lots drawn out of a box. When a divine answer was forthcoming, it could consist only of one of the two alternatives propounded explicitly or implicitly by the questioner. This mechanical consultation of the deity, although the ark, or sacred box, is still mentioned by Jeremiah (3:16), became obsolete about the middle of the ninth century, at least for kings.

Like the Roman sibyls (cf. Vergil, *Aeneid* 6:40 ff.), the prophets believed that, in moments of inspiration, the deity or its spirit entered their body and spoke through their mouth (cf. I Kings 22:19-23). Convinced that they were physically *inspired*, the prophets uttered the word of God saying, "Thus saith the Lord." Some of the inspired utterances of the ninth century prophets (Elijah, Elisha, and Micaiah the son of Imlah) have been accidentally preserved in the Books of Kings; but, as far as we know, Amos (*ca.* 750) was the first prophet whose oracles were collected in a book.

In principle, this book of Amos constituted sacred scripture, since it purported to embody divine revelations; as a matter of fact, it was not officially canonized, as part of the word of God in written form, until five and a half centuries later. In the time of Amos, the concept of inspired scripture did not exist: the divine revelation was always oral, through the mouth of the prophet as earlier through the mouth of the priest interpreting the sacred lots. The notion of inspired scripture is a contribution of Judaism and appears somewhat later in other religions such as Zoroastrianism, Hinduism, Buddhism, as well as in those derived from Judaism (Christianity and Islam). How did the Israelites come to believe that God not only spoke but also dictated a book?

It is clear from what precedes that the notion of inspired scripture has its roots in prophecy (see W. R. Arnold, JBL 42 [1923] 1-21). Even if the priestly responses, obtained by drawing lots, had been collected in writing—which was not the case—they could hardly have been regarded as inspired utterances having permanent validity. The priests also codified the law (chiefly religious, although to some extent also civil), but no matter how permanently valid were such codes, in the opinion of the people, they were never regarded as divinely inspired until after the Exile (except possibly the ritual decalogue, Ex. 34:28). Since the prophetic and priestly oracles were the only media of divine communication known in Israel,[1] the notion of inspired scripture must have grown out of prophecy for it could not develop from priestly responses and legal decisions.

1. The Deuteronomic Code

The evidence furnished by the Old Testament itself confirms this conclusion that the idea of inspired scripture having canonical standing was inspired by prophecy. In the eighteenth year of Josiah (621 B.C.), when Hilkiah the chief priest opened the collection box in the Temple at Jerusalem to draw funds for the repairs of the edifice, he found in it "the

---

[1] On what evidence O. Eissfeldt (*Einleitung in das Alte Testament*, p. 615. Tübingen, 1934) asserts that "in Israel there are four different types of utterance that are regarded as Word of God" (namely, the instruction [Torah] of the priest, the oracle of the prophet, the song of the singer, and the proverb of the wise man) is not clear. The case of the Decalogue (Ex. 34:28; 24:12; 31:18; 32:15-16) is unique. Laws, songs, and proverbs were eventually deemed divinely inspired by regarding their authors as prophets: as a result, these compositions came to be considered prophetic oracles and were included in the collection of sacred scriptures.

book of the law (*Torah*)." After the prophetess Huldah had declared that
Jehovah would fulfill the threats of punishment contained in the book,
the king read it to the people "and made a covenant before Jehovah . . .
to keep his commandments and his testimonies and his statutes [cf. Deut.
6:17] . . . to perform the words of this covenant that were written in
this book" (II Kings 23:3).

Two inferences can safely be made from the account of these epoch-
making events, given in II Kings 22-23: in the first place, this book, unknown before being discovered by Hilkiah, was regarded by Huldah, by
King Josiah, and by the people in general as being Jehovah's word; in
the second place, the prescriptions of the book were at once enforced by
the government, and automatically it became the constitution of the
nation. For the first time in the history of mankind, a book was canonized
as sacred scripture.

It is incredible that this book—the charter of the covenant between
God and his chosen people, the cornerstone of Judaism—should have disappeared while Judaism survived. If it has been preserved as part of the
Hebrew Bible, it must be looked for within the Pentateuch (since there
is no "book of the law" outside of it). In spite of isolated dissenting voices
in recent years, critical opinion agrees with W. M. L. De Wette (1805)
in identifying the book that came to light in 621 with Deuteronomy (or
rather with the bulk of Deut. 5-26 and 28). No other part of the Pentateuch fits the situation so perfectly: the reforms of Josiah (II Kings 23)
which removed Canaanitic and Assyro-Babylonian sacred objects from
the Temple and closed all other sanctuaries—those of foreign gods as
well as those of Jehovah; the celebration of the Passover "as it is written
in the book of this covenant" (II Kings 23:21); the conception of the relationship between God and people as a formal *covenant*; and matters of
detail, are found together only in Deuteronomy.

The one prescription of Deuteronomy (18:6-8) that Josiah found impracticable (II Kings 23:9) was that the priests of the closed "high
places" should be allowed to officiate at Jerusalem. Incidentally, II Kings
14:6 quotes Deut. 24:16 as part of "the book of the law of Moses," obviously the same as "the book of the law" found in the Temple. Deuteronomy is called "the book of the law" in Deut. 29:21 (H. 29:20);
30:10; 31:26 (cf. Josh. 1:8; 8:34), passages that did not stand in the
original edition of the book; and Deut. 17:18-19 contains, in prophetic
form, an account of the preparation of the book of the law for the benefit
of the king.

If the original edition of Deuteronomy (most of chs. 5-26 and 28
written a few years before 621 B.C.) was the first book to be canonized
as sacred scripture, then the notion of sacred scriptures was unquestionably inspired by the records of prophetic utterances rather than by

a collection of priestly laws. The objection to be anticipated is that this document found in the Temple (the D Code) was regarded by Josiah and his contemporaries as "the book of the law (of Moses)" and modern critics currently speak of it as a code of laws, if not a *corpus juris*. Although it is now recognized that Josiah erred in attributing the book to Moses, his misconception of its character, in regarding it as a code of laws and not as a prophetic oracle, has by no means been generally discarded. These two initial notions have in considerable measure given to Judaism its legalistic character: the divine revelation (through Moses) is primarily a divine law, not prophetic teaching; the ideal Jew is marked by obedience to the law rather than by faith.

It was not the intention of the author of the Deuteronomic Code to codify the law but rather to redact, in writing, the final prophetic oracle of Moses in the plains of Moab. Moses appears in D in the role of a prophet (Deut. 18:18; cf. Hos. 12:14; Num. 11:24-30), not lawgiver (Ex. 15:25b) nor priest obtaining oracles through the manipulation of sacred lots. The D Code is a sermon of Moses, having the standard division into three parts: introduction (Deut. 5-11), exposition (12-26), and peroration (28). After stating the basic principles of the religion (5:6-21 [H. 5:6-18]; 6:4-5), the introduction presents the motives for obeying God's commandments (8-11); the main part of the sermon lists the divine commandments in detail (12-26); the peroration contains the practical application, consisting of a description of the blessings that follow obedience to the commandments (28:1-14) and of the curses resulting from disobedience (28:15-68).

From beginning to end, the style is that of a pulpit orator. In impressive elaborate sentences and flowing rhythmical language, through insistent reiteration and restatement, the preacher pleads, exhorts, warns, with a warmth of feeling, tender solicitude, and glowing fervor totally at variance with the serene objectivity, limpid conciseness, and impersonal aloofness of a jurist compiling a code of laws. The manner in which the author of D rewrites actual laws in oratorical style can be seen in 15:12-15 where the old law of Ex. 21:2 is adapted to pulpit delivery:

If thy brother, a Hebrew man or a Hebrew woman, be sold unto thee, and serve thee six years; then in the seventh year thou shalt let him go free from thee. And when thou sendest him out free from thee, thou shalt not let him go away empty: thou shalt furnish him liberally out of thy flock, and out of thy floor, and out of thy winepress: of that wherewith Jehovah thy

If thou buy a Hebrew servant, six years shall he serve; and in the seventh he shall go out free, without payment.
(Ex. 21:2)

God has blessed thee thou shalt give
unto him. And thou shalt remember
that thou wast a bondman in the land
of Egypt, and Jehovah thy God redeemed thee: therefore I command
thee this thing this day.
> (Deut. 15:12-15)

This example illustrates not only the differences in style and tone, but
also the philanthropic ideals and religious motives that D injects into
purely civil legislation. Similar illustrations will be found in the treatment
of the law of asylum for unintentional murderers (Deut. 19:1-13; Ex.
21:12-14), in the law about seduction (Deut. 22:25-29; Ex. 22:16-17 [H.
22:15-16]), and in the law against kidnaping and selling into slavery
(Deut. 24:7; Ex. 21:16). Actual law, whether already statutory or merely
customary, was interpreted by the author of D in the spirit of the reforming prophets. Law ceases to be custom and becomes a divine commandment, God's will being, since Amos, the standard of the right. God is particularly concerned with the rights and welfare of the weaker members
of society and condemns actions which are technically legal but cause
severe hardship on widows, orphans, and resident aliens.

Obedience to God's commandments is dictated by both self-interest
and a sense of gratitude. In D the dominant thought, both in civil and in
religious prescriptions, is the maintenance of the right relationship between Israel and Jehovah, according to the terms of the covenant which
the two parties have ratified. Just as the civil law becomes religious and
humanitarian in spirit, so the ritual law regulating the worship is presented with prophetic overtones. In the regulations for the festivals (ch.
16), for instance, two aspects are stressed, gratitude toward Jehovah and
kindness toward the poor and helpless. The author was unquestionably a
priest attached to the Temple in Jerusalem, and well acquainted with civil
and priestly law. But he had been strongly influenced by the prophetic
movement. His doctrine of God (cf. Deut. 5:6-10; 10:12-18, etc.), his conception of religion, following Hosea, as love for God (6:5; cf. 10:12 f.;
11:1, 13, 22; 13:4; 19:9) manifested in doing his will, the polemic against
the worship of the Baals at the high places (ch. 12), the stressing of
ethical and humanitarian duties (*passim*), are clearly derived from the
teachings of the reforming prophets.

It is true that the author did not go so far as Amos or Isaiah in minimizing the significance of sacrificial worship, but he strove to sterilize the
ritual by eliminating popular superstitions and giving it a spiritual meaning: his compromise between priestly and prophetic religion, which was
necessary to assure success to his reformation, leans decidedly toward the
prophets. That is why Jeremiah welcomed the book and at first was

active in his support of the reforms of Josiah (Jer. 11:1-8), although he soon realized that the possession of "the Law of the Lord" was giving rise to new aberrations (8:7-9).

The misgivings of Jeremiah were well founded. The author of D, inspired by the earlier books of Amos, Hosea, Isaiah, Micah, and others, circulating at the time, supplied a prophecy of Moses which did not exist before. This prophetic oracle of Moses, necessarily in written form, was intended as a divinely revealed book, and received as such. But certain results of the canonization of the book must have disappointed the author, if he was still alive. He had advocated a religion of the heart, but his oracle of Moses was taken to be a book of the law, and thus furthered the religion of observance prevailing in Judaism. Centralization of the worship at Jerusalem conferred on the Temple a new significance. The mere presence of the Temple was regarded as a token of divine protection (Jer. 7:3 ff.). Possession of the transcript of divine revelation gave to the literate an exaggerated sense of their wisdom (Jer. 8:8). To the Deuteronomic covenant based on a book, Jeremiah opposed a "new covenant" based on a law written not in a book but in the hearts of the people (31:31-34). And finally, running counter to the author's intentions (Deut. 18:15-19), the transcript of the initial revelation of God to Moses made the sporadic divine revelation through the prophets superfluous.[2] For a time (Jer. and Is. 40-55) prophecy continued to assert itself beside the incipient Bible, but beginning with Ezekiel, Haggai, Zechariah, and Malachi it became either subservient to the written Law or, ceasing to be oral, a transcript of apocalyptic visions. The Deuteronomic Code was the outgrowth of prophecy but marked its doom, by substituting a book for inspired speech, as the ultimate divine authority. Of course, the average prophet was at the time a dreamer of dreams (Jer. 23:9 ff.), and there was some justification for the hostility to prophecy expressed in Deut. 13:1-5 (H. 13:2-6), a passage added in later times to the book found in the Temple.

In any case, prophecy with Ez. 40-48 and Is. 40-66 was no longer oral. It is true that Haggai, Zechariah, and the author of Malachi were preachers as well as writers, but with them went the old spirit. Joel, the last prophet whose name is known, was so conscious of the end of prophetic inspiration that he looked forward to a day when God's spirit would be poured upon all Jews and their servants, so that they would all prophesy (Joel 2:28 f. [II. 3:1-2]). Prophets were still to be found in Jerusalem in the time of Nehemiah (Neh. 6:5-14), but soon after the spirit of prophecy departed from Israel:[3] "there is no more any prophet" (Ps. 74:9).[4]

---

[2] Cf. J. Wellhausen, *Prolegomena zur Geschichte Israels,* pp. 402 f. 6th ed. Berlin, 1905.

[3] Tosefta *Soṭah* 13, 2; *Sanhedrin* 11a; Josephus, *Against Apion* 1:8 (§41).

[4] Cf. I Macc. 4:46; 9:27; 14:41.

2. The Pentateuch

The canonization of the Deuteronomic Code in 621 B.C. marks the beginning of a process rather than its end. The book was regarded as holy scripture, but not as the complete and final transcript of divine revelation. Instead of ending, it rather stimulated literary activity; nor did it decrease the popularity of historical and prophetic writings in circulation at the time. The great national epic, edited about 650 B.C., including JE and the old sources from Josh. 1 to I Kings 2, recited the achievements of Israel under Jehovah's guidance, from Abraham to David's death. It was as dear to the nation as Homer was to the Greeks. This national history was the ultimate source of that sense of superiority over the Gentiles, of that nationalistic pride, which was peculiar to the Jews at the time, and from which even an idealist such as the author of D could not free himself.

About 550 B.C., the Deuteronomic Code was inserted into this national history immediately before the account of Moses' death, and the history was carried down to a period shortly after the fall of Jerusalem in 586. The Books of Kings had been written in harmony with the religious teaching of Deuteronomy (ca. 600 B.C.) and the Book of Judges was re-edited in the same spirit (ca. 550). The prophetic literature was likewise preserved, re-edited, and augmented after 621.

Incidental codification of civil and ritual law in the Deuteronomic Code proved itself insufficient. Ezekiel's program of restoration (Ez. 40-48) was visionary. However Utopic, it was not without influence. The Holiness Code, or H (Lev. 17-26), a codification of priestly law in a homiletic setting like D, was published about 550. Between 500 and 450, the ritual practice of the Second Temple (completed in 516) formed the basis of the Priestly Code, or P, comprising the book of Leviticus and other parts of the Pentateuch.[5]

According to the untrustworthy account of the Chronicler (Ezra 7:14), Ezra came from Babylonia with the Law of God in his hand in 458, and in 444 read the book before the congregation in Jerusalem which pledged itself through a solemn covenant to observe the prescriptions of that law (Neh. 8-10). The historicity of these events is too doubtful to infer therefrom the origin and canonization of the Priestly Code. In any case, the Chronicler did not have in mind the Priestly Code, as some modern critics believe,[6] but the entire Pentateuch which he dated back to the time of Moses.

[5] In the opinion of C. C. Torrey, *Ezra Studies* (Chicago, 1906) pp. 196 f., the "Priestly Code" never existed as a separate lawbook.

[6] Among the most recent is A. Lods, *Les prophètes d'Israël*, p. 344 (Paris, 1935; English translation: *The Prophets and the Rise of Judaism*, 1937).

It seems certain, however, that the Priestly Code comprising laws, genealogies, and accounts of the origin of sacred institutions and of the partition of Canaan (P ends with the book of Joshua) was composed during the fifth century in Palestine, and could not obtain canonical standing until it had been incorporated into the embryo Pentateuch (JED). As a matter of fact, it seems obvious that much of the P material (notably in the narrative parts) never had any independent existence but was only a commentary or supplement to JED. Thus out of Deuteronomy, through successive enlarged editions, the Pentateuch in its present form finally took shape. There is no reason to doubt that as soon as the final edition of the Pentateuch was issued it was received as canonical. The Pentateuch is merely an enlarged edition of the book found in the Temple and is therefore in principle the prophecy of Moses. Actually, it was taken to be the Law of God, and studied as such by Jews, individually and in groups, whatever countries they lived in.

The canonization of the Pentateuch was an epoch-making event, but its date is conjectural. It is apparent that the Pentateuch was the Bible of Judaism about 250 B.C., when it was translated into Greek (Septuagint Version) and regarded by the Chronicler as divinely revealed to Moses. The date of the Samaritan Schism would give us a positive clue as to when the Pentateuch was canonized, for when the Samaritans seceded from Judaism the Pentateuch remained their Bible, to which nothing was added later. In a veiled allusion to the break with the Samaritans (Neh. 13:28 f.), the Chronicler puts the schism in the time of Nehemiah (432), but Josephus (*Antiquities* 11:8, 2 [§§306-312] and 4 [§§321-324]), in a romantic tale, dates the building of the Samaritan temple on Mount Gerizim a century later, in the time of Alexander the Great. The first explicit gesture of contempt from a Jew for the Samaritans, after the Chronicler's disguised sneers, is that of Ben Sira (Ecclus. 50:25 f.) about 180.

Such are the flimsy chronological data at our disposal. The most probable canonization date of the Pentateuch is about 400 B.C. At that time, the five books of the Law (*Tōrâh*), ending with the account of Moses' death, were separated from the four historical books (Josh., Judg., Sam., Kings) with which they had formed a great historical corpus. The Pentateuch alone was regarded as inspired scripture and always retained a higher degree of authority and prestige than the rest of the Old Testament, which failed to receive canonical status for centuries.

Henceforth, no Jew could ignore the prescriptions of the Pentateuch, as the Jews living in Elephantine (an island of the Nile facing Assuan) in the fifth century ignored the prescriptions of Deuteronomy when they reared a temple to Jehovah in that distant outpost, even asking for permission to rebuild it (408 B.C.) after it had been demolished. Circulated to an unprecedented extent among all Jewish communities, wherever they might be, the edition of *ca.* 400 became necessarily the final one. Not long after its publication, it began to be read regularly in the synagogues erected for this very purpose, and hence could never again be supplemented with new layers of legislation.

3. The Former Prophets

About two centuries after the canonization of the Law, the collected edition of historical and prophetic books attained its final stage. The eight volumes grouped as "Prophets" in the Hebrew Bible are divided into "Former Prophets" (Josh., Judg., Sam., Kings) and "Latter Prophets" (Is., Jer., Ez., the Twelve [Minor Prophets]). Originally, each of these two divisions was a single work in four volumes, but in the English Bible there are six books in the first division and fifteen in the second. Although the two divisions attained canonical status at the same time, their previous vicissitudes are quite distinct.

As we have seen, when the Law was canonized in 400, it was severed from the historical corpus (Gen.-Kings) which had been edited *ca.* 550 by the Deuteronomists. The priestly account of the division of Canaan was then added to Joshua between 550 and 400 and, during the two centuries following the canonization of the Law, numerous additions and changes were made to Joshua-Kings in order to encourage successive generations in observing the Law and to enhance their pride in the nation's glories.[7]

With a complete lack of historical sense these annotators present, like the Chronicler, a completely distorted picture of the past. The sharp contours of persons and events are hidden in a fog of wishful thinking and pious ignorance, Levitical institutions are dated back to the beginning, and the ancient heroes of Israel are turned into devout seekers after the righteousness of the Law. This total misconception of past ages begins soon after the end of the monarchy in 586. The author of the Deuteronomic Code, found in 621, was still aware that the legislation revealed to Moses was unsuitable to nomadic life and would go into effect only after his death, in the towns and villages of Canaan. But the Deuteronomic editors of 550 passed judgment on the men of the past according to the Law of 621 and, worse still, the Priestly author in the fifth century naïvely believed that the sacred institutions of his day were observed by Aaron at the foot of Sinai. The misunderstanding of the past thus attained the dignity of religious dogma, and the annotation of the historical books in the same vein helped in no small measure to give them the status of holy writings.

---

[7] For additions to the Books of Samuel see R. H. Pfeiffer, *Midrash in the Books of Samuel* (*Quantulacumque,* edited by R. P. Casey, Silva Lake, and Agnes K. Lake, pp. 303-316. London, 1937).

Another consideration led to the canonization of these historical books: their connection, actual or fictitious, with prophecy. The books of Samuel and Kings contain stories about real or (as in the case of the seer Samuel) supposed prophets. The Deuteronomic editors first in Kings, then in Judges, had used the historical accounts as illustrations of the prophetic teaching that God would punish the nation for its sins. And finally in 250 B.C. the books of Samuel and Kings were attributed to a succession of prophetic writers (I Chron. 29:29; II Chron. 9:29; 12:15; 13:22; 20:34; 26:22; 32:32). God himself is said to have written the specifications of the Temple of Solomon and of its ritual (I Chron. 28:19). In conclusion, the popularity of these books (a requirement for their preservation), their religious and patriotic significance, and their supposed prophetic authorship brought about their canonization about 200 B.C.

4. The Latter Prophets

After the Deuteronomic Code of 621 B.C. had restated the noble theology and ethical religion of the great prophets of earlier days, and by skillful amalgamation of prophetic and priestly religion had made it possible for prophetic ideals to influence the religion of the masses, popular interest in prophetic literature remained faint. The Law of Moses (D) was considered both primary and final, the prophets were regarded merely as witnesses to the old truth in time of apostasy. Even the books of Ezekiel and Second Isaiah (Is. 40-55), whose influence on Judaism in two different directions was incalculable, were not placed on the same level with the book of Moses. Circulating among a limited number of readers, the prophetic books were at first less popular than the historical volumes, with their strong nationalistic appeal. The gloomy and stern tone of the prophets before the catastrophe of 586 was ill-suited to a prostrate nation, and their contempt for the ritual worship ran counter to the prevailing trend.

The dazzling pictures of a glorious restoration, painted in contrasting veins by Ezekiel and the Second Isaiah, probably stimulated (in the fifth century) a certain amount of interest in the old prophetic writings. These two prophets of the sixth century turned the eyes of the nation from the wretched present to a glorious Utopian future and contributed in transforming prophecy—originally a divine message for the present—into prediction. The prophetic books were henceforth eagerly scanned for an augury of events still in the remote future, because it was generally thought, as an interpolation in Amos (3:7) explicitly states, that "surely the Lord Jehovah will do nothing without revealing his secret unto his servants, the prophets." Ezekiel (38:17) and the Second Isaiah (Is. 40:21; 41:26; 42:9; 44:7; 45:19; 46:10; 48:3) were already convinced that God had announced his plans far in advance. Zechariah goes one step further.

in the past, God revealed his statutes and Law to the prophets (1:6; 7:12), but the people did not hearken to their words (1:4; 7:12) and were therefore punished for their sins (1:6; 7:12); let the living generation therefore ponder those ancient revelations (7:7, LXX).

The fall of Jerusalem in 586 had vindicated the truth of the old prophetic oracles; as the voice of living prophets was gradually fading into silence, prophetic literature became the object of a deepening veneration and a more zealous study. The canonization of the Pentateuch, about 400, tended to make of Judaism a religion of the book and to increase reverence for the written word. Just as the picture of the nation's history was retouched and improved in editions of the historical books, so the glories of the future were magnified in the prophetic books, henceforth regarded as predictions of Israel's future supremacy over all nations.

The glosses added to the books of the prophets during the period 500-200 B.C. prove the popularity of this literature. They illustrate two aspects of their attraction: hostility toward foreign nations and faith in the ultimate glorification of Israel.[8] These two attitudes of mind are merely extremes of the nationalistic feeling which appeared with a new intensity in the Deuteronomic Code and, with the downfall of the kingdom, became a conviction that God would intervene in the future to establish a Jewish empire. The prophetic books were brought up to date by means of countless interpolations, in which the nations were denounced as idolatrous and as objects of the divine wrath. On the other hand, these supplements announced the restoration of Israel and victory over its oppressors under the leadership of the Messiah or through miraculous intervention of God. Such promises were usually inserted into the old oracles immediately after threats of ruin and doom.

The volume of Isaiah and that of the Minor Prophets, which contain the earliest prophetic oracles, were subjected to the greatest amount of antiforeign and eschatological annotation; much less was required for Jeremiah, and practically none for Ezekiel. From time to time collections of prophetic writings were prepared, until at last, when it became clear that prophetic inspiration was extinct, the final editor after diligent search collected all prophetic manuscripts available, and prepared the extant edition of the prophets in four volumes. This was made canonical soon after its issue. There was then a popular demand for a prophetic corpus.

The final editions of the four historical books (Josh., Judg., Sam., and

---

[8] R. E. Wolfe ("The Editing of the Book of Twelve," ZAW N.F. 12 [1935] 90-129) has made a careful and minute analysis of the editorial strata of the book of the Twelve Minor Prophets. Although his chronological conclusions concerning the twelve editorial strata discovered in the book may be questioned, owing to insufficient evidence, the study deserves serious consideration.

Kings) or Former Prophets, and that of the Latter Prophets (Is., Jer., Ez., and the Twelve), likewise in four volumes, were issued about 200 B.C. The historical books had been in circulation since 550 and reached their present form and canonical status before the prophetic books. Except for minor changes made later, the Chronicler in 250 had available our Former Prophets in their final form; but he did not yet regard them as canonical scriptures, for he took great liberties in rewriting the history, making additions and corrections, particularly to Samuel and Kings.

In the collection of prophetic writings the presence of sections dating unquestionably from the third century and the absence of the Book of Daniel (dating from 164 B.C.) fix the ultimate date of the final collection (*ca.* 200). The evidence supplied by Ben Sira (Ecclus. 44-49) proves that about 180 B.C. the Bible consisted of "the Law and the Prophets." In his eulogy of the fathers, he briefly summarizes the books from Genesis to Kings and the four prophetic volumes: the Pentateuch in Ecclus. 44-45; Josh. in 46:1-10; Judg. in 46:11-12; Sam. in 46:13-47:11; Kings in 47:12-49:5; Is. in 48:20-25; Jer. in 49:6-7; Ez. in 49:8-9; and the Twelve in 49:10. It is particularly significant that Ben Sira read the Second Isaiah as part of the volume of Isaiah and the Twelve in a single scroll, for this arrangement of the material is characteristic of the final edition. Ben Sira therefore had the four canonical prophetic volumes.

Since Ben Sira passed from the Pentateuch to the Prophets without interruption, it is difficult to escape the conclusion that he regarded the Prophets as no less canonical than the Law. But he did not regard the category of sacred scripture as definitely closed, for he refers to Psalms, Proverbs, Ezra-Nehemiah, and perhaps to Job, and even considered his own book as prophetically inspired (24:33; cf. perhaps 50:28 f.).

Daniel 9:2, in 164, already quotes Jer. 25:11 ff. as Scripture, and in 132 the grandson of Ben Sira refers three times in the preface of his Greek translation of Ecclesiasticus to "the Law and the Prophets." Also he is familiar with their translation into Greek. Before the beginning of our era, selections from the Prophets, in addition to the Law, were read in the synagogues (cf. Luke 4:16-17; Acts 13:15, 27). At that time the Bible was called "The Law and the Prophets" (Matt. 5:17, etc.).

5. *The Writings*

The third division of the Hebrew Bible, following the Law and the Prophets, is simply called the "Writings" (Hebrew, *Ketûbîm*) or "Hagiographa" (sacred writings), because it consists of a miscellany of independent books. The first canon consisted of a single work in five volumes containing all that was attributed to the pen of Moses; the second consisted of two works of four volumes each; but the third consisted of a collection of ten works (one of which, Chron.-Ezr.-Neh., comprises two volumes in Hebrew and four in English), with nothing in common except alleged inspiration. These books are grouped as follows in the Hebrew Bible: 1. Poetical Books (Ps., Prov., Job); 2. The Five Scrolls (Cant., Ruth, Lam., Eccl., Esth.);[9] 3. Prophecy (Dan.); 4. History (Ezra, Neh., Chron.).

The canonization of the Writings necessarily differs from that of the Law and the Prophets. The two first canons consisted of complete and final editions of certain types of literature, presumably meant for canonization. But in the third canon, each of the ten literary works had to achieve canonical status independently; each circulated privately until it was attracted, like a satellite, into the orbit of prophetic literature.

Two factors helped in elevating each book of the Hagiographa to canonical dignity. The first was mere survival. In ancient times, when books had to be copied laboriously by hand on papyrus or parchment, no literary work could survive for a few centuries unless it had attained considerable circulation. Only books were copied for which there was a demand and, among Jews and Greeks likewise, any book which ceased to be copied eventually disappeared, like the Hebrew text of I Maccabees and Ecclesiasticus, until the discovery (1896) in the genizah of Old Cairo of more than half of the Hebrew text of Ecclesiasticus. Each book must needs have possessed some intrinsic value in the eyes of the Jewish public in order to remain in circulation. It had to have a religious or a nationalistic appeal. Since popular literary taste is somewhat capricious, survival was thus accidental. We may wonder, for instance, why Esther should have survived among the Jews, while Judith perished, since the appeal of both was mainly patriotic.

The second requirement for canonization was anonymous authorship. With the exception of the prophets, who collected their public addresses in their books, only one writer in ancient Hebrew literature named himself in his writings, Ben Sira (Ecclus. 50:27-29). Pride of authorship is Greek and Western, not Oriental. Among the Jews, interest in the authorship of books arose on account of the question of their inspiration and not, as M. Jastrow, Jr., believes, on account of Hellenic influence. As we have seen, prophetic inspiration was thought to have come to an end immediately after the time of Ezra, and therefore no book later than Ezra could be regarded as inspired. No book could become canonical if positively *known* to have been written after Ezra. Books like I Maccabees, relating the history of a later period, or like Ecclesiasticus, written by Ben Sira who was known to have lived after the cessation of prophetic

---

[9] The five scrolls (*Megillôt*) were grouped together because it became customary in ·Talmudic times to read them in the synagogue at Passover, Pentecost, the ninth of the month Ab [anniversary of the destruction of Jerusalem in 586], Tabernacles, and Purim, respectively. See L. Blau, in *Jewish Encyclopedia* VIII, 429 f.

inspiration, could not be deemed inspired. All anonymous books apparently not later than Ezra could be attributed to some ancient prophet, even though, like Daniel, they were actually written in the second century. Had the authors of most of Psalms and Proverbs, of Canticles and Ecclesiastes, been known, so that their attribution to David and Solomon would have been impossible, they would have remained outside the canon of Scriptures, like Ecclesiasticus.

The earliest witness to this theory of inspiration and canonicity is Josephus (*Against Apion* 1:8 [§41]), about A.D. 90. After speaking of the canonical books, Josephus says: "From the time of Artaxerxes [i.e. Artaxerxes I Longimanus, 465-424 B.C.] to our own time, each event was recorded, but these writings are not deemed equally trustworthy with those written before them because the exact succession of prophets no longer existed."[10] According to IV Esd. 14:45-46 and *Baba Bathra* 14b-15a, all canonical Scriptures were in existence in the time of Ezra.[11]

Within the limitations imposed by this convention, selection was dictated by popular taste rather than by official authority. The Writings were recognized as being canonical only gradually, book by book, and not always unanimously. The process of canonization began soon after the closing of the prophetic canon in 200. Ben Sira (47:8-10) already knew a Davidic Psalter existing about 180 B.C., and I Macc. 7:17 (*ca.* 100 B.C.) already quotes Ps. 79:2-3 (a Maccabean psalm) as scripture. It seems likely that the Psalter was attaining canonical status about the middle of the second century, and was thus forming the nucleus of the third canon which remained in a fluid state for over two centuries.

In addition to the Law and the Prophets, there was in 132 a rather indefinite third group of sacred writings. Ben Sira's grandson, in the preface to his Greek translation of Ecclesiasticus, refers vaguely to this third group in the following manner: "the Law, and the Prophets, and *the others who followed after them*"; "the Law, and the Prophets, and *the other books of our fathers*"; "the Law itself, and the Prophecies, and *the rest of the books.*" What these "other books" were, in addition to the Psalter, can only be surmised, but there is no reason to doubt that Proverbs

---

[10] Cf. *Seder Olam Rabba* 30: "Up to this point [the time of Alexander the Great, who is the rough he-goat of Dan. 8:28], the prophets prophesied through the Holy Spirit; from this time onward incline thine ear and listen to the sayings of the wise." According to Jewish chronology, Ezra lived just before Alexander. The same principle is expressed in *Tosefta Yadaim* 3:5: "The Gospel and the books of the heretics are not canonical [literally, "do not make the hands unclean"]; the books of Ben Sira and whatever books have been written since his time are not canonical."

[11] Whether the much-cited but baffling passage II Macc. 2:13, according to which Nehemiah collected in a library "the books about the kings and the prophets, and the books of David, and letters of kings about sacred gifts," has any bearing on the canonization of the second canon (history and prophecy) and of the Psalms, is extremely questionable; in any case this passage does not state that the Biblical canon was closed by Nehemiah.

and Job were included in the list. The immense popularity of Daniel must have raised it to the dignity of holy writ comparatively soon after its publication in 164: I Macc. 2:59 f. (and possibly 1:54) already refers to it about 100 B.C.—though not explicitly as scripture.

Interest in the history of postexilic restoration led to the separation of Ezra-Nehemiah from the rest of the work of the Chronicler, and to its canonization before that of I-II Chronicles (in the Hebrew Bible I-II Chron. incongruously come after Ezra-Neh.). Of the five scrolls, the two earliest ones, Ruth and Lamentations, reached canonical status before the other three (Cant., Eccles., Esth.), the canonical standing of which raised serious doubts (cf. G. F. Moore, *Judaism,* Vol. I, pp. 242-246). At the beginning of our era, most of the books of the third canon were generally included in the Bible, although before A.D. 90 there is only one other reference to the threefold division of the Scriptures ("The Law of Moses," "The Prophets," "and the Psalms"; Luke 24:44). No significance should probably be attached to the failure of Philo of Alexandria to quote Ezekiel, the five scrolls, Daniel, and Chronicles (although Ezra is cited as scripture), and to the lack of references to Canticles, Ecclesiastes, Esther, and Ezra in the New Testament. At most, this negative evidence confirms the doubts already mentioned concerning Canticles, Ecclesiastes, and Esther.

At the close of the first century of our era, following the fall of Jerusalem in 70 and the resulting disorganization of Judaism, the Council at Jamnia (*ca.* A.D. 90), under the leadership of Johanan ben Zakkai, fixed for all times the canon of scriptures. Controversies with the Christians, who accepted the authority of writings not included in the Hebrew Bible, made such a step imperative. With the closing of the third canon, the Hebrew Bible was limited to twenty-four books: five in the Law of Moses, eight in the Prophets, and eleven in the Writings (counting Ezra-Neh. as one book and I-II Chron. as another). This Bible of twenty-four books is first mentioned by IV Ezra 14:44-46 (*ca.* A.D. 90). About the same time, Josephus (*Against Apion* 1:8 [§41] disregarded the three canons of the Hebrew and followed the topical arrangement in the Greek version. He counted twenty-two books (combining Ruth with Judges and Lamentations with Jeremiah) and arranged them as follows: 1. The Law of Moses (5 books); 2. The Prophets (13 books); 3. Hymns to God and Practical Precepts to Men (4 books; presumably: Ps., Cant., Prov., Eccles.).[12]

---

[12] Origen (in Eusebius, *Ecclesiastical History* 6:25), Epiphanius (*de mensibus* 10), and Jerome (*Prologus galeatus* [introduction to Sam.-Kings]) likewise count 22 books in the Old Testament, according to the number of the letters of the Hebrew alphabet. However, Jerome knew that among the Jews many counted 24 books (*Praefatio in Danielem; Prol. galeatus*), and he also refers to the fanciful reckoning of 27 books (corresponding to the 22 Hebrew letters and to the 5 additional "final" letters)

With the canonization of the entire Old Testament, the Pentateuch retained its central and unique position. Judaism had no idea of a progressive revelation and regarded as complete and final the revelation to Moses, i.e., the written Torah (Pentateuch) and the "tradition of the elders" (Mark 7:3-13; Josephus, *Antiquities* 13:10, 6) transmitted orally until codified in the Mishnah (*ca.* A.D. 200).[13] The books of the second and third canons are considered "tradition" (*qabbalah*): they preserve and explain the Torah. "Moses received the Law [written and unwritten] from Sinai and delivered it to Joshua, and Joshua to the elders, and the elders to the prophets, and the prophets delivered it to the men of the Great Synagogue" (*Pirqê Abôth* [*Sayings of the Fathers*] 1:1).[14]

The limitation of the Biblical canon to twenty-four books and the supreme authority of the Torah were axiomatic in normative Judaism since at least A.D. 100. But in some Jewish circles the notions were not so stringent. Even in the Talmud, where *Baba Bathra* gives the official list of canonical books, Ecclesiasticus of Ben Sira is cited as canonical three times (*Berakot* 48a, *Erubim* 45a, *Baba qamma* 92b); and IV Esd. 14, in addition to the twenty-four books to be circulated among the public, speaks of seventy esoteric revealed books.

Jewish sects and esoteric circles had secret books of a quasi-canonical standing: for the Essenes we have the testimony of Josephus (*War of the Jews* 2:8, 7 [§142]). The sect of "The New Covenant," or of the Zadokites at Damascus, possessed a legal book for the guidance of the leaders (The Book of the Hago [*sefer ha-hago*]) and, in spite of their reverence for the Torah, seem to have recognized the authority of noncanonical writings.[15]

6. *The Alexandrian and Christian Canons*

The apocalyptic writings, that appeared from the Maccabean period to the end of the first century of our era, were completely ignored (except for Daniel) by the rabbinical leaders, but in some circles they enjoyed considerable popularity during these centuries. It is obvious that the authors of these pseudonymous revelations and their readers did not restrict the idea of inspiration to the Scriptures but held rather elastic

---

obtained by dividing Sam., Kings, Chron., Ezr.-Nehem., and Jer.-Lam. (*Prol. gal.*). For the order of the books of the Old Testament in the ancient lists, manuscripts, and printed editions see *Jewish Encyclopedia* III, 143 f.

[13] For this "unwritten Law" see G. F. Moore, *Judaism*, Vol. I, pp. 251-262. For Philo's acquaintance with it see S. Belkin, *Philo and the Oral Law*. For the Apocrypha, cf. R. Marcus, *Law in the Apocrypha*. New York, 1927.

[14] For the reverence shown the Torah in Judaism see *Jewish Encyclopedia* III, 149 f.; and the entry Torah (or Tora) in the indices of L. Ginzberg, *The Legends of the Jews*, and of Strack-Billerbeck, *Kommentar zum Neuen Testament*.

[15] G. F. Moore, *Judaism*, Vol. I, pp. 202 f. R. H. Charles (editor), *The Apocrypha and Pseudepigrapha of the Old Testament*, Vol. II, pp. 789 ff. Oxford, 1913.

views on canonicity. Finally, among the Greek-speaking Jews in the Dispersion, particularly at Alexandria, the Biblical canon was likewise considerably enlarged.

All these tendencies toward giving canonical standing to Jewish writings outside of the Scriptures were contemptuously ignored by the Jewish authorities, and never affected normative Judaism in the least. Conversely, their influence on early Christianity was incalculable (notably in the case of the apocalypses and Alexandrian Judaism). The Christian Bible was considerably larger than the Jewish. The New Testament quotes noncanonical writings as Scripture: Matt. 27:9, according to Jerome (ad. loc.), quotes an apocryphal writing of Jeremiah; I Cor. 2:9 and Eph. 5:14 quote, according to Origen and Epiphanius, respectively, the Apocalypse of Elijah;[16] Jude vv. 14-16 quotes Enoch 1:9; the sources of the quotations of John 7:38, Luke 11:49, and James 4:5 f. are not known. The writers of the New Testament also used the following apocryphal writings without quoting them as scripture: Ecclus. 5:11 (James 1:19); II Macc. 6-7 (Hebr. 11:35 f.); the Assumption of Moses (Jude v. 9, according to Origen, De principiis 3:2, 1); the Book of Jannes and Jambres (II Tim. 3:8; cf. Origen, ad Matt. 23:37; 27:9).[17] It is likely that Hebr. 11:37 ("they were sawn asunder") refers to the Martyrdom of Isaiah.

The Christian Church had already received its Old Testament Scriptures in Greek from Judaism when the rabbis, about A.D. 90, fixed at Jamnia the extent of the sacred canon. Before then differences of opinion about the matter still prevailed among Jews, for Palestinian sectarians, apocalyptic dreamers, and Hellenistic Jews of Alexandria accepted as scripture books of questionable canonicity. After A.D. 100, in spite of sporadic discussions of a purely academic character, no true Jew ever entertained the slightest doubt concerning the exact bounds of the Law, the Prophets, and the Writings; even the memory of earlier vagaries and aberrations eventually disappeared. With the solitary exception of Ecclesiasticus, still read and copied by Jews in its original Hebrew text as late as the twelfth century, all the extant noncanonical Jewish literature from 200 B.C. to A.D. 100 was preserved by the Christians.

It is not easy to reconstruct opinions on the canon held by Jews outside the main current of Judaism from mere echoes in Christianity. The apocalypses and related writings had a brief vogue in some Jewish circles. But incipient Christianity, awaiting the imminent return of Christ, found in them nourishment for its hopes. The main current of Christianity, represented by the Greek and Roman churches, soon moved away from millenarian speculations, but the surviving translations of Jewish apoca-

---

[16] See E. Schürer, *Geschichte des Jüdischen Volkes*, Vol. III, pp. 369, 363, 365. 4th ed. Leipzig, 1909.

[17] E. Schürer, *op. cit.*, Vol. III, pp. 303 and 304.

lypses into Syriac, Ethiopic, Coptic, Armenian, Georgian, Arabic, and Slavonic bear witness to the more lasting interest of the Oriental churches in this type of literature, even when it was not formally canonized.

It is generally assumed that the Old Testament of the Christian Church is that of the Hellenistic Jews at Alexandria, although this cannot be proved. We have only indirect information about the Biblical canon of the Hellenistic Jews from 250 B.C. to A.D. 100, except for the Law and the Prophets, which were translated into Greek between 250 and 150 B.C. (see preface to the Greek translation of Ecclesiasticus). Ben Sira's grand-child does not tell us what other books were part of the Greek Bible in 132 B.C., when the category of the "Writings" was still in a fluid state.

Several circumstances contributed to make the Hellenistic Jewish canon more inclusive. In Palestine, where all literature was written in Hebrew or Aramaic, the distinction between sacred and profane writings in those languages had been clear-cut since the canonization of the Pentateuch. Eventually, the rule that prophecy had ended in the time of Ezra automatically excluded from canonization any recognized later writing.

Conversely, at Alexandria all profane literature was in Greek; the Law and the Prophets and other sacred books had been translated in Alexandria from the Hebrew, and it was natural to consider all writings translated from the Hebrew or Aramaic as sacred. This tendency was strengthened by a theory of inspiration which did not, like the Palestinian, have a chronological limitation in the time of Ezra. According to Philo,[18] inspiration is not confined to ancient days: not only the translators of the Law into Greek, but every truly wise and virtuous man is inspired and thus enabled, through the Spirit of God, to announce what is hidden to the ordinary eye. For Philo, for the author of the Letter of Aristeas,[19] and for the Alexandrian Jews in general, the Pentateuch occupied a place of unique authority; all other sacred books were subordinate to it and belonged to a group whose boundaries had not been fixed.

In spite of the statement of Ben Sira's grandson, the line of demarcation between "Prophets" and "Hagiographa" was not generally recognized. Even Josephus, who, as we have seen, accepted the Palestinian theory of the canon, completely disregarded this cleavage. Moreover, Josephus used the Greek (Septuagint) Bible, containing additions to the text of Esther, as well as entire books (I Esd., I Macc.) wholly lacking in the Hebrew. In his use of this apocryphal material,[20] Josephus apparently regards it as

[18] *De Cherub.* 9 (p. 112 D); *de migratione Abrah.* 7 (p. 393 C). Cf. A. Gfrörer, *Philo und die alexandrinische Theosophie*, Vol. I, pp. 46-68. Stuttgart, 1831.

[19] The Letter of Aristeas (*ca.* 100 B.C.) is the first book to quote the Pentateuch as "Scripture" or *graphé* (§§155, 168).

[20] For references see H. Bloch, *Die Quellen des Fl. Josephus in seiner Archäologia*, pp. 8 ff. Leipzig, 1879; H. B. Swete, *An Introduction to the Old Testament in Greek*, p. 378.

equally authentic with the canonical books, in opposition to Philo, whose quotations are limited to the Law, Prophets, and Writings (he fails to quote Ez., the five scrolls, Dan., and Chron., although Ezra is cited as Scripture).[21]

The Septuagint Greek version (LXX) is generally considered the Bible of the Jews at Alexandria. Presumably this is correct, although most copies and fragments of the Septuagint and all lists of books in it are Christian. But what was the Septuagint before ca. A.D. 130, when it was condemned in Judaism, and a new literal Greek translation of the twenty-four books canonized at Jamnia (ca. A.D. 90) was prepared by Aquila? We do not know positively, but we may surmise that it differed considerably in text, contents, and arrangement from the Hebrew Scriptures, the wording of which was fixed before A.D. 130 under the leadership of Rabbi Akiba. As long as the Biblical books were copied individually on papyrus rolls, the order and contents of the Scriptures remained uncertain until fixed by such official action, and to the best of our knowledge none was ever taken at Alexandria.

The earliest known copies of the Greek Bible in book (codex) form belong to the fourth century, and there is no reason to believe that the entire Old Testament or even large sections were copied on vellum codices before the third century.[22] The books are arranged without uniformity, and their number varies in the uncial manuscripts of the Bible and in the lists prepared by Church Fathers and councils (see the conspectus of these lists in H. B. Swete, An Introduction to the Old Testament in Greek, pp. 201-214). However, it seems certain that in the Bible of the Jews at Alexandria during the first century A.D. the clear-cut separation between the Prophets and the Writings was disregarded and these books were arranged topically and chronologically (cf. Josephus, Against Apion 1:8). Interspersed among them were the Apocrypha, which the rabbis never considered canonical (except possibly, in some circles, Ben Sira's Ecclesiasticus).

Presumably the conspectus of the Hellenistic Jewish Bible was as follows:[23] 1. The Pentateuch. 2. Historical Books: Joshua, Judges, Ruth, I-II

---

[21] The fact that Philo quotes the books of Ps., Prov., Job, and Ezra as Scriptures militates against the view of O. Eissfeldt (*Einleitung in das Alte Testament*, pp. 626 f.), according to whom the Jews of Alexandria recognized only the Law as canonical and regarded the other Biblical books as works of religious edification not sharply separated from mundane books.

[22] In Palestine (see *Baba Bathra* 13b; cf. F. Buhl, *Kanon und Text des Alten Testaments*, p. 40. Leipzig, 1891), the three divisions of the Hebrew Bible seem to have been copied on separate scrolls at an earlier date; a volume containing the 8 books of the prophets is mentioned at the end of the first century; after some misgivings, Rabbi Judah (ca. 200) sanctioned a copy of the whole Bible in one volume.

[23] The Apocrypha are *italicized*. *The Prayer of Manasses*, usually reckoned among the Apocrypha, was not part of the Greek and Latin Bible in the time of Jerome,

Kings (= I-II Sam.), III-IV Kings (= I-II Kings), I-II Chronicles, *I Esdras* ("Greek Esdras"), II Esdras (= Ezra-Neh.). 3. Poetical and Didactic Books: Psalms, Proverbs, Ecclesiastes, Canticles, Job, *Wisdom of Solomon, Ecclesiasticus of Ben Sira.* 4. Story Books: Esther (with *additions*), *Judith, Tobit.* 5. Prophetical Books: The Twelve, Isaiah, Jeremiah, *Baruch,* Lamentations, *Epistle of Jeremy,* Ezekiel, Daniel (with *The Song of the Three Children, The History of Susanna,* and *Bel and the Dragon*). 6. *I and II Maccabees* (seldom also *III and IV Macc.*). Except for the omission of I-IV Maccabees, this is the order and contents of the great Vatican Manuscript (Codex Vaticanus, Gr. 1209), or Codex B, of the middle of the fourth century, and of most printed editions.

The Septuagint Greek Bible (LXX) was the Old Testament of the Christian Church from the beginning, although there were always differences of opinion about the canonicity of some or all of the books of the Apocrypha. The Bible of the Syriac Church (the Peshitta) originally lacked the Apocrypha and Chronicles; Theodore of Mopsuestia omitted also Ezra-Nehemiah, Esther, and Job; but the Nestorians recognized Job, and even Ben Sira and the additions to Daniel (some Monophysites also added Esther). Eventually, however, these books were included: the Codex Ambrosianus (in Milan), which is a Peshitta manuscript of the sixth century, contains not only the Old Testament with the Apocrypha (except 1 Esd., Tob., and the Prayer of Manasses), but also the apocalypses of Baruch and Ezra, as well as Josephus, *War of the Jews,* Book 7.

The Greek Church generally accepted the Apocrypha, although Melito of Sardis and Origen[24] knew that they did not appear in the Bible of the Jews, and some Church Fathers objected to their inclusion into the canon. The Council *in Trullo* (692) recognized the Apocrypha as canonical, but that of Jerusalem (1672) accepted only four of them (Tob., Jud., Ecclus., Wisd. of Sol.).

In spite of Jerome's strong objections, the Roman Church accepted the Apocrypha, following the usage of Augustine and the African churches. The synods of Hippo (393) and Carthage (397), with some variations in the order, adopted the books of the Hellenistic Jewish Bible as listed above (with III-IV Esd., and I-II Macc. at the end). The Council of Trent (1546), confirmed by the Vatican Council (1870), declared the Apocrypha canonical, but placed III-IV Esdras and the Prayer of Manasses in an appendix at the end of the New Testament. Jerome's plea for the recognition of only the Hebrew canon, excluding the Apocrypha, was thus disregarded in the Roman Catholic Church but eventually found acceptance in Protestantism.

---

although it is found after Psalter in the Codex Alexandrinus (A) dating from the fifth century; this manuscript contains also 3-4 Maccabees.

[24] Eusebius, *Ecclesiastical History* 4:26 and 4:25, respectively.

Luther, in his translation of the Bible (1534), relegated the Apocrypha to the end of the Old Testament, regarding them as inferior to the Holy Scriptures, but "good and useful for reading."

The Apocrypha are likewise included in the early English translations of the Bible (except, of course, for Tyndale's, whose translation of the Old Testament is confined to the Pentateuch [1530] and Jonah [1531]): Wycliffe (*ca.* 1382, revised 1388), Coverdale (1535), "Thomas Matthew" (1537), the Great Bible (1539), the Genevan Bible (1560), the Bishops' Bible (1568), and the Authorized Version (1611). But beginning with 1629, the Apocrypha were omitted in some editions of the English Bibles, and since 1827 the British and Foreign Bible Society excluded them from all printings of the Bible. Although most Protestant editions of the Old Testament now contain only the books of the Hebrew canon, the arrangement is still that of the Greek and Latin Bibles (which disregard the distinction between the "Prophets" and the "Writings"), thus obliterating all trace of the last two stages in the canonization of the Old Testament.

CHAPTER V

TEXT AND VERSIONS OF THE OLD TESTAMENT

~~~~~~

1. The Hebrew Text

A. Before A.D. 90

The original drafts of the Old Testament writings perished within a century or two, but we still possess authentic information on the preparation of one of these lost "first editions." According to Jer. 36, Baruch wrote Jeremiah's oracles under dictation on a scroll (patently of papyrus), using pen and ink. This Book of Jeremiah, and other ancient Biblical books, differed from their modern Hebrew editions in regard to the writing material and the script—besides the obvious differences in contents and text, the lack of vowel signs, and the modern use of the printing press.

Papyrus scrolls used for writing were prepared in Egypt during the Old Kingdom (*ca.* 2780-2270 B.C.), if not earlier, by cutting longitudinal strips of the pith of sedges (*Cyperus papyrus*) growing in marshes and pressing two (or three) layers together crosswise (cf. Pliny, *Naturalis Historia* 13:11). Egyptian papyrus books of the end of the third millennium (e.g., the Instructions of Ptah-hotep and Kagemni) are still extant. As early as the eleventh century, at least, papyrus rolls were exported from Egypt to Gebal in Phoenicia (*Story of Wen-Amon* II, 41; see A. Erman, *The Literature of the Ancient Egyptians,* p. 182). In Greek, Gebal was accordingly called *Byblos,* meaning "papyrus" (Herodotus 2:92). The word *biblos* was used in the sense of "book" even when its sheets were of parchment (Herodotus 5:58); from *biblia* (little books) comes our word "Bible." The largest papyrus scroll in common use was about thirty feet long and nine or ten inches high—sufficient for the Hebrew unvocalized text of the Book of Isaiah—although exceptionally the Egyptians used such enormous scrolls as the Papyrus Harris (133 feet long, 17 inches wide) and a Book of the Dead (123 feet long, 19 inches wide). The use of the standard papyrus scrolls necessitated the division of the Hebrew Pentateuch into five books. The Books of Samuel, Kings, and Chronicles (and presumably Genesis and Isaiah) were divided in Greek into two books, because Greek, owing to the writing of the vowels, required more space than Hebrew.

71

The text was written with a sharpened reed pen (Jer. 8:8; Ps. 45:1 [H. 45:2]; III Macc. 4:20) and ink (Jer. 36:18), on the side where the papyrus fibers ran horizontally. The writing was divided into columns (Jer. 36:23) separated (according to the Talmud) by the space of one thumb or two fingers; the margins at the top and bottom were from two to four fingers wide. Ample space for annotations was thus provided. Only rarely were scrolls inscribed on both sides (Ez. 2:10).

It has been assumed here that at first the Hebrew scrolls were made of papyrus—not of leather or parchment. Decisive evidence on this point is, however, lacking. The LXX version in Jer. 36 takes it for granted that Jeremiah's scroll was made of papyrus (*chártēs* or *chártion* renders *megillah* [scroll] throughout the chapter)—and with good reason, for when Jehoiakim burnt that scroll (Jer. 36:22-25), the stench would have been intolerable had it been of leather or parchment. But leather and parchment scrolls of the Hebrew Scriptures were also in circulation, at least when the Letter to Aristeas (§§176-179) was written, about 100 B.C. In this passage the Pentateuch seems still to be copied on five parchment scrolls, but later (as now) the copies read in the synagogues were written on a single scroll of parchment or leather obtained from clean animals, domestic or wild. The substitution of the book (*codex*) for the scroll (*volumen*) was first made by the Christians and is unknown to the Jews before the second or third century A.D.

Modern editions of Biblical books differ from the Hebrew manuscripts —at least until 200 B.C.—in a second important respect: the form of the letters. The old Phoenician alphabet was used for books until after the time of Nehemiah and for coins even in A.D. 132-135. The current printed Hebrew type, called "square Hebrew," is a modification of the Aramaic characters and appears for the first time in the inscription *ṭwbyh* (Tobiah)[1] at ʿArâq el-Emîr in Ammon (see the photograph in H. Gressmann, *Altorientalische Bilder zum Alten Testament*. 2nd ed., Fig. 608. Berlin and Leipzig, 1927). This inscription apparently dates from about 180 B.C. The Pentateuch was written in square characters in the first century B.C.; the reference of Jesus to *yod* or *y* ("jot") as the smallest of all letters (Matt. 5:18) is correct with regard to square characters but not with regard to the old Phoenician alphabet. The oldest Hebrew Biblical manuscript, the Nash papyrus (S. A. Cook in PSBA 25 [1903] 34-56), is written in square Hebrew. It contains only the Ten Commandments (Deut. 5:6-21 [H. 5:6-18]) and the *shemaʿ* (Deut. 6:4 f.), in a text closer to the LXX than to the Masoretic. It is generally dated in the second cen-

---

[1] This inscription is generally ascribed to Hyrcanus, the grandson of Tobiah (son of the high priest Onias II), who lived in a stronghold in Transjordania from 183 to 176 B.C. (Josephus, *Antiquities* 12:4, 11).

tury of our era, although W. F. Albright (JBL 56 [1937] 145-176) would date it in the period of 165-37 B.C.

The origin of the old Phoenician alphabet—from which all alphabets in current use have been ultimately derived—is obscure.[2] To judge from recent discoveries of early inscriptions, it was invented about 1500 B.C. or even before. The Israelites adopted it from the Canaanites and used it both for commercial purposes (as shown by the ostraca from Samaria written during the reign of Ahab [875-853 B.C.]) and for the Scriptures (as we may infer from the Samaritan Pentateuch, written in an ornate form of the Phoenician letters). According to a Jewish legend (cf. L. Ginzberg, *The Legends of the Jews*, Vol. VI, pp. 443 f.) accepted as true by Origen, Epiphanius, and Jerome, Ezra introduced from Babylonia the new square Hebrew characters. In reality it seems probable that the Jews, when Aramaic gradually became their vernacular in the fourth century, adopted the Aramaic script (from which the square characters were derived) and probably began to copy the Scriptures first in Aramaic and then, after 200 B.C., in square characters. Accordingly, the Greek version (with the exception of the Pentateuch translated about 250 B.C., for which see J. Fischer, Beih. ZAW 42, 1926; AA X: 2, 1929) was made from manuscripts written in a cursive Aramaic or a nearly square Hebrew alphabet. The confusion of *j* and *w*, of *b* and *m* (inexplicable in the old script) is extremely rare in the Pentateuch, but not infrequent in the rest of the Greek Bible (cf. J. Fischer, Beih. ZAW 56, 1930; S. R. Driver, *Notes on the Hebrew Text of the Books of Samuel*, pp. lxiv ff., 2nd ed., Oxford, 1913; H. M. Orlinsky in JQR N.S. 30 [1939] 37-39). We may also infer from certain differences between the Hebrew and Greek texts that the manuscripts from which the LXX was translated had no vowels and few "mothers of reading" (i.e., consonants used to mark a long vowel); it usually lacked all indications of the end of words (such as a space, a dot, and the peculiar form of the final letters *k, m, n, p, ts*), and contained abbreviations such as Y' for Jehovah; for examples see S. R. Driver, *op. cit.*, pp. xxvii-xxxiii, lxii-lxiv, lxix, n.2; C. Steuernagel, *Einleitung in das Alte Testament*, p. 76-79.

B. From A.D. 90 to 135

The differences in contents are far more important than these external differences between our printed Hebrew text and its original form. The text of a literary work during its manuscript transmission is always more or less fluid, unless strict measures are taken to ensure that every fresh copy will be an exact reproduction of the original. The importance of

---

[2] For recent publications on the subject see the present writer's review in *Amer. Jour. of Archaeol.* 41 (1937) 643 f. and the article of J. W. Flight in the *Haverford Symposium on Archaeology and the Bible*, pp. 111-135. New Haven, 1938.

guarding the text of the Scriptures against all change dawned only gradually on the Jews. The earliest allusions to their interest in the matter are
Deut. 17:18 f.; Josh. 1:8; Ps. 1:2; II Chron. 17:9. Their concern with the
letter of God's word led them to take steps, increasing in effectiveness, to
preserve the text intact; but when they finally succeeded it was too late
to recapture the wording of the original writings. Although we are ill-
informed on the matter, we may distinguish three main stages in this
concern about the text: the canonization of the books and the activity of
Rabbi Akiba (d. *ca.* A.D. 132); the work of Talmudic rabbis; and the
labors of the Masoretes.

Before the books of the Old Testament reached their canonical standing—the Pentateuch in 400 B.C., the Former and Latter Prophets in 200
B.C., and the Writings in A.D. 90—they were circulating more or less
privately. The owners of manuscripts felt free to annotate them; such
glosses were inserted into the text of later copies. Moreover, through
accidental or deliberate modifications, each new manuscript was a new
edition and, as will be shown in the analysis of the individual books,
scribes and scholars issued from time to time enlarged editions of the
ancient books, containing either quotations from other writings (most of
which are now lost) or contributions of their own. When the Scriptures
were eventually canonized in the three stages mentioned above, a first
step was taken to save the individual books from further change at the
hand of scribes and editors (cf. Josephus, *Against Apion* 1:8). Nevertheless, accidental and deliberate modifications in minor matters continued
to be made by copyists and, more important, editorial changes could still
be made. This may be seen in the differences between the Hebrew and
the LXX texts, between the Hebrew and Samaritan Pentateuchs, and
between parallel texts in the Bible (Genesis-Kings and Chronicles; I Sam.
22 and Ps. 18; II Kings 18-20 and Is. 36-39; etc.). An imposing list of
some three thousand textual errors has been compiled by Friedrich
Delitzsch (*Die Lese- und Schreibfehler im Alten Testament.* Berlin,
1920) from the apparatus of Kittel's *Biblia Hebraic* (2nd ed.).[3] More
important is the classification of textual variants compiled by A. Sperber

---

[3] A similar, independent conspectus of textual errors in the Old Testament is available in English: James Kennedy, *An Aid to the Textual Amendment of the Old Testament* (edited posthumously by N. Levison), Edinburgh, 1928. In spite of typographical errors and of the questionable validity of some suggested emendations, a
discriminating student may use the book profitably. An important classification of
textual errors, illustrated with typical examples, will be found in the suggestive and
original book of F. Perles, *Analekten zur Textkritik des Alten Testaments,* Neue Folge,
Leipzig, 1922. P. Ruben (*Recensio und Restitutio,* London, 1936) has attempted to
recover the original text of certain corrupt passages, which he believes to have assumed their present form through ancient emendation of texts preserving a multiple
recension. See J. Reider, in *HUCA* VII (1930) 285-315.

(HUCA XIV [1939] 161-175) by comparing two ancient recensions of the same text.

In view of the innumerable manuscript variants and of the differences between the Hebrew and LXX texts, about A.D. 100 (when the scriptural canon had been fixed for all time) the rabbis felt the urgent need of fixing a standard text of the Scriptures, and particularly of the Pentateuch. At that time two factors contributed to focus attention on the dangers lurking in the variety of textual recensions: the controversy with the Christians and primarily the recognition that the whole system of Jewish faith and practice rested on the authority of the Scriptures—on the very letter of the sacred texts.

Christian polemics were more important for fixing the canon than the text. When the Jewish authorities assembled at Jamnia (*ca.* A.D. 90) defined the canon of Hebrew Scriptures, they officially declared, "The Gospel and the books of the heretics are not sacred Scripture" (cf. G. F. Moore, *Judaism,* Vol. I, p. 243). But until the final separation of the Nazarenes (Judeo-Christians) from the Synagogue after Bar-Cocheba's rebellion (A.D. 132-135) under Hadrian, the rabbis were forced to defend Judaism on two fronts. The exclusion of "the Gospel" from the canon did not prevent the Nazarenes, who were still worshiping in the synagogues, from finding in the Hebrew Bible arguments to prove that Jesus was the Messiah and from seeing in the destruction of Jerusalem in A.D. 70 a divine punishment for the rejection of the Christ (Moore, *op. cit.,* p. 90). As for the Gentile Christians, they found in the Greek Bible (the LXX) their defensive and offensive weapons in the controversy with the Jews. For instance, they proved the virgin birth of Jesus through the incorrect Greek rendering of Is. 7:14 (cf. Matt. 1:23). On the basis of the Greek text they did not hesitate to accuse the Jews of falsifying the Scriptures by expunging from it much that favored the Christians (Justin Martyr, *Dialogue with Tryphon* [written *ca.* 155-160] §§71-73). Such accusations were of course without foundation. But Justin (*loc. cit.*) quotes *in extenso* passages from Ezra and Jeremiah which presumably never stood in any edition or version of these books; erroneously he claims that the Jews have expunged Jer. 11:19 from their Bible (cf. F. C. Burkitt in JTS 33 [1931-1932] 371-73); and without warrant adds to Ps. 96:10 (LXX and Vulgate 95:10) the following words in italics, "Say among the nations, The 'Lord has reigned *from the wood* [i.e., the Cross].'" Even Jerome (*ad* Gal. 3:13), noticing that Paul omitted the mention of God in quoting Deut. 21:23 in Gal. 3:13, could seriously deem it possible that the Jews had added the reference to the deity in Deut. 21:23 to insult the Christians.[4]

[4] A comprehensive study of the polemic between Jews and Christians during the first three centuries remains to be written. For a summary of Christian attacks on

A standard Biblical text was not only essential to repel the attacks of the Christians, but even more for the discovery of God's will revealed in every word—nay, in every letter—of the Scriptures. When the Jews became convinced that Judaism in every last detail had been divinely revealed in the canonical Scriptures and that no word or letter therein was devoid of significance, it became necessary to formulate the rules of interpretation for discovering in individual clauses, words, and even letters God's revelation of his character and requirements. Seven rules were formulated at the beginning of our era and attributed to Hillel; they were expanded into thirteen rules by Rabbi Ishmael in the early part of the second century (for the literature see G. F. Moore, *Judaism*, Vol. III, p. 73). Ishmael's colleague Akiba (d. *ca.* 132) apparently realized more keenly than the other rabbis how essential the fixation of the text was for Jewish apologetics, polemics, and particularly for halakic and haggadic exegesis (on Akiba see L. Finkelstein, *Akiba.* New York, 1936).

The exact contribution of Akiba and his colleagues to the fixation of the Hebrew text is unknown, but it is certain that definite measures inspired by him were taken early in the second century. One of his mottoes was, "*Masôreth* [meaning probably tradition, i.e., the correct transmission of the text] is a fence for the Torah" (*Sayings of the Fathers* 3:18) and he was later praised for deriving from every single "thorn" or stroke (the "tittle" of Matt. 5:18) of the Pentateuch "heaps and heaps of legal norms [halakahs]" (G. F. Moore, *Judaism*, Vol. III, p. 76; L. Ginzberg, *Legends of the Jews*, Vol. II, pp. 325 f.; Vol. III, p. 115). Developing the verbal exegetical method of his teacher Nahum of Ginzo in opposition to Ishmael's logical method, Akiba discovered through incredible ingenuity a hidden meaning in apparently insignificant Hebrew particles.[5] Thus *eth*, which merely introduces a determined accusative but cannot be distinguished in form from the preposition meaning "with," allegedly conceals hidden direct objects: in Gen. 1:1 "*eth*—the heavens" implies also

---

Judaism and abundant bibliographical references see: J. Juster, *Les Juifs dans l'empire Romain* (Vol. I, pp. 43-76, Paris, 1914). The Jews did not compose tracts attacking the Christians before 300, but their rabbinical literature contains more or less veiled polemical allusions to Christianity; see, for typical examples, H. L. Strack and P. Billerbeck, *Kommentar zum Neuen Testament*, Index *sub voce* "Polemik gegen Christliches." Some Christian claims of Jewish falsification of the scriptural text are discussed by E. König (*Einleitung in das Alte Testament*, pp. 86 f., Bonn, 1893); cf. the remarks of N. Peters (*Der Text des Alten Testaments und seine Geschichte* [Bibl. Zeitfragen V: 6-7], p. 28, Münster, 1912) on Pss. 16:10; 22:16 [H. 22:17].

[5] Philo of Alexandria had already declared that the Law contains no superfluous words and had discovered hidden meanings in isolated words and constructions: so the phrase "eating you may eat" (i.e., you may freely eat) in Gen. 2:16 refers for him to a spiritual nourishment of the soul accompanied by a realization of the causes of things (*Leg. alleg.* 1:31); see for other instances C. Siegfried, *Philo von Alexandrien als Ausleger des Alten Testaments*, pp. 168 ff.

"sun, moon, and stars"; in Deut. 10:20 "thou shalt fear *eth*—Jehovah" means "the teachers of the Law along with Jehovah."

Obviously textual variants and dubious readings would preclude interpretations based on such insignificant particles or even on peculiarities of spelling, and Akiba must have endeavored to standardize the text in its minutest components. It was inevitable that the LXX Greek version used by Hellenistic Jews, often differing radically from the Hebrew text, should be regarded as corrupt (Justin Martyr, *Dialogue with Tryphon* §71), particularly when the Christians used it to prove the tenets of their faith. Consequently, Aquila, a pagan from Sinope who became a Jew after his conversion to Christianity, on his having learned the exegetical methods of his teacher Akiba, prepared (about 130) a new literal Greek version of the standard Hebrew text of the Scriptures (see J. Reider, *Prolegomena to a Greek-Hebrew and Hebrew-Greek Index to Aquila*. Philadelphia, 1916). Hellenistic Jews still used it in the sixth century, under Justinian. "A slave to Hebrew idiom" (Origen), Aquila regularly translated the accusative particle *eth* by "with," and otherwise reproduced literally every Hebrew word in Greek, with no concern about Greek syntax. To the horror of the Christians, in Is. 7:14 Aquila rendered "young woman," and not "virgin" as it is in the LXX (Justin Martyr, *Dial. with Tryph.* §§67, 71, and 84); Irenaeus [d. *ca.* 202], *Against Heresies* [Stieren edition] 3:21, 1 [others 3:24], also attacks this rendering of Theodotion and Aquila.

Early in the second century (probably before Aquila, cf. H. M. Orlinsky in JQR N.S. 27 [1936] 143), Theodotion revised the LXX in order to bring it into harmony with the Hebrew text then current. He was not a follower of Akiba nor a slave of the letter and, despite the criticism of Irenaeus just mentioned, his version attained great popularity among Christians. For Daniel all extant Greek manuscripts except one (the Chigi manuscript—Holmes and Parsons 88) give Theodotion's text. Theodotion incorporates in his version of Daniel parts of an earlier Greek version, known through quotations in the New Testament and in other writings of the first century (cf. J. A. Montgomery, *Daniel* [ICC] pp. 46-50, and the investigations quoted there).

Akiba's emphasis on the letter of the text inspired not only Aquila's Greek version, but also the earliest known Aramaic versions, or *Targums*. The original Palestinian Targums of the Law and the Prophets (those of the Writings are late), dating from the second century, were edited in Babylonia in the third century and have come down in late recensions.[6]

---

[6] On the Targums see, for general summaries and bibliographies, W. Bacher in *Jewish Encycl.* XII, 57-63; E. Schürer, *Geschichte des Jüdischen Volkes*, 3rd and 4th edit., Vol. I, pp. 147-156, Leipzig, 1901; T. Walker, in Hastings' *Dictionary of the Bible*, IV, 678-683. The word *"targum"* means "translation" (cf. Ezra 4:7).

The official Targum to the Pentateuch, according to legend, was dictated to Onkelos by Eliezer and Joshua, contemporaries of Akiba. Scholars generally recognize that the unknown author of this Targum was erroneously confused with Aquila and that *Onkelos* is merely an Aramaic spelling of Aquila (*Akylas*). Onkelos seems to be a revision of an old Palestinian Targum. Through this revision the differences between the original Targum and Akiba's official Hebrew text were eliminated in Onkelos. Onkelos is strictly literal, except for some paraphrases of the poems and some prose sections. Nevertheless, anthropomorphisms in reference to God are eliminated regularly through circumlocutions; out of reverence for Moses, his "Ethiopian wife" in Num. 12:1, becomes his "beautiful wife." The periphrastic Palestinian Targum of which Onkelos seems to be a revision has also survived in a late enlarged edition called "Jerusalem Targum" and, in a slightly different recension, "Targum of Jonathan." The latter name rests on a misunderstanding of the abbreviation "T.J." (Jerusalem Targum), and moderns refer to it as "Pseudo-Jonathan." The surviving edition of the latter cannot be earlier than the seventh century, since it names (*ad* Gen. 21:21) a wife and daughter of Mohammed; nevertheless, it may be surmised that its nucleus is earlier than Onkelos. A third (incomplete) Targum to the Pentateuch (the "Fragment Targum") may represent another recension of the old Palestinian Targum (W. Bacher) or less probably a collection of glosses added to it (A. Geiger). Newly discovered fragments of the Jerusalem Targum have been published by P. Kahle (*Masoreten des Westens*, Vol. II. Stuttgart, 1930; cf. A. Marmorstein in ZAW N.F. 8 [1931] 231-242).

The official Targum to the Prophets (Joshua-Kings, Isaiah-Minor Prophets) is said to have been delivered orally by Jonathan the son of Uzziel, a pupil of Hillel, in the first century. After being revised in Palestine, this Targum was rewritten in Babylonia in the fourth and fifth centuries. It paraphrases the text far more than Onkelos. Fragments of a different recension of this Targum have survived in the Codex Reuchlinianus (edited by P. de Lagarde in 1872): this *Targum Yerushalmi* (Jerusalem Targum) contains revisions which are later than the Jonathan Targum.

On the basis of circumstantial evidence—furnished by Akiba's exegetical method and the new Greek and Aramaic versions or revisions inspired by him—we may conclude that in the first quarter of the second century the rabbis took definite measures to fix the authorized Hebrew text. Their efforts were not entirely successful. Although it may be said that "from the second century of our era the Jews had a standard Hebrew text which was transmitted with great fidelity" (G. F. Moore, *Judaism*, Vol. I, p. 101), it would be an error to imagine that this ancient text was identical in all details with that of our printed editions. P. de Lagarde (*Anmer-*

kungen zur griech. Uebersetzung der Proverbien, pp. 1 f. 1863) tried to prove that after A.D. 130 all copies of the Scriptures conformed to an archetype (selected shortly before that time) and reproduced all its minute graphic peculiarities. But this theory has been disproved by the studies of H. L. Strack, C. D. Ginsburg, and particularly now through the work of P. Kahle and his students. It is clear from the variants that still persist in all the ancient versions made after 130,[7] that the official text of Akiba, if we may call it so, did not entirely eliminate other textual recensions circulating at the time, and that copyists of the standard text continued to make some unwitting or deliberate slight changes. Consequently, when the Masoretes undertook to fix the text in all its minute eccentricities, they were confronted with variants which were too well attested to be summarily suppressed (cf. P. Kahle in TSK 81 [1915] 399 ff.; J. Hempel in ZAW N.F. 7 [1930] 187-198; A. Sperber in HUCA XIV [1939] 153 f.).

C. From 135 to 500

A number of deliberate changes were apparently introduced in the text between Akiba and the completion of the Talmud (135-500). Some changes are purely graphic, others reflect religious ideas.

Subdivisions in the text and diacritical marks belong to the first group. In the Hebrew manuscripts from which the LXX was translated the single words were not separated by a space or a mark, but written continuously, as also in ancient Greek manuscripts. As a result, in a number of cases the words are divided differently in the Hebrew and in the LXX (cf. S. R. Driver, *Notes on Samuel,* 2nd ed., pp. xxviii f.). For instance, in I Chron. 17:10 the difference between the Hebrew ("and I tell you") and the LXX ("and I will magnify you") rests entirely on reading the consonants *w'gdlk* as one word (LXX) or as two (Hebrew); the doubling of the *d* (LXX) or of the *g* (Hebr.) was not yet indicated by a dot (called

---

[7] For the differences between the Targum Onkelos and the Hebrew text see A. Sperber in Proceed. Amer. Acad. for Jewish Research 6 (1934-35) 309-351; for Targum Jonathan on the Prophets see P. Churgin, *Targum Jonathan on the Prophets,* pp. 55-65 (New Haven, 1907). The main deviations from the Hebrew in Jerome's Vulgate are listed by W. Nowack, *Die Bedeutung des Hieronimus für die alttestamentliche Textkritik.* Göttingen, 1875 (cf. A. Sperber in HUCA XII-XIII [1937-38] 124-127). For variants in the Talmud, Midrashim, and even later rabbinical writings, see A. Aptowitzer, *Das Schriftwort in der Rabbinischen Litteratur*: (I and II) Sitzungsberichte der Akademie der Wissenschaft in Wien 153 (1906), Abhandlung VI; 160 (1908), Abh. VII; (III) XVIII. Jahresbericht der israel.-theologischen Lehranstalt in Wien, 1911, pp. 95 ff. (cf. the list of variants in the Mishna and in the Talmud in H. L. Strack, *Prolegomena Critica in Vetus Testamentum Hebraicum,* pp. 94-111. Leipzig, 1873). Despite this evidence, R. Gordis (*The Biblical Text in the Making,* pp. 45-49. Philadelphia, 1937), still maintains that the archetype of the Scriptures was chosen *before* A.D. 70.

dagesh). In some cases (e.g., Gen. 49:19 f.; I Kings 19:21; Am. 6:12), the Hebrew and the versions all agree in adopting a wrong word division.

It would seem that the word division was introduced in the text some time before 500. The Targum, the Syriac, and Jerome differ rarely from the Hebrew in word division and in every instance they agree with the LXX and may have been influenced by it (cf. the table in C. D. Ginsburg, *Introduction to the Masoretico-Critical Edition of the Hebrew Bible*, p. 159. London, 1897). In any case, the word division is assumed by the Masoretes, who list variants differing merely in the word division (Ginsburg, *op. cit.*, p. 163; A. Sperber, in HUCA XIV [1939] 175). Such variants prove, moreover, that at the time the elongated shape of the letters *k m n p ts* at the end of words was not yet in general use, although according to *Jerus. Megillah* 1:9 (translated in Ginsburg, *op. cit.*, pp. 297 f.) they are mentioned, apparently as something new, in the time of Akiba. Jerome is already familiar with these five *litterae duplicae* (*Prologus Galeatus*).

The earliest subdivisions of Hebrew books are the verses and the synagogue lessons. It is sometimes said that the verse division was originally used for poetic lines or stichs, and subsequently introduced in the prose parts of the Scriptures (F. Buhl, *Kanon und Text des Alten Testamentes*, p. 223. Leipzig, 1891; and M. L. Margolis in *Jewish Encyclopedia* XII, 423). But in our Hebrew Bible one verse often included more than one line of poetry, indicating that the verse was not always identified with the stich. It seems more likely that the verse division originated in the practice of reading successively brief sections of the Hebrew Scriptures in the synagogue and translating each into Aramaic. This custom is first mentioned in the Mishnah (A.D. 200), but it may be considerably earlier (cf. G. F. Moore, *Judaism*, Vol. I, pp. 303 f.). The Mishnah (*Megillah* 4:4) actually prescribes that a single verse (*pāsûq*) of the Pentateuch will be read to the *methûrgemān* ("dragoman" is derived from the same root) for his translation, but three verses of the Prophets may be translated together. As these oral translations (which should not be read from a manuscript, *Jerus. Megillah* 4:1) tended to become standardized, they were eventually committed to writing in the Targums and the verse division became fixed. The two dots (:) marking the end of every verse, or *sôph-pāsûq*, are only mentioned after A.D. 500. For centuries the verse division current in Palestine and in Babylonia varied considerably (cf. Ginsburg, *Introduction*, pp. 68-108). Finally, the greatest of the Masoretes, Aaron ben Moses ben Asher (often called "ben Asher"), in the first half of the tenth century, edited the text with the current verse division, according to which the Pentateuch comprises 5,845 verses (previously in Babylonia the number was 5,888 and in Palestine 5,842).

The current division of the Hebrew books into chapters is relatively recent, being first mentioned about 1330 (Ginsburg, *Introduction,* p. 25). It was first adopted for the Latin Bible in the thirteenth century, presumably by Stephen Langton, Archbishop of Canterbury (d. 1228); cf. G. F. Moore in JBL 12 (1893) 73-78. On the contrary, in the New Testament the chapter division of Langton is older than the verse division (first introduced by Robert Stephanus in his fourth edition of the New Testament, Geneva, 1551).

Two kinds of divisions of the Hebrew text into pericopes are, however, ancient: one follows the natural subdivisions of the text; the other is liturgical. According to the first, the Pentateuch is currently subdivided into 290 "open" and 379 "closed" *perashiyôth* (sing. *parashâh*, section). The open (marked by a *p*) are paragraphs beginning a new line; the closed (marked by an *s*) are briefer and are preceded by a blank space in the line. The Mishnah, about A.D. 200, mentions the *perashiyôth* of the Pentateuch and of the Prophets, but the distinction between open and closed sections is first made in the Talmud (*ca.* 500). Jerome's Hebrew text (cf. his remarks on Mic. 6:9) showed these subdivisions plainly. Only rarely (as in Ex. 6:28; Hag. 1:14; Is. 56:9) does this accepted subdivision of the text do violence to the real meaning of the words.

The liturgical division of the Law and the Prophets into synagogue lessons is equally ancient. The synagogue originated between 400 B.C. and the Maccabean rebellion (168-165 B.C.) as the meeting place where sections of the Pentateuch were read in public. It is possible that the Chronicler's description of Ezra's reading from the Law of Moses (Neh. 8) was inspired by the synagogue practice of his day; if so, this is our earliest source (about 250 B.C.) on the subject. Before A.D. 70 a section of the Prophets was added to the Torah lesson (Luke 4:16-21). Eventually the Sabbath lesson from the Law (*sēder*) and from the Prophets (*haphṭārâh*) became fixed, perhaps in the third century since the Mishnah does not regulate the matter (G. F. Moore, *Judaism*, Vol. I, p. 300). According to the Babylonian Talmud (*Megillah* 29b and 31b), in Palestine the Pentateuch was read in the course of three years (and was accordingly divided into 154 [or 158, 167] *sedārîm* or weekly lessons), whereas in Babylonia it was finished in one year (and therefore divided into 54 *perashiyôth*). The Babylonian yearly cycle prevailed everywhere among the Jews, except in some localities like Old Cairo, where the triennial cycle continued until the thirteenth century. The Babylonian list of weekly lessons is printed in English in the Jewish Publication Society translation of the Bible. The earliest synagogue homilies (*midrashîm*) are based on the lessons from the Law and the Prophets and follow the obsolete triennial cycle; see Jacob Mann, *The Bible as Read and Preached in the Old Synagogue* (Vol. I: Genesis and Exodus. Cincinnati, 1940. This monumental work will be completed in three volumes). The reading of Biblical pericopes in the synagogues and the singing of Psalms in the Temple led to the addition of some verses of good augury (see K. J. Grimm, *Euphemistic Liturgical Appendixes in the Old Testament.* Leipzig, 1901).

A diacritical mark which was originally unrelated to the vocalization and the accents of the Masoretic Bible, originated before A.D. 500. *Sifre,* a juristic commentary on Numbers dating from the early part of the third century, lists (in a note on Num. 9:10) dots placed over words or letters in the following ten passages of the Pentateuch (cf. Ginsburg, *Introduction,* pp. 318-334): Num. 9:10; Gen. 16:5; 18:9; 19:33; 33:4; 37:12; Num. 21:30; 3:39; 29:15; Deut. 29:28. In addition, the Masora adds five instances from the Prophets and the Writings: II Sam. 19:20; Is. 44:9; Ez. 41:20; 46:22; Ps. 26:13. These dots mark words or passages which are textually, grammatically, or exegetically questionable, in the opinion of ancient scholars (see the discussion of each in Ginsburg, *ibid.*). The use of such a dot in Num. 9:10 is attested in the Mishnah (*Pesachim* IX, 2), and in Gen. 19:33 by Jerome.

Another diacritical mark, called *pāsēq* (divider) or *pesîq* (divided), is a vertical line occurring about 480 times in our Hebrew Bible. The term, which occurs only after the tenth century, reflects the Masoretic view that the sign had the purpose of preventing two letters or words from being pronounced together. In a late addition to a Masoretic book (*Diqduqe ha-Teʿamim* §28), appearing for the first time in a manuscript of the year 1448, five uses of the paseq are named: separation of identical consonants (cf. I Chron. 22:3, 5) and identical words (cf. Gen. 39:10; Ex. 24:6), of a divine name from a word adjoining it (cf. Ps. 139:19, 21), of two words which in meaning do not belong together (cf. Ps. 68:21 [English 68:20]), of two words apparently joined by the accents (cf. Num. 3:38, *bis*).

In reality, however, many of the occurrences of the paseq line cannot be explained in this manner. Some modern scholars believe that it had originally another purpose and regard it as pre-Masoretic, as would be the case if the Masoretes no longer knew its original significance. But P. Kahle (in H. Bauer and P. Leander, *Historische Grammatik der Hebräischen Sprache,* Vol. I, pp. 157-162. Halle, 1922) infers from a study of the early manuscripts and from the silence of the Talmud that it was introduced only shortly before its first mention in the *Midrash Rabba ad Ex.* 3:4 (eleventh or twelfth century), according to which the paseq occurs when the names Abraham, Jacob, and Samuel are repeated, but not with "Moses Moses." Although the paseq is still the most mysterious of the signs in the Hebrew Bible, it seems probable that it was used before the Masoretes by a few scholars to call the attention of copyists to textual errors which should not be corrected in transcription: it would thus correspond to *sic*![8]

The inverted *n* (written thus "[" instead of thus "]") is probably an early diacritical mark, and seems to be a bracket used to indicate passages which are out of place. It occurs nine times in our Bible: before and after Num. 10:35 f. (cf. *Sifra, ad loc.; Shabbath* 115b-116a) which in the LXX precede Num. 10:34, and in each verse of Ps. 107:23-28, 39 (cf. Ginsburg, *Introduction*, pp. 341-345; Krauss, ZAW 1902, p. 57 ff.). The Masora adds a tenth occurrence in Gen. 11:32.

The Masoretes punctiliously recorded the peculiar writing of certain letters and we may surmise that, at least in some cases, such eccentricities had a critical purpose. This practice originated before 500 B.C. The following instances occur in our Masoretic text: *a.* Raised letters (cf. Ginsburg, *Introduction*, pp. 334-341); the suspended *n* in "Manasseh" (Judg. 18:30) was added to the original text, which read "Moses," "for the sake of Moses' fair name" as Rashi said (cf. for Talmudic and other references G. F. Moore, *Judges* [ICC], pp. 401 f.): a letter *'ayin* is raised in Ps. 80:14 either to mark a variant reading (Ginsburg, *op. cit.*, pp. 338-340) or to indicate the middle of the Psalter (*Kiddushin* 30b); the *'ayin* in the word for "wicked" in Job 38:13, 15 is raised to indicate variant readings (omitting this letter), i.e., either "poor" or "chiefs" (Ginsburg, *op. cit.*, pp. 340 f.). *b.* Large letters (cf. H. L. Strack, *Prolegomena*, pp. 92 f.) are used to indicate: the beginning of the book (the large initial *b* in Gen. 1:1, cf. A. von Gall in ZAW 1911, pp. 74 f.), the middle letter of the Pentateuch (Lev. 13:33 [*Kiddushin* 30b] or 11:42 [*Soferim* IX]), important passages (Deut. 6:4; Ex. 34:7; Num. 14:17), and other matters (Num. 14:17; Deut. 29:27; Ps. 80:16, etc.). *c.* Small letters occur in Gen. 2:4; 23:2; Lev. 1:1; Deut. 32:18; Prov. 28:17. For the large and small letters in Esther 9:7-10 see L. B. Paton, *Esther* [ICC], p. 284. For lists of large and small letters, see B. Walton, *Biblia Polyglotta*, Vol. I, p. 46 (London, 1657), and C. D. Ginsburg, *The Massorah*, Vol. IV, pp. 40 f. *d.* The broken *waw* (w) in Num. 25:12 may indicate a variant reading. *e.* A *q* in Ex. 32:25 is closed. *f.* The "closed" (final) *m* in Is. 9:6 (English 9:7) seems to indicate that *lm* should be omitted (cf. LXX and Targum) or read as a separate word. *g.* Ordinary letters occur at the end of words, in place of the final letters: an *m* in Neh. 2:13 and an *n* in Job 38:1.

[8] Cf. P. Kahle (*op. cit.*, Vol. I, p. 161); J. Olshausen, *Lehrbuch der Hebräischen Sprache*, Vol. I, p. 86 (Braunschweig, 1861); W. Wickes, *A Treatise on the Accentuation of the Twenty-one so-called Prose Books of the Old Testament* (Oxford, 1887); F. Praetorius, "Pāsēq" (ZDMG 53 [1899] 683-692); H. Grimme, "Paseqstudien" (BZ I [1903] 337 ff.; 2 [1904] 28 ff.) and *Psalmenprobleme* (Freiburg, Schweitz, 1902); James Kennedy, *The Note-Line in the Hebrew Scriptures commonly called Pāsīq* (Edinburgh, 1903); Hugo Fuchs, "Pesiq ein Glossenzeichen" (*Vierteljahrsschrift für Bibelkunde, Talmud, und patristische Studien* 3 [1907] 1-66, 97-181).

Finally a blank space (*pisqâ*) was left in the middle of twenty-eight verses, e.g., Gen. 4:8; 35:22; I Sam. 14:19; Ez. 3:16, in some cases to mark an omission. In Gen. 4:8 we should in reality add after "his brother" the words, "Let us go to the field" (so the Samaritan text, the LXX, Syriac, and the Old Latin; similarly the Jerusalem Targum and the Vulgate); and in 35:22 the LXX reads after "Israel" the words "and it was grievous in his sight." On the *pisqâ* see in particular H. Graetz in MGWJ 1878, pp. 481 ff.; 1887, pp. 193-200.

Although the exact transmission of the text, even when it seemed to be doubtful, is thus generally enjoined, the rabbis of the Talmud knew that in a few cases the scribes had deliberately changed the received text. They officially approved such corrected readings, whether made in writing in the text or, without changing the consonants, orally.

Early in the third century, the halakic commentary on Exodus (*Mekilta, ad* Ex. 15:7) lists eleven "corrections of the scribes" (*tiqqûnê sôferîm*) occurring in Num. 11:15 ("*thy* [God's] evil" changed to "*my* evil"); Num. 12:12 (originally "*our* flesh . . . *our* mother"); I Sam. 3:13 (originally "his sons cursed *me* [God]"); II Sam. 20:1 ("to his *gods*" changed into "to his *tents*"; cf. I Kings 12:16 and II Chron. 10:16, quoted in later lists); Jer. 2:11 ("*my* [God's] glory" changed to "*his* glory"); Ez. 8:17 ("*my* [God's] nose" changed to "*their* nose"); Hab. 1:12 ("*thou* [God] wilt not die" changed to "*we* shall not die"); Zech. 2:12 (English 2:8) ("*my* [God's] eye" changed to "*his* eye"); Mal. 1:13 ("you sniff at *me* [God]" changed to "at *it*"); Ps. 106:20 ("*his* [God's] glory" changed to "*their* glory"); Job 7:20 ("a burden to *thee* [God]" changed to "a burden to *myself*"). In the early midrash on Numbers and Deuteronomy (*Sifre* 22b, *ad* Num. 10:35), likewise dating from the early part of the third century, a similar list is given, in which I Sam. 3:13; II Sam. 20:1; Mal. 1:13; Ps. 106:20 are omitted. Conversely the final Masoretic list of corrections (cf. Ginsburg, *Introduction,* pp. 347-363) includes eighteen items, adding to the eleven of Mekilta the two parallels to II Sam. 20:1 mentioned above and the following five corrections: Gen. 18:22 (originally "Jehovah was yet standing before Abraham"); II Sam. 16:12 (the original "*his* [God's] *eye*" was corrected to "*my* iniquity" which was eventually read [*qerê*] "my eye"); Hos. 4:7 ("*my* [God's] glory they turn to shame" changed to "*their* glory I shall turn to shame"); Job 32:3 ("they condemned *God*" changed to "they condemned *Job*"); Lam. 3:20 ("*thy* [God's] soul is dissolved" changed to "*my* soul is dissolved").

This list of eighteen corrections is neither exhaustive nor entirely correct, but it is significant. It will be noted that, with a single exception (Num. 12:12), all changes have the purpose of removing from the Scriptures expressions lacking the proper reverence for the deity, either because they ascribed to God human organs and imperfections, or because a human being appeared to be equal or superior in rank to God, or because the diction was deemed blasphemous. In some instances we may doubt that the alleged original reading ever stood in the text, but in some instances an ancient version bears witness to these original readings (I Sam. 3:13; Zech. 2:8 [H. 2:12]; Ps. 106:20; Job 7:20) or to the uncertainty of the text (Ez. 8:17; Hab. 1:12; Lam. 3:20).

Without changing the written text, rabbinical authorities took steps to remove obscenities by prescribing that euphemistic expressions be read in their place. In *Megillah* 25b (cf. *Tosefta Meg.* IV) the following instances are listed (see Ginsburg, *Introduction,* pp. 345-347): "to lie" (with a woman) instead of "to ravish" (Deut. 28:30; later lists [*qerê*] include Is. 13:16; Jer. 3:2; Zech. 14:2); boils associated with unnatural sexual practices, changed to hemorrhoids (Deut. 28:27; cf. *qerê* in I Sam. 5:6, 9, 12; 6:4 f.); an unknown word denoting some unpalatable food (or, according to A. Geiger, human excrements), changed to dove's dung (II Kings 6:25); excrements, changed to a less vulgar word of the same meaning (II Kings 18:27; Is. 36:12), and similarly in the case of "backhouses" (II Kings 10:27); urine, changed to "water of the legs" (18:27; Is. 36:12). In Is. 19:18 the name of an Egyptian city was changed from "City of Righteousness" (so the LXX) to "City of the Sun" which in turn became "City of Destruction" (see Ginsburg, *Introduction,* pp. 406 f.).

Less significant textual changes are recorded in a passage of the Talmud (*Nedarim* 37b-38a; cf. Ginsburg, *Introduction,* pp. 307-312). "A [peculiar] pronunciation of the scribes, the removal [of the letter *w*] by the scribes [*iṭûr sōferîm*], words read but not written and written but not read, are a prescription of Moses at Sinai." *a.* The pronunciation of the word for "earth" (with the lengthening of the initial vowel following the article) and those for "Egypt" and "heaven" (with the ending characteristic of the dual). *b.* The letter *w* (*we,* meaning "and") is to be left out of the text of Gen. 18:5; 24:55; Num. 31:2; Pss. 36:7 and 68:26, where it is expected and is actually found in some manuscripts and versions. *c.* Read but not written (*qerê welô' kethîb*): "Euphrates" (II Sam. 8:3; cf. LXX and I Chron. 18:3); "a man" (II Sam. 16:23, "as if *a man* inquired"); "are coming" (Jer. 31:38, "the days *are coming*"; so Mss and the versions); "for her" (Jer. 50:29 [H. 31:37] "let there be no survivors *for her*"; omitting the word, with the LXX and Vulgate, "let none escape"); the accusative particle *eth* (before "all that thou hast done" in Ruth 2:11; the meaning is not affected and the Masora disregards this correction); "unto me" (Ruth 3:5, 17, after "thou sayest" and "he said"). The Masora adds the following words in italics to the preceding list (cf. Ginsburg, *Introduction,* pp. 313-315): "*the children* of Benjamin" (Judg. 20:13); "*forasmuch* [*kēn* is required] as the king's son is dead" (II Sam. 18:20); "the Lord *of hosts*" (II Kings 19:31; cf. Is. 37:32); "*his sons* smote him" (II Kings

19:31; cf. Is. 37:38). *d.* The words in italics are written but not read (*kethîb welô' qerê*) (Ginsburg, *Introduction,* pp. 315-318): the second "may Jehovah *please* pardon thy servant" (II Kings 5:18); "*and* [*we-eth*] the law" (Jer. 32:11, disregarded by the Masora); "bend *bend* his bow" (Jer. 51:3); "the south side . . . five *five* hundred" (Ez. 48:16); "it is true that [omitting *'im*]" (Ruth 3:12). In addition to these instances, all of which except possibly the first are actual errors, the Masora rightly omits: *'im* (as in Ruth 3:12 above) in II Sam. 13:33; 15:21; Jer. 39:12; and the accusative particle *eth* in Jer. 38:16.

In other instances it is clear that words with blasphemous or pagan connotations were often changed without being noted by rabbinical and Masoretic scholars; the original reading seldom appears in the early versions. A. Geiger (*Urschrift und Übersetzungen der Bibel in ihrer Abhängigkeit von der innern Entwickelung des Judenthums.* Breslau, 1857) was the first to make a systematic investigation of the subject (particularly *op. cit.,* pp. 267-299 and 313-345; see also Ginsburg, *Introduction,* pp. 363-367), but his great ingenuity frequently discovered deliberate euphemism in accidental errors. Blasphemous expressions were eliminated in several ways: *a.* By the addition of one or more words, bracketed here, as "for they despised [*the offering of*] Jehovah" (I Sam. 2:17; cf. the Syriac); "why have you despised [*the word of*] Jehovah?" (II Sam. 12:9); "you have greatly despised [*the enemies of*] Jehovah" (12:14; a similar addition in I Sam. 25:22 is omitted in Codices A and B of the LXX). *b.* By substituting for an expression meaning "to blaspheme or curse God" the expression "to bless God" (I Kings 21:10, 13; Ps. 10:3; Job 1:5, 11; 2:5, 9); in Ps. 10:3 the original text ("he despises") and the euphemism ("he blesses") are both preserved in the text, showing perhaps that the correction was written originally between the lines over the objectionable word. *c.* By other changes: in Jer. 23:17 the text is vocalized to read, "They say *to my* [Jeremiah's] despisers, *'Jehovah has spoken'* "; but the LXX and the Old Latin (cf. the Syriac), without changing the consonants, read what was really intended, "They say *to the despisers of the word of Jehovah.*" In I Sam. 3:13 not only was "to them" substituted for "Elohim" (cf. LXX), as was recorded in one of the "corrections of the scribes" listed above, but a substitute was provided for public reading, "for the iniquity which he knows" ("for the iniquity of his sons," in the LXX; "namely that these sons of his dishonored the people," in the Syriac). In II Sam. 6:21 the expression, "I have exposed myself before Jehovah" was corrupted and annotated (W. R. Arnold, *Ephod and Ark,* p. 42).

This last verse is one of the "numerous passages in the Old Testament where the scribes have preferred nonsense to an utterance which was objectionable on dogmatic or religious grounds" (Arnold, *op. cit.,* p. 14, n. 2). The text in which Zechariah (6:9-15) described the ill-fated coronation of Zerubbabel as the Messiah has been willfully curtailed and corrupted—Zerubbabel is not even mentioned! We shall see that the P sections of Joshua describing the territory of Ephraim and Manasseh have suffered great damage at the hand of an anti-Samaritan fanatic. In accordance with the Jewish dogma that there was in Israel a single "ark of the covenant" (said to have been made in the days of Moses), whenever other arks or divination boxes were mentioned in ancient writings the word *ephod* (meaning a linen apron) was generally substituted for *ārôn*, ark (Judg. 8:27; 17:5; 18:14, 17 f., 20; I Sam. 2:28; 14:3; 21:9 [H. 21:10]; 22:18; 23:6, 9; 30:7; cf. Hos. 3:4), as W. R. Arnold has shown (*op. cit.*). But in some passages the text was willfully corrupted or curtailed because the objectionable word "ark" had been accidentally allowed to stand: I Sam. 14:18, where the LXX has, however, "ephod" (Arnold, *op. cit.*, pp. 12-17); Judg. 18:27; I Sam. 2:28 and 21:9 [H. 21:10], and 30:7 (in Codex B of the LXX); and 15:23, where "iniquity" was substituted for "ark" (*op. cit.*, pp. 130 f.).

The horror of the Synagogue for heathenism in all its forms inspired the elimination of terms referring to pagan gods or objects from the text in public reading and even in manuscript copies. The divine names Astarte (so often in the LXX) and Melek were regularly read *bosheth* (shame) and are vocalized Ashtoreth (plural, Ashtaroth) and Molech (in the later Greek versions Moloch, cf. Acts 7:43; the LXX usually translates ruler or king); similarly Topheth (*Tapheth*, variously spelled, in the LXX; *Tappath* in the Syriac). In proper names, "Baal" (meaning "master" and used innocently in ancient times for Jehovah) was changed occasionally to *bosheth*, particularly in Samuel (the only exception is I Sam. 12:11; contrast II 11:21). A gloss in Hos. 2:16 [H. 2:18] announces the future elimination of the word *baal* from the Hebrew language. Accordingly we find in Samuel the names Jerubbesheth (II Sam. 11:21), Ishbosheth, and Mephibosheth instead of the original forms Jerubbaal (Judges and I Sam. 12:11), Ishbaal (cf. the later Greek versions and the Old Latin in II Sam. 3-4, and I Chron. 8:33 and 9:39), and Meribaal (I Chron. 8:34; 9:40). In Jer. 3:24; 11:13 (where both *bosheth* and *baal* occur in the Hebrew, but only *baal* in the LXX) and Hos. 9:10, *bosheth* is a surrogate for *Baal* (similarly in the LXX in I Kings 18:19 and 18:25, "the prophets of *shame*") and, as A. Dillmann has shown (*Monatsberichte der Kön.-Preuss. Akademie der Wissenschaften*, 1881, pp. 601-620), the use of the feminine article with Baal in the LXX (regularly in Jeremiah; Hos. 2:10 and 13:1; cf. Rom. 11:4) indicates that *aischyne* (shame) was substituted for Baal in reading. Sometimes *el* (divine being) was substituted for Baal (Beeliada [I Chron. 14:7] and Eliada [II Sam. 5:16; I Chron. 3:8]; Baal Berith [Judg. 8:33; 9:4] and El Berith [9:46]). The term *shiqqûts* (abomination) is used in Am. 5:26 as an oral surrogate for the names of the

Babylonian gods Kaiwanu and Sakkut, which were vocalized accordingly (but not yet in the LXX; cf. Acts 7:43); this word appears also as a written substitute for the *elohim* (gods) of pagans (I Kings 11:5, 7; II Kings 23:13, etc.) and, in the famous expression "the abomination of desolation" (Dan. 9:27; 11:31; 12:11; cf. Matt. 24:15; Mark 13:14), for the Baal of heaven, the Semitic name of the Olympian Zeus (see E. Nestle in ZAW 4 [1884] 248). Even the word for the ancient stone pillars was avoided by the Chronicler and willfully corrupted in ancient texts (cf. JBL 43 [1924] 236 f., notes 45 and 51, where other surrogates for heathen matters are likewise listed; see also, *Quantulacumque,* Studies presented to K. Lake, p. 307, n. 10).

The full extent of dogmatic revision of the Old Testament text is not known, but new investigations will undoubtedly bring unsuspected instances to light. Thus M. G. Slonim (in JQR 29 [1939] 397-403) has recently discovered that the substitution of masculine pronominal suffixes (in the second and third persons plural) for the feminine, appearing about 350 times in the Bible (except for some of the Minor Prophets), was apparently made deliberately and often serves to express reverence for sacred objects and institutions (cf. JQR 32 [1947] 139-158).

D. From 500 to 1200

The textual labors of the scribes and the Talmudic scholars were brought to completion by the Masoretes. The triumph of Christianity in Palestine forced many Jewish scholars to migrate to Babylonia, where they transplanted the Jewish learning in the second century and established in the third century the academies of Nehardea, Sura, and, after the destruction of Nehardea in 259, Pumbedita. Biblical studies were pursued in Babylonia until the tenth century. The Moslem conquest of Palestine (638) brought about a revival of the Palestinian schools. The school of Tiberias achieved prominence in the eighth and ninth centuries and after the decline of the Babylonian schools in the tenth century it became the center of Biblical studies and fixed the authorized text of the Scriptures, both consonantal and vocalic, for Judaism in general. In India such labors for the preservation of a sacred text had been carried forward long before. "As early as about 600 B.C. we find that in the theological schools of India, every word, every verse, every syllable of the Veda, had been carefully counted" (Max Müller, *Selected Essays,* Vol. XI, p. 119).

The contribution of the Babylonian schools, formerly known merely from a list of "Eastern" (*madinchae*) variants in contrast with Palestinian or "Western" (*ma'arbae*) readings,[9] has become better known in recent times through the discovery of manuscripts and the research of P. Kahle

[9] See Ginsburg, *Introduction,* pp. 197-240; R. Gordis, *The Biblical Text in the Making,* pp. 70-80.

and his school.[10] The Babylonian variants from recently discovered manuscripts (chiefly from Yemen, in Arabia, and Old Cairo) are quoted in the
apparatus of the third edition of R. Kittel's *Biblia Hebraica* (edited by
A. Alt, O. Eissfeldt, and P. Kahle. Stuttgart, 1929-1937).

   In general, however, the Masoretic school at Tiberias was destined to
prevail over the Babylonian academies in the transmission of the sacred
text. The Masoretes, as their name seems to indicate, were chiefly concerned with the preservation of the traditional text and its pronunciation,
rather than with a critical search for the earliest known textual recension.
With meticulous care they noted the peculiarities of the consonantal text,
which have been listed above, and transmitted them to us. On the whole,
the consonantal text was standardized, but variants still appeared here
and there. In many cases the Masoretes found themselves unable to choose
between two variants, equally well attested, and refrained from discarding
one in favor of the other. They ingeniously succeeded in transmitting
both readings either through an anomalous consonantal spelling or
through a pronunciation (fixed in the vowel signs) out of harmony
with the consonantal text: significant examples of both methods are
pointed out in the Aramaic portions of Daniel and Ezra by C. C. Torrey
(in JAOS 43 [1923] 229-238), and in Samuel by O. H. Boström (*Alternative Readings in the Books of Samuel.* Augustana College, Rock Island,
Illinois, 1918). In other cases the two readings were written separately,
producing a conflate text. R. Gordis (*The Biblical Text in the Making,*
pp. 41 f.) cites the following instances of both types (conflate spelling
and double text): Ex. 6:4; 16:35; Lev. 20:10; Josh. 2:7; 18:19; II Sam.
15:8; 19:32; Jer. 2:11; Ez. 3:15; 9:8; Lam. 5:18; Eccl. 6:10; Esth. 9:19.

   With regard to the consonantal text, the contribution of the Tiberian
Masoretes was chiefly negative: they succeeded in preserving the received
text of about A.D. 500 substantially intact and in transmitting it to future
generations without any important changes. In regard to the pronunciation and vocalization of the text, on the contrary, their contribution was
epoch making: faced with a variety of pronunciations of the Hebrew,
they devised the eclectic system which is the foundation of Hebrew
grammars.

   Before vowel signs were added to the consonantal text in the seventh
century of our era, the vocalization was not fixed and had varied considerably through the centuries and in various countries. Not seldom the
LXX reads the consonants of the Masoretic text but vocalizes them differently (see, for instance, the list for Ezekiel in G. A. Cooke, *Ezekiel*

---

   [10] P. Kahle, *Masoreten des Ostens* (BWAT 15), Leipzig, 1913; *Untersuchungen
zur Geschichte des Pentateuchtextes* (TSK 88 [1915] 399-439); *Die hebräischen
Bibelhandschriften aus Babylonien* (ZAW 46 [1928] 113-137, 70 photographs); "Der
Alttestamentliche Bibeltext" (Theol. Rundschau N.F. 5 [1933] 227-238).

[ICC] I, xliii; for other ancient versions cf. F. Buhl, *Kanon und Text,* p. 239). Jerome (cf. A. Sperber, in HUCA XII-XIII [1937-38] 118; Ginsburg, *Introduction,* pp. 446-449) observes that a word (written then without vowels) may have several meanings, as *metta* (stick or couch) and *sabee* (seven, oath, or abundance). It is now possible to distinguish several systems of pronunciation earlier than the Masoretic (F. X. Wutz, *Die Transcriptionen von der Septuaginta bis Hieronimus I.* Stuttgart, 1925) and to note how greatly the pronunciations exhibited in the LXX, in Origen's transcription of the Hebrew text in Greek letters, in Jerome's transcriptions, in the early Palestinian and in the Babylonian vocalizations differed from that recorded in our Masoretic text (cf. P. Kahle, *Masoreten des Westens,* Vol. I, pp. 43-50). Moreover, A. Sperber (*Hebrew Based upon Greek and Latin Transliterations.* HUCA XII-XIII, pp. 103-274) has proved that the grammatical structure of Masoretic Hebrew differs materially from that presupposed in transliterations antedating the Masoretes. We are driven to the conclusion that the Masoretic school of Tiberias (and likewise the Babylonian Masoretes) in fixing the pronunciation of Hebrew for the public reading of the Scriptures, substituted for the current pronunciation, which they regarded as degenerate, another which was to some extent artificial (P. Kahle, *op. cit.,* pp. 50, 55) and differed even from that indicated in the Samaritan Pentateuch and that of the Talmud (A. Sperber, *op. cit.,* pp. 151 f., 146 f.). This Tiberian system, according to Sperber (*op. cit.,* pp. 140-142), combines various ways of pronouncing Hebrew.

The new pronunciation was meticulously fixed in writing through the system of Tiberian vowel points used in our printed Hebrew Bibles. This system (having seven vowel signs) was introduced at the end of the eighth century and is a decided improvement over the earlier Palestinian system (having six signs written over the consonants), which was perhaps derived from the early Babylonian signs and is related to the simpler Samaritan system of five supralinear signs. The Babylonian system (likewise supralinear) was derived from the Syriac Nestorian system and evolved from a simpler to a more elaborate notation of the vowels, but eventually was discarded in favor of the Tiberian system.[11]

The elaborate system of accents was introduced in two different forms, in Babylonia and Palestine, together with the vowel signs. In both countries the accents of the three poetical books (Psalms, Proverbs, Job) differed from those of the other twenty-one books of the Bible. The accents contribute to indicate the correct reading of the text by marking the stressed syllable, by serving as punctuation signs to separate words

---

[11] For further details see P. Kahle, *Masoreten des Westens,* Vol. I, pp. 23-36; *Masoreten des Ostens,* pp. 157-170; in Bauer and Leander, *Histor. Gram. der Hebr. Sprache,* Vol. I, pp. 81-85, 91-114; Theol. Rundschau N.F. 5 (1933) 232-238.

(disjunctive accents or "masters," subdivided into "emperors, kings, dukes, and counts") or to join them together (conjunctives or "servants"), and also as a no longer understood musical notation of the melodies according to which the text was chanted in the synagogues.[12]

It may be said in conclusion that the Masoretic text is a compromise, in both its consonants and its vowels, between two or more traditional recensions. Essentially conservative and cautious, the Masoretes lacked both the inclination and the authority for the preparation of a truly critical edition of the Scriptures.

After the fixation of the written and pronounced text in the minutest details, the second great task of the Masoretes was to ensure its exact transmission to future generations. Since earlier measures had proved inadequate, the Masoretes took infinite pains to preclude the slightest modification of the standard text. The results of their labors were assembled in monographs and in annotations to the Bible.

The earliest manuals still extant seem to be the *Masseket sefer torah* (published by Kirchheim in *VII libri Talmudici*, Frankfurt, 1851) and its later expansion, the *Masseket soferim* (published by J. Müller, Vienna and Leipzig, 1878), dating probably from the seventh century, before the invention of the vowel points (Ginsburg, *Introduction*, p. 451). These Palestinian manuals, giving exact instructions to the scribes for preparing acceptable copies of the Scriptures, were incorporated in the treatise *Soferim* (scribes), dating from the eighth century, intended primarily for synagogue readers (cf. *Jewish Encycl.* VIII, 370; XI, 426-429). Aaron ben Moses ben Asher of Tiberias (first half of the tenth century) not only prepared the manuscript of the Bible marked with vowels and accents which became standard, but composed a number of Masoretic and grammatical manuals, published under the title *Diqduqe ha-Teʻamim* (grammatical rules of the accents) by S. Baer and H. L. Strack (Leipzig, 1879; cf. Ginsburg, *Introduction*, pp. 281 ff., 983 ff.) and a list of eighty homonyms. A similar treatise was published by Jos. Derenburg (*Journal Asiatique*, 1870, pp. 309 ff.). Later manuals, of which the most famous is the *Ochlah we-Ochlah* (so called from the two initial entries, "eating [I Sam. 1:9], and eat thou [Gen. 27:19]"), were compiled on the basis of the annotations in the text after the work of the Masoretes was completed (see E. Ehrentreu, *Untersuchungen über die Massora.* Hannover, 1925). The most copious edition of the Masora is that of C. D. Ginsburg (*The Massorah Compiled from Manuscripts*, 4 vols. London, 1881-1905).

The Masoretic annotations to the Biblical text are usually classified as follows: initial Masora (surrounding the first word of a book); small

---

[12] See W. Wickes, *A Treatise on the Accentuation of the Three Poetical Books of the Old Testament*, Oxford, 1881; *A Treatise on the Accentuation of the Twenty-one Prose Books of the Old Testament*, Oxford, 1887; and the larger Hebrew grammars.

Masora (written on the side margins, rarely between the lines); large Masora (written on the lower and upper margins); and final Masora (written at the end of a book).

The small Masora is probably the earliest. It consists of abbreviations giving statistics about the occurrence of similar expressions or spellings, and of peculiarly written letters. Thus on Gen. 1:1 it states that "in the beginning" occurs five times in the Bible, of which three are at the beginning of the verse; the large Masorah quotes the actual occurrences: at the beginning in Gen. 1:1; Jer. 26:1; 27:1, in the middle of a verse in Jer. 28:1; 49:34. On the same verse the small Masora remarks that "God created" occurs three times, "the heavens and the earth" three times, and "the earth" three times at the end of a verse (the large Masora adds that in these three occurrences, Gen. 1:1; Is. 24:4; and Hos. 2:23 [English 2:21], "the earth" is followed by "and the earth"). On Gen. 1:6 the small Masora states that "and God said" occurs three times "with the same accent" [i.e., *zakef qaton*].

Besides elucidating the small Masora, as just noted, the large Masora deals more fully with similar matters, citing the individual passages by quoting characteristic expressions in them. The final Masora contains longer rubrics on the same topics and is arranged alphabetically, and often refers to the marginal Masora.

In general, the Masora deals with the following topics: the consonants, the vowel points and accents, the spelling of the words (with or without the letters *h, y,* and *w* marking long vowels), variant readings, and corrections of the text. The Masoretes noted the large, small, suspended, inverted, or otherwise irregularly shaped consonants which have been listed under C, above; and they counted the letters of each book, noting also the central letter of each book and of the Pentateuch. Thus, for instance, the note at the end of Genesis reads:

Be strong! The number of the verses of the Book of Genesis is 1534. Its sign [menomonic symbol] is *'k ld* [' = 1000, *k* = 500, *l* = 30, *d* = 4]. And its middle is, "And by thy sword shalt thou live" [27:40]. And its pericopes [*perashiyôth*] are 12; the sign is, "*This* [*zh* = 7 + 5] is my name forever" [Ex. 3:15]. And its sections [*sedarim*] are 43; the sign is, "*Yea* [*gm* = 3 + 40] he shall be blessed" [Gen. 27:33]. And its chapters are 50; the sign is, "O Lord be gracious unto us, we have waited *for thee* [*lk* = 30 + 20]" [Is. 33:2]. The number of open *perashiyôth* is 43, and of the closed 48; the total is 91 *perashiyôth*; the sign is, "*Go* [*s'* = 90 + 1] thou and all the people that is after thee" [Ex. 9:8].

In this form, as it appears in printed editions, this note (as shown by the indication of the chapters) is modern; in the text of Aaron ben Moses ben Asher, printed by Kahle in the third edition of Kittel's *Biblia Hebraica*, only the number of the verses (1,534) is given.

Vowel points, accents, and the spelling were punctiliously noted when-

ever they seemed to be unusual. Thus, for instance, in Num. 23:18, 24
and Judg. 1:15 the notes call attention to a long *a* where, according to
the accent, a short one would be expected; while on the contrary a short
a occurs with the *atnach* (marking a pause in the middle of the verse
and usually lengthening the vowel) in Judg. 1:10, 28 and with the *sōph
pāsûq* (at the end of the verse, where vowels are lengthened) in Judg.
1:30, 33, 35.

The Masora notes the diacritical dots over certain words and letters,
which have been listed in a preceding page, but enumerates a much
larger number of variants and emendations than the rabbis of the Talmud,
omitting, however, the variant readings which, as we have seen, were
indicated by unusual spellings. The variants listed are of two types: the
sebîrin (conjectures) and the *qerē* (read) as distinguished from the
kethib (written). Although occasionally a *sebir* is called *qere* in some
manuscripts, and vice versa (cf. Ginsburg, *Introduction*, pp. 187-189), in
general the *qere* was mandatory and the *sebir* more or less optional. In his
editions of the Masoretic text (London, 1894; 1926), C. D. Ginsburg has
edited from manuscripts some 350 *sebirin* (some of them being questionable), and he believes that in many instances they "preserve the primitive
textual readings" (*Introduction*, p. 193). The *sebirin* in Gen. 49:13; Ex.
6:27; 25:39; 36:31; Num. 11:21; 23:8; Josh. 1:15; I Sam. 18:25; I Kings
1:18; II Chron. 21:2 are actually supported by manuscripts, the Samaritan
text, or some ancient versions (cf. Ginsburg, *op. cit.*, pp. 190-193; Kittel's
Biblia Hebraica) and are accepted by some modern critics.[13]

The origin and significance of the Masoretic *kethib-qere* is still in dispute among critics. Even their number is uncertain: it varies from 848
(E. Levita) or 1,314 (F. Buhl) to 1,548 or 1,566 (counted by L. Cappellus in Jacob ben Chayyim's Rabbinical Bible, Venice, 1524-1525 [1,353,
according to Ginsburg], and in the Antwerp Polyglot published in 1569-
1572, respectively); Gordis lists 1,350. The *kethib* (written) is the consonantal text; the *qere* (read) is an accepted reading differing from the
consonantal text. At first the vowels in the *kethib* were written on the
margin, while the text was left unvocalized. In most modern editions,
following Jacob ben Chayyim, the consonants of the *qere* are given on
the margin while its vowels are incongruously written in the *kethib*, with
the result that the latter is printed as a hybrid word, with the consonants
of one word and the vowels of another.[14] The most common and earliest
instance, the "perpetual *qere*" disregarded in the marginal notes, is the

---

[13] For further details see J. Reach, *Die Sebirin der Massoreten von Tiberias*. Breslau,
1895; cf. R. Gordis, *The Biblical Text in the Making*, pp. 26 f.

[14] Ginsburg, following an earlier procedure, gives both *kethib* and *qere* on the
margin, with their vowels, leaving the word unvocalized in the text of his Masoretic
Bible (London, 1926).

pronunciation *adōnāy* (LORD; actually "my lordship") for the divine name *Yahweh*. Accordingly, the consonants of the *kethib*, YHWH, were vocalized *YeHoWaH* (with the vowels of *adōnāy*). From this hybrid spelling, the significance of which was known to every Jew, came the divine name *Jehovah*, current in English and other modern languages. This erroneous Hebrew pronunciation "Jehovah" was introduced by Christians at least as early as the fourteenth century and became current since the sixteenth.[15] Whatever may be said of its dubious pedigree, "Jehovah" is and should remain the proper English rendering of *Yahweh*, the God of Israel who revealed his name to Moses in the burning bush. The original pronunciation of this name, which is not Hebrew but belongs to an otherwise unknown Semitic dialect, was unquestionably *Yahwe*.[16] We do not know when this pronunciation ceased to be current among the Jews, but we may surmise that when with the Second Isaiah (about 540 B.C.) Jehovah was recognized to be the sole God in existence, it was felt more and more that it was incongruous to refer to him by a personal name. In any case the process was under way in the time of Nehemiah (444-432) and was completed by the middle of the third century B.C.

The reading *adonay* for *Yahweh* is attested in the LXX of the Pentateuch (*ca.* 250 B.C.), where *YHWH* is rendered regularly with *kyrios* (lord).[17] In the same period the Chronicler wrote regularly *YHWH* for *adonay* (as we write *i.e.* and pronounce *that is*) as shown from the fact that *adonay* (with reference to God) never occurs in his writings (whereas Nehemiah distinguishes *YHWH* [1:5; 5:13] and *adonay* [1:11; 4:14, H. 8]) and that he reproduces *adonay YHWH* (II Sam. 7:18 f.) with *YHWH elohim* (I Chron. 17:16 f.): both expressions were pronounced in his day *adonay elohim*, for following *adonay*, to avoid a repetition, YHWH was

[15] See G. F. Moore in *Old Testament and Semitic Studies in Memory of W. R. Harper*, Vol. I, pp. 145-163 (Chicago, 1908); AJT 12 (1908) 34-52; cf. AJSL 25 (1909) 312-318; 28 (1911) 56-62.

[16] See especially W. R. Arnold in JBL 24 (1905) 107-165 (particularly pp. 152 ff.); cf. W. F. Albright in JBL 43 (1924) 370-378; 44 (1925) 158-162; J. A. Montgomery in JBL 25 (1906) 49-54; D. D. Luckenbill in AJSL 40 (1924) 277-283. The first suggestion of the pronunciation *Yahwe* was made by Mercerus (d. 1570), cf. Moore (first reference in note 15, above, p. 157).

[17] In his monumental work, *Kyrios als Gottesname und seine Stelle in der Religionsgeschichte* (edited posthumously by O. Eissfeldt, Giessen, 1926-1929), W. W. Baudissin claims that the substitution of "Lord" for "Yahweh" began among Hellenistic Jews and passed from them to the Jews who read the Scriptures in Hebrew. This theory, which seems false to the present writer, does not vitiate the outstanding importance of this work. A. Geiger (*Nachgelassene Schriften*, Vol. III, p. 261) believed that before 250 B.C. the Jews (like the Samaritans and the rabbis of the Talmud) read "the Name" instead of YHWH and that the reading *adonay* was an imitation of the *kyrios* of the Hellenistic Jews. See in general G. Dalman, *Der Gottesname Adonaj und seine Geschichte*, (Berlin, 1889); *The Words of Jesus*, pp. 179-183. On substitutes for the divine names in rabbinical Judaism see H. L. Strack and P. Billerbeck, *Kommentar zum Neuen Testament*, Vol. II, pp. 308-329.

pronounced *elohim* (deity) and is vocalized accordingly. We may conclude that the *qere* "Lord" (instead of the *kethib* "Yahweh"), was current in 250 B.C. if not before. Incidentally, the Authorized Version follows the *qere* (the LORD) and the Revised the *kethib* (Jehovah).

But "the employment of the ordinary synagogue surrogate for YHWH, namely adonay, was from the nature of the case impossible" in Ex. 3:14, where God revealed his name Yahweh to Moses; "to prevent the utterance of the ineffable name in this one passage," by the change of two letters YHWH became 'HYH (*ehyeh;* I am, or I shall be) which a glossator tried to explain with the words in 3:14a, "God said to Moses, I am that I am [or, I will be whatever I choose]" (so W. R. Arnold, JBL 24 [1905] 133 ff., 162).

To avoid the utterance of the name Yahweh, both before and after the adoption of the qere, other devices were employed. In some cases *adonay* was written in the text (so in Dan. 9:9 where the Babylonians wrote YHWH); in Pss. 42-83 *elohim* (deity) is substituted for *Yahweh*; in Am. 5:16 *adonay* (missing in the LXX) and in Pss. 59:5 (H. 59:6); 80:4, 19 (H. 80:5, 20); 84:8 (H. 84:9) *elohim* are interlinear substitutes for YHWH, which were mechanically copied into the text (see W. R. Arnold, *Ephod and Ark*, pp. 31, 38, 145-147). We even find in the text late substitutes for Yahweh: "Heaven" (Dan. 4:26 [H. 4:23]; cf. Is. 14:13, LXX; the Kingdom of Heaven" in Matthew) and "the Name" (Lev. 24:11, 16). In the Aramaic portions of Daniel 2-7, not only are substitutes for Yahweh regularly employed, but the verbal form YeHeWeH (he is or will be), which occurs regularly in the Elephantine papyri, to avoid confusion with the ineffable name YHWH was changed to LeHeWeH (similarly the plurals *lehewon, lehewyan*).

Long after the introduction of the *qere* "Lord" for YHWH (6,823 times in the Old Testament according to the Masora), but before A.D. 500, vulgar expressions in the text, as we have seen, were removed by substituting a euphemism in the reading (qere). Equally ancient are the instances of "read but not written" and "written but not read" listed above. Except for these instances mentioned in the sources which are earlier than 500, the great mass of kethib-qere readings belongs to a later period, probably to the eighth century.[18] Before we can hope to gain a clear notion of the origin and significance of these Masoretic variant readings, much critical research is required. In some cases the difference between the kethib and the qere is purely graphic and does not change the pronunciation of the word; in other cases kethib and qere record two different pronuncia-

---

[18] Like W. F. Albright (JBL 57 [1938] 223 f., cf. 329-333), H. M. Orlinsky (JAOS 60 [1940] 30-45), P. Kahle (OLZ 42 [1939] 25-29), and others, the present writer cannot accept the new theory of R. Gordis (*The Biblical Text in the Making*) in regard to the date of the qere-kethib.

tions of the same word, without changing the meaning; and finally in another group the qere suggests an entirely different word or modifies the meaning profoundly by a mere change of the vocalization.

The instances in which the meaning is not affected are of great significance for the history of Hebrew spelling and grammar. Our standard Hebrew text (substantially that of ben Asher, first half of the tenth century) exhibits eclectic notions of Hebrew morphology and syntax. Side by side with archaisms it gives the forms regarded as normal by the Tiberian grammarians, whose reverence for the text prevented a thorough normalization of spellings and grammatical forms. Before the Masoretes, other grammarians had been at work sporadically in normalizing the grammar. This appears, for instance, in the fact that only in the Pentateuch (Gen. 24; 34; Deut. 22) is the masculine *na'ar* (youth) used for a maiden (an anomaly which does not occur in the Samaritan text and is regularly corrected in the qere) and that in the Pentateuch, except for rare exceptions, "he" is used for "she" consistently (the Samaritan text has "she"), whereas in the rest of the Bible only a few sporadic instances occur in I Kings, Isaiah, Job 31:11 (a gloss in which "she" is used for "he"), Jeremiah, Ezekiel (ten times). A. Geiger notes that the Babylonians wrote "he" outside of the Pentateuch in some passages where the Tiberian Masoretes wrote the correct "she" (*Urschrift,* p. 236). We can now gain some notion of these diverse grammatical traditions from A. Sperber's classification of variants occurring not only in the *kethib-qere,* but also in parallel recensions of the same text, such as the Masoretic and Samaritan Pentateuchs, parallel passages in the Bible, *sebirin,* and Eastern-Western readings (HUCA XIV [1939] 153-249). A perusal of his lists proves that when the kethib-qere has close parallels in two distinct recensions of the same text we must consider the qere an ancient manuscript variant.

In individual cases, unless evidence such as has been collected by Sperber or that of manuscripts and ancient versions is available, it is difficult to determine whether the qere is a variant attested in manuscripts available to the Masoretes or a Masoretic correction of the received text. Let us consider, for instance, three qere readings which modern critics regard as definitely superior to the received text. In Am. 8:8 the kethib reads "the land . . . will be watered," but the qere "the land . . . will sink" (so the versions, some manuscripts, and the parallel Am. 9:5; cf. Jer. 51:64). In I Sam. 14:32 the kethib reads, "and the people *prepared to* spoil"; but the qere, supported by ancient versions and obviously correct (cf. 15:19; in both cases, however, the vocalization of the verb is erroneous), reads, "and the people *flew* at *the* spoil." In II Sam. 23:20 the kethib has "son of a *living* man," whereas the qere, supported by I Chron. 11:22 and by all the versions, has "son of a man of *valor*," which is manifestly right. It is safe to say that in all three cases the kethib is wrong and the qere is right; but whether the qere is a correction based on common sense and the Biblical parallels noted or actually a variant in manuscripts available to the Masoretes can manifestly not be determined. Quite often, on the contrary, the kethib is preferable to the qere: so in Job 9:30, where it reads, "if I wash myself with snow" (so the LXX); the qere, the Targum, and the Syriac read *with waters of snow.*" The reverse change is made in Is. 25:10 (kethib, "in the waters of a dunghill"; qere, "in a dunghill"), where the kethib is likewise better, although some versions support the qere. It should always be kept in mind, however, that the better reading is not necessarily the original one; on the contrary, the more difficult reading should be presumed a priori to be the earliest.

In the first half of the tenth century the two rival authorities at Tiberias, ben Naphtali and ben Asher prepared the two standard copies of the Masoretic Bible. The differences between them (for which see Ginsburg, *Introduction,* pp. 241-286) are usually confined to minor points that do not affect the meaning of the passages. Through manuscripts that have been investigated recently (cf. P. Kahle, *Masoreten des Westens,* Vol. II, pp. 45*-68*. Stuttgart, 1930) and particularly through the list of discrepancies between them compiled soon after their death by Mishael ben 'Uzziel (published in L. Lipschütz, *Ben Ascher-Ben Naftali. Der Bibeltext der tiberinischen Masoreten.* Eine Abhandlung des Mischael ben 'Uzziel. Bonner Orientalistische Studien, XXV. Stuttgart, 1937), ben Naphtali's text is now better known.

The standard edition of ben Naphtali is lost, but a copy of that of ben Asher is in the possession of the synagogue of the Sephardim at Aleppo. The autograph itself was taken to Old Cairo when Jerusalem was plundered in 1099 and was apparently studied there by Maimonides (d. 1204), who declared that the official standard text of the Scriptures was ben Asher's. The Aleppo manuscript, which unfortunately has not been made accessible to scholars, according to the colophon was written by Solomon ben Buyâ'a (in the first half of the tenth century) and reproduced the Masoretic text of ben Asher (see P. Kahle, *Masoreten des Westens,* I, 1-23. Stuttgart, 1927; cf. Ginsburg, *Introduction,* pp. 241-243). A later copy of ben Asher's text was made in Old Cairo in 1008-1010 by Samuel ben Jacob for the priest Merodak (known as Ben Ozdad). This important manuscript of the whole Bible is in Leningrad (Codex B 19a) and has been edited by P. Kahle in the third edition of R. Kittel's *Biblia Hebraica* (Stuttgart, 1929-1937).

E. After 1200

The text of ben Asher, through the authority of Maimonides and other scholars, was eventually recognized as the standard one; in transmission, however, it suffered contamination, in minor points, from the Ben Naphtali recension.

Most of the Hebrew manuscripts are comparatively late, hardly any being earlier than A.D. 900. The most important are described by Ginsburg (*Introduction*, pp. 469-778) and by P. Kahle (in his works mentioned in note 10, above). The fullest collections of manuscript variants are published in the following editions of the Masoretic text: B. Kennicott, *Vetus Testamentum Hebraicum cum variis lectionibus*. (2 vols. Oxford, 1776, 1780; gives variants only for the consonantal text). J. B. de Rossi, *Variae lectiones Veteris Testamenti ex immensa manu scriptorum editorumque codicum congerie haustae* (4 vols. Parma, 1784-1788); *Scholia critica in V. T. libros seu supplementa ad varias sacri textus lectiones* (Parma, 1798; includes variants in the vowels and accents). C. D. Ginsburg, *The Twenty-Four Sacred Books* (Hebrew title) (2 vols. London, 1894); and *The Old Testament, diligently Revised according to the Massorah and the Early Editions, with the Various Readings from Manuscripts and the Ancient Versions* (4 vols. London, 1926; text of Jacob ben Chayyim and critical apparatus).

The earliest printed edition of a portion of the Hebrew Bible is the Psalter (with David Kimchi's commentary) issued in 1477 (perhaps at Bologna).[19] The first edition of the Pentateuch (with Onkelos and Rashi's commentary) appeared at Bologna in 1482. The Former and Latter Prophets (with Kimchi's commentary) were first published at Soncino near Milan in two volumes (1485-1486) and there the first edition of the complete text of the Bible appeared on February 23, 1488. Before then the Writings (with various commentaries) had appeared at Naples (3 parts, 1486-1487) and the Pentateuch at Faro in Portugal (1487). The *editio princeps* of the Bible (1488) was followed by a new edition (in which Masoretic peculiarities were disregarded) published by another Soncino printer, Gerson ben Moses (Brescia, 1494): this is the Hebrew text translated by Martin Luther, whose copy is at Berlin. This text was reproduced substantially in D. Bomberg's manual editions (Venice, 1516-1517, 1521, 1525-1528), and in the editions of S. Münster (Basel, 1536) and R. Stephanus (Paris, 1539-44).

A different recension appears in the first Christian edition of the Hebrew Bible, the *Complutensian Polyglot*, printed under the auspices of Cardinal F. Ximénes de Cisneros at Alcalá (*Complutum*) in 1514-1517 but issued to the public through papal sanction only after 1520. The first four volumes contain the Old Testament, and give Jerome's Vulgate in the central column, between the Hebrew and the LXX (with a Latin intralinear version), "like Jesus between the two thieves"; Onkelos (with Latin

---

[19] For detailed descriptions of the most ancient printed editions of the Hebrew Bible see C. D. Ginsburg, *Introduction*, pp. 779-956.

translation) is printed at the bottom. The fifth volume contains the New Testament; and the sixth, dictionaries and a grammar.

Far richer are the contents of the three other great polyglots, but their Hebrew text is unimportant (being derived from the Complutensian and from Jacob ben Chayyim). The *Antwerp Polyglot* was published at the expense of Philip II (and is therefore called *Biblia Regia*) under the editorship of B. Arias Montanus, and printed by C. Plantin at Antwerp in 1569-1572. For the Old Testament (vols. 1-4) it gives the Hebrew text, the Targums (except for Daniel, Ezra-Nehemiah, and Chronicles) with a Latin version, the LXX (following the Complutensian text) with a Latin version, and the Vulgate. The other volumes contain the New Testament (vol. 5, in the original Greek, in the Vulgate, and in Syriac with a Latin version; vol. 6, in Greek with the intralinear version of Montanus), and philological and archaeological monographs (vols. 6-8).

The costs of the *Paris Polyglot* (Paris, 1629-1645) were supplied by G. M. Le Jay. The chief editors for the Oriental texts were J. Morinus, who published the Samaritan Pentateuch and its Targum (according to a manuscript brought to Europe in 1616 by Pietro de La Valle, the discoverer of the cuneiform inscriptions at Persepolis) and G. Sionita, who edited the Syriac (Peshitta) text. Volumes 1-4 reproduce the Old Testament and its versions as given in the Antwerp Polyglot; vols. 5-6 give the New Testament (including the Syriac and Arabic versions); vols. 7-10 contain the Samaritan Pentateuch with its Targum, the Peshitta, and the Arabic versions of the Old Testament, all of which are translated into Latin.

The *London Polyglot*, the first work published in England through public subscription, was edited by Brian Walton (Bishop of Chester from 1660 to his death a year later) and appeared in 1657.[20] The six folio volumes of the Polyglot are supplemented in vols. 7-8 (1669) with the *Lexicon heptaglotton* of E. Castellus (a dictionary of Hebrew, Aramaic, Syriac, Samaritan, Ethiopic, and Arabic; with a separate Persian vocabulary and a comparative Semitic grammar). The most comprehensive and important of the great Polyglots, this monumental work is still invaluable to Biblical students, both for Walton's learned prolegomena in vol. 1 and for the editions of Biblical versions (some of which are supplied with

---

[20] In the preface at the beginning of Vol. I in the original printing, Walton pays his respects to Oliver Cromwell, "*D. Protectore,*" as one of the principal patrons of the work. But after the death of Cromwell on September 3, 1658, when Charles II was crowned in 1660, Walton dedicated the work to Charles II. In the new preface, which took the place of the other, Walton complained that Cromwell, "that great dragon" (*Draco ille magnus*), had hindered the publication until it was dedicated to him. The present writer is the fortunate owner of a copy of the original "republican" edition, in which the royal dedication is inserted in loose leaves; quite apart from this bibliographical curiosity, this London Polyglot has been invaluable in the preparation of the present volume.

a critical apparatus of variants in vol. 6) which it contains. The New Testament comprises vol. 5 (Greek [with the Latin version of Montanus]; Vulgate; the Syriac, Ethiopic, Arabic texts and, for the Gospels only, the Persian are supplied with Latin renderings). The London Polyglot gives for the Old Testament (vol. 1-4): the Hebrew with Latin intralinear version, the Samaritan Pentateuch and Targum, the LXX (reproducing the Roman edition of 1586, with variants from the Codex Alexandrinus), fragments of the Old Latin, the Vulgate, the Peshitta, the Arabic, the Targums (including Pseudo-Jonathan and the Jerusalem Targum), the Ethiopic version of Psalms and Canticles, and the Persian for the Pentateuch (all non-Latin texts with a Latin version).

More important than the two recensions of the Hebrew text published in the Soncino and Complutensian Bibles, is that of *Jacob ben Chayyim*. After publishing his first Rabbinical Bible (edited by Felix Pratensis, a Jewish convert to Christianity) at Venice in 1516-1517, D. Bomberg sponsored a second one (likewise in four volumes), edited by Jacob ben Chayyim and issued at Venice in 1525-1526. Prepared from manuscripts and the best printed editions, ben Chayyim's text, in spite of the fact that readings of ben Naphtali occasionally mar the ben Asher recension, has remained the standard one and is unsurpassed among the early editions. It was often reprinted in the sixteenth century and was used (unfortunately with tacit emendations) in the Bibles of R. Kittel (first and second editions, 1905 and 1912, with variants from the ancient versions) and C. D. Ginsburg (1894 and 1926). Ben Chayyim printed for the first time the Masoretic notes (though not exhaustively); in addition to the Targums, he gave for individual books of the Bible (except Chronicles) the commentaries of at least two of the following exegetes: Saadia, Rashi, Ibn Ezra, Kimchi, and Levi ben Gerson.

The received Hebrew text of our standard editions is substantially that of ben Chayyim. The manual edition of J. Buxdorf (Basel, 1611), based on ben Chayyim and on the Complutensian Polyglot, was revised through collation with the Soncino and other texts by J. Athias and J. Leusden (Amsterdam, 1661 and 1667). This edition was critically edited by D. E. Jablonski, Berlin, 1690 and 1712; J. H. Michaelis, Halle, 1720; and by Raphael Chayyim Basila (together with Norzi's commentary), Mantua, 1742-1744. But it was in the less scholarly reprint of E. Van der Hooght (Amsterdam, 1705) that the Athias-Leusden text was destined to become generally accepted, particularly in the widely circulated editions of A. Hahn (1832, 1833, and 1868) and of M. Letteris (Vienna, 1852; reprinted since 1866 by the British and Foreign Bible Society).

In addition to the Hebrew Bibles of C. D. Ginsburg and R. Kittel (first and second editions) already mentioned, the only modern editions which are critically important are the following. S. Baer and Franz

Delitzsch have published in separate parts the individual books of the Old Testament (except Exodus-Deuteronomy) according to manuscripts and Masoretic books (Leipzig, 1869-1895). In "The Sacred Books of the Old Testament" edited by P. Haupt, a series begun in 1893 but not completed, a revised Hebrew text of the individual books is published without vowels and with critical notes (English translations have also appeared). Finally, in the third edition of R. Kittel's *Biblia Hebraica* (Stuttgart, 1929-1937), P. Kahle has printed the ben Asher text in its purest form and other scholars have contributed a critical apparatus giving selected variants from manuscripts and the ancient versions.

F. The Samaritan Pentateuch

The date of the Samaritan schism is uncertain, but must fall within the century 432-332 B.C. We may infer, therefore, that the Samaritan community adopted the Pentateuch as its Bible soon after its canonization about 400 B.C. The script of the Samaritan Pentateuch, which is a modification of the old Phoenician alphabet discarded by the Jews for their Torah soon after 200 B.C., and the fact that the Prophets (canonized about 200 B.C.) were never included in the Samaritan Bible, prove that the Pentateuch was unquestionably their Bible well before 200 B.C.

Neither the Masoretic nor the Samaritan Pentateuch has preserved intact the text canonized about 400 B.C. In the course of their manuscript transmission both were modified accidentally or deliberately—without mutual influence. The measures taken by the rabbis about A.D. 100 to fix the Biblical text, for instance, had no effect whatsoever on the Samaritan text. The Masoretic and Samaritan texts (in spite of their variants) were recensions of the final edition of the Pentateuch, as also the LXX. Jews and Samaritans made slight retouches to the Torah, but its sacredness after 400 B.C. prevented major changes.

First published in the *Paris* and *London Polyglots*, together with its Targum, the Samaritan Pentateuch has now been issued in a critical edition by A. von Gall (*Der Hebräische Pentateuch der Samaritaner,* 5 vols. Giessen, 1914-1918). It differs from the Masoretic text in some 6,000 instances, in 1,900 of which it agrees with the LXX against the Masoretic (P. Kahle, in TSK 88 [1915] 399-439). The principal variants are listed and discussed in the *London Polyglot* (Vol. VI, parts iv-v) by B. Walton, E. Castle (or Castellus), and J. Lightfoot, and are also given in the apparatus of the Kittel Bible. Although further research is required before we can fully appreciate the significance of these variants and utilize them for a reconstruction of the earliest text of the Pentateuch, some facts are by now well established.

It is obvious that both the Jews and the Samaritans have willfully tampered with the text in the interests of their opposite claims in regard

to the sole place on earth chosen by Jehovah as the seat of his worship
(cf. John 4:20). To remove scriptural support for the Samaritan claims
that the temple on Mt. Gerizim was the only legitimate sanctuary of
Jehovah, both before and after the schism had become incurable, the Jews
changed the crucial passages (cf. E. Meyer [and B. Luther], *Die Israeliten
und ihre Nachbarstämme,* pp. 543-547. Halle, 1906; C. C. Torrey, *Ezra
Studies,* pp. 321-333. Chicago, 1910). The following anti-Samaritan additions, made before the schism, were curiously allowed to stand in the
Samaritan Pentateuch—so great was their slavish reverence for the sacred
text. With utter disregard for geographical reality, the gloss in Deut. 11:30
removes Gerizim and Ebal from the vicinity of Shechem (still attested in
the reference to the terebinth of Moreh) to the Jordan valley at Gilgal,
near Jericho (cf. 27:12, "when you have passed over the Jordan"); similarly
in Josh. 8:30-35 the altar was built on Gerizim (*sic!*) while the Israelites
were still encamped at Gilgal. The early account of the origin of the cult
at Shechem (Deut. 11:29; 27:11-25) was thus first given a Deuteronomistic interpretation (in 11:26-28, 31 f.; 27:7-10), then the scene was removed
to Gilgal and connected with the famous stones there (27:1-4, 8), and
finally, after the Samaritan schism, "Gerizim" was changed into "Ebal"
in Deut. 27:4 (where the Samaritan Pentateuch still reads "Gerizim")
and in Josh. 8:30.

For their part the Samaritans likewise retouched the text for dogmatic
reasons. To enhance the prestige of their temple on Gerizim, they did
not hesitate to add at the end of the Ten Commandments (after Ex. 20:17
and Deut. 5:21 [H. 5:18]) a long interpolation reproducing substantially
Deut. 27:2, 3a, 4-7; 11:30. We may detect a similar purpose in a less
obvious change: in all the twenty-one occurrences of the phrase "the
place which Jehovah your God *will choose*" (Deut. 12:5, 11, 14, 18, 21, 26;
14:23-25; 15:20; 16:2, 6 f., 11, 15 f.; 17:8, 10; 18:6; 26:2; 31:11; it occurs
elsewhere only outside of the Pentateuch) the Samaritan text reads
". . . *has chosen*" (by omitting the initial y and thus changing the imperfect into perfect). Shechem *had been chosen* as a sanctuary of Jehovah
in the time of Abraham, but Jerusalem *would be chosen* long after Moses,
in the time of David. The Chronicler (II Chron. 3:1) and later Jewish
tradition identified the place of the sacrifice of Isaac (Gen. 22:2, 14) with
Zion (cf. J. Skinner, *Genesis* [ICC], pp. 328 f., 330 f.; L. Ginzberg,
Legends of the Jews, Vol. 5, p. 253), but with no better warrant than the
Samaritans had in identifying it with Shechem (Skinner, *op. cit.,* p. 329).
Other interpolations in the Samaritan Pentateuch, such as those in Num.
10-27 (taken from Deut. 1-3, cf. G. B. Gray, *Numbers* [ICC], p. xl) and
those after Ex. 18:24; 20:19 and elsewhere, have no polemic purpose,
serving only to increase the clarity and impressiveness of the Scriptures.
Occasionally some obvious errors in the Hebrew are corrected, as in Gen.

2:2, "And on the *sixth* [Hebrew "seventh"] day God finished his work" (cf. LXX, Syriac, etc.).

In other instances the Samaritans made orthographic and grammatical revisions which do not affect the meaning of the words (see E. König, *Einleitung in das Alte Testament*, p. 96; and in Hastings' *Dictionary of the Bible*, Extra Volume, pp. 69 f.). They changed the anomalous "he" into "she" and "boy" into "girl" (cf. the *qere*) with reference to a woman, made abundant use of the "mothers of reading" (consonants indicating a long vowel), and eliminated some unusual spellings and constructions. But in many of the variants listed by A. Sperber (HUCA XIV [1939] 161-248) it is not always easy to determine whether the Hebrew or the Samaritan text is more original. Moreover, Sperber (HUCA XII-XIII [1937-38] 151 f.) may be right in explaining some important grammatical differences through the hypothesis that the Samaritan Pentateuch preserves North Israelitic dialectal peculiarities (being the "Israelitish or Samaritan recension") while the Masoretic text preserves the recension in the Judean dialect. The problem of the differences in the dates given by the Hebrew, the Samaritan, and the LXX in Gen. 5 and 11 is extremely complex and will be discussed in connection with the chronology of the Priestly Code (Part II, Chap. VI).

After due allowance is made for accidental and willful textual changes in the Samaritan Pentateuch, it cannot be gainsaid that in some verses the Samaritan has preserved a better text than the Masoretic and is therefore a valuable aid in emending erroneous readings, particularly when it is supported by the LXX or other ancient versions. Thus, for instance, the following words in italics, preserved in the Samaritan text, should be restored to the Hebrew text: "And Cain said to Abel his brother, '*Let us go into the field*'" (Gen. 4:8; so LXX, Syriac, Old Latin; similarly the Vulgate and Targum Pseudo-Jonathan); "and the Girgashite, *and the Hivvite*, and the Jebusite" (15:21; so LXX); "not circumcised in the flesh of his foreskin *on the seventh day*" (17:14; so LXX); "also the son of the handmaid will I make a *great* nation" (21:13; so LXX, Syriac, Vulgate); etc. In other instances, accepting the Samaritan readings, slight corrections should be made in the Hebrew text: "and behold a ram behind" (22:13) should be read "and behold *one* ram" (so the principal versions and some manuscripts); "were gathered all the *flocks*" (29:3, 8) should be read "were gathered all the *shepherds*" (so the Arabic in the first instance and the LXX in the second); "Anah, the *daughter* of Zibeon" (36:2, 14) should be read "Anah, the *son* of Zibeon" (so LXX and Syriac; cf. 36:24 f.; I Chron. 1:40); "*Dodanim*" (10:4) should be "*Rodanim*" or Rhodians (so LXX and I Chron. 1:7); etc. These few instances chosen at random in Genesis may suffice to show the value of the Samaritan Pentateuch in the search for the earliest Hebrew text. On the Samaritan Targum, which is less important in textual criticism, see L. Goldberg, *Das Samaritanische Pentateuchtargum* (Bonner Orientalische Studien, XI, 1935).

2. The Ancient Versions

A. The Greek Versions (LXX, etc.)

An adequate presentation of the results of the vast and detailed investigation of the Greek Bible would require several volumes. Here, in a volume dealing with the literary history of the Hebrew Bible, the Greek text is important chiefly as preserving in many instances a better and more primitive reading than the Masoretic recension. The intrinsic importance of the Greek Bible, its historical, literary and philological interest, its outstanding influence on the development of Christianity, lie beyond the scope of this work, as do also the technical investigations on its origin, earliest text and later recensions, and the varied vicissitudes of its manuscript transmission. The curious reader may supplement this brief sketch by a perusal of the excellent survey of the subject by H. B. Swete (*An Introduction to the Old Testament in Greek*. Cambridge University Press, 1900 [quoted here]. 2nd ed., 1902. Revised by R. R. Ottley, 1914).[21]

The earliest and most important translation of the Old Testament into Greek is called "The Septuagint" (LXX) or in full "Interpretation of the Seventy Men (or Elders)." The origin of this name, which originally was applied only to the Greek Pentateuch, is unknown and probably antedates the legendary explanation given in the *Letter of Aristeas* (*ca.* 100 B.C.), according to which the Pentateuch was translated by seventy-two elders, six from each tribe of Israel, brought to Alexandria from Palestine under the auspices of Ptolemy II Philadelphus (285-246 B.C.). A fragment from the writings of Aristobulus, a Jewish Alexandrian philosopher who wrote in 170-150 B.C., preserved by Eusebius (*Praeparatio Evangelica* 13:12) and Clement of Alexandria (*Stromata* 1:22, 148) and printed in W. N. Stearns, *Fragments from Graeco-Jewish Writers* (Chicago, 1908), pp. 78 f., gives, if authentic, an earlier version of the story. Aristobulus claims

---

[21] A more popular treatment will be found in A. S. Geden, *Outlines of Introduction to the Hebrew Bible,* pp. 165-217 (Edinburgh, 1909); and in R. R. Ottley, *A Handbook to the Septuagint* (London, 1920). See also the articles of E. Nestle in Hastings' *Dictionary of the Bible* (IV [1902] 437-454) and F. C. Burkitt in Cheyne's *Encyclopaedia Biblica* (IV [1903] 5016-5022); the introductions to the Old Testament; the Biblical commentaries; F. Buhl, *Kanon und Text des Alten Testament,* pp. 109-160 (Leipzig, 1891). Bibliographies of earlier monographs will be found in the book of Swete, in Nestle's article, and in E. Schürer, *Geschichte des jüdischen Volkes,* Vol. III, pp. 429-434. For recent literature see: F. Kenyon, *Recent Developments in the Textual Criticism of the Greek Bible* (Schweich Lectures for 1925. London, 1933); G. Bertram (*Theol. Rundschau* N. F. 3 [1931] 283-296; 5 [1933] 173-186; 10 [1938] 69-80, 133-159); P. L. Hedley (HTR 26 [1933] 57-72); and the article of H. M. Orlinsky, "On the Present State of Proto-Septuagint Studies" (to be published in JAOS, June, 1941), the manuscript of which has been generously placed at my disposal by Dr. Orlinsky.

erroneously that Homer, Hesiod, Pythagoras, Socrates, and Plato were familiar with portions of the Pentateuch and that a Greek translation was available "before the conquest [of Egypt] by Alexander [332 B.C.] and by the Persians [525 B.C.]." He adds, more plausibly, that "the complete translation of the whole of the Jewish Law was made in the time of the king who was surnamed Philadelphus [Ptolemy II] . . . through the efforts of Demetrius of Phalerum." Later Philo (*Life of Moses*, 2:5-7), Josephus (*Antiquities*, Preface §3; 12:2, 1-15), and the Church Fathers beginning with the second century (cf. Swete, *Introduction*, pp. 13-14) repeat the story of Pseudo-Aristeas, the Fathers even applying it to the whole Bible. Philo (*loc. cit.*) adds the interesting information that an annual festival was celebrated on the island of Pharos in commemoration of the translation.

The only historical fact which we may derive from these stories is that the Pentateuch was translated into Greek at Alexandria about 250 B.C. But under whose auspices the version was made and for what purpose remains debatable. According to Aristobulus and Pseudo-Aristeas, the translation was made at the suggestion of Demetrius under the auspices of Ptolemy II, presumably for the enlightenment of Gentile readers. This notion of the genesis and purpose of the LXX is easily explained by the apologetic aims of Aristobulus and Pseudo-Aristeas, eager to impress the Greeks with the unsurpassed value of the Law of Moses. Modern critics, however, generally regard the undertaking as a strictly Jewish one. If such was the case, two purposes of the translation are conceivable. It could have been prepared to impress and convert the heathen, or to supply the religious needs of the Alexandrian Jews who spoke Greek and no longer understood Hebrew. The first of these views is already advanced by Philo (*Life of Moses*, 2:5 and 6): "Some persons, considering it dreadful that the laws [of the Jews] should be known to a half portion of mankind—solely to the barbarian [portion]—while the Greek [portion] remained wholly ignorant [of them], turned their attention to their translation"; and "their laws . . . will obscure all others, as the rising sun obscures the stars." A. Bertholet (*Die Stellung der Israeliten und der Juden zu den Fremden*, p. 262. Freiburg and Leipzig, 1896) and J. Juster (*Les Juifs dans l'empire romain*, Vol. I, p. 253. Paris, 1914) are inclined to see some truth in this view. Nevertheless, the Hebraisms and barbarisms in the LXX, incomprehensible to the Greeks—whether scholars seeking information or simple souls seeking inspiration—militate against such a purpose (cf. F. Buhl, *Kanon und Text*, pp. 114 f.; Swete, *Introduction*, p. 19).[22] It seems certain that the LXX was prepared by Jews for

---

[22] It should be noted, nevertheless, that some renderings seem to presuppose Gentile readers. The Hebrew word for "hare" in Lev. 11:6 and Deut. 14:7 was not rendered with the usual word *lagos* but with *dasypous*, out of respect for the founder of the Ptolemaic dynasty in Egypt, Ptolemy I Lagos. Typically Greek terms (Titans, Sirens,

Jews, either for public reading (cf. H. St. John Thackeray, *The Septuagint and Jewish Worship* [Schweich Lectures for 1920]. London, 1921) or for private study. It seems obvious, from the characteristics of the vocabulary of the Greek Pentateuch (cf. Swete, *op. cit.*, p. 21), that the translators were Alexandrian and not (as Pseudo-Aristeas claims) Palestinian Jews. In the Pentateuch, as in the books translated later, several hands were at work, frequently at each half of a book.

It may be surmised that the translation of the Pentateuch, superior in many respects to the rest, was sponsored by the Jewish authorities at Alexandria as an official undertaking: this would explain perhaps the public celebration of its anniversary. This official character is more questionable in the case of the rest of the books. It seems likely that soon after a work attained canonical standing or at least considerable popularity in Palestine, it was rendered into Greek, generally under private auspices. The grandson of ben Sira came from Jerusalem to Egypt in 132 B.C. and translated there his grandfather's book (Ecclesiasticus), which had been written half a century before. He tells us (*Prologue to Ecclesiasticus*) that in 132 "the Law itself, and the Prophecies, and the rest of the books" had been translated into Greek, but adds that these renderings differed considerably from the Hebrew originals. The "Prophecies" (Joshua-Kings, Isaiah-Minor Prophets) had been canonized about 200 B.C. and were obviously translated not more than half a century later by a group of interpreters who took far greater liberties than the "Seventy" had taken with the Pentateuch. While the historical books are well translated on the whole and at times, as notably in the case of Samuel, from a far better Hebrew prototype than our Masoretic text, the prophetic books proved often too difficult and many passages (notably in Isaiah) were wholly misunderstood, or freely paraphrased. Unfortunately, the grandson of ben Sira did not list "the rest of the books" which had been translated into Greek before 132. The most important among the Writings were probably available in Greek at that time and all of them certainly before the Christian era, if not by 100 B.C. (cf. Swete, *Introduction*, pp. 24-27). Among the Writings, some books are translated accurately (Ezra, Chronicles) or even literally (Canticles) after the manner of Aquila (Ecclesiastes); others, like Job, with capricious license, utilizing reminiscences of Greek poets.

The Septuagint soon acquired immense authority among the Hellenistic Jews. The Jewish inscription of Rheneia (Delos)—a prayer in Greek to "God the highest, the Lord of spirits and of all flesh," begging him to avenge the murder of Heraclea—bears witness to the wide circulation of the Septuagint outside of Egypt about 100 B.C. (cf. A. Deissmann, *Licht*

Greek coins, cemetery, etc.) are used occasionally to render Hebrew words (see JBL 56 [1937] 96).

vom Osten, 4th ed., pp. 351-362. Tübingen, 1923). The *Letter of Aristeas* not only quotes the Greek Pentateuch (§§57-58, 96-99, 228) but, for the first time in extant records, speaks of it as "Scripture" (§§155, 168). Philo considers the translators to have been inspired prophets (*Life of Moses,* 2:7). Hellenistic Jewish writers disclose a knowledge of the Greek Bible between 200 and 50 B.C. (see Swete, *Introduction,* pp. 369-372); it is frequently quoted (except for a few Biblical books) by Philo, Josephus, and the writers of New Testament (Swete, *op. cit.,* pp. 372-405). But having become the Bible of the Christian Church, it lost all authority among the Jews soon after A.D. 100. Nearly all Mss of the LXX extant are Christian. As we have seen (1: B, above), the radical differences between the LXX and the Hebrew text[23] induced Aquila (*ca.* A.D. 130) to prepare a literal translation of the Bible into Greek, and Theodotion to revise the LXX according to the Hebrew (cf. Swete, *op. cit.,* pp. 31-49). Both disregarded the Apocrypha, as also a third translation circulating among Christians before Origen (d. *ca.* 254): it was prepared by Symmachus who, apparently shocked by the frequently incomprehensible literal renderings of Aquila, revised his version with the help of the LXX and Theodotion, striving, as Jerome says, to render the sense rather than the letter (cf. Swete, *op. cit.,* 49-53). Origen knew likewise three other versions of individual Biblical books, chiefly of those in poetry according to Jerome; being anonymous, they are simply called the fifth, sixth, and seventh (*quinta, sexta, septima*). Although Jerome attributes them to "Jewish translators," they are probably Christian (cf. Swete, *op. cit.,* pp. 53-56). Later Greek translations have no value whatsoever for the critical reconstruction of the Hebrew text.

Strictly speaking, the Septuagint (LXX) about which we have been speaking is an unknown entity. It is uncritical to speak of the printed editions of the Greek Bible or even of the Greek text preserved in manuscripts as "the LXX," although this practice is well-nigh universal. In the first place, the LXX is not a unified translation, even in the Pentateuch, but the work of many hands. The Bible of the Alexandrian Jews during the last centuries before the Christian Era, which alone should be called the LXX, no longer exists; demonstrably it differed considerably from the Greek Bible of the Christians which was derived from it, as shown from quotations and allusions to the LXX in Philo (cf. C. Siegfried, *Philo und der überlieferte Text der LXX,* in *Zeitschr. f. d. wissensch. Theolog.,* 1873, pp. 217-238, 411-428, 522-540; H. E. Ryle, *Philo and the Holy Scriptures,* London, 1895) and in Josephus (cf. A. Mez, *Die Bibel des Josephus untersucht für Buch v-vii der Archäologia.* Basel, 1895). The New Testament does not offer decisive evidence for fixing the text of the Christian

---

[23] Some interpretations of the LXX are criticized by Talmudic rabbis (see A. Geiger, *Urschrift und Übersetzungen der Bibel,* pp. 436-447).

LXX in the first century. Apart from the critical problems inherent in the New Testament text itself, the evidence is not uniform. It appears that in the Synoptic Gospels the LXX is closer to Codices A and Aleph than to Codex B (occasionally Theodotion is preferred to the LXX), but at times the quotation differs both from the LXX and from the Masoretic text (Swete, *Introduction,* pp. 395-398). John's Gospel, Acts, the Catholic Epistles, Hebrews, and Paul's Epistles seem likewise to quote a recension closer to Codex A, Lucian, and Theodotion than to the standard LXX text of Codex B (Swete, *op. cit.,* pp. 398-403). Revelation quotes Daniel in a text resembling Theodotion (Swete, *op. cit.,* p. 48). But in many instances the text seems to be quoted from memory and offers no help to the critic. According to A. Sperber ("New Testament and Septuagint," in JBL 59 [1940] 193-293) two Greek versions, known as the LXX, are quoted in the New Testament.

By the time of Origen, in the first half of the third century, the text of the LXX not only differed from the Hebrew text but had become corrupt through manuscript transmission. Indeed, manuscript variants and textual corruptions are already attested in Philo's writings (cf. Swete, *op. cit.,* pp. 478 f.). Origen was seriously concerned with "the great difference in the manuscripts, due either to the negligence of the scribes, or to the ill-advised daring of some in revising what is written, or even to those who add or omit in the revision whatever seems right to them" (*Commentary on Matthew,* Vol. XV, Chap. 14 [Lommatzsch ed., Vol. III, p. 357]). He therefore took steps to remedy the textual corruption—but only increased the confusion.

Like Jerome later, Origen was convinced that the Hebrew text was correct (Jerome called it *Hebraica veritas*). He was misled by the fact that the consonantal Hebrew text had become more or less fixed before his time, and by the remarkable agreement of available Hebrew manuscripts. To recover the unadulterated text of the Greek Bible, which was for the Christians the transcript of divine revelation, Origen felt impelled first to learn Hebrew in order to familiarize himself with the original text of the Scriptures, and in the second place to compare carefully the Greek Bible with the Hebrew and with the other Greek versions. In his letter to Africanus (Lommatzsch ed., vol. XVIII, §5), written about 240, Origen says:

Nor do I speak thus because I am unwilling to investigate even the Jewish Scriptures and to compare all of ours with theirs, and to notice their variants. This, if it be not arrogant to mention it, I have already done to the best of my ability, striving laboriously after the sense in all the recensions and their variants, particularly in connection with the labor of interpreting the LXX. . . . I strive not to be ignorant even in regard to their [Hebrew] text, in order that in disputation with the Jews I do not adduce what does not stand in their copies and in order that I may be able to use what they adduce even if it does not stand in our own books. For, since I am thus prepared for them in our discussions, they will not despise nor, as is their wont, ridicule the Gentile [Christian] believers for being ignorant of the true [readings] as they are recorded with them.

In his great *Hexapla*, the result of twenty years of labor, Origen provided the Christian Church not only with "a text-book wherewith to learn the Hebrew language" (H. M. Orlinsky, JQR 27 [1936] 149), but also with the textual apparatus for "curing" the "discrepancy in the [LXX] manuscripts of the Old Testament . . . using as a test the other recensions" (*Comment. on Matthew*, Vol. XV, Chap. 14 [Lommatzsch ed., Vol. III, p. 357]). In six parallel columns Origen copied the text of the three principal recensions of the Old Testament, in this order: the Hebrew consonantal text and its transcription in Greek letters (according to the current pronunciation); the literal Greek version of Aquila and its revision by Symmachus; the LXX and its revision by Theodotion. Some notion of the contents and appearance of the Hexapla may be gained from the reproduction of Ps. 46:1-3 (from a palimpsest discovered in Milan by G. Mercati) in Swete, *Introduction*, pp. 62 f. (on "The Columnar order of the Hexapla" see H. M. Orlinsky, *loc. cit.*, pp. 137-149). Omitting the two Hebrew columns, Origen prepared also a *Tetrapla*:

"After collecting all these [Greek recensions] in the same [work], dividing them in sections and placing them side by side, together with the evidence of the Hebrews, he left us the manuscripts of the so-called Hexapla, having prepared also a separate edition of Aquila, Symmachus, and Theodotion, together with that of the LXX, in the Tetrapla" (Eusebius, *Ecclesiastical History*, 6:16).[24]

The Hexapla was a monumental work. If it had been written on papyrus scrolls, it would have comprised 150 large volumes; if in the form of a codex, it would have filled nearly seven thousand pages. Its size alone prevented its reproduction as a whole. The original copy was preserved in the library of Pamphilus at Caesarea in Palestine, where Jerome studied it. But after the Moslem conquest of Palestine in 638 this great manuscript mysteriously disappeared, presumably being forgotten and allowed to decay. Most of the extant fragments of the Hexapla have been collected by F. Field in his great work, *Origenis Hexaplorum quae supersunt, sive Veterum Interpretum Graecorum in totum Veterum Testamentum fragmenta.* Vol. I: Prolegomena, Genesis-Esther; Vol. II: Job-Malachi; indices (Oxford, 1875). For material which has come to light

---

[24] In the Psalter, Origen added three more columns, giving the *fifth* and *sixth* and *seventh* Greek versions (Eusebius, *loc. cit.*); the first two (or one of them) occurred for other books, so that the terms "Heptapla" and "Octapla" are occasionally used.

after Field's researches, see E. Schürer, *Geschichte des jüdischen Volkes* (Vol. III, p. 430, n. 13).

Assuming that the LXX had been translated from a Hebrew text identical with the current one, Origen revised it by marking the passages of the LXX lacking in the Hebrew by means of an *obelos* (−), *lemniscus* (÷), or *hypolemniscus* (⨪) at the beginning, and a *metobelus* (: or/.; ⏌ in the Syriac) at the end. Conversely, the beginning of passages in the Hebrew which were not in the LXX (supplied from Theodotion or another Greek version) was marked with an *asterisk* (※; in the Syriac ⨯), and their end by a *metobelus*. When Origen found differences in the order, he transposed entire sections in the LXX (so in Ex. 35-40; I Kings 4-11, 20-21; Jer. 25-50) according to the Hebrew sequence, with the exception of Proverbs, where the divergent arrangement was indicated by diacritical marks. The orthography of proper names and minor differences between the LXX and the Hebrew were tacitly corrected in accordance with the Hebrew text. Other variants were allowed to stand.

This revised edition of the LXX in the fifth column of the Hexapla was published separately by Pamphilus (d. 309) and Eusebius (d. 339), attaining wide circulation in Palestine in the fourth century (Jerome, *Preface to Chronicles*). This recension, called Hexaplaric, differed according to Jerome from the standard LXX (*koinē* or *vulgata*), but he regarded it as the genuine LXX, *incorrupta et immaculata* (Epistle 106, to Sunnia and Fretela). In reality, instead of giving us the pure LXX, Origen corrupted it by additions and changes made, with the help of the other Greek versions, in order to bring it into harmony with the current Hebrew text. Origen's diacritical marks, which warned scholars of some of these alterations, were eventually omitted by copyists. Although only few of the manuscripts preserved the Hexaplaric recension more or less intact (cf. Swete, *Introduction*, p. 482), most manuscripts show its influence. For the reconstruction of the Hexaplaric recension, one of the most valuable records is its literal translation into Syriac made by Paul, Bishop of Tella (Mesopotamia), in 616-617 (cf. Swete, *Introduction*, pp. 112-114; A. Baumstark, *Geschichte der Syrischen Literatur*, pp. 186 f. Bonn, 1922), in which Origen's signs were retained punctiliously and references to variants in the other Greek versions were noted on the margin. Most of the Old Testament (without Genesis-Kings, Chronicles, Ezra-Nehemiah, Ruth) in this so-called Syro-Hexaplaric version was edited from a manuscript in Milan by A. M. Ceriani (*Monumenta Sacra et Profana*, Vol. VII. Milan, 1874); the rest of the manuscript was known to A. Masius (1574), but has since disappeared. A. M. Ceriani published Gen. 1:1-Ex. 33:2 (*Monumenta*, Vol. II, 1868); P. de Lagarde (*Bibliotheca Syriaca*. Göttingen, 1892) published most of the other books according to manuscripts in London and Paris. The Syro-Hexaplaric text is the sole witness, apart from the Greek Chigi manuscript, to the LXX of Daniel, for Theodotion was substituted for Daniel in all other Greek manuscripts.

In addition to Origen's Hexaplaric recension, two other editions of the LXX were circulating in the fourth century, according to the witness of Jerome:

"Alexandria and Egypt in their LXX praise Hesychius as its author; Constantinople as far as Antioch approves the copies of Lucian the martyr; the provinces between these read Palestinian codices[25] which, edited by Origen, were popularized by Eusebius and Pamphilus; and the whole world is in a state of mutual strife about this threefold variety" (*Preface to Chronicles* [ed. Vallarsi, Vol. IX, pp. 1405 f.]).

Hesychius may be the Egyptian bishop of that name who died a martyr in 311 (Eusebius, *Eccl. Hist.*, 8:13, 7); a year later, likewise, Lucian, born in Samosata and presbyter at Antioch, was put to death for his faith (Eusebius, *op. cit.*, 8:13, 2; 9:6, 3).

The principal clue for the reconstruction of the Hesychius and Lucian recensions are patristic quotations: according to Jerome's statement translated above, the Church Fathers in Egypt quoted the LXX in the Hesychius recension; those in Syria and Asia Minor, Lucian's. Our principal witness for Hesychius is Cyril of Alexandria (d. 444), while Chrysostom (d. 407) and Theodoret (d. ca. 457) quoted Lucian. Thus, for instance, A. Sperber (JBL 54 [1935] 73-92) has collated and compared the Greek text of the Minor Prophets used by Cyril and Theodoret, respectively, in their commentaries, presenting thus a classification of the differences between two Greek texts, presumably those of Hesychius and Lucian.[26] Assuming that Cyril and Theodoret have preserved a fairly pure form of the text, it is then possible to collate the manuscripts and determine which ones preserve Hesychian readings and which Lucianic. Thus, in theory, it seems possible to fulfill the task first envisaged by P. de Lagarde: the reconstruction of the three recensions named by Jerome. In practice, however, the available evidence is too confused and fragmentary to allow critics to reach final and undisputed conclusions. Some notion of the bewildering complexity of the problems involved may be gained by a perusal of J. A. Montgomery's article in JBL 44 (1925) 289-302. It is not surprising that the attempt of C. H. Cornill to determine the Hesychian recension of Ezekiel (in his outstanding work, *Das Buch des Propheten Ezechiel*. Leipzig, 1886) should now be considered at

[25] P. de Lagarde would read *Palaestinae* instead of *Palaestinos*; the meaning would then be, "the Palestinian provinces between these read codices which . . ."

[26] In contrast with the majority of critics, A. Sperber (*op. cit.*) follows his teacher P. Kahle (cf. TSK 88 [1915] 410-426) in regarding the texts of Hesychius and Lucian not as recensions of the LXX but as independent translations. He also believes that "as late as the days of Origen two different translations of the Old Testament into Greek were known as LXX" (JBL 59 [1940] 279).

least in part "fallacious" (Montgomery, *op. cit.*, p. 294, n. 6). Even sharper has been the criticism of P. de Lagarde's famous edition of Lucian (*Librorum Veteris Testamenti canonicorum pars I graece edita*. Göttingen, 1883), including the Pentateuch and the historical books (i.e., Genesis-Esther): see G. F. Moore, "The Antiochian Recension of the Septuagint" (AJSL 29 [1912-13] 37-62). "It should be clearly understood that Lagarde's text of the Octateuch should not be quoted in any circumstances whatever, and that it is perilous to cite it for Samuel and Kings, or Chronicles. . . ." (P. L. Hedley, HTR 26 [1933] 59).

Manuscripts of the Greek Bible are of course the chief basis for a critical reconstruction of the LXX, if possible, in addition to patristic quotations and versions based on the LXX. The fullest catalogue of the Greek manuscripts of the LXX is that of A. Rahlfs (*Verzeichnis der griechischen Handschriften des Alten Testaments*. Mitteilungen des Septuaginta-Unternehmens, Vol. II. Berlin, 1914), which despite its size is not exhaustive (see also, for the principal manuscripts, Swete, *Introduction*, pp. 122-170). The earliest manuscripts are papyrus fragments from the second and third centuries of our era; the John Rylands papyri are dated by the editors in the second century B.C.[27] These ancient scraps of the Greek Bible are valuable in affording us a glimpse—more direct than the quotations in Philo, Josephus, the New Testament, and the Apologists—into the text of the LXX before Origen. But every edition of the Greek Bible must ultimately rest on the great uncial manuscripts containing originally the whole Bible (both Old and New Testaments).

The most important of these is Codex B or *Vaticanus* (Vatican Library, Gr. 1209), written about the middle of the fourth century. It never contained I-IV Maccabees, and is now defective at the beginning (lacking now Gen. 1:1-46:28), in the middle (lacking II Sam. 2:5-7, 10-13; Ps. 106:27-138:6b [Gr. 105:27-137:6b]), and at the end (breaking off at Hebr. 9:14 and lacking I-II Timothy, Titus, Philemon, Revelation). This famous manuscript probably offers for the Old Testament as a whole the best text of the LXX, although for Judges it gives an Egyptian version made early in the fourth century (G. F. Moore, *Judges* [ICC], pp. xlv f.), and Theodotion for Daniel and (as shown by C. C. Torrey, *Ezra Studies*,

---

[27] H. A. Sanders, *The Old Testament Manuscripts in the Freer Collection* (University of Michigan Studies, Humanistic Series, 8). H. A. Sanders, and C. Schmidt, *The Minor Prophets in the Freer Collection and the Berlin Fragment of Genesis* (University of Michigan Studies, Humanistic Series, 21. Ann Arbor, 1927). F. Kenyon, *The Chester Beatty Biblical Papyri*, Fascicules I ff. (London, 1933 ff.). C. H. Roberts, *Two Biblical Papyri in the John Rylands Library* (Manchester, 1936). A. C. Johnson, H. S. Gehman, and E. H. Kase, *The John H. Scheide Biblical Papyri* (Princeton, 1938). For the significance of these newly published texts for the transmission of the LXX see: A. Allgeier, *Die Chester Beatty Papyri zum Pentateuch* (Studien zur Geschichte und Kultur des Altertums, XXI:2. Paderborn, 1938). Some of these papyri are collated in the apparatus of Kittel's *Biblia Hebraica* (third edition).

pp. 66 ff. Chicago, 1910) for Chronicles-Ezra-Nehemiah; the text of Chronicles-Nehemiah is, moreover, notoriously corrupt. Beginning with the third printing of the Greek Bible, the Roman or Sixtine edition (published at Rome under the auspices of Sixtus V in 1586 [1587 in most copies]),[28] nearly all printed editions are more or less based on Codex B. This great manuscript was edited by Cardinal A. Mai (1828-1838, issued in 1857; in a corrected edition in 1859; reproduced several times); by C. Vercellone, J. Cozza-Luzi, and others (under the auspices of Pius IX, 1868-72; the commentary appeared in 1881); and it was issued in a photographic reproduction by J. Cozza-Luzi in 1890. The text of Codex B is Egyptian, and at least in part reproduces a pre-Origenic text.

Another important uncial manuscript is Codex A, or *Alexandrinus*, in the British Museum (Royal I. D. v-viii), written in Egypt in the fifth century. Except for some lacunae (particularly in Genesis, I Samuel, and Psalms), it gives the Old and New Testaments. Its text in general (and particularly for the historical books) seems to follow closely Origen's Hexaplaric edition of the LXX, preserving, however, some earlier readings. Codex A was collated in the *London Polyglot* (1657) and edited by J. E. Grabe (4 vols., Oxford, 1707-1720; re-edited by F. Field, Oxford, 1859); a facsimile reproduction was published at London in 1881-1883 in three volumes.

The Codex *Sinaiticus* or *Aleph* (now in the British Museum) is better preserved in the New Testament than in the Old, where only the poetic and prophetical books, Esther, Judith, Tobit, I and IV Maccabees are fairly complete, while only fragments of Genesis, Numbers, I Chronicles, II Esdras are extant. Its text in general resembles that of Codex B, but in Tobit it differs radically from it and not seldom it is closer to Codex A than to Codex B. It was written at the end of the fourth or early in the fifth century. The fragments were published at different times by C. von Tischendorf, and were collated by E. Nestle in a supplement to the sixth and seventh editions of Tischendorf's *Vetus Testamentum Graece* (Leipzig, 1880, 1887).

The other uncial and minuscule codices contain only limited portions of the Old Testament. Collations of a large number of them are given in the critical apparatus of the great edition (still indispensable) of R. Holmes and J. Parsons (*Vetus Testamentum Graece cum variis lectionibus*, 5 vols., Oxford, 1798-1827), and in the "Larger Cambridge Septuagint" edited by A. E. Brooke and N. McLean which is nearing completion (vol. I, part I: Genesis. Cambridge, 1906; etc.). The text is that of H. B. Swete's

---

[28] With some revisions and the addition of a textual apparatus the Sixtine edition has been often reprinted (cf. Swete, *Introduction*, p. 182). According to M. L. Margolis (JBL 38 [1919] 51 f.), the "copy" used by the printers of the Sixtine was the Aldine edition (Venice, 1518-1519) on which the variants of Codex B had been entered (cf. the error in Josh. 22:25).

manual edition of the LXX (3 vols., Cambridge, 1887-1894, and later editions), which generally gives the text of Codex B, with some variants of other uncials.

The four primary printed editions of the LXX are the following: *a*. The *editio princeps*, in the *Complutensian Polyglot* (1514-1517), is based on manuscripts obtained from Rome (*Vat. graec.* 330 and 346, i.e., Holmes and Parsons 108 and 248) and Venice (S. Marc 5, i.e., Holmes and Parsons 68); other manuscripts utilized are now lost. The text of this edition seems to be closely related to Lucian's recension. The text of the Complutensian is followed in the Antwerp (1569-1572) and Paris (1629-1645) Polyglots. *b*. The *Aldine Edition*, prepared by A. and F. Asulanus and published at Venice by Aldus the elder and his father-in-law Andreas in 1518-1519, was based on manuscripts in Venice (including Holmes and Parsons 29, 68, 121). Its text is said to be on the whole close to the Hesychian recension. *c*. The *Roman*, or *Sixtine, Edition* (1586) is based, as stated above, on the Vatican Codex. This edition, reproduced by B. Walton (*London Polyglot*, 1657), by Holmes and Parsons (1798-1827), by Tischendorf (Leipzig, 1850, and later editions), and others, may be regarded as the vulgate text of the LXX. *d. Grabe's Edition* of Codex A (Oxford, 1707-1720).

No critical edition of the LXX is available. The new manual text published by A. Rahlfs (*Septuaginta*, 2 vols., Stuttgart, 1935) is based primarily on the Vaticanus, the Sinaiticus, and the Alexandrinus; selected variants from other witnesses are given in a small critical apparatus. Rahlfs died before he could complete his great critical edition sponsored by the Göttingen Academy, of which, aside from many learned monographs, only three parts have appeared: *Ruth* (Stuttgart, 1922; cf. his important *Studie über den Griechischen Text des Buches Ruth*, Berlin, 1922), *Genesis* (Stuttgart, 1922) and *Psalms with the Odes*[29] (*Psalmi cum Odis*. Göttingen, 1931). Only one other book has been issued in an admirable critical edition: *The Book of Joshua in Greek*, edited by M. L. Margolis (Parts I-IV [reaching Josh. 19:38], Paris, 1931-1938).

B. Translations from the Greek

For the reconstruction of the original text of the LXX in so far as possible, critics utilize, in addition to manuscripts and patristic quota-

---

[29] The Odes, or *cantica*, following the Psalms in many Greek manuscripts, are psalms occurring in the Old and New Testaments outside of the Psalter. Codex A, for instance, gives the psalms in the following chapters: Ex. 15, Deut. 32, I Sam. 2, Is. 26, Jonah 2, Hab. 3, Is. 38, the Prayer of Manasseh, Dan. 3 (apocryphal additions in the LXX), Luke 1:46-55; 2:29-32; 1:68-79, and the Morning Hymn (the *Gloria*, beginning with Luke 2:14; for its text see E. Hennecke, *Neutestamentliche Apokryphen*, 2nd ed., p. 599. Tübingen, 1924). The Greek and Roman churches still sing some of these psalms at Lauds and other services.

tions, also the ancient versions which were made from the Greek into Latin and Oriental languages. These versions are of course all of Christian origin.

Christianity flourished in North Africa, in the regions around Carthage, from the second to the seventh century (see E. Buonaiuti, *Il Cristianesimo nell'Africa romana*. Bari, 1928). The Christians there were descendants of Roman colonists and therefore spoke Latin. The greatest in their midst—Tertullian (d. *ca.* 230), Cyprian (d. 258), and Augustine (d. 430) —wrote their works in Latin and quoted the Bible in a Latin version or versions. Nothing is known of the origin of this Latin Bible: it seems probable that the Latin version quoted by Cyprian was prepared in Carthage shortly before 200, but Tertullian's text often differs radically from it. Although Augustine laments the *infinita varietas* of Latin inter- preters (*De Doctrina Christiana,* 2:11)—Greek translators may be counted, but not the Latin (*loc. cit.*)—it is now generally thought that he had reference to innumerable discrepancies between manuscripts (at- tested by Jerome, in his preface to Joshua and elsewhere) rather than to numerous independent versions (cf. F. C. Burkitt, *The Old Latin and the Itala,* p. 5. Cambridge, 1896; Kennedy, Hastings' *Dictionary of the Bible,* III, 48 f.; Swete, *Introduction,* p. 89). On the basis of a reference of Augustine, this "Old Latin" (*vetus latina*) is sometimes called *Itala* (see Burkitt, *op. cit.*). The fragments of this version have been collected, chiefly from patristic quotations, by P. Sabatier (*Bibliorum sacrorum Latinae versiones antiquae, seu Vetus Italica et caeterae . . . ,* 3 vols., Rheims, 1739-49; 2nd ed., Paris, 1751). U. Robert (*Pentateuchi versio latina anti- quissima e codice Lugdunensi.* Paris, 1881) has published the Lyons man- uscript of the Pentateuch; for other manuscripts and their editions see Swete, *Introduction,* pp. 93-97; Kennedy, *op. cit.,* pp. 49-51. The Greek text from which the Old Latin was translated is said by many to agree with Lucian's recension. Since Lucian is later than this version, we must conclude that both Lucian and the Old Latin have preserved some read- ings of the LXX in a pre-Origenic recension.

Native Egyptians unfamiliar with Greek began to be converted to Christianity about 200 and a century and a half later most of them were members of the *Coptic* (Arabic pronunciation of "Egyptian") Church. Translations of the Bible into Coptic dialects began to be made early in the fourth century. The writing used is not the old Egyptian, but the Coptic alphabet, derived from the Greek. The earliest version, probably completed about 350, is in *Sahidic* (from the Arabic *eṣ-Ṣa 'īd*, Upper Egypt), the dialect of Thebais (Southern Egypt). Portions of the Scrip- tures are also preserved in *Akhmimic* (from the city of Akhmim, ancient Chemmis, in Upper Egypt), in *Fayumic* (in Middle Egypt), and in

Bohairic, the dialect of Alexandria and the Western Delta.[30] All of them, even the Bohairic version, which is the latest (*ca.* 650) and shows the influence of the Sahidic, were made from LXX texts of the fourth century but bear witness occasionally to some earlier readings; the Sahidic fragments of Job, for instance, are said to be pre-Origenic. See, in general, H. Hyvernat, in RB 5 (1896) 427-433, 540-569; 6 (1897) 48-74; H. S. Gehman, in JBL 46 (1927) 279-330; Fr. H. Hallock, in AJSL 49 (1933) 325-335.

Christianity was introduced into Abyssinia by Syrian missionaries in the fourth century. About the middle of the fifth century (in 340 according to H. S. Gehman) the Kingdom of Axum, whose inhabitants were descended from South Arabian immigrants speaking a Semitic dialect (Geez or *Ethiopic*), became Christian through the conversion of its king Tazana (or Ezana). The Bible was gradually translated by many hands between the fifth and the eighth century: it lacked I-IV Maccabees and Revelation, but included in turn a number of Pseudepigrapha, notably Enoch and Jubilees (the complete text of which is preserved only in Ethiopic) and IV Ezra. The oldest manuscript (containing the Pentateuch, Joshua, Judges, and Ruth) dates from the thirteenth century and is textually corrupt. The Biblical text was accordingly revised in the fourteenth century with the help of Arabic translations (particularly Saadia's), and again later.[31] Consequently the Ethiopic text is not critically important for the LXX and the Hebrew.

Reference has already been made, in connection with the Hexapla, to Paul of Tella's *Syriac* translation of Origen's edition of the LXX (*Syro-Hexaplaric* version). An earlier Syriac version from the Greek is attributed to the Nestorian Patriarch Mar Abbas (d. 552), but except for some possible echoes (cf. A. Baumstark, *Geschichte der Syrischen Literatur*, p. 119. Bonn, 1922) it has perished completely. Little is known of two other incomplete Nestorian translations from the Greek. Polycarp (*ca.*

---

[30] For an account of Coptic literature see W. D. Dawson, in Asiatic Review N.S. 17 (1921) 342-351; J. Leipoldt, in *Geschichte der Christlichen Litteraturen des Orients*, pp. 132-183 (Litteraturen des Ostens, VII: 2). Leipzig, 1907. For editions of Coptic Biblical texts, see Swete, *Introduction*, p. 107; A. Vaschalde, *Ce qui a été publié des versions coptes de la Bible*, Paris, 1922 (also RB 28-31, 1919-1922); Ida A. Pratt, *Ancient Egypt*, pp. 382-384. New York Public Library, 1925.

[31] On the Ethiopic Bible see: Swete, *Introduction*, pp. 109 f.; E. Littmann, in *Gesch. der Christl. Litterat. des Orients*, pp. 223-228. The published portions include: Genesis-II Kings (A. Dillmann; Leipzig, 1853-1855, 1861-1872); Apocrypha (Dillmann; Berlin, 1894); Joel (Dillmann, in A. Merx, *Die Prophetie Joels*; Halle, 1879); Psalms and Canticles (*London Polyglot*); Obadiah, Malachi, Lamentations, and Isaiah (J. Bachmann; Halle, 1892, 1893); Jonah (W. Wright, *Jonah in Four Semitic Versions*. London, 1857); Daniel (O. Löfgren; Paris, 1927); Jonah, Nahum, Habakkuk, Zephaniah, Haggai, Zechariah, and Malachi (Löfgren. Vilh. Ekmans Universitetsfond, Vol. 38. Uppsala, 1930); on the text of I Kings see H. S. Gehman, in JBL 50 (1931) 81-114.

507), under the auspices of Philoxenus of Mabug, is said to have translated the Psalter, but nothing remains of this version; fragments of a version of Isaiah apparently made by him have, however, been published by A. M. Ceriani (cf. Swete, *Introduction*, pp. 115 f.; Baumstark, *op. cit.*, p. 144; A. Mingana, in Exp. 19 [1920] 149-160). Jacob of Edessa (d. 708) prepared a revised edition of the Old Testament, based on the Peshitta and the Hexaplaric LXX, of which some fragments are extant (cf. Swete, *op. cit.*, p. 116; Baumstark, *op. cit.*, p. 251). Finally the Palestinian Christians, after they severed their former relations with the Monophysites of Edessa after the Council of Chalcedon (451), prepared in the late fifth or early sixth century a translation of the LXX into their dialect (cf. F. Schwally, *Idioticon des Christlich Palästinischen Aramaeisch.* Giessen, 1893; C. Brockelmann *Grundriss der vergleichenden Grammatik der Semitischen Sprachen,* Vol. I, pp. 15 f.), of which some fragments are extant (cf. Swete, *op. cit.*, pp. 114-115).

It was only with the rapid expansion of Islam beyond the limits of Arabia, which occurred after the death of Mohammed (632), that the Bible was translated into *Arabic*. Partial translations may have been prepared in the seventh century, but the first one of which there is a record is that of John, Bishop of Seville, made in 724, twelve years after the Moslem conquest of Spain; Christians in the Near East must also have had Arabic versions at that time. The first and most important Arabic translation among the Jews is that of Saadia Gaon (d. 942), which was of course based on the Hebrew text. Only the Pentateuch, Isaiah, the Minor Prophets and portions of other books (Judges, Psalms, Job, Proverbs, Daniel) are extant; the Pentateuch was published in Hebrew characters at Constantinople in 1546, and in Arabic characters in the Paris (1645) and London (1657) Polyglots; some of the other books individually (cf. F. C. Burkitt, in Hastings' *Dictionary of the Bible*, Vol. I, p. 137). With the exception of the Pentateuch and Joshua, none of the other books in the Arabic Bible printed in these Polyglots was translated from the Hebrew (cf. B. Walton, *London Polyglot*, Vol. I, pp. 96 f.; Burkitt, *loc. cit.*). The London Polyglot reproduces the text of the Paris Polyglot with a few revisions and adds some of the Apocrypha (none of which appeared in the earlier work). Some of the books in these editions (based on a sixteenth century manuscript from Egypt) were translated from the Peshitta (Judges, Samuel, Kings, Chronicles, and Job), others from the LXX (the Prophets, Psalms, and Proverbs; likewise of course the Apocrypha). According to A. Vaccari ("Le versioni Arabe dei Profeti," *Biblica* 2 [1921] 401-423; 3 [1922] 401-423; cf. 4 [1923] 312-314) the text of the prophetic books in the Paris Polyglot was translated at Alexandria by the priest El-'Alam (ninth or tenth century) from a Greek text close to Codex A. A careful study of the Arabic Daniel in these Polyglots has convinced

H. S. Gehman (JBL 44 [1925] 327-352) that the Arabic represents the Hexaplaric text of Constantinople in a recension superior to Codex A and all other witnesses. Vaccari also observes that the text of Isaiah, Jeremiah, and Ezekiel in the London Polyglot is a revision of the Paris text on the basis of a translation from the Syriac (made by Pethion in the ninth century). As for the Pentateuch, two Christian Arabic versions were current in Egypt: a version from the Bohairic used by the Jacobites and one from the Sahidic used by the Melchites; both were influenced by the Hebrew and Samaritan texts (see J. F. Rhode, *The Arabic Versions of the Pentateuch in the Church of Egypt*. Dissertation at the Catholic University of America. St. Louis, 1921).[32]

Like the Coptic versions, the *Armenian* Bible arose from nationalistic as well as religious aspirations. At the beginning of the fifth century Sahak (d. 428), the Patriarch, and Mesrop (d. 441), the inventor of the Armenian alphabet, began a translation of the Scriptures and of the liturgy into the national language, as a reaction against the prevailing use of Syriac in the worship—a language which the common people did not understand. According to Moses of Chorene (said to have been a nephew of Mesrop), this incomplete translation was made from the Syriac. But Koriun relates that Mesrop began his translation at Edessa (*ca.* 397), with the help of a Greek scribe, commencing with Proverbs. Another Armenian historian of the fifth century, Lazar of Pharphi, asserts that the translation was made from the Greek—a view adopted by F. C. Conybeare (Hastings' *Dictionary of the Bible*, Vol. I, p. 152). In any case, the definitive official translation, dating from about 430 or later, was made from the LXX (using manuscripts obtained from Constantinople and Alexandria), but clear traces of the Peshitta appear in numerous passages. In general the Armenian Old Testament follows exactly the Hexaplaric recension, although occasionally (notably in Jeremiah) the text was revised in accordance with the Syriac, but not, as is sometimes asserted, the Hebrew (F. Macler, in Handēs Amsorya 1927, cols. 609-616).[33]

According to Moses of Chorene, Mesrop was also the author of the *Georgian* version. The truth in this legend is that before the Georgian Church separated from the Armenian at the end of the sixth century, the influence of Armenian Christian literature on the early Georgian writings was dominant, so that the Georgian Bible has been called "the twin sister of the Armenian" (H. Goussen). It is now certain that "the whole

[32] A selected bibliography on the Arabic versions is given by H. S. Gehman (JBL 44 [1925] 327 f.). For these versions, and Christian-Arabic literature in general, see: G. Graf, *Die Christlich-Arabische Literatur bis zur Fränkischen Zeit* (Strassburger Theol. Studien, VII: 1) Freiburg i. B., 1905.

[33] A brief bibliography and general summary will be found in Swete, *Introduction*, pp. 118-120. For fuller details see: H. S. Gehman, "The Armenian Version of the Book of Daniel and its Affinities" (ZAW N.F. 7 [1930] 82-99).

Bible must have been translated into Georgian by the end of the sixth century" (R. P. Blake, JTS 26 [1927] 50-64). The original version, made by several hands, had an Armenian-Syriac foundation but discloses some Septuagint influence (Blake, *loc. cit.*); it is not a version from the Greek containing Armenian and Syriac readings, as F. Zorell (Handēs Amsorya 1927, cols. 669-680) believed. The *editio princeps* (Moscow, 1743), based on lost manuscripts that were probably recent, discloses traces of a scholastic revision in the Prophetic books and in Kings, while other parts preserve a relatively pure form of the original text; but the Books of Maccabees (still unknown in the old Georgian) were translated from the Slavic. It is critically important as a witness to early readings, being on the whole more archaic than the current Armenian Bible (which has subsequently been further revised according to the LXX).[34] Eighth century fragments of Jeremiah from the Old Cairo Genizah preserve a text going back to an Armenian original, but have also been affected by a strongly Hexaplaric Greek text (R. P. Blake, in HTR 25 [1932] 225-272; cf. P. L. Hedley, in JTS 34 [1933] 392-395).

The *Slavonic* version was made by Cyril (d. 869), who translated the Psalter, and Methodius (d. 885), who carried the work to completion. Except for fragments embedded in the official Slavonic Bible, the original translation has perished. It seems certain that it was based on Lucian's recension of the LXX, although in the present Bible some books are translated from the Hebrew or the Vulgate (Swete, *Introduction,* pp. 120 f.).

The *Gothic* Bible, prepared by Ulfilas about 350, is also based on Lucian's recension. Only a few fragments of the Old Testament (verses in Genesis, Psalms, and II Ezra) survive (cf. Swete, *Introduction,* pp. 117 f.) and have been edited in: W. Streitberg, *Die gothische Bibel*; Erster Teil: *Der gothische Text und seine griechische Vorlage* (Germanische Bibliothek, Untersuchungen und Texte, III, i). Heidelberg, 1908; 2nd ed., 1919.

C. Translations from the Hebrew (Peshitta and Vulgate)

The Jewish translations from the Hebrew have already been mentioned: the LXX, the Aramaic Targums, Aquila's Greek version, and Saadia's Arabic Bible. The Samaritans made Greek, Aramaic, and Arabic translations of their Pentateuch (cf. C. Steuernagel, *Einleitung in das Alte Testament,* pp. 43 f. Tübingen, 1912).

The Christians, besides the Greek and other partial versions previously

[34] See also: Swete, *Introduction,* p. 120; R. P. Blake, "Ancient Georgian Versions of the Old Testament" (HTR 19 [1926] 271-297); "The Athos Codex of the Georgian Old Testament" (HTR 22 [1929] 33-56); on the text of IV Ezra (HTR 19 [1926] 299-375; 22 [1929] 57-105); "Catalogue of the Georgian Manuscripts in the Cambridge University Library" (HTR 25 [1932] 207-224).

mentioned, prepared two great translations from the Hebrew: the Peshitta and the Vulgate.

The Bible of the Syriac Christians was called *Peshitta* (i.e., simple, presumably to distinguish it from the Syro-Hexaplaric) since the ninth century; in the fourth century Syriac theologians called it "our edition." Like the LXX, the Peshitta is obviously the work of many hands, as Ephraem Syrus (d. 373) and Jacob of Edessa (d. 708) well knew. Its origin, or rather the origin of its several parts, is, however, still as unknown to us as it was to Theodore of Mopsuestia. It may be surmised that soon after the birth of the Syriac Church (about 150) at least parts of the Bible were provided, but how many of the Biblical books were translated by 200 is uncertain (Chronicles, Ezra-Nehemiah, Esther, and the Apocrypha were added later); at least Tatian's harmony of the Gospels (*Diatessaron*) dates back to about 160, but whether the separate Gospels were translated at that time is unknown. It seems that the Pentateuch was the first part of the Old Testament to be translated; its text follows closely the Masoretic Hebrew and resembles the Targum Onkelos. In fact, some critics believe that the Syriac Pentateuch (if not the whole original Peshitta) was of Jewish (or at least Jewish Christian) origin.[35] It seems obvious that even if the translators were Christians they utilized for the Pentateuch (and some other books) Jewish Targums and followed, like Jerome, the Jewish interpretation. The text of the Syriac Pentateuch is quoted in other parts of the Old Testament and in the New. Of course the tradition that the Peshitta originated in the time of Solomon or was prepared by the priest (Asa) sent to Samaria after 722 B.C. (II Kings 17:28) is too fantastic to give any support to the theory of the Jewish origin of this translation.

In view of the conflicting evidence, the most likely opinion is that of F. Buhl (*Kanon und Text des Alten Testaments*, p. 187), according to whom the Peshitta "owed its origin to Christian efforts: in part older individual Jewish translations were utilized, in part the remainder was commissioned to Jewish Christians for translation." This original Peshitta, as it existed in the third century, was variously revised and supplemented. The books of Chronicles, Ezra, Nehemiah, and Esther, as well as the Apocrypha, were soon added. The translation of Chronicles has the characteristics of a Targum; it freely paraphrases, avoids anthropomorphic expressions with reference to God, and is conformed to the text of Samuel and Kings. According to S. Fraenkel (JPT 1879, 508-536, 720-759), Chronicles was translated by Jews in Edessa in the third century; according to

---

[35] Cf. J. Perles, *Meletemata Peshittoniana* (Breslau, 1859). J. M. Schönfelder, *Onkelos und Peschitto* (Munich, 1869). F. C. Burkitt, *Encyclopaedia Biblica*, Vol. IV, col. 5025. J. Bloch, in AJSL 35 (1919) 215-222. A. Baumstark, *Geschichte der Syrischen Literatur*, p. 18.

Th. Nöldeke (*Die Alttestamentl. Litteratur,* p. 263. Leipzig, 1868), it was actually a Jewish Targum. The Jewish character of the Peshitta of Chronicles cannot, however, be proved, as Nöldeke (*loc. cit.*) and others believe, by the words added to I Chron. 5:2, "out of Judah will come the King Messiah" (in one manuscript: *"has come . . . ,"* which is a Christian revision). Far from being a Jewish denial that the Messiah had come in the person of Jesus, the statement could well be a prophecy of Christ's coming placed into the mouth of the Chronicler. With the exception of Sirach's Ecclesiasticus, most of which was translated from the Hebrew (although there are revisions according to the LXX), the Apocrypha were translated from the Greek.

Some Biblical books were revised to conform with the LXX, the official Christian Bible. This revision was not systematic, and is especially conspicuous in Genesis (cf. 47:31), Isaiah (cf. 7:14, "the virgin"; 30:20, "and he will no longer gather those that mislead you, and your eyes will see those that mislead you"; etc.), the Minor Prophets, and the Psalms (cf. W. E. Barnes, in JTS 2, 186 f.; J. F. Berg, *The Influence of the Septuagint on the Peshitta Psalter.* New York, 1895. J. Hänel, *Die aussermasoretischen Übereinstimmungen zwischen der Septuaginta und der Peschitta in der Genesis* (Beih. ZAW 20). Giessen, 1911; J. Bloch, in AJSL 36 [1920] 161-166). Christian influence can also be detected here and there: Is. 9:6 (H. 9:5); 52:15; Jer. 31:31 ("a new testament"); Hos. 13:14 ("Where is thy victory, O death? Where is thy sting, O nether-world?" Cf. I Cor. 15:55); Zech. 12:10 ("they will look upon me by means of the one whom they have pierced").

The *editio princeps* of the Peshitta is that of Gabriel Sionita in the *Paris Polyglot* (1645), based on a manuscript written only a few years before; this edition was reproduced in the *London Polyglot* (1657), which in turn was published, omitting the Apocrypha and without improvements, by S. Lee (London, 1823). The Nestorian recension was edited by J. Perkins (Urumiah, 1852) and the Apocrypha were published by P. de Lagarde (Leipzig and London, 1861). The Dominicans in Mosul published the Peshitta in 1887-1891.[36] By far the most important text of the Peshitta is that of a sixth or seventh century codex in the Ambrosian Library in Milan, edited in photographic facsimile by A. M. Ceriani (*Translatio Syra Pescitto . . .* Milan, 1879-1883). Few individual Biblical books have been published in critical editions or provided with a critical apparatus: Psalms (by W. E. Barnes, 1897 and 1904), Isaiah (G. Dieterich, 1905), Song of Songs (J. Bloch, AJSL 38 [1922] 103-139), Ezra (C. A. Howley, *A Critical Examination of the Peshitta Version of the Book of Ezra.* New York, 1922), etc. See in general, L. Haefeli, *Die*

[36] For an appraisal of these editions of the Peshitta, cf. J. Bloch, in AJSL 37 (1921) 136-144.

*Peshitta des Alten Testamentes mit Rücksicht auf ihre textkritische Bear-
beitung und Herausgabe* (AA XI, 1). Münster, 1927.

No Christian translation of the Old Testament played a greater role
than the Latin *Vulgate*, at least before the Protestant Reformation; it is
still the official Roman Catholic Bible. In its famous decree issued on
April 8, 1546, the Council of Trent declared that this Latin Bible, "*haec
ipsa vetus et vulgata editio*," should remain the official Bible of the Roman
Catholic Church, and that "none should dare or presume to reject it
under any pretext whatsoever."

The Vulgate is the greatest of the works of Jerome (d. 420):[37] he
translated the Old Testament books in the Jewish Canon from the Hebrew
and for the New Testament he revised the text of the Old Latin (*vetus
latina*) on the basis of the Greek (changing the received text as little as
possible and even retaining in I Pet. 3:22 a half verse lacking in the
Greek). The Apocrypha, which Jerome (*Prologus Galeatus,* his preface
to I Samuel-II Kings; cf. his preface to the Books of Solomon) relegated
inter apocrypha because they are not "in the canon," were only translated
in part: he retained the Old Latin text for Baruch, Wisdom of Solomon,
Sirach's Ecclesiasticus, and I-II Maccabees; he reluctantly and carelessly
translated Tobit and Judith from "Chaldee" (i.e., Aramaic) texts which
had apparently been translated from the LXX (for Judith, cf. E. E. Voigt,
The Latin Versions of Judith [Yale University Dissertation], Leipzig,
1925); for the other books of the Apocrypha he revised the Old Latin
text. So slight was his interest in the Apocrypha that his work on Judith
was completed in a night, that on Tobit in a day.

At first Jerome, following the instructions of Pope Damasus, intended
merely to revise the text of the Old Latin, which had become corrupt
and varied greatly in the available manuscripts, to make it conform to
the Greek text. For the New Testament (completed in 391) he never
went beyond emendation of the Old Latin through its collation with the
Greek, revising only passages "which seemed to change the meaning"
(*Preface to the Gospels*). In the Old Testament, he began with a cursory
(*cursim*) revision of the Psalter, according to the LXX, without, however,

[37] Jerome (*Eusebius Sophronius Hieronimus*) was charged by Pope Damasus with
the revision of the Old Latin in 382 and before he left Rome (following the death of
Damasus) in 385 he had revised the Gospels and the Psalter (*Psalterium Romanum,*
following the LXX). The Old Testament was translated from the Hebrew, with the
help of Jewish scholars, in Palestine (390-405); his partial edition of the Apocrypha
dates from the same period. For the life of Jerome see: F. W. Farrar, *Lives of the
Fathers,* Vol. II, pp. 150-207 (Edinburgh, 1889). G. Grützmacher, *Hieronimus,* 3
vols. (Leipzig, 1901-1908.) For numerous publications on Jerome on the occasion of
the fifteen hundredth anniversary of his death (1920), see A. Vaccari in Biblica I
(1920) 379-396, 533-562. In general, see on Jerome and the Vulgate the excellent
manual of F. Stummer (*Einführung in die lateinische Bibel.* Paderborn, 1928); cf
F. Kaulen, *Geschichte der Vulgata* (Mainz, 1838). For additional recent monographs
see O. Eissfeldt, *Einleitung in das Alte Testament,* pp. 717 f.

correcting some serious divergences between the Old Latin and the LXX (cf. A. Rahlfs, *Der Text des Septuagintapsalters*, pp. 223, 225. Göttingen, 1907). The LXX text used was apparently Lucianic (*op. cit.*, pp. 65, 72 f.). This edition of the Psalter, called *Psalterium Romanum* was used exclusively in the liturgy at Rome until Pius V (1566-1572), and has remained the text used in St. Peter's at Rome, in St. Mark's at Venice, and at Milan.

A second phase of his work began during his residence at Bethlehem (after 385), from where he could journey to Caesarea to study Origen's Hexapla. He made a new revision of the Psalter, according to the Hexaplaric text, which was adopted in the liturgy of the churches in Gaul (hence its name, *Psalterium Gallicanum*) and subsequently in all Catholic churches (except those mentioned above); the Anglican Psalter, on the whole, is a version of the Gallican Psalter. It was inserted into the official text of the Vulgate and of the Breviary. Again Jerome avoided changing the wording of the Old Latin, revising it in general only when the meaning differed from Origen's recension; occasionally, however, he followed the Hebrew and columns 3, 4, and 6 of the Hexapla. Finally, Jerome prepared a third Latin Psalter, which is a translation from the Hebrew (*Psalterium juxta Hebraeos*); it has been edited by P. de Lagarde, *Psalterium juxta Hebraeos Hieronimi*. Leipzig, 1874. In the official editions of the Vulgate, the Psalter is the Gallican Psalter and is therefore the only part of the Old Testament (except the Apocrypha) which was not translated from the Hebrew.

From some statements of Jerome (cf. Swete, *Introduction*, p. 102) it would appear that he revised the whole Old Testament after the manner of the Gallican Psalter: "the edition of the Seventy interpreters which is found in the scrolls of the Hexapla was accurately translated by us into the Latin speech" (Epistle 106, to Sunnia and Fretela). The prefaces to the books of Job, Proverbs, Ecclesiastes, Canticles, and Chronicles in this Hexaplaric Latin Bible are extant, but only the text of Job (edited by P. de Lagarde [Mitteilungen II, 189-237. Göttingen, 1887] and by C. P. Caspari [*Das Buch Hiob (1:1-38:16) in Hieronimus' Übersetzung . . .* Christiania, 1893) has survived, together with some fragments of Proverbs, Ecclesiastes, and Canticles (S. Berger, in *Notices et extraits des manuscripts de la Bibliothèque Nationale et autres Bibliothèques*, Vol. 34, part 2, pp. 140 f. Paris, 1895; A. Vaccari, in *Civiltà Cattolica* 1913, pp. 190-202; 1915, pp. 290-297).

While engaged in this revision of the Latin Bible—nay, while still in Rome—Jerome had secured portions of the Hebrew Bible and had begun to plan its translation into Latin. This great task—the third phase of his work on the text—was begun in 390 and completed in 405, during Jerome's residence in Palestine. It would seem, from the *Prologus*

Galeatus, that Jerome commenced with the books of Samuel and Kings in 390; by 393 he had completed, besides these, Job and the Prophets (Epistle 49, to Pammachius; Migne, P. L., vol. 22, p. 512) and apparently also his Psalter according to the Hebrew; from 394 to 396 he translated Ezra, Nehemiah, and Chronicles; in 398 he translated Proverbs, Ecclesiastes, and Canticles—in three days after a long illness, as he says in the preface; in 405 he began his work on Genesis and completed the Pentateuch, Joshua, Judges, Ruth, and Esther, together with Tobit and Judith.

Since Origen, no Christian scholar had laboriously learned Hebrew and studied the Hebrew text of the Bible. His learning so impressed his contemporaries that Augustine could say, "What Jerome does not know, no mortal ever knew." Judged by the standards of his day, Jerome's Latin translation of the Hebrew Bible is a notable achievement: "the work as a whole has always been recognized by unbiased judges as eminently successful" (J. Wellhausen). His purpose, as he states in a note after Esth. 10:3, was to render "with complete fidelity what stands in the Hebrew"; his method since boyhood was to render *non verba sed sententias* (Epistle 57, to Pammachius), not the letter but the meaning, for "if we follow the syllables we lose the understanding" (Epistle to Sunnia and Fretela).

Jerome was, however, prevented from adhering steadfastly to this purpose and method. He was not only a scholar, but also a Christian theologian and clergyman, eager to provide the Church with an uncorrupted record of God's word. He was forced to compromise, in order not to shock the religious feelings of the faithful whose Bible had been the Old Latin. After admitting in his *Preface to Ecclesiastes* (Migne, P. L., vol. 22, pp. 1011 f.) that in translating from the Hebrew he utilized the LXX (particularly where it did not differ greatly from the Hebrew), Aquila, Symmachus, and Theodotion, he says that he did not wish, on the one hand, to hinder the reader by excessive innovation nor, on the other, to follow, against his own conscience, the opinion of mere rivulets (i.e., these versions) disregarding "the source of truth" (i.e., the Hebrew text).

Accordingly, in the historical books (Josh.-Kings, Chron., etc.), where Christian doctrines were not conspicuous, he generally exhibited his skill and originality as a translator, following the exegesis of his Jewish teachers (if not that of Aquila),[38] although occasionally showing dependence upon Symmachus (cf. for Samuel, S. R. Driver, *Notes on the . . . Books*

[38] A curious example of Jerome's dependence upon Aquila is found in Ex. 34:29, where he rendered "the skin of his [Moses'] face *shone*" with "his face was *horned* (*cornuta*)" (cf. Aquila)—a blunder which induced Michelangelo to carve horns on his famous statue of Moses in S. Pietro in Vincoli. For examples of Jerome's dependence upon Jewish interpretation, see F. Stummer, *Einführung in die lateinische Bibel*, pp. 105-110, and the bibliography on p. 90.

of *Samuel*, 2nd ed., pp. lxxxi f.). But in the books of the Prophets and in the Psalter, as he recognized in numerous passages of his commentaries (cf. W. Nowack, *Die Bedeutung des Hieronimus*, p. 13), he often deliberately accepted the rendering of the Greek versions (cf., for individual instances, F. Stummer, *Einführung in die lateinische Bibel*, pp. 99-105). The vital significance of these books for the Church, since New Testament times, dictated this reverence for the traditionally accepted interpretation. He retained from the LXX the "virgin" in Is. 7:14 and the seventh gift of the Spirit in Is. 11:2 f. (translating the first "fear of the Lord" with *pietas* and the second with *timor Domini*). He read Messianic prophecies in Gen. 49:10; Is. 11:10; 45:8; 62:1 f.; Jer. 23:6; 33:16; Hab. 3:18 (*in Deo Jesu meo*); Zech. 9:6 (*separator*, i.e., the Christ); Mal. 3:8 (*affiget, configitis, configimus* refer to the Crucifixion).

In spite of Jerome's respect for the traditional text of the Christian Bible, his version from the Hebrew was no more acceptable to the Church for public reading than the Old Testament in J. Moffatt's "New Translation" (New York, 1922) or in the "American Translation" (Chicago, 1927) at the present time. Rufinus (d. 410) at once declared it heretical, and even Augustine (d. 430) questioned its necessity, writing to Jerome that his rendering of Jonah's gourd (Jonah 4:6) with "ivy" (*edera*) instead of "pumpkin" (*cucurbita*, in the Old Latin) had caused a riot (Epistle 88, to Jerome). Gradually, however, after it was used by such churchmen as Vincent of Lerins (*ca.* 450) and Gregory the Great (d. 604), the Vulgate became the Bible of the Roman Church, but in the process its text became seriously contaminated with that of the Old Latin Bible, quite apart from the corruptions caused by scribal negligence. Accordingly, several recensions of the text were made from time to time, notably those of Cassiodorus (d. 570), Alcuin (d. 804) on instructions of Charlemagne, Theodowulf of Orleans (c. 800), Lanfranc (d. 1089), and Stephen Harding (d. 1134). In the thirteenth century lists of textual variants (*correctoria*) were prepared.[39]

The first printed edition of the Vulgate, the *Bible of 42 Lines*, or Mazarin Bible (issued before August 15, 1456), is attributed on insufficient evidence to J. Gutenberg (d. 1468), the reputed inventor of printing. The second printing of the Vulgate is the *Bible of 36 Lines*, or Bamberg Bible (1462); ninety other editions were printed before 1500.[40] These

---

[39] On the history of the text of the Vulgate in the Middle Ages see: S. Berger, *Histoire de la Vulgate pendant les premiers siècles du Moyen Âge* (Paris, 1893); cf. F. Stummer, *Einführung in die Lateinische Bibel*, pp. 125-221, and the bibliographical references given there.

[40] On the fifteenth century Latin Bibles see: W. A. Copinger, *Incunabula Biblica: The First Half Century of the Latin Bible*, London, 1892; Dom H. Quentin, *Mémoire sur l'établissement du texte de la Vulgate*, 1re partie: Octateuque (Collectanea Biblica Latina, Vol. VI), pp. 75-208 (Rome and Paris, 1922). This latter work includes the editions published before the Vulgate of Clement VIII (1592).

early editions are merely the reproduction of various single manuscripts, usually late, and are of slight critical value.

In the sixteenth century the following editions represent an attempt to improve the text of the Vulgate: the *Complutensian Polyglot* (1514-1517), the Bible of A. Osiander (1522), the combination of these by J. Petreius (1527). Critical editions, if they may be so called, are those of T. Kerver (1506), A. Castellanus (1511), G. Laridius (1530; some accretions from the Old Latin are omitted), J. Benedictus or Benoit (1540), and particularly R. Stephanus or Etienne (his first edition is dated 1528; his last, 1557) and J. Hentenius or Henten (1547). After some preliminary labors, an official edition was issued under the auspices of Sixtus V (Rome, 1590), but such strong objections were raised against it, particularly by the Jesuit (later Cardinal) R. F. R. Bellarmine, that a new edition was issued in 1592 by order of Clement VIII and (in its reprints, in which typographical errors were corrected) became the official Bible of the Roman Catholic Church.[41]

The need of a text representing better the work of Jerome than the Clementine edition has prompted a vast undertaking. The task of preparing a critical edition of the Vulgate was appropriately assigned by Pius X (in 1907) to the Benedictine Order, specifically to a commission headed by Cardinal A. Gasquet. Dom H. Quentin, appointed as editor of the text, has explained his critical methods in a learned monograph on the Octateuch (cf. above, note 40; his method has been criticized by F. C. Burkitt in JTS 24 [1922-23] 406-414; M. J. Lagrange, in RB 33 [1924] 115-123; E. K. Rand, in HTR 17 [1924] 197-264), and in two books (*La Vulgate à travers les siècle et sa revision actuelle.* Rome, 1925; *Essais de critique textuelle,* Paris, 1926). The first volumes of this critical edition of Dom Quentin appeared in 1926 (comprising the Book of Genesis) (cf. Dom D. De Bruyne, Revue Benedictine 39 [1927] 222-225; A. Vaccari, Biblica 7 [1926] 449-455; F. Stummer, in ZAW N.F. 4 [1927] 141-150) and in 1929 (Exodus and Leviticus); Joshua, Judges, and Ruth were issued in 1939. In innumerable details this new text is far more correct than the Clementine Vulgate. Already utilized for Genesis in the third edition of Kittel's *Biblia Hebraica,* it will be of service in the critical restoration of the Hebrew Bible—a task which will for a long time engage the attention of scholars without ever being brought to a successful realization.

[41] The best available edition of this Vulgate is M. Hetzenauer, *Biblia Sacra vulgatae editionis, Oeniponte* (Innsbruck, 1906; 2nd ed., 1922). The fullest collection of manuscript variants is in C. Vercellone, *Variae lectiones Vulgatae Latinae Bibliorum editionis,* 2 vols. (Rome, 1861, 1864.) Unfortunately it includes only the books from Genesis to Kings.

PART II

THE PENTATEUCH

CHAPTER I

GENERAL CONSIDERATIONS

~~~~~~

The first five books of the Old Testament (Gen., Ex., Lev., Num., and Deut.) were called, after their canonization about 400 B.C., "the law of Moses" (II Chron. 23:18; 30:16; cf. 33:8) or "the book (*sepher*) of Moses" (35:12; cf. 25:4).[1] Later, one simply said "the Law" (Hebrew *Tôrâh*, Greek *nomos*); this term is so used by the grandson of Ben Sira, in his preface to the translation of Ecclesiasticus, and also in the New Testament (e.g., Luke 10:26), Philo of Alexandria, and Flavius Josephus. The word "Pentateuch" (from the Greek *pente*, five; *teuchos*, scroll) is first found in Origen's commentary on John 4:25 ("the pentateuchal [book]"), but it was probably used by the Hellenistic Jews of Alexandria during the first century, as the equivalent of the Talmudic expression "the five fifths of the Law" (meaning the Pentateuch written in five volumes; when written on one scroll, it is called "the Book of the Law").

In Hebrew the titles of the five books of the Pentateuch are simply the initial words of each. The English titles are derived from the Greek through the Latin, indicating the initial subject of each book. The Greek titles, except for Numbers, are already used by Philo. Thus Philo also attests the division of the Pentateuch into five books. Although we lack earlier evidence, this partitioning was certainly made in the Septuagint Greek version (*ca.* 250 B.C.) and in fact must go back to the first Hebrew edition of the work.

The lines of demarcation between books actually mark topical and chronological divisions of subject matter, and yet the partition of the work into five volumes was originally dictated by purely practical considerations. The largest papyrus scrolls available accommodated roughly but one-fifth of the Torah. It was only later that a single large parchment scroll, being of stouter material, sufficed for the entire Pentateuch.

However, the Pentateuch is a single work in five volumes and not a collection of five different books, although Deuteronomy was originally (as the D Code) a separate book. In fact, it is only the first part of a work

[1] Cf. Ben Sira, Ecclus. 24:23, "All these things are in the book of the covenant of the Most High, the Law which Moses commanded. . . ." Although there is no unanimity of opinion about the authorship and meaning of Ezr. 3:2; 6:18; 7:6; Neh. 8:1-2, 18; 9:3; 13:1, it seems clear that in these passages from the pen of the Chronicler "the Law of Moses" is the whole Pentateuch and not the Priestly Code.

in nine volumes (Gen.-Kings) describing the history and institutions of Israel and extending from the creation of the world to the events immediately following the fall of Jerusalem in 586 B.C. The first five volumes, comprising the history to the death of Moses and the Mosaic legislation, were separated from the last four and canonized as the Law of Moses about 400 B.C.; the four historical books that followed (Josh., Judg., Sam., Kings) were not recognized as sacred scripture until two centuries later.

The term "Hexateuch" (meaning the Pentateuch and Joshua) was introduced by modern scholars; the terms "Heptateuch" (Gen.-Judg.) and "Oktateuch" (Gen.-Sam.) are found in Ambrose (*ad* Ps. 118) and in a manuscript in Naples, respectively. None of these groups of six, seven, or eight books was ever considered a unit by the Jews, who were acquainted with Genesis-Kings before, and Genesis-Deuteronomy and Joshua-Kings after, 400 B.C. The reason for speaking of a Hexateuch is that the Priestly Code (P) runs through the Pentateuch and comes to an end with the account of the partition of Canaan in Joshua.

The contents of the Pentateuch may be summarized under nine divisions, as follows:[2]

I. *The origin of the world and of the nations of mankind* (Gen. 1-11). 1. The first account of creation (Gen. 1:1-2:4, P). 2. The second account: creation of Adam (2:5-7, S), planting of Eden (2:8-17, S), creation of Eve and of animals (2:18-25, S). 3. The fall of Adam and Eve (3, S). 4. Cain and Lamech (4:1-24, S). 5. The descendants of Seth (4:25 f., S; 5, P). 6. The giants (6:1-4, S). 7. The Flood (6:5-9:17, S^2 and P). 8. The descendants of Noah (9:18-10:31, S, S^2, and P). 9. The tower of Babel (11:1-9, S). 10. The ancestry of Abraham (11:10-32, redactional).

II. *The Patriarchs* (Gen. 12-50). 1. Abraham and Isaac (12-26): *a.* Abraham in Canaan and in Egypt (12, J [P]); *b.* Abraham and Lot separate (13, J [P]); *c.* Abraham defeats the four kings of the East (14, S and S^2); *d.* God's covenant with Abraham (15, E); *e.* Hagar (16, J [P]); *f.* God's covenant with Abraham and the institution of circumcision (17, P); *g.* promise of a son to Sarah (18:1-15, J); *h.* Lot and the destruction of Sodom and Gomorrah (18:16-19:38, J and S); *i.* Abraham at Gerar (20, E); *j.* birth of Isaac and expulsion of Hagar (21, J and E); *k.* sacrifice of Isaac (22:1-19, E); *l.* the family of Nahor (22:20-24, redactional); *m.* death and burial of Sarah (23, P); *n.* Isaac marries Rebekah (24, J); *o.* children of Keturah (25:1-6, redactional); *p.* death of Abraham

---

[2] The chief sources that modern critics have identified in the Pentateuch are indicated by the following symbols: S (a Southern source, probably of Edomitic origin [S^2 indicates additions to S]: see ZAW N.F. 7 [1930] 66-73); J (the Yahwistic or Jahvistic source); E (the Elohistic source); D (the Deuteronomic source); H (the Holiness Code); P (the Priestly Code). The analysis given here is for general orientation and not exhaustive as in the following chapters.

(25:7-11, P); *q*. descendants of Ishmael (25:12-18, P); *r*. Rebekah's children (25:19-34, J, E, and P); *s*. Isaac at Gerar (26, J and E).

2. Jacob (27-36): *a*. Jacob obtains the birthright and the blessing (27, J-E; 27:46-28:9, P); *b*. Jacob's dream at Bethel (28:10-22, E [J]); *c*. his marriage with Leah and Rachel (29-30, J [E, P]); *d*. Jacob's flight from Laban (31, J-E); *e*. at Mahanaim and Penuel (32, J-E); *f*. reconciliation with Esau (33, J-E); *g*. Simeon and Levi attack Shechem (34, S); *h*. at Bethel and Hebron (35, E, P [S]); *i*. the descendants of Esau (36:1-19, 40-43, P; the kings of Edom: 36:20-39, S).

3. Joseph and the other sons of Jacob (37-50): *a*. Joseph's dreams and his coming to Egypt (37, J-E); *b*. Judah and Tamar (38, S); *c*. Potiphar's wife (39, J-E); *d*. Joseph interprets dreams in prison (40, J-E); *e*. Joseph interprets Pharaoh's dreams and becomes his grand vizier (41, J-E); *f*. Joseph's brothers in Egypt (42-45, J-E); *g*. Jacob comes to Egypt (46-47, J-E, P); *h*. Jacob blesses Manasseh and Ephraim (48, E and P); *i*. the blessing of Jacob (49:1-27, ancient poem); *j*. death of Jacob and of Joseph (49:28-50:26, P [E]).

III. *Moses and the Exodus from Egypt* (Ex. 1-18). 1. The oppression of the Israelites in Egypt (Ex. 1:1-22, J, E, and P). 2. The birth of Moses and his flight to Midian (2, J, E, and P). 3. The burning bush (3, J-E). 4. Divine instructions to Moses; his return to Egypt (4, J-E). 5. Pharaoh's refusal of Moses' request (5:1-6:1, J-E). 6. Divine commission to Moses and Aaron (6:2-7:7, P). 7. The plagues of Egypt (7:8-11:10, J, E, and P). 8. The first Passover (12:1-51, chiefly P). 9. Unleavened bread, first-born, firstlings (13:1-16, chiefly P). 10. The crossing of the Red Sea (13:17-15:21, J, E, P, and poetry). 11. The journey to Sinai (15:22-18:27, J, E, and P).

IV. *The divine revelation at Sinai* (Ex. 19-40). 1. The Decalogue and the Covenant Code (19-24): *a*. the theophany (19, J-E); *b*. the Ten Commandments (20:1-17; cf. Deut. 5:6-21 [H. 5:6-18]); *c*. the Covenant Code (introduction: 20:18-22; the laws: 20:23-23:19; conclusion: 23:20-33); *d*. the solemn covenant (24, J, E, and P). 2. Instructions concerning the Tabernacle and priesthood (25:1-31:17, P). 3. The golden calf (31:18-33:23, E and E²). 4. The ritual decalogue (34, J narrative, RᴰD legislation). 5. The execution of the instructions contained in 25-31 (35-40, P).

V. *The Levitical legislation at Sinai* (Lev. 1-27, P). 1. Sacrifices (1-7): *a*. burnt offering (1); *b*. meal offering (2); *c*. peace offering (3); *d*. sin offering (4:1-5:13); *e*. guilt offering (5:14-6:7 [H. 5:14-26]); *f*. duties and prerequisites of the priests in sacrificing (6:8-7:38 [H. 6-7]). 2. Priesthood (8-10): *a*. ordination of Aaron and his sons according to Ex. 29:1-37 (8); *b*. their assumption of the priestly office (9); *c*. miscellaneous regulations regarding the priesthood (10). 3. Purifications from ritual impurity

(11-15): *a.* dietary laws on clean and unclean animals (11); *b.* childbirth (12); *c.* leprosy (13-14); *d.* sexual causes of impurity (15). 4. The Day of Atonement (16). 5. The Holiness Code (H) (17-26): *a.* regulations about slaying, sacrificing, and eating animals (17); *b.* incest and unchastity (18); *c.* religious and moral duties (19); *d.* penalties for religious and moral offenses specified in 18 and 19:3, 31 (20); *e.* holiness laws concerning priests (21:1-22:16) and offerings (22:17-33); *f.* the calendar of sacred days (23); *g.* daily provision of the lamps (24:1-4) and weekly provision of the shewbread (24:5-9); *h.* blasphemy, murder, an eye for an eye, etc. (24:10-23); *i.* the Sabbatical year (25:1-7, 20-22) and the year of jubilee (25:8-19, 23-55); *j.* idolatry and the Sabbath (26:1-2); *k.* conclusion: blessings and curses (26:3-46). 6. On vows and tithes (27).

VI. *The last events and laws at Sinai* (Num. 1:1-10:10, P). 1. The census of the tribes and their disposition in the camp at Sinai (1-4): *a.* census of the tribes exclusive of the Levites (1); *b.* position of the tribes in the camp and on the march (2); *c.* census and functions of the Levites (3-4). 2. Miscellaneous laws (5-6): *a.* leprous and unclean excluded from the camp (5:1-4); *b.* special emoluments of the priests (5:5-10); *c.* ordeal for woman suspected of unfaithfulness (5:11-31); *d.* the Nazarite vow (6:1-21); *e.* the priestly benediction (6:22-27). 3. The gifts of the twelve princes of the tribes to the sanctuary (7:1-89). 4. Supplementary ritual ordinances (8:1-10:10): *a.* the sacred lamps (8:1-4); *b.* ordination of the Levites and their age limit (8:5-26); *c.* Passover and supplementary "Little" Passover (9:1-14); *d.* cloud signals for marching and halting (9:15-23); *e.* trumpet signals (10:1-10).

VII. *The journey to the plains of Moab* (Num. 10:11-22:1). 1. From Sinai to Paran (10:11-14:45): *a.* departure from Sinai (10:11-28, P); *b.* Hobab and the ark guide the Israelites (10:29-36, J-E); *c.* the fire at Taberah (11:1-3); *d.* murmurings of the people, appointment of 70 elders, Eldad and Medad, the quails (11:4-34, J-E); *e.* revolt of Aaron and Miriam (12, J-E); *f.* the report of the spies and the punishment of the people (13-14, J, E, and P). 2. From Paran to Kadesh (15:1-20:13): *a.* supplementary laws on the sacrifices (15:1-31, P); *b.* punishment of a Sabbath-breaker (15:32-36, P); *c.* law on the tassels (15:37-41, P); *d.* the rebellion of Korah, Dathan, and Abiram (16:1-50 [H. 16:1-35; 17:1-15], chiefly P); *e.* Aaron's budding rod (17 [H. 17:16-28], P); *f.* duties and revenues of the priesthood (18, P); *g.* purification, after defilement with a corpse, by means of the ashes of a red heifer (19, P); *h.* death of Miriam and murmurings of the people for water at Kadesh (20:1-13, J, E, and P). 3. From Kadesh to the plains of Moab (20:14-22:1): *a.* Edom refused passage through its territory (20:14-21, J-E); *b.* death of Aaron on Mount Hor (20:22-29, P); *c.* victory at Horma (21:1-3, J); *d.* the brazen serpent (21:4-9, E); *e.* itinerary to Pisgah, song of the well (21:10-20, E and ancient poems); *f.* victory over Sihon and Og (21:21-22:1, J-E. and ancient poem).

VIII. *Events in the plains of Moab* (Num. 22:2-36:13). 1. Balaam (22:2-24:24, J-E and ancient poems). 2. The worship of Baal Peor (25, J-E and P). 3. The second census (26, P). 4. Inheritance of daughters (27:1-11, P). 5. Moses was commanded to view Palestine before his death and to make Joshua his successor (27:12-23, P). 6. Schedule of public sacrifices, supplementing Lev. 23 (28-29, P). 7. Vows, particularly of women (30, P). 8. War against the Midianites and law on the distribution of the booty (31, P). 9. Allotment of the territory east of the Jordan to Gad, Reuben, and half of Manasseh (32, J-E and P). 10. Itinerary from Rameses to the plains of Moab (33:1-49, P). 11. Instructions for the allotment of the territory west of the Jordan (33:50-34:29, P). 12. Levitical cities and cities of refuge (35, P). 13. Law regulating the marriage of heiresses (36, P; cf. 27:1-11).

IX. *The last discourses of Moses and his death* (Deut. 1-34, D, D^s, etc.). 1. Introduction (1:1-5). 2. The first discourse (1:6-4:43). 3. The second discourse (4:44-29:1): *a.* superscription (4:44-49); *b.* exordium (5-11); *c.* exhortation to obey God's laws (12-26); [*d.* instructions concerning the acceptance of the code, 27:1-13; twelve anathemas, 27:14-26;] *e.* peroration: blessings and curses (28:1-68; 29:1 [H. 28:69]). 4. The third discourse (29:2-30:20). 5. Appendices (31-34): *a.* last words of Moses and appointment of Joshua (31); *b.* the Song of Moses (32, late poem); *c.* the Blessing of Moses (33, ancient poem); *d.* the death and mysterious burial of Moses (34, J-E and P).

There is no reason to doubt that the Pentateuch was considered the divine revelation to Moses when it was canonized about 400 B.C. Since then and until recent times, the opinion that Moses was its author has prevailed in Judaism, Christianity, and Islam. That Moses not only delivered the children of Israel from Egypt but bestowed upon them divinely revealed laws was ancient tradition, the earliest trace of which is found in the J document (*ca.* 850 B.C.). Moses wrote on two tables of stone "the ten words" which Jehovah had revealed to him on Mount Sinai (Ex. 34:28). According to the E document (*ca.* 750 B.C.), Jehovah "gave unto Moses . . . two tables of stone written with the finger of God" (Ex. 31:18).[3]

Except for the story of Ex. 18:13-26 (J-E), this is all the early evidence we have for the tradition, which may or may not be true, that Moses gave laws unto the children of Israel. We can surmise, however, that at least in priestly circles all current laws were attributed to Moses about 650 B.C., and this belief became general among the Jews when the Deuteronomic Code, found in the Temple in 621, was officially accepted at once as the

[3] See further my article, "The Oldest Decalogue," in JBL 43 (1924) 294-310.

transcript of a divine revelation to Moses. The author of this code would not have incorporated in his prophetic oracle of Moses current civil and ritual laws unless he had reason to believe that their Mosaic origin would not be questioned.

The Pentateuch is only an enlarged edition of the Deuteronomic Code. The latter was called, in *ca.* 550, "the Law of Moses" (I Kings 2:3; II Kings 23:25, cf. 21:8; Mal. 4:4 [H. 3:22]) or "the book of the Law of Moses" (Josh. 8:31; 23:6; II Kings 14:6) or simply "the book of the Law" (22:8; Josh. 8:34). It was therefore perfectly natural to use the same titles for the whole Pentateuch. As we have seen, the Chronicler, in writing about 150 years after the canonization of the Pentateuch, called it "the Law of Moses" or "the Book of Moses." It is obvious that both the belief in the Mosaic authorship of the Pentateuch and the conception of it as "Torah" (law) are derived from similar notions with regard to the Deuteronomic Code in 621 B.C.

In the Pentateuch itself, Moses is considered the author of particular sections. In J and E, he is made responsible only for a decalogue. Later, he is called the author of the denunciation of Amalek (Ex. 17:14), of the Covenant Code (24:4), of the itinerary from Rameses to the plains of Moab (Num. 33:2), and of the Deuteronomic Code, consisting of the bulk of Deut. 5-30 (Deut. 31:9-13, 24-26).

After 400, the Mosaic authorship of the Pentateuch became an article of faith as well as an axiomatic truth. If the Pentateuch was divinely revealed scripture, Moses had perforce to be its author. All Jewish law in theory originated with Moses: it was transmitted either in writing through the Pentateuch or orally through an unbroken chain of witnesses, as the "tradition of the elders" (Matt. 15:2, 3, 6; Mark 7:3, 5, 8 f., 13), codified and committed to writing in the Mishnah about A.D. 200 (cf. *Sayings of the Fathers* [*Pirqê Abōth*] 1:1). Such was the general opinion in Judaism and in early Christianity.

No one doubted that Moses wrote the Pentateuch: this is expressly stated, after the Chronicler, by Ben Sira (Ecclus. 24:23), Daniel (9:11, 13), Philo (*Life of Moses*, 3:39 [M II, 179]), Josephus (*Antiquities*, 4:8, 48), and the authors of the Gospels (Matt. 19:8; Mark 12:26; Luke 24:27, 44; John 7:19, 23).[4] Philo and Josephus state positively that Moses wrote the story of his own death in Deut. 34:5-12, whereas the Talmud (*Baba Bathra* 14b) ostensibly attributes this passage to Joshua when it says, "Moses wrote his book, the section on Balaam [Num. 22-24], and Job; Joshua wrote his book and eight verses in the Torah." It was even said that whoever denied the Mosaic authorship of the Pentateuch was excluded from Paradise (cf. A. Westphal, *Les sources du Pentateuque*, Vol I, p. 25. Paris, 1888).

[4] See also Acts 13:39; 15:5; 28:23; I Cor. 9:9; II Cor. 3:15; Hebr. 9:19; 10:28.

Nevertheless, the Mosaic authorship of the Pentateuch was attacked in the early centuries of our era by religious sectarians.[5] As we have seen, the author of Fourth Ezra (*ca.* A.D. 90) believed that the entire Old Testament, including the Torah, had been lost and was dictated by Ezra, under divine inspiration, to five secretaries during forty days, besides seventy new esoteric books (II [IV] Esd. 14). This story made an impression on Irenaeus (d.*ca.* 200), Clement of Alexandria (d.*ca.* 220), and Tertullian (d.*ca.* 230). With equal equanimity Jerome (d. 420) could regard either Moses as the author or Ezra as the editor. The Nazarenes denied the Mosaic authorship, and the Clementine *Homilies* saw in the Pentateuch a corrupt and radically different transcript of the oral teaching of Moses. Celsus not only denied the Mosaic authorship of the Pentateuch but questioned its literary unity. Similarly, Ptolemy, a Valentinian Gnostic, distinguished Mosaic sections from the additions of the elders.

In Judaism, the first misgivings as to the Mosaic authorship appear about A.D. 500 in the famous passage of *Baba Bathra* already quoted, according to which Joshua was the author of the last eight verses of Deuteronomy. During the Middle Ages, some Jewish scholars discovered in the Torah expressions obviously pointing to a time long after the age of Moses. Ibn Ezra (1088-1167) stated that Rabbi Isaac (possibly Isaac of Toledo [982-1057]) dated Gen. 36:31 in the reign of Jehoshaphat and, although denouncing this view most acrimoniously, he pointed out in cleverly equivocal language four verses (Gen. 12:6; 22:14; Deut. 3:11; 31:9) and "the mystery of the twelve" (i.e., Deut. 34:1-12) no less puzzling, to say the least, in a work of Moses than the words "beyond Jordan" (Deut. 1:1) to indicate the side where Moses stood.

In the time of the Reformation, both Catholic and Protestant scholars pointed out similar difficulties. A. B. Carlstadt (1520) noted that style and diction before and after the death of Moses remain the same, therefore "Moses was not the writer of the five books"; and he remarked that no one except a lunatic (*nemo nisi plane dementissimus*) would regard Moses as having written his own obituary. The Catholic A. Masius (Du Maes), in his commentary on Joshua (1574), conjectured that the Pentateuch was compiled by Ezra from ancient documents. He pointed out that the cities of Dan (Gen. 14:14; Deut. 34:1) and Hebron (Gen. 13:18; 23:2, etc.) received these names after the death of Moses; in his time they were called Laish and Kirjath-arba, respectively. The Spanish Jesuit B. Pereira in his commentary on Genesis (1594-1600) believed that the greatest part of the Pentateuch had been written by Moses, but recognized later retouches; similar views were presented by J. Bonfrère (1625;

[5] See: J. E. Carpenter and G. Harford, *The Composition of the Hexateuch*, pp. 34 f. London, 1902; H. Holzinger, *Einleitung in den Hexateuch*, pp. 11-12, 25 ff. Freiburg and Leipzig, 1893.

1631). Episcopius (d. 1643) believed that Ezra was responsible not only for additions in Deuteronomy, but also for Num. 12:3; Gen. 35:19; 49:7, etc.

Th. Hobbes in his *Leviathan* (1651) carried forward the bold criticism of Masius. Moses "wrote all that which he is there said to have written"; not, however, anachronisms like Gen. 12:6; Num. 21:14; Deut. 34:6. In two anonymous works published in 1655, Isaak de La Peyrère (Peyrerius), a Calvinist, saw in the Pentateuch not an "autograph" of Moses, but a "transcript of a transcript" (*apographum apographi*) and pointed as proof to Num. 21:14; Deut. 1:1; 2:3, 8; 3:11, 14, to discrepancies (as between Ex. 4:20 and 18:2-3), and to anachronisms. B. Spinoza, in his *Tractatus Theologico-politicus* (1670), noting again the troublesome passages listed by Ibn Ezra, observed "that in these five books precept and narrative are jumbled together without order, that there is no regard to time, and that one and the same story is often met with again and again, and occasionally with very important differences in the incidents"—in other words, we have "materials for history rather than the digested history itself." He came to the conclusion that out of a mass of ancient documents (including some by Moses), Ezra wrote the history of his nation from the creation of the world to the destruction of Jerusalem, interpolating Deuteronomy, which according to Spinoza was the code promulgated by Ezra (Neh. 8).

Richard Simon, a priest of the Congregation of the Oratory (1678), regarded the Pentateuch as a compilation from a great number of documents of different dates, some (the divine commandments) inspired by God, others (the historical narratives) of human origin. In his criticism of Simon, Jean Le Clerc (1685) went one step further. From Gen. 1-11, he concluded that the author of the Pentateuch must have been in Babylonia (therefore he lived after 722 B.C.) but writing before Ezra, because the Samaritans accepted the Torah. The priest mentioned in II Kings 17:28 fills all the conditions. He wrote after the eighteenth year of Josiah, and incorporated into his book the Law found in the Temple which was then sanctioned in Jerusalem because it was found to agree with the law of Judah.

The results of the investigations during the seventeenth century had been chiefly negative: it was noticed that the Pentateuch contained numerous statements that Moses could not have written, since they obviously belonged to a later period; but although it was surmised that the Torah was compiled out of different documents, no hint for their identification was found. The critical analysis, which passed through four principal stages, began when Astruc in the eighteenth century discovered a clue suggesting separate sources of the Pentateuch.

I. *The First Documentary Theory.* After some hesitation, Jean Astruc, a French physician (d. 1766), published anonymously in French a book entitled, *Conjectures on the original memoirs which Moses seems to have used in composing the Book of Genesis* (Brussels, 1753). The clue discovered by Astruc is not only obvious but given in plain language in Ex. 6:2-5 (although he did not notice it there). In the Book of Genesis, the divine names *Yahweh* (Jehovah) and *Elohim* (God, deity) are *not* used interchangeably. One predominates in some sections, the other in others. According to Astruc, those sections using Elohim belonged to an A source; those using Yahweh, to a B source.[6] Furthermore, what remained in Genesis in addition to the two sources consisted of the remnants of ten sources of Midianite or Arabian origin.

J. G. Eichhorn, in his introduction to the Old Testament (3 vols., Leipzig, 1780-1783), reached conclusions similar to those of Astruc, although he knew his book only through the criticisms of J. D. Michaelis and J. F. W. Jerusalem; but he also proceeded to characterize the style and thought of the Elohist and Jahvist sources in Genesis. However, his analysis of the other books of the Pentateuch remained in a rudimentary stage. K. D. Ilgen (1798) anticipated the discovery of Hupfeld that the "Elohist" consisted of two distinct documents (now called E and P), but failed to identify them correctly.

II. *The Fragment Hypothesis.* The English Catholic priest, Alexander Geddes (1792 and 1800), believed that the Pentateuch was compiled from numerous documents written in the time of Solomon; these fragmentary documents originated from two circles of authors, using Elohim and Yahweh, respectively. J. S. Vater (*Commentary on the Pentateuch*, 3 vols., Halle, 1802-1805) carried forward the work of Geddes and divided the Pentateuch, which in his opinion was not finished until the Exile, into numerous disconnected fragments. Unlike his predecessors, W. M. L. De Wette (*Contributions to the Introduction of the Old Testament*, 1806 and 1807) did not confine himself to literary analysis but attacked the historical problems. A comparison of Kings and Chronicles convinced him that many of the Pentateuchal institutions were not yet in force during the early monarchy; the Pentateuch contained legislation of various periods. Among his brilliant guesses, one was epoch-making, viz., the Deuteronomic Code was the book found in the Temple in 621 B.C.[7] In a general way, he combined the documentary with the fragment hypothesis: Genesis and Exodus are a theocratic epic, Leviticus is a collection of late

---

[6] H. B. Witter in his *Jura Israelitarum in Palaestina* (1711) recognized that Gen. 1-2:4 and 2.5-3:24 are parallel accounts, and that different divine names occur in them. This observation was, however, totally forgotten until A. Lods (*Jean Astruc et la critique biblique au XVIIIᵉ siècle.* Paris, 1924) brought it to the attention of modern scholars.

[7] This theory was regarded as certain by Lessing; cf. ZAW 55 (1933) 299, n. 1.

laws, Numbers is a miscellaneous supplement. L. Bertholdt (1812-1819) dated the "fragments" much earlier, and considered Samuel as the author.

In opposition to the preceding views, G. H. A. Ewald (1823) stressed the unity of plan and authorship of Genesis (which Vater had broken up into 39 fragments). F. Bleek (1822 and 1831), who admitted the Mosaic authorship of a number of chapters, recognized two main redactions: the first by the author of Genesis in the time of the united kingdom, and the last by the author of Deuteronomy, shortly before 586. A. T. Hartmann (1831) dated the Pentateuch *in toto* during the exilic period and none of its parts before Solomon. P. von Bohlen (1835) believed Deuteronomy, dating from the reign of Josiah, to be the oldest part of the Pentateuch. C. P. W. Gramberg (1829) dated Genesis and Exodus between David and Hezekiah, Leviticus and Numbers at the beginning, and Deuteronomy at the end, of the Exile. W. Vatke (1835) believed that the Deuteronomic Code, published *after* the reforms of Josiah, reproduced the essence of the older legislation (Ex. 13; 19-24; 32-34) and that in general the Torah, like canon law, was not the law of a state but originated in a country already equipped with civil laws.

J. F. L. George (1835) divided Hebrew literature into three periods: the age of myth (Gen. and parts of Ex. and Num.), the age of poets and prophets (Deut.), and the age of reason (theocratic legislation). E. Bertheau (1840) arranged the laws of Exodus-Numbers into seven groups of seven decalogues each, and considered them Mosaic in origin even if not written down by Moses.

III. *The Development Hypothesis.* The theory that there is in the Pentateuch a basic document supplemented by other material had already been adumbrated by De Wette, without attracting much attention. It was, however, clearly presented by H. Ewald, in his review of J. J. Stähelin's "Critical investigations on Genesis" (1830) in TSK 4 (1831) 595-606. Whereas Stähelin recognized two main sources, the Elohistic from the time of Saul and the Jehovistic from the time of David, Ewald found in the Pentateuch an Elohistic source (incorporating earlier material like the Decalogue and the Covenant Code), starting from the Creation and continuing after the death of Moses into Joshua, and supplemented with fragments of the later Jehovistic source and other writings.

Going one step further, Bleek (1836) denied the independent existence of the Jehovistic source and identified the Jehovist with the redactor who supplemented the Elohistic source by his own additions. This theory, claiming that a fundamental source was supplemented by literary fragments of various dates, received its classical treatment in F. Tuch's commentary on Genesis (1838) and was adopted by De Wette (1840 and 1845), C. von Lengerke (1844), and Franz Delitzsch (1852). H. Ewald in his history of Israel (three editions, 1843-1864) abandoned the theory that he had advocated in 1831 and regarded the Pentateuch not as the result of additions to an original document but an amalgamation of five or six separate works. This view was presented more simply by A. Knobel (1861). E. Schrader (1869) recognized two Elohistic sources, one annalistic, from the time of David, and the other theocratic, dating from the period after the division of the kingdom. They were amalgamated during the reign of Jeroboam II by the Jehovistic author, who added much from his own pen.

IV. *The New Documentary Theory.* Although vaguely suggested by Ewald, the current theory of Pentateuchal composition in its rudimentary form was first presented by H. Hupfeld (1853). He distinguished three independent sources in Genesis (the original Elohist, the later Elohist, and the Jehovist) skillfully combined into an organic whole by a redactor. The outstanding followers of Hupfeld were A. Dillmann (1875 ff.) and Franz Delitzsch (1880), whose learned commentaries on Biblical books are still important. The chief weakness of Hupfeld's theory was the chronological sequence of his three sources. It was eventually found that the order was not P, E, J, as Hupfeld had it, but J, E, P.

Only gradually was the relative lateness of the "First Elohist" or "Fundamental Writing" (*Grundschrift,* now called Priestly Code or P) recognized. E. Reuss, in a university course during 1834, recognized that the legislation of the "First Elohist" was by no means the earliest; J. F. L. George and W. Vatke, through their study of the development of Israel's institutions, had reached the same conclusion independently. But it was only through K. H. Graf's study of *The Historical Books of the Old Testament* (1866) that the lateness of Levitical legislation was convincingly demonstrated. Graf proved that Deuteronomy (621 B.C.) knew the stories of the Jehovist, or J-E (and therefore of the Second Elohist [E] which he considered earlier than J), but neither the laws nor certain stories of the Grundschrift (P), which he dated in the time of Ezra. The narrative portions of P were shown by J. W. Colenso, Bishop of Natal (1862-1879), to be unhistorical and late; and W. H. Kosters (1868) proved that the Deuteronomist was not acquainted with them.

Without accepting Graf's theory, T. Nöldeke (1869) determined the character of P and admitted its lateness, while A. Kuenen (d. 1891) finally proved conclusively that the Grundschrift as a whole, both in its legal and in its narrative parts, was postexilic in date. The brilliant publications of J. Wellhausen (chiefly 1876-1884) led the majority of critics to accept the "Graf-Wellhausen" theory of the sources of the Pentateuch.

This theory in its simplest form, may be summarized as follows: the J document (*ca.* 850) and the E document (*ca.* 750) were combined as JE by a redactor (R^{JE}) about 650; the Deuteronomic Code of 621 (D) was added by R^D about 550, and the Priestly Code (*ca.* 500-450) by R^P

about 400, when the Pentateuch attained substantially its present form. It was soon recognized, however, that none of the four great sources (J, E, D, P) is really a literary unit. Schrader, Reuss, and Kuenen had doubted the unity of J before K. Budde (1883) distinguished J[1] and J[2] in it; R. Smend (1912) regarded J[1] and J[2] as distinct sources running through the Pentateuch, and O. Eissfeldt (1922) proposed for them the symbols L ("Lay source") and J; the present writer (1924 and 1930) has attempted to show that certain sections of Genesis (notably most of J[1]) constitute an ancient source from the South (indicated with the symbol S), probably Edomitic in origin.

Kuenen distinguished E[1] and E[2]: it is clear that the original E has been supplemented by later hands. The same is true of the code found in the Temple in 621 (D) which, through additions (D[s]), has grown to the present Deuteronomy. In P, Graf identified a separate code, the Holiness Code or H (P[H]) in Lev. 17-26; as early as 1862, J. Popper proved that Ex. 35-40 and Lev. 8-10 are later than Ex. 25-31, and it is clear that both in the laws and in the narratives there are earlier and later strata of P (P and P[s]).

The fullest presentations of the Graf-Wellhausen Pentateuchal theory are the following: A. Westphal, *Les sources du Pentateuque*. H. Holzinger, *Einleitung in den Hexateuch*. J. E. Carpenter and G. Harford-Battersby, *The Hexateuch According to the Revised Version* (London, 1900). J. E. Carpenter and G. Harford, *The Composition of the Hexateuch* (London, 1902). See also: O. Eissfeldt, *Hexateuch-Synopse* (Leipzig, 1922).

Although the Graf-Wellhausen theory with variations in detail generally prevailed after 1880, its acceptance was by no means unanimous. The postexilic date of the Priestly Code was contested by A. Dillmann, R. Kittel (in his early books), H. L. Strack, W. W. Baudissin, and others. Baudissin and E. König date E before J. The dating of D in 621, the foundation stone of the Graf-Wellhausen theory, has again been questioned in recent years (for the literature see A. R. Siebens, *L'origine du code deutéronomique*. Paris, 1929. R. H. Pfeiffer, HTR 27 [1934] 308-310).

H. M. Wiener, E. Naville (cf. R. H. Pfeiffer, HTR, *ibid.*, 304-305), and W. Möller have even championed the Mosaic authorship of the Pentateuch as a whole; A. Šanda (*ibid.*) believes that Moses wrote Genesis, and that Exodus-Numbers are based on his diaries, and J. G. Duncan attempts to prove, through archaeological evidence, that the documents incorporated in the Pentateuch are contemporary with the events described therein. A. Klostermann believes that a body of Mosaic legislation was the kernel around which the Pentateuch gradually grew. Although holding divergent views, B. D. Eerdmans and J. Orr have rejected the critical analysis of the Pentateuch identifying its four sources. J. Dahse and H. M. Wiener base their opposition on the uncertainty of the Hebrew text,

which differs from the Septuagint Greek version in the use of Yahweh
and Elohim, and on other details. Volz and Rudolph regard E as a series
of redactional notes to J.[8] D. B. Macdonald (*The Hebrew Literary Genius.*
Princeton, 1933) and U. Cassuto (*La questione della Genesi.* Florence,
1934), in sharp contrast to the Graf-Wellhausen theory, emphasize independently the unity of thought and style of Genesis. The author of this
book was for them a man of outstanding genius, who created a single,
complete, organically unified work out of miscellaneous materials (oral
traditions, according to Cassuto; the documents, "E, J, P and the rest,"
according to Macdonald).

Broadly speaking, the Graf-Wellhausen hypothesis is adopted as fundamentally sound in the following analysis of the Pentateuch. In some
points, however, the views presented here differ from all others, particularly in beginning the J document with the call of Abraham in Gen. 12
and in postulating the existence of a non-Israelitic source in Genesis (indicated by S:South or Seir). This fifth source of the Pentateuch differs
materially from J[1] or L. O. Eissfeldt's L (or Lay) source begins with
Gen. 2 and continues, beyond the borders of the Pentateuch, into Judges
and Samuel. It is characterized in the Pentateuch by archaic traits, exaltation of nomadic life, a certain coarseness, a primitive conception of the
deity, and the lack of organic unity between the several stories. But after
the end of Genesis, these characteristics fade away more and more, and
it is often difficult to know on what criteria Eissfeldt separates J and L
in the books from Exodus to Samuel.

J. Hempel (*Die althebräische Literatur.* Wildpark-Potsdam, 1930-1933)
distinguishes three phases in J: J[1] (the story from Abraham to the conquest of Canaan, written in the early years of David's reign), J[2] (the novel
about Joseph), and J[3] (the primeval history, omitting P, in Gen. 2-11),
corresponding to the divisions of the Book of Genesis (1-11; 12-36; 37-50).
The differences in mood and outlook between the three sources of Hempel
are more obvious than the imperceptible evanescent differences between
the bulk of L and J in Eissfeldt. Nevertheless, in spite of undeniable peculiarities in the Joseph stories, it seems hardly necessary to detach them
from J.

[8] P. Volz and W. Rudolph, *Der Elohist als Erzähler; ein Irrweg der Pentateuch-*
kritik? (Beih. ZAW 63, Giessen, 1933.) W. Rudolph, *Der "Elohist" von Exodus bis*
Josua. (Beih. ZAW 68, Giessen, 1938.)

CHAPTER II

THE J DOCUMENT

In the story of Abraham's call (Gen. 12:1-4a), the theme of the J document is set forth at the very beginning in sonorous language with patriotic and religious fervor. In ordering Abraham to leave the country of his birth, Jehovah promises him, "I will make of thee a great nation, . . . and in thee shall all the families of the earth be blessed." And later, in the Land of Promise, a third prophecy was made by God, "Unto thy seed will I give this land" (12:7). With epic scope and dramatic intensity, the author of the J document portrays the humble beginnings, slow growth, and final triumph of Israel under the guidance of its god Jehovah. The three divisions of the work correspond to the three initial promises: the first part shows how the twelve tribes of Israel grew out of Abraham's seed (Gen. 12-33), the second how, through Joseph, the Egyptians and other peoples were saved from starvation (Gen. 37-50), the third how, after being delivered by Moses from Egyptian bondage, Israel conquered Canaan, the Land of Promise (Ex. 1-Judg. 1).

J is both an epic and a drama. It is an epic in style and subject: both reflect the passionate religious and patriotic fervor of the author. Jehovah is the god of Israel, Israel the people of Jehovah (cf. Gen. 12:3): this axiom sums up his faith and his national pride. Israel, once a wretched mob of slaves in Egypt, succeeded in conquering a land flowing with milk and honey; famished Bedouin tribes in the desert, they established a powerful kingdom in a cultured country. How? Because Jehovah was with them in every step of the way, fighting their battles and conquering their foes. The glorious destiny of the people is the unfolding of a providential plan, the fulfillment of divine promises to Abraham. But the achievement was not easy: with dramatic suspense the author shows how, again and again, apparently insurmountable obstacles barred the way, how the nation's very existence was threatened more than once, how often everything seemed lost. But always at the last moment, when all human means had failed, Jehovah intervened, literally a *deus ex machina*, to cut the Gordian knot and change defeat into victory.

The J author achieved dramatic unity with material drawn from miscellaneous legends of Israelitic origin and memories of the dawn of their national history as well as from the stories told at the Canaanitic sanc-

tuaries about the origin of the several shrines. He built up a harmonious
and organic structure in which each ornamental detail enhanced the
beauty of architectural lines. In spite of wealth of anecdote and descriptive detail, he never loses the main thread of the narrative, and joins all
incidents into an unbroken chain of cause and effect. The charm of his
individual stories is matched by an unerring sense of the march of events
toward the fulfillment of divine promises.

In the patriarchal stories of Gen. 12-33, the narrative leads up to the
birth of the sons, the condition *sine qua non* of the continuation of
Abraham's line and its growth into a nation. *Tantae molis erat Romanam
condere gentem!* At Jehovah's behest and trusting in his promises, Abraham leaves his father's country and comes to Canaan (Gen. 12:1-4a, 7-9).
The future line of Abraham was first threatened in Egypt, when Pharaoh
took Sarah for his harem, after Abraham had deceitfully assured him that
she was his sister; but through divine intervention she was returned intact
to the Patriarch, to whom this inauspicious adventure brought considerable wealth (12:10-20; 13:1-2).

When Abraham found it necessary to separate from Lot and allowed
him to choose his dwelling place, he would have lost the Land of Promise
if Lot, the ancestor of Moab and Ammon, had not chosen the territory
of Sodom (13:4 f., 7a, 8-10a [11-18]). "Now Sarai, Abram's wife, bare him
no children" (16:1): How could a great nation grow from his unborn
seed? The dramatic suspense is heightened when Hagar, an Egyptian
handmaiden, after bearing Abraham a son, fled into the wilderness on
account of Sarah's harshness, and received there the promise that her yet
unborn son, Ishmael, would grow to manhood (16:1-2, 4-6, 7a, 8, 11-14).
At last, when Sarah was too old to bear children, Jehovah appeared to
Abraham by the oaks of Mamreh, promised him a son by his wife
(18:1-15), and announced the punishment of Sodom (18:16-33; 19:27 f.).
"And Jehovah visited Sarah as he had said, and Sarah conceived and bare
Abraham a son in his old age" (21:1a, 2a; 21:7, 33).

When Isaac grew up, Abraham sent his servant to fetch a wife for him
from the land of his kinsmen, lest the line be contaminated through
Canaanitic blood, and through divine guidance Rebekah was chosen (24)
—but she also was barren. Again through divine intervention she conceived twins. "And the children struggled together within her"—an omen
of the rivalry between the two nations (Israel and Edom), destined by
Jehovah to grow out of their descendants (25:21-26a). Although Esau
(Edom) was the first-born, the future pre-eminence of Jacob (Israel) was
recognized by the ease with which Jacob obtained Esau's birthright in
exchange for a dish of lentil soup (25:27-34) and deceitfully robbed him
of his father's blessing (27, JE).

The vague figure of Isaac, about whom oral tradition knew little, in J is merely the shadow of his great father and re-enacts some of his experiences (26:1-33 [in part]; cf. 12:10-20; 21:22-34). Conversely, the full-blooded personality of Jacob and his astute schemes for acquiring wealth are related in J with vividness and wit. Jacob's dream at Bethel was told in J, but the story, except for a remnant (28:10, 13-16, 19a), has been sacrificed by redactors in favor of the fuller account in E. That auspicious beginning of Jacob's flight prepares the reader for the successful outcome of what seemed at first a serious setback to the fulfillment of the promises to Abraham. Through his sagacity and energy, but ultimately through the favor of Jehovah, Jacob returns from Harran with two wives (Leah and Rachel), two concubines (Bilhah and Zilpah), eleven sons, and much wealth, after setting at naught the dangerous threats of Laban and Esau (29:2-14, 26, 31-35; 30-32, where J and E are closely interwoven; 33:1-17).

The second act of the drama unfolds in Egypt, whither Joseph, until the birth of Benjamin in Canaan the only son of Jacob's favorite wife Rachel, had been taken as a slave and rose from prison to the position of grand vizier. In Joseph's adventurous career, the story as before seems to lead to a catastrophe until the crisis is victoriously overcome through divine intervention. In ways often obscure to mortals, Jehovah was fulfilling his plans, and through Joseph he saved not only the family of Jacob, but also the Egyptians, from starvation. Thus the seed of Abraham became a blessing to "all families of the earth."[1]

When the curtain goes up on the third act, after the passing of obscure centuries, the fortunes of Israel have fallen to the lowest ebb. The descendants of Jacob have been enslaved in Egypt under brutal taskmasters, and although Pharaoh could not check their increase, their position was utterly and hopelessly abject (Ex. 1:6, 8-10 is all that can be certainly assigned to J in ch. 1). But at the end of the drama, the Israelites have not only been freed by Jehovah from Egyptian bondage but in returning to Canaan as conquerors are in firm possession of some parts of the country. During each and every interval when all seemed lost Jehovah triumphantly intervenes.

The champion of the Israelites enslaved in Egypt was Moses. He appears abruptly in J as the slayer of an Egyptian taskmaster and a fugitive before the wrath of Pharaoh (Ex. 2:11-23a). But Jehovah had not forgotten his people in their misery. In Midian, where Moses had found refuge with a priest whose daughter Zipporah he married, Jehovah spoke to Moses out of the burning bush (3:2-4a, 5, 7, 8aα [18?]). Reluctantly obedient to the divine command Moses returned to Egypt with his fam-

---

[1] The story of Joseph in J is found in Gen. 37 (JE); 39:1-23; 41-42 (JE); 43:1-13, 15-34; 44:1-34; 45 (JE); 46:1a, 28-34; 47:1-4, 5a, 6b (12-27a), 29-31; 48:2b, 10, 13-14, 17-19; 50:(1-11), 14.

ily (4:19-20a) and was saved by Zipporah when Jehovah unaccountably sought to slay him (4:24-26).

The first attempt of Moses in persuading Pharaoh to allow the Israelites to depart only resulted in harsher measures against them (5:1-2, 5-23, omitting "Aaron" in this and in the following chapters). Thereupon, to break down the stubborness of Pharaoh, Jehovah sent seven plagues which Moses announced in advance: the death of the fish in the Nile which made the water foul (7:14, 15a, 16, [17a], 18, 21a), frogs (8:1-4, 8-15a [H. 7:26-29; 8:14-11a]), flies (8:20-24, 28-32 [H. 8:16-20, 24-28]), cattle murrain (9:1-7), hail (9:13, 17 f., 23b, 24b, 25b-29a, 33 f.), locusts (10:1a [3-10], 13aβ, 14aβ, 15a, 16-19), and finally the death of all first-born among the Egyptians (11:4-8). At last, broken in spirit and without waiting for morning, Pharaoh allowed the people to go at once (12:29-33, 38). So they went into the Wilderness, guided by Jehovah through a pillar of cloud by day and a pillar of fire by night (13:21 f.).

At the very moment of deliverance a new crisis arose. Reversing his decision, Pharaoh pursued the Israelites, and they believed the hour of their doom had arrived (14:5-6 (?), 10abα, 11 f.). But through an east wind Jehovah pushed back the sea, and after the Israelites had crossed, the Egyptians were drowned in the returning tide (14:13 f., 19b [20], 21a, 24, 25b, 27aβb, 28b, 30). No single event in their history made a deeper impression on the Israelites than the crossing of the Red Sea; Deuteronomy and the Psalms repeatedly refer to the deliverance from Egypt. As a matter of fact, the faith of the J author in the glorious destiny of his people under the guidance of Jehovah virtually originated at that time, together with the unparalleled cohesion between Jehovah and his people. From the Red Sea the Israelites marched to Marah, where the bitter waters were made sweet by means of the tree pointed out by Jehovah (15:22-25a, 27), and soon they arrived at Kadesh.

J's account of the events at Kadesh had been so disarranged and curtailed by redactors that it is impossible, from remnants extant, to gain any clear conception of the contents of this section of J. It is possible that J material was utilized in Ex. 16-18 for the stories about the manna and the quails (16), about Massah and Meribah (17:1-7), the victory over Amalek at Rephidim (17:8-16), and about the visit of the father-in-law of Moses (18). But the repetition of some of these stories in Num. 10:29-32 (J; the father-in-law of Moses), 11:4-34 (mostly JE; manna and quails), 20:1-13 (JEP; the waters of Meribah) indicates the extent of the confusion wrought in J at this point.

We may surmise that in J the period from the Exodus to the invasion of Canaan was spent for the most part at Kadesh and not at Sinai (or Horeb) as in later sources. Historians have questioned the likelihood of the journey to Sinai and of the revelation of the Law there. The only traces of a J story about the revelation on Sinai exist in Ex. 19:2b, 18, 20a, 21 (if these disconnected remnants are really J) and in 34:1a, 2, 4, 28 (omitting a few words: see JBL 43 [1924] 294-298), the J story of the writing of the Decalogue on two tables of stone.[2] However, we do not know how the J story in Ex. 34 came to be embedded within the Kadesh stories, with which it has no connection. J seems to pass from Ex. 18 to Num. 10 with no perceptible break. Guided by Hobab (the father-in-law or brother-in-law of Moses), the Israelites set forth from Kadesh (Num. 10:29-32), and near the borders of Canaan they sent spies into the Promised Land (13:17b, 19, 22a, 28, 30 f.); but on hearing the report the people refused to enter it on account of the strength of its defenses (14:1b, 3 f., 31 f., 40-45 seem to be JE).

The chaotic state of J prevailing in the Kadesh-Sinai sections continues in the following sections dealing with the conquest of Canaan. J's story of the death of Moses was discarded (Deut. 34:4 may preserve an echo of it) and that of the conquest of Canaan was deliberately suppressed in favor of the less historical but more romantic account of E. Of J's account of how each tribe (or small group of tribes) fought its way to precarious foothold east and west of the Jordan, only scattered references in Numbers and Joshua are left and a late summary of J inserted in Judg. 1. Hardly any of this J material is preserved intact. J's story of Hormah was the source of Num. 21:1-14 (and also of 14:40-45 and Judg. 1:16 f.). The conquests of East Manasseh in Gilead are summarized in Num. 32:39, 41 f. (cf. Deut. 3:14 f.; Josh. 13:30); and those of Gad and Reuben in the same region are retold, possibly from a J account, in Num. 32:1-38 (cf. Deut. 3:16 f.). In Joshua, 13:13; 15:13-19, 63; 16:10; 17:11-18; 19:47 represent the conquest of Canaan as a slow, haphazard, and incomplete process (like the summary of J in Judg. 1) and are therefore generally attributed to J by the critics: these verses are more likely echoes of J. It is doubtful whether J included a story of Israel's covenant with the Hivvites (Josh. 9:6 f.) or the Gibeonites (Josh. 9); Josh. 5:13-15 (Joshua and the captain of Jehovah's host) and Josh. 10 (Joshua's victory over Adonizedek at Gibeon,[3] cf. Judg. 1:5-7) are likewise in question. Most regrettable is the wretched condition of these remnants of J, from the time of the Exodus from Egypt to the conquest of Canaan, caused by redactors who held different views on the revelation at Sinai and the work of Joshua. From

---

[2] J. A. Bewer (*The Literature of the Old Testament*, p. 66. New York, 1922) denies that according to J the Israelites went to Sinai and finds no J material what soever between Ex. 18:11 and Num. 10:29. Cf. also J. Wellhausen, *Prolegomena zur Geschichte Israels*, pp. 341 ff. (6th Ed.). E. Meyer, *Geschichte des Altertums*, Vol. II, Pt. 2, p. 210 (2nd Ed., Stuttgart, 1931).

[3] See Dr. Beatrice L. Goff, "The Lost Jahwistic Account of the Conquest of Canaan," JBL 53 (1934) 241-249.

the literary and historical points of view, the loss of these pages of J is inestimable.

Without doubt, J contained a story of the conquest of Canaan, for *Capture of Canaan* aside from the evidence of its deplorable fragments, the Israelitic occupation of the Land of Promise constitutes the goal of the whole epic from the very beginning (Gen. 12:7). The only question is whether J ended with the account of the several tribes' first onslaught and their precarious occupation of scattered bits of territory. On this point opinions vary, and no decisive evidence is available. It is conceivable that after describing the preliminary conquest, J continued by narrating how, through the exploits of the "Judges," the Israelites gained a firmer foothold in some parts of Canaan. He may then have concluded his history with the union of the tribes under the scepter of Saul, and finally with David's creation of a short-lived empire.[4]

However, if the J document did not contain the ancient poems in Gen. 49 (the blessing of Jacob), Num. 24:3-9, 15-19 (the "J" oracles of Balaam), and Gen. 9:25-27 (the blessing of Noah), only vague references to David's glorious reign can be detected in the genuine pages of J which have survived. Gen. 27:29 in its present form is hardly J, Gen. 36:31 is S; the allusions to David's conquest of Edom (II Sam. 8:13 f.) in Gen. 25:23 (J) and to Edom's subsequent rebellion (Gen. 27:40, JE or redactional) can scarcely prove that J contained the story of David.

The question whether J ended with the account of the conquest of Canaan summarized in Judg. 1 or with the death of David and the accession of Solomon (I Kings 1-2) must be left open. The third possibility, namely, that J contained the stories of the Judges but not those of Saul and David, seems to be excluded by the close connection between Judges and Samuel.

This uncertainty about the extent of J prevents us from determining its date accurately. If David's biography in Samuel was written by the author of the J document in the Hexateuch, then the date of J could be fixed in the first half of the tenth century, during the reign of Solomon. But if J was written by a different author, its date could be either *ca.* 950 or *ca.* 850 B.C., i.e., in the reign of Solomon (*ca.* 970-935) or of Jehoshaphat (*ca.* 875-851).

An earlier date than Solomon or a later one than Jehoshaphat is inconceivable. If, as seems certain, the author of the J document was a Judean and not an Ephraimite, his firm assurance in the glorious destiny of his people could only have arisen at a time when the kingdom of Judah was either at the height of its power (as under Solomon) or at least enjoyed a

---

[4] T. Klaehn (*Die sprachliche Verwandtschaft der Quelle K der Samuelisbücher mit der Quelle J des Heptateuch.* Borna-Leipzig, 1914) has attempted to prove, through linguistic arguments, that J continued through the books of Samuel. Part of his evidence is, however, vitiated by a questionable analysis of the sources.

degree of security and prosperity that boded well for the future (as under Jehoshaphat). Although the author's patriotism is national rather than provincial, it cannot be inferred that he lived before the division of the kingdom (ca. 935), for in E and in D, written long after the schism, Israel was still one, at least in principle.

Neither J nor E makes the slightest allusion to the divided kingdom. Political vicissitudes had no influence on the national feeling of Israel because it rested on religious faith. Whether Israel consisted of separate tribes in the desert or in Canaan, whether the nation had been irretrievably divided into two hostile kingdoms did not matter: Israel was one because it was the people of Jehovah. God and his people were inseparable, their fortunes mutually interdependent, Israel's triumphs conceived and realized by Jehovah. This combination of religion and patriotism, which inspires the J document from beginning to end, already animates the triumphal ode of Deborah (Judg. 5, dating from the twelfth century), and was kindled in Israel by Moses after the crossing of the Red Sea, to prove itself imperishable. This national pride whose root was in complete trust in Jehovah, although not created by the author of the J document, received through him its classical expression and permanent validity in Israel.

Thus J created the nationalism of Israel—a nationalism without parallel in the ancient world before the Greeks and Romans—the nation's sense of superiority over other peoples, pride in past achievements under the guidance of its god, and faith in its glorious future. Nothing could shake this pride, neither the fiery denunciations of Amos, who declared that Jehovah would bring ruin to Israel, nor the complete downfall of the two kingdoms of Israel. It was ultimately from J that the Deuteronomist derived the daring notion that Israel was the chosen people of God, a notion which later led to the division of mankind into Jews and heathens.

The shortcomings of nationalism, namely, contempt or hatred for aliens, are not very apparent in the great-souled author of J. However, a close scrutiny will disclose a bias against the Canaanites (Gen. 24:3, 37), the Edomites, whom he regards as uncouth simpletons (Gen. 25:27-34), and the Bedouins of the desert, represented by Ishmael, "a wild-ass of a man, with his hand against everyone and everyone's hand against him" (Gen. 16:12). The attitude toward the Arameans is less simple. Although he distrusted them, and related how the Aramean Laban tricked Jacob by giving him Leah instead of Rachel in marriage (Gen. 29:25), yet he admired them, and he made a point of connecting, while deliberately distorting the facts, the ancestors of Israel with the Arameans of the North (Gen. 24 and 29) rather than with the Bedouins of Northwestern Arabia (according to the more plausible view of the E document). If the S document was Edomitic in origin, as there is reason to believe, its author reciprocated J's unfriendly attitude toward Edom by his unflattering portraits of the eponym heroes of four tribes of Israel (Judah, Gen. 38; Simeon and Levi, Gen. 34; and Reuben, Gen. 35:21 f.), although he disclosed no trace of J's intense nationalism.

The patriotism of the J author did not blind him to the failings of his own people and of its heroes of old; he did not, however, depict them as rascals after the manner of S. The noble Abraham did not hesitate to resort to lies when his life seemed endangered (Gen. 12:19), and he allowed Sarah to deal so harshly with Hagar that the latter fled into the inhospitable desert (16:6). Likewise Isaac lied about Rebekah (26:7-10). Jacob took advantage of Esau's hunger to obtain his birthright (25:29-34) and became rich at the expense of Laban (30:37-43). Moses killed an Egyptian (Ex. 2:11-15).

In all these cases, deceit or assault was perpetrated against foreigners (Esau and Laban represent Edom and Aram, respectively). In the ancient practice of the desert, moral duties extended only to members of one's clan or nation, so that deceit or spoliation of foreigners was not condemned. In the case of Jacob, however, we find a man with no scruples whatsoever where his own interests were concerned. He not only deceived his brother, father, and uncle without compunction but, when fearing Esau's assault, he placed his women and children as a barrier between himself and his brother (Gen. 33:1-2). Even more shocking is the intention of Joseph's brothers to kill him, and their heartlessness in selling him as a slave on the advice of Judah (Gen. 37:23, 25-27). In dealing with foreigners, Jehovah is also an Israelite. He punished Pharaoh for innocently taking Sarah after Abraham had untruthfully said she was his sister (Gen. 12:17-20) and he also sent Moses to ask Pharaoh for permission to celebrate an Israelitic festival in the wilderness, with the tacit assumption that they would return in a few days (Ex. 5:1). The partiality of Jehovah for Israel and its ancestors pervades J: nothing could be more explicit than his words to Abraham, "And I will bless them that bless thee, and curse him that curseth thee" (Gen. 12:3a). There are, however, indications in J both of an earlier and of a later religious stage. In two archaic stories, far from showing kindness to men of his own clan, Jehovah viciously attacks them with intent to kill, acting more like a malignant demon of the wilderness than a national god (Gen. 32:22-28 [in part]; Ex. 4:24-26).

Our author allowed such sagas of a bygone age to stand, even when their import must have been repulsive. Although his religion was profoundly nationalistic and his god the God of Israel, the author of J seems to have conceived long before Amos a far more advanced religion, freed from national limitations, from emphasis on external worship. Occasionally Jehovah concerned himself with the welfare of all nations, rather than that of Israel alone (Gen. 12:3b, in opposition to the immediately preceding clause quoted above; and Gen. 18:25; 24:3, 7, [LXX], if the verses are really original in J). In contrast with his sources, the J author, ostensibly expressing his own religious attitude, described how the Patriarchs built altars but never implies that they sacrificed thereon.[5] Prayer, in J, takes the place of animal sacrifice.

The J author was ardently, but not rabidly, patriotic. His nationalism did not blind him to the worth of foreigners and Israel's failings; his God is more than the God of Israel. Abraham's appeal for the wicked city of Sodom (Gen. 18:22b-33a) exhibits a noble religious and ethical viewpoint which seemingly has no parallel before Jeremiah. However, it is not certain that this story belongs to J. It is characteristic of our author to accent the noble generosity of Esau (Edom) in forgiving his brother Jacob (Israel) when he had him at his mercy (Gen. 33:1-4, 6-10, 11b-17).

Pacifist

Fundamentally J is a pacifist: in the idyllic picture which he paints of the patriarchal age, the ancestors of Israel settled inevitable conflicts with their neighbors without having recourse to arms. The difficulties of Abraham with Pharaoh and Lot, of Isaac with Abimelech, and of Jacob with Esau and Laban were all solved amicably and left behind no bitter feelings. This friendship among men corresponds to that between Jehovah and the Patriarchs. God guides and protects them on their way, intervenes at critical moments to overcome their difficulties, appears to them in human form, and even accepts their hospitality (Gen. 18:1-16). On a larger scale the same familiarity prevails when Moses repeatedly interceded before a long-suffering deity for an ungrateful, cowardly, and complaining people.

The author of J composed his national epic out of stories circulating orally among the Israelites of his day; his original contributions were the style, selection, arrangement, and modifications dictated by his own conviction, by which he constructed a great work of art out of miscellaneous material.

When the Israelites entered Canaan, they brought memories of ancestral exploits, related and handed down from one generation to another in the form of songs and stories. Other stories current in Canaan eventually became part of the sagas of Israel. But not all of Canaan's traditions became part of the cycles of stories cherished by Israel. Whatever unconsciously offended the patriotism and religion of the conquerors was forgotten. The stories of the Book of Judges, for instance, are tales of victory and represent only the Israelitic side of the picture. Canaanite triumphs celebrated in stories that survived among the latter until their extinction (the last Canaanites being completely absorbed in the reign of Solomon) were eventually forgotten.

[5] Gen. 12:7, 8; 13:18; 26:25; cf. 21:33.

Through an accident, certain of the Canaanite stories unflattering to the Israelites have survived in a collection of myths and tales compiled outside of Israel. The S source containing these tales was eventually incorporated by an antiquarian into the writings of Israel. The stories of Gen. 34; 35:21 f.; 38 illustrate the Canaanitic tales which ancient Israel did not relish. The first two were current in Judah at the time of the united kingdom (Gen. 49:4-7) when the hostility between Judah and North Israel that resulted in the schism was already at work. But the third story must have been told among the Edomites or other unfriendly neighbors of Judah since, in the time of Deborah, North Israel still ignored Judah.

Before becoming a united nation and kingdom, through the achievements of Saul and especially David, Israel consisted of separate tribes. The Song of Deborah (Judg. 5) knows only ten. Later, thirteen were listed and, after the division of Solomon's kingdom exclusive of Judah into twelve fiscal districts, their number was reduced to twelve, by counting Ephraim and Manasseh as one [Joseph] or by omitting the landless Levi. Tribal traditions, except for Joseph's deliverance from Egyptian bondage through Moses, did not reach back beyond the settlement in Canaan (Judg. 1). Memory of earlier vicissitudes of the tribes in the Wilderness was a blank, and it was easy to imagine that all the tribes had been in Egypt with the Joseph group.

When the traditions, as we know them, began to be sifted and organized during the united monarchy, the people had achieved national unity and consciousness, and they projected this unity (disregarding the smoldering rivalry between the Judah and Joseph groups) into the dim past by means of the artificial genealogical tree of the Patriarchs who had been transformed from heroes of sacred legends into tribal and national ancestors.

This genealogical scheme, identical in J and E, antedates the composition of J. Israel (as distinguished from Jacob) and his sons were originally mere personifications of nation and tribes. Only Joseph becomes in popular fancy the hero of a romantic tale in which his brothers play minor roles—a tale in which he is a full-blooded individual and not, as Simeon, Levi, Reuben, and Judah in the slanderous stories of Gen. 34; 35:21 f.; 38 (cf. Gen. 49:4-7 for the first two), a thinly veiled symbol of a tribe.

The genuine traditions of ancient Israel are confined to the stories of Joseph, Moses, and the invasion of Canaan. The rest is an adaptation from Canaanitic and other sources. Since the Canaanitic stories were in circulation among the Israelites long before they were collected in J, they have lost so much of their original character that the author of J could regard them as genuine Israelitic traditions. Nevertheless, there is reason to believe that the characters of the Patriarchs originated in Canaan. The names of Asher, Ephraim, and Gilead [Gad] were those of the territories occupied later by these tribes; Jacob appears about 1470 on a Palestinian list of Thotmes III (as *y-ʿ-q-b-ʾ-r*, Jacob-el);[6] the name of the city of Samhuna, mentioned in the letters of Tell el-Amarna (fourteenth century) may be the prototype of Simeon. Asher, Gad, and Edom are also known as names of gods.

That most of the Patriarchs have names of probable Palestinian origin is less significant than their connection with the sacred shrines of ancient Canaan. Abraham received a revelation at Shechem (Gen. 12:6), and built an altar there; as also between Bethel and Ai (12:8), and at Hebron (13:18), where Jehovah appeared unto him and accepted his hospitality (18:1 ff.). He planted a tamarisk at Beersheba (21:33, J; cf. 21:22-24, 27, 31, E) which, like the terebinth (cf. 18:4) of Mamre (13:18; 18:1; cf. 14:13), was venerated as sacred before the coming of the Israelites. It is generally recognized that Abraham was originally connected with the shrine at Hebron, and only secondarily with the others. Isaac dug wells in the valley of Gerar (26:17, 19-22, J; cf. 20:2, E) and at Beersheba (26:23-25), where he had a divine revelation. Jacob was regarded as the discoverer of the famous sanctuary of Bethel (28:10 ff., JE; 35:1-8, 14, E) and connected with the shrines at Mahanaim (32:2 [H. 32:3], E) and Penuel (32:24-32 [H. 32:25-33], JE), both east of the Jordan, and with the ones in Canaan proper at Shechem (33:18b-20, E) and Ephrath (incorrectly identified with Bethlehem in the gloss 35:19b; see 35:16-20, E). In the oldest tradition Abraham is connected with Hebron, Isaac with Beersheba, and Jacob with Bethel and possibly with Transjordanic sites.

The Israelites were aware that their shrines were originally Canaanitic (Deut. 12:1 ff.; Ez. 20:28; for Bethel cf. Judg. 1:22-26, omitting the misleading gloss in v. 23b; for Shechem cf. Judg. 9; for Hebron cf. Josh. 15:13 ff.; Judg. 1:10-20; Amos 5:5, cf. 8:14, denounced the sanctuaries of Bethel, Gilgal, and Beersheba). If these shrines were Canaanitic, the stories telling of their origin must have been pre-Israelitic. This is confirmed by evidence not entirely obliterated, showing that other gods (*numina loci,* Hebrew *el,* pl. *elohim*) were worshiped in these shrines before the Israelites dedicated them to the worship of their god Jehovah. El Roi, the deity of the spring called Beer-lahai-roi, saved Hagar in the desert (Gen. 16:13 f., J); El Olam was the god of Beersheba (21:33, J), El Berith of Shechem (Judg. 9:46; also called Baal Berith: 8:33; 9:4), El Bethel of Bethel (Gen. 35:7, E; cf. 31:13, E, "the El Bethel"; but cf. the LXX and the Targums; for the literature on these two passages see

[6] That *y-š-p-ʾ-r* on the same list (No. 78) is the prototype of Joseph is uncertain. In one of his campaigns in Southern Syria, Ramses III reports the conquest of Levi-el (A. Lods, *Israël,* p. 61. Paris, 1930). A "field of Abram" is mentioned in the list of Pharaoh Shishak (PEFQS [1905] 7). In the hymn of Merenptah (1225-1215) even "Israel" is a nation in Canaan.

U. Cassuto, *La questione della Genesi*, p. 72, n. 8), and perhaps El Elyon of Jerusalem (Gen. 14:18-20, 22. S²).

El Shaddai (Gen. 49:25), the name by which, according to P, Jehovah revealed himself to the Patriarchs (Gen. 17:1; Ex. 6:3) cannot be localized; the suggestion that El Pahad (or Pahad Isaac, the fear of Isaac) was the god of Mizpah in Gilead (Gen. 31:42, 53, JE?) has not been generally accepted. In a passage which has been willfully corrupted, Amos (8:14) seems to allude to the local deities of Bethel, Dan, and Beersheba. In the Israelitic versions of the Palestinian sacred legends, the local deities are of course identified with Jehovah, who at Shechem bore the title *El Elôhê Yisra'el*, or El the God of Israel (Gen. 33:20, E; cf. Josh. 8:30).[7]

Not only the shrines and their deities, but also the sacred objects revered in the several sanctuaries and the rites there employed in the worship, were Canaanitic in origin. At Bethel, the cult object was a sacred stone, a *maṣṣebah* or stone pillar upon which libations of oil were poured (Gen. 28:18; 35:14, E). At Shechem, there was a sacred terebinth called "terebinth of Moreh" [perhaps meaning "of the diviner"] (Gen. 12:6a, J; cf. Deut. 11:30), possibly identical with the "terebinth of the diviners" (Judg. 9:37); and another one called "terebinth of the maṣṣebah" (*sic;* 9:6). At Hebron, there was the "terebinth of Mamre" (Gen. 13:18; 18:1, J; the plural "terebinths" is a Jewish correction: cf. 18:4 and LXX), at Beersheba, a tamarisk is said to have been planted by Abraham (21:33, J), and at Bethel the "oak of weeping" on the grave of Deborah, Rebekah's nurse (35:8, E). The sacred spring of Lahai-roi (16:14, J) has already been mentioned.

The Palestinian origin of the sanctuary legends is indubitable, notwithstanding their far-reaching adaptation to Israel's nationalistic and religious ideals. Other elements in the patriarchal stories are of doubtful origin. It is probable that some of the Oriental folklore utilized in the stories was likewise Canaanitic, although we have no evidence to determine where the folk tales originated regarding Jacob's ruses by which he defrauded Esau and Laban (Gen. 25:29-34, J; 30:37-42, mostly J), the deception of his father (27:6-25, JE), and Rachel's use of mandrakes to facilitate conception (30:14-16). In view of E's obvious dislike of these pranks, a non-Israelitic origin is likely.

The extraordinary interest in folk etymologies of names of persons and places, and the delight in puns disclosed in J (and to a lesser degree in E), may be genuinely Israelitic, although certain of these place names could be connected with the Canaanitic sanctuary legends and local lore. We have no way of telling whether some of the characters in the patri-

---

[7] For a different theory on the gods of the Patriarchs, see A. Alt, *Der Gott der Väter*. Stuttgart, 1929.

archal stories were already regarded as the ancestors of Palestinian ethnic groups, and to what extent tribal history was told in the form of tales about eponym heroes in Canaan; nor can we determine the mythological substratum, if any, of these stories. The tale of Jacob and Esau may have some connection with the Phoenician myth of the hostility between Ousoos the hunter and his brother Sameroumos ("high heaven"),[8] though hardly with the duel between the two brothers Aleyan and Moth in a Ras Shamra mythological poem of the fourteenth century B.C.

The Joseph stories in J disclose not only a notable acquaintance with Egyptian customs and institutions but seem to utilize the plot of Egyptian stories. A correct Egyptian background has been detected in the fiscal and agrarian measures of Joseph (Gen. 47:13-26);[9] in the reluctance of Egyptians to eat with foreigners (43:32); in the career of a foreigner like Joseph, whose rise to power has been compared to that of Dudu in the time of Ikhnaton;[10] and in the embalming and burial of Jacob (50:2-11, mostly J).[11] It is true that in some details the Hebrew author is mistaken, but significantly the most obvious errors, such as the assumptions that camels were used in Egypt in ancient times (12:16, J; Ex. 9:3, J?)[12] and that straw was used in making bricks in the Nile valley (Ex. 5:5-19, mostly J),[13] are outside the Joseph stories. It is clear that the J author possessed a very superficial knowledge of Egypt. He had listened to a Hebrew version of the Egyptian tales which he used in the Joseph stories, being obviously unable to read them in the original.

There is no reason for doubting that the episode of Potiphar's wife (Gen. 39:7-20, J; J does not name Joseph's master) has been inspired, possibly at several removes, by the Tale of the Two Brothers, extant in a copy dating from the end of the thirteenth century B.C.[14] Indeed, the plot of the Joseph stories, in its main outline, has been found in the Story of the Seven Sages,[15] written in the twelfth century. It would be idle to guess how the author of J became acquainted with Egyptian tales; but that he could have done so without leaving Palestine is certain.

Before the J epic was written, Canaanitic sacred legends and folk tales, Egyptian stories, anecdotes explaining the origin of names and customs,

[8] M. J. Lagrange, *Etudes sur les religions sémitiques*, pp. 416 f. (2nd ed., Paris, 1905.) The text of this myth, preserved by Eusebius (*Pr. Ev.* I, 10), may be found in C. Müller, *Fragmenta historicorum graecorum*, Vol. III, pp. 563 ff. (Paris, 1883).

[9] E. Peet, *Egypt and the Old Testament*, p. 96. Liverpool, 1922.

[10] A. Erman-H. Ranke, *Aegypten und aegyptisches Leben im Altertum*, pp. 118 f. Tübingen, 1923.

[11] W. Spiegelberg, "Die Beisetzung des Patriarchen Jakob im Lichte der altaegyptischen Quellen," *Oriental. Literaturzeit.* 26 (1923) 421-424.

[12] Erman-Ranke, *op. cit.*, p. 586.

[13] Peet, *op. cit.*, pp. 99 f.

[14] English translation in A. Erman, *The Literature of the Ancient Egyptians*, pp. 150 ff. London, 1927.

[15] Cf. A. Lods, *Israël*, pp. 181 f.

mythological narratives, Israelitic historical traditions, and miscellaneous tales were circulating orally among the Israelites, and were thus being molded by popular imagination into an embryonic national literature. The narrative material varied at first according to the locality, although the most popular stories soon circulated far from their place of origin. A certain selection was unconsciously being made. The stories told at Bethel and Shechem in the North and at Hebron and Beersheba in the South proved to be the most popular, while those from other places, such as Shiloh, for instance, attained neither wide circulation nor immortality.

Gradually two principal cycles of stories, one Ephraimitic (Shechem and Bethel) and the other Judahite (Hebron), took shape. The J document drew its material from both, the E document exclusively from the Ephraimitic, which ignored Hebron but contained stories about Beersheba (Isaac) because it was a place of pilgrimage for the Northern Israelites (I Kings 19:3; Am. 5:5, cf. 8:14).[16] Early in the process, the legendary Canaanitic heroes became Israelites, or at least ancestors of the nation. This is still seen in the identification of Jacob with Israel (at Penuel, Gen. 32:28 [H. 32:29], J; at Bethel, 35:10, P). Later, Abraham was presented as the ideal and Jacob as the real Israelite; the first became the embodiment of moral virtues and religious faith, the second of mundane shrewdness and success (this development continued between J and E, and reached its climax with Philo).

Joseph is a sort of combination of the two, whereas Isaac was completely neglected. Abraham, probably a Southern hero, was the great pilgrim and founder of shrines in the South; Jacob, a Northern hero, played a similar role in the North, although the two cycles, through the activity of wandering storytellers and bards ("those that speak in proverbs," Num. 21:27) did not remain mutually impervious. Indeed, in the time of the united monarchy a national systematization and selection was in process.

But before the traditions of North and South could have been cemented in a national epic the division of the kingdom, an incurable breach, caused two epics to be written instead of one, a Judahite (J) and an Ephraimite (E). The synthesis begun during the united monarchy, however, left an indelible impress on the material used by J and E: it was during the united monarchy that the genealogical scheme was devised and the Patriarchs, originally with little in common, were joined together into a single family; it was then, or shortly before, that Jehovah had taken the place of the local deities of Canaanitic legends and that events of past history, relations with neighboring nations, and pride in national achievements were read in the adventures of legendary heroes.

Over this slowly crystallizing mass of literary material the author of the

[16] The Southern story about Hagar, contained in E, is connected with Beersheba.

J document blew the breath of life. The epic scope, dramatic structure, superb style and religious and national fervor animating the whole are the contributions of his genius. The gigantic figure of Abraham was his creation: he visualized Abraham as the embodiment of Israel. Entering Palestine from the north, Abraham traversed this country from north to south, with stops at Shechem and between Ai and Bethel (Gen. 12:1-9, J with glosses in vv. 4b-5, 6b). Then to Egypt whence, after a harrowing experience, he returned enriched by worldly goods, to settle in Hebron, and triumph over Lot, the father of Moab and Ammon (13:1-18, mostly J).

Thus Israel's conquest of the Promised Land, even Joseph's conquest of Bethel and Judah's conquest of Hebron (Judg. 1, late summary of J), is not only promised by Jehovah to Abraham but already realized symbolically in his wanderings, just as later, in E, Jacob's journey from Harran to Bethel and Shechem foreshadows Joshua's victories but completely ignores Judah's invasion from the south. This injection of the future conquest of Canaan into the patriarchal stories by means of divine promises and significant itineraries is probably a contribution of the J author, although he may have found some suggestions in his sources. In any case, the central thought, dominant motive, and focus giving unity to miscellaneous narrative, are in J the gradual growth and progress of Israel under the guidance of Jehovah.

Great literature consists of great thoughts clothed in matchless form. The epic scope of J's subject—the birth and triumph of a nation under the aegis of its god—corresponds to the superb literary form. J's style, like that of the Iliad, combines nobility with simplicity—a paradoxical combination that is extremely rare. Nobility is found in the mature, full-grown literary masterpieces of civilized nations; simplicity belongs to the works of simple, uncultured peoples or to works written for simple persons, like books for children. A combination of the two requires a set of conditions seldom realized: a period of transition from primitive to advanced culture, during which a literary genius is capable of molding the simple literary utterances of his people into a finished majestic monument.

These conditions were never realized as fully as in the Iliad and in J. In English literature, for instance, Chaucer has simplicity without majesty, Milton (and in a different way Shakespeare) majesty without simplicity. Perhaps the closest approach to the combination is in the *chansons de geste*, like the *Chanson de Roland*. But these are inferior in rank to the Iliad and J. The author of J was highly cultured and sophisticated, but he succeeded in injecting his great thoughts into the simple folk tales of his people without spoiling their charming pristine naïveté, as did the author of E. With consummate literary art, he spans the bridge from the sublime to the ridiculous, from the noble faith of Abraham to the rustic pranks of Jacob, without shocking the reader. The skill by which his great thoughts about the glorious destiny of Israel are presented in the account of a trivial incident can be seen in Gen. 24:1-9, a classic example of this combination of nobility and simplicity.

The magic of J's prose eludes dissection. Its style has the admirable quality of being unobtrusive and transparent. Unless the reader is engaged in literary investigations, he notices not the words but only the picture or thought behind them. The J author excels in the portrayal of scenes and characters. The picture of the women fetching water from the well has a peculiar fascination for him, and he portrays it three times, with variations in detail but with extraordinary charm: Gen. 24:15-20 (Rebekah at the well), 29:2-12 (Rachel at the well), Ex. 2:15-21 (Zipporah at the well). These scenes are re-created with a minimum of actual description. *They live.*

With equal directness and sharp delineation, the J author parades before us the characters of his story. Only rarely, when an understanding of the narrative requires it, does he give a brief and pointed characterization of his heroes. Thus, for instance, he writes, "And Esau was a cunning hunter, a man of the field; and Jacob was a plain man dwelling in tents" (Gen. 25:27; cf. the characterization of Ishmael in 16:12). Descriptions of physical traits, such as the beauty of women (12:11, 14; 24:16; 26:7) or men (39:6), or physical defects (27:11), are introduced only when relevant. As a rule, it is only through the vividness of the dialogue and the course of events that his characters stand out in three-dimensional reality: the dignified and generous Abraham, the outspoken and nagging Sarah, the quiet and serene Isaac, and the versatile and ambitious Jacob so akin to Rebekah, his resourceful mother; the brilliant, upright, and fortunate Joseph, the inspired and persistent Moses patiently overcoming his inferiority complex—all, except the last, the creation of a fresh and glamorous imagination—stand forth before the reader no less actual than Achilles, Agamemnon, and Hector.

All of J's characters have a monumental stateliness, heroic stature, towering strength; even Hagar, who flees defiantly and faces probable death rather than submit to humiliating treatment. In E, on the contrary, she is a pathetic figure, driven away and helplessly leaving her son to die. None, not even Moses, is a brooding, introspective, dismayed figure tossed about by events. They are all conscious of being figures of destiny, heirs of divine promises.

J's evocative, plastic, poetic style not only portrays concrete scenes and characters, dramatic episodes and vivid action, but also background and atmosphere. It is the idyllic background of a pastoral existence,[17] in

---

[17] Occasionally, the author forgets that he is dealing with shepherds and herdsmen, and introduces the products and life of a settled agricultural community: fine meal (Gen. 18:6), lentil soup (25:34), wine (27:25), the wheat harvest (30:14).

which the grim search for pasturage and water is transmuted into a pilgrimage from shrine to shrine. It is an atmosphere of peace and good-will among men in which armed conflicts have no place. Not until the author passes from the golden age of legend to the real world of history, in the time of Moses, does the dreamy atmosphere give way to the struggles, fears, hardships, and bitter complaints of tribesmen of flesh and blood, whom a man of vision, Moses, had brought out of degrading slavery to precarious freedom at the gate of the Land of Promise.

CHAPTER III

THE S DOCUMENT

~~~~~~

R. Smend[1] recognized in 1912 that four strands could be distinguished in the narrative portions of the Hexateuch, and he used for them the symbols J[1], J[2], E, and P. Ten years later, O. Eissfeldt,[2] accepting Smend's conclusions in a general way, substituted for J[1] and J[2] the symbols L and J, respectively. According to him, L ("Lay source" in contrast with P, "the Priestly Code") ran parallel to J from the Creation to the death of David.

The chief objection to Eissfeldt's theory is that, outside of Genesis, his L and J either supplement each other or consist of mere snatches of narrative or isolated stories, hence, unless we suppose that large portions are lost, no "sources" or "documents" can be reconstructed out of this literary debris. Since it is doubtful that a convincing analysis can be achieved by a hypothetical and subjective reconstruction of lost material, it seems preferable to recognize the fact that there are in the books from Exodus to Samuel, in addition to the primary sources, not only brief glosses but also bits of poetry and prose which have at some time been added to the text, either from books now lost (such as anthologies of poetry or books of law and history) or freely composed *ad hoc* (II Sam. 7 is a good example of a lengthy interpolation composed for the context).

In the Book of Genesis, the situation is different. After J, E, and P have been removed, the remnant consists of not only redactional material and isolated fragments but a series of stories with such well-defined characteristics that it is not unreasonable to consider them a separate document. This writing is so different from J[1] and L that a special identifying symbol has been suggested by the present author (S, from South or Seir, the probable place of its origin).[3] The S source is divided into two parts: the mythical account of the origin and early development of mankind (Gen. 1-11, omitting P) and the legendary account of the origin of the peoples in Southern Palestine and Transjordania, concluding with a summary of

---

[1] *Die Erzählung des Hexateuch auf ihre Quellen untersucht.* Berlin, 1912.

[2] *Hexateuch-Synopse.* See also his *Einleitung in das Alte Testament.* Tübingen, 1934.

[3] R. H. Pfeiffer, "A Non-Israelitic Source of the Book of Genesis," ZAW N.F. 7 (1930) 66-73.

the history of Edom before the time of David (parts of Gen. 14-35; 38; 36).

As an obvious characteristic of this material, it ignores the tribes of North Israel and in the case of the Leah tribes located in the South (Reuben, Simeon, Levi, Judah) discloses a decided hostility against them. In Gen. 1-11 the S material is inserted into P (elsewhere in Gen., P is added to JE); therefore, neither of the two strands in this primeval story (called J¹ and J² or L and J; here they are indicated with S and S²) can be identified with J unless it is supposed that in contrast with his regular procedure elsewhere, the author of J incorporated without change several long sections from a book. In any case, as P knew JE without this primeval history, he wrote one that has no connections whatever with S and parallels S² only in the Flood and in genealogies. In thought and form, S-S² in Gen. 1-11 is totally at variance with J. In Gen. 14-38, the S material has been abruptly inserted into JEP and consists of sections easily identified, as they are isolated within their present context; they cannot be attributed to J² or E² because they are indifferent or hostile to Israel and its religion.

The contents of S may be summarized as follows:

I. *The primeval mythological history of mankind.* 1. The story of creation (Gen. 2:5-9;[4] 15-25). 2. The expulsion from the Garden of Eden (3).[5] 3. Cain and his descendants (4:(1), 17-24). 4. The birth of the giants (6:1-4).[6] 5. Noah and his sons (9:20-27). 6. The Tower of Babel (11:1-9).

II. *The legendary history of Southern Palestine and Transjordania.* 1. Abraham's victory against the kings of the East (14:1-17, 21-24). 2. Lot's deliverance from Sodom (19:1-26), and the birth of Moab and Ammon (19:30-38). 3. Simeon and Levi's treacherous attack on Shechem (34; 35:5). 4. Reuben's incest (35:21-22a). 5. The annals of Edom (36:9-39 or only 36:20-39, the rest being possibly S²). 6. Judah and Tamar (38).

The contents of S², consisting of redactional additions and isolated stories, follow:

1. The four rivers flowing out of Eden (2:10-14). 2. Cain and Abel (4:1-16; possibly a revised S story). 3. Seth (4:25 f.). 4. The Flood (5:29; 6:5-8; 7:1-5, 7-10, 12, 16b, 17b, 22 f.; 8:2b-3a, 6-12, 13b, 20-22). 5. The descendants of Shem, Ham, and Japheth (10:1b, 8-19, 21, 24-30). 6. The descendants of Terah (11:28-30)[?]. 7. Melchizedek (14:18-20). 8. The descendants of Keturah (25:1-4).

The sections called S² represent additions made to S at various times

---

[4] Probably the order was 2:5-7, 9a, 8, 9b.
[5] 3:20, 23 may be glosses.
[6] 6:3 may be a gloss.

during the two centuries 600-400 B.C. Some are merely erudite annotations (2:10-14; 10:1b ff.; 25:1-4) or transitional clauses (4:25 f. harmonizes the story of Cain and Abel with the P genealogy of Seth in 5:3 ff.; 11:28-30 is an introduction to the Abraham stories that follow). Neither S nor JE contained long genealogies. If 36:9-30 is S rather than S², a difficult question to decide, the inclusion into S of Horite and Edomitic genealogies is a clue to its place of origin. The only important sections of S² are the story of Cain and Abel and the story of the Flood. In its present form, the story of Cain and Abel can hardly be an original part of S, but the tradition is old that Cain was a murderer, for there is an allusion to it in the ancient poem of Lamech (4:24). The S² story of the Flood has suffered severe disarrangement and loss through its insertion into the P story; S² represents, however, the earliest Hebrew transcript of the Babylonian flood story in the Gilgamesh Epic.

Curiously enough, although P has parallels to S², he shows no acquaintance whatsoever with S. The materials of S² were collected in circles not unlike those producing the narrative sections of P, although S² discloses no great interest in legal matters. S² may have originated in priestly circles at Jerusalem. It makes sacrifice the point of the Cain-Abel story, whereas the original version probably had an entirely different motive for the murder, and preserves from the Babylonian account the sacrifice of Noah (8:20-22) omitted in the Flood story of P. The Melchizedek episode (14:18-20) also shows an interest in ritual matters, such as tithes, and seems to be a late midrash written to glorify the priesthood of Jerusalem (cf. Ps. 76:2); Ps. 110:4 uses Melchizedek to provide a legitimate ancestry for the non-Levitical Hasmonean high priests.

The S document consists of a dozen stories, some of which may have been joined originally in separate cycles (for instance, the stories of Creation, of the Garden of Eden, and of the Tower of Babel). The stories are different in character and origin and were brought together, without being welded into an organic whole, by an editor expressing a definite philosophical viewpoint. With the exception of Gen. 36:31-39 (a summary of the genuinely historical annals of Edom), they are rather primitive and childish myths and legends, and were used by the editor, as was the popular tale of the long-suffering Job by the author of Job, as vehicles for his philosophy of history.

In so far as possible, the viewpoint of the stories and that of the editor should be kept distinct. The initial stories relate the birth and early history of mankind, and explain in mythical manner some puzzling features of human life and culture (Gen. 2-11); in the second part (14-38), they give a legendary account of the regions around the Dead Sea leading up to the history of Edom (Gen. 38 probably preceded Gen.

36 before the insertion into JEP). After the manner of the so-called "primitive mind" (which displays an intellectual curiosity anything but "primitive") the stories of Gen. 2-11 undertake to explain why man has a body and soul (2:7),[7] why man and woman are different and yet are one in matrimony (2:21-23), why serpents have no legs and must crawl in the dust (3:14), why women give birth in great pain (3:16), why the cultivation of the soil is laborious and precarious (3:17-19) ever since man's expulsion from the earthly paradise (3:23); how the giants originated (6:1-4), and how the various crafts (4:20-22) and nations speaking different tongues (11:1-9) came into being. Likewise the story of Cain and Abel (4:1-16), in a more primitive form, may have been an explanation of the feud between nomadic Bedouins and settled peasants.

Passing on to the historical period, the stories relate with malicious glee how Canaan was destined to be conquered by Philistines and Bedouins (9:20-27), how the great ziggurat of the Temple of Marduk in Babylon was but the vestige of a miserable failure (11:1-9), how Sodom, whose sin has become proverbial, came to its catastrophic end (19:1-26), and how the proud nations of Moab and Ammon were the issue of incestuous unions (19:30-38), how Simeon and Levi were cutthroats (34; 35:5; cf. 49:5-7), how Reuben committed incest (35:21 f.; cf. 49:4) and Judah was duped by Tamar in the guise of a harlot (38)—a most unsavory collection of scandal. In this unattractive gallery, only Cain, the ancestor of the Kenites (4), Shem and Japheth (9:26 f.), Abram the Hebrew (Ḫabirû of the Amarna letters), the victor over the four kings of the East (14:1-17, 21-24), and the Edomites (36:9-39) are presented in a favorable light.

The stories originated in different environments over a considerable area around the Dead Sea, but were apparently collected in Edom. The story of the Garden of Eden (ch. 3) (and possibly the Creation story in ch. 2 and the story of the Tower of Babel in ch. 11) arose in an agricultural community and expressed the stolid resignation—with occasional bitter outbursts—of the peasant contending with thorns and thistles, and by the sweat of his brow wearily extracting a meager sustenance from a soil that seemed accursed (3:17-19).

Conversely, the story of Cain and his descendants reflects a Bedouin background, and it is connected artificially with the preceding stories. Cain could not have been the son of the first man, or he could never have

---

[7] As in the case of similar primitive myths, there seems originally to have been an explanation in the story of Gen. 2-3 of why man must die: somehow, man failed to eat the fruit of the "tree of life" (2:9; 3:22, 24). The editor practically suppressed this element in favor of the story of man's theft of the fruit of the tree of knowledge, which marks the passage from a state of happy, idle savagery to the painful, exacting, and godless climb toward an ever higher civilization. The connection between the tree of knowledge and death (2:17; 3:3) is entirely spurious (3:4 f.).

found a wife (4:17). According to one version, he was condemned to be a "fugitive and a vagabond," to whom the soil would not yield its produce, because he murdered Abel (4:12). According to another, however, he is the proud ancestor of the line of tent-dwellers who introduced the refinements of civilization (4:17-22)—haughty desert tribesmen boastful of their deeds of valor and revenge (4:23 f.), who would never have regarded their lot as inferior to that of the tillers of the soil.[8]

Without attempting to produce a unified and well-organized book, the editor of S, by careful selection and arrangement of these miscellaneous stories, has succeeded in conveying to the reader some notion of his philosophy of history. Obviously conscious of a progress of civilization, he distinguishes five eras: 1. The primitive age: men were naked and lived from the fruits of the trees (Gen. 2). 2. The beginning of civilization: the use of garments of leaves (3:7) or skins (3:21), and the cultivation of the soil (3:17-19). 3. The development of arts and crafts: the making of tents [weaving], and of musical instruments; the working of metals (4:20-22).[9] 4. The age of the giants (6:1-4). 5. The present age: the planting of vineyards and the making of wine (9:20 f.); the distinction of nations and languages, the building of cities (11:1-9).

This scheme represents a development from the early myth of the lost paradise, current in ancient Greece and elsewhere, in which there are two periods only, a happy existence in Eden and a life of toil and suffering outside. The classical series of the four ages (gold, silver, brass, and iron) comes later. The age of the giants has been inserted into it from another system. Hesiod (*Works and Days* 5:109-201) likewise interpolates the age of the heroic demigods in the fourth place, and has five ages instead of four; similarly, he is acquainted with the more primitive division into two eras, the rule of Kronos (period 1) and the rule of Zeus (periods 2-5). The interpolation of the Flood into the early eras of mankind, made by S[2], is first found in Ovid (*Metamorphoses*, 1:89-162) in classical authors.

Both in S and in Hesiod there is the pessimistic observation that cultural progress is accompanied by increased wickedness and unhappiness. The Stoics developed this conception of a progressive moral deterioration, and Aratus (*Phaenomena*, 97-140) presents this notion plastically in his three ages of mankind: during the Golden Age, Dike (justice) lived among men; during the Silver Age she withdrew to the mountains; during the Brass Age she ascended to heaven and became a star. On the contrary, the Epicureans believed in a triumphant progress of mankind

---

[8] Another contrast between the stories of Adam and of Cain is that the background of the Adam story is approximately the Stone Age while that of Cain's descendants is the Bronze Age.

[9] The building of cities (4:17b) seems premature and may be a later addition.

to ever higher achievement, without moral disintegration. This view received its classical presentation in the great poem of Lucretius (*On Nature* 5:925-1457).

Not only did the editor of S hold a theory about stages in the technical progress of mankind, corresponding to an increasing moral disintegration, but he traced its beginning to a godless act—the eating of the fruit of the tree of knowledge, which "opened the eyes" (Gen. 3:7) of Adam and Eve. The theft of knowledge on the part of the first man is a myth familiar also to the author of the Book of Job (Job 15:7 f.). The deity, in the stories of Eden and the Tower of Babel, wished to keep mankind on a level little above that of the animals. Jealous of his own prerogatives, God forbade the eating of the fruit of knowledge and prevented the building of the tower by which men intended to scale the divine mansions. After man ate of the fruit of knowledge, God said, "Behold man is become as one of us, to know good and evil; and what if now man were to put forth his hand and take also of the tree of life, and eat, and live forever!" (Gen. 3:22.)

Thus it is in open defiance of the deity that man takes the first step upward, from primitive barbarism toward an ever higher level of civilization. The eating of the forbidden fruit of knowledge gave to man both the urge and the capacity for cultural advancement. At the same time, it created a state of hostility between man and his Maker. The sad lot of mankind, whether in city, farms, or deserts, is a punishment for its daring boldness in attempting to ascend from the level of brutes to that of gods. The underlying thought is not unlike that expressed in the myth of Prometheus who, by his theft of fire, made possible the progress of arts and crafts among men.

It is probable that the editor of S believed the acquisition of knowledge, with its resulting divine curses, human suffering and wickedness, to be preferable to the placid stupidity and moronic innocence which man could have enjoyed in Eden, in accordance with the wishes of the deity. It is probable that the editor admired the rebel Cain, setting out in the trackless wilderness to create a civilization, more than he did the meek frightened Adam, struggling with an unyielding soil and thwarted in returning to the Garden, as he obviously wished to, by the flaming sword and the Cherubim. Like Lucifer in Milton's *Paradise Lost*, man in Eden and at Babel is defeated by God but, armed with his newly purloined knowledge, refuses to surrender and marches on, godless and bold, to new tragedies, new discoveries, new iniquities.

A later thinker of the same school, the author of Job, was forced to admit that man is at the mercy of a deity who may torment him without reason, ever unable to attain the cosmic wisdom hidden from him by the deity. Ecclesiastes finally, after losing all his illusions, could see no purpose in the unequal fight and, recognizing the inanity of man's toil and suffering, advocated passivity and desertion from the battlefield until, as S said, man returns to the dust from which he came (Gen. 2:7; 3:19; Eccl. 3:20; 12:7).

The stories of Eden and Babel, as well as others in S, are pervaded by an atmosphere of gloom and a sense of God's indifference to human beings. It is only in the stories of the mark of Cain (Gen. 4:9-15) and Lot's deliverance from Sodom (19:1-26), which are different from the rest and may have been retouched in the vein of S[2], that the deity manifests kindness for an individual and his family. Elsewhere, human misdeeds (unless they infringe on divine prerogatives) do not come under the scrutiny of the deity and are not punished (except 38:7, 10); if the difficult verse 6:3 is original, it probably reports another measure of the deity to prevent mortals from becoming like divine beings through an infusion of God's spirit (J. Wellhausen, *Die Composition des Hexateuchs*, pp. 305 f. 3rd ed. Berlin, 1899). Since divine intervention in the human world usually brought only disaster in its wake, the deity could inspire in man only a feeling of fear (3:10) and a desire to remain aloof from its presence (4:16), exactly as in the Book of Job (7:19). Traces of a pagan polytheism have not been entirely eliminated from the stories of S (3:22; 11:7).

The picture of human life throughout S is pessimistic in the extreme: after the expulsion from Eden, man draws a precarious sustenance from the soil by the sweat of his brow, woman is subject to the labors of childbirth, enmity prevails between mankind and animals like the serpent, the battle for existence is incessant, evil impulses lurking at the door of man's soul are uncontrolled and lead to deeds of violence, incest, and sexual abominations; and even divine beings are subject to lust. Rape, murder, and war form the plot of most of the stories; religion neither soothes human pain nor checks the wickedness of the human heart. Progress in the arts and crafts fails to ameliorate the morals of men and their mutual relationships. The theme of S is "Paradise Lost," and an era of peace on earth and goodwill among men does not even appear as a comforting chimerical hope.

The editor of S was not a creative literary craftsman. He was a thinker and a collector of ancient mythical and legendary tales. His style is concise and lucid, but not brilliant. The abiding charm and pathos of some stories were inherent in his sources, which have the unadorned simplicity and polish, and occasionally the coarse vigor, of the folk tales told repeatedly in the course of generations. The editor did not attempt to write a unified organic story, merely collecting detached episodes in chronological order (Gen. 38 should precede Gen. 36). His philosophy of history dictated the selection and arrangement of the popular tales; it gave to the whole a certain unity apparent in the geographical background, in the pessimistic mood, and withal in the satisfaction of contemplating the human family battling with a world in which it receives no favors and gives no quarter.

From the viewpoint of both form and content, the masterpiece in S is the story of the Garden of Eden (Gen. 3), which incidentally has played an outstanding role in theological thought.[10] As a story, Gen. 3 is superb: it has dramatic suspense, vivid characterizations of each protagonist (including the serpent), excellent dialogue, and a nobly poetic diction in the divine curses against serpent, woman, and man. No other parts of S, as we know them today, can match it in literary distinction and dignity.

To speculate about the date of the sources of S would be idle, and even the editor's date can only be conjectural, for the only datable historical allusion (Gen. 36:31) may be redactional (R[s]) and is not perfectly clear. The eight kings of Edom ruled "before a king of the Children of Israel ruled" over either Israel or Edom, in other words, before either Saul or David (who conquered Edom). The difference is unimportant. If the list of the kings of Edom formed part of the S document, as seems certain, one would date the editor not earlier than Saul or David. In view of the rather archaic character of S, the most likely date is the time of Solomon in the tenth century.[11] Curiously, although Ezekiel and the Second Isaiah in the sixth century are acquainted with S (Ez. 28:1-19 alludes to the story of Eden and 32:27 to the giants; Is. 43:27 to Adam's sin), the Priestly Code early in the fifth century ignores it completely, unless P in Gen. 1-11 was written as a substitute for S. Conversely, the later strata of Deuteronomy (2:8-25; 29:23 [H. 29:22]) derive information from S (Gen. 14:2-8; 19:24 f.).

If S was written in Israel, its unfriendly attitude toward the tribes of Simeon, Levi, Reuben, and Judah and its silence about the tribes of North Israel can hardly be explained. The editor's philosophy and his religious attitude are totally at variance with those of Israel at any time of its history, and they are closely related to the teaching of the Book of Job, which is saturated with the wisdom of Edom if not of Edomitic origin. The geographical background of S, centered in Edom, and the friendly attitude toward Cain and his descendants (the Kenites) as well as

[10] In Ecclesiasticus (25:24) and in the Wisdom of Solomon (2:23 f.) death "entered into the world" as a result of the sin of Adam and Eve. Rabbinical Judaism taught the same doctrine, which is found in the first century of our era in IV Ezra 3:7, 21; 7:116-126 and in Syriac Baruch 23:4; 54:15. Whether Paul, who also taught this doctrine, believed that a sinful nature has been transmitted to mankind by Adam's Fall is not certain (Rom. 5:12-21); however, the doctrine of original sin became through Augustine an important teaching in the Western Church, and particularly in some Protestant churches.

[11] J. Morgenstern (HUCA XIV [1939] 94, n. 114) dates, however, "The J strata in Gen. 1-11" in the period 516-485 B.C.

toward Edom, the one nation about which genuinely historical information is given (in the list of early kings of Edom), confirm the Edomitic origin of S. Supplemented with S^2 (a Jewish midrash to it), S was incorporated into the Pentateuch after the insertion of P, not long before the final edition of the "Law of Moses" was issued about 400 B.C.

CHAPTER IV

THE E DOCUMENT

About the middle of the eighth century, during the reign of Jeroboam II (785-744), when the Northern Kingdom of Israel reached the acme of its power and prosperity before its end in 722, a Northern Israelite (possibly a priest of Bethel) composed an epic, similar to the J document. It is called the Elohistic (or E) document because of its use of *Elohim* (deity) for Jehovah (*Yahweh*) in the patriarchal stories, and frequently also after Moses, although the name Yahweh was revealed to Moses on Horeb. This use of Elohim was not due, as was true later on, to a deliberate avoidance of the name "Yahweh" lest it be profaned through abuse or unconscious disrespect. It was due to a vernacular usage: very likely, the priests of Bethel and other sanctuaries of Jehovah simply called their god "Elohim," i.e., the deity, God, in the same way as the appellatives "the King, the President, the Mayor" are currently used for proper names, when no ambiguity is possible.

Like J, E began its narrative with Abraham. The actual beginning of E, presumably telling how God called Abraham (cf. Gen. 20:13) from his home in "the land of the people of the East" (29:1), is lost; it is clear that E connected Abraham with the Eastern Bedouins rather than, as J did, with the Arameans in the North. The story of E, as we know it, opens after Abraham had come to Canaan, trusting in the divine promise. There, in a vision of the night, God renewed the promise of a glorious line of descendants (Gen. 15:1-3, 5 f., 11, 12a, 13 f., 16; the rest of the chapter is redactional, and even in these verses there is evidence of editorial rewriting).

At Gerar, Abraham's wife and half-sister Sarah was taken by Abimelech. However, he was restrained, through divine revelation in a dream, from committing adultery with her (20:1-17); Abraham and Abimelech made a covenant at Beersheba (explained as "well of the oath" [in J² as "well of the seven," 21:28-30], 21:22-24, 27, 31). After the birth of Isaac, Sarah asked Abraham to cast out his concubine Hagar and her son, Ishmael; Abraham did so after God had commanded him to hearken to Sarah's voice. An angel appeared to Hagar, and she found water in the wilderness (21:6a, 8-21). To test Abraham's faith (cf. 15:6), God ordered him to sacrifice Isaac but sent his angel to stop him when he was on the point of slaying the boy (22:1-13, 19; the rest of the chapter is redactional).

The E stories of Isaac's marriage with Rebekah, the birth of the twins, and how Jacob obtained the primogeniture belonging to Esau (see 24-27) are either lost or closely interwoven with J. It is only in Gen. 27 (the story of how Jacob obtained his father's blessing) that there is reason to believe E represents a substantial part of JE. E's story of Jacob's dream at Bethel was probably fuller than the J story now combined with it (E: 28:11 f., 17 f., 20-22). The story of Jacob's stay with Laban is imperfectly preserved (29:1, 15-18 [18-23, 25, 27, 28a, 30]; 30:1-3, 4b-8, 17-20a, 21, 22b-23, 26, 28 [31-35, 38-40, JE]).

Greatly enriched, through divine favor rather than his own cleverness (cf. 31:9), Jacob fled from Laban who, after being warned by God not to harm Jacob, made a covenant with him in spite of the fact that Rachel had stolen his *teraphim*[1] (31:2, 4-11, 13-17, 19, 24, 25a, 26, 28-31a, 32-35, 36b-37, 41-43; E[2]: 31:45, 47, 49 f., 54 f.; 32:1 f. [Engl. 31:55; 32:1 f. = H. 32:1-3]). Jacob then sent a present to Esau (32:13b-21; H. 32:14b-22) and fought with the angel at Penuel (32:23a, 24a, 25a, 26b, 27 f., 31 f.; H. 32:24a, etc.), and after a friendly meeting with his brother (fragmentary: 33:5, 11a), settled in Shechem (33:18aαb, 19 f.). From there he made a pilgrimage to Bethel (35:1-4, 6b-7, E[2]), where he buried Deborah (35:8) and poured a libation on the pillar of stone (35:14). At Ephrath, Rachel died giving birth to Benjamin (35:16-20).

In the Joseph stories, E is more explicit than J when showing God's hand and purpose in the adventures of the hero (45:5-8; 50:20). E relates how at the very beginning Joseph's rise to power was predicted in his dreams, which aroused the envy of his brothers (37:5a, 6-11 [12-18, JE], 19 f., 22, 24, 28aαb-30, 32-34a, 35b). Sold by Midianite merchants to Potiphar in Egypt (37:36), Joseph was assigned by his master to serve two royal eunuchs placed by Pharaoh in Potiphar's charge (40:2-3a, 4, 5a) and he interpreted their dreams correctly (40:6-15a, 16-23). As a result, he was called to explain Pharaoh's dreams, became second in power in the kingdom, and administered provisions during the famine (41; all E except traces of J in 41:14a, 21a, 29-31, 35b, 36b, 42a, 43b, 45b, 49, 54, 56a, 57; 41:46a is P).

When Joseph's brothers came to Egypt, he accused them of being spies, allowed them to go back to fetch Benjamin, keeping Simeon as hostage, and placed in their bags the money they had paid, so that they

---

[1] See M. Burrows, JAOS 57 (1937) 259-276. S. Smith, JTS (1932) 33-36. C. Gordon, *Biblical Archaeologist* 3 (1940) 5-7. The meaning of *teraphim* is still unknown (cf. G. F. Moore, *Judges* [International Critical Commentary], pp. 381 f.). The most plausible guess is that of W. R. Arnold (*Ephod and Ark*, p. 136. Cambridge, Mass., 1917) who is inclined to identify them with the sacred lots used in divination.

found it upon arrival at their home. Leaving Reuben as a hostage with Jacob, they returned at once to Egypt with Benjamin (42:1, 3, 4a, 8-26, 29-37, with possible traces of J; 43:12a, 13 f., 15aβb, 23b). At last Joseph made himself known to his brothers, who brought Jacob down to Egypt (45:1b, 3, 5aβb, 7a, 8, 9a, 13, 15-18, 20 [21], 24b, 25-27; 46:1b) after he had received a revelation in a vision of the night (46:2-5a). In Egypt, Jacob blessed Pharaoh (47:7) and, shortly before his death, Joseph with his sons Ephraim and Manasseh (48:1, 2a, 7-9, 11 f., 15 f., 20-22). Joseph made his brothers swear that when their descendants went to Canaan they would take his body along for burial there (50:15-26).

After subjecting the Israelites to forced labor, Pharaoh ordered the two Hebrew midwives to slay the male children at birth. But they contrived to deceive him (Ex. 1:11-12, 15-22). The infant Moses, found by Pharaoh's daughter in an ark on the bank of the Nile, was brought up by her (2: [1], 2-10). While pasturing the flocks of his father-in-law Jethro, Moses came to the sacred mountain Horeb, where he received a revelation of Jehovah (3:1, 4b, 6, [9-22]; 4:1-17, [21-23]). Moses took leave of Jethro, met his brother Aaron at the sacred mountain, and returned to Egypt (4:18, 20b, 27-31). When Moses and Aaron requested Pharaoh to allow the Israelites to go into the wilderness and celebrate a festival, he refused (5:3 f. and fragments in 5:6-19).

In the stories of the plagues of Egypt, E differs from J in attributing the miracles to the staff of Moses and in reporting growing concessions on the part of Pharaoh after each of the five (seven in J) plagues (7:15aβb, 17b, 20b; 8:25-27 [H. 8:21-23]; 9:22, 23a, 25a (35); 10:8 f., 11 (12-15), 20-27; 11:1-3; 12:35 f.). Finally, the Israelites were allowed to go and departed under the guidance of God (13:17-19). Moses divided the sea, the Israelites crossed, and the Egyptians pursuing them were drowned (14:[5-7], 15 f., 19a, 20a, 21a, 22a (23), 25a, 31). Miriam intoned the song, praising Jehovah for his deliverance (15:20 f.).

In the stories that follow (Ex. 16-18), J and E cannot be separated. Both seem to have included accounts of the provision of water and food (manna and quails) and of the battle against the Amalekites. Originally, the E document contained no laws. However, it did relate how Moses received from God the two tables of stone inscribed with the Decalogue (24:12 f., 18b; 31:18). Meanwhile, the people were celebrating an orgiastic festival at the foot of the mountain (32:5b, 6, 15-19a, 25-29); the rest of the chapter, containing the story of the golden calf, belongs to postexilic times [E²?].

Driven from the holy mountain of Horeb by an indignant deity (33, where an E kernel has been wholly rewritten by later redactors), the Israelites set forth for Kadesh, guided by the ark (Num. 10:33, 35 f.).[2]

---

[2] According to W. R. Arnold (*Ephod and Ark,* p. 139, n. 2), the formulae of Num. 10:35 f. are probably interpolated.

The stories of Taberah (11:1-3), of the appointment of the seventy elders (11:16 f., 24), of Eldad and Medad (11:25-30), and of the rebellion of Aaron and Miriam (12) seemingly belong to E² rather than to E. The J and E stories of the sending out of spies, supplemented with a P account, cannot be disentangled in Num. 13 f. The story of the rebellion of Dathan and Abiram (16:1b, 2a, 12-15, 25 f., 27b-34) is generally assigned to JE. Miriam died at Kadesh (20:1b). Moses failed to obtain permission to cross the territory of Edom (20:14-21; 20:19 f. may be a remnant of J). While circling the borders of Edom, the Israelites were attacked by snakes, and Moses made the brazen serpent (21:4b-9); they then continued their journey east of Moab (21:11b-15) and defeated Sihon king of the Amorites (21:21-25), and Og king of Bashan (21:33-35, JE).

The stories about Balaam are generally divided between J and E, although the poetic oracles contained therein were not composed by the authors of these documents (22:2-21, 35b-41; 23:1-30; 24:25, with minor omissions, are usually assigned to E). The Baal Peor incident seems to be JE (25:1-5), as also the allotment of Gad and Reuben's territory in Transjordania (32: [1-5], 16 f., 20-27, 34-41). Moses made Joshua his successor (Deut. 31:14 f., 23) and died in Moab, over against Peor (34:3, 5 f., 10, in part). The E story of the conquest of Canaan is told in the first half of the Book of Joshua.

Like the J author, the writer of the E document used the Canaanitic sanctuary legends and Israelitic traditions circulating orally in North Israel, but either intentionally or accidentally omitted the stories of Abraham at Hebron, which were typically Judean. Although there is no valid reason for doubting that the E author knew the J document,[3] since he clearly corrected the outspoken objectivity and crass humor of the earlier document, he used the oral tradition rather than J as his source. Thus, in some cases, he has preserved it in a purer form. E makes Abimelech king of Gerar (Gen. 20:2) not, with the glaring anachronism of J, king of the Philistines (26:1b), who in reality appeared in Palestine nearly a millennium after the time of Abraham. J's story of Abraham in Egypt (12:10-19) impresses one as being an invention of J: following the current tradition, E properly omits it. In connecting the Patriarchs with the Eastern Bedouins (29:1) rather than with the Arameans of distant Harran (as J did in 24), and in locating Laban's home not far from Gilead (in J, Laban overtook Jacob in Gilead after seven days, 31:22 f.; in E, after one day 31:24, 25a), E is more faithful to the oral tradition than J. Another instance of his fidelity is the retaining of Reuben (changed to Judah for patriotic reasons by J) as the brother who tried to save

---

[3] So B. Luther, in E. Meyer, *Die Israeliten und ihre Nachbarstämme*, p. 169, Halle, 1906. On the contrary, O. Procksch, *Die Elohimquelle*, pp. 305-307 (Leipzig, 1906), argues for the literary independence of E with respect to J.

Joseph and later became the spokesman of the brothers in pleading with Jacob (37:22; 42:37, E; contrast 37:26; 43:3; 44:16; 46:28, J).

Most of the traditions common to J and E were North Israelitic, more specifically Ephraimitic, in origin. The prominence of Joseph, his mother Rachel (more beloved than Leah), Shechem, and Bethel make this perfectly clear. As a patriotic Judean, the J author was not only inclined to emphasize Judah, he also omitted mention of Northern shrines with purely local significance, such as the tombs of Rachel (lovingly mentioned by E, Gen. 35:16-20; 48:7; cf. I Sam. 10:2; Jer. 31:15) and of the nurse Deborah (35:8, E). Likewise the graves of Joseph, Joshua, and Eleazar are mentioned only by E.

Since the author of E was unquestionably an Ephraimite, he had no occasion to make any changes in his Ephraimitic sources for nationalistic purposes. But even though Bethel, the great religious center of Ephraim, was presented both in the oral sources and in E as the holiest of shrines, the only one with a temple to which tithes were brought (Gen. 28:22), the role of Shechem, capital of Manasseh, was not minimized in E, and Manasseh's primogeniture was freely admitted (41:51). As a matter of fact, Ephraim in Canaan far surpassed Manasseh in territory and population. To explain this, the Ephraimitic tradition reversed the normal order and related that Jacob had blessed Ephraim before his older twin brother Manasseh. The E document considers this reversal as perfectly natural (48:20), but J found it puzzling enough to require an explanation (48: 13 f., 17-19).

A few of the differences in terminology between J and E are probably to be explained by the environment of their authors. We do not know enough about the dialectic characteristics of Hebrew in Judah and Ephraim to ascribe positively to them the differences in vocabulary and grammatical forms between J and E (for which see the books on the Hexateuch by Holzinger, and Carpenter and Harford),[4] although the linguistic differences must have exceeded in scope Ephraimitic peculiarities of pronunciation, one of which is attested in Judg. 12:6. It is likely, however, that such terms as "Canaanites" in J and "Amorites" in E rest on local usage, since the Amorites are first attested in the fourteenth century in the North. The same probably applies to "Sinai" in J and "Horeb" in E, for Horeb is the term used in the Elijah stories, known to have been written in North Israel (I Kings 19:8), although Sinai occurs in a northern poem (Deut. 33:2; in Judg. 5:5 "that is Sinai" is a gloss).

In the patriarchal stories the use of Jehovah (Yahweh) in J rests on the connection of the Judeans with the Kenites and Judah's acquaintance with this god before Moses and independent of him. Conversely, the

[4] The most conspicuous differences in vocabulary are the two words for "handmaid" (shifḥah, J; amah, E) and the two for "small" (saʻir, J; qaton, E).

Joseph tribes became acquainted with Jehovah through Moses in Egypt, and E preserves the Northern tradition according to which the name "Yahweh" was unknown to the Israelites before Moses.

The variations which J and E present in the reproduction of Ephraimitic traditions are not only to be explained, as has been seen, by the dissimilar interests of Judah and Ephraim, but also by the peculiar religious viewpoint and individuality of the authors of J and E.

Divergent views, current in Judah and Ephraim respectively, on how Jehovah became god of Israel have been noted. Other dissimilarities in the religious conceptions of the two documents reflect the convictions of the authors, at least in part. The J author disclosed his dislike for ritual acts of worship by omitting from the traditional stories all accounts of sacrifices—although incongruously preserving reports on the building of altars—and all mention of the sacred stone pillars (*maṣṣebôth*) in the shrines of Canaan, upon which libations of oil were poured (contrast Gen. 28:18; 35:14, E). Here the J author presaged the teaching of the reforming prophets, in preferring prayer to sacrifice as a means of communion with God. This attitude explains the omission of the beautiful story of the sacrifice of Isaac (Gen. 22:1-13, 19, E) in J.

Conversely, the interest in ritual, disclosed in E, is so pervasive that we may surmise its author was a priest, presumably at Bethel. E (or R^JE) explains in mythical terms why the eating of the ischial nerve was forbidden (Gen. 32:32 [H. 32:33]). Its priestly background appears in the reference to temples which exacted tithes (28:22) and stone pillars upon which libations of oil were poured (28:18; 35:14); as also in emphasis on the priestly functions of Moses (cf. G. Hölscher, *Die Propheten*, pp. 109 f. Leipzig, 1914) appearing in Ex. 19:14 f.; 24:6-8; 33:5 f. (though not intact, these texts contain an E kernel).

At the time E was written the priests of Bethel naturally regarded the attacks of Amos against the government and the ritual worship as seditious and heretical (Am. 7:10-13), and it is not surprising that no trace of the teachings of the reforming prophets can be detected in E. It is absurd to call E (and J) "prophetic" documents, as some have done. However, the prophets of the school of Elisha had given their active support to the bloody revolution of Jehu (II Kings 9:1-14; cf. I Kings 19:16), and such prophets were probably not unpopular during the reign of Jeroboam II, a descendant of Jehu. This explains why in spite of opposition to Amos, the priesthood in the time of Jeroboam II was not hostile to prophecy, which, at least since the time of Ahab, had become the recognized organ of divine revelation in place of the old priestly oracle by means of the "ark," or sacred box.

Moreover, this historical situation suggests a reason why the author of the E document invented an ark, not mentioned in his sources, for the time of Moses, but significantly enough, instead of describing it as the instrument of priestly divination, he called it a symbol of God's presence (Num. 10:33, 35 f., omitting "of the covenant" in v. 33). On the other hand, Abraham (Gen. 20:7), Miriam (Ex. 15:20), and Moses (if Deut. 34:10 is E) are called prophets in a laudatory sense and high praise of prophecy is expressed by Moses in Num. 11:25-29 (E or E²). The E story of Balaam (Num. 22-23) is also highly significant in this connection. Amos was not more representative of contemporary prophets than Luther of contemporary monks. Friendship for prophecy did not in the least imply acceptance of the ideas of Amos—quite the contrary.

Pride in national achievement, a sense of security and power, and the assurance of divine guidance which E has in common with J, are all in the sharpest possible contrast to the fiery denunciations of Amos and his proclamation of imminent, irretrievable, national ruin. In E, a prophet seems to be simply a person receiving divine revelations, usually through dreams and visions as in the case of Abraham, and directly in the unique case of Moses, who spoke mouth to mouth with the deity (Ex. 33:11; Deut. 34:10; cf. Num. 12:6-8, E or E²).

This distinction between Moses and ordinary mortals, totally foreign to J and heightened in D and P, has far-reaching effects in E. With painstaking consistency, the E author eliminated from his story all physical appearances of the deity to mortals, except to Moses alone. The anthropomorphic apparitions of God to the Patriarchs, current in the oral tradition and J, are discarded in E not, as is commonly believed, because of progress in theological thinking, but to place Moses in a class by himself. A truly spiritual conception of the deity would scarcely have tolerated the crass anthropomorphism that appears in E's story of Moses (Ex. 31:18b). Whenever possible, the deity reveals itself to men other than Moses in dreams and visions, as a rule in the nighttime (Gen. 15:1; 20:3, 6; 28:12; 31:11, 24; 46:2; Num. 22:9, 20, E; in J: Gen. 26:24; in 21:12; 22:1, E, the divine word probably also came in a dream; cf. in E the prophetic dreams in the Joseph stories). When God wished to communicate to mortals during their waking hours, he made use of an angel speaking from heaven (Gen. 21:17; 22:11, E).

Another characteristic difference between Moses and other men is that Moses alone is a miracle-worker. When God intervenes providentially to help other men, as in enriching Jacob at the expense of Laban (Gen. 31:7-16), he does not use supernatural means. With his wonderful rod, Moses, however, performs miracles. In E, the plagues of Egypt are not merely announced previously by Moses as in J, but produced instantly before Pharaoh by means of the rod (Ex. 7:20b; 9:23a; 10:12, 13a, 21 f.), with which he also divided the Red Sea (14:16), brought water out of the rock at Meribah (17:5 f.; Num. 20:11), and defeated Amalek (Ex.

17:8-13).[5] Other miracles performed by Moses without the rod include changing the bitter waters of Marah (Ex. 15:22-27, JE), healing the people through the brazen serpent (Num. 21:4b-9) and, through intercession, quenching the fire at Taberah (11:1-3) as well as cleansing Miriam of her leprosy (12:11-15, E or E[2]).

Thus, in E the character of Moses loses much of the historical reality typical of J. From the romantic story of his birth and childhood in Egypt (Ex. 2:2-10) to the account of how he was buried by Jehovah (Deut. 34:5 f.), the story of E is a collection of legends leading up to the conclusion: "And there arose not a prophet since in Israel like unto Moses, whom Jehovah knew face to face" (Deut. 34:10). The general impression of E's inferiority to J as a historical source for the life of Moses and for the conquest of Canaan is not weakened in the least by the topographical (Pithom and Raamses, Ex. 1:11) and chronological (Gen. 15:13; 29:18, 27; 31:41, 45:6) details, nor by added names of secondary characters such as the midwives Shiphrah and Puah (Ex. 1:15), Hur (17:10), Nadab and Abihu (24:1). Even Aaron and Miriam were unknown to J, and Jethro, father-in-law of Moses, was probably unnamed in the original text of J. In the patriarchal stories, E names Eliezer, Deborah, Potiphar, and others.

Such learned material is of doubtful historical value, but it confirms our surmise that the author of E was a priest. The chief interest of J was the achievement of Israel under the guidance of its god; that of E was rather the religious history of his people. It has been noted by many that E recognized three stages in the religious development: that of the kinsmen of Abraham (with "teraphim" in the house, Gen. 31:19b, 30, 32-35; cf. 35:2-4; Josh. 24:2, E[2]), that of Abraham, the prophet (20:7), and that of Moses, who was more than a prophet, to whom the divine name Yahweh was first revealed (Ex. 3:15).

In conformity with this scheme, Abraham and his descendants are idealized more than in J, and questionable actions in their career are justified as divine commands or otherwise made to appear innocent. Contrast, for instance, Gen. 20:1-17 (E) with 12:10-20 (J); 21:12 (E) with 16:6 (J); 31:5-16 (E) with 30: 37-43 (J); 42:13, 32 (E) with 44:20 (J). In these passages, in which he corrects J, the author of E takes pains to explain that Abraham did not lie when he said that Sarah was his sister, and did not dismiss Hagar because of Sarah's nagging but in obedience to a divine command; that Jacob did not acquire his wealth through clever tricks but through divine blessing; that Joseph's brothers did not

---

[5] The story of Ex. 4:1-4, in which the rod is changed into a snake, cannot be J, as many critics suppose; if it is not E, it must be E[2] (so O. Procksch, *Die Elohimquelle*, p. 64).

utter the blunt untruth that Joseph was dead, but used a vague expression, "he is not."[6]

E is distinguished from J in various hallmarks of professional concern, if not expertness, in priestly matters. Interest in the sacred institutions of Israel, a sense of progress in revelation culminating in Moses, research detectable in such details as names and numbers coupled with a fanciful reconstruction of history in accordance with religious tenets—these and other characteristics of E may be considered germs destined to develop into the theoretical and systematic outline of Israel's history down to the conquest of Canaan presented in the narrative portions of the Priestly Code (P).

Looking at the E document as a whole, we note that it lacks the epic scope, dramatic progress, and organic unity of J, without, however, being merely a collection of unrelated episodes like S. E has a definite plan, solid structure, logical arrangement of material, a symmetry and consistency of the whole which does not quite achieve the finished, living oneness of J. J is sculpture, E is architecture; J is like a river, E like a canal. The rational scaffolding has not been wholly removed from E's structure, although it is not as obtrusively manifest as in P. In a word, E's plan is systematic rather than organic.

E's language is classical Hebrew at its best, although subtly different from that of J. Similar to J in subject, in pride of national achievement, and in assurance of the glorious future of his nation under protection of its god, E nevertheless reflects a more advanced civilization, a more refined environment, a more thoughtful age. The style of E is less transparent, less spontaneous, less objective than that of J. It is more consciously artistic, although not yet rhetorical like the Deuteronomic prose, more deliberately musical, more delicately emotional. The subtle, elusive differences between the classicism in J and the romanticism in E may perhaps be compared to those between the *Iliad* and the *Odyssey*.

In E, the simplicity and nobility of J are lost to some degree. So are the vivid scenes depicted by J, the feeling for the charms of nature, and the delightful idylls near the wells at sunset. E is more detailed but less lucid, more prolix but less direct. One illustration may suffice:

And Jehovah said unto Jacob, Return unto the land of thy fathers, and to thy kindred; and I will be with thee.

Gen. 31:3 (J)

And the angel of God spake unto me in a dream (saying), Jacob; and I said, Here am I. And he said, . . . I am the God of Beth-el, where thou anointedst the pillar, where thou vowedst a vow unto me: now arise, get thee out from this land, and return unto the land of thy kindred.

Gen. 31:11-13 (E)

[6] In J (Gen. 37:26 f.), Joseph was sold into slavery by his brothers; in E, he was kidnaped by Midianites (37:22, 28a).

Occasionally, however, E is laconic to the point of obscurity. In Gen. 20:3-7, the author is so concerned with the moral issues at stake that he forgets to mention an essential point, namely, that Abimelech and his harem had been stricken with some disease (cf. 20:17). The necessary transitions are omitted in Ex. 10:20-24. The clause, "each one of us dreamed according to the interpretation of his dream" (Gen. 41:11b), is too concise for lucidity.

The characters in E are more prone to outbursts of joy and sorrow than those of J. Driven out by Abraham and weeping desperately in the wilderness, Hagar is a pathetic figure in E (Gen. 21:14-16). On the contrary, in J she is a valiant and proud Bedouin woman who rebels against humiliating treatment (16:4-7a, 11-14). In contrast with the callousness of Joseph's brothers selling Joseph to the Ishmaelites (37:25-27, J), Reuben gives expression to profound grief when he fails to find Joseph (37:29 f., E). The irritation of Leah and Rachel against their father (31:14-16), the remorse of Joseph's brothers (42:21 f.) and Joseph's uncontrollable tears (42:24; 45:15), Jacob's joy at hearing that Joseph is alive (45:26 f.)— these and other expressions of deep emotion are feelingly described by the author of E. His masterpiece is the story of Isaac's sacrifice (Gen. 22:1-13, 19). With admirable restraint but dramatic intensity and underlying pathos, the author paints a vivid picture of the scene with just enough concrete detail to make the reader feel the unexpressed anguish of a father preparing to slay his son in obedience to a divine command.

CHAPTER V

THE BOOK OF DEUTERONOMY

The expectations of a continued, uninterrupted prosperity and power for the kingdoms of Judah and Israel, which inspired the authors of J and E to write their proud epics, were not fulfilled. The rapid expansion of the Assyrian Empire, which began with Tiglath-pileser III (745-727 B.C.), swept away the Kingdom of Israel in 722 B.C. and reduced Judah, after it had been devastated by Sennacherib in 701, to the status of a vassal kingdom. The power of the Assyrian Empire in Western Asia was invincible until the death in 625 B.C. of Ashurbanipal (Sardanapalus; Asnapper in Ezra 4:10), the last great king of Assyria.

It was only through complete submission to Assyria that the Judean kings of this period (700-625) saved their kingdom from the fate of Samaria in 722. Manasseh (692-639), in particular, not only paid his tribute punctually, as we know from the inscriptions of Esarhaddon and of Ashurbanipal (cf. JBL 47 [1928] 185 f.) but, to strengthen the bond with Assyria and promote good relations with his suzerain, encouraged the introduction in Jerusalem of Assyrian culture, particularly the religious practices for which there is alone documentary evidence.[1] The "abominations" housed in the Temple of Jehovah at Jerusalem, according to Jeremiah (7:30), were principally Assyrian cult objects, such as the altars on the roof for the Babylonian astral deities (II Kings 23:12) and horses for the chariot (a throne on wheels) of the sun-god Shamash (23:11). The astral cults were popular among the masses (Zeph. 1:5; Jer. 8:2; 19:13; 32:29; cf. Jer. 7:18; 44:15-19); Ezekiel (8:14, 16) still refers to ceremonies in the Temple in honor of Tammuz and Shamash.

In paying their respects to the gods of the emperor, neither Manasseh nor his subjects had the slightest intention of forsaking the worship of Jehovah, their own god. The urgent appeals of the reforming prophets failed to convince them that Jehovah did not tolerate the worship of other gods, and their viewpoint was that of the Judeans who fled to Egypt after 586 (Jer. 44:15-30). This introduction of alien cults did not exclude a frantic effort to secure the favor of Jehovah who (as they believed) in his wrath had allowed his nation to come to grief.

What did Jehovah require of his worshipers? The people still answered

---

[1] Unless the "foreign apparel" of Zeph. 1:8 refers to Assyrian styles in dress.

"sacrifice"; the prophets said "rectitude" (the two opposite views are contrasted in Mic. 6:7 f.). Since ordinary sacrifices had not brought about desired results, many Judeans in those troubled days revived the long obsolete sacrifice of the first-born, believing that, by giving to the deity the most precious thing on earth, its wrath would be allayed. Accordingly, the first-born of both sexes were sacrificially slain and cremated (after the manner of the proposed offering of Isaac) in a shrine called Tophet, just outside Jerusalem in the valley of Hinnom.

This shrine was erected in honor of "Molech" (i.e., *mélech*, king: both *tapheth* [or *tephāth*] and *mélech* were read as *bosheth*, shame, and vocalized accordingly). Molech (or Moloch) is not an alien god, but Jehovah "the king" or "the (divine) ruler." Even if Ahaz (735-720) really "offered his son by fire" (II Kings 16:3), he did not inaugurate the abominable "Molech" rites which, whether instituted by Manasseh or not (the historicity of II Kings 21:6 is in doubt), flourished in the seventh century (Jer. 7:31; 19:6, 13; 32:35). Although officially abolished by Josiah in 621 (II Kings 23:10), this horrid cult was not extirpated at that time (Jer. 11:10-13; Ez. 16:20 f., 36; 20:16, 31; 23:27, 29; Lev. 18:21; 20:2a).

The policy of Manasseh and the superstitious practices of the masses called forth denunciations from the reforming prophets. Two types of religion, apparently irreconcilable, were offering a ray of hope to a despairing people. The aping of Assyrian fashions for political motives, and revival of the ancient barbaric rite of human sacrifice, which in civilized nations had survived only among the Phoenicians and Carthaginians, would in the long run have deprived Judah of that religious uniqueness which alone was to keep national feeling alive after the downfall of the state in 586.

But the teaching of the great prophets, beginning with Amos, was too revolutionary to make the slightest impression on the masses. The essence of all ancient religions, including that of Israel, was the acts of worship and particularly the various sacrifices. On the contrary, the prophets asserted that sacred ceremonies had no significance for a god who demanded unswerving devotion to the right. At the time when the nation, faced by a choice between the old religion of cult and the new one of conduct, had discarded the latter and was sinking rapidly into insignificance, a man inspired by the prophet's ideals but simultaneously well aware of the current trend and of practical possibilities, effected a compromise between the two antagonistic religions and thus became the founder of Judaism. This man was the author of the book of Moses found in the collection box of the Temple at Jerusalem in 621 B.C., a book which now forms the kernel of Deuteronomy.

The author of D, or the Deuteronomic Code, was a priest in Jerusalem upon whom the prophetic teaching had made a deep impression. He realized that an agreement between priests and prophets, representing the two types of religion contrasted in Mic. 6:7 f., could only be effected through mutual concessions. Unfortunate as it may seem, no religious reformation based on the highest principles has ever achieved success without making important concessions to the religion of the masses; every important church represents such a compromise.

In the case of the Deuteronomist, the spiritual religion and exacting morality of the prophets was codified in a series of concrete enactments. On the other hand, popular worship was sterilized of its heathen elements and given spiritual significance. Amos (5:24) had said, "Let judgment run down as waters, and righteousness as a mighty stream." The Deuteronomist, however, defines righteousness, which for Amos was merely a principle, as observing to do "all these commandments before Jehovah our God, as he has commanded us" (6:25). For the Deuteronomist, as for Hosea, love for God is the essence of true religion (Deut. 6:5), but this love consisted primarily in keeping the divine commandments, (7:9; 10:12 f.; 11:1, 13, 22; 19:9). The traditional ceremonies of the cult, such as festivals and sacrifices, were no longer to be regarded as a gift or tribute paid to God, but merely as the expression of religious feeling, particularly gratitude for God's blessings, and rejoicing (Deut. 5:15; 12:11 f., 18; 14:26; 16:1-15; 26:10 f.).

The author of D not only sensed precisely the form in which prophetic ideas could become acceptable, but he timed the appearance of his book to ensure it a favorable reception. During the reign of Manasseh, D would have been consigned to the flames, like Jeremiah's book later on (Jer. 36:23), for the desecration of Assyrian holy objects would have been considered an act of open insurrection by the imperial government during the height of its power. But the Scythian invasion (ca. 626 B.C.) reaching as far as the border of Egypt and threatening Judah without actually harming it, although Jeremiah (4:5-31; 5:15-17; 6:1-8, 22-26) had foreseen a complete devastation, broke down the power of the Assyrian Empire. When Ashurbanipal died (625), Assyria collapsed, coming to its end soon after the fall of Nineveh (612).

The reaction against Manasseh's religious policy, after his death, the downfall of Assyria, the revival of optimism in Judah after the unexpected deliverance from the Scythian scourge, and the burst of nationalism voiced in Nahum's ringing hymn of hatred against Assyria and, less sonorously but no less intensely, in the Deuteronomic Code (a nationalism which sent Josiah to his death at Megiddo in 609 and brought about the end of the kingdom in 586)—all these circumstances contributed to the success of the reformation of religion and national life advocated by the D author in the book which he contrived to have discovered in 621 B.C.

It has been tacitly assumed here that the "book of the *Torah*" found in the Temple in 621, upon which Josiah based his religious reformation (II Kings 22:3-23:25), was the bulk of Deuteronomy. This assumption, which is older than Jerome[2] and has generally been considered axiomatic by most critics since the time of De Wette, has recently been disputed by competent scholars.[3] But their arguments are not convincing. No other theory does justice to the facts so well as the view still generally held.

All measures which Josiah took after having pledged the elders and people by solemn covenant to keep Jehovah's commandments (II Kings 23:3, cf. Deut. 5:1-3; 7:12 f.; 8:18; 29:1 [H. 28:69]) were enforcements of prescriptions contained in Deuteronomy (and in most cases in no other codes of the Old Testament).[4] The only exception was II Kings 23:9 (contrast Deut. 18:6-8). Josiah removed from the Temple in Jerusalem the paraphernalia of the Assyrian cults; namely, the horses and chariot of the sun-god Shamash (II Kings 23:11) and the roof altars dedicated to the astral deities (23:12; cf. 23:5), according to Deut. 17:2-5 (cf. 4:19). The Asherah (a sacred wooden post) was burned in the Kidron valley (23:6) conforming with the order to destroy the Canaanitic pillars and posts (Deut. 12:3; 16:21); while the house of the hierodules was demolished (23:7; cf. Deut. 23:18 f.).

Josiah defiled Topheth, where first-born infants were sacrificed to Molech (23:10; cf. Deut. 12:31; 18:10; Lev. 18:21; 20:1-5), the shrines of foreign deities on the Mount of Olives (23:13; cf. Deut. 5:7; 6:14; 8:19; 11:16, 28; 13:2 f., 6-9, etc.), and all the "high places" of the kingdom, from Geba to Beersheba, where the Judeans offered sacrifice to Jehovah (23:8; cf. Deut. 12:2 f.).

But the desecration of Bethel and other shrines of "Samaria" related in a late redactional passage (23:15-20) can hardly be historical. After thus closing all sanctuaries of Jehovah within the Kingdom with the sole exception of the Temple at Jerusalem (according to the law of Deut. 12), Josiah brought the provincial priests to the capital (23:8). But it was patently impracticable for them to officiate at Jerusalem with the local priesthood (the sons of Zadok), as Deut. 18:6-8 had ordered. Josiah, however, allowed these dispossessed priests to "eat of the unleavened bread among their brethren" (23:9).

[2] Cf. E. Nestle, ZAW 22 (1902) 170 f. 312 f.
[3] For the vast literature on this subject, and discussion of the various theories, see A. R. Siebens, *L'origine du code deutéronomique*. Cf. also HTR 27 (1934) 308-310; O. Eissfeldt, *Einleitung in das Alte Testament*, pp. 188-191; J. A. Bewer, L. B. Paton, G. Dahl, "The Problem of Deuteronomy. A symposium," JBL 47 (1928) 305-379.
[4] Cf. Paton, JBL 47 (1928) 325 f., for a list of parallels between II Kings 22-23 and Deuteronomy.

Finally, Josiah "commanded all the people, saying, Keep the Passover unto Jehovah your god, as it is written in the book of this covenant" (23:21). The celebration of the Passover in conjunction with the Feast of Unleavened Bread as a national festival at the unique sanctuary ("in Jerusalem," 23:23) was unknown before the publication of the law of Deut. 16:1-8. Even the abolition of pagan divination and idolatry, which an editor adds to the list of Josiah's pious works (23:24), was definitely prescribed in Deut. 18:10b-12 (magic and divination, cf. Lev. 19:26b, 31; 20:6, 27) and 12:3; 16:22, cf. 5:8, etc. (idolatry).

If the account of Josiah's reforms is substantially historical, and the book found in the Temple has been preserved in the Pentateuch, parts of Deut. 5; 12; 16-18; 23 were included in that book; the consternation of Josiah, after hearing it read (II Kings 22:11), seems to indicate that at least some of the curses of Deut. 28 were part of it.[5] The canonical book of Deuteronomy represents the last stage of the long process of editing and supplementing the book of Josiah, and it attained its present form about 400 B.C., more than two centuries after D was found in the Temple. Modern research can hope to determine only approximately the original contents of D. Deuteronomy professes to contain the last exhortations of Moses to Israel, delivered in Moab shortly before the invasion of Canaan. Omitting the introductions to addresses and the narrative portions in 4:41-43; 10:6-9, 27, 31, 34, there are three distinct speeches (1:6-4:40; 5-26; 28; 29-30), each one of which has a special introduction (1:1-5; 4:44-49; 29:2 [H. 29:1]); the main address, 5-26; 28, is provided with a narrative ending in 29:1 (H. 28:69). In addition to the three speeches there are two poems (32; 33) which Moses recited before the people, according to the narrative introductions in 31:16-21 (31:22 and 32:44 are the *two* endings of the poem) and 33:1; the Blessing of Moses (33) is enclosed within a poetical framework (33:2-5, 26-29).

Deuteronomy 31-34 are miscellaneous appendices added in part when D was joined to JE in 550 and later supplemented. Deuteronomy 30:15-20 is the eloquent end of the last edition of D as a separate book outside the Pentateuch.

Deuteronomy 1-30 has more than one author: there is clear evidence of editorial rearrangement and addition. The collection of the special laws (12-26) is inserted into a framework (11:26-30; 27) which, even though accommodated to its context, originally refers not to the address of Moses in the plains of Moab but to the promulgation of the Law by

---

[5] As we have seen, some of Josiah's reforms could have been inspired by the Holiness Code (Lev. 17-26), but only in Deuteronomy is it clearly and repeatedly stated that Jehovah is to be worshiped exclusively in one place. The theory that the Holiness Code (H) was the book found in the Temple (G. R. Berry in JBL 39 [1920] 44-51) has not found favor among critics.

Joshua at Shechem (Josh. 8:30-35; 24:22-27). The tradition according to which Joshua inaugurated a covenant and published a law (presumably the Covenant Code) at Shechem circulated in the Northern Kingdom before 722 B.C. (E. Meyer [and B. Luther], *Die Israeliten und ihre Nachbarstämme,* pp. 542-555. H. Gressmann, ZAW N.F. 3 [1926] 308). Although we must seriously question the historical truth of this story, which is probably a legendary embellishment of the apparent Shechemite origin of the Ten Curses of Deut. 27 and of the Ritual Decalogue of Ex. 34 (cf. JBL 43 [1924] 309), it was not forgotten even after the publication of D. Unable to suppress it, a redactor found it necessary to subordinate this significant act of Joshua to the supreme work of Moses by means of the interpolations in Deut. 11:26-30 and 27. Going a step further, the Priestly Code later transferred all covenants and legislation to Sinai, disregarding entirely the covenant of Moses in the plains of Moab (D) and that of Joshua at Shechem. Consequently, the Covenant Code, which according to some critics occupied originally the place of D before the death of Moses (Deut. 34) but in reality was probably Joshua's legislation at Shechem (cf. HTR 23 [1931] 109), after being transmitted and edited for centuries outside the Pentateuch was finally inserted in Ex. 20:22-23:19 and thus artificially connected with the Sinaitic legislation divinely revealed to Moses.

The original introduction and conclusion of Deut. 12-26 are not intact. The introduction (4:44-11:25) is the result of successive additions and redactions: the original title of D may have been merely 4:44, and 4:45-49 may be editorial expansion (although a geographical indication like that of 1:5 must have stood after 4:44). The long historical digression about the revelation of the Decalogue and the sin of the Golden Calf (9:1-10:11, including two narrative interpolations, 10:6 f., 8 f.) does not belong to this context and should precede the historical recapitulation in 1:6-3:29, which takes up the story where 10:11 leaves off. It should be noted, however, that 9:1-10:5, 10 f. is in itself the product of successive amplifications: the historical narrative is taken from JE (including E²) as edited with notes by R^JE (*ca.* 650)[6] but also supplemented with midrashic references to the ark in 10:1-5, and with homiletic passages (9:1-6), prayers (9:25-29), and glosses, to the utter confusion of some parts of the text. Although expanded and annotated, 4:44-8:20; 10:12-11:25 belong substantially to D.

Aside from glosses (5:5; 7:22) and repetitions (11:18-21 repeats 6:6-9; 7:16, 25 f. repeats 7:1-5) contributed by the scribes, the editors of the Deuteronomic school, according to the characteristic procedure so obvious in the Deuteronomistic books of Judges and Kings, have supplied even

[6] Cf. JBL 43 (1924) 295 f.

small sections with introductions and conclusions.[7] The author of D had unquestionably used this system for his book as a whole and, as in the case of Hammurabi's Code more than a millennium before, provided a framework for his code of special laws in 12-26. To what extent the D author framed important individual sections of his book in similar manner is uncertain, but there is reason to doubt that he was entirely responsible for the introductions and conclusions now enclosing the Ten Commandments (5:1-5, 22-33 [H. 5:19-30]), the great summary of the law (6:1-3, 20-25; cf. 6:20 ff. with Ex. 12:26 f.; 13:14 f.), and the exhortation to gratitude in ch. 8 (8:1, 20). The present introduction and conclusion of the whole section 5-11 (4:45-49; 11:31 f.) if not completely editorial, have certainly been expanded; the same is true for the code of special laws itself (12:1; 26:12-15, notably the latter).

In D's third part, or peroration (28), later expansion is likewise obvious: the original series of blessings and curses ended clearly with the summing up in 28:45 f. and probably lacked 28:25-42, for, as L. Horst ("Etudes sur le Deutéronome," *Rev. de l'Hist. des Relig.* 16 [1887] 60; cf. 18 [1888] 328) first noticed, there is a close parallelism between blessings (28:1-14) and curses (28:15-24, 43-46). Three interpolations of postexilic date occur: 28:25-42 (28:26 is taken from Jer. 7:33; 28:32 f., 36 f. refer to the Exile); 28:47-57[8] (the siege and destruction of Jerusalem in 586, and the ensuing woes, are clearly depicted); and 28:58-68 (D is no longer the address of Moses but a *book*, presumably with canonical standing: 28:58, 61; cf. 29:20 f., 27 [H. 29:19 f., 26]; 30:10; 31:24, 26; contrast 17:18; 28:63-68 knows not only the Exile but also the Jewish dispersion).

The enlarged edition of D contained in Deut. 4:44-29:1 [H. 28:69] was provided with an additional introduction and conclusion by an editor who was interested in history. The introductory historical retrospect, as we have seen, probably began with Deut. 9:7-10:11 (with 9:1-6 as a homiletic prelude) summarizing the JE story of the revelation at Horeb and the Golden Calf, continuing in 1:6-3:29 with events following the departure from Horeb up to the arrival at Beth Peor in Moab, the time and place where Moses is speaking to the Israelites.

After the great address of Moses, the story is taken up again without a break in 31:1-8. The divine order to appoint Joshua as his successor (given in 3:28) is carried out by Moses in 31:7 f.; the style of 1-3 is very

[7] The Nash Papyrus (published by S. A. Cook in PSBA 25 [1903] 34-56; cf. A. S. Geden, *Outlines of Introduction to the Hebrew Bible*, pp. 57-59. Edinburgh, 1909), dated by W. F. Albright (JBL 56 [1937] 145-176) in the Maccabean period (165-37 B.C.) and by others in the second century A.D., as well as some manuscripts of the LXX, provide a brief introduction for the "Shema'" (Deut. 6:4). This text, which may have been omitted accidentally in the Masoretic Bible, is practically identical with Deut. 4:45.

[8] See W. A. Irwin, "An Objective criterion for the dating of Deuteronomy," AJSL 56 (1939) 337-349, particularly pp. 346 f.

similar to that of 31:1-8. On the other hand, 31:14 f., 23, in which Jehovah himself gives his instructions to Joshua, are by a different and probably earlier hand (E?). It is possible that the author of these historical résumés also composed 31:9-13, according to which Moses wrote the law, delivered it to the Levites and elders, and ordered them to read it to the people every seven years on the Feast of Tabernacles. The parallel account (31:24-27), coming later, is reminiscent of the glosses in 10:1-5: in 10, Moses places the tables of stone inside the ark, in 31 the Levites place there the book of the law.

The rest of Deut. 31 contains two introductions (31:16-21, 30; 31:24-27) and two conclusions (31:22; 32:44) for the Song of Moses in Deut. 32. Strangely enough, there is also an introduction (31:28 f.), with a conclusion in 32:45-47, for a missing address of Moses, which seems to have been displaced by his song (according to A. Dillmann, this address consisted of Deut. 4; 29 f. in their original form).

The historical framework contained in Deut. 9:1-10:11; 1-3; 31:1-13, although generally written in the typically homiletic Deuteronomistic style, is plainly the work of a later author (R^D?) probably living about the middle of the sixth century. He uses the J and E sources in late editions, although before their union with P: his chief sources are a Judean edition of E (E^2) and R^{JE}'s annotated combination of J and E. If the learned archaeological and topographical glosses in 1-3 (2:10-12, 20-23; 3:9-11, 13b-17) are not interpolated, this author draws information from S (Gen. 14:5 f.; cf. Deut. 29:23 [H. 29:22] which refers to Gen. 14:2, 8; 19:24 f.). The author contradicts certain of D's statements in attributing a friendly attitude to the Moabites (2:29; contrast 23:4 f.), and in declaring that the generation living at Horeb had died before Moses made his last speeches in Moab (1:35, 39; 2:16; contrast 5:3; 11:2-7).

This Deuteronomic historian is, in some respects, a forerunner of the Priestly author, even though his oratorical style (1:19-21, 30-31, etc.) is totally different from the dry and sober prose of P. The author of the historical retrospects in Deuteronomy devoted much attention to archaeological, topographical, chronological (2:14), and statistical details— matters of scholarship that have nothing to do with religion. Furthermore, three details of his narrative, for which JE had no parallel, are found in P: the *twelve* spies, one for each tribe (1:23; cf. Num. 13:2-17, P), the *seventy* souls that went down to Egypt with Jacob (10:22; cf. Gen. 46:27; Ex. 1:5, P), and the use of *acacia* wood in making the ark (10:3; cf. Ex. 25:10, P).

Another postexilic framework for D, hortatory in character and later than the historical one just considered, is found in 4:1-40; 29 f. Chapter 4 has no connection with the preceding ones but is a homiletic and theological commentary on ch. 5; 4:13, refers to the Ten Commandments, and

4:16-19, 23 f., 25-28 (cf. 29:17 f., 26 [H. 29:16 f., 25] 30:17) are an exposition of the First and Second Commandments (5:7-10); 4:10 agrees with 5:2-5 in saying that the hearers of the last speeches of Moses had witnessed the revelation at Horeb (in contrast with 1:35, 39; 2:16); as in 6:7, 20-25; 11:19, religion is something which can be learned and should be taught children (4:9 f.). But chs. 4 and 29 f. stress the intellectual element in religion far more than D: the principles of true religion are accessible in a book (29:20 f., 27 [H. 29:19 f., 26] 30:10); nothing should be added to or detracted from the words of Moses (4:2).

It is even more significant that, according to 4:6, the law of Moses constitutes the peculiar wisdom of the Israelites (cf. Ezra 7:25), a notion which became commonplace in Judaism after Ben Sira (Ecclus. 24) early in the second century B.C.[9] The influence of the wisdom literature on these chapters is notable: in 29:29 (H. 29:28) the author distinguishes the metaphysical wisdom of Job 28, known only to God, from the revealed wisdom of Prov. 8, which consists in fulfilling the law; the latter is neither hidden nor remote, neither in heaven nor beyond the sea (like the inaccessible wisdom of Job 28, which is in no part of the world) but near at hand (30:11-14). In his theology, this author follows Second Isaiah (Is. 40-55, ca. 540 B.C.) who, by combining the conception of God in non-Israelitic wisdom (as presented in Job) with that of the prophets, had attained real monotheism (cf. JBL 46 [1927] 193-206). Following the Second Isaiah, he declares that Jehovah is the creator of man (4:32, an echo of Is. 45:12; note the use of the verb bārā', to create, which occurs first in the Old Testament in Ps. 104:30, in Ez. 21; 28, and in Second Isaiah (19 times in Is. 40-65); only later in P (11 times in Gen. 1-6 and elsewhere; never in Job) and that there is no god beside him (4:35, 39; cf. Is. 44:6, 8; 45:5 f., 14, 21 f.). The gods of the nations are the heavenly bodies (4:19, cf. 32:8) or mere idols of wood and stone (4:28; 29:17 [H. 29:16]; cf. 28:36, 64; cf. Is. 44:15-17, 19; 45:20) that "neither see, nor hear, nor eat, nor smell" (4:28).

In regard to the good life, the doctrine of the two ways (Jer. 21:8 calls them the way of life and the way of death), which in its national application (Deut. 28) was implicit in D, is clearly formulated in 30:15-20. Applied to the individual, the doctrine became pervasive in the Book of Proverbs. The Deuteronomic philosophy of history (most clearly set forth in Judg. 2:7-23), with its rhythm of righteousness-prosperity and wickedness-ruin, is not unfamiliar to our author. The punishment of the Exile (4:25-28; 29:15-28 [H. 29:14-27]) is followed, after true repentance, by a national restoration (4:29-31; 30:1-14). These allu-

---

[9] See G. F. Moore, *Judaism* (Cambridge, Mass., 1927) Vol. I, pp. 263-266. J. Fichtner, *Die altorientalische Weisheit in ihrer israelitisch-jüdischen Ausprägung*, pp. 79-97 Giessen, 1933.

sions to the historical situation (note also references to the Jewish dispersion in 4:27; 30:3 f.) fall logically into the period 500-450, thus confirming a date later than Second Isaiah indicated by their theological point of view.

In conclusion, our Book of Deuteronomy represents the final result of a series of editorial expansions beginning in 621 and ending about 400 B.C. Leaving out of account the miscellaneous appendices in Deut. 31-34 and reserving for a later analysis the code of special laws in 12-26, we may summarize this editorial process in its main lines as follows:

1. The edition of 621 (D in its original form): Introduction (4:44-8:20; 10:12-11:25); Special Laws (12-26); Conclusion (28:1-24, 43-46; 29:1 [H. 28:69]).

2. The edition of 600-550: addition of 11:26-30; 27, preparing for Joshua's covenant and legislation at Shechem.

3. The edition of *ca.* 550 (R^D): Historical Introduction (9:1-10:11; 1:6-3:29) and Conclusion (31:1-13).

4. The edition of 500-450: Introduction (4:1-40) and Conclusion (29:2-30:20 [H. 29:1-30:20]), in which the Law is identified with wisdom.

The latter incorporates an earlier section (30:15-20), which eloquently closed the last edition of D as a separate book (*ca.* 550).

5. Redactional: 1:1-5; 4:41-43; 11:31 f.; etc.

CHAPTER VI

THE PRIESTLY CODE (P)

~~~~~~

The Priestly Code is a fifth century midrash, or historical commentary, on the embryonic Pentateuch (JED), including a series of narratives often illustrating legal precedents, and a codification of ritual laws based on earlier codes. Reserving treatment of the legislation of the P Code for a later chapter, we will consider here only the narrative portions of this learned *corpus* without noting their occasional juristic purport. The contents of P may be summarized as follows:

1. From the Creation to Noah. *a.* "This is the genealogy of heaven and earth, when they were created" (Gen. 2:4a) is the misplaced title (supplemented with the gloss in 2:4b) which belongs at the beginning of the account of the creation of the world in six days (1:1-2:3). *b.* "This is the document of the genealogy of Adam" (5:1a): a list of the eight first-born descendants of Seth, son of Adam, with exact chronology of their fantastically long lives, ending with the three sons of Noah (5:1b-28, 30-32, reading "Noah" instead of "a son" in 5:28; cf. the story of the descendants of Cain in 4:17-22, S).

2. From Noah to Abraham. *a.* "This is the genealogy of Noah" (6:9aα) is the title of the story of the Flood (6:9-22; 7:6, 11, 13-16a, 17a, 18-21, 24; 8:1-2a, 3b-5, 13a, 14-19; 9:1-17, 28 f.). *b.* "And this is the genealogy of the sons of Noah: Shem, Ham, and Japheth" (10:1a) is the title of the table of the nations of mankind, classified as "The sons of Japheth" (10:2-5), "The sons of Ham" (10:6 f., 20), "The sons of Shem" (10:22 f., 31): they are the nations that populated the earth after the Flood (10:32). *c.* "This is the genealogy of Shem" (11:10aα) introduces the list of the first-born descendants of Shem, ending with the sons of Terah: Abram, Nahor, and Haran (11:10-26).

3. From Abraham to Moses. *a.* "And this is the genealogy of Terah" (11:27aα) introduces the story of the journey of Terah and his family from Ur of the Chaldees to Haran (11:27, 31 f.). *b.* Abraham and Lot (12:4b-5; 13:6, 11b-12); the birth of Ishmael (16:1a, 3, 15 f.). *c.* God's covenant with Abraham (17:1-8), the institution of circumcision (17:9-14), the prophecy concerning Isaac and Ishmael (17:15-22), and the circumcision of all males in Abraham's household (17:23-27). *d.* The deliverance of Lot (19:29). *e.* The birth of Isaac (21:1b, 2b-5). *f.* The

death and burial of Sarah (23:1-20) and of Abraham (25:7-11a). *g.* "And this is the genealogy of Ishmael . . ." (25:12) introduces a list of twelve Arabian tribes and localities, "sons of Ishmael," and a résumé of the latter's life (25:13-17). *h.* "And this is the genealogy of Isaac, son of Abraham" (25:19a) introduces a few data about Isaac and his family (25:19b-20, 26b). *i.* Esau (26:34 f.). *j.* Jacob (27:46-28:9; 29:24, 28b-29; 30:4a, 9b, 22a; 31:18aβb; 33:18aβ; 35:6a, 9-13, 15, 22b-29; 37:1). *k.* "And this is the genealogy of Esau (i.e., Edom)" (36:1) introduces the list of his sons born in Canaan (36:2-5), an account of his migration to Seir (36:6-8), and a list of the chiefs of Edom (36:40-43). *l.* ("This is the genealogy of Jacob," 37:2aα): Joseph (37:[1]-2; 41:46a). *m.* The Children of Israel in Egypt (46:6 f.; the list of the "seventy souls" of the house of Jacob in 46:8-27 is secondary in P, cf. Ex. 1:1-5; Gen. 47-5b [LXX], 6a, 8-11, 27b-28). *n.* The blessings of Jacob; his death and burial (48:3-6, [7]; 49:1a, 28b-33aαb; 50:12 f.).

4. <u>Moses and Joshua</u>. *a.* The oppression of the Children of Israel in Egypt (Ex. 1:1-5, 7aαb, 13-14aα; 2:23aβb-25). *b.* Jehovah's revelation to Moses 6:2-12, [13, 28-30]). *c.* "These are the heads of their fathers' houses" (6:14a), i.e., the sons of Reuben (6:14), the sons of Simeon (6:15), and the sons of Levi (6:16-27; 6:13-30 is secondary in P). *d.* Jehovah's instructions to Moses and Aaron (7:1-13). *e.* The plagues of Egypt (7:19-20aα, 21b-22; 8:5-7, 15-19 [H. 8:1-3, 11-16]; 9:8-12; 11:9 f.). *f.* The institution of the Passover and the Exodus (12:1-28, 40-51; 13:1 f., 20; 14:1 f., 4, 8 f., 10bβ; and, in part, 14:15-18, 21-23, 26-29). *g.* The manna (16:1-36, for the most part). *h.* The journey to Sinai (17:1abα; 19:2a). *i.* The revelation to Moses on Sinai (24:15b-18a): instructions for making the Tabernacle (25:1-31:17), the divine glory reflected by the face of Moses (34:29-35, Ps), and the making of the Tabernacle (35-40, Ps). *j.* The Sinaitic Levitical legislation: the sacrifices (Lev. 1-7), the priest-hood (8-10), the purifications (11-15), the Day of Atonement (16), the Holiness Code (17-26), the vows and tithes (27). *k.* The organization of the camp as the foot of Sinai, including miscellaneous legislation (Num. 1:1-10:10, mostly Ps). *l.* The departure from Sinai (10:11 f., P; 10:13-28, Ps). *m.* The sending out of the spies and their depressing report on Canaan (13:1-17a, 21, 25-26a, 32abα; 14:1a, 2, 5-7, 10; and, for the most part, 14:26-38). *n.* Miscellaneous laws (15:1-41). *o.* The rebellion of Korah (16:1a, 2aβb, 3-11, 16-24, 27a, 35-50; 17:1-13 [H. 16:36-17:28]; P, Ps, and RP). *p.* Prerogatives of priests and Levites (18:1-32). *q.* Purification through the ashes of a red heifer (19:1-22, Ps). *r.* The miraculous waters of Meribah at Kadesh (20:1aα, 2, 3b-4, 6-8a [omitting "take the rod"], 10, 11bβ, 12 f.); death of Aaron on Mount Hor (20:22-29); itinerary (21:4a, 10-11a; 22:1). *s.* In the plains of Moab: Phinehas kills an Israelite and a Midianite woman (25:6-18, Ps); the second census (26:1-65 [H. 25:19-

26:65], Ps); precedent for the inheritance of daughters (27:1-11, Ps); divine announcement of the death of Moses and appointment of Joshua (27:12-23, Ps); miscellaneous laws (28:1-30:16 [H. 30:17], Ps). *t.* War with Midianites (31, Ps). *u.* Allotment of the Transjordanic territory (32:1a, 2b, 4a, 6-15, 18 f., 28-33, mostly Ps); Moses writes the itinerary of the Israelites in the desert (33:1-49, Ps for the most part); instructions for the allotment of the land of Canaan (33:50-34:29, Ps) and provision of cities of refuge (35, Ps); supplement to the regulation of the inheritance of daughters in 27:1-11 (36, Ps). *v.* The death of Moses (Deut. 32:48-52; 34:1-4 [in part], 7-9). *w.* The conquest of Canaan (Josh. 4:10, 16, 19; 5:10-12 [with glosses]; 9:15b, 17-21, 27a [in part redactional]). The list of the 31 kings whose lands Israel occupied (12:1-24) seems to belong, at least in its second part, to P. *x.* The partition of the land among the tribes of Israel (13:15-33; 14:1 f., [3-5]; 15:1-12, 20-62; 16:4-8; 17:1-6 [partly secondary]; 18:1-28; 19:1-51 [expanded]; 20:1-21:42; 22:9-34 [Ps]).

1. God and His Holy Congregation

This bare outline of the contents of the Priestly Code, including both its oldest parts (P) and later accretions (Ps), shows that it is a skeleton history of the origin of the chosen people and their sacred institutions, beginning with the creation of the world and ending with the settlement in Canaan. At the same time, it is a juristic codification of its ritual laws. Reserving the analysis of the legal portions of P and Ps for a later chapter, we must note that, although the compilation of the Priestly Code was based on a great variety of sources, both historical and juristic, the selection and treatment of the material as a whole was dictated by the same fundamental principles. The purely historical sections, the strictly legal parts, and the stories which purport to have the validity of legal precedents, whether belonging to P or to Ps, in spite of notable differences in detail, have the same purpose and point of view.

As will be shown more fully in dealing with the legislation of P and Ps, during the fifth century, when the Persian Empire allowed the Jews every opportunity for religious development and organization but tolerated no attempts to regain political independence, the compilers set out to make a holy nation of the Jews, a church within the empire, a Kingdom of God realized not in a future Messianic age, but in the present. More realistic than the apocalyptic dreamers of the time, whose expectation of a divinely promulgated Jewish Empire brought them at times into conflict with the civil authorities, the Priestly authors, like the Pharisees later, carefully avoided interference with the civil administration. They succeeded in creating for the Jews the kind of theocratic state which could cause no uneasiness to foreign rulers.

In principle, the P Code made of the Jews a sort of monastic order, living in the world but apart from outsiders and under their own rules, theoretically impervious to political vicissitudes. The legal sections of P and Pˢ formulate the constitution and statutes of this theocratic state; the historical parts describe the steps by which God brought it into being in the days of Moses and Joshua.

The aim of the Priestly Code is to show how the only God in existence became the invisible sovereign of the Jewish community. From the moment when God created heaven and earth, his one purpose, according to P, was to separate Israel from the other nations, reveal his Law, give his covenant, and provide a country for it. In other words, the Priestly Code is just as dogmatic and detached from reality as the apocalypses. The only difference is that, whereas the apocalypses dreamt of a political Kingdom of God in the age to come, the Priestly Code dreamt of a purely ritualistic ideal Kingdom of God, belonging to the dim past.

In practice, however, the exact pattern of the theocratic state, presented by P as an ideal to be realized at once, in every detail, had a far greater influence on the life of the Jews than the visionary expectations for the future, which on the whole were to become real through miraculous intervention of God in human affairs, whenever the situation of the Jews became intolerable. The first Utopia was, after all, a program of life within the realm of possibilities, whereas the other was a dream which only God could fulfill in supernatural manner. The first was in essence the Jerusalem of the fifth century, the second was the heavenly Jerusalem, far more wonderful but quite beyond human reach.

It seems that both Utopias, the one normative Judaism strove to put into practice and the one to be realized in a Messianic era, had their roots in the plan of restoration of Ezekiel 40-48, which combined practical suggestions and chimerical dreams at the same time. Ezekiel was the fountainhead of both legalism and apocalypse. Augustine, similarly, was "the father of the Roman Church and of the Reformation" (A. Harnack): in his prayer *da quod iubes, et jube quod vis* he, like Ezekiel, joins together the concepts of divine help and divine law. *Jube quod vis* (command what you wish) is entirely in the spirit of the Priestly Code, in which God is conceived primarily as the invisible ruler of man and the universe.

The Priestly Code could be given the title of Augustine's greatest work, *The City of God (De civitate Dei)*, for both books depict the rising of a spiritual commonwealth on the ruins of the old order; both are philosophies of history, rather than history, which exercised an incalculable influence not only on their times but on later centuries. Even though some of the characters in P's story, like Moses, are genuine, the work as a whole is dogmatic rather than historical. It is an account of the establishment of an imaginary Utopia, planned and organized by God, on this earth. This ideal commonwealth, like the earthly ones, has a sovereign, a people, a country, and a body of laws.

The supreme and absolute sovereign of the ideal Jewish Commonwealth is God, the one and only god in existence. This conception of God in P combines, somewhat illogically, three distinct notions: the God of Israel, as conceived by Moses and Deborah, and of Canaan; the international God of justice proclaimed by Amos, fulfilling his plans in human history; and the creator of heaven and earth, the source of all life (Job, Ps. 104). More directly, the Priestly authors were indebted for their theology to the Second Isaiah, who had identified the lord of the physical world with the lord of history and thus came to the conclusion that there was no other god in existence besides Jehovah (cf. JBL 46 [1927] 193-206). Nevertheless, Ezekiel's notion of the holiness of God was also decisive in its influence on P. It cannot be gainsaid, however, that the Priestly authors molded a synthesis out of these originally distinct conceptions, bequeathing to later generations the noblest conception of God in the Old Testament, the one nearest to that of modern Christian theologians.

This lofty point of view of P appears clearly in the contrast between Gen. 2 (S), with its God strolling through the Garden in the cool of the evening, and Gen. 1 (P), with a transcendental deity creating the world by divine fiat. The theological progress between these two chapters, which are contiguous in Genesis but separated by nearly five centuries in time, is due, on the one hand, to the contributions of the Reforming Prophets (notably Amos) and the Deuteronomic Code and, on the other, to the teachings of sages indebted directly (Ps. 104) and indirectly (Job) to the wisdom literature of the Egyptians. The P account of the Creation (Gen. 2:4a [b]; 1:1-2:3) is based on an earlier version. There is an obvious discrepancy between the source utilized by P, probably a non-Israelitic mythological poem, and his own philosophy. As early as 1798, K. D. Ilgen (*Urkunden des Jerusalemischen Tempelarchivs*, pp. 433 f.) noted this discrepancy between the eight creative acts and the six days in which they were performed.[1]

Without attempting to reconstruct the original version, some of its characteristics may be noted. The chaos (*tōhû wābōhû*, "waste and void," 1:2), the primeval ocean (*tehôm*, 1:2), and darkness (1:2) were not

[1] See on Gen. 1: K. Budde, *Die Biblische Urgeschichte*, pp. 470-492 (Giessen, 1883). J. Wellhausen, *Die Composition des Hexateuchs*, pp. 186 ff. (Berlin, 1885; 2nd ed., 1889); *Prolegomena*, pp. 295-297 (6th ed., Berlin, 1905). B. Stade, *Biblische Theologie des Alten Testaments*, pp. 349 (Tübingen, 1905). H. Gunkel, *Genesis*, pp. 116-131 (Göttinger Handkommentar; 3rd ed., 1910). K. Budde, "Wortlaut und Werden der ersten Schöpfungsgeschichte," ZAW 35 (1915) 65-97. J. Morgenstern, "The Sources of the Creation Story—Gen. 1, 1-2, 4," AJSL 36 (1920) 169-212. W. E. Barnes, "Who Wrote the First Chapter of Genesis?" *Expositor* 22 (1921) 401-411. G. von Rad, *Die Priesterschrift im Hexateuch* (BWANT IV, 13). Stuttgart, 1934.

created by the deity, but existed before the work of creation began. Over this chaotic liquid mass, the *rudis indigestaque moles* of Ovid (*Metamorphoses* 1:7), the spirit of the deity brooded like a bird on an egg (1:2b). Similarly, in the Phoenician cosmology attributed to Sanchuniathon by Philo Byblius (quoted by Eusebius, *Praeparatio Evangelica* 1:10; text in C. Müller, *Fragmenta historicorum graecorum,* Vol. III, p. 565) from the union of the primeval "Spirit" and "Chaos"—a union which is called "Desire"—there arose "Mot," the cosmic egg from which, after it was divided into heaven and earth, sprang all things.[2]

The work of creation consisted of eight distinct acts—nine, if the creation of man at the end is separated from that of animals; ten, if vegetation is considered a separate act. In the first four works, God made the elements; in the last four their respective inhabitants. God separated light from darkness (1:4b; cf. Job 38:19 f.); he made the firmament to separate the upper from the lower waters (1:7; cf. Ps. 104:2b-3a; Job 37:18); he collected the waters below the firmament in their gathering place so that the dry land appeared (1:9 in the LXX; cf. Ps. 104:5-9; Job 38:4-11) and brought forth vegetation (1:12; cf. Ps. 104:14-16). Thus out of chaos, by separating elements previously in utter confusion, God made the four parts of the world: light, firmament, seas, and land.

In every part of the world God now placed appropriate inhabitants. The dwellers of light are the heavenly bodies attached to the firmament. They are conceived as divine beings (cf. Job 38:7; Ps. 19:4-6 [H. 19:5-7]): they rule (cf. Job 38:33) respectively over the day (the great luminary, i.e., the sun) and over the night (the small luminary, i.e., the moon) (1:16-18, in part; cf. Ps. 104:19). The air below the firmament he populated with birds, and the seas with marine animals and mythical dragons (1:20-22, in part; cf. Ps. 104:12, 17, 25 f.). Finally, the earth brought forth living creatures: God made wild animals, cattle, reptiles (1:24 f.), and finally man (1:26 f.).

The expression "Let us make man in our own image," (1:26; cf. 1:27; 5:1, 3; 9:6) is doubly archaic: it presupposes, as Philo (*De Opificio Mundi* I, 24 [I, 16-17M]) already recognized, the presence of other divine beings besides the Creator; and it conceives of God in the form of a human being. Equally archaic is the conception of a golden age, similar to that pictured in the story of the Garden of Eden, when men and animals were exclusively vegetarian (1:29 f.); in P, the eating of meat begins after the Deluge (9:1-5), although the distinction between pure and impure animals was not known before the revelation to Moses.

The Priestly authors of the story of creation in Gen. 1:1-2:4 re-edited this old mythical account without eliminating all matter incongruous

---

[2] On the cosmic egg in Greek mythology see O. Gruppe, *Griechische Mythologie,* Vol. I, pp. 420 ff. München, 1906.

with their own views, but injecting into the final redaction the tenets of Judaism. Owing to conflicting interpretations of 1:1, it is debatable whether the deity in P created the world *ex nihilo*, out of nothing (see Philo, *De creat. princ.*, 7 [II, 367M], and perhaps II Macc. 7:28) or from existing materials (as in Wisd. of Sol. 11:17). In either case, God's absolute sway over all that exists and his transcendent exaltation over the works of creation are taken for granted. God brought the world into being "not with hands, not with labor, nor needing any collaborators" (Josephus, *Against Apion* 2:22 [§192]), but by fiat. "By the word of the Lord were the heavens made; and all the host of them by the breath of his mouth. . . . For he spoke, and it came into being; he commanded, and there it stood" (Ps. 33:6, 9). "Through ten words [i.e. Gen. 1:3, 6, 9, 11, 14, 20, 22, 24, 26, 28, 29] was the world created" (*Sayings of the Fathers* [*Aboth*] 5:1).

The notion that the Creator of the world was not a vanquisher of dragons, as in the Babylonian myth, nor yet an artificer, as in the substratum of Gen. 1 and in Gen 2, but a spiritual being creating by his word alone, became normative in Judaism (cf. G. F. Moore, *Judaism*, Vol. I, pp. 382, 415), Christianity (Rom. 4:17; II Cor. 4:6; Hebr. 11:3, etc.), and Islam (Koran 2:111) through the teaching of the Priestly authors in Gen. 1. Although they gave its classical formulation to this doctrine, they did not originate it. They obviously derived it from the Second Isaiah (cf. Is. 41:4; 44:26; 45:12; 48:13 f.), from whom they obtained their conception of God in general. In turn the Second Isaiah had read in Job 38:11 that God had confined *through his word* the primeval ocean within its bounds (cf. Is. 44:27; 50:2). It remains doubtful whether the author of the Book of Job was familiar with those vague allusions to the creation by fiat which have been discovered in the ancient writings of Egypt (cf. A. Erman, *Die Religion der Ägypter*, p. 92, n. 1. Berlin, 1934) and Babylonia (cf. M. Jastrow, Jr., *Hebrew and Babylonian Traditions*, pp. 122 f. [New York, 1914] and the Hymn to the god Sin, in R. W. Rogers, *Cuneiform Parallels to the Old Testament*, pp. 141-147. New York, 1912).

From the Second Isaiah, the Priestly authors also derived the verb "to create" (*bārā'*), used exclusively of divine effortless activity. For the word does not occur in the Old Testament before the Second Isaiah; Ex. 34:10 and Num. 16:30, where the word has another connotation, cannot be attributed to J, and are hardly earlier than 550 B.C. It is significant that the word is not used in Job. The substratum of P in Gen. 1 seems to have used either a definite word, such as "to divide," or, in general, the verb "to make."

In addition to a more exalted conception of the deity, the Priestly authors contributed to the old account of creation the connection of Jewish festivals with the works of God. One purpose of the luminaries in the firmament was to fix the calendar, in particular the sacred seasons of the Jews (1:14; cf. Ps. 104:19a). By compressing the eight creative acts of the original document into six days of twenty-four hours each, the authors were able to give to the Sabbath a cosmic primeval origin— the resting of God on the seventh day (2:1-3; cf. Ex. 20:11; 31:17). Unaccountably, in 2:2a God finished his work on the seventh, not on the sixth day; the Samaritan text, the LXX, and the Syriac correct the text and read "sixth." The arrangement into six days is shown below in tabular form.[3]

Creative Acts	Days	Elements	Creative Acts	Days	Inhabitants
1	1	Light	5	4	Luminaries
2	2	Firmament	6	5	Birds
3	3	Seas	7	5	Fishes
4	3	Land, vegetation	8	6	Animals, man

By this arrangement in six days, P spoiled the correlation between the elements and their respective inhabitants which was obvious in the earlier document. He joined together the third and fourth elements, and the inhabitants of the second and third. Perhaps he failed to notice the intended correlation, but in any case he regarded it as less significant than the institution of the Sabbath. Inconsistently, in Ex. 31:12-17 the Sabbath is revealed to Moses as an eternal sign between God and the Children of Israel. The detailed instructions in Ex. 16 concerning the gathering of the manna on the first six days of the week seem to indicate that, according to P, men did not observe the Sabbath before the revelation to Moses, although God had instituted it at the time of creation. When the shining glory of God was manifested to Moses on the seventh day, after it had been hidden by a cloud for six days (Ex. 24:15b-18a), God sanctified the seventh day again, as he had done after the creation of the world.

In the majestic proemium to P in Gen. 1, the Priestly authors have not only set the stage for what is to follow, but furnished an account of the origin of the world that is both scientific and religious. In harmony with the most advanced scientific thought of their day, as expounded poetically in Job, these authors conceived "heaven and earth" quite differently from modern astronomers. It is idle to look for any foreknowledge of the geological and biological discoveries of our day, and to regard, as many have done, the six "days" as six geological epochs. Nor does it seem per-

[3] U. Cassuto, "La creazione del mondo nella Genesi" (*Annuario di Studi Ebraici* I [1935, for 1934] 9-47), has attempted to show that the creative acts described in Gen. 1 are the six following: 1. Light; 2. Seas and heaven; 3. Earth with vegetation; 4. Heavenly bodies; 5. Fishes and birds; 6. Terrestrial animals and man. He concludes that the arrangement in six days was not an afterthought but an integral part of the original account.

tinent and sensible to interpret those lapidary words, " 'Let there be light!' And there was light" in the sense that God's word could make the electrons rotate within the atom and thus produce in the ether the light waves (E. König, *Theologie des Alten Testaments*, p. 204. 3rd-4th ed. Stuttgart, 1923).

But whereas the views about the world in Gen. 1 are essentially those of a science now obsolete, the spirit animating the writers is religious rather than scientific. Profoundly religious is the thought that the Creator, exalted above all limitations and obstacles, was primarily concerned with man. Every created thing was good—perfect in itself, as part of the whole, and for the fulfillment of God's purposes. This optimistic conviction that the world is good springs from a profound faith in God, as also from the certitude that all the world was created for man, who has the divine image and is to fulfill the purposes of God under his guidance. Neither Job nor Ecclesiastes believed, like P, that man is the king of creation, the climax and goal of God's activity, nor that Jewish institutions such as the festivals and the Sabbath had the validity and scope of laws of nature divinely established from the beginning. Unlike Job and Ecclesiastes, the authors of P had neither mental struggles nor doubts. Their religious convictions have the granitic solidity required of the cornerstone on which the Jewish Church was built.

In Gen. 1, the Priestly authors introduce the reader to the exalted supreme sovereign of the world. Believing firmly, however, that the sole God of the world was peculiarly the invisible king of the Jewish commonwealth, the authors were confronted by a serious problem. How could the universal God be exclusively the Jewish God? In other words, they had to reverse the theological development carried on by the great prophets. Amos and his followers elevated a purely national god, Jehovah, to the level of an international god of justice, directing the course of human history according to his great principles. The P Code, on the contrary, had to reduce the universal God of all nations and all creation to the stature of a Jewish God.

The idealistic and poetic solution of the Second Isaiah was obviously repulsive to the Priestly authors. That the universal God should select Israel as the sacrificial lamb offered up for the redemption of all the Gentiles no later Jew could believe, to the best of our knowledge, least of all the sacerdotal class. In strict logic, however, as the author of Job had realized (cf. Ps. 104), the Creator of the world and the animator of all living beings is as concerned with dumb animals as with mankind. He is not partial to the latter. It may be that to counteract this heresy, the Priestly authors emphasized the creation of man alone in the divine image. But even so, it remains to be explained why the Creator of all men singled out Israel as his own peculiar people—and no rational explanation is possible.

Like other theologians faced by a problem without a logical solution, the Priestly authors were forced to be irrational, although they obviously devoted much thought to this matter. Their ultimate conclusions, as in Islam and in strict Calvinism, was that God is an arbitrary despot whose actions are capricious when judged by human standards, or, to say the least, incomprehensible. The Priestly authors reached a point at which human reason ceases to function, accepted inconsistencies without hesitation and thus established a successful church. Cold reason is poison to religion.

On the assumption of the arbitrary enactments of God, it was simple enough to show how he became sovereign of the Jews and their proselytes, and lost interest in the rest of mankind. In his inscrutable, inexplicable decision God selected Israel from all nations, descended from heaven to take up his abode in their midst (Ex. 29:43-46, probably influenced by Ez. 43:7-9), and revealed his Law unto Moses. These three points, particularly the first and last, determine the philosophy of history characteristic of P, and form the chief topic of the whole work. For P deals primarily with the subjects of God and the meaning of citizenship in his spiritual commonwealth. Citizenship has inconsistently a double meaning in P—racial and religious. Each of these phases may be treated separately.

Racially, the origins of Israel were traced back to Adam. At the same time, purity of stock was secured by a succession of eliminations, in the course of which the interest of God, at the beginning embracing all creation, was gradually focused on the sons of Jacob.

In other words, the racial history of Israel in P is like a funnel comprising ten rings of decreasing size, down to the extremely small but all-important tube at its bottom—the theocratic community. This racial history is purely genealogical and chronological—nothing else matters in vital statistics. The ten genealogies constitute ten chapters provided with titles, "these are the generations of . . ." In the center, at the end of the fifth genealogy, stands Abraham, who marks a new epoch: J and E began their history of Israel with Abraham.

The first five genealogies are the following: heaven and earth (Gen. 2:4; 1:1-2:3), Adam (5), Noah and his three sons (6:9aα; 10:1a, 2-7, 20, 22, 23, 31 f.), Shem (11:10-26), Terah (11:27, 31 f.). The last five are: Ishmael (25:12-17), Isaac (25:19 f., 26b), Esau (36:1-8, 40-43), Jacob (37:2), and his sons (35:22b-26; Ex. 1:1-5). In each generation, the firstborn is selected and the chosen line continued through him. As a matter of fact, only the eldest son is mentioned in the genealogy leading from Adam to Noah (Gen. 5). Israel is the first-born among nations! The ancestors of Israel, by strict avoidance of mixed marriages, secured the desired racial purity but those, like Esau, who failed in this respect became outcasts (26:34 f.; 27:46-28:9). The line of Adam (Gen. 5) and that of Shem (Gen. 11:10-26) both end with the birth of triplets.

Finally, in supplements to P Levi was singled out among the sons of Jacob and Leah (Ex. 6:14-26); among the sons of Levi (Num. 3:14-39), the high priest Aaron and his line (3:1-4) marked the exact center of the concentric circles beginning with heaven and earth, and simultaneously the climax of Israel's racial history.

Israel is not only a pure race, but the body of true believers. Religious progress in P runs parallel to racial refinement. Combining the prophetic doctrine of divine revelation with the Deuteronomic idea of the divine covenant, P divides human history into four eras, each of which begins with a divine revelation accompanied, in the second and third, with a divine covenant.

During the first era, going from Adam to Noah, God was known as "Elohim" (deity), men and animals were vegetarian (Gen. 1:29 f.), God instituted the Sabbath (2:2 f.), and in his revelation commanded that men should multiply and have dominion over the earth and animals (1:28). In the second era, going from Noah to Abraham, God was still known as Elohim. In his revelation following the Deluge, he allowed men to eat meat, but without the blood (9:3 f.), and prohibited murder (9:5 f.). In the covenant which God made at that time with human beings and all other living creatures, he promised that they would not perish again through a deluge, and placed his bow in the clouds (the rainbow) as a sign of this eternal covenant with all flesh (9:8-17). In the third era, going from Abraham to Moses, God was known as "El Shaddai" (the meaning is obscure; the usual translation "Almighty" goes back to the LXX), a divine name common in Job. The revelation to Abraham contains the noblest ethical saying in P: "I am El Shaddai: walk in my presence and be blameless" (17:1). The covenant with Abraham is a promise to give to his seed the land of Canaan (17:2-8) and required on the part of his descendants the circumcision of infants on the eighth day (17:9-14). The fourth era begins with the revelation to Moses, in which God made known for the first time his name "Yahweh" (Jehovah in English) and, recalling his covenant with Abraham, sent Moses to deliver the children of Israel from Egyptian bondage (Ex. 6:2-8); in subsequent revelations, God instructed Moses in the building of the Tabernacle, ordination of the clergy, details of ritual worship, and requirements of the Levitical law.

According to P, these four revelations and two covenants are sufficient. The covenant with Noah embraced all living beings; the one with Abraham selected Israel out of all nations to be God's chosen people, his holy congregation. The sign in the heavens (the rainbow) and the sign in the flesh (circumcision) attest forever the benevolence of the Creator toward the human race in general and toward Israel in particular. The four revelations disclose two types of Judaism. The first three, culminating with Abraham, reflect the religion of the Jews in their Babylonian Exile, consisting of a moral life, avoiding murder and meat with blood, and the two rites later characterizing the Jews in the eyes of the Romans (Sabbath and circumcision). The patriarchal period for P was religiously akin to the Exile in lacking Temple worship and being limited to private observances. The religion revealed to Moses is that of the Second Temple, with its elaborate sacrificial worship and priestly hierarchy.

Since the divine oracles concerning Isaac and Ishmael (Gen. 17:15-22) and the oracles to Jacob at Bethel (35:9-13) are secondary, the principal revelations are precisely four. This is not accidental. The ancient tradition of the four ages of the world, symbolized by the four metals—gold, silver, bronze, and iron (Hesiod, *Works and Days* 5:109 ff.; Ovid, *Metamorphoses* 1:89 ff.)—seems to have been known to the author of the earliest parts of Gen. 1-11, as we have seen in describing the S document, and it is obviously familiar to the author of Dan. 2:31-45 (cf. 7 and 8:22; see also Zech. 1:18-21 [H. 2:1-4]). The Priestly authors were not only influenced by the notion of the four ages, but even preserved an echo of their original connection with cultural development. The first era is vegetarian, the three others carnivorous. This initial age when men ate no meat (Gen. 1:29 f.) still retains a characteristic of the Golden Age and of the story about the Garden of Eden (cf. Gen. 2:16). In apocalypses, this era of peace during which no animals were slaughtered for food is relegated to the end of history (Is. 11:6-8). In antiquity the notion of the four ages is so widespread that there is no occasion to assume that P borrowed from Babylonian myths (E. Schrader, *Die Keilinschriften und das Alte Testament*, pp. 535 f., 542 f., 3rd ed. by H. Zimmern and H. Winckler. Berlin, 1903) or from Parsee notions (*Dinkart* 9:7, in *Sacred Books of the East*, Vol. XXXVII, p. 180).

Although the fundamental notion is commonplace, P is highly original in depicting four stages of religious progress instead of four steps in increasing moral decay. And yet, in spite of its triumphant optimism that places, at the beginning, a world recognized by God as good and, at the end, a glorious revelation of his ordinances for his kingdom on earth, P unobtrusively records mankind's increasing wickedness through the steady decrease in the span of human life. In the first age, men lived from seven to ten centuries (except Enoch, whose years were 365), in the second from two to six, in the third from one to two, and in the fourth age, which is the present one, only seventy or eighty years. We may interpret this decreasing scale in the words of Prov. 10:27, "The fear of the Lord prolongs the days, but the years of the wicked will be shortened."

There is another hint in P as to the growth of human iniquity. Adam and his four immediate descendants, as shown by their enviable longevity, were regarded as paragons of virtue. Sinfulness apparently began with the sixth generation (Jared, a name which may mean "descent") and became so prevalent that the Flood was needed to purify the earth. When we read that Enoch, in the seventh generation "walked with God, and he was not; for God took him" (5:24) we may infer that he and Noah were the only righteous men from the sixth to the tenth generation. God saved Enoch from the Flood by snatching him alive out of a wicked world in his 365th year, and Noah by instructing him in the building of the ark. The other three, in the sixth to tenth generations, perished in the Flood (according to the chronology of the Samaritan text) or before (only Methuselah perished in the Flood, according to the Masoretic text). According to the Samaritan chronology, all ten antediluvian patriarchs witnessed the translation of Enoch; in the Masoretic text, however, Adam was already dead, and Noah had not yet been born.

We are now confronted with the vexing problems of the P chronology.[4] The basic data are furnished by the genealogies of Adam (Gen. 5:1-32) and of Shem (11:10-26), the data about Abraham, Isaac, Jacob, and Joseph (12:4; 16:3; 17:1, 24 f.; 21:4 f.; 23:1; 25:7, 20, 26b; 26:34; 35:28; 47:9, 28; 50:22, 26), and the period of 430 years' residence of the Israelites in Egypt (Ex. 12:40). According to I Kings 6:1 (R^D), the Temple of Solomon was built 480 years after the Exodus. Thus P furnished an unbroken chronology—needless to say, entirely fictitious—from the Creation to the Exodus (2,666 years, according to the Masoretic text). The creation of the world is dated on Oct. 7, at 11 h. 11 1/3 m. P.M., 3761 B.C. by the Jews, who still use that year as the beginning of their era. According to the Jewish era of Creation, A.D. 1939-40 is the year 5700.

According to the reckoning of Bishop James Ussher (1581-1656), whose dates are printed on the margin of many editions of the Authorized Bible, the date of the Creation is 4004 B.C. (for computation of this date cf. S. R. Driver, *Genesis*, p. xxviii, n. 2. 6th ed., 1907).

The first difficulty in connection with the P chronology arises from differences in the figures given in the Masoretic Hebrew text (reproduced in the English versions), in the Samaritan text, and in the Septuagint Greek version (LXX), with its manuscript variants, not to mention the Book of Jubilees and Josephus. From the creation of Adam to the Flood, the Masoretic text reckons 1,656 years; the Samaritan text and the Book

---

[4] See, on the chronology of P, the articles on "chronology" in the Biblical and theological encyclopaedias, the commentaries on Genesis (particularly A. Dillmann [1892], S. R. Driver [1904], H. Holzinger [1898], J. Skinner [1910], H. Gunkel [1910], E. König [1925]) and the following monographs: K. Budde, *Die Biblische Urgeschichte.* A. Bosse, "Die Chronologischen Systeme im Alten Testament und bei Josephus," *Mitteil. d. Vorderasiat. Gesellsch.* 13 (1908) 2. F. Bork, "Zur Chronologie der biblischen Urgeschichte," ZAW 27 (1929) 206-222. A. Jepsen, "Zur Chronologie des Priestercodex," ZAW 27 (1929) 251-255.

of Jubilees 1,307; the LXX and Josephus 2,262 (LXX-Lucian and Codex A 2,242, dating the birth of Lamech 20 years earlier). These totals are obtained by adding together the ages of the patriarchs when they begat their first-born son. The Samaritan reduces the Masoretic dates of Jared, Methuselah, and Lamech by 100, 120, and 129 years respectively, while the LXX adds a century each to the first five patriarchs and to Enoch, and six years to Lamech. The LXX-Lucian increases the numbers of the Samaritan by one hundred years, with the exception of Noah, whose life span remains the same, and Lamech, to whose life span 135 years are added (LXX adds 120 to Methuselah).

From the birth of Arpachshad in the year of the Flood[5] to the birth of Abraham (Gen. 11:10-26) the Masoretic text reckons 290 years, the Samaritan 940, and the LXX (Codex A) 1,070 (Lucian, adding four years to Peleg, 1,074). With the exception of Shem and Terah, the Samaritan and the LXX add a century to each generation but only 50 years to Nahor; in addition, the LXX interpolates Kainan, with 130 years, before Shelah. Josephus lacks Kainan and reckons 981 years.

It is generally recognized that for this second genealogy, following the Flood, the Masoretic provides the more original figures. For it would be strange if Abraham had abandoned hope of begetting a son when he was a centenarian if his ancestors had, as in the Samaritan and LXX, regularly begotten sons at 130 years of age or older. Opinions are divided, however, as to whether the Masoretic or the Samaritan contains the best text for the antediluvian patriarchs, although it seems probable that the figures of the Samaritan, which are increased both in the LXX and in the Masoretic text, represent the oldest textual tradition.

If we follow the Masoretic text for the second list and the Samaritan for the first, Arpachshad was born in the year 1310 after the creation of the world (two years after the Flood in 1307-1309), Abraham in 1600, Isaac in 1700, Jacob in 1760, Joseph in 1850; the Israelites were in Egypt from 1890 to 2320, and the Temple of Solomon was begun in the year 2800 (i.e., 480 years after the Exodus, I Kings 6:1). These round figures do not seem accidental, and it would not be unnatural for the Priestly authors to make the building of Solomon's Temple the goal and climax of their chronological scheme (cf. A. Jepsen, ZAW 27 [1929] 253), 400 weeks of years after the Creation.

On the assumption that this was the genuine P chronology, Jepsen has ingeniously explained the modifications introduced in the extant versions. In the Samaritan text, the year 2800 after the Creation is the fifth or sixth year after the invasion of Canaan; the Samaritans presumably dated in

---

[5] Since Shem was begotten in Noah's 500th year, one hundred years before the Flood, and Arpachshad was begotten in Shem's 100th year, the "two years after the Flood" as the date of Arpachshad's birth in 11:10 are puzzling.

that year the building of their Temple on Mount Gerizim (cf. Deut. 27:4, where the Samaritan text reads Gerizim instead of Ebal). In the Masoretic text, we find the following dates according to the creation of the world: Flood, 1656; Exodus, 2666 (if Arpachshad was born in the year of the Flood), or 2669 (if he was born three years after the Flood); beginning of the building of Solomon's Temple, 3146 or 3149. Adopting the latter date, Jepsen reckons that the Second Temple was dedicated in the year 3600, and regards this as the climax of the revised chronology (3600 is a *sar*, a basic figure in the Babylonian sexagesimal system). Omitting Terah and the two years between the Flood and the birth of Arpachshad, A. Bosse (MVAG 13 [1908] Part 2) discovers in the Masoretic text two chronological systems. One reckons by generations of forty years and counts fifty generations (2,000 years) from the birth of Shem to the end of the Exile. The other reckons with a Great Month of 260 years (the number of weeks in five years) and, including Terach, gives for the dedication of Solomon's Temple the year 3166 ($12 \times 260 + 46$, a Great Year) after creation. Such a complicated and subtle chronological system commends itself to us less than the simpler one of Jepsen.

The basis for the system of dates in the LXX has never been satisfactorily explained. The Temple of Solomon, dedicated according to the LXX in the year 4260, may be the goal in this chronology. Bosse explains 4260 as a Great Year composed of twelve Great Months of 355 years (355 is the number of days in the lunar year). F. Bork (ZAW 27 [1929] 214 f.) supposes that the LXX operates with the Iranian "World-year" of 3200 years: Terah was born in the year 3242 of the Creation, a thousand years after the Flood.

The third concomitant of the Jewish theocratic commonwealth is territory. In this matter, the Priestly Code is no less unhistorical and dogmatic than in dealing with the sovereign and subjects of this ideal kingdom. Actual historical events and solid reality vanish in the account of how Israel acquired its land. Facts are sacrificed on the altar of theory. When God chose Abraham and his seed as his own people, he gave them at the same time, through a solemn covenant, "the whole land of Canaan for an everlasting possession" (Gen. 17:7 f.; cf. 28:4; Ex. 6:4).

Since it is the Creator of heaven and earth who assigns Canaan to the Israelites, there can be no gradual and laborious conquest of Canaan on the part of the Israelites. Through a miracle, the Israelites simply cross the Jordan and, tribe by tribe, are assigned their land by Joshua, as if Canaan had been entirely depopulated. By a stroke of the pen the Canaanites ceased to exist. No battles were fought. The conquest becomes an act of God: "And I will bring you into the land, concerning which I did swear to give it to Abraham, to Isaac, and to Jacob; and I will give it to you for a heritage: I am the Lord" (Ex. 6:8). After the land was subdued,[6] the whole congregation of Israel gathered in Shiloh and set up the Tabernacle (Josh. 18:1). Then Eleazar the priest, Joshua, and the family heads assigned by lot the land of Canaan west of the Jordan to the nine and a half tribes, just as Moses had assigned the land east of the Jordan to two and a half tribes (Josh. 14:1-2). The Priestly Code ends by defining exactly the boundaries of the territory of each tribe (Josh. 13-21, in part).

Since God endowed Israel with its land, the title was clear. The divine decree gave the Israelites legitimate, unimpeachable possession of the country, whose ultimate and absolute owner was God. The premises of P make this indisputable. But the authors of P, through another of these inconsistencies typical of many theologians, added a legal deed to the divine grant, in order to make the title doubly certain. The authors were priests and lawyers at the same time. When Abraham acquired the cave of Machpelah for a tomb for Sarah, he made a legal contract with Ephron. He refused to accept it as a gift, and insisted on paying the full price demanded for the property (Gen. 23). "And the field, and the cave that is therein, were made sure unto Abraham for a possession of a burying place by the sons of Heth" (23:20). We may surmise that the punctilious legal language used in the conveyance of this property to Abraham and the insistence on the clear title given to Abraham by its former owner and the local community afforded the juridically minded authors of P the satisfaction of knowing that the conquest of Canaan was not highhanded robbery but legitimate acquisition resting on a valid ancient contract.

After P has dealt with the sovereign, subjects, and territorial possessions of his ideal commonwealth, nothing remained except to give the statutes and ordinances regulating the relations and duties of the subjects to their divine sovereign. This legal part of P, most important of all, will be considered in the chapter dealing with the codes of law in the Pentateuch.

2. *Sources and Style*

The authors of the Priestly Code were not only priests and lawyers, but scholars—the most erudite writers in the Old Testament. Their work is based on a careful examination of available literary sources. Whereas the J and E documents had produced epics out of material from the oral traditions of their people, the P authors searched with scholarly patience for written documents alone, and obviously looked with suspicion on information conveyed to them by word of mouth.

The indebtedness of P to the great Pentateuchal sources (J, E, D) is

[6] A few scattered verses dealing with the conquest of Canaan (Josh. 4:10, 16, 19; 9:15b, 17-21, 27a) and the list of the 31 kings whose land Israel occupied (12:1-24) are generally assigned, at least in part, to P. Nevertheless, it is extremely doubtful if P contained a real account of the conquest. In any case, no battles were described in P.

well known (cf. J. E. Carpenter and G. Harford, *The Composition of the Hexateuch,* pp. 230-234). Something has been said of the influence of the Second Isaiah and Ezekiel on the theology of P. But the most difficult problem in this connection is P's use of sources which, except for such as he has preserved, are lost. A good example of P's method in the use of written sources not available to us is Gen. 1, where we have identified a mythical Creation story so completely rewritten by the Priestly authors that it is no longer possible to reconstruct it in its original form.

The list of antediluvian patriarchs descended from Adam is clearly based on a written source. This line of Adam through Seth in P (Gen. 5) is similar to the line of Adam through Cain (Gen. 4:1a, 17 f., S), in spite of differences in the order and spelling of names; Seth, Enosh, and Noah are missing in the Cainite line of Gen. 4. On the other hand, a certain parallelism has been detected between Gen. 5 and the list of ten prediluvian kings of Berossos (translated in R. W. Rogers, *Cuneiform Parallels to the Old Testament,* pp. 78 f.; text in C. Müller, *Fragmenta historicorum graecorum* Vol. II, pp. 499 f. See also P. Schnabel, *Berossos und die babylonisch-hellenistische Literatur.* Leipzig, 1923). In their corrupt Greek form, the names in Berossos were seen to be derived from ancient Babylonian originals (cf. E. Schrader, *Die Keilinschriften und das Alte Testament,* pp. 530 ff.) even before the discovery of two ancient Babylonian lists from Larsa (dated about 2000 B.C.).[7]

But the disfigurement suffered by the Babylonian names, first when rewritten in Greek by Berossos and then through his excerptors and copyists, placed recovery of the originals beyond the reach of philological speculation. In Berossos, ten kings ruled no less than 432,000 years; in the first Larsa list, eight kings, ruling over five cities, piled up the respectable total of 241,200 years; in the second Larsa list, ten kings (two of whom were spuriously added as kings of Larsa by local patriotism) ruling over six cities attained a total of 456,000 years of reign. As we have seen, the longevity of the antediluvian patriarchs in P is extremely modest in comparison. Not even Methuselah had succeeded in reaching a mere millennium.

The dependence of Berossos on genuine ancient Babylonian lists like these from Larsa is now beyond question. And the fact that such material was available to him in the middle of the third century enhances the probability that in some unknown manner the authors of P could have had access to such lists two or two and a half centuries before. Although the Hebrew names are still more at variance with the Babylonian than

[7] The texts were published in the cuneiform and in English by S. Langdon (*Oxford Editions of Cuneiform Texts,* Vol. 22, 1923). See also S. Smith, *Early History of Assyria,* pp. 17-25 368 f. London, 1928; G. A. Barton, *The Royal Inscriptions of Sumer and Akkad,* pp. 340-355. New Haven, 1929.

the Greek names of Berossos, some sort of influence of the Babylonian lists on Gen. 5 cannot be gainsaid. But whereas the list of S (Gen. 4:17 f.) is earlier than that of P (Gen. 5), P is unquestionably closer to the Babylonian originals, even though these are adapted in both cases to Hebrew traditions, and P must have derived some of the names from S.

It is extremely doubtful, however, that P's chronology is directly dependent on that of Berossos, as J. Oppert ("Die Daten der Genesis," in *Nachrichten von der Königl. Gesellsch. der Wissensch. zu Göttingen*, 1877, p. 201) attempted to prove. He reckoned that the 1,656 years of P, from Adam to the Flood, correspond to the 432,000 years of Berossos if one Biblical week is regarded as the equivalent of sixty months, or five years, in the Babylonian chronology.

The story of the Flood in P (parts of Gen. 6-9) is another example of the direct or indirect acquaintance which the Priestly authors had with Babylonian writings.[8] The technical details of dates and measurements, the close connection with P's four revelations, and the dry, schematic style contrast sharply with the S² incomplete story of the Flood with which it is now combined. As in Gen. 1, the authors of P make their source conform with their norms and principles and use an old story to explain the origin of legal prescriptions (Gen. 2:2 f.; 9:1-6).

A divine covenant is ushered into the Flood story wholly unwarranted by the sources (6:18; 9:9-17) and also a reference to man's creation according to the image of God (9:6; cf. 1:27). Apropos of the oracle in 1:28-30 which prescribed vegetarianism, the authors of the Flood story extended permission to eat meat (9:1-3), without, however, distinguishing between pure and impure animals (as in S², 8:20) since the dietary laws were first revealed to Moses. Similarly, P omits Noah's sacrifice, the climax of both the Babylonian and S² (8:20-22) stories, because no legitimate sacrifices could be offered before the ritual laws were revealed to Moses.

P's use of earlier written sources is clear in another instance—the list of nations descended from Shem, Ham, and Japheth (Gen. 10:1a, 2-7, 20, 22 f., 31 f.). Here again, as in the list of antediluvian patriarchs (Gen. 5) already considered, the authors of P may have known S² (the rest of ch. 10), but did not make use of it as their primary source. The descendants of Shem, Ham, and Japheth are quite different in P and S², and in the two lists identical names occur in different relationships.

---

[8] The various cuneiform versions of the Flood story are published with a translation by A. T. Clay (*A Hebrew Deluge Story in Cuneiform*. New Haven, 1922). His attempt to prove that the story is of "Hebrew" (Amoritic) origin is not convincing. Most of the Babylonian texts are also translated in R. W. Rogers, *Cuneiform Parallels to the Old Testament*, and in G. A. Barton, *Archaeology and the Bible* (7th ed., Philadelphia, 1937). The landing of the ark on Ararat (Urartu, Van, in Armenia) finds its parallel only in the recension of the Flood story given by Berossos.

The Table of Nations in P is perhaps the most striking instance of
the authors' erudition and historical research. Unquestionably it reflects
the international situation not of the middle of the fifth century B.C.,
when these authors lived, but of the seventh century (about 710-610), as
has been shown elsewhere by the present writer (JBL 56 [1937] 91-94).
The amazingly exact knowledge of seventh century Greek colonization
in the Mediterranean, when ancient Phoenician settlements in Cyprus,
Tartessos (Tarshish), and Rhodes (10:4) were Hellenized, must have
been derived from written sources ultimately of Anatolian or, less probably, of Phoenician origin. The cuneiform sources, judging from those
known to us, do not furnish all the information accessible to P. In addition to the Greeks, the sons of Japheth include nations in Asia Minor
and the Medes in the period 710-610 (10:2 f., note particularly the Cimmerians and the Scythians, i.e., Gomer and Ashkenaz).

Mention of Ethiopia (Cush) before Egypt (Mizraim), among the sons
of Ham (10:6), reflects the Twenty-fifth (Ethiopian) Dynasty of Egypt
(712-663). Similarly, mention of Assyria rather than Babylonia among
the sons of Shem (10:22) points to the century preceding the fall of
Nineveh (612). The omissions from the table suggest the same date.
Omission of the Hittites and Philistines precludes an earlier date; that of
Persia (Ez. 27:10; 38:5), whose place is taken by Elam (destroyed as a
kingdom by Ashurbanipal in 640), and that of the Arab Bedouins (Jer.
25:24) by the side of the South Arabian kingdoms (named in 10:7) preclude a later one. It is significant that P lists no less than twelve Bedouin
tribes classed as Ishmaelites in Gen. 25:12-18 but ignores them in Gen. 10.
The Judeans came into contact with the Arabs after 586 B.C., and particularly in the fifth century and after.

How the priestly authors obtained this information about those nations
which flourished during the seventh century from the Black Sea to Gibraltar and from South Arabia to Asia Minor must remain a mystery.
Obviously, however, it was accessible to them in written documents of
which there is no trace elsewhere in the Old Testament.

These examples, by far the clearest, suffice to illustrate P's erudite use
of more or less recondite written sources in the narrative portions of his
work.[9] The legal parts of P and the codes of law utilized in them will be
considered elsewhere. As we have seen, the authors of P did not hesitate

[9] Other traces of written sources have been detected in P. God's bow set in the
cloud (9:13-37) is the echo of a myth. The circumcision of Ishmael (17:23) contradicts the statement that circumcision was the sign of the covenant with Abraham
and his seed (i.e., the Israelites only, 17:1-8). One of the sources of P in Ex. 25-30
manifestly describes God giving Moses not only oral instructions for building the
Tabernacle, but also a model of it (25:9, 40; 26:30; 27:8; cf. Wisd. of Sol. 9:8; II
Macc. 2:4-8; Apoc. of Baruch 4:5; Acts 7:44b; Hebr. 8:5); see also L. Ginzberg,
The Legends of the Jews, Vol. VI, p. 67, n. 346. Philadelphia, 1928.

to rewrite these sources entirely removing whatever conflicted with their theories and adding whatever was needed to integrate their work. In the lists of antediluvian patriarchs and nations descended from Noah's sons, the authors seem to have made few changes. The story of Abraham's purchase of Machpelah (Gen. 23) was apparently reproduced from an earlier source with only minor retouches: except for the beginning and end (23:1 f., 17-20), where P's pedantic style is obvious, the story is more vivid and lifelike than any other in P.

No part of the Old Testament has a more systematic arrangement than the narrative passages of P. As the outline at the beginning of the chapter shows, the history is divided into four periods beginning respectively with Adam, Noah, Abraham, and Moses—the only men to whom God revealed his Law. The first three parts are divided into chapters bearing standardized titles: "These are the generations of . . ." (Gen. 2:4a [originally placed before 1:1]), 5:1; 6:9; 10:1; 11:10, 27; 25:12, 19; 36:1, [9]; 37:2). Even the subdivisions are sometimes marked. The Table of Nations, for instance, has a title (10:1) and a concluding remark (10:32); moreover, each of its three subdivisions has a special title (10:2a, 6a, 22a) and concluding remark (10:5, 20, 31).

The title "generations" is appropriate for these chapters, since before Moses P is for the most part a skeleton history in which entire periods are condensed into genealogical lists. In Genesis, the only real stories are the Creation (1:1-2:4), the Flood (parts of 6-9), the divine covenant with Abraham and the institution of circumcision (17), Abraham's purchase of Machpelah (23), and the blessing of Jacob (27:46-28:9). For the rest and except for genealogies, P in Genesis consists merely of brief annotations and supplements to the JE stories. P is often incomprehensible when removed from its context, and should therefore be considered a framework of JE rather than a separate work added to JE (cf. ZAW N.F. 7 [1930] 67).

In the rest of the Pentateuch and Joshua, P is no mere commentary and usually self-sufficient without JE. Nevertheless, it may have been composed primarily as a supplement to JE. Moses, for instance, is introduced abruptly in P with these words, "And God spoke unto Moses and said unto him, 'I am Jehovah'" (Ex. 6:2). A knowledge of the preceding JE stories about Moses is clearly presupposed. In general, the narrative portions of P inject into the old stories of JE the ritual and doctrines of normative Judaism dating from the first half of the fifth century. P is on the whole more a midrashic commentary than an independent midrash like Chronicles.

The purpose, contents, and general character of P explain the style of the work. It is only occasionally (Gen. 17:15-22; 23; 28:1-9; 47:7-10), when P is probably rewriting an earlier source, that his style is picturesque, dramatic, and colorful; here it has some of the freshness and vividness of J and E. However, in general, the authors write like a notary public drawing up a legal document or a scholar engaged in erudite research. The bleak, monotonous style is due primarily not to their dislike of literary charm or even elegance, but rather to the nature of their book— a constitution of the Jewish theocratic state. The stories in P are not related for their own sake, as in J and E, but either because they furnish legal precedents or are otherwise essential for understanding the origin and organization of the holy congregation.

In a document of this sort (the charter of Judaism) the authors naturally strove after juristic lucidity and completeness rather than literary charm.[10] As in any legal document, the style of P is exact in dates, measurements, and genealogical relationships; precise and complete in catalogues of things and persons; punctilious in its definitions and choice of words. At the same time it is elaborate in dealing with essential details, and extremely concise in more or less irrelevant matters. But generally speaking, it is a stereotyped style, repetitious, intolerably explicit, pedantic, erudite, colorless, and schematic. In some places it reads like a municipal register of vital statistics (5; 11:10-26) or like a real-estate deed (23:17 f.); in others, like a textbook of botany and zoology (1:11 f., 20 f., 24 f.). And yet there are in P words sublime in their majesty, lapidary in their conciseness: " 'Let there be light (*fiat lux*)': and there was light" (Gen. 1:3) is the outstanding instance; see also Gen. 1:1 f., 26; 9:13; 17:1b, 4; 47:9; Ex. 7:1; Num. 6:24-26.

In particular, P selects the right term or phrase and unfailingly repeats it without change, in similar circumstances. A perusal of P's characteristic words and expressions (listed in English by J. E. Carpenter and G. Harford in *The Composition of the Hexateuch*, pp. 408-423; for a Hebrew list see H. Holzinger, *Einleitung in den Hexateuch,* pp. 339-349) will show that such tedious repetitions are not confined to technical terms (i.e., assembly, congregation, to create, covenant, the Dwelling, generations, possession, inheritance, testimony, etc., besides many ritual terms), but extend to other formulae as well. Instead of merely saying that a person died, P says that he "expired and died; and was gathered unto his people" (Gen. 25:8, 17; 35:29; 49:29, 33; Num. 20:24, 26; 27:13; 31:2; Deut. 32:50). Other standard phrases invariably repeated are: "And Jehovah spake unto Moses saying, 'Speak unto the children of Israel' " or "unto Aaron and his sons" (Ex. 14:2, 15; 25:2; Lev. 1:2; 4:2, and frequently); "This is the thing which Jehovah has commanded" (Ex. 16:16, 32; Lev. 8:5, etc.); "And . . . did as Jehovah had commanded . . . , so did he" or "they" (Gen. 6:22; Ex. 7:6; 12:28, 50, etc.).

Moreover, P reports the execution of an order in full, repeating the

[10] Cf. H. Gunkel, *Genesis,* pp. xcii-xcix.

diction of the command (Gen. 1:11 f.; Ex. 7:9 f.; 8:1 f., 12 f., etc.). After the manner of lawyers, he delights in the use of exhaustive and precise expressions. He is not satisfied with saying "These are the names of the chiefs [issued from] Esau," but adds "according to their families, after their places, by their names" (Gen. 36:40; cf. 36:43). Similarly in the Table of Nations: "These are the sons of Ham after their families, after their tongues, in their countries, in their nations" (10:20; cf. 10:5, 31). Pharaoh is regularly identified as "the king of Egypt" (Gen. 41:46; Ex. 6:11, 13, 27, etc.), Sarai as "Abram's wife" (Gen. 16:1, 3, unnecessarily, after 11:31; 12:5). Canaan and Egypt are punctiliously called "the land of Canaan" and "the land of Egypt." A good example of redundant emphasis on the obvious is found in Ex. 12:18-20, a fivefold injunction to avoid leaven and eat only unleavened bread; another in Ex. 2:23-25; see also Gen. 1:26; 6:19-22; 7:15 f.; 21:3; Num. 14:26-35.

As J. Wellhausen said (*Prolegomena zur Geschichte Israels.* pp. 348 f. 6th ed. Berlin, 1905), "P has a veritable passion for classifications and schematisms; when he has once subdivided a genus into several species, every time he talks of the genus we must again be told every single species. . . . Whenever possible he prefers prolix expressions, he never tires of repeating the obvious in full for the hundredth time (Num. 7 [Pˢ]), he detests pronouns and all abbreviating substitutes. What is interesting is skipped over, what is indifferent is described exactly . . ."

CHAPTER VII

THE CODES OF LAW IN THE PENTATEUCH

Seven distinct codes of law can be identified within the Pentateuch: the Covenant Code (Ex. 20:22-23:19 [with an appendix, 23:20-33]), the Ritual Decalogue (34:10-26 and 22:29b-30 [H. 22:28b-29] 23:12, 15-19), the Twelve (originally ten) Curses (Deut. 27:14-26), the Ten Commandments (Deut. 5:6-21 [H. 5:6-18] and Ex. 20:1-17), the Deuteronomic Code (Deut. 12-26), the Holiness Code or H (Lev. 17-26), and the Priestly Code or P, the legal portions of which, in addition to Leviticus *in toto*, are scattered throughout Exodus and Numbers. All these were enforced as soon as they were promulgated and, although codified in the course of the eight centuries preceding the final publication of the Pentateuch about 400 B.C., all are attributed to Moses. No Hebrew law, whether oral or written, was regarded as binding unless of Mosaic origin, and the ritual prescriptions of Ez. 40-48 were never enforced as such, even though they had a profound influence on the practices of the Second Temple.

The Priestly author knows of laws antedating Moses (the Sabbath, Gen. 2:3; the prescriptions to Noah, 9:3-6; the rite of circumcision ordained to Abraham, 17:10-14; see also 32:32 [H. 32:33] where a custom is said to have originated with Jacob), but since these laws were revealed by God, as in the case of Moses, their authority was in no way impaired by an earlier date. As a matter of fact, the Priestly author is only the first known instance in Judaism of a tendency to date certain laws before Moses—a tendency particularly marked in the Book of Jubilees (cf. G. F. Moore, *Judaism,* Vol. I, pp. 274 f.). Purely human legislation (such as royal edicts), even though it must have played an important role in the time of the monarchy (cf. I Sam. 30:23-25), was frowned upon after the promulgation of the Deuteronomic Code in 621, and either implicitly (I Sam. 8:11-18; cf. Deut. 17:14-17) or explicitly (Mic. 6:16) denounced.

The divine origin of the law, whether communicated by God through the prophets (Zech. 1:6) or through Moses (Mal. 4:4 [H. 3:22]), is an article of faith whose validity does not concern historical research. The historian's task is to determine as far as possible the date of promulgation of the several codes, their antecedents and characteristics, contemporary cultural background and mutual relationships. Such an objective study shows that none of the Pentateuchal codes could have been promulgated by Moses (even if Ex. 18:13-27 is historical), since they all reflect Palestinian conditions, not excepting the Holiness Code, written in Babylonia (the Ten Commandments in their present form are no exception). Moreover, of the narrative sources of the Pentateuch, only D and P, combining history and legislation, contained originally any laws whatsoever.

1. The Covenant Code and the Ritual Decalogue (Ex. 20:22-23:33; 34)

The Covenant Code, as we have it, is not much earlier than the Pentateuch in its final edition. Like the other Hebrew codes of law, even down to the Mishna, the Talmud, and later Jewish codifications, it is a medley of civil and criminal legislation (Ex. 21:1-22:20 [H. 22:19]), ritual rules (20:24-26; 22:28-31 [H. 22:27-30]; 23:10-19), and humanitarian prescriptions (22:21-27 [H. 22:20-26]; 23:1-9). The book closes with a paraenetic peroration (23:20-33) loosely connected with the preceding laws and probably penned by one of the last editors of the Covenant Code, who was also the author of the brief introduction (20:22 f.).

The Covenant Code (called Book of the Covenant in 24:7) is the result of successive enlarged editions (see for details my article in HTR 23 [1931] 99-109). The original nucleus was *the ancient ritual decalogue*, preserved in the late copy of Ex. 34 and in a much earlier but partly disarranged text in 22:29b-30 [H. 22:28b-29]; 23:12, 15-19 (cf. my article in JBL 43 [1924] 294-310). This decalogue was supplemented at various times by editorial additions and laws; the humanitarian prescriptions were added partly before and partly after the publication of Deuteronomy in 621; and the civil and criminal legislation, although the earliest part of the book, was inserted about the middle of the fifth century.

The juristic formulation of *civil and criminal laws* varies. The standard form, likewise current in the Babylonian Code of Hammurabi (about 1800 B.C.), in the Assyrian laws (about 1350 B.C.), and in the Hittite Code (about 1350 B.C.),[1] is that of precedents in case law (Hebrew *mishpāṭim*, judgments; cf. the title in Ex. 21:1). The articles of law consist of a series of conditional sentences in the third person singular, of which the first is a general one introduced by *kî* ("assuming that," "in the case that"; often preceded by *wᵉ*, "and," "but") and those following are subordinate and specific conditional sentences introduced by *'im* ("if," with or without "and"). For instance: "And in case an ox gore a man or a woman to death, the ox must be stoned to death. . . . But if the ox has been goring

---

[1] For English translations of these codes see G. A. Barton, *Archaeology and the Bible*. J. M. P. Smith, *The Origin and History of Hebrew Law*. Chicago, 1931. German translations in *Altorientalische Texte zum Alten Testament*. Herausgegeben von H. Gressmann, Berlin, 1926.

previously and its owner has been warned . . . the ox will be stoned and also its owner will be put to death . . ." (21:28-32). In other words, the law considers first a general case and then different exceptional instances of it, each of which can in turn be analyzed into a number of particular cases, and so forth.

The following laws in the Covenant Code are formulated in this casuistic manner: sale of a daughter into slavery (21:7-11), murder (21:14), assault and battery (21:18-27, omitting the *lex talionis* in 21:23-25; cf. A. Alt, *Ursprünge des israelitischen Rechts*, pp. 34 f.; J. Morgenstern, *The Book of the Covenant*, Vol. II, pp. 68-71, omits only 21:23b-25), the goring ox (21:28-32), animals falling into a pit (21:33 f.), an ox killed by another (21:35 f.), theft (22:1, 4, 3b; 22:2, 3a [H. 21:37; 22:3, 2b; 22:1, 2a]), damage to crops (22:5 f. [H. 22:4 f.]), deposits and loans (22:7 f., 10-15 [H. 22:6 f., 9-14]), rape (22:16 f. [H. 22:15 f.]).

To this group of laws, presented objectively in the correct juristic formulation, we must add a few others in which the formulation has been accidentally or willfully altered: laws on the manumission of a Hebrew slave (21:2-6), reading "in case a man buy" instead of "in case *thou buyest*" (21:2, cf. A. Jepsen, *Untersuchungen zum Bundesbuch* (1927), Vol. I, p. 56; J. Morgenstern, *The Book of the Covenant*, (Pt. II, p. 38 [HUCA 7, 1930]), since the third person singular is used correctly in 21:4, 6 ("his master," not "thou"); or we should rather read, on the basis of Deut. 15:12, "in case a Hebrew man sells himself [into slavery]" as proposed by A. Alt (*Die Ursprünge des israelitischen Rechts*, p. 19. Leipzig, 1934). The phrase "unto the Elohim and" in 21:6 is omitted in the Deuteronomic revision of these laws (Deut. 15:12-18) and is probably a gloss that has been variously understood. "The Elohim" could mean either deity or household gods; the LXX renders "the tribunal of God"; the Onkelos Targum and the Syriac translate "the judges."[2] We have, then, in 21:2-22:17 [H. 22:16], omitting those laws in 21:12-17, 23-25; 22:9 [H. 22:8] which have no juristic formulation of case law, remnants of the oldest civil legislation of the Israelites.

It is extremely probable that other fragments of the ancient code from which these laws were taken have been preserved in a revised form in Deuteronomy. There are two reasons for this assumption. In the first place, outside of the Covenant Code, Deuteronomy alone (with the possible exception of Lev. 19:20) contains a number of civil laws in which the original juristic case law formulation has not been entirely obliterated by later revision (cf. J. Morgenstern, *The Book of the Covenant*, Vol. II, pp. 123-241). In the second place, marriage law, which is missing from the Covenant Code except for a vestige in 22:16 f. [H. 22:15 f.] (cf. Deut. 22:28 f.), takes up the bulk of the laws of Deuteronomy which are re-

[2] Cf. C. H. Gordon in *JBL* 54 (1935) 139-144.

visions of old case laws. That the Deuteronomist rewrote such ancient precedents in a religious spirit has already been noticed in Deut. 15:12-18 (cf. Ex. 21:2-6) and 22:28 f. (cf. Ex. 22:16 [H. 22:15]).

Except for these two close parallels, the civil laws in Deuteronomy supply those missing in the Covenant Code, particularly in the case of the marriage laws of Deut. 22:13-29. That the two codes are supplementary appears most clearly in the case of the laws on rape and seduction:

Subject	Deut	Cov. Code (Ex.)
Seduction of betrothed virgin	22:23 f.	
Seduction of unbetrothed virgin:		
Her father consents to marriage		22:16 [H. 22:15]
Her father refuses his consent		22:17 [H. 22:16]
Rape of betrothed virgin	22:25-27	
Rape of unbetrothed virgin	22:28 f.	

From this group of four laws against seduction and rape, of which Deuteronomy has three and Exodus two, with a single one in common, it appears clearly that Deuteronomy could not have used the Covenant Code as its source (nor, of course, vice versa), and that both these codes of laws derive most of their civil legislation from an ancient code exhibiting the strictly juridical formulation.[3] Since it is obvious that Deuteronomy has preserved some laws from this ancient code not in Ex. 21:2-22:17 [H. 22:16] (omitting 21:12-17, 23-25), which is obviously an incomplete code, an attempt to gain a better idea of the original code by putting together its remnants both in that section of Exodus and in Deuteronomy is quite legitimate.

In spite of the disarrangement of the laws in Deuteronomy and of the less drastic rearrangement in Exodus (where the original order is much better preserved), it seems that the main divisions of the lost code corresponded to those of the Code of Hammurabi (for which cf. my analysis in AJSL 36 [1920] 310-315). The main divisions of the Code of Hammurabi are the law of procedure, (§§1-5), the law of property (§§6-126), and the law of persons (§§127-282), corresponding to the *jus actionum, jus rerum,* and *jus personarum* in Roman jurisprudence. In the Covenant Code the law of procedure is missing, but in Deut. 19:16-20 it is preserved, at least in part. The law of persons (except for the displaced family law in Ex. 22:16 f. [H. 22:15 f.]) precedes the law of property. It would seem that in the lost code, as in Roman law, the order of the

[3] I cannot subscribe to the suggestive theory of J. Morgenstern (*The Book of the Covenant*, Vol. II, pp. 249-256), according to which the laws in the Covenant Code are taken from a corpus of laws of the Northern Kingdom (compiled by Ahab in 865-854 B.C.) and those in Deuteronomy from a corpus of the Southern Kingdom (dating from the first half of the eighth century).

three parts of Hammurabi's Code was reversed and that its original arrangement was substantially as follows:

I. LAW OF PERSONS

1. *Liability.*
 a. Liability arising from contract (Hammurabi §§228-282):
  Purchase of male slaves, Ex. 21:2-6.
  Purchase of female slaves, Ex. 21:7-11.
  Purchase of slaves of both sexes, Deut. 15:12-18.
 b. Liability arising from tort (Hammurabi §§194-227):
  [Murder?]
  Bodily injury or death caused by persons:
   To free men, Ex. 21:18f.
   By a woman, Deut. 25:11f. (cf. Assyrian Code I, 8)
   To free women, Ex. 21:22.
   To slaves, Ex. 21:20f., 26f.
  Bodily injury or death caused by a vicious ox, Ex. 21:28-32.

2. *The Family.*
 a. Inheritance (Hammurabi §§162-193): Deut. 21:15-17.
  Punishment of wicked son, Deut. 21:18-21 (cf. Ex. 21:15, 17).
 b. Marriage (Hammurabi §§127-161):
  Virginity of the bride, Deut. 22:13-21.
  Adultery, Deut. 22:22.
  Seduction of betrothed virgin, Deut. 22:23f.
  Seduction of unbetrothed virgin:
   marriage allowed, Ex. 22:16 (H. 22:15).
   marriage forbidden, Ex. 22:17 (H. 22:16).
  Rape of betrothed virgin, Deut. 22:25-27.
  Rape of unbetrothed virgin, Deut. 22:28f.
  Incest(?) (only in later codes).
  Divorce, Deut. 24:1-4.
  Levirate marriage, Deut. 25:5-10 (cf. Assyrian Code I, 30, 31, 43;
   Hittite Code II, 79).

II. THE LAW OF PROPERTY

1. *Ownership of property* (Hammurabi §§53-65ff.).
  Recovery of damages done to:
   Cattle, Ex. 21:33f., 35f.
   Crops, Ex. 22:5, 6 (H. 22:4, 5).

2. *Possession of property.*
 a. Illegal possession (Hammurabi §§6-25):
  Kidnaping, Deut. 24:7 (cf. Ex. 21:16).
  Theft of cattle, Ex. 22:1, 4, 3b (H. 21:37; 22:3, 2b).
  Theft of household goods, Ex. 22:2-3a (H. 22:1-2a).
 b. Legal possession (Hammurabi §§120-126):
  Deposit of valuables, Ex. 22:7f. (H. 22:6f.).
  Deposit of cattle or sheep, Ex. 22:10-15 (H. 22:9-14).

III. THE LAW OF PROCEDURE

False witness (Hammurabi §§3-4), Deut. 19:16-20.
Administration of lashes to offender, Deut. 25:1-3.

Like the other ancient Oriental codes, this old code of civil law consists of collections of juristic precedents (*mishpāṭîm*). If we disregard the revision of the old laws in Deuteronomy, there is nothing in the code that discloses the national self-consciousness of the Israelites and their peculiar institutions, evident in all the later codifications. Even the term "Hebrew" (Ex. 21:2), which many critics, following Deut. 15:12 and Jer. 34:9, 14, regard as a synonym of "Israelite," has no narrow racial or ethnic connotation in the original code (cf. A. Alt, *Die Ursprünge des israelitischen Rechts,* pp. 19-23). This much seems certain, although the exact original meaning of "Hebrew" and *ḫabirū* (in the cuneiform records) is still obscure to scholars (cf. E. Chiera, AJSL 49 [1933] 115-124; E. A. Speiser, *Annual of the Amer. Schools of Orient. Research XIII* [1933] 34-46; J. Lewy, in HUCA XIV [1939] 587-623; XV [1940] 47-58).

The unshatterable bond between Israel and its god Jehovah, since the birth of the nation in the time of Moses, was always the essential element in national feeling and Jehovah therefore the source of all Israelite laws and customs. In the ancient code reconstructed above, this bond is totally missing. In Ex. 22:11 [H. 22:10], "Jehovah" was substituted for the general term *elōhîm*, (deity, applied to any god), occurring in 21:6, 13 (both probably secondary) 22:8 f. [H. 22:7 f.]. In similar connections, for oaths and declarations in the name (or in the presence) of the deity, the Code of Hammurabi (§§103, 107, 120, 126, 131, 227, 240, 249, 266, 281) employs "god" (*ilu* in the singular) with the same indefinite meaning as the Hebrew plural *elōhîm*. Religion, which among the Israelites could not be dissociated from right and law, is absent in this code, just as in Hammurabi's the piety of the nonlegal prologue and epilogue contrasts with the religious neutrality of the code itself.

The attribution of this code to Moses (cf. Ex. 21:1), which is still defended, among others,[4] by A. Jirku (*Das weltliche Recht in Alten Testament,* pp. 52 f. Gütersloh, 1927), is clearly absurd if one considers its characteristics. "Its origins must be sought outside of Israel" (A. Alt, *Ursprünge des israelitischen Rechts,* p. 24) among the population which the Israelites found in Canaan (*ibid.,* pp. 25 ff.). Apparently it was not the code of an individual locality, but, as general references to the deity indicate, of some Canaanitic region; dating from before 1200 B.C., it was adopted by the Israelites after their invasion into Canaan but before the coronation of Saul (i.e., in the century 1150-1050 B.C.).

[4] H. Schmökel (JBL 52 [1933] 224 f.) believes that the case law in Exodus and Deuteronomy is "the remnant of a larger Kenite code of law in force at the sanctuary of Kadesh" in the time of Moses.

Not only was this ancient code preserved in writing until nearly 621, when the Deuteronomist rewrote extracts from it in his book, but considerably later, when some portions were copied, substantially verbatim, into the late edition of the Covenant Code which we now have (cf. HTR 23 [1931] 101). If the civil legislation had been part of the Covenant Code before 621 B.C., it is difficult to explain how it escaped the Deuteronomistic revision obvious in other parts of the book. In any case, the author of Deuteronomy, who used other parts of the Covenant Code, derived the civil legislation from a copy of the old code and not from the Covenant Code: with the exception of Deut. 15:12-18; 22:28 f., the civil legislation of Deuteronomy has no analogy with that of the Covenant Code.

Seemingly, the Deuteronomist selected from the old code such laws as suited his purpose, and later an editor with antiquarian propensities added to the Covenant Code the laws of the old code not included in the D Code. That would explain this editor's insertion of only the last two laws on seduction and rape (Ex. 22:16 f. [H. 22:15 f.]). In order to complete the law on seduction and rape, reproduced only partially in Deut. 22:23-29, this editor preserved two omitted laws (Ex. 22:16 f. [H. 22:15 f.]); cf. above, pp. 213 f. The other duplication of Deuteronomic laws (Ex. 21:2-11; cf. Deut. 15:12-18) is less obvious but quite understandable. The Deuteronomist not only added his philanthropic retouches to the law on the manumission of the Hebrew slaves, but passed over the laws on the bondwoman, merely equating her treatment to that of male servants (Deut. 15:12, 17b) contrary to the tenor of the old law (Ex. 21:7). Strictly speaking, our editor could merely have added the laws on the bondwoman, but he inserted before them the laws on male slaves for the sake of completeness, to emphasize the difference in the treatment of male and female slaves in the old law.

The criteria guiding the Deuteronomist in this matter can easily be surmised. His main purpose was to transform his nation into "a holy people unto Jehovah" (Deut. 7:6; 14:2, 21; 26:19) living up to the ideals of the prophets. The realization of such an ideal could come only through the creation of a general state of mind dominated by love for God and man, and by the elimination of profane, unholy, impure, and ungenerous actions. Consequently, within the realm of the old case laws, only those having a social, philanthropic, or moral implication (or at least allowing such a nonjuristic interpretation) were germane to the aim of the book. All laws fixing property rights, unrelated to social and moral principles, were *ipso facto* excluded: laws fixing monetary or other compensation for bodily injuries (Ex. 21:18-22, 26-32) were omitted, but a related law dealing with a grossly obscene action was mercilessly enforced (Deut. 25:11 f.).

Of the family laws, the only one omitted dealt with monetary compensation for seduction of unbetrothed virgins (Ex. 22:17 [H. 22:16])—obviously most distasteful to the Deuteronomist; the laws on recovery of damages done to cattle or crops, theft, and compensation for loss of property in storage (21:33-22:15 [H. 22:14], omitting 22:9 [H. 22:8]), involving neither social nor moral matters, were omitted *in toto*, but the theft of persons for sale into slavery was regarded as an evil so defiling that it could be purged only with death (Deut. 24:7). The sale of a daughter into permanent slavery, allowed with some restrictions in the old law (Ex. 21:7-11), was rigidly abrogated in Deut. 15:12, 17b.

The civil laws chosen by the Deuteronomist either protected the rights of the oppressed and weak members of the community and provided for their welfare (Deut. 15:12-18; 21:15-17; 22:13-19, 26-29; 25:1-3, 5-10) or kept the community free from pollution of what was an abomination in the sight of Jehovah (24:1-4) by prompt punishment of the evildoers (19:16-20; 21:18-21; 22:20-22, 23-25; 24:7; 25:11 f.). The usual form of execution for violators was stoning (21:21; 22:21, 24; cf. for religious crimes 13:10 [H. 13:11]; 17:5), a most efficient method for removing the contagion of evil.

The Deuteronomist leaves no doubt as to his reasons for selecting the laws in the latter group by adding to the old law some standard phrases of his own: "thine eye shall not pity" (19:21; 25:12; cf. 7:16; 13:8 [H. 13:9]; 19:13); "and all Israel shall hear and fear" (with some minor variations: 19:20; 21:21; cf. 13:11 [H. 13:12]; 17:13; 31:13); "so shalt thou put away the evil from the midst of thee" (19:19; 21:21; 22:21 f., 24; 24:7; cf. 13:5 [H. 13:6]; 17:7, 12). The old laws in Deuteronomy dealt with criminal law to a considerable extent, those in Exodus with property law, which is why reference to the judges who imposed the sentence is found only in Deuteronomy. Usually (as we know was the case even during the monarchy; cf. I Kings 21:5-13), the elders of the town sat in judgment (21:19 f.; 22:15-18; 25:7-9; cf. 19:12), although there is also mention of judges (19:17 f. [omitting "before Jehovah, before the priests"]; cf. 17:9, 12). In Ex. 21:22 the *pelilîm* are not, strictly speaking, "judges" but private arbitrators.

The Deuteronomist used the juridical formulation also in purely religious laws which never stood in the old code and are probably altogether new in his book, namely, the laws in which the worship of other gods (or the mere inducement thereto) and the adoption of heathen religious and magical practices were made capital offenses (13:1-18 [H. 13:2-19]; 17:2-13; cf. 18:9-11). At the end he used the same formulae which he added to his revisions of the old case laws involving the death penalty (13:5, 8, 11 [H. 13:6, 9, 12]; 17:7, 12 f.). This also applies to the laws on murder (19:11-13; 21:1-9, 22 f.), where these formulae appear once

(19:13). The law on murder (Ex. 21:12-14), on kidnaping (21:16; cf. Deut. 24:7), and on smiting or cursing one's parents (Ex. 21:15, 17; cf. Deut. 21:18-21) are interpolated, in a nonjuristic formulation, into the case laws of the Covenant Code. Since they occur with variations among the case laws of Deuteronomy they may well have stood in a form no longer known in the old code. The other "case laws" in Deuteronomy (21:10-14; 22:6-8; 23:9-14 [H. 23:10-15]; 24:5) are Israelitic or Deuteronomistic and had no place in the old code.

In addition to the old Canaanite code of civil laws in the juristic formulation, the Covenant Code has preserved also remnants of one or more genuinely Israelitic codes earlier than Deuteronomy and derived in part from the ancient Bedouin law of the desert which the Israelites brought with them into Canaan (cf. A. Alt, *Die Ursprünge des israelitischen Rechts,* pp. 33-71). We have already observed that the laws in Ex. 21:12-17, 23-25 have no casuistic formulation and do not belong to the old code in which they are now embedded. Some of these (21:12, 15-17), and others elsewhere, have a characteristic form: they list capital offenses with impressive lapidary brevity; the Hebrew text is always limited to five words in slow rhythm: after an active participle followed by its object comes the formula *môth jûmath* ("he shall surely be put to death"). This characteristic formulation occurs in the following laws. Translated literally, they read as follows:

One smiting a man mortally must be put to death (21:12).
One smiting his father or his mother must be put to death (21:15).
One cursing his father or his mother must be put to death (21:17).
One stealing a man and selling him must be put to death (21:16).[5]
One lying with a beast must be put to death (22:19 [H. 22:18], omitting "everyone" at the beginning).
One sacrificing to other gods must be put to death (22:20 [H. 22:19], revised text).
One doing work on the Sabbath must be put to death (31:15b, with the omission of three words).

A series of such laws, in a different formulation and with many additions, although still recognizable by the words "he must be put to death," is found in Lev. 20:2, 9-13, 15 f.; 24:16 f., 21b, and perhaps 20:27, condemning the necromancer. Since the list includes three of the laws in the preceding series—cursing one's parents (Ex. 21:17; Lev. 20:9), bestiality (22:19 [H. 22:18]; Lev. 20:15 f.), and murder (Ex. 21:12; Lev. 24:17, 21b; cf. the axiomatic formulation in Gen. 9:6 and the various specifications in Num. 35:16-18, 21, 30 f.)—it is possible that, like the Twelve Curses in Deut. 27, these laws formed a single collection. We note, however, that some of them look like fairly late supplements to a

[5] Omitting the gloss "and he is found in his hand."

code which in its original form may go back to the nomadic period of
the Israelites. Obviously the execution of the worshiper of other gods
(Ex. 22:20 [H. 22:19]), of the Sabbath breaker (31:15b), and of the
Molech worshiper (Lev. 20:2) is hardly conceivable before 621 B.C. at
the earliest; we may hesitate in regard to the laws against the necromancer
(20:27) and the blasphemer (24:16), which could have been in force
among the Israelites ever since the invasion of Canaan. However, the
four laws in Lev. 20:10-13 dealing with adultery, incest, and homo-
sexuality, together with the first five of Exodus, could date back to the
early period of the history of Israel (cf. Gen. 26:11, J). Deuteronomy
contains no laws of this type because their brevity was ill-fitted to its
eloquent discourse and because their apodictic and absolute phrasing
could not be adapted to the tone of exhortation and warning, which
pervades the book.

The law on murder, which is accidentally missing in the remnants of
the old Canaanite code of laws, went through an interesting evolution in
the laws of Israel. The axiomatic principle that the murderer must be put
to death was stated in the code described above and quoted several times
either simply or with specifications. Some of the capital crimes listed in
this code, including murder (Deut. 27:24), form the subject of the
anathemas in Deut. 27:15-26. With classical simplicity, the same principle is stated by the Deuteronomist in his characteristic hortatory form
in the Sixth Commandment, "Thou shalt not kill" (Deut. 5:17 = Ex.
20:13). But such general statements were obviously inadequate in a more
advanced state of civilization.

Since time immemorial, the old law of the desert was the *lex talionis*
which demanded "life for life, eye for eye, tooth for tooth, hand for
hand, foot for foot, burning for burning, wound for wound, stripe for
stripe" (Ex. 21:23b-25; cf. Deut. 19:21; Lev. 24:20a); the execution of
a murderer was only a specific application of this more general law. Only
in particular instances is the old *lex talionis* still valid in the Hammurabi
Code (§§196, 197, 200; cf. §§116, 210, 230); but it no longer appears in
the Assyrian and Hittite codes. In the old Canaanite Code it is likewise
obsolete, for a monetary compensation is allowed even in the case of
death caused by an ox known to be vicious (Ex. 21:29 f., as in Hammurabi §251; cf. also 22:2 f. [H. 22:1 f.]) unless 21:31 means that the
son or daughter of the owner of the ox goring a boy or a girl is to be put
to death (as in Hammurabi §200; cf. §§116, 230).

But among the Israelites, who never forgot their desert origin, such
old nomadic institutions lingered even when they adopted Canaanite
civilization and law. "Life for life" in its absolute form is the principle of
the desert law of blood-revenge, which expressed the inviolable sacredness of the ties of kinship. The whole clan is responsible for the life of

each of its members, the tribal god demands restitution for the loss of any one of its worshipers. If a member of the clan kills his kinsman, the other members either drive him away (Gen. 4:14) or kill him (II Sam. 14:4-7); if the slayer belongs to another clan, the dead man's family or a member of his clan must kill him (Judg. 8:18-21; II Sam. 3:27) to appease the anger of the deity (II Sam. 21:1-9; cf. 14:9). This religious significance of blood-revenge is also manifest in the law of Deut. 21:1-9, according to which, when the murderer is unknown, the elders of the town nearest the place where the corpse was found must clear themselves before Jehovah by means of a sacrifice. In the primitive conception, the blood of the slain cries unto the deity from the ground (Gen. 4:10) unless it is covered up (Job 16:18; Is. 26:21; Ez. 24:7 f.).

This ancient barbarity of blood-revenge, well illustrated by the proud song of the Bedouin braggart Lamech (Gen. 4:23 f.), yielded to the refining influence of Canaan's higher civilization in two respects: the king could stop its course (II Sam. 14:8-11) and the right of asylum was given to the unintentional manslayer (in its original form, blood-revenge did not discriminate between murder and accidental manslaughter). Immediately after the old general law of Ex. 21:12 (decreeing the death penalty for all killers) come the laws, characteristically in the very midst of the code in participial form, discriminating between intentional (21:14) and unintentional (21:13) killing (the order of the laws in the text should be reversed), and providing the right of asylum only in the latter case. Like most laws of Israel, these are regarded as divinely revealed: "thou shalt take him from *my* altar"; "*I* will appoint thee a place." These laws may have existed as early as Solomon's reign: in any case, Solomon regarded Joab as a murderer and applied to him the principle of Ex. 21:14 (I Kings 2:28-34). The later codes explicitly recognize the right and duty of blood-revenge in the case of deliberate murder: Deut. 19:11-13 announces the procedure to be followed in applying the law of Ex. 21:14; Num. 35:14-34 expounds Ex. 21:13 f. with considerable detail. Special cities of refuge for unintentional slayers are provided in Deut. 4:41-43 (three cities east of the Jordan) and 19:1-10 (three cities west of the Jordan); Num. 35:6, 11-15 and Josh. 20:1-9 (21:13, 21, 27, 32, 38 [H. 21:36]): six cities in all.

The editor who, shortly before the final edition of the Pentateuch about 400 B.C., inserted the laws of the old Canaanite Civil Code, which had no parallel in Deuteronomy (Ex. 21:2-11, 18-22; 21:26-22:17 [H. 22:16]) either found in his copy the portions of old Israelitic codes appearing in 21:12-17, 23-25 or placed them there himself. In any case, he reproduced the old laws faithfully without editorial revision, having been fortunate in discovering a text transmitted through several centuries without additions and modifications. That such careful transmission of an old document

more or less unknown to the general reader was not impossible is shown
by the preservation of II Sam. 9-20 outside of the Deuteronomistic edition
of the books of Samuel, which enjoyed popular support and was therefore
abundantly annotated and revised. The old civil laws and the story of the
scandals at David's court have come down substantially intact, because
they were inserted where we find them shortly before the canonization
of the Pentateuch and Samuel respectively, after obscure circulation for
centuries. Following the canonization of these books, a thorough revision
of the old documents was no longer possible.

Another code of laws in the Covenant Code is Canaanitic in origin and
dates from before 1200, like the old code of civil laws; it was adopted
by the Israelites soon after their invasion into Canaan. This is *the old
ritual decalogue,* preserved in a late Deuteronomistic edition (*ca.* 550
B.C.) in Ex. 34:10-26 and, in a disarranged but earlier text in the Covenant Code (see my article in JBL 43 [1924] 294-310 and cf. HTR 23
[1931] 102-105). From the available material, the oldest form of this
decalogue may be reconstructed as follows:

I. THE FESTIVALS

1. Six days thou shalt do thy work, but on the seventh day thou shalt desist
   (Ex. 23:12a; cf. 34:21a [20:8-11; Deut. 5:12-15]).
2. The Feast of Unleavened Bread shalt thou keep at the appointed time in
   the month of Abib (Ex. 23:15aα in part; cf. 34:18a in part [13:3-10; Deut.
   16:3-8; Lev. 23:6-8; Ex. 12:14-20; Num. 28:17-25]).
3. And the Feast of Harvest, the first fruits of thy labors (Ex. 23:16aα; cf.
   34:22a [Deut. 16:9-12; Lev. 23:15-20 (21); Num. 28:26-31]).
4. And the Feast of Ingathering at the exit of the year (Ex. 23:16bα; cf.
   34:22b. [Deut. 16:13-15; Lev. 23:34b-36, 39-43; Num. 29:12-38]).
5. Three times in the year shall all thy males see the face of the Lord [not
   Jehovah, but *hā-'ādōn*] (Ex. 23:17, omitting "Yahweh"; cf. 34:23, omitting "Yahweh the God of Israel" [Deut. 16:16; Ex. 23:14; 34:24]).

II. THE SACRIFICES AND OFFERINGS

6. The first-born of thy sons shalt thou give unto me; thus shalt thou do to
   thy ox, thy sheep, (and thy ass; cf. LXX) (Ex. 22:29b-30a [H. 22:28b-
   30a]; cf. 34:19-20bα [Deut. 15:19-23; Ex. 13:2, 11-16; Num. 18:15]).
7. Thou shalt not sacrifice with leavened bread the blood of my sacrifice (Ex.
   23:18a; cf. 34:25a [Deut. 16:3; Lev. 2:11; 6:16f.]).
8. Neither shall there remain all night the fat of my feast until morning (Ex.
   23:18b; cf. 34:25b [Deut. 16:4; Ex. 12:10; Num. 9:12]).
9. The first of the first fruits of thy ground shalt thou bring into the house
   of thy god (Ex. 23:19a; cf. 34:26a, omitting "Yahweh" [22:29a (H.
   22:28a); Deut. 14:22; 18:4; 26:1-11; Lev. 23:10-20; 2:14-16; Num.
   15:17-21; 18:13]).
10. Thou shalt not boil a kid in its mother's milk (Ex. 23:19b; cf. 34:26b
    [Deut. 14:21b]).

In contrast with the civil legislation of the Covenant Code, which had no influence on the Deuteronomic Code (only Ex. 21:2-6 and 22:16 [H. 22:15] have parallels in Deut.), the influence of the ritual decalogue on all later Pentateuchal codifications cannot be overestimated (cf. the references to later codes given within brackets above). These old Canaanitic regulations for the worship formed the original kernel around which the Covenant Code gradually grew. They were not only revised and supplemented in that code in the spirit of the religion of Jehovah, but re-edited in the Deuteronomic Code shortly before 621, and in Ex. 34 about 550, and likewise brought up to date in the Holiness Code and in various strata of the Priestly Code.

Before Saul, the Israelites adopted this old ritual decalogue, which apparently originated at Shechem, by inserting the name of their god in 23:17, 19, and they added to it the prescriptions for building altars (Ex. 20:24-26) and for the observance of the Sabbatical year (23:10 f., omitting "that the poor of thy people may eat," a clause added, with another humanitarian gloss in 23:12b and the interpolations in 23:15aβb, about 650 B.C.). The archaic instructions for building the altar were observed in ancient Israel and, although disregarded by Solomon if he really placed the brazen altar in the Temple, were considered valid after the Exile. It is significant that tradition remembered the building of an altar of unhewn stones at Shechem soon after the Israelitic invasion of Canaan, connecting it with the writing of the law (Deut. 27:4-8; Josh. 8:30-32). The altar of the Second Temple, even in Herod's rebuilding of it, was of unhewn stones (see E. Schürer, *Geschichte des Jüdischen Volkes*, Vol. II, p. 344, n. 21, 4th ed., 1907).

The antiquity of the Sabbatical year is likewise beyond doubt. Not only is the prescription for leaving the land fallow in the seventh year repeated in later codes (Lev. 25:2-7, 20-22; 26:34 f., 43) and practiced in postexilic times (Neh. 10:32; II Chron. 36:21; I Macc. 6:49, 53; Josephus, *Antiquities* 14:10, 6; 15:1, 2; cf. Tacitus. *Hist.* 5:4), but it is probably connected with the release of enslaved debtors on the seventh year (Ex. 21:2-7; Deut. 15:12-18; cf. 15:1-6).

Outside the Covenant Code, the old ritual decalogue passed through two editions: in Deuteronomy (published in 621 B.C.), where, like the civil laws, the ten rules were scattered; and in Ex. 34 (about 550), where they were kept together. But even in Deuteronomy the arrangement of the laws in the old decalogue is not completely obliterated: laws 2-5 are found in their correct order in Deut. 16:3-16 and laws 7-8 in Deut. 16:3 f., where they were connected with the celebration of the Passover, of which there is no trace in the old decalogue. The other laws were placed by the Deuteronomists in suitable contexts: law 1 in the Ten Commandments (5:12-15); law 6 (15:19-23) immediately before laws

2-5 and after the law of the seventh year of release (law 6, which is out of place in Ex. 22:29b-30a [H. 22:28b-30a], was already displaced in the copies of the decalogue used by the Deuteronomist and by the editor of Ex. 34); laws 9 and 10 are placed among the laws about the revenues of priests and the dietary laws, respectively.

It has long been obvious that the author of D is not only dependent on the old decalogue, occasionally quoting it verbatim (e.g., 14:21b), but that often, as in the case of the civil laws already discussed, he amplified its concise diction with the hortatory and homiletic clauses characteristic of his style, introducing important modifications suitable to his time. Of course, he suppressed entirely that ancient barbaric rite of Canaan, the sacrifice of human first-born.

His most important innovation is the official sanction of the Passover, attached to the Feast of Unleavened Bread, as one of the three great annual festivals (cf. W. R. Arnold in JBL 31 [1912] 9). The Feasts of Harvest and of Ingathering he called the Feasts of Weeks and of Booths, respectively, injecting his humanitarian ideals into their observance (16:10-12, 14) and making joy and gratitude to God the keynote of their celebration (16:10, 15, 17). He laid stress on the unique place of worship, "the place which he shall choose" (i.e., the Temple in Jerusalem) (14:22 f.; 15:20; 16:2, 6 f., 11, 15 f. and often elsewhere), whereas the old law of Ex. 20:24b read (before the text was corrected) "in every place where I record my name," implying a multiplicity of sanctuaries belonging to Jehovah. The Sabbatical year of the land (Ex. 23:10 f.) is extended to the cancellation of debts in Deut. 15:1-6.

The Covenant Code, as edited about 650 B.C., contained the old ritual decalogue in its Israelitic edition, together with the old laws on the altar and Sabbatical year but not, as we have seen, the old civil legislation which came into the Deuteronomic Code (621 B.C.) from another source. The humanitarian motives, so conspicuous in Deuteronomy, make their appearance in this edition for the first time not only in glosses to the old ritual laws (Ex. 23:11aβ, "that the poor of thy people may eat"; 23:12b, omitted with all philanthropic considerations in Ex. 34 although included in the Deuteronomic Sabbath law, Deut. 5:14), but also in the new humanitarian prescriptions added in this edition (Ex. 22:21a, 23, 25a, 26 f. [H. 22:20a, 22, 24a, 25 f.]; 23:1-3, [4 f.?], 6-8). The gloss connecting the Feast of Unleavened Bread with the Exodus from Egypt (23:15aβ; and also 23:15b which is found in Deut. 16:16 and Ex. 34:20) was found here by the Deuteronomist (Deut. 16:3, 6; cf. 16:1). Like the old ritual laws, these humanitarian prescriptions are couched, in Exodus as well as in their Deuteronomic reproduction, in the second person singular, whereas the later ones take the second person plural. In the Deuteronomic Code they are rewritten in the following passages:

Subject	Exodus	Deuteronomy
Oppression of a stranger	22 : 21a 23[H. 22 : 20a, 22]	24 : 17f.
Usury	22 : 25a [H. 22 : 24a]	23 : 19f. [H. 23 : 20f.]
Pledges	22 : 26f. [H. 22 : 25f.]	24 : 10–13
False witness	23 : 1	5 : 20
Perversion of justice	23 : 2f., 6–8	16 : 19f.
Kindness to animals	23 : 4f.	22 : 1–4

As has been shown elsewhere (JBL 43 [1924] 294-310; HTR 23 [1931] 99-109), the copy of the old ritual decalogue in Ex. 34 (usually called *the J Decalogue*) comes later than Deuteronomy (621 B.C.) and dates from about 550 (R^D). In spite of the fact that the terminology of the laws in Ex. 23 is unmistakably more archaic than that of the parallel in Ex. 34, it is still the prevalent opinion of critics that Ex. 34 is an integral part of the J document (not later than 850 B.C.) and that Ex. 23 is a redactional copy thereof. Recently a new theory about Ex. 34 has been presented with much learning by J. Morgenstern ("The Oldest Document in the Hexateuch," HUCA IV [1927] 1-138). He has identified a "Kenite document" ("K") containing a biography of Moses, stressing particularly his relations with the Kenites, and ending with the settlement of the Judeans and Kenites in Southern Palestine (Judg. 1). This document reaches its religious climax when the Kenite god Yahweh manifests himself to Moses, and reveals the laws of Ex. 34, the Tabernacle, and the priestly oracle (Ex. 33). The Kenite book was written before 899 B.C., and inspired the religious reforms of Asa (I Kings 15:9-15; cf. II Chron. 14:1-4; 15:1-18).

However attractive or suggestive this theory, the fact remains that the laws in Ex. 34 are not only demonstrably later in formulation than those in Ex. 23, but written under the influence of Deuteronomy: note in particular the name "Feast of Weeks" (34:22), taken from Deut. 16:9 f., 16 (contrast Ex. 23:16); the mention of the Passover (34:25b; cf. Deut. 16:1-8; contrast Ex. 23:18); and omission of the sacrifice of the first-born of men (Ex. 22:29b [H. 22:28b]).

The law on the sacrifice of first-born animals in 34:19 f., providing for redemption as in the late law Ex. 13:12 f., is unquestionably later than Deut. 15:19-23. Following Deut. 5:13, Ex. 34:21 says, "thou shalt labor," whereas Ex. 23:12 says "thou shalt do thy work"; in contrast with Ex. 23:18 and Deut. 16:2, which use the old Semitic term for "to sacrifice" (*zābaḥ*), 34:25 uses the technical term current in the Levitical legislation (*šāḥaṭ*). In Ex. 23:16 the third annual festival is dated "at the exit of the year," according to the old Canaanitic calendar in which the year began on September 21, but 34:22 substitutes the "revolution of the year," an expression found elsewhere only in II Chron. 24:23. The latter phrase, which could be applied to any of the four changes of season, was used because about 600 B.C. the Jews adopted the Babylonian calendar in which the year began on March 21.

Morgenstern regards such marks of late date, in Ex. 34, as editorial changes of the text (cf. for "feast of weeks" in 34:22, HUCA IV, 73-79), but only proves that a late text, which is a revision of an early one, may be changed by emendation into its prototype. Exodus 34 is both Deuteronomistic in language and provided with a typical Deuteronomistic introduction (34:6 f., 10-17).

Moreover, Ex. 34 was inserted into a J story (34:1a, 2, 4, 28) already revised about 650 B.C. by the JE redactor, who added 34:1b and the words "like the former ones" in 34:4. This story did not yet contain any laws when it was rewritten in Deut. 10:1-4, 10. Therefore, it hardly seems expedient to revise the late text of Ex. 34 to conform with the early text of Ex. 23—and then pronounce it earlier. The only conclusion which is in harmony with the facts is that reached also by A. Alt (*Die Ursprünge des israelitischen Rechts*, p. 52, n. 1), who sees in it only "a secondary compilation" (*ein sekundäres Mischgebilde*).

As we have seen, the edition of the Covenant Code issued in 650 was an important source of the Deuteronomic Code and may be regarded as its immediate precursor although, of all the great ideas of Deuteronomy, only humanitarian concern for oppressed members of the community (and even for animals) appears in it. There is no trace of the prophetic theology, of the Deuteronomic centralization of worship, nor of a divine covenant with Israel.

It was therefore inevitable that, after the publication of the Deuteronomic Code and Josiah's reforms in 621 had profoundly modified the religion of Israel, paving the way for the birth of Judaism, a new edition of the Covenant Code, giving expression to the religious aspirations and practices of the exilic period, should be issued by editors of the Deuteronomistic school. This edition, dating from about 550 (R^D), was provided after the manner of the Deuteronomists, with a suitable introduction (20:22 f.) and conclusion (23:20-33, where verses 28-30 may have been taken from another source), in which the transcendence of Jehovah (20:22b), denunciation of idolatry in general (20:23) and of the Canaanite religion in particular (23:24, 33), previously missing in the book, received adequate emphasis.

At the same time, the humanitarian prescriptions were supplemented with others easily recognized from the second person plural (the only exception is 23:9a, quoted from 22:21a [H. 22:20a]) instead of the singular used in 650. Following Deuteronomy (10:18; 14:29; 16:11, 14; 24:17-21; 26:12 f.) this editor adds to the resident alien (23:9a) the widow and the fatherless (22:22 [H. 22:21]) as typical of the oppressed. Influenced by Deut. 23:19 [H. 23:20], he supplements the prohibition of usury with the prohibition of interest (22:25b [H. 22:24b]). Exactly like the Deuteronomist, he quotes the bitter experience of Israel in Egyptian bondage as a reason for kindness to the underprivileged (22:21b [H. 22:20b]; 23:9b; cf. Deut. 5:15; 10:19; 24:18, 22) and threatens dire divine punishment on violators of these laws (22:24 [H. 22:23]; cf. Deut. 28:15 ff.). Like Deuteronomy, he calls his god Yahweh, not Elohim (20:22; 23:25). In the old ritual decalogue, the words "which thou sowest in the field" and "when thou gatherest in the labors out of the field" (23:16), missing in Ex. 34, seem to have been added in the edition of 550 or a later one.

The final editor of the Covenant Code (ca. 450 B.C.) inserted the ancient codes of civil law (21:2-22:17 [H. 22:16]) attaching a title at the beginning (21:1) and three laws at the end (22:18-20 [H. 22:17-19]). The first one of these commands the execution of witches, and the other two were part of the code in participial form apparently joined to the old Canaanite laws by this same editor.

This editor also added a few glosses to the ritual decalogue. Their date may be fixed about 450 by two facts. In the first place, they are missing from the transcripts of the old decalogue in Ex. 34 and in Deuteronomy (Ex. 22:28, 29a, 30b, 31 [H. 22:27, 28a, 29b, 30]; 23:13 f.); in the second place, in thought and expression they all betray the influence of the Priestly Code (500-450). The word for "ruler" in 22:28 [H. 22:27] is not found before Ezekiel and P; the word "bounty" (of crops) in 22:29a [H. 22:28a] occurs in P (Num. 18:27), but has a different and earlier meaning in Deut. 22:9; the offering of the first-born of animals on the eighth day after birth (22:30b [H. 22:29b]) is paralleled in Lev. 22:27, but not in Ex. 34 and Deuteronomy; 22:31 [H. 22:30] lays emphasis on ritual holiness after the manner of H and P (never in D) and, like H and P, forbids the use of the meat of animals dying in the field (Lev. 11:39; 17:15; 22:8; cf. 7:24). Note the contrast in Deut. 14:21, where such flesh was still allowed resident aliens or foreigners. To prohibit the mere mention of "other gods" (23:13) was inconceivable before the fifth (or at most the sixth) century; the Hebrew word "times" in 23:14 is not the ordinary word occurring in 23:17, but an unusual expression found only in the Balaam episode (Num. 22:28, 32 f.) and apparently quoted from there; the verb "to keep a feast" does not occur elsewhere before P, except for Deut. 16:15 and perhaps in Ex. 5:1. Most of these verses have thus the characteristics of priestly annotations.

2. The Anathemas in Deut. 27:15-26

Strictly speaking, the twelve solemn curses, which Moses commanded the Levites to utter before the Israelites when they would cross the Jordan and come to Shechem, are not a code of laws but a liturgy in which the congregation participated by pronouncing "Amen" after each curse. But while these curses are not laws in form, in substance they are a summary of civil, humanitarian, and religious legislation dealing with offenses committed in secret and therefore known only to God, who alone can punish the offenders: the community can only utter curses against them.

The origin of these anathemas is obscure. They are contained in a chapter added to the Deuteronomic Code of 621 by a later redactor. Hence, as in the case of the Covenant Code, no clue to their date is to be sought in their present context. More significant is the geographical setting: Moses orders six tribes to stand on Mount Gerizim for the curse and six on Mount Ebal for the blessing (27:11-14). The tradition connecting Shechem (the present Nablus, located in the valley between these two mountains) with the giving of the law (Josh. 8:32; 24:25-27; Deut. 11:29; 27:2-8) seems to have an historical basis: it not only contradicted the doctrine which derived all legislation from Moses at Sinai, but confirmed the claims of the Samaritans in regard to exclusive legitimacy of the Temple of Jehovah on Gerizim (John 4:20). The latter doctrine was so heretical to the Jews that they did not hesitate to change "Gerizim" into "Ebal" in Deut. 27:4 (where the Samaritan text and the Old Latin version still read "Gerizim") and probably in Josh. 8:30 (see in general the important study of B. Luther and E. Meyer in E. Meyer, *Die Israeliten und ihre Nachbarstämme*, pp. 542-561).

But even if we believe, as most critics do, that the curses were actually pronounced in a solemn meeting at Shechem soon after the conquest of the land, we cannot determine for certain whether they were originally a Canaanite or a genuine Israelitic ritual. In form and content the resemblance of these anathemas to the code on capital offenses couched in participial form seems to favor an Israelitic origin for the list of curses. The first and last curses (27:15, 26) define the offense by means of a relative sentence and are clearly later additions, but the other ten use the participle like the other code; the repetition of "accursed" at the beginning corresponds to "he will certainly put to death" in the other code. In the "participial" criminal code, each law has five words, in the curses each one has four words,[6] although interpolations are now present in both codes. In Deut. 27, we must not only omit vv. 15 and 26, but also the following clauses: in v. 19, the Deuteronomistic list of "stranger, fatherless, and widow" (cf. Deut. 24:17) represents an expansion, and the original only had one term, probably "stranger" (we have seen that "fatherless and widow" were added in the Covenant Code in 550); "because he has uncovered his father's shirt" (v. 20; cf. 23:1); "the daughter

---

[6] The standard formulation of the ten curses is: "Accursed—one despising—his father—and his mother."

of his father or the daughter of his mother" (v. 22; cf. Lev. 18:9; 20:17); "to slay an innocent person" (v. 25; cf. Lev. 24:17; Deut. 19:10).

We may classify the curses as follows:

1. Criminal offenses punishable by death according to the "participial code": contempt for parents (v. 16; cf. Ex. 21:17; Lev. 20:9); incest with father's wife (v. 20; cf. Lev. 18:8; 20:11); bestiality (v. 21; cf. Ex. 22:19 [H. 22:18]; Lev. 18:23; 20:15 f.); and probably incest with a sister (v. 22; cf. Lev. 18-9; 20:17) and with a mother-in-law (v. 23; cf. Lev. 18:17; 20:14) which, though preserved in Leviticus in a different formulation, may have belonged to the old participial code; criminal assault presumably with fatal results (v. 24; cf. Ex. 21:12; Lev. 24:17, 21b).

2. Acts of dishonesty: moving landmarks (v. 17; cf. 19:14); perversion of justice (v. 19; cf. 24:17; Ex. 22:21-24; 23.9); accepting bribes (v. 25; cf. Ex. 23:8; Deut. 16:19). These three deceitful acts are frequently denounced by the prophets, and in the wisdom books of Egypt and the Old Testament (cf. J. Fichtner, *Die Altorientalische Weisheit* u.s.w., pp. 25 f., 28 f Beih. ZAW 62).

3. Misleading the blind (v. 18; cf. Lev. 19:14).

In its present form, Deut. 27:15-26 is fairly late: the curse on the idol-maker, particularly in the words of 27:15, is unquestionably later than the publication of the D Code in 621 and even of Is. 40-55, about 540 (cf. JBL 43 [1924] 229-240); 27:26 obviously refers to the D Code; these two verses and the other glosses probably belong to the fifth century. The original list of curses must be later than the "participial" code (which may be earlier than the period of the settlement in Canaan) and possibly though not probably antedates the monarchy; 27:17-19, 25 presupposes the complete change in the Israelites' mode of life, from nomadic to agricultural. A date in the ninth or eighth century seems to be in harmony with the characteristics of these curses.

3. The Ten Commandments

The Ten Commandments appear in two editions, a Deuteronomistic one in Deut. 5:6-21 (H. 5:6-18) and a Priestly one (Ex. 20:2-17). The chief difference between them is the motivation for the observance of the Sabbath:[7] a rest for the laborers, including farm animals, granted in gratitude for deliverance from Egyptian bondage in Deut. 5:14 f.; but in Ex. 20:11 (cf. Gen. 2:2 f., P) sanctification of the day on which God rested after creating the world in six days.

The second of these editions (Ex. 20) is unquestionably later. It is clear that Ex. 20:11 cannot be dated earlier than 500 B.C.; it probably belongs to the second half of the fifth century. Like the Covenant Code,

---

[7] For minor differences see S. R. Driver's *Commentary on Deuteronomy*, and commentaries on Deuteronomy and Exodus in general.

the copy in Ex. 20 was inserted into the Sinai stories in the latter part of the fifth century, possibly by the same redactor. The Ten Commandments break the connection between Ex. 19 and 20:18 and their insertion occurred later than that of the old ritual decalogue into Ex. 34, since there the words written on the two stone tables are the old ritual decalogue, "the words of the covenant" (34:28) and not, as in Deut. 5:19; 10:4, the Ten Commandments. Judging from Ex. 20:11, RP was the redactor who inserted the Ten Commandments in Ex. 20 after the middle of the fifth century.

It is even questionable whether the Ten Commandments were an original part of Deut. 5 (since 5:22 [H. 5:19] could be the sequel of 5:4) and whether they were in the D Code which was found in the Temple in 621. However, the style and ideas of the Ten Commandments are so thoroughly Deuteronomic that, in their present form, they can be attributed only to the author of the D Code, or to the Deuteronomists of 550 B.C. Broadly speaking, the first alternative is preferable in view of the ethical and religious nobility of this Decalogue.

Typical Deuteronomistic expressions follow: "Jehovah thy god, who brought thee out of the land of Egypt, from the house of bondage" (5:6; cf. 5:15); "other gods" (5:7); "likeness" (5:8); "a jealous God" (5:9; cf. Ex. 34:14; Deut. 4:24; 6:15); "to bow down and serve [other gods]" (5:9); "to love [God]" (5:10); "keep my commandments" (5:10); "thy stranger that is within thy gates" (5:14); "maidservant" (5:14, 21); "thou, thy son," etc. (5:14; cf. 12:18; 16:11, 14); "remember" (5:15); "through a mighty hand and by a stretched out arm" (5:15); "as Jehovah thy god has commanded thee" (5:12, 16); "that thy days may be lengthened" "and that it may go well with thee" "in the land which Jehovah thy god gives thee" (5:16).

All these expressions, except those in 5:12, 15 and "that it may go well with thee" (5:16), occur also in Ex. 20. Although both versions are obviously Deuteronomic in style, the difference between them brings up the question of the genuineness of Deuteronomic expressions listed. Are they to be considered redactional amplifications of a much shorter original text?

We have seen that in Ex. 34 a Deuteronomic edition exists of the old ritual decalogue, a much earlier version of which can be reconstructed through comparison with Ex. 22-23. But in the case of the Ten Commandments we lack all documentary evidence for a previous shorter version. As shown by the divergent results attained by critics who have reconstructed the supposed original version of this code,[8] such attempts

---

[8] The following publications present a few typical examples of reconstructions of the Decalogue: B. Stade, *Biblische Theologie des Alten Testaments*, Vol. I, pp. 249 f. O. Procksch, *Die Elohimquelle*, pp. 88 f. C. Steuernagel, *Einleitung in das Alte Testa-*

to reach an original non-Deuteronomic text are necessarily subjective. The fact remains that even H. Schmidt, who takes the greatest liberties with the text and actually eliminates the two Commandments on respecting one's parents and on the Sabbath, cannot obliterate the Deuteronomic idioms entirely from his alleged original decalogue. And this fact stubbornly precludes the attribution of the Ten Commandments to Moses.[9] For not only is the language Deuteronomic but also the ideas, no matter how much they may be condensed.

The Ten Commandments, we are often told, are a compendium of prophetic religion. This is only partly true. Like the prophets, the Fifth to the Tenth Commandments make of morality an integral part of religion; but whereas for the prophets religion was primarily an attitude of mind (righteousness, loyalty, faith) expressing itself in right living rather than in worship, the Decalogue, in Commandments one to four, endeavors to purify the worship of Jehovah from heathen contamination, and emphasizes the holiness of the Sabbath day, while in Commandments five to ten it lists a number of sins which are partly criminal acts punished by the state and partly mere ethical transgressions. The prophets did not codify the will of God, which is the standard of moral conduct, in this manner; nor did they concern themselves with purely ritual matters, such as the use of sacred images or the observance of the Sabbath. On the contrary, they consider the latter as one of the festivals distasteful to God (Is. 1:13; Hos. 2:11 [H. 2:13]).

No, the Ten Commandments do not represent the prophetic teaching in its inspired purity, but rather a Deuteronomic compromise between the prophetic religion of right motives and the priestly religion of ritual observances. In contrast with the great affirmations of the prophets, all the Commandments, except two (keeping the Sabbath and honoring one's parents) are negative in form. The conception of God is identical with that of the Deuteronomic code. Jehovah is the God of Israel (Deut. 5:6; cf. 6:4, "Jehovah is our god, Jehovah alone"); he is a jealous god (5:9; cf. 6:15) and tolerates neither strange gods (5:7; cf. 6:14; 7:4; 8:19; 11:16, 28; 13; 17:2 f., etc.) nor sacred images of any sort (5:8-10; cf. 12:2 f.); he is at the same time just and merciful, and demands of his worshipers a love that expresses itself in keeping his Commandments (5:9 f.; cf. 6:5-19, etc.).

---

ment, p. 260. Tübingen, 1912. W. Nowack, Festschrift für Baudissin (Beih. ZAW 33), pp. 381 ff. Giessen, 1918. J. A. Bewer, The Literature of the Old Testament, pp. 30 f. H. Schmidt in Eucharisterion (Festschrift für H. Gunkel), Vol. I, p. 107. Göttingen, 1923. R. Kittel, Geschichte des Volkes Israel, Vol. I, pp. 383 f. (7th ed.). Stuttgart, 1932. G. A. Barton, Semitic and Hamitic Origins, p. 352. Philadelphia, 1934.

[9] Among the authors mentioned in the preceding note, Procksch (pp. 227 f.), Nowack, Schmidt, and Kittel attribute the shorter decalogue to Moses. For the date of the Decalogue, see Sh. Spiegel in HTR 27 (1934) 140 f.

As to a Mosaic origin of the first four Commandments, it must be regarded as a guess without historical basis. Moses could conceivably have forbidden the worship of other gods (although Elijah is the first to protest against it) and the profane use of Jehovah's name (for magical purposes?), but it can positively be asserted that he was concerned neither with images nor with the Sabbath. There is no trace of animus toward idols before Isaiah (cf. JBL 43 [1924] 229-233), and the Sabbath is a Canaanitic institution (connected with the agricultural festivals in the old ritual decalogue and in Hos. 2:11 [H. 2:13]). The Sabbath is inconceivable among the nomads of the desert: either they are raiders, and then every day is a Sabbath when they are not on a foray, when no Sabbath would be observed, or they are shepherds, and their work cannot be interrupted one day in seven, as in farm work.

In regard to the last six Commandments, the situation is different: except for the tenth, they concern offenses against the civil law. There is no parallel in the Bible for the tenth ("thou shalt not covet . . ."), which can be interpreted either as referring to the superstitious fear concerning the evil effects of envious admiration for the property of another, still current among the Moslem (cf. E. W. Lane, *The Manners and Customs of the Modern Egyptians,* ch. 11, p. 256, Everyman's Library ed.), or to covetousness leading to unlawful expropriation, as in Mic. 2:1 f. In either case, an attribution to Moses is purely hypothetical. Commandments five to nine deal with offenses condemned in every code of laws from time immemorial, particularly in the case of the three basic crimes (murder, adultery, theft).

The Decalogue, as A. Alt (*Die Ursprünge des israelitischen Rechts,* pp. 52-59) has shown, represents a later stage in the juristic development than the codes previously discussed. There is a chronological succession in Israelitic laws from the axiomatic "one doing this shall surely be put to death" to the anathema "accursed be one doing this," and finally to the hortatory (typical of the Deuteronomic Code) "do not do this" in the Ten Commandments (where, however, the formulation is not rigidly standardized). The source of Commandment four (the Sabbath) is the old ritual decalogue (Ex. 23:12; 34:21); Commandments five to nine are derived from the other codes, as shown in this table (Deut. 5:17-21 correspond to 5:17 f. in the Hebrew).

Under the circumstances, there is no reason for supposing, as some critics do, that the Ten Commandments were known to David (II Sam. 11), Elijah (I Kings 21:9), the J author (Ex. 34), the E author (Ex. 20), Hosea (4:2),[10] or even to Jeremiah (7:9), although in the last case there

[10] Sh. Spiegel (HTR 27 [1934] 105-144) discovers "The earliest, definite and dated, literary attestation of the decalogue" in a reconstructed text of Hos. 6:5 (p. 142) and dates the Ten Commandments before 730 B.C.

Commandment	Ten Commandments	Canaanitic Code	Participial Code	Curses Deut. 27
5. Parents	Ex. 20 : 12 Deut. 5 : 16	. . . . . .	Ex. 21 :17 Lev. 20 : 9	27 :16
6. Murder	Ex. 20 : 13 Deut. 5 : 17	?	Ex. 21 : 12	27 : 24
7. Adultery	Ex. 20 : 14 Deut. 5 : 18	Deut. 22 : 22	Lev. 20 : 10	. . . .
8. Theft	Ex. 20 : 15 Deut. 5 : 19	(Ex. 22 : 1–4 [H. 21 : 37–22 : 3])	. . . . . .	. . . .
9. False witness	Ex. 20 : 16 Deut. 5 : 20	Deut. 19 : 16–20 (cf. Ex. 23 : 1)	. . . . . .	. . . .

is no chronological impossibility. There never was a time in the history of Israel when murder, adultery, perjury, theft, and the like were not considered offenses of the first magnitude and punished first according to customary common law and later according to written codes. The first actual allusion to the Ten Commandments in the Bible is Lev. 19:2-4, 11-13, dating from about 550 B.C. Composed by the author of the Deuteronomic Code of 621, the Ten Commandments were not yet regarded as the law written by Moses on the two tables of stone by the redactor who inserted the ritual decalogue into Ex. 34 about 550, but they were used at that time by the author of the Holiness Code in Lev. 19—his summary of the ethical principles of early Judaism.

4. The Deuteronomic Code (Deut. 12-26)

Strictly speaking, the book of the law found in the Temple in 621 B.C. was not a legal code but a long address of Moses contained substantially in Deut. 5-26; 28. The main part of this sermon, however, is the miscellaneous collection of laws (in Deut. 12-26) which Moses exhorts the people to keep: this body of legislation, being part of an address, is couched in oratorical, homiletic style.

Although certain broad divisions may be detected in Deut. 12-26, no logical arrangement is followed in the order of individual prescriptions; in fact, the disorder is so extreme that one would almost call it deliberate, unless it arose as a result of successive additions of new material. The contents of the code may be summarized as follows:

1. Religious institutions. *a.* Centralization of worship at a single sanctuary, which involves the destruction of the "high places" and the slaughtering of animals without sacrifice (12:2-28). *b.* Warning against

imitation of Canaanite religious practices, and punishment of apostasy and its advocates (12:29-13:18 [H. 13:19]). *c.* Warning against pagan mourning customs (14:1 f.). *d.* Dietary prescriptions (14:3-21). *e.* Tithes (14:22-29).

2. Cancellation of debts (15:1-11) and manumission of Hebrew slaves (15:12-18) on the seventh year.

3. Offerings and festivals. The sacrifice of unblemished firstlings (15:19-23). The three annual festivals (16:1-17).

4. The local judges (16:18-20).

5. Prohibition of sacred pillars and posts (16:21 f.), blemished sacrificial victims (17:1), and worship of astral deities (17:2-7).

6. Civil and religious authorities. *a.* The highest court (17:8-13). *b.* The king (17:14-20). *c.* The revenues of the Levitical priests (18:1-8). *d.* Prohibition of Moloch worship, divination, and magic (18:9-14). *e.* True and false prophets (18:15-22).

7. Judicial procedure. *a.* The right of asylum for unintentional slayers, but not for murderers (19:1-13). *b.* Moving of landmarks (19:14). *c.* Witnesses (19:15-21).

8. Warfare. *a.* The army chaplain (20:1-4). *b.* Exemptions from military service (20:5-8). *c.* Appointment of officers (20:9). *d.* Investment of hostile cities (20:10-20).

9. Judicial procedure. Inquest for unsolved murder (21:1-9).

10. Family laws. *a.* Marriage with woman captured in war (21:10-14). *b.* Primogeniture (21:15-17). *c.* Rebellious son (21:18-21).

11. Judicial procedure. Burial of hanged criminal (21:22 f.).

12. Consideration for persons and animals. Restoration to owner of lost animals (22:1-3); help to animals in distress (22:4).

13. Wearing apparel of opposite sex forbidden (22:5).

14. Consideration for persons and animals. *a.* Mother bird not to be taken (22:6 f.). *b.* Roofs to be provided with parapets (22:8).

15. Mixtures forbidden: different seeds in vineyard (22:9); ox and donkey on the same plow (22:10); different materials in cloth (22:11). Tassels on corners of upper garment (22:12).

16. Marriage laws. Virginity of the bride (22:13-21); adultery (22:22); seduction and rape (22:23-29); incest with stepmother (22:30 [H. 23:1]).

17. Exclusion from citizenship of: eunuchs (23:1 [H. 23:2]); bastards (23:2 [H. 23:3]); Ammonites and Moabites (23:3-6 [H. 23:4-7]); but not of Edomites and Egyptians in the third generation (23:7 f. [H. 23:8 f.]).

18. Hygienic rules for the camp (23:9-14 [H. 23:10-15]).

19. Kindness to runaway slave (23:15 f. [H. 23:16 f.]).

20. Prostitutes and sodomites (23:17 f. [H. 23:18 f.]).

21. Interest allowed only with strangers (23:19 f. [H. 23:20 f.]).

22. Payment of vows (23:21-23 [H. 23:22-24]).

23. Eating, not stealing, of a neighbor's grapes or corn (23:24 f. [H. 23:25 f.]).

24. Marriage laws. Divorce (24:1-4); release from war and other obligations for one year after marriage (24:5).

25. Millstones not to be taken as pledges (24:6).

26. Kidnaping (24:7).

27. Leprosy (24:8 f.).

28. Humanitarian prescriptions. Consideration for debtors (24:10-13) and hired servants (24:14 f.); the family of the criminal is not to be punished with him (24:16); consideration for the stranger, the fatherless, and the widow (24:17-22).

29. Judicial procedure. Limitation of number of strokes administered to a malefactor (25:1-3).

30. Consideration for animals. The threshing ox is not to be muzzled (25:4).

31. Marriage laws. Levirate marriage (25:5-10).

32. Assault and battery. Punishment of immodest woman (25:11 f.).

33. Commercial laws. Honest weights and measures (25:13-16).

34. Amalek to be annihilated (25:17-19).

35. Ritual and liturgy for the presentation of first fruits (26:1-11) and tithes of the third year (26:12-15). [Conclusion, 26:16-19.]

These 35 subdivisions can be grouped as follows:

I. Religious laws: 1, 3, 5, 6c-e, 8a, 22, 35 (cf. 13, 15; 20, 27).

II. Humanitarian laws: 1. Warfare: 8b, 18 (cf. 10a); 2. Consideration for strangers, widows, orphans, slaves, and other persons: 14b, 19, 21, 23, 25, 28 (cf. 2, 29); 3. Consideration for animals: 12, 14a, 30.

III. Civil laws: 1. Law of persons: a. liability, arising from contract: 2; arising from tort: 32; b. the family: 10, 16, 24, 31. 2. Law of property: 7b, 26, 33. 3. Law of procedure: 4, 6a, 7ac, 9, 11, 29.

IV. The state: 6b, 8cd, 17, 34.

The following passages have been questioned by some critics, and may not have stood in the original edition of the D Code: 12:8-12, 15 f., 25; 14:4-21aα; 15:4-6; 17:14-20 (cf. I Sam. 8:4-18; Deut. 31:9, 26); 18:14-19 (?); 20 (?); 21:5.

The religious laws comprise nearly half of the code (150 out of 340 verses). In part they represent, as we have seen, a rewriting of the old ritual decalogue (except for the Sabbath law placed in the Ten Commandments). These old laws are found in section 3 (cf. also 14:22-29; 18:4) with one important innovation: the Passover is combined with the Feast of Unleavened Bread (16:1-8). Far more revolutionary is the law commanding centralization of worship in a single sanctuary—"the place that Jehovah shall choose"—i.e., according to the interpretation of Josiah which is obviously correct, the Temple in Jerusalem. Recent attempts to show that "the place that Jehovah shall choose" really meant a number of legitimate sanctuaries, are utterly unconvincing (cf. A. R. Siebens, *L'origine du code deutéronomique,* pp. 103-118; J. A. Bewer in JBL 47 [1928] 306-321).

The original formulation of the new law centralizing the worship at Jerusalem forbade the presentation of burnt offerings (12:13 f.) and of other sacrifices (12:17-19; 15:19-23), and the celebration of the three annual festivals (16:1-17) except at the unique sanctuary. The corollaries of this law are the destruction of all the high places (the old Canaanitic shrines dedicated to Jehovah) throughout the land (12:2 f.; cf. 16:21 f.; the D Code avoids the use of the term *bāmôth* [high places], common in later Deuteronomistic writings like Kings); permission to slaughter animals for food in the villages, without sacrifice (12:20-24), which is contrary to the old custom in which butchery involved sacrifice (cf. Lev. 17:3 f.; I Sam. 14:32-35); conversion of tithes into money to facilitate the payment at the central sanctuary every third year (14:22-29); permission to priests in provincial sanctuaries to come to Jerusalem and officiate there in the Temple (18:6-8)—a Utopically generous provision that Josiah could not enforce (II Kings 23:8 f.); reorganization of the judicial system (16:18; 17:8-13) to take the place of the courts at the local sanctuaries (Ex. 22:8 f. [H. 22:7 f.]); and finally provision of three cities of refuge offering asylum to unintentional slayers in place of the destroyed local sanctuaries (19:1-13). The ritual for the presentation of first fruits and tithes at the central sanctuary is given in 26:1-11, 12-15.

As appears also in Josiah's reforms based on the D Code, the purpose of the law centralizing worship at Jerusalem was primarily to purify the worship of Jehovah from Canaanitic and other heathenish practices considered abominable in the eyes of Jehovah, and at the same time to prevent the worship of other gods on the part of the Judeans. Another view of this law is presented by G. F. Moore (*Encyclopaedia Biblica* 1 [1899] 1091 f.): the author of the code instinctively felt that multiplicity of places of worship was not consistent with monotheism, and might lead the people to believe that the Jehovah of one sanctuary was different from that of another. Three considerations compel rejection of this view held by this eminent scholar. First, there is no trace of monotheism in Deuteronomy outside of ch. 4 (which is postexilic); second, nowhere, even in the vaguest way, does the author forbid the worship of "other Jehovahs," but only of "other gods"; and third, the translation of 6:4 as "Yahweh our god is *one* Yahweh" sounds less plausible than "Yahweh is our god, Yahweh alone" (so Ibn Ezra, C. Steuernagel, etc.), which summarizes the fundamental Deuteronomic doctrine of exclusive worship of Jehovah on the part of the Judeans.

These two inseparable aims of the law of centralization, namely, purification of worship and its sole consecration to Jehovah, are apparent in most of the other religious laws of the book. Purification of worship implies not only the removal of shrines and sacred objects of alien origin, such as the "high places" with their altars, pillars and posts, and idols (12:2 f.; 16:21 f.) but also scrupulous avoidance of what is ritually defiling (12:16, 23-25; 14:3, 21 [4-20]; 15:23; 21:1-9, 22 f.; 23:9-14, 17 f. [H. 23:10-15, 18 f.]; 24:8) including such small matters as victims with a blemish (15:21; 17:1) and mourning customs (14:1; cf. 26:14).

This interest in details of an external and nonmoral nature indicates how conservative and ritually minded the author was in some matters. Particularly significant is the list of "abominations" to the Lord (16:21-17:1; 18:9-12; 22:5; 23:18 [H. 23:19]; 25:13-16), ranging all the way from child sacrifice in Moloch worship (18:10) down to wearing the garments of the other sex (22:5; the strange laws in 22:9-12 are probably to be classed with it).

To preserve Jehovah's children (14:1 f., 21; cf. 7:6; 26:19), the holy chosen people, from contamination, severe measures such as these were to be taken. The Canaanites were to be exterminated (12:29 f.; cf. 7:1-4, 16; 20:16-18)—a bloody program that fortunately was not carried out when there were Canaanites to be slaughtered and that was mere wishful thinking in 621. This applies also to the Amalekites (25:17-19; cf. the old poem in Ex. 17:14-16). Why the author decreed that Edomites and Egyptians could be admitted to the nation, but never Moabites and Ammonites (23:3-8), remains an insoluble riddle.

No less severe than the laws against the heathen were the laws against apostasy, dooming both those who induced Judeans to worship other gods and such individuals or cities as had forsaken Jehovah (12:29-13:18 [H. 13:19]; 17:2-7; 18:20; cf., on the worship of other gods, 4:19; 5:7; 6:14; 7:4; 8:19; 11:16, 28; 18:9-14; 28:14, 36). The only religious laws not directly connected with the main purpose of the book are those on vows (23:21-23 [H. 23:22-24]), on the regular revenues of Levitical priests (18:1-8), on the marks of the true prophet (18:15-22), and, if authentic, on the army chaplain (20:1-4).

Prescriptions for humane conduct fall into three groups: laws on warfare, consideration of the needy, and kind treatment of animals. The incredible exemptions from military service in time of war for anyone who had just built a house, planted a vineyard, betrothed a woman, and even for every coward in the ranks (20:5-8), are so Utopian and impracticable (even if they go back to early magical conceptions) that they have been regarded as postexilic dreams by some critics. The Judeans could hardly have followed these rules while they had a state of their own and waged wars. However, exemption of the newly married also occurs in 24:5, and idealistic chimerical legislation is not in the least alien to the spirit of the D Code. Nor does one expect logic in this book. Recognition of the rights of a female captive and permission to marry her (21:10-14) is hardly consistent with the destruction of the Canaanites and provision for the purity of Judean blood prescribed elsewhere (cf. 7:3). Other laws on warfare, such as negotiations preceding an attack and the sparing of fruit trees belonging to the enemy (20:10-20), have a practical rather than a humanitarian purpose.

The philanthropic spirit animating the code finds its best expression in pleas to respect the rights of weaker members of the community and to treat even domestic and wild animals kindly. As we have seen, the author of the code received some inspiration from the humanitarian prescriptions in the Covenant Code, edited about 650. Hence, the generous motivation of the Sabbath law (5:14) is derived from Ex. 23:12b and a humanitarian motive is likewise injected independently of the Covenant Code into the celebration of other festivals and ritual duties in the D Code (Weeks, 16:11; Booths, 16:14; first fruits, 26:11; tithes, 14:28 f.; 26:12 f.). The Covenant Code's injunction to deal justly and kindly with the resident alien (Ex. 22:21a, 23 [H. 22:20a, 22]) and the poor (23:3, 6) in a court of law is applied to the resident alien, the fatherless, and the widow (Deut. 24:17 f.; cf. 27:19). The humane treatment of debtors in Ex. 22:25a, 26 f. (H. 22:24a, 25 f.) is rewritten in Deut. 23:19 f. (H. 23:20 f.); 24:6, 10-13; cf. 15:1-11. The Deuteronomic laws on impartial justice (16:19 f.) and kind treatment of animals (22:1-4) have antecedents also in the Covenant Code (Ex. 23:2 f., 6-8 and 23:4 f.), but contain novel enactments (Deut. 22:6 f.; 25:4; cf. 5:14).

Other new laws of a humane nature in the D Code provide for the needs of the landless Levite (12:12, 19; 14:27, 29; 16:11, 14; 26:11-13), the rights of hired servants (24:14 f.), sheltering of a runaway slave (23:15 f. [H. 23:16 f.]), feeding the poor in general (15:7-11; 24:19-22; cf. 23:24 f. [H. 23:25 f.]), and even for humanity toward a criminal (25:1-3) and his family (24:16; cf. 7:10; Jer. 31:29; Ez. 18:2; II Kings 14:6, in contrast with Deut. 5:9; Ex. 34:7; Num. 14:18). The most curious of the new laws orders that parapets be placed at the edge of roofs to prevent accidents (22:8).

The civil legislation in the D Code was not derived from the Covenant Code, which did not yet contain the civil laws in 621, but from the old Canaanitic Civil Code. The author of D selected the laws which seemed appropriate for his purpose, and many of those that had been omitted were added later to the Covenant Code. The only parallels between D and the Covenant Code are Ex. 21:2-11; cf. Deut. 15:12-18; and Ex. 22:16 (H. 22:15), cf. Deut. 22:28 f., which were placed in the Covenant Code because the Deuteronomist had omitted important clauses of the old law.

The Deuteronomist was concerned with personal rights and duties, and entirely omitted the old law of property, with the significant exception of one type of theft—kidnaping (24:7); that is, unless this law was not taken from the old Canaanitic Code but from the "participial" Israelitic Code (Ex. 21:16), from which the author may also have derived the laws inflicting death penalty on those worshiping, or advocating the worship of, other gods (17:2-7; 13:6-11 [H. 13:7-12]; cf. Ex. 22:20 [H. 22:19]), on the murderer (19:11-13; cf. Ex. 21:12), and on the rebellious son (21:18-21; cf. Ex. 21:15, 17).

The only other laws on property in D are the one on moving the land-marks (19:14), possibly derived from the list of anathemas in Deut. 27 (27:17), and the law on honest weights and measures (25:13-16). The latter may have been inspired by Am. 8:5 and is given a strongly religious character (as in Prov. 20:10, where it is summarized). From the list of anathemas, some of the laws on persons and procedure may have been derived: such as laws on incest with the stepmother (22:30 [H. 23:1]; cf. 27:20), on the perversion of justice (24:17; cf. 27:19) and acceptance of bribes (16:19; cf. 27:25; see, however, Ex. 23:8). As noted, most of the other laws on persons come from the old Canaanitic Code, to wit: the laws on the manumission of slaves (15:12-18), on obscenity in assault and battery (25:11 f.), on the family (21:15-21; 22:13-29; 24:1-4; 25:5-10). The new laws display the humanitarian spirit of Deuteronomy: release from debt (15:1-11), marriage with a woman captured in war (21:10-14), and military exemption for the newly married (24:5).

In the law of procedure, the law on witnesses (19:15-21, including a quotation of the old *lex talionis* added from another source) and that limiting the number of lashes administered to malefactors (25:1-3) are taken from the old Canaanitic Code. The new laws prescribe the organi-zation of the courts (16:18-20; 17:8-13), provide cities of refuge for the unintentional slayer (19:1-10; 19:11-13 are probably based on an old law), specify the purifications required in the case of unsolved murders (21:1-9), and order that the hanged body of a criminal be buried before night (21:22 f.). New also are the laws on the state (17:14-20; 23:1-8 [H. 23:2-9]; 25:17-19, although the last is based on the old poem in Ex. 17:14-16). As a matter of fact they could hardly have stood in D, for it is difficult to believe that in 621, when the Judeans still had a king, the only laws about the monarchy, then the symbol of national unity, should pre-scribe that the king instead of following in Solomon's footsteps should make himself a copy of the D Code and study it. We may compare this with I Sam. 8:4-18, which likewise regards the monarchy as an institution burdensome to the people and displeasing to Jehovah. Both passages are obviously postexilic.

5. The Holiness Code (Lev. 17-26)

In 1877, A. Klostermann recognized (cf. p. 140) a separate code of laws within the Priestly Code in Lev. 17-26 and gave it the appropriate name of Holiness Code. The contents of this legislation may be summarized as follows:

1. The eating of meat. No animal may be slaughtered privately, but must always be sacrificed to the Lord (never to "satyrs," 17:7) at the door of the "tent of meeting" (17:1-9, in sharp contrast with the permission of private slaughtering in Deut. 12:15, 20-22). Blood is not to be eaten, since it is the seat of life and provides atonement (17:10-14). After the eating of animals found dead in the fields, a purification is required (17:15f.; cf. 11:40; 22:8; Ez. 44:31; contrast Ex. 22:31 [H. 22:30]; Deut. 14:21). [References to "the camp" (17:3) and to "the door of the tent of meeting" (17:4-6, 9) are additions by the Priestly redactor.]

2. Marriage and chastity laws. The customs of the Egyptians and Canaanites are forbidden (18:1-5). Incestuous marriage with the following relations is forbidden (18:6): mother (18:7), stepmother (18:8; cf. 20:11; Ez. 22:10; Deut. 22:30 [H. 23:1]; contrast II Sam. 16:22), sister or half sister (18:9; cf. 20:17; Deut. 27:22; contrast Gen. 20:12; II Sam. 13:13), granddaughter (18:10), half sister (18:11; cf. 18:9), paternal aunt (18:12), maternal aunt (18:13), wife of a paternal uncle (18:14; cf. 20:20), daughter-in-law (18:15; cf. 20:12; contrast Gen. 38), sister-in-law (18:16; cf. 20:21; contrast Deut. 25:5-10), mother and daughter or grandmother and granddaughter at the same time (18:17; cf. 20:14; Deut. 27:23), two sisters at the same time (18:18; contrast Jacob's marriage to Leah and Rachel). Various forms of unchastity (18:19f., 22 f.) and the Moloch worship (18:21) are similarly forbidden. Hortatory conclusion (18:24-30).

3. Religious and ethical duties (ch. 19). *a.* Parallels to the Ten Commandments (19:2-4, 11 f., 30a). *b.* Ritual prescriptions (19:5-8 [connected with 22:29 f.], 30b). *c.* Prohibition of heathen practices (19:19, 26-29, 31). *d.* Moral (19:16-18, 20-22, 35-37) and philanthropic (19:9 f., 13-15, 32-34) prescriptions. *e.* Miscellaneous (19:23-25, connected with 25:1-7). The verse 19:20 (glossed in 19:21 f.) belongs to the civil legislation in 20:10 (Dillmann) or more probably in 24:18-21.

4. Penalties for violations of the laws in chs. 18-19: Moloch worship (20:1-5; cf. 18:21), necromancy (20:6-8, 27; cf. 19:31), cursing parents (20:9; cf. 19:3a), incest and unchastity (20:10-21; cf. 18:6-23). Hortatory conclusion (20:22-26). [There are editorial expansions in 20:2-6; 20:9 is connected with 24:16; 20:25 f. with ch. 11.]

5. The priesthood (chs. 21-22). *a.* Priests in general must avoid defilement in mourning (21:1-6) and in marriage (21:7-9). *b.* The chief

priest likewise in mourning (21:10-11) and in marriage (21:13-15); he shall not leave the sanctuary (21:12). *c.* Blemishes that disqualify for the priesthood (21:16-24). *d.* Neither ritually defiled priests (22:1-9) nor persons not belonging to a priest's family (22:10-16) shall eat of the holy consecrated offerings. *e.* The acceptable burnt (22:17-20) and peace offerings (22:21-25); the sacrifice of young animals and thank offering (22:26-30). *f.* Closing exhortation (22:31-33). [There are minor redactional glosses.]

6. The festivals. *a.* Sabbath (23:1-3). *b.* Passover and Unleavened Bread (23:4-8); wave sheaf of first fruits (23:9-14); Weeks or Pentecost (23:15-21; gleanings of harvest to be left for the poor, 23:22); New Year (23:23-25); the Day of Atonement (23:26-32; cf. ch. 16); Tabernacles or Booths (23:33-43); conclusion (23:44). [The following sections belonging to P or P^s are additions to the Holiness Code: 23:4-8, 13 f., 21, 23-38, 39b; in 23:18 f. the original text reads "And ye shall present with the bread two he-lambs one year old as a sacrifice of peace offerings" (the rest is interpolated); 23:22 is quoted from 19:9 f.].[11]

7. The sacred lamp (cf. Ex. 27:20 f.); the twelve loaves of shewbread for each Sabbath (24:1-9; cf. Ex. 25:30-40 [P^s?]).

8. Punishment of a blasphemer; laws on blasphemy, murder, and injuries (24:10-23; *lex talionis,* 24:20). [In part P^s, notably 24:10-14, 23.]

9. The Sabbatical year (25:1-7; cf. Ex. 23:10 f.). The year of jubilee (25:8-55): *a.* General rules for the fiftieth year (25:8-13). *b.* Honesty in buying and selling land (25:14-17) is rewarded through safety and abundant crops (25:18 f.). *c.* Food will not be lacking on the Sabbatical year when the land lies fallow (25:20-22). *d.* The land must revert to its previous owner on the jubilee year because it belongs to the Lord (25:23 f.). *e.* The land of the poor must either be redeemed by kinsman or owner, or restored to the latter in the year of jubilee (25:25-28). *f.* Regulations for the sale of houses in cities (25:29 f.), in villages (25:31), and of houses belonging to the Levites (25:32-34). *g.* The needy Israelite should be helped without exacting interest from him (25:35-38). *h.* Israelites sold into slavery for debt are to be treated like hired servants and must be redeemed on the year of jubilee (25:39-43). *i.* Non-Israelitic slaves, however, are perpetual bondsmen (25:44-46). *j.* Israelitic slaves purchased by resident aliens are to be redeemed by their kinsmen and, in any case, freed on the year of jubilee (25:47-55). [The following sections belonging to P or P^s were added to the Holiness Code: 25:8-13, 15 f., 26-34, 40b-41, 50-52, 54; the year of jubilee, which even the rabbis admit was counted but not observed, is a "paper law." P. H. Schaeffer (*The Social Legislation of the Primitive Semites,* pp. 165-

---

[11] See, on Lev. 23, J. Morgenstern in HUCA X (1935) 29-72.

181. New Haven, 1925) has failed to prove its observance in pre-exilic or exilic times.]

10. Conclusion. *a.* Laws on idolatry and Sabbath observance (26:1 f.). *b.* Blessings resulting from the observance of the law (26:3-13). *c.* Curses following the violation of the law (26:14-45, with references to the Exile in 26:34-44). *d.* Colophon of the Sinaitic legislation as a whole (26:46).

11. Appendix on vows, devoted things, and tithes (27, Ps), with another colophon (27:34; cf. 26:46).

Some critics have suggested that part of Lev. 11-15 and Num. 5-6, and other sections (Ex. 31:13-14a; Num. 15:37-41), originally belonged to the Holiness Code, but, outside of Lev. 17-26, only Lev. 11:43-45 has the characteristics of thought and expression of our book and may be the conclusion of a lost catalogue of unclean animals which it once contained (see 20:25).

Like the Deuteronomic Code, the Holiness Code (H) is a sermon of Moses (or a divine oracle through Moses) consisting, to a great extent, of old legislation in hortatory form, and ending with a peroration emphasizing the practical value of observing the divine law (Lev. 26:3-45; cf. Deut. 28). It is from this peroration and other homiletic sections scattered throughout the book (18:1-5, 24-30; 19:37; 20:22-26; 22:31-33; 25:18-22) that we gain an idea of the purpose and style of the author of H. This writer lived not only after the publication of D in 621, but also after the destruction of Jerusalem in 586, since allusions to the Exile are unmistakable (26:34-44; cf. 26:27-32).

His style in this chapter is influenced by Jeremiah (II Chron. 36:21 actually quotes Lev. 26:34 as a saying of Jeremiah), Deuteronomy, and Ezekiel (J. Wellhausen, *Prolegomena zur Geschichte Israels,* pp. 381-383, 6th ed.). The image of the uncircumcised heart (26:41) occurs elsewhere only in these three books. The close connection between the peroration in ch. 26 and the preceding chapters appears clearly, *inter alia,* in the allusion to 25:2-4 in 26:34 f.; in style and thought, the homiletic parts and the legal sections, in which the author has rewritten or supplemented older laws, are so closely parallel (cf. J. E. Carpenter and G. Harford, *The Composition of the Hexateuch,* p. 281) that one is convinced the author of the homiletic sections is identical with the compiler of the legal sections, most of which were taken from existing codifications. In all sections of the book the most characteristic expressions of this author are: I am the Lord; for I, the Lord, am holy; to observe and to do; my statutes and my judgments; and thou shalt be afraid of thy God; etc. (see S. R. Driver, *Introduction to the Literature of the Old Testament,* pp. 49 f. 7th ed., Edinburgh, 1898).

Our author and Ezekiel have a number of typical expressions in common: (I am the Lord) that sanctify you [them]; whoever (*'ish 'ish*);

I will cut off from the midst of his [its, their] people; to walk in the statutes; to profane the name of the Lord (or the like); my Sabbaths; his blood shall be upon him (or the like); etc. (see Driver, *ibid.*, and especially pp. 145 ff.). The relation between H and Ezekiel is so close that L. Horst (*Leviticus xvii-xxvi und Ezekiel*, p. 96. Colmar, 1881) and others concluded Ezekiel was the redactor of our book—a view which has been justly relinquished.

While it seems certain to most critics that the compiler of H and Ezekiel wrote in the sixth century, they do not agree which one of the two is earlier. B. Baentsch, author of the most elaborate monograph on H (*Das Heiligkeits-Gesetz.* Erfurt, 1893; cf. his commentary on Exodus-Numbers in Nowack's *Handkommentar.* Göttingen, 1903), perhaps in desperation, gave up the unity of the book and dated H^1 (the parts of Lev. 18-20; 23-25 belonging to H) before Ezekiel, and H^2 (H in 21-22), H^3 (H in 17), and Lev. 26 ("an anthology from Ezekiel") after Ezekiel. There are no compelling reasons for such a drastic procedure. In view of the striking uniformity of thought and diction, the unity of 17-26, after the P and P^s material has been removed, cannot successfully be gainsaid[12] (in spite of numerous repetitions, resulting to a great extent from the sources utilized by the compiler). Recognizing the unity of H as indubitable, we face the difficult problem of deciding whether the compiler of H was influenced by Ezekiel or whether, on the contrary, Ezekiel knew it. L. B. Paton (*Presbyterian Review* 7 [1896] 98-115), S. R. Driver (*Introduction,* pp. 145 f.), G. F. Moore (*Encycl. Bibl.* III, 2791), C. C. Torrey (*Pseudo-Ezekiel,* p. 91. New Haven, 1930), and others have maintained that Ezekiel was acquainted with H, but a number of other critics have defended the opposite thesis.

Although lacking evidence for settling the problem, the present writer has reached the conclusion, with some hesitation, that Ezekiel was acquainted with some of the laws incorporated in H, but that the compiler of H wrote after Ezekiel, about the middle of the sixth century. The author of H was inspired to write his book by Ezekiel's prophecies both positively, to inculcate the prophet's conception of holiness as the essence of Judaism, and negatively, to correct the prophetic liberties Ezekiel allowed himself in matters of traditional law and which led him, in the opinion of the H author, to commit errors of omission and commission in legal matters.

The author of H agrees with Ezekiel in making holiness the dominant element in the relation between the Lord and his people, while for the prophets and the Deuteronomic Code righteousness and love represented the right attitude of the people toward their God. Both Ezekiel and H

---

[12] Although S. Kuchler (*Das Heiligkeits-Gesetz.* [Dissertation.] Königsberg, 1929) has recently contested the existence of a "Holiness Code" as a separate book.

(Lev. 26) retained the Deuteronomic doctrine of the "Covenant" between God and people. But Ezekiel (and H under his influence) stressed ritual purity as a condition for its fulfillment, without, however, entirely disregarding moral factors (as later the P Code tended to do), and in his eagerness to transform the nation into a church, ignored the state. He aspired to a holy people unto the Lord (cf. the additions to D in Deut. 7:6; 14:2, 21; 26:19; 28:9, and to the Covenant Code in Ex. 22:31 [H. 22:30]), "a holy flock" of "human sheep" (Ez. 36:38), a people cleansed with pure water (36:25). The holiness of Israel was demanded by the holiness—physical purity and awful majesty—of the Lord. God in his sanctity had punished his people for profaning his holy name and defiling the land; in his sanctity he would later restore them to their land so as to vindicate his name among the scoffing nations (36:22 f.). This prophet, in his plan of restoration (Ez. 40-48), not only took extraordinary precautions to prevent future defilement of the land and people, as well as confusion between sacred and profane (22:26; 44:23), but made of the Temple service the agency for the removal and expiation of all profanation, notably through the sin offerings to be brought on both New Year's days (March 21, September 21), on the Passover, and on the fifteenth of the seventh month (45:18-25).

The author of H was not, like Ezekiel, a prophet of great originality and freedom (though of priestly stock), but a priest deeply devoted to sacerdotal traditions and customs. He adopted eagerly Ezekiel's fundamental concept of the holiness of God (Lev. 19:2; 20:7, 26; 21:8), which demanded the holiness of his people (*ibid.*), subordinating both the ritual (20:7 f., 26; 21:6-8, 15, 23; 22:9, 16, 32) as well as the moral (19:2) laws to this principle (cf. Ez. 20:12). He refused, however, to follow Ezekiel's innovations in matters of traditional law, for he was not, like the prophet, giving the people a program of restoration received through divine inspiration, but the laws which Moses had proclaimed at Sinai (25:1; 26:46).

As a result, the legislation of H is often more archaic than that of Ezekiel, although this is no argument for dating H before Ezekiel. One might just as plausibly argue that the P Code was codified before Ezekiel. Ezekiel's innovations were never taken seriously by experts. Long before Hananiah ben Hezekiah "supplied with three hundred jars of oil sat in his upper chamber and explained" the discrepancies between Ezekiel and the Pentateuch (Talmud, *Shabbath* 13b), thus saving the prophet's book from withdrawal, an irreverent reader wrote on the margin of Ez. 45:20 these words, "From [the pen of] a man mistaken and foolish" (cf. A. B. Ehrlich, *Randglossen zur hebräischen Bibel*. Leipzig, 1908-1914. *Ad loc.*).

The author of H (cf. 17:8), basing his codification on actual practice in pre-exilic times, knows nothing of the sin and trespass offerings mentioned by Ezekiel (40:39; 42:13; 43:19 ff.; 44:27, 29; 45:17 ff.; 46:20) for the first time (Lev. 23:19 being a priestly gloss from Num. 28:27). He ignores Ezekiel's distinction between priests and Levites (44:9-16), adopted later with some modifications by the P Code. The original H law on the annual festivals in ch. 23 not only disregards the new festivals introduced by Ezekiel (45:18-25) and his fixed dates for the feasts (*ibid.*), but in some respects is even more archaic than Deut. 16 (cf. J. Morgenstern, HUCA 10 [1935] 36). H mentions the Feast of Weeks, which Ezekiel omits, perhaps accidentally. Ezekiel's provision that the priests should sit in judgment in criminal cases (44:24) is another innovation with no basis in the practice of earlier times, and is naturally omitted in H.

The stricter rules for the priest "who is greater than his brethren" (21:10), or the head of a priestly family in charge of a sanctuary, are not found in Ezekiel; whether they are based on ancient practice or, on the contrary, developed later than Ezekiel in the direction of the Aaronic high priest is uncertain. In no case do they make it necessary to place H before Ezekiel. However, H is unquestionably more archaic than Ezekiel in refraining from a polemic against the "high places" of Canaan, which plays such a prominent part in D, Ezekiel, and the Deuteronomists in Kings (if this argument from silence be valid), as also in maintaining (in Lev. 26:36, 39) the traditional theory of the punishment of children for the sins of their fathers (Deut. 5:9; Ex. 20:5) against Ezekiel's new theory (anticipated in Jer. 31:29 ff.; Deut. 24:16) about individual responsibility (Ez. 18, especially 18:20).

Passing on to moral and civil rules of conduct, we find that Ezekiel and H have much in common, but it cannot be shown that one is borrowing from the other. In a list of sins and virtues in 18:5-9 (cf. 18:10-13, 14-17), Ezekiel mentions worship at the "high places" of Canaan, idolatry (cf. Lev. 19:4; 26:1), adultery (cf. Lev. 18:20; 20:10), commerce with a woman in her impurity (cf. Lev. 18:19; 20:18), oppression (cf. Lev. 19:13, 33; 25:14, 17), restoring pledges for debt (not in H), robbery (cf. Lev. 19:13), helping the needy (cf. Lev. 19:9 f.; 23:22), refusing to lend on interest (cf. Lev. 25:35-37), refraining from iniquity, executing true justice (cf. Lev. 19:15, 35), and walking in God's statutes (cf. Lev. 18:3; 20:23; 26:3). In most cases, we find parallels in the Covenant Code and D.

In addition to some of these sins and virtues, Ezekiel in 22:6-12 enumerates shedding blood (judicial murders?), contempt for parents (cf. Lev. 20:9), despising holy things (cf. Lev. 19:8; 22:15), profaning God's Sabbaths (cf. Lev. 19:3, 30; 26:2), slander (cf. Lev. 19:16), unchastity (cf. Lev. 18:17; 19:29; 20:14), incest with stepmother (cf. Lev. 18:7 f.; 20:11; Deut. 22:30 [H. 23:1]; 27:20), with daughter-in-law (cf. Lev. 18:15; 20:12), with sister (cf. Lev. 18:9; 20:17; Deut. 27:22), and bribery for murder (cf. Ex. 23:8; Deut. 16:19; 27:25). Note that the sexual offenses mentioned by Ezekiel parallel those in H and Deut. 27, and that the last offense in the preceding list occurs in Deut. 27 and not in H.

Other miscellaneous laws in Ezekiel concern eating meat with blood (33:25 [some read "blood" for "on the hills" in 18:6]; cf. Lev. 19:26), honest weights and measures (45:10; cf. Lev. 19:36; Deut. 25:13-15). Regulations for the clergy include avoidance of pollution through contact with a corpse except in the case of near relatives (44:25; cf. Lev. 21:1-3; both lists, strangely enough, omit the wife) or through mourning customs (44:20; cf. Lev. 21:5, which has some important differences). It should be noted that Jer. 16:6 f. speaks of such customs without the slightest objection, whereas Deut. 14:1 and Lev. 19:27 condemn them even for laymen. Leviticus 21:10 f. makes these rules more stringent in the case of the chief priest. The marriage restrictions of Ezekiel (44:22) are more drastic than Lev. 21:7, 14. The dietary restrictions (44:31; cf. 4:14) forbid priests the meat of animals found dead or torn by beasts as in Lev. 22:8. Previously such flesh was allowed to resident aliens (Deut. 14:21), later it was declared unfit for all (Ex. 22:31 [H. 22:30]; Lev. 7:24 f.); in Lev. 17:15 f. [H?] (cf. 11:40) a purification was required for Israelite or alien after such consumption.

In Ezekiel and H idolatry[13] is stressed among the religious sins, notably idolatry after the manner of Egypt (Ez. 20:7 f., 18, 31; 23:7, 30; 36:18; 37:23; Lev. 18:3) and of Canaan (*hammânîm* images, Ez. 6:4, 6 and Lev. 26:30; *gillûlîm,* 39 times in Ezekiel and elsewhere only Lev. 26:30; Deut. 29:17 [H. 29:16]; Jer. 50:2). Other religious offenses decried are the violation of God's Sabbaths (Ez. 20:12 f., 16, 20 f., 24; 22:8, 26; 23:38; 44:24; Lev. 19:3, 30; 26:2), the drinking of blood (Ez. 33:25 and, according to the emended text, 18:6, 11, 15; 22:9; Lev. 17:10-14; 19:26), and child sacrifice, particularly in Moloch worship (Ez. 16:20 f.; 20:26, 31; 23:37-39; Lev. 18:21; 20:2; Deut. 12:31; 18:10).

These are the chief parallels in matters of law between Ezekiel and the Holiness Code; and exhaustive enumeration would not add materially to the picture. The similarity is too striking to be accidental; if one author did not borrow from the other, they both made use of common sources. The latter view seems the most probable: no analogy can be detected in the arrangement of the laws, because both authors disregarded the original order in their common sources (in H, for instance, the laws from the "participial" code on capital punishment are found in both Lev. 20 and 24). Moreover, the parallelism is confined to the laws and does not include the homiletic additions of authors.

[13] The numerous references of Ezekiel to idolatry are listed in JBL 43 (1924) 234, n. 34; for H see Lev. 19:4; 26:1.

B. Baentsch (*Das Heiligkeits-Gesetz,* p. 87) is clearly in error when he says that Ezekiel (in chs. 18, 20, 22, 33) found the individual articles of law to which he refers in a fixed order, identical with that of Lev. 18-20, because the separate clause "I am the Lord your god" is never found elsewhere in his book. Once the actual facts, not furnished by Baentsch, are examined, this argument becomes specious. The formula "I am the Lord your god" occurs only in Ez. 20:5, 7, 19; v. 5 is a reference to the revelation of Jehovah to Moses, in v. 19 the formula occurs at the beginning (in H it occurs at the end of a section), as in the redactional verse Judg. 6:10, and only v. 7 is a real parallel to H (Lev. 18:30), although not particularly close. Baentsch also states that Ez. 20:6, 15 must be derived from Lev. 20:24, and not vice versa. The most striking parallel between these passages is the familiar phrase "a land flowing with milk and honey" which in both authors is obviously a reminiscence of the D Code (where it occurs four times). How such a stereotyped cliché—a favorite of Deuteronomistic redactors in Exodus and Numbers (8 times, never in the original J or E), and in Deut. 27:3; 31:20; Josh. 5:6; Jer. 11:5; 32:22 (all Deuteronomistic)—could be seriously regarded as good evidence of Ezekiel's dependence on H is incomprehensible.

Concluding this comparison of Ezekiel with H, the H legislation is given in a form earlier than in Ezekiel (except for the priestly additions in H) but the homiletic sections of H (notably Lev. 26) clearly disclose the influence of the prophet's style and thought. Bishop J. W. Colenso (*The Pentateuch and Book of Joshua Critically Examined,* Part VI, p. 9. London, 1871) recognized this long ago when he wrote, "It is surely extravagant to suppose that a writer so profuse and so peculiar, as this prophet [Ezekiel] is acknowledged to be, should have studied so very closely this particular chapter of Levit. (26) out of the whole Pentateuch, as to have become thoroughly imbued with its style and familiarized with its expressions—so thoroughly, indeed, as to have adopted nearly fifty of them as his own, of which eighteen . . . occur nowhere else in the Bible." It is obvious that unless we give up the unity of H, which seems established beyond reasonable doubt, we must recognize that some of the codes of law excerpted in H were familiar to Ezekiel.

Our next task is to determine, if possible, these legal sources of H. Plainly, the compiler of H not only knew some of the codes preserved in the Pentateuch (an early edition of the Covenant Code, the D Code, and the list of anathemas in Deut. 27), but also some of the lost codes, notably the "participial" code on capital offenses. A striking difference between the Covenant Code, D, and H is that the Covenant Code contains extracts of both the Canaanitic Civil Code and the "participial" code, whereas D contains only extracts from the first, and H from the second, of these ancient codes (with some possible echoes from the first).

Although H contains no laws in the juristic formulation of the old Canaanitic code of civil laws, possible rewriting of certain laws from that code in H should not be excluded a priori. It is barely possible that the following laws may have belonged originally to the Canaanitic Code where they exhibited at one time the juristic formulation. The law on the seduction of a betrothed bondmaid (Lev. 19:20) may possibly supplement Deut. 22:23 f. The law on the indemnity due the owner of an animal that has been killed (Lev. 24:18, 21a) may possibly be part of the law on damages to cattle (Ex. 21:33 f., 35 f.). Less probably, some of the laws on incest (Lev. 18:6-18; 20:11 f., 14, 17, 19-21), of which there are only traces outside of H (Deut. 27:20, 22; 22:30 [H. 23:1]), might have belonged to the Canaanitic Code, although none of these laws has the juristic formulation. Hammurabi's Code, however, contains laws on incest (§§ 154-158) and prescribes death by burning in the case of incest with one's mother (§ 157), just as does Lev. 20:14 for incest with mother-in-law.

The indebtedness of H to the Covenant Code has been much exaggerated by B. Baentsch and later critics. A number of parallels pointed out between the two codes are spurious for one of three reasons. In the first place, some of the laws in the Covenant Code are later than those of H (Ex. 22:28 [H. 22:27] is later than Lev. 24:15 f.; Ex. 22:30b [H. 22:29b] is later than Lev. 22:27; Ex. 22:31 [H. 22:30] than Lev. 17:15; 22:8). In the second place, laws like the *lex talionis* (Ex. 21:23b-25; Lev. 24:19 f.; cf. Deut. 19:21) and three "participial" capital sentences (Lev. 20:9, 15 f.; 24:17, 21b; Ex. 21:17; 22:19 [H. 22:18]; 21:12), have a common source in an older code. Finally, owing to the extensive use made of D, it is more probable that the H laws were derived from D rather than from the Covenant Code: thus, for instance, the law on usury (Ex. 22:25 [H. 22:24]; Deut. 23:19 f. [H. 23:20 f.]; Lev. 25:35-37).

Except possibly for the requirement of fair judgment to the poor (Ex. 23:3; Lev. 19:15) and of fair treatment to the resident alien (Ex. 22:21a [H. 22:20a]; 23:9; Lev. 19:33), I can find no law of H that is unquestionably derived from the Covenant Code. The old ritual decalogue, forming the core of the Covenant Code, is entirely ignored in H, like the civil legislation added to the Covenant Code after H was written. The ritual laws of H are entirely different from those of the ritual decalogue and, if the author of H was acquainted with it, he felt free to alter it. More likely he ignored it and revised the parallel laws in D: for D was then sacred scripture, enjoying an immense prestige, whereas the Covenant Code was still circulating privately (even Malachi, in 460, acknowledged nothing but D as the law of Moses).

The far-reaching dependence of H on D appears first in a number of laws without parallel elsewhere in the Pentateuch: condemnation of sacred prostitution (Lev. 19:29; cf. 21:9; Deut. 23:17 [H. 23:18]), prompt payment of hired servants (Lev. 19:13b; Deut. 24:14), permission to the poor to glean (Lev. 19:9 f.; 23:22; Deut. 23:24 f. [H. 23:25 f.]; 24:19-22), prohibition of miscellaneous mixtures (Lev. 19:19b; Deut. 22:9-11; the word *ša'atnez* [cloth of mixed materials] occurs only in these two passages), just weights and measures (Lev. 19:35-37; Deut. 25: 13-16), prohibition of sacred stone pillars (Lev. 26:1b; Deut. 12:3; 16:21), of soothsaying and necromancy (Lev. 19:31; 20:6, 27; Deut. 18:10b-11), of Canaanitic "abominations" (Lev. 18:24-30; Deut. 18:9), of drinking blood (Lev. 17:10-14; 19:26a; Deut. 12:23-25; cf. 12:16; 15:23; also in later P laws), of Moloch worship (Lev. 18:21a; 20:1-5; Deut. 18:10a; cf. 12:31b), and of mourning customs (Lev. 19:27 f.; cf. 21:5; Deut. 14:1 f.). Finally, if Num. 15:37-41 belongs to H, specifications for the garments of laymen (Deut. 22:12). Moreover, the compiler of H prefers to use D even when earlier laws were available; e.g., in the law on usury, already mentioned, in the prescriptions for the three annual festivals (Lev. 23; Deut. 16) and for the Sabbath (called "the seventh day" in the ritual decalogue, but "Sabbath" in the Ten Commandments and in H).

In some cases, H corrects D, as in forbidding marriage with a sister-in-law (Lev. 18:16), implied in the levirate marriage ordained by D (Deut. 25:5-10). Some of the enactments of H are stricter than those of D: the permission to resident aliens, granted in Deut. 14:21, to eat of animals found dead is repealed (Lev. 17:15 f.); love for resident aliens is enjoined (Lev. 19:33 f.; cf. Deut. 10:18 f. which is not D) and practical equality of rights and duties is now granted to them (Lev. 17:8-16; 18:26; 20:2; 22:18, 24 f.; 24:16, 22; 25:6, 35; cf. Deut. 29:10 f., outside D, where the resident alien is a member of the group with which God makes his covenant). Unless H reflects a pre-Deuteronomic stage in religion, his prohibition of private butchery without sacrificial rights (Lev. 17:1-9), which is explicitly permitted in Deut. 12:15, 20-22, cannot be explained. H is similarly more archaic than D in the ritual of the three annual festivals (Lev. 23, omitting the P material): "It would seem almost as if this H legislation, with its sanction of these old folk-ceremonies and their observance at the home, was designed consciously to repeal the Deuteronomic legislation for the observance of these festivals at the central sanctuary" (J. Morgenstern in HUCA X [1938] 36).

The compiler of H was also familiar with the Ten Commandments, an integral part of D (Lev. 19:3 f., 11 f.); and with the Ten Anathemas, an addition to D, with which it has in common certain laws on incest (Lev. 18:8 f., 17; 20:11, 14, 17; Deut. 27:20, 22 f.; cf. 22:30 [H. 23:1]), and cruelty to the blind (Lev. 19:14; Deut. 27:18). In addition to these laws, which are without parallel elsewhere, all the other laws of Deut. 27:16-25 occur in H with the exception of 27:17, 25. H also preserves a fragment of the old Israelitic *lex talionis* (Lev. 24:19 f.; cf. Ex. 21:23-25; Deut. 19:21) and a considerable portion of the "participial" code on capital offenses: three of the articles are identical with three in Exodus (Lev. 20:9; Ex. 21:17; Lev. 20:15 f.; Ex. 22:19 [H. 22:18]; cf. Deut. 27:21; Lev. 24:17, 21b; Ex. 21:12; cf. Num. 35:16-18, 21, 30 f.), six others, concerning Moloch worship, sexual offenses, and blasphemy, stand only in H (Lev. 20:2, 10-13; 24:16).

To conclude, it is apparent that the compiler of H made use of the codes of law existing in his time, with the exception of the old Canaanitic Civil Code (as far as it is preserved) and the old Canaanitic ritual decalogue (was he aware of their foreign origin?) although he probably used some philanthropic exhortations of the Covenant Code. Thus, on the whole H, like D, represents actual law. Besides legislation which is attested elsewhere, however, there are in H not a few enactments of unknown origin—some with a parallel in Ezekiel, others original. It is not unlikely that H utilized and modified a lost code, known also to Ezekiel, which was used in a sanctuary other than Jerusalem before the publication of D in 621, and which became obsolete after the official ratification of D in 621.

To this lost code we may tentatively assign not only the majority of parallels between H and Ezekiel already noted, but also certain ritual prescriptions of H, that are without parallel elsewhere. The priesthood in this code was neither Levitical as in D (Levites appear in H in the glosses 25:32-34), nor Zadokite as in Ezekiel, nor Aaronic as in P and in the priestly glosses in H (Lev. 17:2; 21:1, 17, 21, 24; 22:2, 4, 18; 24:3, 9). It was a provincial priesthood, officiating at one of the local shrines desecrated by Josiah in 621. The head of this local priestly family was called "the priest that is greater than his brothers" (21:10), and he is entirely different from the Aaronic high priest of P.

The functions of "the priest," as he is called, are described in 17:5 f.; 21-22; 23:10 f., 20. According to ancient practice, all animals slaughtered for meat must be sacrificed at this local sanctuary under supervision of the priests (17:1-9), but the three annual festivals (Lev. 23, omitting P), after the first fruits had been brought to the priests, were celebrated at home and were agricultural in character. The combination of the Passover with the Feast of Unleavened Bread (23:5-8) does not seem to belong to the original code. Originally a set of rules for the priesthood, this code laid particular emphasis on ritual cleanliness and avoidance of defilement on the part of priests and laymen (cf. 17:15 f.; 19:5-8; 20:25 f. [cf. 11:1 ff.]; 21:1-4, 11; 22:4-8, 17-30). If the laws in regard to the land's periodic rest (25:1-7, 18-22; 19:23-25) belonged to this code, they may also be understood as ritual taboos for laymen. It is difficult to determine whether the laws on sexual offenses in chs. 18 and 20, not quoted from other codes, should be attributed to the compiler's aim at completeness in these matters, or whether they were already in the sanctuary Torah which we have been reconstructing. It is certain, however, that the compiler was responsible for the emphasis on the holiness of the Lord, for the attribution of the code to Moses, and for the transformation of what was, to a great extent, a priestly manual into a rule of life and worship for the layman living not in the Babylonian land of exile, like the author, but in the Land of Promise "flowing with milk and honey."

When the Holiness Code, as it left the hands of the compiler about 550 B.C., was incorporated into the P Code during the first half of the fifth century it was edited with numerous additions in the vein of the P Code to harmonize with a subsequent point of view. If the Priestly Code was solemnly read and ratified in 444 B.C., the Holiness Code was an integral part of it, for Neh. 8:14-18 refers specifically to Lev. 23:33-43 as part and parcel of the Law of Moses.

6. The Legislation of the Priestly Code (P)

In the Priestly Code (P), the legislation is presented in two forms, narrative and juristic. On the one hand, there are stories recounting the origin of a prescribed institution and other stories with the implied force of legal precedents. On the other hand, the juristic sections are in the form of commandments.

The following are those P narratives with a legislative purpose:

I. Genesis. 1. The story of the Creation (Gen. 1:1-2:4), leading up to the origin of the Sabbath (2:2 f.).

2. The story of the Deluge (6:9-22; 7:6, 11, 13-16a, 17a, 18-21, 24; 8:1-2a, 3b-5, 13a, 14-19; 9:1-17, 28 f.), containing the laws which prohibit the eating of "meat with its soul" (i.e., with the blood) and murder (9:4-6).

3. The story of the covenant of God with Abraham (Gen. 17), requiring the circumcision of all male infants eight days after birth (17:9-14; cf. 17:23-27; 21:4).

4. The story of Abraham's purchase of the cave at Machpelah as the grave of Sarah (23), furnishing his descendants with a legal title to the land of Canaan (see also 25:7-10; 49:29-33).

5. The stories of the marriages of Esau and Jacob (26:34 f.; [27:46]; 28:1-9), furnishing a precedent for the prohibition of mixed marriages.

II. Exodus. 6. The story of Israel's deliverance from Egypt (Ex. 11:9-12:20, 28, 40-51; 13:1 f.), with the ordinances for the celebration of the Passover and the Feast of Unleavened Bread (12:1-20 [24-27a]), for the night of watching (12:42), and for the divine ownership of every first-born (13:1 f.).

7. The story of the manna and of the quails (16), illustrating the observance of the Sabbath (16:23-30).

III. Leviticus. 8. The story of the ordination to the priesthood of Aaron and his sons (Lev. 8, Ps), in accordance with the law of Ex. 29:1-37.

9. The story of the inauguration of the priestly functions of Aaron and his sons (9, omitting 9:23 f.), a concrete precedent for the ritual followed in a solemn sacrificial service.

10. The story of the dire punishment of Nadab and Abihu (sons of Aaron) for offering strange fire (10:1-5), with a warning that they should not be mourned by the priests (10:6 f., Ps). This story was followed originally by prescriptions regulating the entrance of the high priest into the Holy of Holies (Lev. 16:1-4, 6, [11], 12 f., 23, 24a, 34b, Ps), now combined with the ritual of the day of atonement.

11. The story of an error of Eleazar and Ithamar, the surviving sons of Aaron (10:16-20, Ps). Since the blood of the people's sin offering was *not* brought into the Tabernacle (according to the law of Lev. 4; cf. 8:14-17; Ex. 29:10-14) the flesh should have been eaten by the priest (according to 6:24-29 [H. 6:17-22]) and not burnt outside the camp (6:30 [H. 6:23]; 9:11).

12. The story of the stoning of a blasphemer of the (divine) "Name" (24:10-14, 23, Ps), a precedent for the injunction in 24:16aβb ("all the congregation . . ."), 22a.

IV. Numbers. 13. The census of the twelve tribes (Num. 1:1-47) exclusive of the Levites (1:48-54, Ps); their arrangement in the camp (ch. 2), a confused and irregular precedent for their geographical location in Canaan; the census and functions of the Levites (3:1-4:39, Ps); the census of first-born males (3:40-51, Ps).

14. The gifts of the princes of the twelve tribes to the priesthood (7:1-89, Ps), a commendable example of pious generosity.

15. Purification and installation of the Levites (8:5-22, Ps), who were to serve from their 25th to their 50th year (8:23-26, Ps)—a modification of 4:3, 23, 30, where the service began in the 30th year.

16. The second celebration of the Passover, on the 14th of the first month one year after the Exodus, with the provision of a "Little Passover" one month later for those prevented by uncleanliness or absence from celebrating the first (9:1-13, Ps); resident aliens likewise will celebrate the festival (9:14, Ps).

17. Ten of the twelve spies sent into Canaan reported pessimistically, and the people, in spite of the favorable report of Joshua and Caleb, murmured against the Lord and were condemned (with the exception of Joshua and Caleb) to die in the Wilderness without entering the

Promised Land; the ten spies were struck dead by the Lord (13:1-17a, 21, 25-26a [to "Paran"], 32abα; 14:1a, 2, 5-7, 10, 26-29 [30-33], 34-38). This story is a warning against ingratitude and mistrust toward the Lord.

18. Stoning of a Sabbath-breaker (15:32-36, Ps).

19. The fire of the Lord consuming Korah and his 250 followers. They had protested, either as laymen against the monopolistic priestly prerogatives of the tribe of Levi (16:1a, 2aβb-7a, 18, 23 f., 27, 35, P) or as Levites claiming equal ecclesiastical rank with Aaron and his sons (16:7b-11, 16 f., 19-22, Ps). The murmuring nation was punished and duly impressed (16:42-50; 17:12 f. [H. 17:6-15, 27 f.], P). The priestly prerogatives of Aaron were confirmed through the miraculous budding of his rod (17:1-11 [H. 17:16-26], probably Ps). The obvious juristic import of both stories is explicitly stated in 18:2a, 4, 5, 7b, 22 (laymen excluded from the service; P) and in 18:1, 2b, 3, 6-7a, 8-21, 23-32 (subordination of the Levites to the sons of Aaron, the priests; Ps).

20. Moses and Aaron, on account of their incredulity at Meribah, shall not enter the Promised Land (20:1aα, 2, 3b, 4, 6-8a [omitting "take the rod" in v. 8], 10, 11bβ, 12 f.).

21. Death of Aaron on Mount Hor and ordination of Eleazar as his successor (20:22-29; cf. 33:38 f.).

22. Phinehas the son of Eleazar rewarded with "the covenant of an everlasting priesthood" for slaying Zimri, who had taken unto himself a Midianite woman (25:6-18, Ps), an act of apostasy.

23. A second census of the children of Israel taken in the plains of Moab (25:19-26:65 [H. 26:1-65], Ps omitting the glosses in 26:8-11, 58a).

24. The case of the daughter of Zelophehad furnishing a precedent for inheritance on the part of daughters, when there were no sons (27:1-11, Ps).

25. Moses ordered to look at the Promised Land, which he could not enter (cf. 20:1 ff.), and to appoint Joshua as his successor (27:12-23, Ps; cf. Deut. 32:48-52; 34:[1-3], 7-9, P).

26. The war of vengeance against the Midianites (cf. 25:16-18) furnishing a precedent for the law regulating the distribution of booty (31, Ps; cf. I Sam. 30:24 f.).

27. Allotment to the tribes of Reuben and Gad (the half of Manasseh is an afterthought) of their Transjordanic territory after they promised to fight with the other tribes for the territory in Canaan (32:1a, 2b, 4a, 6-15, 18 f., 28-33, in part [notably 32:6-15], Ps; cf. also Josh. 13:15-33; in both sections the P material has been re-edited).

28. Instructions of Moses for the conquest and allotment of the land of Canaan (34, P and Ps), prefaced with an exhortation (in the style of H) to exterminate the Canaanites (33:50-56, Ps).

29. Allotment to the Levites of 48 cities (35:1-8, Ps). of which 6 were

to be cities of refuge for unintentional manslayers (35:9-15, P), with the law on murder and unintentional homicide (35:16-29, P) and the procedure in dealing with such cases (35:30-34, Ps). How the Levitical cities were allotted is described in Josh. 21:1-42 [H., lacking 21:36 f., 21:1-40], a secondary Ps list reproduced in I Chron. 6:54-81 [H. 6:39-66.]

30. Supplementary restrictions to the provisions for the inheritance of the daughters of Zelophehad (see 27:1-11), specifying that they must marry within their tribe (36, Ps).

The legislation proper in the Priestly Code, revealed to Moses at Sinai (Ex. 25:1-31:17; cf. 35-40, Lev., and the laws in Num. 1:1-10:10), on the journey from Sinai to Kadesh and at Kadesh (Num. 15:1-13, 37-41; 19), and in the plains of Moab (Num. 28-30), may be summarized as follows:

I. Exodus. 1. Instructions given to Moses for the building of the Tabernacle (Ex. 25-27) and the organization of the priesthood (Ex. 28-29), with a Ps appendix (30:1-31:17). I. *a.* Introduction (25:1-9). *b.* The ark (25:10-22). *c.* The table for the shewbread (25:23-30). *d.* The candlestick (25:31-40). *e.* The Tabernacle (26). *f.* The altar (27:1-8). *g.* The court of the Tabernacle (27:9-19). *h.* The oil for the lamps (27:20 f., Ps, quoting Lev. 24:1-3). II. *a.* The vestments of Aaron the high priest (28:1-39). *b.* The vestments of the priests (28:40-42); closing instructions (28:43). *c.* Ordination of Aaron and his sons (29:1-37). *d.* The daily burnt offerings (29:38-42, Ps). *e.* Conclusion (29:43-46). III. *a.* The altar of incense (30:1-10, a Ps supplement to 25-27). *b.* The tax of half a shekel per person (30:11-16, Ps; cf. Neh. 10:32 [H. 10:33], where the yearly tax is one-third of a shekel). *c.* The laver of brass (30:17-21, Ps). *d.* The aromatic anointing oil (30:22-33, Ps). *e.* The incense (30:34-38, Ps). *f.* Bezalel and Oholiab appointed to make the Tabernacle and the holy objects (31:1-11, Ps). *g.* The Sabbath law (31:12-17, Ps).

2. Execution of the instructions given in Ex. 25:1-31:17, largely repeated verbatim, but with additions, omissions, summaries, and in a different order (Ex. 35-40, Ps). The Greek version in 36-39 differs in arrangement; two distinct translators are responsible for the LXX in 25-31 and 35-40, respectively. The Hebrew text underlying the Greek of 35-40 antedates the Masoretic text. The differences between 25-31 and 35-40 (in Hebrew and Greek) are conveniently tabulated in Driver's *Introduction to the Old Testament* (pp. 40 f. of the 7th ed.) and in Carpenter and Harford, *The Composition of the Hexateuch* (pp. 469 f.). Ex. 35-40 is later than Ps in Ex. 30:1-31:17. This section omits from 25-31: 27:20 f.; 28:30; 29 (cf. Lev. 8); 30:6-16, but 35:10-29; 36:2-7; 38:21-31; 39:32-43; 40 are additions to 25-31. The Greek version omits the altar of incense (37:25-28 and in 35:15; 39:38), lacks 35:8; 40:11, 28, 29b; and summarizes 36:8-34; 38:1-7.

II. Leviticus. 3. The five sacrifices (Lev. 1:1-6:7 [H. 1-5]). *a.* The ritual of the burnt offering, to make atonement (Lev. 1). *b.* The ritual of the meal offering, as a votive or freewill offering (Lev. 2): fine wheat flour (2:1-3), unleavened cakes mixed with oil or unleavened wafers smeared with oil (baked in the oven, 2:4), cakes baked in a griddle (2:5 f.) or fried in a pan (2:7-13), first fruits (2:14-16). *c.* The ritual of the peace offerings: the fat and the blood belong to the Lord, the meat is eaten anywhere by the worshiper (3). *d.* The ritual of the sin offering, expiating inadvertent transgressions of the chief priest (4:1-12), the congregation (4:13-21), the ruler (4:22-26), or an ordinary Jew (4:27-35); a supplement specifies cases requiring a sin offering (5:1-6, Ps) and provides for the impecunious (5:7-13, Ps). The law of Lev. 4 appears to be later than that of Ex. 29; Lev. 8-9; Num. 15:22-31; although inserted late and revised (so that sin and trespass sacrifices are confused), 5:1-13 is based on ancient law. *e.* The ritual of the trespass offering (always a ram), in expiation of illegal appropriation of property belonging to another or to the Lord (5:14-6:7 [H. 5:14-26]); in 5:17 and elsewhere the sin and trespass offerings are confused.

4. Instructions for the officiating priests (Lev. 6:8-7:38 [H. 6-7]; 10: 8-15). *a.* The burnt offering (6:8-13 [H. 6:1-6]). *b.* The meal offering (6:14-18 [H. 6:7-11]). *c.* The daily meal offering (6:19-23 [H. 6:12-16], Ps, omitting the erroneous gloss "on the day when he is anointed" [6:20; H. 6:13]). *d.* The sin offering (6:24-30 [H. 6:17-23]; 6:29 f. [H. 6:22 f.] belong to Ps). *e.* The trespass offering (7:1-6, with a Ps appendix in 7:7-10). *f.* The peace offering, presented as a thank offering (7:11-15) or as a vow or freewill offering (7:16-21). *g.* The Israelites shall not eat the fat and the blood (7:22-27, Ps). *h.* In a peace offering the priest shall have the "wave-breast" (7:28-34, Ps; a glossator in 7:32, 34 adds the "heave-thigh"). *i.* Conclusion (7:37, expanded with the Ps additions in 7:35 f., 38). *j.* Supplementary instructions: the officiating priests shall abstain from drinking wine (10:8 f., Ps; cf. Ez. 44:21) and discriminate between holy and profane (10:10 f., Ps: a misplaced fragment, cf. 11:47; 20:25; Ez. 44:23 f.); prescriptions concerning the priests' share of the meal and peace offerings (10:12-15, a supplement to 7:28-34 or 9:21, with the similar interpolation of the "heave-thigh").

5. Laws on clean and unclean things; purifications (Lev. 11-15). *a.* Clean and unclean animals: animals fit and unfit for food (11:1-23 [cf. Deut. 14; see S. R. Driver, *Deuteronomy* [ICC], pp. 158 f.]): quadrupeds, 11:2-8; aquatic animals 11:9-12; birds, 11:13-19; winged insects, 11:20-23; [creeping insects and reptiles, 11:41 f., Ps;] pollution through contact with unclean animals or their carcasses (11:24-40), exhortation (11:43-45, apparently taken from the Holiness Code), conclusion (11:46 f.). *b.* Uncleanness after childbirth (12; 12:2 presupposes 15:19 and 12 probably followed 15 in the original code). *c.* Leprosy (13-14): symptoms by which

leprosy may be distinguished from ordinary skin diseases (13:1-28), symptoms of ringworm (13:29-37), tetter (13:38 f.), baldness and leprosy (13:40-44), segregation of the leper (13:45-46a; 13:46b is redactional). Leprosy (i.e., mold) in garments (13:47-59, Ps). The cleansing of a leper who has recovered (14:1-8aα); supplementary sacrifices and purifications (14:8aβ-20, Ps), with a later reduction in cost for the benefit of the poor (14:21-32, Ps). Leprosy (i.e., mold) in a house (14:33-53, Ps). Subscription (14:57b, expanded with the addition of 14:54-57a, Ps). *d.* Secretions (15) of men (15:1-8) and women (15:19-30); conclusion (15:31-33; originally only 15:32a).

6. The Day of Atonement (Lev. 16). Prescriptions for the entrance of the high priest into the Holy of Holies, as we have noted, belong after 10:1-5; the rest of the chapter is still composite but difficult to analyze. The law on the Day of Atonement, based on very ancient custom, is to be found chiefly in 16:29b-33, Ps (an expanded original introduction now combined with the superscription in 16:34a, cf. 16:29a) and in 16:5a, 7-10, 15 (omitting, "and do with that blood . . . bullock"), 16a, 18-22a, 26-29a. The remaining clauses in these verses are for the most part editorial notes.

III. Numbers. 7. Miscellaneous laws (Num. 5-6). *a.* The leprous and unclean excluded from the camp (Num. 5:1-4, Ps). *b.* A supplement to the law on the trespass offering (Lev. 6:1-7 [H. 5:20-26]) providing for payment to the priest of the fraud compensation when the injured party dies leaving no kinsmen (5:5-10, Ps). *c.* The law of ordeal for a wife suspected of adultery (5:11-31). This extremely ancient custom was legalized by P and edited with Ps supplements; according to B. Stade (ZAW [1895] 166-178) and others, two separate sources are combined into one; see the detailed study of J. Morgenstern (in *Hebrew Union College Jubilee Volume*, pp. 113-143, Cincinnati, 1925; cf. HUCA VII [1930] 114 ff.). *d.* The Nazarite vow (Ps): conditions for its fulfillment (6:1-8), purification from defilement through accidental contact with a corpse (6:9-12), completion of the vow (6:13-21). *e.* The words of priestly blessing (6:22-27).

8. Ritual laws. *a.* Instruction for placing the seven lamps on the golden candlestick (8:1-4, Ps; cf. Ex. 25:31-37). *b.* Supplementary instructions for oblations and libations which accompany animal sacrifices (15:1-16, Ps; probably based on the Holiness Code; cf. Lev. 17:10, 13, 15; 19:23; 23:9 f.; 25:2). *c.* Heave offering of the first dough of the year (15:17-21, Ps; "cake" in 15:20 is a gloss; cf. Ez. 44:30; Neh. 10:37 [H. 10:38]). *d.* The sin offering of the congregation (15:22-26, Ps) and of the individual (15:27-31, Ps): this law is probably earlier than Lev. 4 but later than Lev. 5:1-13. *e.* Tassels (or fringes) worn on the corners (or borders) of the dress (15:37-41; cf. Deut. 22:12; an old law, sometimes attributed to

H; 15:40 is a gloss). *f.* Purification, after defilement with a corpse, by means of the ashes of a red heifer (19:1-13, P^s; with a supplement in 19:14-22; there are vague references to it in 31:19-23). *g.* An elaboration of the calendar of festivals in Lev. 23 (Num. 28:1-29:40 [H. 30:1], P^s; 28:3-8 repeats Ex. 29:38-42; new moons, 28:11-15, are lacking in Lev. 23). *h.* An elaboration of the law on vows (cf. Lev. 27; Num. 6), dealing particularly with the validity of vows made by women (30:1-16 [H. 30:2-17], P^s).

The Priestly Code, the charter of the new Jewish Church, originated between Haggai and Nehemiah, but the story describing Ezra the scribe coming from Babylonia in 458 with the Law of God in his hand (Ezra 7:14, 25 f.) hardly contains an element of truth. Writing two centuries later, the Chronicler exaggerates the role of Ezra so fantastically that it is difficult to recapture the true historical picture of his contribution out of the misty haze of imagination. One thing seems certain: if Ezra brought the book of the law from Babylonia, it was *not* the Priestly Code (and much less the Pentateuch *in toto*). It could only have been the Holiness Code, apparently composed in Babylonia about 550. For the Priestly Code is definitely a product of Jerusalem and not of Babylonia. It codifies in stereotyped and idealized form the current practices of the Second Temple, about 500 or perhaps in the next half-century. It is not, like Ez. 40-48, a visionary glimpse of the Temple of the future, nor yet, like the Holiness Code, a mere program for the future reflecting ancient usage, but an accurate description of current ceremonies, some reaching back to immemorial antiquity, while others were but of yesterday and were projected back artificially into the ancient days of Moses and Aaron.

More credible than the story of Ezra coming from Babylonia with the book of the Law in his hand (if it is identified with P) is the story, likewise from the Chronicler's fanciful pen, of the reading of the Law before the whole congregation in 444 (or a few years later), when Nehemiah was governor of Judea (Neh. 7:73b-9:38 [H. 10:1]), and of the religious reformation that followed (Neh. 10:28-39 [H. 10:29-40]). Whether this is historical or an invention of the Chronicler, patterned on the reading of the Deuteronomic book of the Law in 621 B.C. (or conceivably on the synagogue service), it has long since been recognized that the reforms of Nehemiah presuppose at least in part (if historical) the P Code, just as those of Josiah were based on the D Code. Since the Chronicler always regarded the finished Pentateuch as the Law of Moses, and the book read in the days of Nehemiah was obviously considerably shorter, judging from the time required for reading, its content is unknown, although it contained Lev. 23 (Neh. 8:13-18 alludes to Lev. 23:39-43). The account of Nehemiah's reforms (Neh. 10:30-39 [H. 10:31-40]) is of little help in determining the nature of the book. Some measures are based on P; others have no parallels in the Pentateuch; again others are based on earlier codes.[14] We must conclude that the book in question contained more than the separate Priestly Code, and that therefore little or nothing can be inferred from the Chronicler's account in Ezra-Nehemiah in regard to the origin and promulgation of the Priestly Code. It is possible that a fragmentary papyrus from Elephantine (Sachau, No. 6), dated 419 B.C., contains instructions for the Jews of Elephantine to celebrate the Passover according to the prescriptions of Ex. 12:1-20 (P), as if these were something new and hitherto unknown (cf. W. R. Arnold, JBL 31 [1912] 1-33). Supposing this interpretation to be correct, we have here the first allusion to the Priestly Code.

The Priestly Code, like all legislation, notwithstanding its deliberate timelessness and fictitious Mosaic background, bears the earmarks of its age, the first half of the Persian period (538-331). More precisely, P seems to have been written either toward the end of the reign of Darius I (521-485), some years after the rebuilding of the Temple in Jerusalem (516), or during the reign of his successor Xerxes I (485-465). Just as the Deuteronomic Code reflected the downfall of Assyria and the prophetic movement, so the P Code presupposes the capture of Babylon by Cyrus (538) and the rebuilding of the Temple (516). The enlightened policy of Cyrus and Darius, tolerant of all religions and favorable to the development of local cultures, gave to the empire a co-ordinated and just provincial administration which anticipated in a way the Pax Romana.

Such a great empire was a condition for the early phenomenal diffusion of the three great universalistic religions, Judaism, Christianity, and Mohammedanism. It is difficult to conceive the transformation of that miserable Jewish community in Jerusalem during the time of Haggai and Zechariah (520) into the enthusiastic and aggressive, reborn congregation of Nehemiah (444), growing in strength until it was able to withstand the vicious onslaught of Antiochus Epiphanes in 168, without the favorable and peaceful environment of the Persian Empire. The vigorous repression of revolutionary movements and the reorganization of the empire into twenty satrapies (Herodotus 3:90-94) by Darius I had a decisive

[14] Neh. 10:30 [H. 10:31], excluding intermarriage with the Canaanites, has a parallel in Deut. 7:3; Ex. 34:16 [R^D], but no definite enactments in P (unless Gen. 26:35; 28:1-9; Num. 25:6-15 be regarded as statutory precedents); the expression "to do all the commandments of Jehovah our Lord, and his ordinances, and his statutes" in Neh. 10:29 [H. 10:30] is Deuteronomistic; the law of the Sabbatical year (Neh. 10:31b [H. 10:32b]) is that of Deut. 15:1 f. The prohibition of market transactions on the Sabbath (Neh. 10:31a [H. 10:32a]) and provisions of a Temple tax of one-third of a shekel (Neh. 10:32 [H. 10:33]; half a shekel in Ex. 30:13, P^s), of deliveries of wood by lot (Neh. 10:34 [H. 10:35]), and for the collection of tithes by the priests or by the Levites in the presence of a priest (Neh. 10:37 f. [H. 10:38 f.]) are unknown in the Pentateuch. The only parallels with P or P^s exist in Neh. 10:33 [H. 10:34] (cf. Lev. 24:5-8; Num. 28:3-29;38; Lev. 4, etc.) and 10:35-37 [H. 10:36-38] (cf. Num. 18:11-19).

influence on the character of the Priestly Code, and through it determined the subsequent development of Judaism. The imperial organization of Western Asia was far more integrated and permanent than that of earlier empires, which ruled over nations and kingdoms by force of arms and were concerned more with the collection of tribute than with the welfare of their subjects.

After the ill-fated proclamation of Zerubbabel as the Messianic King of the Jews by Zechariah (see p. 603), resulting in the immediate intervention of the Persian officials of Darius I, the Jews realized the futility of attempting to become independent through a *coup d'état*. They were forced either to confine their nationalistic aspirations to apocalyptic, Utopian dreams, or accept the *status quo* as permanent and reorganize their community as a church within an empire—a community willingly forsaking all hope of political independence but becoming a religious group impervious to assimilation. The compilers of the Priestly Code were not dreamers but realists, and they chose the second course. Their God was no longer a national deity—the God of apocalypse whose Messiah would create a Jewish empire—but a universal God. Their community was no longer, even in aspiration, an independent state but a universal church to which members of all nations were welcome. The convert, or *ger*, now on an equal footing with the native Judean, is to be loved as a native (so already in H, Lev. 17:8-16, 18:26; 19:33 f.; 20:2; 22:18, 24 f; 23:22b; 24:16; 25:6, 35; for P see Ex. 12:45; Num. 15:29; for Ps see Num. 9:14; 15:14-16; 35:15; cf. Deut. 29:10-12 [H. 29:9-11]. Moreover, in that extraordinary document in Gen. 10, all civilized nations of the world are recognized to be a single family in a sense that even Herodotus, in his remarkable list of the twenty satrapies of Darius, never imagined.

Eduard Meyer in his classical history of ancient Persia (*Geschichte des Altertums*, Vol. III, pp. 167-174. Stuttgardt, 1901) clearly recognized that one of the most profound and far-reaching results of the Persian Empire was the transformation of the national religions into personal and universal types of worship offered to deities no longer localized, but cosmic in scope. With the cessation of political independence, nationality could have only a cultural, and particularly a religious, meaning. The national gods, formerly unable to preserve the individual states, had to become patrons of the Persian kings. Marduk of Babylon, according to his priests (R. W. Rogers, *Cuneiform Parallels to the Old Testament*, p. 381), and Jehovah, according to Second Isaiah and the Chronicler, had chosen Cyrus. Marduk had selected him as ruler of the world, Jehovah as his shepherd and anointed (Is. 44:28-45:4; cf. II Chron. 36:22 f. = Ezr. 1:1-3a). The deity in the Priestly document (Gen. 1) is that of Second Isaiah—the Creator of the world and God of all nations; but at the same time, with glaring inconsistency, the invisible ruler of the Jewish community.

The problem which the Priestly authors face and solve in the Book of Genesis is not how the God of Israel became the only God in existence (an article of faith proclaimed by Second Isaiah with the zeal and eloquence appropriate to a new doctrine), but rather how it happened that the Creator of heaven and earth, the universal God of Adam and Noah, could graciously consent to become (through the covenant with Abraham and the revelation to Moses) the peculiar God of the Jews. Another solution to the same problem is given in additions to the Deuteronomic Code dating from the Persian period (Deut. 4:19 f.; 32:8 f.); more startling is the assertion of Mal. 1:11 that the heathen are (unconsciously) worshiping Jehovah. The Priestly document, although recognizing in principle that God was king of the universe, inevitably presented him primarily as the king of Israel. And this theological antinomy, which appears already in an acute form in Second Isaiah, together with the antinomy of Judaism as both a national and a universal religion, became a permanent characteristic of the theology and religion of the Jews. Judaism never developed into a completely denationalized church, like the Christian. In Roman law, for instance, the Jews were regarded as a nation and as such given peculiar privileges.[15]

The Priestly Code is the law of a holy nation, a theocracy (Ex. 19:6, redactional), whose absolute ruler is the God of the world. Since the Persian Empire had assumed responsibility for maintaining law and order and constituted the political state, secular matters could find no place in the priestly legislation. Only in ordinances for taking the census of Israel's tribes (Num. 1:1-47; 25:19-26:65), arranging them in the camp (Num. 2), and allotting to them the Promised Land (Josh. 13-21, in part), in which cities of refuge for unintentional manslayers are provided (Num. 35:9-34; Josh. 20:1-9), does P encroach on the functions of secular authorities. But it was essential to define, ethnically and geographically, the holy congregation to whom the sacred law was binding. For the rest, it is only in supplements to P (Ps) that ordinances regulating civil matters are to be found: the inheritance of daughters (Num. 27:8-11, with a restrictive supplementary clause in 36:1-12), the ordeal for a wife suspected of adultery (5:11-31), and the sparing of virgins captured in war (31:15-18). P deals in a typically ritualistic way with such matters as theft (Lev. 6:1-7 [H. 5:20-26], with a Ps supplement in Num. 5:5-10), accidental homicide and murder (Num. 35:9-29, with a Ps supplement in 35:30-34), and false witness (Lev. 5:1, 5 f.); thus even ancient civil laws become sacred ordinances.

In contrast with the reforming prophets, who considered the ceremonies of the cult insignificant before God, in comparison with right living, P regards ritual correctness as supreme and takes justice and mercy,

[15] See in general J. Juster, *Les juifs dans l'empire romain.* (2 vols.) Paris, 1914.

which are still paramount in the Deuteronomic Code and Holiness Code (cf. Lev. 19), for granted. It cannot be gainsaid that P shifts the emphasis from ethics to the cult and is only interested in one sphere of life: religion understood as recognition of the rights of God. God is conceived as a sort of supergovernment: the relations of the average Israelite with his invisible and absolute ruler are substantially identical, in principle, with those of subjects to their despotic dictator, whose might is irresistible and whose will is law. In both cases, the absolute government is theoretically owner of the persons and property of the subjects; its enactments, whether sensible or arbitrary, are to be obeyed blindly under penalty of exile or death; even criticism of the ruler or his agents is inexorably punished. The ruler, however, is exclusively devoted to the national interests and gives to his people, in reward for unquestioned obedience, protection against external aggression and internal disturbance.

The law of P thus established a holy state within a state, a church within an empire, an entity as independent theoretically from political vicissitudes as the Vatican, which it patently resembles. Only priests who were lawyers could have conceived of religion as a theocracy regulated by divine law fixing exactly, and therefore arbitrarily, the sacred obligations of the people to their God. In so doing they were wholly unconscious of having sanctified the external, obliterated from religion both the ethical ideals of Amos and the tender emotions of Hosea, and reduced the universal Creator to the stature of an inflexible despot.

Is this Priestly Code "the climax of the whole prophetic teaching" as L. Finkelstein (*The Pharisees*, Vol. II, p. 462. Philadelphia, 1938) maintains? If so, we must admit with him that "there was only one loss in the substitution of legalism for prophecy; poetry was replaced by prose" (*ibid.*, p. 463)—a rather fundamental change in religion. Regulation took the place of spontaneity, discipline stifled freedom, solemnity displaced joyousness in the festivals, holy sacraments were substituted for the religious exercises of the laity. Nevertheless, P preserved the Jews from assimilation and did not entirely throttle other types of religion (as can be seen from the Psalms), any more than Scholasticism eliminated the religion of St. Francis. In reality, by making the ancient rites and customs mere empty forms, P sterilized the pagan elements of the religion of Israel and made obedience to the divine Law the supreme test of piety.

The contribution of the Priestly Code is the fixation of the ritual ordained for public and private devotions. It presents in its purest form the priestly point of view, and is by no means representative of all religious tendencies of the Persian period, for such books as Ruth, Jonah, Proverbs, and Psalms betray at times a radically different notion of religion. In reality, the conflict between a religion of observance and one "in spirit and in truth" persists to the present day in Judaism and Christianity.

Notwithstanding a very advanced conception of God, derived from the Second Isaiah, and some innovations in the ceremonial worship, the Priestly authors of the code, like priests in general, were extremely conservative and even reactionary, not unlike the Sadducees who in a later period opposed the progressivism of the Pharisees.

From immemorial custom P derived the two fundamental notions which characterize it: physical holiness and arbitrary law—archaic conceptions which the reforming prophets had discarded in favor of the noble ideals of a spiritual holiness and a moral law. These two principles, the physical sacredness implied in divine ownership of everything and the inflexible authority of the Law, no matter how unreasonable some of its ordinances may appear, explain the whole theocratic system of P.

Within the borders of Israel everything belonged to God. Such a principle carried to its logical conclusion would involve the immediate death of all Jews unable to obtain the necessities of life without theft; but common sense, introducing the notion of arbitrary enactment, tempered theoretical requirements and allowed the Jews to obtain these necessities on condition that an arbitrary portion be set aside for the exclusive use of the deity, and that taxes and donations be gathered from the remainder. This principle and its practical adaptation to actual conditions in human life was applied to land, time, persons, and possessions.

In principle the Lord said, "The land is mine, for ye are strangers and sojourners with me" (Lev. 25:23, H or P), but in reality he allowed the Israelites to use the land provided they fulfill certain conditions. They must reserve for God a limited territory. The camp of the Israelites at the foot of Sinai (Num. 2), a miniature model of the land of Israel, was divided into four zones of increasing sanctity: the secular zone (Num. 2); the forecourt of the Tabernacle reserved for priests and Levites (Ex. 27:9-19), into which laymen entered only when they offered private sacrifices; the Holy Place reserved for the priests (Ex. 26:31-33, 35); and the Holy of Holies (26:34) where, according to Lev. 16:1-4 (Ps), only the high priest could enter (perhaps only on the Day of Atonement), although an earlier law of P (Num. 18:7) admitted all priests. The Levites encamped between the court of the Tabernacle and the secular tribes, as a protective insulation against their contact with the dangerous holy presence of the deity (Num. 1:53).

The assignment of forty-eight important cities to the priests and Levites (Josh. 21; cf. Num. 35:1-8, Ps) was a late afterthought, born in the fancy of a priest but never put into practice; it contradicts the earlier laws in Num. 18:20 f. (cf. 26:62, Ps). Private individuals might "own" a piece of land on condition that they allow it to "rest" (i.e., lie fallow) on the Sabbatical year (Lev. 25:1-7, H), restore the land to its former owners on the jubilee year (25:23 f., H, a provision not enforced), and pay a sort of rent by bringing the firstlings, first fruits, tithes, and other agricultural offerings to the sanctuary (Num. 18:8-19, 21-32; cf. Lev. 23:10-20; in Ps: Ex. 13:1; Lev. 27:26 f., 30-33).

The festivals were a tax paid to God for the use of the time, which in principle belonged to him. Rest from work on the Sabbath and the joyful celebration of the feast days in ancient times had been a privilege; in P they become a solemn duty, a sacred debt to be paid, an ascetic abstention from professional work on the festivals (Lev. 23:7 f., 21, 25, 35 f., P; cf. Num. 28:18, 25 f.; 29:1, 12, 35, Ps) and from any kind of work (except eating, Ex. 12:16) on the Sabbath (Ex. 16:23; 31:15-17; 35:2 f.; Lev. 23:3; Num. 15:32-35, Ps; cf. Gen. 2:2 f.; Ex. 20:11, P) and on the Day of Atonement (Lev. 16:31; 23:28-32). On the Sabbath and the Day of Atonement one must "afflict one's soul" and any manner of work was a capital offense. A "solemn convocation" was called on the Sabbath (Lev. 23:3), and on these seven yearly festivals: the first and seventh day of Unleavened Bread (Ex. 12:16; Lev. 23:7 f.; Num. 28:18, 25), the Feast of Weeks (Lev. 23:21; Num. 28:26), the old New Year in the fall, i.e., the first day of the seventh month (Lev. 23:24; Num. 29:1), the Day of Atonement (Lev. 23:27; Num. 29:7), the first and the eighth day of the Feast of Tabernacles (Lev. 23:35 f.; Num. 29:12-35).

These festivals are now dated exactly and have lost their connection with agriculture or shepherding: they are either memorials of historical events or mere sacramental celebrations. The Passover, celebrated immediately before the Exodus from Egypt, when the sacrificial system had not yet been revealed to Moses on Sinai, ceased to be a sacrifice and became a celebration in the family (Ex. 12:3-14). In a sense, the Sabbatical and Jubilee years were not only a payment of rent on the land but also on the use of one's time.

All the Israelites belonged to the Lord, they were his servants whom he acquired by liberating them from Egyptian bondage (Lev. 25:42, 55, H). They must therefore be a nation consecrated to God and ritually pure: they must submit to circumcision (Lev. 12:3; cf. Gen. 17:10-14; 21:4; Ex. 12:48), which was a sign of the divine covenant with Israel, and to numerous purifications and atoning sacrifices, to remove all pollution from the holy congregation. A special code incorporated in P (Lev. 11-15) dealt with the various types of pollution caused by food, childbirth, diseases of the skin, mold on garments or buildings, and natural secretions, and specified the various purifications required in each case. Some of these purifications are attested in ancient times (e.g., II Sam. 11:4). In D there are also laws on the clean and unclean (e.g., Deut. 23:10-14 [H. 23: 11-15]), as also in H (Lev. 17:10-16; 20:25 f.; 21:1-7, 11; 22:1-9). Supplementary laws on this subject are found in Ps: Lev. 3:17; 5:2-6; 7:22-27; 10:10; Num. 9:1-13; 19.

As slaves of God, the Israelites could not be held in actual serfdom (Lev. 25:39-40a, 42 f., 47-49, 53, 55, H) and must be freed in the Jubilee Year (25:40b-41, 44-46, 50-52, 54, Ps). In a special sense, all first-born males belonged to God (Ex. 13:2, Ps; cf. the ancient law in Ex. 22:29 [H. 22:28]) and must therefore be redeemed (Ex. 13:13-16; 34:19 f., redactional; Num. 18:15, Ps) at the cost of five shekels, according to a late supplementary law (Num. 18:16). However, in general every Israelite, from the age of twenty must give "a ransom for his soul unto the Lord" amounting to a yearly half-shekel "to make atonement" for his soul (Ex. 30:11-16, Ps; cf. Neh. 10:32 [H. 10:33]). But in addition to this individual ransom, the Israelites must consecrate the clergy to the exclusive service of the deity in order to obtain release; in addition, a layman might consecrate himself to the deity for a limited period through the Nazarite vow (Num. 6:1-21, Ps).

In D, the terms "Levites" and "priests" were synonymous (Deut. 17:9, 18; 18:1, etc.), but the priests of sanctuaries outside of Jerusalem left stranded by the desecration of all the "high places" were allowed to come to Jerusalem and live off the revenues from the Temple (Deut. 18:6-8)— a generous provision which Josiah could not put into practice (II Kings 23:9). Consequently, the situation of the provincial priests became desperate (I Sam. 2:36). Ezekiel saw in their plight a divine punishment (44:4-16) and decreed that only the sons of Zadok should officiate at Jerusalem, whereas the other "Levites" should perform the menial tasks in the sanctuary: thus for the first time the *de facto* distinction between Zadokite priests and their servants, the Levites, was declared to be *de jure*. Although the H Code ignored this distinction, the P Code ratified it with an important modification. According to P, of all the sons of Levi only Aaron and his sons—a much more comprehensive group than the sons of Zadok in Ezekiel—were to be priests (Ex. 28:1; Num. 18:7b, etc.; Ex. 29:9b; Num. 3:10; 25:10-13, etc., Ps) and the Levites were to be their servants (Num. 3:5-9, Ps).

Although the Priestly authors were forced to admit numerous members of non-Zadokite priestly families to holy orders, as appears also from the fictitious but significant totals of 4,289 priests and only 74 Levites who returned with Zerubbabel from Babylonia (Ezr. 2:36-40), they reserved for first-born descendants of Zadok the office of high priest. In P, the Zadokites were the descendants of the oldest son of Aaron, Eleazar; the other priests were the descendants of a second son, Ithamar. The title of "high priest" is still unknown to P and later parts of the Pentateuch. H uses a descriptive expression, "the priest that is greater than his brethren" (Lev. 21:10). Instead of "high priest," P says "the anointed priest" (Lev. 4:3, 5, 16; 6:22), because only the chief priest was anointed (Ex. 29:7-9) and not all the priests, as in the later legislation of Ex. 28:41b;

30:30; 40:15; Lev. 7:36 (Ps); or, more often, simply "the priest." But Aaron and, after him, Eleazar in P were virtually high priests in function, although not in name (cf. J. Wellhausen, *Prolegomena*, pp. 142-145. J. Morgenstern, "A Chapter in the History of the High Priesthood," AJSL 55 [1938] Nos. 1, 2, 4).

The high priest was not only the holiest of men and spiritual head of the congregation but also a substitute for the former kings and superior to the highest lay authorities (Num. 27:21, Ps). The laws of P concerning the priests, "Aaron and his sons," dealt with their vestments and ordination (Ex. 28-29; cf. Num. 20:25-29; the ordination is described in Lev. 8, Ps), Aaron's performance of a solemn sacrifice (Lev. 9), contrasted with an illegitimate one (10:1-5), the priest's portion in a meal offering and peace offering (10:12-15), regulations in regard to the entrance of Aaron into the Holy of Holies (Lev. 16, combined with the law on the Day of Atonement), ending with the various taboos prescribed for the priests in the Holiness Code (Lev. 21-22) and the priestly emoluments (Num. 18:8-32). The laws on sacrifice (Lev. 1-7) deal incidentally with the duties of the priests.

The priests were the only sacred persons absolutely belonging to God. Not so the Levites who were not consecrated to God through a solemn rite: they were merely the servants of the priests, presented to them by the Lord (Num. 18:6) to perform menial tasks in the sanctuary. In Num. 16-18, P emphasized the distinction between clergy (priests and their servants, the Levites) and laity, but Ps stressed the abyss separating priests from Levites. Elsewhere in Ps their humble duties were specified (Num. 1:48-54; 4:1-49) without leaving their servile status in doubt (3:5-9). They were offered by the Israelites to the Lord (i.e., to the priests) as ransom for the first-born (Num. 3:11-13; 8:16). Since the first-born were 22,273 and the Levites only 22,000, 273 first-born had to be redeemed at the cost of 5 shekels apiece (Num. 3:39-51). Nay, as if they were mere objects, the Levites were presented by Aaron as a wave offering from the children of Israel, to make atonement for them (Num. 8:5-22). The Levites were not consecrated to the Lord like the priests, but merely purified (8:5-8, 21). They were not only forbidden to officiate in the worship but also to touch sacred vessels under pain of death, and could only carry them after the priests had carefully covered them (Num. 4:15, Ps; cf. 18:1-7, P).

In addition to the cultivated land, all other property belonged, in principle, to the Lord, and the Israelites had to pay him a tribute for using most of it for their own benefit. These sacred dues were partly reserved by God for his own exclusive use, thus particularly the blood and the fat in all animal sacrifices as well as the whole victim in burnt offerings, and partly assigned to the priests and Levites. To the priests, Aaron and his sons, belonged all the heave offerings, meal offerings, sin offerings, trespass offerings, wave offerings, the first fruits and the choice produce of the fields, the first-born of man and beast, of which the first-born of man and unclean animals had to be redeemed (Num. 18:8-15, 17-19, Ps). To the Levites, who like the priests possessed no fields (18:20, 24b), the Lord gave the tithes of the Israelites (18:21, 24a); with the proviso, however, that the Levites shall pay to the high priest "a tithe of the tithe" or the best tenth of their revenues (18:25-32).

It is thus clear that the cardinal principle of the P Code, divine ownership of everything, was purely theoretical and that in practice the Lord was satisfied with a token payment, fixed arbitrarily—a concrete sign that the rights of the divine landlord were honored. The arbitrary character of priestly legislation appears not only in the adaptation of a Utopian ideal to the actual conditions of human life, but also in the recognition that even these gracious enactments admitting the necessities of human life might prove difficult in practice, and that some provision must be made for sins of omission or commission by which the Law had been unintentionally violated.

The whole sacrificial system of the P Code, except for purely optional offerings, was a more or less conventional and arbitrary scheme intended to preserve the correct relation between the Lord and Israel, to balance the books without a deficit, and to preserve the delicate equilibrium on which the very existence of the nation depended. The sacrifices and offerings required by the Lord were partly taxes and partly fines, either national or private in scope; the amount of these dues, while fixed arbitrarily, was no more a subject of discussion, in view of the absolute authority of the divine law, than the taxes and fines imposed by a dictator upon his subjects.

The taxes paid by individual Israelities for the support of the Temple and clergy have been listed above; they were considered as financial obligations with no sacrificial or sacramental character whatsoever. In a general way, private sacrifices, which at least until the reforms of Josiah were by far the most common, have nearly disappeared in P. Conversely, national taxes paid to the Lord were strictly sacramental. The most important was the *tāmîd* (i.e., regular, perpetual; the word is used alone for the daily sacrifice in Dan. 8:11-13; 11:31; 12:11), which consisted of the daily burnt offering of a yearling lamb, a cereal oblation, and a libation of wine presented to the Lord every morning and evening (Ex. 29:38-42; Num. 28:1-8, Ps). In Ez. 46:13-15, the burnt offering and oblation were offered only in the morning, but Ezra 9:4 mentions the evening meal offering (cf. II Kings 16:15). The libation of wine, not mentioned by Ezekiel, may have been a supplementary rite; even later was the daily offering of incense (Ex. 30:7, Ps). The late law of Num. 28:9-29:38 provided for additional sacrifices on the Sabbath, the new moons, and annual festivals. However, the presentation of a sheaf of barley and a yearling lamb at the Passover (Lev. 23:9-12, H) and two loaves and two yearling lambs at Pentecost (23:15-20, mostly H) are survivals of ancient rites. Similarly, the provision of shewbread (Ex. 25:30; Lev. 24:5-9) rests on ancient custom (I Sam. 21:4-6 [H. 21:5-7]).

The other public and private sacrifices prescribed may be classed as fines. Just as governments punish crimes with death or exile, but misdemeanors with fines, so in the holy commonwealth, whose constitution was the Priestly Code, deliberate and impertinent violations of the sacred law (Lev. 10:1-5, P; Lev. 24:10-23 [H and Ps]; Num. 15:32-36 [Ps]; 16-18 [P and Ps]; 25:6-18 [Ps]; cf. D, H, and earlier codes) were summarily punished with death to remove the taint at once from Israel (Num. 15:30 f., Ps). But less flagrant, more or less unintentional, offenses were atoned for with a sacrificial fine.

For the nation as a whole, the P Code provides an annual ceremony of expiation for all sins, on the Day of Atonement (the tenth day of the seventh month). Ezekiel (45:18-20) had ordained that the atonement of the sanctuary fall on the first day of the first and seventh months. Originally, the Day of Atonement was merely a day of repentance observed with fasting, Sabbath rest, and offerings decreed for feast days (Lev. 23:26-32, P; cf. 16:29-34, Ps). Numbers 29:7-11 (Ps), however, prescribes the sin offering of a he-goat, in addition to other sacrifices on that day, although the ceremonies of fasting and repentance on the twenty-fourth of the seventh month described in Neh. 9:1-4 included no sacrifices. The later observance of the Day of Atonement, described in the composite and late law of Lev. 16, consisted of the sin offering of a bullock (the burnt offering of a ram is secondary) for the high priest and the priesthood (16:3, 6) and the burnt offering of a ram for the people (16:5, where a sin offering of two he-goats is added).

In addition to these sin offerings, the great annual expiation of the sins of the people was accomplished by means of an extremely archaic rite, magical rather than sacrificial in character. The high priest, after placing both hands on the head of a goat, thus transferring to it all the sins of the people, sent the goat with a messenger out into the wilderness to Azazel (16:8, 10, 21 f., 26). This ancient pagan magical rite, with parallels among many primitive peoples (cf. James G. Frazer, "The Scapegoat," in The Golden Bough, Vol. IX. 3rd ed., New York, 1935), was incorporated into Judaism by the Priestly authors who combined with it the sin offering (to the Lord) of another goat, chosen by lot from two (16: 7-9, 15-19).

Analogous to this transference ceremony of sin or evil was the cleansing of a leper (Lev. 14:4-7) or a house (14:49-53) by means of two birds;

Zechariah (5:5-11) saw wickedness transported, in a vision, from Palestine to Babylonia. Other rites, private in character and seemingly survivals of ancient magic rather than sacrifices, are the burning of the red heifer, whose ashes were mixed in a potion used for the purification of those polluted by contact with a corpse (Num. 19, P⁵), and the ordeal of a woman suspected of adultery, by means of the "water of bitterness" containing dust from the floor of the Sanctuary (Num. 5:11-28, P⁵).

Besides the ceremonies of the Day of Atonement, the Priestly Code prescribes a number of other sacrifices which, like fines, serve to atone for sin: the sin offerings of a he-goat on new moons and festivals (Num. 28:15, 22; 29:5, 11, 16, 19, 22, 25, 28, 31, 34, 38, P⁵; Lev. 23:19a, redactional); the sin offerings of a bullock at the consecration of priests (Ex. 29:14, 36, P and P⁵, respectively; Lev. 8:2, 14, P⁵), followed by the sacrifice of a ram as a burnt offering (Ex. 29:18, 25, P; Lev. 8:18, P⁵) and of another ram, the "installation ram," as a heave offering (Ex. 29:19-28, P and P⁵; Lev. 8:22-32, P⁵); the blood of the afore-mentioned bullock served also to purify the altar (Ex. 29:36 f.; Lev. 8:15, P⁵; cf. Ez. 43:18-21), which a late law (Ex. 30:10) erroneously regarded as the altar of incense; the sin offering of a bullock and the burnt offering of another for the atonement of the Levites when they assumed their office (Num. 8:8-12, P⁵); occasional sin offerings of the high priest to atone for inadvertent transgressions committed by himself (Lev. 4:1-12), the congregation (4:13-21), the ruler (4:22-26), or a private individual (4:27-35; cf. the earlier law in Num. 15:22-31, P⁵).

These last two laws, after prescribing the congregational atonement for involuntary transgressions, dealt with sin offerings required of individuals who had "sinned through error" (Lev. 4:27-35; Num. 15:27-29). The sin offering (*haṭṭāth*) was required of individuals as atonement for unconscious violations of certain taboos, both ceremonial and moral (Lev. 5:1-6, P⁵), for involuntary failure to observe certain laws (Num. 15:22-29, P⁵), and for specific purification of those polluted through childbirth (Lev. 12:6), organic secretions (15:14 f., 29 f.), leprosy (14:10-20, erroneously called a trespass offering), or contact with carcasses of unclean animals (5:2 f., P⁵). In the case of a Nazarite, the sin offering was prescribed both as a purification in case of his accidental proximity to a corpse (Num. 6:9-12, P⁵, omitting the trespass offering in 6:12) and in conclusion of this vow (6:14-16, P⁵). The usual victims in a sin offering were, according to the circumstances, a he-goat, she-goat, ewe lamb, or kid (Lev. 5:6, P⁵). Less expensive offerings were accepted from people of small means: two doves (5:7-10, P⁵) or, from the poorest, a cereal oblation (5:11-13, P⁵).

The trespass, or guilt, offering (*āshām*) should not be confused with the sin offering, although the two are more or less equated in the late law of Lev. 5:5-7. The trespass offering of a ram atoned for illegal retention or misappropriation of property belonging to God (Lev. 5:14-16) or to man (6:1-7 [H. 5:20-26]), after restitution, plus one-fifth, had been made (*ibid.* and Num. 5:6 f., Ps). If the defrauded person had died leaving no heirs, restitution was made to the priest (Num. 5:8, Ps). In place of the ram, which was regularly prescribed (Lev. 5:15 f., 18; 6:6 [H. 5:25]; 19:21 f.; Num. 5:8; cf. Ezra 10:19), late laws (Lev. 14:12, 21; Num. 6:12) substituted a lamb. The female lamb or kid of the goats in Lev. 5:6 (Ps) and the doves allowed as a substitute for the poor in 5:7-13 were not trespass, but sin, offerings. In some late laws a trespass offering was prescribed for offenses not connected with misappropriation of property (Lev. 5:1-6, 17-19; 19:20-22). The ritual for the trespass offering is described in Lev. 7:1-6 (7-10).

Private sacrifices called burnt offering (*'ōlâh* or *kālîl*) and peace offering (*shelem*), constituting the principal offerings in ancient times, lost their significance in the priestly legislation, which took away from the laity most of the initiative and all active participation in Temple worship. Only the Passover festival, celebrated in the family circle, survived in the Priestly Code as an isolated remnant of the ancient private worship with a sacred meal as its central rite (Ex. 12:1-18, 43-50, P and Ps; Lev. 23:4-8, P; Num. 9:1-14; 28:16, Ps). However, in these laws the sacrificial character of the celebration became more and more obliterated.

The other private sacrifices became purely optional, works of supererogation (Num. 29:39, Ps). The burnt offering (Lev. 1:1-17) was presented in payment of a vow (22:17-20, H; Num. 15:3, 8, Ps) or freewill offering (Num. 15:3); the same applied to the peace offering (Lev. 3; 7:11-34; 22:21-25; Num. 15:8-15), except that in Lev. 7:12-15; 22:29 a third type of peace offering (*tôdâh*) was added. A vegetable or meal offering (*minḥâh*) consisting of flour and oil either kneaded together or variously cooked (Lev. 2), was the concomitant of certain sacrifices or else an independent offering. Cereal oblations (and also wine libations) were required for the daily burnt offering (*tāmîd*) in the Temple both on ordinary days (Lev. 6:19-23 [H. 6:12-16]; Ex. 29:38-42; 40:29; Num. 4:16, Ps) and holy days (Lev. 23:13, 16 [18], 37, H and P; Num. 28-29, Ps); and they were part of the sacrifices for the consecration of priests (Lev. 9:4, 17) and the purification of Levites (Num. 8:8, Ps). They could also be offered independently by the priests (Lev. 6:14-18 [H. 6:7-11]).

As part of the private worship, oblations were made independently, either as substitutes for burnt offerings (Lev. 5:11-13), in the ordeal for jealousy (Num. 5:15) or, ostensibly, as vows or freewill offerings (Lev. 2; Lev. 7:9 f.; Num. 7, Ps). They were, however, required with sin offerings (Num. 15:24, Ps), with burnt and peace offerings (15:1-16), in the purification of a leper (Lev. 14:10, 20 f., 31), and in terminating the

Nazarite vow (Num. 6:15, 17, Ps). Wine, incense, and salt were used only in connection with sacrifices and oblations, not independently.

The arbitrary character and absolute authority of the Priestly Code appear not only in the exact amounts specified for these sacred tributes and fines, but also in the failure of the legislators to give a rational explanation of how and why such sacrifices and offerings produced the results ascribed to them. The legislators demanded blind, unquestioning obedience rather than intelligent understanding—exactly like military officers or authoritarian states. The old rites had become empty forms, meaningless in themselves but essential because prescribed by God for his inscrutable, unsearchable purposes. No attempt was made to explain rationally the ceremonial system as a whole, but occasional explanations of individual rites occurred—without, however, being systematized in the least. Some rites, as we have seen, were treated as pure and simple magic —efficacious in themselves without divine intervention; other ancient practices, conversely, acquired a new profound religious meaning, like the Sabbath and circumcision—practices with nearly a cosmic scope and significance.

As a whole, the sacrificial system was conceived partly as payment of sacred dues and partly as a means of expiating sin; or, as Philo (*De Victimis* 4 [M II, 240]) says, there are sacrifices for God alone, who must be honored for his own sake, and sacrifices for the benefit of the worshiper, either for safety and improvement of his situation or for cure of the offenses of his soul.

Two general terms, used in P with reference to sacrifices, express this twofold purpose. The general term for sacrifice in P is *qorbān*, possibly a loan word from the Aramaic, meaning "gift"; this term, in the sense of gifts to the sanctuary, occurs no less than twenty-eight times in Num. 7 (Ps) and the related term *qurbān* is used in Neh. 10:34 [H. 10:35]; 13:31 in the sense of contributions (of wood) for the Temple; *qorban*, meaning any kind of sacrifice or offering, appears only in Ez. 20:28; 40:43 and in the various strata of P in Leviticus and Numbers (cf. in the New Testament Matt. 5:23 f.; 8:4; 23:18 f., where the word is translated. and Mark 7:11, where it is transcribed as *korbán; korbanás*, in Matt. 27:6, means the Temple treasure). In P, the word obviously evolved from meaning a free gift to God to a prescribed tribute; the corresponding word in ancient Israel, *minḥâh* (meaning gift to man or God, tribute), was used in P only for cereal oblations.

The other technical term in P expressing the main purpose of sacrifice is *kipper*: this verb is probably connected with the Assyrian *kuppuru* (to erase, wipe off, hence to cleanse persons or things, to perform a lustration) rather than with the Arabic *kafara* (to cover up; cf. Gen. 6:14). In Hebrew the verb never occurs in a physical sense but, before P and Ezra, only in the sense of propitiating, securing remission, atoning, while in Assyrian the verb is used for the ritual purifications and expiations performed by the *âshipu* priest. In the technical priestly language (Ez. 43-45; P; Neh. 10:33 [H. 10:34]; I Chron. 6:49 [H. 6:34]; II Chron. 29:24) the verb denoted expiation or atonement which the priest performed by means of blood (Lev. 17:11), sin offerings (4:20; 10:17, etc.), trespass offerings 5:16), other animal sacrifices (1:4; 14:20), oil (14:18), the goat for Azazel (16:10), service of the Levites (Num. 8:19), priestly rites (I Chron. 6:49 [H. 6:34]), burning of incense (Num. 16:46 f. [H. 17:11 f.]); and even the slaughter of a sinner (25:13) or the execution of a murderer (35:32 f), and the offering of jewelry (31:50). So dominant is this idea of expiation that even the poll tax was regarded as a means of expiation (Ex. 30:16, Ps)!

Thus obviously, in spite of the old principle expressed in Lev. 17:11, "it is the blood that makes atonement by reason of the life [that is in it]," the Priestly authors held no theory on how sacrifices and offerings expiated sin. They were evidently obsessed by the idea of sin (cf. Num. 32:14, Ps): for them it was not confined, as with the prophets, to transgressions of the moral law, but included any infringement, even unwitting, of ceremonial rules and prescriptions concerning the defilement of persons or inanimate objects. This rather physical conception of sin rests on the idea of holiness as a mysterious power, somewhat akin to electricity, which automatically becomes contagious (Ex. 29:37; 30:25-33, Ps; Lev. 6:13 f. [H. 6:20 f.] cf. Ez. 44:19; 46:20) and kills instantly not alone through contact but even by mere sight (Num. 4:15-20).

The God of holiness separated Israel from all nations and made it holy (Lev. 20:8; 21:8; 22:32 f., H; Ex. 31:12-17, Ps). Israel was "a kingdom of priests, a holy nation" (Ex. 19:6; redactional; cf. Is. 61:6) and could only exist as such: it was therefore a matter of life and death to observe the prescriptions of the divine law faithfully and punctiliously no matter how incomprehensible, lest the holy anger of the Lord be inflamed once more against his people and destroy them from the face of the earth. Whatever opinion one may hold of the "legalism" of the Priestly Code, it fulfilled its purpose in preserving the Jews as a peculiar nation to the present day.

CHAPTER VIII

THE POEMS IN THE PENTATEUCH

On the metrical form of Hebrew poetry much has been written since the time of Josephus (*Antiquities* 2:16, 4; 4:8, 44; 7:12, 3). Jerome (*Prologue to Job*) remarked that the verses of Job were hexameters, composed of a variety of feet, determined not by the number of syllables but by their quantities (*tempora*). Certain scholars like him have regarded the *quantity* of the syllables as essential in Hebrew meters as in Greek and Latin meters; others instead counted the syllables. Finally, in a learned and conclusive study of "The Rhythms of the Ancient Hebrews" (*Old Testament and Semitic Studies in Memory of William R. Harper,* Vol. I, pp. 167-204. Chicago, 1908), W. R. Arnold accepted the theory of Aristoxenus of Tarentum, a colleague of Aristotle, that rhythm in poetry is "a period of time divided into two commensurate parts . . . sustaining to each other one of three ratios, 1:1, 2:3, or 1:2" (p. 193). Arnold has proved that only the 1:1 ratio occurs in Hebrew poetry and that "the only time lengths that can contribute to the rhythm of Hebrew poetry are the intervals between accents" (p. 194).

In brief, a Hebrew verse consists of two equal parts which are divided by the stress accents into two, three, or four feet. In the elegiac (*qînâh*) line a pause takes the place of the last foot (4:3 accents in Lam. 1-4). The most common Hebrew verse has four accents in each half-line (4:4) and its meter corresponds exactly to that of these verses of Coleridge:

The lóvely lády Christabél, / Whom her fáther lóves so wéll,

What mákes her ín the wóod so láte, / A fúrlong from the cástle gáte?

As in Hebrew, here the number of syllables is variable (7 to 9 in a half-line) and a word like Christabel may take two accents. The following line (Gen. 49:10) may serve to illustrate this 4:4 meter:

lô'–yāsúr shébhet mîhúdháh / úmeḥōqéq mibbén raghláw

The scéptre shall not páss from Júdah / nor the stáff from betwéen his féet.

The following line (Ex. 15:3) has a 3:3 meter in the Hebrew:

Jehóvah is a mán of wár / Jehóvah ís his náme.

Finally, Miriam's song (Ex. 15:21), has a 2:2 meter:

Síng to Jehóvah / for he tríumphed glóriously

The hórse and its ríder / he cást into the séa.

The poetry contained in the Pentateuch spans the whole period between 1200-400 B.C., but does not contain the three great masterpieces of classical Hebrew poetry (Judg. 5; II Sam. 1:19-27; Nah. 1:10-3:19). The authors of the ancient narrative sources of the Pentateuch (S, J, E) may be the authors of the poetic divine oracles, blessings, and curses, which are an integral part of their stories; but in all probability they quoted the longer poems from poetic anthologies or from the mouth of the bards (Num. 21:27). The names of two ancient anthologies are preserved, *The Book of the Wars of Jehovah* (Num. 21:14) and *The Book of the Upright* or, rather (reading *sh-y-r* [song] for *y-sh-r* [upright], according to the LXX in a passage following I Kings 8:53, missing in the Hebrew), *The Book of Poetry* (Josh. 10:13; II Sam. 1:18).

Although no assurance can be reached in the matter, one must not overlook the possibility that considerable portions of the stories of Genesis were sung in verse by minstrels before they were retold in prose by the authors of the S, J, and E documents. If such was the case, the extant poetic sections of the stories may be a survival from some preliterary stage. It is, however, not to be excluded that the compilers of S, J, and E, like the authors of the *Arabian Nights*, occasionally lapsed into verse.

These incidental poems in the narratives may be considered first. In their written form they cannot be later than the documents in which they were embedded. Those in J and S may be dated in the century 950-850 B.C., those in E in the following century, although it is impossible to say whether they had been transmitted orally by ballad singers long before. The poetic form was demanded by their subject, since they are divine oracles or human blessings and curses.

In the S document the curses of God against the serpent in Eden (Gen. 3:14 f.), against the first woman (3:16), and against Adam (3:17-19) are noble and rhythmical in diction, but not always strictly metrical; the curse of Cain (4:11) is similar, but may be a later imitation. The divine promise to Noah (8:22) is a postexilic addition to S.

A great many of the divine oracles in the prophetic books are likewise eloquently rhythmical without being exactly metrical. The words of Adam after the creation of the woman (2:23, S) are in 2:2 meter. The poetic blessing of Abram by Melchizedek (14:19), in 2:2 meter, belongs to the latest strata of S and, as the advanced theology shows ("God Most High, maker of heaven and earth"), is to be dated in the fifth century.

In the J document, the divine oracles are not curses, as in S, but blessings and promises of a glorious future. The initial divine oracle to Abram (Gen. 12:1-3) is sonorous and majestic; the 2:2 meter is not carried out consistently, but most of the verses rhyme in *khā*. The other divine oracles in verse included in the J document are: the promise to Hagar concerning Ishmael (16:11 f., 2:2 meter); the oracle to Rebekah concerning the enmity between the two nations which would be born of her (25:23, 2:2 meter); the promise to Isaac (26:24, 4:4 meter); the oracle to Jacob (28:13 f.) is not metrical.

Several human blessings have a certain oracular character and occur in verse: the blessing of Rebekah by her brother and mother (24:60, 2:2 meter); Isaac's blessing of Jacob, whom he mistakes for Esau (27:27-29, 2:2 meter) is generally divided by critics between J (27:27, 29aɑb) and E (the rest), but the poem seems to be a unit and may be older than either document; it is by the same author who wrote the corresponding curse on Esau (27:39 f., 2:2 meter; 27:40b may be an addition) which is later than the conquest of Edom by David but earlier than Edom's successful revolt under Jehoram (i.e., *ca.* 1000-850). Since J and E are closely inter-woven in Gen. 27, it is no longer possible to determine with assurance whether the last two poems constituting the climax of the story were originally a part of J or E.

In the E document, the only blessing in poetry is Jacob's blessing of Ephraim and Manasseh (Gen. 48:15 f., probably 4:3 meter; 48:20, 2:2 meter). The oracle to Abraham in 15:18b (2:2 meter, omitting the last two words) is redactional and not earlier than 600 B.C., for it extends the ideal borders of Israel to the Euphrates. The words of Moses, upon hearing the tumult at the festival for the Golden Calf (Ex. 32:18), are in 2:2 meter.

Incidental poems are also included in the Priestly document in Genesis; they probably date from the fifth century. Nearly all of them are divine oracles. The P story of Creation contains not only an oracle of verse (Gen. 1:28, 2:2 meter), but seems to be the revision of a poem describing the eight acts of Creation; at least 1:27 is still in 2:2 meter. The divine sentence against murderers (9:6) is in 3:3 meter; the oracle to Noah (9:1-7), of which it is a part, and the words of the covenant with him (9:8-16) have a stately rhythm without being exactly metrical. The revela-tion to Abraham (17:1 f., 4 f.) is in 2:2 meter.

The original poems inserted into the Pentateuch can be dated only by internal evidence; the date of the document in which they are acci-dentally located is entirely irrelevant. There is no reason whatsoever to suppose that the writers of the narratives had anything at all to do with their composition. Some may have been quoted by the authors of the S, J, and E sources, others were inserted by redactors at various stages of the Pentateuch's growth. They may be grouped chronologically into four periods: nomadic and premonarchic (*ca.* 1250-1050), the united monarchy (*ca.* 1050-950), the Northern Kingdom of Israel (*ca.* 950-722), early Judaism (650-400).

1. 1250-1050. Two early poems still preserve the flavor of Bedouin desert life in all its pristine savagery and simplicity, devoid of that aura of noble idealism carried in the memory of the Israelites in Canaan. The song of Lamech (Gen. 4:23 f., 4:4 meter) is the wild boast of a vindictive Arab; its grim ferocity contrasts sharply with the humorous victory song of Samson (Judg. 15:16), reflecting a peasant rather than Bedouin background. To regard this song, as some critics do, as a "sword song" celebrating the discovery of the working of metal by Tubal-cain, son of Lamech (Gen. 4:22), is wholly unwarranted. The other desert poem is the song of the well (Num. 21:17 f., 3:3 meter), similar to the Arabic song heard by A. Musil (*Kuseyr Amra,* p. 298, 1907):

> Spring up, O well, flow copiously
> Drink and disdain not, with a staff we dug it.

Of the war songs ascribed by their present setting to the time of Moses, only one belongs indubitably to that time, the triumphal hymn of Miriam, composed immediately after the crossing of the Red Sea (Ex. 15:21, 2:2 meter). Either it consisted of only two lines, perhaps sung antiphonally, or else its beginning alone has been preserved. A late psalmist used this song as the text and exordium for his pretentious poem (Ex. 15:1-18). A fragmentary poetic list of localities in Moab (Num. 21:14 f., 3:3 meter?) was inserted from *The Book of the Wars of the Lord* into the itinerary of the Israelites' march on the borders of Moab. This poem and a sarcastic elegy on the devastation of Moab (Num. 21:27-30, omitting "to Sihon king of the Amorites" in 21:29; 3:3 meter), are of uncertain date, although hardly from the time of Moses. The same applies to the oracle against the Amalekites (Ex. 17:14, 4:4 meter) and declaration of eternal war against them (17:16, 4:4 meter). These poems and the liturgies for bringing the ark into battle (Num. 10:35 f., 4:4 meter) can hardly be put earlier than the eleventh century although apparently earlier than 950; W. R. Arnold (*Ephod and Ark,* p. 139, n. 2), however, is inclined to regard the formulae on the ark as redactional.

The poems in the Book of Genesis generally antedate the narratives which preface them. This is particularly obvious in the case of the curse and blessings of Noah (Gen. 9:25-27, 2:2 meter) according to which Japheth is to occupy the tents of Shem—an event for which the introductory story (9:20-24) gives no explanation. In the poem and story, Noah is the father of Shem, Japheth, and Canaan, i.e., the ancestor of the nations living in Canaan when the poem was composed. He is not yet, however, the hero of the Deluge nor has he become through his sons.

Shem, Japheth, and Ham (cf. the harmonistic glosses in 9:18, 22), the father of the three races of mankind (9:18 f.). In its general lines the historical situation presupposed by the poem is clear. The Canaanites (Canaan[1]) have become the "servants of servants" of the Israelites (Shem; cf. 10:21 where Shem is the ancestor of the Hebrews and Arameans) and of the Philistines (Japheth; cf. 10:2-5 where Japheth is the ancestor of the Aegean and Anatolian nations). But the Philistines are beginning to "dwell in the tents" of Israel. They were part of the Aegean "Peoples of the Sea" defeated in 1190 by Ramses III of Egypt. With the Israelites they invaded Canaan from opposite sides after the year 1200 B.C. The poem presupposes, on the one hand, certain spectacular victories of the Israelites over the Canaanites, such as that celebrated in the Song of Deborah (Judg. 5), and, on the other, the beginning of Philistine pressure over the Israelites, which forced the tribe of Dan to migrate en masse to the extreme north of the country (Judg. 17-18). It is, however, earlier than David's deliverance of Israel from the Philistine yoke. We may therefore date this poem in the century 1150-1050 B.C., which makes it the earliest record in the Old Testament dealing with the history of Canaan as a whole.

2. 1050-950. During the glorious period of David and Solomon (about 1013-933 B.C.), when the tribe of Judah became not only an integral part of Israel but enjoyed its brief period of hegemony over the whole nation, several poems, predicting the lasting supremacy of Judah over Joseph (lost after the division of the kingdom about 933), were composed to celebrate the achievements of David. From an historical and literary viewpoint, the most important of them is the "Blessing of Jacob" (Gen. 49:2-27, 4:4 meter). In the form of predictions, the poem describes the vicissitudes of the twelve tribes of Israel (Joseph represents Ephraim and Manasseh) and their characterization in the period of the Judges or earlier, when each tribe usually fought its own battles. Only the oracle about Judah (49:8-12) belongs to the reign of Solomon. The oracles about Reuben, Simeon, and Levi (49:3-7) refer to events earlier than the time of Moses, related in the S source (Gen. 35:22; 34), and are maledictions rather than blessings.

Except for the one about Judah, the others reflect the situation after the settlement in Canaan but before the coronation of Saul. The oracle about

---

[1] Canaan, in 10:15, is the ancestor of the Phoenicians (Sidon) and the Hittites. In Egyptian records, in the Tell el-Amarna letters of the fourteenth century, and in 10:19, Canaan is Southern Palestine. In the fifteenth century (tablets from Nuzi), "Canaan" (*kinaḫḫu*) means red purple dye—from the native name of Phoenicia at the time; the Greeks used their word for this dye (*phoinix*) to indicate the country, Phoenicia, where it was manufactured (E. A. Speiser, in *Language* 12 [1936] 121 ff.; R. H. Pfeiffer and E. A. Speiser, "One Hundred New Selected Nuzi Texts," *Annual of the Amer. Schools of Orient. Research*, XVI [1936] 121 f.; D. Cross, *Movable Property in the Nuzi Documents*. Amer. Orient. Series 10, pp. 48 f. New Haven, 1937).

Joseph (49:22-26) is often dated after Solomon, in the period of the divided monarchy, because Joseph is called the *nāzîr* (consecrated one, prince) of his brothers, and the "archers" who will harass him are identified with the Arameans of Damascus. But the *nāzîr* is not necessarily a king: he could be a champion (and Joseph was the leading group of tribes in ancient Israel); the identity of 49:26b and Deut. 33:16b (dated two centuries later) may cast some doubt on its authenticity. As for the "archers," they fit the raiding Bedouins who robbed Joseph until "a mighty one" (Gideon) broke their bow (49:24, revised text, cf. LXX), much better than the powerful chariotry of Damascus.

With intense patriotism, the poet surveys in retrospect the struggles of the Israelites in Canaan. Forgetting occasionally that he was placing predictions in the mouth of Jacob, he makes it clear that he is referring to events in the past (49:6b, 9, 15, 23 f.). He is familiar with the Song of Deborah (Judg. 5) and applies to Zebulon (49:13) Deborah's reproach of Asher (Judg. 5:17), but he cannot recapture the poetic passion and dramatic reality of the older ode. Jehovah is not only the god of war, as in Deborah, but also the god of fertility. However, a martial spirit pervades this ode in vivid contrast to the idyllic serenity of the J document. The poet extols Benjamin, living like a wolf of slaughter and prey (49:27), but pours contempt on Zebulon dwelling peacefully by the sea (49:13) and on Issachar who, according to his name (*'ish-sakhar*, hireling), like a loaded donkey adapted himself to humiliating service (49:14 f.). He admires the fighting valor of Judah (49:8 f.), Joseph (49:23 f.), and even of Dan (49:17) who, treacherous as a serpent, conquered an unsuspecting city (Judg. 18:27-29).

The poet puns on the names of several tribes (cf. Japheth in the blessing of Noah, Gen. 9:27) either explicitly (Dan "judges" [*jādîn*], 49:16; Gad "a robber band will rob him," 49:19; Judah "they will praise thee," 49:8) or implicitly, as in the above-mentioned case of Issachar (also Zebulon, 49:13; cf. Gen. 30:20; Asher, 49:20, means "happy"). All the names (except Benjamin) receive similar etymologies in Gen. 29:31-30:24. According to the style of predictive oracles, the author is deliberately mysterious. But for the sagas of Genesis and the stories of Judges, we would often fail to understand his obscure illusions. Particularly puzzling is the mention of "Shiloh" in the oracle about Judah (49:10, where most of the ancient versions read *shellô*, "which belongs to him"), usually understood in a Messianic sense but which seems originally to have been an enigmatic reference to David or Solomon.

This poem is not a collection of separate tribal oracles circulating independently, as some critics have suggested, but the work of a poet living about 960 B.C. That, of course, does not exclude his use of early tribal traditions. In some cases, as we have seen, the traditions utilized have been preserved in the S document and in the Book of Judges. But the unity of the poem appears in the etymological puns on the names of six tribes, and in the comparison of six different ones (Judah, Issachar, Dan, Naphtali, Joseph, and Benjamin) to animals, usually wild and fierce. Judah, Issachar, and Dan are characterized by puns and animals as well; Reuben, Simeon, and Levi, whose oracles are derived from S sagas, suggest neither puns nor animals to the poet.

The unity is also apparent in the order of the tribes (nearly identical with that of Gen. 29:31-30:24). First come the six Leah tribes, then the four Zilpah and Bilhah tribes (the two Zilpah tribes are inserted between the two Bilhah tribes), and finally the two Rachel tribes. The geographical arrangement is likewise deliberate. First come the four Southern tribes, then five Northern tribes and Gad across the Jordan, and finally the two Central tribes. The poet is responsible for fictitiously placing these oracles in the mouth of the dying Jacob—explicitly in the case of the four longer pieces (Reuben, Simeon-Levi, Judah, and Joseph)—who is not the Patriarch but united Israel as a whole (cf. 49:6, 7b, 16).

The poet's national pride in the military victories of the single tribes and in unification of all under the scepter of Judah does not blind him to some of the darker aspects of their history. On the whole, however, he sings of heroic deeds in epic style. Less refined than J, less reflective than S, less photographic than Deborah, he has succeeded in preserving the flavor of the treacherous cunning and barbaric ferocity of Israel's conquest of Canaan. This ancient poem was inserted at the end of the patriarchal stories of Genesis by a redactor in the sixth or fifth century; he uses (49:1b) the late eschatological expression "at the end of time."

The earliest of the oracles ascribed to Balaam (Num. 24:3-9, 15-19, 4:4 meter; in part textually corrupt) are included in the J document. Like the Blessing of Jacob, they are Judean in origin and only a little later in date (about 950 B.C.). Their author is likewise ardently patriotic, although less heroic and epic in tone (note the idyllic descriptions in 24:5 f.). The poet knew Gen. 49 (24:9 quotes Gen. 49:9b) and, although not mentioning individual tribes, he uses the figures of the lion (24:9, Judah in Gen. 49) and the wild ox (24:8; cf. Joseph in Gen. 49) to indicate the might of Israel. David, the "star" arisen out of Jacob to establish his scepter in Israel, has conquered Moab and Edom (24:15-19) and the nation is now at peace, resting like a lion that no one dares arouse (24:9).

The three oracles on Amalek (Num. 24:20), Cain (24:21 f.) and the destruction of "Asshur" and "Eber" through the ships of Kittim (Cyprus) (24:23 f.) are considerably later in date. The third of these is particularly mysterious, and may allude to the conquest of the Persian Empire (i.e.,

Asshur and Eber[2]) by Alexander the Great (Kittim, originally Cyprus, comes to mean Macedon, cf. I Macc. 1:1; 8:5), according to the interpretation of the oracle in I Macc. 1:1. Daniel 11:30 seems to understand the oracle as referring to the Roman (Kittim) opposition to Antiochus Epiphanes at the time of his second Egyptian campaign in 168 B.C.

3. 950-722. These poetic predictions of Jacob and Balaam, composed in Judah in the first half of the tenth century, have their counterpart, two centuries later, in the North-Israelitic (Ephraimitic) Blessing of Moses (Deut. 33, 4:4 meter) and the oracles of Balaam included in the E document (Num. 23:7-10, 18-24, 4:4 meter), respectively.

The original and ancient part of the Blessing of Moses (Deut. 33:6-25), depicting, like Gen. 49, the vicissitudes of the individual tribes, has been enclosed within an exordium (33:2-5), describing the appearance of the Lord in power and the giving of the Law through Moses, and a peroration (33:26-29) depicting the triumphs and prosperity of Israel under the protection of its God. As C. Steuernagel has rightly observed (*Einleitung in das Alte Testament*, p. 259), these two additions to the original poem constitute the two parts of a single postexilic psalm. If, as it seems, the blessing was inserted into the Pentateuch in conjunction with this psalm, it could not have been an integral part of the E document, which is contemporary, but must have been added, like Gen. 49, in the fifth century.

The historical situation depicted in Deut. 33:6-25 is considerably later than that of Gen. 49. Simeon has been absorbed by Judah and, having lost its tribal existence, is no longer mentioned. The tribe of Levi is no longer cursed for its bloodthirsty deeds but has become the priestly tribe, while still eking out a scanty living. Reuben, east of the Jordan, is on the point of disappearing. The other tribes no longer fight for their territory and are free from foreign domination. The struggles of the Judges and the conquests of David are long since past: Judah, separated from the rest of Israel (33:7), and Joseph (Ephraim and Manasseh, 33:17), prosperous and victorious as the leading group (33:13-17), are now distinct kingdoms (after about 933 and before 722 B.C.). The weakness of Judah, in need of help against adversaries, contrasts sharply with the peace and prosperity of the Joseph tribes (the Northern Kingdom), at the height of their power presumably under Jeroboam II (785-744), whose decisive victories over the Arameans of Damascus gave Gad, across the Jordan, a breathing spell (33:20).

The oracle on Levi (33:8-11) in its present form cannot, however, date from the time of Jeroboam II and seems to be a postexilic priestly

---

[2] Presumably "Eber" stands for *'ēber hā-nāhār* (I Kings 4:24 [H. 5:4]; Ezra 8:36; Neh. 2:7, 9; 3:7 and, in Aramaic, in Ezra 4:10-7:25), "beyond the river," i.e., in Persian times, the land west of the Euphrates, or Syria in the wider sense. Asshur in Ezra 6:22 is equivalent to the Persian Empire.

substitution for an earlier oracle: v. 8 refers obscurely to Aaron, the high priest with the Urim and Thummim of the Priestly Code (Ex. 28:30; Lev. 8:8), and alludes with some confusion to Num. 16, Ex. 17:7, and Num. 17:1-13; v. 9 is probably a reminiscence of Ex. 32:27-29; v. 10 is Deuteronomistic and Priestly; hardly anything except 33:11 can be original. The author of Deut. 33 was familiar with Gen. 49 (Deut. 33:13-16, 22 contains reminiscences of Gen. 49:22-26, 9) but reflects a time of safety and affluent ease, distinguished from the warlike tension and dangers of the older poem. The eleven tribes are listed geographically, from south to north. The glowing patriotism of Deut. 33 is that of a Northern Israelite of the Joseph tribes (Ephraim and Manasseh), who regards the division of the kingdom under Jeroboam and Rehoboam (about 933) as a defection of Judah from Israel rather than, as Deuteronomic historians believed, a religious schism of the ten Northern tribes, led astray by "the sin of Jeroboam."

The oracles of Balaam in Num. 23:7-10, 18-24 have a much closer connection with the J and E stories of Barak, king of Moab, and the seer Balaam, whom he hires to curse Israel, than the oracles in Num. 24 which, except for the standardized introductions (24:3 f., 15 f.), have no connection with Balaam. The oracles in Num. 23 are more general in tone and lack the specific historical allusions of those in 24. Although it is difficult to assign them to a specific date, they are probably contemporaneous with the E document (about 750), of which they are an integral part, and perhaps by the E author. The influence of the oracles of Num. 24 on those of Num. 23 appears in the quotations of 24:8 in 23:22, and in the simile of a lion (24:9) in 23:24; with the difference, however, that in 24:9 Israel is like a resting lion conscious of its strength (in the peaceful and glorious reign of Solomon), whereas in 23:24 Israel is like a lion pouncing on its prey (like North Israel during the victorious wars against the Arameans in the early part of the reign of Jeroboam II, 785-744). The oracle in 23:7-10 (23:10b may be a gloss) contemplates not only the prodigious numerical growth of Israel, but also its separation, as the chosen people, from other nations. The second oracle (23:18-24, omitting perhaps 23:23b) predicts the invincible progress of Israel under the mighty and loyal protection of Jehovah.

4. 650-400. The latest poems in the Pentateuch belong to the period of the decline and end of the kingdom of Judah and the two centuries following. The poetic oracle in which Jehovah rebuked Aaron and Miriam for claiming equality with Moses in the matter of divine revelations (Num. 12:6-8, 4:4 meter, textually not intact) is generally dated about 750 and considered part of the E document. More probably this oracle is Judean in origin and belongs to the time about 650 (E^2), when, after Isaiah lent new prestige to the prophetic calling, Moses began to be regarded as the

greatest of the prophets. Accordingly, his prophetic oracle (D, found in 621) was on the point of being written.

The beautiful words with which the priests bless the people (Num. 6:24-26) are not strictly metrical but rise to a rhythmical climax: the three verses have 3, 5, 7 words, respectively. It is difficult to determine whether this famous blessing belongs to the sixth or the fifth century.

The Song of Moses (Deut. 32:1-43, 4:4 meter; the final clauses in 32:14, 15, 39 disturb the meter and are spurious) is provided with two late editorial introductions (31:16-21, 30; 31:24-27) and conclusions (31:22; 32:44) which seem to indicate that the poem was inserted by the Priestly redactor late in the fifth century. Although this has no bearing on the date of the poem, thought and language point clearly to the first half of the fifth century as the date of composition. The poem is a didactic psalm; it is "doctrine" (leqah. 32:2).

After a majestic exordium (32:1-3), the poet introduces his theme (32:4-6a): can the righteous God forgive his crooked, foolish, and unwise people? As a father, Jehovah has abundantly blessed Israel in the past (32:6b-14), but that ungrateful nation has repaid him by forsaking its God for strange gods and demons (32:15-18). Consequently, Jehovah has, in his holy anger, punished Israel through a "no-people" (barbaric hordes) (32:19-22) and horrible calamities (32:23-25). God would have annihilated them utterly were it not for the subsequent taunts of the enemy (32:26 f.)—a people wholly devoid of understanding, sprung from the seed of Sodom and Gomorrah (32:28 f., 32 f.; the gloss in 32:30 f., misunderstanding the context, speaks of Israel instead of its enemy). But the day of divine vengeance upon those wicked foes (32:34 f.) and of Jehovah's merciful concern for the miseries of Israel (32:36) is at hand: then God will prove to his people that no other god can help (32:37-39) or avenge them of their foes (32:40-42). The brief peroration invites all nations to praise Israel for these mighty deeds of their God (32:43).

This psalm excels in neither originality of thought nor literary quality, but is an illuminating historical document for the religion of the first half of the fifth century, between Zechariah and Nehemiah. Written at a time when Jerusalem was still in a wretched state and the Jewish nation, surrounded by enemies, close to extinction (32:26), it nevertheless expresses an invincible tenacity, an unconquerable faith in the power and mercy of Jehovah, a firm assurance in the triumphant survival of the nation, in spite of its manifold past apostasy, through the glorious theophany in which Jehovah will avenge himself of his adversaries and remove the guilt of his people. Like Haggai and Zechariah, in contrast with the earlier pessimism of Habakkuk, the poet expects a miraculous deliverance and rebirth of his people after the extermination of their foes.

The poem is hardly a "compendium of prophetic theology," as many say following C. H. Cornill, even though the conception of a just and merciful God is ultimately derived from Amos and Hosea. The poet does not threaten the nation with a future punishment—the blow has already fallen—but announces an imminent restoration of the fortunes of Israel. His allusions to the writings of Hosea, Isaiah, Micah, and more particularly Jeremiah, Ezekiel, Second Isaiah, and the Deuteronomists, are combined with the early apocalyptic expectations and with the teachings of the sages. Like other writers of his time, the author is obsessed with idolatry and utter contempt for the Gentiles. The intense religious and nationalistic spirit animating this psalm is characteristic of early Judaism, and reappears later in a prayer from the time of the Maccabean rebellion (Ps. 79), which presents some striking resemblances to this song.

The ringing invitation of Miriam, "Sing unto Jehovah, for he has triumphed gloriously!" (Ex. 15:21) was taken up more than seven centuries later by a well-intentioned versifier who composed the prolix expansion of her song which we read in Ex. 15:1-18 (irregular 3:3 meter). This pious Jew of the second half of the fifth century begins boldly, "Let me sing unto Jehovah, for he has triumphed gloriously." But being a peace-loving soul utterly devoid of martial fire, a townsman who had never seen a battle, he chose a model that he could not emulate and wrote not a miniature epic, like Miriam, but a homiletic and devout paraphrase thereof. Imitating the historical psalms, without succeeding in carrying out the correct meter, this pseudo-poet praises the Lord for his glorious deeds but, forgetting that his poem was supposed to have been sung at the Exodus from Egypt, he also summarizes the conquest of Canaan (15:13-18) and even refers to the Temple in Jerusalem (15:17)—not Solomon's but the Second Temple, completed in 516. About 250 B.C. the Chronicler placed an echo of this poem in the mouth of Ezra (Neh. 9:11). From careful examination of thought and language, A. Bender (ZAW 23 [1903] 1 ff.) has proved its postexilic origin. The psalm enclosing the Blessing of Moses (Deut. 33:2-5, 26-29) resembles the poems in Deut. 32 and Ex. 15 in a general way and like them belongs to the fifth century, probably to the second half.

CHAPTER IX

THE REDACTORS OF THE PENTATEUCH

As the critical analysis has shown, the Pentateuch is the final result of the amalgamation of five narrative sources (J, S, E, D, P) besides a number of poems and legal codes. The editorial work by which these diverse elements were combined in a single book with each unit previously subjected to revision and addition, began about 650 B.C. if not earlier, and ended about 400 B.C., when the Pentateuch was issued to the Jews in their widely scattered settlements as a definitive edition of the Law of Moses. This editorial process is so complicated that it can be identified only along its main lines. Any attempt to reconstruct it is perforce a simplification of countless individual changes. Moreover, some critics seem to forget that the legal portions of the Pentateuch went through an editorial process which had no connection with the amalgamation of JEDPS or with the insertion therein of poems quoted from other sources. Having examined the development of the laws and dates of the poems in earlier chapters, we shall confine ourselves to the fusion of the great narrative sources.

The first important step was the joining of J (dating from 950-850) to E (about 750). The redactor, to whom we owe JE (Wellhausen's *Jehovist*), was active about 650 B.C., and he is now indicated by the symbol R^{JE}. His date is fixed, on the one hand, by the E^2 elements which had attached themselves to E during the century following the publication of this document and, on the other, by the fact that the D Code of 621 shows acquaintance with both J and E in their separate forms as well as with R^{JE}. Apparently the two separate documents disappeared from circulation soon after the destruction of Jerusalem in 586; at least no trace of their presence can be detected later.[1]

It has been noticed that from the migration of Abraham to the death of Moses J and E ran parallel. The most important events were related by both, with differences in detail, but in each document were a number of stories lacking entirely in the other. These circumstances compelled R^{JE} to employ a variety of methods in fusing the two documents into a single narrative. Stories occurring alone in either J or E, the redactor preserved intact if they seemed too valuable to be omitted. Thus we have master-

---

[1] The J account of the conquest of Canaan was still circulating after 400 B.C., but lies beyond the limits of the Pentateuch.

pieces of J, such as the fetching of Rebekah (Gen. 24), and of E, the sacrifice of Isaac (Gen. 22:1-13, 19), as well as two entirely different stories about Moses before his call (Ex. 2:11-22, J; 2:1-10, E). He frequently adopted the same method when the two sources differed so substantially in reporting the same event that R^JE failed to discern a parallel in the two stories. The two tales of Sarah's fascination in the eyes of foreign kings (Pharaoh in Gen. 12:10-20, J; Abimelech in 20:1-17, E) must have had a common source in oral tradition.

The task of R^JE became much more difficult when confronted with J and E's divergent accounts of one and the same event. For, unless R^JE simply eliminated both stories, he was faced with the choice of one of four possible procedures, and on occasion he did use all four. He could omit one story entirely in favor of the other, amalgamate both into a single narrative (or write a new story based on the two accounts), supplement one story given in full with a few details taken from the other, or even reproduce both stories, making them appear to be reports of successive and not identical events.

The judicious use of these four methods, with free variations, shows that this redactor was no mere hack writer, and explains the extraordinary success of his edition of JE. Applying the first method, at the beginning he suppressed E's story of Abraham's migration to Canaan (to which 20:13, E, alludes), but for obvious reasons at the end of the work he omitted J's true but unflattering story of Israel's conquest of Canaan in favor of E's more fantastic tale. In Ex. 7-19 J and E are closely interwoven, and in Numbers the two sources are usually rewritten as a single narrative and can no longer be disentangled. On the contrary, in Genesis J and E are reproduced more or less *in toto* side by side, with J prevailing in the stories about Abraham, and E in the Joseph stories.

A good example of this third method, by which scattered fragments of one source (J) supplement the story of another (E), is furnished by the Joseph stories, particularly chs. 37, 40, 42. The most striking examples of the fourth method are the stories of Hagar and the revelation of the Decalogue. In order to preserve both the J (Gen. 16:1 f., 4-6, 7a, 8, 11-14) and the E (21:8-21) stories of Hagar's separation from Abraham, R^JE explains that after she fled a first time she was sent back by an angel so that she could be regularly dismissed (16:9 f.). Similarly, after R^JE had told how Moses received the tables of the Decalogue (according to E, Ex. 24:12 f., 18; 31:18), he had Moses break the tables (32:19b) in order to prepare for the J story about the *second* revelation of the Decalogue (34:1 f., 4, 28, with the harmonistic notes of R^JE in 34:1 [beginning with "like the former ones"] and 34:4 ["like the former ones"]; cf. JBL 43 [1924] 294-298).

The contributions from R^JE's pen may be classed in the following groups:

1. In Gen. 16:9 f. and in Ex. 32:19b; 34:1, 4 the redactor was forced to explain that J and E's stories are not reports of the same event but of successive incidents. Similar harmonistic glosses from his pen are found in: Gen. 12:9; 13:1, 3 f.; 21:32b, 34; 26:1, 2b, 15, 18; 39:1 ("Potiphar, an officer of Pharaoh's, the captain of the guard"); 39:20aγ; 40:3b, 15bβ; 46:1 ("and he came to Beer-sheba"); Ex. 18:2 ("after he had sent her [Zipporah] away"); Num. 23:13b, 23.

2. This redactor also contributes explanations and notes to the stories. In Gen. 20:18 he supplies the nature of the plague that struck Abimelech's household, which E had absentmindedly omitted. His explanation in 22:14 is obscure, although he erroneously attempted to locate the sacrifice of Isaac on the hill of Zion. In 28:21b he adds "Jehovah will be my God and," because Jacob's vow in E only mentioned the stone of Bethel. The interesting explanation of a dietary law in 32:32 [H. 32:33] may have come from his pen. He facilitates Jacob's journey to Egypt by supplying him with wagons provided by Pharaoh himself (45:19 f.; "wagons according to the command of Pharaoh and he gave them" in 45:21; 46:5b). See also 25:6; Ex. 4:14aβ-16; 9:19-21.

3. R^JE in accordance with the spirit of his time, shortly before the Deuteronomic reformation of 621, laid particular stress on the religious elements of JE. In eloquent style, which in a measure anticipated the grandiose oratory of D, he composed a prayer of Jacob (Gen. 32:9-12 [H. 32:10-13]) and some divine oracles to Abraham (13:14-17; 22:15-18), Isaac (26:3b-4, 24-25a), and Jacob (28:14; 46:3b), in which proudly the future greatness of Israel is foretold. An oracle to Hagar (16:10) and one to Moses (Ex. 4:21-23) are also from his pen. The following of his annotations also have a religious character: Ex. 3:20; 7:17a; 8:10b [H. 8:6b]; 9:14b-16, 29b; 10:1b. He adds to Moses "Aaron the Levite" (particularly in Ex. 4:14-16, 27-31) and is perhaps the redactor who prematurely mentioned the priests in Ex. 19:22-24.

The second important stage in the growth of the Pentateuch was the addition of the Deuteronomic Code (D) to JE. Since D was a prophetic oracle of Moses, it was natural to find a place for it in JE's biography of Moses, just before the story of his death (Deut. 34). The editorial expansion of D to our Book of Deuteronomy had begun before the addition of D to JE and continued thereafter. The editor who attached D to JE (R^D) is identical with the Deuteronomist of Joshua, Judges, and Samuel, and with the Second Deuteronomist of Kings. He is responsible for the edition of the books from Genesis to Kings (omitting Leviticus and the rest of P) issued about 550 B.C. In the Pentateuch, aside from the addition of D to JE, he made only insignificant changes, but his hand is most evident in Joshua and Judges.

In style and thought, R^D is deeply influenced by the D Code. The Deuteronomic doctrine of the covenant of Jehovah with Israel is traced back to Abraham (Gen. 15:18-21), who kept God's commandments (26:5) according to the terms of the covenant. In his edition of the old ritual decalogue found in Ex. 34 (see in particular 34:6-17, 24), this redactor has given a summary of the ethics, theology, and ritual of D. In Num. 10:33; 14:44 he has added "of the covenant" to "ark" (cf. "the words of the covenant" in Ex. 34:28). He reiterates the Deuteronomic warning, that obedience to God's law will bring prosperity to the nation, and vice versa (Ex. 15:26; 19:3b-8 [in part]; 32:7-14; Num. 14:11-24;[2] cf. Ex. 16:28). Like D, he regards the deliverance of Israel from Egypt and the conquest of "a land flowing with milk and honey" as outstanding manifestations of Jehovah's loving-kindness for Israel and fidelity to his promise to the Patriarchs (Ex. 3:8, 17; 13:5; 23:23, 28; 33:1b-3a; 34:10 f.). He lists the nations of Canaan which Jehovah drove out before the Israelites (Gen. 15:19-21 [probably expanded by a later redactor]; Ex. 3:8, 17; 13:5; 23:23, 28; 33:2; 34:11) and, living after the end of the Judean Kingdom, like other postexilic writers, he can allow his fancy to picture the territory of Israel as extending from the river of Egypt to the Euphrates (Gen. 15:18). Historical notices (Num. 21:33-35; 32:20-23, 25-27, 33a, 40, in part) and ritual prescriptions (Ex. 12:24-27a; 13:3-16) are occasionally contributed by this redactor. Some parts of the framework of Deuteronomy, as has been said above in Ch. V, may also be attributed to him.

The third main stage in the growth of the Pentateuch was the addition of the Priestly Code to JED. The redactor responsible is referred to by the symbol R^P. Here our problem is less simple than in the case of R^JE and R^D. Despite frequent assumption, it is by no means certain that P was a separate historical and legal work joined to JED by R^P. On the one hand, the history and law in P are closely intertwined (since many narratives have the force of legal precedents) and present consistently, both in thought and in diction, the ideal of the theocratic community; the unity of authorship can therefore hardly be doubted. But, on the other hand, certain of the narrative sections, particularly in Gen. 12-50, although an integral part of P, are incomprehensible aside from JED, and seem to be a supplement rather than an independent work (cf. ZAW N.F. 7 [1930] 67).

The evidence is too contradictory to warrant a hard and fast solution—

---

[2] His argument that Jehovah should forgive or save his people for the sake of his honor or prestige among the Gentiles (Num. 14:15-17) is characteristic of the sixth century (cf. Ez. 20:9 ff.; 36:16-36; 39:21-29; Is. 48:11; 52:5 f.).

P either a commentary or an independent book. It may be mentioned that P was compiled for the purpose of being united with JED, which enjoyed a certain canonical authority at the time, so as to bring that older work into harmony with the tenets of Judaism in the fifth century. However, some parts of P, particularly the codes of law and portions of the narrative, circulated as separate works before being amalgamated with JED. It is therefore extremely difficult to differentiate sharply between the authors' work in certain parts of P (and of Ps) and in RP. We shall nevertheless use the symbol RP for whoever accomplished the fusion of JED and P. The symbol Ps must be retained because in some cases Ps is demonstrably later than JEDP and therefore distinct from RP (as in Num. 33:1-49; 34:13-15).

The authors of P had prepared an introduction (P in Gen. 1-11) and appendix (P in Josh. 13:15-19:51) for JED. These could be attached by RP to the work without additions or changes, and it is therefore idle to seek, as numerous critics do, anything therein from the pen of this redactor. Whatever is not P in these two sections was certainly added later than RP, even when taken from much earlier writings. Curiously enough, critics do not see the absurdity of asserting that RP, whose task was the fusion of P with JED, added "J" to P in Gen. 1-11. For if "J" in Gen. 1-11 was a part of JED, P would have been added to it as elsewhere; but since this so-called J in Gen. 1-11 was not included in JED, it is hardly conceivable that RP, with his manifest reverence for P, would have spoilt the well-knit texture of P by the intrusion of alien material, much of which is fragmentary and decidedly poor in quality. The same applies to Gen. 36 and 49.

The task of RP, writing about 430 B.C., was by no means an easy one. JE and P are poles apart in their views of life and religion in ancient Israel. The authors of P, and RP, would obviously have preferred to substitute P for JED as the charter of Judaism, but such was the popularity and authority of JED in the fifth century (Mal. 4:4 [H. 3:22] still regarded D, not P, as the Law of Moses) that P could become part of the Scriptures at that time only by being fused with JED. The method of RP was dictated by this circumstance. In his dealings with JED he was forced to use the greatest circumspection and reverence. That he would dare omit any conspicuous part of JED in favor of P is extremely doubtful. The stories of the birth of Ishmael, the construction of the ark of the covenant, and others, which some critics believe were omitted from JED, were probably never in JED at all. On the contrary, RP does not hesitate to preserve the JED version of events which he thought P had reported much more accurately. So in the case of the covenant with Abraham (Gen. 15, JED; 17, P), the call of Moses (Ex. 3-4, JED; 6-7, P), the revelation of the Law at Sinai (JED in Ex. 19:1-24:14, omitting the

Covenant Code which was added after R^P; 32-34; and P in 25:15-31:18; 35:1-Num. 10:10), etc. In spite of the fact that P consistently ignored Hagar's expulsion (Gen. 17:20; 25:9, 12-17), R^P even allowed the two accounts of the separation of Hagar from Abraham to stand.

Our redactor made no attempt to harmonize fully JED and P—an impossible task—and permitted himself only the slightest changes in JED. Thus he consistently adopted in Gen. 11-16 the spellings "Abram and Sarai" because, according to P, the names "Abraham and Sarah" were first revealed in Gen. 17:5, 15. Likewise he changed "Israel" in J (32:29-35:10) into "Jacob" on account of 35:10. Through slight retouches in Gen. 24, R^P substituted the death of Sarah for the death of Abraham (assumed by the servant in 24:65), this to conform with P's chronology, according to which Abraham lived thirty-five years after the marriage of Isaac (25:20; cf. 17:1, 21; 25:7). Well aware of the inconsistency between Gen. 27:43-45 (J), where Jacob after receiving Isaac's blessing is urged by Rebekah to flee from the wrath of Esau, and 28:1-9 (P), where Jacob is blessed and sent away by Isaac, R^P inserted 27:46 (cf. 26:35, P) to reduce with a fine touch the clash between JED and P. In Gen. 15:7 R^P names Ur of the Chaldees (an expression which cannot be earlier than the seventh century when the Chaldeans first conquered Ur), following P in 11:31; 11:28 is R^S; cf. also Neh. 9:7). Other minor additions of R^P have been identified in Ex. 9:35b; 11:9 f.; "the tables of the testimony" in 31:18; 32:15; 34:29; Num. 10:34; and reference to the Midianites in 22:4, 7.

This redactor was even less inclined to modify the text of P than that of JE. Such changes in P are extremely rare. In Gen. 49:31 R^P omitted "Rachel" after Leah because the well-known tradition of Rachel's tomb at Ephrath (Gen. 35:19 f.; I Sam. 10:2; Jer. 31:15) could not be reconciled with P's theory that the Patriarchs and their wives were buried at Machpelah. As the Deuteronomic diction in a P passage shows, this redactor recast Ex. 6:6-9 (P). In Ex. 16 and Num. 20:1-13 he even sacrificed some of the P material. Although in general he preserved both JED and P intact, simply copying them side by side, he occasionally combined JED and P into a single narrative. The most conspicuous examples of such a fusion are Ex. 16; Num. 13-14; 16; 20:1-13; 32.

According to popular view, R^P edited the Pentateuch substantially in the form which has reached us, except for certain later additions (P^s) and the textual changes then not yet made in the prototype of the LXX version.[3] Differing from this conclusion, the present writer has attempted

---

[3] At least in Gen. 47:5-6 LXX represents an earlier recension. In the following passages the Hebrew and Greek texts present important differences: Gen. 31:47-52; Ex. 20:13-15; 35:8-40:38; Num. 1:24-37; 6:22-27; 26:15-47. As we have seen, the Masoretic, Samaritan, and Greek texts differ in the P chronology.

to show that the source which he calls S, with its editorial accretions (S²), was inserted into the Pentateuch *after* P (ZAW N.F. 7 [1930] 66-73), or between 430 (the approximate date of Rᴾ) and about 400, when the Pentateuch reached its final form and was canonized. We may use the symbol Rˢ for the redactor who inserted S enlarged with the S² annotations. A scholar with antiquarian propensities, in spite of occasional divergence from the teachings of P, he was a pious Jew and was eager to include in JEDP an ancient document whose foreign origin was obscured by its Jewish supplements (S²).

When confronted by the necessity of curtailing either JEDP or S, this editor chose perforce the second alternative. As a result, P has survived fully in Gen. 1-11, while S and S² appear at times to be fragmentary: the Creation story begins abruptly in Gen. 2:5, and the note of Rˢ in 2:4b may replace its original beginning; only 4:25 f.; 5:29 are left of the genealogy of Seth; the Deluge story and the Table of Nations (S² in Gen. 7-10) consist of disconnected fragments. How much of S-S² was omitted by Rˢ we cannot tell, nor is it always possible to distinguish his contributions from those of S². Only editorial notes that are harmonistic or disclose the influence of JEDP can be safely attributed to him.

By means of slight retouches, Rˢ adapts the language of S and S² to that of P. Typical P expressions used by Rˢ are conspicuous in S-S²: "man, as well as beast, and reptile, and fowl of the air" (Gen. 6:7; 7:23; cf. P in 7:14, 21, etc.); "male and female" (7:3, 9; cf. P in 1:27; 5:2; 7:16, etc.); "whom I have created" (6:7; cf. P in 1:1, etc.; contrast "I have made" [S²] in the same verse); "and his sons, and his wife, and his sons' wives with him" (7:7; cf. P in 7:13); in 9:18 (and in the gloss "Ham, the father of" in 9:22) Rˢ attempts to reconcile the list of the sons of Noah according to P (Shem, Ham, and Japheth) with that according to S (Shem, Canaan, Japheth); 10:24 (Rˢ) is based on 11:12-14 (P); "Ur of the Chaldees" (11:28; cf. P in 11:31); according to P, Abraham and Sarah are called "Abram and Sarai" by Rˢ (11:29); "And these are the generations of Esau, the father of Edom, in Mount Seir" (36:9; cf. P in 36:1); "these are the names of Esau's sons" (36:10, redundant after the preceding title; imitating P in 25:12 f.).

In combining the data on Edom in S-S² (36:9-39) with P's genealogy of Esau (36:1-8, 40-43), Rˢ became involved in insurmountable difficulties. By trying to reconcile divergent data he only increased the inherent confusion. In 36:1-5 he substituted Esau's wives according to S-S² (cf. 36:9-14) for those listed by P (26:34; 28:9). Against P's statement that Esau is identical with Edom (36:1, 8), he added to P a note making Esau the father of Edom (36:43; cf. 36:9), and to S-S² a note making Esau identical with Edom (36:19), contradicting 36:9. To S-S² he added a thirteenth (illegitimate) son of Esau, Amalek (36:12, 16). He allowed, however, P to assert that Esau's sons were born in Canaan (36:6-8) and S-S[2] to place their birth in Seir (36:9). His chronological note in 36:31 is ambiguous, meaning either before Israel had a king (i.e., before Saul) or before a king of Israel ruled in Edom (i.e., before David), although the second alternative is the more probable.[4]

The following passages were presumably written, or at least revised, by R[s]: Gen. 3:20; 4:25 f.; 5:29; 6:4 ("and also after that"); 9:18 f.; 10:9, 14 ("out of whom came the Philistines," a gloss to Caphtorim, the Cretans; cf. Am. 9:7); 10:16-18a, 24; 11:9;[5] 11:28-30; 14:12 ("Abram's brother's son, and he was living in Sodom"); 18:17-19, 22b; 25:6.

Shortly before 400 B.C., when R[s] had completed his work, other editors inserted into JEDPS the Covenant Code in its latest edition and some recent elements of P[s]. Thus, after an editorial process of several centuries, the Pentateuch attained canonical status and, except for minor textual changes, its final form—the Law of Moses, the supreme norm of religion and life in Judaism and one of the most influential books in the history of mankind.

[4] For a historical analysis of Gen. 36 see E. Meyer, *Die Israeliten und ihre Nach-barstämme*, pp. 328-389.

[5] In 11:9, by a fanciful etymology, R[s] derives the name "Babel" from the verb *bll* giving to it its Aramaic meaning (mix, confuse); in Hebrew the verb means "to moisten, to smear [with oil]". The anomalous form *nābelāh* in 11:7 is usually derived from the same root ("let us confuse"). More probably it is either a *Pi'el* of *blj* [*blh*] ("let us ruin" their speech) or a *Qal* of *nbl* (and their speech "will wither" there).

PART III

THE FORMER PROPHETS

CHAPTER I

THE BOOK OF JOSHUA

~~~~~~

The sixth of the nine volumes comprising the legal and historical corpus from Genesis to Kings is called "Joshua" not after the name of its author but after that of the hero whose achievements it relates. Describing the vicissitudes of the Israelites, from the death of Moses to that of Joshua, it deals with the invasion and conquest of Canaan (1-12) and the distribution of territory among the various tribes (13-24). Irrespective of the sources identified in it, its contents may be summarized as follows:

1. Preparatory events (1-5). Jehovah orders Joshua to cross the Jordan and take possession of the Promised Land (1:1-11). The two and a half tribes that had settled east of the Jordan promise their co-operation (1:12-18). The two spies sent to Jericho are saved by Rahab, a harlot (2). Joshua leads the Israelites across the Jordan (3) and sets up twelve memorial stones at Gilgal (4). There he circumcises the Israelites (5:1-9), celebrates the Passover (5:10-12), and sees the captain of the Lord's host (5:13-15).

2. The conquest of Canaan (6-12). Jericho is destroyed and placed under the interdict (6). But Achan's theft of part of the forbidden booty results in defeat at Ai (i.e., "the ruin"), and the culprit is stoned in the valley of Achor (7). Ai is taken through a military stratagem (8). By a ruse, the Gibeonites make a compact with Joshua (9). The rest of Southern Canaan is conquered through the victory at Gibeon—celebrated by the famous poem addressed to the sun and moon (10:12)—against Adoni-Zedek of Jerusalem (cf. Judg. 1:5-7) and his allies (10). Northern Canaan is subdued through the victory by the waters of Merom over Jabin, king of Hazor (cf. Judg. 4) and his allies (11:1-15). A general summary of the conquests of Israel in Canaan (11:16-23) and a list of the kings defeated east of the Jordan in the time of Moses (12:1-6) and west of the Jordan in the time of Joshua (12:7-24) concludes the first part of the book.

3. The allotment of territory (13-21). After an introduction (13:1-7) listing still unconquered regions (13:2-6), after recalling the allotment of Transjordania to Reuben, Gad, and half of Manasseh (13:8-33), and after a new introduction (14:1-5), Joshua assigns by lot the land of Canaan to the following tribes: Caleb (14:6-15) and Judah (15), Ephraim (16) and Manasseh (17), Benjamin (18; with a digression about

293

the tent of meeting at Shiloh, 18:1-10), Simeon (19:1-9), Zebulon (19:10-16), Issachar (19:17-23), Asher (19:24-31), Naphtali (19:32-39), Dan (19:40-48). Then Israel gives Joshua an inheritance (19:49 f.) and the division is completed (19:51). Six cities of refuge are provided for unintentional murderers (20) and 48 cities allotted to the Levites (21).

4. The final acts and speeches of Joshua (22-24). The Transjordanic tribes are dismissed by Joshua with a blessing (22:1-8), but an altar which they erect at the Jordan causes great perturbation until they explain that it is simply a memorial and would not be used for sacrifices in violation of the law of Deut. 12 (22:9-34). In the first of his last addresses (23), Joshua exhorts the Israelites to keep the Deuteronomic Law; in the second (24:1-15), he reviews God's blessings and draws the conclusion that they should serve no other god; thereupon the people pledge themselves and erect a stone at Shechem (24:16-28). The book closes with accounts of the death and burial of Joshua (24:29-31), the burial of Joseph's bones (24:32), and the death and burial of Eleazar, son of Aaron (24:33).

According to the traditional view, first recorded in the pages of the Talmud (*Baba Bathra* 14b), Joshua was the author of this book, but to modern critics this is just as untenable as the ascription of the Pentateuch to the pen of Moses. The book itself contains no reference to Joshua as its author, although it speaks of a description of Canaan prepared in book form at Joshua's orders (18:9), of Joshua's redaction of a "Book of the Law of God" (24:26), and of a "copy of the Law of Moses" on stones (8:32).

The Book of Joshua, as we have it, was written a considerable period after the time of Joshua. Not only does it contain an account of the death of Joshua and of subsequent events (24:29-33), but the expression "unto this day" (4:9; 5:9; 6:25; 7:26; 8:28 f.; 9:27; 10:27; 13:13; 14:14; 15:63; 16:10) could only have been written long after the incidents narrated. The Book of Jashar ("The Upright," or, reading *sh-y-r* for *y-sh-r* with the LXX after I Kings 8:53, "The Book of Song"), from which the poetic appeal to the sun and moon at the battle of Gibeon is quoted (10:13), cannot be earlier than the time of David (II Sam. 1:18) or even, according to the text of the LXX just quoted, of Solomon. In fact, 9:27 refers clearly to the Temple of Solomon with the Deuteronomic expression "the place which 'Jehovah' [so the versions] will choose" (6:19, 24 also refer to the Temple in Jerusalem). The conquest of Laish (Leshem in Josh.) by the Danites (19:47; cf. Judg. 18:27-29) cannot have taken place before the death of Joshua. In fact, as we shall see, other identical events are related both in Joshua and in Judges, and some of them occurred after the death of Joshua.

Not only must our book be dated after Joshua's time, but it cannot be regarded as a literary unit composed by a single author. It betrays traces of composition, juxtaposition of different narratives, and sources divergent in the conception of the conquest of Canaan. A few examples of glaring inconsistencies and incompatible statements may suffice here. According to 4:9, the twelve stones were erected in the middle of the Jordan "and they are there unto this day"; according to 4:8 they were carried from the river bed to the western bank and set up at Gilgal (4:20) as a perpetual memorial (4:21-24; cf. 4:7).[1]

There are at least two entirely different accounts of the fall of Jericho in ch. 6. According to one, the army of Israel encircled Jericho ominously and silently seven times; then, at the blowing of the ram's horn and Joshua's command, they shouted the war cry and stormed the city (6:3a, 5, 7, 10, 16b, 17). According to the other version, a solemn religious procession, led by seven priests holding trumpets and preceding the ark, encompassed the city once a day for six days, whereupon on the seventh, when the priests blew the trumpets, the walls of Jericho fell to the ground (6:3b, 4, 6). The result of combining these two accounts into one story and of adding numerous harmonizing glosses is utter confusion in the Masoretic text, and slightly less in the better text of the LXX.[2]

There are other examples of such confusion. The Israelites stoned and burned Achan (7:25bα); thereupon they stoned him and his family (7:25bβ, omitted in the Syriac and the Vulgate). In the story of the capture of Ai, Joshua stationed 30,000 (an error for 3,000?) chosen men in ambush, west of Ai, on the evening before the battle (8:3), yet on the next morning he dispatched 5,000 men to the same place for the same purpose, as if his men had not lain there in ambush all night (8:12; the LXX corrects the inconsistency).

The preceding instances show that the Book of Joshua is a compilation from separate sources. It is natural to assume that those are a continuation of the Pentateuchal sources, that would scarcely end with the death of Moses. In fact, the J, E, and P sources (the D document is, of course, confined to Deut.), as well as the various redactors who combined them, look forward to the settlement of the Israelites in Canaan as the climax of their story and cannot have closed abruptly with the death of Moses. Even the S source, although it had no interest whatsoever in the nationalistic aspirations of Israel, tells of an attempt of Simeon and Levi to conquer Shechem (Gen. 34)—and seems to gloat over its dismal failure. Beginning with Abraham, Jehovah promises to give Canaan to the Israelites: Gen. 12:7; 24:7, J; 13:14-17, R^{JE}; 15:13-16, redactional; 17:6-8, P; 26:3b, R^{JE} or R^D; 28:13-15, R^{JE}; 35:11 f.; 48:4, P; Ex. 3:8, 17, R^{JE}(?); 6:4, 8, P; 13:5, 11, R^D; 23:20-31; 32:13; 33:1b, 3a, redactional;

---

[1] Cf. K. Möhlenbrink in ZAW N.F. 15 (1938) 256 f.
[2] Cf. Möhlenbrink, ZAW N.F. 15 (1938) 258 f.

Lev. 23:10; 25:2, H; Num. 15:18, Ps; 27:12, redactional; 32, JE, P, redactional; 33:50-54; 34-35, Ps and redactional; Deut. 1:38; 3:21 f., 28; 27:1-8; 31 [for the most part], Ds; 31:14 f., 23, E.

Although it is thus certain that J, E, and P recounted, in their original form, the story of the settlement of the Israelites in Canaan—the chief topic of the Book of Joshua—their identification is much more difficult in Joshua than in the Pentateuch, where they are preserved more or less intact. In Joshua the author of the first edition of the book (RD, about 550 B.C.) practically left J out of account and to a considerable extent rewrote the stories of E. Later editions were supplemented with P and Ps material (particularly abundant in Josh. 13-22), with scattered fragments and summaries from J, and redactional annotations and changes which ceased only when the book was canonized about 200 B.C., two centuries after the final edition of the Pentateuch. The framework of the Pentateuch is furnished by the P Code, whereas Joshua and Judges are Deuteronomistic books, with annotations and extracts of ancient sources added during the period 550-200 B.C. The P material, however, ends with Joshua and is not present in Judges; and in Judges the "J" source is far more abundant.

1. The Conquest of Canaan in J

Of the Israelites' invasion into Canaan and of their initial struggles for the possession of parts of the country, little or nothing remains in J, in its original form. We have only more or less corrupt and interpolated fragments of a late epitome of J, and perhaps a few echoes from J in unabridged form (5:13 f.; 9:6 f.; 10:12-13a; their attribution to J is, however, extremely doubtful). It is clear that the Deuteronomistic historians who compiled the first edition of the books of Joshua and Judges suppressed the J account of the settlement in Canaan practically *in toto* because its portrayal of historical facts—tragic failures and limited achievements—could not be reconciled to the later idealization of the time of Joshua.

From the dry summaries and meager fragments extant we can gain only a vague idea of J's epic of the conquest of Canaan. We may group the fragments scattered in Numbers, Joshua, and Judges as follows.[3] The beginning of the narrative is lost. As it opens abruptly, Judah was designated by the oracle, patently obtained through manipulation of the lots in a sacred box. In conjunction with Simeon, Judah invaded the land (from the south), defeated and captured Adoni-Zedek (Josh. 10:1, 3; Judg. 1:5-7 has erroneously Adoni-Bezek) king of Jerusalem (Judg. 1:1

---

[3] Cf. A. Lods, *Israël des origines au milieu du VIIIe siècle*, p. 380, n. 1. Paris, 1930 (English translation, London, 1932). R. Kittel, *Geschichte des Volkes Israel*, Vol. I, pp. 396-400. 6th and 7th ed., Stuttgart, 1923 and 1932.

[omitting "and it came to pass after the death of Joshua"]; 1:2 f., 5-7; cf. Josh. 10:1-11). Thus the Judeans occupied the Highlands, but could not dispossess the inhabitants of the plain and the Jebusites of Jerusalem (Judg. 1:19, 21; Josh. 15:63; Judg. reads erroneously Benjamin instead of Judah). Caleb drove three giants out of Hebron (Josh. 15:13 f.; Judg. 1:20, 10b), married his daughter to Othniel as a reward for his capture of Debir, also called Kirjath-sepher, and provided her with a dowry (Josh. 15:15-19; Judg. 1:11-15; on Othniel, cf. Judg. 3:9 [R^D]). The children of Hobab the Kenite, father-in-law of Moses (read so in Judg. 1:16, according to some mss. of the LXX and to 4:11, cf. Num. 10:29), marched southward and destroyed Zephath, which was henceforth called Hormah (Judg. 1:16 f., omitting the references to Judah and Simeon). Another story explaining the origin of the name Hormah ("devoted [city]," from *herem*, ban, interdict; the actual meaning was probably "inviolably sacred") is found in Num. 21:3. Hormah was in Southern Judah, near the border of Edom (Josh. 15:21, 30; Num. 14:45; Deut. 1:44; cf. I Sam. 30:30); accordingly the fragmentary and misplaced delineation of the Edomitic (not of the Amoritic) border in Judg. 1:36 should probably be placed after 1:16 f.

After Judah's occupation of territory south of Jerusalem, the Joseph tribes (Ephraim, Manasseh, and Benjamin) invaded the mountain of Ephraim in Central Canaan and took Bethel (Judg. 1:[22], 23-26). But they could not penetrate into the plain of Jezreel, to the north (Judg. 1:27 f.; Josh. 17:11-13; cf. 17:16-18a, 15b), nor conquer Gezer, to the south (1:29; Josh. 16:10). Half of Manasseh had already occupied thirty towns in Gilead, called Havvoth-jair, east of the Jordan (Num. 32:39, 41 f.; cf. Judg. 10:4), without, however, becoming masters of Geshur and Maacah in the north (Josh. 13:13; cf. 12:5; Deut. 3:14). In the time of David, Geshur was an Aramaic kingdom (II Sam. 13:37; 14:23, 32; 15:8) which, if we may believe I Chron. 2:23, eventually dispossessed East-Manasseh (Machir) of Havvoth-jair.

North of the plain of Jezreel, the tribes of Zebulon, Asher, and Naphtali (Issachar is accidentally or deliberately omitted) settled among the Canaanites wherever they could find room, without conquering any cities (Judg. 1:30-33). The tribe of Dan at first was crowded in the district of Zorah and Eshtaol, between Ephraim and the Philistines (Judg. 13-18), unable to occupy the cities in the plain (Judg. 1:34 f.). The story of the migration of the Danites and their conquest of the city of Laish, which they renamed Dan, is preserved in the full original text of J, extant in a late edition with a running commentary (Judg. 17-18), and in a brief summary similar to the others under consideration (Josh. 19:47; the LXX has a fuller and older text).

The war of Northern tribes (perhaps Zebulon and Naphtali) against

Jabin king of Hazor, which has been interpolated in the story of the victory over Sisera (Judg. 4:2a, [7], 17b, 23 f.) and is magnified into Joshua's conquest of Northern Canaan in Josh. 11:1-9, may have been described summarily in this document after Judg. 1:30-33. It would be a fitting parallel to Judah's victory over Adoni-Zedek of Jerusalem, similarly magnified into Joshua's conquest of Southern Canaan. We surmise that the conclusion of this summary of the invasion into Canaan is imperfectly preserved in Judg. 2:23a; 3:2a, 5a, 6 (cf. Ex. 23:29 f.; Deut. 7:22 f., where another reason for the incomplete conquest is given), rather than in Judg. 2:1a, 5b (so R. Kittel, *Geschichte des Volkes Israel*, Vol. I, p. 400).

The close parallels between parts of Judg. 1 and scattered verses in Josh. 15-17—Josh. 15:13-19, 63; 16:10; 17:11-13 being substantially identical with Judg. 1:10-15, 20, 21, 29, 27 f.—are best explained by their derivation from a common source, such as the one summarized above. The text in Joshua is at times more original and less altered than that of Judges (in Judg. 1:10, 20, 19, 21 the text, as seen from the parallels in Josh., has been deliberately annotated and changed by late editors). It contains material missing in Judges (so Josh. 13:13; 19:47, LXX), which could hardly have been based on Judg. 1. On the other hand, it is difficult to see how Judg. 1 could have been constructed out of the scattered and intrusive verses in Josh. 15-17, for some of its passages constitute a unit in spite of some displacements. The only conjecture justified by the facts is that a document summarizing the precarious initial settlement of individual tribes of Israel in Canaan furnished isolated quotations for the Book of Joshua. This document was edited in Judg. 1 with late annotations and alterations, probably dating from the third century. Judg. 1:1b-2:5 has been inserted abruptly at a late date between Josh. 24:27 and Judg. 2:6-10, which in an earlier edition were obviously contiguous, as shown by the identity of Josh. 24:28-31 and Judg. 2:6-9.

Notwithstanding its imperfect preservation, this document furnishes us with the most reliable information on the settlement of the Israelites in Canaan. It was compiled from the earliest sources available, and in its original form antedated all other stories of the conquest of Canaan (including that of E). Since the J document must have contained a story of the settlement in Canaan, of which no traces exist elsewhere, it was natural to regard Judg. 1 and the parallels in Joshua, as the J story of the conquest. This view was first advanced by E. Schrader in the 8th edition of W. M. L. De Wette's *Lehrbuch der histor.-krit. Einleitung in die . . . Bücher des Alten Testaments* (p. 327), published at Berlin in 1869, and has been generally accepted by many later critics.

But serious objections against the ascription of this document to J were soon raised by E. Bertheau (*Richter*, 2nd ed., 1883, p. xviii, in the

Kurzgef. Exeg. Handbuch zum Alten Testament); A. Kuenen (*Historisch-critisch Onderzoek*, Vol. I, p. 357. 2nd ed., Leiden, 1885, 1887); W. W. Baudissin (*Einleitung in die Bücher des Alten Testaments*, pp. 231 f.); J. E. Carpenter and G. Harford (*The Composition of the Hexateuch*, pp. 353 f.). Recently O. Eissfeldt (*Hexateuch-Synopse; Einleitung in das Alte Testament*, pp. 283 f.) assigned this material mainly to his source L, but also, in part, to J, E, and P. After careful examination of the evidence, Dr. Beatrice L. Goff (JBL 53 [1934] 241-249) in a new study of the problem comes to the conclusion that J's account of the invasion into Canaan has perished except for a few possible traces in our document, which, however, is based for the most part on another early source.

For two reasons it is hardly credible that so important a part of the J document, that great epic of Israel, should have been successfully suppressed by the Deuteronomists and later dogmatic historians, and that hardly a trace of it should remain. The early sections omitted by the Deuteronomists in Judges and Samuel (Judg. 5; 9; 16-21; I Sam. 28; II Sam. 9-20) were somehow preserved for centuries outside the Deuteronomic histories and were eventually inserted where we now find them. Moreover, the J account of the conquest could not have been more distasteful to the Deuteronomists than the story under discussion, which not only survived but was eventually inserted in both Judges and Joshua.

There is reason to believe that parts of the J document continued being copied after the publication of the Deuteronomic histories (550 B.C.), but we may surmise that the story of the settlement in Canaan which it contained became increasingly unpopular. It would have been natural, under the circumstances, to preserve only a brief summary thereof, with (or without) the kind of annotations we have in Judg. 1. These glosses were added to remove some of the stigma of failure. We find the same kind of biased notes in Judg. 17-21, part of which (17 f.) had been summarized in this document (Josh. 19:47, LXX) ostensibly for the unattained purpose of suppressing the unabridged story.

Unfortunately, from this single instance, in which we possess both the original and the summary, we cannot say whether the former (Judg. 17 f.) was part of the J document or of the early source in the Books of Samuel (cf. W. R. Arnold, *Ephod and Ark*, p. 99). It is still uncertain whether the same author wrote the early narratives from Abraham to the accession of Solomon (cf. T. Klaehn, *Die sprachliche Verwandschaft der Quelle K der Samuelisbücher mit der Quelle J des Heptateuch*) or whether J and the biographer of David were different writers.

Aside from Josh. 19:47 (cf. Judg. 17 f.), however, the document under consideration deals with the first settlement of the tribes in Canaan and not, as in this case, with their subsequent vicissitudes. Josh. 19:47 may

well be a summary of material outside the scope of the J document, but
for the rest our summary seems to be based on lost J material. In the
process of summarizing, editing, and copying, the characteristics of J,
and particularly the classical beauty of its language and dramatic suspense of its stories, were naturally lost by the wayside, as we may see in
comparing Josh. 19:47 with Judg. 17 f. A bare outline of a literary masterpiece can never be great literature. Moreover, the textual variants between the parallel passages in Joshua and Judges indicate sufficiently the
fluctuation of the diction through deliberate alterations or accidents of
transmission. Such radical modifications explain those profound differences between our text and the original J document, which Dr. Goff
adduces as proof that our summary cannot be based, for the most part,
on J. After making every allowance, we can hardly escape the conclusion
that our summary is at least a faint echo of that epic account of how the
tribes of Israel gained a foothold in the Land of Promise, which formed
the climax to the J document in the Pentateuch.

Next to the Song of Deborah (Judg. 5), which reflects a somewhat
later historical period, the J history of the conquest is an invaluable historical source, even in its abridged, mutilated, and textually corrupt form.
It permits us to recognize the fanciful and idealized description given
of the conquest in all later sources, and to gain at least a glimpse of the
historical reality. Of course we cannot expect to find in it the accurate
historicity of a contemporary document, such as the Song of Deborah,
or II Sam. 9-20. J wrote more than two centuries after the events narrated—his earliest possible date is the reign of Solomon—and had no
access to written contemporary sources. But it is clear that he set out to
write an objective and unbiased history. He utilized the oral traditions
of the several tribes when such were available: his account of the
achievements of Judah, Caleb, Joseph, as well as other exploits seems to
be based on tribal reminiscences. Of course, tribes are inclined to forget
past failures. J's frank admission that they were unsuccessful in the
occupation of fortified cities and fertile plains, and that certain tribes,
notably those in Galilee, were forced to settle precariously in the midst
of the native population, is not based on the oral tradition but on his
own inferences from the situation before David's conquests.

The extant summary of J is unhistorical in certain details, but it is
difficult to determine whether such lapses are due to J or to his excerptors.
J himself often tells fanciful tales. He delights in imaginary stories explaining the etymology of place names. That he might, in his enthusiasm,
have told two different stories about the naming of Hormah (Num. 21:1-3
and Judg. 1:17) must not be excluded a priori. One could have been
traditional and the other original with him. Another etymological story
about Hormah is found perhaps in Num. 14:45; Deut. 1:44.

In still other cases, several unhistorical details may be safely attributed to excerptors from J: Joshua as the chief of Israel (Josh. 17:14-18); Israel conceived as a united nation rather than a group of separate tribes (Judg. 1:1, 28; Josh. 13:13); the tribes setting forth from Jericho or Gilgal to conquer their territory (Judg. 1:1-4, 16, 22; cf. 2:1; Josh. 13:13) and not from the south (cf. Num. 13:22; 21:1-3), as Judah and its allies certainly did. Unless "lot" in Judg. 1:3 simply means "portion," without implying Joshua's allotment of the land (cf. R. Kittel, *Geschichte des Volkes Israel*, Vol. I, p. 408), the editors have introduced into J's summary in Judg. 1 (as also in Josh. 15:13; 17:14, 17) an unhistorical picture of the distribution of the land prevailing in later accounts from the pen of the Deuteronomists and the Priestly authors.

In conclusion, J's story of the conquest of Canaan, which survives in a meager and revised summary, without being strictly accurate in all details is our main source for a period of Israel's early history as obscure as it is important for the nation's later achievements.

2. The E Stories

In proceeding from J to E in Joshua we pass from a solid sense of reality, with all its harshness and failures, to a vision of events as they should have been. We have noted that the unhistorical notions appearing sporadically in late revisions of J's summary are dominant in E. Joshua, who was apparently not even mentioned in the genuine J, becomes the protagonist of the E narrative. If Joshua was historical he was an Ephraimitic hero, and his glorification at the hand of the Ephraimitic author of the E document is not surprising. In E, Joshua becomes nearly a second Moses—a divinely inspired commander and legislator. In E, the tribes do not proceed individually to find a *pied-à-terre*, but receive their territory by lot. Nor is the conquest a series of more or less successful exploits of individual tribes scattered over Canaan; it is a brilliant military campaign of united Israel under the leadership of Joshua. All the tribes entered Canaan from the east, crossing the Jordan miraculously —none came up from the south. They remained together until they dispersed to their allotted territories.

Other general characteristics of E are a relish for miraculous tales, such as the crossing of the Jordan and fall of the walls of Jericho, and the special interest in Ephraim as shown in the role of Joshua, in detailed descriptions of exploits on the mountain of Ephraim, and in the mention of monuments within the territory of the Joseph tribes (4:7, 20; 5:3, 9; 7:26; 8:30 f.; 24:26 f.). E's story of the conquest, a continuation of E in the Pentateuch, was written about 750 B.C., probably at Bethel.

Little of the original E in Joshua has, however, been preserved intact. But more than a brief summary—such as we have for J—has survived.

The text of E has been repeatedly edited and rewritten by the editor of JE (about 650 B.C.), Deuteronomists (about 550), and numerous annotators and redactors down to 200 B.C. Hence it is hardly possible to determine what parts of Josh. 2-11 and 24 belong to E—for, except perhaps in 14:6-14 and 19:49 f., there seems to be no trace of E elsewhere in the book— much less to feel any assurance that the original diction has been preserved. On the whole, the style of the sections usually attributed to E is not that of the admirable E prose at its best in the Pentateuch, but that of the pious, prolix, and rhetorical Deuteronomists. Even Rahab the harlot, talking to the two spies (2:9-13), expresses herself with the pulpit eloquence of a Moses addressing all Israel (cf. Deut. 31:1-6).[4]

Such being the case, to determine exactly what parts of Joshua belong to E is futile. Critics have reached divergent and uncertain results in their efforts to trace the original E source, and never succeeded in finding E material entirely free from Deuteronomistic contamination. Deuteronomistic diction is so pervasive that its removal leaves only disconnected words and expressions belonging to E's language. Nevertheless, there is an E substratum in the stories of 2-11 and in the speech of Joshua in 24. In E, the Israelites camped at Shittim (Num. 25:1); from there Joshua sent two spies to Jericho (Josh. 2:1) and set forth to cross the Jordan (3:1). The E substratum is present in 2:1-9, 12-23, in the story of the two spies and of Rahab. However, two narrative strands are interwoven in these verses, as likewise in the story of the crossing of the Jordan (3-4), where one of these strands probably derives from an E story.

But in both accounts the prominent role played by the imaginary "ark of the covenant" hides the E story from us. This sacred object, unknown to the Israelites before they settled in Canaan, was first mentioned by the early sources (with the possible exception of Num. 10:35 f.; 14:44, reflecting later usage) in the time of the Judges. Nothing but a miraculous crossing and the setting up of twelve stones as a memorial can be attributed to E in chs. 3-4. In ch. 5, the circumcision of the Israelites, erroneously explaining the etymology of Gilgal, which really means "circle [of stones]," or cromlech, may belong to E (5:2 f., 8 f.); the vision of the captain of the Lord's host (5:13 f.), often attributed to J or E, is of unknown origin.

The story of the fall of the walls of Jericho (6) also rests on two strands, each of which again features the ark. It is difficult to say whether, according to E, the walls fell when the warriors of Israel uttered the war cry (6:3a, 5, 7, 10, 16b, 17) or when the priests blew a fanfare on

---

[4] On the Deuteronomistic coloring of style and ideas in the E sections of Joshua, see O. Procksch, Die Elohimquelle, pp. 239-247.

their trumpets (6:3b, 4, 6, 11-13a, 14-16a). In any case, the first account can hardly be J, as J. Wellhausen believed. It is possible that the stories of the sin of Achan (7) and the capture of Ai (8) contain an E or JE kernel, but the analysis of chs. 7-8 is very uncertain; the LXX contains a shorter text in ch. 8. The story of the capture of Ai ("the Ruin") by a military stratagem is unhistorical and was inspired by Judg. 20:29-41. From the historical viewpoint, the compact made by the Gibeonites with the Israelites (9) is the best documented story in the whole book. With the exception of Beeroth, from which the Gibeonites were expelled (II Sam. 4:2b-3) ostensibly by Saul (cf. II Sam. 21:1-5), they were left in possession of the four cities mentioned in 9:17 (cf. I Sam. 6:21; 7:1; II Sam. 21:2, 6) after they became worshipers of Jehovah. The story seems to disclose some traces of J (9:6b-7, the compact of the Hivvites with the Israelites, omitting "unto him and" in v. 6), but belongs substantially to E (9:3, 6a, [8-11], 14, 15aα), with Deuteronomistic and Priestly additions. In J the victories of Joshua against Adoni-zedek at Gibeon (10) and Jabin by the waters of Merom (11) are minor tribal exploits. In their Deuteronomistic form, these two stories become decisive national victories through which Joshua conquered Southern and Northern Canaan, respectively. Whether this telescoping of the lengthy conquest into two battles was already done by E, in stories no longer recognizable under their thick layer of Deuteronomistic language, must remain in doubt, but we may assume the presence of an E substratum in some of the picturesque details (10:6, 16-24, 26 f.; 11:1-9, in part).

Few traces of E can be detected after ch. 11 until the final address of Joshua in ch. 24:1-27. This speech has not been edited by the Deuteronomists, who prepared another final address of Joshua in ch. 23, and it was probably lacking in the Deuteronomistic edition of about 550 B.C.[5] Added subsequently in its present form, it is substantially E—with redactional annotations of a Deuteronomistic nature written after 550. The recapitulation of Joshua in 24:2-15, from the migration of Abraham to the settlement in Canaan, is valuable as a summary of the E document. Emphasis on the worship of "other gods" in place of Jehovah (24:2, 14 f.) and the solemn covenant by which the Israelites pledged themselves to worship Jehovah exclusively (24:16-27) do not seem to belong to E in its original form and can be dated about the time of the publication of the D Code in 621. The closing verses of the book (24:28-33, except 24:31, quoted from Judg. 2:7) belong substantially to E and reappear in part (24:28-31) at the beginning of the Deuteronomistic Book of Judges (Judg. 2:6-9).

---

[5] So W. W. Baudissin, *Einleitung in die Bücher des Alten Testaments*, p. 177. Leipzig, 1901. G. F. Moore, *Encycl. Bibl.* 2, 2605.

3. *The Deuteronomistic Edition*

The Deuteronomistic Book of Joshua ended with 24:31; 24:32 f. was added from E. The close connection in the Deuteronomistic edition between the end of Joshua (24:28-31) and the beginning of Judges (Judg. 2:6-9) is emphasized in the additions at the end of Joshua in the LXX. After the account of the death and burial of Eleazar (24:33) the Greek text adds, "In that day the children of Israel, having taken the Ark of God, carried it about in their midst. And Phinehas exercised the priestly office in place of Eleazar his father until he died, and he was buried in Gabaar [error for *gibeah*, hill] which belonged to him. The children of Israel went each one to his place and to his city [cf. Judg. 2:6]. And the children of Israel worshiped Astarte and Astaroth and the gods of the nations round about them [cf. Judg. 2:13 f.]. And the Lord delivered them into the hands of Eglom [error for Eglon] king of Moab, and he ruled over them eighteen years [cf. Judg. 3:12-14]."

Joshua was subjected to a more thoroughgoing revision than the other volumes of the Deuteronomistic corpus Genesis-Kings, published about 550. Not only was the book provided with a freely composed Deuteronomistic introduction (1) and conclusion (23), as in Judges in this edition (Judg. 2:6-3:6; I Sam. 12), but the stories of E were substantially rewritten, as we have seen, in the characteristic flowing and rhetorical style of this school. Because it is impossible to obtain a pure E text by merely removing the Deuteronomistic material, C. Steuernagel (*Joshua*, HKAT, 1899. *Einleitung in das Alte Testament*, p. 275), following A. Dillmann (2nd ed. of A. Knobel's *Numbers-Joshua*, p. 600 in the Kurzgef. Exeget. Handbuch, 1886), posits the existence of an independent Deuteronomic source based on E. However, the intimate connection of the Deuteronomistic Joshua with Deuteronomy and Judges in the same edition precludes the assumption that it ever existed separate from the Deuteronomistic corpus Genesis-Kings. This hypothetical "source" is a finished book, not material added to a book; it had no more independent existence outside our book than the Deuteronomistic material of Judges contributed by the same school.

In its present form, our book is closely connected with secondary parts of Deuteronomy, some of which may have been written by the same Deuteronomists. The instructions in Deut. 27 (cf. 11:26-32) are fulfilled in Josh. 8:30-35. The conquests of Joshua are predicted in Deut. 1:38 f.; 3:21 f., 28; 31:1-8, 14, 23. The divine instructions to Joshua in Josh. 1:3-9 actually quote Deut. 11:22-25 (cf. 1:3 f. with 11:24; 1:9 recalls Deut. 3:21 f.; 31:6-8, 23); the address to the Transjordanic tribes in 1:12-18 refers to Deut. 3:18-20. Just as the introduction in ch. 1 shows close relations with Deut. 1-3 and 31, so the conclusion in ch. 23 reveals parallelisms with Deut. 28-29. The author knows our Deuteronomy as the "book of the Law of Moses" (23:6; cf. 1:8; 8:31, 34; and see Deut. 28:58, 61; 29:20 f., 27 [H. 29:19 f., 26]; 30:10; 31:24, 26), and refers to the blessings and curses in Deut. 28 (23:15; cf. in particular Deut. 28:63). Although its style is less vigorous and its diction more commonplace, the homiletic tone resembles that of Deut. 29.

This dependence of Josh. 1 and 23 on the framework of Deuteronomy,[6] and the triteness of style are signs of secondary Deuteronomistic redactions, later than 550 B.C. Although several critics have attempted to distinguish the two redactions in detail, their results are not conclusive. It seems certain, however, that the Deuteronomists did not stop with the publication of the edition of 550. The facts of the case are better explained by the assumption of successive retouches of the edition of 550 than by O. Eissfeldt's hypothesis of two separate Deuteronomistic editions combined in our book (*Einleitung in das Alte Testament*, p. 285).

The Deuteronomistic Book of Joshua, published about 550, consisted of the following parts: 1-4; 6:1-8:29; 9:1-16; 9:22-13:12; 14:6-14; 16:1-3; (18:2-10); 21:43-45 (H. 21:41-43); 22:1-6; 23; 24:28-31. The brief glosses included have not been indicated here. The Deuteronomists' sources were chiefly JE (about 650 B.C.) in ch. 2-9, and in 10-11 E alone. JE practically suppressed J, and made E the basis of the narrative. In 10-11, J is merely the ultimate source entirely rewritten by E and perhaps also retouched by the editor of JE, so that actually E is here the Deuteronomists' source. After ch. 11, the Deuteronomists composed freely and their sources cannot be determined with any certainty.

The Deuteronomists (R[D]) were not interested in history per se, whether tribal as in J or national as in E. Their chief concern was religious. They stressed the religious teaching of the D Code: Jehovah made a covenant with Israel by which he would bless the nation only if it fulfilled the divine Law revealed to Moses. Consequently genuine historical events were either described according to the narratives of JE or E, with pious revisions and additions, or merely presented concisely in bare outlines devoid of picturesque details but with repeated emphasis on Jehovah's decisive intervention in behalf of his people (10:14, 42; 23:3, 10). In 10:28-42 Jehovah is responsible only for the victory; in 11:16-20 he is responsible, first, for arousing the resistance of the kings of Canaan and then for their utter destruction.

In contrast with the meagerness of historical narrative in R[D], the homiletic discourses, whether they be exhortations (as in 1; 22:1-5; 23) or confessions of faith (2:9-11; 9:9-11; 14:6-14), are oratorical, expansive,

---

[6] Another instance of this influence of the framework of Deuteronomy on Joshua may be found in references to the "Ark of the Covenant" (3:3, 17; 4:7, 18; 6:8; 8:33; cf. Deut. 10:8; 31:9. 25 f.), which is ignored entirely in the D Code of 621 B.C.

and sonorous. Obedience to the Law of Moses is inculcated not only through exhortation (1:7 f.; 22:5; 23:6) but also through example. Contrary to the actual facts—which RD did not entirely conceal (11:22b; 13:1-6; 23:4-13)—Joshua is said not only to have conquered all of Canaan (10:40-42; 11:16 f., 23; cf. 12:7-24) but also, according to explicit statements in the Book of the Law (Deut. 4:38; 7:16; 9:3-5; 11:23; 18:12), to have expected the total dispossession of all the inhabitants through Jehovah's future intervention (13:6; 14:12; 23:5; in 24:18 the dispossession is finished). We read, moreover, that Joshua utterly destroyed them through the ban (2:10; 6:17; 8:26; 10:28, 35, 37, 39; 11:11 f., 20 f.), in obedience to the command in the Book of the Law (Deut. 2:34; 3:6; 7:2; 13:15; 20:17). The story of Achan (7) illustrates the dire consequences of a transgression of the divine covenant and the right way of "putting away the evil" from the midst of Israel. In 8:30-35 Joshua performs the ceremonies ordered in Deut. 27. Briefly, Joshua "left nothing undone of all that Jehovah had commanded Moses" (11:15).

As in Deuteronomy, the cardinal principle of the law is to love (22:5; 23:11; cf. Deut. 5:10; 6:5; 7:9; 10:12; 11:1, 13, 22; 13:3 [H. 13:4]; 19:9; 30:6, 16, 20) and fear (4:24; 22:25; cf. Deut. 6:2, 13; 7:21; 10:17, 20; 13:4 [H. 13:5]; 25:18; 28:58; 31:12, etc.) Jehovah with all one's heart and soul (22:5; cf. Deut. 4:29; 6:5; 10:12; 11:13; 26:16; 30:2, 6, 10, etc.), avoiding worship of all other gods (23:16; 24:20; cf. Deut. 7:4; 8:19; 11:16; 13:2, 6, 13, etc.).

4. The Priestly Code

Like the Deuteronomists, the authors of the Priestly Code have no real interest in the actual history of ancient Israel. Their reconstruction of the past is even more theoretical and theological. Their purpose is no longer, as with the Deuteronomists, to inculcate the noble tenets of the religion of the D Code, but to organize solidly the Jewish theocracy and trace its statutes and origins to the times of Moses and Joshua. In the period of Joshua the significant event for P is not (as in J and E, and even for RD) the conquest of Canaan, but the exact fixation of the territory divinely assigned to the holy Jewish commonwealth. P has thus extremely little to say about the initial occupation of Canaan, but goes into great detail in fixing the extent and borders of the territory allotted to each tribe of Israel.

Since the P Code mentions not a single battle, it apparently conceived the conquest as a miraculous event. It almost looks as if P wiped the Canaanites off the map by a stroke of the pen. East of the Jordan, P ignores the victory over Sihon and Og (Num. 21:21-32, JE), which evoked such pride in the Deuteronomists (Deut. 3:8-17; 4:46-49; Josh. 2:10; 9:10, etc.). He gives merely a bare itinerary, ending with the arrival in the plains of Moab, on the Jordan opposite Jericho (Num. 22:1), and an account of the allotment of the territory east of the Jordan to Reuben and Gad, with the understanding that they would accompany the other Israelites over the Jordan (P in Num. 32 or, more probably, in Josh. 13:15-33).

The description of the battle with the Midianites (Num. 31) is a later supplement to P. He considered the stories of the conquest inconsequential and irrelevant and, conversely, the exact account of the land allotment of paramount importance. Hence, long before Joshua led the Israelites across the Jordan, P placed in the mouth of Moses instructions regarding the borders of the territory to be distributed (Num. 34:1-12), naming punctiliously the twelve tribal princes who were to assist Eleazar and Joshua in the allotment (34:16-29) and listing the cities of refuge in Canaan (35:9-29).

Hastening toward the climax—the allotment of Canaan—the Priestly authors made only a few additions to the stories of the conquest in Josh. 1-12. Having quickly crossed the Jordan on the tenth day of the first month (4:10, [16 f.], 19), because of the imminence of the Passover, the Israelites camped at Gilgal and celebrated the festival on the fourteenth (5:10-12). In the story of the Gibeonites, P was interested in the verdict that allowed the Gibeonites to live, but characteristically sentenced them to be "hewers of wood and drawers of water" (in the Temple at Jerusalem) for the Jewish congregation (9:15b, 17-21). With dogmatic unconcern for facts and magnificent inconsistency, P blithely allots to Benjamin (18:25-28) the four cities wherein the Gibeonites had been permitted to dwell in peace (9:17 f.), according to the oath of the princes of the congregation.

There is no reason to assume, as some critics do, that P's account of the conquest of Canaan is lost. It never existed. All memory of the heroic struggles of the Israelites, to gain a precarious foothold in Canaan in the midst of a large native population, is completely missing in P. As we have seen, the recollection of the facts was fading rapidly from the time of J, when it was still vivid, to E, JE, and R^D. It would have seemed blasphemous to the Priestly authors to suspect for an instant that Jehovah, Lord of the world, should need human co-operation in carrying out his plans. What obstacles could the Omnipotent encounter in giving to his holy nation the land which he had chosen for it? His decision had been taken long before (Gen. 17:8; Ex. 6:4-8). A word from his lips sufficed to give his people a great flourishing land devoid of inhabitants except for some Gibeonite temple slaves. God gives the land to Israel "as an inheritance," and Israel needs only to receive it from him. This theoretical and idealized notion of the occupation of Canaan already appears in Deuteronomy (12:9 f.; 15:4; 19:3, 10; 20:16; 21:23; 24:4, etc.) and was developed by Ezekiel (47:13 f., 21 f.; cf. 45:1; 48:29), from whom it passed to P, where it is taken for granted. The immediate complete possession of the land is indicated by the fact that only four days after crossing the Jordan the Israelites could celebrate the Passover without fear of attack and that, beginning with the fifth day the manna ceased and they lived from the produce of Canaan (5:10-12).

P's account of the allotment of land to the several tribes begins with the words, "And the whole congregation of the children of Israel assembled together at Shiloh, and set up the tent of meeting there. And the land was subdued before them" (18:1, out of place in our text); and ends as follows, "These are the inheritances which Eleazar the priest, and Joshua the son of Nun, and the heads of the fathers' houses of the tribes of the children of Israel distributed by lot for inheritance in Shiloh in the presence of the Lord at the entrance of the tent of meeting. So they finished allotting the land" (19:51). Within this introduction and conclusion, P described exactly the borders and principal cities of the territory allotted each tribe. Parts of this important document are, however, imperfectly preserved in our text.

Opinion is divided on the original location of 13:15-33 (omitting the references to Sihon, Balaam, and Og in 13:21 f., 30 f.). Some critics place it immediately before, others immediately after, 18:1. But this account of the allotment of Transjordania to Reuben, Gad, and half of Manasseh has really no place in Joshua. Made by Moses before his death, it rightly belongs at the end of Numbers (before 34:13-15), together with the parallel JE account in ch. 32, containing P interpolations. In the introduction to the account of the allotment of Canaan (14:3) the allusion to Josh. 13:15-33 proves that this Transjordanic apportioning was reported in P before the death of Moses.

After the brief introduction in 18:1; 14:1 f., 5 comes P's report of the allotment of Canaan to nine and a half tribes in the following order: Judah (15:1-12, 20-44, 48-62);[7] the sons of Joseph (16:1-4, redactional), i.e., Ephraim (16:5-8) and Manasseh (17:1a, 7-10); Benjamin (18:11-28); Simeon (19:1-8); Zebulon (19:10-16); Issachar (19:17-23); Asher (19:24-31); Naphtali (19:32-39); Dan (19:40-46, 48). The account of the allotment ends with the concluding remarks in 19:51 (cf. 13:32 and the LXX in 13:14b).

In an appendix, P lists the three Canaanitic cities of refuge for unintentional murderers (20:1-9, with a gloss from Deut. 4:41-43 in 20:8 and an interpolation still lacking in the LXX in 20:4-6), according to the prescriptions of Num. 35:9-29 (cf. Deut. 19). In the third century, a Levite who

---

[7] The names of 11 cities of Judah have been accidentally omitted from the Hebrew text of 15:59 and are preserved in the LXX.

was a kindred spirit of the Chronicler (cf. I Chron. 6:54-81 [H. 6:39-66])
protested against the ancient practice (officially sanctioned by P in Num.
18:20 f., 24) depriving priests and Levites of territorial possessions. He
assigned on paper thirteen cities to the priests and thirty-five to the
Levites (all in the vicinity of Jerusalem), listing them (in Josh. 21:1-42
[H., lacking 21:36 f., 21:1-40); cf. 14:4; Num. 35:1-8, Ps) as a fitting supplement to P's provision for asylum cities in Josh. 20.

Another supplement to P, by the pen of an equally late interpolator,
is found in 22:7-34 (22:7 f. are secondary). This midrash, comparable
to Num. 31; 32:6-15 and the late commentary interpolated in Judg. 20,
apparently wished to explain that the numerous ancient shrines, where
Jehovah was worshiped before Josiah's reforms in 621, were merely
memorial altars on which no sacrifices whatever were ever offered.

For the history of Palestine, the most valuable source contained in the
Book of Joshua is paradoxically P's account of the allotment of territory to
the several tribes (Josh. 15-19, in so far as they belong to P). Although
the topographical information contained therein is worthless for the time
of Joshua, it is nevertheless invaluable. P's description of Canaan, dating
from the fifth century B.C. but embodying earlier data, is the earliest and
most detailed available. This ancient miniature "Baedeker" formed the
basis of the topographical studies embodied in the *Onomastikon* of Eusebius, re-edited by Jerome, and for the modern investigations of A. Alt
and others.[8]

Besides the accidents of textual transmission, several factors have contributed to the confusion prevailing in a considerable part of P's description of the tribal territories. P used conflicting sources of an earlier date.
It is generally recognzied that E's account of the partition of Canaan,
fragments of which are preserved in P, was based on the catalogue of
cities in seven parts fictitiously dated during the time of Joshua (18:9).
A fragment of this book seems to be preserved in the list of fortified cities
of Naphtali (19:35-38) and traces which we can no longer identify with
certainty appear in the other lists of cities in P (perhaps in 19:15, 18b-22
[in part], 25b, 28a, 30). In some cases, it is clear that P's lists are derived
from more than one source, for the same city is ascribed to both Judah
and Benjamin (Beth-arabah, 15:6; 18:22) or to Judah and Dan (Beth-
shemesh, 15:10; Ir-shemesh, 19:41), and all the cities of Simeon (19:1-8)
are reckoned as part of Judah (15:21 ff., in a different order), an incon-

---

[8] A. Alt, BWAT 13 (1913) 1 ff.; PJ (1925) 100 ff.; *Sellin Festschrift* (1927), pp.
13 ff.; ZAW N.F. 4 (1927), 59 ff. M. Noth, ZDPV (1935) 185 ff. W. F. Albright,
ZAW N.F. 3 (1926) 225 ff.; and in AASOR II-III (1923); IV (1924); etc. K.
Elliger (PJ 30 [1934] 47-71) has investigated the topography of Josh. 10:28-39. For
full biographies from 1895 to 1934 see Peter Thomsen, *Die Palästina-Literatur* (5
vols.).

sistency explained in 19:9. Similarly, certain cities of Ephraim are said to have stood within the borders of Manasseh (16:9; cf. 17:8 f.) and certain cities of Manasseh to be situated in Issachar and Asher (17:11).

Besides utilizing at least two lists of cities, P had at his disposal more than one outline of the tribal borders. The sentence "this will be your southern border" (15:4) is the remnant of a JE delineation of the borders of Judah presented in the form of an address—in contrast with P's "notary public" style. From one of these outlines, possibly in E, is quoted a description of the southern border of Joseph (16:1-3; cf. 17:14-18 where Joseph, regarded as a single tribe, received one inheritance); from another is taken the delineation of the separate borders of the two Joseph tribes, Ephraim and Manasseh (16:5-8; 17:7, 9 f.). P, in fact, regarded them as two tribes (Gen. 48:5) and placed Manasseh before Ephraim (17:1a; cf. 14:4). Besides, the same source would hardly fix the southern border of Joseph twice, first describing it westward from the Jordan to the sea (16:1-3) and then, with slight variations, eastward from the sea to the Jordan (16:5-8).

The text of P, which was apparently inconsistent from the start, owing to different sources utilized, was confused still more by later additions and curtailments. The following passages are clearly interpolated into P: 15:13-19, 43-47, 63; 16:10; 17:3-6, 12; 19:49 f. The allotment in two stages, first to Judah, Ephraim, and Manasseh and then to seven other minor tribes (18:2-10) is totally foreign to P, where the division is made in a single act (18:1; 19:51); numerals indicating the order of the lots of the seven tribes have been added to P (except for the first, 18:11) in 19:1, 10, 17, 24, 32, 40. The most important omissions occur in the description of the territory of Ephraim and Manasseh (16-17). Although it covered the principal part of the land of Israel, its description is conspicuously brief in comparison with the description of Judah (15). The list of the cities of Ephraim, presupposed by 16:9 and 17:9 (in part), which allude to those within Manasseh without listing them, is completely omitted, as well as the borders of Ephraim to the east, west, and north. The borders of Manasseh are given, but the list of its cities, except for those in Issachar (17:11), is also missing. J. Wellhausen (*Composition des Hexateuchs*, p. 133) is probably right in his surmisal that such lacunae are due to deliberate curtailment by a fanatic anti-Samaritan redactor, who may likewise have been responsible for the deliberate change of Shechem, metropolis of the Samaritans, to Shiloh (in the text from which the LXX of 24:1, 25 was translated). Shechem could not have been omitted from a list of the cities of Ephraim (cf. P in 20:7). A similar abridgment occurs in Josh. 1-12, where only the conquest of the South and of the North is reported, omitting entirely the mountain of Ephraim in the center.

5. *The Successive Editions of the Book*

The redaction of the Book of Joshua began with the writing of J, about the middle of the tenth or ninth century, and continued until about 200 B.C. when the prophetic canon, of which it was the first volume, was published. The lamentable condition in which J and E have reached us in the book makes an investigation of the oral traditions, rewritten by the J and E authors, much more precarious than in the case of Genesis. The results of such a study are necessarily conjectural.[9]

The two primary sources, J (about 950-850) and E (about 750), were re-edited jointly in JE about 650. This book discarded most of J and was originally a new edition of E, like JE in the Book of Numbers. It was quite impossible to harmonize two radically different notions of the conquest of Canaan. In J, this conquest appeared partial and uneven since the tribes went into action individually; in E, Joshua at the head of a united Israel conquered the whole country through a few decisive victories.

It is difficult to discover how far the JE editor revised E and how much he added from other sources (such as the so-called J[2] material of various date and origin that has nothing to do with J) or from his own pen. Harmonistic notes, concluding statements, and other annotations may be tentatively attributed to him (although a later date is possible). R[JE] may be responsible for 2:17; 5:15; 6:15b, 17b, 24b; 10:43; 11:23b; 14:15; 15:13; 19:49 f.; 22:7 f. In 7 and 24, this redactor seems to be particularly in evidence.

About 550 the Deuteronomists (R[D]) issued JE in a thoroughly revised edition. They provided the book with an introduction (1) and conclusion (the final address of Joshua in 23, which they substituted to ch. 24), added pious speeches, and rewrote much of JE. Thus they radically changed its character. What had been a history of the conquest of Canaan became a sermon exhorting the nation, through lessons from its past achievements and failures, to respect the covenant with Jehovah.

The Deuteronomistic revision of Joshua was not completed about 550, but continued at least until 400, as in Deuteronomy, and even later. We have observed that the late Deuteronomistic additions to Joshua disclose familiarity with the fifth century additions to Deuteronomy, and there is no reason to doubt that some were written in the fourth century. For instance, the advanced theology of Deut. 4, derived from the Second

---

[9] The latest study of the "sagas" of Josh. 1-11; 22; 24 is that of K. Möhlenbrink in ZAW N.F. 15 (1938) 238-268, where many of the relevant German publications are quoted. The author comes to the conclusion that two cycles of traditions (the Ephraimitic cycle from Shiloh and the Gilgal traditions of Benjamin, Reuben, and Gad) were combined, giving preference to the first, before J and E were written. J or, more probably, E substituted Shechem for Shiloh in 8:30 ff.; 9; 24. Such speculations are more suggestive than convincing.

Isaiah (about 540) and dating from the fifth century, is ascribed to Rahab (2:11), who quotes the words of Deut. 4:39, "Jehovah, he is God in heaven above and upon the earth beneath." These late Deuteronomists inserted again 24:1-31 (omitted in the edition of 550) together with their own annotations (such as 24:1bα [cf. 23:2], 13 [cf. Deut. 6:10], 18b-22, 26a). They added "of the covenant" to "the ark" in 3:3 ff. In two cases (3:14, 17), the addition of "the covenant" to "the ark" (with the article) renders the Hebrew ungrammatical (cf. also 3:11 where "the covenant" is ungrammatical before "the Lord . . ."). Priestly redactors added "of the testimony" to "the ark" in 4:16. Under the influence of J's increasing popularity after 550, later Deuteronomists admitted, in contrast with R^D, that Joshua's conquest of Canaan was not complete (11:22, 13:1bβ-6; 23:4 f., 7, 12 f.).

The P material was added to R^D's Book of Joshua at the end of the fifth century. The doubtful traces of R^P (who inserted P into Joshua) may be later glosses to P (13:14, 21aβ-22, 27 ["the rest of the kingdom of Sihon king of Heshbon"], 29-31, 33; 14:3 f.; 15:45-47; 17:1b, 3-6; 19:9). P's account of the land allotment to the tribes, a single act, was adapted at the time of its insertion to JE's notion of an allotment in two stages, first to Judah and Joseph, then to the other seven tribes. Accordingly, 18:1 was removed from before 14:1 to its present place. R^D remained the framework of Joshua after the addition of P, whereas in the Pentateuch P furnished the framework. It is therefore probable that P was inserted into Joshua later than into the Pentateuch, and hence it was possible to preserve in Joshua P's account of the allotment of Transjordania made by Moses (13:15-33), which had its logical place in Num. 32-34 but had been omitted in favor of the JE account in Num. 32.

In the fourth or the early third century, additions of various kinds were made in the book. Some of the late Deuteronomic glosses already mentioned cannot antedate the insertion of P. Thus the typically Deuteronomistic gloss, "to the place which he will choose" (9:27; cf. Deut. 12:5, 14, 18, 21 and often in Deut. 12-26; 31), meaning the Temple of Jerusalem, seems to have been added incongruously to a verse already retouched by Priestly redactors ("for the congregation," cf. 9:21); cf. the LXX. In some cases, there are Deuteronomistic glosses in P sections. The references to Sihon and Og are secondary in 13:15-33 (P) and, to judge from their frequency in Deuteronomistic passages alone (Deut. 1-4; 29; 31; Josh. 2:10; 9:10; 12:1-6), may safely be termed Deuteronomistic. Similarly, P in 20:1-9 has been supplemented not only with a quotation of Deut. 4:43 in v. 8, but with the gloss in 20:4-6, based on Deut. 19 (cf. the interpolation of "unawares" from Deut. 19:4), which is still lacking in the LXX.

In this period we may also date the addition of scattered quotations from a late summary of J and a late edition of JE. Quotations from the abridgment of J (also found in an even later edition in Judg. 1) were inserted, usually in P, in their proper place (13:13; 15:13-19, 63; 16:10; 17:11-18; 19:47). Similarly, some parts of JE (mostly E), which R^D had not included in the edition of 550 B.C., were replaced where they belonged originally: 5:2 f., 8 f. (with the late interpolation 5:4-7, P^s?); 5:13-15 (a JE torso of unknown origin); 8:30-35; 19:49 f.; 24:1-27, 32 f. In the LXX, 8:30-35 appear after 9:1 f. One may raise the question whether ch. 6, which is a much interpolated JE story without clear traces of R^D, was not also added at this time.

The willful anti-Samaritan curtailment of the sections dealing with Ephraim probably dates from the fourth century. The JE story of the conquest of Central Canaan in chs. 1-12 and some essential parts of chs. 16-17 were drastically omitted at that time.

The latest important additions to Joshua were made in the third century. They are the P^s sections on the priestly and Levitical cities (21:4-42 [H. 21:4-40]) and on the memorial altar erected by the Transjordanic tribes (22:9-34). Some of the glosses (5:4-7; 6:3-5; 20:4-6, etc. See J. Hollenberg, *Der Character der alexandr. Übersetzung des Buch. Josua und ihr textkritischer Wert*. Mörs, 1876; the best edition of the LXX for Josh. is that of M. L. Margolis) are lacking in the LXX and can hardly be earlier than the third century. It is clear that minor modifications were introduced into the text even after the book was canonized about 200 B.C.

CHAPTER II

THE BOOK OF JUDGES

The Book of Judges is a history of the period between Joshua and Samuel. Its title, which occurs already in Origen and in the Talmud (*Baba Bathra* 14b; cf. Ben Sira's *Ecclus.* 46:11 and Philo, *De confus. ling.* 26:1) is taken from the name of the leaders whose stories it relates. The Hebrew word, translated "judges" (*shōphetîm*), has a wider meaning than in English. In our book (2:16-19; cf. Ruth 1:1; II Sam. 7:11 [I Chron. 17:10]; II Kings 23:22; I Chron. 17:6; Acts 13:20) it does not refer to arbitrators or to the presiding officers of a court of justice (as in 11:27), but to the men performing a twofold function. First they heroically delivered their people from the oppression of their enemies (2:16, 18; cf. I Sam. 8:20; Neh. 9:27), then they ruled dictatorially until their death without, however, founding a dynasty, except for Gideon (9:2). In this second capacity of "rulers," (for which see 4:4; 10:2 f.; 12:7-14; 15:20; 16:31; I Sam. 4:18; 7:15), *shōphetîm* corresponds to *shupetim* or regents of Phoenicia (Josephus, *Against Apion* 1:21) and the *sufetes* or chief magistrates of Carthage, akin to the Roman consuls (for references see Z. S. Harris, *A Grammar of the Phoenician Language,* p. 153. New Haven, Conn., 1936). In this dual meaning, the word "judges" is Deuteronomistic.

The Deuteronomists, in their great history edited in 550, first conceived of the time from Joshua to Saul as the period of the judges, a transition epoch between the complete conquest of Canaan (in reality accomplished by David) and the founding of the monarchy. The Deuteronomistic Book of Judges began with the introduction in 2:6-3:6 and ended with the final address of Samuel (I Sam. 12), including Eli and Samuel among the "judges."

Our book consists of three well-defined parts: 1. A preliminary survey of the partial occupation of Canaan after the Israelitic invasion (1:1-2:5). 2. The story of the judges (2:6-16:31). 3. An appendix comprising the stories of the migration of the Danites (17-18) and of the war against the Benjamites (19-21). These three parts may be summarized as follows:

1. The initial occupation of Canaan. *a.* Judah and Simeon (1:1-8, 17 f.), Caleb and Othniel (1:9-15, 20), and the Kenites (1:16) in Southern Canaan, where certain districts remained unconquered (1:19, 21). *b.* Central Canaan: Joseph at Bethel (1:22-26); unconquered cities (1:27-29).

314

c. Northern Canaan: limited conquests of Zebulon (1:30), Asher (1:31 f.), and Naphtali (1:33). *d.* Dan in the South (1:34 f.). *e.* The border of the Edomites (so, with some recensions of the LXX, instead of Amorites; 1:36), an isolated fragment more appropriate if following 1:17 or 1:16. *f.* A denunciation by an angel at Bochim (2:1-5).

2. The Judges. *a.* Introductory religious characterization of the whole period (2:6-3:6). *b.* Othniel of Judah delivers Israel from Cushan-rishathaim (3:7-11). *c.* Ehud of Benjamin assassinates Eglon king of Moab (3:12-30). *d.* Shamgar slaughters the Philistines (3:31). *e.* Deborah and Barak at the head of Zebulon and Naphtali defeat Sisera and subdue Jabin king of Hazor (4), an exploit celebrated in Deborah's triumphal ode (5). *f.* Gideon (Jerubbaal) of West Manasseh delivers Central Canaan from the depredations of the Bedouins (Midianites and Amalekites) (6-8). *g.* Abimelech is made king of Shechem and then destroys it (9). *h.* Tola of Issachar (10:1 f.). *i.* Jair of Gilead, or East Manasseh (10:3-5). *j.* Jephthah delivers Gilead from the Ammonites (10:6-12:7). *k.* Ibzan of Bethlehem in Zebulon, (12:8-10; Josh. 19:15). *l.* Elon of Zebulon (12:11 f.). *m.* Abdon of Pirathon in Ephraim or Benjamin (12:13-15). *n.* The exploits of Samson the Danite against the Philistines (13-16).

3. Appendix. *a.* The Danites, after carrying away the priest and sacred objects of Micah, conquer Laish and rename it Dan (17-18). *b.* Following the outrage at Gibeah against the concubine of a Levite, the tribe of Benjamin is nearly wiped out in an Israelitic crusade (19-21).

Like Joshua, Judges is essentially a Deuteronomistic book dating from about 550. Nevertheless, there are far-reaching differences in the structure and substance of the two books. In Joshua, the Deuteronomists edited extensively in the style of Deuteronomy the stories of JE, which were E for the most part, and by pious speeches gave to the book a pervasive religious character. But in Judges, where J material abounds in JE, they contented themselves with religious introductions and conclusions to the stories. The easily recognized Deuteronomistic framework and late glosses may be removed without difficulty, and J and E readily separated in most cases making it possible to reach J and E stories in practically unadulterated form. The literary excellence of these stories, particularly those in J, makes of Judges a book far superior to Joshua as literature and history. Indeed, it is second only to the most ancient, most brilliant pages of Samuel and Genesis, which with Judges contain the best prose in the Old Testament.

The use of the symbols J and E, to indicate the two old strands of narrative in Judges, is merely a matter of convenience and need not imply that the same authors wrote J and E in Judges as well as J and E in Genesis, respectively. Identity of authorship is rejected by some critics and cannot be proved. We have seen that J and E continue without a break from the Pentateuch to Joshua, and they could have closed with the occupation of Canaan, as P actually did. On the whole (except for Judg. 1), J and E in Judges are more closely connected with the two sources of Samuel than with J and E in Joshua, although Judg. 17-18 is summarized in Josh. 19:47.

1. J in Judges

The J narratives preserved in Judges have come down through different channels. Some parts of J originally excluded from the Deuteronomistic book were added from J as a separate book, in a late postexilic edition (1:1-2:5; 17-21); or from JE, where J appeared either with (9) or without E (5; 16). Other parts of J were copied into the Deuteronomistic Book of Judges from JE (J in 3:16-4:24; 6:1-8:35; 10:6-12:7, where it is combined with E, and in 13-15, where there are no traces of E). As a result of these vicissitudes in transmission, the original place of 17-18; 19-21 cannot be surmised, and in general the stories of J are now disarranged and variously supplemented or glossed. The secondary material, either E or glosses, is lacking in the stories of Samson (13-16) and in the Song of Deborah (5), assuming of course that the latter was part of J. In its most corrupt and glossed form, J appears in ch. 1.

The summary of J's account of the occupation of Canaan (1:1-2:5), notwithstanding the historically absurd initial gloss, "And it came to pass after the death of Joshua" (1:1aα), logically belongs to the Book of Joshua. As we have seen in the preceding chapter, the full account of these events given in J was suppressed, leaving only a meager epitome. Excerpts were quoted, in their appropriate place in Joshua, to supplement P's account of the allotment of Canaan, and in the late fourth or third century a partly rewritten and annotated edition was inserted at the beginning of Judges, thereby breaking the natural connection between Josh. 24:28-31 and Judg. 2:6-9. The text of the J summary is purer in Joshua, where no trace of late rewriting and glossing such as we have in Judg. 1 can be detected.

These late editors of Judg. 1 substituted Judah for Caleb in 1:10 (contrast 1:20b; Josh. 15:13-19) and Benjamin for Judah in 1:21 (contrast Josh. 15:63), according to subsequent notions of territorial divisions. They also inserted general summaries (1:4, 9) and, with utter disregard for well-known historical facts, attributed to Judah, at the time of the invasion, the conquest of Jerusalem (1:8; cf. 1:7b and contrast 1:21), which was first taken by David, as well as the conquest of the Philistine cities of Gaza, Ashkelon, and Ekron (1:18, contradicting 1:19). In 2:1-5, only the first and last words are attributed to J, "And the angel of Jehovah went up from Gilgal to Bethel [so with the conflated LXX instead of Bochim] . . . and they sacrificed there to Jehovah." The rest, explaining the origin of the name Bochim (i.e., "Weepers"), may be safely regarded as an expression of our editor's indignation for the failure of the Israelites to exterminate all the Canaanites. The Deuteronomic editors of Judges patently knew this summary of J (2:23a; 3:2a, 5a, 6), although they did their best to suppress it.

The J stories of the judges in 3:16-16:31, whether combined with E or not, are notably free from the late postexilic commentary so conspicuous in 1:1-2:5 and 17-21. In the central part of the book, J relates the deeds of the tribal leaders of Israel and of Samson, a folk-tale hero. Ehud (3:15aβ-29; the beginning and end are partly rewritten by R^D), a left-handed Benjaminite, was sent east of the Jordan bearing the tribute of his tribe to Eglon king of Moab. After assassinating Eglon, Ehud escaped and defeated the Moabitic army of occupation west of the Jordan. Aroused by Deborah and Barak, the tribes of Israel north and south of the plain of Jezreel defeated Sisera, who was struck dead with a hammer by Jael while drinking the milk she had offered him (5, the Song of Deborah, probably included in J).

The presence of E and of editorial material in the stories of Gideon and Jephthah (6-8; 10:6-12:7) raises some difficulties as to the identification of J. On the contrary, all attempts to discover E material in the story of Ehud have led to questionable results.

The J story of Gideon (called Jerubbaal in E, although the two names are used indiscriminately in JE) must have begun with an account of the raids of the nomadic Midianites—camel-riding Bedouins—who carried off the harvest of the farmers in West Manasseh (6:2-6a, JE). The angel of Jehovah (i.e., Jehovah himself) appeared to Gideon at Ophra, assuring him of divine help in the war against the Midianites both by word and through a miracle; Gideon erected an altar and called it "Yahweh— Shalom," meaning "Jehovah is safety" (6:11-24, omitting the glosses of R^{JE} in 6:13b, 17b, 20, 21bβ). He blew his horn, summoned his clan Abiezer to battle (6:34), and encamped early in the morning opposite his foes (7:1). Creeping into the enemy camp that night, Gideon heard a Midianite tell a dream that foreshadowed Israel's victory (7:9-15; omitting 7:12, R^{JE}, and some slight editorial retouches). Surrounding the enemy camp, Gideon's men, at his signal, broke the earthen jars in which lighted torches had been hidden, and shouted the battle cry. The Midianites fled in terror (7:16-22, JE; J's remnants are found in 7:16bβ, 17a, 19bβ, 20aβb, 21 and part of 7:22b). In hot pursuit across the Jordan, Gideon was refused food for his men by the chiefs of Succoth and Penuel (8:4-9; 8:10aβb is a gloss of R^{JE}). After capturing the two kings of the Midianites, Zebah and Zalmunna (8:11 f.), Gideon punished the men of Succoth and Penuel on the way back (8:13-17) and slew Zebah and Zalmunna to avenge his brothers killed in the raid (8:18-21). From the golden earrings among the spoils yielded by the defeated Bedouins, Gideon made an ephod weighing 1,700 shekels, or about 65 pounds (8:24a, 25, 26a, 27aα; the rest of vv. 24-27 has been added by R^{JE} and R^D). The word "ephod" does not refer to an idol, as the Deuteronomist assumed in 8:27aβb, but is a surrogate for "ark," or sacred box used by the priests in divining (W. R. Arnold, *Ephod and Ark,* pp. 125, 128).

In the dramatic story of the brief reign of Gideon's son, Abimelech, over Shechem, R^{JE} primarily utilized the E narrative but inserted into it a solid block of J (9:26-41). Perhaps in 9:1-6, 21, 42-54 there is a J substratum in the E narrative. But if such is the case, it has been so thoroughly rewritten that it is now unrecognizable. However, in style and historical objectivity, Judg. 9 is one of the outstanding remnants of the ancient literature of Israel.

As in the story of Gideon, J and E are so closely intertwined in some parts of the Jephthah narrative ([10:17 f.] 11:1-12:7) that the separate stories are only imperfectly preserved. According to the J narrative, Jephthah, driven from his home because of his illegitimate birth, collected a band of outlaws at Tob (northeast of Gilead) and became a freebooter (11:1a, 3). Attacked by the Ammonites, the Gileadites promised to make him their ruler if he delivered them from their enemies (11:4, 5b-11). "And the spirit of Jehovah came upon Jephthah . . . and from Mizpah of Gilead he went over to the Ammonites [the rest of 11:29 is R^{JE}] . . . to fight with them. And Jehovah delivered them into his hand. And he smote them from Aroer to the approach to Minnith" (11:32aβb, 33aα; the rest is E, JE, and R^D). On the pretext that they had not been summoned to battle, the Ephraimites crossed the Jordan and threatened Jephthah; but he defeated them and, seizing the fords of the river, slew those who betrayed their Ephraimitic origin by pronouncing "*shibbōleth*" (meaning an ear of grain or, rather, a flood) as "*sibbōleth*" (12:1-6, omitting the unintelligible gloss in 12:4bβ, "because they said, etc."). The number of fallen Ephraimites at the end—42,000—is of course a redactional exaggeration.

The Samson stories (13-16) belong to J except for 13:1; 15:20; 16:31b, R^D's framework, and a few insignificant glosses in 13:3bβ ("but you shall conceive, etc."), 19bβ ("and Manoah and his wife, etc."); "and his mother" in 14:2 f.; 14:4b (cf. 15:11); "and his father and mother" in 14:5a; 14:6b; "to take her" in 14:8; "his father" in 14:10a, 11a; 16:2aβ; the lacuna in the Hebrew text between 16:13 and 16:14 should be restored from the LXX (extant in two recensions). That these stories, although possibly of various origin, form a single cycle and obviously belong to the oldest stratum of the book is certain. The arguments advanced by critics favoring an E authorship or an analysis into two sources are unconvincing.

The Samson cycle is well arranged in structure, narrating the adventures of the hero in chronological order, from birth to death. Samson's birth was divinely announced in advance to his mother, who was barren, with strict injunctions to observe certain abstentions until his arrival, and to make him a Nazarite devotee as soon as he came (13:2-14). Her husband, Manoah, who was next told, offered a sacrifice (13:15-23), and eventually Samson was born, with the spirit of Jehovah in him (13:24 f.).

The first group of Samson's adventures resulted from his determination to marry a Philistine woman of Timnath (14-15). On the way to visit her, he killed a lion, and on a later journey found the carcass occupied by bees (14:1-9). At the wedding festivities he propounded a riddle suggested by the lion and the bees (14:10-14). The thirty companions of the bridegroom learned the answer from the bride-to-be (14:15-18) and Samson, killing thirty men to obtain their raiment, paid his forfeit. But his bride was married to one of the companions (14:19 f.). To avenge himself, he burned the standing grain of Timnath; the Philistines in retaliation burned the bride and her father, whom Samson avenged with great slaughter (15:1-8). The Judeans, among whom Samson had escaped, brought him bound to the Philistines (15:9-13). But he killed a thousand of them with the jawbone of an ass at Ramath Lehi, which J interpreted as "The Throwing of the Jawbone," but which really means "The Height of Lehi" (15:14-17). To quench his thirst, God "clave the Mortar (*Maktesh*) which is in Lehi," and the miraculous spring was called *En ha-qōrē*, interpreted by J as the "Spring of the Caller," although the actual meaning was probably "Partridge Spring" (15:18 f.). After Samson had lodged with a harlot at Gaza, he escaped from a Philistine ambush by carrying away the city gates to a hill near Hebron (16:1-3).

The stories of Samson and Delilah and of his death (16:4-31a) close the cycle. Importuned by Delilah, who had been bribed by the Philistines to discover the source of his strength, Samson deceived her three times (16:4-15) but finally disclosed to her that he was a Nazarite from birth and that his strength depended on his hair which had never been cut (16:16 f.). The Philistines, after cutting his hair and blinding him, set him to work at a hand mill in prison (16:18-22). Brought to the Temple of Dagon during a festival, Samson, whose strength had returned, overthrew the two pillars supporting the roof and died in the ruins along with the Philistines (16:23-31a).

In a literary analysis of the stories of Samson, it is essential to distinguish the oral sources utilized by J from the contribution made by the brilliant author. In their preliterary stage, these stories were a cycle of folk tales of great interest to comparative folklorists on account of their antiquity. They are well-nigh unique in early literatures as examples of rustic fiction. The great epics of India, the *Iliad*, and J represent material sung by bards at court or in polite circles. The stories of Samson are instead told by wandering storytellers to rustic village audiences. The hero lacks the refinement of a Joseph or an Achilles, but possesses traits dear to simple and healthy rural folk. Always brawling and excelling all rivals in muscular strength, this uncouth fellow is no match for feminine wiles. But under the rough exterior there is a witty if untutored mind, quick at repartee, an instinctive devotion to his own people, and a dogged determination in avenging wrongs, which culminates in a self-inflicted heroic death. Samson is a sort of irresponsible and uncontrollable Till Eulenspiegel or Peer Gynt.

Without denying that certain traits of solar mythology may have indirectly contributed something to the adventures and character of Samson, it must be said, in view of the numerous mythological interpretations of the Samson sagas,[1] that both the popular storytellers and J believed the hero to be a man of flesh and blood, although endowed with fabulous strength. Whether they went so far as to consider Samson a historical character we cannot say. In any case, like all good raconteurs, they spun their tales vividly, as actual happenings. The brilliant personality of the J author would be much clearer to us if we knew whether he regarded Abraham, Joseph, and Samson as no less historically real than David and Solomon—an academic question which, for lack of clues, must remain unanswered.

In any case, J placed Samson in a definite geographical and historical environment—near Zorah, in the century 1150-1050 B.C. When the pressure of the Philistines became intolerable, the tribe of Dan, to which Samson and his father Manoah belonged (13:2), migrated from Zorah and Eshtaol (18:2, 8, 11), less than 20 miles west of Jerusalem near Beth-shemesh, to Laish (Dan) in the extreme North of Palestine. It is probable that in the oral tradition Samson was already a symbol of the early stages of the ineffective Israelitic resistance to Philistine domination. The political situation, however, is usually secondary in fairy tales. It was this minor element in the stories, the unremitting singlehanded battle of Samson with the Philistine masters of Israel, which induced J to incorporate them into his epic of Israel, making of Samson a sort of precursor and shadow of Saul (13:5; cf. J. Wellhausen, *Die Composition des Hexateuchs*, p. 231). The contribution of J was the patriotic fervor and divine calling of Samson. J infused the dominant thoughts of his epic into these crude rustic tales, without spoiling their pristine freshness. He combined in superb fashion great ideals with superlative art. His

---

[1] On the mythological interpretation of Samson, see G. F. Moore, *Judges* (ICC), pp. 364 f. For the older literature, see H. Stahn, *Die Simsonsage*, 1908. See also A. Smythe Palmer, *The Samson-saga, and Its Place in Comparative Religion*, 1913. P. Carus, *The Story of Samson*, Chicago, 1907. C. F. Burney, *The Book of Judges*, pr 391-408. 2nd ed., London, 1920.

noble religious and patriotic spirit is particularly conspicuous in the story of Samson's birth (13), which came substantially from his pen, as W. Böhme (ZAW 5 [1885] 251-274) has shown, and in the tragic end of the cycle (16:23-31a). Elsewhere, J limited himself to light touches. The long hair, which in the popular tales constituted the secret of Samson's strength, was connected by J with the Nazarite vow (13:5, 7; 16:17; cf. I Sam. 1:11; Num. 6:5). In addition, however, J frequently attributed the mighty exploits of Samson not to the mysterious power of the hair but to a sudden infusion of divine spirit (14:6, 19; 15:14; cf. 13:25; 15:18 f.; 16:20), as in the case of other heroes (6:34; I Sam. 11:6, etc.). This trait was apparently lacking in the old stories (15:8; 16:9, etc.), where nothing was known of a Nazarite vow taken by the hero. The hand of J also appears in other references to Jehovah's participation in human affairs (14:4a; 15:18 f.; 16:20, 28 f.); in the tales loosely connected with Samson (15:17-19) giving fictitious etymologies of place names, a favorite device of J, and in the frank admission of the humiliating Philistine oppression and Judah's resignation (15:9-13)—but not without allusion to future deliverance through Saul and David (13:5).

The two stories following the Samson sagas, in the appendix to the Book of Judges (17-18 and 19-21), are radically different from the rest of the book but belong to its oldest stratum, which we have called J. They should not be analyzed into several sources but, according to the conclusions of W. R. Arnold (*Ephod and Ark*, pp. 95-122), into an ancient narrative, a late commentary incorporated into the text, and scattered glosses. His analysis is substantially adopted here.

In their original form, these ancient narratives were written by the author of the early source of Samuel (Arnold, *Ephod and Ark*, p. 99). This brilliant historian, who may or may not be identical with J, regarded the monarchy as the crowning achievement of Israel's glorious progress, in contrast with later writers who condemned it as an apostasy. The shocking stories of public and private lawlessness in Judg. 17-21 are told for the purpose of showing how urgent was the need for a king's central authority: "in those times there was no king in Israel" (18:1; 19:1). To be sure, a king could not have prevented crime itself, but such a state of anarchy among the separate tribes, who acted without regard to a national policy, would at least not have existed under a monarchy. The late glossators, however (17:6; 21:25), were less impressed by the autonomy of the tribes—inconceivable to them, since they regarded Israel as a united theocratic "congregation" (20:1; 21:10, 13, 16)—than by the impertinent violations of the Law of Moses.

Primarily, the story of Judg. 17-18 relates the origin of the sanctuary and clergy at Dan, and incidentally the migration of the Danites. Since the Levite seems to be the protagonist, it was probably preserved by his descendants, the priests of Dan. As such, the record is of inestimable value historically, and presents the earliest information on the priesthood in ancient Israel. The original story has been interpolated by a Jew who, long after the Deuteronomic law of 621 had condemned as illegitimate all sanctuaries of Jehovah outside of Jerusalem, wished to show that at Dan they worshiped an idol made of stolen silver (17:2-4 and all references to "graven and molten image" in 17-18).

As this story goes, a prosperous farmer in the Highlands of Ephraim named Micah owned a private shrine and hired a passing Levite as his priest (17:1-13, omitting 17:2-4, 6, 7bβ, 10b). Five scouts were sent out by the Danites, hard pressed by the Philistines at Zorah and Eshtaol, to find a suitable territory elsewhere. The spies obtained from Micah's Levite a favorable oracle, which was gained through the "ephod and teraphim," i.e., the manipulation of lots in the sacred box (18:1-6, omitting 18:1bβ, 2 ["of their family" "men of valor"], 3 ["and what hast thou here"]). They reached Laish, a city isolated and secure, and reported that its conquest would be easy (18:7-10, omitting 7 ["how they dwelt in security after the manner of the Sidonians" "and there was no magistrate . . . in any thing"], 9bβ, 10). On their way northward, the Danites, comprising six hundred fighting men, carried off Micah's Levite with his "ephod and teraphim" (18:11-26, omitting 18:12 [beginning with "in Judah"], 14 ["Laish" "and a graven image and a molten image"], 16b, 17 [from "(and) came in thither"], 18 ["and when these . . . Micah's house" "the graven image of" "and the molten image"], 20 ["and the graven image"]). The Danites then captured Laish, slaughtering the inhabitants and, calling it Dan, settled there (18:27-29, omitting 18:28 ["and it was . . . Beth-rehob"], 29 [from "after the name of Dan"]; in 18:27 add, after "and they took" the words "the ephod [i.e., the ark] and the teraphim").

Two chronological notes have been added at the end of this story. According to the first (18:30), which is earlier than the second, the nameless Levite was Jonathan, grandson of Moses (by the insertion of a suspended "n" in the Hebrew, a horrified reader changed "Moses" into "Manasseh," the detested name of the idolatrous king of Judah), and his descendants continued to officiate until "the depopulation of the land" (perhaps in 734; cf. II Kings 15:29). According to the second note (18:31), the image of Micah remained in the temple of Dan while there was a Temple in Shiloh. Although we do not know exactly when Shiloh was devastated, everything indicates that its sanctuary was destroyed by the Philistines before the reign of David.

The story of Judg. 19-21 deals with the outrage at Gibeah and the resulting war against the Benjamites. A certain Levite residing in the Highlands of Ephraim went to Bethlehem in Judah, thence to bring back his concubine. On his return, he obtained lodging for the night at Gibeah in the house of an old man (19:1-21, omitting 19:6 ["and they drank"], 9 ["behold the day groweth . . . merry" "that thou mayest go home"], 12 f. [from "that is not of . . ."], 16aβb). When some degenerate rascals of the town demanded that the Levite come out to satisfy their sodomitical lust, he surrendered his concubine; the next morning he found her dead (19:22-27, omitting 19:24). From his home, the Levite dispatched parts of her body throughout Israel to urge the punishment of this crime (19:28-30, omitting 19:30 [cf. Codex A of the LXX]). The Israelites assembled in Mizpah and resolved to punish the lawless Benjamites in Gibeah (20:1-11, omitting 20:1 ["and the congregation was gathered from Dan . . . Gilead"], 2a ["of all the people *even*" "in the assembly of the people of God"], 2b, 3a, 3b ["the children of Israel"], 6 ["of the inheritance" "lewdness and"], 9-11). Demands for the surrender of the culprits were refused by the Benjamites, who prepared for war (20:12-17, omitting 20:15-17). The Israelites were defeated in battle (20:18-25, omitting 20:18, 20-23, 24 ["the second day"], 25a ["eighteen thousand" is a correction of the original smaller figure], 25b). Encouraged by a favorable oracle obtained at Bethel, they surrounded Gibeah in ambush, captured it, and slaughtered the Benjamite army as well as the civilian population (20:26-48, omitting 20:26 ["and all the people" "and wept and fasted that day" "and peace offerings"], 27 ["of the covenant"], 28 ["And Phinehas . . . in those days"], 30 ["on the third day . . . times"], 31 ["*and* were drawn away . . . of Israel"], 32-35, 43, 36a, 44b, 45 f., 47 ["four months"]).

The Israelites had sworn not to give their daughters in marriage to the Benjamites but, lest the tribe perish, provided four hundred virgins from Jabesh in Gilead, a town that had not taken part in the war, for four hundred of the six hundred survivors of Benjamin (21:1-14, omitting 21:2-5, 7 ["for them that remain"], 8b, 10 [all but "and they sent thither"], 11, 12 ["by lying with any male" "to Shiloh which is in the land of Canaan"], 13 ["the whole congregation"], 14 ["at that time"; read "had been" for "they had saved alive"]). On the advice of the Israelites, the remaining two hundred Benjamites hid in the vineyards at the time of the festival at Shiloh, and when the maidens came out to dance they each snatched himself a wife and made off for their homes (21:15-25, omitting 21:15-18, 19aβb, 24 f.).

Freed from later accretions, the J narratives in the Book of Judges fall into four groups: the initial occupation of Canaan by the separate tribes (preserved only in a late summary, 1:1-2:5 and scattered verses in

Josh.); the successful wars, under tribal leaders, for consolidation of the conquest (J in 3:16-12:7); the sagas of Samson—a fictional account of the obscure beginnings of the Philistine conflict (13-16); the origin of the sanctuary of Dan (17-18) and the war against the Benjamites (19-21), glaring instances of the state of anarchy which, together with the Philistine subjugation of Israel, made the unification of Israel under a king indispensable for the preservation of the nation. The first two groups of narratives are closely connected with the Book of Joshua, the latter two with the Books of Samuel: J knows nothing of a separate period of the "Judges."

Omitting the stories of Samson, manifestly fiction, the J narratives are invaluable as historical sources. Writing some centuries after the events narrated, and patently lacking any written contemporary documents with the exception of the Song of Deborah, the J author made excellent use of oral traditions still alive among the Israelites of his time. But he could not write a history accurate in all details. As he receded into the past, these oral traditions became more and more legendary, and no historical facts should be expected in the stories about Abraham, Isaac, and Jacob. But the epic struggles for the possession of Canaan did not soon vanish from the memory of the people. In the meager summary of the situation, after the several tribes had gained a foothold, we recognize both the echo of actual tradition and inferences drawn by J from conditions at a later period. For tribal memory remembered only successful operations and soon forgot the failures. J's picture of the sadly incomplete conquest has the purpose of enhancing by contrast the achievements of David and is furnished by his own conclusions, not by tradition.

For the wars with the native population and Bedouin invaders which followed the invasion, J can give us only one side of the picture, the story of successful exploits through which the Israelites consolidated their position. If the Canaanites had survived as a nation, their traditions would have furnished the other side of the picture, the occasions in which Israel was worsted.

The five stories told by J about Ehud, Deborah (Barak), Gideon, Abimelech, and Jephthah are substantially historical, but represent only snapshots of tribal heroic deeds, and not the history of the long period which they cover, with its alternation of peace and war in individual tribal territories. In these stories, as well as in those of chs. 17-21, even though many of the specific details be merely the product of J's vivid imagination and superb literary art, we have not only a fairly accurate report of actual events but an amazing feeling for emotions and characters, besides a genuine picture of social and religious conditions in the somewhat barbaric age when "there was no king in Israel."

2. The Song of Deborah

Although the Song of Deborah (Judg. 5) was probably a part of J, it must be considered separately.[2] This magnificent triumphal ode celebrating the defeat and death of Sisera in the plain of Jezreel, by the brook Kishon near Megiddo, was composed immediately after the victory (about 1150-1100 B.C.). It is therefore one of the earliest extant monuments of Hebrew literature; only a few short poems in the Pentateuch may belong to more ancient times. It is the only important historical source, contemporary with the events described, before the time of David. Deborah, whose enthusiasm stirred Barak and the Israelite tribes to valiant combat, did not compose the ode, as the editorial superscription (5:1, R[JE]) claims. The only basis for such attribution is the Masoretic text of 5:7 ("until I, Deborah, arose"), the LXX and the Latin, however, read, "until she, Deborah, arose," and the Hebrew should probably be rendered, "until thou, Deborah, didst arise." In any case 5:12 ("awake, awake, Deborah") and 5:15 ("and the princes of Issachar were with Deborah") militate against Deborah's authorship.

The ode contains a double exordium: 5:2, which is obscure and corrupt, may be editorial; 5:3, calling upon the kings to hear Jehovah's praises is probably the original beginning. The poem has three main parts: vv. 4-11 (introductory), 12-18 (praise or reproach for the tribes of Israel), and 19-30 (the victorious battle and death of Sisera). It closes with a curse against the enemies and a blessing on the friends of Jehovah (v. 31a; 31b belongs to R[D]'s chronological framework of the book).

From the sacred mountain in Northern Arabia, Jehovah comes forth to battle, marching over the land of Edom (5:4 f., omitting "this is Sinai," an explanatory gloss, in v. 5; cf. Deut. 33:2; Hab. 3:3). At that time, the Israelites on the edges of the Jezreel plain, harassed by the Canaanites, could not send forth their caravans and were forced to abandon their unprotected villages (5:6-8, omitting "in the days of Jael" in v. 6; the text of 5:7a, 8a is corrupt). The following verses (5:9-11), hopelessly corrupt and unintelligible for the most part, may either have taken up again the praise of Jehovah from v. 3 or, if 5:11b is really the conclusion of this section, they may have described the preparations for battle.

After a spirited appeal to Deborah and Barak (5:12) comes the roll call of the ten tribes of Israel (5:13-18), which does not yet include Judah, Simeon, and Levi in the South. In spite of the serious textual corruption in 5:13-15, it is still possible to see that only six tribes, Ephraim,

---

[2] G. F. Moore (*Judges* (ICC), pp. 127-173), in the opinion of the present writer, has given us the best study of the Song of Deborah. Except in minor points, his views have generally been adopted here. C. F. Burney (*The Book of Judges*, pp. 94-176) supplements Moore in numerous matters of detail, has a good bibliography and a careful study of the meter of the song.

Benjamin, Machir (Manasseh) (5:14), south of the Jezreel plain, and Zebulon (5:14, 18), Issachar (5:15a), and Naphtali (5:18) north of it, valiantly came forth to fight Sisera. Remote from the field of operations either east of the Jordan—Reuben (5:15b repeated by mistake in 5:16b) and Gilead (Gad) (5:17)—or far north of the plain—Dan and Asher (5:17)—the other four tribes, not being involved directly in the *casus belli*, refused to lend their aid.

The chariots of Sisera and of his vassals charged the Israelites "at Taanach by the waters of Megiddo." But Jehovah intervened in behalf of his people. "The stars in their courses fought against Sisera" and, swollen by a heavy rainstorm, "the brook Kishon swept away" the foes (5:19-22).

After cursing the village of Meroz for not halting the flight of the vanquished foes, the poet blesses Jael for killing Sisera (5:23 f., omitting "the wife of Heber the Kenite," a gloss from 4:17, in 5:24). In his flight, Sisera had stopped at the tent of Jael to ask for a drink of water. She gave him a cup of sour milk and, as he raised it to his lips, she struck a deadly blow on his temple with a mallet or heavy club (5:25-27).

Unaware that her son was lying dead at the feet of Jael, the mother of Sisera peered anxiously out of the window awaiting his return, while her princesses suggested that he had been detained by the wealth of spoils to be divided (5:28-30). In closing, the poet addressed to Jehovah his wish that all Jehovah's enemies might perish like Sisera, and all his friends be like the sun, rising in its glory at dawn (5:31a).

The Song of Deborah is the finest masterpiece of Hebrew poetry and deserves a place among the best songs of victory ever written. The consummate literary art manifested therein is spontaneous and unconscious, and the genuine inspiration of the poet is evident. His burning passion, patriotic as well as religious, fired his thoughts to white heat, while an instinctive literary sense simultaneously molded them into patterns of arresting beauty. With fine dramatic sense the poet sketches a series of separate scenes, each of which is self-contained, to break off abruptly at the climax, leaving to the reader's imagination a vision of the inevitable sequel. Yet these abrupt individual scenes with their natural movement are molded into one dramatic whole, from the coming of Jehovah to help his people in distress and the rising up in arms of the tribes to the divinely sent storm, that brought victory against the dreaded chariots of iron, and the tragic end of Sisera, whose return is vainly awaited by a mother filled with premonitions of disaster.

The textual corruption of the central part of the poem, apparently due to a defective manuscript, is earlier than the Greek translation and probably antedates the insertion of the ode in our book. Even the better-preserved portions at the beginning and end have presented serious difficulties to students of Hebrew meters. We can safely assert, however, that the prevailing rhythm is the usual Hebrew rhythm, the verse being of a variable number of syllables with four beats to the half-line. For instance:

′   ′   ′   ′   ′   ′   ′   ′

Water he asked, milk she gave / In a lordly bowl she offered sour milk.

In some cases, however, the regularity of this rhythm is marred by the presence of a third half-line, notably in 5:3, 7, 15a, 21, 27. In most of these cases, we may assume that the text has suffered conflation or loss, although the drastic emendations required to restore the correct rhythm can never pass beyond the stage of conjecture and inevitably mar the beauty and power of the style. It is characteristic of many of the lines of this poem that the second half-line picks up the thought from the middle or end of the first half-line and brings it to completion (cf. C. F. Burney, *The Books of Judges,* pp. 169-171). This so-called "climactic" parallelism may be schematically represented thus: a-b / b-c. For instance:

From heaven fought the stars / From their courses they fought against Sisera.

Aside from literary charm, the Song of Deborah is invaluable as a contemporary source, furnishing us with a unique touchstone in gauging the credibility of other sources for the early stages of the history and religion of Israel. When the poem was composed, the tribes of Israel had, several decades after their invasion of Canaan described in Judg. 1, established themselves firmly in the hilly regions north and south of the plain of Jezreel. But the Canaanites still controlled the great plain through the strategic fortifications at Taanach, Megiddo, and Bethshean. Thus they were able to cut off communications over the great roads, and even to drive the Israelite farmers from their villages. We may surmise that the victory against Sisera, significant and portentous though it was, brought only temporary relief to the Israelites, who did not become masters of the plain until the time of David, after the Philistines had gained control over it.

Historically, however, the ode is more significant for its implications than for the victory it celebrates. The bond uniting the ten autonomous and scattered tribes was the worship of Jehovah, "the God of Israel (5:3). Israel was not yet a state but already "the people of Jehovah" (5:11, 13). Jehovah did not yet reside in Canaan but in the distant sacred mountain, somewhere in Northern Arabia, where Moses discovered his presence in a burning bush and whither Elijah went to hear his "still small voice" (I Kings 19:12). Thus this ancient *Te Deum* in praise of Jehovah, the God of Israel, confirms the work of Moses beyond the shadow of a doubt. By instilling in certain tribes of Israel an undying loyalty to the god of a remote mountain, a god willing and able to discomfit their foes, Moses simultaneously created a national feeling and religious faith, inseparable and imperishable, impervious to attack up to the present day.

3. E in Judges

The E stories in Judges possess neither the qualities of style nor the historicity of the J stories. The judges are no longer tribal leaders but national rulers like Joshua (in E) and the first three kings of Israel. It may be surmised that the E stories were originally written in the Northern Kingdom about 740 B.C. or soon after, although, to a lesser degree than in Joshua, they have been supplemented and revised by later hands or closely interwoven with J. A clue to the contents of E in Judges is furnished by I Sam. 12:11, which belongs to its later strata: "And Jehovah sent Jerubbaal, and Bedan [read "Barak" with the LXX and the Peshitta], and Jephthah, and Samuel, and delivered you out of the hand of your enemies on every side, and ye dwelt in safety." Except for the omission of Abimelech, which causes no surprise, this may be considered a summary of E in Judges and I Sam. 1-12. In contrast with J, it is significant that Gideon is called Jerubbaal, that Barak is mentioned instead of Deborah, and that Ehud and Samson are missing.

J had no introduction to his collection of stories, and it is by no means certain that E had such an introduction in its original form, as most critics assume. For Judg. 2:6, 8 f., which belongs to E or E², really marks the end of E's account of the final address of Joshua at Shechem (Josh. 24:28-31; Judg. 2:7 = Josh. 24:31 is Deuteronomistic), and the account of the nation's apostasy following in 2:10, 13, 20 f., and often attributed to E together with other parts of 2:6-3:6, is closer to D than to E. At most, it may be regarded as E².

The story of the victory of Barak over Sisera in Judg. 4 (E) has been contaminated, by RJE and RD, through allusions to J's account of the exploit of Zebulon and Naphtali against Jabin king of Hazor. An echo of the latter survives in the late text of Josh. 11:1-9; cf. Judg. 4:1-3, 23 f. (RD). We may attribute to RJE the references to Jabin (4:7, 17) and to Kedesh in Naphtali (4:6, 9, 10 f.), the natural rallying point for an attack against Jabin. Even later is the gloss in 4:5, which locates Deborah's residence in Ephraim, near Bethel, confusing our Deborah with Rebekah's nurse (Gen. 35:8) who had the same name.

The account of the defeat and death of Sisera (4:4-22, E, omitting the above-mentioned additions), told of Deborah's appeal to Barak (4:4-9), his victory at the head of Zebulon and Naphtali over Sisera at Mount Tabor (4:10-16), and the latter's death, in his sleep, at the hand of Jael (4:17-22). This story differs in important details from the Song of Deborah (5): here only two, not six, tribes take part in the war (4:10) and Sisera was pierced through the temple by Jael while sleeping (4:21), not savagely hit on the head while drinking sour milk outside the tent. Several particulars given in the prose account of E are missing in the ode: the name of Deborah's husband (4:4), the number of Barak's men (4:10, 14) and Sisera's chariots (4:13), the name of Sisera's capital (4:13, 16), and the mustering of the Israelites at Mount Tabor (4:6, 12, 14). It is therefore highly improbable that E's version is derived from the poem. The prose account is substantially based on oral tradition circulating some centuries after the poem was composed. It is therefore instructive to note, in this one instance when both a contemporaneous report and a later tradition are extant, how faithful tradition could be in the essential facts, yet how fanciful in a number of details.

The E stories of Jerubbaal (Gideon in J) contain E^2 material, i.e., pious denunciations and exhortations in the vein of Deuteronomy, although somewhat earlier (about 650). Thus, at the beginning of the story, Jehovah sent a prophet to the Israelites oppressed by the Midianites to rebuke them for disregarding the law forbidding worship of the gods of the Amorites (6:7-10, E^2; cf. 2:1b-5a; 10:11-16; I Sam. 7:3 f.; 10:17-19; 12:6-25; Ex. 20:2 f.). Later editors omitted the end of the address. In E^2 this divine oracle was followed by its practical application. That very night, Jehovah ordered Gideon to destroy the altar and the sacred post of Baal belonging to his father, and to offer sacrifice on Jehovah's altar which he was to build. Upon discovering this sacrilege, the villagers wished to put Gideon to death (6:25-30, omitting 6:28b). But his father Joash rescued him by remarking, "Will ye contend for Baal? Or will ye save him? If he be a god let him contend [*yareb*] for himself" (6:31; the other words of Joash are spurious). Accordingly, Gideon was called "Jerubbaal," interpreted as meaning, "Let Baal contend," although the real etymology may be quite different (6:32; cf. G. F. Moore, *Judges* [ICC], *ad loc.*).

The story of the divine call to Gideon to deliver his people in E has been omitted by R^{JE}, who preferred the J account in 6:11-24, except for its conclusion in 6:36-40. Likewise, E's account of the raids of the Midianites and of the mustering of the Israelites under Gideon's command, except for possible traces, is lost. We pick up the thread of E after a large body of Israelites has been mobilized. Jehovah, however, did not allow such numerous forces to go into battle, lest they attribute the victory to their own power rather than to divine intervention. After eliminating those cowards (the majority) who drank water from their hands, only the three hundred who lapped water like dogs were retained (7:2-8; in 7:6 the gloss "with their hands to their mouth" belongs at the end of the verse). Although the story is substantially E, the hand of R^{JE} may be detected throughout.

According to E, Gideon threw the Midianite camp into panic by surrounding it at night with three hundred men, who at a given signal blew a fanfare of trumpets and shouted, "For Jehovah and for Gideon!" But E's story (7:16-21) has been confused by R^JE, who combined it with J's story in which the Israelites at a given signal shattered jars concealing lighted torches. Gideon pursued the Midianites and had the Ephraimites cut off their retreat; the two chiefs of the Midianites, Oreb ("Raven") and Zeeb ("Wolf"), were captured and slain (7:22-25, omitting the editorial notes in 7:22aα, 23, "and also the Jordan" in 7:24; "beyond the Jordan" in 7:25). Gideon then tactfully appeased the anger of the Ephraimites, who resented having been called in only after the victory had been won (8:1-3). When the Israelites offered the royal crown to Gideon and his descendants, he piously refused, regarding the monarchy as an apostasy (8:22 f., E²; cf. I Sam. 8:7; 10:19; 12:12). "And Jerubbaal the son of Joash went and dwelt in his own house" (8:29) concludes the E story.

The finest of the E stories in Judges is that of Abimelech, son of Gideon (9:1-25, 42-57). Aided by his mother's kinsmen in Shechem, he slew the seventy sons of Gideon, except Jotham, and made himself king in their place (9:1-6). From the top of Mount Gerizim, Jotham denounced Abimelech and the Shechemites by reciting the fable of the trees which offered the crown to the useless boxthorn after worthier trees had refused it (9:7-21). E probably did not find this charming fable in the traditional story of Abimelech but obtained it from folk wisdom—source of the similar apologue in II Kings 14:9. He inserted it here to voice his indignation against Abimelech's highhanded and dastardly act, if not to contest (as E² does; cf. 8:23 above) the divine sanction of the monarchy in general. The practical application of this fable in E (9:16a, 19b, 20), foreshadowed in 9:15, questioned the mutual loyalty and good faith of Abimelech and the Shechemites and foresaw the tragic results of their later discord. R^JE, however, inconsistently disregarded the clear purport of the fable and questioned the Shechemites' loyalty to Jerubbaal and his house (9:16b-19a, 56 f.), not to Abimelech. As punishment for their evil deeds, God sent a spirit of mutual treachery between Abimelech and the Shechemites, and the latter proceeded to raid passing caravans (9:22-25; 9:22, 24 look like expansions by R^JE). On the day following the report of these raids (9:25b), Abimelech by a military stratagem defeated the forces of the Shechemites and destroyed their city (9:42-45).

When the people of the Tower of Shechem sought refuge in the crypt (?) of the temple of El Berith (or Baal Berith; cf. 9:4: numen or Baal of the covenant), Abimelech burnt the temple over their heads so that none escaped (9:46-49). Finally he attacked Thebez, where a woman on the walls threw an upper millstone on his head. Mortally wounded, he ordered his armor-bearer to slay him (9:50-55). The lesson drawn from this story in 9:56 f. (cf. above) could be assigned to E or E², but probably comes from the pen of RᴶᴱE.

In the E story, Jephthah is not an illegitimate son who becomes a bandit, as in J, but the respected owner of a house in Mizpah where he lived with his daughter. The notice in 11:1, "and Gilead begot Jephthah," is, however, editorial and rests on a confusion between his tribe (Gilead) and parentage. The account of the futile negotiations of Jephthah with the king of "the Ammonites" in 11:12-28 (E² or RᴶᴱE) refers exclusively to relations with the Moabites. It is therefore probable that E told of Jephthah's war with the Moabites and that, in harmony with the J story, RᴶᴱE changed "Moabites" to "Ammonites" throughout the E story. Otherwise 11:12-28 must be considered a late interpolation intended to defend Israel's title to the land betwen the Arnon and Jabbok (G. F. Moore, *Judges* [ICC], p. 283).

After promising Jehovah the life of "whatsoever" came out of his house when he returned victorious (11:30 f.), Jephthah defeated the "Moabites" (11:32aα, 33b; E's account, combined with J's and interpolated, is mostly lost). When he returned in triumph, his daughter came from the house dancing joyfully. Brokenhearted, the father had to sacrifice his daughter, his only child. She submitted stoically, asking only for two months' respite to bewail her virginity. Thus originated the custom for the women of Israel to lament the sad fate of Jephthah's daughter every year for four days (11:34-40). In E, the story of Jephthah explains primarily the annual rite of mourning observed by the Gileadite women. A mythological interpretation of the story, suggested by the vaguely similar sacrifice of Iphigenia by her father Agamemnon, is farfetched. In any case, the E author had no notion of an underlying myth in which a god died and was ritually mourned; his purpose in telling this story, as in that of the sacrifice of Isaac (Gen. 22:1-13, 19), also from his pen, was to discourage the sacrifices of first-born.

In the E stories there is far greater emphasis on morality and religion than in J, where the tone is frankly patriotic and religion essentially nationalistic. In E there are echoes of the prophets' teachings, particularly of Hosea who, like Jotham, considered most kings a liability for the nation. At his best, in the stories of Abimelech and the vow of Jephthah, E is less virile and more tender than J. Tribal discords leading to slaughters in J (12:1-6; 20) are settled amicably in E (8:1-3). In its later strata (E²), E approaches the horror which the Deuteronomic Code felt for the cults of Canaan, and anticipates its assurance that Jehovah's blessings on his people are conditioned by the fulfillment of the divine will.

4. The Successive Editions of Judges

If E² had already been added to E (as there is reason to believe) when J and E were united by the JE redactor (RᴶᴱE) into a single book, the date of R^{JE} is about 630-600 B.C. Otherwise it could be as early as 650. This edition had a general introduction, which was substantially that of E^2 (2:6, 8-10, 13, 20 f.), perhaps with some expansions of R^{JE} in other parts of 2:6-3:6 (particularly 2:23; 3:2a, 4-6), and contained the stories of Ehud (3:15-29), Deborah and Barak (4:4-22; 5:2-31a), Gideon (6:7-8:28; it is possible, however, that 8:4-21, J, was left out by R^{JE} and R^D), Abimelech (9), Jephthah (11:1-12:6), and Samson (13:2-16:31a, omitting 15:20). In addition, JE contained the brief standardized stories of the five "minor judges" in 10:1-5; 12:8-15, who governed Israel a total of seventy years. Nothing is said of their exploits. Information about them is confined to their name and locality, length of rule, and place of burial, with the exception of Jair, Ibzan, and Abdon for whom the number of sons and grandsons and evidence of affluence are also given. The names of these minor judges occur elsewhere (except for Ibzan and Abdon) as clans.

The period of seventy years during which they ruled consecutively has no place in the chronological scheme of the Deuteronomistic book, although J. Wellhausen (*Prolegomena*, p. 226) has noted that this period corresponds almost exactly with the total of the oppression periods separating the individual major judges (71 years). Moreover, the Deuteronomistic rhythm of oppression and deliverance is excluded in the time of the minor judges. It is therefore clear that they were not included in the Deuteronomistic book but were added later to obtain a total of "twelve" judges. There is, however, no reason for assuming that the minor judges were not included in JE, but the source of these stories beyond this point is entirely unknown.

In all probability the stories of the judges were supplied in JE with introductions and conclusions. This is particularly obvious in the case of the story of Abimelech (9), omitted in the Deuteronomistic edition. The conclusion of R^{JE} is still intact (9:56 f.), and there are obvious traces of his introduction in R^D's substitute for ch. 9 in 8:30-35. We may surmise that the Deuteronomistic introductions in 3:12-15a; 4:1-3; 6:1-6; 10:17 f., and conclusions in 3:30; 4:23 f.; 8:28; 12:7, are in part based on JE material.

In combining J and E, R^{JE} used different methods. Sometimes, as in ch. 9, he reproduced both sources substantially intact, dovetailing them. At other times, he amalgamated fragments from J and E so inextricably that the resulting narrative is utter confusion (7:16-21; 11:32 f.). Occasionally, he contaminated an E narrative with J (4) or revised E (7:2-8; 9:16-25; 11:12-28), but fortunately in general he gave preference to J. From J he reproduced the stories of Ehud and Samson in full (with some contaminations from another source in the Ehud story). However, he omitted the J stories in 1 and 17-21 and possibly 8:4-21, to judge from its present awkward position.

While most of the additions of R^{JE} are merely harmonistic (e.g., references to Kedesh in 4:6, 9, 10 f.; and 4:17b; 6:35b; 7:25), this editor occasionally discloses his moral and religious point of view, notably in 6:13b; 7:2b; 9:16b-19a, 24, 56 f. In the general introduction to the book, it is difficult to determine whether the explanation of the incomplete conquest as a test of Israel's faith (2:22) belongs to E^2 or R^{JE}, since their viewpoints are often similar.

The Deuteronomistic edition of Judges (R^D) was prepared after the tragic events of 586, when Jerusalem with its Temple was destroyed and part of the nation taken captive to Babylonia. The purpose of the book was to convince the bewildered and helpless Judeans that this national calamity was not the result of Nebuchadnezzar's imperialistic policy, but Jehovah's punishment for the sins of the people, notably their violation of the Deuteronomic Code. The Deuteronomists endeavored to show that the recent tragedy was neither unprecedented nor necessarily fatal. In their opinion, the nation's entire history proved that its prosperity or misery derived only from Jehovah, who rewarded loyalty to his covenant, and punished apostasy and violation of his Law.

According to the Deuteronomistic introduction (2:6-3:6, in which R^D used earlier materials but wrote at least 2:7, 12, 14b, 15, 18 f.) as well as the Deuteronomistic framework of the stories about individual judges (3:12-15a, 29 f.; 4:1-4, 23 f., 5:31b; 6:1-6; 8:33-35; 10:6-16; 12:7; 13:1; 15:20; 16:31b), the period of Judges is but a rhythmical succession of identical cycles: apostasy, oppression, repentance, and deliverance through a judge. When the Israelites forsook Jehovah for other gods, he delivered them into the hand of their enemies; when in their distress they cried out to him for help and repented, he sent them a deliverer, during whose lifetime they remained loyal to Jehovah. At the death of the judge, the same cycle was repeated. To illustrate better this lesson from history, the Deuteronomists concocted the typical story of Othniel's deliverance of Israel from the oppression of Cushan-rishathaim (meaning "Nubian of double villainy"), at the same time furnishing Judah with a judge (3:7-11; cf. 1:13).

The Deuteronomists made a selection of the JE stories which could be fitted into their scheme of religious pragmatism. The J stories in 1:1-2:5 and 17-21, already omitted in JE, were naturally disregarded although they may well have been known to these editors. They omitted the Song of Deborah (5) as superfluous after the prose story in ch. 4, the story of Abimelech (9)—for which a brief summary (8:30-35) was substituted —as refractory to their historical theories, the summaries about the minor judges (10:1-5; 12:8-15) because they were not deliverers and finally the unedifying story of Samson's sad end through a woman's betrayal (16:1-31a). Shamgar's deliverance of Israel from the Philistines (3:31) is a pure invention of a later editor who was familiar with 5:6 and II Sam. 23:11 f. (cf. Judg. 15:14-16) and ostensibly desirous of substituting a more fitting hero for Abimelech in the roll of the "twelve" judges.

The Deuteronomistic Book of Judges did not end abruptly in the middle of the stories about Samson but, continuing into I Samuel, found fitting conclusion in Samuel's farewell address (I Sam. 12), just as the Pentateuch, in the same edition, concluded with the great address of Moses in Deuteronomy, and the Book of Joshua with R^D's parting speech of the hero (Josh. 23). Thus we may assign to this edition of Judges, dating from about 550, the following sections: 2:6-3:30; 4; 6-8; 10:6-12:7; 13:1-15:20; 16:31b; also I Sam. 1-12, where R^D's hand is noticeable in I Sam. 4:15, 18b; 7:2 (also in the addition "of the covenant" to "ark" in 4:3-5).

The Deuteronomist's schematic presentation of history as a series of cycles divided into well-defined, recurring periods tended to make an exact chronology, like that previously given for the minor judges, much more essential than in the Pentateuch or in Joshua. Such a chronology is actually found in the Deuteronomistic framework for the individual stories and for the two last judges, Eli and Samuel, in I Sam. 4:15, 18b; 7:2. Omitting the data for Abimelech (9:22) and the minor judges (10:2 f.; 12:9, 11, 14), which do not belong to this edition, we have the following figures. The rule of the individual judges comprised 226 years (Othniel: 40; Ehud: 80; Barak-Deborah: 40; Gideon: 40; Jephthah: 6; Samson: 20) and the periods of oppression preceding their respective deliverances total 111 years (8, 18, 20, 7, 18, 40 years). The whole period from the death of Joshua to that of Samson therefore lasts 337 years.

Several schemes have been proposed to fit the chronology of Judges into the 480 years which, according to R^D, elapsed from the time of the Exodus from Egypt to the building of the Temple of Solomon (I Kings 6:1, R^D).[3] Needless to say, this figure, probably representing twelve generations of forty years each, is artificial (cf. I Chron. 6:3-10 [H. 5:29-36], where Azariah in the time of Solomon is the thirteenth high priest after Phinehas, grandson of Aaron). It resembles the data in Judges where, with the exception of Jephthah, the judges rule eighty, forty, or twenty years. It could be surmised that the twelve generations from the Exodus to the building of the Temple, in addition to the six represented by the judges, are those of Moses, Joshua, Eli, Samuel, Saul, and David. As a matter of fact, six of these twelve leaders are said to have ruled

---

[3] See G. F. Moore, *Judges* (ICC), pp. xxxvii-xliii. C. F. Burney, *The Book of Judges*, pp. l-liv. M. Thilo, *Die Chronologie des Alten Testaments dargestellt* u.s.w. Barmen, 1917.

forty years. But counting the periods of oppression, the chronology in Judges cannot be explained on this basis. If we add the three years of Solomon (I Kings 6:1) to the total period of Judges, 337 years, we obtain 340. The additional 140 years, to make the total of 480, are the forty years of Moses, when Israel was in the Wilderness (Deut. 2:7; 8:2, 4; 29:5 [H. 29:4]; cf. Ex. 16:35 [P]; Num. 14:33 [JE?], 34 [P] 32:13 [Ps]), the forty years of Eli (I Sam. 4:18, RD; the LXX has 20 years), the twenty years of Samuel (if we may so interpret I Sam. 7:2, RD), and the forty years of David (II Sam. 5:4; I Kings 2:11, both RD).

It will be noticed that no pertinent data in RD have been disregarded, and none from other sources utilized. We must assume that the chronology of RD was self-contained and self-sufficient. The proposed scheme differs from most of the others in completely eliminating Joshua and Saul. As a matter of fact, they are actually ignored in the RD chronology. It is clear that RD believed that Joshua conquered all of Canaan with lightning speed, within a year after the death of Moses (cf. Josh. 2:24; 5:1; 10:28-42; 11:10-20, etc.), so that the period of the conquest could be disregarded. But the period from the completion of the conquest to the death of Joshua, "a long time" according to RD in Josh. 23:1, was likewise, inconsistently, left out of the reckoning. Otherwise its exact length would have been given. Obviously the Deuteronomists did not take into consideration the statement of E according to which Joshua died at the age of 110 years (Josh. 24:29; Judg. 2:8) and must therefore have lived forty to fifty years after the death of Moses. On the contrary, they considered him an old man before the land was conquered, as does the author of Josh. 13:1. Everything indicates that RD, for whatever reason, regarded the period of Joshua's leadership as so brief that it could be omitted from the chronological reckoning.[4] For different reasons, the reign of Saul was likewise disregarded. RD failed to give a chronology for Saul, as he did for Eli and David, because Saul was deposed by Samuel. The latter ruled Israel during his lifetime (I Sam. 7:15) and anointed David as king in place of Saul (I Sam. 15:28; 16:13). A later editor wished to give the chronology for Saul (I Sam. 13:1), but left the

---

[4] The time of Joshua is likewise omitted by the late glossator, who reckoned 300 years from the settlement of the Israelites east of the Jordan in the time of Moses to Jephthah (11:26). Adding up the figures given in Judg. 3:8-10:8 (including two minor judges in 10:2 f.), he obtained a total of 319, from which he subtracted 18 years of Ammonite oppression (10:8): 301 years is the result. Since Abimelech in the Deuteronomistic and in the late editions of the book was not reckoned as a judge (cf. the insertion of Shamgar in 3:31 to obtain 12 judges without him), this editor probably left out of his reckoning the 3 years of Abimelech (9:22), counting 298 years from the beginning of the oppression of Cushan-rishathaim (3:8) to Jephthah. Accordingly, the Transjordanic settlement, before the death of Moses, was made two years before this oppression. In those two years Moses died, Joshua conquered Canaan, and ended his life.

figures blank, apparently because he could not obtain the necessary information from historical books.

The Deuteronomists completed the transformation of the historical tribal leaders of J into "judges" ruling over united Israel (a development which had begun with E). By the exact chronological scheme, events in various parts of the country, presented without chronological sequence, as individual military exploits in J and E, were welded into an unbroken history of Israel in Canaan, after the whole country had been theoretically conquered by Joshua. The religious pragmatism, by which the Deuteronomists explained the Israelites' varying fortunes during this heroic period, was dimly foreshadowed in E and particularly in E^2 and JE, but drastically forced upon the stories in this edition. The aim was to change a patriotic record of valiant deeds into a religious tract.

The Book of Judges reached its present form, except for subsequent minor textual changes, during the three centuries from 500 to 200 B.C. The most important editorial changes in the Deuteronomistic book of 550 B.C. were the addition of omitted portions of JE and of the stories of J at the beginning and end of the book which were not even included in JE. It is probable that the JE additions were made before the J additions not only because the JE stories have been inserted in their proper place while those from J merely served as a foreword and appendix, but also because the late abundant annotations and commentaries marring the J stories are conspicuously absent from the JE stories in 5; 9; 10:1-5; 12:8-15; 16. It appears that these JE stories were copied into the Deuteronomistic book from a JE text transmitted not alone with fair accuracy but with fewer glosses than we find in the Deuteronomistic book. The latter had obviously taken the place of JE in popular favor and was much copied and read, each new copy being slightly different from its prototype. On the contrary, after 550 JE must have circulated only within a small group of scholars, so that its text suffered only slight modifications of an accidental character and was not annotated in a religious vein.

Under the circumstances, we must assume that the Song of Deborah (5:2-31a, with the editorial superscription in 5:1), and the stories of Abimelech (9), the minor judges (10:1-5; 12:8-15, inserted before and after Jephthah), and the end of Samson (16, with a repetition of R^D's conclusion [15:20] in 16:31b) were added to the Deuteronomistic book comparatively early and perhaps in the fifth century. The editor who inserted the stories did not object to the inclusion of Abimelech in the list of the judges (10:1), as did a later editor, who added Shamgar (3:31) as a substitute for Abimelech. This dating is confirmed by the similarity of diction of 8:30-32 with the Priestly Code if, with K. Budde (*Die Bücher Richter und Samuel* u.s.w., pp. 119-122. Giessen, 1890) and others, we see in these verses our editor's introduction to ch. 9. He left the JE stories intact and, with the exception of the few introductory remarks already noted (5:1; 8:30-32), apparently contributed nothing of his own. If 8:4-21 was also lacking in R^D's edition and added by our fifth century editor, he apparently added the gloss with the impossible figures in 8:10aβb. Such fantastic statistics are characteristic of the latest strata in the Pentateuch (P^s; cf. Ex. 12:37; 38:25-29; Num. 1-3 [partly P]; 25:9; 26; 31), and of much later glosses in Judges (1:4; 12:6 and the late commentary in 20-21; cf. 20:2, 10, 15, 17, 21, etc.) and Samuel (I Sam. 4:10; 6:19; 11:8b; 15:4b; II Sam. 24:9, 15, etc.).

Another editor, who followed probably in the late third century, added the J material at the beginning (1:1-2:5) and at the end (17-21) of the book. Paradoxically, these sections comprise the earliest and latest prose in the book. A late commentary was scribbled on the margins of the old J stories in 17-21 "by a Jewish scribe of no earlier date and far less literary ability than the Chronicler [about 250 B.C.]" (W. R. Arnold, *Ephod and Ark*, p. 101).

It is unlikely that the editor who inserted 1:1-2:5 and 17-21 was at the same time the author of the late commentary and glosses found therein. He probably used an edition of J extant at the time, in which the story of the conquest had been abridged and annotated (1:1-2:5) and the stories of the Danites and Benjamites (17-18; 19-21) previously annotated. This late material has already been listed in the description of J. All of it is not necessarily by the same hand, although it belongs *in toto* to the late third century. In ch. 1, the notes fantastically exaggerate the conquests of Judah before David's time (1:4, 8, 18). In chs. 17-18, the scribe's purpose is to cast contempt on the ancient sanctuary of Dan, the origin of which was told in J's narrative, by transforming its instruments of divination ("ephod and teraphim," presumably the sacred box and lots), into "graven and molten images" manufactured by a smith out of Micah's stolen 200 shekels of silver (17:2-4, a gloss written in six sections passing from the right to the left margins of the column [a-b, c-d, e-f] and mechanically copied by a later scribe vertically, first the right margin [a-c-e], then the left [b-d-f]; cf. Arnold, *Ephod and Ark*, p. 105).

By a stroke of the pen, the commentary in chs. 19-21 transforms historical events into an imaginary tale—a tale of what would have taken place had the Israelites at that time been not a group of warlike tribes still conscious of their wild Bedouin antecedents, but the pious theocratic congregation of Jews which the Priestly Code boldly dated back in the time of Moses. Thus, these closing chapters of the Book of Judges, in which the two main elements were written seven centuries apart, present in striking contrast the early days of Israel's history and the final metamorphosis of the nation, after many vicissitudes, into the Jewish Church.

CHAPTER III

THE BOOKS OF SAMUEL

~~~~~~

The two books of Samuel, like the two books of Kings, were originally in Hebrew a single volume, as we know from the Talmud (*Baba Bathra* 14b), Eusebius (*Hist. eccl.* 7:25, 2), and Jerome (*Prologus galeatus*).[1] The division into two books was introduced in the Greek version (LXX) because the Greek, in which vowels are written, required one and three-quarters more space than the Hebrew, in which no vowels were used until after A.D. 600. Thus one large scroll sufficed for the Hebrew, while two were required for the Greek. The division was introduced into the Hebrew text for the first time in Daniel Bomberg's first edition of the Hebrew Bible (Venice, 1516-1517) and thereafter became current. In the Greek and Latin Bibles, the four books of Samuel and Kings are called I, II, III, IV "Kingdoms" ("Kings" was preferred by Jerome), respectively.

The traditional ascription of I and II Samuel to Samuel (*Baba Bathra* 14b) requires no refutation, since Samuel's death is reported in I Sam. 25:1 and the evocation of his ghost in 28, and since all the events narrated in I Sam. 25-31 and II Samuel took place after his burial.

The books of Samuel may be summarized as follows:

1. *The priests and the ark of Shiloh; Samuel* (I Sam. 1:1-7:1). *a.* The birth and childhood of Samuel, and the end of the priests of Shiloh, Eli and his sons (1:1-4:1a, including the Song of Hannah [2:1-10]). *b.* The vicissitudes of the ark of Shiloh in the war against the Philistines (4:1b-7:1).

2. *Samuel and Saul* (7:2-15:35). *a.* Samuel as judge of Israel defeats the Philistines (7:2-17) and vainly opposes the people's demand for a king (8:1-22). *b.* Saul anointed king three times: first, secretly by Samuel (9:1-10:16); second, publicly by Samuel at Mizpah, after Saul was selected by lot (10:17-27a); third, by the people at Gilgal (10:27b, LXX; 11). *c.* Samuel, in his farewell address, lays down his office of judge (12). *d.* Saul's initial success in the war against the Philistines: the outbreak of the war (13:1-7), Saul deposed by Samuel for offering a

---

[1] The Masoretic note, provided for every book of the Hebrew Bible, is found at the end of II Samuel. It calls our book "The Book of Samuel" and treats it as a unit, giving as the central verse I Sam. 28:24.

sacrifice (13:8-14), the difficult situation of the Israelites (13:15-23), victory over the Philistines at Michmash resulting from Jonathan's heroic boldness (14:1-46), summary of Saul's reign (14:47-52). *e.* Saul's victory over the Amalekites and his second deposition by Samuel (15).

3. *Saul and David* (I Sam. 16-31; II Sam. 1). *a.* David at the court of Saul: Samuel anoints David (16:1-13); double first meeting of David with Saul as a harpist (16:14-23) and after the slaying of Goliath (17:1-18:5); Saul, jealous of David's popularity (18:6-16), promises him his daughter Merab as wife (18:17-19); but when David produces one hundred Philistine foreskins, gives him Michal in marriage (18:20-30); Jonathan temporarily persuades Saul to spare David's life (19:1-7) but, threatened again by Saul, David escapes for good, first when his wife deceives Saul's messengers (19:8-17) and he goes to Samuel at Ramah, where Saul follows him but falls into a prophetic frenzy (19:18-24); and a second time when secretly warned by Jonathan (20:1-42 [H. 20:1-21:1]). *b.* David as a freebooter: David is helped by the priests of Nob (21:1-9 [H. 21:2-10]); he feigns insanity at Gath (21:10-15 [H. 21:11-16]); and becomes chief of a robber band (22:1-5); Saul orders the priests of Nob slain, but Abiathar flees to David (22:6-23); David delivers Keilah from the Philistines (23:1-6), but escapes thence before Saul, to Ziph (23:7-14), where Jonathan makes a third covenant with him (23:15-18); Saul is called back by a Philistine attack (23:19-28); David spares Saul's life at Engedi and Saul, upon David's remonstrations, ceases to pursue him (23:29-24:22 [H. 24:1-23]); Samuel dies (25:1; cf. 28:3a); when Nabal, who refuses to pay David for "protection," dies of a stroke, David marries his widow Abigail (25:2-42; David's other wives, 25:43 f.); David spares Saul's life at Ziph (26:1-25). *c.* David as a Philistine vassal (27; 28:1 f.; 29-30; 28:3-25 belongs after 30): David with his band offers his services to Achish king of Gath (27:1-4), receives Ziklag as his fief (27:5 f.), and pretends to be raiding Judah while raiding other peoples (27:7-12); when David presents himself at the mustering of the Philistines against Saul (28:1 f.) he is sent back (29:1-11); meanwhile, however, the Amalekites have raided Ziklag (30:1-6), but David overtakes them (30:7-31). *d.* Saul's end (I Sam. 28:3-25; 31; II Sam. 1): beset by premonitions of disaster, Saul consults the ghost of Samuel (28:3-25); defeated by the Philistines at Gilboa, Saul takes his own life (31); David slays the Amalekite who deceitfully claimed to have killed Saul (II Sam. 1:1-16), and composes an elegy over Saul and Jonathan (1:17-27).

4. *David as king of Judah* (II Sam. 2-4). The Judeans anoint David as king (2:1-7) but Abner makes Ishbaal king of Israel (2:8-11) and fights against David (2:12-3:1); list of David's sons (3:2-5); Abner

makes a compact with David but is killed by Joab (3:6-39); assassination of Ishbaal (4).

5. *David as king of Israel* (II Sam. 5-24). *a.* Anointed king of Israel (5:1-3), David captures Jerusalem (5:4-25, including summaries on David's reign [5:4 f.] and family [5:13-16]) and brings there the ark of Shiloh (6). *b.* Nathan prophesies the endless duration of David's dynasty (7). *c.* Condensed lists of David's wars (8:1-14) and principal officials (8:15-18). *d.* David's domestic and national troubles (9:1-20:22): David's kindness toward Meribaal (9); war with the Ammonites (10:1-11:1); David's adultery with Bathsheba (11:2-4), the killing of her husband Uriah and the king's marriage with Bathsheba (11:5-27); Nathan's de-nunciation (12:1-15a); death of the first child of Bathsheba and birth of Solomon (12:15b-25); conquest of Rabbath Ammon (12:26-31); Amnon killed by Absalom for his rape of Tamar (13:1-38); David's reluctant reconciliation with Absalom (13:39-14:33) and Absalom's rebellion (15:1-12); flight of David (15:13-30); Absalom follows Hushai's advice instead of Ahithophel's, and as a result is defeated and killed (15:31-18:18); David mourns Absalom (18:19-19:8 [H. 18:19-19:9]) and returns to Jerusalem (19:9-43 [H. 19:10-44]); the rebellion of Sheba (20:1-22). *e.* David's officials (20:23-26; cf. 8:15-18). *f.* Blood revenge of the Gibeonites against Saul's sons (21:1-14). *g.* Exploits of David's heroes, first part (21:15-22). *h.* A psalm of David (22 = Ps. 18). *i.* "Last words" of David (23:1-7). *j.* Exploits of David's heroes, second part (23:8-39). *k.* The census and the pestilence (24).

Evidences of composition, which appear even from such a bare out-line, are more conspicuous in I Samuel than in any other of the books of the Genesis-Kings historical corpus. The same incidents are reported twice or three times with considerable differences in detail. The sudden end of Eli's house is announced twice (2:31-36; 3:11-14). Saul is anointed king privately by Samuel (9:26-10:1) and twice, on different occasions, in public (10:17-24; 11:15). Likewise Saul is twice deposed from the throne (13:14; 15:26-29), but continues to rule, his legitimacy unchal-lenged to the day of his death. As for David, he is introduced twice to Saul (16:14-23; 17:55-58), he is twice offered a daughter of Saul in mar-riage (18:17-19, 22-29a; a third time in 18:21b), twice he escapes from Saul's court, never to return (19:12; 20:42b [H. 21:1]); although Saul is at once cognizant of the first flight (19:17) he wonders why David is not present later at dinner (20:25-29); twice David has Saul in his power and spares his life (24:3-7 [H. 24:4-8]; 26:5-12), three times he makes a covenant with Jonathan (18:3; 20:16, 42; 23:18), twice he seeks refuge with Achish king of Gath (21:10-15 [H. 21:11-16]; 27:1-4). Goliath is slain both by David (17; cf. 19:5; 21:9 [H. 21:10]; 22:10b, 13) and Elhanan, one of David's heroes (II Sam. 21:19). This last contradiction troubled the Chronicler, who solved it by saying that Elhanan slew *"Lahmi, the brother of Goliath"* (I Chron. 20:5).

No less significant as clues to the composite character of our book are the differences in the viewpoint, long since observed in I Samuel. The most obvious is the diametrically opposed attitude to the monarchy in the two accounts of its origin. In 9:1-10:16; 10:27b-11:11, 15 Jehovah himself, in order to deliver the Israelites from the Philistine yoke, orders Samuel to anoint Saul, who has by mere chance visited him. But in 7:2-8:22; 10:17-27a; 11:12-14; 12, on the contrary, the monarchy is considered not only a national calamity but also an apostasy from God, according to the manner of the heathen. It is only in his anger against the nation's ingratitude that Jehovah here accedes to their demand for a king. In the first account, Samuel is an obscure clairvoyant consulted for a small fee about the whereabouts of stray donkeys; in the other, he is a second Moses, ruler of Israel, who delivers his people through prayer from the Philistines, and who can anoint and depose kings.

Finally, the radical differences in style between various parts of the work may easily be verified by comparing II Sam. 7, written in a prose as wretched and inept as that of the worst written parts of the Old Testament,[2] with II Sam. 9-20, the unsurpassed prose masterpiece of the Hebrew Bible.

In view of these unmistakable signs of composition, critics have generally come to the conclusion that Samuel comprises at least two principal sources, an early and a late one. Their relationship is similar to that of J and E in the Pentateuch and Judges, but it is by no means certain, as K. Budde believed, that they are really a continuation of J and E in the Pentateuch or part of the same works. T. Klaehn (*Die sprachliche Verwandtschaft der Quelle K der Samuelisbücher mit der Quelle J des Heptateuchs*) has collected much linguistic evidence to prove the same authorship of the early source of Samuel and J, but a final solution of the problem is perhaps impossible. What seems certain is that the early sources of Judg. 17-21 and Samuel were written by the same hand (W. R. Arnold, *Ephod and Ark,* pp. 99, 110 ff.).

In the main the following analysis[3] rests on the conclusions of K. Budde, J. Wellhausen, and their school. Here, as elsewhere, I have been unable to accept the new three-source theory of O. Eissfeldt (*Einleitung in das Alte Testament,* and his earlier writings) who has discovered in Samuel, as in the preceding Biblical books, the L, J, and E sources

---

[2] Even the Chronicler, who is not among the most brilliant writers in the Old Testament, when he copied II Sam. 7 in his work (I Chron. 17), felt impelled to remove some of the worst infelicities of that chapter.

[3] Cf. my paper "Midrash in the Books of Samuel" (*Quantulacumque*, pp. 303-316). Studies presented to K. Lake, edited by R. P. Casey, S. Lake, A. K. Lake. London, 1937.

"which are probably the continuation of the three narrative threads of the Hexateuch" (*ibid.*, p. 306). The books of Samuel are regarded here as the result of successive additions—first of the secondary source, and then of later materials—to the superb early history of the origin of the monarchy and of the reign of David (to the accession of Solomon, I Kings 1; 2:13-46a).

1. The Early Source of Samuel

The early source in Samuel, beginning with I Sam. 4:1b, is not the continuation of Judg. 17-21, which belonged to the same document in an earlier part, but of Judg. 13-16, relating the legendary and fabulous beginnings of the conflict with the Philistines. Here, in 4:1b-7:1, the author continues the story of the same conflict on solid, historical ground. It is not certain, however, that the stories of Samson (Judg. 13-16, J) belonged to this document. Judges 17-18, in which the Danites move to Laish-Dan, relates later events than the stories of Samson, in which the Danites are still in the South, close to the Philistines. And yet I Sam. 4:1b has a better connection with Judg. 13-16 than with 17-21, which the author wrote to impress the reader with the urgency of the monarchy, but relating events of a much earlier time than I Sam. 4.

Even though the connection of the early source of Samuel with that of Judges is not entirely clear, there is no reason to suppose that much material has been lost between the two books. For 4:1b, restored to its original form with the help of the LXX, indubitably marks the beginning of a story in the usual manner of our author: "And it came to pass in those days that the Philistines came together for war against Israel [LXX], and Israel marched against them [so LXX] for battle" (cf. Judg. 19:1). Moreover, it is clear that the sacred divining box ("ark") of Shiloh has not been mentioned by this author before 4:3 f. (W. R. Arnold, *Ephod and Ark*, pp. 37-40).

With more boldness than wisdom, the Israelites accepted the challenge of the Philistines and met them in a pitched battle in the open field at Aphek, with disastrous results. After the defeat, in which about four thousand Israelites were slain, the elders decided to "fetch from Shiloh the box of Jehovah. . . . So they sent to Shiloh and brought from thence the box of Yahweh Sebaoth [Jehovah Militant] and the two sons of Eli with the sacred box, Hophni and Phinehas" (4:2-4, omitting some glosses).

The arrival of the sacred box raised the spirits of the Israelites and caused a moment of panic among the Philistines, but it failed to produce the desired effect. The second battle ended in a defeat worse than the first. Hophni and Phinehas fell valiantly, defending their sacred trust, but the box was taken by the Philistines (4:5-11, omitting 4:8, 10b and

"Hophni and Phinehas" in 4:11). When the news was brought to Eli at Shiloh, he died instantly, killed by the shock. The widow of Phinehas, overcome by the tragic report, died giving birth to Ichabod [meaning, "Without Glory" or "Alas for the Glory!"] (4:12-22, omitting "Hophni and Phinehas" in 4:17, and 4:15, 18b [R^D], 20b, 21aβb).

The sacred box wrought havoc among the Philistines. It overthrew the statue of Dagon at Ashdod (5:1-5, omitting 5:5) and the pestilence which broke out in the city was attributed to its presence (5:6 f., omitting "Ashdod and the borders thereof" in 5:6). When the box was sent to Gath, the plague followed it, so that later Ekron refused to admit it, and the five city "rulers" (*serānîm*, possibly akin to Greek *tyrannos*, "tyrant") of the Philistines sent it back to the Israelites on a new cart drawn by two milk kine, together with a votive gift consisting of five golden tumors and five golden mice (5:8-6:11, omitting "the hand of Jehovah" in 5:9; 5:10bα; 6:5aα, 6, 11b). Contrary to their natural instincts, the cows forsook their calves and took the box straight to Beth-shemesh, where the people received it with a joyful burnt offering (6:12-18, omitting 6:15, 17 f). But the men of Beth-shemesh, in their curiosity, irreverently gazed inside the sacred box, and seventy of them died of the plague (6:19 f., omitting "and he smote of the people fifty thousand men" in 6:19). Finally the box, which could not be returned to Shiloh because that shrine had presumably been razed by the Philistines (cf. the references to its destruction in Jer. 7:12, 14; 26:6, 9),[4] was deposited in the house of a Gibeonite of Kirjath-jearim named Abinadab, where it was forgotten until David (II Sam. 6:3) decided to bring it to Jerusalem (6:20-7:1).

Leaving the sacred box in its seclusion, where it remained twenty years, according to the late but credible notice in 7:2, our author now proceeds to relate the story of the origin of the monarchy. The conflict with the Philistines, of which the beginnings have just been told, was much graver than the local struggles related in the Book of Judges, when a temporary leader at the head of his tribe could at times achieve victory and deliverance. From their five cities on the coastal plain, these invaders from the Aegean world set out to subject the hinterland and, by their conquest of the strategic fortifications in the plain of Jezreel, made themselves masters of Israel. Thus the Philistine menace threatened not only the conquests, but the very existence of Israel. According to our author, Jehovah did not raise up a judge as heretofore, but chose Saul, son of Kish, to be the king of all the tribes. A modern historian would say that the Philistine attack aroused the Israelite national self-consciousness, both political and religious, to such a pitch that the autonomous tribes were inevitably united into one kingdom.

---

[4] Archaeological excavations have confirmed the destruction of Shiloh at this time. See Hans Kjaer, *The Excavation of Shiloh, 1929*, pp. 19 ff., 23. Jerusalem, 1930.

The story of how Saul became king, told in the sections belonging to the early source in chs. 9-11 and 13-14, is analyzed by A. Lods (Les sources des récits du premier livre de Samuel sur l'institution de la royauté israélite in *Etudes de théologie et d'histoire . . . en hommage à la faculté de théologie de Montauban . . .* pp. 259-284. Paris, 1901; cf. *Israël*, pp. 408-413) into two mutually exclusive parallel narratives. According to one, the "seer" source, Saul (reading Saul instead of Jonathan in 13:3) started a rebellion against the Philistines by overthrowing the stela (*neṣib*) which they had erected at Geba, and was made king after his victory at Michmash, which resulted from Jonathan's boldness (13:3-5, 23; 14:1-20, 23a, 24b, 25-30, 36-46, in part). The account of the actual coronation in Geba (or Gibeah) is lost, but 14:47a alludes to it. According to the other, the "Jabesh" source, Saul was proclaimed king at Gilgal, following his deliverance of Jabesh in Gilead from the Ammonites, after which he attacked the Philistines (11; 13:2, 3a, 17 f.; 14:15, 21 f., 23b, 24, 31-35, in part). Both these sources were preceded by a legendary tale about Saul's youth. The "seer" source was introduced by the folk tale of young Saul going out to find his father's donkeys and meeting Samuel (9:1-10:12), the "Jabesh" source by the legendary story of Saul's (not Samuel's) birth (1).[5]

This attractive conjecture by Lods unquestionably removes some of the incongruities in these stories as part of a single document and is not per se impossible. It is far less complicated than the attempt of I. Hylander (*Der Samuel-Saul-Komplex*) to reconstruct out of scattered fragments of verses the individual traditions utilized by the authors of Samuel, and the several stages through which these traditions passed. But Lods is forced to admit that the climax of the "seer" source has disappeared (14:47a, belonging to the Deuteronomistic summary 14:47-51, can hardly furnish evidence for a lost account of Saul's coronation). He is forced to make serious emendations to the text. In general, he magnifies the significance of undeniable historical and literary inconsistencies of our text. It is not to be expected, however, that the author of the early source of Samuel, relying for Saul on oral traditions of diverse origin, could produce a history no less accurate and consistent than the biography of David in II Sam. 9-20, based on accounts of eyewitnesses. Since the disjointed materials at his disposal were partly historical and partly

---

[5] A. Lods, *Israël*, p. 411. It is of course a fact that 1:20, 28 contains puns on the name "Saul" rather than "Samuel." Saul (*shā'ûl*) means either "asked for" (1:20; cf. 1:27) or "lent" (1:28), while Samuel means "name of God." The difficulty was perceived by Kimchi, who suggested that the author derived "Samuel" from "shā'ûl mē'ēl" (asked of God). I Sam. 1 is regarded as a birth story of Saul by: A. Bernstein (cf. M. Jastrow, Jr., in JBL 19 [1900] 83 f.); J. Hempel, *Die althebräische Literatur* u.s.w., p. 91. Wildpark-Potsdam, 1930 ff.; I. Hylander, *Der literarische Samuel-Saul-Komplex*, p. 13. Uppsala and Leipzig, 1932; R. Press in ZAW N.F. 15 (1938) 189.

legendary, he could not in transcribing them produce a continuous and coherent story.

An historical event like the deliverance of Jabesh in Gilead, bringing Saul into prominence and resulting in his coronation, was long remembered, particularly by the inhabitants of that city (I Sam. 31:11-13; II Sam. 2:4b-7; 21:12). Similarly, Saul and Jonathan's initial success against the Philistines at Michmash. But, as often happens with great men, popular imagination supplied charming legends, such as I Sam. 9:1-10:16, for the obscure period of the hero's youth, before he had attained national prominence. In collecting and rewriting such varied popular traditions about Saul, our author could not have achieved uniform historicity and flawless consistency, even if he had attempted it. What is characteristic of him is uniform good faith, objective impartiality, and fine literary sense—qualities that cannot be attributed to later writers in Samuel, with the exception of the author of I Sam. 1.

In the story of Saul's first meeting with Samuel (9:1-10:16, omitting the glosses in 9:9, 15-17; 10:8, 9aβ, 12 and perhaps 10:16b), it is difficult to disentangle the various legendary strands and separate fact from fancy. There may be only a historical kernel in this story (an actual meeting of Saul with Samuel and Saul's susceptibility to prophetic trances when exposed to the frenzy of ecstatics). But in any case, the picture of ancient Israelite village life is genuine, even though most of the details in the narrative may be imaginative. Even when the author draws on his fancy or on popular legends, he is close enough to the period described to give a genuine picture of a sacred meal at the "high place" and of the bands of ecstatics roaming the countryside in wild transports, in contrast with the later glossators (9:9), who had not the slightest idea of what a "seer" (clairvoyant) was and confused him with a prophet.

Although Saul had been recognized by Samuel as the man of the hour and made into "another man" (10:6, 10) by his prophetic experience, he kept his counsel and returned to his usual agricultural pursuits. According to Samuel's advice (10:7), he awaited his opportunity, which was not long delayed. "And it came to pass about a month later" (10:27b, LXX) that Nahash, king of the Ammonites, threatened to put out the right eye of every man in Jabesh-Gilead upon their surrender, and had contemptuously allowed them one week's time to send for help to the Israelites across the Jordan. Saul alone, among the Israelites shedding futile tears for the unfortunate city, leaped into action. With such suddenness that the Philistines could take no hostile action, he collected an army through a dreadful threat, surprised the Ammonites, and delivered the people of Jabesh in Gilead. The returning Israelite forces, after crossing the Jordan, proclaimed Saul king of Israel at Gilgal (11, omitting "and after Samuel" in 11:7; 11:8b, 12-14, and "peace offerings" in 11:15).

The story continues without a break in 13:2, although the author seems to be unconscious of the inconsistency of presenting Saul in ch. 9 as a bashful young man and in 13:2 as a mature man with a son (Jonathan) old enough to command a detachment of troops.

Saul's first act after his coronation was to retain three thousand men under arms and to send the rest who had fought at Jabesh back to their homes (13:2). Emboldened by his success, he was ready to face the Philistines, of whom most of the Israelites were then subjects. Open rebellion broke out when Jonathan overthrew a commemorative stela which the Philistines had erected in Gibeah [Geba] or, according to other interpretations of the word *neṣib* (which means "pillar, stela" in Gen. 19:26, "governor" in II Sam. 8:6, 14, and "garrison" in I Chron. 11:16), slew the Philistine prefect or garrison (13:3 f., omitting "and Saul blew the horn throughout all the land" and reading "the Hebrews have revolted" [LXX] for "Let the Hebrews hear" in 13:3; "to Gilgal" at the end of 13:4 is a harmonistic gloss).

When the Philistines mustered their forces at Michmash, the civilian population among the Israelites hid in terror (13:5-7a, omitting from "thirty thousand" to "in multitude" in 13:5). And of Saul's army of three thousand, only six hundred remained (13:15b). Feeling themselves masters of the situation, the Philistines left a corps of troops at Michmash, facing Saul at Gibeah, and sent three companies to raid the countryside (13:16-18). The garrison at Michmash occupied a strategic position on the pass of Michmash (13:23).

By a bold attack on an advance post of the Philistines, Jonathan and his armor-bearer slew twenty men (14:1-14a, omitting 14:3a and "first" in 14:14a). The resulting panic among the Philistines, increased by an earthquake (14:15), was observed by Saul's watchmen (14:16). While Saul vainly sought a divine oracle through the lots in the sacred box carried by Ahijah (14:17-19; on 14:18 cf. Arnold, *Ephod and Ark*, p. 16), and finally ordered the attack (14:20), the Israelites in the Philistine army and those hiding in the hills threw themselves against the enemy and routed them as far as Beth-horon (14:21-23).

In hot pursuit of the Philistines, Saul took a vow for himself and his men not to eat until sunset, but Jonathan unwittingly broke it by eating some honey (14:24-30, omitting 14:28b). The Philistines were driven from Michmash to Aijalon (14:31). In their frenzy, Saul's famished and exhausted men began to eat the flesh and blood of hastily butchered sheep and oxen after sunset. Saul stopped this sacrilege by sacrificing the animals on a stone, so that their meat could be eaten without offense to the deity (14:32-35a).

Saul decided to continue the attack at that same time, but when he could obtain no response from the sacred divining box he inferred that someone had offended the deity. By renewed consultation, the lots pointed out the sinner. The army, however, refused to let Saul slay Jonathan. They ransomed him by killing, as a substitute, either a man or an animal (14:36-45; in 14:41 read, "Saul said, 'Jehovah, God of Israel, etc.'"). But the battle was not continued that night or the following day (14:46).

In the third part, following those about the sacred box of Shiloh and the coronation of Saul, the early source deals with David at the court of Saul and as an outlaw. As the author has shown, Saul was intensely emotional, subject to prophetic trances and religious paroxysms. Utterly devoted to his people, he must soon have realized with a sense of frustration and despair that he could not free Israel from the Philistines. In a man of such emotional instability and tension, awareness of failure inevitably produces fits of acute mental depression alternating with violent explosions of anger. In accordance with the medical conceptions of the time, our author diagnosed this condition as possession of an evil spirit sent by Jehovah (16:14). Nevertheless, such was Saul's unselfish devotion to the national interests that he retained not only the respect but also the affection of his subjects to the day of his death. He was never confronted, like David, with serious rebellions against his rule.

Concerned with the king's despondency, the courtiers suggested that music might bring him some solace and, with his consent, brought to court a harpist named David, son of Jesse the Bethlehemite (16:15-23, omitting 16:18aβb and "who is with the sheep" in 16:19). David's natural charm was irresistible. Jonathan became much attached to him, gave him garments and weapons, and made a compact of friendship (18:3 f.). When Saul promoted David to the command of a corps of troops, he not only proved his military ability, but became very popular among the men (18:5) as well as the women, who used to sing antiphonally, "Saul has slain his thousands but David his myriads" (18:6 f., omitting "when David returned from the slaughter of the Philistine" in 18:6). Saul was naturally vexed, and henceforth looked upon David with envy and suspicion (18:8 f.).

When Saul's daughter Michal became enamored of David (18:20), Saul conceived a plan to rid himself of a possible rival. Upon his instructions, the courtiers suggested to David that he ask for Michal's hand, for Saul would accept one hundred Philistine foreskins in lieu of a dowry. Similarly, Agamemnon offered to Achilles one of his daughters in marriage as a return for his military assistance (*Iliad* 9:141-148). But David did not perish in battle, while collecting this gruesome gift, as Saul had hoped, and thus married Michal (18:22-30, omitting 18:26b, 29b-30, and

"and they gave them in full number to the king" in 18:27, where we should read "one hundred" instead of "two hundred." Most of these omissions are actually lacking in the much briefer LXX text of chs. 17-18).

In uncontrollable anger over the failure of his plot to rid himself of David, Saul sent his guards to arrest David on the wedding night but, through a ruse on the part of Michal, David made good his escape (19:11-17; in 19:11 read "to watch him, in order to slay him [omitting the preceding "and"] in the morning"). The priests of Nob, who had no reason to believe that David was *persona non grata* to Saul, assisted him in his flight (21:1-9 [H. 21:2-10], omitting "though it was but a common journey" in 21:5 [H. 21:6] and "whom thou slewest in the vale of Elah" in 21:9 [H. 21:10]). With the single exception of the priest Abiathar, who fled to David with the sacred divining box (cf. 23:6) and became his priest, they were slain at Saul's order by Doeg (22:6-23, omitting "who was set over the servants of Saul" in 22:9, "linen" in 22:18, and 22:19).

David and his men then delivered Keilah, hard pressed by the Philistines (23:1, 5 f.). But David hid in the wilderness when Abiathar obtained through the sacred box a divine oracle to the effect that the people of Keilah would deliver him into the hand of Saul (23:7-14a, omitting 23:10 f. except "Then David said, 'O Jehovah God of Israel, will Saul come down, as thy servant has heard? I beseech thee, tell thy servant.' And Jehovah said, 'He will come down.'" And in 23:14a omit, "and remained in a mountain in the wilderness of Ziph").

Our author tells with great charm and picturesque detail the story of an adventure during David's career as a freebooter. When David heard that a rich herdsman named Nabal (meaning "Fool") was shearing his sheep at Carmel, he sent ten men to request Nabal to pay him for having left his flocks and shepherds unharmed. Nabal insolently refused. David forthwith set out with four hundred armed men but, when met by Nabal's comely wife Abigail with apologies, entreaties, and gifts, he desisted from his murderous intent and accepted her presents. When Nabal awoke the next morning from a drunken stupor and was informed by Abigail of his narrow escape at the hand of David, he suffered a paralytic stroke and died ten days later. David, whose first wife, Michal, had been married by Saul to another man, had wedded Ahinoam. Nevertheless, he promptly wooed and married Abigail, Nabal's widow (25:2-44, omitting "and he was a Calebite" in 25:3, "the enemies of" in 25:22, and 25:28-31).

The story immediately following is no less picturesque and illuminates David's character. On the only occasion when Saul went out in person to seize David, according to the early source, David stealthily entered the tent in which the king was sleeping and carried away his spear and water pitcher, refusing to allow one of his men to slay "Jehovah's anointed"

(26:1-12, omitting, with codices A B of the LXX, "where Saul had pitched: and David beheld the place" in 26:5; 26:1-3, expanded in 23:19-24, are not intact). From a safe distance David upbraided Abner, Saul's commanding officer, for neglecting to protect his king (26:13-16) and, addressing Saul, maintained his innocence (26:17-20; in 26:20b read, in accordance with the LXX, "For the king of Israel has gone forth to seek my life, as a vulture pursues a partridge in the mountains"). Saul admitted his error, and David offered to return the spear and pitcher (26:21 f.). With a final blessing and prediction of David's success, Saul returned to his home (26:23-25; 26:23 f., with their unctuous tone, seem to be a later addition).

In spite of Saul's encouraging words and friendly attitude, David remembered Saul's instability and still felt in peril. In the long run, his chance of escaping from Saul, to whom the Israelites were absolutely loyal to the end, was no better than that of a partridge in the hills fleeing from a vulture or an eagle (26:20b; cf. above). In this predicament David, preferring to sacrifice his honor rather than risk his life, forsook his people and offered his services as a *condottiere* to one of the five Philistine rulers, Achish of Gath (27:1-4, omitting 27:3b). Later sources attempted to erase this dark blot from David's character (cf. 21:10-15 [H. 21:11-16] and 22:5). David's loyalty to Achish was, however, only superficially sincere. Thinking of the future, he pretended to raid his own people in Southern Judah whom, on the contrary, he constantly befriended (cf. 30:26; 27:7-12, omitting 27:6b, [7?], 8b, 11; cf. 30:26). Thus he deceitfully won the full confidence of Achish and received from him the town of Ziklag as his fief (27:5-6a).

The contradiction between 27:5-6, in which David resides in Ziklag, and 27:7-12, in which he is still in Gath with Achish, requires no excision of one section or the other, as some critics believe, but is solved by simply transposing their order. It is most unlikely that Achish would have placed David immediately at the head of one of his towns, before he proved the definite break from his own people, as stated in 27:7-12. David asked for a town only after he was certain of having "found favor" in the sight of Achish (27:5) through his successful schemes. The account of David's residence in Ziklag should immediately precede 28:1 f.; 29-30, where it is presupposed. It is also quite clear that 28:3-25 should be placed between chs. 30 and 31. The consultation of the witch at Endor (28:3-25) took place on the day preceding the battle of Gilboa (28:19) described in 31, and the position of the Philistines at Shunem (28:4) is subsequent to the general initial mustering of their forces at Aphek (29:1) and to their march to the plain of Jezreel (29:11).

When the Philistines mustered their force for a decisive attack against Saul, Achish without demur summoned David and his men to join him in fighting the Israelites (28:1 f.). But upon remonstrations from the other Philistine rulers, who from past experience had reason to mistrust the loyalty of the Israelites (and of David in particular), Achish reluctantly sent David and his men back to Ziklag (29, omitting the second "the princes of the Philistines" in 29:4; 29:5).

Returning to Ziklag after an absence of three days, David found the town thoroughly plundered and ruined by the Amalekites. In accordance with a divine response obtained through Abiathar, David pursued the marauders and surprised them in their camp at night, rescuing the women and children and recovering the booty (30, omitting 30:5, 9b, "and upon that which belongs to Judah and upon the Negeb of Caleb" in 30:14, "and out of the land of Judah" in 30:16; 30:18b, 19b, 25, 27-31).

In the meantime, when the Philistines encamped in Shunem, Saul took position in the vicinity, by Mount Gilboa. Beset by dark forebodings, Saul was unable to obtain a divine oracle either through dreams, the priestly box, or the mouth of a prophet. In desperation, he consulted the ghost of Samuel, brought up from the underworld by a witch at Endor. The dead seer confirmed his worst presentiments (28:3-25, omitting 28:3, 17 f., 19b). On the following day, Saul's fears were realized in tragic fashion. The Israelites were routed by the Philistines, Jonathan and two other sons of Saul lost their lives in battle, and Saul, devoted to his people to the end, refused to save himself by flight. Like a great captain, he went down with his ship. When his own armor-bearer refused to slay him, Saul threw himself upon his sword. The Philistines hung the bodies of Saul and his sons on the walls of Bethshan, but the men of Jabesh in Gilead, remembering how Saul had delivered them, stole the bodies and buried them in their city (31:1-13, omitting "men with the bow" in 31:3a, the second "and thrust me through" in 31:4, "also all his men" in 31:6, the additions to 31:7 lacking in I Chron. 10:7; in general the text of 31 is more corrupt than I Chron. 10:1-12).

News of the disastrous battle reached David at Ziklag two days after he returned from his raid on the plundering Amalekites. An Amalekite, hoping for reward, brought to David the crown and bracelet of Saul and falsely claimed to have slain the king at his request (II Sam. 1:1-10, omitting "after the death of Saul" in 1:1, "from Saul" in 1:2, "and they died" in 1:4, "that told him" in 1:6; 1:8). David mourned Saul and the fallen Israelites, and ordered the immediate execution of the Amalekite (1:11-16).

Observing that the account of Saul's death by his own hand in I Sam. 31 cannot be reconciled with the story of the Amalekite in II Sam. 1, according to which he had killed the king, critics have generally concluded that the same author could not have written both accounts. On the contrary, after giving the true version of Saul's death in I Sam. 31, the author has a right to assume that the reader will recognize the false-hood of the Amalekite's report in II Sam. 1. It is, in fact, characteristic of our author that oral reports are not always in harmony with the actual facts as he has previously presented them. Thus, for instance, Doeg maliciously states, without warrant (I Sam. 21), that Ahimelek the priest of Nob had given David a divine oracle (I Sam. 22:10; cf. 22:13)—an accusation that Ahimelek indignantly rejects, "Have I begun to-day to inquire of God for him? Far be it from me!" (22:15; most of the exegetes, however, interpret the words as an admission that the allegation is true).

Both Doeg and the Amalekite lied deliberately for their own ends. In other cases, as when David claimed to have killed the Amalekite with his own hands (II Sam. 4:10), whereas he was killed by one of David's men (1:15), the lie is rhetorical exaggeration. Our author, like later Greek and Roman historians, composed the speeches and conversations of his characters with such literary art that even when a soldier repeats an order of David he does not reproduce it verbatim (II Sam. 18:5, 12), as would have been the case had the history been done by a more accurate and less brilliant writer. To seek clues for identifying the various sources in the differences between facts and reports seems to reveal a radical misunderstanding of the author's literary manner.

David composed a moving elegy over the death of Saul and Jonathan (II Sam. 1:17-27; 1:18a is part of the textually corrupt beginning of the poem in 1:19-27; 1:18b is editorial; the meter is 4:4). His authorship of the poem is unquestionable. The deep pervading emotion shows that it was composed immediately after the battle of Gilboa, under the first shocking impression of the calamity. The poet was a man who reverenced Saul as the king "anointed with oil" (1:21, omitting the slanderous "not") but loved Jonathan as a brother and cherished his friendship more than love of women. The poet's grief is intense and sincere, but nevertheless virile. For he was clearly a military man who did not allow his lament to become sentimental or unctuous. Moreover, the dirge is a pure and simple expression of deep sorrow, without religious reflections and no mention of God.

Dating shortly before 1000 B.C., it is, like the Song of Deborah (Judg. 5), one of the earliest masterpieces of Hebrew poetry. Both were so radically different from the Psalms of Judaism that they were never used in the liturgy of any sanctuary. The only other genuine poem of David extant is his brief elegy over Abner (3:33 f.), in which the mood is more one of irritation than profound grief.

The fourth chapter of this history deals with David as king. The death of Saul marked the end of David's life as bandit chief, either independent or at the command of a Philistine ruler. He at once moved to Hebron, where the Judeans anointed him as their king (2:1-4a). In a friendly but ill-timed message to Jabesh in Gilead, he delicately hinted that he stood ready to serve also as king of Israel (2:4b-7), obviously still unaware that Israel had remained faithful to the house of Saul. After the defeat at Gilboa, Abner, Israel's commander in chief, had crowned Saul's son Ishbaal (i.e., "man of Baal"; the synagogue reading is "Ishbosheth," "man of shame") at Mahanaim in Transjordania, for the Philistines were masters of Canaan (2:8 f., omitting the list in 2:9 beginning with "and over the Ashurites").

There followed a series of futile minor conflicts between the men of David, under Joab, and the men of Ishbaal at the orders of Abner (2:12-3:1, omitting 2:16b, the second "and he died" in 2:23, and "died" in 2:31). Irritated by Ishbaal, Abner came to terms with David, but was treacherously killed by Joab (3:6-28, omitting 3:6a, 9 f.; "saying, 'Whose is the land?'" in 3:12; 3:14; "Ishbosheth" in 3:15; 3:18b; "the servants of David and" "and brought in great spoil with them" in 3:22). David's indignation at this assassination, which not only brought negotiations with the Israelites to an end but placed him in a most unfavorable light, was uncontrollable. He cursed Joab publicly with such vile and obscene words that the text was perforce corrupted and obscured (3:28-30, omitting 3:30). He took special pains to give Abner a decent burial, even composing an elegy for him, lest he be suspected of connivance in his death (3:31-39). Eventually, however, Ishbaal was assassinated by two of his officers, who instead of receiving a reward from David were ordered to be executed (4:1-12, omitting 4:2b-3, 6 [cf. the variant in the LXX], 7 [to "bed-chamber"]; 4:4, unless it be authentic before 9:1 or 9:4, is a gloss). So the elders of Israel came to Hebron and anointed David as their king (5:1-3, omitting 5:1 f.).

David's first act as national king was the conquest of Jerusalem, which became his capital (5:6-12, omitting "saying, 'David cannot come in hither'" in 5:6, "the same is the city of David" in 5:7, 5:8 from "and the lame and the blind" to the end; "[the] God [of]" in 5:10; 5:11 f.). The Philistines attacked David but were repulsed (5:17-25, omitting 5:20-24 and "so" in 5:25). David succeeded in delivering Israel from the Philistines not through pitched battles in the plain, for previous experiences showed the Israelites to be at a disadvantage here, but through guerrilla warfare, of which nothing is known except the anecdotes told by our author in 21:15-22; 23:8-39 (omitting "again" in 21:15, reading "Elhanan the son of Jair the Bethlehemite" in 21:19; omitting 23:13b-14a). These two displaced sections may have stood originally immediately before or after II Sam. 6.

After making Jerusalem his capital, David brought thither the sacred divination box of Shiloh ("The Ark") which our author had left in the house of Abinadab, a Gibeonite of Kirjath-jearim (I Sam. 7:1; II Sam.

6:1-23; for the original form of II Sam. 6, after the glosses have been removed, see W. R. Arnold, *Ephod and Ark,* pp. 40-67).

The account of David's census and of the pestilence that followed (II Sam. 24) seems to be the sequel of this story about the ark, inasmuch as it culminates in the building of an altar on the threshing floor of Arauna, presumably the site of the Temple of Solomon. The story of the census has been elaborated by later hands, and as a whole is not in the manner of our author. Even if we remove as glosses 24:1a, 11a, "the prophet" (in 24:11b), and the fantastic figures in 24:9, 15, the legendary character of the story, notably of 24:10-19, is still apparent. We may surmise, however, that II Sam. 24 is based on a story in the early source.

Early in his reign, David had an excellent opportunity to rid himself of possible rivals to the throne by allowing, under the guise of piety, the execution of Saul's surviving sons by the Gibeonites (21:1-15, omitting 21:2b, "and David said to the Gibeonites" in 21:3; 21:7; "at the beginning of the barley harvest" in 21:9). This unsavory account of the usual wiping out of the old dynasty by Oriental usurpers, must have been followed by II Sam. 9 (omit vv. 12 f.), where David takes pains to discover any surviving descendants of Saul. Upon tracing Meribaal son of Jonathan (Mephibosheth, according to the synagogue reading), David invites him to eat daily at the royal table. Did David hope by this theatrical act of kindness to a descendant of Saul to offset the silent indignation of the Israelites after the slaughter of Saul's sons? The rebellions led by Absalom and Sheba show that David never became as popular among the Israelites as Saul had been.

With candid objectivity our author relates the subsequent events of David's life and reign in II Sam. 10-20; I Kings 1; 2:13-46a. In this dramatic story, the author shows the mutual interplay of David's personal history, his family history, and national events. The separate episodes in this story are clearly marked by their initial words, "And it came to pass after this . . ." (10:1; 13:1; 15:1; the formula is not used for the last episode beginning I Kings 1:1).

The first episode describes a successful war against the Ammonites, whose king had insulted the ambassadors of David. During the third campaign, David fell in love with Bathsheba and arranged to have her husband, Uriah the Hittite, killed in battle (10:1-12:31; omitting "a thousand men and the men of Tob" in 10:6; "[of] the mighty men" in 10:7; "and the men of Tob" in 10:8; 10:15-19a; "all" in 11:9; "and Judah" in 11:11; 11:21aα [as far as "at Thebez"]; 12:7b-8; "the word of" in 12:9a; 12:9b-12; "the enemies of" in 12:14).

The second episode is a sort of prelude to the third. Amnon, son of David, violated the virginity of his half sister Tamar, and two years later her full brother Absalom, at a sheep-shearing festival, had his servants slay Amnon in vengeance. Absalom fled to his grandfather, king of Geshur. Three years later, by means of the fictitious story a woman of Tekoa told the king, Joab induced David to recall Absalom. But it was only after two years that Absalom, by burning up the barley crop on Joab's field, could force the old general to obtain an audience for him with the king (13:1-14:33; omitting "that ministered unto him" in 13:17; 13:18a; "the sons of the king" in 13:32; 13:34a, 37b-38a; 14:14bβ; "for it was at every year's end that he polled it" in 14:26a; "two hundred shekels" [about six pounds] as the weight of Absalom's hair is absurd in 14:26b; 14:28b). All of 14:25-27 may be redactional; 14:27 contradicts 18:18, but, according to an addition in the LXX of 14:27 and to I Kings 15:2, Tamar or Maacah, daughter of Absalom, was the wife of Rehoboam and thus became the ancestral mother of the kings of Judah.

The third episode is the rebellion of Absalom and its aftermath. By his vacillations, David had alienated his son Absalom. By his national policies he had failed to gain the Israelites' affection, and even lost the support of the Judeans, who apparently resented the substitution of Jerusalem, the Jebusite city, for Judah's principal city, Hebron, as capital. Such were the seeds of the rebellion against David which began in Judah and ended in North Israel. The seditious movement, with headquarters at Hebron, was led by stanch Judeans, Ahithophel, the statesman, and Amasa, the soldier. Soon it attracted Absalom, heir apparent to the throne, and the Northern Israelites, to whom Absalom made alluring promises (15:1-6).

Four years (read so in 15:7 according to some versions of the Greek text) after Absalom's restoration to favor, Absalom proclaimed himself king at Hebron (15:7-12). David, taken by surprise, considered the defense of Jerusalem impossible (15:13-18). Like Napoleon, he could depend on the utter devotion of his veterans, particularly foreign mercenaries (15:19-23) and personal friends, but in his self-seeking aloofness he had failed to win over his subjects en masse.

In his flight to the Jordan, David sent his two priests, Abiathar and Zadok, back to Jerusalem with the sacred box of Shiloh, and also Hushai his friend, that they might keep him informed through Ahimaaz, son of Zadok, and Jonathan, son of Abiathar, of Absalom's plans (15:24-37; in 15:24 omit "and all the Levites with him" "of the covenant" and transpose "and let Abiathar go up" [sic] to 15:27, after "in peace"; 15:25 f.). Ziba, the servant of Meribaal (cf. ch. 9), met David with gifts, and accused his master of treason (16:1-4), while another member of Saul's household, Shimei, cursed him for the slaughter of Saul's sons (16:5-14, omitting "at him and cast dust" in 16:13).

Meanwhile, Absalom had come to Jerusalem and ostentatiously took possession of David's harem (16:15-23, omitting "the people" in 16:15, "and all the men of Israel" in 16:18, and probably 16:23). Refusing to adopt the excellent plan of Ahithophel, which called for an immediate attack with available troops, Absalom followed the deceitful advice of Hushai and delayed until a general mobilization could be carried out (17:1-14, omitting the moralizing reflection in 17:14b). Through Ahimaaz and Jonathan, who eluded pursuit, Hushai reported to David, who at once crossed the Jordan (17:15-22, omitting 17:17 [from "and they went . . ."]). Shrewdly realizing that the delay would be fatal to the rebellion, Ahithophel took his own life (17:23).

David was welcomed in Mahanaim, as previously Abner and Ishbaal (2:8-9a), because the Israelites in Transjordania were doomed to extinction without help from the kings of Israel. In the decisive battle near Mahanaim, Absalom's undisciplined troops could not withstand the attack of David's trained cohorts and fled in panic. Absalom, caught in a tree by his head, was killed by Joab (17:24-18:18, omitting 17:25b and 18:15, 18). But David, mourning his son, did not rejoice over the victory and did not thank his men until Joab, that old watchdog of the monarchy, forced him to appear in public (18:19-19:8bβ [H. 19:9bβ], omitting "the king's servant and" in 18:29, the second "the Cushite" in 18:31, the second "the king" in 19:4 [H. 19:5]).

As a matter of fact, there was no real enthusiasm for David, particularly in Judah where the rebellion had started. The Northern Israelites were the first to take steps to bring back their king. The Judeans remained morose until David appealed to their elders through Zadok and Abiathar, and showed them special favor in appointing Amasa as his commander in chief instead of Joab (19:8bγ-15 [H. 19:9bγ-16], omitting the second "to his house" in 19:11 [H. 19:12] and transposing 19:11b [H. 19:12b] to the end of the preceding verse). Wisely the king forbore to avenge himself on Shimei and Meribaal (19:16-30 [H. 19:17-31]). Barzillai, David's host in Transjordania, declined the invitation to reside at court in Jerusalem, sending his son instead (19:31-39 [H. 19:32-40], omitting "over Jordan" in 19:36 [H. 19:37]).

No sooner had the king reached Gilgal than a quarrel broke out between Judeans and Israelites (19:40-43 [H. 19:41-44], omitting "and also half of the people of Israel" in 19:40 [H. 19:41] and "and all David's men with him" in 19:41 [H. 19:42]). Led by the Benjamite Sheba, the Israelites, who (except for some Benjamites) had been forestalled by the Judeans in bringing David over the Jordan, again raised the standard of revolt (20:1f.). David put Amasa at the head of the levies of Judah and Abishai in command of the mercenaries. But Joab slew Amasa and speedily put down the revolt (20:3-26, omitting 20:23-26; cf. 8:16-18). The seeds of disunion, sown by David's policies, however, eventually brought about the division of the kingdom after the death of Solomon.

The final episode in this ancient history followed soon after these events. David was old and feeble (I Kings 1:1-4) and, after the death of Amnon and Absalom, Adonijah was tacitly recognized by the king as the heir apparent. He had the support of Joab, Abiathar, and most of the royal princes. But Benaiah, commander of the bodyguard, and Zadok the priest, who were rivals of Joab and Abiathar, respectively, connived with Nathan and Bathsheba. Through palace intrigue they succeeded in crowning Solomon, son of Bathsheba, as king shortly before the death of David (I Kings 1:5-53). Secure on the throne, Solomon soon found excuses for ordering the execution of Adonijah, Joab, and Shimei and for exiling Abiathar to Anathoth (so that Zadok became ancestor of the priests of Jerusalem). In this manner "the monarchy was established in the hand of Solomon" (2:13-46, omitting 2:24, 27b).

The early source of Samuel, as the present writer conceives it, has been outlined at some length because, once freed from later additions, it is the outstanding prose writing and historical masterpiece of the Old Testament; this outline also shows what a well-organized literary unit it is. Many critics assume that it is a collection of several documents. Evidence proving uniform authorship drawn from the terminology and style of the original Hebrew is too technical to be presented here, but is partly available in W. R. Arnold, *Ephod and Ark* (pp. 110-122).

This history gives an account of the events from the first battle between the Israelites and Philistines up to the accession of Solomon. The narrative is generally vivid and picturesque, but becomes more absorbing and unmistakably historical in the latter part of David's reign, notably in II Sam. 9-20 and I Kings 1-2, the most brilliant and accurate part of the work.

Obviously, the sources of information available to the author are more detailed and reliable for David than for Saul (Samuel the clairvoyant is mentioned only incidentally in connection with Saul). Indeed, we get the impression that the story of Absalom's rebellion is based on accounts of the persons involved, nay, that it was written by an eyewitness. Already the Chronicler (I Chron. 29:29) attributed the biography of David to three of his contemporaries, Samuel, Nathan, and Gad. But though this guess need not be taken too seriously, it is not entirely futile to look for our author among the persons mentioned in the story of Absalom's rebellion.

The two most probable candidates that have been suggested are Abiathar (B. Duhm, *Das Buch Jeremia,* p. 3, KHC, 1901) and Ahimaaz, son of Zadok (A. Klostermann, *Die Bücher Samuelis und der Könige,* pp. xxxii f. 1887). Since David's biography was obviously not written by his secretary or official recorder, its author may well have been a priest, for the priests at the time were generally the only learned and literate persons in Israel. If, as everything indicates, the story in II Sam. 17:17-21 (cf. 15:27-29) is a record of actual happenings, it indubitably rests on the reminiscences of either Jonathan, son of Abiathar, or Ahimaaz, son of Zadok. No one else could have told it in this fashion, least of all the only other eyewitness to their concealment in the well, the unnamed peasant woman. But, in view of II Sam. 18:19-32, we may safely eliminate Jonathan, for this second story actually follows the footsteps of Ahimaaz from Joab, where he has witnessed the death of Absalom, to David, before whom he hides the tragic news brought soon after by a Negro courier.

Another consideration confirms Klostermann's surmise that Ahimaaz is our author. It has been inferred with great probability (W. R. Arnold, *Ephod and Ark,* pp. 61 f.) that Zadok's name originally stood in II Sam. 6:3 f. in place of "Ahio" ("his brother") and that he was accordingly the son of the Gibeonite Abinadab, in whose house the sacred box of Shiloh remained for many years. If such is the case, detailed knowledge of the vicissitudes of the "ark" (I Sam. 4-6; II Sam. 6), on our author's part, is readily explained assuming that he be Ahimaaz the son of Zadok.

Ahimaaz, or whoever wrote the early source in Samuel, is "the father of history" in a much truer sense than Herodotus half a millennium later. As far as we know, he created history as an art, as a recital of past events dominated by a great idea. In this sense, history did not exist at the time, although historical writing, unknown to the ancient Egyptians and Babylonians, had previously originated among the Hittites in the form of annals as well as in the autobiography or apology of Hattushil. David's biographer was a man of genius. Without any previous models as guide, he wrote a masterpiece, unsurpassed in historicity, psychological insight, literary style, and dramatic power.

As G. F. Moore has observed (*Encycl. Bibl.* 2 [1901] 2075), "the making of history precedes the writing of history." Memorable events, such as a victorious war and the foundation of a powerful kingdom, give to a nation a new sense of its greatness, heighten its national pride, and thus furnish the impulse for historical writing. The far-reaching conquests of Sargon of Akkad, about the middle of the third millennium B.C., provide the first example of the impact of political events on literature. However, the result was not genuine history but a romantic *chanson de geste.* In Egypt, likewise, the victorious campaigns of Thothmes III and Ramses II were recorded in fantastically imaginative language. But the consolidation of the Hittite kingdom, Assyrian conquests, the Persian wars in Greece, and the second Punic war in Rome mark the beginning of genuine historical writing among these peoples.

The struggle with the Philistines, who, far superior to the Israelites and Canaanites in military equipment and organization, had imposed their yoke on Israel, stimulated the latter to a national consciousness and unity which even Deborah could not create. The union of the tribes under

Saul, the first native king of Canaan, the wars through which Israel achieved its independence from the Philistines, and the campaigns of conquest resulting in the founding of a short-lived Israelitic empire (1000-740 B.C., the only time, except for the brief Maccabean period, when no great kingdom was capable of dominating Palestine)—these glorious achievements stirred the soul of the people and were celebrated in song and story. The Canaanites never had the occasion to write a national epic; the Philistines, like the Crusaders later, coming from the West, were gradually absorbed after a striking initial success. Instead, the Israelites, who only shortly before had been slaves in Egypt or Bedouins in the desert, entering Canaan as scattered tribes, found themselves masters of Canaan. The kingdom they ruled seems small to us in comparison with the Egyptian or Babylonian empires, but to David's contemporaries it was immense. The wealth, leisure, and power of Solomon's time created a first-rate literature of which the prose masterpiece is the early source of Samuel.

The author's method is biographical. His story centers around the main characters, and national events are narrated in connection with personal history. Thus the war with the Ammonites is told in some detail to explain how David married Bathsheba, mother of Solomon. This method explains why the author neglects to speak of David's greatest achievement—the deliverance once and for all from the Philistines—limiting himself to a few anecdotes of Philistine campaigns and to lists of David's heroes (II Sam. 5:17-19, 25; 21:15-22; 23:8-39), which are mere summaries or copies of military records. Likewise, the conquest of Jerusalem (II Sam. 5:6-9) is reported, not per se but merely as an introduction to the transportation thither of the ark (II Sam. 6), in which our author is deeply interested.

In comparison with other Old Testament historians, our author (like J in the Pentateuch and Judges) is remarkable for his strict objectivity and impartiality. There is a striking absence of all moralizing reflections, homiletic developments, and "philosophy of history." His only bias is his pride in the nation's achievements. He regards the monarchy as a divine gift—not, as Hosea, E, and the Deuteronomists, as an apostasy and insult to God. His religion and patriotism are one, but his faith in Jehovah, God of Israel, intense though it be, does not color his narrative. Divine interventions in human events are confined to oracular responses through the priestly box.

David, from the moment he appears on the scene, is the hero of the story. The author greatly admired him, and lovingly relates instances of his chivalry, generosity, and religious enthusiasm. He is not, however, blind to David's faults, and paints a lifelike portrait of his hero. He makes it perfectly clear, by psychologically revealing incidents, that David lacked Saul's selfless devotion to national interests and could never gain, through his rather theatrical exhibitions of generosity, grief, and indignation (some of which would now be called "publicity stunts"), the loyalty and intense affection that the Israelites had for Saul. David's blackest deed—not his adultery with Bathsheba and the murder of her husband, but his willingness to join the Philistines in fighting Saul at Gilboa—is related by the author candidly and without comment.

It is only in Nathan's denunciation of David (II Sam. 12:1-7a, 9a, 13-15) that our historian transcends history. Long before Elijah (I Kings 21:17-19) and Amos, he proclaimed that Jehovah would not tolerate criminal actions and that his worship involved moral conduct. Such a doctrine was truly revolutionary in the time of Solomon, when Jehovah was merely champion of Israel and still approved of bloody deeds as treacherous as those of Ehud (Judg. 3:20 f.) and Jael (5:25 f.), and even later, through Elijah and Elisha, sanctioned the assassination of kings (I Kings 19:15-17; II Kings 9). Since there are, however, no valid reasons for assuming the Nathan incident to be a later addition to the early source of Samuel, we must regard our author and, in a different way, J in Genesis—unless they be the same—as precursors of Amos—men of genius who dimly foreshadowed certain phases of the prophetic religion, in which morality was essential.

The style of the early source of Samuel (notably in II Sam. 9-20) is unsurpassed in the whole range of Hebrew prose literature. The author's expert use of syntax and appropriate idiomatic expressions, his classic Hebrew, ranging from the noblest to the coarsest expressions, his vivid descriptions and characterizations, and his lively dialogues have seldom if ever been surpassed in the literature of mankind. "It is the misfortune of this great man that his writings have come down to us within the bounds of an ecclesiastical canon of Holy Scripture; otherwise, students of the humanities would hardly continue to ignore a prose which, for combined simplicity and distinction, has remained unmatched in the literature of the world, and which the progressive sophistication of mankind has long since rendered forever unapproachable" (W. R. Arnold, *Ephod and Ark*, p. 118, n. 8).

2. The Late Source

The protagonist of the secondary source is Samuel; Saul and David were the principal characters of the early source. This document begins with the birth of Samuel (I Sam. 1) and ends with his death (I Sam. 25:1a), being confined to parts of I Sam. 1-24. The first half (I Sam. 1-12), dealing with Samuel as a judge, closed the JE and R^D Book of Judges; the second part (13-24) presents Samuel as a prophet, during Saul's reign.

The story opens with the charming idyll of Samuel's birth (I Sam. 1, omitting 1:6, "so she vexed her" in 1:7, "and after drinking" in 1:9, 1:11bβ, "and Hannah conceived" in 1:20, "and his vow" in 1:21). Although not historical, this story is engagingly written, with a fine feeling for the religious observances in ancient Israel. As literature, it is the best part of the late source of Samuel. Immediately following it (in the LXX after 1:28a), an editor has inserted a psalm of thanksgiving for national deliverance, with a Messianic allusion in 2:10 (expanded by the LXX with the addition of Jer. 9:23 f. [H. 9:22 f.]), dating probably from the fourth or third century B.C. (2:1-10, omitting 2:2aβ, 8b). This psalm, whose meter is 4:4, was not composed *ad hoc* for Hannah, but was quoted from some anthology because 2:5ba seemed appropriate to Hannah. It became the prototype of the *Magnificat* (Luke 1:46-55).

In accordance with his mother's vow, young Samuel became a model temple servant at Shiloh, which was in charge of Eli and his two sons, Hophni and Phinehas. The heroic death of Hophni and Phinehas in battle, while defending the ark, was interpreted by the late source as divine punishment for taking their portions of sacrificial victims before Jehovah's share had been burnt on the altar (2:11-26, omitting "the offering of" in 2:17; 2:22b, where the sons of Eli are maliciously accused of brazen obscenity, and "these . . . evil things" in 2:23). In 2:27-36 an editor supplied a spurious prophecy of the exclusive monopoly attained by the sons of Zadok in the Temple of Jerusalem.

After Samuel received a divine revelation concerning the impending end of Eli and his house, on account of their sins, he became a prophet with a national reputation (3, omitting "and he arose" in 3:6; and perhaps 3:20 f.). We should read in 3:13b "for his sons were cursing the deity and he restrained them not"; this blasphemous statement has been removed in our text by changing "deity" into "themselves," and by the substitute "for the iniquity which he knew." As a judge succeeding Eli, Samuel through prayer delivered for all time the Israelites from the Philistines (7:3-17, omitting "and the Astartes" in 7:3 f., "whole offering" in 7:9; 7:12; "Israel" in 7:16). Reluctantly and after an earnest warning about the evils of monarchy, he acceded to the wish of the people for a king (8), for his sons were unworthy to succeed him. At Mizpah, he selected Saul as king by lot (10:17-27a; 11:12 f.; omitting 10:18 f., the second "again" [A.V. "yet"] in 10:22; 10:23b [cf. 9:2b]).

In resigning as judge in favor of King Saul (contradicting 7:15), Samuel made a farewell address in which he defended his administration and warned the people that, as their past history showed, Jehovah would punish disobedience to his will. Then he compelled nature to manifest Jehovah's displeasure for his people, who had wickedly asked for a king, through a sudden thunderstorm in harvesttime (12; this chapter is R^D's conclusion of the Deuteronomistic Book of Judges).

Although no longer in power, Samuel remained the *de facto* ruler. As a prophet, Samuel was a sort of vicar of God on earth, with the authority to depose Saul, the legitimate king, in favor of David. Saul was deposed for not awaiting Samuel before offering sacrifice during the Philistine war (13:7b-15a, possibly a late midrash), and a second time for not destroying all the Amalekites and their flocks in accordance with the ban (15, omitting "200,000 footmen and 10,000 men of Judah" in 15:4; 15:27-29; on 15:22 f. cf. Arnold, *Ephod and Ark*, pp. 130 f.). Samuel forthwith anointed as king David, youngest son of Jesse (16:1-13, probably a late midrash).

David now takes the center of the stage. While still a boy, David slew Goliath (17:1-54; omitting "which [belongs] to Judah" in 17:1; "this" [A.V., "that"] and "and he had eight sons" in 17:12; "went" in 17:13; 17:13b, 15; "Goliath the Philistine his name from Gath" [*sic*] in 17:23; 17:38b; "with the shepherd's thing which he had" in 17:40; 17:41, 48b, 52b, 54; the LXX contains a much shorter text in chs. 17-18). David immediately joined Saul's retinue and became Jonathan's friend (17: 55-18:2, 6aα).

Envious of David's popularity, Saul tried to kill him (18:10 f.) and sent him out with the troops (18:12-16, omitting 18:12b, "and Judah" in 18:16). Saul promised David the hand of Merab, but married her to another man (18:17, 21a, 18 f., possibly a later midrash; 18:21b is stupidly harmonistic). In spite of Jonathan's good offices, Saul tried to kill David again (19:1-10, omitting "even to the wall" in 19:10, and 19:2 f., 7a). So David fled to Samuel at Ramah where Saul's guards and the king himself became raving ecstatics (19:18-24). From "Naioth" (the coenobium of the prophets?) in Ramah (19:18 f., 22 f.; 20:1) whither he had fled, David went to see Jonathan and made a compact with him. Upon being informed of Saul's determination to kill him, David escaped for good (20:1-42 [H. 20:1-21:1]).

Fearing king Achish in Gath, David feigned insanity by successfully imitating the wild transports of the prophets of Ramah (21:10-15 [H. 21:11-16], omitting "the king of the land" in 21:11 [H. 21:12]). At Adullam, he collected a band of about 400 desperadoes (22:1-5, omitting 22:5). Jonathan comforted David with a prediction that he would be king after Saul, and made another covenant with him (23:14b-18). On the point of capturing David, Saul was recalled by a Philistine raid (23:19-28, omitting from "in the hill" to the end in 23:19). On a later occasion, David spared Saul's life, and the old king, deeply moved, promised David that he should be king, only begging him to spare the royal offspring (23:29-24:22 H. 24, omitting 24:13 H 24:14). Verses 24:5-8 (Eng. 4-7) were written on the margins, first right then left, thus:

Instead of reading correctly, from top to bottom, first the right column and then the left, the next copyist zigzagged between the two as indicated by the arrows. Of course, the inverse alternative is also possible: the first writer may have zigzagged, and the copyist following may have read down the columns.

It is uncertain whether the brief notice of Samuel's death in 25:1a (cf. 28:3a) belonged to this source or was added later. In any case, the late source closes with Saul in tears, virtually handing his crown to David.

In contrast with the lucid and objective presentation of historical events and personalities which characterizes the early source, the late source, like E and E² particularly in Joshua, is clouded with legends and distorted by theories. The sparse dramatic unity and uniformity of style in this material points to multiple authorship. Few of the stories achieve the literary distinction of E in the Pentateuch and Judges: only the charming legend of Samuel's birth (I Sam. 1), the finest story of all, could have been written by one of such subtle literary taste as the author of E (750 B.C.). The famous story of David and Goliath (I Sam. 17) is second best, but the text is too uncertain to warrant a verdict about date and authorship. We may date I Sam. 1 with some assurance about 750 B.C. (probably in the Northern Kingdom) and tentatively I Sam. 17 and 20, in their original form, somewhere in the following century. The rest seems to belong to the century 650-550 B.C.

In general, the late source represents a correction of the early source. Historical facts are sacrificed on the altar of two dominating theories: monarchy is an apostasy from Jehovah, and good or bad fortune among mortals is an exact divine retribution for human conduct. Regarding these theories as axiomatic, the authors of the late source proceeded to rewrite history as it should have happened had Jehovah (or his human vicar) really been at the head of the government and in his absolute justice had actually balanced the books of each human life by rewarding saints and punishing sinners on earth.

Like E² in Judges (Judg. 8:22 f.), I Sam. 8:7; 10:19; 12:12, 17, 19 regard the monarchy as rebellion against God. Moreover, in order to disprove the earlier and unquestionably correct view (I Sam. 9:16), that the monarchy was indispensable for deliverance from the Philistines, the author concocted the story of Samuel's miraculous and final deliverance of Israel from the Philistine yoke (I Sam. 7:3-17, particularly 7:10, 13 f.). Not only is the monarchy as such sacrilegious and unnecessary, it is also a bitter source of woe for the nation. The evils of monarchy include the drafting of men and women in the king's service, militarism, heavy taxation, and expropriation of landed property (cf. 22:7)—in a word, national slavery (I Sam. 8:11-17). This indictment of the monarchy is far more severe and comprehensive than Deut. 17:14-20, which is chiefly directed against several of Solomon's practices, and than Hosea's denunciations of royal usurpations and assassinations (Hos. 7:7; 8:4a, 10; 10:7, 15b).

The second dogmatic theory, though not so explicitly stated as the first, has had an even greater corrosive effect on historical truth. Like the friends of Job, the authors of the late source infer from the Deuteronomic theory of divine retribution for national sin and virtue—a doctrine already individualized here as in Proverbs—that a fortunate man must needs be a saint, whereas an unfortunate one can be safely regarded as a reprobate. Thus the noble figures of Saul, Eli, Hophni, and Phinehas, who died violent unnatural deaths, are depicted as God-forsaken sinners. To take their place, Jehovah chose David and Samuel, conceived as saints because of their good fortune.

In the early source, as in actual life, good and evil are inextricably mixed in human character: Saul and David pass alternatively from the noblest to the basest deeds. In the late source, as in the Psalms, there are but two classes of men, saints and sinners, saved and damned. In the early source, Saul rose to the throne suddenly through an heroic deed and thereafter devoted himself—unsuccessfully, to be sure—to the liberation of his people. He is therefore a nobler—if more tragic—figure than David, who attained the throne deviously, through his wits and fortunate circumstances, and was never oblivious of his personal aims and ambitions. In the late source and later glosses, it is sheer perversion of the facts, dictated by religious dogma, to depict Saul as a divinely accursed, illegitimate, and deposed ruler, and David as God's chosen national hero "sans peur et sans reproche," already on the way to become the "sweet psalmist of Israel" (II Sam. 23:1), the pious organizer of the musical liturgies in the Temple (Chronicles), and prototype of the future Messiah.

With the supercilious indifference to facts typical of some theologians, the authors of the late source glibly proceed to concoct stories and speeches glorifying Samuel and David and vilifying Hophni, Phinehas, and Saul, suppressing when possible or disguising when necessary Saul's noble acts, Samuel's obscure position as a village clairvoyant, and David's detestable actions, which are honestly reported in the old source. The story of Saul's victory over Agag king of the Amalekites (I Sam. 15) is the only one that may be based on facts and, if so, supplements information given by the early sources. The mist of legend and the compelling authority of dogma conspire to produce in the late source an atmosphere of make-believe and the illusion of a mirage.

How the early and late source were joined together is not perfectly clear. In any case, the result is quite different from the union of J and E in Genesis and Judges. In no cases are the two sources closely woven into a single narrative, and little if anything has been lost in the process of combining them. Moreover, no effort was made to harmonize the divergent characterizations and stories of the two documents or to explain, as RJE does, the presence of parallel accounts of identical events, such as the coronation of Saul, the first meeting of David and Saul, and the final escape of David from court.

It is true that in numerous harmonistic notes an attempt is made to eliminate some of the worst inconsistencies, but these notes lack the finesse of RJE's explanations as to why Hagar was driven out twice by Abraham (Gen. 16:9) and why Moses twice received the tables of the Law (Ex. 34:1b, etc.). As a matter of fact, these harmonistic notes in Samuel (listed in *Quantulacumque*, p. 316) do not seem to have been penned by an editor eager to reconcile two conflicting documents. They are far too abrupt, clumsy, and obvious to be editorial. They are merely marginal annotations jotted down by bewildered generations of readers. Only I Sam. 10:8; 11:14, whose purpose is to harmonize the imaginary coronation of Saul at Mizpah (10:17-27a) with the historical coronation at Gilgal (11:15), are worthy of an editor.

Under the circumstances it is by no means certain, as many critics believe, that the two sources of Samuel were joined together after the manner of J and E. Another possibility, which has much to commend it and seems preferable to the present writer, is that the late source is merely a supplement to the early source, after the manner of P in Genesis. Even though parts of the late source may rest on popular tradition and legend, it seems as a whole a deliberate attempt to correct the early history, which faithfully described conditions of an earlier day shocking to later generations, and to bring it into harmony with the theocratic conception of the state and the doctrine of divine retribution for human deeds. This hypothesis would explain the fact that the early source has dramatic unity and is apparently preserved in full, whereas the late source is not only more episodic and disjointed but has obvious lacunae. The revelation to Samuel of the impending doom of Eli and the other priests of Shiloh (I Sam. 3:11-14), harmonized by a later hand with the midrash in 2:27-36 (cf. "For I have told him . . ." in 3:13), belongs to the late source but lacks an account of its fulfillment. If the late source were an independent history, it would indubitably have related the fulfillment of the prophecy in a section now lost. If, however, the late source is merely a supplement to the early one, it would be natural to provide an explanation, through narratives and a divine oracle, for the sudden and tragic death of the priests of Shiloh (4:11-22), which in the old source was told in connection with the capture and return of the ark of Shiloh

The author of the early source in I Sam. 4:1-7:1 is primarily interested in the ark, which became the most sacred object in the Temple of Solomon, and not in the fortunes of the priesthood or sanctuary at Shiloh. There is, therefore, no need to suppose, with B. Stade (*Encycl. Bibl.* 4 [1903] 4279, and elsewhere) and others, that the old source contained after 7:1 an account (now lost) of the destruction of Shiloh by the Philistines, and that Jeremiah (7:12) still read it there. The fate of Shiloh is irrelevant after the ark had left it for good, and the author of the early source is too masterful to lose the main thread of the narrative by following up topics which, though of some interest, are unrelated to the main subject. Besides, the destruction of Shiloh, which Jeremiah still considered a major tragedy, was an incident too sad and humiliating to be described in full by our author unless it were, like the defeat at Gilboa, a necessary link in the succession of events narrated.

In conclusion, it seems better to regard the late source not as a separate and independent document, even though several of its stories may have been in circulation before being incorporated in our book, but as the inception of that pious tampering with ancient historical records of which Chronicles, three or four centuries later, is the classical example. Apparently, however, the authors of the late source did not, like the Chronicler, feel compelled to write a separate work, but, like the authors of the narrative sections in the Priestly Code, preferred to add their corrections and improvements to the original history, blissfully unaware of the havoc and confusion thereby wrought on one of the greatest books ever written.

3. The Deuteronomistic Edition

The addition of the late source to the classic history of Ahimaaz (if he is the author) made it unnecessary for the Deuteronomists, who edited the books from Genesis to Kings (without P, S, and other later additions) about 550 B.C., to subject the books of Samuel to a thorough revision. They found some of their great religious tenets adequately presented in the late source. On the other hand, the material did not lend itself, as in Judges and Kings, to the insertion of introductions and conclusions for individual stories. But the chief reason for the perfunctory character of the Deuteronomic edition of Samuel, in contrast with Judges and Kings, is that the fundamental Deuteronomic doctrine—failure to worship Jehovah exclusively and correctly brings national disaster—was not applicable to the history of the first two kings of Israel. It is only in I Sam. 1-12, the last part of the Deuteronomic Book of Judges, that the Deuteronomists, for whom Eli and Samuel were the last of the "Judges," could to a slight degree apply their method.

The Deuteronomists provided not only a general introduction to the history of the "Judges" in Judg. 2:6-3:6, but also a special one of considerable length (found incongruously in Judg. 10:6-16) for the period of the Philistine oppression, unrelieved by Samson's exploits and brought to an end, according to I Sam. 7, by the last judge, Samuel. Just as in Joshua the Deuteronomists substituted for Joshua's final address in E (Josh. 24) an address from their own pen (Josh. 23), so they added to Samuel's final address in the late source (I Sam. 8) another one in I Sam. 12. This latter address of Samuel's, presenting in retrospect Jehovah's dealings with Israel since the deliverance from Egypt (including his punishments and deliverances during the period of the judges) furnishes the counterpart to the introduction in Judg. 2:6-3:6, as a fitting conclusion to the Deuteronomistic Book of Judges.

But after I Sam. 12 there was no scope for Deuteronomistic moralizing of history. For during the reigns of Saul and David there could be no such national violation of the Deuteronomic law, as occurred in the period of the judges by forsaking Jehovah during peacetime and worshiping the gods of Canaan (the Baals and Astartes), reputedly the givers of agricultural bounty (cf. Hos. 2:8-13 [H. 2:10-15]). Nor was there the opportunity offered by the history of the later kings of denouncing the adoption of alien gods and rites, the worship of Jehovah at the "high places" after the building of Solomon's Temple, not to speak of "Jeroboam's sin" in setting up golden bulls in the northern sanctuaries of Dan and Bethel. On the contrary, the Philistine oppression incited not only an outburst of nationalism but also a religious revival, one of whose symptoms was the outbreak of ecstatic fervor manifested in the transports of the early prophets. As in past wars, the Israelites in their uprising against the Philistines relied on Jehovah, and both Saul and David, whatever their faults, were wholeheartedly devoted to the national god. Before Solomon's Temple was built, the Deuteronomists dared not even resent the worship of Jehovah in the "high places." These ancient village sanctuaries Deuteronomic theory declared illegitimate immediately after the building of the Temple, although actually they were only condemned after the reforms of Josiah in 621.

There is reason to believe that the Deuteronomists suppressed certain parts of Samuel, as also of Judges, deemed unworthy of a religious book. They might endanger the reader's morals and piety. K. Budde (*Die Bücher Richter und Samuel* u.s.w.; and in later books) has noted that redactional summaries (I Sam. 7:13-17; 14:47-51; II Sam. 8) which he rightly attributes to the Deuteronomists, mark the end of the biographies of Samuel, Saul, and David. Consequently, the story of Saul's war against

Agag, king of the Amalekites (I Sam. 15), and David's family history
(II Sam. 9-20; 21-24), which follow the concluding remarks for Saul and
David respectively, must have been left out of the Deuteronomic edition
of 550 and added later; the same applies to I Sam. 28:3-25 (Saul's consultation of the ghost of Samuel).

In every case, even if Budde's omissions are made, the concluding
summaries occur some little time before the hero's death and are followed
by stories concerning him. We may, however, regard II Sam. 8 as a summary prepared to replace the following suppressed material, as I Kings
2:1-12 is a substitute for the rest of I Kings 1-2, omitted by the Deuteronomists. Similarly, Judg. 8:30-35 is a brief Deuteronomistic surrogate
for the deleted story of Abimelech in ch. 9. But there seems to be nothing
in I Sam. 15 to which the Deuteronomists could object. On the contrary,
the religious moralizing in 15:22-30 is much in their vein, and some parts
of 15:24-30 are actually written in their style.

Budde is right, however, in his view that I Sam. 28:3-25; II Sam. 9-20
and 21-24; I Kings 1; 2:13-46a were lacking in the Deuteronomistic
edition of Samuel. It is obvious that these sections belonging to the
old source, omitting the two psalms, II Sam. 22 and 23:1-7, which are
later in date than the Deuteronomists, are out of place, except I Kings
1-2; I Sam. 28:3-25 should follow 30, and the order of the stories of the
early source in II Samuel must have been originally 1-6; 21:15-22; 23:8-39;
24; 21:1-14; 9-20; I Kings 1; 2:13-46a. It is only 21:15-22 and 23:8-39 that
may be in doubt. They could have stood only before or after II Sam. 6,
but neither place is entirely appropriate. In any case, such radical displacements within the early source are best explained first through the
suppression of these sections, which for obvious reasons were objectionable to the Deuteronomists (for I Sam. 28 cf. I Chron. 10:13), and secondly through their later insertion either in a slightly wrong place (I Sam.
28:3-25), or, like Judg. 17-21, at the end of the book (II Sam. 9-20; 21-24).
It is probable that II Sam. 9-20 was inserted before 21-24 and from a better
manuscript. Not only does 21-24 contain late psalms, but 24:10-19 is
clearly a late rewriting of the early source.

Everything indicates that the Deuteronomic Book of Samuel ended with
II Sam. 8, followed by I Kings 2:1-12. When II Sam. 9-20 was added, the
last verses of ch. 8 (8:16-18) were repeated, with some interesting variants, at the end of 20(20:23-26); cf. I Kings 2:12b, 46b. Likewise, the
chronological note for Samson in 15:20 ending the Deuteronomistic Book
of Judges was repeated with variants in 16:31b, when ch. 16 was again
introduced.

The Deuteronomists carried on the chronological scheme begun in
Judges, which has been discussed in connection with that book. The
chronological notes in I Sam. 4:15, 18b; 7:2; 27:7; II Sam. 2:10 f.; 5:4 f.; I

Kings 2:11 were contributed by the Deuteronomists. The reign of Ishbaal (II Sam. 2:10) seems to have been willfully shortened (if the text is intact) to two years from seven years and six months. Since his reign corresponded exactly to David's rule in Hebron (II Sam. 2:11), it was finally ignored (cf. I Kings 2:11). The Deuteronomists had no chronology for Saul, whose reign, considered illegitimate, was presumably included in the time of Samuel and David. A later editor in I Sam. 13:1 introduced the formula for Saul's chronology (after the manner of Kings) but left the numbers blank. All we can say in regard to the absolute chronology of the events related in Samuel is that in 1000 B.C. David was king.

We may surmise that the historical and statistical summaries for Saul (I Sam. 14:47-51) and David (II Sam. 3:2-5; 5:13-16; 8 [20:23-26]) come from the pen of the Deuteronomists, although their dry style and accurate information, derived from excellent sources, have nothing in common with the moralizing eloquence characteristic of this school. The two longer passages in which the Deuteronomists really composed freely, without excerpting older sources and condensing them, are the last words of Samuel (I Sam. 12) and the last words of David (I Kings 2:1-12). The style of the first of these passages corresponds to that of the framework of Judges; that of the second is unmistakably Deuteronomistic (notably in I Kings 2:2-4). No other passages in our book can be attributed with equal assurance to the Deuteronomic school. Some passages resembling the typical Deuteronomic style seem to belong either to recent strata of the late source, being more or less contemporary with the publication of Deuteronomy in 621 (for instance, I Sam. 7:2-4, 15; 8), others are lucubrations penned long after 550 (I Sam. 2:27-36; 10:18 f.; II Sam. 7).

4. The Midrash in Samuel

There is, of course, a great variety of opinion about I Sam. 2:27-36 and II Sam. 7. These obscure, involved, and badly written prophecies about the eternity of Zadok's priestly family and that of David's dynasty have a strange fascination for Bible students.

The first of these oracles is generally considered Deuteronomistic (J. Wellhausen) or at least "Deuteronomistically recast" (K. Budde), but H. P. Smith (Samuel [ICC], pp. xix f.) regards it as an integral part of the early source. In a detailed study of I Sam. 2:27-36, C. Steuernagel (BWAT 13 [1913] 204-221) concludes that its original form predicted the slaying of Nob's priests, with the exception of Abiathar (I Sam. 22), a calamity foreshadowed by the death of Eli's sons on the same day. A first revision transformed it into a sentence of unending misery for the house of Eli, while a second (Deuteronomistic) converted it into a prediction of Josiah's reforms in 621, according to which only the sons of Zadok could be priests in Jerusalem.

Likewise, although less simply, I. Hylander (*Der literarische Samuel-Saul-Komplex*, pp. 41 f., 51-62) regards the oracle as a Zadokite revision, utilizing I Sam. 3, of a prophecy against Nob. Such elaborate critical studies seem wasted on so insignificant and inferior a piece of writing which required but one author. A well-intentioned reader living demonstrably after the publication of the Priestly Code, if not after the codification of the Pentateuch about 400 B.C., could not resist the impulse to put on paper his muddled ideas about the vicissitudes of the priesthood in ancient Israel. Hence this confused oracle somehow found its way into the Scriptures. In conformance with the teachings of the Priestly Code, he regarded all the priests of Israel as descendants of Aaron and, contrary to the general practice until well after Solomon, believed that sacrifice was their chief and exclusive function (2:27 f.).

To show his erudition, the ancient rite (obsolete in the author's time, as when Deut. 10:8; 31:9, 25 f. were written) to "bear the [divination] box [*sic,* for 'ephod'] before" Jehovah (2:28) is punctiliously mentioned by our glossator. But by doing so he betrays his ignorance of the fact that divining and sacrificing *together* were never functions of the priests of Israel. He makes Eli not only a descendant of Aaron (presumably through Ithamar, cf. Josephus, *Antiquities* 5:11, 5), an assumption wholly unwarranted in the older sources, but also the ancestor of all the priests mentioned in Samuel, with the sole exception of Zadok (2:27).

In this fantastic view he agrees with the spurious genealogy given in a gloss (I Sam. 14:3a) whose purpose is to trace the descent of Nob's priests back to Eli. W. R. Arnold (*Ephod and Ark*, pp. 14 f.) has conclusively proved the absurdity of this connection (maintained by some modern scholars) between the priests of Shiloh and those of Nob. The Jewish dogma that all priests are kinsmen is utterly unfounded in pre-exilic times, when the several sanctuaries were supervised by separate priestly families without mutual blood relationships.

To punish the sacrilegious behavior of Eli's sons, countenanced by their father (2:29 f.), Jehovah first destroys Eli's house, leaving in it no old man but only an infant, Ichabod (2:31 f.; cf. 4:11-22). Later, all his descendants at Nob were massacred, except Abiathar (2:33). As a token, Hophni and Phinehas die on the same day (2:34). Even the last survivor of Eli's house, Abiathar, comes to grief (2:33) when Jehovah selects another, Zadok, as a "faithful priest" and ancestor of the priestly family officiating for the kings of Judah forever (2:35; cf. I Kings 2:27). Finally, through Josiah's reforms (621 B.C.), all living survivors of Eli (officiating outside of Jerusalem) are reduced to the status of paupers, begging a morsel of bread from Zadok's proud descendants in Jerusalem (2:36).

This seems to be the purport of the spurious oracle of an anonymous man of God who, like other such imaginary personages (Judg. 6:7-10; I

Kings 13:1-10), was invented for the occasion and after finishing his speech disappears without a trace. The chaos in this oracle is due not to interpolations but to the muddled mind of its author, who wavered between genuine information of the early source and the theoretically reconstructed history of the priesthood penned in the Priestly Code.

The Chronicler may possibly have read I Sam. 2:27-36 in the book but, in his eagerness to reach David's reign, he omitted the stories about Eli, Samuel, and Saul, and ignored this oracle *in toto.* In fact, he not only eliminated Eli from his list of high priests, but through a sleight of hand, utilizing an accidental textual corruption in II Sam. 8:17, he substituted Zadok for Abiathar as the son [really grandson; cf. I Sam. 22:20] of Ahitub (I Chron. 6:8, 52 f. [H. 5:34; 6:37 f.]; 18:16; Ezra 7:2). Thus he made of Zadok—contradicting the whole point of this oracle—a member of the priestly family at Nob and, implicitly, a descendant of Eli. In view of this it becomes doubtful that the Chronicler read I Sam. 2:27-36 in his copy of the Book of Samuel and it is not to be excluded that this section was written after the time of the Chronicler (i.e., in the period 250-200 B.C.).

The Chronicler, on the contrary, attached the greatest importance to Nathan's oracle in II Sam. 7, although in reproducing it (I Chron. 17) he felt impelled to improve the bad grammar and dreary style (truly "monkish drivel," as W. R. Arnold [*Ephod and Ark,* p. 42, n. 3] calls it) of a glossator even more ignorant and amateurish—if possible—than the author of I Sam. 2:27-36.

Aware that, according to I Sam. 2:35, the descendants of Zadok would remain forever the priests of the Davidic dynasty and that the point of II Sam. 7 was the eternity of this dynasty, J. Wellhausen (*Composition des Hexateuchs,* p. 257. 2nd ed., 1889) attributes both oracles to one author living in the reign of Josiah (638-609 B.C.). Although most critics (e.g., A. Kuenen, C. H. Cornill, K. Budde, J. A. Bewer) accept the seventh century, C. Steuernagel (*Einleitung in das Alte Testament,* p. 325) dates II Sam. 7 in the time of David, admitting, however, that the author of the early source and later editors revised it. Conversely, B. Stade (*Encycl. Bibl.* 4 [1903] 4278) and H. P. Smith (*Samuel* [ICC], pp. 297 f.) favor an exilic or postexilic date.

The chief argument for a pre-exilic date is the eternity of the Davidic dynasty. Undeniably, before 586 a Judean like Solomon could rhetorically express a hope that David's dynasty would never cease (I Kings 2:33, 45). But it does not follow that such an expectation could *only* be entertained before the dynasty came to its end. Quite the contrary. When the Jews, having lost their independent state, were living under alien imperial rulers, they clung tenaciously to the hope of a future revival of their state. Those to whom the monarchy was as distasteful as to Hosea and the authors of the late source, with utter indifference for political independence, set about organizing the Jews into an invisible kingdom of God—a theocratic, ritually pure congregation (the Priestly Code). But others refused to resign themselves to foreign rule and with fanatic faith proclaimed a restoration of the throne of David.

Under the Persian and Greek rule, particularly from 520 to 200 B.C., this hope for a restoration of David's throne was widespread among the Jews, as shown by additions to the books of the ancient prophets (Hos. 1:11 [H. 2:2]; 3:5; Am. 9:11 f.; Zech. 9:9; 12:7-10; 13:1; Is. 9:6 f. [H. 9:5 f.]; 11:1, 10; Jer. 30:9; 33:14-26; Ez. 34:23 f.; 37:24 f.) and some Psalms (89; 122:5; 132:10-12, 17 f.). This hope arose soon after 586, if Jer. 23:5 f. (repeated in a spurious passage in Jer. 33:15 f.) is authentic, and in any case was strong in 520 (Hag. 2:23; Zech. 3:8; 6:12 [quoting Jer. 23:5]) when Zerubbabel, a descendant of David, was hailed by some as the Messiah, only to be removed at once from circulation by the Persian authorities. Less than a century later, Nehemiah was falsely accused of encouraging the Messianic prophets in Jerusalem (Neh. 6:7).

The above-mentioned glosses (in the prophetic books) and Psalms are undoubtedly later than Nehemiah and belong, for the most part, to the fourth and the first half of the third centuries. Nathan's oracle in II Sam. 7 is demonstrably earlier than the Chronicler (about 250 B.C.) and was probably written during the preceding century.

The logic of modern critics who date II Sam. 7 before 586 is disproved by Psalm 89, utilized in Ps. 132. This psalm (disregarding the nature hymn in 89:5-18 [H. 89:6-19], and also 89:46-48 [H. 89:47-49], apparently the conclusion of Ps. 88), proves that some Jews believed in the eternity of David's dynasty after it fell in 586. Psalm 89 was written, according to the explicit statements in 89:38-45 [H. 89:39-46], *after* the crown of David's sons lay in the dust and their throne was cast to the ground. And yet this psalm reveals not only the hope for a restoration of the dynasty (89:20-27 [H. 89:21-28]), but gives the clearest possible expression to the doctrine of the eternity of that crownless dynasty (89:3 f., 28-37 [H. 89:4 f., 29-38]).

Belief in the eternity of something that has ceased to exist is characteristic of Judaism in its early stages, and furnishes one of the secrets of its extraordinary vitality. In general, the vigor of a religion seems to be proportionate to its disregard of reason and logic. When a faith ceases to cry out defiantly *Credo quia absurdum* and becomes rational, its days as a vital, inspiring force in the lives of men are numbered.

It is therefore clear that the only argument adduced for the early date of II Sam. 7—assertion of the eternity of the Davidic dynasty—is wholly irrelevant. Moreover, the general assumption that Ps. 89 is in part "a poetic paraphrase" of sections of II Sam. 7 (B. Duhm, *Psalmen*, KHC, p. 222) should be seriously questioned. A comparison of II Sam. 7:8-10 with Ps. 89:20-22 [H. 89:21-23] and of II Sam. 7:13-16 with Ps. 89:26-33

[H. 89:27-34] proves the literary relationship of these verses, but surely also, the dependence of the oracle on the psalm. Why did the author of the dreary prose in II Sam. 7 lapse into verse in 7:8-16 (cf. H. P. Smith's commentary [ICC] *ad loca*), for which alone there are parallels in Ps. 89, and not elsewhere? And, since his point was to develop the pun, "David shall not build a house [i.e., a temple] for Jehovah, but Jehovah shall build a house [i.e., a dynasty] for David," if Ps. 89 was not in his mind, why did he use "seed" for "dynasty" in 7:12 instead of "house," as in 7:11 (cf. 7:18 f., 25-27, 29, where there is no connection with Ps. 89)? If Ps. 89 was a paraphrase of I Sam. 7, why was "house" never used for "dynasty"? And how could any lucidity in Ps. 89 be derived from the muddle in II Sam. 7? Does "thy seed" in 7:12 mean Solomon, as it does if 7:13 is original and as the Chronicler understood it (I Chron. 17:11)? Or does it symbolize the whole dynasty, as most modern commentators believe, omitting v. 13, on the basis of 7:14 (where, however, the beginning is referred to Solomon in I Chron. 22:10; 28:6)? This confusion is hopeless because it existed in the author's mind. He was troubled by David's failure to build the Temple and so hit on the bizarre explanation derived from the double meaning of "house." In the literal sense, the "house" will be built by Solomon (7:13); in the figurative sense, by Jehovah (7:11). Finding in Ps. 89 a clear statement of the latter point— Jehovah permanently establishes David's line—he made free with it, but in so doing he went off on a tangent, losing track of the original problem, why Solomon built the Temple and not David. Not only that, but by ineptly giving a double meaning to "David's seed," first Solomon (7:12 f.), then David's "house" or dynasty (7:14-16), he sank into a mire of unintelligible verbiage. Although the issue was already confused in his mind, the lure of Ps. 89 was fatal.

His style is consistently wretched, whether he writes freely or paraphrases Ps. 89. As examples of his own miserable diction, the following may suffice: "I [Jehovah] was walking about [from locality to locality] in a tent and a tabernacle" (7:6); "and I shall make thee a great name like the name of the great ones who are on the earth" (7:9); "on account of thy word and like thy heart thou hast done all this greatness to cause thy servant to know" (7:21); the worst instance of illiterate inanity is probably 7:23. In more than one way our would-be author succeeds in spoiling the sections of Ps. 89 which he quotes. He is prolix (cf. Ps. 89:20-23 [H. 89:21-24] with II Sam. 7:8-11a); he is banal, as when he transforms "He will cry unto me, 'Thou art my father, O my God, and the rock of my salvation.' Also I shall make him my firstborn" (Ps. 89:26 [H. 89:27 f.]) into "I shall be to him for a father, and he will be to me for a son" (7:14). Likewise Ps. 89:33 [H. 89:34], "But my loyalty I shall not shatter away from him" (literally "from with him") becomes in II Sam. 7:15, "But my loyalty I shall not remove [so with I Chron. and the

versions; the Masoretic text has "will not pass away"] from him." The
author of II Sam. 7 repeats himself *ad nauseam*. Whereas in Ps. 89:28 f.,
36 f. (H. 89:29 f., 37 f.) six different expressions are used to convey the
eternity of David's dynasty, in II Sam. 7:13b, 16 "forever" is repeated
three times: cf. the triple repetition of the same verb in 7:15.

These facts do not exhaust the evidence, but they suffice to prove that
II Sam. 7 cannot antedate Ps. 89. Since the Psalm is explicitly dated after
the Exile of 586, and II Sam. 7 comes earlier than about 250, when the
Chronicler copied it in his book, II Sam. 7 was undoubtedly written
somewhere between those dates. The character of the language places it
closer to the later than to the earlier period, probably in the late fourth
century.

More space than they deserve has been devoted to I Sam. 2:27-36 and
II Sam. 7 in order to illustrate, through the two most elaborate instances,
the character of the midrashic additions to Samuel, and the literary and
historical worthlessness of these oracles, frequently quoted as authorities
on the religion of pre-exilic Israel. The numerous other glosses and annotations to Samuel have been listed in the preceding summaries of the
early and late sources and have been classified in *Quantulacumque* (pp.
305-316). In general, they date from 400 to 200 B.C. and reveal a complete misunderstanding of the religion in the period of Saul and David,
which they try to harmonize with Judaism after 400 B.C. These authors
magnify the glory of David's kingdom (according to II Sam. 24:9 it had
an army of 1,300,000 men) and exaggerate *ad absurdum* a tendency in
the late source to depict Samuel and David as saints, and Eli's sons and
Saul as reprobates. Much of this midrash is merely exegetical but fails to
contribute anything of value to an understanding of the ancient parts of
the book.

As firsthand evidence of dogmatic or stupid exegesis—deliberate or
foolish misunderstanding of Biblical words—these earliest instances of
the misinterpretations which have persisted through the centuries to our
own day are not only historically instructive but should spur modern
interpreters to "go and sin no more."[6]

---

[6] The appendices to Samuel in II Sam. 21-24 (cf. Judg. 17-21) were added in
three stages. First, two omitted stories from the early source (21:1-14; 24, originally
preceding, in inverse order, II Sam. 9) were added at the end of the book; next,
between them, the roster and deeds of David's heroes (21:15-22; 23:8-39); and,
finally, two postexilic psalms (22 = Ps. 18 and 23:1-7) were inserted between the
two preceding sections. The Psalm in II Sam. 22 (Ps. 18), wrongly attributed to
David, is a congregational song of thanksgiving, praising God for his deliverance of
his people; the Deuteronomistic and legalistic tone in 22:21-25 dates it after 400 B.C.,
although the nature hymn in 22:8-16 may be considerably earlier. The sententious
"last words of David" in 23:1-7, in which David regards himself as divinely inspired,
show kinship with II Sam. 7 and Ps. 1; they probably date from the late fourth century. David would hardly have penned such sanctimonious inanities.

CHAPTER IV

THE BOOKS OF KINGS

The two Books of Kings, like the two Books of Samuel (cf. the beginning of the chapter on Samuel), were originally, in the Hebrew, a single volume. They relate the history of Israel from the last days of David (about 973 B.C.) to the release of Jehoiachin from his Babylonian prison in 561 B.C.

This history is divided into three main parts: 1. Accession and reign of Solomon (I 1-11). 2. Division of the kingdom (I 12:1-24) and the reigns of the kings of Israel and Judah to the end of the Northern Kingdom (I 12:25-II 17:6), with an appendix on the mixed race and religion of North Israel (the later Samaritans) after 722 B.C. (II 17:7-41). 3. History of the kings of Judah from 722 to 561 B.C. (II 18-25).

1. *Solomon* (I 1-11). The first two chapters of I Kings are the sequel of II Sam. 9-20 and mark the end of the early source of Samuel (see above). The history of Solomon centers around the building of his palace and the Temple (6-7); the account is introduced by his negotiations with Hiram of Tyre preparatory to building operations (5:1-18 [H. 5:15-32]), and concluded by the dedication of the Temple (8), divine promises and warnings (9:1-9), and payment to Hiram (9:10-14). Brief notices about Solomon's other activities precede and follow the story of the building of the Temple. At the beginning: his marriage with the daughter of Pharaoh (3:1), his sacrifice and dream at Gibeon (3:2-15), his wise decision in the litigation about the two infants (3:16-28), the administration and power of his kingdom (4:1-28 [H. 4:1-5:8]), and his learning and wisdom (4:29-34 [H. 5:9-14]). At the end: Solomon's military and other buildings (9:15-24), his sacrifices (9:25), his naval expedition to Ophir (9:26-28), the visit of the Queen of Sheba (10:1-13), his wisdom and wealth (10:14-29), his harem (11:1-13), his foreign and internal foes (11:14-40), and an editorial conclusion (11:41-43).

2. *The kings of Israel and Judah* (I 12-II 17), with an introductory account of the division of the kingdom (I 12:1-24) and a concluding account of the origin of the Samaritans (II 17:7-41).

The following Judean (Jud.) and Ephraimitic (Ephr.) *stories about prophets* are included in the history of the kings. Ahijah the Shilonite, under Jeroboam I (I 11:29-39; 12:15 [Jud., 550 B.C.]; 14:1-18; 15:29 [Jud.,

600 b.c.]. On the text of the LXX see E. Meyer, *Die Israeliten und ihre Nachbarstämme*, pp. 363-370). An anonymous Judean prophet[1] and an old Ephraimitic prophet under Jeroboam I (I 12:32-13:32 [late Jud.; cf. I 13:2 f. with II 23:15-20]). Shemaiah under Rehoboam (I 12:21-24 [Jud., 550 b.c.]). Jehu, son of Hanani, under Baasha (I 16:1-4 [7]; cf. 16:12 [Jud., 600 b.c.]). Elijah under Ahab (I 17-19; 21; cf. II 9:25 f. [Ephr., *ca.* 800 b.c.]; under Ahaziah, II 1:2-17 [perhaps Ephr. in a late revision]). Elisha under Joram, Jehu, and Joash (II 2:1-8:15; 13:14-21; cf. I 19:19-21; II 9:1-13 [Ephr., 750 b.c.]). An anonymous prophet under Ahab (I 20:13 f., 22, 28 [late Jud.]). An anonymous member of the prophetic fraternity under Ahab (I 20:35-43 [late Jud.]). Micaiah, son of Imlah, and the other prophets of Ahab (I 22:5-28 [early Ephr.]). Jonah, son of Amittai, under Jeroboam II (II 14:25 [Jud., 550 b.c.]; cf. the Book of Jonah). Isaiah, son of Amoz, under Hezekiah (II 19:1-20:19, reproduced with variants and additions in Is. 37-39 [Jud.]). Anonymous prophets under Manasseh (II 21:10-15; cf. 21:7-9 [Jud., 550 b.c.]). Huldah, the prophetess, under Josiah (II 22:14-20 [Jud., 550 b.c.]).

THE KINGS OF ISRAEL

Jeroboam I, son of Nebat (933-912 b.c.): I 12:20, 25-32; 13:33 f.; 14:19 f.; cf. 11:26-28; 12:1-19 and the prophetic stories in 11:29-40; 12:33-13:32; 14:1-18; 21:22; II 9:9.

Nadab, son of Jeroboam (912-911): I 15:25-31.

Baasha, son of Ahijah (911-888): I 15:33 f., 32; 16:5 f.; cf. the prophetic story 16:1-4, 7 and I 21:22; II 9:9.

Elah, son of Baasha (888-887): I 16:8-14.

Zimri, a usurper (one week in 887): I 16:15-20; cf. 16:9-12.

[Tibni, son of Ginath, a rival of Omri (887): 16:21 f.]

Omri, a usurper (887-875): I 16:23-28; cf. 16:16-22.

Ahab, son of Omri (875-853): I 16:29-34; 20 (including prophetic legends); 22:1-38 (including the story of Micaiah, son of Imlah), 22:39 f. Cf. the stories of Elijah (I 17-19; 21).

Ahaziah, son of Ahab (853-852): I 22:51-53 (H. 22:52-54); II 1:1, 18; cf. the Elijah story in II 1:2-17a.

Joram, son of Ahab (852-843): II 1:17b; 3:1 (with conflicting chronologies); 3:2 f.; 3:4-27 (including a story of Elisha); the other stories of Elisha in II 2:2-8:15 are placed within his reign. The concluding remarks on Joram are missing (but see 9:16-24).

Jehu (843-816), son of Jehoshaphat, son of Nimshi (so II 9:2; son of Nimshi in I 19:16; II 9:20): II 9:1-10:36; cf. Hos. 1:4.

---

[1] If we may accept the testimony of Josephus (*Antiquities* 8:8, 5) and Jerome (*ad* Zech. 1:1), who call him Jadon and Addo, respectively, he is to be identified with the seer Jedo, of II Chron. 9:29.

Jehoahaz, son of Jehu (816-800): II 13:1-9.

Joash or Jehoash, son of Jehoahaz (800-785): II 13:10-13, 22-25; 14:15 f. (the last passage repeats 13:12 f., which is a gloss); cf. the Elisha story in 13:14-21.

Jeroboam II, son of Joash (785-744): II 14:23-29; cf. Am. 7:9-11.

Zechariah, son of Jeroboam (six months in 744): II 15:8-12.

Shallum, son of Jabesh (one month in 744): II 15:13-16; cf. 15:10.

Menahem, son of Gadi (744-738): II 15:17-22; cf. 15:14, 16.

Pekahiah, son of Menahem (738-737): II 15:23-26.

Pekah, son of Remaliah (737-732): II 15:27-31; cf. 15:37; 16:5; Is. 7:1-9; 8:6.

Hoshea, son of Elah (732-722): II 17:1-6.

THE KINGS OF JUDAH TO 722 B.C.

Since, with exception of Athaliah, Jehoiakim, and Zedekiah every king of Judah beginning with Rehoboam was the son of his predecessor, the name of the father is omitted.

Rehoboam (933-917): I 14:21-31; cf. 12:1-24; 15:6.

Abijah or Abijam (917-915): I 15:1-8.

Asa (915-875): I 15:9-24; cf. I 22:46 (H. 22:47).

Jehoshaphat (875-851): I 22:41-50 (H. 22:41-51); cf. 22:2-33.

Jehoram or Joram (851-844): II 8:16-24.

Ahaziah (844-843): II 8:25-29; cf. 9:16-28. 9:29 repeats 8:25 with a different year of accession.

Athaliah, mother of Ahaziah and daughter of Ahab and Jezebel (843-837): II 11.

Jehoash or Joash, son of Ahaziah (837-798): II 11:21-12:21 (H. 12:1-22); cf. 11.

Amaziah (798-780): II 14:1-22; cf. 13:12.

Azariah or Uzziah (780-740): II 15:1-7; cf. Is. 6:1; Zech. 14:5.

Jotham (740-735): II 15:32-38; cf. 15:5.

Ahaz (735-720): II 16:1-20; cf. 20:11 (Is. 38:8) 23:12; Is. 7.

THE KINGS OF JUDAH AFTER 722 B.C. (II 18-25)

Hezekiah (720-692): II 18:1-20:21 (18:13, 17-37; 19:1-20:19 are reproduced with variants in Is. 36-39, where a psalm has been added in 38:9-20); cf. 21:3; Jer. 26:18 f.

Manasseh (692-639): II 21:1-18; cf. 23:12, 26; 24:3; Jer. 15:4.

Amon (639-638): II 21:19-26.

Josiah (638-609): II 22:1-23:30; cf. I 13:2; Jer. 1:1-3; 3:6; 22:10a, 15b-16, etc.; Zeph. 1:1.

Jehoahaz or Shallum (three months in 609): II 23:31-34; cf. 23:30; Jer. 22:11 f.

Jehoiakim or Eliakim, son of Josiah (609-598): II 23:34-24:7; cf. Jer. 22:18 f.; 25:1 f.; 26:1-24; 35:1; 36; 45:1; 46:2.

Jehoiachin, Jeconiah, or Coniah (three months in 598-597): II 24:8-17; cf. 25:27-30 = Jer. 52:31-34; Jer. 22:24-28; 24; 27:20; 28:4; 29:2.

Zedekiah, son of Josiah, originally called Mattaniah (597-586): II 24:18-25:21; cf. Jer. 21:1-7; 24:8; 27:2-28:17; 29:3; 32:1-5; 34:1-12; 37-39. II Kings 24:18-25:30 (except 25:22-26) are reproduced in Jer. 52 (52:28-30 is lacking in the LXX and in Kings), where the number of exiles is smaller.

After the end of the Judean kingdom in 586, Gedaliah was appointed governor by Nebuchadnezzar (more correctly Nebuchadrezzar) but was murdered by Ishmael, a descendant of David, two months after the destruction of Jerusalem. Some Judeans fled to Egypt, forcing Jeremiah to go with them (II 25:22-26, a brief summary of Jer. 40:7-43:7). In 561, Jehoiachin was delivered from his prison in Babylonia by Evil-merodach (Amel-Marduk), son and successor of Nebuchadnezzar (II 25:27-30 = Jer. 52:31-34).

1. The First Edition of Kings

It is obvious that, in its present form, Kings cannot have been written before the liberation of Jehoiachin from prison in 561 B.C., the latest incident narrated at the end (II 25:27-30). But A. Kuenen, in the second edition of his great *Historisch-critisch Onderzoek* (Vol. I, p. 2, 1887; German translation, 1890), and G. Wildeboer (*De Letterkunde des Ouden Verbonds,* Groningen, 1893. German translation: Göttingen, 1894) made it clear, as did most of the later critics, that the book was originally written about 600 B.C. and re-edited with additions half a century later. The chief difference between the two editions is that the first knows nothing of the destruction of Jerusalem in 586 or the Exile, whereas the second makes unmistakable allusions to these disastrous events. The original author recognizes that the worship of Jehovah on the high places outside of Jerusalem was legitimate before the building of the Temple of Solomon (I 3:2; cf. Deut. 12:8-11). On the contrary, the later editor condemns Solomon for offering sacrifice at Gibeon (I 3:3), and takes pains to regularize this ritual offense by adding a legitimate sacrifice before the "ark of the covenant of the Lord" in Jerusalem (I 3:15).

The date of the original edition can be fixed without misgivings between Josiah's reforms in 621, based on the finding of Deuteronomy, and the destruction of Jerusalem in 586. The enthusiasm for the reforms and zeal of Josiah in advocating strict observance of the Deuteronomic law dominate the author's thought, and the language and style of Deuteronomy color his own writing extensively (cf. the list of phrases in S. R. Driver, *Introduction to the Old Testament,* pp. 200-202), although they are not

noticeable in some of the sources he quotes. He has set forth his fundamental, Deuteronomic principles in I 2:3 f.; 3:14.

On the other hand, Solomon's Temple (destroyed in 586) was still
standing in his day, as he explicitly states in I 8:8, and David's dynasty
had not yet come to its utter end in 586, according to I 9:21; 12:19; II
8:19, 22; 16:6; cf. II 17:41, which mentions only two generations from
722 to the time of the author. In these passages, the significant expression
"unto this day" does not belong to the sources utilized but to the author
of Kings, with the possible exception of II 8:22; 16:6.

It is more difficult to determine the exact date of the book within the
period 621-586. The author's assurance that Josiah's reforms and obedience to the Deuteronomic law would save Judah from the fate of the
Northern Kingdom in 722, his optimistic outlook, and his assurance of a
glorious future for his nation seem to indicate that he wrote before
Nebuchadnezzar captured Jerusalem and deported the leaders of the
people in 597. But the chief problem remains: did he write before or
after the death of Josiah at the battle of Megiddo (II 23:29) in 609—an
event which would have shocked him deeply? The tragic end of the
most pious of kings (II 23:25a) was in complete disagreement with the
Deuteronomic doctrine of earthly rewards for fulfilling the law of Moses
—the cardinal tenet of his religion (I 2:3 f.; 3:14).

Owing to later additions, the evidence is obscure. According to II 24:5,
the History of the Kings of Judah, that is so frequently mentioned by
our author, contained an account of the reign of Jehoiakim (609-598).
Therefore, unless this lost history was supplemented after being used by
our author—which (as in the case of Kings) is perfectly possible—he
must have written the book after the death of Jehoiakim as well as that
of Josiah. Conversely, there are some who infer from Huldah's prophecy
of Josiah's peaceful death (II 22:20) that our book was written before
609. However, Huldah's oracle (II 22:15-20) merely signifies that Josiah
would not witness the impending ruin of Jerusalem, which is clearly
alluded to even in II 22:20. This oracle cannot therefore come from the
original author, who knows nothing of the events of 586, but from the
later editor.

To judge from the introductory statement for Josiah, which is entirely
in the style of our original author, he must have written *after* Josiah's
death, since he knew that Josiah reigned for thirty-one years (II 22:1).
This information on the length of his reign cannot be attributed to a
later edition for, in the verse following, Josiah's conduct is praised in a
manner leaving no doubt as to his death. That verdict on Josiah in
II 22:2 and the concluding remark referring the reader to the history of
the kings of Judah for further information about Josiah (II 22:28) prove
that our author wrote after 609.

Nevertheless, I believe that the author deliberately made no mention of the well-known story of Josiah's heroic death on the battlefield of Megiddo. The untimely and violent end of this king of Judah, so obedient to the Deuteronomic law of Moses, could hardly have been reported by our author without disproving the Deuteronomic teaching of earthly rewards for good deeds, the lesson for which the book was designed. If, to maintain his theory, he had explained that Josiah's death was a punishment for some wicked act, as the Chronicler did later (II Chron. 35:21 f., according to which Josiah refused to heed a divine oracle that had come to Necho), the king responsible for the Deuteronomic reforms would have ceased being a paragon of virtue, as the author regarded him (II 23:25a). Faced by this dilemma, the author preferred, after the manner of some theologians, to ignore the facts contradicting his dogma rather than to modify the dogma to suit the facts. Thus he ended his book with a high-sounding note of praise for Josiah (II 23:21-25a) and a reference to the History of the Kings of Judah for further information about his deeds (II 23:28).

In the intervening verses (23:25b-27), the later editor explains why Josiah's piety did not suffice to avert the calamity of 586. He also adds an extremely concise report of the death and burial of Josiah (23:29 f.) and relates the events from 609 to 561 (II 23:31-25:30).

In dating the first edition of the Book of Kings about 600 B.C., after the death of Josiah in 609 and before the first capture of Jerusalem in 597, we cannot be far wrong. Such a date provides a fitting end for the book at II 23:25a, 28 and best fits its general spirit. The glamour of Josiah's reforms (621) had not yet wholly faded, one could still hope that obedience to the Deuteronomic law would keep Judah from going the way of the Northern Kingdom, and the mood of optimism had not yet been replaced by the dismal despair of Jeremiah and Ezekiel nor by the bitter resignation of Habakkuk.

The Book of Kings is accordingly the first of the Deuteronomistic histories. The author is the first to use historical materials illustrating the philosophy and religion of Deuteronomy, and to convince the Judeans that their survival as a kingdom, and even as a nation, depended on fulfilling the terms of the covenant by which Jehovah had chosen Israel to be his peculiar people. It was natural to apply first the doctrine of Deuteronomy to the period from Solomon to Josiah, because the central teaching of that code (Deut. 12)—exclusive worship of Jehovah in the Temple at Jerusalem—was made possible through Solomon's construction of the Temple.

The Deuteronomists began to prove the validity of the new law of 621 by applying it to the historical period ending with its discovery. In Kings, they produced not an objective history but a theological treatise on the Deuteronomic doctrines of centralization of worship and divine retribution of human deeds. These were illustrated in the course of historical events. In the first edition of Kings, the primary issue was the worship at the "high places," instead of at Jerusalem exclusively, and only occasionally the adoption of heathen gods and practices (as in the time of Manasseh). In Judges, later Deuteronomists were, however, preoccupied with worship of the deities of Canaan, the Baals and Astartes, instead of Jehovah alone; before the building of Solomon's Temple, worship at the village sanctuaries was of course regarded as legitimate (I 3:2; Deut. 12:8-11).

The authors (or author) of Kings were impelled to write their Deuteronomistic history because the period covered was particularly suited to test the teachings of the Law. But there was another reason: while there was in circulation, before 600 b.c., a JE history from Abraham to the accession of Solomon (parts of Gen., Ex., Num., Josh., Judg., Sam.), no similar history of the period from Solomon to Josiah was available.[2] The three books on the history of Solomon, the kings of Israel, and the kings of Judah, together with biographies of individual prophets, then in circulation, seemed insufficient. Later Deuteronomists had only to provide a framework (with a few scattered sermons) for the JE histories in existence. On the contrary, in the case of Kings, for which no history like JE was available, the authors had to provide the compilation itself, based on the existing political histories of the period.

Thus Kings, and Kings alone, is from its very origin a Deuteronomic history. Although in appearance it is a chronicle of the kings and, through the loss of earlier histories, our only source of information on all the kings of Israel and Judah, in reality it is a religious and not a historical work. The author had no intention of displacing available histories through his book, and constantly refers the reader to them for historical information about each king. However, in order to point his moral, he had to mention every single king. Wishing to teach a religious lesson, he dealt at length only with kings who were religiously significant: whether they were saints or reprobates did not matter. Just as in a history of the Christian Church the most important emperors are the devout Constantine, the wicked Nero, and Julian the Apostate (all of them of secondary political importance in comparison with many other emperors), so in the Deuteronomic history of the kings much more attention is given to Solomon, Jeroboam I, Ahab, Jehu, Hezekiah, Manasseh, Joash, and Josiah than to the two outstanding kings in the political history, Omri and

[2] The assumption, which gained great popularity among critics, that a pre-Deuteronomic book of Kings existed (cf. G. Hölscher in *Eucharisterion* for H. Gunkel, Vol I, pp. 158-213; and O. Eissfeldt, *Einleitung in das Alte Testament*, pp. 335-337), rests on a confusion between the pre-Deuteronomic sources and the Deuteronomic book of Kings. No clear traces of R[JE] can be detected.

Jeroboam II, whose reigns are dismissed in a few words (cf. the list of
kings in the preceding outline of the book).

The author passes judgment on every king according to his obedience
to Deut. 12, the law centralizing worship at Jerusalem and ordering
destruction of the high places. According to this standard, all the kings
of Israel are denounced *ipso facto* for doing "what was evil in the sight
of Jehovah" by not departing from the sin of Jeroboam I, who made Dan
and Bethel the royal and national sanctuaries of the Northern Kingdom.
Jeroboam's sanction of the worship of Jehovah outside of Jerusalem,
rather than setting up two golden bulls in these ancient sanctuaries, is
in the author's eyes the chief offense.[3]

In the case of the kings of Judah, only Hezekiah (II 18:3-5) and Josiah
(II 22:2-23:25a) are praised unconditionally for removing the "high
places." Strangely enough, the author regards David as the ideal king (cf.
I 2:1-4; 11:34, 38; 15:5abα) and exalts his descendants for following in
his footsteps. In the case of Asa (I 15:11-14), Jehoshaphat (I 22:43 [H.
22:43 f.]), Jehoash (II 12:2 f. [H. 12:3 f.]), Amaziah (II 14:3 f.), Azariah
or Uzziah (II 15:3 f.), and Jotham (II 15:34 f.), praise is restricted by
the remark that the "high places were not removed." All the other kings
of Judah are unreservedly condemned—Solomon for worshiping the deities
of his alien wives in his old age (I 11:4-6), the others for violating the
Deuteronomic law either by erecting high places and worshiping there or
by the adoption of alien cults and deities (e.g., I 14:22-24; II 16:3 f.;
21:2 [cf. 21:3-9]; 21:20-22).

In passing verdict on each king, the author obviously intended to prove
that obedience to the Deuteronomic law brought prosperity, and vice
versa. Unfortunately, the doctrine of just retribution for human conduct
on this earth, which our author accepted blindly from Deuteronomy, has
always conflicted with actualities. Obviously, the author is struggling
desperately with the known facts, in order to make them fit his theory.
Why was the reign of the pious Hezekiah beset by such trouble and
disaster while his son Manasseh, most wicked of the kings of Judah,
enjoyed fifty-five years of peace and prosperity? Why did the reformer
Josiah meet death at the battle of Megiddo while the heretical Omri
and Jeroboam II were eminently successful in peace and war? Such facts,
if frankly admitted, would force a man of common sense to question the
universal application, if not the actual validity, of the theory. But to a

[3] According to the original author, Jeroboam was concerned with preventing his
subjects from going to worship in Jerusalem—something they had never done. The
dedication of the two bulls is less significant than the reorganization of the worship
at Dan, Bethel, and other sanctuaries (I 12:26-31; 12:32 is a later addition). In
contrast with our author (II 17:18, 21-23), the second editor (II 17:7-17) lays the
emphasis not on worship at the "high places" outside of Jerusalem but on idolatry.

man whose belief in this doctrine was absolutely unshakable, reality had to be sacrificed to theory.

In the case of Hezekiah, whose ill-fated rebellion against Sennacherib in 701 brought extreme misery to his people, the author could write serenely that "Jehovah was with him; and he prospered whithersoever he went forth, and he rebelled against the king of Assyria and served him not" (II 18:7). Then, instead of reporting, from official annals confirmed by the Assyrian records, the humiliating surrender of Hezekiah to Sennacherib (II 18:14-16),[4] he showed how the Lord rewarded Hezekiah's faith in Isaiah's oracles by the miraculous destruction of the Assyrian army in one night and the subsequent assassination of Sennacherib (II 19:35-37). Note also that he appears to say nothing of Josiah's untimely death in battle.

The problem was easier in the case of the wicked kings, such as Manasseh and Omri. Nothing compelled the author to mention their successful rule, so he simply neglected to mention it. There is reason to believe that all he said about these two kings was limited to the standardized introductions and conclusions characteristic of him (II 21:1 f., 16-18; I 16:23, 25-28). Later writers added details to the general statement of Manasseh's wickedness (II 21:3-9) and through it explained the ruin of Judah half a century after his death (II 21:10-15). The reference to the founding of Samaria by Omri in I 16:24 is a later addition from an excellent ancient source. It is out of place in the middle of our author's introductory statement. In some cases, the author explained the apparent contradiction of facts with his theory by reference to God's compassionate concern for his people, notably in the case of Jeroboam II, whose spectacular victories brought the Northern Kingdom to the height of its power (II 14:24-27).

Whenever possible, the author gratuitously attributed the rooting out of the line of heretical kings of North Israel to a divine sentence (I 14:1-16; 16:1-5). The inconsistency apparent in the unbroken line of the kings of Judah, many of whom were denounced for their wickedness, is explained by a later Deuteronomist as a divine reward for the extraordinary and unparalleled piety of David, founder of the dynasty (I 11:31-36; 15:4 f., omitting at the end the note of a reader who, correctly and in contradiction to the author, regarded David's virtue as spotted "in the matter of Uriah the Hittite" [cf. II Sam. 11]; II 8:19). This latter conception resembles the Roman Catholic doctrine of the treasury of the

---

[4] These verses which frankly state the depressing facts are lacking in Is. 36-39 in which the rest of II Kings 18:13-20:19 is reproduced, and can therefore hardly have stood in the first edition of Kings. For other views on the matter and a full discussion of the subject, see L. L. Honor, *Sennacherib's Invasion of Palestine*. New York, Columbia University Press, 1926. On the LXX of the parallel accounts in Kings and Isaiah see H. M. Orlinsky in JQR 30 (1939) 33-49, to be continued.

Church, consisting of the merits laid up by Christ and the saints, upon which later generations may draw.

It seems clear from all this that the doctrine of retribution was for our author still national in scope, as in Deuteronomy, and that he hardly applied it consistently to single individuals as did the friends of Job and the authors of Proverbs. Even so, although the theory of retribution in its collective form less patently contradicts the facts, our author was not unaware of the difficulties inherent in his convictions.

Our author begins the history with Solomon, who, as builder of the Temple, receives more attention than any other king. The conclusion of the early source of Samuel in I 1; 2:13-46a (omitting 2:27, a midrashic addition akin to I Sam. 2:27-36) was not a part of his book but added later. As a kind of introduction he composed the deathbed words of David (I 2:1-9)[5]—a shocking example of unctuous perfidy more characteristic of the author's mentality than of David's—and a brief account of David's death and Solomon's accession (2:10-12). The author was familiar with Solomon's "purge" at the beginning of his reign (2:13-46a; cf. 2:5-9), but the repetition of 2:12b (in different language) in 2:46b shows that he did not copy 2:13-46a into his book.

The history of Solomon in I 1-11 has suffered in transmission. The LXX, in Codex B and Lucian, differs radically in content and arrangement from the Hebrew text and is the result of two recensions combined: the same passages occur after 2:35, 46; 12:24, and elsewhere. The Hebrew and the two Greek recensions are derived from a prototype variously supplemented and edited. Under the circumstances, the original form of the text cannot be reconstructed with full assurance.

Our author used the Book of the Acts of Solomon (I 11:41), a history of his life containing also an account of his wisdom. This work was based partly on official annals and Temple chronicles, and partly on folk tales and the writer's fancy. Extracts from this history, the style of which has no trace of the Deuteronomic language of our author, are quoted sometimes abruptly in describing Solomon's magnificence and wisdom and the construction of the Temple and other buildings.

Solomon's wisdom, one of the principal topics in his biography (I 11:41), has several connotations. Like his magnificence, it was promised to him by God in a dream (3:4-14, a section of this biography rewritten by the author of Kings). Here his wisdom consists of statesmanship and judicial shrewdness. An Oriental folk tale, which probably had nothing to do with Solomon originally (cf. H. Gressmann in *Deutsche Rundschau* 33 [1907] 175-191), illustrates his wisdom as a judge in a difficult case about the true mother of an infant (3:16-28). In another sense, Solomon's

---

[5] A. Lods (*Israël*, pp. 425f.) is one of the few scholars who regards I 2:1-9 (or at least I 2:5-9) not merely as part of the early biography of David, but also as historical.

wisdom was scientific learning in botany and zoology, proverbial wisdom (cf. Prov. 1:1; 10:1; 25:1) and (cf. Song of Songs 1:1) poetic inspiration (I 4:29-34 [H. 5:9-14]).

Among the "kings of the earth who heard of his wisdom" and came to listen to it (4:34 [H. 5:14]) was the fabulous Queen of Sheba (10:1-10, 13, partly rewritten by our author in a religious spirit). These scattered sections may have been joined together in the history of Solomon, although they do not seem to have been written by the same man, and probably represent successive additions. The author of Kings gives his own conception of Solomon's wisdom in 5:12 [H. 5:26]; 10:23 f., and in his revision of 3:4-14; 10:1-10.

The story of the Queen of Sheba seems to mark the transition from Solomon's wisdom to his wealth and magnificence. He married the daughter of Pharaoh and received the ruined city of Gezer as her dowry (3:1; 9:16, 24). In addition, he had 700 wives of royal blood and 300 concubines, in contrast with Song of Songs 6:8 (11:1-13, rewritten entirely in a Deuteronomistic vein by our author, who is responsible for 11:1b, 2, 3b, 4b, 5 f., 11-13; the second Deuteronomist added 11:9 f.; cf. 9:1-9).

The ancient list of Solomon's highest officials (4:1-6) and the roll (4:7-19; 4:27 f. [H. 5:7 f.]) of the governors whom he appointed over twelve administrative districts—quite distinct from the "twelve" tribes— are ultimately taken from official documents (as also the fragments 9:23; cf. 5:16 [H. 5:30]; II Chron. 8:10) and are valuable sources (cf. A. Alt, Israels Gaue unter Salomo, in *Alttest. Studien R. Kittel dargebracht*, pp. 1-19. BWAT 13, Leipzig, 1913). But they are introduced merely to exemplify the glory of Solomon's court: each governor provides the royal food for one month of the year (4:7, 27 [H. 5:7]). The daily rations for the court are specified in 4:22 f. [H. 5:2 f.]. Solomon had 4,000 (*sic*, not 40,000; cf. II Chron. 9:25) chariot horses and 12,000 cavalry horses (4:26 [H. 5:6]). Except for these misplaced notices in 4:22 f., 26 [H. 5:2 f., 6], the rest of 4:20-26 [H. 4:20-5:6], which is clumsily inserted into the roll of governors, is Deuteronomistic.

Solomon's fabulous riches comprise a second element in his proverbial glory (cf. Matt. 6:29; Luke 12:27). The author of Kings or a later glossator sets the yearly income from taxation at an incredible amount, 666 gold talents, or more than 25 million gold dollars (10:14), in addition to the toll raised on peddlers and caravans crossing his country, and the tribute of the Arabian kings (10:15, revised text). Unquestionably, Solomon knew how to take advantage of unique historical circumstances in developing the international trade of his realm to a degree never attained before or after his time. At the same time he entered into close diplomatic relations with neighboring kingdoms. Since his country had neither industries nor large exports of grain, Solomon improved on the geographical location and became an international middleman. Solomon's agents purchased horses in Kue (Cilicia) and Muzri, in the Taurus (cf. Ez. 27:14), and sold them to the Hittite and Aramean rulers of Syria (I 10:28 f., revised text; cf. 4:26 [H. 5:6]). Incidentally, Solomon's stables at Megiddo have been brought to light by archaeologists (cf. 9:19; 4:12; 9:15).[6]

Moreover, with the help of Hiram, king of Tyre, Solomon developed commerce at sea. He equipped a fleet at Ezion-geber (Elath on the Red Sea, in the land of Edom), sending it to the mysterious Ophir (South Arabia, East Africa, or India?) every three years. On the return journey, these ships brought back gold, *almug* wood (sandal wood?), precious stones, apes, ivory, and peacocks (?) (I 9:26-28; 10:11 f., 22; cf. W. E. Clark, AJSL 36 [1920] 103-119; W. F. Albright, AJSL 37 [1921] 144 f.). In exchange for these wares, Solomon may have delivered horses, slaves, and copper from the mines in Edom.[7] These passages are derived from Solomon's biography but have been revised by the author of Kings and later editors (10:12 in particular was no part of the biography).

The third element in Solomon's magnificence consists of his buildings, primarily on Zion in Jerusalem, but elsewhere too. The account given in 5:1-9:25 (H. 5:15-9:25) is one of the most difficult sections in the Old Testament. First, owing to scribes who failed to understand architectural terms and the obscure descriptions of the original author who was neither an architect nor a clear writer, the text has been greatly corrupted. Second, the account has endured successive additions and revisions. The Temple with its furniture was of extraordinary interest in postexilic times. After the Temple was destroyed in 586, scribes and editors were prone to identify the first Temple as much as possible with the second (finished in 516) which was more familiar to them. Ezekiel's fanciful description of the ideal Temple of the future (Ez. 40-43), far more lucid and skillful, gives a better idea of Solomon's Temple than the Chronicler's late revision of the account in Kings (II Chron. 1:13-7:22, where nothing is said of the royal palace [I Kings 7:1-12] of which the Temple was a part).

The report of the buildings begins and ends with descriptions of negotiations with Hiram of Tyre, from whom Solomon obtained the skilled craftsmen and many of the materials needed for construction (5:1-18 [H. 5:15-32] and 9:10-15). The first of these sections has been rewritten in a Deuteronomic vein by the author of Kings. Only 5:7a, 8-11 [H. 5:21a, 22-25], more or less intact, and 5:13-18 [H. 5:27-32], with a revision of the colossal figures, may belong to the biography of Solomon; the rest is

[6] P. L. O. Guy, *New Light from Armageddon*. Oriental Institute Communications, No. 9; pp. 37-48. R. S. Lamon and G. M. Shipton, *Megiddo I. Strata I-V*. Oriental Institute Publications, Vol. 42, pp. 8-61.

[7] Cf. N. Glueck, in AASOR XV, pp. 48-53. Cf. J. P. Hyatt, JBR 8 (1940) 27-30.

clearly from the pen of the author of Kings. The report closes (9:10-25) with a collection of miscellaneous notices of various origin.

To Solomon's biography we may ascribe the recountal of the final payment given Hiram, consisting of twenty towns in Galilee (9:11b-14; 9:14 is, however, suspect), as also the misplaced summary of great historical value, listing Solomon's fortifications, garrisons, and stables (9:15-19), the number of overseers (9:23, where we should read 250 instead of 550), and 9:24 (cf. 3:1; 7:8; 9:16). The hand of the author of Kings may be seen in 9:10-11a, 25. A late glossator, contradicting 5:13 f. [H. 5:27 f.]; 11:28; 12:4, patriotically claims that Solomon did not impose corvée and forced labor on any Israelite but only on the remnants of unassimilated Canaanites (9:20-22).

In our text, the Temple is by far the most important of Solomon's buildings, and is described in detail (6:1-38) together with the sacred objects belonging to it (7:13-51). Conversely, the royal palace, more imposing and requiring thirteen years to build—six more than the Temple (6:37-7:1)—is dismissed with a few words (7:1-12), and little is said of its rich furnishings (10:16-20a). We have nothing but a bare list (9:15-19) for Solomon's buildings outside of Jerusalem.

Unless we assume that the original account has been radically changed by expanding the description of the Temple and drastically curtailing the account of the other buildings, we must conclude that these sections were written by a priest in Jerusalem better acquainted with the Temple than with the rest of Solomon's buildings. This writer was entirely familiar with the interior of the Temple but, with the exception of the golden shields and ivory throne (10:16-20a), had apparently not seen the inside of the royal apartments. He could hardly have lived during the reign of Solomon or in that of his immediate successors. Solomon's contemporaries were unquestionably more impressed by the royal palace than by the Temple itself.

On the other hand, our writer must have lived before the reign of Ahaz (735-720), when important changes were introduced in the Temple. He knows nothing of the new altar which Ahaz ordered, a replica of the one he saw in Damascus (II 16:10-16), nor of the removal of the twelve brazen oxen supporting the laver (II 16:17), nor of the mysterious remodeling mentioned in a corrupt and unintelligible text (II 16:18).

It is also significant that the most important sacred object in Solomon's Temple, the altar, is neither described nor mentioned. Following J. Wellhausen (*Composition des Hexateuchs*, p. 266), it is generally assumed that the description of the altar was willfully omitted, because, after the publication of the Priestly Code, it was natural to expect Solomon to use the (imaginary) brazen altar made by Moses. This hypothesis is contradicted not only by the fact that the explicit reference which the author of Kings made to Solomon's altar (9:25aα; the rest of the verse is hopelessly corrupt) has been allowed to stand, but also by an allusion in II Chron. 4:1, long after the publication of the Priestly Code, to the brazen altar installed by Solomon (not by Moses).

Indeed, everything indicates that the original altar in Solomon's Temple was the native rock rather than a brazen altar of Phoenician workmanship —the very stone, presumably by the threshing floor of Arauna (II Sam. 24:15-25; cf. II Chron. 3:1), over which the Dome of the Rock (*Qubbet es-sahra*), incorrectly called the Mosque of Omar, now stands. The author of Kings declares that on the day in which the Temple was dedicated sacrifices were offered not on the brazen altar but on the ground "in the middle of the forecourt" (I 8:64). The brazen altar, known to the author of Kings (cf. Ez. 9:2) but not to the author of Solomon's biography, was placed in the Temple before the reign of Ahaz (II 16:14 f.), after that biography was written. Probably, therefore, the biographer was a priest of Jerusalem between 850 and 750 B.C.

According to Solomon's biography, the Temple was built during the seven years from the fourth to the eleventh of Solomon's rule (6:37 f., omitting the postexilic gloss "which is the eighth month"). In the LXX, this date stands more correctly at the beginning of the description of the Temple, before 6:2 and in place of 6:1 (the chronological note of the Deuteronomistic editor who provided the chronology of Judges and Samuel about 550 B.C.). In the biography, the description of the Temple is confined to 6:2-6, 8, 10, 15-17, 20 (omitting "overlaid with pure gold"), 23-27, 31, 33 f., 36. The author of Kings is responsible for legendary touches enhancing the glory of the Temple (6:7, 9, 29 f., 32a, 35a) and for a divine oracle in Deuteronomistic style (6:11-14). Later scribes went further in adorning the interior of the Temple, by covering the walls, altar, cherubim, and doors with genuine gold leaf (parts of 6:20-22, 28, 30, 32, 35).

The description which follows that of the Temple (in I 6) does not include the sacred objects belonging to it (I 7:13-40) but the several edifices of the royal palace (7:1-12). This order has seemed incongruous to the authors of the LXX (who transferred 7:1-12 after 7:51), and to many others since then. Nevertheless, it is obviously original. In Solomon's biography, the Temple was still recognized as part of the royal palace. The "great court," enclosed within a great wall, surrounded both palace and Temple and made of them one great architectural unit (cf. 7:9, 12). The "inner" court (6:36; 7:12; also called the "upper" court, cf. Jer. 36:10, because the Temple was higher than the palace south of it, Jer. 26:10), and the "central court" (II 20:4, revised text) surrounding the apartments of the king and his wives (7:8, 12) were both within the "great court." This close connection between palace and Temple (cf. II 11:4-12) was regarded as sacrilegious by Ezekiel (Ez. 43:7 f.).

In the biography of Solomon the royal buildings are described briefly from south to north as follows: the "House of the Forest of Lebanon" (7:2-5) the Hall of Pillars (7:6), the Judgment Hall or Throne Room (7:7), and, within the "central court," the residence of the king east of the palace of Pharaoh's daughter (7:8). The account is introduced by a chronological note according to which the palace was completed in thirteen years (7:1), either including the seven during which the Temple was built or, as the author of Kings believed (9:10), additional to them. Remarks about the building material (7:9-11) and the "great court" (7:12) conclude this chronicle.

The biography continues with an account of the metalwork in the Temple fashioned by a Tyrian craftsman named Hiram (7:13 f.) or perhaps Huram-abi (II Chron. 2:13 [H. 2:12]): the two pillars called Jachin and Boaz (7:15-22; cf. 7:41 f.; Jer. 52:21-23 = II 25:17; II Chron. 3:15-17) after the manner of the two stelae in Melkart's Temple at Tyre (Herodotus 2:44), the "molten sea," a large basin filled with water resting on twelve brass oxen (7:23-26), the ten brass basins supported by bases on four wheels (7:27-39), and the small vessels and shovels (7:40). The following brief repetition of this inventory (7:41-46) has been inserted from another source by an editor. A later scribe, perhaps identical with the one who used gold leaf so freely in ch. 6, disregarded both inventories as too sordid and, drawing on his imagination after the manner of the Priestly Code (he is familiar with Ps), made up a list of sacred objects fashioned from pure gold (7:47-50). The early account in Solomon's biography is concluded in 7:51.

The original narrative of the dedication of the Temple at the time of the Feast of Tabernacles (in the eighth month, Bul [6:38], not in the seventh, Ethanim [8:2]; cf. 12:32) has been thoroughly revised and is found in parts of the following sections: 8:1-5 (cf. the LXX), 12 f., 65aα. In 8:1-11 it is difficult to identify the successive layers of editorial expansion; some additions to the original text, notably the reference to the Tabernacle of Moses (not to the tent of David of II Sam. 6:17; I Kings 1:39; 2:28-30) in 8:4, are present in the briefer and more original text of the LXX.

Solomon's dedication speech (8:12 f., revised according to the LXX) was a brief poem preserved in the "Book of Song" (shîr, not yashar, "the upright"), which contained also Joshua's (Josh. 10:12) and David's (II Sam. 1:18-27) poems. Solomon's poem reads as follows (cf. the LXX after 8:53):

Jehovah has placed the sun in the heavens,
But he said that he would dwell in darkness.
I have built thee a house of habitation,
A place for thy dwelling for all time.

The author of Kings could not let such an important occasion pass
with only this brief and, to him, religiously insignificant utterance. He
therefore composed an eloquent prayer in the language and spirit of
Deuteronomy—a noble invocation which has no equal among the Psalms
in its confident optimism and assurance of Jehovah's readiness to forgive
and help his people in distress (8:22, 23-40, 53). The exilic editor of 550
B.C. has supplemented this prayer with unmistakable references to the
Exile of 586 (8:44-52), and with a parallel to the Second Isaiah's expectation that all nations would someday worship Jehovah (8:41-43). He has
also added another address of Solomon explaining why he, and not
David, built the Temple (8:14-21). Solomon's blessing of the people from
the pen of the author of Kings (8:54a ["And it came to pass . . . that he
arose"], 55 [omitting "and he arose"], 56-58) has likewise been expanded
by the exilic editor (the rest of 8:54-61; 8:60, with its monotheistic doctrine, may be a later addition).

The account of the celebration of the "feast" (i.e., Tabernacles) in
8:62-66 is mostly by the author of Kings, although the fantastic figures
in 8:63 look like later midrashic exaggeration. The exilic editor could not
close this imposing ceremony without a divine revelation (9:1-9) supplementing the oracle at Gibeon (3:4-14; cf. 9:2) and assuring Solomon
that Jehovah had hallowed the Temple just dedicated to him, but that
eventually it would be destroyed (in 586) because of the worship of
alien gods.

After rearranging the narratives in Solomon's biography illustrating his
wisdom, wealth, and glory so as to bring out the central importance of
the Temple, the author of Kings gives an account of Solomon's religious
infidelity and explicitly points out his moral that sin is followed by punishment (11:1-13). In this manner, the author reconciles his admiration
of the builder of the Temple with his resentment at Solomon's violations
of the Deuteronomic law, giving the reader the erroneous impression that
in a first period of his life Solomon served Jehovah and prospered, while
in his latter years he forsook his god and suffered reverses.

The biography of Solomon related that he had many wives, a great
number of them foreign, who were allowed to continue worshiping their
gods, and that he built, for instance, an altar for Kemosh, god of the
Moabites, on the Mount of Olives (11:1, 3, 7a, 8, in part). This furnished
evidence of his magnificence and glory. But in the revision of the author
of Kings (11:1-13, in which 11:9-10 are penned by the exilic editor)
such latitude is regarded as a violation of God's will.

The stories about Solomon's three enemies, Hadad the Edomite (11:14-22, 25aβb), Rezon of Damascus (11:23-25aα), and Jeroboam the Ephraimite, later king of Israel (11:26-40), although presented here as evidences of Jehovah's displeasure with Solomon, are ultimately derived from a good source (the first one perhaps from Solomon's biography, the others, in part, from the History of the Kings of Israel). They are in the main historical. Although they depict events belonging to the beginning of Solomon's rule (11:21, 25a, 27; cf. 9:24), they are placed at the end of his life in order that the picture of the glorious inception of his reign be left unmarred. This incongruity, in regarding events long past as punishment for Solomon's sins in his old age is wrongly attributed to the author of Kings. After his account of Solomon's sin (11:1-8), the author of Kings concludes the story of his reign with the usual formula (11:41-43), and in the following chapter shows how the divine punishment was inflicted. It seems clear that 11:14-40 was inserted by the exilic Deuteronomist of 550. The introductory formulae (11:14, 23) are like those of the framework in Judges (550) rather than Kings (600). The prophecy of Ahijah of Shiloh to Jeroboam (11:29-39) is Deuteronomistic in style (cf. 11:32-39), but not necessarily after the manner of the author of Kings. The purpose of the oracle, which is somewhat confused (Ahijah tears his cloak into twelve pieces and gives ten to Jeroboam, leaving *one* [!] for David's house: 11:30-32), is to explain why Solomon's punishment followed his death—a puzzle already solved by the author of Kings in 11:11-13. The author of 11:1-13 could therefore not have written 11:29-39. Finally, the expectation that the Davidic dynasty would go on forever (11:36; cf. 15:4 f.; II 8:19), as we have seen in discussing II Sam. 7, is found primarily (and almost exclusively) in texts written *after* the dynasty came to its end in 586. In any case, about 550 B.C., when 11:39 was written, the Davidic dynasty was a hope rather than a reality.

The story of Hadad, who became king of Edom after the death of David (11:14-22, 25aβb) is so interpolated (cf. E. Meyer, *Die Israeliten und ihre Nachbarstämme,* pp. 359-363) that H. Winckler (*Alttestamentliche Untersuchungen,* pp. 1-15. 1892) believed it to be a combination of two stories, one about Hadad the Edomite and the other about Adad the Midianite. Its conclusion in 11:25aβb, revised with the help of the LXX (after 11:22), should read, "And Hadad returned to his country. And he oppressed Israel and reigned over Edom. This is the evil which Hadad did."

The story of Rezon, founder of the Aramaic kingdom of Damascus (11:23-25aα), has been inserted into that of Hadad by accident; the LXX makes matters worse by placing it in 11:14. In becoming king of Edom, which had been conquered by David, Hadad reduced the extent of

Solomon's kingdom, even though the latter must have retained control at least of the harbor of Ezion-geber (Elath) and of the road leading to it. Conversely, David had never conquered Damascus (in spite of II Sam. 8:5, 6a), but that kingdom proved eventually more dangerous to Israel than Edom.

Jeroboam (11:26-28, 40) was appointed by Solomon as the head of the forced levies of laborers from the ten Northern tribes, but started an abortive rebellion when the king undertook the work of the Millo ("the filling")—not the construction of an edifice, but "the building of the causeway, the closing of the gap of the City of David" (11:27; cf. W. R. Arnold, *Ephod and Ark*, pp. 46-49). Jeroboam and other proud Israelites revolted at the unheard-of labor of *filling* in with earth the small gully separating the Temple Hill in the north from the stronghold of Zion (or City of David) in the south. From Egypt, where he fled from Solomon, Jeroboam returned after the king's death, to found the Northern Kingdom of Israel.

In the second part of his book (I 12-II 17), the period of the divided kingdom (933-722), the author of Kings had to use a new method. His plan required that he mention every king of Israel and Judah in chronological order. He could have finished the series of rulers in one kingdom before taking up the other series. But he preferred to shuttle back and forth between the two, completing the history of each king with his death and picking up the thread of the other line where it had been dropped, and so down to the end of the last monarch crowned during the reign of the contemporary king of the other line.

The two series start simultaneously with Jeroboam of Israel and Rehoboam of Judah, and merge again when Jehu kills the Joram of Israel and Ahaziah of Judah on the same day (II 9:23-27). At this latter point, the author is forced to abandon his usual scheme: he leaves off in the middle of Joram's reign (II 3; 9) to deal with Jehoram (II 8:16-24) and Ahaziah (II 8:25-29) of Judah, in order to make ready for the massacres of Jehu. Only in one instance (II 13:10 f.; 14:1-22) does he deal simultaneously with a king of Israel and a king of Judah.

Following the pattern of Deuteronomy, which furnishes the body of legislation (Deut. 12-26) with an introduction and conclusion, our author prefaces and closes each reign (except Athaliah's, II 11) with stereotyped introductions and conclusions.[8] This framework was imitated half a century later by the Deuteronomistic editor of Judges.

A. Introductions for the kings of Judah:

[8] The author of Kings has given part of the standardized conclusion for David (I 2:10-12), part of the introduction (I 3:2) and the conclusion (I 11:41-43) for Solomon, and the conclusion only for Jeroboam I (I 14:19 f.). The full framework begins with Rehoboam and Nadab.

1. The date of accession according to the reigning year of the contemporary king of Israel (synchronism): "Now in the eighteenth year of king Jeroboam the son of Nebat began Abijam to reign over Judah" (I 15:1). Similarly for his successors down to Hezekiah (II 18:1). 2. The age of the king at his accession: "Jehoshaphat was thirty and five years old when he began to reign" (I 22:42); omitted for Abijah and Asa. 3. The length of reign: (I 14:21; 15:2, 10, etc.). 4. The name of the king's mother (I 14:21; 15:2, 10, etc.); omitted for Jehoram and Ahaz (II 8:17; 16:2). 5. A brief verdict of his religious practices, with reference to the observance of the Deuteronomic law and the good example of David. "And he did that which was right in the eyes of Jehovah, according to all that David his father had done. He removed the high places . . ." (II 18:3 f.; cf. II 22:2). Such unqualified approbation is limited to Hezekiah and Josiah (cf. Ecclus. of Sirach 49:4). The praise of Asa, Jehoshaphat, Jehoash, Amaziah, Azariah, and Jotham is not unreserved, because "the high places were not removed" (I 15:14; 22:43 [H. 22:44]; II 12:3 [H. 12:4], etc.). All the others are denounced severely as unregenerate sinners, unfaithful to Jehovah.

B. Introductions for the kings of Israel:

1. The synchronism of the accession with the contemporary king of Judah (I 15:25, 33; 16:8, etc.); for Nadab (I 15:28) and Elah (I 16:10) the date of death is also given. 2. The length of reign (I 14:20 [in the conclusion]; 15:25, 33; 16:8) and the royal residence (omitted for Jeroboam I and Nadab), which was Tirzah until Omri built Samaria. 3. The verdict: "and he did that which was evil in the sight of Jehovah" usually with the addition "for he walked in all the way of Jeroboam the son of Nebat, and in his sins wherewith he made Israel to sin. . . ." Except for Shallum, this sweeping condemnation (or a similar one for Elah and Zimri) is applied to all kings of Israel. For Jehu (as for Jeroboam I) no formal introduction is provided, but the length of his reign is given in II 10:36 and the adverse verdict is 10:28-31. The name of the king's father is also given in the introduction, except for Zimri and Omri.

C. Conclusions for the kings of Judah:

1. "Now the rest of the acts of . . . , and all that he did, are they not written in the book of the chronicles of the kings of Judah?" (I 14:29; 15:7, 23; 22:45 [H. 22:46]; II 8:23; 12:19 [H. 12:20]; 14:18; 15:6, 36; 16:19; 20:20; 21:17, 25; 23:28; 24:5; cf. I 11:41. Esther 10:2 is a late and fanciful imitation of the formula.) 2. "And . . . slept with his fathers and was buried with his fathers in the city of David" (see one or more verses following the above references). 3. "And . . . his son reigned in his stead" (same verses as No. 2).

These concluding formulae are entirely omitted for Ahaziah, Jehoahaz,

Jehoiachin, and Zedekiah, whose reigns were cut short by assassination or captivity and who were not succeeded by a son. The phrase "and he slept with his fathers" is omitted when the king met a violent death (II 12:21 [H. 12:22]; 14:20; 21:26). As we have seen, the account of the death and burial of Josiah (II 23:29 f.) was probably not included in the first edition of Kings. Until the time of Ahaz the royal tombs stood in the City of David, later in the garden of Uzzah. In the case of the two most pious kings (Hezekiah and Josiah), the place of burial is not, given, because of later objections to the proximity of the tombs in the garden of Uzzah to the Temple (cf. Ez. 43:7). In the case of Jehoiakim (Jer. 22:19) it is omitted because presumably he was buried near the battlefield on which he fell.

D. Conclusions for the kings of Israel:

1. "And the rest of the acts of . . . , behold, are they not written in the book of the chronicles of the kings of Israel?" (I 14:19; 15:31; 16:5, 14, 20, 27; 22:39; II 1:18; 10:34; 13:8 [12]; 14:15, 28; 15:11, 15, 21, 26, 31). 2. "And . . . slept with his fathers, and was buried in. . . . And . . . his son reigned in his stead" (cf. the verses following the above references). The last clause is of course omitted whenever a king's successor was a usurper. The entire conclusion is omitted in the cases of Joram and Hoshea, because their end is described in full. The second part (No. 2) is used only for kings who died a natural death and for Ahab (I 22:40). The place of burial, which is Samaria except for Baasha (Tirzah, I 16:6), is omitted in I 14:20; 22:40; II 14:29; 15:22. Of the two conclusions for Joash (II 13:12 f.; 14:15 f.) the first one, not quite according to pattern, was interpolated.

To historians the information of greatest importance in this framework is the chronology. The name of the mother of the kings of Judah and the name of the father in that of the kings of Israel are less valuable. There are two sets of chronological data, disregarding the age of the kings of Judah at the time of their accession which is of no use for fixing absolute dates: the regnal periods and the synchronisms. It is obvious that the regnal periods were given in the two sources used by the author for the period after Solomon: the History of the Kings of Judah and the History of the Kings of Israel. There is no reason to suppose that these histories likewise contained the synchronisms, for in neither kingdom would an event be dated according to the regnal year of the other kingdom. In dating the books of Amos and Hosea (Am. 1:1; Hos. 1:1) the addition of the kings of Judah to the kings of Israel is patently redactional (contrast Is. 1:1; Mic. 1:1).

When the author of Kings decided to combine the history of the two kingdoms by finishing each reign and then taking up the contemporary king of the other kingdom, he was forced to calculate the synchronisms[9] by adding up the regnal periods of the two kingdoms. There is no reason to assume that after computing the synchronisms he omitted them from his book, or to believe with C. H. Cornill, R. Kittel, I. Benzinger, and others that they were inserted by the exilic editor of 550. The chronology of the histories of the kings of Judah and Israel—the regnal periods—and that of the author of Kings—the synchronisms—are genuine, though not .errorless; but the chronology of the exilic editor in Judges and Kings is purely fictitious. He assumes that Solomon began building the Temple 480 years after the Exodus from Egypt (I 6:1), or twelve generations of forty years each. He may have revised the regnal periods of the kings of Judah in order to obtain 430 years from the beginning of its erection to its destruction in 586, or exactly 480 (adding the 50 years 586-536) to the end of the Exile. Hence the Chronicler (I Chron. 6:4-15 [H. 5:30-41]; cf. 6:50-53 [H. 6:35-36]) lists twelve high priests from the Exodus to the building of the Temple (12 × 40 = 480) and eleven from its construction to its destruction. Adding one high priest for the exilic period, we again obtain twelve generations, or 480 years, from the time the Temple was built to the end of the Exile. In reality, the period from the Exodus to the construction is probably about 250 years, and from the construction to the end of the Exile about 430 years.

The chronology based on the synchronisms is of course less reliable than the one based on the regnal periods, since the synchronisms were figured from the regnal periods. Neither chronology is wholly accurate. The period from the division of the kingdom to the accession of Jehu, identical for both kingdoms, comprises 95 years for Judah, 98 for Israel, and 88 according to the synchronisms (actually probably 91 years). The period from the accession of Jehu to the fall of Samaria (843-722, 121 years) comprises 165 years for Judah, 143 years and 7 months for Israel, and 170 years according to the synchronisms. The total for both periods is 260 years for Judah, 241 years and 7 months for Israel, and 258 years according to the synchronisms. Although 136 years elapsed from the end of the kingdom of Israel (722) to that of the kingdom of Judah (586), as we know from data furnished by cuneiform records, Kings reckons 139 years and 6 months from the accession of Hezekiah to 586, dating the fall of Samaria (722) in the sixth year of Hezekiah (I 18:10); however, in I 18:13, the year 701 is the fourteenth of Hezekiah. In reality, Hezekiah

---

[9] An instructive parallel is furnished by cuneiform inscriptions. The so-called Synchronistic Tablet from Asshur (H. Gressmann, *Altorientalische Texte zum Alten Testament*, pp. 333-335) listing in parallel columns 82 kings of Assyria and 98 kings of Babylonia (c. 1850-625 B.C.) is not exact because the synchronisms were not calculated. On the contrary, the "Babylonian Chronicle" (*ibid.*, p. 359), covering the period 745-668 and written in 499, in which the synchronisms are calculated and given, is accurate and closely resembles the framework of Kings.

came to the throne in 720, since his father Ahaz was crowned in 735 and ruled sixteen years.

In spite of these discrepancies, inaccuracies, and errors, the chronology of Kings is not fantastic, like that of the Priestly Code in Genesis, nor artificial, like that of the Deuteronomist in Judges. The exact data furnished by cuneiform records beginning with 854, when Ahab and his allies fought against Shalmaneser II at Qarqar, have not overthrown the chronology of Kings but only rectified it here and there. The original data in the histories of the kings of Israel and Judah must have been fairly accurate but, aside from accidental errors of transmission, may have been deliberately revised. At any rate, errors are not of sufficient magnitude to warrant the conclusions of J. Wellhausen (*Prolegomena*, pp. 270 f.) that the chronology is essentially artificial.

The many complicated attempts to explain the discrepancies between synchronisms and regnal periods through the use of divergent chronological systems (two according to I. Benzinger, *Die Bücher der Könige*, pp. xviii-xxi. Freiburg, 1899; four according to C. Steuernagel, *Einleitung in das Alte Testament*, pp. 353 f.; five according to J. Begrich, *Die Chronologie der Könige von Israel und Juda* u.s.w. Tübingen, 1929) have not yielded convincing results because the data are inaccurate. The discrepancy between the regnal periods of Judah and Israel seems to have been present in the sources used by the author of Kings. He attempted unsuccessfully to correct this by means of the synchronisms.

2. *The Sources Utilized*

Just as the author of Kings derived most of his information about Solomon from his biography, so for the later parts of the book his principal sources are the royal histories. In his standardized conclusions (see above) he refers the reader for additional information on the monarch in question to the histories of the kings of Israel or Judah.

It is probable that, beginning with Solomon, the chief public acts of the kings, particularly their wars and building operations, were recorded for posterity in official annals similar to the Hittite and Assyrian annals, still extant in the original cuneiform tablets,[10] and to the Phoenician annals, of which Josephus (*Against Apion* 1:17 f., 21; *Antiquities* 8:5, 3; 9:14, 2) has preserved some extracts derived by Alexander Polyhistor from Menander of Ephesus and others. Such annals, whether merely chronicles narrating bare facts or eulogistic reports of royal deeds, are precious historical sources for the chronology of each reign and for

---

[10] For the earliest annals (Babylonian and Hittite before 1200) see H. G. Güterbock, *Die historische Tradition . . . bei Babyloniern und Hethitern bis 1200* (Leipzig dissertation, 1934; reprinted in enlarged form in *Zeitschr. f. Assyriol.* N.F. 8). For the Assyrian annals see A. T. Olmstead, *Assyrian Historiography* (Univ. of Missouri Studies, Social Science Ser., III, 1. 1916).

information on important events. But they are not real histories or biographies. There is no parallel in antiquity to the superb biography of David in the early source of Samuel.

It is now recognized that the two books mentioned so often by the author of Kings are not the official annals of the kings of Israel and Judah but histories based on them. The Hebrew title, literally "the book of the things of the days of the kings . . ." means book of the events of (past) time or book of history of the Kings . . . In I Chron. 27:24 and Neh. 12:23, let alone the title of Chronicles ("things of the days"), this expression cannot possibly mean official annals. These lost histories derived, however, much of their information from the official state chronicles. But as we have seen, the chronological data of the histories were no longer accurate when used by the author of Kings. Moreover, these histories contained matter that an official annalist would hardly have recorded: the treacherous conspiracies by which Zimri and Shallum gained the throne (I 16:20; II 15:15) and the sin that Manasseh sinned (II 21:17).

In spite of the last reference, the tone on the whole was patriotic rather than religious, like that of Kings. We may surmise that their authentic information on the following events was derived from the royal annals: the wars of Jeroboam I (I 14:19), of Jehoshaphat (I 22:45 [H. 22:46]), of Joash against Amaziah (II 14:15; cf. the gloss 13:12), and of Jeroboam II against the Arameans (II 14:28, textually corrupt; cf. 14:25); the cities built by Asa (I 15:23), the pool and the aqueduct of Hezekiah (II 20:20), probably identical with the tunnel in which the Siloam inscription was carved (for its text see G. A. Cooke, *Text-book of North-Semitic Inscriptions,* p. 15. Oxford, 1903); and the ivory house, some of the ivory carvings of which have come to light (see J. W. and Grace M. Crowfoot, *Early Ivories from Samaria.* London, 1938), and the cities built by Ahab (I 22:39).

As history and literature, the book on the kings of Israel was far superior to that on the kings of Judah. To a great extent, this is due to the subject matter. The kingdom of Israel ranked high above Judah not only in size but in culture, power, splendor, foreign relationships, commerce, and even religion, for (except for Amos, who, however, delivered his message in the Northern Kingdom) the prophetic movement before Isaiah is confined to North Israel. Even the pious Judean author of Kings, who had no love for North Israel, unwittingly admits this. Only three kings of Judah were praised in their history for military valor (Asa, I 15:23; Jehoshaphat, I 22:45 [H. 22:46]; and even the unlucky Hezekiah, II 20:20). In contrast with this modest number, twice as many kings of Israel are so praised (Baasha, I 16:5; Omri, I 16:27; Jehu, II 10:34; Jehoahaz, II 13:8; Joash, II 14:15 [cf. 13:12]; and Jeroboam II, II 14:28 [textually corrupt]). without including the valiant Ahab (for whom the explicit reference is lacking in I 22:39). This disproportion is the more striking when we note that Judah's kings ruled 136 years longer than Israel's.

We may surmise that certain authentic and brilliant stories, which unquestionably present the viewpoint of the Northern Kingdom and do not conceal contempt or hostility for Judah, are derived, with hardly any abridgment or change, from the history of Israel's kings.[11] The first one tells of the selection of Jeroboam as first king of North Israel (I 11:26-28, 40; 12:1 f., 3b-14, 16, 18-20, 25, omitting "Jeroboam and" in 12:12). Then come two stories about Ahab, his victory over Ben-hadad of Damascus (I 20:1-12, 15-21, 23-27, 29-34; the rest of the chapter is either legendary or possibly, in the case of 20:35-43, derived from another source) and his death at the siege of Ramoth in Gilead (22:1-38, omitting 22:28b [quoted from Mic. 1:2 by a reader who identified Micaiah, son of Imlah, with Micah]; 22:35bβ, 38).

The core of the stories describing the unsuccessful campaign of Jehoram and Jehoshaphat against Mesha, king of Moab (II 3:4-27), the miraculous deliverance of Samaria from a siege (6:24-7:20), and less probably 13:14-21, may be derived from this source. But in their present form these stories belong to the cycle of the Elisha legends. Conversely, in spite of the mention of Elisha at the beginning, the story of the revolution of Jehu, one of the most vivid and dramatic in the book, belongs to the Israelitic royal history (II 9:1-10:27, omitting 9:7-10a, 14 f., 28 f., 36 f.; 10:6b, 10).

Finally, the story of the victory of Joash over Amaziah (II 14:8-14) is clearly derived from this source. In this narrative the contempt of the Northern Israelites for the Judeans (cf. Abner's surly question, "Am I a Judean dog's head?" II Sam. 3:8) receives its classical formulation in a fitting apologue (II 14:9).

In this last instance, the author of Kings, a patriotic Judean, explicitly states that the tale was related in the history of the kings of Israel and, by implication, that he omitted it entirely from his book (II 14:15; cf. the gloss in 13:12). Also, it is extremely improbable that the above-mentioned stories about Jeroboam I and Ahab were included in the first edition of Kings. Written by a Northern Israelite, these stories present Jeroboam and Ahab in a favorable light, whereas the Judean author of Kings expresses his detestation for both monarchs in clear and forcible language (I 12:26-31; II 17:21-23; I 16:30-33).

Moreover, our author's succinct reference to the death of Ahab (I 22:40) shows conclusively that he did not reproduce the complete ac-

---

[11] These stories are generally ascribed by critics to separate Ephraimitic documents. Since one of them certainly belonged to the history of the Kings of Israel (see below), the others were probably included. This does not imply common authorship.

count of Ahab's death given in the history of the kings of Israel (22:1-38). With this sole exception, he never uses the formula (and . . . slept with his fathers . . .") in the case of kings who, like Ahab, met a violent death. On the contrary, our author maliciously reported the story of Jehu's revolution and massacres, adding several sanguinary touches of his own (II 9:7-10a, 36 f.). For he saw in Jehu's bloody deeds not a dastardly crime, that horrified Hosea (Hos. 1:4), but the fulfillment of the divine vengeance on Jezebel, on Ahab's house, and on the worshipers of the Tyrian Baal in Samaria (I 21:20bβ-22, 24; II 10:28-31).

In addition to these stories, nothing remains of the history of the kings of Israel except brief snatches or summaries (ultimately derived from the royal annals) preserved by the first or second Deuteronomist (12:25; 15:27; 16:9-11a, [15], 16-18, 21 f., 24, [34]; II 1:1; 13:7 [?]; 13:22 [cf. LXX: Lucian], 24 f.; 14:25a; 15:[10, 14], 16, 19 f., [25], 29, 30a). In most cases, the language of the source is not intact in these brief notices.

If, as the author of Kings testifies (II 15:31), the History of the Kings of Israel reached to the end of Pekah's reign (737-732) but not beyond, it was written about 730 B.C., at the end of the classical period of the prose literature of North Israel (850-730). This history is the swan song of the Northern Kingdom, penned just before its downfall in 722.

The authors of the stories about Jeroboam I, Ahab, Jehu, and Joash were outstanding as historians and as writers. Although they cannot equal the greatest and earliest Old Testament historian, David's biographer, they rank above all other Judean historians except J. They were interested in the prophets of the old school (I 22:5-28; II 9:1-6, 10b), but not in the least influenced by the words of Amos and Hosea.

Like Oriental historians in general, the author of the History of the Kings of Israel quoted his sources in extenso without distinguishing between his own writing and that of others. We may therefore assume that the stories about Jeroboam I, Ahab, Jehu, and Joash were written by separate authors in the ninth and the early eighth century.

The History of the Kings of Israel was supplemented at the end with an account of the events following 732: Hoshea's reign ending disastrously with the capture of Samaria by Sargon of Assyria (722), after Shalmaneser V had besieged the city during three years (II 17:3-6; cf. the account in the History of the Kings of Judah in II 18:9-11). According to his own inscriptions, Sargon deported 27,290 Israelites. In their place he settled immigrants from Babylonia and Syria, to whom he sent back an Israelitic priest to teach them the worship of Jehovah (17:24-28); this foreign settlement is dated in the time of Esarhaddon (681-668) by Ezra 4:2. The author of Kings explains the downfall of North Israel as divine punishment for persisting in the sin of Jeroboam (17:21-23) and regards the religion of the mixed population of Samaria after 722 as a combination of Jehovah worship and foreign idolatry (17:29-34a, 41). The postexilic Deuteronomist adds to the sins of North Israel those of Judah under Ahaz and Manasseh (17:7-17) and refers to the downfall of Judah in 586 (17:19 f.). A later scribe dismissed the wretched religion of the inhabitants of North Israel after 722 as an unforgivable violation of God's written Law (17:34b-40); in 17:37 the divine Law is already a book—perhaps the canonical Pentateuch after 400—but in 17:13 it is still oral.

The History of the Kings of Judah lacks the brilliance of the Israelitic history. Neither the authors of its sources nor the final compiler were outstanding writers and historians. The difference in viewpoint may be seen in the accounts of the same events (II 12:17 f. [H. 12:18 f.], Jud., cf. 10:32, Israelitic; II 16:7-9, Jud., cf. 15:29 f., Isr.; II 18:9-11, Jud., cf. 17:3-6, Isr.). The Israelitic history was essentially political; the Judean was instead primarily a chronicle of the Temple in Jerusalem; in both, the prophets are mentioned only incidentally.

To the best of our knowledge, the information presented objectively in the History of the Kings of Judah is derived from two main sources: the official annals of the kings of Judah and a Temple chronicle. Both works were in the nature of diaries, supplemented from time to time, as occasion demanded. The notice in the royal annals, that Edom shook off the dominion of Judah "unto this day" (II 8:22), was undoubtedly written before II 14:7. Similarly, the detailed description of Solomon's Temple (I 6; 7:13-51), which is rightly ascribed to the Temple chronicle by J. Wellhausen, was obviously written before Ahaz made certain innovations in the sacred edifice (II 16:10-18).

Most of the data in the History of the Kings of Judah derived from the royal annals were summarized or omitted by the author of Kings, whose chief interest was religious. In addition to chronological and other data about each king used in the standardized introductions, the royal annals gave accounts of wars (I 22:45 [H. 22:46]; cf. I 15:23; II 20:20) and building operations (I 15:23; II 20:20). The royal annals seem to be the ultimate source from which information about purely secular matters in the following sections is derived: I 22:47-49 (H. 22:48-50); II 8:20-22; 3:28 f. (inserted by the first Deuteronomist in 9:14 f.); 14:7, 19-22; 15:5; 18:13, 17-19:8, 36 f. (cf. Is. 36:1-37:8, 37 f.) (omitting "tartan and rabsaris and" [i.e. commander in chief and chief of the eunuchs] in 18:17; cf. Is. 36:2 [18:22, 25, 32]; 21:23 f.).

Among these stories, the account of the deliverance of Jerusalem from Sennacherib's army in 701 (18:13, 17-19:8, 36 f.) is the most important; it has, in fact, no equal in interest among the extant remains of Judean royal history (on II 18:13-19:37 see L. L. Honor, *Sennacherib's Invasion of Palestine*). It is now combined with two other stories: an account of the submission of Hezekiah to Sennacherib (18:14-16, lacking in Is. 36), closely paralleling Sennacherib's own report and ostensibly quoted from the Temple chronicle, and a legendary story of the slaying of 185,000 Assyrians in one night by the angel of the Lord, i.e., the bubonic plague (19:9b-35; Is. 37:9b-36), which corresponds to the onslaught of field mice on the army of Sennacherib when he attacked Egypt (Herodotus 2:141).

This story of 19:9b-35, in which Jehovah, as in Second Isaiah, is the only God and creator of heaven and earth (19:15) while the other gods are nothing but "the work of men's hands, wood and stone" (19:18), is unhistorical and was written after 500 B.C. Both oracles of Isaiah which it contains (19:21-31, 32-34) are spurious prophecies after the event, but the second (19:32-34) seems to be earlier than the first, which is poetic utterance in the style of Second Isaiah (19:21-28), supplemented with a prophecy in the apocalyptic vein (19:29-31).

The reference to "Tirhakah king of Ethiopia" who ruled Egypt from 688 to 663 (19:9a) raises serious, and indeed, insoluble problems. Tirhakah was not yet ruling when Sennacherib (705-681) besieged Jerusalem in 701;[12] nor is there (aside from Herodotus 2:141) any knowledge of a later attack on Egypt by Sennacherib. Whether 19:9a was an integral part of 18:13, 17-19:8 or, more likely, a gloss intended to fulfill the prophecy "and he will hear a rumor and he will return to his own land" (19:7; the rest of the prophecy is fulfilled in 19:36 f.), the reference to Tirhakah is an anachronism without historical basis.

In regard to the historicity of the three stories in 18:13-19:37, the most probable of the conflicting conjectures is that 18:14-16, which is confirmed by the Assyrian sources (on which cf. R. P. Dougherty, JBL 49 [1930] 160-171), is substantially historical, whereas the other two are more or less legendary elaborations of the facts. Hezekiah was regarded as one of the most pious, and therefore successful, kings of Judah (18:5, 7). Consequently, his abject submission to Sennacherib related in 18:14-16, which contradicted the Deuteronomic doctrine of earthly rewards for obedience to the Law, was suppressed by the author of Kings in favor of 18:13, 17-19:8, (9a), 36 f., and is consequently lacking in Is. 36 and II Chron. 32.

This second account, probably taken from the History of the Kings of Judah, is well written and substantially historical, as far as it goes. By omitting Hezekiah's heavy payment to Sennacherib, it could interpret the sudden deliverance of Jerusalem and the assassination of Sennacherib as due to divine intervention in behalf of the pious king of Judah. The

[12] It is true that Tirhakah held an official position during the reign of Shabataka, his uncle and predecessor on the throne (cf. C. F. Lehmann-Haupt, *Israel* u.s.w., p. 114. Tübingen, 1911), but he was not commander of the Egyptian forces defeated by Sennacherib at Eltekeh in 701 as E. König (*Das Buch Jesaja*, p. 21. Gütersloh, 1926) claims. A renewed Egyptian attack after that battle is unlikely in any case.

"rumor" causing Sennacherib to lift the siege can hardly have been the menacing advance of Tirhakah (19:9a), but rather a report from Baby· lonia, where Bel-ibni (703-700), placed on the throne by Sennacherib instead of the Chaldean Merodach-baladan, joined the Chaldeans in their inveterate anti-Assyrian plotting.

Two reasons, the payment of Hezekiah's tribute (amounting to more than 5 million gold dollars) and the report of seditious plots in Babylonia, adequately explain the lifting of the siege of Jerusalem and the return of Sennacherib. A third reason, the plague, is given in the third account (19:9b-35). In spite of indirect confirmation in Herodotus 2:141, this catastrophic end to Sennacherib's campaign of 701 is extremely unlikely. This third account is a legendary elaboration of the second. Its author did not consider Sennacherib's withdrawal and later assassination as sufficient manifestation of divine wrath for his blasphemous taunts of Jehovah and attack against the city housing his Temple. So he pictured the angel of the Lord dramatically wiping out the Assyrian army in a single night.

The following stories of Hezekiah's illness (20:1-11; cf. Is. 38) and of Merodach-baladan's embassy to him (20:12-19; cf. Is. 39) may ultimately rest on facts reported in the royal annals, but in their present form they cannot be earlier than 19:9b-35 (dating from after 500 B.C.). Both events are said to have occurred during the siege of Jerusalem in 701 (20:6, 12), but Merodach-baladan could only have sent his embassy when he ruled Babylon (721-710) in the time of Sargon or, at the latest, during the six months in which he reoccupied the throne at the beginning of Sennacherib's reign (704-703). Even more significant is the idealization of Hezekiah and David (20:3, 6) and the clear allusion to the Exile of 586 (20:17 f.). The author of these tales completely ignores the payment of Hezekiah's tribute (18:14-16), after which no treasure was left in Jerusalem; if the inspection of 20:13-15 took place before this payment, Isaiah should have predicted the delivery of the treasures to Nineveh rather than to Babylon (20:16).

The author of the history of Judah's kings seems to have found his information, apart from the royal annals, in a Temple chronicle written by priests. This document must have begun with the account of the building of Solomon's Temple and a description of the sacred edifice and its furnishings, now found in I 6:2-37; 7:13-51, although not originally a part of Solomon's biography. To this source we may ascribe the stories disclosing a special interest in the Temple: accounts concerning restoration or refurnishing (II 12:4-16 [H. 12:5-17]; 15:35b; 16:10-18), an enemy's plundering of the Temple (I 14:25-28, and perhaps II 14:14, which concludes a story from the History of the Kings of Israel), spoliation of the Temple treasures to provide funds for a heavy tribute, a war indemnity, or gift to a foreign king (I 15:16-22; II 12:18 f.; 16:5-9 [16:6 may come from the royal annals]; 18:14-16). The story of Athaliah (II 11) is taken from the Temple chronicle (11:1-12, 18b-20, omitting 11:6, 10, "all the people of the land" in 11:19, and premature references to the king in 11:7, 11) but has been supplemented by a fragmentary parallel from an unknown source (11:13-18a, omitting the harmonistic glosses "the guard [and]" in 11:13 and "the captains of hundreds" in 11:15).

It is possible that some references to religious reforms (I 15:12 f.; 22:46 [H. 22:47]) may be derived from this source but, while II 21:17 suggests that the History of the Kings of Judah contained an account of the "sin" of Manasseh, the extant account of his religious syncretism (II 21:3-16) has been written by the second Deuteronomist (21:7-15) and later scribes (21:3-6). Only the framework (21:1 f., 17 f.) and perhaps 21:16 were written by the author of Kings.

The same author, writing about twenty years after the events and drawing in part on his own memories, composed the original account of the discovery of the Deuteronomic Code in 621 and Josiah's reforms (II 22:1-23:30). Our text, however, has been revised and supplemented by later hands. The "priest" became the "high priest" (22:4, 8; 23:4); 22:4b, 5a, 6 f. were added by a scribe who remembered II 12:9-15 [H. 12:10-16]; the oracle of Huldah (22:15-20) has been thoroughly rewritten by the postexilic Deuteronomist, who through a strange slip of the pen made the prophetess predict a peaceful death for Josiah (22:20 in contrast with 23:29).

The account of Josiah's reforms (23:4-27) has suffered particularly at the hand of editors: the second Deuteronomist added 23:25b-27 at the end; 23:4 f. have been revised by a late editor (who considers the Asherah a goddess and not, as in 23:6, the sacred post). Although historically correct to a great extent, 23:8b, 10, 14, 24 exhibit traces of stylistic revision; on the contrary the desecration of Bethel (23:15) and the shrines of Samaria (23:19 f.), over which Josiah had no jurisdiction, are historically absurd. Even more fantastic is the story in 23:16-18, which alludes to the late legend of I 13.

The authors of the Temple chronicle were priests. They reported with complete objectivity events affecting the Temple. They make it perfectly clear that at the time the Temple was nothing but a royal chapel—not yet a national shrine (as in I 8)—and that its priests were mere servants of the king. Had we their account of the religious policies of Manasseh, it is unlikely that we would read in it a single word of disapproval for this king—not to speak of the fiery indignation of the first and second Deuteronomists and, if we believe II 21:17, even of the author of the History of the Kings of Judah. Everything indicates that the royal annals and Temple chronicle, which were utilized in composing the history of the Kings of Judah, did not reach beyond the death of Amon (638 B.C.).

Our Book of Kings contains two important North Israelitic biographies which, on the whole, did not belong to the history of the kings: the life of Elijah (I 17-19; 21 and perhaps II 1:2-4, 17aα; cf. II 1:5-16; 2) and the life of Elisha (II 2; 3:4-8:15; 13:14-21; cf. I 19:19-21; II 9:1-6, 10b). Although considerably earlier than the first edition of Kings, the stories of Elijah (except II 21) and those of Elisha (except II 9) were not included. In the first edition, I 16:29-34 was immediately followed by 21 and 22:39 f., II 1:18 by 3:1-3. There is no trace of the first Deuteronomist between II 3:1-3 and 8:16-19; and II 13:14-21 is manifestly intrusive. We do not know when these stories were inserted in our book: Malachi (Mal. 4:5 [H. 3:23]), about 460 B.C., presumably read the Elijah stories in Kings, just as the Chronicler (II Chron. 21:12) unquestionably did two centuries later, although he did not reproduce them. In the LXX, II 21 follows 19.

The stories about Elijah (I 17-19; 21) date from about 800 B.C. Like the early stories concerning Jeroboam I, Ahab, Jehu, and Joash, they are masterpieces from the best period of North Israelitic prose literature. The author of the Elijah stories has full command of the resources of Hebrew style, and with simple means obtains brilliant effects. He thus conveys to the reader a vivid picture of the misery and suffering caused by a three-year famine, not by describing the people starving and by depicting gruesome scenes like that of II 6:25-30, but indirectly. Elijah is fed miraculously by the ravens (I 17:2-7), through the inexhaustible earthen jar of meal and cruse of oil belonging to the widow at Zarephath (17:8-16), and by an angel (19:5-8); Ahab himself and his major-domo, Obadiah, go through the land looking for pasturage to keep the horses and mules alive (18:3-6).

The author is particularly effective in dialogues (18:7-15, 17 f.; 21:2 f., 5-7) and in the description of scenes, whether charmingly simple (19: 19-21), intensely dramatic (18:20-40), or even spiritually infused with the divine presence (19:9-14). His apposite use of irony and sarcasm is unexcelled (18:27). But his greatest achievement is the living portrait of the gigantic figure of Elijah, a second Moses (cf. Mark 9:4 f.) with moments of heroic grandeur, as on Carmel (18:36-40), followed by moods of abject fear and utmost despair (19:2-10).

The similarity between the Elijah cycle and the political stories from the history of Israel's kings, mentioned above, is confined to literary excellence. Their authorship and character are wholly different. The political stories present the point of view of the court and nobility, and are the work of able historians; the Elijah stories reflect a plebeian viewpoint (notably I 21) and, originating on the lips of the common people, were redacted by an admirer of the prophet endowed with great literary talent. The first are factual and objective, the second legendary. In these stories, Elijah does not appear as a mere "man subject to like passions as we are," according to the prosaic characterization of James (5:17), but as a superman of heroic stature, contemplated by a reverent popular imagination through the haze of legend, the only champion of the God of Israel defying in solitary grandeur Ahab's displeasure and Jezebel's fury.

It is true that Elijah was a real historical character, that the dreadful famine in the time of Ahab actually occurred (cf. Menander of Ephesus in Josephus, *Antiquities* 8:13, 2), and that the conflict between Jehovah and Baal, which furnished the pretext for Jehu's successful revolution, was epoch-making in the religion of Israel. Even Obadiah (18:3-16) may be a historical character, conceivably the owner of a seal inscribed "'bdyhw [Obad-Jahu or Abdi-Jahu] servant of the king" (cf. ZDPV 37 [1914] 173). Nevertheless, what marks the Elijah stories as legends is the supernatural background manifested in numerous miracles (17:2-7, 8-16, 17-24; 18:38; 19:5-8), in Obadiah's belief that the prophet might be carried to distant places by the spirit of Jehovah (18:12), and in the divine presence at the prophet's side.

Their folk character also appears in the obvious exaggerations: Ahab allegedly permits the slaying of Jehovah's prophets by the hundred (18:13, 22; 19:14), whereas he actually kept many at court for consultation (22:5-28). Moreover, as shown also by the names of Ahab and Jezebel's children (Ahaziah, Joram, Joash, and Athaliah), all of which contain the name of Jehovah (-Jah, Jo-), Ahab remained a worshiper of Jehovah all his life, without the slightest intention of making Jezebel's god, Melkart (the Baal of Tyre), to whom he merely erected a temple in Samaria, the sole god of Israel. Ahab probably could see no reason for Elijah's dilemma—either Jehovah or Baal (18:21)—and regarded it as the product of a fanatical mind. Before Elijah, Jehovah's jealousy and exclusiveness had never been proclaimed.

In any case, the worship of Baal at the time of the revolution of Jehu had made such slow progress that all the worshipers of this god could be gathered in the temple at Samaria and slain by eighty guards (II 10: 18-25). Nothing could show more clearly how extravagant was Elijah's conviction that he was the sole surviving worshiper of Jehovah, or how inadequate the number (7,000) of Israelites who had not bowed to Baal and kissed his image (I 19:18).

The stories of Elijah are incomplete—the original beginning and end are lost—but, as in an ancient Greek torso, what remains seems somehow to have taken on the virtue of what is lost. The beginning of 17:1, by its very abruptness and suddenness, achieves an artistic effect and instantly conveys an impression of the swift, unpredictable appearances and disappearances of the prophet.

The story of Naboth (I 21) is a separate episode and not the conclusion. The main part (17-19) has dramatic unity but lacks a denouement. Jehovah on Horeb gives three commissions to the prophet: he shall anoint Hazael as king of Damascus, Jehu as king of Israel, and Elisha as the prophet who will succeed him (19:15-18). Only the fulfillment of the third commission is told at the end (19:19-21). But according to the original form of the story Elijah must have carried out the other two. Thus the climax was reached in the final triumph of Jehovah over Baal and of the prophet over Ahab and his house. But in this dramatic denouement, in which Elijah was erroneously connected with the wars waged by Ahab and Joram against Damascus and with Jehu's revolution, the author attributed to Elijah the deeds of Elisha.

However, noting that in II 9:1-10 (which stood in the edition of 600 B.C.) Elisha anointed Jehu through an emissary, and that elsewhere he promised to Hazael the throne of Damascus (II 8:7-15, belonging to the Elisha stories), the postexilic editors who inserted into our book the stories of Elijah and Elisha simply suppressed the end of the Elijah stories, without removing the clue to its contents in 19:15-18. At the same time, they added the Elijah legend in II 1:2-17aα; of which only 1:2-4, 17aα could possibly have belonged to the original cycle.

A few glosses and editorial additions can be detected in the Elijah stories. To concur with Ex. 16:8 (which may be an echo of I 17:6), we should probably read "and the ravens brought him bread in the morning and meat in the evening" (17:6; cf. some recensions of the LXX). Late glossators have added the "four hundred prophets of the Asherah" in 18:19 (cf. 18:40), and in 18:31-32a (in which Gen. 35:10, P, is quoted) they have provided an incongruous variant to 18:30b (in the LXX, this gloss precedes 18:30b). The magnificent theophany on Horeb is marred by the unfortunate addition of 19:9b-11aα ("and behold the word of Jehovah . . . stand on the mount before Jehovah"); in 19:14 (the prototype of 19:10) "they have forsaken thy covenant" is a Deuteronomistic revision of "they have forsaken thee," which still stands in both passages in some recensions of the LXX and Syriac, and in the Old Latin text. The original text of the story of Naboth's vineyard ends abruptly in 21:20abα, "and he answered, 'I have found (thee)'" (in 21:1-19 we should omit "that were in his city" in 21:8; the second "the men of Belial" and "(even) against Naboth" in 21:13; and the second "Ahab" in 21:16). The end of the story has been supplemented with a sentence against Ahab and his dynasty (21:20bβ-22, 24), written by the first Deuteronomist; with a sentence against Jezebel (21:23), inferred from II 9:30-35 and quoted in the late verses II 9:36 f. (cf. 9:10a); with a condemnation of Ahab's conduct (21:25 f.); and finally with an oracle, explaining why the sentence against Ahab was not carried out during his lifetime (21:27-29), written by the second Deuteronomist.

The author of Kings omitted the stories of Elijah in I 17-19 because their point of view differed radically from his own. For him the earthly abode of Jehovah was the Temple in Jerusalem (I 8:27-30; 14:21), not Horeb, the one place outside of Israel where Elijah thought he could receive an oracle of his God (I 19:8, 11b-18). He necessarily regarded Elijah's sacrifice on Carmel (I 18:30, 32b-38) as a violation of Jehovah's law in Deut. 12, and the prophet's lament over the destruction of the altars of Jehovah in the Northern Kingdom (I 19:14) as blasphemy against the same law ordering their desecration.

The story of Naboth (I 21), however, did not conflict with the Deuteronomic law, and it presented Ahab in a much darker light—as a puppet of Jezebel sanctioning murder to obtain a vineyard—and furnished a suitable setting for our author's fiery denunciation of Ahab and his dynasty (21:20bβ-22, 24). The style and language of this oracle prove that it was written by the author of Kings. He reproduces it with slight changes when the sentence is carried out by Jehu (II 9:7-9); he refers in both passages to similar oracles from his pen against Jeroboam I (I 14:1-16; cf. 15:29) and Baasha (I 16:1-4; cf. 16:11 f.), and in all three instances uses the vulgar circumlocution for "all males" (I 14:10; 16:11; 21:21; II 9:8) which David had used in a moment of rage (I Sam. 25:22, 34) but which occurs nowhere else in the Bible.

The expression "shut up and left" (probably meaning "ritually pure and impure") occurs only in these passages (I 14:10; 21:21; II 9:8) and in later ones (II 14:26; Deut. 32:36). The presence of an addition by the first Deuteronomist in I 21 proves that the story of Naboth was included in the first edition of Kings; in I 17-19, on the contrary, there is no trace of his pen.

Paradoxically, Elisha is a more historical and also a more legendary character than Elijah: more historical because his share in Jehu's annihilation of the dynasty of Omri is attested incidentally in a document of unimpeachable historicity and objectivity (II 9:1-6, 10b-13). At least in this one instance, Elisha's personality is so inextricably interwoven with the political events of his time that his historicity cannot be doubted. On the contrary, appearing suddenly from his remote hiding places to fulminate against Ahab, Elijah left no tangible impression on the course of events. Nevertheless, there is a substratum of fact in the legends about Elijah (particularly in the story of Naboth, I 21) more solid than in most of the stories about Elisha.

It is true that Elisha is introduced in the narratives of genuine occurrences, such as the war against Mesha king of Moab (II 3:4-27) and the

Aramean wars (6:24-7:20; 8:7-15; cf. 5:1-27; 6:8-23; 13:14-21). It should be noted that the three stories just mentioned (3:4-27; 6:24-7:20; 8:7-15) differ from all other Elisha stories (in 2:1-25; 3:4-8:15; 13:14-21) in two respects: they have an historical background (as of course II 9, which does not belong to the Elisha cycle) and, contradicting Elisha's patriotism and friendliness to the king of Israel in the other stories, they depict the prophet as an irreconcilable enemy of the ruling king of Israel. This hostility is revealed when the throne of Damascus is promised to Hazael, archenemy of Israel (8:7-15). The other two stories (3:4-27; 6:24-7:20) relate events preceding the accession of Jehu and Hazael (843-842), when one of Ahab's sons was still on the throne and the prophet's hatred for the king was inevitable. They contain such excellent historical narratives (3:4-8, 26 f.; 6:24-30; 7:3-15, which have nothing to do with Elisha), that J. Wellhausen was inclined to attribute them to the brilliant author of I 20 and 22. Although this connection has been generally rejected, it seems probable that in these two stories (and in 8:7-15 to a lesser extent [see 8:15]), good historical narratives were rewritten as Elisha legends, whereas all the other Elisha stories (II 9 excepted) are mere legendary fiction.

With the exception of these three stories, the genuine factual core of which may have been derived from the History of the Kings of Israel (as II 9 was), the Elisha narratives fail to attain the literary brilliance, dramatic power, and sense of reality which characterize the stories of Elijah (despite the supernatural events). The Elisha cycle is an artificial literary product, not an echo of the overwhelming impression made upon popular imagination by a titanic personality such as Elijah. None of them appears to have been handed down from the oral tradition, even if I. Benzinger (*Die Bücher der Könige*, pp. 129, 137-139) is right in regarding II 4:8-37 as the amalgamation of two sources.

Like the writer of the Book of Jonah, the author of the Elisha stories composed a volume of fiction about a real prophetic personality. He deliberately provided a sequel to the Elijah cycle: his story of Elijah's ascension at the beginning (II 2) marks a transition between the two works. Moreover, his imitation of the Elijah stories is obvious and, like all imitations of a masterpiece by a second-rate craftsman, pathetically artificial. The stories about the widow's miraculous pot of oil (4:1-7), and the resurrection of the son of a woman offering hospitality to the prophet (4:8-37) have their prototypes in I 17:8-24.[13] In fact, Elisha is an *editio*

[13] G. Hölscher (*Die Propheten*, p. 177, n. 1), on the contrary, is of the opinion that Elisha's deeds were subsequently ascribed to Elijah, and that a good part of the Elijah stories was originally told of Elisha. It is obvious, of course, that the growth of legend around a heroic figure tends to endow him with achievements of later times: the legends about Moses are particularly significant in this respect. So Jehu's massacre of the Baal worshipers is prematurely ascribed to Elijah on Carmel. Never-

minor of Elijah, fulfilling the latter's commissions in selecting Hazael as king of Damascus (I 19:15; II 8:7-15) and inheriting a double portion of the spirit (II 2:9 f., 15; cf. Deut. 21:17), the mantle (2:13), and the sonorous title (2:12; 13:14) of his great predecessor. In both cycles, the protagonist is frequently called "man of God." The Elisha stories were written in the Northern Kingdom, presumably half a century after the Elijah stories, or about 750 B.C.

The Elisha stories are a series of anecdotes without much cohesion, let alone the dramatic unity of I 17-19. All of them deal with miracles. But while the supernatural atmosphere in the stories of Elijah seemingly furnished the inevitable background for the titanic figure of that prophet, in the Elisha stories it becomes a theatrical *mise en scène*: not so much a manifestation of the deity's presence as more or less magical (notably 4:31; 13:20 f.) performances. The primary intention was to clothe the influential politician, inspiring the revolution of Jehu, with the awful majesty of a superhuman miracle-worker who annihilated the irreverent (2:23-25; 7:18-20), of an exalted person whose very corpse restored the dead to life (13:20 f.).

The editor who inserted the Elisha stories into the Book of Kings did not respect their original order; and seems to be responsible for most of the confusion and contradictions of our text, although even the original version probably lacked a consistent and chronological arrangement. Critics have pointed out a number of contradictions. In the story of Naaman (II 5), Israel and Damascus are at peace; in a later story (6:8-23), after they have waged war with one another, Elisha miraculously (but fictitiously, as in the case of Samuel's final deliverance of Israel from the Philistines [I Sam. 7:13 f.]) delivers Israel from the Aramean raids forever, although the war is continued immediately afterward (6:24-7:20). In fact, its results prove increasingly disastrous for Israel (8:12), and even the death of the prophet (13:14-19) does not end the war. In 5:27, Gehazi became an incurable leper, but in 8:1-6 he converses with the king, ostensibly after the death of Elisha (cf. 8:4), as if completely healed. In some stories, Elisha resides at Gilgal and Jericho at the head of a prophetic fraternity (2:1-22; 4:1-7, 38; 6:1-7); in others he lives in Samaria (2:25; 5:3; 6:24-7:20; 13:14).

The editor who inserted the Elisha stories into our Book of Kings placed some of them in a wrong period. All the legends, with the exception of the account of the prophet's death in the reign of Joash (800-785) (13:14-21), are dated between the accession (II 1:17; 3:1) and death (9:24) of Joram (852-843). The activity of Elisha was presumably con-

---

theless, as a literary document the story of Elijah is based on popular legends in circulation long before the Elisha cycle took shape, and it was written without question before the anecdotes about Elisha were collected in a book.

fined to the reign of Joram—first, because he was the only king actually named in the stories (3:6) and, second, because the only king of Damascus named was Joram's contemporary, Ben-hadad II (6:24; 8:7, 9), killed by his successor, Hazael, in 842 (8:10-15). However, while Joram's reign lasted twelve years (3:1) or less, the Elijah stories cover a period of at least fourteen years (seven years at least elapsed between 4:16 and 4:18, and a seven-year famine came later, 8:1-6). Moreover, the friendship of Elisha for the king disclosed in 4:8-37 + 8:1-6; 5; 6:8-23 is inconceivable in the reign of Joram, a son of Jezebel, and clearly points to the reign of Jehu (cf. 9:1-3) and his son Joash (13:14-19). If the original author observed any chronological order at all, he placed the stories of Joram's time (3:4-27; 6:24-7:20) before the accessions of Jehu and Hazael (9:1-6; 8:7-15) in 843-842, and the rest later. The editor has broken the original connection between 4:8-37 and 8:1-6 by filling in the intervening period of seven years with the events related in 4:38-7:20 regardless of their sequence in time: the famine announced in 8:1-6 was already raging in 4:38 and 6:25.

In conclusion, the author of Kings writing about 600 B.C. used as his sources three Judean books (the acts of Solomon, History of the Kings of Judah, and the Temple chronicle) plus one North Israelitic book (History of the Kings of Israel). He left out of account the two North Israelitic biographies of Elijah (except I 21) and Elisha (except II 9). This first edition began with I 2:1-12; 3:1 and ended with II 23:25a, 28, but was considerably shorter than the present text. Later editors added not only their own brief annotations and longer reflections or narratives, but also generous extracts from ancient sources, particularly North Israelitic.

The following extracts from the history of Israel's kings were added (with editorial additions) to the first edition of Kings by the second Deuteronomist (550 B.C.) or by later editors: I 11:26-40; 12:2-25 (Jeroboam I); 20; 22:1-38; (Ahab); II 14:8-14 (Joash). Several summaries in this history were added by the second Deuteronomist, usually with pious reflections: I 16:34 (the rebuilding of Jericho); II 1:1 (rebellion of Moab); 13:22-25 (Joash); 14:25-27 (Jeroboam II). The stories of Elijah (I 17-19; II 1:2-17) and Elisha (2; 3:4-8:15; 13:14-21) were likewise added in the edition of 550 B.C. or in a later one.

Conversely, little ancient material of Judean origin was added to Kings after 600: the end of the early biography of David (I 1; 2:13-46a); some annotated extracts from Solomon's biography (4:20-26 [H. 4:20-5:6]; 4:29-5:1 [H. 5:9-15]; 9:15-24; 11:14-25); a quotation from the Temple chronicle (II 18:14-16); late revised transcriptions from the History of the Kings of Judah (II 19:9b-35; 20:1-19); and brief notices outside the framework of the first Deuteronomist (I 14:30 = 15:6; 15:7b, 23b; 22:46-49 [H. 22:47-50]; cf. the gloss 15:32 taken from 15:16).

3. The Second Edition of Kings and Later Supplements

The exilic Deuteronomist published not only the book of Kings in a new edition about the year 550 B.C., but edited the books of the Pentateuch (except Leviticus, which is later) and the three other historical books (Josh., Judg., Sam.) at the same time. As we have seen, his contribution is particularly conspicuous in Joshua, where he rewrote most of the stories and added Joshua's address in ch. 23, and in Judges, where he furnished the framework of the book. In Kings, he continued the history down to the liberation of Jehoiachin from prison (in 561) and his death (alluded to in II 25:30 but explicitly mentioned in the parallel Jer. 52:34), adding II 23:25b-28, 29-37; 24-25 at the end of the first edition. This Deuteronomist therefore wrote between 561 (or a few years later, the date of Jehoiachin's death being unknown) and the conquest of Babylon by Cyrus in 538 (still unknown to him), marking the end of the "Exile."

His source for the account of Josiah's death (II 23:29 f.), theologically explained by him in 23:25b-27, for Jehoahaz (609; 23:31-35), and for Jehoiakim (609-598; 23:36-24:7), was a supplement to the History of the Kings of Judah (cf. 24:5). This source was lacking for Jehoiachin (598-597), Zedekiah (597-586), and the events from the destruction of Jerusalem in 586 to the liberation of Jehoiachin in 561. However, he had reliable written sources of information for the period 598-561.

The excellent statistics of exiles preserved in Jer. 52:28-30 (omitted in the LXX), which were disregarded in Kings, indicate what accurate records were kept in these troubled times. For Jehoiachin (24:8-17) a fragment of his source is preserved in Jer. 29:2 (cf. 24:15 f.; 24:13 f. is a priestly addition). For the time of Zedekiah (24:18-25:21) the source is partially preserved in Jer. 39:4-13. His own account, including the gloss to 25:13 in 25:16 f., is reproduced in Jer. 52:1-27. In 25:22-26, his story of the assassination of Gedaliah, governor of Judah under Nebuchadnezzar, is a brief epitome of the circumstantial and accurate account in Jer. 40:7-43:7; 25:22-26 is omitted in Jer. 52. Finally, the story of the liberation of Jehoiachin (25:27-30) is reproduced in Jer. 52:31-34.

Besides bringing the history of Judah down to his own day, the exilic Deuteronomist inserted into Kings a number of the extracts and summaries from ancient sources which, as we have seen, were not in the first edition of the book. He clearly left his mark on these insertions (as in I 4:20-26 [H. 4:20-5:6]; 11:14-40; 12:2-25; II 13:22-25; 14:25-27); for other additions it is impossible to determine whether he or a later editor copied them into the book.

Imitating the author of Kings, this exilic editor composed several of the prophetic oracles in the book. The different attitude toward North Israel

in these two writers makes it possible to distinguish their respective contributions. In 600, when Judah gloried in its survival 122 years after the
downfall of North Israel and ignored warnings of its imminent collapse
uttered by Jeremiah and other prophets, the first Deuteronomist considered the kingdom of Israel completely reprobate and accursed, as its
miserable end testified. Accordingly, after the manner, but without the
literary and religious genius, of Amos, he composed oracles proclaiming
the inevitable doom of certain kings of Israel and their dynasties: Jeroboam I (I 14:1-18; 15:29), Baasha (I 16:1-4, [7], 12), Ahab (I 21:20bβ-22,
24; cf. II 9:7-9). He shed no tears over the end of the kingdom in 722,
since he saw in this calamity a just punishment for persistence in the sins
of Jeroboam (II 17:21-23).

But after the destruction of Jerusalem in 586, the second Deuteronomist
could no longer contrast the virtue and security of Judah with the woe
and sinfulness of Israel. In his day, the prayer of the publican, "God, be
merciful to me a sinner," was more appropriate than that of the Pharisee,
"God, I thank thee, that I am not as other men are." It was natural to conclude, as Ezekiel did (Ez. 23), that the two kingdoms had come to the
same tragic end because they had both been sinful: in II 17:17, for
instance, the exilic Deuteronomist attributes to North Israel Manasseh's
abominable child sacrifices to Moloch. Jeremiah (Jer. 3:6-11) even regards
Judah as worse than Israel. Moreover, as the two kingdoms shared a
common fate in the past (II 17:7-20; 21:13), would they not both experience a future restoration together? Ezekiel and Second Isaiah, about this
time, firmly believed so.

Thus the exilic Deuteronomist discloses a friendly attitude toward
North Israel (cf. Jer. 3:12-19) inconceivable either half a century before
(in the first Deuteronomist) or later, after the Samaritan schism. Intervening between the contempt and fanatical hatred for North Israel in the
minds of the author of Kings and of the Chronicler, there was a feeling of
solidarity with North Israel during the "Exile," a sense of national unity
between the two kingdoms, graphically expressed by Ezekiel in joining
together a stick for Judah and one for Joseph (Ez. 37:15-28).

The exilic Deuteronomist is not immune from this changed attitude
toward North Israel. He seems deliberately to correct some of the first
Deuteronomist's implacable oracles against North Israel. In the writings
of the latter, Ahijah the Shilonite pronounces the doom of Jeroboam and
the whole kingdom (I 14:1-16; 15:29; the last clause in 14:2 is harmonistic). On the contrary, the second Deuteronomist has Ahijah promising him the bulk of David's kingdom (11:29-39; 12:15). Moreover,
Shemaiah, the man of God, ordered Rehoboam to desist from his attack on
Jeroboam's subjects, "your brethren the children of Israel" (12:21-24).
Apropos, our editor mollifies (21:27 f.) Elijah's pitiless oracle against

Ahab, written by the first Deuteronomist (I 21:20bβ-22, 24). After Ahab repented and wore mourning garments, Jehovah announced that the punishment would not be inflicted upon the king during his lifetime, as also in the case of Solomon (I 11:11-13, written by the original author).

Contrasted with the merciless severity of Jehovah toward the Northern Kingdom in the writings of the first Deuteronomist, our editor of 550 B.C., like the Second Isaiah, stresses the compassion of the deity for his sinful but afflicted people in both Judges and Kings. On several occasions, Jehovah sent a "deliverer" (II 13:5; cf. Judg. 3:9, 15; 6:36; 12:3), because he heard their petition in times of distress (II 13:4-6) and showed them compassion remembering his covenant with Abraham, Isaac, and Jacob (13:23), and because he had not decided to "blot out the name of Israel from under heaven" (14:25-27). There is a striking similarity between these passages (cf. also II 17:7-20) and the framework of Judges, written by the same editor.

The realization that Judah and Israel were equally false to Jehovah induced our editor not only to soften the harshness of the oracles for Israel but also to sharpen the oracular denunciations of Judah by unequivocal announcements of the national ruin of 586. In the divine utterance to Solomon, when Israel and Judah were still united (I 9:1-9; cf. 11:9), through the prophets to Manasseh (II 21:7-15), and through Huldah to Josiah (22:14-20; cf. 23:26 f.), the destruction of Jerusalem and the deportation of the Judeans are predicted (after the event) in no uncertain terms, as also in additions to Solomon's prayer (I 8:41-52) and elsewhere (II 17:19 f.).

Between the edition published in 550 and its canonization in 200 B.C., the four historical books constituting the canon of the Former Prophets (Josh., Judg., Sam., and Kings) were annotated by readers and scribes. Several glosses were still unknown to the Chronicler in 250, and even to the LXX (200-150 B.C.). Some of these notes disclose familiarity with the Priestly Code (and Ps) and were inserted ostensibly soon after the canonization of the Pentateuch in 400: "to him (belong) the towns of Jair the son of Manasseh, in Gilead" (I 4:13, omitted in the LXX; cf. Num. 32:41 and Josh. 13:30); 4:19b; references to gold-leaf overlay in the interior of the Temple in I 6; "as far as the Holy of Holies" (I 6:16); 7:47-50; reference to the Tabernacle in 8:4 and other glosses in 8:1-11; 8:54; 12:32 f.; 16:7; 18:31 (cf. Gen. 35:10); II 12:16 (H. 12:17). Other longer or shorter additions are dated even later: I 2:27 (cf. I Sam. 2:27-36); I 13 and II 23:15-20 which refers to I 13; I 20:13 f., 22, 28; II 1:5-16, 17b-18; 17:34b-40; 22:4b, 5a, 6 f.; 23:4 f., 8b, 10, 14, 24.

Our Book of Kings spans the history of less than four centuries and a half, but it is a repository of documents ranging from the days of Solomon to those of Judas Maccabeus—a period of eight centuries during which time almost all of the Old Testament was written.

PART IV

THE LATTER PROPHETS

CHAPTER I

THE BOOK OF ISAIAH

~~~~~~

Since J. C. Doederlein published his commentary on this book (*Esaias.* 1775; 2nd ed., 1780), it is generally recognized that it comprises two distinct works. The first is the "Book of Isaiah" (Is. 1-39), the second, now called the "Second Isaiah" (or Deutero-Isaiah), is an anonymous work written about 550 B.C. or later (Is. 40-66).[1] The second accidentally became part of the volume of Isaiah when the prophetic oracles extant about 200 B.C. were issued in four volumes (Is., Jer., Ez., and "The Twelve" [Minor Prophets]).

This comprehensive edition of prophetic writings, called "The Latter Prophets," was copied on four scrolls of papyrus almost equal in length: only two consist of the works of individual prophets (Jer. and Ez.), with later additions; the others are anthologies. Anonymous prophecies in Is. 40-66 filled up the space left on the first scroll after the Book of Isaiah was copied. Owing to their anonymity and to the fact that Is. 1:1 was naturally taken to be the title of the complete scroll (cf. Luke 4:17), the oracles of Is. 40-66 were attributed to Isaiah despite mention of Cyrus king of Persia (Is. 44:28; 45:1), who conquered Babylon two centuries after Isaiah began his prophetic ministry.

Of course this anachronism offers no difficulty to those who believe that God predicted through Isaiah's pen what was to happen two centuries later, Josephus (*Antiquities* 11:1, 2) glibly states that Cyrus read the prediction about himself in the book which "Isaiah had left behind two hundred and ten years before," or in 748; Josephus reckoned for the Exile "seventy years" instead of 48 (586-538); he is more accurate when he says (*ibid.*) that "Isaiah foretold these things one hundred and forty years before the Temple was destroyed." In 726, 140 years before 586, Isaiah was unquestionably active in his prophetic ministry. Isaiah 40-66 is already quoted as "Isaiah" by Ben Sira (Ecclus. 48:24 f.) about 180 B.C., and likewise regularly in the New Testament: Matt. 3:3 = [Mark

[1] Ibn Ezra (d. 1167) is the first to express, in carefully veiled language, some doubts about Isaiah's authorship of Is. 40-66; see his commentary on Is. 40; 49; 53; cf. A. Geiger, *Wissensch. Zeitschr., f. Jüd. Theol.* 2 [1836] 553-557; J. Fürst, *Der Kanon des Alten Testaments*, p. 16. Leipzig, 1868.

1:2 f.] = Luke 3:4-6; cf. John 1:23; Matt. 8:17; 12:18-21; Luke 4:17-19; John 12:38; Acts 8:28-33; Rom. 10:16, 20; 15:12b.

Whatever conclusion may be reached as to the authorship and date of Is. 40-66, the differences in style, historical background, and theological thought between Is. 1-39 and 40-66 are so marked that it is preferable to treat them as separate books.

I. ISAIAH 1-39

The first part of the Book of Isaiah may be summarized as follows:

1. Oracles against Judah and Israel; predictions of a glorious future (1-12). The title of the book (1:1).

a. The sin, punishment, and salvation of Jerusalem (1:2-31). Judah's ingratitude to Jehovah (1:2-4) and desolate state (1:5-9); Jehovah does not demand sacrifices (1:10-15) but right living (1:16 f.) in order to give prosperity to his people (1:18-20); Jerusalem's sinfulness (1:21-23) and future purification (1:24-26); redemption after the annihilation of evildoers (1:27-31). Glosses: 1:1, 4b; "and it is desolate as overthrown by strangers" in 1:7; "as a besieged city" in 1:8; "very small" in 1:9; "or of lambs" in 1:11; "and your appointed feasts" in 1:14; "of your doings" in 1:16; "but now murderers" in 1:21; "with water" in 1:22; "the lord" (*ha'-ādôn*) in 1:24; 1:27-31 entire. Read the last two words in 1:12, and 1:13, thus, "Do not continue to tread my courts. The presentation of oblations is an abomination unto me; new moon and sabbath I cannot (endure), (nor) fasting [LXX] and festive assembly."

b. Specific sins of the Judeans, their punishment, and the future glory of Zion (2:1, new title; 2:2-4:6). The Hill of Zion will become the religious center of the world (2:2-5 = Mic. 4:1-5). Jehovah will appear in power to humble Judah's pride (2:6-22). The wicked judges and other leaders shall be removed, and anarchy prevail (3:1-15). Ruin and disgrace will fall upon the patrician ladies of fashion (3:16-4:1). The survivors of this judgment will be holy and gloriously happy (4:2-6). Glosses: 2:1, 2-4, (5), 8b, 9, 11; "high and lifted up" in 2:13; "on that day" in 2:17; in 2:18 "and the idols" is all that remains of the original text (cf. JBL [1924] 232, n. 21); 2:20-22; "for" and "the lord" in 3:1a; 3:1b, 6-8; "like Sodom" in 3:9; 3:10 f., 15b, 18-23; 4:1, 2-6.

c. Biographical accounts, including prophetic oracles (6:1-9:7 [H. 6:1-9:6]); for chapter 5 see under *d,* below). Isaiah beholds Jehovah on his throne and is called to the prophetic office (6:1-13). Isaiah warns Ahaz against an alliance with Assyria when he is attacked by Pekah king of Israel and Rezin king of Damascus: words of encouragement from Isaiah, accompanied by his son Shear-jashub ("A remnant [only] shall return") (7:1-9); the sign "Immanuel" (7:10-17); Judah shall be devastated by Assyrians and Egyptians (7:18-25); the ruin of Samaria and Damascus is foretold by the birth of Isaiah's son Maher-shalal-hash-baz ("Swift-Spoil Quick-Prey") (8:1-4); Isaiah assures his disciples that neither the coming invasion of Judah (8:5-8 [9 f.]; cf. 7:17) nor the people's disbelief (8:11-15) has shaken his faith in Jehovah (8:16-18); obscure and fragmentary remarks about necromancy (8:19 f.), someone in the darkness (8:21 f., and the last words of 8:20), and better times coming to Galilee (9:1 [H. 8:23]). The birth and righteous rule of the Messiah (9:2-7 [H. 9:1-6]). In this section, only 6:1-11 was unquestionably written by Isaiah; 7:15, 18-25; 8:9 f., 19-22; 9:1-7 [H. 8:23; 9:1-6] belong to a much later period; in the rest of 7-8 a genuine kernel has been expanded.

d. Denunciations against Judah, North Israel, and Assyria, followed by Messianic prophecies (5; 9:8-12:6 [H. 9:7-12:6]). The oracles in 5; 9:8-10:4 [H. 9:7-10:4] are manifestly disarranged and will be grouped more suitably. α. Oracles against Judah: the song of the vineyard (5:1-7, omitting the gloss, with a well-known pun, in 5:7). β. Oracles against North Israel. The seven "Woes" (which may have inspired the Beatitudes of Jesus, Matt. 5:3-11) in 5:8-24 and 10:1 f. (omitting 5:9 f., 12 f., 15-17, 24; "and ye dwell alone" in 5:8; 5:23 seems to belong after 10:1; 5:14, if authentic, is apparently the end of a missing "woe" against Samaria). Despite a series of disasters, Ephraim remains proudly obdurate in its evil ways; therefore "for all this his [God's] anger is not turned away; but his hand is stretched out still" (a refrain repeated five times in the poem, 9:12, 17, 21 [H. 9:11, 16, 20]; 10:4; 5:25): 9:8-21 [H. 9:7-20]; 10:3 f.; 5:25, omitting the glosses in 9:13, 15 f., 18 [H. 9:12, 14 f., 17]; 10:4a; 5:25a. γ. Oracles on Assyria: the swift, irresistible advance of the Assyrian army (5:26-30, omitting 5:30); "Alas, Assyria, the rod of mine anger!" (10:5-27); the rapid advance of the Assyrians against Jerusalem (10:28-34). In 10:5-34 the following glosses should be omitted: 10:10-12; "for he saith" in 10:13; "as if the rod should shake those that lift it, as if the staff should lift something which is not wood [i.e., lift a man]" in 10:15; 10:16-27a, 33 f.). δ. Concluding apocalyptic oracles (11-12): the Messianic king, a David reborn, will rule in righteousness and usher in the Golden Age (11:1-9); the Gentiles (11:10) and the Jews of the Dispersion (11:11-16) will join with a reunited Ephraim and Judah (11:13) in this restoration of David's kingdom (11:14); the redeemed will sing two songs of praise (12:1-4, 4-6), which are a sort of concluding doxology for Is. 1-11. Nothing in chapters 11-12 was written by Isaiah.

2. Oracles against foreign nations (13-23, except 20 and 22 which concern Jerusalem). Not much in these chapters was written by Isaiah.

a. "The Burden of Babylon," or Oracle against Babylon (13:1-14:23). The mustering of Jehovah's host (13:2-5), the terrors of "the day of the Lord" (13:6-16), the final and complete destruction of Babylon by the Medes (13:17-22). The restoration of Israel (14:1-4a, interpolated prose introduction), the sarcastic dirge over the king of Babylon hurled down into the underworld: "How art thou fallen from heaven, O Lucifer, son of the morning!" (14:4b-21); eternal devastation of Babylon (14:22 f., interpolated prose conclusion).

b. Jehovah decrees the downfall of Assyria (14:24-27).

c. "The Burden" against the Philistines, dated in the year Ahaz died (ca. 720 B.C.). Their rejoicing over the death of an oppressor is premature, for a worse enemy will arise from his roots (14:28-32).

d. "The Burden of Moab" (15:1-16:14, imitated in Jer. 48). A lament on the ruin of Moab (15:1-9aα; 16:7-11), annotated in a contemptuous and hostile spirit (16:1-6, 12) and changed into a prediction of doom (15:9aβb), to be realized more fully in three years (16:13 f.).

e. "The Burden of Damascus" and especially of North Israel (17:1-11). The original oracle (17:1-3) proclaims the impending ruin of Damascus and Israel; later oracles announce the misery of Israel (17:4-6), the end of idolatry and the conversion of mankind to Jehovah (17:7 f.), and the futility of Adonis worship to save Israel from ruin (17:9-11).

f. The Gentiles roar like the sea, but shall suddenly be dispersed by Jehovah (17:12-14).

g. In dismissing the envoys of "the land beyond the rivers of Cush" (Ethiopia?), Jehovah proclaims, in obscure language, the ruin of an unnamed nation (18:1-6). The added appendix announces that Ethiopia (?) shall send gifts to the Temple in Jerusalem (18:7).

h. "The Burden of Egypt" (19). Jehovah shall provoke civil war in Egypt and deliver the country into the hand of a "cruel lord" (19:1-4). The Nile shall dry up, bringing ruin to fishermen and flax workers (19:5-10); Egyptian princes and sages are foolish (19:11-15). The Egyptians shall fear Jehovah and Judah (19:16 f.). Five cities in Egypt shall speak Hebrew (19:18), and an altar and sacred stone pillar shall be dedicated to Jehovah in Egypt (19:19-22). Egyptians and Assyrians shall worship Jehovah (19:23) in friendly intercourse and, joined with Israel, become a blessing for all the world (19:24 f.).

i. As a portent of Assyria's conquest of Egypt and Ethiopia, Isaiah goes about for three years half-clad and barefoot (20:1-6).

j. "The Burden of the Desert of the Sea." Babylon, with all her idols, falls into the hands of the Medes and Elamites (21:1-10).

k. "The Burden of Dumah" or, with the LXX, of Edom. A voice from Edom asks, "Watchman, what of the night?" The watchman answers that morning and also night have come; let inquiry be made again later (21:11 f.).

l. "The burden of ba'rāb [?]," hardly "Arabia" (Authorized Version) in the original. The caravans of the Dedanites should hide in the thickets, and the inhabitants of Tema (Teima in northwestern Arabia) provide nourishment for war refugees (21:13-15). This oracle, no less enigmatic than the one preceding, was interpreted as signifying the doom of Kedar, or the Bedouins of the Syrian desert (21:16 f.).

m. "The Burden of the Valley of Vision" (a title derived from 22:5). Although Jerusalem is tumultuously exultant (22:1-2a)—presumably because Sennacherib has failed to capture it in 701 B.C.—the prophet weeps over the dead warriors (22:2b-3) and the dreadful Day of the Lord which is to come (22:4 f.), when Elam and Kir shall invest the city (22:6 f.). Frantic attempts to fortify the city (22:8-11, omitting perhaps 22:9b-11a) are of no avail: although Jehovah called the people to mourning, they continued to feast—"for tomorrow we die" (22:12 f.). Jehovah shall not forgive them as long as they live (22:14).

n. "Against Shebna, the major-domo" (22:15b, probably the title). Shebna, a high official of Hezekiah (cf. 36:3), is denounced for hewing out of the rock a tomb for himself (22:15 f.)—a useless labor since he is to die in exile (22:17 f.). His post shall be given to Eliakim (cf. 36:3), who shall be as firmly established as a tent peg (22:19-23). A later oracle predicts that the "wall-peg," heavily loaded with miscellaneous articles, shall fall—i.e., Eliakim's shameless nepotism shall bring about his downfall (22:24 f.).

o. "The Burden of Tyre." A sarcastic elegy celebrating the destruction of Tyre and Sidon (23:1-14, omitting 23:5, 13) was applied to Alexander's capture of Tyre in 332 in a later appendix (23:15-18) predicting the rebuilding of Tyre after seventy years, in order that its commercial gains might enrich the Jews and their Temple.

3. Apocalyptic vision of the final judgment and God's kingdom on earth (24-27, much later than Isaiah).

a. Preparatory stages (24). Heaven and earth are fading away; mankind has violated the eternal ordinances; gladness is gone, few are left (24:1-13). Joy over a new dawn for mankind is premature (24:14-16a), for it shall be first thrown into a panic (24:16b-18a); the sluices of heaven shall be opened (24:18b), the earth quake and be broken (24:19 f.), and the Lord shall judge the hosts on high and kings of the earth (24:21-23a). Then only shall the Lord be enthroned on Zion (24:23b).

b. The Kingdom of God (25-27; the hymns and songs will be grouped together under the next subdivision). The Lord shall spread a banquet for all nations on Zion, he "will swallow up death in victory, and . . . wipe away tears from all faces" (25:6-8). Israel shall hide in its chambers while the Lord goes forth in his indignation to punish the inhabitants of the earth, and slay the three dragons—either heathen empires (cf. 24:21-23) or mythical monsters hostile to God (26:20-27:1). When the great trumpet is blown, the Lord shall gather one by one the Israelites scattered in Egypt and Assyria (27:12 f.).

c. Hymns of praise and vengeance in 25-27. The Lord is praised for destroying a pagan-fortified city (Samaria?; cf. 24:10, 12) and protecting the humble (25:1-5). He has crushed Moab (25:9-12). The Lord is a mighty fortress for the "righteous nation," but destroys a lofty citadel (Samaria?) (26:1-6). He rewards the pious (26:7-9), but consumes the wicked (26:10-12), particularly alien tyrants ruling over the Jews (26: 13 f.). He has enlarged the borders of Israel (26:15) when the nation was in sore straits (26:16-18); his dead ones shall live again, those that lie in the dust shall awake and sing (26:19, the earliest reference to the resurrection of the dead in the Old Testament). The Lord tends his vineyard (Israel) but burns up the thorns and thistles (27:2-6). The Lord's judgments against Israel aim at improvement and not, as in the case of the heathen, at destruction (27:7-11).

4. Oracles on Judah and Assyria (28-31, containing some genuine writings of Isaiah).

a. The impending end of the Northern Kingdom, which fell in 722 (28:1-4, with a comforting conclusion interpolated in 28:5 f.).

b. An indictment of the religious and political leaders of Jerusalem (28:7-29). Priests and prophets utter childish oracles under the influence of wine (28:7-13). The Judean ruling classes feel secure because they have made "a covenant with death" (meaning either a compact with Assyria or a magical ceremony), but it will not stand; in its stead Jehovah has laid in Zion a firm cornerstone as a foundation (cf. Rom. 9:32 f.; I Pet. 2:6-8) so that only "he that believes will not be *moved*" (conjectural revision; the LXX has "will not be ashamed") (28:14-22). God's methods vary, just as a farmer's work changes with the seasons and the crops (28:23-29, a comforting gloss).

c. Jerusalem threatened and saved (29). "Woe to Ariel, to Ariel the city against which David encamped!" (i.e., Jerusalem, heretofore besieged by David, II Sam. 5:6-8). Jerusalem is besieged, but suddenly its enemies are dispersed (29:1-8, of which 29:5-8 is interpolated). The people are blind (29:9-12; omitting "the prophets" and "the seers" in 29:10; and 29:11 f.); neither the external hypocritical worship (29:13 f.) nor the secret intrigues of the diplomats (29:15, to which 29:16 has been added) can save the nation. A later writer has added a promise that Israel shall be redeemed in a short while (29:17-24).

d. Denunciation of an alliance with Egypt (30:1-5), to which a "Burden of the Beasts of the Southland" (30:6 f.) has been added.

e. Against the crafty, diplomatic intrigues of the rebellious nation, which can only lead to ruin, Isaiah asserts the principle, "In quietness and in confidence shall be your strength" (30:8-17). Later writers have appended to this gloomy oracle a picture of a forgiven and prosperous nation (30:18-26), and of the Lord appearing majestically in a storm to humble Assyria (30:27-33).

f. In another fiery protest against negotiations with Egypt (cf. *d* above), Isaiah points out their futility by stating that "the Egyptians are men, and not God; and their horses flesh, and not spirit" (31:1-3). Again the denunciation was changed into assurance of salvation for Jerusalem (31:4 f.) and ruin for Assyria (31:6-9) by later annotators.

5. Oracles depicting the future Messianic age (32-35), written long after Isaiah and collected as a fitting conclusion of his book in one of its stages of growth.

a. The righteous future ruler (32:1-5). The appendix (32:6-8), by a different author, is written in the style of the wisdom literature.

b. An invitation to the thoughtless women of Jerusalem (cf. 3:16 f.) to weep and mourn over the coming ruin of Jerusalem (32:9-14), followed by a vision of the spirit's outpouring and national prosperity (32:15-20; this section has perhaps no connection whatsoever with the one preceding).

c. A psalm (33), written in times of distress (33:2), expressing the assurance that the Lord shall destroy the host of the heathen (33:1-13) and sinners in Jerusalem (33:14-16), to reign triumphantly in Zion (33:17-24).

d. A short apocalypse in the style of the Second Isaiah (34-35). The Lord shall judge all nations (34:1-4) and pour out his wrath particularly upon Edom, whose land will become pitch and brimstone, a dwelling of demons and wild beasts (34:5-17). Conversely, the land of Israel shall be transformed into an earthly paradise and the Jews of the Dispersion shall return to Zion on a holy highway, singing and rejoicing (35).

6. The deliverance of Jerusalem from Sennacherib's siege (36-39) in 701. But for minor textual changes this historical narrative is taken bodily (e.g., 38:21 f. should follow 38:6), from II Kings 18:13-20:19, except for the omission of its most historical part, 18:14-16, suppressed in the first edition of Kings. The editors of the Book of Isaiah have added to the story in Kings a psalm in 4:3, or elegiac, meter, entitled "*Mikhtam* [so for *mikhtab*, writing] of Hezekiah king of Judah, when he had been sick and had recovered from his sickness" (38:9-20). This psalm, quoted from an anthology, is actually the lament of a man sick unto death (38:10-15) followed by a prayer for divine help in recovery (38:16-20). The patient in the psalm is not a king, however, but apparently a Levitical singer; his terror of death and the underworld is due primarily to his abrupt removal from the Temple worship ("see the Lord," 38:11) and its music (38:18-20). This psalm of Hezekiah resembles Ps. 6 (a prayer for recovery from illness), 30 (a hymn of thanksgiving for recovery), and 88 (the lament of a sorely afflicted man).

1. Isaiah and His Times

Isaiah was born about 770-760 B.C. and died not long after 700 B.C. His name means "Jehovah is salvation" or "the salvation of Jehovah." Since the name of his father, Amoz (1:1; 2:1; 13:1; 20:2; 37:2, 21; 38:1), meaning "strong," was identical in Greek with that of the prophet Amos, Isaiah's father was erroneously identified with the prophet from Tekoa (Clement of Alexandria, *Stromata* 1:327). In reality, Amos may have been only ten or fifteen years older than Isaiah. This identification was hardly possible for the Jews, to whom the different spelling in the Hebrew was obvious, but they sometimes (Bab. *Megillah* 10b; Rashi *ad* 1:1) regarded Amoz as the younger brother of King Amaziah, because of the similarity of names. Nothing, however, indicates that Isaiah was, like Zephaniah, related to the Davidic dynasty.

Isaiah was born in Jerusalem and lived there all his life. There is no indication that he visited any foreign country, and it is even uncertain whether he went to Samaria (like Amos) to deliver his sermons on the Northern Kingdom. His imagery is derived from scenes in Jerusalem and the vineyards in its immediate vicinity. He is familiar with the Temple (6:1-7; cf. 1:12; 8:18; 28:16) and its ritual (1:11-15), and the waters of Shiloah (8:6) emptying into the pools at the foot of Zion (7:3). He has walked through the vineyards (1:8; 5:1-6) and in the orchards (1:8) outside the city walls, and has seen donkeys and oxen in their stables (1:3).

His urban metaphors differ no less from the pastoral similes of Amos than Paul's metropolitan background from the feeling Jesus had for the beauties of the Galilean landscape. On the whole, Isaiah's interest is confined to the city proper. When cities are depopulated and their houses emptied, the country becomes utterly abandoned (6:11), as if the entire population dwelt in cities. In the city Isaiah noticed houses of brick and others of cut stone (9:10 [H. 9:9]), men clad in scarlet or crimson (1:18), street minstrels (5:1), elegant ladies parading "with outstretched necks, ogling with their eyes, tripping along as they go, and jingling with their feet" (3:16).

Nothing is known of Isaiah before his call to the prophetic ministry, "in the year that King Uzziah died" (6:1), about 740 B.C. He was then between twenty and thirty years old, and had grown up in Jerusalem during a time of national peace and prosperity. After an initial victory over Edom, through which Amaziah (798-780) had conquered Sela (II Kings 14:7), Azariah or Uzziah (780-740) subjected Edom in its entirety. For he recovered Elath on the Red Sea (II Kings 14:22) and like Solomon furthered the economic prosperity of Judah by exploiting the copper mines in the Arabah. Sailing from Ezion-geber laden with copper, Uzziah's ships returned from Arabian harbors with Oriental merchandise,[2] and the Judean merchants accumulated the wealth that evoked Isaiah's sarcastic reproaches (2:7, 16; 3:14, 16; 5:11, 14, 22 f.).

Another factor in this enrichment of Judah's upper classes during the reign of Uzziah was the current prosperity of the Northern Kingdom during the reign of Jeroboam II (785-744)—a wealth and luxury vividly depicted by Amos (3:15; 4:1; 5:11; 6:4-6) and Isaiah himself (9:10 [H. 9:9]; 28:1; cf. 17:4). The power and wealth of Israel and Judah during the reigns of Jeroboam II and Uzziah were the direct result of the international situation. During the eighth century, Egypt was torn by dissensions and weakened by anarchy, while Assyria, during the forty years preceding the accession of Tiglath-pileser III in 745, was governed by incompetent kings, too feeble even to attempt effective domination of Syria and Palestine. The call of Isaiah in 740 marked the approaching end of Israel's and Judah's power and prosperity.

Like Amos, Isaiah had a premonition of disaster during the period of peace and prosperity when he was summoned by Jehovah to prophecy in 740 B.C., unless he wrote the account of this call (6:1-11; 6:12 f. is spurious) some years later, after storm clouds had gathered overhead. He tells us that he saw Jehovah seated on a lofty throne, the train of his robe filling the whole Temple. Seraphim having six wings praised the holiness and glory of Jehovah in tones so loud as to make the thresholds tremble. The apparition of the deity sometimes proved fatal and Isaiah, conscious of being "a man of unclean lips," cried out in anguish and terror. But one of the seraphim touched his mouth with a glowing stone taken by tongs from the altar, and thus removed his iniquity. Then Jehovah asked, "Whom shall I send and who will go for us?" And Isaiah, with none of the hesitation which Moses and Jeremiah showed, promptly offered himself. He received a tragic commission: to make his people so blind, deaf, and witless as to render them unable to mend their ways and be healed. Isaiah cried out in dismay, "How long, my Lord?" The answer was utterly hopeless: until cities and houses had become uninhabited and the country be made entirely desolate.

This dismal outlook (6:9-11), which certain clumsy annotators in later centuries attempted to brighten (6:12) and rectify by means of unintelligible verbiage (6:13), may actually have been a brilliant intuition at the beginning of Isaiah's career, unless it is merely the summing up of his hopeless mission, written in old age. In any case, the sixth chapter of Isaiah is not only a classic account of an overwhelming religious experience, but also the most revealing page he ever wrote. The enthroned,

---

[2] See, on this commerce in the Red Sea, N. Glueck's reports of his archaeological explorations in Edom, particularly in the Annual of the American Schools of Oriental Research, Vol. XV, pp. 48-53. New Haven, 1935; and also *The Other Side of the Jordan*, pp. 84-87. New Haven, 1940.

awe-inspiring God, glimpsed for a breathless moment after which the prophet looked deliberately elsewhere, is a king thrice holy, whose glory is the contents of the whole earth. Exalted in his sanctity far above human limitations and sinfulness, yet by means of his manifested glory Jehovah is present everywhere on earth—nay, his shining glory is the very "filling" of the whole earth. This sublime deity, "Yahweh Militant," resides significantly in the Temple on Zion, although his sway embraces not only Israel (1:2 f.; 5:1-7), as before Amos, but the entire earth.

Like other great religious leaders in later times—for instance, St. Paul and Luther—Isaiah is acutely conscious of his own sinfulness, particularly the sins of thought and word indicated by the expression "unclean lips." But he also experienced symbolically the ethical purification enabling him to carry out a divine mission. It is generally thought that Isaiah's readiness in accepting his commission, his subsequent ease in addressing kings, his tone of authority in berating high officials (22:15-25), all prove that he was a nobleman. Although the evidence on this point is not conclusive, such may well have been the case. While championing the cause of the impoverished and oppressed lower classes, he displays the horror of the well-bred man, belonging to an ancient family, at the sight of a youth behaving rudely toward his elders, or a plebeian of low birth showing disrespect for a gentleman of high rank (3:5b). In later times the Greek poet, Theognis (6th century B.C.), gave classical expression to a similar, although more passionate, "snobbishness."

Isaiah may have been married at the time of his vision, but if not he married soon after. The name of his wife is not given; Gomer, the wife of Hosea, is the only wife of a prophet whose name is recorded. Isaiah referred to her as "the prophetess" (8:3), not because she had trances and moments of inspiration but, according to the custom prevailing in Germany where courtesy accords a wife her husband's title, simply because she was married to a prophet. We see that the term "prophet," which in earlier days was occasionally used contemptuously (in the sense of "lunatic"), had by now acquired the dignity of an honorific title.

That Isaiah married shortly before or after 740, the probable date of his vision, is certain, because in 735 he had a young son, presumably three to five years old. We may infer from the symbolical name of the boy (cf. Hos. 1), "Shear-jashub," meaning, "A remnant will return," that he was born *after* Isaiah's call to his ministry. Opinions vary about the significance of this name, for the meaning is indeed ambiguous: we may interpret it either as a promise (a remnant will escape the coming disaster) or as a threat (nothing but a remnant will survive the impending calamity). The latter meaning finds some support in the dire words of Jehovah to Isaiah at the time of his call (6:9-11)—unless they be a reflection of Isaiah's later experiences—and in Amos 3:12, where the "remnant" is compared to two legs and a piece of an ear rescued by a shepherd out of the mouth of a lion.

In giving to his first-born this emblematic name at the very beginning of his ministry, Isaiah wished to sum up the import of his message. He was already convinced that Israel and Judah were doomed. At the same time, he could not force himself to see the doom as complete and final, like Amos who sang a dirge over Israel, which he envisaged as prostrate in death (Am. 5:2). The catastrophe would serve to remove the dross, leaving a remnant of pure metal; Jerusalem would become a city of righteousness (1:24-26) after the ordeal. In thus naming his son "Shear-jashub," Isaiah was filled with conflicting emotions: righteous anger at his people's wickedness, awe before the just sentence of doom pronounced by the God of holiness, and withal a glimmer of hope that a small remnant of the people would finally return to Jehovah.

But when his second son was born in 735-734, not more than five years after Shear-jashub, Isaiah gave him an ominous name of unambiguous meaning, "Maher-shalal-hash-baz" ("Swift-Spoil, Quick-Prey" or "Swift is the spoil, speedy is the prey"). To the relief of the Judeans, however, Isaiah interpreted this as signifying the imminent destruction, not of Judah itself, but of the two enemies of Judah, Damascus and Samaria (8:1-3). For at this critical time, the prophet still had hopes for Judah's survival.

The peaceful and prosperous period marked by the reigns of Jeroboam II and Uzziah did not continue long after Isaiah's call in 740. Uzziah had been stricken with leprosy a few years before his death in 740, and his son Jotham had ruled as regent in his place. Just before Jotham's death in 735, the storm broke. The new king, Ahaz (735-720), faced a situation that would have sorely taxed the ingenuity and energy of a much abler ruler.

After a period of feeble inaction, the great Tiglath-pileser III (745-727) restored the fortunes of Assyria. When he conquered Arpad (10:9; cf. 36:19; 37:13) in 740, after a siege of three years, his sway in Syria was unchallenged: Rezin of Damascus, Menahem of Israel (744-738), and other Syrian princes paid him tribute in 738. But while Tiglath-pileser was occupied in his campaigns in Media and Armenia (737-735), Rezin organized a coalition against Assyria. After assassinating Pekahiah (738-737), who had continued the pro-Assyrian policy of his father Menahem, Pekah (737-732) allied himself to Rezin and joined him in demanding that Jotham lend his support to the contemplated rebellion. Jotham refused and died soon after, leaving Ahaz to deal with an attack from Pekah and Rezin; they threatened to place "the son of Tabeel" (i.e., Rezin) on David's throne (7:1-7). Taking advantage of Judah's plight, the Edomites lost no time in capturing Elath on the Red Sea (II

Kings 16:6, text revised according to II Chron. 28:17). This permanently ended Judah's exploitation of the copper mines in the Arabah and the sea commerce with Arabia which had enriched the kingdom in the days of Solomon and Uzziah.

In his extremity, Ahaz disregarded Isaiah's plea (7:1-7) and hastily appealed to Tiglath-pileser for help against Pekah and Rezin, sending as tribute the treasures of the Temple and the royal palace (II Kings 16:7 f.). In 734, the Assyrian king attacked Israel; after part of the population had been deported, Galilee and Gilead became Assyrian provinces (II Kings 15:29). In the two years following, Damascus was invested; in 732 it was taken, and its king, Rezin, executed (II Kings 16:9). Thus ended the Syro-Ephraimitic war against Judah. Ahaz went in person to Damascus to congratulate Tiglath-pileser and pay his tribute (II Kings 16:10). He had delivered his kingdom from the threat of Pekah and Rezin at the cost of its own independence, for during the following century Judah was to be a tributary of Assyria.

Thus Isaiah witnessed the realization of the ominous import of his second son's name, Maher-shalal-hash-baz, although not so swiftly as he had anticipated in 735. For Damascus fell in 732 and Samaria in 722, both some years *after* (not *before*; cf. 8:4) the child was old enough to say "My father and my mother." Reduced to Ephraim in 734, the Northern Kingdom rebelled in the reign of Hoshea (732-722) immediately after the death of Tiglath-pileser (727). Shalmaneser V (727-722) besieged Samaria during three years, but the city was taken after his death by his successor Sargon (722-705), who deported 27,290 Israelites, settled foreign colonists in their stead (II Kings 17:6, 24; 18:11), and placed the country under Assyrian governors.

Hezekiah probably followed Ahaz on the throne two years after the fall of Samaria, or in 720 (in 727 according to II Kings 18:10 and in 715 according to 18:13), reigning until 692. Reversing Ahaz's policy, Hezekiah was eager to shake off the Assyrian yoke. It is doubtful, however, if he defied Assyria openly before the death of Sargon in 705. Twice under Sargon certain parts of Syria and Palestine lifted the banner of rebellion, but nothing in the extant records indicates Hezekiah's participation in these ill-fated movements.

In 720, under the leadership of the king of Hamath in the North and the king of Gaza (supported by an Egyptian army) in the South, the first rebellion broke out; even the Assyrian provinces of Damascus, Samaria, Arpad, and Simirra revolted. But Sargon, through his victories at Qarqar and Raphia, promptly subdued the rebels.

In 713-711, Ashdod became the focus of a second rebellion. By a *coup d'état*, a certain Iatna or Iamani (i.e., "Ionian"), presumably a Greek adventurer, seized the throne of Ashdod and sent inflammatory messages "to the kings of the lands of Philistia, Judah, Edom, Moab," tributary to Assyria, in an attempt to secure their co-operation against Sargon. But he was soon driven to flight by an Assyrian general and arrested on the border of Egypt to be delivered into the hands of Sargon. Sargon's accounts of these events are translated by D. D. Luckenbill in his *Ancient Records of Assyria and Babylonia* (Chicago, 1927; see especially Vol. II, pp. 13 f., 31 f., 40, 105 f.).

When Iamani's embassy came to Jerusalem and induced Hezekiah to participate in the rebellion against Sargon, Isaiah was so disturbed that he went about barefoot and half-clad in the guise of a captive, for thus, said the prophet, would Sargon lead away the captives of Egypt and Ethiopia. Isaiah retained this scanty attire for three years, until the fall of Ashdod (713-711), hoping in this graphic manner to impress on king and people the futility of a revolt counting on help from Egypt and Ethiopia (20:1-6). Significantly he joins Ethiopia to Egypt because at that time (712) the Ethiopian Shabaka, king of Napata, had conquered Egypt and had founded the Twenty-fifth Dynasty. Whether Hezekiah was impressed by Isaiah's startling costume or not, he apparently resisted the impulse to become actively involved in Iamani's revolt. At any rate, in his inscriptions, Sargon did not consider him a disloyal vassal.

It seems probable that the embassy of the Chaldean Merodach-baladan II (king of Babylonia in 721-710 and in 703), which aroused the ire of Isaiah (II Kings 20:12-19; Is. 39), came to Hezekiah not in 720 but 703, after the death of Sargon. The real purpose of the embassy was unquestionably to stir up in Syria and Palestine a movement against Assyria of such magnitude that Merodach-baladan could maintain himself in power; and it is hardly conceivable that Hezekiah would have compromised himself by plotting with Babylonia during Sargon's reign.

This embassy of Merodach-baladan achieved its purpose and brought about the third and gravest international crisis involving the kingdom of Judah during Isaiah's lifetime. Owing to the unexpected turn of events in Babylonia and the prompt, energetic measures of Sennacherib (705-681), son and successor of Sargon, Merodach-baladan failed dismally. To forestall his seizure of the Babylonian throne, a native ruler had been installed at the New Year festival of 704. Thus Merodach-baladan's hand was forced prematurely, before a concerted rebellion could break out simultaneously in Babylonia and Palestine. Even though he drove out the new Babylonian ruler after one month and became king in his place, within a year Merodach-baladan was forced to flee before the armies of Sennacherib.

The anti-Assyrian movement in Palestine, originally instigated by Merodach-baladan, had gained too much momentum to end suddenly with his failure. Egypt took the place of Babylonia in stirring up the rebellion. With the connivance of Shabaka, the Ethiopian Pharaoh (712-700), the princes of the Delta were intriguing in Palestine with such success that Hezekiah in 702 sent an embassy to Zoan (Tanis, in the Eastern Delta, about 40 kilometers west of the Suez Canal) and Hanes (probably Heracleopolis Magna in Middle Egypt, west of Beni-Suêf). In spite of its extreme secrecy, the plot (29:15) became known to Isaiah, who denounced this alliance with Egypt in the strongest terms (30:1-5; 31:1-3, and perhaps 18:1-6), correctly anticipating Egypt's inability to supply effective military assistance against Assyria.

Dominated by the anti-Assyrian party in Jerusalem and deaf to Isaiah's warnings, Hezekiah joined Tyre and other Phoenician cities, most of Philistia, Ammon, Moab, and Edom, in open defiance of Assyria. The rebellion began with the attack on Philistine governors and princes who refused to join the coalition against Assyria. Hezekiah invaded Philistia (II Kings 18:8) and assisted in the overthrow of the kings of Askelon and Ekron, as also of the governor of Ashdod, bringing Padi king of Ekron back to Jerusalem in chains.

In 701, Sennacherib intervened at the head of a large army. He invested Tyre and, although unable to take this island city, he drove its king Luli (Eluleus) to Cyprus, where he died. After the capitulation of Sidon, the Phoenician cities promptly surrendered, and most of the allied princes came to Lachish to pay tribute to Sennacherib. Askelon and the fortresses around it were swiftly taken, while Ekron was invested before the Egyptian forces could reach it. The Egyptians were routed at Eltekeh, Ekron was taken, and after the rebel leaders there had suffered particularly gruesome punishments, Padi was reinstated as king.

Thus Judah was left alone to face the Assyrian army. When Hezekiah had failed to appear with the other princes to submit to Sennacherib at Lachish, the latter had dispatched three high officers, the *tartan* (commander in chief), *rab-saris,* and *rab-shaqe* (literally chief cup-bearer), at the head of a body of troops, to demand Hezekiah's surrender (II Kings 18:17-19:8; Is. 36:2-37:8). Upon Hezekiah's refusal, Sennacherib invaded Judah after his victory at Eltekeh. Strengthened by undisciplined Arab mercenaries, the Judean troops were brought to Jerusalem in expectation of a siege.

Sennacherib reports that he took forty-six walled cities of Judah (all the cities, according to II Kings 18:13 and Is. 36:1), captured 200,150 inhabitants (incredible number!), and shut up Hezekiah "like a caged bird, in Jerusalem, his royal city." Realizing the futility of further resistance, Hezekiah finally capitulated. According to Sennacherib's account, Hezekiah sent 30 talents of gold and 800 talents of silver, together with many precious objects and members of the court, to Nineveh; according to II Kings 18:14-16, he sent 30 talents of gold and 300 talents of

silver to Sennacherib at Lachish. This discrepancy as to locality may be
only apparent: Hezekiah could have sent his ambassadors to Lachish to
negotiate terms for his surrender, paying the tribute later at Nineveh.
We need hardly add that neither surrender nor payment would naturally have taken place in 701 if the army of Sennacherib, supposedly
comprising 185,000 men, had been smitten in one night at the gates of
Jerusalem by the angel of Jehovah (II Kings 19:9-35 = Is. 37:9-36, a
later legendary account). The account of Sennacherib's death in II Kings
19:36 f. = Is. 37:37 f. is based on fact, but it actually occurred twenty
years after the siege of Jerusalem.

So disastrous for Judah were the results of this ill-fated rebellion in
703-701 that the kingdom never again attempted to shake off the yoke of
Assyria. In vivid language Isaiah has given a picture of the utter ruin
left behind by the Assyrian army of Sennacherib (1:5-9). Like a person
ill unto death, drained of all courage and covered with festering sores
from head to foot, the land of Judah was utterly desolated, its cities
burnt, the countryside invaded by foreigners! Nothing remained except
Jerusalem, solitary in the midst of this devastated land, like a booth in a
vineyard. But Isaiah's faith did not falter. Even at the end of his ministry
and despite the calamity that had overcome his people, he could still
find comfort in the thought that Jehovah had left a few survivors, had not
utterly destroyed Judah like Sodom and Gomorrah (1:9). Perhaps with
the approach of death, the prophet was at peace in the assurance that
Jehovah would never allow his people to perish entirely from this earth.

2. The Prophetic Oracles of Isaiah

The international events just described, and occasional mentions of
kings of Judah (6:1; 7:1; 14:28; 20:1) are our only clues for dating the
prophecies of Isaiah. Consequently, the date of a number of his oracles
unrelated to the political situation must remain conjectural.

The first period of Isaiah's prophetic ministry extends from the death
of Uzziah (about 740 B.C.) to the fall of Samaria in 722. In his first
prophetic trance (about 740) he saw his God sitting on a throne and
was called by him to proclaim the divine sentence against the nation
(6:1-11). Even though this account of his vision may not have been committed at once to writing, it is conceivably the first of his written oracles,
and possibly the introduction to the little autobiographical section 6:1-9:7
(H. 6:1-9:6) (omitting glosses) prepared soon after 734.

Following the description of his vision (6), Isaiah tells (first in the
third, then in the first person) of his activity during the Syro-Ephraimitic
war in 735-734. When, threatened by Pekah king of Israel and Rezin king
of Damascus, Ahaz was inspecting the defenses and water supply of
Jerusalem, Isaiah went to meet him accompanied by his small son,

Shear-jashub ("A remnant will return"). Isaiah assured the king that his two foes, "these two tails of smoking firebrands," could not prevail against Jehovah. Therefore he should remain calm and have faith in God: "If you do not believe in me [sic] you will not abide" (7:1-8a, 9). Isaiah could see that Ahaz did not rely on Jehovah implicitly and offered him a sign, which the king refused with a pious excuse. Irritated with the king, Isaiah proclaimed the sign: "When the young woman [LXX and Matt. 1:23 render incorrectly "the virgin"] will conceive and bear a son, she will call him Immanuel ["God with us"; meaning either "God be with us!" or "God is with us!"]." Before the infant could distinguish between right and wrong, Israel and Damascus would be devastated; but Judah would also suffer (7:10-14, 16 f., omitting "the King of Assyria" in 7:17).[3] A later author (in 7:18-25) explains Judah's ruin as resulting from the raids of Egyptians and Assyrians.

Further to encourage the Judeans to have confidence in their God and cast off fear of their threatening foes, Isaiah wrote on a large tablet the words "Belonging to Maher-shalal-hash-baz," and named his second son according to this ominous phrase, which means "Swift-Spoil, Quick-Prey." Before the child could talk, Assyria would plunder Damascus and Samaria (8:1-4). The oracle in 17:1-3 (with a later supplement in 17:4-11) also proclaimed the impending destruction of Damascus and Samaria and belongs likewise to the year 734.

When king and people put their trust in Tiglath-pileser and not in Jehovah, Isaiah anticipated that the Assyrians would overwhelm Judah like a flood (8:5-8, supplemented by a later writer with a triumphant hymn beginning with "Immanuel" at the end of 8:8 and ending with the same word in 8:10). As a result of this unbelief, Jehovah would become a stumbling stone and snare for both kingdoms of Israel (8:11-15); but Isaiah, whose faith could not be shaken, entrusted his teaching to his disciples, and with his two sons stood as a portent of Jehovah's abiding presence on Zion (8:16-18). Later writers are responsible for the concluding oracles of this section (8:19-9:7 [H. 8:19-9:6]).

Isaiah's genuine oracles in 6:1-8:18 can unquestionably be dated in the earliest period of his activity (740-732). Although other early

[3] The numerous other interpretations of the "Immanuel sign" cannot be discussed here, nor can a full bibliography of the vast literature on the subject be given. The following are some of the significant recent publications: K. Fullerton, "Immanuel" (AJSL 34 [1918] 256-283). H. C. Ackerman, "The Immanuel Sign and its Meaning" (AJSL 35 [1919] 205-214). A. A. Schelven, "De Immanuels prophetie" (GTT 1920/21, 368-375). R. Kittel, Geschichte des Volkes Israel, Vol. II, p. 361 (7th ed., 1925). E. G. Kraeling, "The Immanuel Prophecy" (JBL 50 [1931] 277-297). K. Budde, "Das Immanuelzeichen" u.s.w. (JBL 52 [1933] 22-54). W. C. Graham, "Isaiah's Part in the Syro-Ephraimitic Crisis" (AJSL 50 [1934] 201-216). A. von Bulmerincq, "Die Immanuelweissagung (Jes 7) im Lichte der neueren Forschung" (Acta et Commentationes Universitatis Tartuensis B 37, 1 [1935] 1-17).

prophecies can be assigned only a tentative date, it seems certain that the genuine oracles assembled in the collection 2:1-5:7, bearing the redactional title "The word which Isaiah the son of Amoz saw concerning Judah and Jerusalem," were uttered not later than the fall of Samaria in 722, during the reign of Ahaz (735-720) or shortly before his accession. While the collection 6:1-8:18 was biographical and concerned with Judah's international relations, 2:1-5:7 contains denunciations of Judah's domestic abuses, notably the corruption of the upper classes and general disloyalty to Jehovah. Pride is Jerusalem's basic sin.

The keynote in these early oracles is sounded in a poetic parable, a "love song" (*sic*, 5:1) which Isaiah chanted, in the guise of a minstrel, for his beloved, concerning his vineyard (5:1-6; 5:7a, in which Israel and Judah are distinguished and Judah is Jehovah's favorite, and 5:7b, which consists of a rather prosaic pun, are spurious). Jehovah planted his vineyard—his people—and cared for it; but since it produced only revoltingly inedible grapes, he would abandon it.

What are these rotten fruits with which Judah has rewarded Jehovah's past solicitude? The first oracle (2:6-8a, 10, 12-19, omitting a few brief glosses) announces the divine Day of Judgment (cf. the "Day of the Lord" in Am. 5:18-20) upon everything enhancing the pride of the Judeans—nothing but mundane things: foreign customs and soothsayings (2:6), wealth (2:7), idols (2:8a). Before Jehovah's terror and majesty, when he comes to crush whatever is proud and lofty, men will hide in the dust and in caves (2:10, 12-19).

The second oracle (3:1a, 2-5, 9, 12-15a) shifts its focus from men of wealth to men of authority. Public officials and rulers, high and low, will be removed by God because they have despoiled and crushed the poor. In their place, riffraff, babes, and women will be at the helm. The third one (3:16 f., 24, omitting "and it shall come to pass" in 3:24) inveighs against ladies of fashion; it inspired a prosaic reader to draw up a catalogue of twenty-one articles of women's finery (3:18-23). The concluding poem (3:25 f.) is a lament (possibly inspired by Am. 5:2) over the daughter of Zion, sitting bereft upon the ground after her warriors have fallen in battle. A statistically minded editor concluded from this decimation of males that there would be at that time seven women to one man (4:1).

The first chapter of the book, a miniature anthology of oracles pronounced by Isaiah from the beginning to the end of his public career, contains prophetic utterances belonging to the reign of Ahaz. The influence of Amos, particularly noticeable in Isaiah's early period (cf. 2:12-19; 3:25 f., above), appears clearly in Isaiah's rejection of the acts of worship when divorced from right living (1:10-17, omitting the brief glosses noted in the summary of the book; cf. Am. 5:21-24). In lamenting the degeneration of Jerusalem and its authorities (1:21-23), Isaiah adopts the elegiac (*qînah*) meter from Amos (Am. 5:2) and the figure of the harlot from Hosea.

The expectation of a future moral and political regeneration of Jerusalem (1:24-26) may have been inspired, at least in part, by Hosea (Hos. 2:6 f., 14, 19 f. [H. 2:8 f., 16, 21 f.]). Isaiah did not wholly exclude the conversion of Judah. Appealing to his hearer's reason (which is the meaning of "speak to her heart" [i.e., mind, not emotions] in Hos. 2:14 [H. 2:16]), he argues that scarlet or red sins cannot become white as snow or wool (the Authorized Version, failing to recognize the rhetorical questions, interprets the verses in the opposite sense), but repentance and obedience will restore the people's fortunes (1:18-20).

During the last years of the Northern Kingdom (735-722), Isaiah pronounced a number of denunciations against the Ephraimites. These have been greatly disarranged by the editors of the book. In a series of brief oracles beginning with "Woe unto . . . !" the prophet inveighs against the upper classes of the kingdom of Israel. In all probability the superscription of these seven "woes" is "Woe unto the proud crown of the drunkards of Ephraim and to the fading flowers of its glorious beauty . . ." (28:1-4). Although in the opinion of many critics the "seven woes" were addressed to Judeans, they are in reality more appropriate to the opulent Ephraimites. As we know from Amos, the evils of landlordism, drunkenness, skepticism, reversal of the moral values, and worldly wisdom were far more glaring in Samaria than in Jerusalem; moreover, in denouncing the upper classes of Judah, Isaiah does not specify these particular offenses. Woe, cries the prophet, unto those who join house to house and field to field, expropriating insolvent proprietors (5:8; cf. Am. 2:6)! Woe unto those who drink wine from early morning to night (5:11, 14; cf. Am. 2:8; 4:1; 6:6)! Woe unto those who with their sins, as if with ropes, draw upon themselves the divine punishment, which they sneeringly consider a delusion (5:18 f.; cf. Am. 5:18)! Woe unto those who change morals into self-interest and light into darkness (5:20)! Woe unto those who are proud of their mundane wisdom and diplomatic cleverness (5:21)! Woe unto those heroic at guzzling wine, valiant in mixing drinks (5:22)! Woe unto those who decree oppressive laws and dictate harmful decisions, justifying the guilty for a fee and frustrating the rights of the poor (10:1; 5:23; 10:2; cf. Am. 5:10 f.)! The remaining material in 5:8-24 is editorial expansion.

In another oracle against the Ephraimites, Isaiah proclaims the imminence of divine punishment (9:8-12, 14, 17, 19-21 [H. 9:7-11, 13, 16, 18-20]; 10:3, 4b; 5:25). With its refrain repeated five times (9:12, 17, 21 [H. 9:11, 16, 20]; 10:4b; 5:25), this poem is inspired by one of Amos's (Am. 4:6, 7aα, 8b, 9aαb, 10, 11, 12a), also with a refrain repeated five

times and recalling five calamities by which Jehovah has tried to warn
the Northern Israelites. Isaiah reminds these Israelites of their past misfortunes—loss of territory, decimation of the populace, civil strife—and
declares that, because they have not come to their senses, their God will
bring against them a storm from afar (the Assyrians) and exterminate
them.

With the exception of 17:1-3 and 28:1-4, Isaiah's oracles uttered before
722 B.C. are all contained in chapters 1-12 of the book bearing his name.
This first section of the book is made up of separate collections, all of
which show evidence of late editing. The earliest of these is 6:1-9:7
(H. 6:1-9:6), but curiously enough this autobiography did not constitute
the original nucleus of the book. Instead, it was inserted rather clumsily
within another collection, thoroughly disarranged in the process, namely,
5:8-30; 9:8-12:6 (H. 9:7-12:6). The other two collections in 1-12 consist
of ch. 1, placed at the beginning as a sort of noble overture, and 2:1-5:7.

Since oracles of Isaiah later than 722 are found only in ch. 1 and 5:8-30;
9:8-12:6, and since ch. 1 was placed at the beginning of one of the
postexilic editions of the book, it seems probable that the collection
5:8-30 and 9:8-12:6 (H. 9:7-12:6) (omitting perhaps the later oracles in
11:10-12:6) formed the nucleus around which the whole book gradually
grew: first 6:1-9:7 (H. 6:1-9:6) was inserted into it, then 2:2-5:7 was
placed before it, and the resulting collection 2:2-11:9 was provided with
the title in 2:1. If our assumption is correct that 5:23 originally belonged
after 10:1 and 5:25 after 10:4, these displacements probably occurred
before 6:1-9:7 (H. 6:1-9:6) was inserted between chs. 5 and 10. The
two oracles, to which 10:1; 5:23; 10:2, on the one hand, and 10:3, 4b;
5:25, on the other, belong respectively, had been clumsily joined together
before 6:1-9:7 (H. 6:1-9:6) was added. The poems on Assyria in 5:26-29
and 10:28-32 likewise originally belonged together.

The second period of Isaiah's activity corresponds to the reign of Sargon
of Assyria (722-705). Only two of Isaiah's oracles are definitely dated in
these years: 14:28-32 ("In the year that King Ahaz died, i.e., probably
720) and 20:1-6 ("In the year that the *tartan* [commander in chief]
came to Ashdod, when Sargon the King of Assyria sent him," i.e., in 713).
Many critics believe, however, that the first of these oracles was pronounced in 705, and J. A. Bewer (*Old Testament and Semitic Studies in
Memory of W. R. Harper*, Vol. II, pp. 224-226. Chicago, 1908)[4] reads in
14:28, "In the year of the King's [Sargon's] death I saw this oracle."
Unfortunately, the "rod" that smote the Philistines which, to their joy, is
now broken, cannot be identified with certainty; nor can we determine

---

[4] See also his article in AJSL 54 (1937) 62, and C. C. Torrey in JBL 57 (1938)
110-114. Torrey regards 14:28-32 as the conclusion of 20, dating both (as all of
13-23) in the Hellenistic period.

whether the "smoke" from the north that will overwhelm Philistia is Sargon in 713-711 or Sennacherib in 701; it can hardly be, as B. Duhm thought, Alexander the Great. Despite traces of editorial revision, there are no decisive reasons for rejecting the date given in the text (720).

The second oracle (20:1-6) is unambiguous: to restrain the Judeans from joining the Philistine rebellion against Sargon, Isaiah went about for three years (713-711) barefoot and half-clad, to portray the fate of the Ethiopians and Egyptians on whose help the Philistines were counting.

During the reign of Sargon, the Judean kingdom was quietly submissive to Assyria—whose power had been demonstrated in the conquest of the Northern Kingdom—and its history is unknown. Except for the two oracles just mentioned, we cannot identify any which Isaiah unquestionably pronounced during these obscure years.

On the contrary, the stormy period at the end of Isaiah's life (705-700) is known best of all. Our detailed knowledge of the political vicissitudes, summarized in a preceding section, sheds great light on Isaiah's activity and teaching, particularly at the time of the siege of Jerusalem by Sennacherib (701).

Isaiah did his utmost to restrain Hezekiah from participating in the widespread anti-Assyrian movement in Phoenicia and Palestine, which broke out soon after the death of Sargon (705) and was actively instigated first by Merodach-baladan, Chaldean ruler of Babylonia, and later by Egypt. With biting sarcasm, the prophet condemned the secret negotiations of Hezekiah with Merodach-baladan in 703 (II Kings 20:12-19; Is. 39) and with Egypt in 702. As in an earlier crisis more than thirty years before (7:4, 9), for Isaiah the basic principle in foreign policy remained strict neutrality under the protection of Jehovah: "In turning back and in rest lies your salvation, in quietness and in confidence lies your strength" (30:15; cf. 28:16). The prophet thundered with vehemence and passion against secret plots and military alliances with Egypt and Ethiopia. Such foreign entanglements were for him clear signs of distrust of Jehovah's ability to save his people, and open rebellion against the rule of the divine king. Such a policy was foolish and disastrous, for Egypt's help at the critical moment would prove to be illusory (18:1-6; 28:7-22; 29:1-5, 9-15; 30:1-5, 8-17; 31:1-3; cf. 1:19 f.).[5]

Isaiah's appeals to faith and common sense availed him nothing against the growing war hysteria. Carried away by popular enthusiasm, Hezekiah became one of the leaders in the rebellion against Sennacherib, and plunged his country into a disastrous war in which only Jerusalem was

[5] The oracles of the year 702 have been collected and edited with notes in the little volume Is. 28-31. An earlier oracle against Samaria (28:1-4, with the regular editorial happy ending in 28:5 f.) has been placed at the beginning either accidentally or deliberately.

spared. When Sennacherib set out at the head of a large army against the Phoenician and Palestinian rebels in 701, Isaiah in two superb poems, the first of which is a masterpiece in Hebrew literature, described the swift pace of the invincible Assyrian army (5:26-29, followed by an editorial note in 5:30), and the itinerary of its march against Jerusalem (10:28-32; cf. W. F. Albright in AASOR IV [1924] 134-140).

But this vivid picture of the impending Assyrian attack made no impression. The spirits were too excited to consider the menacing situation calmly. As Isaiah had said in the previous year, the people were drunken, but not with wine, roused to wild enthusiasm by blind leaders (29:9 f.), confident in the efficacy of a hypocritical religion divorced from true faith (29:13), following the pernicious leadership of shrewd diplomats plotting in the dark (29:14 f.), and priests and prophets uttering childish oracles in a disgracefully intoxicated condition (28:7-13). Now Isaiah's fury against the political leaders focused on one of them, Shebna, Hezekiah's major-domo. The prophet spied him inspecting the excavation of an elaborate sepulchral chamber for himself. With burning invective Isaiah predicted his death in a distant land of exile (22:15-18). As for his successor Eliakim (cf. 36:3), the weight of his brazen nepotism would crush him to the ground (22:19-25).

The attitude of Isaiah during the siege of Jerusalem by Sennacherib's forces has given rise to considerable discussion on the part of critics. The problem embraces two phases, his attitude toward Judah and that toward Assyria. According to the traditional and legendary view, Isaiah suddenly ceased his denunciations and became a nationalistic champion of his people, proclaiming the doctrine of Zion's inviolability (I Kings 19:6 f., 21-34 = Is. 37:6 f., 22-35; 31:8 f.). Although such a sacrifice of religious and ethical principles on the altar of patriotism under the influence of war hysteria is easily conceivable—it is actually commonplace in our day—nothing in the authentic oracles of Isaiah indicates that it ever took place.[6] Such a lapse is most unlikely in a man of Isaiah's stature and character, so utterly devoted to his God and dedicated to his divine mission. He could never have said, "My country—right or wrong"; on the contrary, his motto would have been, "Let thy will be done, though heaven fall." In the midst of the crisis, Isaiah could only have counseled humble acceptance of the calamity as a divine and well-deserved punishment, submission to Assyria, repentance, and reliance on God. Even if such words of Isaiah had actually been preserved in writing, they were naturally suppressed by the editors of the book, as contradicting the legends

---

[6] Even R. Smend (*Lehrbuch der Alttestamentliche Religionsgeschichte*, pp. 219-224. Freiburg, 1893), who believes that Isaiah became a nationalist in 734 under the pressure of Assyrian domination, has to regard this lapse as a passing phase of his convictions. He admits that such an outburst of patriotism contradicts the prophet's early and late oracles.

that soon distorted historical facts. A century later, in the days of Jeremiah, the people already believed that Hezekiah had turned to Jehovah in prayer and that Jehovah had repented of the evil he had pronounced against them (Jer. 26:19). It was only a step further to say that Sennacherib's army had been destroyed in a night by the angel of the Lord (37:36: cf. 10:24-27; 14:24-27). The true attitude of Isaiah, either during or immediately after the siege, is exhibited in 1:2-9. One of the most drastic and bitter of Isaiah's oracles, it was preserved accidentally outside the main body of the book in the little anthology (ch. 1) placed at the beginning in one of the later editions.

When at last the Assyrians withdrew, the people of Jerusalem went insane with joy and celebrated the deliverance with wild abandon. On the contrary, Isaiah was shocked at the tumult and banqueting, and saw in this thoughtless revelry a sign of the incurable wickedness of a people already doomed to divine punishment and unable to realize the horrible truth of those words spoken in jest, "Let us eat and drink, for tomorrow we die." In the midst of gaiety, the prophet sat alone, weeping over the future plundering of the daughter of his people (22:1-14).

While Isaiah stood firm as God's champion against Judah, his attitude toward Assyria underwent a change. Ever since Ahaz had become tributary of Assyria and defied Isaiah, the latter had opposed all rebellions against that country. He had never uttered a word against that military empire and had come to regard it as the instrument in God's hand for the chastisement of Judah and Israel. But after Sennacherib had devastated Judah and left only Jerusalem "as a booth in a vineyard" (1:7-9), Isaiah expressed his flaming indignation in a magnificent oracle. Proud of his achievements, the Assyrian had not gone forth as "the scourge of God" against a wicked nation, but "to destroy and cut off nations not a few." "Shall the ax boast itself against him that heweth therewith?" (10:5-9, 13-15.) But the predictions of Assyria's doom (10:24-27a; 14:24-27; 30:27-33; 31:4-9), which editors placed in the mouth of Isaiah, do not harmonize with his utterances: he was not concerned with what would take place a century later, but with expounding the problems of his day *sub specie aeternitatis*.

3. The Teaching and Style of Isaiah

The unique influence of the Book of Isaiah on Judaism and Christianity has given to Isaiah himself the highest rank among prophets, in the traditional views of Jews and Christians. However, while Isaiah ranks with Amos in literary quality, he is not his equal as an original thinker. Isaiah, in the first place, adds little to the new, epoch-making, theological teaching of Amos, who transformed the God of Israel into the international God of justice. Profoundly influenced by Amos, as we have seen,

Isaiah is far less radical and revolutionary than his great predecessor. Inflamed by his new notions of God's character, purpose, and requirements, Amos had lighted the fuse of the bomb which blasted traditional worship and beliefs. His task was negative, destructive: the old must be swept away before the new could arise, phoenixlike, out of its ruins.

Isaiah continued Amos's revolutionary work but, having seen with his own eyes the realization of divine judgment performed against Israel and Judah by Assyria, the rod of God's anger, he laid the foundations of a new order: "Behold I lay [*sic*] in Zion a foundation stone, a tested stone . . ." (28:16). Isaiah deduced from the teaching of Amos regarding the sway of Jehovah over all nations and his power to punish iniquity anywhere on earth that the basic sin against God was pride in human wisdom and confidence in human means (2:12; 5:21; 9:9 f. [H. 9:8 f.]; 10:13; 28:1, 3, etc.)—nothing but foolishness and blindness (6:9 f.)—and that confidence in God's power (faith) was the essence of religion (7:4, 9; 28:16; 30:15).[7] Thus Isaiah goes one step further than Amos in identifying religion not with ritual worship but with an attitude of mind—complete trust in God after loyally carrying out his will.

Besides defining religion positively, Isaiah, in the second place, is more constructive than Amos in regarding the divine judgment not as the extinction of the people but as the dawn of a better day, as Hosea had hoped early in his ministry. A small "remnant" will survive the catastrophe and "will return" to Jehovah (Shear-jashub, 7:3), new authorities in Jerusalem will replace the corrupt leaders of the prophet's day, and Zion will be known as "the city of righteousness, the faithful city" (1:24-26). Descriptions of the righteous rule of the Messianic king (particularly 9:2-7 [H. 9:1-6]; ch. 11), however, could only have been penned after 586, when the Davidic dynasty lost its throne.

And in the third place, Isaiah took constructive measures for perpetuating his teachings and planting the seeds of the righteous "remnant" of the future. He organized a group of disciples and gave them written transcripts of certain of his oracles (8:16). Thus he not only passed on the torch to later generations, but separated from the corrupt body of the people a tiny nucleus of true believers, anticipating in a vague way individual salvation, substitution of a church for the nation, and separation of the redeemed from the worldly mass of apparent believers. Thus Isaiah unwittingly was laying the foundation stone of both Judaism and Christianity.

It is unfortunate that Isaiah's oracles should have come down to us in

[7] Even if J. Böhmer ("Der Glaube und Jesaja" in ZAW 41 [1923] 89-93) is right in denying that Isaiah used the technical term "faith" in an absolute sense and in dating 7:9b (cf. II Chron. 20:20) and the last clause in 28:16 in the third century B.C., it remains clear that Isaiah regarded trust in God as fundamental.

a much more imperfect state than those of Amos. The textual corruption of some, the fragmentary state of many others, and the pervasive jungle of editorial matter in which all genuine prophecies are now hidden constitute serious obstacles to a literary appreciation of Isaiah. Nevertheless, enough gold can be extracted from the dross to prove the greatness of his poetical genius. His mastery over the resources of Hebrew style appears in the clear and straightforward account of his vision and call (6:1-12), the vivid picture of the worthless vineyard (5:1-6), the epic description of the Assyrian advance, a poem worthy of Nahum and as exciting as a cavalry charge (5:26-29), and in the pathetic lament over the ruin of Judah (1:4-9). These four compositions, perhaps the best of Isaiah's fairly well-preserved writings, suffice to give their author a place among the best of the ancient Hebrew classic poets.

4. Messianic and Apocalyptic Oracles in Is. 1-39

Concerned with the problems of the living generation of his people, Isaiah did not attempt to pierce the mystery of the future, if the preceding analysis of his oracles is valid. He merely assured his people that Jehovah, their divine king, would not allow Assyria to overstep its function—punishment of the nation (10:5-9, 13-15)—and bring Judah to its complete extinction. Jerusalem would be resurrected—after a faithful remnant, surviving the catastrophe, had returned to Jehovah—as a city of righteousness under the rule of new authorities (1:24-26).

Numerous modern scholars, however, are certain that Isaiah not only proclaimed the imminence of the Day of the Lord, in which the nation would be punished for its sins, and the subsequent survival of a converted remnant—as every student must admit—but also the coming of a Messianic king, the inviolability of Zion, and the end of Assyria.[8]

None of the three other volumes of the prophets (Jer., Ez., The Twelve) enjoyed popularity equal to that of the Book of Isaiah, and none was more zealously annotated and supplemented with other oracles during the period from 500 to 200 B.C. In these centuries, under Persian and Ptolemaic rule, many Jews were dreaming of divine intervention to restore David's kingdom or create a Jewish world empire. The ancient prophecies of Amos, Hosea, Micah, and especially Isaiah were supplemented with "happy endings," promises of a dazzlingly glorious future (Am. 9:9-15;

[8] A sane and full discussion of this problem, leading to conclusions substantially similar to those advanced here, has been published by K. Fullerton ("Viewpoints in the Discussion of Isaiah's hopes for the future," JBL 41 [1922] 1-101), with a bibliography up to 1921. Among later publications, these deserve special mention: an article of K. Budde (ZAW 40 [1923] 154-203), the commentaries on Isaiah by E. König (1926) and O. Procksch (1930), the introductions to the Old Testament by J. Hempel (1930-1934) and O. Eissfeldt (1934), and E. A. Leslie, The Prophets Tell Their Own Story (New York, 1939).

Hos. 14:1-9 [H. 14:2-10]; Mic. 4-5. Mic. 4:1-5 has been also inserted in Is. 2:1-4).

In Is. 1-35, some of these additions were taken from collections of Messianic oracles, others composed for the context in which we find them. In any case, scarcely a single genuine oracle of Isaiah has escaped annotation of some kind. Disregarding the minor glosses listed above in the summary of the book, we note that the additions are of two types: threats of destruction against "sinners" among the Jews (the object of innumerable invectives and menaces in the Psalms); promises of the triumph of Jews over heathens (either spiritually, after the manner of Is. 40-55, or politically). Single oracles and collections of oracles in Is. 1-35 have been supplemented in this manner, according to the following tabular summary:

a. Ch. 1. Threats: 1:28-31. Promises: 1:27; 2:2-4 [5].

b. 2:1; 2:6-4:6. Threats: 2:8b, 9, 11; 3:6-8, 10 f., 18-23; 4:1. Promises: 4:2-6.

c. 6:1-9:7 (H. 6:1-9:6). Threats: 6:12 f.; 7:18-25; 8:19-22; 9:1 (H. 8:23). Promises: 8:9 f.; 9:2-7 (H. 9:1-6).

d. 5:1-30; 9:8-12:6 (H. 9:7-12:6). Threats: 5:9 f., 12 f., 15 f., 24, 25a, 30; 9:13, 15 f., 18 (H. 9:12, 14 f., 17). Promises: 10:10-12, 16-27a, 33 f.

e. The entire little book 1-10. Promises: 11-12.

f. Genuine individual oracles of Isaiah in 13-23: 14:28-32 (promises: 14:24-27); 17:1-3 (threats: 17:4-6, 9-11; promises: 17:7 f., 12-14); 18:1-6 (promises: 18:7). Similar additions are lacking in chs. 20 and 22, which are out of place.

g. The book of oracles against foreign nations (13-23) was supplemented by a complete brief apocalypse, containing threats and promises (24-27).

h. Genuine individual oracles of Isaiah in 28-31: 28:1-4 (promises: 28:5 f.); 28:7-22 (promises 28:23-29); 29:1-4 (promises: 29:5-8); 29:9 f., 13-15 (threats: 29:16; promises: 29:17-24); 30:1-5 (threats: 30:6 f.); 30:8-17 (promises: 30:18-26, 27-33); 31:1-3 (promises: 31:4-9).

i. Comforting conclusion appended to 28-31. Threats: 32:6-8, 9-14. Promises: 32:1-5, 15-22; 33.

j. Apocalyptic conclusion, containing threats for Edom and promises for Israel, attached to the whole of Is. 1-33:34-35 (unless they are the beginning of 40-66).

In contrast to Isaiah, these later authors preferred promises to threats. Such additions as are menacing in tone are few and not particularly important. In some of these, Jewish "transgressors and sinners" are compared to trees that are cut down, or to their branches destroyed in the flames (1:28-31; 5:24; 6:13). They will be humiliated (2:9, 11; 5:15 f.). The country will be invaded (7:18-25), the people exiled (5:12 f.), anarchy will prevail (3:6-8; 9:13, 15 f., 18 [H. 9:12, 14 f., 17]), the land will be desolated and subjected to various other calamities (5:9 f., 25a, 30; 6:12; 8:19-22; 9:1 [H. 8:23]; 17:4-6, 9-11; 32:9-14). Women will also be variously afflicted (3:18-23; 4:1; 32:9-14). Two passages (3:10 f.; 32:6-8) are not in the style of oracles but in that of the wisdom literature; they contrast, like Ps. 1 and many of the Proverbs, the happiness of the righteous to the misfortunes of the wicked.

As the preceding list shows, the promises of a glorious future in Is. 1-35 include brief oracles and three separate apocalyptic tracts (24-27; 32-33; 34-35). These tracts contain both negative and positive phases of the apocalyptic hope and will be considered apart, after the others.

In its earliest form, the vision of better days to come was confined to Palestine and the Jews; and, as already in Isaiah's own writings (1:24-26), implied both a political and a religious regeneration of the nation, protected by Jehovah from Assyria's attacks (cf. 10:5-9, 13-15). Strangely enough, neither Isaiah nor the early oracles attached to his writings connected the curbing of Assyria's power with Judah's revival; later, however, these two phases became inseparable.

Going beyond Isaiah's denunciation of Assyrian pride and selfishness (10:5-9, 13-15), the secondary prophecies in his book, supplementing this genuine oracle (10:10-12, 16-19, 24-27a, 33 f.) or else standing independently (14:24-27; 30:27-33; 31:4 f., 6-9), proclaim the final destruction of Assyria, usually alluding to the legendary annihilation of Sennacherib's army before Jerusalem. These prophecies may have been written soon after 612 B.C., when the Assyrian Empire actually ceased to exist. None of them, however, has the feeling for reality as well as for drama characteristic of Nah. 2-3. After Assyria had become but a memory, the prophecies predict in more general terms the destruction of inimical hosts of the "nations" or heathen (8:9 f.; 17:12-14; 29:5-8). This divine victory would make possible the return of "the remnant of Jacob" (10:20-23; 11:11-16).

Although presupposing Judah's recovery of political independence and power, peace and prosperity, the visions of a golden age to come in Is. 1-31 (disregarding for the moment 24-27) stressed particularly more spiritual phases of the restoration: obedience to God, honesty and kindness, and personal righteousness and piety. For even when a Messianic descendant of David ruling in Zion became a prominent feature of the restoration (9:2-7 [H. 9:1-6]; 11:1-9 [10]; cf. 32:1-5; the gloss 7:15 identifies Immanuel with the Messiah), he was a prince of peace and righteousness rather than a conquering hero. It is not surprising that these magnificent visions of the ideal king of the future, filled with the divine spirit, made such a deep impression on the early Christians (cf. Matt. 3:16; 4:15 f.; Luke 2:11; Rom. 1:3; Eph. 5:8, 14; Rev. 5:5, etc.), and that modern critics cling so tenaciously to their Isaianic authorship.

In other descriptions of the future Kingdom of God on earth the figure of the Messiah is missing and Zion "redeemed with justice" (1:27) and true to Jehovah (17:7 f.), becomes the religious center of mankind (2:2-4 [5] = Mic. 4:2-5; 18:7; 28:5 f.) as well as a safe and joyful haven for redeemed Jews (29:17-24; 30:18-26). Thus will the wonderful wisdom of Jehovah be manifested (28:23-29) and hymns of thanksgiving sung in his honor (12:1-3, 4-6, based in part on Ex. 15 and Ps. 105; cf. the hymns in 26-27). The parable describing various agricultural labors and their several purposes in 28:23-29 shows that Jehovah alternately uprooted and planted, saving a remnant—thus proving the organic unity of threats and promises.

The oracles collected without a logical plan in 32-33 are closely related to preceding ones; 32:6-8, 9-14, which are a disturbing note, have already been considered among the threatening oracles. Again we have a picture of the righteous Messianic king (32:1-5), the outpouring of the spirit from on high (cf. 11:2; 28:6) bringing peace and prosperity to the country (32:15-20), the triumph of Jehovah over the hosts of heathen (33:1-13) and over the sinners of Jerusalem (33:14-16), and finally God's Kingdom on earth (33:17-24).[9]

On the contrary, the following poem (34-35) is a unit in two parts. Written in dithyrambic and imaginative style, which resembles to some extent that of the Second Isaiah (to whom C. C. Torrey [*The Second Isaiah*. New York, 1928][10] attributes it), this oracle is an apocalytic vision of Jehovah's final triumph. The two acts of the drama are sharply distinguished. First comes the "day of vengeance," a dreadful *dies irae* in which the land of Jehovah's enemies—"Edom," either literally, or symbolically for all unconverted heathen—will be turned, after the slaughter of its inhabitants, into a wilderness of pitch and brimstone, with ruined palaces populated by ghouls, goblins, and nocturnal beasts and birds (34). The counterpart of this terrestrial hell is an earthly paradise: the desert blossoms as the rose, its wild animals disappear, streams flow through it, and the redeemed march over it on "The Way of Holiness," returning to Zion with songs on their lips and everlasting joy in their hearts (35).

The two little books in 32-33 and 34-35 can hardly be earlier than the fifth century, and may belong to the fourth. The apocalypse in 24-27 is even later. Theology and historical background, as well as the general characteristics of language and style,[11] point to the third century as the

[9] H. Gunkel (ZAW N.F. 1 [1924] 177-208) regards Is. 33 as a "prophetic liturgy," but is not certain that it was actually sung in Temple worship.

[10] R. B. Y. Scott (AJSL 52 [1936] 178-191) and A. T. Olmstead (AJSL 53 [1937] 251-253) likewise attribute ch. 35 to the Second Isaiah. On ch. 34 see J. Muilenburg in JBL 59 (1940) 339-365.

[11] Numerous puns and verbal repetitions usually farfetched and in questionable taste occur in 24-27 (particularly in 24:1-23; 25:1; 26:3, 5). In 24:16b, all five

period in which Is. 24-27 was written. The apocalyptic character is more pronounced here than in any other parts of Isaiah: the blowing of the great trumpet to gather God's elect from the four winds (27:13; cf. Matt. 24:31; I Cor. 15:52; I Thess. 4:16), the resurrection from the dead (26:19; cf. Dan. 12:2), and the divine judgment of angels (24:21a, 22 f.), either fallen or (as in Dan. 10:20 f.) patrons of heathen nations, are clear signs of late composition. Moreover, when ch. 27 was written, the Jewish Dispersion was extensive and widely scattered (27:12 f.) and the Seleucid and Ptolemaic kingdoms, enigmatically named Leviathan and the dragon, respectively (27:1; cf. 27:13), were the chief obstacles to Jewish independence.

Isaiah 24-27 marks the transition from the nationalistic expectation of a revived kingdom of David to the apocalyptic visions of cosmic upheavals and rebirth of the whole world. The hymns of joy and hatred (25:1-5, 9-12; 26:1-6, 7-19; 27:2-6, 7-11) still stress the nationalistic aspirations. In the destructive phase the Lord annihilates the enemies of Israel (25:1-5, 9-12; 26:5 f., cf. 27:4, 7 f., 10 f.), the wicked in its midst (26:10-12), and its heathen rulers (26:13 f.). In the constructive phase the Lord is a mighty fortress for the pious Jews (26:1-4), whose path he has smoothed (26:7-9); he has widened the borders of Israel in time of distress (26:15-18) and will raise from the dust the pious dead (26:19); the Lord cares for his vineyard, Israel, and destroys the weeds (27:2-6), for he will allow Israel again to take root and blossom, while its foes will be consumed like the boughs of a withered tree set on fire by the women (27:7-11).

The horizon of apocalyptic sections (24; 25:6-8; 26:20-27:1, 12 f.) is much wider than in these hymns, although to assume a different authorship for hymns and oracles is unnecessary. The apocalypse is concerned not merely with restoring the Jewish community in Jerusalem and protecting it from internal and external enemies, but with the whole world—mankind and the physical universe. Through increasing deterioration, humanity as well as heaven and earth have reached a stage of decrepitude and are under a curse (24:1-13). Some are already rejoicing over the dawn of a new and happier day (24:14-16a), but the author looks forward to worse evils: men fleeing from the scene of panic will fall into the pit, and those escaping from this pit will be caught in a trap (24:16b-18a); inundated by heavenly cataracts, the earth itself will reel and be shattered (24:18b-20). Then the Lord will judge the angelic hosts and the kings of the earth, casting them into a dungeon (24:21-23a), and reign gloriously on Zion (24:23b).

---

words are derived from the root *bgd*; similar repetitions occur in 27:7. In 24:17 f., there is a pun on the words *pahad, pahat,* and *pah* (fear, pit, and snare). Rhymes occur in 27:3-5.

To usher in the new world, the Lord will invite all nations to a rich feast on Zion: he will destroy death and wipe the tears from all eyes (25:6-8). Israel should go into hiding during the final judgment, when the Lord will slay with his sword Leviathan, that swift and tortuous serpent (Syria), and the dragon (Egypt) (26:20-27:1). Thus it will be possible for the Jews, scattered widely throughout Egypt and Syria, to come and worship the Lord on Zion when the great trumpet is blown (27:12 f.).

The hymns are loosely connected with the apocalypse. They are like the voice of the chorus in a Greek drama, although, since they do not interpret the action but express the feelings of Israel, far less organically related to the drama. The hymns could have been written before the apocalypse and been added to it, but there is no proof that they were not an integral and original part of it. A characteristic of most of the later apocalypses is chaotic arrangement, and the lack of logical structure in Is. 24-27 is not necessarily a sign of composite authorship.

5. *The Oracles against Foreign Nations (Is. 13-23)*

The first three prophetic books contain a collection of denunciations of foreign nations, both the immediate neighbors of Judah and the great empires of Mesopotamia and Egypt: Is. 13-23; Jer. 46-51; Ez. 25-32. Although such anathemas against the heathen were inaugurated by Amos (Am. 1-2, in part spurious), they reflect on the whole not the moral indignation of the great pre-exilic prophets, but rather the nationalism of the "false prophets" and of the later Jews chafing for centuries under alien rule. The masses did not rise to the idealistic universalism of a Second Isaiah, nor even to the friendly attitude of toleration for foreigners that animates the books of Ruth and Jonah. Ardently nationalistic and fanatically intolerant, postexilic Jews found some relief by gleefully anticipating divine vengeance on their enemies and oppressors. Nahum's classic paean on the fall of Nineveh is one of the earliest and by far the best of these outbursts of hatred for the heathen kingdoms.

The book Is. 13-23 contains some genuine oracles of Isaiah (14:28-32; 17:1-3; 18:1-6; 20:1-6; 22:1-14, 15-25) and later additions to the same (14:24-27; 17:4-14; 18:7) which have already been discussed. The rest of the book consists of prophecies of doom addressed to foreign nations, written long after the time of Isaiah.

The first prophecy (13:1-14:23) is directed against Babylon. In the original oracle (13:17-19), Babylon is still mistress of the world, as it could be called hyperbolically between 605 and 538 B.C.; but soon the Medes will destroy it and, according to the supplementary prediction in 13:20-22, it shall remain forever uninhabited. The original oracle was written before Cyrus conquered Babylon in 538, presumably about 550.

This historical situation is beclouded by apocalyptic fantasy in the introduction (13:1-16), dealing with "the Day of the Lord"—God's triumph over the hordes of his foes.

The second part of the oracle against Babylon (14:1-23) is much less explicit. The poem (14:4b-21), enclosed within an editorial introduction and conclusion (14:1-4a, 22 f.), describes a heathen emperor's fall into Hades. The editor who placed the poem here evidently identified this ruler with a Babylonian king, either the great Nebuchadnezzar (605-561) or one of the two last rulers of the Neo-Babylonian empire, Nabonidus and his son Belshazzar (ruling jointly during the latter part of the reign of Nabonidus [555-538]). In reality, however, the poem is so deliberately vague and mysterious that, in spite of concrete details in 14:19-21 (the body of the king was left unburied and his nation ruined), we cannot determine whether the poet had in mind a historical character, or described allegorically through the figure of a tyrant the downfall (past or future?) of a detested world empire. Consequently, we cannot fix the date of this poem: it was written some time within the period 580-250 B.C.

In 14:12-14, the poet allegorically identifies the dead tyrant with a semidivine being, Halel ben Shahar (Lucifer, son of the morning, 14:12) who, filled with "ambitious aim against the throne and monarchy of God" (Milton), attempted to place his throne above God's and was precipitated into the lowest pit. This ancient myth, reappearing in Christianity in the form of Satan's fall, could have inspired Ez. 28:11-19 (which resembles Is. 14), although that passage may be interpreted as a version of the lost Paradise myth (Gen. 3).[12]

The second oracle is directed against Moab (15:1-16:14). Like the author of Jer. 48, the writer quoted verbatim, but with some omissions, an earlier non-Israelitic poem. This piece is of particular interest because, except for the "Moabite Stone" commemorating the reign of Mesha about 850 B.C. (published with a translation and notes in G. A. Cooke, A Textbook of North-Semitic Inscriptions, pp. 1-14), it is the only remnant of Moabitic literature now extant. The Moabitic language differed from Hebrew only slightly. This poem (15:1-9aα; 16:7-11; Jer. 48:15, 18, 37, 38a, 34a, 31, 34b, 5, 34d, 36c, 29, 30b, 36b, 32cba, 33, 36a; Is. 15:7b-9a are not in Jer. 48) is a touching elegy, bewailing with true feeling and poetic beauty the ruin of Moab. One night, Bedouins from the Syrian desert invaded the central part of Moab from the east, and with a surprise attack captured Ar-Moab on the Arnon and Kir-hareseth (modern Kerak) south of it. In their panic, the Moabites fled southward into Edom. The Arabs invaded the lands of Edom and Moab during the sixth and fifth

---

[12] For the latest discussion of the mythological background of Is. 14, see J. Morgenstern in HUCA 14 (1939) 29-126, and especially pp. 107-112.

centuries and this dirge, lamenting a particularly tragic phase of this movement, probably dates from 550-450 B.C.

In contrast to the Moabitic poet weeping over his country's desolation, the Jewish author of the oracle against Moab slyly changed the elegy into a prediction (15:9aβb). In obscure language he then seems to have invited the Edomites to give shelter to the fugitives (16:1-4a) because a Messianic righteous king was ruling in Zion (16:4b-5). He condemned the pride of Moab (16:6), and declared that no acts of piety could save it (16:12). Finally a later editor announced that this ancient prediction would be realized by the Lord within three years (16:13 f.).

The third prophecy is directed against Egypt (19). The first part of the chapter is in verse (19:1-15), the second, obviously later, in prose (19:16-25). The first part describes a series of calamities that will afflict Egypt after Jehovah flies thither on a cloud (19:1): civil war (19:2 f.), tyranny under a "cruel lord" (19:4), drying up of the Nile (19:5-7), bringing ruin to fishermen (19:8) and flax weavers (19:9 f.), helpless confusion of Pharaoh's ministers and provincial princes (19:11-15). Such natural and political disasters have occurred frequently in ancient Egypt, and offer no clue to the date of this oracle or series of oracles. Nor can the "cruel lord" be identified with any assurance: most critics see in him Psamtik I (663-609), founder of the Twenty-sixth Dynasty; others suggest the Assyrian (Esarhaddon [681-668] or Ashurbanipal [668-625]) or Persian (Cambyses [530-521], Xerxes I [485-465], or Artaxerxes III [358-338]) conquerors of Egypt. It is not unlikely that the author had a vague notion of conditions in the Nile Valley, and composed this "burden of Egypt" without a definite historical situation in mind. If such is the case, the date of the poem must remain uncertain; it probably falls within the period 600-300 B.C.

Nor can the second part (19:16-25) be dated, although it is later than the first; its epilogue (19:23-25), predicting the conversion of Egypt and Assyria (i.e., the Ptolemaic and Seleucid kingdoms) to the worship of Jehovah, is not original. The allusions (in 19:16-22) to Jews frightening the Egyptians, settling among them in five cities where Hebrew will be spoken, and erecting a sanctuary of Jehovah in Egypt are utterly obscure. The first recorded settlement of Jews in Egypt occurred soon after 586 (Jer. 42-43), unless we accept the testimony of the Letter to Aristeas (§13), according to which Psammetichus (presumably Psamtik II [593-588]; cf. Herodotus 2:30) sent Jewish mercenaries against the Ethiopians. If such was the case, they could have been permanently garrisoned at Elephantine, where Cambyses found them in 525. This military colony of Jews at Elephantine had erected a temple to Jehovah before 525. After its destruction in 411 B.C. it was never rebuilt, in spite of the efforts of the

Jews there.[13] The oracle in Is. 19:19 *could* possibly refer to this temple "at the border" of Egypt, and would then date 525-411. The only other Jewish temple known in Egypt is that of Leontopolis, erected by Onias III about 163 B.C. and destroyed in A.D. 73. (see E. Schürer, *Geschichte des Jüdischen Volkes* u.s.w., Vol. III, pp. 42, 49, 144-148. 4th ed., Leipzig, 1909). According to Josephus (*Antiquities* 13:3, 1), Onias justified the building of the temple by quoting Is. 19:19; nevertheless, some critics regard our oracle as an insertion made in the Book of Isaiah *after* Onias built his temple. In conclusion, the date of 19:16-22 is unknown. The present writer believes that this oracle alludes in imaginative language to the Jewish community in Alexandria in the third century.

The fourth prophecy is another oracle against Babylon (21:1-10). The strange title, "Burden of the Desert of the Sea" is generally regarded as corrupt and "of the sea" is usually omitted (with the LXX), although "wilderness of the sea" might well be a translation of (*mât*) *Tamtim* (literally "land of the sea") or Sealand frequently mentioned in Babylonian records (cf. R. P. Dougherty, *The Sealand of Ancient Arabia*, pp. 169 f. New Haven, 1932). Like the other oracle against Babylon (13:17-19; cf. also ch. 47), this poem was composed shortly before Cyrus conquered the city in 538, or about 550, but by a different author (in 13 the Medes take Babylon, here Elam and the Medes).

From B. Duhm to O. Eissfeldt, nearly all the interpreters have discovered in the oracle an introspective account of the psychology of prophetic trance: the author objectifies his alter ego, his psychic self (called "the seer" in 21:6), separating it from his normal self. J. Obermann (JBL 48 [1929] 307-328), however, has plausibly analyzed the oracle as a dramatic dialogue in which the characters and their words are as follows: the seer (21:1), Babylon (21:2abα), the seer (21:2bβ, beginning with "Go up, O Elam"), Babylon (21:3-5a), a voice (21:5b), Babylon to a messenger (21:6 f.), the seer to God (21:8-9a), the seer to the Babylonian messenger (21:9b-10).

The fifth and sixth oracles (21:11 f., 13-15, [16 f.]) are mysterious and bear the puzzling titles "Burden of Dumah" (LXX: Edom; J. Obermann [JBL 48, 1929, 325] renders, "Oracle of silence" in contrast with 21:1 where he reads "oracle of a speaker") and "Burden of *ba 'rab*" (omitted in LXX). Nothing indicates that either oracle was written by a Judean or Jew, and they may well be of Edomitic origin. The language of the first, and to a lesser degree of the second, is a mixture of Hebrew and Aramaic words. Neither oracle was originally a denunciation. The first (21:11 f.) exhibits the simplicity and charm of folk poetry, the second (21:13-15)

---

[13] On the temple at Elephantine, see the letter which the Jews there addressed to Bagoas, the Persian governor of Judea, in 408 (A. Cowley, *Aramaic Papyri of the Fifth Century*, pp. 108-119; cf. 119-126. Oxford, 1923).

the genuine background of war and hospitality in the Arabian desert. A Jew has interpreted the second as a prediction of the ruin of Kedar (Bedouins of the Syrian desert) within a year (21:16 f.). The original poems probably date from the fifth or the fourth century; the prose appendix to the second could have been added in the third century.

The seventh and final foreign oracle is addressed to Tyre and Sidon (23). The chief problem raised by this prophecy is the alternation of the names Tyre (23:[1], 5, 8, [15, 17]) and Sidon (23:2, 4, 12). Ostensibly, the oracle predicts the destruction of Tyre (23:1-14, omitting 23:5, 13) and its rebuilding after seventy years in order that its wealth may enrich the Temple at Jerusalem and the Jews (23:15-18). This second part is clear: its author interpreted the original oracle as a prophecy of the conquest of Tyre by Alexander in 332 and added a prediction of its restoration seventy years later. The "seventy years" may have been inspired by Jer. 25:11; 29:10, or else are merely a round number; as a matter of fact, Tyre languished under the rule of the Ptolemies (286-197), whose great harbor was Alexandria, but only fifty-eight years after Alexander's victory Tyre was sufficiently revived to start a new era, when Ptolemy II granted autonomy to the city in 274. One should not reject a priori this interpretation of the first part of the oracle (in which "Tyre" should then be read for "Sidon" in 23:2, 4, 12).

Most critics, however, follow B. Duhm, who regards the original oracle as a sarcastic elegy over the destruction of Sidon by Artaxerxes III in 348; the later author of 23:15-18 applied the poem to Tyre (23:1), adding 23:5 and changing "Sidon" into "Tyre" in 23:8 (though not in 23:2, 12). Such a view is more plausible than the theory of O. Procksch (in his commentary on Is. 1-39, 1930): a poem on Sidon (23:1-4, 12-14), composed by Isaiah, was united with a much later one on Tyre (23:5-11). The text is so vague that no definite historical situation can be precisely identified; that a writer of uncertain date (550-300) should compose a sarcastic dirge over the ruin of Phoenicia in general is a real possibility. Only the appendix (23:15-18) may be dated with some accuracy: it was written shortly after 274 B.C.

6. The Origin of the Book of Isaiah

The first part of Isaiah (1-39) is not an organically constructed work but a collection of separate little books. All these (except 36-39, which is an extract from Kings) were circulating as separate collections of oracles, repeatedly edited, before they were copied together on a single scroll of papyrus. It was only because sufficient space remained on the scroll that the final editor of the four prophetic volumes (Is., Jer., Ez., and The Twelve)—which are really a comprehensive edition of all prophetic oracles accessible in 200 B.C.—copied Is. 40-66 (then circulating as a separate book) after Is. 1-39. Thus about 200 B.C. originated our Book of Isaiah, for which the first attestation is found in Sirach (Ecclus. 48:24 refers to Is. 40:1; 61:2 f. as part of Isaiah's book), about 180 B.C. With respect to the structure of the whole, as a miniature library rather than a book, Isaiah is not essentially different from the Book of the Minor Prophets, and could nearly be regarded, like Psalms and Proverbs, as an anthology or rather a "collection of collections."

Unlike Jeremiah, Isaiah did not himself prepare a book of his prophecies: he merely wrote down some of his experiences and oracles from time to time. His earliest writing is 6:1-9:7 (H. 6:1-9:6), in its original form; his second 2:1-5:7. Near the end of his life he wrote 5:8-30; 9:8-10:32 (H. 9:7-10:32) and ch. 1. The first three of these four collections were carelessly thrown together in a book (2-12) entitled "The word that Isaiah the son of Amoz saw concerning Judah and Jerusalem" (2:1) after the prophet's death. Later, ch. 1 was used as a preface of an enlarged book of his oracles and presumably 2:2-5, the comforting appendix to ch. 1, was removed to its present place. When 2-12 was prepared as a book, its editor either lacked or else disregarded the Isaianic oracles in 28-31, a collection which may have been originally prepared by Isaiah himself. The scattered genuine oracles of Isaiah in 13-23 apparently survived on separate sheets of papyrus and were not collected by the prophet.

The second book in Isaiah, after 2-12, is a collection of foreign oracles (13-23) with its apocalyptic supplement (24-27, originally a separate booklet). It hardly seems likely that the genuine prophecies of Isaiah scattered in 13-23 formed the original nucleus of this collection; on the contrary, they appear to have been added at random to save them from oblivion. Conversely, the third book (28-31, with its apocalyptic supplement, 32-33) grew up around genuine Isaianic oracles.

The editor who combined these three books (2-12; 13-27; 28-33) may have placed ch. 1 at the beginning as a preface, and 34-35[14] at the end as a general eschatological conclusion. The extracts from Kings in 36-39 were probably added to the book 1-35 (or 1-33) in the third century, for about 250 the Chronicler (II Chron. 32:32) read them both in Kings and in the Book of Isaiah (unless the reference to Isaiah is spurious). On the other hand, even allowing for the additions made shortly before 200, the book 1-35 contains so much late material that it cannot be much earlier than 300 B.C. After 200 B.C., when the book as a whole attained the rank of canonical Scriptures, only a few scattered clauses were added to Is. 1-66.

---

[14] Of course 34-35 may have been originally an introduction to 40-66 or, as C. C. Torrey maintains (JBL 57 [1938] 126 ff.), "the beginning of the word of 'Second Isaiah.' "

II. ISAIAH 40-66

The second part of the Book of Isaiah may be summarized as follows:

1. Introduction (40:1-11): *a.* Jerusalem, after paying double for her sins, is forgiven (40:1 f.); *b.* a highway is prepared in the desert for the return of the exiles (40:3-5); *c.* the author receives the theme of his book (40:6-8); *d.* Zion bears the good tidings to the cities of Judah (40:9-11).

2. Jehovah's work of salvation (40:12-48:22).

a. The unique greatness of Jehovah (40:12-31). Jehovah, the creator of the world (40:12-17), cannot be compared to idols (40:18-20), for he rules nature and history (40:21-26) and renews the strength of those who hope in him (40:27-31). The inaneness of idol manufacture and worship is sarcastically pictured in 40:18-20; 41:6 f.; 44:9-20 (cf. the glosses 41:24b, 29; 42:17; 45:16, 20b; 46:1 f., 6 f.; 48:5b); this attack on idolatry is imitated in Jer. 10:2-5, 9, 14 f.; Hab. 2:18 f.; Ps. 115:4-8 = 135:15-18.

b. It is Jehovah that has stirred up Cyrus (44:28; 45:1) the Persian (550-530 B.C.) and led him to the conquest of nations and kingdoms (41:1-5, 12-28; cf. 44:24-45:13). The manufacture of idols (41:6 f.; cf. *a*).

c. Israel is the beloved of Jehovah (41:8-20): his servant (41:8-10), whose enemies will perish (41:11-13); though only a worm, Israel will thresh the mountains to dust (41:14-16); for Israel Jehovah will provide in the desert abundant water and pleasant vegetation (41:17-20).

d. Jehovah, not the heathen gods, predicted the conquests of Cyrus (41:21-29, omitting the gloss on the idols in 41:29; cf. *a*).

e. The merciful mission of "The Servant of the Lord" (42:1-4, 6 f.); the other "Servant" songs are in 49:1-6; 50:4-9; 52:13-53:12; cf. 41:8-16; 42:5-7, 18-25; 43:10; 44:1 f., 21, 26; 45:4; 48:20; 50:10; C. C. Torrey would add 61:1 ff. Israel is "the light of the nations" (42:5-9). "Sing to the Lord a new song" in commemoration of his future victories (42:10-13) and of his gracious intervention in Israel's behalf (42:14-17). For Israel had been abandoned to spoilers on account of its sins (42:18-25).

f. The redemption of Israel (43:1-44:5): other nations shall be given by Jehovah as the ransom for Israel (43:1-7); Israel is the proof of Jehovah's triumph over the false gods (43:8-13); Jehovah destroys Babylon (43:14 f.) in order to save his people (43:16-21), graciously forgiving their past sins (43:22-28) and pouring water on the desert and his spirit upon Israel (44:1-5).

g. Jehovah is the only God and predicts the future (44:6-8), but the other gods are but idols of wood and metal (44:9-20; cf. *a*).

h. Exultation over Israel's redemption (44:21-23).

i. Through Cyrus, his servant and his anointed, Jehovah manifests his power and restores the fortunes of Judah (44:24-45:13; cf. *b*). As a consequence heathen nations will dedicate themselves to Jehovah (45:14-25).

j. The fall of Babylon, presumably into the hands of Cyrus in 538 (46-47): the gods of Babylon are helpless (46:1 f.), being only idols (46:5-7), but Jehovah remains the same (46:3 f.), fulfilling his predictions (46:8-11) and saving Zion (46:12). The "virgin daughter of Babylon" shall sit in the dust; the mistress of kingdoms shall become a wretched handmaid as a punishment for her fastidiousness, inhumanity to Israel, self-complacency, conceited wisdom, and superstition (47).

k. Israel has transgressed from its birth and, after testing the nation through affliction, Jehovah for his own sake saves it through Cyrus from the Babylonian captivity (48:1-16). If they had previously hearkened to their God the Israelites would not have been decimated (48:17-19). Now, however, the time of redemption is at hand and they will go forth from Babylon (48:20-22).

3. The new Israel (49-55).·

a. Israel, the Servant of the Lord, becomes the light of the nations (49:1-6; cf. 2: *e*).

b. Israel, the despised servant of tyrants, will triumphantly return to its land (49:7-13). Zion in her misery has given up all hope, but Jehovah will force the nations to become solicitous servants of Israel (49:14-23) and make the oppressors eat their own flesh (49:24-26).

c. Jehovah has not divorced his bride, Israel (50:1-3).

d. The Servant of the Lord bears unflinchingly the humiliating torments of his calling, trusting in Jehovah's help (50:4-9; cf. 2: *e*); and God's voice proclaims his vindication (50:10 f.).

e. Zion's restoration is imminent (51:1-52:12): God blessed Abraham (51:1-3) and his salvation goes forth to the nations (51:4-6); the people in whose heart is God's law (cf. Jer. 31:33) have nothing to fear (51:7 f.); a jubilant appeal to God (51:9-11; cf. 51:17; 52:7 f.) receives a divine answer (51:12-16); the cup of God's wrath that Zion has drunk will be placed into the hands of her persecutors (51:17-23; cf. Jer. 25:15); the bearers of good tidings proclaim the restoration of Zion (52:1-12).

f. The Servant of the Lord, "a man of sorrows and acquainted with grief," suffers death for the sins of mankind (52:13-53:12; cf. 2: *e*): the divine promise (52:13-15); the confession of the Gentiles (53:1-10); the divine vindication (53:11-12).

g. The new Zion (54): its enlarged population (54:1-8); the renewal of the covenant with Noah (54:9 f.); the wealth and might of Zion (54:11-17).

h. Concluding exhortation (55): invitation to enter into the divine covenant by which Israel, now without kings, inherits the promises made to David (55:1-5); God's word is always fulfilled (55:6-11; cf. 40:6-8); and it will bring the Exiles back to Zion (55:12 f.; cf. 40:1-5, 9-11).

4. Warnings (56-59) and promises (60-66).

a. Proselytes and eunuchs will be admitted into the Jewish congregation, provided they keep the Law, observe the Sabbath, and offer sacrifices; "for my house shall be called a house of prayer for all peoples" (56:1-8).

b. Denunciations against the worthless winebibbing leaders (56:9-12), and the apostate and superstitious masses, indifferent to the fate of the pious (57:1 f.), practicing obscene fertility cults in the country (57:3-6) and idolatrous rites in the city (57:7-13).

c. God will bring back the Exiles and promises "peace to those far and near" (57:14-21).

d. A sermon on fasting: the current practice of fasting is detestable in the sight of Jehovah, who requires in its place deeds of kindness and philanthropy (58:1-12).

e. Admonition to keep the Sabbath (58:13 f.).

f. Israel's sins (59:1-8) are confessed by the people in distress (59:9-15a).

g. Conclusion of 56:1-59:15a: Jehovah will reward all according to their deserts and come to redeem Zion (59:15b-20), and place his spirit upon his people forever (59:21).

h. A hymn on the New Jerusalem, which is the lamp (60:1-4, 19-22) and the treasury (60:5-18) of the nations.

i. Jehovah's messenger brings comfort to the afflicted (61:1-3) and promises that the Jews in their homeland will be priests, and aliens their servants (61:4-7), that Jehovah in his justice will bless the Jews scattered among the nations (61:8 f.), and that Jerusalem, clothed with salvation, will exult in her God (61:10 f.).

j. The messenger cannot keep silent until Jerusalem's glory is manifested (62:1-3); then she will be Jehovah's bride (62:4 f.). The watchers remind Jehovah that the walls of Jerusalem should be rebuilt (62:6 f.). Jerusalem will never again be plundered (62:8 f.). A song of the Jews of the Dispersion marching to Zion (62:10-12).

k. Jehovah returns from Edom in blood-stained garments after devastating that land (63:1-6, possibly the conclusion of 59:15b-20, [21]).

l. A hymn of praise for Jehovah (63:7-9), a confession of sins (63:10), a yearning remembrance of the time of Moses (63:11-14), and a prayer for Jehovah's manifestation in power in behalf of his people (63:15-19; 64:1-12 [H. 63:15-19a; 63:19b-64:11]).

m. The divine answer: in vain has Jehovah waited for his apostate people to return to him (65:1-7), but for the sake of the faithful he will not destroy the whole nation without leaving "a scion out of Jacob" in possession of the land (65:8-12). After fixing the opposite destinies of the reprobates and of the pious (65:13-15), Jehovah will create a new heaven and a new earth (65:16 f.) in which Jerusalem will be a city of exultation

(65:18 f.) where long-lived inhabitants will prosper and the most fero-
cious animals will become tame (65:20-25).

n. Jehovah needs neither temple nor sacrifices, but considers the man
who is humble and fears his word (66:1-4).

o. Conclusion: after the elimination of the apostate Jews (66:5 f.), Zion
will give birth to many children (66:7-11). The wealth of the nations
will flow to Jerusalem (66:12-14) but Jehovah will slay the apostates
who worship in the gardens and eat the meat of swine, vermin, and mice
(66:15-17). The Jews of the Dispersion will carry out missionary work
among the most distant nations (66:18 f.) and from among those who
come to Zion Levitical priests will be chosen (66:20 f.). The Jews shall
abide forever (66:22). To the worshipers from all mankind in Jerusalem,
the corpses of the apostate Jews will be exhibited on New Moons and
Sabbaths (66:23 f.).

1. Authorship and Date of Is. 40-66

Critics are now agreed, with rare exceptions,[15] that Is. 40-66 was not
written by Isaiah the son of Amoz (active in the period 740-700 B.C.),
but their opinions on the date, unity, and authorship of these chapters
differ radically.

Written anonymously,[16] composed more or less disjointedly in brief
sections, containing few clear allusions to datable historical events, Is.
40-66 lacks the decisive evidence which enables us to reach definite conclusions in regard to the authorship and date of the genuine writings of
the prophets from Amos to Jeremiah and, later, of Haggai and Zechariah.
All that can be reasonably inferred with some assurance is that the historical situation, the theological thought, and the peculiarities of style
and diction manifestly place the composition on these chapters, whether
by a single or by several authors, in the period after 586. Such a general
conclusion is obvious and now generally adopted. But beyond this point
the evidence is contradictory and critical opinion is still sharply divided.

The following problems have taxed the ingenuity of scholars. Is the
book a collection of separate poems, an anthology, or a structural unit?
Is it the work of a single author or of several? When did the author or
authors of the book write? Where did he, or they, live? Who was "The

[15] Franz Delitzsch (in his *Commentary on Isaiah.* Leipzig, 4th ed., 1889) supposed
that in 40-66 Isaiah, forgetting the present, lived in imagination in a period more than
a century and a half in the future. Among recent critics the following still defend the
Isaianic authorship of Is. 40-66: Herzog ("Zum Verständnis des Propheten Jesaja,"
Schweitz. Kirchenzeit. 1915, 136-138); J. J. Lias ("The Unity of Isaiah," BS 72 [1915]
560-591; 75 [1918] 267-274); A. Kaminka ("Le développement des idées du prophète
Isaïe et l'unité de son livre," REJ 80 [1925] 42-59, 131-169; 81 [1925] 27-48).

[16] The principal author, to whom at least Is. 40-48 or 40-55 is generally attributed,
is currently called the "Second Isaiah" or, if Greek terminology is preferred, "Deutero-
Isaiah."

Servant of the Lord"? The solutions offered by critics may be classified as follows:

A. The Structure and Authorship of Is. 40-66

a. Unity of Is. 40-66. The most emphatic defender of the homogeneous unity of Is. 34-35; 40-66 is C. C. Torrey (*The Second Isaiah*), who divides the work in twenty-seven poems "written down in the order in which we now find them" (p. 53). The unity of Is. 40-66 is also defended by E. König (*Das Buch Jesaja*), L. Glahn (L. Glahn and L. Köhler, *Der Prophet der Heimkehr*, Vol. I. L. Glahn, *Die Einheit von Kap. 40-66 des B. Jesaia.* Giessen, 1934) and L. Finkelstein (*The Pharisees*, Vol. II, pp. 627-629). George Dahl (JBL 48 [1929] 362-377) seems to be the only critic who subscribes to all the conclusions of C. C. Torrey; G. A. Barton (*The Haverford Symposium on Archaeology and the Bible*, p. 61 and n. 53 on pp. 76 f. Edited by E. Grant. New Haven, Conn., 1938) adopts Torrey's views in the main. Following W. F. Albright (*The Archaeology of Palestine and the Bible*, p. 218. New York, 1932), Fleming James (*Personalities of the Old Testament*, p. 363. New York, 1939) regards Is. 40-66 as a unit and dates it in the period 540-522 B.C.

b. The separation of Is. 56-66 from Is. 40-55. Friedr. Bleek (d. 1859) believed that "perhaps after ch. 58 and more certainly in the case of the last four chapters, 63-66" we have prophecies of a later date, though written by the same author (F. Bleek, *Einleitung in das Alte Testament*, pp. 345 f. 4th ed. by J. Wellhausen, Berlin, 1878). B. Stade (*Geschichte des Volkes Israel*, Vol. II, p. 70, n. 1. Berlin, 1888) denied that 56:9-57:13a; 58:13-59:21, and also 62-66, "at least in their present form," could have been written by the Second Isaiah. According to A. Kuenen (*De godsdienst van Israël*, Vol. II. Haarlem, 1889), Is. 50-51; 54-66 was written for the most part in Palestine by the "school" of the Second Isaiah. K. Budde (ZAW 11 [1891] 242) dates 56-59; 61 (?); 63-64 later than the rest of 40-66. Finally B. Duhm (*Jesaia*, HKAT, 1892) and K. Marti (*Der Prophet Sacharja*, p. 40. Freiburg, 1892), apparently independently, presented the theory that has been generally adopted: the Second Isaiah wrote 40-55 (with or without the "Servant" poems) in Babylonia shortly before 538, and the Third Isaiah (Trito-Isaiah) wrote 56-66 after 538 in Palestine.

c. The composition of Is. 40-55. The unity of this section has been variously attacked. F. Rückert (*Hebräische Propheten u.s.w.* Leipzig, 1831) divided chs. 40-55 into two parts (40-48; 49-55) on the basis of 48:22 (which occurs in similar form in 57:21; 66:24). A. Kuenen (*Historisch-critisch Onderzoek*, Vol. II, pp. 137-145. 2nd ed., Leiden, 1889) dated 50-51; 54-55 (and perhaps 49) *after* 536, though written at least in part by the Second Isaiah. W. H. A. Kosters ("Deutero- en Trito-Jezaja,"

TT 30 [1896] 577-623) affirmed that 49:12-26; 51:1-52:12; 54-55 were written in Palestine; including the Servant poems, he denies that the Second Isaiah wrote anything in 49-55 (similarly T. K. Cheyne, Isaiah in the "Polychrome" Bible. New York, 1898). L. Seinecke (*Der Evangelist des Alten Testaments.* Leipzig, 1870), R. Kittel (6th ed. of Knobel's commentary, 1898), and R. Levy (*Deutero-Isaiah,* pp. 12, 220. London, 1925) believe that 49-55 were written in Palestine after the return of the Exiles in 536 (a return that, according to Kosters, never took place). E. Sellin at first (*Serubbabel.* Leipzig, 1899) dated 49-55 between 515 and 500 B.C., but later (*Einleitung in das Alte Testament.* Leipzig, 1910) after the conquest of Babylon by Cyrus in 538 but before the return of the Exiles; this latter view is also that of C. H. Cornill (*Einleitung in die kanon. Bücher des Alten Testaments.* 7th ed., Tübingen, 1913), W. W. Baudissin (*Einleitung in die Bücher des Alten Testaments*), and W. Staerk (BWAT 14, Leipzig, 1913).

The division of Is. 40-55 into two books from the pen of the Second Isaiah has been attacked, from the point of view of H. Gunkel's "Gattungskritik," by H. Gressmann (ZAW 34 [1914] 254-297), L. Köhler (Beih. ZAW 37. Giessen, 1923), S. Mowinckel (ZAW N.F. 8 [1931] 87-112, 242-260), and P. Volz (*Jesaja II,* KAT, Leipzig, 1932). They conceive Is. 40-55 as a collection of detached poems composed by the Second Isaiah, arranged without strict logical order.[17] The number of separate units is reckoned at 49 (Gressmann), 70 (Köhler), and, not counting the Servant poems, 41 (Mowinckel) or 50 (Volz). According to Volz, the arrangement is due to the Second Isaiah; according to Mowinckel, to a disciple of his, identified by K. Elliger (BWANT 63. Stuttgart, 1933) with the Third Isaiah, who wrote considerable parts of 40-55.

d. The Servant poems. Usually the poems on the Servant of the Lord are identified with 42:1-4; 49:1-6; 50:4-9; 52:13-53:12. Some critics add 42:5-7 (or 42:5-9); 49:7-9a; 50:1-3 [10 f.]. C. C. Torrey (cf. *a,* above) considerably extends the list of Servant passages to include other parts of 40-55 and even 61-62. Some critics attribute the last poem (52:13-53:12) to a different author, either because its style and diction are like that of the Third Isaiah (E. Sellin, NKZ 41 [1930] 73-93, 145-173; ZAW N.F. 14 [1937] 207; K. Elliger, BWANT, 11. Stuttgart, 1933) or because of its contents (P. Volz, *Jesaja II,* KAT, Leipzig, 1932). On the relation of the poems to the Second Isaiah five different views have been de-

---

[17] See also: S. Mowinckel, "Neuere Forschungen zu Deuterojesaja, Tritojesaja" u.s.w., *Acta Orientalia* 1 (1937) 1-40. W. Caspari, *Lieder und Gottessprüche der Rückwanderer* (*Jes. 40-55*). Beih. ZAW 65. Giessen, 1934. Caspari assigns the individual poems to separate authors. O. Eissfeldt (*Einleitung in das Alte Testament,* pp. 377-381) recognizes the "Gattungen" represented in the poem of Is. 40-55, but defends the common authorship of the whole.

fended: 1. They were written by the Second Isaiah as part of his book (e.g. E. König, *The Exiles' Book of Consolation.* Edinburgh, 1899; G. Füllkrug, *Der Gottesknecht des Deuterojesaja.* 1899; K. Marti, *Jesaja,* KHC, Tübingen, 1900; J. Ley, in TSK [1901] 659-669; E. Sellin, *Mose.* 1922; S. H. Blank, in HUCA XV [1940] 20). 2. They were composed by the Second Isaiah before the rest of his book and were inserted by him into it (e.g., T. K. Cheyne, *Introduction to the Book of Isaiah.* London, 1895. A. Condamin, RB [1908] 162 ff. E. Sellin, *Einleitung in das Alte Testament,* p. 77. R. Levy, *Deutero-Isaiah,* pp. 138. London, 1925). 3. They were composed by the Second Isaiah after his book and added by him to it (M. G. Glazebrook, *Studies in the Book of Isaiah.* Oxford, 1910. J. Fischer, *Is. 40-55 und die Perikopen des Gottesknecht,* AA VI, 4-5. Münster, 1916. W. Rudolph, in ZAW N.F. 2 [1925] 90-114. J. Hempel, ZST 7 [1929-30] 631-660). 4. They were composed by an earlier author and inserted by the Second Isaiah into his book (e.g., C. J. Bredenkamp, *Der Prophet Jesaja erlaütert.* 1886-1887. J. Wellhausen, *Israelitische und Jüdische Geschichte,* p. 152, n. 1. W. Staerk, *Die Ebed-Jahwe-Lieder in Jes. 40 ff.,* p. 138. 1913). 5. Written by a later author, they were added to the book by a redactor (B. Duhm, *Jesaja.* M. Schian, *Die Ebed-Jahwe-Lieder in Jes. 40-66.* 1894. A. Bertholet, *Zu Jes. 53.* 1899. R. Kittel, *Zur Theologie des Alten Testaments,* pp. 22 f. 1899. L. Lauc, in TSK [1904] 319-379. R. H. Kennett, *The Servant of the Lord.* London, 1911. F. Feldmann, *Isaias II.* Exeg. Handbuch z. A. T. Münster, 1926).

e. The composition of Is. 56-66. With variations in the date, the following critics follow B. Duhm in attributing these chapters to Third Isaiah: E. Littmann, *Über die Abfassungszeit des Tritojesaja* (1899). A. Zillessen, "'Tritojesaja' und Deuterojesaja," ZAW 26 (1906) 231-276. G. E. Box, *The Book of Isaiah* (1908). K. Elliger, *Die Einheit des Tritojesaja.* BWANT III, 9. Stuttgart, 1928; "Der Prophet Tritojesaja," ZAW N.F. 8 (1931) 112-141; *Deuterojesaja und sein Verhältnis zu Tritojesaja.* BWANT IV, 11. 1933. H. Odeberg, *Trito-Isaiah* (Uppsala, 1931). E. Sellin in NKZ [1930] 73-93, 145-173.

Others, on the contrary, attribute the separate parts of Is. 56-66 to individual writers: T. K. Cheyne, *Introduction to Isaiah; Jewish Religious Life after the Exile,* p. xvi (New York and London, 1901). W. H. A. Kosters, in TT 30 (1896) 577-623. K. Cramer, *Der Geschichtliche Hintergrund der Kap. 56-66 im Buch Jesaja* (Dorpat, 1905). K. Budde, *Geschichte der althebräischen Literatur,* p. 177 (Leipzig, 1909). M. Buttenwieser, in JBL 38 (1919) 94-112. J. Marty, *Les chap. 56-66 du livre d'Esaïe* (Paris, 1924). R. Levy, *Deutero-Isaiah,* pp. 30-32. R. Abramowski, "Zum literarischen Problem des Tritojesaja" (TSK 96/97 [1925] 90-143). P. Volz, *Jesaja II* (KAT. Leipzig, 1932). A. Lods, *Les prophètes d'Israël,* pp. 309 f.

B. The Date of Is. 40-66

a. The date of Is. 40-48. With the exception of C. C. Torrey (cf. above), who dates Is. 34-35; 40-66 about 400 B.C., and of the rare critics who still attribute Is. 40-66 to the prophet Isaiah, it is generally recognized that the Second Isaiah wrote chs. 40-48 shortly before the armies of Cyrus of Persia took Babylon in 538. In 1870 L. Seinecke inferred from 44:26 that Cyrus had already conquered Babylon and had issued his decree allowing the Jews to return to Jerusalem, but in view of the abundant evidence for a slightly earlier date, this theory has been generally rejected. The historical background of Is. 40-48 seems clear, unless the most significant items are spurious, as C. C. Torrey has attempted to prove.

It is evident that Is. 40-48 was written after the destruction of Jerusalem in 586 B.C. Judah's capital and other cities had been destroyed and depopulated (44:26, 28; cf. 49:8, 19; 51:3). Israel had been deported from its land and scattered to the four winds (41:8 f.; 42:22; 43:5 f.; 45:13; cf. 49:5 f., 19-21; 52:9). In his holy anger Jehovah had thus punished his people for their sins (40:2, 27; 42:24 f.; 43:28; 48:10; cf. 50:1; 51:17-52:12; 54:7 f.), but now he has forgiven them and is on the point of restoring their fortunes (40:1 f., 9-11; 41:9-14; 42:14-16; 43:1-8; cf. 49:5 f., 13; 54:7 f.). Moreover, it was Babylon, still the mistress of the world (47) as she was in the period 605-538, whose power had crushed Judah (47:6) and brought the Jews captive to Babylonia (43:14; 48:20). Therefore Jehovah's vengeance will soon overtake disastrously the great city of the Chaldeans (43:14; 47; 48:14).

It is obvious from all this that the tragedy of 586 is some years in the past and that the Second Isaiah is addressing the exiles in Babylonia. He is convinced that the sufferings of the Jews are at an end and that Cyrus (44:28; 45:1) will deliver them from exile. Cyrus king of Anzan deposed his sovereign Astyages of Media about 550, conquered Lydia in 546 and Babylon in 538. Before 546, the Second Isaiah could not have regarded Cyrus as the restorer of the fortunes of the Jews. For it is clear that Cyrus had initiated his great conquests (41:2 f.; 45:1-4; 46:11; 48:14 f.) and is on his way toward Babylon (41:25; 43:14). But since the conquest of Babylon is still in the future (47; 48:14), most critics have concluded that the Second Isaiah wrote Is. 40-48 between 546 and 539, either at one time (about 540) or, according to J. Ley (*Historische Erklärung des 2. Teils des Buches Jesajas.* 1893), G. Füllkrug (*Der Gottesknecht* u.s.w.), and W. B. Stevenson (BZAW 66 [1936] 89-96), in successive years during the period 546-539 (or 555-539, 547-538). J. Begrich (*Studien zu Deuterojesaja,* BWANT IV, 25. Stuttgart, 1938) says that the Second Isaiah wrote between 553 and 546. M. Haller (*Festschrift für H. Gunkel,* pp. 261-277) believes that Is. 41-42; 44-46; 48 are a series of oracles addressed to Cyrus and presented to him personally by the Second Isaiah himself, who was (like Nehemiah later) a courtier of the king of Persia.

b. The date of Is. 49-55. The historical background of these chapters is far less obvious than in the preceding ones. It is true that the Jews are still pining for a restoration, living in foreign lands (49:5 f., 19-21; 52:9), as a divine punishment for their sins (50:1; 51:17-52:12; 54:7 f.), but looking forward to an imminent act of God in their favor (49:5 f., 13; 54:7 f.). But no reference is made again to the conquests of Cyrus, to the fall of Babylon, and to the deliverance of the Jews from Babylonian captivity. The language of chs. 49-55 is so vague that there is less unanimity in fixing their date. It has been inferred from the passages just listed and from others (49:26) that Cyrus's conquest of Babylon in 538 is still in the future. J. Fischer (Isaias II. *Die Heilige Schrift des Alten Testaments,* p. 6. Bonn, 1939), C. Steuernagel (*Einleitung in das Alte Testament,* p. 524), and others conclude that all of Is. 40-55 was written at the same time, before 538. On the contrary, Cornill, Baudissin, Sellin, and Staerk, as we have seen (cf. A: *c*) would date chs. 49-55 after the fall of Babylon but before the Exiles returned to Jerusalem, or in 538-536. As a matter of fact, the triumphal march of the Exiles to Zion, on a smooth highway through a desert miraculously transformed into an oasis, is predicted in both chs. 40-48 (40:3-5; 41:18 f.; 43:19 f.; 48:20 f.) and chs. 49-55 (51: 10 f.; 52:7-12; 55:12 f.), but these imaginative descriptions of a New Exodus are more in the nature of pilgrim songs than actual reports of an historically questionable return to Zion of numerous Jews, soon after 538. As B. Duhm clearly saw, "the vessels of Jehovah" in 52:11 are not necessarily the Temple vessels taken to Babylonia by Nebuchadnezzar and restored, if we believe the Chronicler, by Cyrus.

Later dates for the composition of chs. 49-55 have also been proposed. According to G. Füllkrug (*Der Gottesknecht* u.s.w.), the Second Isaiah wrote 49:1-52:12 in Babylonia shortly after 538, 52:13-53:12 upon his arrival in Palestine with the returned Exiles; 54-55 were written, after the departure of the Exiles, by a Jew who remained in Babylonia. R. Kittel (cf. A: *c*), though ascribing chs. 49-55 to the Second Isaiah, dates them later than 536, as also W. H. Kosters and T. K. Cheyne (cf. A: *c*), who deny that they were written by the author of chs. 40-48. In general there is a tendency to accept this opinion of Kittel (so recently P. Volz, *Jesaja II,* p. xxxiv). In reality, however, there are no positive clues for the date of chs. 49-55. They deal with the present misery and future glory of Zion, to which Jews dispersed to the ends of the earth will come after their God has transformed the deserts into well-watered luxuriant gardens. Such apocalyptic dreams could have been written at any time between 586 and 444, to encourage the Jews during one of the most depressing periods of their history.

c. The date of the Servant poems (42:1-4; 49:1-6; 50:4-9; 52:13-53:12). As we have seen (A: *d*) these poems have been variously assigned to the pen of the Second Isaiah, or to authors living in an earlier or a later period. Here again we lack all evidence for an exact date within the period 586-444 B.C.

d. The date of Is. 56-66. The critics who attribute these chapters to a single author (see A: *e*), assign them to the following periods: after 536 (L. Glahn, *Der Prophet der Heimkehr*), about 516 (K. Elliger, E. Sellin), about 457-445 (B. Duhm, 1892; E. Littmann, 1899, and many others [Cheyne, Kosters, Kittel, Gressmann, Marti, Cornill, Budde, Zillessen, etc.]), a few years before 400 (H. Odeberg), or about 400 (C. C. Torrey).

The critics who consider Is. 56-66 as a collection of poems of different authors vary likewise in their dating. The following periods have been suggested: 700-400 (R. Abramowski), 600-400 (K. Budde, in E. Kautzsch, *Die Heilige Schrift des Alten Testaments,* 4th ed. Tübingen, 1922), 515-200 (except for 56:9-57:21, which may be exilic; K. Cramer), 538-445 (J. Marty), 500-400 (S. Mowinckel). How the single poems are dated may be illustrated through the conclusions of two recent critics. P. Volz (*Jesaja II,* p. 200) distributes the separate sections as follows: 56:9-57:13 (pre-exilic); 63:7-64:12 (H. 63:7-64:11) (about 585); 66:1 f. (about 520); 63:1-6 (500-450); 56:1-8; 57:14-21; 58:1-14; 59:9 ff.; 61 (500-400); 65; 66:3-24 (after 331). O. Eissfeldt (*Einleitung in das Alte Testament,* p. 387) would date chs. 56-66 in general about 520-516, but admits that individual sections may belong to other periods: 57:1-13 (before 587); 63:7-64:12 (H. 63:7-64:11) (soon after 587); 66:1-4 (before 538); 65 (400-200).

The variety of opinion exhibited in this necessarily incomplete conspectus shows that Is. 56-66 contains no definite clue for exact dating within the Persian and Hellenistic periods (538-200). From the fact that whoever wrote 57:1-13; 65:1-15; 66:15-17 saw with his own eyes Jews practicing idolatry, it cannot be inferred that these sections were written before 586 (in the case of 57) or after 331 (in the case of 65; 66), as Volz and Eissfeldt conclude, for we know that the attraction of heathenism persisted in some Jewish circles at least until the Maccabean period. Nor is there any conclusive reason for identifying these idolatrous Jews with the Samaritans (so C. Steuernagel, *Einleitung in das Alte Testament,* pp. 526 f.) or with their half-heathen ancestors (so A. Lods, *Les prophètes,* p. 311). This clear-cut division of the Jewish congregation into the pious and the wicked, which is attested in the Psalms and the Proverbs, is too vague an indication of date to be utilized. Since the Temple seems to be standing (56:5, 7), we are in the period after 516; but the reference to the walls of Jerusalem (62:6) is too vague to determine whether it was

written before or after the rebuilding of the walls in 444. In general, however, the period 450-350 seems the most appropriate for most of Is. 56-66.

C. The Place of Origin of Is. 40-66

a. The Second Isaiah lived, according to the generally held view, in
Babylonia. Other countries have, however, been regarded as his domicile:
Northern Phoenicia or the Lebanon (B. Duhm, *Jesaja*, HKAT, 1892.
A. Causse, *Les dispersés d'Israel*, p. 35. Paris, 1929); Egypt (H. Ewald,
Die Propheten des alten Bundes. 1840-1841, 2nd ed. 1867-1868; *History of
Israel*, Vol. V, p. 42. London, 1874. K. Marti, *Jesaja*, p. xv. G. Hölscher,
Die Propheten, pp. 321 f., 373); Palestine, or more precisely Judea (L.
Seinecke, *Der Evangelist des Alten Testaments*, 1870. W. H. Cobb,
JBL 27 [1908] 48-64. J. A. Maynard, JBL 36 [1917] 213-224; *The Birth of
Judaism*, pp. 25-38. London, 1928. M. Buttenwieser, JBL 38 [1919] 94-112.
C. C. Torrey, *The Second Isaiah*, p. 53. S. Mowinckel, ZAW N.F. 8 [1931]
244. L. Finkelstein, *The Pharisees*, Vol. II, p. 629. S. H. Blank, in HUCA
XV [1940] 29, n. 55). M. Haller (FRLANT 19 [1923] 1, p. 277) surmises
that the Second Isaiah lived at the court and camp of Cyrus. Some critics,
as we have seen (A: *c*), believe that the Second Isaiah wrote chs. 40-48
in Babylonia and 49-55 either in Babylonia before the return of the Exiles
or in Palestine after it. These scholars, who place the residence of the
Second Isaiah outside of Babylonia, attribute to him all of chs. 40-55 (with
the possible exception of the Servant poems).

b. The Third Isaiah, or the various authors of Is. 56-66, according to
the consensus of critics, lived in Palestine; according to G. Hölscher (*Die
Propheten*, pp. 374-379), however, these chapters were written in Egypt,
like the rest of Is. 40-66.

D. The Servant of the Lord

In an attempt to identify the protagonist of the four Servant poems
(42:1-4; 49:1-6; 50:4-9; 52:13-53:12) almost every conceivable possibility has been suggested by critics. The various theories fall into two
groups: those in which the Servant is the personification of Israel or its
noblest part and those in which he is an individual. The first type of theory
is more prevalent in Judaism, the second in Christianity. If the word
"Israel" in 49:3 is a gloss, as many exegetes believe, it is the earliest trace
of the first type of interpretation, which is also attested in the LXX of
42:1 ("*Jacob*, my servant . . . *Israel*, my elect . . ."). It was defended
by Jews in the time of Origen (*Contra Celsum* 1:55) and prevailed with
Rashi (d. 1105), Ibn Ezra (d. 1167), and later Jewish scholars. Nevertheless, the individualistic (Messianic) interpretation of Is. 53 also is
attested in ancient Judaism (Enoch 38:2; 46:4; 47:1, 4; 53:6; 62:5 f.; the

Targum of the Prophets dated in the third century A.D.).[18] Whether Jesus identified himself with the Servant of the Lord or not (Luke 4:17-21; 7:22 = Matth. 11:5; cf. C. C. Torrey, JBL 48 [1929] 31 f.; on various modern views on the question see H. J. Holtzmann, *Lehrbuch der Neutestam. Theologie*, Vol. I, p. 358, n. 3. 2nd ed. Tübingen, 1911), it is certain that the Suffering Servant of Is. 53 was identified with Jesus by members of the apostolic church (Acts 8:32-35; Hebr. 9:28; I Pet. 2:22-25; cf. J. H. Ropes, JBL 48 [1929] 37-39).

a. The Servant is Israel. This theory was defended by a number of German scholars between 1900 and 1922 (see the list in E. König, *Jesaja*, p. 463), but with the exception of E. König (pp. 453-463) and O. Eissfeldt (*Der Gottesknecht bei Deuterojesaja*. Halle, 1933; *Einleitung in das Alte Testament*, pp. 381-383) it seems to have been abandoned in Germany in recent years. It is prevalent, however, in English-speaking countries: e.g., C. G. Montefiore, *Lectures on the Origin and Growth of Religion*, etc., p. 276. 3rd ed. London, 1897. W. E. Addis, *Expos. Times* [1906-1907] 6. R. H. Kennett, *The Servant of the Lord*, pp. 10, 92. G. A. Smith, *Isaiah* (Expositor's Bible), Vol. II, pp. 256 ff. London, N. D. A. C. Knudson, *The Religious Teaching of the Old Testament*, p. 301, New York, 1918. H. J. Cadbury, *National Ideals in the Old Testament*, pp. 202 f. New York, 1920. J. A. Bewer, *The Literature of the Old Testament*, pp. 208-213. E. A. Leslie, *Old Testament Religion*, p. 227. B. D. Cohon, *The Prophets*, pp. 193-197. New York, 1939.

b. The Servant is an individual.

1. A historical character of past or contemporary history. E. Sellin, in the course of forty years, has successively identified the Servant with Zerubbabel, Jehoiachin (cf. L. A. Baehler, *De messianische Heilsverwachting*, 1893), Moses, and the Second Isaiah (cf. *Serubbabel*, 1898, and ZAW N.F. 14 [1937] 177). In addition to these, the following characters are said to be the Servant: Jeremiah (Saadia Gaon, d. 942; L. Seinecke, *Geschichte des Volkes Israel*, Vol. II, p. 71. Göttingen, 1876), Josiah (Abrabanel), and others. According to S. H. Blank (HUCA XV [1940] 18-32), the Servant represents Israel, but the tragic career of Jeremiah inspired some of the traits of the Suffering Servant.

2. An unnamed contemporary of the author: a teacher of the Torah afflicted with leprosy (B. Duhm, on 42:1, in his commentary of 1892), an exilic martyr (M. Schian, *Die Ebed-Jahwe-Lieder*), or a pious sufferer (A. Marmorstein in ZAW N.F. 3 [1926] 265). A. Bertholet (*Zu Jes 53*. 1899) saw in 53:1-11a, which he considered interpolated, an allusion to the scribe Eleazar, who died a martyr about 168 B.C. (II Macc. 6:18-31).

[18] See G. Dalman, *Der leidende und der sterbende Messias*, pp. 27 ff. 1888. H. L. Strack and P. Billerbeck, *Kommentar zum Neuen Testament aus Talmud und Midrasch*, Vol. I, pp. 481-485. Munich, 1922. E. Seidelin, in *Zeitschr. f. d. Neutest. Wissensch.*, 35 (1936) 194-281.

3. The Second Isaiah himself. The autobiographical interpretation of the Servant poems was considered possible by the Ethiopian eunuch of Acts 8:34. After this notion had been advanced for 50:4-9 by some Jews in the time of Jerome and for 49:1-6; 50:4-9 by Rashi, it was revived by S. Mowinckel (*Der Knecht Jahwäs.* Giessen, 1921). Although he soon modified his views (ZAW N.F. 8 [1931] 245-257), his theory has been adopted by H. Gunkel (*Ein Vorläufer Jesu.* Bern, 1921; "Knecht Jahwes" in *Religion in Geschichte und Gegenwart.* 2nd ed., Tübingen, 1927-1932), M. Haller (FRLANT XIX, Pt. 1, pp. 261-277; *Schriften des Alt. Test. in Auswahl,* Vol. II, Pt. 3, p. 32. 2nd ed. Göttingen, 1925), E. Balla (FRLANT XIX, Pt. 1, pp. 245-247), H. Schmidt (*Gott und Leid im Alten Testament,* pp. 30 f. Giessen, 1926), E. Sellin (NKZ 41 [1930] 73-93, 145-173; ZAW N.F. 14 [1937] 177-217), K. Elliger (*Deuterojes. in seinem Verhältnis zu Tritojes,* BWANT IV, 11. Stuttgart, 1933), and P. Volz (*Jesaja II*).

4. The Messiah. J. W. Rothstein (*Die Genealogie des Königs Jojachin,* p. 156. 1902) regards the Servant as the Davidic dynasty. C. von Orelli (*Jesaja und Jeremia,* p. 174. Nördlingen, 1887) says that the Servant is "the genuine Israel, . . . a living individual figure, . . . the mediator for the redemption of Israel and of the foundation of the Kingdom of God." W. Rudolph (ZAW N.F. 2 [1925] 91; 5 [1928] 156-166) believes that the author recognized in a contemporary personality the promised Messiah (cf. R. Kittel, *Geschichte des Volkes Israel,* Vol. III, pp. 222-257). The following critics see in him the future Messiah in general, or in particular Jesus Christ: J. Ley (TSK [1899] 163-206; [1901] 663 f.), G. Füllkrug (*Der Gottesknecht* u.s.w.), L. Laue ("Die Ebed-Jahwe-Lieder," TSK [1904] 376-378), A. Condamin (*Le livre d'Isaïe,* pp. 338 ff. Paris, 1905), F. Feldmann (*Der Knecht Gottes* u.s.w., pp. 189 ff. Freiburg, 1907), D. S. Margoliouth (*Exposit. Times* [1908] p. 482; cf. 1909-1910, p. 3), E. Ziemer (*Jesajas 53 in der neueren Theologie,* 1912), J. Fischer (*Isaias 40-55 und die Perikopen vom Gottesknecht,* p. 198. AA 7, 4-5. Münster, 1916; *Wer ist der Ebed* u.s.w., pp. 80 ff. AA 8, 5. 1922; *Das Buch Isaias.* pp. 18 ff. Bonn, 1939), C. Bruston (Beih. ZAW 41 [1925] 33-44), J. S. van der Ploeg (*Les chants du Serviteur de Jahvé.* Paris, 1936).

5. The dying and resurrected god of vegetation (Tammuz-Adonis or Eshmun). H. Gressmann (*Der Ursprung der israelitische-jüdische Eschatologie,* pp. 324 ff.; *Deutsche Literaturzeit.* [1908] 1171) believed that a hymn in honor of Tammuz-Adonis inspired Is. 53 (cf. H. Gunkel in *Religion in Geschichte und Gegenwart,* col. 1543). W. Staerk (ZAW N.F. 3 [1926] 259 f.) sees in Is. 53 a mystery-cult hymn. A. Jeremias (*The Old Testament in the Light of the Ancient East,* Vol. II, p. 278. New York, 1911) sees in the Servant "a figure of Tammuz embellished by the prophet." G. H. Dix (JTS 26 [1925] 241 ff.) is inclined to accept this

theory, and L. Dürr (*Ursprung und Ausbau der isrealit.-jüdisch. Heilands-erwartung*, pp. 125 ff. Berlin, 1925. ZDMG [1924] lxvii f.) believes that the Babylonian New Year festival influenced the notion of the Servant. S. Mowinckel (ZAW N.F. 8 [1931] 256 f.) comes to the surprising conclusion that the Servant was the Second Isaiah himself who, after his martyrdom, was celebrated by his disciples as a cult-hero, and thus was regarded as a divine being, like Adonis.

c. The Servant is both Israel and an individual. Franz Delitzsch (*Bibl. Kommentar über den Propheten Jesaja*, p. 432. 4th ed., 1889) conceives the Servant under the figure of a pyramid in which the basis is Israel as a whole, the middle levels are Israel according to the spirit, and the apex is the Redeemer (cf. the 6th ed. of Knobel's commentary revised by A. Dillmann and R. Kittel [1898], pp. 459 f.). C. C. Torrey (*The Second Isaiah*, pp. 135-150) regards the conception of the Servant as "shifting" from a collective to an individual meaning: the Servant is Israel, Israel's representative, Abraham, Jacob, a personification "of the present Jewish nation," "the coming leader who is destined to 'restore Jacob and gather Israel,'" the Messiah. S. A. Cook (*Cambridge Ancient History*, Vol. III, pp. 492 f.) likewise regards "the conception of the Servant as, on the whole, a fluid one." M. Löhr (*Alttestamentliche Religions-Geschichte*, p. 119. 2nd ed., Berlin, 1919) believes that the Second Isaiah erroneously considered the Servant as a personification of Israel but that the author of the Servant poems really conceived him as an individual.

In conclusion, it is clear from this conspectus of critical opinion that several of the problems raised by Is. 40-66 are insoluble owing to the lack of definite data. All the solutions proposed are possible, though some are less probable than others. All that seems certain is that Is. 40-66 was written between 586 and 350, by one or more writers, in Babylonia or Palestine (or both). The present writer is inclined to prefer the theory of B. Duhm to that of C. C. Torrey, and to ascribe chs. 40-55 to the Second Isaiah, dating 40-48 in Babylonia shortly before 538 and 49-55 shortly after that year. Whether this second part was written in Palestine, as has been inferred, for instance, from 52:11, or in Babylonia, is uncertain. Chapters 56-66 seem to have been written in Palestine in the period 516-400, either by one author, the Third Isaiah, or by several.

2. The Style of Is. 40-55 (and 56-66)

The differences in style, diction, and thought between the genuine writings of Isaiah and Is. 40-55 are so obvious and have been listed so often that it seems unnecessary to present the evidence again. It is sufficient to say that the conciseness, variety, and concreteness of Isaiah's poetry contrast sharply with the eloquent verbosity, repetitiousness, and vagueness of Is. 40-55. Isaiah belongs to the golden age of Hebrew literature, Is. 40-55 to its silver age. The difference is that between naïve, unconscious art and deliberate striving for majestic eloquence by means of rhetorical devices. A similar difference in prose can be noted between the simplicity of J or of II Sam. 9-20 and the sonorous and ample sentences of Deuteronomy. It should perhaps be noted that we are here concerned with the original Hebrew text and not with the English versions. The magnificent grandeur of Is. 40-55 and of Deuteronomy lent itself particularly well to rendition into superb Elizabethan prose. Accordingly, Is. 40-55 and Deuteronomy are more impressive literary masterpieces in the Authorized Version than in the original Hebrew.

The Second Isaiah (Is. 40-55) was a theologian and a poet rather than a prophet, although in 40:6-8 (omitting the gloss "surely the people is grass" at the end of 40:7) he seems to report poetically his prophetic call. This "call," however, lacks the psychological reality of the initial experiences through which the prophets from Amos to Jeremiah, and even Ezekiel, became heralds of the divine word. This disembodied "voice" (40:3, 6) is even more abstract than the spectral voice that spoke similarly to Eliphaz (Job 4:12-21), whom no one would consider a prophet. In all probability the Second Isaiah wrote this account of his "call" more under the influence of Eliphaz than of the great prophets.

The Second Isaiah is more important as a thinker than as a poet. But he was unquestionably a genuine poet, though hardly, even in his own sphere, "supreme and unrivalled among the great poets of the world" (C. C. Torrey, *The Second Isaiah,* p. 91). *Mutatis mutandis,* the Second Isaiah is the Milton of Hebrew poetry, while the author of the Book of Job is its Shakespeare. "Paradise Regained" could well be the title of Is. 40-55.

The Second Isaiah employs a singing style. He lifts up with strength (40:9) "a voice of singing" (48:20), "a voice like a trumpet" (58:1) and listens to "the voice of melody" (51:3). Again and again impassioned hymns burst from his lips (45:8): he calls on the heavens and the earth to sing (44:23; 49:13), he cries, "Sing unto the Lord a new song" (42:10-13), and even desolate Zion is invited to lift her voice in song (52:7-12; 54:1-10). The dominant note in chs. 40-55 is rapturous enthusiasm, triumphant joy, in spite of other moods expressed in melancholic reminiscence (43:22-28), bitter sarcasm for the idol worshipers (40:19 f.; 41:6 f.; 44:9-20), earnest exhortation for Israel (48), imaginary forensic debates (41:1-5, 21-24), mock lamentation for Babylon (47), and the inexpressible pathos of the Servant's vicarious suffering (52:13-53:12). But even in these passages the underlying note is one of exultation for Jehovah's invincible sway and imminent triumph. The work as a whole is a rhapsody.

This enthusiasm, which gives to our poet's style a dithyrambic quality, is connected with another characteristic of his poetic genius, an extremely vivid imagination. This is so pronounced that, on the one hand, it robs him of a clear perception of reality and, on the other, creates a world of fancy more actual to him than his surroundings. This partial blindness to actuality and this vision of imaginary scenes explain the inability of critics to determine accurately and convincingly the date and habitation of the author.

In his portrayal of Jews and Gentiles alike the Second Isaiah draws on his imagination rather than on his observations. With poetic license it could perhaps be said that Israel was scattered to the ends of the earth, at the four points of the compass (43:5 f.; 49:12, where we should read "from the east" instead of "from afar," and "land of Sewēnîm" [i.e., Syene or Assuan in the extreme south of Egypt; cf. Ez. 29:10; 30:6] instead of "land of Sinim"). But whether in Palestine or in the lands of their Dispersion, the Jews were assuredly no longer "a people robbed and spoiled," hiding in holes and pining in dungeons (42:22; cf. 42:7; 49:9, 24 f.; 51:14; 52:2). The poet's fancy pictures their condition in the darkest colors in order to enhance the brilliance of their coming triumph: the "worm" Israel becomes "a new threshing-sledge" that will reduce the mountains to dust (41:14 f.). Moreover, if Israel is the Servant suffering and dying vicariously for the salvation of mankind (as the present writer believes), its present misery and plight must needs be magnified beyond the bounds of actual fact.

The same fanciful hyperbole obliterates prosaic actuality in the description of the Gentiles. His incandescent imagination carries him to fantastic extremes. On the one hand, the heathen are such utter fools that they prostrate themselves in worship before a wooden figure which their hands have carved (44:9-20). On the other hand, Cyrus the Persian is a worshiper of Jehovah, the only true God (41:25), and becomes the instrument of God for the annihilation of Gentile kingdoms (41:2, 25; 45:1-3), particularly Babylonia (44:28; cf. 43:14; 47), and the glorification of Israel (44:28; 45:4, 13). One is tempted to say with Isidore Loeb (*La littérature des pauvres dans la Bible*, p. 223. Paris, 1892) that this idealized Cyrus is "a kind of pagan Messiah by the side of the Jewish Messiah."

In his enthusiasm our poet becomes unaware of the logical inconsistency between his expressions of hatred and contempt for the Gentiles and his expectation that they will soon be converted to the true God. On the one hand, the heathen are subordinated to Israel and have no value in comparison with the Jews: Egypt, Ethiopia, and Saba are paid out as ransom for the deliverance of Israel (43:3 f.), the Gentiles have oppressed Israel without cause (52:3-5; cf. 47:6), and will soon carry them, as if beasts of burden, back to Jerusalem, lick the dust of Jewish feet (49:22 f.), and become the chained slaves of Israel (45:14; see, however, B. Duhm's emendation in his commentary); no uncircumcised and unclean person will ever enter Jerusalem again (52:1). At the other extreme, the poet envisages the day in which every knee shall bend before Jehovah and every tongue shall swear in his name (45:23 f.). Our poet bequeathed to Judaism the contradictory notion of Jehovah as both the King of the Jews (43:15) and the sole universal God of all mankind (45:6, 22; cf. 42:10-12).

The poet's imagination is so vivid that he lives in the magnificent future rather than in the depressing present. The glorious redemption of Israel blinds him to his actual environment. God rushes into battle like a hero (42:13), idolaters and idols flee before him and go into captivity (46:1 f.), the Jews, redeemed by their God, are to flee from Babylon (48:20; 52:11 f.) and will march to Zion over a fantastic highway across the desert, which is miraculously changed into a garden of Eden (40:3-5; 41:17-20; 42:16; 43:1 f., 19-21; 48:21; 49:9b-13; 51:9 f.; 52:12): truly a spectacle to call forth the astonished delight of heathen and wild beasts (42:10-13; 43:20) and the jubilant hymns of Zion (54:1)—and of heaven, earth, mountains, and forests (44:23; 49:13).

The poet's intense enthusiasm, fanciful Oriental imagination, and burning passion lift him above the world of reality to the realm of fantastic dreams. He creates this Utopia by means of imaginative flashes and not, like some of the later apocalyptic writers, according to careful architectural plans and elevations, nor, like the authors of the Priestly document, according to the juristic corollaries of theological principles. It is in vain that one looks for logical sequence and arrangement in his poems, much less for a unified structure, such as Dante's amazing architectural arrangement of the invisible world. His book is an incoherent succession of ecstatic shouts; his thoughts are poured out glowing and fluid, like molten metal before it has hardened into a definite shape.

Consequently, the dilemma posed by critics—is the work a unit or an anthology of separate poems?—is meaningless. In his rushing flow of words, in his passionate outbursts, a few identical great thoughts and hopes reappear constantly without rational order, like stars shining intermittently through clouds carried onward by the wind. Isaiah 40-55 is neither a literary unit like the Book of Job nor an anthology like Lamentations: it is a passionate and effusively incoherent rhapsody in which the emotional moods, the dominant thoughts, and the prevalent style furnish the only bond uniting detached poems into a whole, just as rocks and earth are joined ephemerally into an avalanche precipitating downward on an Alpine slope. Like the momentum which throws the materials of an avalanche into chaotic confusion, so the enthusiasm of the author prevents an orderly and logical presentation of ideas, although there is occasionally an appeal to reason by means of dialectic arguments.

"A whirlpool of thoughts, a deluge of declarations, is poured out . . ."
(L. Köhler, *Deuterojesaja stilkritisch untersucht*. Beih. ZAW 37 [1923]
119).

When we pass from the general to the specific characteristics of the
Second Isaiah's style we note that they are also highly individual, although less unique. The originality consists chiefly in combining individual literary devices used separately by other authors.

The Second Isaiah is fond of figures of speech. He personifies not only
cities (Jerusalem: 51:17; 52:1 f.; 54:1; Babylon: 47) and Israel (the
Servant), but also nature (44:23; 49:13; 55:12; cf. 52:9), the points of
the compass (43:6), God's arm (40:10; 51:9), and his word (55:11). The
vicissitudes of Zion are graphically depicted under its personification: as
a bride (49:18; 54:5; cf. 62:5); as a wife forsaken (54:6 f.), though not
divorced (50:1); barren (54:1), and yet abundantly blessed with children (51:1-3); as a mother (49:17, 22 f.; 51:18-20) bereaved of her
children (49:20 f.; 51:20), and yet suddenly surrounded by far more
children than she had lost (49:20 f.; cf. 60:4 f.); and finally as a widow
whose husband is restored to her (54:4 f.).

Such personifications contribute to give to the poem a dramatic character. God, the author, Israel personified (49:1-6, etc.), Zion, mysterious
voices (40:3, 6; cf. 57:14), imaginary watchmen (52:8; cf. the guardians
in 62:6) are the principal *dramatis personae* speaking in dialogues or
monologues on the stage.

Like the personification of Zion as a bride, a mother, and a widow,
some of the imagery of the Second Isaiah is derived from family life
and expresses the author's intense emotional nature (49:15-18; cf. 61:10b;
62:5; 66:13). Other metaphors and similes likewise express deep pathos
(40:6-8, 11, 24; 42:3; 47:1-3, 8 f.; 50:9; 51:8; 53). Extreme exaggerations
in opposite directions, the infinitesimal and the immense, are inspired by
the author's unchecked imagination (40:15, 22, 31; 41:4 f.; 48:18 f.; 51:23).
A good example of his fancy, in addition to the previously noted transformation of the desert into the garden of Eden, is the picture of the New
Jerusalem with foundations of beryl and sapphires and with walls and
battlements of other precious gems (54:11 f.).

The diction and syntax of the Second Isaiah have peculiarities which
belong to the silver, rather than the golden age (before 586 B.C.) of
Hebrew literature. Characteristic expressions are listed by T. K. Cheyne
(*Introduction to the Book of Isaiah*, pp. 255-270), S. R. Driver (*Introduction to the Old Testament*), E. König (*Das Buch Jesaja*, pp. 331 f.), and
many others. Only a few striking examples need be mentioned here. In
the vocabulary the following words are particularly significant: *bārā'*
(to create, the technical term of P in Gen. 1) occurs twelve times in Is.
40-55 and three times in 56-66 but never in Job and other writings earlier

than 595 B.C., as also *'iyyîm* (islands and shores of the Mediterranean).
Some words occur for the first time in our author, at least in the meaning
which he gives to them: *pāṣaḥ* (to burst into song, 5 times in chs. 40-55;
elsewhere only Is. 14:7 and Ps. 98:4), *hālal* (in the technical sense of
praising God in song), *ḥēpheṣ* (in the sense of God's plan), *bāḥar* (referred to God's choice of Israel; cf. "my chosen one"), *ephes* (nothing),
"the arm of Jehovah," and others.

In the realm of syntax, the midrash *Wayyiqra' Rabbah* (ch. 10, §2)
already noted that the prophet, in his enthusiasm, often repeated his outcries: "Comfort ye, comfort ye my people" (40:1; see also 41:27; 43:11,
25; 48:11, 15; 51:9, 12, 17; 52:1, 11; cf. 57:6, 14, 19; 62:10; 65:1).

It has not been sufficiently recognized that <u>the language and thought
of the Second Isaiah were profoundly influenced by the Book of Job.</u>
Leaving the theological indebtedness of our author for a later section, we
may classify the linguistic influence of the Book of Job as follows:

1. Vocabulary. *a. Nouns and verbs*, in special meanings, which the
Second Isaiah took over from the Book of Job, have been classified and
listed by the present writer in JBL 46 (1927) 203. We should also add: *śûś*
or *śîś* (to exult) and *tohû* (emptiness, chaos). *b. Prepositions and other
particles* with an archaic or peculiar orthography: *minnî* (instead of *min*,
from; Is. 46:3 [*bis*], Judg. 5:14 [*bis*], seven times in the Psalms, and 19
times in Job), *bemô* (instead of *be*, in; Is. 43:2; 44:16, 19; cf. 25:10
(*kerê*), Ps. 11:2, and five times in Job), *'adê* (for *'ad*, as far as; Is. 26:4;
65:18; Num. 24:20, 24, six times in the Psalms, and twice in Job), *hēn*
(for *hinneh*, behold; 23 times in Is. 40-66, three times in late parts of Is.
1-39, 22 times in Job, and less frequently in other parts of the Old Testament), *lāmô* (for *lahem*, unto them; five times in Is. 43-53, ten times in
Job, 21 times in the Psalms, and occasionally in Deut. 32-33, Is. 16-35,
Hab., Prov. Lam.). *c. Aramaic words*: *'atāh* (to come; seven times in
Is. 40-56, four times in Job, occasionally in Deut. 33, Is. 21, Jer., Mic., Ps.,
Prov.).

2. Syntax. *a. Adverbs and conjunctions*: It is possible that the Second
Isaiah's characteristic liking for the negative particle *bal* (not; four times
in Is. 40-44; Job 41:15; ten times in Is. 14-35; often in the Psalms, rarely
elsewhere) and for the conjunction *aph* (also; 14 times in Is. 40-48, five
times in Is. 26-35, four times in Job, often in the Psalms, occasionally elsewhere) was influenced by Job. On the contrary, the Second Isaiah's excessive use of conjunctions (such as *lema'an*, in order that, 16 times),
peculiar negative particles (*ephes*, five times in Is. 40-56; Job 7:6), and
adverbs (*le'ōlām, tāmîd*, always) is foreign to Job's more poetic style.
Such abstract words indicating syntactical relations lend to the Second
Isaiah's style the tone of argumentation, of a legal plea, but detract from
poetic freshness, vividness, and charm. The discussion in Job is less

frenzied and less scholastic than in Is. 40-66, but far superior in literary beauty and distinction.

b. Participial sentences. One of the peculiarities of the Second Isaiah has often been noted without, however, perceiving that it is derived from the Book of Job: the series of clauses beginning with a participle and expressing the attributes of the deity. In Job, Ps. 104, and Is. 40 ff., these participles are used indiscriminately with or without the article. As a matter of fact, the article is frequently omitted in poetry when it would be required in good prose. This type of incompleted sentence may be illustrated with 40:22, "The one sitting upon the circle of the earth," etc. There is neither an antecedent for "the one sitting" nor a finite verb completing the sentence; the translation "it is He that sitteth" is unwarranted. With the article this construction occurs in: 40:22 f.; 43:16 f.; 44:26b-28; Job 5:10a; 9:5-7; Ps. 104:3, 10; Am. 5:9; 9:5 f. Without the article we find it in: 44:24-26a; 45:7, 18; 46:10 f.; 51:13, 15; cf. 56:8; 63:12 f.; Job 5:9, 10b, 12 f.; 9:8-10; 26:7-10; Ps. 104:2, 4, 13, 14; Am. 4:13; 5:8; Jer. 10:12. This list includes the clearest instances noticed by the present writer, but is not necessarily exhaustive. The expressions "thy [or Israel's] maker, creator, savior, redeemer," common in Is. 40-55, are irrelevant in this connection.

The Second Isaiah adopted this participial clause under the influence of the Book of Job. From Is. 40 ff. and Job it passed on to the late authors of Jer. 10 and of the doxologies of Amos. Ultimately the construction seems to be of Egyptian origin. It is hardly an accident that we find it in Ps. 104 and in its model, Ikhnaton's Hymn to Aton (text in N. de G. Davies, *The Rock Tombs of El Amarna*, Vol. VI, pp. 29 ff. London, 1908; translation in J. A. Breasted, *A History of Egypt*, pp. 371-376. New York, 1905; A. Erman, *The Literature of the Ancient Egyptians*, pp. 288 ff. London, 1927), lines 18-19: "The one who creates (*šhpr;* literally "the one who causes to become") the child (lit. "seed") in woman, the one who makes (*'ir*) the seed in man, the giver of life (*s'nh*) to the son in the body of his mother, the one soothing (*śgrḥ*) him so that he weep not, a nurse (*mn't*, noun) within the body! Giver (*dyw*) of breath to animate all that he has made!" A similar participial construction appears in much earlier Egyptian hymns (see A. Erman, *The Literature of the Ancient Egyptians*, pp. 137-149; 282-288).

3. Style. A number of figures of speech in Is. 40-55 seem to be derived from the Book of Job. God is a *gō'ēl* (kinsman, redeemer; Job 19:25), human life is military service (40:2; Job 7:1; 10:17; 14:14), men are like the grass that withers (40:7 f.; Job 8:12) or like worms (41:14, according to Duhm's emendation; Job 25:6), or like a garment which moths devour (51:8; Job 13:28). The Second Isaiah, however, fails to recapture the terse vividness and the superb diction of Job. Like most imitators, he

weakens the expressions of his model by unnecessary expansion. Job had said, "Shall any teach God knowledge?" (Job 21:22); but the Second Isaiah, opening wide the cataracts of his words, says, "With whom took he counsel, and who instructed him, and taught him the right path, and *taught him knowledge,* and caused him to know the way of understanding?" (40:14) Other instances of such rhetorical and pompous inflation of Job's transparently concise expressions will be found in 41:20 (cf. Job 12:9); 40:22; 45:12; 48:13; cf. 44:24 (cf. Job 9:8); 51:17, 20, 22 (cf. Job 21:20); 51:15 (cf. Job 26:12). In 53:9b, however, the Second Isaiah condenses Job 16:17 and 6:30.

Some scholars have discovered a Babylonian influence on the style of the Second Isaiah. If he lived in Babylonia about 540 B.C., an indirect contact on his part with Babylonian literature, through oral channels, is not impossible. A number of parallel expressions have been pointed out in the following publications: R. Kittel (ZAW 18 [1898] 149-162). A. Jeremias, *Das Alte Testament im Lichte des Alten Orients,* pp. 605 ff. (3rd ed., Leipzig, 1915). A. Jirku, *Altorientalischer Kommentar zum Alten Testament,* pp. 202 ff. (Leipzig, 1923). L. Dürr, *Ursprung und Ausbau der israelitischen-jüdischen Heilandserwartung,* pp. 125 ff. W. Rudolph (ZAW N.F. 2 [1925] 105, n. 2). F. Stummer (JBL 45 [1926] 171-189).

Less probable than the presence of echoes of Babylonian writings in Is. 40-55 is the alleged influence of Zoroastrianism on the thought of our author. A. von Gall (*Basileía toû Theoû,* pp. 175-188. Heidelberg, 1927) believes that our author derived his idea of the Kingdom of God from the teaching of Zoroaster and that the Servant of the Lord is a reflection of Gojomart, the Persian "Adam." C. E. Simcox (JAOS 57 [1937] 158-171) has noted some parallels between our book and the Avesta.

The striking similarity—obvious to every reader—between the style of 40-55 and 56-66 makes a special analysis of the latter section unnecessary. The differences between the two parts are more of subject matter than of expression. We note in 56-66 the same fantastic pictures of the future, the same enthusiasm, the same prolixity of diction. If anything, the less attractive features of the style of the Second Isaiah are intensified. If, as seems probable, the Second Isaiah did not write chs. 56-66, they were written by one or more authors whose thought and diction were dominated by Is. 40-55. Innumerable literary affinities have been pointed out in detail by H. Odeberg (*Trito-Isaiah. A Literary and Linguistic Analysis*). Characteristic expressions of the Second Isaiah will be noticed in 56:1; 57:11; 59:1, 19; 60:4, 9, 13, 16; 61:8, 11; 62:11; 65:17, and elsewhere. One difference may be worthy of notice: the Second Isaiah is chiefly influenced by the Book of Job, and somewhat less by the earlier prophetic books and the Pentateuch; in Is. 56-66 the influence of Job is insignificant compared with the influence of other Old Testament writings.

3. The Teaching of the Second Isaiah

The author of Is. 40-55 addressed his religious rhapsodies to Jews who were dejected, pessimistic, and disillusioned, during the decade 540-530 B.C. In chs. 40-48 he seems to have written especially for the Jews living in Babylonia, in 49-55 he may have contemplated a wider circle of readers, Israel scattered to the four winds and particularly the remnant in Jerusalem. Unless we can visualize in some measure his invisible audience, with its pressing problems and tormenting doubts, we fail to understand the author's purpose and the genesis of his message.

The economic situation of the Jews in Babylonia was steadily improving and was less critical than in Judea. Even the original Exiles of 597, if we believe Jeremiah (Jer. 29:5-7), were allowed free economic and social development in the villages around Nippur where they were settled. They were not slow in taking advantage of the opportunities offered by the richest country of Western Asia in that period—a country described in such glowing terms by an officer of Sennacherib that exile thereto could have seemed a privilege (II Kings 18:32). They soon became prosperous, at first as cultivators of the soil, but soon as administrators, merchants, and bankers.[19] Thus they were able to send contributions to their destitute brothers in Jerusalem (Zech. 6:9-15; the colossal sums mentioned by the Chronicler are fantastic exaggerations of actual gifts). There is no sign, among the Babylonian Jews, of the acute economic distress prevailing in Jerusalem until the time of Nehemiah, and well attested in the writings of Haggai and Malachi.

But in spite of their relative freedom and financial prosperity, the Jews in Babylonia were by no means happy. Some may have been homesick for Zion—though hardly as desperately as a later poet (Ps. 137) imagined. Many, however, were tormented by doubts and misgivings. The recent bankruptcy of the monarchy, the dispersion of the nation, and the cessation of the Temple worship seemed to leave no hope for a national and religious rebirth. The triumph of Nebuchadnezzar, which for Jeremiah was paradoxically a victory of Jehovah (Jer. 25:8 f.), could easily be construed as a humiliation of the national God, a sign of his helplessness before the Babylonian deities. Was he able to snatch Israel from mighty

[19] The business records of the banking firm Murashu Sons at Nippur, published by H. V. Hilprecht and A. T. Clay (The Babylonian Expedition of the University of Pennsylvania. Series A: vols. 9 and 10. Philadelphia, 1898, 1904; University of Pennsylvania. The Museum. Publications of the Babylonian Section II, 1. Philadelphia, 1912), illustrate the commercial activity of Babylonian Jews in the time of Artaxerxes I and Darius II (465-404 B.C.). For translation of significant documents and lists of Jewish names see E. Ebeling, *Aus dem Leben der Jüdischen Exulanten*. Berlin, 1914 (Wissenschaftl. Beilage zum Jahresbericht des Humboldt-Gymnasium).

Babylon (49:24)? Even the Jews who still believed in the overwhelming power of their god wondered why he appeared to have forgotten his people (40:27; 49:14), why he did not vindicate his honor by blotting out the transgression of Israel (43:25) and by preventing its utter annihilation (48:9-11). Admitting that Israel had been punished justly for its sins against Jehovah (42:24 f.; 43:22-28)—which some, however, denied, saying that aliens had oppressed the nation without cause (cf. 52:4)—and that Israel had been tried and refined in the furnace of affliction (48:10), they were, however, convinced that their guilt had been expiated and that in fact the punishment had been twice as great as the sin (40:2). Israel was afraid and dismayed (41:10, 13 f.), its faith was shaken: Jehovah had profaned his inheritance (47:6; cf. 43:28) and allowed his name to be blasphemed (52:5 f.).

Faced with this dejected mental attitude, the Second Isaiah was spurred to action. Being a thinker and a poet, rather than a prophet, he composed a book. His spiritual epic not only inflamed the faith of Israel, but surpassed all other writings of the Old Testament, not excepting the Books of Job and Daniel, in its influence on mankind. Reaching the highest level of Old Testament religion, he passed on the torch to Christianity and the world. By not only dispelling the doubts of his contemporaries, but by formulating religious and theological principles of universal validity, he endowed his words with permanent significance. We may consider separately the message for his day and the message for the future, even though they are not distinguished in his book.

As we have seen, the Jews were troubled by doubts about God's power and solicitude, and about the future of their nation. Though acutely conscious of his people's mental blindness and deafness (42:16-19), the author was deeply touched by their misery. He did not reprove them, as the earlier prophets, but with inexpressible tenderness he exclaimed, "Comfort ye, comfort ye my people, saith your God" (40:1). With extraordinary sagacity and understanding, he did not irritate the doubters with dialectic arguments, but won them over with moving appeals, with alluring hopes, and with impassioned oratory. To question God's power and wisdom was beyond his comprehension: "Do you not realize? Do you not hear? Has it not been told to you from the beginning? Have you not perceived from the founding of the earth? . . ." (40:21-26). But equally absurd was the thought that the almighty Creator of the world has forgotten Israel: "Why sayest thou, O Jacob, and speakest, O Israel, 'My way is hid from Jehovah . . .' Hast thou not known? Nor even heard? . . ." (40:27-31). In this manner the author persuades his readers that the power, wisdom, and kind solicitude of Jehovah are axiomatic eternal verities; to raise any doubts about them is inconceivable.

If Jehovah's ability and willingness to help human beings in their distress is admitted, then the future of Israel is no longer in doubt, provided that Jehovah's abiding loyalty to his people can be demonstrated convincingly. This is, however, the crucial point. At the time several objections were probably raised by disgruntled Jews against the hope of Jehovah's triumphant intervention in behalf of Israel. The unhappy situation of the Jews, particularly in Judea, seemed to indicate that Jehovah was either indifferent or hostile to the Jews. In the second place, the new notion that Jehovah was the Creator and the God of all nations was not easily reconciled with the old notion that Jehovah was partial to Israel. And in the third place, one could wonder if Israel was sufficiently free from wickedness to be worthy of being exalted by Jehovah, the God of justice, to a position of power and glory.

The Second Isaiah was well aware of these difficulties. His ultimate solution belongs not to his message to Israel, which we are now considering, but to his message to mankind. But even on the lower plane of national hopes he had answers for the doubters. Refusing to admit, for reasons that will soon be obvious, that Jehovah could be indifferent to his people's fate, he recognizes frankly that Jehovah has poured out on Israel the fury of his anger because they were not obedient to his Law (42:24 f.; cf. 47:6; 51:17, 21 f.); they have thus received double payment for their sins (40:2). Far from minimizing the iniquity of Israel, the author stresses its gravity from the beginning to the present and, like Jeremiah (Jer. 5:23 f., etc.), he regards it essentially as mental, as rebellion and obduracy of the heart (43:22-24, 27 f.; 46:12; 48).

Why, then, did not Jehovah, in his righteous anger, cut off Israel from the face of the earth, as Amos has proclaimed, particularly since Jehovah knew in advance of Israel's defection (48:4 f.)? Not because Israel has shown any signs of repentance (43:22-24), but because of God's character and purposes. Three characteristics of God make it impossible for him to annihilate Israel: he is loyal, merciful, and intolerant of rivalry or aspersions on his honor.

Jehovah has chosen Israel as his people (41:8 f.; 42:1; 43:10, 20; 44:1 f.; 45:4; 49:7) and called it by name (43:1; 49:1). Why the sole God of heaven and earth should select Israel among all nations is a problem that preoccupied the Second Isaiah much less than the authors of the Priestly Code; he would probably have said either that God's thoughts are inscrutable or that Jehovah loved Abraham (41:8). In any case, Israel is Jehovah's people and Jehovah is Israel's God (40:1, 27; 41:10, 13 f., 16 f., 20 f.; 43:3, 14 f., 20; 44:6; 45:3, 11, 13, 15; 47:4; 48:2, 17; 49:7, 26; 50:10; 51:15, 22; 52:4-7, 9; 54:5 f.; 55:5). Having given his pledge to Israel, Jehovah will keep it eternally (cf. 49:7). For human loyalty fades like the flowers of the field (40:6), but the divine loyalty abides forever: "For the mountains will be removed and the hills will totter; but my loyalty will not be removed from thee, neither will my covenant of peace totter" (54:10). The divine word is not a mere *flatus vocis*, but an invincible power, an irresistible decree that "stands forever" (40:8) and inevitably fulfills its purpose (45:19, 23; 46:10; 55:11; cf. Jer. 1:9 f.; 23:29). Jehovah knows the future: what he predicts inevitably comes to pass (41:22-29; 42:9; 43:9-13; 44:7 f., 24-28; 45:18-25; 46:9-11; 48:3-8, 14-16).

Jehovah is not only faithful to his word, but is also a God of love. The Second Isaiah presents numerous aspects and instances of Jehovah's love for Israel (43:4). He is the father (43:6) and creator (43:1, 15; 44:2, 24; 45:11; 51:13; 54:5) of Israel; he is Israel's husband (50:1; 54:5 f.). His tender affection is like a mother's for her infant child (49:15). He has brought Israel from the ends of the earth (41:9; 42:6; 48:12; 49:1), holding its hand (42:6). In the past he has loved Abraham, Israel's progenitor (41:8; cf. 51:2); he brought Israel out of Egypt (52:12), making a path in the sea and destroying Pharaoh's chariotry (43:16 f.; 51:9 f.), and providing water in the desert (48:21); he was loyal to David (55:3), and took up his residence in Israel (45:14), making the Jews his witnesses (43:10, 12; 44:8). In the present Jehovah has been wroth with his people, but his anger lasts but a moment while his love is eternal (54:7-10). Soon the divine wrath will be turned against the heathen and thus his love for Israel will be manifest (42:14-16: 51:17-23): he will then lead Israel gently, as a shepherd caring for his flock (40:11; 49:9-13), and in his mercy pardon the sinners (55:7; cf. 43:25).

Finally, Jehovah cannot permit the heathen to destroy his people lest their gods be deemed superior to himself and lest he be discredited in the eyes of the nations. How could the sole God in existence allow his glory to be given to another and his praise to the heathen gods, who are nothing but graven images (42:8)? But at present, while Israel is taken away for nought, the foreign rulers "howl" (?) and Jehovah's name is blasphemed (52:5). Therefore, for his own sake, for his own honor, Jehovah must rescue his people (42:14-17; 43:25; 48:9-11; cf. 59:17; 63:1-4; 66:6, 9).

Jehovah's character thus requires the restoration of Israel; his purpose— the manifestation of his glory to the Gentiles and their conversion to his religion—demands it in the immediate future. For Israel, Jehovah's servant, has been called in righteousness and taken by the hand to become the light of the Gentiles (42:6). An era has come to its end: "Behold, the former things have come to pass, and new things I declare: before they spring forth I tell you of them" (42:9; cf. 43:19; 48:3-8). The divine work of salvation embracing both Jews and Gentiles has been initiated. God has chosen Cyrus the Persian to crush Babylon and to deliver Israel (41:2 f., 25; 43:14; 45:1-5, 13; 46:11; 48:14 f.; 49:17). Cyrus himself has been girded by Jehovah although he knew it not (45:5) and having become a worshiper of the true God (41:25) will spread his religion to the ends of the world (45:6). The marvels of Israel's redemption, the triumphant march through a desert that has become a garden, and the dazzling glory of the New Jerusalem have been considered previously, in connection with the style of our author. The conversion of the Gentiles brings us to the second phase of the poet's teaching—the message intended not for Israel alone, but for all mankind.

No one contributed more than the Second Isaiah to the transformation of the national religion of Israel into a religion for all men. The prophets and Deuteronomy, notwithstanding some astonishing statements of Amos, had confined Jehovah's solicitude to his chosen people. But the Second Isaiah looks forward to the day when all men will worship Jehovah as their only God and will be saved by him. Although our poet, as we have seen, is ardently patriotic and believes that only Israel is in possession of the true religion, he is by no means selfishly parochial in outlook. His deepest convictions may be summarized in J. Wellhausen's (*Israelitische und jüdische Geschichte*, p. 152. 7th ed., Berlin, 1914) apt paraphrase of the Moslem creed, "There is no God but God, and Israel is his prophet." For monotheism and Israel's prophetic—nay, atoning—mission to mankind are the two cornerstones which the Second Isaiah provided as the basis of the three universal religions of salvation destined to spring eventually from his teaching, Judaism, Christianity, and Islam.

Monotheism is a self-evident truth for our author. Although he is the first Hebrew writer known to deny categorically the existence of other gods by the side of Jehovah (44:6; 45:5, 14, 18; 46:9; cf. 44:8; 45:6, 21)—similar denials in the Old Testament (Deut. 4:35, 39; I Kings 8:60; II Kings 19:15 [= Is. 37:16]; Ps. 83:18 [H. 83:19]; 86:10; Neh. 9:6; cf. II Sam. 22:32 [= Ps. 18:31, 18:32 in H.]) being demonstrably later than 500 B.C.—he does not believe for an instant that this new doctrine requires a demonstration. How did he come to regard monotheism as axiomatic truth? For some years the present writer has been convinced that when the Second Isaiah identified the unnamed deity of the Book of Job—the sole creator and upholder of physical nature and living beings—with Jehovah (the God of Israel and, for the prophets, the ruler of all human history) he inevitably realized that there could be no other god in existence (JBL 46 [1927] 193-206; cf. ZAW N.F. 3 [1926] 24f.; N.F. 11 [1934] 99-101).

By combining the faith of Israel and of its prophets with the philosophy of Job, by identifying the national God of Israel, the prophetic international God of justice and love, and Job's almighty Creator of all that exists, the Second Isaiah laid the foundations of the eclectic monotheistic theology of Judaism and Christianity. He seems utterly unaware of the inconsistencies in his notion of the deity. His God is, as we have seen, the God of Israel, the nation's creator, father, husband, and king. He is at the same time Amos's God of impartial justice (45:21), punishing his people for its sins (43:27 f., etc.); Hosea's God of love, ready to forgive Israel's iniquity (43:25; 44:22); Isaiah's holy God, "the Holy One of Israel" (41:14, 16, 20; 43:3, 14, etc.), who uses world empires no longer as the rod of his anger (Is. 10:5) but, through Cyrus, as the instrument by which he performs his work of salvation.

And finally Jehovah is the almighty Creator pictured in the Book of Job. The author of that book had depicted with such poetic vividness, scientific knowledge, and profound philosophy the wise and irresistible divine formation and control of the cosmos, that the Second Isaiah felt no need of dealing with the matter in detail. Clearly dependent on this work written by a greater poet and thinker, he confined himself to general summaries and allusions. Jehovah (not God or El Shaddai, as in Job) is the creator of heaven and earth (40:21 f.; 42:5; 44:24; 45:12, 18; 48:13; 51:13, 16), of the stars (40:26; 45:12), of man (41:4; 45:12), in fact, of all things (44:24), both good and bad (45:7; cf. 54:16; it is sometimes supposed that the poet is here attacking the dualism of Zoroastrianism). Our author's dependence on Job can be recognized in his use of particular expressions: God stretched forth the heavens alone (Job 9:8; Is. 44:24) and founded the earth (Job 38:4; Is. 48:13; 51:16; Ps. 104:5); he "stirred up" the sea (Job 26:12; Is. 51:15; cf. Jer. 31:35) and "pierced" the primeval monster of chaos, Rahab (Job 26:12; Is: 51:9; cf. Job 9:13; 26:13; 38:10 f.; Ps. 104:9); he sits on the "circle" of the earth (Is. 40:22) or walks on the "circle" of the heavens (Job 22:14).

Like the Book of Job (Job 9:4; 12:13, 16; 26:12), the Second Isaiah stresses two attributes of God: wisdom and might. No one can teach God knowledge (Job 21:22; Is. 40:14); his mind and deeds are unsearchable (Job 5:9; 9:10; 11:7; Is. 40:28), he is invisible to man (Job 9:11; 23:8 f.; Is. 45:15). "Mighty in strength" (Job 9:4; Is. 40:26), irresistible in action (Job 11:10; 23:13; Is. 43:13), he deals with man as a potter with clay (Job 10:9; Is. 45:9; cf. Jer. 18:2 ff.) and no one can say to him, "What doest thou?" (Job. 9:12; Is. 45:9). He animates men with the breath of life (Job 12:10; Is. 42:5), but controls their destiny, keeping their "way" (fate) hidden (Job 3:23; Is. 40:27), frustrating their devices and making fools of them (Job 5:12; 12:17; Is. 44:25). Nations are as nothing in his sight (Job 12:23; Is. 40:15, 17) and their rulers are abased by him (Job 12:17, 21; Is. 40:23 f.; 41:5; 43:13, 16; 44:25).

In his amalgamation of three entirely different and partly contradictory notions of the deity, the Second Isaiah could utilize the combination of the first two in Deuteronomy. By means of the "Covenant" between Jehovah and Israel, the authors of the Deuteronomic Code (found in

621) were able to join the popular notion of the God of Israel with the prophetic notion of the God of justice and love. For the Covenant, on the one hand, stirred the nationalistic pride of the masses by making of Israel the chosen nation of Jehovah the God of Israel, but on the other, through the divine Law that Israel was to obey in order to fulfill the terms of the Covenant, it stressed the ethical requirements of the God of justice, proclaimed by Amos. Thus the Deuteronomists succeeded in obliterating, in a measure, the sharp contrasts between the popular and the prophetic notion of Jehovah.

The Second Isaiah faced a far more difficult task when he amalgamated the deity of Deuteronomy with that of Job, for their respective attributes were indeed logically irreconcilable. The author of the Book of Job had proved this beyond cavil by showing that the undeserved suffering of the righteous and the unmerited prosperity of the wicked could not be explained if God was both almighty and just. Moreover, the God who once created and now controls the world with wisdom and power could have no more concern for the just retribution of human deeds than nature, which expresses his character. The Second Isaiah did not attempt on philosophical grounds a solution of the problem of theodicy—the contradiction between moral attributes (justice and love) and metaphysical attributes (omniscience and omnipotence) in the sole God responsible for the world as it is—for Job had proved that the problem defies the efforts of human reason (and in fact still does to the present day). On the basis of some vague intuitions of Job and of his own invincible faith, he overcame, however, the logical difficulties within the sphere of religion.

In the first place, he boldly denied the validity of the dilemma posed by Job: God is either almighty or just and merciful, but not both. He cried out enthusiastically that "the Creator of the ends of the earth . . . gives power to the faint" (40:28-31), that Jehovah, Israel's redeemer, is the maker of all things (44:24), that the mysteriously hidden God is Israel's savior (45:15). Any philosophical objection to this faith that attributes to God irreconcilable characteristics is silenced once for all, unanswerably, by admitting that in the last analysis the human mind cannot comprehend God's thoughts and deeds (55:8 f.).

In this manner the Second Isaiah concluded that the God of power who crushed Job and the God of mercy and justice—his witness in heaven— to whom Job appealed (Job 16:19-21) were the same God—Jehovah. But he still faced the problem of the undeserved suffering of an upright God-fearing man like Job. Facing the issue squarely, he discovered a new, profound meaning of suffering. The innocent may voluntarily undergo self-immolation as a sublime vicarious atonement for the sins of others. Israel, like a sacrificial lamb, has given its life for the salvation of the Gentiles (Is. 53).

This brings us to the second, practical part of the creed of the Second Isaiah: Israel is the prophet of the only God of heaven and earth. The conversion of the Gentiles is an obvious corollary of monotheism, at least in principle. Conscious, however, of the practical difficulties of persuading the pagans to become worshipers of Jehovah, the Second Isaiah strategically maps out his missionary campaign from three points of view: theology, history, and the example of Israel.

In the first place, the author presents to the Gentiles a theological apology of the new faith and a polemic against their old religions. As we have seen, he asserts that Jehovah is not only the God of Israel, but the sole God in existence, the creator of heaven and earth, to whom alone the worship of all men is due. As for the gods of the Gentiles, they have no existence by the side of Jehovah, they are nothing but inanimate idols, incapable of perception or motion, helpless and unable to help others (40:19 f.; 41:6 f.; 42:17; 44:9-20; 45:20b; 46:1 f., 5-7; 48:5; for glosses see the summary of ch. 40). Paganism with its false gods, with its idols, with its spurious magic and divination (44:25; 47:9, 11-13), is dismissed summarily as a colossal fraud, as an absurd folly, as an insane aberration. The author adduces but one proof for his allegations: if Jehovah and the pagan gods were brought into court to plead their respective case it would immediately be manifest that Jehovah alone is able to predict the future, having actually done so (41:21-23, 26, 28 f.; 42:9; 43:9-13; 44:7-9; 45:18-22; 46:8-11; 48:3, 5-7, 14-16).

The conversion of the Gentiles is not only a matter of theological argument but is on the verge of becoming an historical fact. The conquests of Cyrus the Persian have been decreed by Jehovah (41:2 f., 25) not only for the redemption of Israel, as we have seen, but also for the conversion of the Gentiles. Jehovah has sworn that "every knee shall bow, every tongue shall swear" unto himself (45:23), a statement triumphantly quoted by the Apostle Paul in Rom. 14:11 and applied by him to Jesus Christ in Phil. 2:10. Jehovah gives Cyrus victory in order that he may know that the God of Israel has called him by name (45:1-3; cf. 48:14 f.); girded by God without his knowledge (45:5), Cyrus is converted to the worship of Jehovah (41:25) and from east to west all will eventually know that Jehovah is the only true God (45:6). The ends of earth should look unto God and be saved (45:22). To him will the pagans turn in confusion (45:24): individuals (44:5), kings (49:7), and nations (51:4 f., reading "peoples . . . nations" for "my people . . . my nation"). "Sing unto Jehovah a new song, his praise from the end of the earth!" (42:10).

Even more than Cyrus, Israel is the instrument for the conversion of the Gentiles—Israel as the possessor of the true religion, Israel to be glorified in the future, but still afflicted in the present.

Since Israel knows righteousness and has God's Law in its heart (51:7;

cf. Jer. 31:33 f.), Israel is the witness (43:10; 44:8), the messenger (44:26; cf. 42:19), and the Servant of Jehovah (41:8 f.; 43:10; 44:1 f., 21, 26a; 45:4; 48:20; 49:3, 5).[20] Endowed with prophetic inspiration (42:1), Israel will bring the true religion to the Gentiles (42:1-4).

In the second place, the restoration of Israel will in itself contribute to the conversion of the Gentiles. Those who will witness the triumphant return of the Jews to Zion will sing hymns in praise of the Lord (42:10-13; cf. 40:5). In fact, Israel's rebirth is only the preliminary stage for the conversion of the Gentiles. It is too small a matter for the God of the world merely to "raise up the tribes of Jacob and to restore the saved ones of Israel"; God's main purpose is to make Israel "a light for the Gentiles" and manifest his salvation to the ends of the earth (49:6; cf. the preceding footnote).

Finally, as the Servant of the Lord, Israel has sacrificed itself for the salvation of the Gentiles. The sad spectacle of Israel, despised of men, abhorred of nations, a servant of rulers, will bring kings and princes to the worship of Jehovah (49:7). Through suffering, courageously and patiently borne, Israel acquires an ear attuned to the divine message and a mouth able to encourage the weary (50:4-9). This sublime self-immolation for a great cause will shock the Gentiles (52:14 f.) until they realize its full meaning. They will then confess that this Servant of Jehovah, loathsome of aspect and despised, a man of sorrows and acquainted with grief (53:1-3), was not divinely accursed, but was wounded for their transgressions and crushed for their iniquities, healing them with his stripes (53:4 f.). Jehovah loaded him with the iniquity of all Gentiles; he was cut off from the land of the living and buried with the wicked although he was innocent (53:6-9). But because he bore the sins of many and made intercession for the transgressors, Jehovah will somehow vindicate him and reward him for his vicarious self-sacrifice (53:10-12, in part textually corrupt and incomprehensible).

In some unexplained manner the martyrdom of the Servant is followed by his triumph. The resurrection from the grave on the part of a Jew living in the days of the Second Isaiah or before would have been an event of such startling magnitude that it could not merely be taken for granted in 52:13 and 53:12. It would have been no less significant than the resurrection of Jesus in the New Testament. Since nothing indicates that the author of 52:13-53:12 held the doctrine of the resurrection from the grave—a doctrine unknown in the Old Testament before the third

[20] Isaiah 49:5 f. has been adduced as proof that the Servant and Israel are separate entities. Isaiah 49:5 should be rendered, "And now Jehovah who formed me from the womb as his servant has decided to bring Jacob back unto himself. . . ." In 49:6 we should omit, with B. Duhm, the words "that you should be my servant." In 53:8, with the addition of a final *m*, we should read "peoples" instead of "my people." See A. Lods, *Les prophètes d'Israël*, p. 277, n. 6. Paris, 1935.

century (Is. 26:19; cf. later Dan. 12:2)—the Servant can hardly be conceived as an historical individual. Even if the author had in mind a mythical figure, a dying and rising god like Tammuz-Adonis, he would of necessity have stressed the central feature of the drama, the return of the deceased hero from the underworld to the realm of the living. The description of the martyrdom and triumph of the Servant, without any reference to resurrection, fits Israel much better than an individual. For one could speak, without violence to historical reality, of the death of the nation (in 586) and of its future glory (after 538). The Exile could be conceived as a residence in the underworld and as a passage from death to life. Significantly Ezekiel, who, like the Second Isaiah, knows nothing of a revivification of individuals after death, saw in a vision the dry bones, filling a valley in Babylonia, being animated by Jehovah into living men, and he interpreted the vision as the restoration of "the whole house of Israel" (Ez. 37:1-14). Both the Second Isaiah and Ezekiel, living in the time of Israel's humiliation, believed firmly in the future resurrection of their nation and depicted it symbolically, although with profound differences in details owing to their extremely divergent poetic and religious natures.

The spiritual epic of the Second Isaiah had a decisive influence on the religion of the Jews and, through Christianity, on the religion of mankind. Isaiah had merely expected that a small remnant, purified in the fire of affliction, would survive the national ruin; Jeremiah had hoped that one day Jehovah would write a new covenant in the hearts of men, and thus save his faithful ones individually as well as nationally; Ezekiel, certain of the restoration of Israel, furnished an ecclesiastical organization for the future community. But it was the Second Isaiah who made of the hope in a fantastically glorious future an essential half of Judaism before A.D. 100. He may therefore be called the father of apocalypse, which after him and until the rise of Christianity was no less characteristic of Judaism than the observance of the Law. Through his agency the Jews were able to lift their eyes from a precarious and depressing present to the mirage of their future sway over the whole earth. Jeremiah had looked forward to a restoration of the Davidic dynasty, but Second Isaiah knows nothing of a Messiah from the seed of David. For him Jehovah is the king of the Jews; the chosen people, after expiating their sins and suffering for the redemption of mankind, will return in triumph to the New Jerusalem and live in their land peacefully and prosperously forever after.

Israel derived from the Second Isaiah the hope in a magnificent future which, no less than the Law, contributed to its survival in times of distress; but the Jews refused to consider themselves the scapegoat for the sins of the Gentiles. The great thought of the atoning effectiveness of suffering and death furnished the interpretation of the death of Jesus on the cross: Christianity cannot be understood without the Second Isaiah. Moreover, he passed on to Christianity, as well as to Judaism, the element of hope in religion, the outlook on a coming Golden Age, the doctrine of the Kingdom of God on earth to which all men, without distinction of race, are called. In addition, the Second Isaiah, with his epoch-making discovery that there is only one God of heaven and earth, furnished the basis for the theology of Judaism, Christianity, and Islam, bequeathing to them the insoluble problem of reconciling in the only God in existence the functions of the creator of the world and those of the just and benevolent ruler of mankind.

4. The Teaching of the Third Isaiah

The purpose of Is. 56-66 is to interpret the Second Isaiah for a later generation. It is a valuable indication of how Judaism understood the great epic of Is. 40-55 and of how it disregarded some parts of its teaching and emphasized others. As could be expected, in a later age the references of the Second Isaiah to contemporary events were no longer significant: nothing is said in Is. 56-66 of the victorious campaigns of Cyrus, of the fall of Babylon, and of the return of the Jews to Zion. Only a few of the Babylonian Jews had actually returned to Judea after 538 (56:8; 57:19), and the magnificent prophecy of the great and triumphant march through the desert had not yet been fulfilled: the promised salvation was still in the future (56:1; 59:14-19) and the Jewish community in Jerusalem was still so small that proselytes and even eunuchs were welcomed to it (56:3-8).

The miserable situation of the Jews is no longer explained as atoning suffering for the sins of the Gentiles, nor is the author in the least concerned with the missionary endeavors of Israel (on the contrary, Jehovah devastates Edom, 63:1-6). The glorious salvation has been delayed on account of the sins of the congregation, particularly the ritual and moral transgressions of the masses and of the leaders (56:9-57:13; 58:1-59:15a). It is only for the sake of the pious Jews that Jehovah does not wipe out the whole nation (63:10-65:15). And yet, under the spell of the contagious optimism of the Second Isaiah, in 60-62 the glories of the New Jerusalem are depicted even more magnificently than in Is. 40-55.

Modern scholars, who believe that Biblical authors should be consistent, have attributed Is. 56-66 to a number of contemporary writers because of its obvious logical contradictions. But in dealing with a highly imaginative work of Oriental origin it is hardly proper to demand clear and self-consistent thought; there is consequently no proof that Is. 56-66 could not have been written by a single writer. The basic inconsistency is already noticeable in Haggai and Zechariah, whose oracles were known to the Third Isaiah. On the one hand, the glorious salvation of the Jews and the establishment of the Kingdom of God on earth is conditioned by the repentance and spiritual revival of the Jews (Hag. 1:5-11; 2:15-19; Zech. 1:3; Is. 59:9-15a). On the other, God will usher in his Kingdom in the immediate future, whether the Jews repent or not (Hag. 2:4-9; Zech. 8:1-17; Is. 59:15b-21; 60-62; 63:1-6; 66:6-14).

Another inconsistency, characteristic likewise of Deuteronomy and Ezekiel, and in fact of Judaism in general, is the failure to discriminate, as the great prophets had done since Amos, between ritual and moral transgressions. The author summarizes the requirements of Jehovah thus (56:2): to keep the Sabbath from profaning it (ritual requirements) and keep one's hand from doing evil (moral requirements); or, to keep the Sabbaths, to choose the things that please God, and to hold fast to Jehovah's covenant (56:4; cf. 56:6). Similarly he denounces the ritual observance of fasting divested from the practice of justice and philanthropy (58:1-12). On the one hand, the observance of the Sabbath (58:13 f.) and the offering of sacrifices (56:7) are considered essential; on the other, we read that Jehovah loves justice and hates robbery with iniquity (61:8), needs no Temple and considers the man of contrite spirit (66:1 f.; cf. 57:15), classing the sacrifices of oxen and lambs with murder and idolatry (66:3 f.). Likewise the sins denounced are partly ritual (57:3-13; 65:1-7, 11 f.; 66:17) and partly moral and social (56:9-12; 57:1; 59:1-8).

A third inconsistency, which like the other two is not found in the Second Isaiah, is connected with the coming salvation. On the one hand, one could believe that, as the Second Isaiah had proclaimed, Israel as a whole would be saved and glorified (57:14-19; 59:21; 60-62); but, on the other, that, before ushering in his Kingdom (66), Jehovah will punish the wicked, rebellious, and apostate Jews and save only the pious (57: 20 f.; 59:15b-20; 65:1-15; 66:5 f., 15-17, 23 f.).

In conclusion, there is more pessimism, more concern with the externalities of religion, more nationalism, more legalistic zeal after the manner of the First Psalm, in the Third Isaiah than in the Second. He is more in touch with the dreary reality, but is less spiritual, less cosmopolitan, less sublimely idealistic than his great master, the Second Isaiah, whose exalted message inspired him. Occasionally (60:1-4) our author seems to capture the spirit of his model, but in general it was inevitable that in supplementing and interpreting Is. 40-55 for the wretched Jewish community shortly before the days of Nehemiah he would, like most epigoni, fail to attain the sublimity of his master and popularize his message almost beyond recognition.

CHAPTER II

THE BOOK OF JEREMIAH

~~~~~~

The Book of Jeremiah is divided into three parts (1-25; 26-45; 46-51) and ends with a historical appendix in ch. 52. It may be summarized as follows:

I. THE WORDS OF JEREMIAH (1-25)

1. Superscription of the book (1:1-3).

2. Jeremiah's call to the prophetic office (1:4-19): *a.* the call and consecration (1:4-10); *b.* two visions (1:11-16); *c.* the promise of divine strength (1:17-19).

3. Early exhortations to Judah and North Israel (2-6): *a.* North Israel, the faithless wife (2; 3:1-5); *b.* an appeal to North Israel (3:6-22a); *c.* repentance (3:22b-25) and conditional restoration (4:1-4); *d.* punishment through the Scythian invaders (4:5-31; cf. 5:15-17; 6:1-8, 22-26; 8:14-17; 10:18-22); *e.* Jerusalem's depravity (5); *f.* the Benjamites are warned to flee from Jerusalem before it is destroyed (6).

4. Jerusalem's wrong religion (7:1-10:25): *a.* the vain trust in the Temple (7:1-15; cf. 26); *b.* the worship of the Queen of Heaven (7:16-20; cf. 44:15-30); *c.* the futility of sacrifices (7:21-28); *d.* the Moloch worship at Tophet in the Hinnom valley (7:29-34); *d.* the worship of astral deities (8:1-3); *e.* moral backsliding (8:4-7); *f.* blind trust in the (Deuteronomic) Law (8:8 f.); *g.* the terrors of the coming doom (8:10-17); *h.* Jeremiah's own anguish (8:18-9:1 [H. 8:18-23]) and longing for a secluded refuge (9:2-11 [H. 9:1-10]); *i.* threat and lament in anticipation of Jerusalem's utter ruin (9:12-22 [H. 9:11-21]); *j.* futility of wisdom and might (9:23 f. [H. 9:22 f.]), as well as of physical circumcision (9:25 f. [H. 9:24 f.]); *k.* an interpolated denunciation of idolatry (10:1-16); *l.* the imminence of the attack on Jerusalem (10:17-22) and a prayer for mercy (10:23-25).

5. Jeremiah's support of the Covenant, i.e., the reforms of Josiah (11:1-12:6): *a.* The Judeans have violated the Covenant (11:1-17); *b.* at Anathoth a plot was hatched against Jeremiah (11:18-23); *c.* "Wherefore doth the way of the wicked prosper?" (12:1-6).

6. Lamentations and warnings (12:7-13:27): *a.* Jehovah has abandoned his heritage (Israel) into the hand of the enemy (12:7-13, with a com-

forting supplement of later date in 12:14-17); *b.* two parables: the buried girdle (13:1-11) and the broken wine jars (13:12-14); *c.* the pride of Judah (13:15-17) and of its royal house (13:18 f.) will be humbled; *d.* Jerusalem's whoredoms will be dreadfully punished (13:20-27).

7. The great drought (14:1-15:9): *a.* suffering caused by the drought (14:1-6); *b.* a prayer for divine help (14:7-9) is rejected (14:10); *c.* Jeremiah should not intercede for the people (14:11-16), but weep over its ruin (14:17 f.); *d.* a second prayer of the people (14:19-22) is also rejected (15:1-4); *e.* proclamation of the punishment (15:5-9).

8. Confessions and speeches (15:10-20:18): *a.* the prophet's laments and the divine answer (15:10-21); *b.* renunciations demanded of Jeremiah: he must refrain from marriage (16:1-4), and from attendance at funerals (16:5-7) and at feasts (16:8 f.); *c.* for Jehovah has forsaken his people (16:10-13, 16-18); *d.* interpolated promises of salvation for Israel (16:14 f.) and for the Gentiles (16:19-21); *e.* sin is a disease of the heart (17:1-11); *f.* a prayer for healing and vindication (17:12-18); *g.* interpolation against breaking the Sabbath by making deliveries (17:19-27); *h.* the potter's work is a symbol of God's procedure (18:1-17); *i.* the plot against the prophet (18:18) and his prayer for vengeance (18:19-23); *j.* the symbol of the broken earthen jar (19:1-15) and Jeremiah's humiliating punishment in being put in the stocks by Pashhur (20:1-6); *k.* inner struggles of the prophet: his complaint against Jehovah who has forced him to utter a message of doom (20:7-12, supplemented with a brief psalm of later authorship, 20:13), and his curse of the day whereon he was born (20:14-18; cf. Job 3).

9. Denunciations of kings and prophets (21-23): *a.* Jeremiah advises Zedekiah to submit to Nebuchadnezzar (21:1-10); *b.* a warning to the house of David (21:11 f.); *c.* a denunciation of the "inhabitant of the valley" (21:13 f.); *d.* a warning to the king to execute justice (22:1-5; cf. 21:11 f.); *e.* prediction of the end of the dynasty (22:6-9); *f.* oracle on Shallum (Jehoahaz) (22:10-12); *g.* oracle against Jehoiakim (22:13-19); *h.* the end of the kings (22:20-23); *i.* Coniah (Jehoiachin) will fall into the hand of Nebuchadnezzar (22:24-30); *j.* a righteous "scion" of David will restore Judah after the nation has been exiled (23:1-8); *k.* denunciation of the false prophets for their wickedness (23:9-15), for announcing a glorious future (23:16-24), and for basing their oracles on dreams instead of revelations (23:25-32); *l.* what is the "burden" (*massâ* in the sense of "oracle") of Jehovah? You (*sic*) are the "burden" (*massâ* in the sense of "heavy load") and I cast you off (23:33-40).

10. Two visions (24-25): *a.* the Exiles of 597 are the good figs, those left behind in Judah are the bad ones (24:1-10); *b.* introduction to the book of Jeremiah's oracles (25:1-14; cf. 36); *c.* introduction to the oracles against foreign nations (46-51, placed after 25:13 in the LXX, where

25:14 is lacking): the Gentiles will drink from the cup of God's fury (25:15-38).

II. THE BIOGRAPHY OF JEREMIAH (26-45)

1. Jeremiah's Temple address (cf. 7:1-15) and its consequences for the prophet (26:1-19); execution of the prophet Uriah (26:20-24).

2. Jeremiah's part in restraining the Judeans in their abortive rebellion against Nebuchadnezzar in 593 (27-29): a. Jeremiah wears bands and bars and warns the ambassadors of neighboring nations (27:1-11, reading "Zedekiah" instead of "Jehoiakim" in 27:1; cf. 28:1), Zedekiah (27:12-15), the priests, and the people (27:16-22) not to rebel against Nebuchadnezzar; b. Hananiah, a nationalistic and optimistic prophet, breaks the wooden yoke from off Jeremiah's neck (28:1-11); Jeremiah replaces it with a yoke of iron (28:12-17); c. letter of Jeremiah instructing the Babylonian Exiles to settle there permanently and to mistrust the false prophets, such as Ahab and Zedekiah, in their midst (29:1-23); d. one of these prophets in Babylonia, Shemaiah, writes a letter to Jerusalem urging the arrest of Jeremiah (29:24-32).

3. Jeremiah's hopes for the future (30-33): a. introduction (30:1-3); b. through the divine judgment on the nations, their yoke will be broken from off the neck of "Jacob," i.e., either North Israel or both Judah and Israel (30:4-11); c. again under a native "prince," Zion shall be restored (30:12-22); d. the storm of Jehovah's wrath against the wicked (30:23 f.); e. North Israel will be restored (31:1-9); f. the nations are warned that Jehovah has redeemed Israel (31:10-14); g. Rachel, the mother of Joseph and Benjamin, should no longer weep over the fate of her descendants (31:15-22); h. Judah shall also be restored (31:23-30); i. the prophecy of the "New Covenant": God's laws will be written in the heart and all will know God (31:31-34); j. Israel is as permanent as the laws of the heavens (31:35-37); k. Jerusalem shall be holy (31:38-40); l. during the siege of Jerusalem, when Jeremiah was under arrest, he purchased a field from his cousin Hanamel (32:1-15), but was later assailed by doubts (32:16-27); m. Jerusalem is to be destroyed on account of her sins (32: 28-35), but will again be restored (32:36-44); n. Jerusalem after its fall will again be glorious (33:1-9), the devastated land of Judah will again revive (33:10-13), a "scion" of David will sit on the throne (33:14-16), the dynasty and the priestly orders will continue unbroken (33:17 f.), firm like the laws of nature (33:19-22), the captivity of Israel and Judah will return (33:23-26).

4. Jeremiah's experiences under Jehoiakim and Zedekiah (34-36): a. oracle to Zedekiah at the beginning of the siege of Jerusalem (34:1-7); b. threatened punishment for the violation of the law ordering the release of Hebrew slaves (34:8-22; cf. Ex. 21:2; Deut. 15); c. contrast be-

tween the Rechabites, who in obedience to their ordinances abstain from wine, and the Judeans, who have disregarded God's words (35); *d.* when Jehoiakim burns Jeremiah's book, the prophet prepares a new edition of his oracles (36).

5. Jeremiah during the siege and destruction of Jerusalem (37-39; cf. 21:1-10): *a.* when a contingent of the Babylonians besieging Jerusalem marched forth to meet an approaching Egyptian army, Jeremiah assured the people that Jerusalem was doomed whatever happened (37:1-10); *b.* Jeremiah, attempting to go to Anathoth to take possession of his portion (perhaps the field that he bought later, 32:1-15), was arrested as a traitor (37:11-15); *c.* in an audience with Zedekiah, the prophet could give the king no hope, but he was allowed to leave the prison and to be confined in the court of the guard (37:16-21; the sequel seems to be 38:24-28a); *d.* some fanatical leaders of the anti-Babylonian party cast Jeremiah into a miry cistern in the court of the guard (38:1-6) but he was rescued with the consent of the king by Ebed-melech, a Negro eunuch (38:7-13; the sequel seems to be 39:15-18); *e.* Jeremiah's last appeal to Zedekiah to surrender to Nebuchadnezzar (38:14-23); *f.* on the advice of the king, Jeremiah lied about the subject of his audience (38:24-28a, belonging perhaps after 37:16-21); *g.* the fall of Jerusalem (38:28b-39:14): the fate of the king and of the people (39:1 f., 4-10, probably spurious; cf. 52 and II Kings 25) and the kind treatment accorded to Jeremiah (38:28b; 39:3, 11-14); *h.* a favorable oracle for Ebed-melech (39:15-18, belonging after 38:7-13).

6. The last years of Jeremiah (40-45): *a.* the assassination of Gedaliah and its aftermath (40:1-41:18; cf. II Kings 25:22-26); Jeremiah, freed by the Babylonians, went to Gedaliah at Mizpah (40:1-6), together with other Judeans (40:7-12); Johanan and others vainly warned Gedaliah against Ishmael (40:13-16), who eventually assassinated him (41:1-3) and also massacred a group of pilgrims from North Israel (41:4-10); Johanan delivered the captives taken by Ishmael and forced him to flee (41:11-18); *b.* Jeremiah assured Johanan and his companions that they had nothing to fear from Nebuchadnezzar (42:1-22), but they forced Jeremiah and Baruch to flee with them to Tahpanhes in Egypt (43:1-7); *c.* by hiding some stones in Pharaoh's house at Tahpanhes, Jeremiah predicted (erroneously) Nebuchadnezzar's conquest of Egypt (43:8-13); *d.* Jeremiah inveighed against the worship of alien gods (44:1-14), but his hearers asserted their trust in the Queen of Heaven (44:15-19); the prophet warned again (44:20-23) and as a sign of their impending punishment foretold the downfall of Pharaoh Hophra (Apries, 588-569 B.C.; 44:24-30; cf. Herodotus 2:163-169); *e.* Jeremiah rebuked his secretary Baruch (in 605, according to 45:1, or later) but predicted that his life would be spared in the impending national disaster (45:1-5).

III. THE ORACLES AGAINST FOREIGN NATIONS (46-51)

"The word of Jehovah which came to Jeremiah the prophet concerning the nations" (46:1).

1. Two oracles against Egypt (46): *a*. Martial song on the victory of Nebuchadnezzar over Pharaoh Necho at Carchemish in 605 (46:2); the Egyptian army in battle (46:3-6); the humiliation of Egypt (46:7-12). *b*. Nebuchadnezzar's devastation of Egypt (46:13-26); the salvation of Israel (46:27 f.).

2. The oracle against the Philistines (47).

3. The oracle against Moab (48; cf. Is. 15-16): the fall of the cities of Moab (48:1-10), owing to the self-confidence of the Moabites (48:11-19), will result in national ruin (48:20-28), in the abasement of Moab's pride (48:29-39), and in general panic (48:40-47).

4. The oracle against the Ammonites (49:1-6).

5. The oracle against Edom (49:7-22, in part identical with Obadiah): exhortation to flee before the coming calamity (49:7-12) in which Edom will be wholly laid waste (49:13-22).

6. The oracle against Damascus (49:23-27).

7. The oracle against Kedar (the Bedouins of the Syrian desert) and the kingdom of Hazor (an unknown community of settled Arabs) (49:28-33).

8. The oracle against Elam (49:34-39), dated at the beginning of the reign of Zedekiah (597).

9. The oracle against Babylon (50:1-51:58, written long after the death of Jeremiah) is supplemented by instructions of Jeremiah to Seraiah: he should sink into the Euphrates, as a sign of Babylon's sinking, the prophet's oracle concerning Babylon (51:59-64).

"Thus far are the words of Jeremiah" (51:64).

IV. HISTORICAL APPENDIX (52)

The history of the fall of Jerusalem in 586 (52), quoted for the most part (except for the valuable statistics in 52:28-30) from II Kings 24:18-25:21, 27-30 (cf. Jer. 39:1 f., 4-10).

The Greek translation (LXX) of Jeremiah differs from the standard Hebrew (and English) text in important respects; not infrequently it preserves an earlier textual recension. Two sections of the Hebrew book stand in entirely different places in the LXX: the oracles against foreign nations come after 25:13 (46:1-51:64 of the Hebrew are 25:14-31:44 in the LXX) and 25:15-45:5 of the Hebrew correspond in a general way to 32:1-51:35 in the LXX. Moreover, the order of the oracles against the foreign nations in the Greek is different: oracles 1-9 (cf. the preceding summary under 46:1-51:64) are in this order in the LXX: 8 (Elam), 1 (Egypt), 9 (Babylon), 2 (Philistia), 5 (Edom), 4 (Ammon), 7 (Kedar),

6 (Damascus), 3 (Moab). The Hebrew order corresponds more to the list in 25:18-26. *Sheshach* in 25:26 [cf. 51:41] is an *athbash* cipher for *Babel* or Babylonia, based on a substitution of letters according to the reversed order of the alphabet (*sh*, the second letter from the end, corresponds to *b*, the second from the beginning; *ch* (*k*) is the eleventh from the beginning, *l* the eleventh from the end).[1] But although the Hebrew order of these oracles may be the original one and is certainly more logical since it groups the nations geographically (Egypt and Philistia; Moab, Ammon, and Edom; Damascus and Kedar; Elam and Babylon), they should come, as in the LXX, after 25:13, or rather after 25:15-38, which seems to be their general introduction.

The Hebrew and Greek texts differ also in regard to the contents. While the LXX has some slight additions to the Hebrew (about 100 words, mostly unimportant), it omits about 2,700 words, or one-eighth of the book. The most noteworthy omissions in the LXX are: 8:10b-12; 10:6, 8, 10; 17:1-5a; 29:16-20; 33:14-26; 39:4-13; 52:28-30.[2] Although it is conceivable that occasionally the LXX translators deliberately condensed the Hebrew when it seemed unduly diffuse and at other times accidentally omitted a section of their prototype, in most cases the "omissions" of the LXX were not an original part of the book, but contributions of editors and readers.

1. The Historical Background

The public ministry of Jeremiah, like that of Isaiah a century before (740-700), covered four dramatic decades (626-586) which were epoch-making in the political history of Judah. As in the case of Isaiah, Jeremiah's words and deeds are so intimately related to the vicissitudes of Judah and to the international political upheavals that without a knowledge of the historical background they would be incomprehensible.[3]

The catastrophic reign of the pious Hezekiah (720-692) was followed by the long peaceful reign of Manasseh (692-639). The latter's subservience to Sennacherib (705-681), Esarhaddon (681-668), and Ashurbanipal (668-625), his Assyrian overlords (cf. JBL 47 [1928] 185 f.),

[1] Another occurrence of this cipher has been detected in 51:1, where (according to the LXX and the Targum) *lb qmy* is to be read *Kśdym* (Chaldeans). For another interpretation of *Sheshach*, see R. P. Dougherty, *The Sealand of Ancient Arabia*, pp. 15 f. L. Finkelstein (*The Pharisees*, Vol. I, p. 338. Philadelphia, 1938) has ingeniously explained Magog (Ez. 38:2; 39:6; cf. Rev. 20:8) as a cipher for Babel. Written backward *mgg* is *ggm*; substituting in *ggm* the preceding letter of the alphabet we obtain *bbl*, Babel.

[2] The differences between the Hebrew and Greek texts are given by W. Rudolph in the 3rd ed. of Kittel's *Biblia Hebraica* (Stuttgart, 1931); cf. his article in ZAW N.F. 7 (1930) 272-286. On the critical problems raised by these differences see, among others, A. W. Streane, *The Double Text of Jeremiah* (Cambridge, 1896).

[3] For a history of the times of Jeremiah see, in addition to the general histories, J. Lewy, *Forschungen zur Geschichte Vorderasiens* (MVAG 29.2, 1925).

his servile adoption of Assyrian religious practices, and his encouragement of ancient popular superstitions, earned for him the opprobrium of
both the patriots and the prophets of Judah, but spared his country the
horrors of war. Popular reaction to his policy inflamed not only the assassins of his son Amon (639-638), but also the authors of the Deuteronomic
Code, which inspired the reformation of Josiah (638-609) in 621.

The success of the anti-Assyrian movement was made possible by the
serious weakening of Assyria. The wars of Ashurbanipal, which sapped
the man power of the kingdom, the revival of Egypt under Psamtik I
(663-609), the founder of the Twenty-sixth (Saïtic) Dynasty, the devastating invasion of the Scythian hordes (630-624), nominally allied to
Assyria, had already impaired the imperial power of Assyria before the
death of its last great sovereign, Ashurbanipal. But his death in 625
marked the beginning of the swift disintegration and sudden end of the
Assyrian Empire. No sooner was Ashurbanipal buried than Babylonia
under Nabopolassar (625-605) and Media under Cyaxares (625-593)
became independent and, after joining forces in the siege and destruction
of Nineveh (612), they divided among themselves most of the territory
of the extinct Assyrian Empire.

The Assyrians, however, made a last stand after the fall of their capital.
Ashur-uballit, at the head of the remnants of the Assyrian army, occupied
Harran. But three years later, at the beginning of 609, the Umman-Manda
(Medes) destroyed the city,[4] and drove Ashur-uballit across the Eu-
phrates. Pharaoh Necho (609-593) marched at once to the help of the
Assyrians. Josiah was defeated and slain, when he heroically met Necho
at Megiddo in a futile attempt to drive him back (609).[5]

Although Necho could not conquer Harran, he subjected parts of Syria
and Palestine. But Ashur-uballit and the Assyrian nation itself ceased to
play an historical role in that year. As for Necho, his Asiatic conquests
were ephemeral: crushingly defeated at Carchemish (605) by Nebuchadnezzar, the Babylonian crown prince, he saw Syria and Palestine become part of the Neo-Babylonian Empire (625-538) and "came no more
out of his land" (II Kings 24:7).

Nebuchadnezzar (605-561) returned to Babylon immediately after the
battle because his father Nabopolassar had died (Berossos, in Josephus,
Against Apion 1:19). His rule over a vast empire was unchallenged and
peaceful, except for his wars against the Judeans and his fruitless siege

---

[4] Nabonidus (555-538) relates in his stela, now at Istanbul, that at the beginning
of his reign he restored the temple of Sin at Harran, which had been destroyed 54
years before, i.e., in 609, by the Umman-Manda (Nabonidus No. 8, Col. X, Line 13,
in S. Langdon, *Die Neubabylonischen Königsinschriften*, pp. 284 f. Leipzig, 1912.

[5] Herodotus (2:159), through an understandable error, wrote "Magdolos" instead
of Megiddo in reporting Necho's victory and says that he then conquered "Kadytis"
(i.e., Kadesh on the Orontes); cf. W. W. Cannon in ZAW N.F. 3 (1926) 63 f.

of Tyre (585-573). He could thus devote his energies to the deeds of piety and the great public works of which he proudly speaks in his inscriptions. The city of Babylon, that so astonished Greek historians with its grandeur and magnificence, was his creation, and he could well have boasted in the words of Dan. 4:30 (Aramaic 4:27), "Is not this the great Babylon, which I have built as a royal house by the might of my power and for the honor of my majesty?"

These epoch-making changes in the international situation from Ashurbanipal to Nebuchadnezzar, when Jeremiah was active, had of necessity profound, and often tragic, repercussions in the kingdom of Judah. Before the death of Ashurbanipal in 625 it does not appear that the seething nationalistic aspirations of the Judeans found expression in overt acts of rebellion against Assyria, then still at the height of its power. Even the assassination of Amon in 638 was not apparently regarded as a seditious act by the Assyrian authorities. But the Deuteronomistic reformation in 621, four years after Ashurbanipal's death when the rapid disintegration of the Assyrian Empire began, was not merely a purification of the worship but, through the desecration of the Assyrian sacred objects in the Temple, an actual declaration of independence.

This independence of Judea, made possible by the downfall of Assyria, was brief (621-609). It could last only as long as the kingdoms of the Nile and the Tigris-Euphrates valleys were too weak or too bewildered to extend their dominion over Palestine, as was the case only in two other periods of ancient history (1000-740 and 142-63 B.C.). When the fragments of the Assyrian Empire crystallized again into great kingdoms, the days of Judean freedom were over.

Aglow with pride in his kingdom's independence and convinced that his God Jehovah, whose worship he had purified in accordance with the divine Law, would stand by him, Josiah took the heroic step of meeting Pharaoh Necho in battle at Megiddo, but paid with his life for his rashness (609). Josiah's body was taken to Jerusalem for burial. The city was profoundly shocked. The king was beloved by his subjects and sincerely mourned (Jer. 22:10a). Even so severe a critic as Jeremiah had words of praise for the pious king (22:15b-16). But the wave of patriotism that had carried Josiah to his death did not immediately abate in the midst of general sorrow and disappointment. "The people of the land" in an outburst of nationalism made a last assertion of independence and, in patent defiance of Pharaoh Necho, anointed Jehoahaz (Shallum) as their king (II Kings 23:30). Jeremiah (22:10-12) seems to have realized the tragic futility of this act.

After three months, Necho summoned Jehoahaz to Riblah, sent him to Egypt in chains (II Kings 23:33 f.), imposed a war indemnity on Judah, and made his older brother Eliakim (609-598) king of Judah, after changing his name to Jehoiakim, as a token of Judah's subjection to Egypt.

Jerusalem did not resign herself to foreign domination. At first the patriotism of the masses, restrained from political manifestations, expressed itself in a renewed enthusiasm for the Deuteronomic reforms of Josiah. Certain of divine favor because it possessed the Temple (Jer. 7:4) and the Law (8:8) of Jehovah, the people were fully convinced that their God would soon change their fortunes as a reward for fulfilling the Law. An enthusiastic assembly gathered in the Temple on a festive occasion soon after the accession of Jehoiakim. In a frenzy of enraged patriotism and of blind superstition they almost lynched Jeremiah for his prediction of the destruction of the Temple and for his outspoken denunciation of their religious hypocrisy and moral depravity (Jer. 7 and 26). Only the intervention of some elders and ministers of the king saved Jeremiah from the fate that befell another prophet, Uriah, executed for uttering speeches in the same vein (26:20-24).

Eventually this popularity of the Deuteronomic reform declined and vanished, as the masses observed that Josiah and, presumably, Jehoahaz had not been saved from a dire fate by their zeal for the Law, and that the expected divine deliverance failed to come. In their fickleness the people, probably encouraged by Jehoiakim, returned to the pagan practices of their fathers (7:18, 31; 8:2; cf. 11:13; 44:17 f.). The majority of the prophets fanned the patriotism of the people by deceitfully optimistic assurances of peace and prosperity (Jer. 6:14 = 8:11; 14:13). Jehoiakim, until the very end of his reign, followed the policy of Manasseh and gave free rein to the superstitions of his subjects while restraining all manifestations of their nationalistic dreams of independence. Jeremiah had nothing but contempt for this king, who built himself luxurious palaces with callous indifference for the misery of his subjects, and ruled them unjustly and despotically (22:13-19).

Jeremiah (or a contemporary poet) celebrated the victory of Nebuchadnezzar over Pharaoh Necho at Carchemish (605) with a triumphant ode (46:1-12). It is probable that Jehoiakim submitted to Nebuchadnezzar at once, and not four years later, as Josephus asserts in *Antiquities* 10:6, 1, presumably on the basis of the questionable and ambiguous statement in II Kings 24:1. But in 598 Jehoiakim refused to pay his tribute to Nebuchadnezzar and was attacked by the Chaldean garrisons, strengthened with bands of Arameans, Moabites, and Ammonites (Jer. 12:7-17; II Kings 24:2). He died during the course of these military operations, possibly in battle. This would explain his unceremonious burial, compared by Jeremiah (22:19; cf. 36:30) to "the burial of a donkey." When Nebuchadnezzar finally arrived at Jerusalem, Jehoiachin (Jeconiah,

Coniah), the son and successor of Jehoiakim, eighteen years of age, promptly surrendered after a reign of three months (597).

The Judean king and his court (cf. Jer. 22:24-30; 27:20; 29:2, and possibly 13:18 f.), together with the "men of valor" (landowners), the craftsmen, and the ironworkers, were exiled to Babylonia; the poorest classes were left in Jerusalem. The number of exiled men was, according to Jer. 52:28, 3,023; the figure is increased to 8,000 in II Kings 24:16 and to 10,000 in 24:14. If the smallest number is considered correct, the Exiles, including women and children, would have been at least 10,000. Jeremiah was allowed to remain. Ezekiel, according to his book, was exiled with the others "by the river Chebar" (Ez. 1:1, 3, etc.), in the vicinity of Nippur. In the mistaken belief that the Judeans, deprived of their leaders, would henceforth submit to his yoke, Nebuchadnezzar placed a third son of Josiah, Mattaniah, on the throne, "and changed his name to Zedekiah" (II Kings 24:17) as a public sign of the new king's vassalage (cf. Ez. 17:13).

Zedekiah apparently intended to remain submissive, but it is questionable whether even a king of far stronger character could have controlled the seething nationalism of his people. The prophets continued to stir the spirits with alluring promises of a triumphant future (Jer. 23:16-24; 27:14-18; 28:1-4, 11). The diplomats, as soon as Pharaoh Necho was dead (593), opened negotiations with the neighboring nations (Jer. 27:3) and planned a general rebellion. They hoped that Necho's successor, Psamtik II (593-588), would not remain at peace with Nebuchadnezzar, as Necho had done after his defeat at Carchemish.[6] This plot, denounced by Jeremiah (27-29), was nipped in the bud, and Zedekiah sent envoys to Babylon to reassert his fealty (Jer. 29:3; 51:59 [LXX]).

As for the masses, the deportation of the upper classes in 597 had produced a result contrary to that expected by Nebuchadnezzar. The poor, taking possession of the lands and houses that had belonged to these wealthy Exiles, acquired, like typical *nouveaux riches*, an exaggerated sense of their importance. For parvenus are usually snobs. Crying joyfully, "The land belongs to us for a possession!" (Ez. 11:15; cf. 33:24), they regarded the former owners as God-forsaken exiles: they themselves were now God's people. Jeremiah did not gain popularity in their midst by declaring that, on the contrary, the good figs had been taken to Babylonia and the bad figs had been left in Jerusalem (Jer. 24)!

Only a spark was needed to turn the inflammable state of mind of Jerusalem into an open conflagration. Few, besides Jeremiah, realized

---

[6] Psamtik actually went to Phoenicia in 590, but it is not certain that, as A. Alt maintains (ZAW 30 [1910] 288 ff.), he had military objectives in view (cf. H. R. Hall, in *Cambridge Ancient History*, Vol. III, pp. 300 f.).

the futility of another rebellion against Nebuchadnezzar. When Pharaoh Hophra (or Apries, 588-569) organized at his accession an expedition into Asia, Judah at once revolted. Hophra (named in Jer. 44:30) attacked Sidon by land and Tyre by sea (Herodotus 2:161; cf. Diodorus 1:69). Thus Tyre, Judah, and Ammon joined Egypt in defying Nebuchadnezzar (cf. Ez. 21:23-37), while Edom and Philistia remained loyal to him (Ez. 25:12-17). Establishing his headquarters at Riblah, Nebuchadnezzar sent a detachment of troops against Tyre and appeared before Jerusalem with the main body of his troops in January 587. Food in the city was scarce, but the fortifications were formidable. Joyous enthusiasm filled Jerusalem in April, when Nebuchadnezzar lifted the siege to repel an Egyptian army sent by Hophra to help the beleaguered city (Ez. 30:20 f.). But Jeremiah still foreboded the worst (except for Zedekiah, 34:4 f.) and urged prompt surrender (21:1-10; 37:1-10; cf. 34:1-3, 6 f., 18-22). He even asserted that only those who went over to the Babylonians would survive (21:9) and was arrested as a deserter when he himself attempted to slip out of the doomed city (37:11-15).

The siege was soon resumed; it lasted one year and a half. Famine prevailed (II Kings 25:3). The torments of hunger are vividly described, perhaps by eyewitnesses, in the pages of Lamentations (2:11 f., 20; 4:3 f., 10). In July, 586, a breach was made in the walls. Zedekiah with a detachment of troops fled by night, but was overtaken near Jericho (II Kings 25:4 f.; Lam. 4:19 f.). Brought to Nebuchadnezzar at Riblah, he witnessed the execution of his sons, was blinded, and brought in chains to Babylonia (II Kings 25:6). After a month of plundering, Jerusalem, with its Temple and palaces, was burned to the ground. According to Jer. 52:29, 832 men (with their families) were exiled to Babylonia; men of the lowest classes were left to tend the vineyards and the fields (II Kings 25:12).

The land of Judah thus ceased to be a kingdom under the dynasty of David and became a Babylonian province. As its first governor Nebuchadnezzar appointed Gedaliah, a grandson of Shaphan, presumably Josiah's scribe. Residing at Mizpah, Gedaliah was beginning to bring order out of chaos when, only two months after the burning of the Temple in August, he was assassinated by Ishmael, a fanatic of David's seed, instigated by the Ammonites. Fearing Nebuchadnezzar's vengeance, a group of Judeans fled to Egypt, forcing the reluctant Jeremiah to accompany them (Jer. 40:1-43:7; II Kings 25:22-26). After a final attempt at insurrection in 582, when 745 men and their families were exiled to Babylonia (Jer. 52:30), the remnant of the Judeans lived miserably and dejectedly until Nehemiah in 444 rebuilt the walls of Jerusalem and revived the Jewish community both politically and religiously.

2. *Life and Character of Jeremiah*

Jeremiah, the son of Hilkiah (1:1), was born at Anathoth (less than two hours' walk, northeast of Jerusalem) about 645 B.C., and died presumably in Egypt shortly after 586. His father belonged to a family of priests living in Anathoth (1:1) and was probably a descendant of Abiathar, the sole survivor of the priests of Nob (I Sam. 22:20). After serving David many years, Abiathar was exiled by Solomon to Anathoth, where he had some fields (I Kings 2:26).[7] Jeremiah's family still possessed landed estates in Anathoth (Jer. 32:6-15).

Anathoth was reckoned to the territory of Benjamin (1:1; 32:8; 37:12) and Jeremiah, although he lived in Jerusalem the better part of his life, always remained at heart a Benjamite—a Northern Israelite rather than a Judean (cf. 29:27). His favorite prophet, whose teaching made a profound impression on him in his youth, was Hosea, the only Northerner among the reforming prophets.[8] Jeremiah urged the Benjamites to escape from the Scythian hordes (6:1) and went to Anathoth to preach in favor of the reforms of Josiah (11:18-23). He remembered with heartfelt emotion the ancestral mother of Benjamin, Rachel, whose grave was reverenced not far from his birthplace (31:15). He recalled the destruction of the Ephraimite sanctuary of Shiloh during the Philistine wars (7:12, 14; 26:6, 9). Early in his ministry Jeremiah addressed two moving appeals to "backsliding Israel" (2:4-3:5 and 3:6-22a; cf. W. R. Arnold, *Ephod and Ark*, p. 76, n. 2, where the spurious material is indicated) and in his old age he still hoped for the salvation of the "virgin of Israel" (31:2-5, 15-22a).

Jeremiah was called to the prophetic mission in 626 (1:2; 25:3), when he was still "a child" (1:6 f.), perhaps not quite twenty years of age; but he believed that Jehovah had selected him even before he came forth from his mother's womb (1:5). Written more than twenty years later, the account of the divine call (1:4-10, 17-19) clearly reveals the polarity of his nature. Naturally of a timid, introspective, sensitive, emotional disposition—distrustful of his own abilities (1:6) and tormented by uncontrollable fear (1:8)—he became through an inner power, which to him was unquestionably divine (1:9 f.), "a fortified city, an iron pillar, and walls of brass, against the whole country, against the kings of Judah, against the princes thereof, against the priests thereof, and against the people of the land" (1:18; cf. 15:20). Jehovah appointed him "over the

---

[7] On the basis of tendentious glosses in Samuel many critics still affirm that Abiathar and the priests of Nob were descendants and relatives of Eli, the priest of Shiloh. The absurdity of this genealogical connection has been demonstrated by W. R. Arnold (*Ephod and Ark*, p. 14 f.).

[8] Cf. K. Gross, "Hoseas Einfluss auf Jeremias Anschauungen" (NKZ 42 [1931] 241-255, 327-343).

nations and over the kingdoms, to root out, and to pull down, . . . , to build, and to plant" (1:10). The long struggle between his native reserve and the ecstatic compulsion to heroism ended with the triumph of the latter. All in all, he was more like an oak than like the weeping willow of popular misconception. He became a warrior, rushing into the thick of battle, oblivious of his shaking knees and chattering teeth. Under the spell of divine inspiration, he boldly defied the world. The erroneous attribution to Jeremiah of the Book of Lamentations has contributed to the current distortion of his character, making his name a byword for unrelieved pessimism (cf. "jeremiad") and qualifying him as the "weeping" prophet.

Soon after his call Jeremiah detected a symbolical meaning in two commonplace sights: a sprig of an almond tree, which (like the basket of summer fruit in Am. 8:1 f.) suggested through a pun (*shāqēd*, almond tree; *shōqēd*, watchful) Jehovah's vigilance (1:11 f.); and a boiling pot, somehow turned northward, which suggested an attack upon Judah by Northern nations (1:13-16).

These Northern invaders are generally identified with the Scythians who, between 630 and 624, came southward along the Mediterranean coast as far as Egypt, whence they were turned back, if we believe Herodotus (1:105), by the bribes of Psamtik I. In a series of poems dating from this period, Jeremiah gave expression to his terror at the advance of an invading host from the north (4:5b-8, 13-17a, 19-26, 29-31; 5:15-17; 6:1-7, 22-26; possibly also 8:14-17; 10:19-22). After Photius had discovered in 6:22-26 an allusion to the Scythians, J. G. Eichhorn (1819) suggested that Jeremiah wrote chs. 4-6 under the overwhelming impression of the Scythian invasion, and this view has become prevalent. F. Wilke,[9] however, has argued that Jeremiah in these poems (as well as Zeph. 1-2; Joel 2:20; Deut. 28:49-57) does not refer to the Scythians, but to the armies of Nebuchadnezzar.

Jeremiah actually composed some poems when the panic over the Scythian menace—which did not materialize in Judah—was at its height. These poems dating from about 626 (comprising a good part of the passages in 4-6 and 8-10 quoted above) were rewritten by Jeremiah more than twenty years later, when Judah was menaced by Nebuchadnezzar,[10] and were supplemented with denunciations of Judah's sins and

[9] Das Skythenproblem in Jeremiabuch, in *Alttestam. Studien R. Kittel dargebracht* (BWAT 13, pp. 222-254. Leipzig, 1913).

[10] The references to chariots (4:13) and to siege operations (6:6) are obviously more appropriate to the Chaldeans than to the Scythians. C. C. Torrey (JBL 56 [1937] 208 f.) identifies the "foe from the north" with Alexander and dates Jer. 1-10 (and much else in Jeremiah) in the third century. He regards the connection that chs. 1-10 have with the seventh century as only "imaginary." J. P. Hyatt (JBL 59 [1940] 499-513) sees in the northern enemy the Chaldeans and Medes who destroyed Nineveh in 612 B.C.

moral reflections appropriate for that time. In their present form, therefore, 4-6 (8:14-17; 10:17-25) contain revised poems on the Scythians
(626), homiletic exhortations by Jeremiah (604-598), and editorial
matter.

When the Deuteronomic Book of Moses was found in the Temple
(621), the prophetess Huldah (II Kings 22:14), and not Jeremiah, was
consulted in regard to its validity. Jeremiah was still unknown to Josiah
and to his advisers, apparently not having yet appeared in public at
Jerusalem to declare the word of Jehovah. The Scythian poems in their
original form are addressed to the Benjamites and were recited at
Anathoth, if delivered publicly at the time of their composition. The
genuine oracles in 2:4-3:22 also were delivered there before 621. But as
soon as Josiah carried out his reforms in accordance with the newly
found book, Jeremiah was ordered by Jehovah to proclaim "the words of
this covenant" in the streets of Jerusalem and in the cities of Judah
(11:1-17). When he did so at Anathoth, Jehovah revealed to him that a
plot was afoot to "cut him off from the land of the living" (11:18-23).
Jeremiah escaped in time (perhaps never to return) but wondered why
Jehovah allowed those wicked people—including his own relatives—to
remain unpunished (12:1-6).

Later, however, Jeremiah realized that the new Law had merely given
the people the illusion of having become "wise" (8:8) and that Josiah's
reformation had cleansed only the outside of the cup (8:4-9). Nevertheless, Jeremiah never doubted the sincerity and high purpose of Josiah.
After the king's death at Megiddo in 609 the prophet praised his righteous
rule (22:15 f.) and exhorted the people to weep not for Josiah but rather
for his ill-fated successor Shallum (22:10-12).

In any case the Deuteronomic Law ceased to be enforced between 609
and 597. Religiously and ethically Jerusalem sank again to the level of
the period before 621, if not lower. Jeremiah was forced to admit that
the "vain pen of the scribes" who prepared copies of the Deuteronomic
Code "had forsooth toiled for naught" (8:8). In his "Temple Address"
(7:1-8:12), pronounced soon after 609, early in the reign of Jehoiakim
(26:1), Jeremiah declared that the Judeans, overlooking the ethical and
religious ideals of that Code, had enforced only some of its insignificant
regulations about sacrifices (7:21-26). They violated both the spirit
(7:23) and the letter (7:6, 9, 17-20, 30 f.; 8:1-3) of Deuteronomy. Having
closed all the sanctuaries of Jehovah except the Temple in Jerusalem (in
accordance with Deut. 12), they regarded the latter as the earthly abode
of their God and consequently believed that its mere presence in their
midst would protect and deliver them (7:4, 10). When Jeremiah declared
that Jehovah would destroy the Temple as he had destroyed the sanctuary
at Shiloh (7:11-14) and cast the Judeans out of his sight, as previously

the Ephraimites (7:15; cf. 26:9), in a burst of indignation the people would have lynched him on the spot if the authorities had not intervened (26).

Twice, in Anathoth and in Jerusalem, Jeremiah's life had been threatened when he proclaimed the divine message. Such terrifying experiences, doubly shattering for his sensitive spirit, would have driven him insane (cf. 20:14-18, where he wishes he were dead) or forced him forever into solitary retreat (cf. 9:2 [H. 9:1]) had not the mysterious overwhelming sense of the presence of Jehovah continually renewed his assurance and persistence (20:7-12). A tragic but undaunted figure, the prophet was torn by a twofold inner struggle—between his longing for peace and his cruel inescapable task, and between his tender love for his people (8:18-9:1 [H. 8:18-23]) and his passionate, occasionally vindictive, denunciation (11:20 = 20:12; 18:18-23)—but he continued to the end as "a man of contention to the whole earth" (15:10), denied even the companionship of a wife and children (16:2). And yet, when a severe drought and famine, perhaps in the early part of Jehoiakim's reign, caused dreadful suffering, Jeremiah wholeheartedly interceded for Judah (14:1-15:9; cf. 7:16; 11:14). We may infer from 18:20 that these oracles were pronounced shortly before the events of 18:1-20:6.

Later in the reign of Jehoiakim, immediately after the battle of Carchemish in 605 (cf. 46:1-12), Jeremiah became convinced that Nebuchadnezzar's yoke over Judah could not be cast off. Jehovah, in whose hands nations are like clay, had decreed it so. Judah was like soft clay, fashioned by the potter into an imperfect vessel and lumped together again (18:1-12; 18:13-17), or like the earthen bottle that Jeremiah shattered symbolically in Topheth, the sanctuary of Moloch (in the valley of the Sons of Hinnom) where infants were sacrificed (19:1 f., 10-13). When Jeremiah explained the meaning of the shattered bottle in the Temple itself, Pashhur, the chief priest, placed Jeremiah publicly in stocks for the night (19:14-20:6) and forbade him, ostensibly, future access to the Temple (36:5).

Late in the same year (605), while in enforced seclusion, Jeremiah was ordered by Jehovah to dictate to his secretary Baruch his prophecies of the preceding twenty years, from the time of his call (36:1-8). About a year later, Baruch read the scroll in the Temple, in the presence of the throngs that had gathered there in December to observe a fast (36:9 f.). Summoned before the royal ministers, Baruch read the scroll again (36:11-15). They advised him and Jeremiah to go into hiding (36:16-20). In his winter house, Jehoiakim, after listening to the reading of the first columns of the scroll, cut it up with a knife and cast it into a burning brazier (36:21-26). During the following years Jeremiah dictated a new version of his book, adding "many like words" to his oracles (36:27-32).

This second scroll became the first edition of our Book of Jeremiah and contained most of the genuine oracles now found in Jer. 1-25.

Now that the king himself was determined to slay Jeremiah, his life depended on successful concealment. How Jeremiah, helped by influential friends, outwitted the royal police during seven years (605-598) is unfortunately not recorded. These years of seclusion, in which Jeremiah could no longer deliver his oracles in public, were nevertheless profoundly significant in his career. When he entered this period of solitary retreat he was tormented, as we saw, by anguish of soul and inner struggles. When he emerged at the end of Jehoiakim's reign, he was truly "an iron pillar and wall of brass" (1:18; cf. 15:19-21), no longer interceding for his people, no longer complaining, no longer arguing with his God.

It seems likely that the "Confessions," into which Jeremiah poured his mental anguish, were written for the most part during these years of silence; a few may be earlier, but none can be later. It is certain, from a study of their contents, that the "Confessions" were not in the first collection of oracles prepared by Jeremiah in 605. But in preparing the second larger edition of his book during the following years of solitude, Jeremiah not only added his "Confessions" (1:4-19; 11:18-23; 12:1-6; 15:10 f., 15-21; 17:14-18; 18:18-23; 20:7-12, 14-18), in some of which (1:4-19; 11:18-23; 12:1-6) he reinterpreted earlier experiences in the light of his present dejection, but he also inserted into some of his earliest poems cries of agony expressing his present mood (cf. the addition of 4:19 to 4:20 f., and 6:11; 8:21-9:1 [H. 8:21-23]).

Daily in danger of detection, aware of the general animosity against him, and helpless to save his beloved nation from irretrievable ruin, Jeremiah during the last seven years of Jehoiakim underwent extreme agonies (15:18) of despair, doubt, and distress. Baruch, his faithful companion, was far from cheerful: he complained bitterly of his fate and was rebuked gently by his master (45). Convinced that his prophetic oracles were not only responsible for his plight (15:18) and isolation (15:17; 16:8; 20:8), but were actually the fire and hammer that would destroy Judah (1:10; 5:14; 23:29), Jeremiah cursed the day of his birth (20:14-18, the most tragic of his words, more bitter than Job 3; cf. 15:10), and even dared to call God to account. Jehovah had deceived him (15:18) and prevailed over him by sheer might (20:7). If he refused to prophesy, the divine word was like a burning fire shut up in his bones (20:9); if he prophesied he aroused antagonism and violent hatred (20:8, 10). And yet Jeremiah far from desiring, like Jonah, a speedy fulfillment of his dire predictions (17:15 f., revised text) had repeatedly interceded for his wicked countrymen (18:20 and likewise probably in 15:11, where the text is corrupt) and now weeps over their ruin (8:21-23). Why, then, does Jehovah allow the wicked to prosper (12:1-6) while Jeremiah, his herald, is persecuted and disgraced?

Jeremiah is the first in the line of mystics who have recorded their inner experiences; the first to argue thus with God and to have ascended *de profundis*, from the slough of despond, to a glorious and triumphant faith. At first he pitifully begs God to heal and save him (17:14) and, in a mood of irritation, to avenge him of his foes (15:15; 17:18; 18:21-23; 20:12). God replies that if he returns and separates in himself what is precious from what is vile, he shall be God's mouthpiece and the people will turn to him (15:19); then God will save him from the hand of evil and violent men (15:20). Finally Jeremiah reached complete trust and harmony with his God: Jehovah is his "hope" (17:14, where "my praise" should be read "my hope") and his strong protector against his persecutors (17:11). Having completely overcome his despair, Jeremiah found his deepest joy in the word of Jehovah (15:16) and became, as God had said at the time of his call (1:18), a wall of brass capable of resisting all attacks (15:20). When the curtain lifts again at the end of Jehoiakim's reign, the prophet came forth from his hiding place as a man of iron, ready to endure, unflinchingly, renewed persecutions at the hand of the leaders and the masses of Jerusalem.

In his first public appearance, at the end of the reign of Jehoiakim (598), Jeremiah praised the Rechabites, who had come to Jerusalem on account of the war (II Kings 24:2), for their steadfast fidelity to their vow of abstinence (35). During the brief reign of Jehoiachin (597) Jeremiah bewailed the tragic fate of this king (22:24-30) and of Jerusalem's upper classes, taken captive by Nebuchadnezzar (13:15-27), but with a strong note of denunciation for the sins of the wicked city.

In his first oracle under Zedekiah in 597-596 he compared the Exiles to good figs and the Judeans left in their country to rotten ones (24). Early in 593 the prophet warned Judah and the neighboring countries against plotting rebellion. He appeared in public wearing a wooden yoke as a sign of submission to Nebuchadnezzar. When Hananiah, an optimistic prophet, broke the yoke from off his neck, Jeremiah replaced it with one of iron (27-28). At the same time he wrote to the Exiles, exhorting them to mistrust the promises of a speedy return (for the Exile would last "seventy years," 29:10; cf. 25:11) and to settle down for a permanent residence in Babylonia (29).

When Nebuchadnezzar besieged Jerusalem (587), Zedekiah consulted Jeremiah but neither the king (21:1-7) nor the people (21:8-10) would follow his advice and surrender. Nevertheless, the prophet promised that Zedekiah would die in peace (34:1-7). Shortly after this the people of Jerusalem released their slaves, in accordance with the Law (Ex. 21:2; Deut. 15:12), hoping to induce Jehovah to help them; but no sooner was the siege lifted on account of the approach of an Egyptian army, than they promptly brought them back into subjection (34:8-22). Consulted again by the king during this respite, Jeremiah declared that the Chaldeans would return and burn up the city (37:1-10). He was arrested as a deserter when he attempted to go to Anathoth to take possession of a field (37:11-15). While incarcerated in the house of Jonathan, Jeremiah was again brought before the king and, although he foretold that Zedekiah would fall into the hands of Nebuchadnezzar, he was allowed to reside in "the court of the guard" (37:16-21). On the advice of the king, Jeremiah lied about the real purpose of this audience (38:24-28a).

Some of the leaders, fearing that Jeremiah's continued warnings to the people to flee from the doomed city would weaken their morale, cast him into a cistern (38:1-6). Zedekiah, who had been forced to consent to this indignity, allowed, however, Ebed-melech, a Negro eunuch, to deliver the prophet from probable death. Henceforth the prophet remained in the court of the guard (38:7-13), and promised that the good Ebed-melech should not be slain when Jerusalem would fall (39:15-18). In his last audience with Zedekiah, the prophet reiterated his advice to surrender at once (38:14-23).[11]

Seeing that his counsel was invariably disregarded, Jeremiah realized that the city and the kingdom were doomed and for a time he seems to have thought that the future of the nation rested entirely on the Exiles of 597 (24; 29). And yet, in the dark days just before the destruction of Jerusalem, Jeremiah purchased a field from his cousin Hanamel, as a sign of better times to come, when houses, fields, and vineyards would again be bought (32:1-15, omitting the redactional introduction in 32:1b-6a). Jehovah confirmed this hope for a better future (32:16, 24 f., 26, 37-44). North Israel will repent and return to its land (31:2-5, 7-8a, 9, 11, 12b-22a). After the removal of the incompetent kings of Judah (23:1 f.), Jehovah will raise up a "righteous scion" of David's house (23:5 f.; cf. 33:14-16). After the passing of the present disease will come healing and the rule of a pious native king (30:4-21); then Jehovah will make "a new covenant" with both Israel and Judah, writing his Law in their hearts, and forgive their iniquities (31:31-34).

Jerusalem was finally taken by the Chaldeans, and Jeremiah was treated with great consideration, upon orders of Nebuchadnezzar (38:28b; 39:3, 11-14, omitting the rest of 39:1-14). When by mistake he was included in a caravan of captives and was recognized at Ramah, he was allowed to go to Gedaliah, the new governor, at Mizpah (40:1-6). But

[11] Some critics have suggested that 37:17-21 and 38:14-27 are parallel accounts of the same audience with Zedekiah, and in fact that a double narrative may be detected in Baruch's biography; cf. the parallel between 39:1-14 and 40:1-6 (see J. Skinner. *Prophecy and Religion*, pp. 258 f., note. Cambridge, 1922). This theory, though not impossible, is unnecessary.

after Ishmael murdered Gedaliah, Jeremiah and Baruch were forced to go to Egypt with a group of fleeing Jews who feared Nebuchadnezzar's vengeance (40:7-43:7). At Tahpanhes (perhaps Tell Defenne, about 2 miles west of el-Kantara on the Suez Canal) Jeremiah hid some stones in the masonry of Pharaoh's palace, as a sign of Nebuchadnezzar's (unrealized) conquest of Egypt (43:8-13) and, in his last preserved oracle, denounced the revival of pagan cults, particularly the worship of the Queen of Heaven, among the Jews in Egypt (44, to a great extent redactional).

There is no reason to suppose that Jeremiah ever returned to his native land. He probably died in Egypt not long after 586, perhaps comforted by the thought that his long tragic mission was at last completed.

3. The Book of Jeremiah

The critical analysis of our book has identified in it three groups of writings: the words dictated or written by Jeremiah himself, a biography of the prophet presumably written by his secretary Baruch, and miscellaneous contributions from the hands of redactors and later authors.

Although Jeremiah began to prophesy in 626, he did not commit his words and deeds to writing until he dictated to Baruch, late in 605, the most telling of his oracles (36:1-8). That this scroll contained only a selection of his addresses is proved by its brevity: in December 604, Baruch read it twice, before a third reading was begun in the presence of Jehoiakim, in the course of the same day. The contents of this scroll, which was consumed by fire immediately after it was read in public, is a matter of conjecture. Keeping in mind that the diction of the destroyed scroll was not preserved intact in its enlarged edition, which was dictated from memory by the prophet and, not being intended for public reading, had a more intimate character, we may tentatively surmise that the first scroll contained the following oracles, listed here chronologically: the symbolical meaning of an almond tree and of a seething kettle, dating from 626 (1:11-16); a sermon urging support for Josiah's reformation in 621 (11:1-17), abundantly revised and annotated); the prophecy of Shallum's exile (22:10-12), in 609; the "Temple Address" (7:1-8:3 considerably expanded) and related denunciations (8:4-9), soon after 609; the announcement of the devastation of Judah and the destruction of Jerusalem (8:18-9:11; 9:15-22 [H. 9:10, 14-21], rewritten by the prophet after 605). The Scythian poems in their original form (about 626) have not been included in this list because the expected invasion had not taken place and Jeremiah rewrote them between 604 and 597, applying them to the Chaldeans. It is unlikely that the oracles on North Israel (2:4-3:22a) and the revelation of the plot of the men of Anathoth (11:18-23) were part of this book, which contained only the oracles "against Jerusalem and against Judah" (36:2, revised in accordance with the LXX; "and against all the nations" is an editorial addition). The Scythian poems were at first addressed to Benjamin and not to Judah.

When Jehoiakim consigned this volume to the flames in December 604, Jeremiah went into hiding for seven years and prepared the new edition, considerably enlarged, which has come down to us in the canonical book. The new volume is characterized by a more subjective tenor, marked by the addition of the introspective "Confessions" of the prophet, and by the free expression of his personal emotions in connection with his past experiences and with national events. In general the tone was probably more bitter than in the first edition. It is likely that the new volume consisted of the following sections: 1:(1-4), 5-19; 2:(1-3), 4-3:22a; 4:5-8, 13-21, 23-26, 29-31; 5:1-17, 20-31; 6:1-9:22 (H. 9:21) (revised by a Deuteronomist); 10:17-22; 11 (revised by a Deuteronomist); 12:1-3, 5 f.; 14:1-15:9 (including glosses); 15:10 f., 15-21; 16:1-9, 16 f.; 17:14-18; 18:1-19:13 (editorially expanded); 20:7-18; 22:1-23; 23:9-32 (?); 25 (?); 46:(2), 3-12.

Like his predecessors, Jeremiah regarded preaching as the primary function of a prophet and became a writer only when he was prevented from delivering his message orally, from 605 to 598. It is therefore probable that after Jeremiah resumed his public ministry in 598 (cf. ch. 35) he left to Baruch the task of supplementing his writings. Even the autobiographical accounts of events from 598 to 587 (35; 24; 27; 32) and the oracles from 597 (13) to 587-586 (21; 23:1-6, but not 30:12-22a; 31:2-5, 15-22a, 31-34) may well have been penned by Baruch rather than dictated by Jeremiah. After 598 it is impossible to separate actual writings of Jeremiah from the biography of Baruch except in 30-31. In ch. 32, for instance, the third person and the first person alternate capriciously, and in 32:6, 26 the Hebrew and the LXX disagree in this matter. Some critics assign ch. 34 to Jeremiah, others to Baruch; and O. Eissfeldt assigns 34:8-22 to Baruch and 34:1-7 to Jeremiah. It is difficult to understand why ch. 27 should be generally assigned to Jeremiah and ch. 28 to Baruch: they are but the two parts of one story and the first and third persons are used in both (first person: 27:2 [not in LXX], 12, 16; 28:1 [in all versions]; third person: 27:1 [not in LXX]; 28:5, 10, 12). It may therefore well be that Jeremiah himself committed nothing to writing after 598, with the exception of the genuine oracles of consolation and encouragement, after the downfall of Judah, contained in 30-31, which are included in the little volume (30-33) predicting the return of the Exiles to their land (30:3, 18; 31:23; 32:44; 33:7, 26). This little volume is probably an expansion of a booklet of comfort prepared by Jeremiah himself (cf. 30:1-3). If this view is correct, the actual writings of Jeremiah are confined to the book prepared in the years 605-598 and to the comforting appendix (parts of 30-31) which he added, as a sort of spiritual testament, in 586.

Although decisive evidence is lacking, everything indicates that the biography of Jeremiah contained in his book was composed by his secretary Baruch. This biography is confined to the years 608-586, and it is probable that the association between the two men was confined to this period. Baruch's book, restoring the original chronological order, comprised the following sections, which describe events that took place in the years indicated: 26:1-19, 24, 20-23 (608). 19:14-20:6 (605). 36 and 45 (605-604). 27-29; 51:59-64 (593). 21:1-10; 34; 37; 38:24-28a; 38:1-13; 39:15-18; 38:14-23 (587-586, during the siege of Jerusalem); 38:28b; 39:3, 11-14; (40:1-5); 40:6-16; 41-44 (586, after the fall of Jerusalem). We should perhaps add: 35 (598); 24 (597); 32 (587-586). For 35 and 24 bridge the gap between 604 and 593, and Baruch is mentioned in 32. It is not to be excluded that the oracles in 13 (597) and 21:11-14 and 23:1-6 (587) were also part of Baruch's book.

These two books, Jeremiah's and Baruch's, probably include all genuine information about Jeremiah's words and deeds. The rest of the canonical book is of questionable authenticity. We may analyze Jeremiah's own writings as follows:

1. WORDS OF JEREMIAH

a. From 626 to 622: two oracles in verse addressed to North Israel, pronounced in Anathoth (2:4-11aα, 11aβ-14, 17-26a, 27-28a; 3:1 f., 3b-5. 3:12-16 [omitting "under every green tree" in 3:13b; "and I will bring you to Zion" in 3:14] and 3:20-22a; 2:2aβb may be original). The poems on the Scythian invasion (4:5-8, 13, 15-17a, 19-21, 23-26, 29-31; 5:15-17; 6:1-5, 22-26; 8:16 f.; 10:17-22); originally addressed to North Israel, they were rewritten by Jeremiah for Judah with reference to Nebuchadnezzar's campaigns against Jerusalem and supplemented with oracles on the sins and punishment of the Judeans (4:14; 5:1-14, 23-31; 6:6-21, 27-30; 8:14 f.); later editors have added 4:3 f., 9-12, 17b-18, 22, 27 f.; 5:18-22; 10:23-25.

b. About 621: oracles from the time of Josiah's reformation (11:18-23 and a small part of 11:1-16).

c. From 620 to 609: sermons on the futility of Josiah's reformation, attached to the Scythian poems (5:1-14, 20-31; 6:6-21, 27-30; 8:4-9. 8:10-12 is quoted from 6:12-15; 8:13-15; see above under a).

d. During 609: the announcement of the captivity of Jehoahaz (22: 10-12).

e. From 609 to 604: oracles denouncing Jehoiakim's despotism (22: 13-19) and Judah's moral and religious depravity (7:1-8:3, expanded by Deuteronomists; 8:18-9:11 [H. 9:10]; 9:15-22 [H. 9:14-21]; 14:2-10, 17-22;

15:1-6, revised; 16:1-9, 16 f.; 25:1-14, revised). An oracle against Egypt after the battle of Carchemish in 605 (46:1-12).

f. From 604 to 598: the "Confessions," dictated to Baruch but never delivered orally in public (11:18-23; 12:1-3, 5 f.; 15:10 f., 15-21; 17:14-18; 18:18-23; 20:7-12, 14-18; cf. 1:4-19; 4:19; 6:11; 8:21-9:1 [H. 8:21-23]).

g. In 598: oracles against Jehoiakim (22:13-19) and Judah (12:7-13 [14-17]).

h. In 597: oracles on Jehoiachin (22:24-30), and on king and nation (13:18-27).

i. From 597 to 586: oracles of doom (10:17-22, based probably on a poem about the Scythians; perhaps parts of 15:5-9 and 17:1-4; 21:11-22:7; 23:9-32); oracles of consolation and hope for North Israel (31:2-5 [7-8a, 9, 11], 12b-22a; cf. ch. 3), for Judah (23:[1-4], 5 f. [= 33:15 f.]; 30:4-21 [in part]; 31:23-25), and for reunited Israel (31:27 f., 31-34). The authenticity of some of these oracles of hope (notably 23:5 f. = 33:15 f.; 31:31-34) is not absolutely certain.

j. Discourses of Jeremiah reported by Baruch: 26:2-6, 9 (608 B.C.). 20:3-6 (605). 36:2 f., 5-7, 28-31; 45:2-5 (605-604). 35:2, 13-19 (598). 24:3-10; 13:1-17 (597). 27:2-22; 28:6-9, 13-16 (a letter to the Exiles: 29:4-23); 29:25-28, 31 f.; 51:61-64 (593). 21:4-10; 23:1-6; 32:3-15, 17-44; 34:2-5, 13-22; 37:7-10, 17-21; 38:2 f., 17 f., 39:16-18; 38:20-23 (587-586). 42:4, 9-22; 43:9-13; 44:2-14, 21-30 (586).

2. EXPERIENCES AND DEEDS OF JEREMIAH

a. Visions: the call (1:4-10); the almond tree (1:11 f.); the seething pot (1:13-16); two baskets of figs (24:1-10); the cup of fury from which the nations are to drink (25:15-29, regarded as spurious by some critics); cf. the vision of the Scythian advance (4:13, 21, 23-26).

b. Hallucinations of hearing (in addition to auditions in the preceding visions); the tumult of the Scythian approach and the cries of the Judeans (4:15, 19, 31; 8:16, 19 f.; 10:22); the weeping of the Northern Israelites (3:21).

c. Physiological repercussions of ecstatic experiences: 4:19; 6:11; 8:21; 15:16; 20:9; 23:9.

d. Inner struggles: see the "Confessions" listed under 1: *f.*

e. Symbolical actions and parables: the girdle (13:1-7); the wine jars (13:12-14); the potter (18:1-12); the shattered earthen jar (19:1-13); bands and bars on the prophet's neck (27:1-11); a wooden (28:1-11) and an iron (28:12-17) yoke; the purchase of a field and the safekeeping of the transfer deed (32:6-15); the offering of wine to the Rechabites (35:2-11); the stones hidden in the walls of Pharaoh's palace (43:8-13); a book of ill omen for Babylon is to be sunk in the Euphrates (51:59-64, spurious).

f. Personal vicissitudes: see the narrative parts of Baruch's book and 11:18-23.

Jeremiah's book (with its appendix in 30-31), and to a less extent Baruch's biography, have been subjected to editorial revision and amplification. Titles of particular sections have been supplied at the beginning of the following chapters: 7; 11; 18; 21; 25; 26; 27; 30; 32; 34; 35; 36; 40; 44; 45; 46; 47; 50, and also in 34:8; 49:34; 51:59. Such superscriptions, occasionally giving the date, may be compared with the historical notes at the beginning of some Psalms of David. The hand of editors can also be recognized in the repetition, more or less verbatim, of verses occurring elsewhere in the book. In five cases the LXX omits the second occurrence (6:12-15 = 8:10-12; 15:13 f. = 17:3 f.; 23:5 f. = 33:15 f.; 46:27 f. = 30:10 f.; 52:7-16 = 39:4-10); in five others it gives both (6:22-24 = 50:41-43; 10:12-16 = 51:15-19; 16:14 f. = 23:7 f.; 23:19 f. = 30:23 f.; 49:19-21 = 50:44-46). Shorter passages and standard phrases are also frequently repeated (see the detailed lists in S. R. Driver, *Introduction to the Old Testament*, pp. 275-277).

There is wide disagreement among critics in regard to the extent of the editorial revisions and additions in Jeremiah's prophecies. At one extreme, B. Duhm (KHC, 1901) asserts that all Jeremiah's oracles were in poetry, his only writing in prose being the letter to the exiles in ch. 29 (similarly W. Erbt [1902]). G. Hölscher (*Die Propheten*) even regards the "Confessions" as later psalmlike compositions. At the other extreme, the majority of the other critics regard most of the material in 1-25 and 30-32 as genuine.

It cannot be gainsaid that there is an abyss between Jeremiah's poetic oracles, frequently marked by great originality and distinction, and the dull, repetitious, and rhetorical prose addresses which are placed on his lips. The list of stereotyped expressions, many of them patently Deuteronomistic, prepared by G. Hölscher (*Die Propheten*, p. 382, n. 2) is impressive. They are especially abundant in the following speeches of Jeremiah: 3:6-12a; 4:1-4, 9 f.; 7:1-27, 30-34; 8:1-3; 9:12-14 [H. 9:11-13]; 9:25 f. [H. 9:24 f.]; 11:1-14, 17; 12:14-17; 14:11-16; 15:1-4; 16:10-15, 18 [17:19-27]; 22:1-5, 8 f.; 23:7 f., 33-40; 30:3. If Jeremiah actually dictated these words, it is difficult to understand how he could, on the one hand, retain to the end his inspired originality and independence of thought and, on the other, imitate so slavishly the diction and thought of Deuteronomy.

The obvious clue to the origin of these Deuteronomistic addresses of the prophet has not been sufficiently recognized. If we compare these speeches with those reported by Baruch (listed above [1:*j*]), we note striking similarities. The Deuteronomistic diction of 7:1-27 and 11:1-14, where it is most conspicuous, reappears in Baruch's book, particularly in the speeches in chs. 32, 34, 44. The following expressions, chosen among many, may serve as illustrations: "to come upon the heart [i.e., into the mind]" (7:31; 44:21); "on the day that I brought them out of the land of Egypt," or the like (7:22; 11:4, 7; 34:13); "hearken unto the voice of Jehovah," or the like (7:23, 28; 11:4, 7; 42:13, 21; 44:23, etc.); "I shall be your God and you will be my people," or the like (7:23; 11:4; 24:7; 30:22; 31:1, 33; 32:38); "which I swore to your fathers to give them a land flowing with milk and honey" (11:5; 32:22); "he sent to you all his servants the prophets, early and often," or the like (7:25; 25:4; 26:5; 29:19; 35:15; 44:4); "other gods whom you [or "they"] have not known" (7:9; 19:4; 44:3).

Since there is no reason to believe that Baruch reproduced Jeremiah's words verbatim (like other ancient historians, he gave the substance of speeches in his own words or even composed them freely), it seems absurd to regard similar utterances of Jeremiah in chs. 1-25 as the prophet's own words. The only plausible explanation of the facts seems to be that Baruch prepared an edition of the Book of Jeremiah, combining the prophet's book with his own, and revising or rewriting entirely many of his master's speeches in his own Deuteronomistic style. Clearly this could have been done only after the death of Jeremiah, or at least without his knowledge: for the prophet could hardly have sanctioned such an extensive adulteration of his diction.

It is hardly an accident that after Jeremiah dictated his oracles in 604-598, so few of them have been preserved intact: only 10:17-22; 13:18-27; 23:9-32 (and the words of consolation in 30-31 that Jeremiah himself dictated as a separate book) of all his utterances from 597 to 586 seem to have escaped the revision of Baruch. All the others from this period have come down to us couched in the pedestrian style of Baruch —a good historian, but no poet.

Baruch had little imagination: the speeches that he put into the mouth of Jeremiah have a monotonous similarity. He occasionally preserved Jeremiah's own thought, as for instance the characteristic reference to the destruction of Shiloh in the Temple Address of 608 (7:12-14; 26:6, 9) and perhaps the allusion to the worship of the Queen of Heaven (7:18; cf. 44:17-19), but for the most part he is merely concerned with violations of the Deuteronomic law and refers to it specifically in 6:19; 9:13 [H. 9:12]; 16:11; 26:4; 32:23; 44:10, 23 (contrast Jeremiah in 8:8).

The book prepared by Baruch was supplemented in later times with the numerous marginal notes such as are found in all prophetic books: e.g., 2:8b, 11aβ, 15 f., 26b, 28b (the last is quoted from 11:13, in which "the altars are for *shame*," i.e., for Baal, is a gloss); 3:3a, 7b-11, 17-19, 22b-25; 4:27; 5:1 ("and see now and know whether you can find a man who seeks truth"); 5:18 f., 22aβbβ; 10:11 (a gloss in Aramaic); 12:4;

16:10-13; 22:8 f.; 24:8 (the last clause). The glosses in the Scythian poems 4-6; 10) have been listed above (1:a). Editors also added longer writings.

Longer interpolations in prose consist of extracts from Kings (like Is. 36-39): 52:1-27, 31-34 (= II Kings 24:18-25:21, 27-30; Jer. 52:28-30 is lacking in the LXX and in Kings, but is historically invaluable); 39:1 f., 4-10 (cf. II Kings 25:1-12; Jer. 52:4-16); of a sermon against the violators of the Sabbath law (17:19-27; cf. Neh. 13:15-21, dating from 432 or later); and of a pun on *massâ*, burden (23:33-40). The prose interpolations attached to poems will be listed below.

The poetic sections added to the Book of Jeremiah as it left the hands of Baruch are far more extensive and significant than the prose additions. The most important is the collection of ten oracles against foreign nations (46-51). Some critics (F. Schwally, B. Stade, R. Smend, B. Duhm, and recently J. Skinner, *Prophecy and Religion*, p. 239, n. 3; P. Volz, *Jeremia*, pp. 378-443, KAT, 2nd ed., 1928) believe that Jeremiah had no hand in the writing of these oracles. Others, though recognizing that the oracle on Babylon (50:1-51:58) is unquestionably a late compilation, have devoted much labor to discovering a genuine kernel in 46-49 and in the prose appendix to the oracle on Babylon (51:59-64).[12] While it must be conceded that Jeremiah *could* have written some verses in 46-49 and less probably in 51:59-64a (the colophon in 51:64b is missing in the LXX and is a late editorial gloss, perhaps to 51:58), the weight of the evidence is against such an assumption. It is certain that 46:1-51:58 formed a separate book, assembled long after Jeremiah's death: in the LXX, as in the books of Isaiah (13-23) and of Ezekiel (25-32), this book of foreign oracles was placed in the middle (after 25:13); in the Hebrew text, at the end. As we have seen, the order of the oracles differs radically in Greek and in Hebrew.

Since the editor of this book compiled his collection with the intention of including it in Jeremiah's book, as shown by his titles in 46:1 f., 13; 47:1; 49:34; 50:1 and the references to Nebuchadnezzar in 46:25 f.; 49:28, 30; 50:17; 51:34, it is obvious that the edition of Jeremiah's book circulating at the time did not contain a series of foreign oracles. However, Jer. 25 (in part) seemed to require foreign prophecies.

Although most of the oracles were written with reference to the period 605-561, only the first oracle on Egypt (46:3-12) was clearly written in those years (46:6 unmistakably refers to the battle of Carchemish in 605) and can be attributed to Jeremiah with some assurance. It resembles, how-

---

[12] H. Bardke (ZAW N.F. 12 [1935] 209-239; N.F. 13 [1936] 240-262) is convinced that Jeremiah prepared a volume of foreign oracles containing the following sections: 1:2, 4-10; 25:15-17; 47; 49:34-39; 46:1, 2b, 18-24; 48; 49:1-6, 7 f., 22, 10 f., 23-27, 28-33; 25:27-29. Jeremiah's oracle on Babylon was suppressed soon after 597 and the oracle in 50-51, from the pen of another author, was inserted after 586.

ever, Nahum's superb ode on the fall of Nineveh, although much inferior to it in literary quality, far more than Jeremiah's own writings. It may not be without significance that two oracles are addressed to Egypt, an early one and a late one. For the rest the other oracles exhibit in varying degree the marks of artificiality and late composition.

The worst example is the oracle on Babylon (50-51), a prolix, disjointed, vacuous literary exercise abounding in reminiscences of late parts of Isaiah's book (Is. 13; 34; 49) as well as of Jer. 6:22-24; 10:12-16; 49: 17-21, 26 (see K. Budde in *Jahrb. f. deutsche Theol.* 23 [1878] 428 ff., 529 ff.). It may well be that this inane poem was concocted to supply the missing book that Jeremiah is said to have sent to Babylon, where it was to be sunk in the Euphrates (51:59-64a), although this story, which contradicts Jeremiah's friendly attitude to Nebuchadnezzar, looks like a midrash, possibly inspired by the letter that Jeremiah sent to the exiles in Babylonia (29). The poem, however, is apparently later than the story.

Two other foreign oracles are clearly elaborations of earlier poems. The long oracle on Moab (48), like the similar one in Is. 15:1-16:14, is a Jewish rewriting of a touching elegy written by a Moabite after an invasion of Bedouin Arabs (about 550-450) brought ruin to his country and drove the Moabites to flight (cf. the discussion of Is. 15-16). The original elegy is better preserved in Is. 15-16, which our writer imitated (cf. especially 48:29-38), adding reminiscences of Num. 21 and 24; Is. 24, and his own lines. Likewise, the oracle on Edom (49:7-22) parallels closely Obad. 5, 1-4 (cf. 49:9, 14-16); K. Budde (*Geschichte der althebräischen Litteratur,* p. 214) is far from plausible in regarding Jer. 49 as the source of Obadiah. Both recensions are free reproductions of an earlier poem (see the analysis of Obadiah in a later chapter). The author of Jer. 49, in addition to describing the horrors of the invasion of the Nabateans into Edom, adds that Jehovah would provide for Edom's orphans and widows (49:11) and that Edom (according to 25:15-29) would be forced to drink from the cup of Jehovah's fury (49:12 f.).

The other six foreign oracles, although less patently imitative, are rhetorical; their date is later than the time of Jeremiah. The second oracle on Egypt (46:13-26, to which the words of comfort for Israel found in 30:10 f. have been added in 46:27 f.) seems to have been written on the assumption that Ezekiel's prophecy of Nebuchadnezzar's conquest of Egypt (Ez. 29:17-21, dated in 571) had been fulfilled through Nebuchadnezzar's victory over Amasis in 567 (recorded in two fragmentary cuneiform tablets, translated in R. W. Rogers, *Cuneiform Parallels to the Old Testament,* p. 367). Actually, whatever may have been the importance of this battle, Egypt remained independent until conquered by Cambyses king of Persia in 525. Even if the oracle was written as early as 567—

which is not impossible, though unlikely—Jeremiah, being, if still alive, over eighty years of age, could hardly have written it.

The oracle against Philistia (and also Tyre and Sidon) in ch. 47 threatens destruction to the coastlands through an enemy coming from the North—presumably the Chaldeans after the battle of Carchemish (605), not, as the editor in 47:1 believed, Pharaoh (Necho). Nothing is known of such a devastation in the time of Nebuchadnezzar, whose siege of Tyre from 585 to 573 ended in failure. Unless the writer was thinking of the conquests of Alexander, it seems that the prophecy is merely an apocalyptic vision like 25:30-38, for the victims are terrified not by human enemies but by "the sword of the Lord" (47:6 f.).

The oracle against the Ammonites (49:1-6, omitting 49:6 with the LXX; 49:3b, like 48:7b, is an echo of Am. 1:15) presents some similarities with the much longer oracle against Moab (48); in 49:3 the Moabitic city of Heshbon is incongruously addressed. The Ammonites encroached on the territory of the Israelites east of the Jordan as early as the time of Amos (Am. 1:13-15); when this poem was written the Israelite settlements in Transjordania were nearly extinct (49:1). But Israel's hatred for Ammon, as expressed in this oracle was more justified in the time of Nehemiah about 444 (cf. Neh. 2:10, 19; 4:3, 7 f. [H. 3:35; 4:1 f.]; 6:17-19; cf. Neh. 13:23; Ezra 9:12) than in the time of Jeremiah, when the Ammonites helped the Judeans (27:3; 40:11); even their connivance with the assassins of Gedaliah (40:13 f.; 41:1-3) was dictated more by hostility against Nebuchadnezzar than against the Judeans.

The brief oracle against the Arameans, predicting the ruin of Damascus, Hamath, and Arpad (49:23-27) is deliberately archaic. It reflects the Assyrian conquests in the second half of the eighth century (cf. 49:27, which quotes Am. 1:4) rather than the time of Jeremiah, when these cities were no longer powerful. This archaizing tendency in epigonic literature begins to be especially prominent late in the fifth century, when such books as Ruth and Jonah were written, and continues later. The Aramaic kingdoms threatened with ruin in these oracles were but a memory in the time of Jeremiah, and this author, writing probably two or three centuries later, displays his erudition and indulges in apocalyptic dreams (like the author of Zech. 9:1-9) but fails to shed any light on the situation of his day.

The following oracle is addressed to the Bedouins in the Syrian desert (Kedar) and their otherwise unknown capital, Hazor (49:28-33). Although the mention of Nebuchadnezzar (49:30) seems to provide a genuine historical background for this poem, we have no information about this campaign. Moreover, 49:30b-31 is an echo of Ez. 38:10 f., an apocalyptic oracle addressed to the fabulous Gog of the land of Magog. It is not impossible that the original poem read "for the Lord has taken counsel against you" in 49:30; cf. 49:20 (the LXX omits "Nebuchad-nezzar"); and that the reference to the Babylonian king is from the hand of the editor who attributed these foreign oracles to the pen of Jeremiah. Although Jeremiah names Kedar (2:10) to indicate the dis-tant East (in contrast with the Mediterranean isles, signifying the West), it was only some centuries later that the Jews had reason to hate these Bedouins (cf. Is. 21:16 f.; Ps. 120:5 f.).

The oracle against Elam (49:34-39) is unique in the Old Testament. As in the case of Damascus, the time of Jeremiah is particularly unsuited for a threat of destruction against Elam. This kingdom was devastated and ceased to exist in 640, after the campaigns of Ashurbanipal, and does not begin to play an historical role until the time of Cyrus (558-529); cf. Is. 21:2. Historically the prediction of the dispersion of the Elamites to the four winds was fulfilled in 646-639 (cf. Ez. 32:24 f.), but our author is not thinking of past history but of apocalyptic times when the Lord will establish the Jewish world empire (49:38). The restoration of Elam at the end of days is not out of harmony with this dream and 49:39 (cf. 46:26; 48:47; 49:6; Ez. 29:14) need therefore not be considered a gloss.

This examination of the individual foreign oracles in Jer. 46-51 has shown that with the exception of the first (46:2-12) they have an apoca-lyptic rather than an historical background, the editorial mentions of Jeremiah and Nebuchadnezzar notwithstanding. Taken as a whole, the nine oracles in 46:13-51:58, covering in fair geographical order the lands between Egypt and Elam or the parts of the Persian Empire most familiar to the Jews, are but a vision of the kingdoms that the Lord will over-throw before establishing his Kingdom on earth—the Jewish Empire envisaged in Messianic dreams. In this collection, the extent of the Mes-sianic kingdom is much greater than in Zech. 9:1-10, where it comprises the territory from Hamath and Damascus in the North to the Egyptian border on the South, and from the Mediterranean coast to the Syrian desert (i.e., the ideal borders of David's kingdom, I Kings 8:65), but it has not yet reached its ultimate extent, "all peoples, nations and lan-guages" "under the whole heaven" (Dan. 7:14, 27; cf. Zech. 14:9). The scope of these visionary dreams is in inverse proportion to the limitations of actual reality. Less than twenty years before Daniel expected immi-nently that the Jewish saints would rule over the whole earth, Ben Sira (Ecclus. 50:25 f.) gave expression to his indignation against the three nations (Edomites, Philistines, and Samaritans) that were hemming in the Jews within their extremely restricted territory.

This eschatological, nonhistorical understanding of the oracles against the foreign nations was given by their first interpreter, who in 25:15-38 prepared an introduction to this collection of prophecies; whether in 25:15-29 he rewrote a genuine vision of Jeremiah or composed freely must remain in doubt. "All the kingdoms of the world, which are upon the face of the earth" are to drink of the cup of God's fury (25:15-29); the Lord will indict the nations (25:30 f.) and like a lion ravaging the flock he will slaughter kings and peoples (25:32-38). Elsewhere (23:19 f. = 30:23 f.) this *dies irae* is depicted as a divine storm raging against the wicked.

The second act of the eschatological drama, following this destruction of the Gentile kingdoms and of the wicked in Israel, presents the glorification of the Jews, when God's Kingdom is established on earth. The oracles against the foreign nations, although chiefly concerned with the negative phase of the events at the end of time, contain a few glimpses of Israel's future glory (46:27 f.; 49:2, 38; 50:4 f., 19 f., 34; 51:10, 36, 45). Other prophecies added to the book edited by Baruch are more explicit. After punishing the wicked shepherds of Israel, the Lord will gather the remnant of his flock and provide for their needs and protection (23:1-4); the Jews will be brought back from all lands and dwell in their own country (23:7 f. = 16:14 f.); the Lord will build and plant instead of destroying (31:28); each one will suffer for his own sins (31:29 f.); the nation will be no less steady than the laws regulating the course of the heavenly bodies (31:35-37); Jerusalem will be rebuilt as a holy city (31:37-40); the Lord will give the people a new heart and according to his everlasting covenant will forever bless them (32:36-44, in prose; possibly written by Baruch); in the rebuilt Jerusalem, the forgiven and redeemed Jews will be feared by the nations of the earth and the Lord will provide for them unbroken lines of Davidic kings and of Levitical priests (33, for the most part in prose).

As for the Gentile nations, Israel's hostile neighbors will be returned to their countries, after being deported, and allowed to remain there if they adopt the religion of Jehovah (12:14-17, in prose; cf. 10:23-25). Another writer, influenced by the Second Isaiah, looks forward to the day when the heathen, casting away their false gods, will come to Jehovah from the ends of the earth (16:19-21). To hasten this conversion of the heathen, another disciple of the Second Isaiah (cf. Is. 44:6-20, 24) has prepared a brief sermon in verse: in each one of the two parts of the address (10:1-7, 8-16, omitting 10:11, a gloss in Aramaic; cf. 16:19 f.) he ridicules the idols (10:1-5, 8-9) and glorifies Jehovah (10:6 f., 10, 12-16). The author of 9:24 f. (in prose) goes so far as to say that circumcision of the flesh is neither peculiar to the Jews nor essential.

The other poetic interpolations in Jeremiah fall into the two principal types of Hebrew postexilic poetry, represented by the books of Psalms and Proverbs, respectively. The following poems are akin to the Psalms: the appearance of Jehovah in power (25:30-38, already considered for its eschatological contents); "Sing unto the Lord, praise him! For he has delivered the soul of the poor from the hand of the evildoers" (20:13, according to the LXX); hymns of praise (16:19 f.; 17:12-14); prayers (10:23-25; 14:8 f.); and a public lamentation (14:19-22) that could have been dictated by Jeremiah.

The following compositions are meditations in the vein of the wisdom literature such as we know it from Proverbs (and some Psalms): one should not boast of wisdom, strength, and wealth, but only of the knowledge of the Lord (9:22 f.); man's destiny is not in his hand (10:23, followed by a prayer); the man who trusts human power is like a tree planted in arid soil, but a man who trusts in the Lord is like a tree planted by a brook (17:5-8; cf. Ps. 1); the human heart (mind) is deceitful but the Lord searches it to reward everyone according to his deserts (17:9 f.); ill-gotten wealth is like eggs hatched by a bird that has not laid them—it must be forsaken in the midst of life by its dishonest possessor, who is thus proved to be a fool (17:11; cf. Prov. 10:2; 13:11; 16:8; 20:21; 21:6; 28:20, 22). The popular proverb about the sour grapes is quoted in 31:29 (cf. Ez. 18:2). Jeremiah 5:22 is a reminiscence of Job 38:10 f.; Jer. 10:23, like Job and especially Ecclesiastes, regards man's fate as inexorably determined.

4. *Jeremiah's Historical Significance*

The verdict on Jeremiah's importance in literature and religion obviously presupposes a determination, such as has been attempted above, of what parts of the book that bears his name were dictated by him or at least correctly reproduce his thought. The critical analysis of the book, as indicated above, presents serious difficulties, and scholarly research has not reached uniform conclusions. Nevertheless, the uncertainty in regard to the genuineness of some individual passages does not preclude the possibility of evaluating his contributions to human culture.

The picture of Jeremiah as a poet and as an orator is blurred, as we have seen, by the prosaic rendition of some of his speeches on the part of Baruch. But if we disregard the Deuteronomistic sermons ascribed to him, as possibly reproducing here and there the teaching of the prophet but not the vigor and freshness of his diction, we will refrain from concluding with C. Steuernagel (*Einleitung in das Alte Testament*, p. 573) that the prophet was *not* a brilliant and powerful orator. In literary quality his poetic oracles and "Confessions" match neither the superb style of Amos and Isaiah at their best, nor the epic brilliance of his contemporary Nahum; but all in all these poems deserve a place—perhaps near the edge —in the golden age of Hebrew literature. The emotional strain, which Jeremiah has in common with Hosea, distinguishes our prophet from the three writers just mentioned. It is only in Am. 5:2 and, to a lesser degree, in Is. 1:7 f. that these prophets are overcome by the tender sadness and compassion so typical of Jeremiah.

Characteristically Jeremiah of Anathoth wept like Amos of Tekoa (Am. 5:2) over the ruin of the people (Jer. 4:31; 8:21 f.; 9:1 [H. 8:21-23]) and not, like Isaiah (1:8), the city man, over the ruin of Jerusalem. Similarly Jesus of Nazareth bewailed the fate of the people of Jerusalem (Matt. 23:37 f.) rather than that of the city itself and its Temple (24:2). Jeremiah disliked the city of Jerusalem profoundly (5:1-5, 26-29; 6:6 f.) and never quite understood the complexities of urban life. But the common people fascinated him. Like Jesus he enjoyed participating in their joys and sorrows (cf. 16:5-9; 25:10), and watched them at work (18:2-4; 6:27-30). His interest ranges from the bride (2:32) to the thief (2:26). He suffered mental anguish when social intercourse was precluded to him, or when he was forced to vent the divine fury, pent up in him, over children and young men (6:11), although in moments of despair he longed for solitude (9:2 [H. 9:1]) or even death (20:14-18).

Compelled to live in the capital, Jeremiah longed for the countryside. His imagery, like that of Amos, is drawn from field and forest, wilderness and desert (2:6 f.). But he had a stronger feeling for nature, in its charming and terrifying aspects, than the earlier prophets—a feeling that in the Old Testament is more intense only in Job, Song of Songs, and some Psalms. His famous contrast between the living waters of nature and the leaky cisterns of the city (2:13) reveals his preference for what is natural to what is artificial. He observed the periodical return of the stork and of other migratory birds (8:7), and described lions emerging from the thickets by the Jordan (4:7; 5:6; 12:8). He is acquainted with the wolves of the steppe (5:6) and with leopards whose spots cannot be changed (13:23; cf. 5:6). He has noticed swift dromedaries (2:23) and jackals (9:11 [H. 9:10]; 10:22; 14:6) in the desert. His description of the suffering of men (14:3 f.) and wild animals (14:5 f.), when a drought had parched the ground, is dramatically vivid.

The wild barren hills and ravines between Anathoth and the Dead Sea —a desolate wilderness—made an abiding impression on the prophet. He was haunted by the horrors of arid, uninhabited, gloomy wastes, by the desolation of the bare hills which he names shephāyîm (3:2, 21; 4:11; 7:29; 12:12; 14:6), a word that is characteristic of our prophet.[13] Out of his memories of these wild hills, which "hear not the lowing of cattle" and from which birds and beasts have fled (9:10 [H. 9:9]), there arose the nightmares of a future desolation of Judah—a veritable chaos (4:23-26).

[13] Except for two doubtful occurrences in corrupt texts (Num. 23:3; Job 33:21), the word is found elsewhere only in the Second Isaiah (Is. 41:18; 49:9), who transforms the dreary wastes of Jeremiah into attractive oases.

Jeremiah excels in the description of gruesome imaginary horrors: the plight of Judah invaded by the Scythians (4:7, 13, 19-21, 23-26, 31; 5:15-17; 6:24-26; 8:15-17; 10:19 f.); the terrors of darkness on "the mountains of twilight" when the way is lost (13:16); the premonition of impending calamity (12:5 f.); the figure of Disaster peering from the north (6:1); Death, presented for the first time in literature as the Grim Reaper, entering through the windows or cutting down children and youths in the streets and letting their bodies lie like rows of grain stalks behind the harvester (9:17-22 [H. 9:16-21]).

Such macabre touches (cf. also the metaphor in 5:16), so revealing of the inner thoughts of the prophet, are unknown in literature before him and, except for an occasional personification of death in Job 18:13 f. and 28:22, are entirely alien to the writers of the Old Testament. Equally original in the lyrics of Jeremiah is the preoccupation with mourning and funerals. He teaches the mourning women their dirge (9:17-22 [H. 9:16-21]); he listens to the lament of mountains and pastures (9:10 [H. 9:9]; a glossator in 4:28 even sees heaven and earth mourning) and beholds the land in mourning (12:11; 23:10; 12:4 is, if not a gloss, the sequel to 12:11); he gently urges Rachel, his tribal mother buried in Ramah, to cease her mourning for the misery of her descendants (31: 15 f.), but conversely invites his nation to mourn and wail (4:8; 6:26; 7:29) and contemplates in reality (22:10) and imagination (14:2) two instances of national mourning. Jeremiah himself mourned bitterly in secret for the nation (9:1 [H. 8:23]; 13:17), but was not allowed to participate in funeral rites (16:5) as a sign that in the future the corpses would be left in the fields as food for wild birds and beasts (16:4, 6 f.). A donkey funeral is predicted for Jehoiakim (22:18 f.).

Such imaginary scenes filled with horror or pathos, coupled with the prophet's forebodings of ruin and moods of hopeless despair, give to his lyrics a characteristic note of intense gloom, tender melancholy, and acute mental anguish. Deeply moving are his pathetic pictures of the cessation of human activity in the midst of silence (7:34; 16:9; 25:10; 33:11), darkness (13:16; 23:12), and chaos (4:23-26).

In his ecstatic states, the future calamity becomes present and its contemplation stirs him to the depths of his being. Overcome by grief, he intercedes for the people until Jehovah must forbid intercession (7:16; 11:14; 14:11)—nay, he even identifies himself with the guilty nation (10:24). And again, in an opposite mood, he asks God to avenge him dreadfully of his persecutors (note the contradiction between 17:16 and 17:18; cf. 11:20; 15:15; 18:19-23; 20:11 f.). This intrusion of his own personal feelings in the proclamation of the divine message is typical of him alone among the prophets. From the literary point of view, some of the words of Jeremiah are a unique combination of denunciation and personal feelings, of sermons and lyrics; some oracles may be called, with G. Hölscher (*Die Propheten,* p. 235), "visions in lyric form."

These two elements, the objective and the subjective, are, however, separated in other utterances of Jeremiah. His moving appeal to North Israel to return to Jehovah (in 2-3) and his hopes for a future regeneration of the nation (in 30-31) are presented objectively, without any reference to his personal feelings; conversely, his "Confessions" are entirely lyrical.

In his "Confessions" Jeremiah is purely subjective, for even his dialogues with the deity are in essence dramatizations of inner struggles between opposite moods and desires, chiefly between fidelity to his arduous duties as a prophet and his personal propensity for a quiet life. In these lyrics he analyzes his states of mind and his motives. He discovers in himself, on the one hand, fear of his foes and bitter hatred of them, dejection arising from his isolation and the public rejection of his message, resentment at the invincible divine compulsion to proclaim the word, and the wish that he had never been born. But, on the other hand, he finds that he has carried out his mission without a vindictive desire for the final punishment of his people, having on the contrary interceded in their behalf; and he discovers that through communion with his God he has gained the victory over himself, renewed his consecration to his mission, and received indomitable strength and ineffable joy.

The literary importance of the "Confessions" is out of proportion to their intrinsic qualities of style, which are not outstanding. They mark the beginning of a new type of devotional—one could even say mystical —poetry, in which a human soul shaken by doubts, tormented by remorse, and distressed by anguish and fear finds peace and joy in the sense of the nearness of God. Jeremiah "is the father of true prayer, in which the wretched soul expresses both its subhuman misery and its superhuman confidence. . . . The Psalms would not have been composed without Jeremiah" (J. Wellhausen, *Israel. und Jüd. Geschichte,* p. 141). Through his own inner struggles and victories, our prophet has created the language of the devout soul in the presence of its Maker.

Jeremiah's influence on the Psalmists is both general and specific. He contributed, as we shall see, in creating a new type of piety, the religion of the spirit which found expression in many Psalms. Ultimately we may trace back to the "Confessions" the assurance of devout Psalmists—distressed either mentally by the success of the wicked or physically by disease and misfortune—that in the communion with their God they will find peace and joy (Ps. 73:26), even without deliverance from their woes. Individual Psalms voicing these various religious experiences are listed in the chapter on the Psalter.

A few illustrations will indicate the literary influence of Jeremiah in matters of detail. No matter how bitterly afflicted, the Psalmists never dared to reproach God in the almost blasphemous manner of Jeremiah (15:18b; 20:7), which has parallels only in Job. Even their most desperate laments (Pss. 22:1 [H. 22:2]; 88:14 [H. 88:15]) express anguish rather than accusation. This and the unmistakable personal touches in the "Confessions" disprove the singular view of G. Hölscher (*Die Propheten*, pp. 396-399), who considers these poems as a collection of late fragmentary Psalms (cf. C. C. Torrey, JBL 56 [1937] 212 f.; S. Mowinckel, *Psalmenstudien*, Vol. V, p. 93, note; Vol. VI, p. 23. Oslo, 1921-1924).

Other emotional outcries of the prophet, which are humanly excusable but religiously regrettable, are, however, echoed again and again. With far less justification than Jeremiah, the Psalmists accuse personal enemies, who are mostly imaginary, of dastardly secret plots against themselves (Jer. 11:19; 18:18, 22b; 20:10; cf. Pss. 10; 21; 35; 36; 38; 41; 52; 140; note particularly the parallel between Jer. 20:10 and Ps. 31:13 [H. 31:14]) and invoke upon them vindictively the most horrible divine punishments (Jer. 11:20b; 12:3b; 15:15; 17:18; 18:21-23; 20:11 f.; cf. the numerous "Imprecatory Psalms," and note the verbal parallels between Jer. 12:3; 18:21, 22 and Pss. 44:22 [H. 44:23]; 63:10 [H. 63:11], and 35:7, respectively). Some expressions in 11:19 became clichés (cf. Is. 53:7-8; Pss. 52:2, 5 [H. 52:4, 7]; 83:4 [H. 83:5]).

Like Jeremiah (12:1-3, 5 f.), some Psalmists are dismayed at the sight of the success of wicked men and, without finding a solution of this problem, seek in the communion with God an escape from distressing doubts (Pss. 37; 49; 73). They believe that God is righteous (12:1, quoted in Ps. 119:137; cf. Pss. 7; 11; 112; 129; 145) and "tries the reins and the heart" (11:20a; 17:10; 20:12; cf. Pss. 7; 26). "A righteous God tries the reins and the heart" (Pss. 7:9 [H. 7:10]) is a particularly striking reminiscence of Jeremiah. Therefore they commit their cause unto God (11:20 = 20:12; cf. Ps. 37:5) in the assurance of their innocence (15:10; 18:20; cf. Ps. 35:12 f., among others, for a close parallel with 18:20) and of being martyrs, suffering reproach for God's sake (15:15; cf. Ps. 69:7 [H. 69:8]). It is clear from this comparison between the "Confessions" and the Psalter that Jeremiah's words (in spite of some exaggerations) reflect actual experiences, while much in the Psalms is mere literary composition of a devotional type.

Just as the "Confessions" are the part of Jeremiah's book which had the most profound literary influence, so they also disclose the chief contribution of the prophet to religious growth, namely, the shift of the center of gravity in Judaism from the nation to the individual, from external acts to an attitude of mind. Perhaps in no less measure than the Second Isaiah, Jeremiah was a precursor of Jesus—although in both these prophets the Gospel of the Kingdom is foreshadowed but partially and inadequately.

Jeremiah does not, strictly speaking, inaugurate personal religion and substitute it for the national. Like the Deuteronomic law, he addresses his message to the nation. His oracles to individual priests, prophets, kings, and friends are generally private in character and personal in scope, without close connection with his religious program as a whole. But the prophet experienced, in the depths of his being, a more intimate and more tempestuous relation with his God than his predecessors did. The earlier prophets had been, according to their own conviction, passive instruments 'n the hand of God—like the ax, saw, or rod (to which Isaiah, 10:15, compares Assyria) which Jehovah used to carry out his purposes. But with Jeremiah the instrument, the channel of the divine word, becomes self-conscious: "the ax" boasts "against him that hewes therewith."

Jeremiah is apparently the first of the prophets to protest against the ruin of his personal life involved in the execution of the prophetic mission, but in any case he is the first to leave to posterity the record of his innermost experiences. The literary imitation of the "Confessions" is proof of their religious influence. The new type of piety disclosed by certain Psalms, describing the longing for the communion with God and its attainment, grew out of Jeremiah's own experiences. Jeremiah's "Confessions" led some devout Jews, bewildered by the interruption of the Temple worship and by Jehovah's ostensible rejection of his people in 586, to discover God in the depth of their own heart. Without deliberately emphasizing, like Ezekiel, individual responsibility (unless we regard 31: 29 f. [cf. Ez. 18] as genuine) and personal relationship to God, Jeremiah contributed to make religion a spiritual communion with God not only through his personal experiences, but also in his teaching.

His disparagement of the gross religious practices of his people is of course a legacy from the earlier prophets beginning with Amos. There is nothing original in his low estimation of sacrificial worship (6:20; 7:21 f.), which prompts him to ask, "Can vows and the holy flesh [of victims] remove thy wickedness?" (11:15, revised according to the LXX), nor in his attacks on the religious (2-3), moral (5:1-5), and social (5:26-29) perversity of his people. But he recognizes more clearly than his predecessors that *in essence* wickedness and piety are mental. What matters most is the condition of the "heart," i.e., the mind. At the root of sin is the "obduracy of the heart," an expression common in Baruch's transcripts of Jeremiah's addresses (7:24; 9:14 [H. 9:13]; 11:8; 13:10; 16:12; 18:12; 23:17; cf. Deut. 29:19 [H. 29:18]; Ps. 81:12 [H. 81:13]) but which expresses exactly the prophet's own thought: "but this people has a rebellious and obstinate heart. . . . Neither say they in their heart, 'Let us now fear Jehovah . . .'" (5:23 f.). Being a disease of the mind, sin becomes no less indelible than the spots of a leopard (13:23). Not circumcision of the flesh, but of the heart (4:4), meaning a cleansing of the mind from evil thoughts (4:14), is required to appease the divine indignation.

With regard to Judah, Jeremiah before 586 incessantly proclaimed utter ruin, to be brought about by Jehovah in his righteous anger. But for our prophet Jehovah was not only the God of justice (as in Amos and Isaiah), but also the God of love (as in Hosea and Deuteronomy): it was therefore inevitable that he should be conscious of a conflict in God between his righteousness and his mercy (12:7 f.). He seems to have solved this strife of divergent impulses in the deity by assuming that justice would execute the punishment and mercy would heal the wounds thus inflicted. This solution is applied first to North Israel, then to the Judean Exiles of 597, and finally to Judah and the whole nation after 586.

North Israel had been punished in 722 and, although Jeremiah was shocked at the persistent religious infidelity of the Ephraimites, far from proclaiming a new outburst of divine anger against them, he tenderly invited them to return to their God who in his mercy would "bear no grudge forever" (2-3, especially 3:12, 19, 22), and even promised that God would in his "everlasting love" (31:3) give them a joyful and prosperous future (31:2-5, 12b-22a).

He exhorts the Exiles of 597 to identify themselves with the Babylonian communities in which they live and look forward to a hopeful future and to uninterrupted communion with their God (29:5-7, 11-14; cf. 24:7).

Finally, when the end of Judah as a kingdom had come, Jeremiah indicated through the purchase of a field, during the siege, that normal times would come again (32:14 f.). After all seemed lost, he looked forward to a rebirth of the kingdom under a scion of the house of David (23:5 f. = 33:15 f., assuming that this oracle is genuine; cf. 30:9) and a national restoration (30:4-21; 31:23-35, if authentic).

As for Israel as a whole, in the future Jehovah will build up instead of tearing down (31:27 f.), and establish the "New Covenant" (31:31-34). In this final oracle—the spiritual testament of the prophet if, as the present writer believes, it was really dictated by him—Jeremiah joins together the new notion of a personal relation of the individual with his God (which had arisen from his own agonizing inner strifes) with the old type of religion based on nationalism. He looks forward to the day when, in establishing a New Covenant (31:31 f.), Jehovah will write his Law in the hearts of Judeans and Israelites (31:33), so that every individual, from the least to the greatest, will know Jehovah, who will forgive and forget their iniquity (31:34).

Jeremiah seems to have discovered, in the moment when his world was crumbling about him, that it is always darkest just before dawn. In the ruin of his people, which he had visualized in advance as a nightmare of death, silence, darkness, and chaos, he recognized the birth pangs of a new and better order—a religion "in spirit and in truth" which he, more than any other man up to his time, had foreshadowed in agony of soul and in flashes of blissful illumination.

CHAPTER III

THE BOOK OF EZEKIEL

~~~~~~

Superficially the Book of Ezekiel resembles, in general structure, the Book of Isaiah. Both are divided into three main parts: oracles against Judah and Israel (Is. 1-12; Ez. 1-24), oracles against foreign nations (Is. 13-27; Ez. 25-32), oracles on the future glory of Israel (Is. 28-66; Ez. 33-48). On closer examination, however, it will be noted that, while Isaiah is an anthology of writings of diverse character and date grouped more or less arbitrarily, Ezekiel is more homogeneous and exhibits a chronological arrangement. The Book of Ezekiel may be summarized as follows:

I. *Denunciations of Judah and Israel* (1-24, dated 593-588 B.C.), announcing the impending ruin of Jerusalem in 586.

1. Visions (1-3) dated in July, 593 (1:1 f.): *a.* Introduction (1:1-3). *b.* Vision of the divine glory (1:4-28a) borne aloft on a "firmament" (1: 22-28a) supported by four living creatures or cherubim (as they are called in ch. 10) which enclose a four wheeled chariot (1:4-21). *c.* The prophetic commission (1:28b-2:7). *d.* The divine message, conveyed symbolically to the prophet through his eating of a scroll inscribed on both sides with lamentations (2:8-3:3). *e.* The divine orders to preach to the Judeans (3:4-9) are confirmed by an audition of the noise of the four creatures' wings (3:12 f.). Ezekiel is sent to the Exiles (3:10 f.) and goes to Tel-abib, but remains silent seven days (3:14 f.). *f.* He is to be a watchman among the Exiles (3:16-21; 3:16b-21 is a parallel of 33:7-9). *g.* After beholding again the divine glory (cf. ch. 1 and 11:22-25), Ezekiel is ordered to remain silent and stay in his house (3:22-27).

2. Symbolical actions and denunciations (4-7). *a* The siege of Jerusalem and the Exile are portrayed symbolically by a plan of the city, drawn upon a brick, which the prophet besieges (4:1-3); by lying on his left side (a symbol of North Israel) 390 (or, with the LXX, 190) days, and on the right (a symbol of Judah) 40 days, to indicate the number of years during which Israel and Judah respectively would be in exile (4:4-6; 4:7-8, however, refer to the duration of the siege of Jerusalem); by subsisting on rationed food and drink during these days of immobility, to indicate the privations caused by the siege (4:9-11; cf. 4:16 f.); by eating barley cakes, cooked revoltingly by using human excrement as fuel, to symbolize the impure food that Israel eats in the lands of exile (4:12-15;

4:16 f. explain 4:10 f.); by cutting his hair and beard, and burning, chopping, and scattering each third of the cuttings, respectively, to symbolize the fate of the inhabitants of Jerusalem at the end of the siege (5:1-4). Of these symbolical actions, 4:1-3, 7 f., 9-11, (16 f.); 5:1 f. refer to the siege, and 4:4-6, 12-15; 5:3 f. to the Exile. *b.* An oracle on the sin and punishment of Jerusalem (5:5-17). *c.* An oracle against the land of Judah ("the mountains of Israel") which has been polluted by the worship at the "high places" (6). *d.* An oracle against Judah ("the land of Israel") describing the dreadful, inescapable disaster to be wrought by the Babylonians (7).

3. Visions (8-11) dated in September 592 (8:1). *a.* Ezekiel, transported in spirit to Jerusalem (8:1-4), beholds in the Temple the "image of jealousy" (8:5) and witnesses idolatrous rites performed by the elders in a dark chamber (8:6-13); he sees women weeping for Tammuz-Adonis (8:14 f.), and twenty-five men worshiping Shamash, the sun god (8:16-18). *b.* Jehovah, standing at the threshold of the Temple after alighting from his throne borne by the cherubim (8:4; 9:3; cf. ch. 1 and 3:23), orders six "men" (i.e., angels of destruction) to slay the sinners whose forehead had not been marked with an ancient Hebrew *T* ($\times$ or $+$) by a seventh "man" (9). This seventh angel is then ordered to cast coals of fire, taken from the chariot of the cherubim, against Jerusalem (10:2-7). Then the glory of Jehovah departs from the Temple on the chariot (10:18 f.; cf. 11:22 f.), which is described again (10:1, 8-17, 20-22; cf. 1:26, 5b-21). *c.* A displaced section, which belongs after 8:18, describes twenty-five men plotting rebellion, and the sudden death of Pelatiah, one of their leaders (11:1-13). The following oracle, taking issue with the pride of the Judeans left in their land in 597, declares that the future of the nation rests on the Exiles of 597 (11:14-21; cf. Jer. 24). *d.* Conclusion of the vision: the glory of Jehovah departs from Jerusalem (11:22 f; cf. 10:18 f.) and Ezekiel is brought back to Babylonia (11:24 f.).

4. *Delenda Jerusalem!* (12:1-19:14, undated.) *a.* Symbolical action: Ezekiel is ordered to enact the departure into exile (12:1-7) to signify the tragic fate of Zedekiah in 586 (12:8-16; cf. II Kings 25:4-7). *b.* Mimic representation of the starvation and terror during the siege of Jerusalem (12:17-20; cf. 4:10 f., 16 f.). *c.* Oracles on prophecy (12:21-14:11): contrary to popular misconceptions, Jehovah's oracles will inevitably be fulfilled (12:21-25) in the immediate future (12:26-28); but the false prophets, "foxes in the ruins," have failed to save Israel (13:1-6), proclaiming peace when there was no peace (13:7-16); the false prophetesses are witches practicing godless magic arts (13:17-23); the idolatrous people will obtain no true oracles (14:1-5) but only deceptive ones (14:6-11). *d.* In principle, only the righteous (like Noah, Daniel, and Job) will escape Jehovah's punishment of the nation's guilt (14:12-20),

but although there are no righteous in Jerusalem, Jehovah will preserve a few from its destruction to prove by their evil conduct that Jerusalem fully deserved its fate (14:21-23; cf. 6:9 f.). *e.* Three allegories (15-17). α. Like the wood of the wild vine, worthless except as fuel (15:1-5), the people of Jerusalem will be consumed in the flames (15:6-8). β. Judah, a foundling girl lovingly chosen by Jehovah as his queenly bride (16:1-14), has ungratefully played the harlot (16:15-34; cf. Hos. 2; Jer. 2-3) and must be put to death as an adulteress (16:35-43), for her guilt has surpassed that of her sisters Samaria and Sodom (16:44-52), who will be restored before her (16:53-59); nevertheles, Jehovah will remember his covenant and the two sisters will become the daughters of Jerusalem (16:60-63; 16:53-63 may be secondary). γ. A great eagle (Nebuchadnezzar) brought the top of a Lebanon cedar (Jehoiachin, II Kings 24:10-16) to a land of commerce (Babylonia) and planted a seed (Zedekiah, II Kings 24:17) by abundant waters (in Palestine; cf. 19:10) so that it became a trailing vine. The vine, however, with no gratitude for the eagle, turned to another great eagle (Pharaoh Hophra; cf. Jer. 37:7; 44:30); but the east wind withered the vine and the first eagle plucked it up (17:1-10); the explanation of the allegory is given in 17:11-21; a Messianic prophecy follows in 17:22-24. *f.* Children do not suffer for the sins of the fathers (18:1-4), but everyone, being responsible for his acts, suffers for his own sins (18:5-20); the repenting sinner is forgiven (18:21-23, 27 f.), but the apostate righteous cannot be saved by his former acts of piety (18:24-26); Israel should therefore repent of its iniquities and live (18:29-32). *g.* Two elegies in allegorical form: a lioness (Judah) reared her two whelps, but one (Jehoahaz; II Kings 23:31-34) was taken to Egypt and the other (Jehoiachin, II Kings 24:8-16) to Babylonia (19:1-9). A vine (Judah) grew a vigorous branch reaching to the clouds (Zedekiah), but after becoming withered the vine was transplanted into the desert and a fire from her branch consumed all her shoots (19:10-14).

5. The indictment and punishment of Israel (20-24, dated in August 591 [20:1] and January 588 [24:1]). *a.* To some elders who had come to consult him (20:1-4), Ezekiel decries the wickedness of Israel in the past (in Egypt, 20:5-9; in the Wilderness, 20:10-17; at the threshold of Canaan, 20:18-26; in Canaan, 20:27-29) and in the present (20:30-32); Jehovah will therefore bring Israel back into the Wilderness for judgment (20:33-38) and, refusing the offerings of the idolaters (20:39), will restore the correct worship in the Temple (20:40-44). *b.* Jehovah's sword (20:45-21:32 [H. 21:1-37]). Like a burning forest Judah will perish (20:45-49 [H. 21:1-5]); its inhabitants, righteous and wicked, will be slain by Jehovah's sword (21:1-7 [H. 21:6-12]), which is placed into the hand of Nebuchadnezzar (21:8-17 [H. 21:13-22]). At the crossroads, hesitating between Jerusalem and Ammon, Nebuchadnezzar consults three

distinct oracles and following their response attacks Jerusalem (21:18-27 [H. 21:23-32]). Jehovah's sword, however, also destroys Ammon (21: 28-32 [H. 21:33-37]; cf. Jer. 27:3 f., 8). *c.* The moral corruption of Jerusalem (22): bloodshed and idolatry (22:1-5) and specific moral and religious crimes (22:6-16; cf. Lev. 18-20) are rampant; Jehovah will smelt the ore (Israel) in the furnace (Jerusalem) and obtain nothing but dross (22:17-22); every class in Jerusalem is guilty and will be consumed by the divine wrath (22:23-31). *d.* The allegory of the two debauched sisters Oholah (meaning "her tent," i.e., having her own [illegitimate] sanctuaries), or Samaria, and Oholibah (meaning "my tent [Jehovah's Temple] is in her"), or Jerusalem (23; cf. 16): they have practiced harlotry (i.e., made alliances) with the heathen (23:1-27), but Jerusalem will soon be punished like Samaria (23:28-35); brought to judgment together, the two sisters will be sentenced to suffer the penalty of adulteresses (23:36-49). *e.* The allegory of the rusty caldron (24:1-14, dated on the day when Nebuchadnezzar began the siege of Jerusalem, in January 588; cf. II Kings 25:1 and Jer. 52:4): the meat of sheep (i.e., the people of Jerusalem) is boiled in a rusty caldron (i.e., Jerusalem) and removed; the caldron's filth cannot be cleansed even by fire. *f.* As Ezekiel must refrain from mourning for his wife, stricken suddenly with a fatal disease, so Israel is not to mourn for the destruction of the Temple (24:15-24); on the day when the report of Jerusalem's fall reaches the prophet, his enforced silence (3:22-27) comes to an end (24:25-27).

II. *Oracles against foreign nations* (25-32, dated 587-571). 1. Four neighboring peoples (25): *a.* Ammon (25:1-7; cf. 21:28-32 [H. 21: 23-27]). *b.* Moab (25:8-11). *c.* Edom (25:12-14; cf. 35). *d.* Philistia (25:15-17).

2. Tyre (26-28, dated erroneously in 587-586 [26:1] but in reality [cf. 26:2 with 33:21] soon after January 585): *a.* Jehovah proclaims the destruction of Tyre (26:1-6). *b.* The city will be taken by Nebuchadnezzar (26:7-14). *c.* Repercussions of Tyre's fall (26:15-18; cf. 27:32-36). *d.* Flooded by the abyss, Tyre will descend to the underworld (26:19-21; cf. 31:14, 16; 32:18, 24, 29; Is. 14:12-21). *e.* A magnificent dirge over Tyre (27): the poem picturing Tyre as a proud ship wrecked by a storm (27:3b-9a, 25b-36) is interrupted by the enumeration of wares brought to Tyre from many countries (27:9b-25a). *f.* The ruler of Tyre, insolently regarding himself as a demigod, will be slain by an attacking army (28:1-10). *g.* A sarcastic elegy over the arrogant king of Tyre—a mythological being residing in Eden, the divine garden (28:11-15)—who will be destroyed by fire (28:16-19). The ruler (28:1-10) and the king (28:11-19) are personifications of the city. *h.* The doom of Sidon (28:20-23) and the glorification of Israel (28:24-26).

3. Egypt (29-32): *a.* The great crocodile (i.e., Pharaoh) is dragged out

of the Nile and slain (29:2-5, dated in January 587 [29:1]); Egypt has always been a broken reed for Israel (29:6 f.) and shall become desolate (29:8-12); after forty years (as Judah in 4:6) a limited Egyptian kingdom will be restored in the southern part of the country (29:13-16). *b.* Unable to take Tyre (contrast 26:7-14), Nebuchadnezzar will conquer Egypt (29:17-20, dated April 571, the latest date in the book), and Israel's power will be restored (29:21). *c.* The Day of the Lord, marking Egypt's doom, is at hand (30:1-19). *d.* Nebuchadnezzar, armed with Jehovah's sword (cf. 21:3, 5 [H. 21:8, 10]; 32:10), will defeat Pharaoh Hophra (30:20-26, dated April 587). *e.* A great cedar of Lebanon [i.e., allegorically, the Pharaoh], the loftiest of all trees (31:2-9), is destroyed (31:10-14); the Pharaoh is mockingly welcomed to the underworld (31:15-18; cf. 26:19-21). Chapter 31 is dated in June 587 (31:1). *f.* A lamentation (32:2, 16), or rather a denunciation, of Pharaoh, who is again likened to a great slain crocodile (32:2-10; cf. 29:2-5) and whose land is laid waste by Nebuchadnezzar (32:11-16; cf. 30:20-26). The date of this poem is March 585 (32:1). *g.* A lamentation over Egypt joining other great nations in the underworld (32:18-32; cf. 31:15-18; dated in March [*sic*] 585 [32:17]).

III.*The future restoration of Israel* (33-48, dated from January 585 [33:21] to October 573 [40:1].

A. *Secular restoration* (33-39). 1. Introduction. The turning point in Ezekiel's ministry when in January 585 (33:21) he hears that Jerusalem has fallen (33): *a.* The prophet is to be a watchman, warning his people of the penalties of iniquity (33:1-9; cf. 3:16-21). *b.* Each individual is responsible for his actions and will be rewarded accordingly (33:10-20; cf. ch. 18). *c.* Upon the arrival of the report of Jerusalem's fall, Ezekiel breaks his long silence (33:21 f.; cf. 3:24-27; 24:26 f.) and denounces the remnants of Judah in Jerusalem (33:23-29). *d.* Ezekiel's hearers will henceforth recognize that he is a genuine prophet (33:30-33).

2. The new government (34; cf. Jer. 23:1-4): *a.* In place of the former selfish shepherds (rulers) of Israel (34:1-10), Jehovah himself will gather his scattered sheep (the Exiles) and pasture them upon the mountains of Israel (34:11-16). *b.* The sheep will be protected against the arrogant rams and he-goats, i.e., the upper classes (34:17-22). *c.* Then a Davidic Messiah will rule (34:23 f.) over a miraculously transformed land (34:25-27), safe from attack (34:28-31).

3. Territorial integrity (35:1-36:15): As a prelude to Israel's future sway over its own land, Edom must be utterly devastated (35; cf. 25:12-14; 36:5); then the mountains of Israel will be secure in the possession of the people of Jehovah (36:1-15).

4. Moral regeneration (36:16-38): *a.* Jehovah redeems Israel not for its own sake, but for his holy name (36:16-23). *b.* He will purify the

Israelites (36:24 f.), give them a new heart (36:26), and by placing his spirit within them, enable them to observe his laws (36:27); thus he will be their God (36:28). *c.* Then the land will be fruitful (36:29 f.) and Israel will repent of its former evil ways (36:31 f.): the desolate land will become like Eden (36:33-36) and the waste cities will be filled with "flocks of men" (36:37 f.).

5. National rebirth (37): *a.* In a vision Ezekiel sees a valley filled with dry bones, which come to life (37:1-10) to signify the resurrection of Israel (37:11-14). *b.* The joining of two sticks (37:15-17) represents symbolically the union of Judah and Joseph under a Davidic king (37:18-28; cf. 34:23-25).

6. Final triumph over the Gentiles (38-39): *a.* At the end of this age Jehovah musters the multitude of Gog's northern horsemen against restored Israel (38:1-9). *b.* Gog, plotting the spoliation of a defenseless people (38:10-13), will march against Israel (38:14-16a). *c.* Jehovah has sent him against Israel (38:16b) in fulfillment of the earlier prophecies (38:17), but will exterminate Gog with all his hosts through earthquake, mutual slaughter (resulting from panic), pestilence, and brimstone (38:18-23). *d.* Jehovah will bring Gog against Israel but will annihilate him with his hordes (39:1-7). *e.* The Israelites will burn Gog's weapons and plunder the would-be plunderer (39:8-10). *f.* During seven months Israel will be occupied in burying the corpses in Abarim (*sic,* 39:11), a gorge east of the Dead Sea, in order to cleanse the land from this pollution (39:11-16). *g.* Birds and beasts will feast on the corpses as if partaking of a sacrificial meal (39:17-20). *h.* Thus will Jehovah's glory be revealed among nations (39:21-24). *i.* The Exiles will be brought back from far countries and recognize Jehovah as their only God (39:25-29).

B. *Religious restoration* (40-48). 1. The Temple (40:1-44:3): *a.* Introduction. Ezekiel is brought to Jerusalem in spirit, on New Year (in October) 573 (40:1 f.). An angel holding measuring instruments explains the following visions to Ezekiel (40:3 f.). *b.* The enclosing Temple wall (40:5), its Eastern Gate (40:6-16), and the Outer Court (40:17-27). *c.* The Inner Court (40:28-31), and its three gates (40:32-37). The tables for the sacrifices, within the Eastern Gate of the Inner Court (40:38-43), and the chambers for the priests adjoining the Northern and Southern Gates of the Inner Court (40:44-46). The altar (40:47). *d.* The Temple (40:48-41:26): the vestibule (40:48 f.); the Holy Place and the Holy of Holies (41:1-5a); the ninety cells (three stories of thirty each) surrounding the Temple on three sides (41:5b-11); the building behind the Temple, west of it (41:12); the general dimensions of the Temple and its environs (41:13-15a); interior decoration of the Temple (41:15b-26). *e.* Two three-story buildings north and south of the Temple (42:1-12) containing holy chambers for the use of the priests (42:13 f.). *f.* Measurements of the whole Temple area (42:15-20). *g.* Jehovah's glory, entering through the East Gate, takes possession of the Temple (43:1-12; Jehovah had previously abandoned the Temple; cf. 10:19; 11:23). *h.* The altar for burnt offerings (43:13-27; cf. 40:47): its dimensions (43:13-17); its consecration (43:18-27; in the LXX a priest, not Ezekiel, performs the ritual. *i.* The Eastern Gate, through which the divine glory has entered (43:1-4), must remain closed (44:1 f.), but the prince is allowed to eat within it (44:3).

2. The Priesthood (44:4-45:17): *a.* Introduction (44:4 f.). *b.* Aliens may no longer minister in the Temple (44:6-9). *c.* Their place is to be taken by the Levites who, having officiated in the "high places," are now degraded to the lowest order of the clergy and are entrusted with menial tasks (44:10-14). *d.* The Levitical priests are now only the sons of Zadok— the clergy of Jerusalem since Solomon (44:15 f.; cf. I Kings 2:27, 35); the vestments of the Zadokites (44:17-19); they shall neither shave the head nor let the hair grow long (44:20); nor shall they drink wine (44:21) and marry a widow whose husband had not been a priest (44:22); their functions include instructing the people on ritual purity (44:23), acting as judges (44:24a), and observing the ritual prescriptions (44:24b); they shall avoid defilement through burial ceremonies except in the case of members of their own family (44:25-27); their emoluments shall consist of certain sacrifices and offerings (44:28-30); they shall not eat meat of animals found dead or torn by wild beasts (44:31). *e.* A certain sacred area must be reserved for the Temple, the priests, the Levites, and the prince (45:1-8). *f.* The duties of the prince (45:9). *g.* Correct weights and measures (45:10-12). *h.* Taxes paid to the prince for the support of the Temple worship (45:13-17).

3. The Temple Ritual (45:18-46:24): *a.* Two semiannual atonement ceremonies in behalf of the Temple at the beginning of the first (March-April) and seventh (September-October) months (45:18-20). *b.* Passover (45:21-24) and Tabernacles (45:25), celebrated at the spring and autumn equinoxes, respectively. *c.* Sabbath and New Moon (46:1-7). *d.* Rules regulating the entrance of prince and people into the sanctuary (46:8-10). *e.* The meal offering (46:11) and the prince's freewill offering (46:12). *f.* The daily burnt offering (*tāmîd*) in the morning (46:13-15). *g.* The prince and the people's inalienable tenure of land (46:16-18, supplementing 45:1-8 and 48:8-15). *h.* The Temple kitchens where sacred meals are cooked (46:19-24, supplementing the description of the Temple).

4. The Holy Land (47-48): *a.* A supernatural stream, flowing out of the Temple hill, turns the desert into a paradise and the Dead Sea into a fresh-water lake abounding in fish, without, however, impairing the supply of salt on its shores (47:1-12). *b.* The borders of Israel's land, west of the Jordan (47:13-20). *c.* The resident aliens are allowed to own land within the territory of the tribes of Israel (47:21-23). *d.* The territory

of the seven tribes north of the Temple (48:1-7). *e.* The "oblation" (cf. 45:1-8) between Judah in the North and Benjamin in the South, comprises the Temple and the priests' domain in the center, and, surrounding them, the Levites' land, the prince's domain, and the city (48:8-22). *f.* The five tribes south of the Temple (48:23-29). *g.* The city (i.e., the new, not the actual Jerusalem) will have twelve gates, named after the tribes, and its name will be *Yahweh shāmmâh*, meaning, *"Jehovah is there"* (48: 30-35).

1. Critical Theories

Until recent years few critics questioned the unity of the book and the data on authorship and date which it abundantly supplies. W. W. Baudissin (*Einleitung in die Bücher des Alten Testaments,* p. 461) unquestionably gave expression to views generally held when he said, "It can hardly be doubted that the Book of Ezekiel was written by one and the same hand. . . . The date of its composition is also certain." Moreover, most critics agreed in saying that "the volume of his [Ezekiel's] prophecies is methodically arranged, evidently by his own hand" (S. R. Driver, *Introduction to the Old Testament,* p. 296). With minor reserves and the admission of editorial expansion in the book, G. A. Cooke at present still defends this traditional opinion in his discussion of "New Views on Ezekiel" (*Theology* 24 [1932] 61-69) and in his commentary (*The Book of Ezekiel* [ICC] 2 vols. New York, 1937). The changed attitude in recent years is well illustrated by G. Hölscher, who in 1914 still maintained substantially the traditional views, but in 1924 regarded more than six-sevenths of the book as editorial supplement (1,103 out of a total of 1,273 verses).

During the years since 1924, however, the unity, exilic date, and Babylonian origin of the book have been increasingly questioned and the most divergent conclusions have been reached by competent scholars. The former unanimity of opinion has given place to irreconcilable theories, the former assurance to uncertainty.[1] The problems which critics have solved in various ways are: Is the book substantially the work of a single author? Are the dates given in the book reliable? Did Ezekiel work and write in Babylonia?

A. The Unity of the Book

The first attack on the integrity of the Book of Ezekiel was made in 1756 by G. L. Oeder, in his *Freye Untersuchung über einige Bücher des Alten Testaments* (published posthumously by G. J. L. Vogel at Halle in 1771).

[1] For recent surveys of Ezekiel research see: Sh. Spiegel in HTR 24 (1931) 245-321. C. Kuhl in *Theol. Rundschau* N.F. 5 (1933) 92-118. O. R. Fischer, *The Unity of the Book of Ezekiel* (unpublished dissertation; Boston University, 1939). The commentaries on Ezekiel by A. Bertholet (1936), G. A. Cooke (1937), and I. G. Matthews (1939).

Oeder regarded Ez. 40-48 as a spurious addition to the genuine book, which ended with ch. 39. H. Corrodi (*Versuch einer Beleuchtung des jüd. und christl. Bibelkanons*, Vol. I. Leipzig, 1792) rejected also chs. 38-39 and has had not a few followers (e.g., G. R. Berry, JBL 34 [1915] 17-40; 40 [1921] 70-75; 41 [1922] 224-232).

An anonymous writer in the *Monthly Magazine and British Register* (5 [1798] 189 f.) finds it impossible to attribute Ez. 1-24, inferior in literary and moral quality, to the excellent and well-informed poet (identified with Daniel; cf. Ez. 28:3) who penned Ez. 25-32 and perhaps 35; 38-39. A century and a quarter later G. Hölscher (*Hesekiel. Der Dichter und das Buch*. Beih. ZAW 39. Giessen, 1924) likewise proceeded to analyze the book on the basis of the quality of the style. Following the method of B. Duhm in his analysis of Jeremiah, and reaching similar results, Hölscher ascribed to Ezekiel only the poems of high quality (sixteen passages) and some brief sections in prose (five passages), 170 verses in all, contained in the following chapters: 1-5; 8-9; 11; 15-17; 19; 21; 23-24; 27-32. The rest of the book was contributed by a Levitical redactor between 500 and 450 B.C. In criticizing these conclusions of Hölscher, W. Kessler (*Die innere Einheitlichkeit des Buches Ezechiel*. Berichte des theol. Seminar der Brüdergemeinde, II. Herrnhut, 1926) stressed the intimate connection between the prose and poetry in the book, and R. Kittel (*Geschichte des Volkes Israel*, Vol. III, pp. 158-163) asserted that Ezekiel was not only a great poet, but also (if, as Hölscher admits, he wrote parts of chs. 16 and 23) an earnest teacher and preacher of repentance who did not disdain to use some of the most repulsively indecent language in the Bible.

The unity of the book was assailed from an entirely different angle by R. Kraetzschmar (*Ezechiel*, HKAT. Göttingen, 1900). Impressed by the parallel texts and doublets, which appear throughout the book, he concluded that two distinct recensions (one in the first person, and a shorter one abstracted from the other in the third person [cf. 1:2 f.; 24:24]) were joined together by a redactor before the translation of the book into Greek. K. Budde (*Geschichte der althebräischen Litteratur*, p. 156) admits that this theory contains some truth and A. Bertholet (*Hesekiel*, HAT, Tübingen, 1936), believing that the prophet left only unfinished sketches and scattered pages, has divided much of the text into two recensions.

J. Hempel (*Die althebräische Literatur*, Handbuch der Literaturwissenschaft. Potsdam, 1930-1934), although not accepting the two-recension theory, holds somewhat similar views: Ezekiel's oracles, circulating orally among the Exiles, were collected and supplemented by several editors before the final edition, which exhibits doublets because it is based on these diverse collections, was prepared before 515 B.C. On the contrary, J. Herrmann (*Ezechielstudien.* Leipzig, 1908; *Ezechiel,* in Sellin's Kommentar. Leipzig, 1924) believes that Ezekiel himself redacted the book out of numerous individual oracles of various date, editing and supplementing repeatedly the first edition of his work (cf. H. Schmidt, *Die Grossen Propheten,* p. 460, in Die Schriften des Alten Testaments, Vol. II, Pt. 2. Göttingen, 1915. P. 460; C. E. K. Kuhl, *Die literarische Einheit des Buches Ezechiel,* p. 20. Tübingen, 1917).

Most critics now recognize that one or more redactors are responsible for considerable portions of the book, some of them, like G. Hölscher (cf. above) and S. Mowinckel (*Zur Komposition des Buches Jeremia,* p. 4. Kristiania, 1914; *Ezra den Skriftlaerde,* pp. 125 ff. Kristiania, 1916) actually ascribing to redactors the greatest portion of the book. We shall see in the two following sections that even books devoting special attention to the date and residence of the original author assign a conspicuous role to the redactors who prepared the final recension of the prophecy.

B. The date of Composition

No other prophetic book, with the exception of Haggai and Zechariah, is provided with such exact and full chronological data. Fourteen dates, giving even the day of the month, are scattered through the book (cf. the summary at the beginning of this chapter). They range from the 5th year of the captivity of 597, i.e., 593 B.C., to the 27th year, or 571. Another date at the beginning of the book, "in the thirtieth year" (1:1), in spite of the ingenuity of the critics (cf. G. A. Cooke, *The Book of Ezekiel,* Vol. I, pp. 3 f., 6 f.; L. Finkelstein, *The Pharisees,* Vol. II, pp. 632-636), has received no satisfactory explanation: it seems to refer to the same year as "the fifth year of king Jehoiachin's captivity" (1:2) and, with the exception of C. C. Torrey (cf. Sh. Spiegel, HTR 24 [1931] 282-289), has not been regarded by critics as an important clue to the true or fictitious chronology of the book.

The date of origin of the book in its original form is fixed exactly if the dates are correct and were penned by the original author. But a number of critics assign them to a redactor and, forced to rely on internal evidence for dating the original prophecy, conclude either that the dates are substantially accurate (I. G. Matthews, *Ezekiel,* p. xvii f.) or that they are entirely imaginary. The views of scholars who reject the validity of these dates must now be considered.

L. Zunz was the first to assert that no part of the book was dated in the period 593-571 B.C. He first presented an array of evidence to prove that Ezekiel's oracles were written in the Persian period, after 538 (*Die gottesdienstlichen Vorträge der Juden,* pp. 157-162. Berlin, 1832) and later concluded that they had been written in 440-400 except for chs. 26-28, alluding to Alexander's conquest of Tyre in 332 (ZDMG 27 [1873] 676-681).

L. Seinecke (*Geschichte des Volkes Israel,* Vol. I, p. 138; Vol. II, pp. 1-20) was far more radical. Subtracting the 430 years mentioned in 4:5 f. from the year 594-593 (1:2), he obtained the year 164-163, when Judas Maccabeus rededicated the Temple which had been profaned by Antiochus Epiphanes (cf. 5:11!), as the date of the book.

Others have dated the book like Zunz in the Persian period (W. Erbt, OLZ 20-22 [1917-1919], dates it between 535 and 523), or like Seinecke in the Hellenistic period (M. Vernes, *Précis d'histoire juive,* p. 811. Paris, 1889). H. Winckler combined the two views, dating most of the book in the period 539-515 (*Altorientalische Forschungen,* Vol. III, pp. 135-155. Leipzig, 1902) but chs. 38-39, in which Gog is said to represent Alexander, considerably later. Two writers have proposed dates later than Seinecke. E. Havet (*Revue des deux mondes,* August 1 and 15, 1889) identifies Gog's hordes with the Parthians and regards chs. 40-48 as a plan for Herod's reconstruction of the Temple. According to G. R. Berry, the territorial arrangement in 45:1-8a; 47:13-48:35 presupposes the conquests of John Hyrcanus in 130-129 (JBL 40 [1921] 70-75), and Gog is Antiochus Eupator, who invaded Palestine in 162 B.C. (JBL 41 [1922] 224-232). In more recent articles, however, Berry has come to regard the whole book as pre-Maccabean. It seems hardly necessary to point out that our book cannot be later than 200, for Ben Sira (Ecclus. 49:8) read it as part of the canonical Scriptures.

The most revolutionary theory in regard to the origin of the book has been advanced by C. C. Torrey.[2] The "original prophecy," comprising the bulk of the book, was composed in Jerusalem about 230 B.C. It purported to be a collection of oracles uttered by one of the prophets (II Kings 21:10-15; 24:2) who denounced the religious abominations of Manasseh (692-639 B.C.). The first oracle is dated in "the thirtieth year" of Manasseh (Ez. 1:1); the others, according to Torrey's revised dates, in the thirty-first, thirty-second, and thirty-fifth years of that king. In other words, the late author of this pseudepigraphic writing "set himself to imagine" what a prophet living more than four centuries before "would have said . . . in describing the sin of the people and predicting the woes that were im-

[2] Notes on the Aramaic part of Daniel (*Transactions of the Connecticut Academy of Arts and Sciences* 15 [1909] 248). *Ezra Studies,* p. 288, n. 8 (Chicago, 1910). *Alexander the Great in the Old Testament Prophecies,* p. 284 (Marti-Festschrift. Beih. ZAW 41. Giessen, 1925). *Pseudo-Ezekiel* (Yale Oriental Series, Researches No. 18. New Haven, 1930). Torrey's theory had been criticized by Sh. Spiegel ("Ezekiel or Pseudo-Ezekiel?" HTR 24 [1931] 245-321; cf. JBL 54 [1935] 145-171) in a long monograph, and more briefly by J. B. Harford (*Studies in the Book of Ezekiel,* pp. 38-53. Cambridge, 1935; cf. *Exposit. Times* 43 [1931] 20-25), W. O. E. Oesterley (*Church Quart. Rev.* 106 [1933] 194) and others. Torrey has replied to Spiegel in JBL 53 (1934) 291-320 (cf. JBL 51 [1932] 179-181).

pending" (*Pseudo-Ezekiel,* p. 113). "Not many years after the original work had appeared" (*ibid.,* p. 102), presumably not later than 200 B.C., an editor of the Chronicler's school converted the book "into a prophecy of the so-called 'Babylonian Golah' [Exile]" (*ibid.*) by means of about fifty interpolations. The editor's purpose, like that of the Chronicler, was to prove the validity of the Temple at Jerusalem against the claims advanced by the Samaritans for their temple on Mount Gerizim (*ibid.,* pp. 102-113).

In his doctoral dissertation (*The Literary Relations of Ezekiel.* Philadelphia, 1925), M. Burrows compares our book with other parts of the Old Testament and finds "that the evidence has converged so very definitely on the very date suggested years ago by Prof. Torrey" (p. 105). He concludes that if the Book of Ezekiel is a unit, it "was written later than I and II Kings and Isaiah 14, after the completion of the Pentateuch, probably later than Haggai, Zechariah, Obadiah, and Isaiah 13, 23, 34 f., 40-55, and 56-66, perhaps later than Joel, the Aramaic part of Daniel, and Zechariah 9:11-11:3 . . . and quite certainly before Sirach . . ." (p. 102). In addition to M. Burrows, only G. Dahl (Crisis in Ezekiel Research; in *Quantulacumque, Studies Presented to Kirsopp Lake,* pp. 265-284. London, 1937) has accepted Torrey's dating of the book of Ezekiel.

Like Torrey, J. Smith (*The Book of the Prophet Ezekiel.* London, 1931) recognizes the fundamental unity of the book, and its historical background in the time of Manasseh, but refuses to consider it pseudepigraphic. He believes that Ezekiel was a Northern Israelite deported in 734 B.C., who preached to his fellow Exiles until his return to Palestine "in the thirtieth year" (1:1) after the fall of Samaria (722), or in 691. After this date he opposed "the Jerusalem priesthood and their cult during the reign of Manasseh" (p. x). Most of the oracles were uttered in Palestine; only three (20:32-44; 36:16-32; 37:11-44) were originally pronounced among the Northern Exiles. The Babylonian setting of 1:1-3; 8:3-4; 11:24 is rejected as secondary.

C. Ezekiel's Residence

Like Torrey and J. Smith, other critics deny *in toto* or in part the Babylonian residence of Ezekiel, without, however, seriously challenging the testimony of the dates given in the book.

V. Herntrich (*Ezechielstudien.* Beih. ZAW 61. Giessen, 1932) and I. G. Matthews (*Ezekiel* in An Amer. Comment. on the O. T. Philadelphia, 1939) agree with Torrey in regarding the "original prophecy" as exclusively Palestinian. According to Herntrich, Ezekiel was active in Jerusalem during the period 593-586 B.C., his audience being the same as Jeremiah's in the same period. But the book took its final shape in Babylonia. We are not informed about the prophet's vicissitudes after 586, since 33:24 is the only allusion to the situation following the destruction of Jerusalem, but it may be conjectured that Ezekiel himself brought it to Babylonia when he went there with one of the last convoys of Exiles; the prophet may have written chs. 38-39 in Babylonia. A Babylonian redactor, or rather a "school," by adding the dates (computed on the basis of Zedekiah's coronation or of Jehoiachin's captivity, either according to the Babylonian or according to the Palestinian chronology) and numerous sections (1:1-2:5; 3:10-16a; 8:2-4; 9-10; 24:25 f.; 25-32; 33:21-23; 40-48) furnished to the Exiles a transcript of divine oracles addressed to them. This revision seems to have been made in 573 (ch. 40:1). The theory of Herntrich is accepted, with minor modifications, by J. B. Harford (*Studies in the Book of Ezekiel*. Cambridge, England, 1935), who argues forcibly that in most of its 83 occurrences in the book the expression "The House of Israel" means the population of Jerusalem and Judah (pp. 77-101); and by W. O. E. Oesterley and Th. H. Robinson (*An Introduction to the Books of the Old Testament*. London, 1934), according to whom Ezekiel was active in Jerusalem between 602 and 597.

The conclusions of I. G. Matthews are similar to those of Herntrich. Although the dates were supplied by the "Babylonian editor" writing between 520 and 500, they correctly mark the period of Ezekiel's activity between 593 and 570. The prophet may have been a Northern Israelite, but lived in Jerusalem; he may have been one of the Exiles of 581 or he may have otherwise visited Babylonia. He was not an ecstatic, but an ethical teacher. The Babylonian editor was a priest living in Babylonia; he compiled chs. 40-48 from two separate sources and thus became "the father of Judaism." Later editors were responsible for the oracles against foreign nations and for the apocalyptic parts of the book.

By limiting Ezekiel's activity to Palestine these critics are forced to postulate a far-reaching revision of the book on the part of a Babylonian editor. Two others, by the simple assumption that Ezekiel exercised his prophetic ministry *both* in Palestine and in Babylonia (cf. J. Smith), reduce the contribution of this editor to modest proportions.

A. Bertholet (*Hesekiel*, HAT), radically modifying his former views (*Hesekiel*, KHC. Freiburg i.B., 1897), recognizes a twofold field of activity of the prophet. He received his initial call (2:3-3:9) in Jerusalem in 593 (cf. 1:2). During the siege he moved ostentatiously to a village in Judah (12:3) where he received the news of the fall of the city in 586 (33:21), leaving soon after for Babylonia. There he received a second call to prophecy (1:4-2:2) in the *thirteenth* (not *thirtieth*, 1:1) year of Jehoiachin's captivity, or in 585. Ezekiel's notes, in several versions (cf. Kraetzschmar's double recension theory), were edited by a redactor who systematically confined the prophet's ministry to Babylonia. Bertholet assigns the following passages to Ezekiel's Judean period: 2:3-3:9; 12:3,

17-20; 14:12-20; 15; 24:1-14; 33:21-29 and probably most of 25-32 (except 29:17-21); the following belong to the prophet's years of exile in Babylonia: 1:1, 4-2:2; 3:10-16a, 22-24a; 11:14-21; 14:4b-6, 7b, 11, 21-23; 17:22-24; 20:33-44; 22:23-31 (?); 33:30-33 (?); 34:1-22, 31, 23 f.; 35:1-6, 8b, 12 f., 15; 36:1-12, 16-36; 37; 39:23-29; 40-48 (except for secondary supplements).

O. R. Fischer (*The Unity of the Book of Ezekiel*) admits, like Bertholet, a double sphere of activity in the life of Ezekiel, but differs considerably in matters of detail. Deported to Babylonia with the captivity of Jehoiachin (597 B.C.), Ezekiel had his initial vision there (ch. 1) and was sent by Jehovah to the "House of Israel," i.e., the Judeans in the homeland (2:3). He returned to Judah after a second injunction (3:4) and witnessed the pagan rites in the Temple (8; 11:1-13). In Jerusalem he delivered his message of woe (2:1-3:9) to the "rebellious" Judeans (4-7; 12-24), remaining in the capital during the siege, the hardships of which caused the death of his wife (24:15-18). He witnessed the looting of Jerusalem after its capture (9) and in a vision saw Jehovah preparing to leave the ruined Temple (10). Though allowed by the Babylonians to remain, he was commissioned by his God to return to the Exiles in Babylonia (3:11), bearing a message of encouragement and hope (34-48). The oracles in the book were arranged topically into distinct sections, such as 25-32, and chronologically within the single sections. The prophet may have edited his book, but it was extensively revised by redactors, whose contributions are particularly conspicuous in ch. 10.

The rapid survey of recent criticism of the Book of Ezekiel shows "a mass of divergences: unity or composition, genuineness or pseudepigraph, poet or prose writer, prophet or pastor, actual prophecy or fiction, Babylonia or Palestine, Samaria or Jerusalem. The task of scholarship is still to lift the Book of Ezekiel out of this crisis to a clear understanding" (C Kuhl, in *Theol. Rundschau* 5 [1933] 115).

2. Ezekiel's Life and Personality

The extreme skepticism of critics who, like C. C. Torrey, regard Ezekiel the son of Buzi as a purely imaginary character, no less fictitious than Noah, Daniel, and Job (14:14, 20), is hardly justified. The wholesale rejection of the historical data in the book is no more scientific than their uncritically blind acceptance. The innumerable difficulties of the book, to some extent due to its wretched textual transmission and to editorial additions, do not hide from an unbiased reader the picture of a definite historical situation and the unique characteristics of a prophet of flesh and blood upon whom the great international crises of his time made an overwhelming impression.

The historical period in which Ezekiel lived is marked exactly not only by the dates appended to his oracles (593-571 B.C.) but also by allusions to contemporary events, known from other sources, and particularly by erroneous predictions of later happenings.

The agitated political history of Western Asia during the century preceding Cyrus's conquest of Babylon (538) and the establishment of the Persian Empire has been reviewed in the chapters on Jeremiah and the Second Isaiah, and need not be repeated here (cf. also W. F. Albright in JBL 51 [1932] 77-106). The historical allusions in the Book of Ezekiel prove that Ezekiel was twenty or thirty years younger than Jeremiah: Jeremiah's ministry lasted from 625 to 585, Ezekiel's from 593 to 571. Consequently, the fall of Jerusalem in 586, which marks the climactic close of Jeremiah's career, divides Ezekiel's into two sharply contrasting periods. Apart from general summaries of past history (20:5-29), Ezekiel alludes only to the events which occurred between 609 and 573: the banishment of Jehoahaz to Egypt after Necho's defeat of Josiah at Megiddo in 609 (19:4; cf. II Kings 23:29 f., 33 f.; Jer. 22:10-12); "Jehoiachin's captivity" in 597 (1:2; 17:12; 19:8 f.; cf. 24:21; II Kings 24:11-16; Jer. 22:26-30); Zedekiah's oath of allegiance to Nebuchadnezzar in 597 (17:13), broken in 588 (17:15-18; cf. II Kings 24:20b); the investment of Jerusalem in 588 (24:1 f.; cf. II Kings 25:1; Jer. 39:1; 52:4); the fall of Jerusalem (33:21, etc.; cf. II Kings 25:8-10; Jer. 52:12 f.) and the captivity of the blinded Zedekiah in 586 (12:12-14; 21:25-27 [H. 21: 30-32]); the ineffective help of Pharaoh Hophra (Apries) during the siege, in 587 (30:20-26; cf. Jer. 37:5-10); the abortive rebellion (Jer. 27:2-8) and prompt submission of the Ammonites in 588 (21:19-23 [H. 21:24-28]); the hostility of the Edomites in 586 and their infiltration into Southern Judah later (25:12-14; 35; 36:5; cf. Obad. vv. 12-14; Ps. 137:7; Lam. 4:21 f.); a similar Philistine penetration at the same time (25:15-17); the exultation and boastful pride of the Judeans left in the land when they occupied the lands formerly belonging to the Exiles (11:15; 33:24).

Thus Ezekiel's allusions to the history of his own people come to an end with the aftermath of the fall of Jerusalem in 586. Like Jeremiah (Jer. 24), Ezekiel (11:14-21) regarded the Exiles as the nucleus of the future restoration. Although the Judeans left in the country were more numerous than the Exiles (cf. 33:24), Ezekiel expected their annihilation or dispersion (5:10; 9:8; 11:13; cf. Jer. 6:9; 8:3; 15:9, etc.). He thus visualized an empty country on which a new Temple, a new city ("Yahwehshammah," quite distinct from Jerusalem) would be erected; the tribal territories are to be restored *de novo ab ovo* on a transformed land patently devoid of inhabitants (40-48). Of what actually took place after 570 there is no inkling in the book: the conquests and liberal policies of Cyrus (538), the rebuilding of the Temple (516), the secular and religious reorganization of Judea accomplished by Nehemiah (444) are beyond the horizon of the book.

Ezekiel's allusions to the history of foreign nations are equally significant for the determination of the date of the book. In a series of oracles against Tyre (26-28) Ezekiel in 585 anticipated its capture by Nebuchadnezzar (26:7-14). In reality Josephus, quoting Philostratus (*Antiquities* 10:11, 1) and Phoenician sources (*Against Apion* 1:21) reports that Nebuchadnezzar vainly besieged Tyre for thirteen years, i.e., probably from 585 to 573, although this second passage (which B. Niese and H. St. J. Thackeray, in their editions of the Greek text, plausibly regard as corrupt, but which G. Hölscher [*Hesekiel*, pp. 20-24] accepts as genuine) dates the siege in 598-586. Accordingly, a later oracle dated in 571, when Nebuchadnezzar had abandoned the siege, states that as a reward for his services against Tyre, for which he received no wages, the Babylonian king would conquer Egypt (29:17-20; cf. 30:10-12).[3] This Babylonian conquest of the Valley of the Nile, anticipated also by Jeremiah (Jer. 43:10-13), remained a dream, although Josephus (*Antiquities* 10:9, 7) reports it as a fact. It is possible that Ezekiel, in his latest dated oracle (29:17-20), was aware of Nebuchadnezzar's plans for the attack on Egypt, which was actually undertaken in 568, according to a Babylonian historical fragment published by T. G. Pinches (TSBA 7 [1882] 218-225; cf. S. Langdon, *Neubabylonische Königsinschriften*, pp. 206 f. Vorderasiat. Bibliot.). But the victory of Nebuchadnezzar over Amasis did not result in a conquest of Egypt; at most it barred the Pharaoh from interference in Palestine. It thus seems clear that the outcome of this campaign of 568 was still in the future when the book was written.

A number of foreign nations are mentioned in 27:10-25a as mercenaries or merchants of Tyre, and in 32:20-32 as having perished and gone down to the underworld. The two lists reflect the historical situation prior to Cyrus (538). After that date it would have been absurd to name "Paras," the Persians (27:10), as mercenaries of Tyre, notably together with "Lud and Put" (presumably Lydia in Asia Minor and Punt on the African coast of the Red Sea; in 38:5 Persia is named with Ethiopia and Punt). Obviously Persia is named here as an obscure nation at the ends of the world (Parsua and Media appear in Assyrian records from 835 on), not yet as the great empire of Cyrus and his successors. Most of the nations listed as trading with Tyre occur also in P's table of nations (Gen. 10, where Persia is omitted). It is significant that Gen. 10, which is so closely related to Ez. 27, reflects the historical situation in the century preceding the fall of Nineveh (612), which marks the end of the Assyrian Empire (cf. JBL 56

---

[3] On the evidence of Babylonian contracts, dating a few years after 571, it may be inferred that Tyre finally capitulated and recognized the authority of Nebuchadnezzar without, however, being stormed and sacked (Sh. Spiegel, HTR 24 [1931] 292 f.).

[1937] 91-94). Assyria is still named in 27:23, but also in the list of kingdoms that have utterly perished (32:22), together with Elam (32:24), whose independence ceased in 640, and Meshek and Tubal (32:26), overwhelmed by the Cimmerians about 650. After these mighty kingdoms of the past come, in 32:29-32, Edom, the princes of the North (i.e., Syria), and the Sidonians (i.e., Phoenicians in general). The hour of Edom and Phoenicia had not yet struck in the time of Ezekiel, for he announces their coming doom (25:12-14; 35, and 26-28, respectively); it is therefore likely that, as some critics believe, 32:29-32 is a later addition.

These historical allusions clearly indicate that Ezekiel was active from 593 to 571, according to the dates given in the book. Babylon is still the mistress of the world, Persia has not yet emerged from its obscurity. The history of Judah and of other nations after 571 is predicted in oracles of doom or of salvation which are not only vague, but never correspond to the actual course of events. If the book had not been finished substantially in its present form soon after 571, and in any case before the rise of Cyrus some twenty years later, the silence over the fate of Babylon would be inexplicable.[4]

To invent, as some modern critics do, a redactor responsible for the Babylonian or for the historical background of the book is not only gratuitous but idle. This editor's ignorance of historical events later than 571 inevitably makes him a contemporary of Ezekiel, in fact his alter ego. On the other hand, one may ingeniously discover some differences between Ezekiel and this redactor. I. G. Matthews, for instance, says that Ezekiel possessed "the ethical insight of the earlier prophets" while the redactor, a Jewish priest in Babylonian exile, was concerned with the Temple and its ritual. But since the publication of the Deuteronomic Code in 621, the dilemma, "either ethics or ritual," that Amos had probably postulated, was discarded. The program of national reconstruction included *both* ethics and ritual (cf. the Holiness Code) and, after the reforms of Nehemiah in 432, this type of religion became normative in Judaism. It therefore seems preferable to recognize in a man like Ezekiel different, nay, conflicting opinions at successive stages of his career, and even with R. Kittel (*Geschichte des Volkes Israel,* Vol. III, p. 164) "two souls in his breast," rather than to impose on such a complex Oriental personality the

---

[4] L. Finkelstein (*The Pharisees,* Vol. I, pp. 335-341) believes, however, that in denouncing Tyre and Egypt, Ezekiel had Babylon in mind, and that the oracle against Gog (38-39) is really addressed to Babylonia: "Write Magog backwards in Hebrew (*Gagam*) and substitute for each letter the one preceding it in the Hebrew alphabet, and it becomes *Babel,* Babylonia" (p. 338). Such an interpretation is, of course, possible, but if the prophet not only employed ciphers, but deliberately expressed himself in language so obscure as completely to mystify the Babylonian secret service, it can hardly be hoped that modern scholars may lift the veil and discover the true meaning of his words.

strait jacket of our logical consistency (see also O. Eissfeldt, *Einleitung in das Alte Testament,* pp. 426 f.).

In our attempt to understand Ezekiel's personality and writings we shall, therefore, assume that his book is substantially trustworthy.

The biographic information on Ezekiel is meager and at times ambiguous. The first event recorded is his vision of Jehovah's glory, in the fifth year of Jehoiachin's captivity (593 B.C.), when he was in Babylonia by the river Chebar (1:2), in the vicinity of Nippur. It may be plausibly inferred from this that Ezekiel went to Babylonia with the first captivity, in 597. He was the son of Buzi and belonged to a priestly family (1:3). It is probable but not certain (in spite of Ezekiel's bias in favor of the Zadokites; cf. 40:46; 43:19 and especially 44:10-16; 48:11) that Buzi was one of the sons of Zadok in charge of the Temple in Jerusalem. His son's expert and professional interest in the ritual of the Temple is thus naturally explained. The call to prophecy in 593 did not obliterate this interest in ritual matters. Jeremiah, on the contrary, who belonged to the priests of Anathoth, vigorously opposed the priesthood of the capital.

At the time of his call Ezekiel was perhaps twenty or thirty years old, having been born between 623 and 613 B.C. (hardly before 630 in any case). J. A. Bewer (AJSL 50 [1934] 96-101) and others infer from the mysterious "thirtieth year" in 1:1 that Ezekiel was thirty years old when he had his first vision, but the following reference to the day of the month militates against this interpretation.

"The heavens opened and I saw visions of God" (1:1) introduces the prophet's account of the hallucination through which he was called to the prophetic ministry. Though some of the details of the vision in ch. 1 are obscure, its fundamental meaning, emphasized by the words just quoted and by some of the later allusions in the book (10:18 f.; 11:22 f.), is that Jehovah has left his polluted and doomed Temple in Jerusalem to go to heaven, whence he would return to occupy a new sanctuary in the midst of a reborn Israel (43:1-9; 44:1-4). The grandiose imagery, coupled with elaborate technical details, was to some extent inspired by Babylonian art and religion (cf. L. Dürr, *Ezechiels Vision von der Erscheinung Gottes u.s.w.* Würzburg, 1917) and stresses the majestic transcendence, cosmic power, and unapproachable holiness of the deity. At the sight of the glory of Jehovah Ezekiel fell senseless to the ground.

The vision (1:4-28) is immediately followed by an audition (2:1-8) and a symbolical hallucination of taste (2:9-3:3), both of which convey to the prophet the commission to go and preach to the rebellious "House of Israel" (2:3-7; 3:4-9) a message of "lamentations, moanings, and woe" (2:10).

The import of Ezekiel's commission depends on the meaning of "House of Israel" (3:1, 4 f., 5, 7) or "Children of Israel" (2:3; the LXX reads

"House of Israel") in 2:1-3:9. The ambiguous expression might mean North Israel, the Judeans in the homeland or those in Babylonian exile, or the whole of Israel. In 593, by the river Chebar, only two possibilities deserve consideration: the Judeans in and around Jerusalem and the Judean Exiles among whom the prophet lived. Several recent critics,[5] in spite of their divergent views, have recognized that in this oracle Ezekiel was sent to the men of Judah and Jerusalem. This seems to be indubitable in view of the stubborn wickedness of his prospective hearers and the message of "lamentations, moanings, and woe" (2:10) intended for them; in view of the entirely different expression used when he is sent to the Exiles, "them of the captivity" (3:11), among whom he is appointed watcher and warner (3:17; 33:1-20) and not denouncer and proclaimer of doom. Only twice (11:15; 37:16), in texts that may not be intact, does "House of Israel" refer clearly to the Exiles.

If then the order, "Go, get thee unto the house of Israel" (3:4) meant, "Go to Jerusalem," did Ezekiel fulfill it? This is perhaps the crucial problem facing his biographer. The fiery denunciations of Jerusalem's iniquity and stubborn rebellion against Jehovah, and the insistent proclamations of its doom, comprising the bulk of chs. 2-24, were either merely committed to writing or first delivered orally. The divine order did not leave the prophet any choice: "*Speak* with my words unto them" (3:4; cf. 2:4, 7; 3:1, 6; 11:5; 12:28; 14:4; 20:3, 27; 21:28 [H. 21:33]; 24:3) can hardly mean "*Write* my words unto them." Moreover, unless Ezekiel, like the earlier prophets, addressed the people orally, there would be no point in the mention of a period of speechlessness (3:24-27; 24:27; 33:22). Did, then, Ezekiel utter his oracles in the presence of the Exiles, having in mind the rebellious Judeans in the homeland? Such is the traditional view. Its latest defender (G. A. Cooke, *Ezekiel* [ICC], Vol. I, pp. xxiii f.) admits that it is perplexing: "No doubt we find it difficult to adjust ourselves to the position of a prophet in Babylonia hurling his denunciations at the inhabitants of Jerusalem across 700 miles of desert." Cooke is forced to conclude that "to a man of Ezekiel's temperament the unseen was more vividly present than the seen"; which may well be true but turns Ezekiel into a Jonah who failed to obey the divine command, "Go, get thee unto the house of Israel."

On the contrary, explicit statements in the book prove that Ezekiel was in Jerusalem before 586. The evidence has been convincingly presented by V. Herntrich (*Ezekielprobleme*) and others. Unless Ezekiel was physically in Jerusalem, some categorical statements in the book must be classed as fiction pure and simple (so G. Hölscher, *Hesekiel*) or be explained through "para-psychic phenomena" (Sh. Spiegel, HTR 24

---

[5] A. Bertholet, O. R. Fischer, J. B. Harford, V. Herntrich, J. Herrmann, G. Hölscher, L. G. Matthews, C. C. Torrey, etc.

[1931] 316). Thus, while Ezekiel (in Babylonia!) was delivering his prophecy contained in 11:4-9, he saw Pelatiah fall dead (in Jerusalem) and instantly cried out in dismay (11:13). Ezekiel could have seen Pelatiah die, through second sight, but how could Pelatiah have died as a result of the denunciations of Ezekiel unless the prophet was present?[6] Obviously the simplest assumption is that he was in Jerusalem, as his instantaneous knowledge of Nebuchadnezzar's investment of the city (24:1 f.), barring telepathic gifts, likewise implies. Similarly the expressions "thou dwellest *in the midst* of the rebellious house" (12:2; cf. all of 12:1-7), "thou shalt burn with fire *in the midst* of the city" (5:2), and *"unto this day"* (20:31: the hearers are obviously in Jerusalem, for the Exiles did not offer sacrifices of any kind) are incomprehensible unless the prophet was actually in the capital during the years immediately preceding 586. The exact knowledge of the religious practices and political events in the city at this time supplies indirect confirmation.

According to the record, Ezekiel arrived in Jerusalem one year and two months (or one year and one month, according to the LXX) after he received his commission to go there (8:1-4). The text, of course, speaks in contradictory fashion of a miraculous journey in the flesh ("and he took me by a lock of the head") and a mere trance experience ("and brought me to Jerusalem *in divine visions*"). This supernatural mode of locomotion does not imply a visionary experience and need not be taken literally. In the case of Elijah (I Kings 18:12; II Kings 2:16) and of Jesus (Matt. 4:1; Luke 4:1) transportation or leading through the spirit of God definitely implies a motion of the body, not a flight of the spirit in a trance; such is the only possible meaning in another passage in Ezekiel, 3:12-15, and presumably in 11:1. If this interpretation of the journey to Jerusalem (8:1-4), and of the similar journey back to Babylonia (11:24), is correct, it may be surmised that the words "in divine visions" in 8:3 (and in the revised text of 11:24) are a misleading gloss taken from 40:2 (in both cases the LXX reads the singular, as also in 1:2), where the words indicate correctly that all of 40-48 represents, like ch. 1 (cf. 1:3 with 43:3), a vision seen in trance. The other instance in which Ezekiel was transported by the spirit (37:1) may likewise be pure rapture. The deciding factor for distinguishing bodily and mental journeys is whether, as in 3:12-15; 8:1-4; 11:1, 24, the prophet witnesses actual occurrences and meets real persons or, as in 37:1; 40:2; 43:5, sees ecstatically only hallucinatory apparitions.

What Ezekiel saw after arriving at the Temple of Jerusalem was not only a second appearance of the glory of God (8:4; cf. ch. 1), but the most sordid reality. The Temple of Jehovah was being desecrated by

[6] Cf. C. C. Torrey, *Pseudo-Ezekiel,* p. 40.

the image of jealousy (8:5; cf. the gloss in 8:3), perhaps Manasseh's idol (II Kings 21:7; cf. II Chron. 33), and by pagan mystery rites (8:6-13), lamentations for Tammuz-Adonis chanted by women (8:14 f.), and worship of the sun-god Shamash (8:16-18). It is surprising, though not incredible, that such heathen cults could still be practiced in Jerusalem after the Deuteronomic reform of 621. The circumstantial description of Ezekiel is, however, one of the most genuinely historical parts of his book and therefore an invaluable source of information on Judean syncretism. L. Finkelstein (*The Pharisees,* Vol. I, pp. 318 f.), who refuses to believe that Ezekiel was in Jerusalem in 592 (as 8:1-4 positively states), sees in the description a reminiscence of what Ezekiel had seen soon after 604 when he was still a boy. Unfortunately the tragic epilogue of this scene, which Finkelstein does not mention, makes his attractive suggestion impossible (unless we believe that Ezekiel was a child prophet, long before his call in 593): Pelatiah, one of the elders engaged in pagan rites, fell dead when Ezekiel, filled with divine fury, decried passionately the political plot of these elders (11:1-13).

After this dramatic beginning of his ministry in Jerusalem in September 592, Ezekiel continued unflinchingly to announce the doom of the city until Nebuchadnezzar began to besiege it in January 588 (24:1). Only one date is recorded within this period of less than four years: in August 591 "certain elders of Israel" (cf. 14:1) came to consult him and he preached a sermon on "the abominations of their fathers," which were still practiced at the time (20:1-32 [20:33-44 cannot be earlier than 586]). The rest of Ezekiel's words and deeds during this period cannot be dated exactly.

In accordance with the words written on the scroll which he symbolically swallowed at the time of his call, his message during this period was one of "lamentations, moanings, and woe" (2:10). A "lamentation" (*qînâh*) over the sad fate of Jehoahaz in 609 and of Jehoiachin in 597 (19:1-9) was probably composed at the beginning of the prophet's residence in Jerusalem (the following poem, 19:10-14, is later than 586). During the early part of his ministry in Jerusalem he seems to have pronounced the oracles, revised by later hands, in 6:1-14 (announcing the devastation of the "high places" and the destruction of the population except for a remnant), 7:1-27 ("an end is come upon the four corners of the land," 7:2), 12:21-14:11 (a denunciation of false prophets, sibyls, and "idols in the mind"), 15:1-8 (the people of Jerusalem are a worthless vine, fit only for fuel), 16:1-52 (Jerusalem has been a faithless bride of Jehovah; 16:53-63 are an addition, possibly by Ezekiel, written after 586), and 23 (allegory of Samaria [Oholah] and Jerusalem [Oholibah], who committed harlotries with foreign kingdoms).

Later, when the siege of Jerusalem was impending, Ezekiel acted a number of pantomimes intended to depict its imminence and horrors: symbolical siege of a miniature city drawn on a brick (4:1-3, 7 f.), the scanty food rations (4:9-11 [16 f.]), symbolical disposal of hair cut from his head and beard (5:1 f.), eating and drinking in anxious fear (12:17-20). After 586 Ezekiel supplemented these symbols of the siege with reference to the Exile (4:4-6, 12-15; 5:3 f.; 12:1-16). In what is perhaps Ezekiel's final address before the siege, pronounced, perhaps, when Nebuchadnezzar was already on the march (21:18-27 [H. 21:23-32], to which 21:28-32 [H. 21:33-37] was added after 586), Ezekiel declared the utter destruction of the city and its inhabitants through Nebuchadnezzar armed with Jehovah's sword (20:45-21:17 [H. 21:1-22]).

On the day when Jerusalem was invested (24:1), in January 588, Ezekiel inveighed against the "bloody city" and composed the parable of the rusty caldron (24:2-14) to signify its ineradicable wickedness and utter destruction. Soon after, in an allegorical parable, he attacked the policy of Zedekiah, who had broken his oath of allegiance to Nebuchadnezzar (17:1-10, followed by its explanation in 17:11-21; the Messianic prophecy in 17:22-24 is obviously later). It was apparently during the siege that Ezekiel's wife died suddenly and was buried without mourning rites (24:15-18),[7] as a sign that when the Temple should be destroyed, the survivors were not to mourn for it and for their dead sons and daughters (24:19-24).

Ezekiel returned to Babylonia some time between January 588 (24:1), when he was still in Jerusalem, and January 585 (33:21), when a messenger brought the news of the fall of Jerusalem (a breach was made in the walls in July 586 and the Temple was burned in August); presumably in 587. A. Bertholet (*Hesekiel,* p. xvi) surmises, on the basis of 12:3, 17-20, that Ezekiel left Jerusalem during the siege and remained in a village of Judah until he received the report of its fall, not in January 585 ("the date of 33:21 is wrong," pp. 116 f.), but on the very day the city was taken (cf. 24:26). O. R. Fischer, in his unpublished dissertation, believes, on the contrary, that Ezekiel stayed in the city until after it was sacked (chs. 9-10 are a symbolic description of looting and destruction) and remained in its vicinity about two months (the oracles in 33:23-32

---

[7] I. G. Matthews (*Ezekiel,* p. 92), by eliminating 24:18 as a gloss, understands "the desire of your eyes" in 24:16 (cf. 24:21) as the Temple and thus removes all reference to the death of Ezekiel's wife. Such a drastic revision of the text is unwarranted. Just as Hosea used his marriage and the emblematic names of his children as symbols of his people's apostasy, so Ezekiel quite naturally equated his personal bereavement with the nation's loss of its sanctuary. Moreover, the Hebrew word for "stroke" in 24:16, used for death of persons through the plague or in battle, could hardly be used for the destruction of a building. J. Herrmann (*Ezechiel,* p. 152) regards 24:15 f. as symbolic and, like Matthews, eliminates the story of Ezekiel's wife's death; for a similar view see G. Jahn, *Ezechiel,* pp. 176-179 (Leipzig, 1905), and G. Hölscher, *Hesekiel,* pp. 130 f.

were pronounced then); he arrived at Tel-abib (3:12-15) a week before the messenger came to report the fall of the city (33:21).

In the midst of ambiguous and conflicting evidence, the only definite fact seems to be that Ezekiel heard of the fall of the city from one who had escaped, five months after the burning of the Temple (33:21); the lapse of time indicates beyond a doubt that Ezekiel was in Babylonia, and not in Judea. If we accept this information and the report of Ezekiel's recovery of speech upon hearing the news (33:22) as historical fact, neither of the preceding theories is tenable. The overwhelming shock in hearing of the city's capture is inconceivable if Ezekiel had been an eye-witness of the plundering five months before (O. R. Fischer) or even if he had witnessed it telepathically in a trance (J. A. Bewer, ZAW 54 [1936] 115). Our attempt to determine, in so far as possible, the vicissitudes of Ezekiel from the death of his wife to his recovery of speech rests on the credibility of 33:21 f. and involves a rearrangement of texts scattered in great confusion in 3:10-27; 9-10; 11:22-25; 24:25-27.[8]

In the death of his wife Ezekiel had recognized a sure omen of Je-hovah's determination to destroy Jerusalem (24:15-18: "I take away from thee the desire of thine eyes . . ." "I will profane my sanctuary . . . , the desire of your eyes"). Since the destruction of the city was the execution of a divine sentence, mourning for it was excluded as a protest against God's just verdict (cf. 24:19-24). The emotional strain following his personal loss, as well as the frightful certainty of the city's doom, sent the prophet into a trance in which his dire premonitions were objectified dramatically in a vision of Jerusalem's end (hardly based on an actual view of the real destruction, as O. R. Fischer believes). In this vision Jehovah orders first the slaying of the sinners in the city (ch. 9), then its burning (10:2-7). Before awaiting the execution of the second order, the glory of Jehovah departed from the doomed Temple (10:18 f.; 11:22 f.) on the heavenly chariot borne by the Cherubim (10:1, 8-17, 20-22; cf. ch. 1).

Ezekiel's mission in Jerusalem was obviously completed. After re-ceiving the order to go to preach to the Exiles (3:10 f.), the prophet reports that he was miraculously carried by the spirit back to Babylonia. Two parallel but irreconcilable accounts of this return journey (which in reality is a bodily, not a visionary, experience) are given: 3:12-14 and 11:24 f. Upon his return to Babylonia, after seven days of silence among the Exiles at Tel-abib (3:15), Ezekiel was appointed as a watchman and warner in their midst (3:16-21; 33:1-9), with instructions to deal with

---

[8] O. Eissfeldt (*Einleitung in das Alte Testament*, p. 419) also rearranges some of these sections, following Rothstein and Sellin, but his conclusions (1:1-3:15; 3:16; 4-5 at the beginning and 3:22-24; 4:4-5, 8; 3:26; 24:26 f.; 33:21 f. at the end of the first part of the book; 3:17-21, 25, 27; 4:6 f. are considered spurious) are quite different.

them as a pastor, individually (33:10-20; cf. ch. 18). Later, in a trance, Ezekiel saw again, in the Babylonian plains, a vision of the glory of Jehovah and, to emphasize the end of his mission to Jerusalem, was told that he would remain in seclusion and speechless (3:22-26, followed by a gloss in 3:27) until he would receive the news of the fall of Jerusalem (24:25-27; read with G. A. Cooke, *The Book of Ezekiel*, Vol. I, p. 273: "in the day [omitting "that"] when the fugitive shall come" [24:26]; if 3:27 is not a gloss, it could follow 24:27). And so it actually came to pass in January 585 (33:21 f.; on the date cf. C. Steuernagel, *Einleitung in das Alte Testament*, pp. 539, 576; in 33:22 omit with G. A. Cooke, "and he opened my mouth against [his] coming").

The shattering impact of the news of Jerusalem's fall produced opposite psychological effects on Ezekiel and the Exiles. A good illustration of such contrasting reactions—resignation or despair—to a final, irremediable calamity, is furnished by the divergent attitude of David and his courtiers when the child of David and Bathsheba died (II Sam. 12:15b-23). David's words may be used to elucidate the feelings of Ezekiel: "While the child was yet alive, I fasted and wept; . . . But now he is dead, wherefore should I fast? Can I bring him back again?" The expectation of the dreadful doom of the city produced in Ezekiel an acute nervous tension and anxiety, causing cataleptic states (4:4-6), speechless dismay (3:15), mutism (3:22-26; 24:25-27; 33:21 f.), hallucinations and ecstatic trances, sometimes followed by fainting spells (1:28; 3:23; cf. 43:3; 44:4).[9] The shock in hearing that Jerusalem had been destroyed instantly released the tension and Ezekiel recovered his speech (33:22). The realization of his worst forebodings, like a thunderbolt suddenly releasing high electrical tension, brought calm serenity to his agitated mind. To the Exiles, who on the contrary had probably hoped for deliverance while Jerusalem was attacked and now gave way to utter pessimism and despair (37:11), Ezekiel was able to bring the assurance of an uninterrupted national existence (33:10 f.). There is reason to believe that Ezekiel was permanently cured of his psychic abnormalities when he received the news of Jerusalem's destruction. Cataleptic states and mutism are no longer mentioned; in 29:21, dated in 571, "opening of mouth" means singing God's praises and has no reference to a recovery of speech (cf. 16:63, where the expression means confession of sins). Of course, after January 585, Ezekiel still had trances, when "the hand of Jehovah" was upon him (37:1; 40:1; cf., before that date, 1:3; 3:14, 22; 8:1; 33:22) and he saw visions (37:1-14; 40:1-4; 43:1-12; 47:1-12). But whereas his

[9] On Ezekiel's abnormal psychological experiences see: A. Klostermann (TSK 50 [1877] 391-439). D. Dieckhoff (*Zeitschr. f. Religionspsychologie* 1 [1907] 193-206). G. Hölscher (*Die Propheten*). H. W. Hines (AJSL 40 [1923] 37-71). H. W. Robinson (ZAW 41 [1923] 1-15). R. Kittel (*Geschichte des Volkes Israel*, Vol. III, pp. 151-158).

previous visions (1; 3:1-3; 9-10; 11:22-24; cf. 12:21-28) had generally an ominous import, the later ones show symbolically the rebirth of the nation (37) and the restoration of its right relations with its God (40-48): the contrast between 10:19; 11:23, and 43:1-12 is characteristic. In the place of the numerous bizarre, grotesque, and at times repulsive symbolical acts recorded during the years preceding the fall of Jerusalem (4:1-3, 9-11; 5:1 f.; 12:3-7, 17-20; 21:11 f.; 24:2, 15-24), all of which are dramatic pictures of the coming calamity, the single act of the second phase of his ministry (37:15-17) is a dignified symbol of the future reunion of Judah and North Israel in their own land.

The radical psychological change in our prophet corresponds to a new conception of his prophetic mission—new in his audience, his methods, his teaching. For his former audience, the citizens of Jerusalem, Ezekiel had nothing but contempt: the "rebellious house" was hopelessly corrupt and doomed to total extinction, with the possible exception of a few saints in its midst. Since they were "hard of forehead and stiff of heart" (3:7), God made the prophet's forehead like "a diamond harder than flint" (3:9). On the contrary, for "them of the captivity, the children of his people" (3:11), his new audience, Ezekiel had deep compassion and affection, and expected from them the rebirth of the nation (33:10 f.). He had no occasion to denounce them for wrong worship of Jehovah, pagan cults, idolatry, international intrigues, violation of compacts, and the other iniquities of which Jerusalem was guilty. Their chief fault was covetousness (33:31). In an illuminating passage (33:30-33) the prophet elucidates his relations with the exilic community. Although the people gossiped about the eccentric man of God in their midst, they were eager to listen to him and, at least with their lips, expressed much love for him. Of course their chief concern was business profits, and the public addresses of Ezekiel were not taken seriously. He was for them as diverting as a gifted minstrel with a good voice and the ability to play a musical instrument. Some recognized, however, that he was a true prophet.

With such an audience it was natural that Ezekiel should change his former methods of work. His symbolical acts of former days would have sent them into peals of laughter. His fiery sermons, his fantastic visions, his ecstatic raptures, and his fanciful allegories would have merely provided an evening's entertainment for good-natured stolid businessmen. Ezekiel, accordingly, preached few sermons to the Exiles: we can identify only five oracles that may have been delivered orally during the eleven years from 585 to 575 (18 and 33:1-20, perhaps two versions of the same address; 34; 35:1-36:15; 36:16-38; 37). All of them contain a note of encouragement and hope, all of them show in Ezekiel a fine perception of what his audience needed and what it would listen to with interest. Nevertheless, his success must have been limited, and he devoted himself more and more to two other tasks: pastoral admonition of individuals (cf. 3:16-21; 14:12-20; 18:20-32; 33:10-20) and drafting for publication old and new oracles. Both these methods of delivering his message, dictated by changed circumstances, are new in his career. Considerable portions of the book, notably chs. 40-48, were composed in writing and were never delivered orally by the prophet. In later sections of this chapter, we shall consider more in detail the literary activity of Ezekiel and the change in his teaching after 585.

Ezekiel is the first fanatic in the Bible. He is completely dominated by an uncompromising zeal for Jehovah's cause and the vindication of his name. He is filled with holy fury against Jerusalem's profanation of Jehovah's earthly abode and for its other insults on the deity. Although he is not devoid of human feelings—twice he cries out in anguish at the thought of the coming destruction, interceding for his people (9:8; 11:13) —he never yielded to them: he was a stern zealot with a forehead hard as a diamond (3:9), whose motto was "for the greater glory of God." Paradoxically, both the destruction of the nation and its resurrection are demanded by God's honor, and therefore inevitably come to pass. Foreign nations are even more insignificant pawns on the checkerboard of history, moved or removed at will that the divine honor may be safeguarded.[10]

Like most fanatics, Ezekiel was dogmatic. Unflinching zeal and doctrinal assurance, often inseparable, tend to produce what Edmund Burke called "a black and savage atrocity of mind," of which there are traces in our prophet, and utter intolerance, deaf to the voice of wisdom and common sense. Dialectic reason, however, is often mustered into the service of dogma. Ezekiel, for instance, presents a logical argument to prove the justice of God (ch. 18), but it is an exaggeration to regard him as "primarily a rational nature" able to act on the emotions "generally only through the medium of reason" (C. Steuernagel, *Einleitung in das Alte Testament*, p. 601). With equal justification one could say with G. Hölscher (*Die Propheten*, p. 303) that "the genuine Ezekiel is anything but a quiet doctrinal preacher. Everything in him breathes passion and wild enthusiasm." In reality both reason and passion, as occasion demanded, were subordinated to his overwhelming zeal for God's cause and his invincible conviction that God's will would inevitably prevail.

Under the obsessing spell of the transcendence and holiness of Jehovah, the invisible world became no less real to the prophet than the visible one. In ecstatic trance he saw visions and heard voices. The visible world and his own personality were more submerged in these raptures than was the case in the earlier prophets. Out of his dogmatic postulates he

---

[10] Cf. R. Kittel, *Geschichte des Volkes Israel*, Vol. III, p. 169; G. A. Cooke, *Ezekiel* (ICC), Vol. I, p. 219.

fashioned an ideal world and was so dazzled by its brilliance that he could no longer perceive reality clearly. So the loss of his wife, which must have affected him profoundly, even though it did not interrupt his work, became so suffused with a halo of imaginary meaning that the woman faded and the doomed Temple took her place in the prophet's mind (24:15-24). So the fall of Jerusalem, about which the prophet must have had authentic information, loses all historical features in a purely imaginary vision of its destruction (9; 10:2-7). Even actual sights (8:5-18; 11:1-13) are reported as visionary experiences—and accepted as such by some modern critics. Actual journeys through the Syrian desert become supernatural flights through the air (8:1-4; 3:12-14; 11:24 f.). This blindness to actuality becomes chronic: the prophet talks of cities under the figure of harlots (16; 23) or caldrons (24:1-4), and of kings under the figure of eagles, tops of cedars, vines (17:1-10), lion whelps (19:1-9), vine branches (19:10-14), or crocodiles (29:2-5). The greatest of these allegories is that of Tyre, pictured as a great ship (27:3b-9a, 25b-36). Finally, near the end of his career, Ezekiel, still obsessed by the memory of his first vision (43:2 f.; cf. ch. 1), in anticipating the future restoration of the Temple and of the nation in its land (40-48) drafted a Utopian plan in many respects beyond the possibility of actual realization, inventing incidentally the heavenly Jerusalem and visualizing concretely the dreamland in which he was living in imagination. Thus, like Dante, he created an unseen world dominated by God and described it with an amazing wealth of technical details.

The three sides of Ezekiel's teaching, which I. G. Matthews (*Ezekiel*) tears apart and attributes to three or more distinct individuals, find their natural explanation in this suggested analysis of his personality. His zeal for Jehovah, conceived as transcendent and holy, inspired his prophetic denunciation of the rebellious nation and of wicked individuals, as well as his program of restoration by which offenses against God's holiness would be prevented by specific ritual institutions, and finally his apocalyptic visions of God's kingdom on earth.

3. The Teaching of Ezekiel

During the first six years of his ministry (593-587) Ezekiel lived in Jerusalem and addressed his oracles to its inhabitants. Following his return to Babylonia in 587, he began his work among the Exiles at Tel-abib in January 585. Upon receiving at that time the news of the fall of Jerusalem, he was again able to speak after a period of mutism, and continued his prophetic activity until at least 571. These two sharply marked periods of his life correspond to the two contrasting phases of his message. In Jerusalem he proclaimed "lamentation, moanings, and woe" (2:10); in Babylonia he announced salvation to the righteous and the rebirth of the nation. All the oracles of the first period are contained in chs. 1-32 of the book (except for parts of 25-32, addressed to foreign nations); those of the second are found primarily in chs. 33-48, but also in parts of chs. 1-24.

In Jerusalem (593-587) Ezekiel's pessimism is even darker than Jeremiah's in the same period, his denunciations are more bitter, his lamentations less sympathetic and more sarcastic. We may distinguish in his message to Jerusalem the indictment and the sentence.

In bringing his charges, Ezekiel does not confine himself to the present, but goes back to the birth of the nation and the early history of Jerusalem. Hosea and Jeremiah had believed that at the beginning Israel was true to Jehovah, although it soon went astray (Hos. 2:15b [H. 2:17b]; 9:10; 11:1, if genuine; Jer. 2:1 f.; 3:4; cf. Is. 5), and Isaiah that Jerusalem in the early days was "full of justice" (Is. 1:21). Such was perhaps the tacit assumption of the Deuteronomic Code. But Ezekiel knows of no time of innocence even in the infancy of his people. Although he does not, like the glossator in Hos. 12:3 (H. 12:4), trace the nation's wickedness to a prenatal stage, he declares that Jerusalem was pagan from birth, her father being an Amorite and her mother a Hittite (16:3, 45). Israel's apostasy (figuratively whoredoms) began in Egypt (20:5-9; 23:3, 19) and had continued unabated ever since (16; 20:1-31; 23).

This indictment of the whole past history of the nation, of which there is no trace in earlier parts of the Old Testament, seems to be an original contribution of Ezekiel. The Deuteronomistic redactors of Joshua, Judges, and Kings a few years later applied this general theory to single periods in the history, and the authors of the framework of the Deuteronomic Code applied it to the Mosaic period (Deut. 1:37; 3:26; 4:21; 9:7-24; 31:27) and to the invasion into Canaan (31:16-21). Even Moses and Aaron were charged with rebellion against Jehovah (Num. 20:12, 24; 27:14; Deut. 32:51, P).

Ezekiel does not accept Job's notion of sinfulness as a taint (cf. Ps. 51:5 [H. 51:7]) from which no human being is free (Job 4:17-19; 15:14-16; 25:5 f.; cf. I Kings 8:46; Prov. 20:9; Eccl. 7:20). This doctrine, already implied in the sin offering required in the consecration of priests (Lev. 8), eventually became normative. Somewhat illogically, Ezekiel regards the nation as a persistently "rebellious house," but admits within it the presence of isolated righteous men (18, etc.). The gulf separating a transcendent holy God from human beings is the common theological basis for the divergent notions of sinfulness presented in the books of Ezekiel and Job, respectively.

Ezekiel's bill of indictment against Judah and Jerusalem includes a general charge of apostasy and specific charges of ethical and ritual transgressions. The "rebellious house" (2:5-8 [correct 2:7]; 3:9, 26 f.;

12:2 f., 9, 25; 17:12; 24:3; only in 44:6 [corrected] after 585; cf. Is. 30:9; Num. 17:10 [H. 17:25]) has constantly outraged Jehovah by ignoring him and worshiping other gods. This disloyalty is manifested in the worship of Jehovah on the "high places," in violation of the law of Deut. 12 (6:3 f., 6, 13; 16:16; 20:27-29; 44:10-12)—a worship which Ezekiel, against the evidence of history, regards as idolatrous (6:3-6; 14:3-11; 16:17-19; 44:10), in the sacrifice of children in the Moloch cult (16:20 f.; 20:26, 31; 23:37-39), in the desecration of the Temple through pagan rites (ch. 8), and its profanation through other forms of pollution (5:11; 23:28 f.; 25:3; 43:7-9; 44:7). Other symptoms of disloyalty have been the "whoredoms" with foreign powers, meaning the international intrigues and alliances (16:26, 28 f.; 23:8-10, 11-21, 30, 40 f.).

The infidelity of Israel to Jehovah, whether religious or political, is regarded by Ezekiel as nothing less than idolatry. This is another instance of his inability to see the historical reality because he lived in an imaginary world. As the present writer has shown elsewhere, the Israelites and Judeans at no period of their history were prone to the use of images, whether in the worship of Jehovah (JBL 45 [1926] 211-222) or of other gods (JBL 43 [1924] 229-240). Ezekiel's obsession with imaginary Judean idols became contagious; he was the founder of the polemic against idolatry in the Old Testament, although the Second Isaiah later surpassed him in literary brilliance when he attacked heathen (not Jewish) image worship (Is. 40:18-20; 41:6 f.; 44:9-20; 45:20; 46:1 f., 5-7) in his argument to prove that Jehovah was the sole God in existence. In his holy rage against Israel's apostasy, Ezekiel coined a new vituperative term for idols, *gillûlîm*, using it 39 times in his book (6:4-6, 9, 13; 8:10; 14:3-7, etc.; the term occurs, in later passages, in Kings; Lev. 26:30; Deut. 29:16; Jer. 50:2). In reality, however, when his invectives against idolatry are examined (cf. the list of passages in JBL 43 [1924] 234, n. 34), it will be found that, aside from the figures carved on the walls of the Temple (8:10), which are never mentioned in historical sources and may be purely imaginary, Ezekiel knows only a single idol, the mysterious "image of jealousy" (8:3, 5), which, according to the Chronicler (II Chron. 33), was none other than "the graven image of the *ashērâh*" set up by Manasseh (II Kings 21:7). With much learning but questionable results, P. S. Landersdorfer (*Der Baal Tetramorphos und die Kerube des Ezechiel*. Paderborn, 1918) has tried to prove that this image was a four-faced Baal and that it inspired the cherubim supporting the divine throne seen by Ezekiel in his visions (chs. 1 and 10). The existence of this idol (whatever may have been its appearance) in the time of Manasseh or of Ezekiel is extremely doubtful.

In dealing with specific national offenses against Jehovah, Ezekiel is similarly theoretical. Among religious transgressions he mentions also the profanation of the Sabbath (20:12 f., 16, 20 f., 24; 22:8, 26; 23:38) and the offenses of the priests (22:26, an expansion of Zeph. 3:4), false prophets (13:1-16; 14:1-11; 22:28 [cf. Zeph. 3:4]; in 22:25 we should read "whose princes" [LXX] instead of "a conspiracy of her prophets"), and prophetesses (13:17-23). Ezekiel inveighs against two definite acts of political dishonesty: the perjury of Zedekiah (17:15-18) and the plot of twenty-five notables (11:2-13). He denounces the princes (22:25 [cf. above]) and nobles (22:27), but in general terms, quoting Zeph. 3:3. A number of ethical offenses are enumerated in 22:1-16, but more fully later, when the prophet is dealing with individuals and not with the nation (ch. 18). The ethical code of Ezekiel resembles closely that of the Holiness Code.

Exactly as Ezekiel, with a theoretical generalization, rhetorically sums up the religious sins as idolatry (or, like Hosea, as whoredoms), so, with considerable exaggeration, he tends to summarize the nation's ethical transgressions as murder, or shedding of blood (7:23; 9:9; 16:38; 22:2-4, 6, 9, 12 f., 25, 27; 23:37, 45; 24:6 f., 9; cf. 18:10; 33:25; 36:18). Ezekiel was probably inspired by the prohibition to slay the innocent, found in laws from the second half of the seventh century (Ex. 23:7; Deut. 19:10 [cf. 19:13; 21:8 f.]; 27:25); the phrase is found also in secondary passages in Jeremiah (Jer. 2:34; 7:6; 19:4; 22:3, 17) and in Deuteronomistic sections in Kings (II Kings 21:16; 24:4) and may have been proverbial in the time of our prophet (cf. later Ps. 10:8; 94:21; 106:38; Prov. 1:11; 6:17; Is. 59:7).

In conclusion, Ezekiel did not derive his material for the indictment of Judah and Jerusalem from actual observation (except for the paganism and plotting described in 8:6-18; 11:1-13) but from his reading and meditation. In imagination he saw a court scene in which the nation and city were tried, found guilty, and condemned to the penalty of adulterous and murderous women, i.e., according to Deut. 22:21 (cf. Deut. 22:22; Lev. 20:10), execution by stoning (Ez. 16:35-43; 23:36-49).

Ezekiel announces the imminent execution of the sentence, i.e., the destruction of Jerusalem and the Exile, through symbolical acts (4:1-5:4; 12:1-7, 17-20; 21:19 f. [H. 21:24 f.]; 24:15-24), allegories and parables (15; 16:1-52; 17:1-21; 19; 23; 24:1-14), prophetic oracles (6-7; 12:8-16; 13:8-16; 20-21; 22:17-31), and visions (9; 10:2-7). Ezekiel's views on the scope of the coming calamity are not entirely consistent. He sometimes says that the destruction will be total (5:12), including righteous and wicked (21:3 f. [H. 21:8 f.]), man and beast (14:13, 17, 19, 21; cf. Zeph. 1:3). But elsewhere, in accordance with his individualized conception of divine retribution (ch. 18), he declares that the righteous will be spared (9:4 f.), and even admits (after 585) that a remnant of the wicked will survive, to serve as a sample demonstrating how richly Jerusalem had deserved its fate (14:22 f.). It is probable that the passages in which a ray of hope shines through the darkness of the coming judgment (16:60-63; 20:40-44) are interpolated, unless they were added by Ezekiel after 585.

In the second phase of his ministry (585-571), following the destruction of Jerusalem, Ezekiel no longer faced the "rebellious house," but a dismayed group of Exiles at Tel-abib. He met the new situation with a radically new message. His task was to convince his audience of the justice of God and of the perpetual survival of Israel, and thus he concerned himself with individuals in the present and with the nation in the future.

The kingdom of Judah had died in 586, the nation itself was apparently dead. Until a miracle of Jehovah revived the monarchy of David (17:22-24; 21:27 [H. 21:32]; 34:23 f.; 37:24 f., passages of questionable authenticity) or restored the nation as a holy congregation (Ezekiel's real hope), only individuals remained alive to receive the prophetic message. So Ezekiel was appointed in their midst as a spiritual adviser, a pastor rather than a preacher. Like a watchman responsible for warning a city, by blowing a horn at the approach of an enemy (33:1-6; cf. Jer. 6:17), so Ezekiel was to be "a watchman unto the house of Israel" (3:17; 33:7) responsible for warning the wicked in the name of Jehovah, lest they die in their iniquity (3:18-21; 33:8 f.). In his ministry to the individual Jew, Ezekiel was concerned primarily with the justification of Jehovah's acts and with the creation of the right religious and ethical conduct in those who constituted the seed of the new Israel.

The theological problem which was raised by the destruction of Jerusalem was the justice in the divine retribution of human deeds. Jeremiah was already aware of some of its difficulties. In contrast with Job, who concluded that in fixing the destiny of a person the deity was not guided by the standards of justice as conceived by men, Ezekiel proved to his own satisfaction the absolute justice of God. Later the Second Isaiah found it unnecessary to argue the point, and inferred from God's justice the imminent glorification of Israel. In the years preceding the fall of Jerusalem, Ezekiel had shown that its doom was fully deserved. But some of the Exiles must have thought that in the wicked city pious persons were present in sufficient number to justify God's sparing it in his mercy. Had not Jehovah assured Abraham that he would forgive Sodom if ten righteous were found in it (Gen. 18:23-33)? Ezekiel, on the contrary, emphatically denied the virtue of the merits of the saints for the benefit of the sinners. According to his theory of strict personal responsibility and retribution, each man receives the just reward for his actions: "the soul that sinneth, it shall die" (18:4; cf. the whole ch. 18). Therefore, even if three famous saints, Noah, Daniel, and Job, had been living in Jerusalem, their piety would not have saved the city but only their own

lives (14:12-20), exactly as Lot and his family were saved from Sodom
(Gen. 19:12-29). The few wicked that escaped from the destruction were
spared to be an object lesson to the Exiles and to demonstrate to them the
incurable wickedness of the city (14:21-23): "and you shall know that I
have not done without cause all that I have done in it, saith the Lord"
(14:23).

In the same manner Ezekiel disposed of another objection to Jehovah's
punishment of Jerusalem. The Exiles, quoting the proverb, "The fathers
have eaten sour grapes, and the children's teeth are set on edge" (18:2;
cf. Jer. 31:29 f.), claimed that the present generation in Jerusalem had
suffered unjustly for the sins of the fathers (18:1-4): "the fathers have
sinned, the children have been smitten" (so the Targum correctly paraphrases the proverb in 18:2). Such was indeed the traditional view of
collective responsibility (Ex. 34:7; Num. 14:18; cf. Ex. 20:5; Deut. 5:9;
Jer. 32:18) which had been attacked before Ezekiel (Deut. 24:16: II
Kings 14:6; Jer. 31:29 f. is probably interpolated), with particular force
in Job 21:19 f.

The third objection to the destruction of Jerusalem was implicit in
the words of the Exiles, "Our transgressions and our sins weigh upon us
and we waste away in them; how then can we recover?" (33:10; cf.
37:11). In the background of this hopeless outlook lurks the thought that,
by destroying Jerusalem, Jehovah had forsaken the land and had averted
his eyes from the plight of his nation, as some people had been saying
years before (9:9).

Ezekiel's reply to these three objections is that of a pastor rather than
that of a theologian. In refuting these attacks on the justice and mercy
of God he is more concerned with the religion of the individual (cf.
3:16-21; 33:1-9) than with the philosophical problem involved, which is
discussed in the Book of Job.[11] Ezekiel does not admit that Jehovah's just
retribution of each man's conduct and his universal benevolence can
possibly be questioned. Each man is free to choose between right and
wrong, whatever his past conduct may have been (18:21-29; 33:12-20)
and is therefore solely responsible for his actions and their inevitable
retribution (18:5-20). Jehovah is not only just in treating each one as he
deserves, he is also merciful: he does not desire the death of the sinner,
but his conversion and salvation (18:30-32; 33:11). Nay, Jehovah not
only invites each one to make himself a new heart (18:31) but promises
to give the people a new heart and put his spirit within them (11:19;
36:26; cf. Jer. 31:31-34; 32:39 f.). To the charge that Jehovah is unjust
the prophet replies, "Is it my ways that are not equitable? is it not your
ways that are unequal?" (18:25, 29; cf. 33:17, 20). To the charge that

---

[11] Ezekiel's inconsistencies are pointed out by G. A. Cooke (*Ezekiel* [ICC], Vol. I,
p. 196); cf. J. Wellhausen, *Israel. und jüd. Geschichte*, p. 146.

God had, without compassion, forsaken his people he replies that Jehovah still invites all to turn from their evil ways and live (18:23, 32; 33:11).

How, then, should the individuals, who accepted the divine invitation to turn from their sins and live, regulate their conduct? Like the Ten Commandments, the Holiness Code, and Jewish laws in general, Ezekiel does not discriminate between ritual and moral transgressions in his lists of acts which the pious Jew should avoid; in Job 31, on the contrary, except for 31:26 f. (31:28 is a gloss), only ethical offenses are listed. In his indictment against Jerusalem, Ezekiel had previously enumerated some of the most glaring sins of the people (22:6-12; 23:37-39). Now, in addressing individuals and in vindicating the justice and mercy of God, he furnishes a fuller list, with greater emphasis on ethical transgressions (ch. 18). The influence of the Deuteronomic Code is visible in 18:7-9, 16, but the parallels with the Holiness Code, which were discussed in connection with it, are particularly striking and seem to indicate that Ezekiel and H utilize a lost collection of laws. Ezekiel obviously assumes that these rules of conduct are familiar to the Exiles.

Of ritual transgressions, Ezekiel mentions the worship at the high places (18:6, 11, 15; 22:9), idolatry (18:6, 12; 22:3 f.; 23:37, 39), the sacrifice of infants (23:37, 39), lack of reverence for holy things (22:8, 26), profanation of the Sabbaths (22:8, 26; 23:38), and defilement of the Temple (23:38 f.).

Ezekiel's social and ethical code is chiefly negative. Of positive virtues he mentions only the restoration of a pledge taken to secure a debt (18:7, 16; 33:15; cf. 18:12), charity for the needy (18:7, 16), and true justice (18:8). The following ethical and social offenses are listed: adultery (18:6, 11, 15; 22:11; 23:37), intercourse with a woman in her impurity (18:6; 22:10; 36:17), unchastity (22:9), various types of incest (22:10 f.), contempt for parents (22:7), informing (22:9), iniquity (18:8), murder (18:10; 22:6, 9, 12, 27; 23:37), robbery (18:7, 12, 16; 22:29; 33:15), usury (18:8, 13, 17; 22:12), and oppression or extortion of the helpless members of the community (18:7, 12, 16, 18; 22:7, 29). The ideal, as in Deuteronomy, is to walk in God's statutes and to observe his ordinances (18:9, 17, 21; cf. 5:6 f.; 11:20, etc.).

In the development of personal religion, which begins after the publication of the Deuteronomic Code in 621 and attains its classical expression in the Psalter, Ezekiel represents an important phase. Jeremiah, through the storm and stress of his inner life expressed in his "Confessions," inspired the emotional, quasi-mystical type of personal relation with God. The early wisdom literature, following Egyptian patterns in the oldest parts of Proverbs, furnished the individual with practical advice for the attainment of happiness and success; later these dictates of common sense were subordinated to religion by being identified with divine Law.

Ezekiel, in the third place, laid the foundations for the doctrine of individual retribution on this earth which, despite the sharp criticism of Job and Ecclesiastes, became orthodox in the later Proverbs, in some Psalms, and in Ecclesiasticus. At the same time Ezekiel had an incalculable influence on the development of so-called legalism—the scrupulous observance of the divinely revealed ordinances, the conformity of the Jews, collectively and individually, to the will of God—which began in 621 and reached its culmination with the Pharisees and their successors.

Ezekiel's concern with the conversion of individual Exiles in the present does not preclude in the least, as some critics believe, his hope for a national rebirth and an ecclesiastical restoration in the future. The personal and national types of religion are not only intimately joined in the Psalter and in the faith and practice of the Pharisees later, but already before our prophet in Jeremiah's prophecy of the New Covenant (Jer. 31:31-34).

Basic in Ezekiel's notion of the relations between Israel and its God Jehovah is the Covenant made by the deity with the nation (16:8)—the most original and influential religious notion in the Deuteronomic Code. Through this Covenant Israel became a peculiar, unique nation. Moab, for asserting that Judah is like all other nations, is to be devastated (25:8 f.; contrast Lam. 4:12). For violating the divine Covenant (44:7; 17:16-19) Judah was conquered and Jerusalem was destroyed. But Jehovah will remember his Covenant (16:60) and establish it anew (16:60; 20:37; 34:25; 37:26; cf. Jer. 31:31-34; the passages in Ez. 16; 20, and 34 may be editorial).

Ezekiel seems to have been aware of a difficulty in this apparently logical view of "thesis, antithesis, and synthesis" (Hegel). How could Jehovah's Covenant remain in force unless the nation were spotless? How could the eternity of Israel, implied in the divine Covenant, be reconciled with the nation's inveterate, still persisting sinfulness? On the other hand, how could Jehovah annihilate his people without being dishonored among the Gentiles (20:14, 22; cf. Jer. 14:7, 21 before, and Is. 48:9, 11; Num. 14:13-17 after Ezekiel)?

Ezekiel's attempt, already noted, to convert the individual Jews was a natural, but impracticable, solution of the difficulty. It must have become clear to Ezekiel, even when he formulated the program of ch. 18, that it was doomed to failure. Practical men, like the authors of the Priestly Code later, proposed the only workable plan: the extirpation of all wicked Jews from the holy congregation. In reality, however, even though Nehemiah took measures to this effect in 432, the congregation remained infested with worldly and unrighteous Jews, against whom the Pious in the Psalter poured out their holy rage. This situation led to the conception of a true Israel according to the spirit, distinct from Israel according to the flesh, appearing already vaguely in the Psalter and concretely realized by the Pharisees.

Ezekiel's fanatic and dogmatic impatience with unpleasant realities, such as the presence of incorrigible wickedness among the Jews, and his tendency to find refuge in an imaginary world, naturally led him to solve the problem in an entirely different manner, on a higher plane, outside the sphere of the historical realities faced by the Priestly Code, Nehemiah, and the Psalmists. Since human means seemed insufficient to create an Israel free from sin and living in accordance with the divine will, and since this ideal Israel was required by the honor of Jehovah's name, he concluded that the Almighty would miraculously create the holy Israel of the future not merely through a moral regeneration of the individuals (as Jeremiah had hoped, in 31:31-34), but by supernatural upheavals in nature and history. Thus was born apocalypse which, despairing of human capacity, relies exclusively on God for the establishment of his Kingdom on earth or in heaven. Ezekiel mechanically and ritually, and the Second Isaiah spiritually, formulated the hopes and dreams of a prostrate nation and thus contributed to save it from extinction.

Jehovah alone is active, according to Ezekiel, in transforming a wicked nation into his Kingdom on earth. Such a purpose implies negative and positive provisions: internal and external obstacles must be removed, and the theocratic state must be created and made invulnerable.

The chief internal obstacle is the sinfulness of Israel. Ezekiel conceives two ways by which Jehovah will remove this taint. Jehovah will simply erase from "the register of the house of Israel" the names of the wicked and keep them out of the land of Israel (13:9). This seems to imply a judgment in which the righteous will be separated from the wicked (cf. the references to the death of the wicked in 3:18 f.; 13:22; 18:20-24; 33:8 f., 12-14). But the only references to a national judgment, which is a prominent feature of later apocalypses (cf. Mal. 3:16-4:6 [H. 3:16-21]), is found in 20:33-39 and 34:17-22, passages of doubtful authenticity. The other method is an inward purification of the sinners: "I shall sprinkle clean water upon you and you will be clean" (36:25); "A new heart also shall I give you . . . and I shall put my spirit within you . . ." (36:26 f.; cf. 11:19; Joel 2:28 f. [H. 3:1 f.]). Unless the outpouring of the spirit follows the judgment, the two measures for the elimination of sinners are irreconcilable.

The external obstacles to Israel's restoration to its former land and safe occupation thereof are the Gentiles. Those of them who, like the Edomites, had taken possession of a portion of Judah shall be driven out (36:1-15 [editorially expanded]; cf. 25:3, 8, 12, 15; 26:2; 35:10). The small nations in the vicinity of Judea (Ammon, Moab, Edom, and Philistia), formerly "pricking briers and piercing thorns" (28:24), will be destroyed (25; on

Ammon cf. 21:28-32 [H. 21:33-37]; on Edom cf. ch. 35 and 32:29), and "they will know that I am the Lord" (25:5, 7, 11, 17; cf. 26:6; 29:9; 30:8, 19, 25 f.; 32:15). The Egyptian Empire will be so reduced and weakened that it shall cease to be a menace (29-32) and Tyre, which had mocked Judah in 586 (26:2), will lose its international commerce and be ruined (26-28). Jehovah's agent of destruction is Babylonia, "the most terrible of nations" (28:7; 30:11; 31:12; 32:12). Ezekiel did not dare prophesy against the Babylonian Empire; on the contrary, he declared that Jehovah had placed his sword (cf. 20:47 f. [H. 21:3 f.]; 21:3, 5 [H. 21:8, 10]; 30:24 f.; 32:10) into the hand of Nebuchadnezzar (21:11 [H. 21:16]; 30:24 f.). In contrast with the Second Isaiah (the first to announce the doom of Babylon, Is. 47), Ezekiel does not look forward to the conversion of the Gentiles to the worship of Jehovah, but only to their recognition of his invincible sway over all kingdoms ("they will know that I am Jehovah"; cf. above).

After the removal of these obstacles, Jehovah proceeds to the revival of Israel as a nation and as a holy congregation: in two visions Ezekiel contemplates the resurrection of his people (ch. 37) and the reorganized Temple worship (40-48).

In ecstasy Ezekiel saw a valley filled with dry bones and by his inspired words brought them together, covered them with flesh, and breathed life into them (37:1-10). Jehovah explains the meaning of this symbol: to sanctify his great name God will bring "the whole house of Israel" out of its grave in the Exile, in the midst of the Gentiles, and lead it back to its land (37:11-14; cf. 11:17; 20:34, 41 f.; 28:25; 29:13; 34:13; 36:24; 37:21; 38:8; 39:27 f.; Jer. 23:3; 29:14; 31:8 f., and the Second Isaiah). "The whole house of Israel" means Judah and North Israel united again, like two sticks firmly joined together, into a nation under one king (37:15-28), "my servant David" (37:24 f.; cf. 34:23), i.e., "the Messiah who shall arise from his seed in the time of salvation" (Kimchi; likewise Rashi). This Messianic prophecy (34:23; 37:24 f.), which could have been inspired by Jer. 23:5 (cf. Jer. 30:9; 33:14-33; Hos. 3:5; Is. 55:3 f.; Ps. 78:70-72, all of which are later than Ezekiel), may be the contribution of an editor. It is not in harmony with the ideal of a theocracy, in which Jehovah himself is Israel's king (34:11-16, 20; cf. 20:33 f., which is perhaps editorial, and the late passages Judg. 8:23; I Sam. 8:7; Mic. 4:7, etc.) and the "prince" plays only an insignificant role (45:9, 16 f.); in the prophecy about the attack of Gog of the land of Magog (38-39), if Ezekiel wrote it, Jehovah is likewise the king of Israel who annihilates this foe without the collaboration of a Davidic king.

These oracles dealing with national restoration are typically apocalyptic and resemble the predictions of Joel and of other early apocalyptic writers. But Ezekiel's vision of Israel living again in its land and **worshiping**

Jehovah in his new Temple (40-48) is a program for the future community rather than an apocalyptic dream, a code in visionary form intended to regulate the life of the holy congregation so as to prevent a future outbreak of Jehovah's anger. The authenticity of this climactic conclusion of Ezekiel's book has been questioned by some critics, but, aside from some interpolations, Ez. 40-48 must be regarded as the prophet's most original and most influential legacy to his people. The ritual and ecclesiastical institutions described here were formulated by a Jew living in Exile before the rebuilding of the Temple (in the period 586-516). This writer lived in a community in which political activity had completely ceased and where the inability to erect a temple and offer the legitimate sacrifices exalted the ceremonial type of religion until the exercise of the divinely revealed worship seemed the supreme task of the community. Moreover, the author was obsessed by the thought of Jehovah's holiness and, in spite of an amazing technical knowledge of Solomon's Temple and of its ritual, presented an ideal plan which was to a great extent Utopic. The details of the plan show that it is later than Deuteronomy and earlier than the Priestly Code (which discloses considerable indebtedness to it). In brief, the author of Ez. 40-48 resided among the Exiles during Ezekiel's lifetime and had in common with him both ideas and style, and, what is even more significant, lived like him in an imaginary world. We may, therefore, assign Ez. 40-48 without hesitation to the pen of Ezekiel.

Ezekiel reports that in October 573 he was brought in spirit to a high mountain in Judea (40:1 f.), where he was shown by a mysterious guide (40:3 f.) the future Temple. The prophet describes in detail the courts (40:5-27, 28-47), the Temple edifice (40:48-41:26), and the sacristies for the priests (42:1-14), and gives exact measurements for the whole Temple area (42:15-20; cf. 45:2). The description and dedication of the altar (43:13-27), which had been merely mentioned in 40:47, the description of the Temple kitchens (46:19-24), and the vision of the Temple spring flowing into the Dead Sea (47:1-12) are either displaced portions of the description of the Temple in 40-42, or supplementary accounts added subsequently by Ezekiel or by editors (47:1-12 would not be inappropriate as the climax of 40-42). The description of the Temple area is concluded with a vision of the glory of Jehovah taking up its permanent abode in this Temple (43:1-12), having previously abandoned the old Temple (10:19; 11:23); 44:1-3 looks like a secondary supplement to 43:1-12.

"The law of the house" (43:12) mentioned at the end of the first part of 40-48 is promulgated in the second part (44-46, omitting perhaps 44:1-3). Critics have surmised that editors have contributed some parts of 44-46, which exhibit traces of disarrangement, but their conclusions are uncertain. These ritual prescriptions deal with the Levites (44:4-14), the

Zadokite priests (44:15-31), the sacred area (45:1-8), the duties of the prince (45:9), the contributions for the support of the worship (45:13-17, with an annotation on the standard weights and measures in 45:10-12), and the correct worship on festivals and ordinary days (45:18-46:15); 46:16-18 is a supplement to 45:1-9, and 46:19-24 belongs to 40-42.

The third part (47-48; 47:1-12 may, however, be the end of 40-42) represents an afterthought. In this appendix Ezekiel, realizing that his program required a transformation of the land of Canaan, describes the borders of the land (47:13-20), its geometrical tribal divisions (47:21-48:29; cf. 45:1-8), and the new capital, Yahweh-shammah, with its twelve gates (48:30-35; cf. 48:15 f.).

In his ministry to the individual Ezekiel had laid emphasis on the justice and mercy of Jehovah and on the ethical duties of the pious Jew. In his plan for the congregation of the future, Ezekiel emphasizes instead the holiness of God and the means of safeguarding it. But this priestly interest in ritual institutions which predominates in chs. 40-48 is by no means new or out of harmony with the earlier teaching of the prophet: he had previously stressed the distinction between the sacred and the profane (22:26), and had regarded the profanation of Jehovah's holy name (20:39; 36:20-22) and holy things (22:8, 26) as one of the capital sins of Jerusalem. The program set forth in chs. 40-48 has the purpose of forever averting another outbreak of the divine anger by forestalling entirely any conceivable profanation of the holiness of Jehovah (43:8).

Obviously such a purpose, requiring the elimination of all possible pollution, implied the isolation of what was holy to prevent its contact with the profane, and the repeated disinfection of the holy from unwitting profanation. In other words, the measures taken by Ezekiel resemble those taken in a modern hospital to prevent infection during a surgical operation. Isolation is secured principally through the architectural plan of the Temple and its surroundings, sterilization through the cultus.

The vital importance of isolating the Temple from all profane contacts is due to its sacrosanct character. It is the place of Jehovah's throne, the place of the soles of his feet, where he will dwell in the midst of the children of Israel forever (43:7). Ezekiel realized that the former arrangements of the Temple could not prevent contact with the profane. He names the following sources of pollution and takes steps to remove them. Previously the royal palace was separated from the Temple by a wall (43:8; cf. I Kings 7:8; II Kings 20:4 [emended]); worse still, the royal tombs were also in the immediate vicinity (43:7; cf. II Kings 21:18, 26); uncircumcised foreigners were employed in a menial capacity in the Temple service (44:7-9; cf. Josh. 9:23, 27). Moreover, the pagan rites described in ch. 8 and the practice of sacred prostitution (43:7; cf. II Kings 23:7) were intolerable profanations.

Radical measures are to be taken to isolate the Temple from external and internal defilement. The future Temple will no longer be located within Jerusalem. The future city, no longer called Jerusalem but Yahweh-shammah ("Jehovah is there"), will be moved bodily more than a mile southward (cf. the sketch in G. A. Cooke, *Ezekiel*, Vol. II, p. 532; or in A. Bertholet, *Hesekiel*, p. 246. KHK, 1897). The twelve tribes are arranged in parallel strips, seven north (Dan, Asher, Naphtali, Manasseh, Ephraim, Reuben, Judah) and five (Benjamin, Simeon, Issachar, Zebulon, Gad) south of the sacred area (48:1-7; 48:23-29). This holy zone or "oblation" (45:1-8; 48:8-22) is a strip 25,000 cubits[12] long and 10,000 wide comprising the domain of the priests with the Temple in the center; north of it is the Levites' domain (10,000 cubits wide), south of it the city, a square of 4,500 cubits per side all surrounded by a strip of open land 250 cubits wide; east and west of the city are its lands—two rectangles 5,000 by 10,000 cubits in size. The whole square, 25,000 cubits per side, comprising the domains of the Levites and priests and the city with its lands is surrounded by the tribal territories of Judah (north) and Benjamin (south), and by the domain of the prince (east and west).

The sacredness of the Temple, entirely surrounded by the priests' domain, is further ensured by being enclosed within two courts, instead of the single court of Solomon's Temple. The external wall separating the holy from the common encloses a square 500 cubits per side (42:20), containing the outer court (40:17-27). Inside of it is the inner court (40:28-37), a rectangle 350 by 200 cubits, within which stands the sanctuary. Laymen worship in the outer court (46:3, 9) and no longer take part in the sacrificial rites. The private sacrifices of the prince are slain by the priests (46:2), those of the people by the Levites (44:11), who also boil the meat (46:24) which the people eat in the outer court. Although Ezekiel's plan of having two courts instead of one was adopted in the postexilic Temple, the laymen did not renounce the immemorial custom of offering their own sacrifices in the inner court (cf. Lev. 1:5, 11, etc.).

The exclusion of uncircumcised foreigners from the sacred precincts, first proposed by Ezekiel (44:9), was on the contrary adopted in later Judaism (Num. 3:10; 16:40 [H. 17:5]; cf. Josephus's *War* 5:5, 2 and the inscription in *Jewish Encycl.* XII, 85). The menial tasks in the Temple, formerly performed by alien slaves, are to be assigned to the Levites, the descendants of priests officiating at the high places before 621. In Deut. 18:6-8 these dispossessed provincial priests were allowed to serve at Jerusalem, but Josiah could not enforce this law (II Kings 23:9). Ezekiel, regarding the worship at the high places as idolatrous, degrades the provincial priests, whom he calls Levites, to a menial position: they minister to the people and not to Jehovah (44:10-14). Thus the sanctity of the

[12] A Hebrew cubit is the equivalent of 17.58 inches or 44.65 centimeters.

Temple is preserved by allowing only members of the clergy to serve in it. Thus beginning with Ezekiel the term Levites, that in Deuteronomy was still the equivalent of priests, acquires a new meaning adopted later in the Priestly Code, where the Levites are likewise the assistants of the priests (Num. 3:5-10; 18:2).

Ezekiel, in contrast with Deuteronomy and the earlier practice, thus reserves the priesthood to a single family, the sons of Zadok of Jerusalem (I Kings 2:27, 35). They alone may enter the sanctuary and minister to Jehovah (44:15 f.). But the Priestly Code, presumably yielding to the pressure of non-Zadokite priests, extended the priestly office to all the sons of Aaron (cf. Lev. 21:1, H), not only to the Zadokites descended from Aaron's son Eleazar, but also to the descendants of Aaron's fourth son Ithamar (Ex. 6:23). But even in P the Zadokites retained a certain superiority (cf. I Chron. 24:1-4), for the high priest belonged to their line. Ben Sira (Ecclus. 51:12, in the Hebrew), long after Ezekiel, still identified the priests with the sons of Zadok and the later term "Sadducees," indicating the followers of the priestly aristocracy, still bears witness to the abiding prestige of the name of Zadok when the high priests were no longer descendants of his.

Being responsible for the preservation of the sanctity of the Temple, the priests are subjected to strict rules intended to keep their own persons from defilement (44:20-27; cf. Lev. 21, R^P). Their contact with holy things requires that they wear holy vestments (44:17 f.) which must, however, be removed and placed in the sacristies before they leave the inner court, lest the common people become impregnated with holiness (44:19; cf. 46:20).

By a number of miscellaneous rules regulating the most minute details of what pertains to the Temple, Ezekiel shows his consuming concern for the prevention of profanation of the holy place. He gives specific rules about animals and vegetables to be offered (e.g., 46:13-15), the materials and cut of the priestly vestments (44:17 f.), the entrance and exit of the prince and the people when they offer sacrifices (46:8-10), the opening and closing of the gates (46:1; cf. 44:1 f.). Such minutiae, which may seem insignificant, are ordered by Jehovah and acquire a sacrosanct character thereby. The authority of arbitrary divine enactment, which is one of the basic principles of the Priestly Code, has its inception with Ezekiel, who regards the rigid observance of such ritual details as an insurance against the outbreak of the divine anger.

Nevertheless, Ezekiel feels no assurance that his program could be fulfilled without the slightest unwitting error, and therefore to remedy any involuntary infraction of the divine will he provided special ritual ceremonies. The prescriptions for the cult deal nearly exclusively with public sacrifices intended to preserve the right relations between the deity and the nation. Private offerings, which had been restricted by the Deuteronomic law, have no important place in his program (44:11; 45:17; 46:2). In his system sacrifices fulfill one of two purposes: the payment of tribute to the deity and the expiation of unwitting transgressions. Thus the cult loses its ancient spontaneity and gladness (still emphasized in Deut. 12:5-7, 11 f., 18; 14:26; 16:11, 14, etc.) and acquires the lugubrious solemnity and punctiliousness characteristic of the Priestly Code. To secure the bond uniting Jehovah and the congregation, every morning a burnt offering of a lamb is to be offered, together with its oblation (46:13-15), with additional victims on feast days (46:4 f., 6 f.). The offering of this daily holocaust, or *tāmîd*, was customary long before Ezekiel; but the burnt offering was presented in the morning and the oblation in the evening (cf. I Kings 18:29, 36). In the Priestly Code, which exhibits the usage in the fifth century, burnt offering and oblation are offered every morning and evening (Ex. 29:38-42; Num. 28:1-8), and such was the later practice (Dan. 8:11-14).

The most important contributions of Ezekiel to the worship are the expiatory rites. To the ancient sacrifices (burnt offering and peace offering) he adds two new ones, the sin and the trespass offerings (40:39; 42:13; 43:19-25; 44:27, 29; 45:17-25; 46:20), of which there is no earlier mention (which does not necessarily exclude their antiquity). A sin offering is presented by the prince on the Passover for himself and the people (45:21-24), and similarly on the Feast of Tabernacles (45:25); the third annual festival (Weeks or Pentecost) is not mentioned. It may be significant that these two annual festivals come on the spring and autumn equinoxes, respectively. Two weeks before these festivals (on the first day of the first and seventh months), a semiannual rite of expiation is performed to "purify the sanctuary" (45:18-20); in reality, a single annual Day of Atonement was observed after 516 on the tenth day of the seventh month (Lev. 16; 23:27-32; Num. 29:7-11), for the same purpose.

By these rites Ezekiel provided the indispensable expiation for unwitting violation of ceremonial rules or for ritual uncleanness, thus preserving the sanctity of God's earthly abode. Such defilement could be contracted not only by the people (45:15, 17), but also by things, such as the Temple (45:20) and the altar (43:20, 26), and in all cases was purged by sacrificial rites. Ezekiel actually seems to regard the whole cult, all sacrifices and festivals, as effective in removing sin and expiating it (45:15, 17).

In conclusion, Ezekiel's teaching is not consistent and uniform. In his life and thought he lived through the transition from ancient Israel (a nation with a country and a state) to Judaism (a holy congregation within an alien empire). The fall of Jerusalem in 586 marked the turning point in his career. Before then he was a prophet with priestly interests, after 586 a priest inclined to apocalyptic dreaming. He thus marks the transition between the oracles of doom of Jeremiah and the apocalyptic hopes of the Second Isaiah, between the ritual institutions of Deuteronomy and those of the Priestly Code, between the national religion of the prophets and the personal religion of the Psalms. His most important contributions to later Judaism are the doctrine of individual retribution, the notion of the holiness of God and its ritual implications, Jehovah's salvation of his people for the sake of his honor, the polemic against idolatry, and the first draft of the ecclesiastical organization presented later in the Priestly Code.

4. The Book of Ezekiel

Available evidence seems to show that Ezekiel, like Jeremiah, prepared an edition of his book. A considerable portion of his book (parts of 1-24, and 33-39; all of 25-32 and 40-48) was never delivered orally. It is possible that about half his book consists of public addresses and half of written compositions. Thus Ezekiel stands between Jeremiah, who was primarily a preacher and a writer by necessity, and the Second Isaiah, who was exclusively a writer. There is no valid reason for denying that Ezekiel in writing a considerable portion of his book failed to include in it a written version of his previously delivered oracles.

An analysis of his book must begin with a determination of the material which was redacted in writing some time after its oral delivery or, in the case of ecstatic or normal experiences, after the event. This material may be arranged topically and chronologically as follows:

1. 593 B.C. The initial vision (1:4-28a) and a twofold commission to go from Babylonia to preach to the Judeans in Jerusalem (1:28b-2:7; 2:8-3:3; the second commission [3:4-9], which parallels 2:1-7, and the title of the book [1:1-3] may have been added when Ezekiel prepared his book).

2. 592 B.C. Arrival in Jerusalem (8:1-4) and sight of pagan mystery cults (8:5-18) and secret plots (11:1-3) in the Temple. The oracle in 11:14-21 was added by Ezekiel when he redacted his book.

3. 591 B.C. Oracle to the Judean elders who consulted Ezekiel in Jerusalem (20:1-32), with later supplements (20:33-39, 40-44).

4. Oracles against Jerusalem and Judah dating from the years 591-588 B.C. (6:1-6, 13 f.; 7:1-27; 12:21-14:11; 22), with later supplements (6:8-12; 13:3 f., 5 f., 9; 22:24, 31 [or all of 22:23-31], and possibly 14:1-11).

5. Allegorical oracles against Jerusalem, Judah, and Judean kings pronounced in 591-588 B.C. (15-16; 19; 23), including later supplements (16:53-63; 19:10-14; 23:36-49).

6. Symbolical acts in the years 590-588 B.C. depicting the imminent siege of Jerusalem (4:1-3, 7 f., 9-11, 16 f.; 5:1 f.; 12:17-20), supplemented

after 585 with references to the Exile (4:4-6, 12-15; 5:3 f., 5-17; 12:1-16).

7. 588 B.C. Last oracles delivered in Jerusalem before (20:45-21:27 [H. 21:1-32]) and immediately after (17:1-21; 24:1-14) the beginning of the siege, with later supplements (17:22-24; 21:28-32 [H. 21:33-37]). The ominous death of Ezekiel's wife during the siege (24:15-27; 24:25-27 may be later than 585).

8. 588-587 B.C. A vision of the slaying of Jerusalem's sinners (ch. 9), of the burning of the city (10:2-7), and of the departure of Jehovah's glory from the doomed Temple (10:18 f.; 11:22 f.), after Jehovah had ordered Ezekiel to return to Babylonia (3:10 f.). Transported (miraculously) to Tel-abib (3:12-15; the parallel account in 11:24 f. may be secondary), the prophet was appointed a watchman among the Exiles (3:16-21; 14:12-23; 14:21-23 may be a supplement; cf. 33:1-9) with instructions to warn them individually (cf. 33:10-20; 18:20-32). The description of the divine chariot in 10:1, 8-17, 20-22, repeating substantially 1:26, 5b-21, may be editorial.

9. 587-585 B.C. In a vision God announced that Ezekiel would be speechless until the arrival of the news of Jerusalem's fall (3:22-26 [3:27 is a gloss]; 24:25-27). When a messenger brought the news in January 585, Ezekiel recovered his speech (33:21 f.).

10. Public addresses and private admonition to the Exiles in 585-575 (18 and 33:1-20, closely parallel; 33:23-29; 34; 35:1-36:15; 36:16-38; 37); a divine oracle of the same period (33:30-33).

The rest of the book (chs. 25-32, 38-39, 40-48) is the fruit of Ezekiel's literary activity during the period 587-571. It is clear from the preceding analysis of chs. 1-24 and 33-37 that some parts are transcripts of actual addresses (cf. 2:4 ff.; 3:17; 11:25; 20:1 ff.; 33:30 ff.) while others are literary compositions in writing. Although our evidence is meager, it may be surmised that Ezekiel wrote extremely little during his ministry in Jerusalem (from 592 to about 587), perhaps only the drafts of some of his addresses. If we believe the statements of the book, the addresses in 14:1-11 and 20:1-32 were delivered extemporaneously in answer to inquiry and could not have been prepared in advance. On the analogy of Jeremiah, about whom more information is available, it would seem that Ezekiel collected his speeches and experiences in a book when his preaching in Jerusalem could no longer be continued.

It is possible that the book of foreign oracles (25-32, with a later addition in 29:17-21) was the first volume prepared by Ezekiel; his second was chs. 1-24 and 33-37 (perhaps with a concluding appendix in 38-39, although the authorship of 38:1-39:24 is uncertain); and his third (dated in 573) the program for the future congregation (40-48).

The oracles against foreign nations (25-32) were written in the years 587-585, except for a late supplement (29:17-21) added in 571, when

Ezekiel was probably preparing the final edition of his works. Aside from this supplement, the oracles against Egypt (29-32) were written partly during the siege of Jerusalem in January (29:1), April (30:20), and June (31:1) of 587, partly after Ezekiel heard that the city was taken, in March 585 (32:1, 17). Although we do not know exactly when Ezekiel left Jerusalem, it is likely that he did so after the death of his wife, when Nebuchadnezzar lifted the siege temporarily to meet the Egyptian forces of Pharaoh Hophra, late in 588. If such be the case, all the foreign oracles were written in Babylonia. It is not to be excluded, however, that Ezekiel left the city after June 587 and composed the earliest of the oracles against Egypt in the city, although owing to the lack of any clear reference to Hophra's defeat no positive inference is possible; 30:20-26, dated in April 587, alludes vaguely and imaginatively to this battle. The only portions of the oracles against Egypt which may not be authentic are 29:13-16 and 32:29-32.

The other oracles against foreign nations (25-28) were written in Babylonia after Ezekiel heard of the capture of Jerusalem, for they denounce the unfriendly attitude of Judah's neighbors (25) and of Tyre (26:2) after Jerusalem's doom (the date in 26:1, 587-586, should therefore be corrected to a date after January 585, when Ezekiel was notified of Jerusalem's fall). The oracles against Tyre (26:1-28:19) were written after Nebuchadnezzar began to besiege this city in 585, but before he withdrew in 573 (cf. 29:17-21), presumably in the early part of this period, when Ezekiel could still look forward to a complete devastation of the city. The catalogue of wares brought to Tyre (27:9b-25a) is out of place and possibly spurious; the concluding oracle on Sidon (28:20-23) is colorless and, if genuine, later than 573; 28:24 marks the conclusion of 25-28 and has been expanded editorially in 28:25 f.

Ezekiel's second volume (1-24; 33-37; [38-39]) was written in Babylonia in the years following 585 and was probably completed before 575, for it is clearly earlier than the third volume (40-48) dated in 573. This dating is certain not only for chs. 33-37 (cf. 33:21), and 38-39, if genuine, but also for 1-24 which contain the account of Ezekiel's experiences and oracles in 593-587. In committing to writing his words and deeds of this period, Ezekiel relied principally on his memory. Like Jeremiah (Jer. 36:32), he edited and supplemented his early oracles, adding to the gloomy words of "lamentations, moanings, and woe" (2:9 f.) the messages of hope characteristic of the period after 585. The following passages in 1-24 refer either to the Exile of 586 or to the restoration of the nation after that date: *a.* the Exile: 4:1-3, 7 f., 9-11, 16 f.; 5:1 f.; 6:8-12; 12:1-16; 14:21-23; 17:1-21; 19:10-14; 21:24-27 [H. 21:29-32]; cf. 21:28-32 [H. 21:33-37]; 22:24, 31; *b.* the restoration: 11:14-21; 16:53-63; 17:22-24; 20:33-44. In addition, Ezekiel's ministry to the individuals, which began in 585, is referred to in 3:16-21; 14:1-20; 18; cf. 33:1-20. It is thus clear that in writing his second volume Ezekiel did not keep the two phases of his ministry, the denunciation of Jerusalem before 585 and the proclamation of a glorious future after 585, sharply separated. It was inevitable that his later attitude of mind should be disclosed in the book which he wrote after 585.

The two parts of the second volume (1-24; 33-37; [38-39]) have been separated by the insertion of the volume of foreign oracles (25-32), thus breaking the natural connection between 24:25-27 and 33:21 f. (33:1-20 is out of place). This second part (33-39), following an introductory chapter (33), consists of oracles assuring the people of the imminence of their national restoration. Some of these may have been delivered orally to the Exiles.

The predictions of the Messianic restoration of David's monarchy (34:23 f.; 37:24 f.) and the apocalyptic oracle against Gog of Magog (38:1-39:24; 39:25-29 has nothing to do with Gog and is the conclusion of Ezekiel's second volume) may have been added to the book by later authors. Critical opinion is sharply divided on the unity, date, and authorship of the oracle against Gog. This mysterious personage has been identified with the Babylonians (G. H. A. Ewald, 1868; Dr. Böhmer, 1901; J. Meinhold, 1932; L. Finkelstein, 1938), with the Scythians (H. A. C. Hävernick, 1843; H. Graetz, 1874; W. F. Lofthouse, 1920; cf. Josephus, *Antiquities* 1:6, 1; Jerome, etc.), with Alexander the Great (H. Winckler, 1898; Th. Nöldeke, 1928 [cf. C. C. Torrey, *Pseudo-Ezekiel*, p. 95, 1930]; C. C. Torrey, 1930), with Antiochus III (Polychronius [d. *ca.* 430]; H. Grotius), with Antiochus Epiphanes (L. Seinecke, 1844), with Antiochus Eupator (G. R. Berry, 1922), with the Parthians (E. Havet, 1891; so already in Enoch 56-57), with Mithridates VI king of Pontus in 120-64 B.C. (N. Schmidt, 1907). Since the oracle depicts purely imaginary events at the end of time (38:8, 16), the author hardly depicted the downfall of a historical character. He selected for his mythical hero the name of Gyges king of Lydia (*ca.* 670-652 B.C.), apparently because his kingdom was in Asia Minor, in the extreme north (38:15; 39:2), where Meshek and Tubal (38:2 f.; 39:1) were located. The Hebrew Gog is the exact equivalent of *Gûgu*, the Assyrian form of the name Gyges. A number of critics have discovered in chs. 38-39 two recensions of Gog's onslaught against Israel, which have been combined into one narrative; but, in spite of some obvious parallels, the analysis into two separate documents is unsatisfactory. Although Ezekiel could possibly have written this apocalypse, it is probably the work of a later author. This attack of the Gentiles on the Jews has no logical place in Ezekiel's hopes for the future. In 34:28 he had said that the Israelites, after returning to their land, would dwell there safely, "and they shall not be a prey to the nations." The reference to the oracles of "my servants the prophets" (38:17; cf. 39:8), who had predicted the coming of Gog, is more than suspicious in the mouth of Ezekiel. Although he was acquainted with the prophetic books, he claims to be inspired and elsewhere never quoted literary authorities. Moreover, the only oracles in which such an apocalyptic defeat of the heathen hosts at the gate of Jerusalem is predicted are considerably later than Ezekiel (Joel; Zech. 12-14); the "Northern One" of Jeremiah and Zephaniah (the Scythians) is an historical, not an apocalyptic foe.

Ezekiel's third volume (40-48) is dated in October 573 B.C. and is therefore, except for 29:17-21 (571 B.C.), the latest part of his writings. This volume, containing the plan for the future ecclesiastical organization of the community, is not intact but, as has been noted, the amount of editorial material is small. One curious gloss expresses a reader's irritation at Ezekiel's deviations from the normative cycle of festivals given later in the Priestly Code. The original text of 45:20, revised according to the LXX read, "And so shall be done in the seventh (month), on the first day of the month, and ye will make expiation for the Temple." A marginal note of a reader, now ungrammatically embodied within this verse, reads, "[written] by a man ignorantly in error, and by a simpleton" (cf. A. B. Ehrlich, *Randglossen zur Hebräischen Bibel.* Leipzig, 1912; *ad loc.*).

It is not possible to determine with any assurance whether Ezekiel joined his three volumes into one or two books or left them separate. We do not know how reliable is Josephus (*Antiquities* 10:5, 1) when he tells us that Ezekiel wrote and left *two* volumes, presumably 1-39 and 40-48 or 1-24, 33-48, and 25-32, but hardly a volume on Jerusalem and one on the Exile, as A. Bertholet (*Hesekiel*, p. xv) suggests. The serious disarrangement apparent in certain parts of the book (3:4-27; 8-11; 40-48), the abrupt insertion of the oracles against foreign nations between chs. 24 and 33, and the numerous parallel sections (e.g., 2:1-8 and 3:4-9; 7:3 f. and 7:6-9; 1:26, 5b-21 and 10:1, 8-17, 20-22; 3:16b-21 and 33:7-9; cf. 18) prove that Ezekiel did not give the finishing touches to his book and justify to some extent the assertion of the Talmud (*Baba Bathra* 15a) that "The men of the Great Synagogue wrote Ezekiel, the Twelve Prophets, Daniel, and Esther." Unquestionably the book as we have it has been edited and arranged by redactors active in the period 560-444 B.C., but an exact determination of their work is beyond the reach of modern criticism.

The *style* of Ezekiel reflects the paradoxical contrasts of his personality. His moods are nearly as varied and contradictory as those of Dante, whose writings range from a dialectic discussion of abstract political and theological problems in the *De Monarchia* to the love poetry of the *Vita Nuova*, and within *The Divine Comedy* from sordid reality to visionary perfection, from abstruse scholastic and scientific discussions to the passionate drama of Francesca and imaginative allegories and symbols. Both Ezekiel and Dante sought escape from the abuses, iniquities, and desolation of reality to a world created by their imagination.

The contrast between the vivid poetry and the dull prose of Ezekiel is even more striking than in Jeremiah. Without doubt in Jeremiah, and perhaps in Ezekiel, some of the most dreary and repetitious prose sections were penned by a secretary or later redactors.

The poetical sections of Ezekiel's book are the following: 15; 16:3-14(?); 17:3-10, 19-20a, 22-24;[13] 19; 21:9-17 (H. 21:14-22) (21:28b-32 [H. 21: 33b-37]); 23:1-27 (?), 32-34; 24:3-5 (6-14), 16 f.; 26:2-6a, 8-14, 17b-18; 27:3b-9a, 25b-36; 28:2-10, 12b-19, (22a, 23a); 29:3-7; (30:2b-19); 31: 2b-9, (10-18?); 32:2b-8, (18-28); (35:3 f., 9a). It is characteristic of Ezekiel that, with rare exceptions, his poems are allegorical. The most significant allegories are the following: the wild vine (15), the un-grateful bride (16), the vulture, the cedar, and the vine (17), the lioness and her whelps (19:2-9) and the uprooted vine (19:10-14), the sword (21), the two unchaste sisters (23), the rusty caldron (24:3-14), the death of Ezekiel's wife (24:16 f.), the ship Tyre (27), the fall of the mythical prince of Tyre (28), the Egyptian crocodile (29; 32), the lofty pine which is cut down (31). Only the poetic descriptions of the destruc-tion of Tyre (26) and of the devastation of Egypt (30) and Edom (35) lack the allegorical form; the threats against Egypt and Edom (30; 35) are composed in rhythmical prose rather than in verse. It is not surprising that even the prophet's hearers complained that he was obscure and said, "Is he not a speaker in parables?" (20:49 [H. 21:5]). Sensitive to this criticism, Ezekiel took pains to explain most of his parables when he prepared them for publication.

From the literary point of view, Ezekiel's allegories are descriptive rather than dramatic, fantastic rather than realistic. Usually they consist of the portrayal of an animal, plant, or thing and picture its destruction. The details of the description are often hyperbolically exaggerated (19:7 [probably corrupt]; 21:15 [H. 21:20]; 27:28; 28:13 f.; 29:4; 31:6, 13; 32:4-8) or otherwise incredible (17:5; 19:14). It is only in the allegories of the foundling girl, reared by Jehovah to become his bride (16), and in the story of the two sisters who became harlots (23) that we find the germs of a dramatic development. The most distinguished and really great poetry, free from exaggerations and distasteful imagery (particularly shocking are the obscenities in chs. 16 and 23), is that of the allegories of the whelps (19:2-6, 8 f.) and of the ship Tyre (27:3b-9a, 25b-36). Here we have Ezekiel the poet at his best, writing with unusual clarity and simplicity, and withal with impressiveness and force. His pictures here are vivid and natural, in fact the details of the ship Tyre are so true

[13] Cf. Louise Pettibone Smith's restoration of Ez. 17 in JBL 58 (1939) 43-50

to life that Ez. 27 is one of the three most important literary sources of our knowledge of ancient navigation (the others being the *Odyssey* and Acts 27).

The prose style of Ezekiel at its best is lucid and adequate, although it does not possess unusual distinction; at its worst it is pedantic, monotonous, and repetitious. Ezekiel in prose as well as in poetry is essentially visual, excelling in descriptions of real or imaginary scenes; however, he lacks restraint, is prone to emphasize technical details, and has more fantasy than creative imagination. As an orator he probably failed dismally—a possible explanation for the puzzling apathy of his listeners, in contrast with the public indignation aroused by Jeremiah's addresses. His discourse on personal responsibility (ch. 18) shows a keen mind and a noble conscience, but no rhetorical skill or stirring eloquence. His best description in prose is that of the bones coming to life (37:1-14), his most involved is that of the divine chariot (ch. 1).

The diction of Ezekiel is postclassical. His Hebrew is tinged with new words and expressions; his vocabulary shows strong influences of the Aramaic and even, to a lesser degree, of the Akkadian languages (cf. Sh. Spiegel, in HTR 24 [1931] 301-306). Despite his limitations as a speaker and as a writer, despite his eccentricities, his daydreaming, his fanatical zeal and dogmatic tone, Ezekiel wrote a book destined to exercise an incalculable influence on the history of his people and indirectly on Western nations.

CHAPTER IV

THE BOOK OF THE TWELVE

~~~~~~

1. Hosea

Hosea, son of Beeri, was called to the prophetic ministry "in the days of Jeroboam [II] the son of Joash king of Israel [785-744 B.C.]" (1:1); the following mention of the kings of Judah from Uzziah to Hezekiah [780-692], which makes Hosea a contemporary of Isaiah, is a Judean interpolation. His call to prophecy must have occurred after that of Amos (ca. 750) but before the death of Jeroboam and his son Zechariah in 744. His first oracle (1:4) predicted divine punishment of Jehu's bloody deeds on the plain of Jezreel (II Kings 10:11), and Jehu's dynasty actually met its doom in the revolution of Shallum in 744.

While Amos's activity ceased before Assyrian power revived with the accession of Tiglath-pileser III (745), Hosea's oracles are dated both before (1-3) and after (4-14) 744. He refers to the period of anarchy and chaos beginning in 744 (7:3, 5, 7; 8:4a): after a month Shallum was assassinated by Menahem (744), whose son Pekahiah was in turn murdered by Pekah (737). In their frantic efforts to save their doomed kingdom from the end that came in 722 with the fall of Samaria (predicted in 13:16 [H. 14:1]), the Israelites turned fitfully to Assyria or to Egypt, alternately, for help (5:13; 7:11; 8:9; 10:3b, 6; cf. 12:1b [H. 12:2b]). It is generally thought that Hosea ceased to prophesy before the Syro-Ephraimitic War (Is. 7), i.e., before 735, but A. Alt (NKZ 30 [1919] 537-568) has tried to show that in 5:10-6:6 Hosea alludes to an attack of Judah upon Ephraim in retaliation for the campaign of Pekah of Israel and Rezin of Damascus against Ahaz.

Hosea was a Northern Israelite, and possibly a member of a priestly family like Jeremiah, as B. Duhm has suggested. He lived in the Northern Kingdom (perhaps in Benjamin; cf. 5:8 f. and Jer. 6:1) and often refers to localities within its borders (1:4; 4:15; 5:1 f.; 6:8 f.; cf. 2:15a [H. 2:17a]; 12:11 [H. 12:12]; 14:5 f. [H. 14:6 f.] which are of doubtful authenticity). He addressed his oracles to "Ephraim" or "Israel" (i.e., the Northern Kingdom); references in his book to the kingdom of Judah are emendations or interpolations of Judean editors, who adapted the book for Southern readers (cf. R. E. Wolfe, ZAW N.F. 12 [1935] 91 f.).[1]

At the time of his call, Jehovah said to Hosea, "Go, take unto thee a wife of fornication and children of fornication; for the country has committed great fornication in forsaking Jehovah" (1:2). So Hosea married Gomer, daughter of Diblaim, who bore him three children to whom Hosea gave emblematic names signifying God's indignation against his people: Jezreel (to proclaim the end of Jehu's dynasty; see above), Lo-ruhamah (she to whom no mercy is shown), and Lo-ammi (not my people) (1:3 f., 6aba, 8 f.; the rest in 1:3-9 is clearly spurious).

Later Jehovah addressed Hosea *a second time* (3:1; '*ôdh* [again, yet] modifies "said," not, according to the usual interpretation, "go") saying, "Go, love a woman beloved by a paramour and adulterous, even as Jehovah loves the children of Israel, although they turn to other gods and like raisin cakes" [used in the worship of pagan gods; cf. Is. 16:7 and the cakes for the Queen of Heaven in Jer. 7:18] (3:1). So Hosea purchased a common streetwalker for the price of an ordinary slave (fifteen shekels of silver and one and a half omers of barley) and kept her in seclusion for a long time as a symbol of Israel's impending loss of king and prince, altar (so LXX) and sacred pillar (3:2-4 [omitting "ephod and teraphim" at the end; 3:5 is spurious without question, 3:4 is doubtful]). There is no valid reason for rejecting all of ch. 3, as do W. R. Smith, P. Volz, K. Marti, P. Haupt, G. Hölscher, and R. E. Wolfe.

These two chapters, 1 (in the third person) and 3 (in the first person), furnish all our information on the prophet's life. In spite of the obvious meaning of Hosea's words summarized above, every conceivable interpretation of these two chapters has been offered (cf. for the early views, W. R. Harper, *Amos and Hosea* [ICC], pp. 208-210, 1905). Some critics cut the Gordian knot by regarding ch. 1 (F. Peiser) or ch. 3 (see above) as unhistorical, or considering either or both stories as pure allegory.[2] If it is admitted that actual experiences underlie both narratives, what is their mutual relationship? Some answer (*mirabile dictu!*) that *the identical experiences* are related by the prophet in ch. 3 and by someone else in ch. 1![3]

With more common sense, most critics admit that 1 and 3 represent *successive* experiences[4] but without justification identify the unnamed

---

[1] A. Alt (NKZ 30 [1919] 537-568) defends the genuineness of the references to Judah in 5:10-6:4. This theory has been accepted by R. Kittel (*Geschichte der Volkes Israel*, Vol. II, p. 334, n. 3, 6th ed.), H. Schmidt, E. Sellin, and others.

[2] A. V. Van Hoonacker; H. Gressmann; E. Day (AJSL 26 [1910] 105-132); C. H. Toy (JBL 32 [1913] 75-79).

[3] C. Steuernagel, R. Kittel, L. Gautier, Th. H. Robinson, O. Eissfeldt.

[4] Regarding the events in ch. 1 as earlier than those in ch. 3. J. Lindblom (*Hosea literarisch untersucht*. Helsingfors, 1927), however, considers the children's birth as following the events of ch. 3.

prostitute in ch. 3 with Gomer, Hosea's legitimate wife. If 3:1 referred to Gomer, the writer would have said "the woman" or "that woman," not indefinitely "a woman." This gratuitous identification presupposes that Gomer was unfaithful to Hosea, that her two younger children were illegitimate (1:3 states positively that this was *not* true of the first child), that after the birth of the third child she forsook Hosea and, following a life of promiscuity and vice, was reduced to the state of a streetwalker until Hosea again (3:1-3) gave her a home.

These assumptions are unfounded, unless, following J. Meinhold, we change the text of 2:1 (H. 2:3) to read, "Then said I to my sons Jezreel and Lo-ammi and to my daughter Lo-ruhamah, 'Plead with your mother, plead; for she is not my wife. . . .'" Moreover, these guesses involve insuperable difficulties. For if the Lord's initial command to Hosea (1:2) really means "marry a prostitute and get illegitimate children," Hosea disregarded it completely, since Gomer was ostensibly unblemished at the time of the marriage and her first son legitimate (1:3). K. Marti's assertion that "woman of fornication" (1:2) means "proleptically" the bad woman she turned out to be some time after her marriage is pure sleight of hand. To say that his domestic tragedy made Hosea a prophet[5] contradicts his declaration that his call came *before* his marriage, and that the name of his first and unquestionably legitimate son came to him through prophetic inspiration. This last difficulty is overcome with extraordinary ingenuity by R. Kittel (*Geschichte des Volkes Israel*, Vol. II, p. 345, note). Before Hosea discovered his wife's infidelity (between 1:8 and 1:9),[6] he had been a "political" prophet; only afterward did he condemn the religion of the Baals and announce God's love; as for God's words in 1:2, they are "not a real but a conventionalized audition that, even though experienced later, was placed at the beginning as a sort of theme." G. Hölscher simply excises the crucial verse (1:2).

It is difficult to understand why modern critics have felt impelled to perpetuate the slanderous insinuations against Gomer's wifely virtue, which Hosea never doubted. The only recent champions of her good name known to me are: G. Hölscher (*Die Propheten*, pp. 424 f.; *Geschichte der israelitischen und jüdischen Religion*, p. 106, Giessen, 1922); W. Staerk, *Das assyrische Weltreich im Urteil der Propheten*, p. 194, 1908; W. R. Arnold (*Ephod and Ark*, p. 126, n. 1); J. Flück (ZAW

---

[5] This view has been presented with psychoanalytic arguments by A. Allwohn, *Die Ehe des Propheten Hosea in psychoanalitischer Beleuchtung* (Giessen, 1926). See also W. O. E. Oesterley and Th. H. Robinson, *An Introduction to the Books of the Old Testament* (pp. 351 f.).

[6] J. Wellhausen (*Die Kleinen Propheten*, 1892) asserts that Hosea became aware of Gomer's faithlessness after the birth of their first child (who, however, was legitimate); H. Schmidt (ZAW N.F. I, [1924] 261), instead, postpones this tragic discovery after the birth of the third.

39 [1921] 283-290); A. Heerrmann (ZAW 40 [1922] 287-312); L. W. Batten (JBL 48 [1929] 257-273). Some earlier writers advocating this view are mentioned by W. R. Harper (*Amos and Hosea* [ICC], p. 209, 1910).

Once the identification of Gomer with the woman of 3:1 is dismissed,[7] her ill repute rests entirely on a misinterpretation of 1:2 (2:4 ff. [H. 2:2 ff.] are addressed to Israel and therefore irrelevant). If Hosea really believed that the deity wished him to degrade himself to the utmost by marrying a whore—quite incredible in view of his conception of God—he would have said so; 3:1; 4:13b, 14aβ and many figurative expressions elsewhere show that Hosea lacked neither the vocabulary nor the candor to express himself plainly and forcibly with reference to indecent matters. The phrasing of 1:2 leaves no doubt with regard to the figurative meaning of the words "woman of whoredoms and children of whoredoms." Not only does "whoredoms" mean religious apostasy elsewhere (2:2, 4 [H 2:4, 6]; cf. the glosses 4:12b and 5:4b, in which the meaning of the expression is explained unequivocally as religious, not sexual, fornication), but, lest there be any doubt in the reader's mind, Hosea explains at once that his wife and children are inevitably in a state of (religious) fornication because the whole land is in such a state.

The point of ch. 1 is not an imaginary domestic tragedy of Hosea but the moral and religious defection of Israel, indicated allegorically in the significant names of Hosea's children and denounced at length in ch. 2. The point of ch. 3, brought out by a symbolical action that has nothing to do with Hosea's family life, is that Jehovah still loves his adulterous nation and will take measures to bring it to its senses (cf. 2:14 [H. 2:16]). This figure of marriage and adultery does not necessarily allude to the Adonis cult.[8]

The book of Hosea is divided into two parts: 1-3 (written before 744), in which the prophet still hoped for a conversion of his people, and 4-14 (written between 744 and 735), in which the nation's condition seems incurable.

Hos. 1-3. In 1:1-9 (see above) the prophet gives his three children symbolical names to announce the downfall of the dynasty of Jehu and of the nation. In 1:10-2:1 (H. 2:1-3) a glossator predicts for Israel a glorious future and its reunion with Judah; he changes the names of Lo-ammi and Lo-ruhamah. In 2:2-13 (H. 2:4-15) (2:8bβ, 11b [H. 2:10bβ 13b] are glosses) using the figure of marriage to describe Jehovah's relations with Israel, Hosea declares that by worshiping the Baals of Canaan and at-

---

[7] With B. Duhm, and the critics just named.

[8] H. G. May ("The Fertility Cult in Hosea," AJSL 48 [1932] 73-98) and E. A. Leslie (*The Old Testament Religion*, p. 184. New York, 1936) have discovered in Hosea allusions to the Adonis myth.

tributing to them the fertility of the land Israel has committed whoredom and adultery against her true husband, Jehovah, and will be punished by him. When the erring wife (Israel) will come to her senses after a period of seclusion (2:14 [H. 2:16]), she will be betrothed anew in abiding love and faithfulness forever (2:19 f. [H. 2:21 f.]); the rest of 2:14-23 (H. 2:16-25) is a postexilic vision of Israel's future glory. By an act of kindness to a wretched prostitute, Hosea symbolizes God, in his abiding love, endeavoring to redeem his wicked people (3:1-4); the national conversion and salvation is described (in wretched Hebrew) by a glossator in 3:5.

Hos. 4-14. The extremely poor textual transmission of these chapters and the large amount of interpolated material which they contain obscure Hosea's own thoughts, which, moreover, are set down in chaotic confusion. In ch. 4, Hosea denounces the current religious worship, which included immoral commerce with temple prostitutes,[9] and Israel's religion in general tolerating gross wickedness and amounting to apostasy; he blames particularly the priests for fattening on the sins of the people (4:3, 5, 10b, 11, 12b, 14aαb, 15aβ, 16 f., 19 are spurious). Therefore judgment will first of all strike priests and dynasty (omit "the house of Israel" in 5:1); Jehovah has forsaken his people (5:2-7, omitting 5:3b, 4b, 5b, 6b as interpolations).

A campaign of Judah against Ephraim will cause great suffering (5:8-14, omitting 5:11), and bring about repentance and a return to Jehovah—but only for a moment (5:15-6:6). Particular criminal acts (6:7-7:1a, omitting "the whoredom of Ephraim" in 6:10; 6:11-7:1a), conspiracies against rulers (7:1b-7, omitting 7:4, 6), international intrigues (7:8-13), and insincere appeals to Jehovah (7:14-16) will inevitably bring ruin. War (8:1-3) for a nation weakened by political anarchy (8:4a) and idolatry (8:4b-6, probably interpolated) will mean complete devastation of the land (8:7-10).

The multiplication of sacrifices on numerous altars will not atone for Israel's guilt (8:11-14, omitting 8:13bβ, 14). Joy at harvest festivals is unwarranted, for the Israelites will soon be exiled to Egypt and Assyria (9:1-7a), even though they persecute the prophets who announce their doom (9:7b-17). The sanctuaries of the land will be desecrated (10:1-8) in a disastrous war (10:9-15). God's love for Israel since her youth has evoked only ingratitude (11:1-7)—and yet how can the God of love give way to anger (11:8-11; 11:10 f. are a postexilic promise of restoration, and 11:8 f. are of doubtful authenticity)? An anti-Samaritan Jew compares Ephraim [Samaria] with its unscrupulous and deceitful ancestor,

---

[9] It would be strange indeed if Hosea had married a "sacred harlot" (Gomer) by command of Jehovah, as H. G. May (JBL 55 [1936] 287 f.) and E. A. Leslie (*The Prophets Tell Their Own Story*, p. 40. New York, 1939) believe.

Jacob, and gloats over its doom (11:12-12:14 [H. 12:1-15]). He may have penned in the same spirit the denunciation of the "calf" worship in 13:1 f.

The final threat proclaims that Jehovah's patience is at an end (13:3-8) and pronounces a death sentence against Israel (13:9-16 [H. 13:9-14:1]). As most critics recognize, the reassurances at the end of the book (14:1-9 [H. 14:2-10]) were not written by Hosea. Probably the editor of his book, who wrote the last verse, was the author of this whole section.

Hosea's style reflects an extremely sensitive, emotional nature, not unlike that of Jeremiah but in sharp contrast to the rugged, unflinching objectivity of Amos. Hosea can describe in tender, warmhearted tones the pathos of Jehovah's love for an ungrateful people (6:4; 11:3 f.), but he can also use vehement and dramatic images to express the burning passion of divine anger (5:14; 13:7 f., 12-14); and he does not hesitate to use harsh and vulgar terms to depict the religious orgies of the time (4:10a, 13, 14aβ). In the most fluent and moving of all his oracles (2:2-13 [H. 2:4-15]), the only one not confined to a few sentences, burning indignation and tender compassion are characteristically blended in a contradictory frame of mind such as we find only in Jeremiah. Otherwise the prophet, in his nervous tension, passes impulsively from mood to mood, from topic to topic without transitions, "quasi per sententias loquens" (Jerome).

Amos had raged against social inequalities and the exploitation of the lower classes, as well as against religious fallacies. Hosea is not interested in the social gospel but thunders only against moral, religious, and political abominations. For him all of these are offenses against the God of Israel—the loving father (11:1, 3 f.) and faithful husband (2:2 ff. [H. 2:4 ff.]) of an ungrateful people. The metaphor of the marriage relation, characterizing the intimate relation between God and worshiper, is the most original as well as the most important contribution of this prophet. Before his time fear was the keynote of all religions and, as a Hittite text expounds in detail,[10] the worshiper stood before the deity as a subject before a king or even as a slave before his master. In Hosea's startlingly new conception, religion becomes more inward and emotional. Instead of the old term for religion "the fear of God," Hosea uses "the knowledge of God" and proceeds to identify it with *hesed*, which means not so much "mercy," according to the usual translation, as "loyalty" (6:6; cf. 4:1; 6:4). Just as Amos had regarded sacrifice as insignificant in comparison with righteousness, so Hosea considers it trivial with respect to loyalty. Israel's basic offense is that her constancy is as ephemeral "as a morning cloud, and as the early dew" (6:4). Instead

---

[10] See A. Goetze, *Kleinasien*, p. 151, in Handbuch der Altertumswissenschaft, III, I, Vol. III (III, 1). München, 1933. G. Furlani, HTR 31 (1938) 251-262.

of being faithful to her divine husband, she has played the harlot and run after lovers (2:5 [H. 2:3]).

She has been unfaithful in three ways. In the first place, the Baals who were worshiped at the old sanctuaries of Canaan—supposed givers of agricultural bounty—lured her away from the divine husband of her youth (2:2-13 [H. 2:4-15]). Even when worship at the "high places" was nominally consecrated to Jehovah (4:15b; 9:4f.), God rejected their offerings (5:6; 8:13) because they did not cry unto him "from their hearts" but merely to obtain grain and new wine; even as they "cut themselves" (so LXX; cf. I Kings 18:28) they were rebellious against him (7:14). God demands loyalty, not sacrifices (6:6). Certain postexilic annotators of the book misunderstood Hosea's denunciations. Instead of numerous local Baals they invented a single Baal for the whole country (13:1b; cf. 9:10b), which is nothing but an idol (2:8bβ [H. 2:10bβ]; cf. 11:2); for them the sin of Israel is the adoration of "the calf of Samaria" (8:5f.; 10:5-6a; 13:2) and of other idols (4:17; 8:4b; 13:2; 14:3aβ, 8 [H. 14:4aβ, 9]). In some cases, it would seem that Hosea's oracles have been edited in the spirit of the law of Deut. 12, forbidding sacrifices outside the Temple at Jerusalem: the multiplication of altars is condemned in 8:11; 10:1b, 2, 8a; 12:11 [H. 12:12], and 9:4f. takes it for granted that in exile far from the Temple the ceremonies of worship cannot be performed.

Israel played the whore not only religiously, but in the second place morally. In a literal sense, this applies to the revolting custom of sacred prostitution in the sanctuaries of Canaan (4:10a, 13, 14a), in a figurative sense, to glaring breaches of elementary moral precepts, particularly murder, highway robbery, perjury, adultery and lying—crimes that are later forbidden in the Ten Commandments (4:2; 7:1; 10:4; cf. 6:7-9). Dishonesty and exploitation of the poorer classes, of primary concern to Amos, do not seem to interest Hosea, but are added to his picture of moral depravity by a glossator (12:6-8 [H. 12:7-9]). Sententiously, after the manner of Proverbs, another glossator contributes a maxim that was divided into two parts in the process of transmission (4:11, 14b); a professional sage likewise penned the last verse of the book.

In the third place, Israel's political institutions and diplomatic intrigues are also a phase of her whoredom. Several critics (J. Wellhausen, R. Smend, W. Nowack, A. Lods) believe that Hosea was opposed in principle to the institution of the monarchy per se, quoting passages like 3:4f. and 13:9-11 (of questionable authenticity) and interpreting "the days of Gibea" (10:9) and even the "wickedness in Gilgal" (9:15) as allusions to the coronation of Saul, their first king.[11] On the contrary,

---

[11] With some exaggeration, A. Causse, P. Humbert, and others say that Hosea was radically opposed to agricultural pursuits and advocated a return to primitive nomadic life. Nothing indicates that Hosea was a Rechabite.

others (K. Marti, G. Hölscher) see in 13:10 a quotation from I Sam. 8:6 ff. and in "the days of Gibea" an allusion to the outrage described in Judg. 19:25. But whether or not Hosea regarded monarchical institutions as offensive to Jehovah, he inveighed in no uncertain terms against usurpations and assassinations of kings (7:3, 5-7; 8:4; 10:3; 13:11) as being one more proof of the nation's religious apostasy. The same verdict is passed on attempts to secure the help of Assyria or Egypt by means of gifts (7:8 f., 11-13; 8:9; cf. 11:12-12:1 [H. 12:1 f.]; and, for the divine punishment, see 5:12 f.; 10:6 and 14:3 [H. 14:4] are later additions). Like Hosea, Ezekiel (ch. 23) nearly two centuries later, speaks of Israel and Judah's relations with Egypt and Assyria as fornication.

Such intolerable conduct has made Jehovah Israel's enemy (7:12 f.; 8:14; 9:9, 15 f.): he will be unto them like a lion, like a panther, like a bear (5:14; 13:7 f.) or, worse still, like a moth and "rottenness" (5:12). The Israelites will be driven out of their country (8:13; 9:3, 6, 17; 11:5) after a foreign army—not apparently the Assyrian, as was actually the case —has invaded and despoiled the land (5:8 f.; 8:1, 3; 10:7 f.; 11:6; 13:16 [H. 14:1]).

At the beginning of his ministry, Hosea seems to have hoped that his people's exile would again turn their hearts to Jehovah in loyalty and love (2:7, 14, 19 f. [H. 2:9, 16, 21 f.]; cf. 3:1-4). Even when he became certain that the nation's corruption was incurable (5:4a) and its repentance in time of trouble only a passing mood (5:15-6:4), even when the ultimate doom of Israel seemed inescapable, Hosea retained his unswerving faith in God's love, despite dark moments in which he thought this had changed into hatred (1:6, 9; 9:15; 13:14), and God's compassion might finally give free rein to his anger (11:8 f.; 13:14). Thus Hosea's early hope for a national conversion gave way to tragic assurance that Jehovah would inevitably be forced, notwithstanding the urgent plea of his love, to execute the death sentence against the people. In sharp contrast to Hosea, the postexilic annotators of his book painted alluring pictures of a national resurrection in the glorious millennium to follow devastation of the land (1:5; 4:3) and deportation of the nation (1:7, 10-2:1 [H. 2:1-3]; 2:15-17, 18, 21-23 [H. 2:17-19, 20, 23-25]; 3:5; 6:1-3 (?); 6:11b-7:1a; 11:10 f.; 14:1-8 [H. 14:2-9]).

2. Joel

Nothing is known about Joel, son of Pethuel, probably the last Hebrew prophet who attached his name to his writing. The little book bearing his name is divided into two parts: 1:1-2:27, describing the divine deliverance, after public repentance, from a visitation of locusts followed by a famine; 2:28-3·21 (H. 3-4), a vision of the outpouring of the divine spirit, of the final judgment over the heathen, and of the millennium.

The locusts have devoured all the produce of the fields (1:2-12); let the priests mourn the lack of sacrifices and libations, and assemble the people in the Temple (1:13 f.). The prophet cries unto the Lord in anguish because a drought has cut men and cattle off from their sustenance (1:15-20). The dreadful "Day of the Lord" (cf. 1:15) is impending: an innumerable new host of fabulous flaming locusts, which shakes the earth and darkens the sun and moon, will overwhelm the country (2:1-11) unless by a wholehearted return to God, with fasting, weeping, mourning, and a rending of hearts rather than garments, as also by public fasting, Jehovah in his mercy might be entreated to spare the nation (2:12-17). Presumably this was done, and Jehovah promised to remove the "Northern" host (the locusts) and restore the fertility of the land (2:18-27).

Upon all Israelites Jehovah will pour the spirit of prophecy (2:28 f. [H. 3:1 f.]) and produce portents in heaven and earth (2:30 f. [H. 3:3 f.]) that presage the coming of the Day of the Lord; but the faithful will be saved on Zion (2:32 [H. 3:5]). The heathen, particularly the peoples of Tyre, Sidon, and Philistia who have sold Jews to the Greeks, will be judged in the valley of Jehoshaphat ("Jehovah judges") (3:1-8 [H. 4:1-8]). In ringing verse they are called to arms and urged to come and battle in the valley of Jehoshaphat, where presumably the angelic hosts (3:11b [H. 4:11b]) will annihilate them, while the heavenly bodies are darkened and the Lord roars out of Zion (3:9-16a [H. 4:9-16a]). Then the Lord will become the refuge of his people, Jerusalem be holy, and the land flourish (3:16b-18 [H. 4:16b-18]); Egypt and Edom will become desolate while Judah abides forever (3:19-21 [H. 4:19-21]).

The problem raised by the juxtaposition of a historical incident and apocalyptic dreams has received various solutions. The locusts of ch. 1 are actual insects; those of ch. 2 are, instead, monsters that look and run like horses, leap mountaintops, and are preceded and followed by flaming fire—similar to the mythical locusts in Rev. 9:3-11 which are described more elaborately. The term "Northerner" (2:20) applied to these locusts undoubtedly indicates their apocalyptic character (cf. for this term Jer. 1:14; Ez. 38:6, 15; 39:2). In its present form, the historical and apocalyptic parts are not sharply divided, although the section ending with 2:27 is mostly historical and what follows mostly apocalyptic: but 1:15; 2:1 f., 10 f. already describe the terrors of the Day of the Lord rather than a natural calamity.

The view advocated by A. Merx, who considers the first part of the book a prediction like the second, is now justly discarded. The solution offered by B. Duhm, who believed that the apocalyptic sections (including the verses just listed) were added to the original oracle dealing with a locust plague, as also the view that the same author wrote the two heterogeneous parts of the book, are still maintained. Since both parts of the book seem to have been written about the same time, there is no compelling reason for attributing them to different authors. In the devastation wrought by the locusts, Joel could have seen a symbol of the dreadful crisis to come, when God would sit in judgment over mankind. Such a keen sense of present-day problems combined with a vivid imagination peering ecstatically into a chimerical, apocalyptic future is by no means singular. Ezekiel, and the authors of the books of Daniel and Revelation offer conspicuous and by no means unique instances of a similar blend of apparently conflicting faculties; compare also Haggai and Zechariah. In Is. 13, a prophecy of the conquest of Babylon by the Medes (Is. 13:17-22) becomes, like the locust plague in Joel, a symbol for the dreadful Day of the Lord ushering in the judgment of the wicked, as well as cosmic convulsions (13:9-13).

The absence of any arrangement in the subdivisions of the Book of Joel is not an argument against unity of authorship, since most of the prophetic books are similarly disordered. For instance, 1:2-12 describes the locust plague, but 1:13-20 gives a vivid picture of a drought and famine having no explicit connection with locusts; real locusts (1:2-12) are followed by mythical insects (2:1-11); the appeal to the people to repent appears in 1:13 f. and again in 2:12-17 but no account is given why Jehovah relented and showed mercy to his people; the prediction of the final judgment is made first in prose (3:1-8 [H. 4:1-8]) and then in poetry (3:9 ff. [H. 4:9 ff.]).

It is only by proving sufficiently divergent dates for the two parts of the book that plural authorship can be convincingly maintained; in reality, according to the scant internal evidence to be discovered, both parts date from around 350 B.C.

The proposed dates for the book, however, range over half a millennium. Some of the early critics, following K. A. Credner (1831), dated it during the first ten years of Jehoash (837-798), when that king was a minor; E. König, in his *Introduction to the Old Testament* (1893), prefers the years immediately preceding or following the death of Josiah (609). A postexilic date was first proposed by W. Vatke (1835), who placed it in the first half of the fifth century, but most of the later critics, following A. Kuenen (1863) and A. Merx (1879), favor a date after Nehemiah (or about 400).

The following allusions to the contemporary historical situation are in harmony with a date around 350. The monarchy is not mentioned; elders and priests are the authorities in Jerusalem (1:2, 13 f.; 2:16 f.). "Israel" is now only Judah, for the descendants of the Northern Israelites are patently outside Jehovah's "heritage" (2:27; 3:2, 16 [H. 4:2, 16]). The people of Jehovah are "scattered among the nations," Israel's land has been divided, and strangers have defiled Zion (3:2, 3, 17 [H. 4:2, 3, 17]).

Such conditions prevailed only after 586. Rebuilt in 520-516, the Temple was again standing on Zion (1:13 f.; 2:15-17), and the whole Jewish congregation could be gathered inside it (1:14; 2:16); for Judah was then limited to Jerusalem and its immediate vicinity, so that the trumpet blown from Zion was heard throughout the land (2:1). Finally, the sale of Jewish slaves to the Greeks (3:6 [H. 4:6]) and the existence of the city wall of Jerusalem (2:9) date the book at least after Nehemiah (444).

Joel's religious viewpoint confirms a dating about 350. In place of the flaming denunciations of specific iniquities, characteristic of pre-exilic oracles, the call to repentance (2:12 f.) mentions no particular sins and urges the performance of ritual ceremonies, i.e., congregational "fasting, weeping, and mourning" (2:12; cf. Neh. 1:4; Esth. 4:3). Moreover (as in Dan. 8:11; 11:31; 12:11), the daily offering and libation in the Temple (i.e., the *tāmîd*) had become not only the main office in religion but an indispensable symbol for the maintenance of correct relations between Jehovah and his people (1:9, 13; 2:14). Jehovah's solicitude was now confined to the Jews (contrast Amos 9:7 and the Second Isaiah). Only upon them would he pour out his spirit (2:28 f. [H. 3:1 f.]), but upon the heathen he would take vengeance in the valley of Jehoshaphat (3:1 ff. [H. 4:1 ff.]); Israel's land would become a paradise (3:18 [H. 4:18]), but Edom's a desolation (3:19), as in Is. 34-35. To Amos, the Day of the Lord was a day of judgment and punishment for Israel (Am. 5:18-20; cf. Is. 2:12 ff.). In that day, according to Zeph. 1:7 ff. (cf. Is. 13), the heathen would carry out the divine sentence against Israel. Jehovah would then burn the wicked Jews and cause the sun of righteousness to shine on the pious (Mal. 3:16-4:3 [H. 3:16-21]). In Joel 3:1 ff., however, it is a day of vengeance against all heathen, and a day of everlasting glory for the Jews, whether good or bad. Such a divine onslaught against the heathen, for the benefit of the Jews, is the burden of the following predictions: Obad. vv. 15 ff.; Zeph. 2:4-15; Is. 34 (against Edom); Ez. 38-39; Zech. 14:1 ff. These oracles (except perhaps Ez. 38-39) belong to a time when possession of the Law of Moses (canonized in the Pentateuch about 400) made the Jews regard themselves as God's favorites and the heathen as rejected by God—a feeling that Joel expresses in no uncertain terms.

The style of Joel is remarkably good—at least for the silver age of Hebrew literature to which he unquestionably belongs. It is far better than that of Haggai or Malachi, who lived in an earlier period. The author obviously nurtured his literary taste in the study of the classical (Amos, Zephaniah, Nahum, the Second Isaiah) and postclassical (Obadiah, Is. 13, Is. 2 = Mic. 4, Ezekiel, Malachi) prophetic oracles. It is not unlikely that Joel's book, one of the earliest of apocalypses, in turn influenced the visions of the end in Zech. 9-14.

3. Amos

About 750 B.C. Amos lived in Tekoa, a mountaintop village situated in the wilderness of Judah, two hours' march south of Bethlehem. He earned his meager livelihood by pasturing sheep (1:1; 7:15; "herdsman" in 7:14 should be read "shepherd" according to the LXX and the Targum). The barren steppe in that region is chiefly suited to pasture sheep and goats (cf. I Sam. 25:2-4), although a limited amount of grain, grapes, and figs was also raised in favored spots (cf. I Sam. 25:18). During part of the year, Amos seems to have gone to the Shephelah, in the western part of Judah, where sycamores grew (I Kings 10:27), to work there as a ripener (by incision) of sycamore fruits (7:14).[12]

It was while pasturing his sheep near Tekoa that Amos received the divine call to go forth and prophesy in the Northern Kingdom, even though he was not at the time a prophet and never became a member of the prophetic fraternity (7:14 f.). If 7:1-6 is genuine, the two visions therein described belong perhaps to the period in Amos's life preceding his call (cf. G. Hölscher, *Die Propheten*, pp. 195 f.).

The call to prophecy came to Amos with irresistible force (3:8), and presumably he left his home in Judah at once for the Northern Kingdom. He seems to have gone from place to place throughout the kingdom of Israel preaching and stirring up men's souls until, according to Amaziah, "the land was unable to endure all his words" (7:10). In the capital, Samaria, he called the ladies of fashion "kine of Bashan" (4:1-3) and inveighed against luxurious living (3:9, 12, 15abα; 6:1a [omitting "in Zion and trust"], 3-6). He may have visited Gilgal (cf. 5:5) and other shrines. But at Bethel, the religious center of the kingdom, his prophetic mission was suddenly brought to an end by Amaziah, chief priest of the royal sanctuary there. Aroused by the ostensibly heretical and seditious utterances of Amos, Amaziah sent a report to King Jeroboam II. In rather vulgar language he forbade Amos to preach further at Bethel and ordered him to return to Judah (7:10-17bα).

It is thus clear that the prophetic mission of Amos was brief, and that the oracles preserved in his book were uttered in the course of a few months; one of the editors quaintly dates them "two years before the earthquake" (1:1; cf. Zech. 14:5). It is certain that Amos carried out his prophetic mission during the reign of Jeroboam II (785-744 B.C.; see 1:1; 7:9-11). The shepherd of Tekoa appeared on the scene for a moment in the latter part of the reign of this victorious king, after his successful

[12] From the fact that sycamore trees do not grow at Tekoa, some critics have inferred that Amos was a North Israelite rather than a Judean, and that he went to Tekoa in exile (H. Oort and others after him; cf. K. Budde, JBL 44 [1925] 81; H. Schmidt [in *Budde Festschrift*]). It is natural to infer from 7:12, on the contrary, that Amaziah regarded Amos as a Judean.

campaigns against the Arameans of Damascus and the Moabites who had invaded Gilead from the south. Thus Jeroboam had "restored the borders of Israel from the entrance of Hamath to the sea of the Arabah" (II Kings 14:25; cf. Am. 6:14; 6:13 refers to the conquest of Lodebar and Karnaim in Gilead).

The ministry of Amos coincides with the last glorious period in the history of the kingdom of Israel, when the Israelites thought that Jehovah was again with them (5:14) and would give them, in the eagerly expected "Day of the Lord," a final victory over all their enemies (5:18). The economic "boom" following the victorious wars had greatly enriched some merchants and speculators, who lived luxuriously in Samaria, and had multiplied the offerings and sacrifices at the sanctuaries of Bethel, Gilgal, and Beersheba (4:4 f.; 5:5, 21-23).

Amos preached during the last years of Jeroboam II, after 760 but unquestionably before his death (744), for he knows nothing of the conspiracies and disorders that then began and were denounced by his younger contemporary, Hosea. In fact, there is no reason to suppose that Amos was still active after the accession of the great Tiglath-pileser III of Assyria in 745, as R. S. Cripps and A. Lods claim. For the revival of Assyrian imperial power and western conquest, then beginning, was hardly surmised by Amos. Unlike Hosea, he never mentions the Assyrians (except for the LXX reading "Ashur" for Ashdod in 3:9) and leaves unnamed the nation destined to devastate the country from north to south (6:14). It is only in glosses that we find predictions of the Israelitic exile to distant regions (5:5b, 27; 6:7; 7:11b, 17bβ)[13]—according to the deportation of hostile populations inaugurated by Tiglath-pileser III.

Amos would not have predicted the end of Jeroboam's dynasty (7:9) after it had already ceased to exist (744). There is no justification for saying that in 8:9 Amos refers to the solar eclipse of 763. The public ministry of Amos is to be dated later than 760 but before 745: the middle of the century (750) cannot be far wrong.[14] That Amos foresaw Israel's miserable end at the moment when she reached the height of her power and prosperity, at a time when Assyria, destined to conquer the kingdom in 722, was still a cloud on the horizon no larger than a man's hand, proves the keenness of his insight and the greatness of his genius.

The Book of Amos is divided into three parts: chs. 1-2, 3-6, and 7-9.

The first section, following the superscription (1:1), which is at least partly editorial, and a motto of questionable authenticity (1:2; cf. Joel 3:16 [H. 4:16]), consists of a series of brief oracles (couched in a stand-

[13] Another gloss (6:2) refers to Sargon's conquests of Calneh and Hamath in 720, and of Gath in 711.

[14] J. Morgenstern (HUCA XII-XIII [1937-1938] 46) dates the address of Amos at Bethel on the New Year (fall equinox) of 751.

ardized form) against seven nations, followed by a longer one against Israel. The oracles against Damascus (1:3-5), the Ammonites (1:13-15), and Moab (2:1-3) are genuine; those against Tyre (1:9 f.) and Edom (1:11 f.), reflecting the aftermath of the destruction of Jerusalem in 586, and against Judah (2:4 f.), are easily recognized as spurious; the oracle against Gaza (1:6-8) has been questioned because 1:7 f. imitates 1:4 f. and because Gath, destroyed in 711 (cf. 6:2), is omitted from the list of the five Philistine cities. The oracle against Israel (2:6-16) in its present form is an expansion of a genuine oracle; 2:10 is a manifest gloss and 2:11 f., 14-16 are of doubtful authenticity.

The middle part of the book is a collection of brief addresses denouncing Israel: three begin with, "Hear this word" (3:1; 4:1; 5:1; cf. 8:4), others with "Woe unto you that . . ." (5:7 [where we must restore "Woe"] 5:18; 6:1). The election of Israel, far from securing her against punishment, requires it (3:1a, 2); the law of cause and effect applies to the prophetic experience: when God speaks, the prophet must needs prophesy (3:3-6, 8; 3:7 is a gloss to the following verse). Luxurious living in the palaces of Samaria, made possible through unrighteous accumulation of wealth, will be ended by Jehovah (3:9-15, omitting the glosses in 3:10 f., 13 f., 15bβ). A terrible fate awaits the frivolous and elegant ladies of Samaria (4:1-3). Ironically, the prophet invites the Israelites to come to Bethel and Gilgal to sacrifice (4:4 f.). Jehovah has warned the nation through famine, drought, mildew, pestilence, and destruction of cities—"Yet have ye not returned to me, saith Jehovah" (a refrain repeated five times, 4:6, 8, 9, 10, 11; cf. Is. 5:25; 9:12, 17, 21 [H. 9:11, 16, 20]): the genuine oracle of Amos is in 4:6, 7aα, 8b, 9aαb, 10 (omitting, "after the manner . . . horses"), 11 (omitting, "as God . . . Gomorrah"), 12a; the rest of 4:6-13 is editorial annotation. As if the nation were already dead, the prophet sings over it a dirge in elegiac (*qînah*), or 4:3, meter (5:1 f.); but in reality, says a glossator, the cities have only been decimated (5:3). To seek Jehovah does not mean to worship at the sanctuaries (5:4, 5a, 6 [omitting "in Bethel"]; cf. the displaced annotation on this in 5:14 f.). "Woe [*sic*] unto them that turn judgment to wormwood!" (5:7, 10-12, 16, 17b). "Woe unto you that desire the Day of the Lord!" (5:18 f.). Religious festivals, with burnt offerings and music, are offensive to God, who demands righteousness instead (5:21-24). The rest of ch. 5 is not by Amos. "Woe unto them that are at ease in the mountain of Samaria!" (6:1 [omitting the rest of v. 1], 3, 4, 5 [omitting "like David"], 6, 8 [omitting "saith the Lord God of hosts"], 12-14). The rest of ch. 6 is spurious.

The third part of the book (7-9) is a series of visions, interrupted by a biographical account of the sudden end of the prophet's public career at Bethel (7:10-17, omitting 7:11b, 17bβ), and by an oracle against wealthy merchants (8:4-7, 14; most of 8:8-13 is spurious). Like the Book of Hosea, this book ends with a postexilic assurance that, after the sinners have been killed, the Davidic dynasty will be restored and the nation, returning from exile, will live forever safely in their fruitful land (9:9-15).

In the first two visions, those of the locusts (7:1-3) and fire (drought?) (7:4-6), the prophet's intercession averts the calamities threatened; but the following three visions, the plumbline (7:7 f.), the basket of summer fruit (8:1 f.; 8:3 is a gloss) (really a pun of *qayiṣ*, summer, with *qeṣ*, end), and the destruction of a temple (9:1-4) make clear that the doom is inescapable. The authenticity of the last three visions, notably the third, is by no means certain. The only unimpeachable parts of chs. 7-9 are 7:1-6, 9, 10-17; 8:4-7, 14 (?); 9:7, 8a. Am. 7:9 is the sequel of 6:14.

First in the line of the great reforming prophets, Amos marks the beginning of a new era in the history of religions. Like other religions of antiquity, the religion of Israel before Amos was national in its appeal. Jehovah was the God of Israel, his jurisdiction limited to the land of Israel, his activity confined to the interests of his people. Amos was the first to extend Jehovah's jurisdiction over all nations. Jehovah punished other nations for atrocities in which Israel was not in the least concerned (2:1), and just as he gave Israel a homeland in Canaan so he assigned countries to Israel's enemies, the Philistines and the Arameans (9:7). In fact, God was no more concerned with Israel than with the Negroes of Africa (9:7); and if he selected Israel as his peculiar people it was only to enforce a more rigid standard of conduct and penalty (3:2). Thus Amos, without discrimination of race or nation, planted the roots of a universal religion, from which were to grow the great monotheistic religions of salvation, Judaism, Christianity, and Islam.

In this revolutionary change of religious conception, Amos had no forerunners—at least our extant sources know none. One century before his time, Elijah and Elisha were the spokesmen and champions of the God of Israel; they were jealous defenders of his sovereignty in the Northern Kingdom, but they knew nothing of his sway over all nations. Indeed, a religious leader of some intelligence like Amaziah of Bethel had obviously never heard any teachings comparable to those of Amos, and could only regard the prophet's words as inflammatory—seditious utterances which the land could not tolerate (7:10). And Amos was so conscious of his unique position that he refused to be identified with the prophetic fraternity (7:14), even though he never doubted for a moment that his words were divinely inspired (3:8; 7:15).

Obviously the convictions of Amos were as different from those of contemporary prophets as the convictions of Luther from those of contemporary monks. And yet, strangely enough, Amos did not know that he was proclaiming an entirely new religion "in spirit and in truth." He did not found a new church but merely endeavored to purify the religion of his day, denouncing its corruption and misconceptions in the name of what he believed to be the ancient, immutable, just requirements of Jehovah. Amos was a reformer—a heretic, if you please—but not a schismatic: he merely changed the center of gravity in religion from the externally correct to the internally moral.

It is in the conception of God and his requirements that Amos differs most radically from his contemporaries: in a negative sense he denationalizes Jehovah; in a positive sense he spiritualizes and moralizes his God. For Amos, Jehovah is not "the god of Israel"—he never uses this expression (4:12b, containing the words, "thy God, O Israel," is a gloss). He is the God of justice, ready to annihilate his people (for in a sense Israel is "his" people, 3:2; 7:15) if the people deserve it (9:8a). He will not, like a purely national god, suffer extinction with the destruction of his nation, for he controls the destinies of other nations (9:7).

At first God mercifully consents to stop the course of justice (7:1-6); but later Israel's doom is sealed. The popular expectation of "the Day of the Lord" when Jehovah would lead his people to victory is but a tragic delusion: it is not a day of triumph but ruin—running away from the lion only to meet the bear (5:18 f.). The coming disaster that will annihilate Israel Amos envisions as a calamitous war: the enemy surrounds the land (3:11), puts the army to flight (2:13-16, in part of questionable authenticity), invades the country, crossing it from north to south (6:14), destroying the sanctuaries and killing the king (7:9), and finally brings the miserable survivors into captivity (4:2 f.; 7:17). All over the land there will be mourning (5:16 f.). The prophet intones the funeral dirge over the Virgin of Israel as if she were already dead (5:1 f.).

This sentence of destruction pronounced against Israel by Jehovah is irrevocable because the nation, warned repeatedly through minor calamities (4:6-12, in part), refuses to return to its God and do his will. Instead of seeking Jehovah (5:4, 6, which a glossator correctly interprets as seeking good and not evil, 5:14), the Israelites have affronted their God first by their iniquities, second by impertinently offering him bribes "to avert his ire." Both affronts rest on a total misconception of the character of the deity. The God of right has been degraded to the level of an unscrupulous "shyster" lawyer, heedless of the knavery of those clients whom he delivers for a fee from a just punishment of their crimes.

For the most part, the moral offenses denounced by Amos violate the common standards of decency recognized in all civilized nations, ancient or modern: dishonesty (8:5, 6b), inexorable ruthlessness (2:6-7a, 8; 4:1; 5:11; 8:4, 6a) in the accumulation of wealth, and venality in the courts of law (2:6-7a; 5:7, 12; 6:12). The herdsman of Tekoa was also shocked at the spectacle of extravagance, luxurious living, and ostentatious elegance in the expensive palaces of Israel's opulent cities (3:12, 15abα; 4:1; 5:11; 6:4-6). And he inveighed against this self-indulgence and debauchery, even when no one seemed to suffer directly thereby, because they revealed the callousness of the rich for the privations of the needy (cf. 6:6): "I abhor the pride of Jacob and detest his palaces" (6:8).

Far from perceiving that this careless indifference to the plight of the poor and ostentatious enjoyment of ill-gotten wealth were offensive to Jehovah, the Israelites serenely based their confidence on their performance of religious ceremonies deemed agreeable to their God. For their religion consisted merely in traditional acts of worship, in the presentation of sacrifices and offerings by which they thought to placate the anger of the deity and preserve its favor. They considered themselves pious when father and son had commerce with the same temple prostitute (2:7), when they stretched themselves by the side of altars on garments taken in pledge from a debtor, when they drank in the sanctuaries the wine extorted as a fine from the poor (2:8). Sarcastically Amos invites them to go to Bethel and to transgress; to Gilgal and multiply their transgressions, and offer ad libitum their sacrifices and vows, seeing that they so loved to do (4:4 f.; cf. 5:4-5a).

For Amos, on the contrary, religion consists not in ritual but in righteousness. Jehovah, God of justice, demands right living, not oblations. God passionately spurns a cult presented in the wrong spirit and entirely divorced from honesty and right living: lavish sacrifices, noisy festal gatherings, and the loud strains of sacred songs and orchestral melodies are no substitute for righteousness (5:21-24).[15] Amos, however, did not, as has been maintained, advocate the abolition of sacrifices: he did not oppose the institution but its misuse, and did not introduce a new order of service. He moralized religion but did not substitute morality for religion.

Our book of Amos has been annotated by a number of hands. R. E. Wolfe (ZAW N.F. 12 [1935] 90-129) has tried to distinguish the individual editors and fix their date, but our evidence is too scanty for such a task. It seems certain that these glossators were Jews of Jerusalem, not Northern Israelites, and that they were active between 500 and 200 B.C. Specific references to Judah and David are found in 1:1 ("in the days of Uzziah king of Judah"); 1:2; 2:4 f.; 6:1 ("In Zion, and self-confident");

---

[15] Although Amos is the first writer in the Old Testament to assert that righteousness is preferable to sacrifices in the sight of God, this view had been presented by Egyptian sages long before. In the *Instructions for King Merikere*, written a millennium and a half before Amos, we read: "More acceptable [to God] is the virtue of one that is just of heart, than the ox of him that doeth iniquity" (A. Erman, *The Literature of the Ancient Egyptians*, p. 83. Translated by A. M. Blackman. London, 1927). Like Amos, Anii (*ibid.*, p. 236) objected to noise in the Temple: "The dwelling of God, it abhorreth clamour."

6:5 ("like David"); 9:11 f. The oracles against Tyre and Edom (1:9-12), against Judah (2:4 f.), and perhaps the one against Gaza (1:6-8) were added to those of Amos in the first two chapters. Similarly, the two early visions of Amos (7:1-6) have been supplemented with three others (7:7 f.; 8:1-3; 9:1-4). Some glosses are merely explanatory (3:7 explaining 3:8; 5:20); in 3:15bβ "houses" (in the sense of "buildings") are misunderstood and thought to be "families." Other glosses refer to stories told in the Pentateuch, such as the destruction of Sodom and Gomorrah (4:11, in part) and the Exodus from Egypt (2:10; 3:1b; 4:10; 5:25), and are presumably later than 400; 6:2 is also reminiscent, and refers to Assyrian conquests later than Amos. The threats of Amos, as if they were not sufficiently dreadful, were intensified, and at times given an apocalyptic coloring in 3:10; 4:7aβ-8a, 9aβ, 10aβ; 5:3, 27; 6:1b, 7, 9-11; 7:11b = 17bβ; 8:3, 8-13; 9:2-4, 5. Worship on the ancient Canaanitic "high places" (3:13 f.; 5:6 ["for Bethel"]; 5:25) and idolatry (2:4; 5:26) are denounced. In the midst of the postexilic Jewish community, the additional pious exhortations (4:12b; 5:4b, 13-15) and glorious promises of apocalyptic blessings (9:8b, 9-15) served to add to the interest and religious value of an ancient book. The cosmological doxologies in 4:13; 5:8 f.; 9:5 f. (9:5 is imitated in 8:8) (cf. F. Horst, "Die Doxologien in Amosbuch," ZAW N.F. 6 [1929] 45-54) may have been inserted for the purpose of public reading, but in any case they brought the theology of Amos into harmony with that of Isaiah 40-55 and are clearly inspired by the Book of Job. Needless to say, the view of R. Gordis (HTR 33 [1940] 239-251), who attributes the whole book (except for 9:13-15) to Amos, seems utterly indefensible to the present writer.

Amos is far from being *imperitus sermone* or unskilled in speech, as Jerome said. On the contrary, his greatness as a religious thinker and reformer is matched by his extraordinary ability as a writer. With the exception of Isaiah at his best, none of the Hebrew prophets equals the purity of his language and the classical simplicity of his style. Whether his book consists of a single address or parts of several addresses, it is one of the best arranged of prophetic books. Far from being untutored, Amos gives evidence of consciously using rhetorical devices, as in the series of oracles against foreign nations all of which are cast in the same mold (1-2), and in a similar series of literary units such as the three "Hear this word" (3:1; 4:1; 5:1), the three "Woes" (5:7, 18; 6:1), later imitated by Isaiah, and the five refrains, "Yet have ye not returned to me, saith the Lord" (4:6, 8, 9, 10, 11).

Amos is particularly apt in the use of imagery, usually taken from his own experiences in the wilderness of Tekoa: the dangers from lions, bears, and snakes (3:4, 8, 12; 5:19); the snares by which birds are caught (3:5); the fishhooks (4:2); the wagon loaded with sheaves (2:13); the locusts eating the new grass (7:1 f.) lend a picturesque rural background to his words. Lacking the Aristotelian terms "cause and effect," Amos succeeds in showing, by a series of images leading up to a climax, that every effect has a cause, and vice versa (3:3-6, 8). A shrewd observer of life, Amos has portrayed most vividly the opulent life of the lords and ladies of the Northern Kingdom (6:4-6; cf. 3:12, 15; 4:1; 5:11; 8:4-6) and their gay and riotous celebration of religious festivities (2:7-8; 4:4 f.; 5:21-23).

The little elegy in 5:2, so tragic in its simplicity, reveals Amos in a new light: no longer the stern prosecutor of his people—with a Bedouin's richness of vocabulary, shrewd common sense, and flaming passion—he sits overcome by grief, and in a quieter mood weeps over the inevitable doom of the Virgin of Israel.

4. Obadiah

Before the fall of Jerusalem in 586 B.C., the attitude of Judeans toward the Edomites was not unfriendly (Deut. 23:7 f. [H. 23:8 f.]; cf. 2:5-8). But when, after the fall of Jerusalem, many Judeans sought temporary refuge in Edom (Jer. 40:11) they were not welcomed; for the Edomites were allied to Nebuchadnezzar (II Kings 24:2). The Edomites, in fact, rejoiced at the overthrow of the kingdom of Judah (Obad. 11-14; Lam. 4:21; Ps. 137:7) and soon seized the opportunity to occupy the Negeb, the southern part of Judah (Ez. 35:10, 12; 36:5). One reason for this occupation was pressure from Arabian tribes, who after invading the land of Edom eventually founded there the Nabatean kingdom. According to Diodorus Siculus (19:98), Southern Judah in 312 B.C. was called Idumaea (after the name of the Edomite immigrants) and the Nabateans were then in possession of the land of Edom, particularly Petra (ibid. 19:94). Naturally, after 586 the Jewish attitude was one of intense hatred for the Edomites (Ez. 25:12-14; 35-36; Is. 34; 63:1-6; Joel 3:19; [H. 4:19]; Mal. 1:2-5, and the passages quoted above; see also Sirach's Ecclus. 50:26).

Such is the historical background of the earliest parts of the oracle against Edom constituting the Book of Obadiah. Unfortunately, the exact date of the Arabian invasion of Edom, certainly later than 586 and earlier than 312 B.C., cannot be determined exactly: the main movement must have taken place between 580 and 480, although it was not yet completed when Mal. 1:2-5 was written (ca. 460).

The oracle of Obadiah consists of a denunciation of Edom (1-14; 15b) and of a prediction of the coming "Day of the Lord" (15a; 16-21); each main division has two subdivisions (1-9, 10-14; 16-18, 19-21); 15b is the conclusion of the first part and 15a the title of the second part.

In spite of her inaccessible mountain shelters and proverbial wisdom, the land of Edom has been invaded by disloyal allies (i.e., the Arabs) and the Edomites have been driven to the border (1-9). This calamity is punishment for the Edomites' disloyal and outrageous behavior when Jerusalem was taken in 586 B.C. (10 f.). An appeal to Edom not to invade Judah in the hour of its doom (12-14) went unheeded: Edom's treachery is thus requited in full (15b).

The day of the Lord is at hand upon all nations (15a): the heathen will drink the cup of God's fury (cf. Jer. 25:15-29; 49:12) and vanish, while Judah, reunited with Joseph, will consume the house of Edom like a flame (16-18) and conquer the Negeb or Southern Judah (already occupied by the Edomites), the Shephelah (occupied by the Philistines), the mountain of Ephraim (in the hands of the Samaritans), and Gilead or Transjordania (inhabited by the Ammonites, reading *benê 'ammôn* instead of Benjamin); the Northern Israelitic Exiles will extend their territory as far as Sarepta (cf. Luke 4:26) in the north, the Judean Exiles as far as the Negeb in the south: thus will begin the Kingdom of God on earth (19-21).

Although small, Obadiah's book is not a unit. The original oracle against Edom is preserved in two editions, both of them considerably rewritten and textually not intact, namely Obad. 1-9 and Jer. 49:7-22. The parallels between the two texts are as follows: Ob. 1 = Jer. 49:14; 2 = 49:15; 3a = 49:16a; 4 = 49:16b; 5 = 49:9; 6 = 49:10a; 8 = 49:7; 9a: cf. 49:22b. Even allowing for willful changes and accidental corruption, neither of the two texts, as we have them, could be derived from the other: the order of the three sections in which the text is divided seems normal in Obadiah but is reversed in Jer. (Obad. 1-4; 5-6; 8; Jer. 49:14-16, 9-10a, 7); Obad. knows nothing of Dedan in North Arabia (Jer. 49:8, 11) and Jer. 49 does not refer to the fall of Jerusalem in 586 (Obad. 10-14); Obadiah emphasizes the human agents of the devastation of Edom (Obad. 7), while Jer. 49:10 attributes the calamity directly to divine intervention. In textual details considerable differences are patent. In most cases, the text of Jeremiah seems better, although occasionally that of Obadiah is preferable (omission of "for" at the beginning of 49:15 in Obad. 2; "thence" in Obad. 4 has a better antecedent than in 49:16b; "steal" in Obad. 5 is more appropriate than "destroy" in 49:9). That both recensions are derived from a lost original is also shown by a comparison of Obad. 8 with Jer. 49:7; the admission in both texts that Edom was celebrated for its sages is derived from a statement in the common source apparently quoted from memory both in Obadiah and Jeremiah. Such an admission was so objectionable to the Jews that in Jer. 49:7 the LXX reads, "there is no longer any wisdom in Teman"; and a glossator declared categorically, with reference to the words, "and understanding out of the mount of Esau" (Obad. 8), "there is no understanding in it!" (Obad. 7).

Not all the clauses in Obadiah missing in Jeremiah should be considered glosses: "and though thou shouldst set it among the stars" (Obad. 4) seems presupposed by the following "thence" preserved also by Jer. 49:16b; "that saith in his heart, Who will bring me down to the ground?" (Obad. 3) may also be considered original. Conversely, the following clauses are probably glosses: "if robbers by night" (the original may have had "in the night"; cf. Jer. 49:9) and "how art thou destroyed!" (Obad. 5); "thy bread" (Obad. 7); "by slaughter" (Obad. 9 [H. "on account of the killing," a gloss to "violence" in the next verse]).

For a determination of the date of Obad. 1-14 and 15b, the relationship with Jer. 49 is entirely irrelevant, since that chapter is not from the pen of Jeremiah. A strange chronological problem is raised by the relationship of Obad. 1-9 to 10-14; 15b: the second section seems to be written soon after the fall of Jerusalem in 586, while 1-9 depicts the Edomites' flight "to the border" under pressure of the Arabian invasion which had not yet run its course in 460 (Mal. 1:2-5). If Obad. 10-14; 15b never existed apart from 1-9, as appears from a study of the text, it must have been written in the fifth century, long after 586, even though it voices so dramatically the indignation of the Judeans against the Edomites at the fall of Jerusalem. The most probable date for the first part of Obadiah's book (1-14; 15b) is a little before or after 460.

The second part is probably later. With 15a; 16-21 we pass from the realm of historical events to that of apocalyptic fancies. Obadiah 16-18 may date from about 400 B.C., for it is clearly earlier than Joel (Joel 2:32 [H. 3:5] actually quotes Obad. 17); 19-21, a geographical comment on the preceding vision of Jewish restoration, is later, for the reference to the Samaritans on the mountain of Ephraim in v. 19 cannot be earlier than the first part of the fourth century.

Both parts of the book are intensely nationalistic. The first voices exultation for the plight of an unfriendly neighbor, the second a hope that he may be completely wiped off the face of the earth. This passionate cry for vengeance is diametrically opposed in spirit to the national self-sacrifice for the benefit of mankind, envisioned in one of the servant poems of the Second Isaiah (Is. 53).

5. Jonah

Unlike the rest of the Book of the Twelve, the Book of Jonah is not a prophetic oracle, but a story about a prophet, Jonah, son of Amittai. According to II Kings 14:25, Jonah, a Zebulonite prophet from Gath-hepher, predicted the conquests of Jeroboam II; the hero of the story is unquestionably intended as that ancient prophet. The insertion of narrative material about a prophet in the Book of the Twelve has a parallel in the insertion into Isaiah of a section taken for the most part from the

Book of Kings (Is. 36-39); but there is no reason to believe, with K. Budde, that our book was part of the midrash used by the Chronicler, or that it stood originally after II Kings 14:27.

The story of Jonah is well known. Ordered by Jehovah to go and denounce Nineveh for its sins, Jonah, anticipating that his announcement of the city's destruction would not be fulfilled (cf. 4:2), sailed from Joppa for Tarshish, near Gibraltar (1:1-3). But Jehovah stirred up a violent storm, and when the frightened sailors drew lots to discover who on board had angered the gods, Jonah was singled out (1:4-10). Upon the prophet's advice, the sailors reluctantly cast him overboard; whereupon the tempest at once subsided (1:11-16). A great fish, prepared by Jehovah, swallowed Jonah (1:17 [H. 2:1]). In the belly of the fish, where he remained for three days, Jonah composed and recited a psalm (2:1-9 [H. 2:2-10], a poem that is obviously interpolated). In accordance with a divine order, the fish deposited Jonah safely on dry land (2:10 [H. 2:11]).

Obedient to a second commission from Jehovah, the prophet went to Nineveh and there proclaimed that it would be destroyed in forty days (3:1-4; 4:5 should probably be read after 3:4). But the king, the people, and even the beasts of Nineveh fasted and put on sackcloth (3:5-9). So Jehovah, seeing their repentance, refrained from carrying out his sentence against the city (3:10). Bitterly disappointed because in his mercy Jehovah had not fulfilled the prophet's dreadful threat, Jonah wished to die (4:1-3). As he was reclining outside of Nineveh, Jehovah made a gourd grow up instantaneously to shelter him from the scorching rays of the sun; but the next morning God sent a worm to blight the gourd, so that Jonah, exposed to the full force of the sun's heat, longed again for death (4:4-8). Using the gourd as an illustration, Jehovah pointed out Jonah's inconsistency in being sorry for the gourd, for which he had not labored, and at the same time in berating the deity for mercifully sparing a city including more than 120,000 innocent infants—"and also much cattle" (4:9-11).

The story of Jonah is neither an account of actual happenings[16] nor an allegory of the destiny of Israel[17] or of the Messiah (cf. Matt. 12:40): it is fiction—a short story with a moral—like the Book of Ruth, which is much less fantastic, or the stories about Daniel. Whether the hero was identified with an actual prophet living in the time of Jeroboam II, which is not to be excluded, or was a legendary character, like Daniel, is totally irrelevant to an understanding of the book. In spite of its abrupt close, as soon as the lesson has been stated, the book is a perfectly good short story—with a beginning, a middle, and an end.

[16] So, e.g., F. W. Mozley in *Bibliotheca Sacra* 81 [1924] 170-200.
[17] So A. D. Martin in *Holborn Review* N.S. 12 [1921] 510-519, and others.

As with Oriental fiction in general (cf. Daniel, Tobit, the *Arabian Nights*, etc.), the supernatural is the *pièce de résistance* of the narrative. The storm at sea, the big fish, the gourd, and the worm are all explicitly said to have been divine miracles. Such coincidences as the cessation of the tempest when Jonah was cast overboard seldom occur in real life. A man's survival for three days in the belly of a fish, or even a whale, which is the only marine animal of sufficient size,[18] is physiologically improbable, to say the least, even if alleged modern parallels are taken into account. The instantaneous and general conversion of Nineveh to the religion of Jehovah could not be taken seriously for a moment by historians of antiquity. They also know perfectly well that no Assyrian king was ever called "King of Nineveh" (3:6), a title no less absurd than "King of London," and that Nineveh was never "an exceeding great city of three days' journey" (3:3), for the circuit of its walls in the time of Sennacherib measured about eight miles.

The author of the story utilized ancient myths and folk tales in his story of the fish (cf. H. Schmidt, *Jona.* 1907). Drawing his main character from II Kings 14:25, he made use of the legendary stories of Elijah and Elisha (compare, for instance, 4:3 with I Kings 19:4b and 4:5, 6 with I Kings 19:4a, 5a) in some incidents of Jonah's career. The author's views on repentance through fasting and sackcloth, followed by divine forgiveness, are obviously derived from Joel (compare 3:5 with Joel 1:13 f.; 3:9 with Joel 2:14; 4:2 with Joel 2:13 [cf. Ez. 34:6]). The strange prescription that domestic animals, as well as human beings, should fast and wear sackcloth as a sign of repentance, finds a parallel in Judith 4:10 and may be a Persian custom: Herodotus (9:24) reports that in mourning for Masistius not only the soldiers but also the horses and oxen were shaved.

Out of such miscellaneous materials, the author has composed a charming story intended to teach the lesson clearly expressed at the end of the book (4:10 f.; cf. 3:9 f.; 4:2), namely, that Jehovah's loving-kindness and compassion are not restricted to the Jews but extend to the heathen as well. Just as the Book of Ruth was not favorable to the narrow nationalism of Nehemiah requiring Jews to divorce Gentile wives, so the Book of Jonah is a protest against the Jews' religious pride following the canonization of the Law of Moses (about 400 B.C.) and their expectation that Jehovah would soon annihilate the heathen for the benefit of the Jews—a bloodthirsty hope, as we have seen, expressed in no uncertain terms in Obadiah.

This contemptible attitude of some Jews in the time of the author, represented by Jonah's bitter disappointment when Jehovah in his mercy failed to destroy Nineveh, is stigmatized in God's stinging rebuke to Jonah

---

[18] Cf. G. Macloskie in *Bibliotheca Sacra* 72 [1915] 334-338.

(4:10 f.). The author's denunciation of the narrow Jewish exclusivism of Nehemiah (cf. the Chronicler) and of the sanguinary apocalyptic dreams of Jehovah's extermination of the Gentiles (Ez. 38-39, Joel, Obad., and the like), shows that the leaven of the prophetic doctrine of Jehovah's universal solicitude did not entirely disappear in postexilic Judaism.

The date of Jonah is obvious from all this: the use of Joel, the fantastic conception of Nineveh, destroyed in 612 and long since a buried city, the legendary and miraculous features of the story, the reaction to nationalistic exclusivism and to Jewish impatience because the heathen were not speedily exterminated, as well as the linguistic characteristics, typical of the late Biblical period, date the book at the earliest in the fourth century and presumably (if Joel was written about the middle of the century) in its second half, at the end of the Persian or at the beginning of the Greek period.

The Psalm of Jonah (2:1-9 [H. 2:2-10]) is not an integral part of the book but was inserted here from some anthology, presumably by the editor of the Minor Prophets (about 200 B.C.). The poem is not a prayer (as 2:1 [H. 2:2] says), but a psalm of thanksgiving by a man saved from drowning. This psalmist cried out "of the belly of hell" (2:2 [H. 2:3]), not that of a fish: he sank to the bottom of the sea with his eyes open and was rescued just as he was about to despair of life. This psalm probably dates from the third century, and was quoted here because it seemed appropriate to Jonah in the belly of the fish: the drowning man was encompassed by the waters, surrounded by the deep, descended to the base of the mountains (2:5 f. [H. 2:6 f.]), and like Jonah was saved by Jehovah.

Besides this psalm, there is little secondary material in the book: "for whose cause this evil is upon us" (1:8); "because he had told them" (1:10); 4:4 (a variant to 4:9a); "to deliver him from his grief" (4:6) are regarded by K. Marti, with some plausibility, as glosses.

6. Micah

Like the books of Isaiah and Zechariah, the book of Micah is composite. In the definitive edition of prophetic books (in four volumes) prepared about 200 B.C., anonymous prophecies (Is. 40-66, Mic. 6-7, and Zech. 9-14) were placed after the oracles of known prophets and subsequently came to be regarded as integral parts of the books immediately preceding. Needless to say, at that time all the oracles from the eighth and seventh centuries (and later ones as well) had been edited in the spirit of postexilic apocalyptic expectations. Accordingly, the Book of Micah consists of his own oracles (1-3) with their comforting interpolations (2:12 f.; 4:1-5:15 [H. 4:1-5:14]), and a later anonymous prophecy (6: 1-7:6), with its own hopeful editorial appendix (7:7-20).

Micah was a native of Moresheth near Gath (1:1) and was a younger contemporary of Isaiah. According to the editorial title (1:1), he prophesied during the reigns of Judah's kings, Jotham (740-735), Ahaz (735-720), and Hezekiah (720-692). There is no reason to doubt the accuracy of the statement of the elders of Judah (a century later) that in the days of Hezekiah Micah the Moreshite prophesied the words of Mic. 3:12 (Jer. 26:17 f.). In contrast to Isaiah, an aristocrat from the capital with access to the court, Micah was, like Amos, a humble villager. His primary concern was the expropriation of the poor for the enrichment of the upper classes.

The book opens with a warning (to all nations) about the impending last judgment: Jehovah's cataclysmic descent from heaven to earth (1:1-4) is caused by Israel's transgressions (1:5a; 1:1-4 or 1:1-5a seem to be an editorial introduction to the whole book). Samaria and Jerusalem are respectively the foci of the sinfulness of Jacob and Judah (1:5b). Therefore Samaria (taken but not destroyed by Sargon of Assyria in 722) will be razed and turned into fields and vineyards and her ruin extend to the very gates of Jerusalem, which was besieged by Sennacherib in 701 (1:6-9, omitting 1:7, a gloss on idolatry). Although Jerusalem was spared, the general devastation of the kingdom is portrayed in a list of towns in Judah, the names of which are puns (in the Hebrew) describing the havoc wrought by the invading enemy (1:10-16).

In a second impassioned oracle (2:1-11, to which a postexilic promise of Judah's reunion with North Israel has been attached, 2:12 f.), Micah denounces the covetousness of the rich, who expropriate the houses and fields of the poor (2:1 f.), sell Judean women and children into slavery, and plunder peaceful wayfarers (2:8 f.); but the time is at hand when they will be despoiled of all their property (2:3-5). To those who would silence this prophet of doom by asking whether Jehovah could ever become impatient and harm his people (2:6 f.), Micah replies with renewed threats (2:10) and the sarcastic remark that only a prophet preaching deceitfully about "wine and strong drink" would be welcome (2:11).

In his third oracle, Micah turns to the leaders of the people with holy indignation (3). They devour the nation in their avarice (3:1-4), the prophets preach prosperity and are well paid (3:5-8), and the magistrates pervert justice on receipt of bribes (3:9 f.). Even though seeking only financial reward, all of them expect Jehovah to protect them from misfortune (3:11). On the contrary, because of them, Jerusalem will be plowed under like a field (3:12).

To counteract the depressing effect of Micah's denunciations and threats of doom, postexilic visions of a restoration (4-5) were attached to his oracles. At the end of time, Zion will become the highest of hills, where pilgrims from all nations will flock to worship Jehovah and learn his Law; under Jehovah's rule, the whole world will enjoy permanent peace (4:1-4a, identical with Is. 2:2-4, where Mic. 4:4a is omitted; 4:4b-5 and Is. 2:5 are probably secondary). On that day, Jehovah will bring back the dispersed Jews and establish his Kingdom in Zion (4:6-8). But for the present there is no king; the daughter of Zion will go into exile to Babylon, and there be saved (4:9 f.). The hosts of nations marching against Zion and eager to see it defiled will be discomfited and their possessions consecrated to Jehovah (4:11-13; 5:1 [H. 4:14] alludes enigmatically to a siege of Jerusalem and, unless read before 4:11, is entirely isolated).

Like his ancestor David, the future Messianic king will go forth from Bethlehem, and until his birth Israel will be given up by God. But this Davidic ruler will restore the fortunes of Israel, for he will rule to the ends of the earth (5:2-4 [H. 5:1-3]; cf. Zech. 9:10; Ps. 89:26-28; Matt. 2:5 f.); "this is peace," adds a glossator at the beginning of 5:5 (H. 5:4). When Assyria attempts to invade the land of Judah, "seven shepherds and eight princes" will come to the rescue (5:5 f. [H. 5:4 f.]); the remnant of Jacob will be like dew to the nations that submit to it, but like a raging lion to those that resist (5:7-9 [H. 5:6-8]). On that day the Lord will remove from Judah all fortifications and weapons, now become useless, and all heathen sorceries and idols. He will turn in wrath against all disobedient nations (5:10-15 [H. 5:9-14]).

The unknown author of 6:1-7:6 denounces the nation as a whole, rather than its leaders after the fashion of Micah, and dramatically presents a court scene in which Jehovah is prosecutor and judge, and Israel the defendant. The style and anonymity of this prophecy suggest a written composition rather than a transcript of public addresses, like those of 1-3. Jehovah presents his argument before the mountains of the earth (6:1 f.). Jehovah has saved the nation from Egyptian bondage and the machinations of Balak king of Moab; in what way has he deserved the nation's neglect (6:3-5)?

Pleading guilty, the nation inquires whether its sins may be atoned with burnt offerings and the immolation of first-born sons; the prophet answers that Jehovah's only requirement is not sacrificial offerings but "to do justly, and to love mercy, and to walk humbly with thy God" (6:6-8). Now Jehovah presents the indictment of the nation: he lists the heartless rapacity of the rich as also the false weights used by merchants (6:9-12), and announces the dreadful penalty he will inflict on the people (6:13-16). Finally, the prophet paints a dark picture of the nation's moral disintegration. Violence, perjury, venality of the courts, and complete dissolution of social and family ties prevail in the land

(7:1-6; 7:4, which alludes to the coming punishment, should perhaps be read at the end).

This dismal lament over Judah's moral collapse is followed without transition by a postexilic vision of national restoration. The punishment has fallen and the penitent community, bearing Jehovah's anger patiently, trusts in the Lord and awaits the vindication that will put Judah's enemies to shame (7:7-10). The prophet promises that Jerusalem will prosper again, but that the world will become desolate (7:11-13). Then he turns to Jehovah, to intervene in behalf of his stricken people against its foes: "May they lick the dust like a serpent!" (7:11-17) The doxology at the end of the book (7:18-20) extols in the vein of Second Isaiah the forgiving mercy of Jehovah.

It is universally agreed that the genuine oracles of Micah (1-3, omitting 1:1-5a and 2:12 f.) date from the last quarter of the eighth century, but some critics place them shortly before the capture of Samaria in 722 and others in 701, when Jerusalem was besieged by Sennacherib. If we could infer from Jer. 26:17 f. that Micah's activity was confined to Hezekiah's reign (720-692), the earlier date would be excluded. As a matter of fact, the later date is preferable for other reasons: it is clear that 1:10-16 and 3 refer to the humiliation of Judah in 701 and the threats of 2 could well have been uttered shortly before.[19]

It is only for 1:5b-9 (omitting 1:7) that a date about 722 could be seriously considered. However, this brief oracle against Samaria predicts not just the capture, but the total destruction of that city (1:6). In 722, 27,290 inhabitants of Samaria were deported by Sargon, but the city was not razed. Moreover, there is no reason to suppose that Judah was attacked in 722, as 1:9 implies. As 1:9 (cf. 1:5b) states, it is only in 701 that Samaria's fate of 722 overtook Judah, so that 1:8 alone severed from 1:6 could be dated back to 722. In conclusion, Micah's genuine oracles, apparently pronounced like those of Amos in the course of a few months, probably date from the days immediately preceding the siege of Jerusalem in 701.

The anonymous prophecy in 6-7 was first dated in the reign of Manasseh (692-639) by G. H. A. Ewald in 1867; J. Wellhausen recognized in 1874 that 7:7-20 was a postexilic addition. The chief reason for placing these oracles in the time of Manasseh is the connection between the sacrifice of first-born in 6:7 and Moloch worship; but in this passage there is no unmistakable allusion to the regular sacrificial burning of infants; on the contrary, this custom is the exceptional and ultimate sacrifice that might restore to a sinful and desperate people God's favor.

Although a date about the middle of the seventh century is not to be

---

[19] The use of Jacob and Israel to indicate Judah in 3:9 (cf. 2:7; 3:1) is inconceivable before the end of the kingdom of Israel in 722.

excluded, a later one is more probable. References to the Pentateuch in 6:4 f. (particularly the mention of Aaron, unknown to the J document or any writings except E before the sixth century), the singling out of Omri and Ahab as conspicuously wicked (hardly probable before Josiah's reforms in 621 or even before the Deuteronomic edition of Kings in 600), as also the state of the Jewish community in Jerusalem, socially disintegrated (7:1-6) and facing economic ruin (6:13-15), indicate a considerably later date during the Persian period, although perhaps before Nehemiah (444). The famous summary of the prophetic teaching in 6:6-8 sounds more like a catechism lesson for the young in the manner of the sages (like Prov. 15:8; 21:3, 27; cf. 16:1-9) than like the inspired utterance of an ancient prophet.[20] Everything considered, a date around 500 B.C. seems likely for Mic. 6:1-7:6.

The rest of the Book of Micah (1:2-5a; 2:12 f.; 4:1-5:15 [H. 5:14]; 7:7-20) is a collection of detached oracles of various dates provided with redactional annotations. All of them are postexilic: Micah's dire threat (3:12) of the utter destruction of Jerusalem as punishment for Judah's sins has been fulfilled in 586 B.C. The "remnant" (2:12; 4:7; 5:3, 7, 8 [H. 5:2, 6, 7]; 7:18) which has survived the catastrophe and perpetuated itself, is looking forward to better times. All these prophecies are addressed to this "remnant"—the impoverished and weak Jewish community in Palestine (or in the Dispersion) during the Persian and early Greek periods (about 500-200 B.C.). By internal organization, codification and enforcement of laws, and military defensive measures, practical statesmen like Nehemiah were giving the Jewish community the cohesion and solidity necessary for its survival.

At the same time, dreamers were lifting the morale of the masses with apocalyptic pictures of a glorious future restoration. Since the middle of the sixth century, hope in some manifestation of Jehovah's power had become basic in Judaism through the magnificent religious epic of the Second Isaiah. Although sitting in darkness and bearing the divine punishment for its sins, the congregation trusted in its God, who was its light, and awaited from him full vindication that would put the enemy to shame (7:7-11, with a marginal annotation in 7:12 f.; this oracle seems to antedate the rebuilding of the walls of Jerusalem in 444). The faith of the congregation found expression in hymns of petition (7:14-17) and praise (7:18-20) to Jehovah.

In some visions, the future restoration was fundamentally religious, in others nationalistic or monarchical. One beautiful idealistic prophecy, inserted both in Mic. 4:1-4a and in Is. 2:2-4, envisioned the Kingdom of God on earth as an era of peace, when all nations would unite in a pil-

[20] That sacrifice was sometimes underrated in postexilic times appears also in the Psalms (40:6 [H. 40:7]; 50:7-15).

grimage to Zion to learn the Law of the Lord; a narrow-minded Jew, however, added a gloss (4:4b-5) denying the heathen's conversion. At that time, the instruments of war and the paraphernalia of heathen ritual, useless when the whole world is at peace and worships the true God, will be removed from Jerusalem (5:8-12 [H. 5:9-13]; again a rabid nationalist added the gloss in 5:13 [H. 5:14]). Similar statements in a universalistic spirit are found in Is. 25:6; 42:1-9; 56:3-7; 60:3; Zeph. 3:9 f.; Zech. 2:11 (H. 2:15); 8:20-23, and elsewhere.

In contrast with this generous invitation to Gentiles to participate in the blessings of the Kingdom of God through conversion to the religion of Jehovah, other Jews regarded the coming Golden Age as restricted to their nation, either with or without a personal Messiah. The restoration of the Davidic dynasty in the person of the coming Messianic king is prominent in some oracles (4:14-5:2 [H. 5:1-3];[21] cf. Is. 9:2-7 [H. 9:1-6]; 11:1-8; Am. 9:11; Hos. 1:11 [H. 2:2]; 3:5; Zech. 3:8; 6:12, etc.).

In most of the eschatological prophecies in Micah and often elsewhere (Is. 29:1-8; Ez. 38-39; Joel 3 [H. 4]; Obad. 16-18; Zeph. 2:5 ff.; Zech. 9:1-8; 14:12-15, etc.), the main feature of the political restoration is the crushing of mighty Gentile nations without the intervention of the Messiah. Jehovah himself descends from heaven to judge the Gentiles (1:2-4; 1:5a is a transitional gloss); he leads the Exiles, Israelitic and Judean together, back to Zion (2:12 f.), thus making the "remnant" again a strong nation with Jehovah at its head (4:6-10), and crushing the hosts of Gentiles (4:11-5:1 [H. 4:11-14]) and the world empire enigmatically called "Assyria" (5:5 f. [H. 5:4 f.]). Even in the Dispersion will the Jews prevail at that time, either peacefully like dew or belligerently like lions (5:7-9 [H. 5:6-8]).

7. Nahum

"The oracle against Nineveh. The book of the vision of Nahum the Elkoshite" (Nah. 1:1)[22] is not a single work, as this title would indicate, but consists of a fragmentary psalm with clear traces of an alphabetic acrostic arrangement (1:2-10) and of the triumphal ode of Nahum on the fall of Nineveh in August 612 B.C. (2:3-3:19 [H. 2:4 ff.]). The intervening material in 1:11-2:2 (H. 2:3) is partly redactional and partly an original section of the ode: the corrupt and editorial end of the psalm and the beginning of the ode are strangely dovetailed.

A redactor living about the year 300 B.C. prefaced Nahum's superb ode, dating from the years immediately preceding the fall of Nineveh in 612, with an alphabetic psalm of his own time. Of this psalm he vaguely re-

---

[21] Micah 5:1 [H. 5:2] is a gloss in which Is. 7:14 is interpreted in a Messianic sense.

[22] According to Jerome, Elkosh was in Galilee.

membered the first part, substituting for the rest remarks of his own, some of which were Biblical quotations quoted from memory (see W. R. Arnold, "The Composition of Nahum 1-2:3," ZAW 21 [1901] 225-265). It is clear that he did not copy the alphabetic psalm from a manuscript but wrote it down as best he could from memory. He had not only forgotten the second part of this poem, but, being unconscious of the alphabetic arrangement of the lines, he paraphrased certain lines, thereby obliterating the original acrostic structure. As reconstructed by Arnold (but without regarding 1:12b as the *shin* verse of the psalm), the first fifteen of the original twenty-two verses of the psalm (from *aleph* to *samekh*) are found in 1:2a, 3b, 4a, 4b, 5a, 5b, 6a, 6b, 7, 3a, 9b, 9c, 9a, 2b, 10. The psalm has nothing to do with the fall of Nineveh but, like the psalms of Hannah, Hezekiah, and Jonah, was inserted because it seemed appropriate to the context. In this poem, Jehovah's appearance during storm and earthquake, as a vengeful and angry God, marks the annihilation of his foes but the protection of those that trust him.

Having forgotten the rest of the psalm, the redactor began to copy Nahum's poem in 1:11, 12, 14; 2:1, 3 ff. (H. 2:2, 4 ff.), inserting within and between these verses his own contributions: "the one who planned evil against Jehovah" (1:11); "thus spoke Jehovah" and "I have afflicted thee *but* I shall afflict thee no longer" (1:12); 1:13; "and Jehovah has commanded concerning thee" and "from the house of thy gods I shall cut off the graven and the molten image" (1:14); 1:15 (H. 2:1); 2:2 (H. 2:3). In 1:12c, 13, 15a (H. 2:1a), the redactor was quoting I Kings 11:39; Jer. 30:8; Is. 52:7, respectively, as he vaguely remembered them. In the destruction of Nineveh so graphically portrayed by Nahum, this pious redactor saw a fulfillment of these prophetic oracles. From the elimination of the Assyrian oppressor he drew a happy omen for the uninterrupted safety of the Jews, and exhorted them to celebrate their festivals and fulfill their vows. In all these glosses, except in 1:11, the redactor was addressing Judah in the masculine, whereas Nahum addressed Nineveh in the feminine.

We owe the preservation of Nahum's magnificent ode to a misunderstanding. As appears in the title, this martial song was considered a prophetic oracle or prognostication against Nineveh, and thus given a place in the Book of the Twelve. In reality, however, to judge from his one extant poem, Nahum was not a prophet—neither a reforming prophet like his contemporary Jeremiah nor an optimistic "false prophet" like Hananiah (Jer. 28). He was a poet. Even though Jehovah himself occasionally threatens Nineveh in the course of the poem (2:13 [H. 2:14]; 3:5 f.), there is nothing specifically religious in this exultant outburst of joy over the inevitable downfall of the Assyrian Empire which had since 701 B.C. crushed the kingdom of Judah. Nahum was both a great poet and a great patriot: his passionate nationalism, his burning hatred for the "city of blood, filled with falsehood, abounding in violence, where rapine never ceased" (3:1), his flaming animosity for the empire that "sold nations for harlotries and peoples for witcheries" (3:4), inspire a superb paean of triumph, matchless in literary power and beauty.

The date of the poem can be easily fixed: it is obviously later than the sack of Thebes (No-Amon, 3:8) by Ashurbanipal in 661, but earlier than the destruction of Nineveh in 612. The rapid decline of the Assyrian Empire began in 625 with the death of Ashurbanipal, and soon after the subject nations shook off the Assyrian yoke. Judean nationalism expressed in this poem flamed up immediately before Josiah's reforms in 621. The openly expressed vindictiveness, implied patriotic fervor, and assurance of Assyria's irretrievable ruin are hardly conceivable before 625. Moreover, Nineveh was not directly threatened before 614,[23] when Cyaxares king of the Medes attacked it without success but captured Ashur before the arrival of Nabopolassar king of Babylonia. The alliance between the two kings resulted in the final assault upon Nineveh in June 612 and its fall in August of that year. The poem was undoubtedly written between 625 and 612, and probably between 614 and 612.

Nahum's poem begins with a brief exordium imperfectly preserved (1:11, 12, 14, omitting the glosses already listed), and contains two main parts: 2:1-13 (H. 2:2-14) (omitting 2:2 [H. 2:3], "like the voice of doves" in 2:7 [H. 2:8], "saith Jehovah" in 2:13 [H. 2:14]) and 3:1-17 (omitting "they stumble over corpses" in 3:3, "Sebaoth" in 3:5; 3:7; "at the top of every street" and "in chains" in 3:10; 3:12; "to thy enemies" in 3:13; "like grasshoppers multiply thyself [like locusts]" in 3:15; "a grasshopper has roamed about and has flown" in 3:16). It closes with an epitaph (3:18 f., omitting "the king of Ashur," a correct gloss to "thy shepherd" in 3:18).

The exordium, disjointed and dovetailed with redactional material, is obviously fragmentary. It begins, "Did not [reading the last word of 1:10 as *halô*] the counsellor of depravity go forth from thee? [cf. 2:13 (H. 2:14); an allusion to II Kings 18:17 ff.]. Though yet intact and ever so many, yet are they mowed down and he passeth on. There shall no longer be sown of thy seed. I shall make thy grave a stench" (cf. Arnold, ZAW 21 [1901] 255 f.).

Each of the two main divisions consists of three parts. In a general way, the sections of one division correspond in import to those of the other, even though the order is different: I. 1. The attack on Nineveh and its frenzied defense (2:1-5 [H. 2:2-6]). 2. The capture and destruction of the city (2:6-10 [H. 2:7-11]). 3. The crimes of Nineveh (2:11-13 [H. 2:12-14]). II. 1. The attack (3:1-3). 2. The crimes of Nineveh and their

[23] Herodotus's account (1:103) of how Cyaxares besieged Nineveh about 623 and was driven away by the Scythians is of questionable historicity.

punishment (3:4-6). 3. The capture and destruction of the city (3:8-17).

The epitaph (3:18 f.) combines a dirge over the fallen city with the joyful shout of subject nations: "Thy shepherd is asleep, thy nobles at rest; thy peoples are scattered upon the mountains—none to gather them. No healing for thy ruin, thy wound is diseased. All that hear thy report clap their hands over thee, for upon whom did not thy crime bear down continually?"

Nahum is the last of the great classical Hebrew poets. His poem ranks with the Song of Deborah (Judg. 5) and the elegy of David over Saul and Jonathan (II Sam. 1:19-27). The vividness of his descriptions is unexcelled: the furious onslaught of cavalry and chariotry (2:3 f. [H. 2:4 f.]; 3:2 f.), the sharp orders of officers (2:1 [H. 2:2]), the capture of the queen surrounded by her distraught maids (2:7 [H. 2:8]), the doom of the plundering Assyrian lion (2:11-13 [H. 2:12-14]), the sack of Thebes of the hundred gates (3:8-10), the breakdown of the defenses of Nineveh and the resulting wild plundering and total ruin (2:8-10 [H. 2:9-11]; 3:11-15, 18 f.), are depicted with a sense of reality, a concise vigor of expression and a concreteness of detail that make these imaginary scenes appear no less true than actual events brilliantly described by an eyewitness.

8. Habakkuk

Like the Book of Nahum, "the burden which Habakkuk the prophet saw" (1:1) is composite: to the prophetic oracles in chs. 1-2, a psalm entitled "a prayer of Habakkuk the prophet, upon Shigionoth" (3:1), has been added in ch. 3. There is no valid reason for attributing both parts of the book to the same author.

The first two chapters are a series of five short and more or less disconnected prophetic utterances. The first (1:2-4) is a complaint because Jehovah allows violence and injustice to triumph in the land. The second (1:5-11) is a divine oracle: Jehovah is arousing the Chaldeans, "a bitter and hasty nation," who will, in their speedy advance, conquer nations and kingdoms. The third (1:12-17) is a renewed appeal to the prophet's God: if Jehovah is righteous and mighty, why does he allow the wicked to devour the righteous? The fourth (2:1-5) is the divine answer which the prophet received on his watchtower: eventually the wicked will be punished, but the righteous Jew "shall live by his faithfulness" (2:4). In the New Testament (Rom. 1:17; Gal. 3:11; Hebr. 10:38) and as the motto of Martin Luther, these famous words acquired a much deeper meaning than they had originally. The fifth oracle (2:6-20, omitting 2:18, a gloss on 2:19) is called a taunting proverb and consists of five "Woes" against the conquering nation that is rapacious, unscrupulous, sanguinary, intemperate, and idolatrous.

Like the fragmentary acrostic psalm at the beginning of Nahum, the "prayer" of Habakkuk (3:1-19; omitting 3:17-19, a liturgical addition) describes the appearance of Jehovah in majesty and power, to punish the heathen and avenge his people. The author implores Jehovah soon to manifest himself (3:2). Coming from Sinai-Horeb, God approaches from the direction of Edom (cf. Judg. 5:4; Deut. 33:2), filling heaven and earth with his glorious brilliance, shaking the mountains and scattering the nations (3:3-7). As God paces the earth in anger, riding over rivers and seas, darkening sun and moon, and splitting the earth, he crushes the heathen for the salvation of his people, his "anointed" (3:8-15). The poet is overcome by the awfulness of this future theophany (3:16). The liturgical appendix (3:17-19) has nothing to do with this psalm: it expresses the pious and joyful confidence of the Jewish congregation in God at a time when crops and herds were a total failure.

The psalm in ch. 3 was taken from a hymnbook and is provided with musical notations: "upon Shigionoth" (3:1), selâh (3:3, 9, 13); the notation at the end, "for the chief musician, with stringed instruments" (so, according to Ps. 4:1; 6:1) probably belonged to the poem immediately following in the hymnbook from which Hab. 3 was taken. This psalm was probably inserted here because in the title it was attributed to Habakkuk, as in the Greek version Pss. 138 and 146-148 are attributed to Haggai and Zechariah. Such attributions are of course devoid of historical value. The author wrote in the fourth or the third century and imitated the ancient poems in Judg. 5 and Deut. 33, using a deliberately archaic style and diction. The epithet, "thine anointed" (thy Messiah) for the Jews (3:13) is an unmistakable clue for a late date. Habakkuk 3:10-15 is imitated in Ps. 77:16-19 (H. 77:18-20). The style is sonorous, rhetorical and majestic, but lacks the noble simplicity of ancient Hebrew poetry at its best.

The critical problems raised by the oracles in the first two chapters are more serious and complicated, and there is no agreement among scholars with regard to unity, authorship, and date. The only clear reference to historical events occurs in 1:5-11: riding on horseback, an invincible army from afar swiftly conquers kingdoms and nations. In our text, these horsemen are identified with the Chaldeans (1:6), who under Nabopolassar became independent from Assyria in 625, conquered Babylonia in 614, and destroyed Nineveh, in conjunction with the Medes, in 612. Under the command of Nebuchadnezzar, the Chaldeans defeated Pharaoh Necho at Carchemish in 605 and destroyed Jerusalem in 586.

The date of 1:5-11, if it refers to the Chaldeans, would be shortly before 600. F. Giesebrecht, J. Wellhausen, K. Marti, and W. Nowack separate this oracle, which they date about 605, from the others in Hab. 1-2, dating the latter in exilic or postexilic times. On the contrary,

S. R. Driver, W. W. Cannon (ZAW 43 [1925] 62-90), and others would date the first two chapters of the book *in toto* about 600, considering these as a dialogue between God and the prophet. Other critics try to remedy the disjointed and disconnected character of the first two chapters by rearranging the five oracles. K. Budde (*Encycl. Bibl.* 2:1921 ff.) would place 1:5-11 after 2:4, referring 1:2-4, 12-17 to Assyria's oppression of Judah, 2:1-4; 1:5-11 to the coming victorious attack of the Chaldeans against Assyria, and 2:5-19 to the violence and lawlessness of the Assyrians; the whole prophecy is then dated about 615. In his *Introduction to the Old Testament*, C. H. Cornill is inclined to follow Budde. R. E. Wolfe (ZAW 53 [1935] 113) adopts the following order: 2:1-3; 1:5-9a, 10, 15ab; 2:5e-7, 8c-13a, 13cd, 15-16c, 17ab (omitting the rest as spurious). C. Steuernagel in his *Introduction* dates 1:2-11 about 605 and 1:12-2:19 during the Exile. M. Lauterburg (*Theolog. Zeitschr. aus der Schweiz* [1896] 74 ff.) instead preserves the unity of chs. 1-2, but dates these about 545 by omitting the "Chaldeans" in 1:6.

A radically different conception of Habakkuk's prophecies was defended by B. Duhm (*Das Buch Habakuk*, 1906), followed by C. C. Torrey (*Alexander the Great in the Old Testament Prophecies.* Festschrift for K. Marti. Beih. ZAW 41 [1925] 281-286).[24] Having corrected "Chaldeans" (*Kasdim*) to *Kittim* (properly Cypriotes, but also used for the Greeks; cf. I Macc. 1:1) they date the book in 331, during Alexander's campaigns in Asia, between the battle of Issus and that of Arbela. O. Happel (*Das Buch des Propheten Habackuk.* 1900) would even come down to the time of Antiochus Epiphanes (about 170), a date which is clearly out of the question, in view of Ben Sira's reference to our Book of the Twelve (including Hab.) in 180.

Fundamentally, our conception of the Book of Habakkuk depends on one word, the "Chaldeans" in 1:6: if it is original, the first two chapters belong to the period 615-600 B.C.; if not, the book may well be an echo of Alexander's conquests. There is no decisive evidence to help us out of this dilemma. Even the concern with the problem of theodicy in 1:12-17 does not preclude the time of Jeremiah at the end of the seventh century. Since the arguments for a dating in the time of Alexander are undecisive, even granting that the description of the invaders on horseback fitted the Macedonians better than the Chaldeans and that 1:10b could conceivably refer to the mole by which Alexander joined Tyre to the mainland before conquering it, it seems preferable to adhere to the traditional dating of the book at the end of the seventh century (605-600).

In 1:5-11 the majority of critics see an allusion to actual historical events. On the contrary, W. Staerk (ZAW 51 [1933] 1-28) recognizes in

---

[24] See also C. C. Torrey, The Prophecy of Habakkuk in *Jewish Studies in Memory of George A. Kohut*, pp. 565-582. New York, 1935.

the invading army a demonic host of apocalyptic horsemen: at the end
of time the Satanic hosts will be defeated by God. Such an interpretation
of Habakkuk in the spirit of the Revelation of St. John is hardly convincing—to say the least. Nor is the proposal of E. Balla (*Religion in
Geschichte und Gegenwart*, Vol. II, pp. 1556 f. 2nd ed.) and E. Sellin (in
his commentary to the Minor Prophets, 2nd-3rd ed., 1929), according to
which our book is a "prophetic liturgy" (a type of literary composition
discovered by H. Gunkel), to be taken too seriously.[25]

9. Zephaniah

Zephaniah was a contemporary of Habakkuk and prophesied a few
years before him: Josiah's reforms in 621 separate the two prophecies. As
the title states, the genuine oracles of Zephaniah belong to the reign of
Josiah (638-609), more exactly to the time of the Scythian invasion along
the Mediterranean coast (between 630 and 624). The prophet is said
(1:1) to have been a grandson of a grandson of a certain Hezekiah—
presumably the king of Judah of that name who ruled from 720 to 692;
Zephaniah was born about one century after King Hezekiah and could
possibly have been his descendant in the fifth generation.

The Book of Zephaniah consists of three distinct parts in which the
spurious material increases steadily. The exordium (1:2 f.) and the concluding practical application (2:1-3) of the principal oracle (1:4-18)
seem to be editorial. In the introduction, Jehovah threatens mankind,
beasts, birds, fishes, and idols with utter extermination (1:2 f.); in the
conclusion, the humble and meek are exhorted to seek the Lord in the
hope of being spared on that dreadful day (2:1-3).

Zephaniah's most impressive oracle (1:4-18) is arranged in two parts.
In the first (1:4-6, 8aβ-13, omitting 1:6, which is a gloss) the prophet
denounces Judah for her religious syncretism—worship of Baal, astral
deities, and Milkom (so for Malcham in 1:5) (1:4-5). He condemns
public officials and the royal house for their extortions and for their adoption or toleration of foreign wearing apparel, as also of alien superstitions such as leaping across the threshold, as (I Sam. 5:5) did the priests
of Dagon (1:8aβ-9). Merchants (1:10 f.) and indifferent Judeans living
at ease in their assurance that Jehovah will not punish them (1:12 f.) are
equally denounced. In the second part of this oracle (1:7-8aα, 14-18),
appalled like Jeremiah (4:5-31; 5:15-17; 6:1-8, 22-26) at the approach of
the Scythian hordes, those veritable scourges of God, the prophet proclaims the imminent coming of the Day of the Lord, the awful *dies irae*.

The second part of the book is a series of oracles against foreign nations,

---

[25] E. A. Leslie (*The Prophets Tell Their Own Story*, pp. 204-226) considers Habakkuk a Temple prophet and singer, attributing to his pen the psalm in ch. 3 (including
the liturgy in 3:17-19).

probably inspired by the irruption of the Scythians. Having devastated
the Philistine cities (2:4-7, omitting the gloss in 2:7 or at least 2:7aαbβ),
the Scythians threatened the Egyptians (2:12), called "Ethiopians"
(Kushites) because the kings of the Twenty-fifth Dynasty, ruling Egypt
from 712 to 663, were Ethiopians. After they were stopped at the Egyptian
border by payment of a great indemnity (Herodotus 1:105), Zephaniah
anticipated that they would turn back and destroy Nineveh (2:13 f.; 2:15
is a gloss written after the destruction of Nineveh in 612). The oracle
against Moab and Ammon (2:8-11), which refers to the unfriendly attitude of these nations at the time of the destruction of Jerusalem in 586,
is clearly spurious.

In the third part of the book (ch. 3) little if anything can be attributed
to Zephaniah with any assurance; even 3:1-7, the only part that could be
regarded as genuine, denounces Jerusalem and its leaders only in the
vaguest and most general terminology, in contrast with the enumeration
of specific religious sins in 1:4-13—the best picture of religious syncretism
prevailing in Jerusalem before Josiah's reforms in 621. The first oracle
in ch. 3 (3:1-7) bewails the sinfulness of Jerusalem which persists in
spite of all divine warnings—a thought apparently inspired by the far
more impressive oracle of Amos 4:6-12a (both in Zeph. and in Am. the
original ending of these oracles, a proclamation of doom, was suppressed
by the editors).

The second oracle (3:8-13) announces the final judgment of God: he
will vent his anger on the nations (3:8), allowing certain heathen, however, to become converted (3:9 f.), and remove the wicked from Israel
so that the pious remnant may abide in peace (3:11-13; cf. Is. 1:21-27).
The final oracle is a paean of praise to God who has defeated the foes
of Israel and ushered in the millennium (3:14-20).

Zephaniah, in his denunciation of religious syncretism and political
corruption, applies the teaching of Isaiah to his own day and derives from
Amos the dismal conception of "the Day of the Lord." His bold, positive,
unflinching nature differs radically from the introspective and emotional
temperament of his contemporary, Jeremiah. The message of the two is
subtly different, even when both are prophesying under the appalling
menace of the Scythian invasion. There is no trace of Jeremiah's distraught panic in Zephaniah. The earnest, sober, vigorous style of this
prophet lacks the poetic brilliance of Amos and Isaiah, but his picture
of the horrors of the *dies irae* (1:15 f.) has become classic.

The Book of Zephaniah, as it finally left the hands of its last editors,
exhibits the editorial arrangement apparent in other books, notably in
Isaiah: indictment of the prophet's own people, denunciation of foreign
nations, and a vision of the future glory of Israel.

10. Haggai

The Book of Haggai consists of four oracles dated exactly near the end of the second year of Darius I, king of Persia (521-485 B.C.), i.e., from the 29th of August to the 18th of December 520 B.C. At that time Haggai and Zechariah (cf. Ezra 4:24; 5:1 f.) induced the people to begin rebuilding the Temple of Jerusalem, which had lain in ruins since 586. The new edifice was completed four years later (Ezra 6:14 f.).

1. On the first day of the sixth month, Haggai told Zerubbabel, the governor of Judea appointed by the Persian authorities, and Joshua, the high priest, that Jehovah had brought crop failure and drought on the Jews because, after building themselves paneled houses, they had failed to reconstruct the Temple (1:1-11, omitting 1:3, a mechanical repetition of part of 1:1). Thus encouraged, Zerubbabel, Joshua, and the other Jews began to rebuild the Temple on the 24th of that month (1:12-15a, omitting the gloss in 1:13 which is based on 2:4).

2. When the work had continued for nearly a month, Haggai on the 21st of the seventh month declared, for the benefit of those who remembered the old Temple and criticized the new one, that the glory of this unpretentious new edifice would exceed that of the former by reason of the Gentiles' munificent gifts (1:15b-2:9, omitting reference to the Exodus from Egypt in 2:5a). That the wealth of nations would pour into Jerusalem is likewise promised in Is. 60:5-11.

3. The third oracle (2:10-19, omitting 2:17, reminiscent of Am. 4:9, and 2:18b) is wrongly dated on the 24th day of the ninth month (instead of the 24th of the sixth month) and is misplaced. This oracle was pronounced by Haggai on the day when work on the Temple was begun, and should come between 1:11 and 1:12. In his final appeal before the inception of the work, Haggai proved to the Jews that the sacrifices offered on the site of the destroyed Temple were ineffective. He elicited from the priests the information that holiness was not contagious, only uncleanliness; therefore the offering of unacceptable sacrifices made the whole nation unclean. But Jehovah would bless the people from that very day, when the cornerstone of the Temple was laid.

4. On the 24th day of the ninth month, Haggai promised that Jehovah would shatter the power of Gentile empires and make Zerubbabel (a scion of the house of David) his signet ring (cf. Jer. 22:24)—meaning Messianic king (2:20-23).

The widespread insurrections and revolutions which Darius I had to overcome at the beginning of his reign, before his authority was recognized throughout the Persian Empire (see his Bisutun [or Behistun] inscription and cf. A. Poebel, AJSL 55 [1938] 142-165, 285-314), stirred in Haggai and Zechariah the chimeric hope that their God was going to shake up the kingdoms of the world and bring not only their wealth to Jerusalem (2:6-9; Zech. 2:8 f. [H. 2:12 f.]) but also restore the kingdom of David under his descendant Zerubbabel (2:23; Zech. 6, where, however, in v. 11 Joshua has been substituted for Zerubbabel after the imprisonment or death of the latter had made the realization of the prophecy impossible). Such nationalistic aspirations, however, led to no open rebellion, for the Jews were too weak at the time. They were not taken seriously by Darius who, in allowing the rebuilding of the Temple, continued the policy of friendship for the Jews which characterizes the Achaemenian dynasty. But the Davidic family lost its prestige and soon disappeared.[26]

Haggai and the prophets following him had little in common with the great Hebrew prophets of the preceding centuries. His great concern was not the moral and religious wickedness of his people, but adherence to the rules of Levitical purity and the fulfillment of ritual acts. For him the present prosperity and future glory of his people depended entirely on rebuilding the Temple. He encouraged his dispirited contemporaries with Utopic dreams of wealth and power as soon as the cornerstone of the Temple was laid. His simple, matter-of-fact, unadorned prose reflects the wretched situation of Jerusalem before Nehemiah came in 444 to revive hope by fortifying the city physically and spiritually against the outside world.

Negligible though this book appears from the point of view of literature and religion, it is of the greatest importance, together with Zechariah, as a historical source. Not only does it permit us to recognize the fallacy of the Chronicler's imaginative description, in the Book of Ezra, of the Jews' return under Cyrus in 538, but it is (with Zech.) the only authentic source that lifts the veil for a moment over the obscure centuries of Jewish history separating the events, told at the end of Kings (561 B.C.), from Nehemiah's activity in 444. Devoid of opulence, refinement, vitality, and enthusiasm, the pitiful Jewish community in Jerusalem in 520 rebuilt the Temple but did not witness the millennium which its prophets were promising. The revival of Judaism was not created by apocalyptic dreams, but by the practical measures of a statesman of common sense, patriotism, and energy, whose name was Nehemiah.

[26] See B. Meissner, *Die Achämidenkönige und das Judentum.* Sitzungsberichten der Preussischen Akademie. Phil.-hist. Klasse, 1938, II, pp. 6-26, particularly p. 17. L. Finkelstein (*The Pharisees,* pp. 500-508) regards Haggai as a revolutionary nationalist and Zechariah as a pacifist urging submission, but the difference between the two prophets is hardly so far-reaching; at most they differed in regard to the method by which God would usher in his kingdom, which they both expected in the immediate future. J. Morgenstern (AJSL 55 [1938] 191; cf. 186, n. 72) believes that Zechariah supported "Zerubbabel's rebellion" before it collapsed between the 24th of the 9th month and the 24th of the 11th month in 520.

11. Zechariah

The prophet Zechariah, son of Berechiah, son of Iddo (1:1, 7; cf. 7:1, 8; these passages, except the first, are probably editorial), or more correctly Zechariah son of Iddo (Ezra 5:1; 6:14),[27] a priest according to Neh. 12:16, was a contemporary of Haggai. Haggai's oracles are dated from the 29th of August to the 18th of December of 520 b.c.; those of Zechariah in November of 520 (1:1), the middle of February of 519 (1:7) and on the 7th of December of 518 (7:1). The Book of Zechariah is confined to chs. 1-8; the anonymous prophecies in Zech. 9-14 are considerably later. The books of Haggai and of Zechariah lack titles.

A. Zechariah 1-8

The Book of Zechariah consists of eight visions of the night, interpreted by an angel and dated on the 24th day of the eleventh month of the second year of Darius (middle of February 519, 1:7-6:8), with an introductory address (1:1-6) and appendix (6:9-15); oracles dealing with the observance of the fasts (7-8) close the book.

In his initial address, dated November 520, Zechariah exhorted his listeners to return to their God in order that he might return unto them, and reminded them of the sad experiences of their forefathers who had disregarded the warnings of former prophets (1:1-6).

The eight visions of Zechariah seem to be arranged in three pairs (2-3, 4-5, 6-7), between the first and the eighth:

1. The rider on the bay horse, standing in the midst of the mountains (so the LXX; Hebrew: the myrtle trees); and the bay, "black," "dappled" and white horses (cf. the LXX and 6:1-3). Although these divine messengers report that the earth is at peace and that there is no sign of the convulsions presaging the approach of the Messianic age, Jehovah declares that the Temple in Jerusalem will be rebuilt, the Jews will prosper, and the heathen become the object of divine displeasure (1:7-17).

2. The four horns (representing the heathen powers) and the four smiths who will break them down (1:18-21 [H. 2:1-4]).

3. The "man with a measuring line in his hand." Jerusalem can have no walls on account of "the multitude of men and cattle therein," and needs none, for Jehovah "will be unto her a wall of fire round about" (2:1-5 [H. 2:5-9]). The following appeal to Exiles in Babylon to flee

---

[27] The insertion of "the son of Berechiah," which makes Zechariah the grandson instead of the son of Iddo, is probably due to a copyist's reminiscence of "Zechariah, son of Jeberechiah" in Is. 8:2. In Matt. 23:35 (cf. Luke 11:51) "Zachariah son of Barachiah" is likewise erroneous: reference is made to "Zechariah the son of Jehoiada" (II Chron. 24:20 f.), whose name was confused with that of our prophet; that the Gospels have reference to "Zacharias the son of Baruch," slain by the Zealots in A.D. 67-68 (Josephus, *War of the Jews* 4:5, 4 [4:335-343]) is unlikely.

before Jehovah comes to judge that city (2:6-9 [H. 2:10-13]), and the song of praise for the conversion of the heathen (2:10-13 [H. 2:14-17]) are, like 1:16 f., reminiscent of prophecies in the books of Isaiah and Jeremiah and, whether written by Zechariah or not, form no integral part of the visions.

4. The high priest Joshua, attired in filthy garments, is accused by Satan (literally, "the adversary") but is acquitted by Jehovah and clothed in rich apparel (3:1-7). An oracle to Joshua announces the imminent coming of *Zemach*, or "Branch" (cf. Jer. 23:5; 33:15; Zech. 6:12), the Messianic scion of the house of David who will usher in the future golden age (3:8-10).

5. The golden candlestick with seven lamps, each of which has a pipe, and two olive trees at the sides thereof (4:1-3). The seven lamps symbolize the eyes of God, the two olive trees the two anointed ones, Joshua and Zerubbabel (4:4-6aα, 10aβ-14, omitting the gloss 4:12 which interrupts the context and introduces new elements in the vision). This explanation of the vision is interrupted by an oracle to Zerubbabel, beginning with the words, "This is the word of the Lord unto Zerubbabel" (4:6aβ), and ending with the words, "and shall see the plummet in the hand of Zerubbabel" (4:10aα): Zerubbabel has laid the foundations of the new Temple in Jerusalem and, in spite of the difficulties looming before him like a mountain, he will set the keystone in place and complete the structure.

6. A scroll inscribed with curses flies over the land and destroys the houses of thieves and perjurers (5:1-4).

7. A woman, symbolizing wickedness, is carried to Babylonia inside a bushel measure by two winged women (5:5-11).

8. Coming out from between copper mountains, four chariots drawn respectively by bay, black, white, and dappled horses, go forth to the four points of the compass to patrol the earth (6:1-8).

The historical appendix (6:9-15) breaks off abruptly in the middle of the last sentence and has been deliberately curtailed and changed, although not sufficiently to obliterate the original import beyond recognition. Zechariah is ordered to make a crown (not "crowns," 6:11; cf. 6:13) out of the gold and silver sent to Jerusalem by the Babylonian Jews and to crown Zerubbabel (not "Joshua," 6:11), the Messianic "Branch" of the house of David (6:12; cf. 3:8; Jer. 23:5; 33:15), who will build the Temple and sit on the throne with Joshua at his side (6:13, where we should read [cf. the LXX], "And Joshua will be priest at his right side, and harmony will prevail between the two"). But while Zerubbabel was presumably crowned in the greatest secrecy, the ceremony did not apparently escape the alert Persian secret service, and Zerubbabel mysteriously disappeared without ever sitting on the throne of David. Two years later (7:1-2) we find a man with a Babylonian name, Bethel-sar-eser (Babylonian *Bīt-ili-šar-uṣur*; cf. J. P. Hyatt, JBL 56 [1937] 387-394), as the leader of the Palestinian Jews in place of Zerubbabel. Thus the prediction had come to naught. To conceal this failure, the text of the passage was later willfully corrupted and in this oracle Joshua, who not being involved in this political plot was not molested, was substituted for Zerubbabel.

The closing oracles of Zechariah (7-8) are dated December 7, 518 (7:1). Darius had nipped the ill-timed Messianic aspirations of Zerubbabel in the bud, but he had no objection whatsoever to the rebuilding of the Temple, according to his pronounced religious liberalism for all cults. But the enthusiasm aroused in Jerusalem by Haggai and Zechariah two years before had died out, since the glowing predictions about the advent of the Messianic age showed no signs whatsoever of early fulfillment. In their disillusionment, the people wondered whether to continue (7:1-3) the observance of the national yearly fast on the 7th day of the fifth month, as a mourning ceremony for the destruction of Jerusalem in 586 (II Kings 25:8 f.; Jer. 52:12 specifies the 10th day), since it would have no place in the Messianic age.

Three other fast days were observed during the exilic period: on the 9th day of the fourth month (8:19), because on that day the Babylonians broke through the walls of Jerusalem (Jer. 39:2); on the 3rd or 24th of the seventh month (7:5; 8:19) because of Gedaliah's assassination (II Kings 25:25; Jer. 41:1 ff.); and on the 10th day of the tenth month (8:19) because it marked the beginning of the siege of Jerusalem (II Kings 25:1).

In a first oracle, Zechariah declared that not fasting but obedience to God's requirements, as proclaimed by the former prophets, was significant in the eyes of Jehovah (7:4-7). Jehovah had asked for justice, mercy, and honesty, and when the earlier generations had refused to listen to the appeals of their prophets, Jehovah in his wrath had scattered the Jews among the nations and ruined their land (7:9-14; 7:8 is a gloss). In a second address, the prophet delivered ten short oracles. In the first seven (8:1-17) Jehovah assured the Jews, who had become discouraged and regarded the fulfillment of the Messianic prophecies as impossible (8:6), that he would dwell in Zion and that Jerusalem would be filled with returned Exiles; the former economic distress would give way to great prosperity but the Jews must be upright in word and deed. In the last three (8:18-23), Jehovah decreed that the four exilic fast days would become joyous festivals (8:18 f.) and declared that the Gentiles, aware that God was with the Jews, would come to Jerusalem to worship Jehovah (8:20-23).

Zechariah is a more complex personality than Haggai. In contrast with

Haggai's "single-track mind" and unswerving purpose, Zechariah os-
cillates between his own deepest convictions and popular Utopic dreams.
He strove to restrain the ferment aroused in the masses by the widespread
rebellions at the beginning of Darius' reign, through assurance that the
whole earth was at peace (1:11) and that the fortifications of Jerusalem
need not be rebuilt (2:1-5 [H. 2:5-9]). But he yielded sufficiently to
popular enthusiasm to announce the destruction of world empires (1:18-21
[H. 2:1-4]; 2:8 f. [H. 2:12 f.]; cf. 6:1-8) and even to participate in the
ill-fated coronation of Zerubbabel as Messianic king (6:9-15, corrected
text). But his support of the militant nationalism of the day was only
halfhearted. His own attitude, derived from the Second Isaiah (Is.
45:21-24), favored the conversion of the heathen to Jehovah's religion
(2:11 [H. 2:15]; 8:20-23) rather than their subjugation and spoliation
(2:8 f. [H. 2:12 f.]; Is. 60:5, 11; Hag. 2:6-9). Moreover, our prophet relied
on divine intervention rather than on political and military devices for
the realization of his hopes (2:5, 13 [H. 2:9, 17]; 4:6).

It is true that Zechariah lent his support, somewhat reluctantly, to
Haggai's movement for the rebuilding of the Temple (1:16; 4:9; 6:12-15;
8:9), but for him external observances and visible symbols did not constitute the essence of religion. Like the great prophets of the past, he
considered sacred rites as religiously insignificant (7:4-7) compared
with the weightier matters of moral living, justice, and mercy (7:8-11;
8:16 f.), and the removal of crime and guilt from the midst of the community (5) as of sin from the high priest (3:1-5).

Zechariah was neither a great writer nor a great thinker. His language
and style lack both brilliance and distinction; his thought, wavering
between the selfish nationalism and crass ritualism of the masses and the
spiritual religion of the great prophets, lacks originality. Nevertheless,
his book is significant not only as a transition between prophecy and
apocalypse, but also as reaffirmation of the noble teaching of the earlier
prophets at a time when prophecy was about to expire.

B. Zechariah 9-14

At the end of the Book of the Minor Prophets, the editors have collected anonymous oracles in three parts, each of which is entitled "An
Oracle" (*massā'*, burden): Zech. 9:1; 12:1; Mal. 1:1. The obscure historical allusions and apocalyptic eschatology of Zech. 9-14, contrasting
sharply with the clear historical background of Zech. 1-8, make it impossible to attribute these chapters to Zechariah. Marked by the title in 12:1,
the two parts of Zech. 9-14 are 9-11 and 12-14, but 13:7-9, which is accidentally misplaced, forms the conclusion of 11:4-17 and should be read
at the end of the first part.

The first part consists of three prophetic poems (9:1-10; 9:11-10:2;

10:3-11:3) and a description of a symbolical action containing some poetic oracles (11:4-17; 13:7-9). After the Lord has pronounced judgment against the cities of Syria (9:1-2a), Phoenicia (9:2b-4), and Philistia (9:5 f.), the remnant of Philistines will become Jewish by adopting the Levitical dietary laws (9:7); the Lord will encamp around the Temple (9:8, a gloss in prose explaining 9:10), and the Messianic king will ride triumphantly into Jerusalem (9:9 f.; 9:9, combined with Is. 62:11, is quoted in Matt. 21:5). The Lord will bring to Zion the Jews of the Dispersion (9:11 f.) and, again uniting Judah and Ephraim, give his people not only victory over the Greeks (9:13-15) but also peace and prosperity (9:16 f.). The Jews should ask rain from the Lord and place no trust in teraphim, soothsayers, and dreams (10:1-2a; 10:2b is a transitional gloss). Enraged against the "shepherds" (i.e., foreign rulers), the Lord will transform his flock into battle steeds and raise up native leaders (10:3-5); he will strengthen Judah and Joseph for battle (10:6 f.) and bring the Jews of the Dispersion back from Egypt and Assyria (i.e., Syria; cf. Mic. 5:4 f.) (10:8-10); thus the power of the Ptolemies and of the Seleucids will be broken (10:11 f.); the cedars of Lebanon and the oaks of Bashan (i.e., the heathen powers) will be consumed by fire (11:1 f.) and the alien rulers wail (11:3).

The allegory of 11:4-17; 13:7-9 alludes to historical events in the immediate past easily recognized by the prophet's contemporaries, but entirely unknown to us. Following a divine command (11:4-6), the prophet becomes a shepherd of the flock to be slaughtered. After slaying three shepherds in one month, he makes unto himself two rods, called Delight and Union (11:7-8a). But when the flock proves hostile, he forsakes it and breaks the staff Delight (11:8b-11). He then casts into the treasury of the Temple the contemptible wages of thirty shekels of silver paid him (11:12 f., quoted in Matt. 27:9 as a prophecy of Jeremiah) and breaks the staff Union to signify the end of the brotherhood between Judah and Israel or, according to the reading of codices Holmes and Parsons 62 and 147 of the LXX, between Judah and Jerusalem (11:14). Finally, the Lord orders him to assume the guise of a foolish shepherd and destroy the flock (11:15 f.). According to the closing oracle, the foolish shepherd and his flock will be smitten leaving only one-third purged by fire and redeemed (11:17; 13:7-9).

The second part (12:1-13:6; 14) consists of two distinct eschatological oracles (12:1-13:6; 14) dealing with the onslaught of the heathen on Jerusalem and the golden age inaugurated after their destruction. After a title and preamble (12:1) comes a series of eschatological pictures. The hosts of heathen nations and rural Judah assemble against Jerusalem (12:2 f.), but are seized by a miraculous panic (12:4). Perceiving thereby that the Lord is the strength of Jerusalem (12:5), the Judeans turn against their heathen allies (12:6) and are saved before Jerusalem (12:7), whose inhabitants gain heroic strength (12:8). On the day when the Lord seeks to destroy the heathen (12:9), he will pour on the house of David and the citizens of Jerusalem a spirit of moving entreaty and they will bitterly grieve for the one they have stabbed (12:10), wailing separately by clans (husbands and wives apart), as at Megiddo in the ritual mourning for Hadad-Rimmon (12:11-14)—meaning presumably Tammuz-Adonis (cf. Ez. 8:14, the "Adonis-plantations" in Is. 17:10, and perhaps Dan. 11:37) rather than Josiah (cf. II Chron. 35:24 f.). A purifying fountain will flow constantly (13:1); idols and prophets will be banned (13:2). If a prophet is discovered, he will either be put to death by his own parents (13:3) or emphatically deny the allegation (13:4-6).

The second oracle (14) describes the capture and sack of Jerusalem by the heathen and the deportation of half the inhabitants (14:1 f.); the other half will escape through a gorge miraculously cut by the Lord in the Mount of Olives (14:3-5). Then will begin the Messianic age, when there shall be neither extremes of heat and cold nor darkness at night (14:6 f.). Two streams will flow out of Jerusalem (14:8), the Lord will rule (14:9), the mountains of Judah become a plain, except for the hill on which Jerusalem is to be rebuilt and which will be higher than before (14:10 f.). As for the heathen who had come against Jerusalem, their flesh and that of their beasts will rot before death, and in their panic men will kill one another (14:12-15; vv. 13-14 interrupt the prophecy and may be a gloss); their survivors must make a pilgrimage to Jerusalem on the Feast of Tabernacles lest the Lord withhold rain from their land or, in the case of Egypt requiring no rain, send a plague (14:16-19). Horses will no longer be used in war, and owing to the immense influx of pilgrims the Temple's sacred vessels must needs be immense basins; nay, every vessel in Jerusalem and Judah will be required for the sacred rites in the Temple; mundane commerce will no longer be tolerated within the sacred precincts (14:20 f.; cf. Matt. 21:12).

In Jewish apocalypses, the great drama at the end of time is in two acts, corresponding to the two phases of a standard drama which Aristotle appropriately named the *désis* (or tying of the knot), leading up to the climax, and the *lýsis* (or denouement) following it. The apocalyptic drama always ends happily through the intervention of the *deus ex machina*. The first act depicts the Jews' intolerable condition growing steadily worse until the crisis is reached, when all seems lost; the second pictures their triumph after their God appears mightily on the scene.

The first act contains elements derived from actual historical situations as well as those purely imaginary events that are the stock in trade of eschatologists. There is a historical basis for expecting the attack on Jerusalem from the north (from Syria, to Phoenicia and to Philistia, in 9:1-7), as in the cases of the Assyrian, Scythian, Babylonian, and Greek attacks; for the rallying of the Jews in Palestine against invaders (9:13), under their native leaders (10:3-5); and for the active participation of the Jews of the Dispersion in the struggle (9:11 f.; 10:8-10). Even the coming of the Lord in a storm from the south (9:14) has its antecedent in the Song of Deborah (Judg. 5:4). But the concentration of hosts of heathen nations against Jerusalem (Joel 3:1-3 [H. 4:1-3]; Ez. 38-39; Obad. 15; Mic. 4:11; Zeph. 3:8; Zech. 12:2 f., 9; 14:1 f.) and their miraculous defeat or annihilation (12:4; 14:12-15; Is. 33:3; Mic. 7:16 f.) are dreams without any historical basis, aside from the fabulous annihilation of Sennacherib's army (II Kings 19:35).

The oracles in Zech. 9-14 present certain features of this crisis not found elsewhere: rural Judah is arrayed against Jerusalem (11:14 [LXX Codd. 62 and 147]; 12:2-7; 14:14); two-thirds (13:8, which belongs to 9-11) or one-half (14:2) of the Jewish population will be slain; the remnant will escape through a chasm cut by the Lord in the Mount of Olives (14:1-5).

The second act of the drama depicts the bliss and glory of the Messianic age. Jerusalem will be forever secure (9:8) either under the rule of the Messianic prince of peace (9:9 f.; Is. 9:6 f. [H. 9:5 f.]; 11:10; Jer. 33:15 f.; Mic. 5:2-5 [H. 5:1-4]; Amos 9:11 f.), whose dominion extends to the ends of the earth, or under the Lord himself (14:9; Mic. 4:7). Palestine will become an earthly paradise (literally like the Garden of Eden, Is. 51:3; Ez. 36:35): the soil will bear prodigiously (9:17; Is. 4:2; 29:17; 30:23-25; 33:16); the mountains of Judah become a plain (14:10; so, presumably, in Ez. 47 f.); two streams (14:8) or a single one (13:1; Ez. 47:1-12; Joel 3:18 [H. 4:18]; cf. Is. 33:21) will flow out of Jerusalem; the climate will become ideally uniform (14:6; cf. Is. 4:6) and the nights be as luminous as the days (14:7; Is. 24:23; 30:26; 60:19 f.; IV Ezra 7:39-42; Rev. 21:23; 22:5).

In this era of peace and safety (14:11; Is. 26:3; 33:20 f.; Jer. 33:12 f.; Mic. 4:3 f.), war horses will disappear (9:10; Mic. 5:10 [H. 5:9]) or be consecrated to religious purposes (14:20); heathen and native superstitions, and even decadent and degenerate prophecy, will disappear (13:1-6 [cf. 10:2]; Mic. 5:12-14 [H. 5:11-13]) because the divine spirit of prophecy will be poured upon all Jews and their servants (Joel 2:28 f. [H. 3:1 f.]); the whole land will be in a state of ritual purity (14:21) and the Temple will become the religious center of the world (14:9; cf. Mic. 4:1 f.) to which the heathen, after their conversion—even the Philistines will observe the Levitical laws of purity (9:7)—will come in pilgrimage to celebrate the Feast of Tabernacles (14:16-19; cf. Zeph. 2:11b; 3:9 f.).

There are five distinct versions of this apocalyptic drama in Zech. 9-14. According to the first (9:1-10), a divinely sent invader (Alexander?)

will devastate Syria, Phoenicia, and Philistia; the conversion of the Philistine remnant and the coming of the Messianic prince of peace will then follow. In the second (9:11-17, with an irrelevant appendix in 10:1 f.), the Jews of the Dispersion will join forces with united Judah and Ephraim and defeat the Greeks; an era of peace and prosperity will result from this victory. The third (10:3-11:3) consists of a successful war for independence in which all Jews (Judah, Joseph, and those living in Egypt and Syria) will break the power of the Ptolemies and particularly that of the Seleucids. The similarities between this imaginary rebellion and the campaigns of Judas Maccabeus and his successors are only superficial. The fourth (12:1-13:6) depicts the deliverance of Jerusalem, when attacked by Judeans and heathen; the city will then mourn for one that has been unjustly killed and, purified by a perennial fountain, be freed from the contamination of heathen superstitions and native degenerate prophecy. The fifth (14) describes the sack of Jerusalem and the miraculous deliverance of half its people; in the ensuing Golden Age climate and soil will be marvelously improved, most of the heathen will rot away, and their survivors will be compelled to celebrate the Feast of Tabernacles in Jerusalem.

It is apparent that supernatural and fantastic elements increase steadily from the first to the fifth. The same author could conceivably be responsible for all five sections, although a few years seem to have elapsed between the writing of the first three and the fourth, and between the fourth and fifth. Nothing indicates, however, that two, three, or five separate authors could not have written these five oracles.

If we knew the historical events inspiring the allegory of the shepherds (11:4-17; 13:7-9) we would have an invaluable clue for dating exactly at least one section of this collection. Attempts to discover the historical background of this mysterious story, either in the decline and fall of the Northern Kingdom of Israel or at the beginning of the Maccabean rebellion, are utterly unconvincing. In view of the fact that no part of the book seems to be earlier than the time of Alexander the Great, it seems likely that the political disturbances, darkly alluded to in this allegory and in 12:10, belong to the third century, during which the history of the Jews is for us a total blank; 11:4-17 is unquestionably influenced by Ez. 34 and 37:16-28.

In dating Zech. 9-14 in the third century, we do justice not only to the general apocalyptic character of these oracles but also to numerous clues of late postexilic origin: the emphasis on ritual observances (9:7; 9:11: the daily burnt offering in the Temple; 14:16-19, 20-21); the allusions to a numerous body of Jews scattered among the nations (9:11 f.; 10:8-11); the decay of the prophetic movement to such an extent that the coming of a true prophet is no longer conceivable (13:2-6); the obvious imitation of parts of Ezekiel, Joel, and (12:1) the Second Isaiah, as also of apocalyptic oracles inserted into the prophetic books. A date later than about 200 B.C. is precluded by the fact that Sirach knew the book of "The Twelve Prophets" (Ecclus. 49:10) substantially in its present form; and it is difficult to see how Zech. 9-14 could have been added later to a volume of canonical Scriptures.

12. Malachi

The Book of "Malachi" was originally anonymous and bore the same title as the two books Zech. 9-11 and 12-14: "An Oracle. The Word of the Lord" followed in Zech. 12:1 with "against ['al] Israel"; and in Mal. 1:1 with "unto ['el] Israel"; the LXX, the Targum, and the Syriac read, however, "against" ('al) in both passages. Eager to present in the volume the books of exactly *twelve* named prophets, an editor added at the end of 1:1 the words "by the hand of Malachi," making a proper name of "mal'ākî" (my messenger) in 3:1. The LXX, however, read "by the hand of *his* messenger [mal'ākô]" inserting, with slight changes, the words of Hag. 2:15, 18 (cf. Mal. 2:2), "Lay it upon your hearts." The Targum understood "Malachi" as "my messenger" and added "whose name is called Ezra the Scribe," according to the tradition (accepted by Jerome) that ascribed the book to Ezra. It is probable that in their original form the three anonymous titles in Zech. 9:1; 12:1; Mal. 1:1 were prefixed by the same editor.

This little book consists of a preamble (1:2-5), a denunciation of the priests that despise God's name (1:6-2:9), four oracles against Jewish laymen (2:10-16; 2:17-3:5; 3:6-12; 3:13-4:3 [H. 3:13-21]), and a concluding warning (4:4-6 [H. 3:22-24]) presumably appended by the final editor of the Book of the Twelve as his parting advice to the reader.

The third oracle against the laymen (3:6-12) seems to break the close connection between the second and fourth, and may originally have stood immediately after the oracle against the priests (1:6-2:9) with which its subject, the payment of tithes, is closely connected. In these oracles, the deity quotes the words of priests and people, and answers their objections and doubts.

In the preamble (1:2-5), the Lord proves the depth and constancy of his love for Israel by pointing to the contrasting fate of Israel and her brother Edom: the land of Edom has been devastated [by a wave of Arabian invaders; cf. above on Obad.] and the attempts of the Edomites to rebuild their ruined homes avail nothing against the decision of the Lord, whose jurisdiction extends beyond the borders of Israel.

In the oracle against the priests (1:6-2:9), the Lord protests against the sacrifice of blemished victims—animals that they would not dare present to their governor—and declares that a complete cessation of sacrifices in the Temple would be preferable to this practice (1:6-10). Nay, the sacrifices that the heathen tender their gods are purer in his sight than these polluted offerings in Jerusalem (1:11)—an instance of religious liberalism unparalleled in the Old Testament; the author would have undoubtedly repudiated the implications of this utterance in a calmer and more reflective mood. Not only do the priests show their contempt for the table of the Lord by offering defective victims, but they perform routine acts of worship in an attitude of supercilious boredom (1:12 f.). Cursed be the layman who pays his vows with worthless sheep (1:14)! Unless the priests, who have violated the divine covenant with Levi and proved themselves unworthy successors of the noble Levites of old (2:5-7), mend their ways, the Lord will pour contempt and disgrace upon them (2:1-9).

Jewish laymen are denounced for marrying Gentile women after divorcing their Jewish wives (2:10-16), for doubting the reality of the just divine retribution for human deeds (2:17-3:5), for failing to pay in full the regular tithes due the Temple (3:6-12, perhaps belonging after 2:1-9), and for thinking that there is no profit in fulfilling the will of God (3:13-4:3 [H. 3:13-21]). In the first of these oracles (2:10-16), two distinct issues are at stake: first, the marriage with heathen wives, daughters "of an alien god," which may be understood literally or, after the manner of Hosea, allegorically for the worship of strange gods (2:11 f., which some think was interpolated), and secondly the divorce of the wife of their youth (2:10, 13-16). The other three oracles deal with specifically religious matters. To the skeptics denying any connection between human conduct and human fate (2:17), as Ecclesiastes did later, and thus feeling justified in neglecting the payment of Temple dues (3:6-9), the author replies that the Lord's appearance in judgment against the evildoers is imminent (3:1-5). He adds that the present crop failure (3:11) will give way to rich agricultural bounty as soon as the tithes are paid in full (3:10, 12), and that far from envying the prosperity of the wicked (3:13-15; cf. 2:17) the pious should rejoice in having their own names written in a divine book (3:16) and in the assurance of salvation at the last judgment, when righteous and wicked will receive their deserts (3:17-4:3 [H. 3:17-21]).

At the end of the volume of the Minor Prophets (4:4-6 [H. 3:22-24]) the editor urges observance of the Law of Moses (probably the Pentateuch rather than the Deuteronomic Code) pending the second coming of Elijah "before the great and terrible Day of the Lord come" (quoted from Joel 2:31 [H. 3:4]). The editor believed that prophecy came to an end with Malachi and understood the divine messenger of 3:1 to be Elijah, who according to II Kings 2:11 had been carried alive into heaven.

The date of the Book of Malachi can be positively fixed in the first half of the fifth century B.C., probably about 460 B.C. Judah is ruled by a governor (cf. 1:8 with Neh. 5:15) and in the second Temple (completed in 516) the priests have been performing ritual ceremonies for a number of years (cf. 1:10; 3:1, 10) and are wearied by them (1:13). The invasion of Arabian tribesmen into the land of Edom, resulting eventually in the organization of the Nabatean kingdom there, cannot be exactly dated but must have begun about the middle of the sixth century; according to 1:2-5, it had already wrought havoc with the Edomites but had not yet driven them into Southern Judah, which was accordingly called Idumea as early as 312.

Some of the abuses corrected by Nehemiah in 432 (possibly after the promulgation and enforcement of the Priestly Code) are still glaringly conspicuous in the time of the author, who knows nothing of Nehemiah's reforms and betrays no knowledge of the Priestly Code. He alludes clearly, however, to the Deuteronomic Code; his contempt for the offering of blemished victims (1:8) rests on Deut. 15:21 ("lame or blind"); 17:1; his demand for the full payment of "tithe and heave offering [terûmah]" (3:8-10) corresponds to the law of Deut. 14:22-29 (tithe and terûmah are mentioned together elsewhere only in Deut. 12:6, 11, 17); the priests are called "sons of Levi" (3:3; cf. 2:4, 8), as in Deuteronomy (21:5), where Levite and priest are synonymous terms, and not "sons of Zadok" (as in Ezek.) or "sons of Aaron" (as in the Priestly Code).

Like the Book of Haggai, the Book of Malachi is of slight religious and literary importance, but an invaluable historical source for the obscure history of the Jews in the Persian period before Nehemiah. Haggai had attributed the wretched condition of the community in Jerusalem in 520 to failure to rebuild the Temple, promising the millennium after it was rebuilt. The Temple was completed in 516, but more than half a century later not only was there no sign of the Golden Age but the situation remained desperate. About 460, when a plague of locusts, "the devourer" (3:11), and a blight in vineyards caused great economic distress, the unknown prophet traditionally called Malachi presented the indictment of the Lord against his people.

Like Haggai, Malachi paints a sordid picture of the economic and spiritual misery of the Jewish community of his day, and believes that the cure lies both in correcting ritual shortcomings and in hoping for the miraculous intervention of the deity which is to follow. The attitude of these prophets in a time of misery is diametrically contrary to that of Amos in a time of prosperity. The latter inveighed against the zeal of the people in bringing sacrifices to their God and against their expectation of his triumphant intervention in their behalf. The enthusiastic optimism of the people in the time of Amos is in sharp contrast with the pessimistic despondency of the postexilic community. "The remnant that are left of the captivity there in the province are in great affliction and reproach" (Neh. 1:3a): such was the report brought to Nehemiah at the Persian court in Susa in 444. In vain did the faithful weep bitter tears on the altar of the Lord (2:13), in vain did they mourn in his presence (3:14).

Since their piety availed nothing and neither priests (1:6 f.) nor laymen (3:7) could discover anything that might explain their plight, they were driven to question both the love (1:2) and the justice (2:17) of the Lord, wondering whether he had changed (cf. 3:6). Some doubted the effectiveness of ritual worship (3:14), others even concluded that the Lord winked at impertinent wickedness (3:15) or actually found pleasure in it (2:17). As a result of these misgivings and doubts, the priesthood had lost all zest in the performance of sacred ceremonies and all reverence for the Lord (1:7-9, 12 f.); and the people, suffering from economic distress, cheated in the payment of vows (1:14) and of tithes due the Temple (3:8).

The congregation was beginning to divide into two groups, the zealous Pious and the indifferent (the scoffers, doubters, and worldly), although at this time the two were not as sharply marked off as in the Psalms and Proverbs. The Pious became utterly discouraged; the worldly enjoyed greater prosperity and success.

Malachi faced a difficult situation. His chief task was to strengthen the tottering faith of the discouraged faithful. He was not a deep thinker. He was addressing simple souls, and his arguments are therefore rather childish. As evidence of God's continued love for his people he reminded his listeners that the Edomites were in a worse state than they (1:2-5)! When they adduced the prosperity of the wicked he could merely assure them that God would soon appear to separate "the righteous and the wicked" (3:18), consuming the wicked with fire and making "the sun of righteousness with healing in its wings" shine upon the righteous (4:1-3 [H. 3:19-21]).

Turning to more immediate and practical matters, the prophet attempted to correct the abuses that had robbed the public worship of dignity and reverence, and to put an end to divorces and mixed marriages. That he failed to attain his objectives, as shown by the measures Nehemiah enforced against these practices, does not detract from his importance as a precursor of Nehemiah's reforms and of the Priestly Code. Our book is invaluable as a picture of a dying church and of the beginnings of the movement giving it a new birth and the energy needed to withstand all attacks to the present day.

PART V

THE WRITINGS, OR HAGIOGRAPHA

CHAPTER I

THE PSALMS

~~~~~~

The English title of the Book of Psalms is derived from the Greek title *bíblos psalmôn* (Luke 20:42; Acts 1:20) through the Latin *liber psalmorum*. In classical Greek, *psalmós* meant the playing of a stringed instrument and the music obtained thereby, but the LXX gave it the meaning of a sacred song (psalm) in translating *mizmôr*. This Hebrew word originally signified a musical composition for stringed instruments, and was later used in the titles of fifty-seven psalms to indicate a hymn with instrumental accompaniment. The Greek *psaltêrion*, meaning originally a psaltery, was used as the title of the Book of Psalms in the Codex Alexandrinus of the LXX and in that connotation (English: The Psalter) it passed into modern languages.

However, in Hebrew the title of the book is *tehillîm* or *tillîm* (Talmud, Origen, Eusebius, Jerome), a masculine plural form used exclusively as the title of this book; the Masoretes use instead the usual feminine plural form *tehillôth*, which means praises (Ps. 78:4, etc.; cf. *Hallelu-jah* = praise ye the Lord). Thus the Hebrew title defines the *contents* of the book, or at least an important part of it, as praises to God (cf. Ps. 106:48, etc.), whereas the Greek and English titles define the *form* of the book as hymns sung to the accompaniment of stringed instruments.

In reality, the present Book of Psalms is a collection neither of doxologies nor of church hymns. The Psalter begins with an introduction in prose (Ps. 1; Ps. 79 is also in prose), it contains a purely secular epithalamium in praise of a royal couple on their wedding day (Ps. 45), wisdom poems hardly composed for singing (Pss. 34:11-22 [H. 34:12-23]; 37; 49; 73; 127; 128; 133), and didactic expositions praising the excellence of the Law of Moses (19:7-14 [H. 19:8-15]; 119; cf. Ps. 1 imitated in Ps. 112).

The current designation of the Psalter as "the hymn book of the Second Temple," is hardly appropriate. Even if the psalms just enumerated and others are eliminated, the remaining collection is not a hymnal in the strict sense. It is perfectly clear that many of the psalms, notably those provided with musical directions, were sung in the service. But the collection we have, based on smaller collections, some of which may have been hymnals for guilds of singers in the Temple, was intended as a devotional anthology of religious poems (Ps. 45 was interpreted Messianically in the Targum and, in a Christian sense, in Hebrews 1:8-9) for the edification of the laity, particularly the lower middle classes.

The final collector probably introduced Ps. 1 at the beginning. In that general introduction, the purpose of the collection is clarified by the contrast between the happy, pious Jew who studies and fulfills the Law of Moses and the careless, worldly Jew who scoffs at wholehearted devotion to God and ardent zeal in fulfilling the minutiae of his law. The Psalter reflects far more the religion of the synagogue than that of the Temple: it expresses the religious emotions of the laity rather than the rituals performed in the sanctuary by the clergy. Even the doxologies, liturgies, and hymns sung in the Temple service, which are included in the Psalter, were selected because they were suitable for private devotion.

The Psalter, in its final edition, cannot truly be understood except as a religious anthology for the reverent Jew, prepared for the purpose of stimulating that personal piety which became characteristic of the Pharisees.[1] It is difficult to refrain from identifying the "righteous" and "sinners" among Jews with the Pharisees and Sadducees respectively, as in the Psalms of Solomon of a slightly later date, or at least with the groups out of which these two parties developed.

The Psalter is the great manifesto of the "Pious," that zealous crusading minority which succeeded in impressing its character on Judaism, even though remaining an *ecclesiola in ecclesia*—an Israel according to the spirit, surrounded by the inert mass of worldly and generally prosperous Jews. With holy indignation, these Pious denounce the "sinners," whom they regard as outcasts (cf. Ps. 139:19-22). Their ideal is a life of intimate communion with their God, in harmony with his will—a life in which simplicity of heart, faith in God, and good conduct are more essential than ritual worship and will eventually be rewarded by God. The intense emotions of these earnest souls, their longing for God's presence, their joyful faith, flaming hatred, agonizing doubts, black hours of despair, all find expression in the Psalter. This book is the voice of those humble believers whose virile hope, in spite of despair, and unyielding tenacity, in the midst of reverses, has kept Judaism alive and militant to the present day.

To be sure, either before or after the final edition, some parts of the Psalter were used for ritual purposes in worship. Within the family circle, the so-called Egyptian *Hallel* (Pss. 113-118) was sung in celebration of the Passover, half before and half after the paschal meal: Mark 14:26 and Matt. 26:30 refer to the singing of Pss. 115-118 after the Passover feast. Pilgrims going up to Jerusalem for one of the annual festivals, or returning therefrom, sang the "Songs of Degrees" or pilgrimage songs

[1] Cf. B. Duhm, *Die Psalmen,* pp. xxiv ff., KHC, 1899.

(Pss. 121-134).[2] Verses of the Psalter were used in public or private prayers. Solomon's prayer in II Chron. 6:41 f. is a paraphrase of Ps. 132:8-10; two of the words addressed to God by Jesus on the cross are from the Psalms: 22:2 (Mark 15:34; Matt. 27:46) and 31:6 (Luke 23:46).

The liturgical use of psalms in Temple worship is well attested since the days of the Chronicler (*ca.* 250 B.C.), who speaks of the musical parts of the ritual with such expert knowledge that very likely he belonged to one of the Levitical choirs. The Chronicler attributes to David the organization of Temple music,[3] both instrumental and vocal. He could not date this institution back to the time of Moses, because the Pentateuch (canonized about 400 B.C.) knows nothing of Temple music except the blowing of silver trumpets by the priests (Num. 10:1-10, one of the latest laws in the Pentateuch).

According to the Books of Chronicles, the three Levitical guilds of Temple singers were descended from Asaph, Jeduthun (identified with Ethan), and Heman, who had been placed in charge of the sacred music by David (I Chron. 25:1, 6; cf. 15:17, 19) and officiated at the dedication of Solomon's Temple (II Chron. 5:12 f.). This connection of the singers with the Levites (cf. I Chron. 6) and their division into three guilds are artificial. Levites, singers, porters, and Temple servants are mentioned separately in Ezra 2:70; Neh. 7:43-46, 73; 10:28 [H. 10:29]; (cf. Neh. 7:1; 10:39 [H. 10:40]; 13:5); Levites and singers in Ezra 10:23 f.; Neh. 12:47; 13:10. At one time, Asaph seems to have been the only singers' guild (Ezra 2:41; 7:7; Neh. 7:44; 11:22; 12:46); the threefold division of singers in Neh. 11:17 is not supported by the LXX (Codices A, B) and is hardly original; in this verse, however (cf. 12:8 f.), Asaph is already reckoned among the Levites.[4] On the other hand, in Neh. 12:27 f. both Levites and "sons of the singers" conduct the musical service.

The process by which the singers attained Levitical status is partly obscure. In the fourth century, an impassable gulf separated the Levites from their superiors, the priests or "sons of Aaron"; but the distinction between the Levites, on the one hand, and singers and gatekeepers, on the other, was vague and tended to disappear.

The complicated history of Korah throws some light on the matter.

[2] Psalms 122 is the typical pilgrim's song. In addition to the "Songs of Degrees," not all of which have the characteristics of Ps. 122, the following Psalms express perhaps the emotions of the pilgrims, who long for Zion and rejoice in its sight: 26; 27 (42-43?); 48; 61; 63; 84; 118; cf. Is. 2:3 = Mic. 4:2.

[3] See on this subject: A. Büchler, "Zur Geschichte der Tempelmusik und der Tempelpsalmen," ZAW 19 (1899) 96-133, 329-44; 20 (1900) 97-135; J. Köberle, *Die Tempelsänger im Alten Testament*, Erlangen, 1899; the articles on "Music" in Hastings's Bible Dictionary and Cheyne's Encyclopaedia Biblica; etc.

[4] According to C. C. Torrey (*The Composition and Historical Value of Ezra-Nehemiah*, pp. 22 f. Beih. ZAW 2, Giessen, 1896; *Ezra Studies*, pp. 236, 278. Chicago, 1910) singers are Levites throughout Chronicles, Ezra, Nehemiah.

Korah was originally an Edomitic clan (Gen. 36:5, 14, 16, 18; I Chron. 1:35), closely related to Caleb (I Chron. 2:43, where Korah is the son of Hebron) and part of the Kenizzite group. After the Korah clan settled near Hebron, it became eventually an integral part of Judah (cf. Josh. 15:13 ff.; Judg. 1:20, 11-13), not of Benjamin, as I Chron. 12:6 absurdly claims. In the original story of Num. 16 (H. 16-17; P), Korah is the representative of lay Israelites who refuse to recognize the exclusive priestly prerogatives of the "Levites" (Moses and Aaron), and he is punished for offering incense. Does this story mark the transition of Korah from a lay to a Levitical clan? In any case, a later writer by alterations and additions to the text, made of Korah the leader of the Levites who arrogated unto themselves the functions of the priests. Finally, a third writer (Num. 26:9-11) took pains to explain the presence of the Levitical guild of Korahites in the Second Temple: the "Sons of Korah" did not perish with their father in the fire from Jehovah.

Before 400 B.C., the Korahites were furnished with an imposing Levitical family tree (Ex. 6:18, 21, 24), their Edomitic origin and lay status long since forgotten. They began their ecclesiastical career as cooks (I Chron. 9:31) and gatekeepers (9:19; 26:19) but eventually became singers (II Chron. 20:19), using a hymnal of their own (Pss. 42-49; 84; 85; 87; 88; Ps. 43 lacks this attribution to the Sons of Korah because it was originally united with Ps. 42). The guild of Heman was probably merged with the Sons of Korah, as I Chron. 6:33-37 (H. 6:18-22) indicates, and Ps. 88 is attributed to both Heman and the Sons of Korah.

The union of Korah and Heman may have been facilitated by the circumstance that both were Edomites before becoming Judeans and later Levites. Heman was a legendary sage (I Kings 4:31 [H. 5:11]) belonging (according to the title of Ps. 88) to the Edomitic clan of Ezrah or Zerah (cf. Gen. 36:13, 17, 33; cf. I Chron. 1:37, 44) which eventually merged also, like other Kenizzite clans, with Judah and was regarded as Judah's son (Gen. 38:30; Num. 26:30; cf. Josh. 7:1, 24; 22:20). In I Chron. 2:6, Heman is the son of Zerah, son of Judah—a thorough Judean. Elsewhere in Chronicles he is not only a Levite of the Levites but, with David, the organizer of Temple music (II Chron. 35:15).

The vicissitudes of Ethan (to whom Ps. 89 is attributed) are identical with those of Heman: from Edomitic sage of the clan of Zerah (I Kings 4:31 [H. 5:11]), to a son of Zerah, son of Judah (I Chron. 2:6), to a Levite through descent from Gershom (I Chron. 6:42 [H. 6:27]) or rather from Merari (6:44 [H. 6:29]; 15:17).

The guild of Jeduthun in Chronicles is identified with that of Ethan. This identification becomes inevitable if we accept Lagarde's etymology of the puzzling name Jeduthun (also spelled Jedithun). Lagarde considers the name a corruption of (*al*) *jedê 'êthan* ([upon] the hands of

Ethan, i.e., in charge of the guild of Ethan).[5] In any case, the name in the titles of two psalms (62; 77) is not that of the author (as in Ps. 39, which is, however, also attributed to David) but of the musical mode, and this may well have been the original meaning of the word. Like Korah, Jeduthun is said to have been the eponym of a guild of gate-keepers (I Chron. 16:42b)—the mythical "father" of Obed-edom (16:38). Obed-edom, a Philistine from Gath living in Gibeonite territory near Kirjath-jearim in the time of David (II Sam. 6:10-12), was adopted by a Levitical guild of gatekeepers as their eponym (I Chron. 15:18, 24; 16:38; 26:4, 8, 15; II Chron. 25:24), manifestly because the ark remained three months in his house. Obed-edom's connection with the ark would inevitably lead to his metamorphosis into a Levite (as in the case of the Ephraimite Samuel; cf. I Chron. 6:28).

Eventually, the gatekeepers of Obed-edom's guild became musicians (I Chron. 15:21; 16:5), and to commemorate their promotion, assumed perhaps at that time the name of Jeduthun (Neh. 11:17 [but cf. LXX]; I Chron. 9:16; 16:38, 41, 42a; 25:1, 3, 6; II Chron. 5:12; 29:14; 35:15) or Ethan. It is clear from these passages, some of which contain the name of Jeduthun interpolated together with Heman, that the Obed-edom guild took special pains to advertise its new name. But even though Jeduthun was called a royal seer (II Chron. 35:15) and his Levitical status taken for granted, he never quite became, in the pages of Chronicles, a person of flesh and blood and, in spite of the facility with which genealogical trees were manufactured to order, Jeduthun's line was not traced back to Levi, even on paper. The best that the interpolator of II Chron. 29:13 f. could do was to add to the three great Levitical families of the fifth century (Priestly Code) named in v. 12, three additional branches of Levi (Asaph, Heman, and Jeduthun; Elizaphan really belongs to the Kohathites; cf. Num. 3:30).

The organization of Temple singers into three distinct guilds, as we find it in the time of the Chronicler (*ca.* 250 B.C.) is comparatively recent; the arrangement of the singers into twenty-four courses, corresponding to those of the priests, came even later (I Chron. 25).[6] When Temple choirs were first employed in the worship, there seems to have been only one guild, that of the sons of Asaph (see above). According to the Chronicler, Asaph was a seer (II Chron. 29:30) living in the time of David and

---

[5] Paul de Lagarde, *Übersicht über die in Aramäischen, Arabischen, und Hebräischen übliche Bildung der Nomina*, p. 121. Göttingen, 1889.

[6] The list of courses in I Chron. 25:9-31 is earlier than the list in 25:2-6; in the latter, the last nine names (beginning with Hananiah in v. 4) are arranged so that the consonantal text reads as a doxology and can be translated as follows, "Have mercy upon me, Jehovah, have mercy upon me! Thou art my god whom I magnify and extol! My help in hardship! Fill me [?] abundantly with visions!" In both lists, these nine names are clearly artificial.

Solomon, and also chief of the Levitical singers (Neh. 12:46; I Chron. 15:17, 19; 16:5; II Chron. 5:12, etc.) although in Ezra 2:41 the Sons of Asaph (or Temple singers) are mentioned apart from the Levites.[7] The hymnal of the Asaph guild comprised Pss. 50; 73-83. Not long after a second guild, the Sons of Korah, officiated with Asaph in the Temple; its hymnal contained Pss. 42-49; 84; 85; 87; 88. The first allusions to the threefold division of Temple singers are found in Neh. 11:17; 12:24.

This complicated and obscure history of the guilds of Temple singers furnishes an important clue to the date of certain collections of hymns incorporated in our Psalter. Even if some individual psalms date from the pre-exilic period, the hymnals used by the various guilds cannot have preceded the guild organization itself. Were there Temple singers before 586? Mention of choir singers of the Asaph guild among the returned Exiles in Ezr. 2:41 = Neh. 7:44 has been adduced as proof of the pre-exilic origin of Temple singers not yet assigned to the tribe of Levi. But the historical value of the lists of returned Exiles, compiled by the Chronicler nearly three centuries after 538, is extremely doubtful. Moreover, the Pentateuch, in its final edition published about the year 400, completely ignores the whole institution of Temple singing, although the ritual in the period 516-400 is described by the Priestly author in great detail.

It is true that in some of the Canaanitic shrines taken over by the Northern Israelites (Amos 5:23) music and song were part of the worship, but the prophet Amos, a Southerner, condemned these practices for which there is no evidence whatsoever in Jerusalem before 400. It is therefore difficult to accept the theory, presented by S. Mowinckel in his *Psalmenstudien*, that many of our psalms were sung during the celebration of certain festivals at an early period in the Temple at Jerusalem. At most, it is conceivable that on very exceptional occasions an especially composed hymn was sung: thus it is possible that Ps. 24:7-10 was sung antiphonally when the ark from Shiloh was installed with due ceremony into the newly built Temple of Solomon. But regular organized Temple singing in Jerusalem was still unknown in 400, although in full operation a century and a half later. It is during the period 400-250 that the guilds of Temple singers were organized and provided with their hymnals; and probably the bulk of our Psalter originated at this time.

The regular use of psalms in temple worship is well attested only at the end of this period. I Chronicles 16:8 ff. illustrates the practice at this time: the Levites sing Pss. 105:1-15; 96:1b-13a, concluding with a doxology (106:1) and an invitation to the congregation to praise God

---

[7] The Asaph guild was given Levitical rank by making Abiasaph a member of the Korah clan (Ex. 6:24 [P]), if we may assume (with W. Robertson Smith) that Abiasaph was the eponym of Asaph.

(106:47 f.); "and all the people said, Amen, and praised [so LXX] the Lord." The liturgical use of psalms is certified already in the Hebrew text, in the titles of Pss. 30; 92, and 100; more fully in the Greek text (LXX) and the Talmudic literature. According to the LXX, parts of the following psalms were sung during the presentation of the daily burnt offering (*tāmîd*) on each day of the week: 24 (Sunday), 48 (Monday), 82 (Tuesday), 94 (Wednesday), 81 (Thursday), 93 (Friday), 38 and 92 (Sabbath). From the LXX we learn that Ps. 29 was sung during the last days of the Feast of Tabernacles (and, according to the Talmudic literature, also Pss. 50:16 ff.; 94:8 ff.; 81:7 ff.; 82:5b ff.; 65); on New Year Ps. 81 and in the afternoon Ps. 29; the *Hallel* (Pss. 113-118) was sung during the slaying of the paschal lamb, and parts of it during the Feast of Tabernacles.[8]

The liturgical use of psalms in the Christian Church is derived from usage in the synagogue.[9] The Hebrew text vouches for the use of Ps. 30 during the Festival of Dedication; we hear from other sources that Ps. 7 was used for Purim, 29 for Pentecost, 83 or 135 for the Passover, 137 to commemorate the destruction of the Temple on the 9th of Ab.

It should be kept in mind, however, that the majority of psalms were not composed for liturgical use, and that the final collection was not a hymnal but primarily a book for private devotions. For instance, Ps. 51, a confession of sin and prayer for forgiveness, was adapted to liturgical use by the addition of vv. 18-19.

The New Testament offers abundant evidence to show how popular the Psalter was among pious Jews: they found in it not only religious inspiration and comfort but also instruction in the fundamental teachings of Judaism. It could fulfill these purposes because it presented not the actual religious level of the average Jew (as, for instance, Proverbs), but an ideal religion worth striving for even if seldom attained.

The Psalter contains exactly 150 compositions. This round number is not fortuitous and was probably obtained by the final editor when he added some of the purely liturgical poems at the end. The number 150 appears significant also because the LXX contains the same total, albeit the two psalms, 116 and 147 of the Hebrew, are four psalms in the LXX (114, 115, and 146, 147, respectively) and, conversely, Pss. 9-10 and 114-115 in the Hebrew correspond to two psalms (9 and 113) in the Greek. Moreover, the Greek Psalter has a spurious 151st Psalm at the

---

[8] See A. Büchler, ZAW 20 (1900) 97 ff.; Jacob, ZAW 16 (1896) 129 ff. and 17 (1897) 48 ff.

[9] The only reference to the synagogue in the Old Testament and the Apocrypha occurs in Ps. 74:8. The earliest reference to synagogue worship comes in an inscription in the reign of Ptolemy III (247-222) found near Alexandria (T. Reinach, REJ 45 [1902] 62; E. Schürer, *Geschichte des 'üdischen Volkes*, Vol. II, p. 500; Vol. III, p. 41. 3rd-4th ed., 1909).

end, which is prefaced as follows: "This psalm was written down by David himself, and is outside the number, when he fought singlehanded against Goliath." As a matter of fact, Pss. 9-10[10] and 42-43 are really two single poems, and Pss. 19; 24; 27; 144 are each the result of the incorrect union of two entirely different compositions. Psalm 40:13-17 (H. 40:14-18) appears also as a separate psalm (Ps. 70), while Ps. 108 combines Pss. 57:7-11 [H. 57:8-12] and 60:5-12 [H. 60:7-14].

The Psalter is divided into five books: I (Pss. 1-41), II (42-72), III (73-89), IV (90-106), V (107-150). Each one ends with a doxology, except for the last, where Ps. 150 serves as a final doxology. This division is already known to the LXX, which translates the doxologies at the end of the books, and to I Chron. 16:36 (where the doxology Ps. 106:48 is freely reproduced). Except for Books IV and V, the divisions between books correspond to those between some of the collections out of which the Psalter grew. However, since there is no justification for the break after Ps. 106, it is likely that, as Hippolytus and the midrash observed, the fivefold division was a mechanical imitation of the division of the Pentateuch.

Some of the original single collections can still be identified by the titles appended to the psalms. When the separate collections were brought together, their respective titles were attached to the single psalms included in them. Thus those belonging to the collection "Psalms of David," were entitled singly "A Psalm of David" or simply "David's." The oldest Davidic collection is Pss. 3-41 (Ps. 10 lacks a title since it is the second part of Ps. 9; the title for 33 occurs in LXX). Psalms 51-72 are a second collection of Davidic psalms, ending with this puzzling colophon, "The prayers of David the son of Jesse are ended" (72:20). Psalms 66, 67 and 71 lack the title "of David" in the Hebrew, but 67 and 71 have it in LXX; Ps. 72 (like 127 in the Hebrew, not in LXX) is attributed to Solomon. The second Davidic collection reproduces some psalms from the first: 14 reappears as 53; 40:13-17 [H. 40:14-18] as Ps. 70; in turn, Pss. 57:7-11 [H. 57:8-12] and 60:5-12 [H. 60:7-14] are later combined in Ps. 108.

This second Davidic collection forms part of the so-called Elohistic Psalter (Pss. 42-83) in which the divine name Elohim (God) occurs more than four times as often as Yahweh (Jehovah, Lord), whereas in the rest of the Psalter mention of Yahweh is twenty times that of Elohim. For unknown reasons, an editor changed Yahweh to Elohim throughout Pss. 42-83, leaving only forty-two occurrences of Yahweh in the text. In

---

[10] Psalms 9-10 are shown to be a single poem by the alphabetic acrostic arrangement of the strophes (even though the central portion is not correctly preserved). Other poems in the Psalter with an acrostic arrangement of the verses or strophes are: Pss. 25; 34; 37; 111; 112; 119; 145.

addition to the second Davidic collection (51-72), the Elohistic Psalter comprises the hymnbook of the Sons of Korah (42-49; 43 lacks the title in the Hebrew, being the second part of 42, but has it incorrectly in the LXX), and the Psalms of Asaph (50; 73-83).

The Elohistic Psalter corresponds to Book II and part of Book III of the Psalter (42-71; 72-83); the rest of Book III (84-89) consists of a miscellaneous supplementary collection comprising a psalm of David (86), four psalms of Korah (84; 85; 87; 88, the last one also attributed to Heman), and a psalm of Ethan (89). Jeduthun (or Jedithun) is mentioned in the titles of two Davidic psalms (39; 62) and a psalm of Asaph (77), once erroneously as an author (39) and twice to indicate how the music of the poem (62; 77) was rendered.

Omitting the first psalm, a prose introduction to the whole Psalter, the first three books (Pss. 2-89) may be considered as the first edition of the Psalter, to which the last two books were eventually added. The earliest collection is that of the Psalms of David in the first book (3-41), which probably dates from the fourth century. According to the obscure and legendary statement in II Macc. 2:13, Nehemiah collected a library containing, *inter alia*, writings of David. In our sources, however, the first references to the Psalms of David belong to the middle of the third century (I Chron. 16:7; II Chron. 29:30; 35:15, etc.), when Ps. 18 was copied in II Sam. 22 and David was called "the sweet psalmist of Israel" (II Sam. 23:1). About 180 B.C. Sirach (Ecclus. 47:8-10) unquestionably had a Davidic Psalter and seems to allude to Ps. 29:9.

Before the guilds of Temple singers had their own special collections of hymns, it was natural to attribute the composition of the earliest hymnal to the great king who was a poet and musician and who, by bringing the ark up to Jerusalem, was indirectly responsible for the later sanctity of Zion. None of the Psalms, however, could have been written by David: even if we disregard anachronisms such as the numerous allusions to the Temple on Zion or even to the Exile (Ps. 69:35 [H. 69:36]), the language, style, and religious conceptions of the Psalms of David are radically different from those of his time.

The second and third books of Psalms (Pss. 42-89) are a supplement to the first, and seem to have formed a separate anthology before being added to the first. There is no reason to doubt that the Elohistic Psalter (Pss. 42-83) was at one time a separate book alongside Pss. 3-41 (from which Pss. 53 and 70 were taken). The original order of the three collections combined in the Elohistic Psalter was presumably as follows: Pss. 51-72 (Davidic, with a Psalm of Solomon, 72, and a colophon at the end); 42-49 (Korah); 50, 73-83 (Asaph). Since the second Davidic collection (51-72) is now inserted into the Asaph collection (50; 73-83), it was probably added to the psalms of Korah and Asaph by the Elohistic editor.

The miscellaneous appendix (Pss. 84-89) was probably added when Pss. 42-83 were attached to Pss. 3-41. Somewhat later Ps. 2, apparently composed for the marriage of Alexander Janneus in 103 (the acrostic of Ps. 2:1-10 reads: *lyny' w'štw*, "For Janneus A[lexander] and his wife"), was placed at the beginning as a counterpart to the end of the book (cf. Ps. 2:7 with 89:27 [H. 89:28]). The Asaph and Korah collections (42-49; 50; 73-83) contain psalms generally recognized as Maccabean in date (Pss. 44; 74; 79; 83), but in a briefer form they probably go back to the first half of the third century. The Elohistic edition, which affected these Maccabean psalms, must be later than the middle of the second century. The collection of Pss. 2-89 existed before 100 B.C. when we find Ps. 79:2 f. quoted as scripture in I Macc. 7:16 f.

If we could infer, from the passage in I Maccabees just quoted, that the Psalter as a whole had attained canonical standing in 100 B.C., we would know positively that Pss. 90-150 had been joined to Pss. 2-89 before that date, and that Ps. 1 had before then been placed at the beginning as a kind of foreword. Although the evidence is meager, hardly allowing any certainty in the matter, it is extremely probable that the Psalter existed substantially in its present form about 100 B.C., and that the last two books (90-106 and 107-150) were in process of being assembled out of existing collections and scattered compositions during the final completion of the first three books.

It is difficult to determine whether Pss. 90-150 were joined to Pss. 2-89 as a complete collection (except for possible later additions of individual psalms), or whether individual collections and separate psalms were gradually added to Pss. 2-89 to form the present Psalter. In any case, it is certain that one of the editors of Pss. 90-150 knew and used the Elohistic Psalter (42-83), because he took from it Ps. 108, which consists of Pss. 57:7-11 [H. 57:8-12] and 60:5-12 [H. 60:7-14] *in their Elohistic redaction*.

Although not so clearly marked by titles as in the first three books, the component collections of Pss. 90-150 may still be identified. Book IV (90-106, to which 107 should be added) begins with "a prayer of Moses the man of God" (90) and contains two Davidic psalms (101 and 103; in the LXX 91; 93-99; 104 are also Davidic); Pss. 92-107 are hymns of praise to God presenting many similarities and apparently constituting a special collection, with 90 and 91 as an appropriate overture and 105-107, which are Halleluiah psalms, as a final doxology. Psalms 108-110 are Davidic, and may have formed a special collection with the Halleluiah psalms 111-118; 113-118 is the so-called "great Hallel," sung at the Passover and other festivals (Ps. 115 lacks the Halleluiah because it may have been originally, as in the LXX, the second part of 114). The third and most characteristic collection is that of the fifteen "Songs of Ascents" (or "of

Degrees")—pilgrimage songs chanted by Jews on the way to Zion (120-134; 122, 124, 131 and 133 are Davidic). This collection, as well as the two preceding and the following, are supplemented with Halleluiah psalms (135, 136).

The last Davidic collection (138-145) is followed by the Halleluiah psalms (146-150), constituting a doxology for the Psalter as a whole, and may in part have been added to obtain the round number 150 for the psalms in the Psalter. Two psalms, 119 and 137, seem to have stood beyond the limits of these four collections and were added in the course of the Psalter's editorial growth before the final editor appended Ps. 1 at the beginning.

Thus it is clear that the Psalter grew out of special collections of psalms during the course of centuries. This process began some time after 400 B.C. and was probably completed about 100 B.C. The quotations from Pss. 96, 105, 106, 130, 132 in I Chron. 16:8-36 and II Chron. 6:40-42 do not help us in fixing the chronology of the Psalter, since these passages may be later than the Chronicler himself and cannot be dated accurately.

The great majority of psalms was presumably written during the assembling of the Psalter, between 400 and 100 B.C. and shortly before, in the fifth century. The real question with regard to the Psalter is not whether it contains Maccabean psalms of the second century, but rather whether any psalms are pre-exilic psalms. On the whole, the Psalter presents the thought, faith, and worship of postexilic Judaism. For the dating of individual psalms, the names of authors mentioned in the titles (Moses, David, Solomon, the sons of Korah, Asaph, Jeduthun, Heman [Ps. 88] and Ethan [Ps. 89]), with the possible exception of the last two (cf. ZAW N.F. 3 [1926] 14 f.) are utterly irrelevant.

During the two most important centuries in the formation of the Psalter (400-200), the history of the Jews is a total blank, with the exception of their rebellion against Artaxerxes III Ochus in 353 (reported by Eusebius, Solinus, and Orosius), which resulted in the destruction of Jericho and deportation of a number of Jews. It is therefore impossible to date accurately any Old Testament writings of this period—notably most of the psalms. As a matter of fact, all our historical information on the Jews for the period reaching from the end of II Kings to the beginning of I Maccabees (*ca.* 550-170) is furnished by the authentic writings of Haggai, Zechariah, and Nehemiah.

This dating of the majority of psalms after 400 B.C. is seriously questioned by competent scholars. For instance, H. Gunkel, in his *Einleitung in die Psalmen* (HKAT, 1928 and 1933) with great force and ingenuity defends the view that the Psalter was completed by 200 B.C., and that the various types of psalms were developed in the time of the Judges or in the early monarchy, reaching their classical stage by 750 and continuing to flourish until 500, when the decadence set in (*ibid.*, pp. 431 f.). One of Gunkel's main arguments for the early date of a psalm is the mention of a king. For example, Ps. 89:1-2, 5-18 (H. 89:2-3, 6-19), he says, was written in the Northern Kingdom before 721 B.C. (on the evidence of vv. 12 and 18). In reality, there is no mention in this psalm of a king of North Israel; moreover, the thought is reminiscent of Job and the Second Isaiah. Other parts of Ps. 89 constitute for Gunkel the last of the royal psalms in which "the last Davidic king, after the fall of the state, lifts up his plaintive voice" (p. 168).

The other royal psalms which Gunkel considers pre-exilic are 2; 18; 20; 21; 45; 72; 101; 110; 132; 144:1-11. But apart from Ps. 45, an epithalamium composed when a king of Israel or Judah married a foreign (apparently Tyrian) princess, none of the poems listed bears the marks of pre-exilic composition. As a matter of fact, the acrostic in Ps. 2:1-10 shows that it was composed in 103 B.C. to commemorate the marriage of Alexander Janneus to Alexandra, and the acrostic in Ps. 110:1-4 (*šm'n*, Simeon), conjointly with the contents of the psalm, shows the poem to have been the oracle by which Simon Maccabeus was solemnly confirmed in the office of leader and high priest in 141 B.C. (see I Macc. 14:41).[11]

The contents and style of the other royal psalms do not favor a preexilic date. They contain no specific allusions to historical events, they deal in generalities of a timeless character, present a view of religion hardly earlier than Deuteronomy, and abound in reminiscences and quotations from parts of the Old Testament comparatively late in date. On the whole, the view of B. Duhm (*Die Psalmen*, KHK, 1899), who dates all of them in the period of the Hasmonean rulers, is more plausible than that of Gunkel. But the clues are so vague that no definite date can be assigned, as in the case of Pss. 2 and 110; at best, we can ascribe them to the postexilic period.

In Ps. 89 (omitting vv. 5-18 [H. 6-19])—an old nature hymn rewritten by a pious Jew—and 132, the rule of David's dynasty has long since come to an end. After reminding God of his promises made to David in the late midrash of II Sam. 7, the authors lament the sad end of his line (89) and assure themselves that God will renew it (132). Psalm 18 (II Sam. 22) and its summary in 144:1-11 were composed as David's own poems, without attaining even the shadow of verisimilitude.

Psalms 20, 21, 72 seem to refer to a contemporaneous monarch, upon whom divine blessings were invoked, or else express assurance that Jehovah would grant him his abiding protection. It is not to be excluded that the kings in question were Achaemenian Persian rulers or even Alex-

---

[11] A former student of the writer, Mr. M. G. Slonim, has detected a possible acrostic in Ps. 4. The initial letters of the verses read from the last to the first spell "*bnr zrwbbl*" (with the lamp of Zerubbabel [?]).

ander the Great. Second Isaiah and the Chronicler regarded Cyrus as a
worshiper of Jehovah, even as "his servant," and it is well known that
the Persian kings favored the Jews (see B. Meissner, *Die Achämeniden-
könige und das Judentum.* Berlin, 1938), and that the latter thrived under
them as under Alexander. It would have been perfectly natural for a Jew
to address poems like these to his sovereign, either on his accession or
on the occasion of some gracious act toward the Jews, as when Cyrus
freed them from Exile, or Darius allowed them to rebuild the Temple,
or Artaxerxes I sent his cup-bearer Nehemiah as governor to Jerusalem
to rebuild the walls of the city. Even the hyperbolic wishes of 72:5-11,
sometimes regarded as Messianic interpolation, would not be out of
place in a poem addressed to a mighty sovereign of Persia or to Alexander.
Still more fantastic expressions are found in Egyptian poems glorifying
the Pharaohs. Finally, this possibility is not to be excluded for Ps. 101, in
which the high principles of Jewish morality and religion are placed on
the lips of a king proclaiming his noble purposes.

If, then, reference to a king is not an absolute criterion for assigning a
psalm to the period of the Judean monarchy, we entirely lack any kind of
objective evidence for dating a psalm before 586 B.C. Relying on internal
evidence of a more or less elusive type, we can accept as final the conclusion of S. R. Driver (*Introduction to the Old Testament,* p. 384), "very
few of the Psalms are earlier than the 7th cent. B.C." Only those psalms
entirely free from the peculiarities of thought and expression of postexilic
Judaism can possibly be dated so early.

Two psalms fulfill these conditions, and apparently only two: Ps. 24:
7-10, an antiphonal hymn celebrating perhaps the entrance of the ark
from Shiloh into the Temple of Jerusalem, and Ps. 45, a secular poem sung
at a royal wedding. In Ps. 45 a few glosses should be omitted: "righteousness" (v. 4; H. 5); "in the heart of the king's enemies" (v. 5; H. 6); "O
God" (v. 6; H. 7); "God, thy God" should be read "Jehovah, thy God" in
v. 7 (H. 8); "in gold of Ophir" (v. 9; H. 10), etc. In the rest of the
Psalter, such magnificent nature poems as 19:1-6 (H. 19:1-7; omitting v. 3
[H. 4]) and 104 (a distant echo of the Tell el-Amarna hymn to Aton by
Amenophis IV), although hardly pre-exilic, are among the earliest, for
they probably antedate the account of Creation in Gen. 1 (P) and perhaps
even Second Isaiah.

Aside from Pss. 19:1-6; 24:7-10; 45; 104, the quality of the psalms is
markedly different from that of early Israelitic religious poetry. The most
ancient Hebrew hymns (Ex. 15:21; Judg. 5:2-5; Is. 6:3) and lamentations
(Am. 5:2) are masterpieces of classical simplicity, conciseness, nobility,
and originality. Conversely, postexilic psalms are characterized by elaborate and rhetorical phrasing, prolixness, artificiality and conventionality.
One need only contrast the vigor and terseness of Ex. 15:21 with the

fifth century turgid and high-sounding elaboration of this old Song of
Miriam in Ex. 15:1-18, or the ringing overture to the Song of Deborah
(Judg. 5:2-5) with the melodramatic imitation thereof concocted by a
postexilic Jew (Hab. 3).

The majority of psalms have much more in common with hymns that
can positively be dated after 200 B.C. (such as Ecclus. [Sirach] 39:14b-35;
42-43; 45:25b-26 [cf. Ps. 8:5b]; 50:22; Tob. 13; Jth. 16; Luke 1), than with
the genuine poetry of ancient Israel. Prolixness in Hebrew prose begins
with Deuteronomy and in poetry with the Second Isaiah (ca. 550). The
latter's work contains characteristic passages in the hymnal style (Is.
42:10-13; 44:23; 49:13; 52:9-10), and prayers for help in times of national distress (51:9-10; cf. 49:14) that are earlier than similar passages in
the Psalter.

Of the psalms found outside the Psalter (Ex. 15:1-18; Deut. 32; I Sam.
2:1-10; Is. 38:9-20; Hab. 3; Jon. 2:2-9; Nah. 1) the first two, being contained in the Pentateuch, must be earlier than 400 B.C., although certainly
postexilic: they may serve as illustrations of the psalms of the fifth century.
The others antedate the canonization of the prophets in 200 B.C., but are
probably later than 400. Thus external evidence confirms our conclusion
that the psalms belong to the postexilic period. Real psalms began to be
written after the middle of the sixth century when the Second Isaiah introduced a new style in Hebrew poetry, and most of the poems in our
Psalter originated in the period 400-200 (practically all in the period
500-100). To the best of our knowledge, no devotional psalms were written before Jeremiah's "Confessions" (600 B.C.).

The question of dating is only one of the problems raised by the Psalter,
on which scholars are sharply divided. Next to dating, the classification
of the Psalms presents serious difficulties with many related and subordinate problems. Two of the latter have been particularly investigated
in recent years: which psalms were used in the Temple services, having
been originally composed for a specific ritual purpose or having been
subsequently adapted to it? Which psalms are congregational and which
individual in character? Our scanty evidence answers neither question.

External evidence for the liturgical use of some psalms has already been
considered: the titles in the Hebrew and the LXX, and the Talmudic
literature attest the ritual use of a limited number; for the rest we must
rely on internal evidence, which is capable of a variety of interpretations.
In contrast with B. Duhm (*Die Psalmen,* p. xxiv), who asserted that "a
large part of the Psalms was probably never sung in the Temple," later
critics like H. Gunkel, J. P. Peters, S. Mowinckel, E. Gressmann, O. Eissfeldt have discovered a great variety of liturgical uses—sometimes on the
basis of unconvincing evidence.

In general, these critics have to assume the pre-exilic date of many psalms—a presupposition hardly warranted, as we have seen, by the general character of the Psalter. For instance, Peters would have us believe that a number of psalms were liturgies used in the sanctuaries of the Northern Kingdom before 721 B.C. (e.g., Ps. 84 was originally a liturgy used at Dan). Mowinckel and other scholars wish to persuade us that after David's reign the Judeans adopted a Canaanitic New Year festival (based on a similar festival in the Temple of Marduk at Babylon), in which they celebrated annually, at the Feast of Tabernacles, the enthronement of Jehovah in his Temple at Jerusalem and sang, besides others, Pss. 47, 93 and 96-99 in his honor. But the fact that postexilic Jews deprived of a Davidic king should in these and other psalms glorify Jehovah as their sovereign, hardly proves the celebration of a religious drama in ancient times. In postexilic times such a pagan festival is, of course, inconceivable. Unless these psalms were composed fairly early in the preexilic period, Mowinckel's theory in so far as it affects the history of the Psalter cannot be maintained. When the title of king was applied to Jehovah by Second Isaiah after the end of the monarchy (Is. 43:15; 44:6), and by later writers (Zeph. 3:15; Ps. 5:2 [H. 5:3]; 84:3 [H. 84:4]), it still meant "king of Israel," as in earlier times (Is. 6:5; Deut. 33:5; Ps. 24:7 ff.), when Jehovah was not yet the one and only God. But in the psalms under discussion Jehovah was already ruler of all nations (47; 96; 99) exalted above all gods (95-97), king (47) and judge (96; 98) of the whole earth, and Creator of the world (93; 95; 96). These theological conceptions, unknown before the Second Isaiah, are found only in late passages such as Jer. 10:7, 10; 46:18; 48:15; Zech. 14:9, 16 f.; Mal. 1:14; Ps. 145:13, etc. The doctrine of God's Kingdom on earth and its future realization is much closer to New Testament times than to the time of David.

With the exception of Ps. 24:7-10, which might have been sung when Solomon brought the ark into the new Temple, there is no psalm that could conceivably have been used in the ritual of the pre-exilic period. The liturgical use of psalms is a question to be raised only in connection with the Second Temple, after 400 B.C., for the Pentateuch published about that time knows nothing of psalmody. Although it is certain that psalms were sung by the Levitical choirs during the sacred services in the Temple at least as early as the time of the Chronicler (*ca.* 250 B.C.), we have no other specific information except that furnished by the titles and Talmudic literature. We are therefore in the dark with reference to the great majority of psalms.[12]

[12] It seems unnecessary to discuss Mowinckel's view that all the psalms, with the exception of two or three (1, 127, and perhaps 112), were composed for ritual use. G. Quell (*Das kultische Problem der Psalmen,* 1926) reaches more plausible conclusions on the matter.

Closely related to their ritual use and even more important for an understanding of the Psalter is the second problem mentioned, namely, the distinction between psalms voicing the religious emotions of the nation or congregation and those that are purely or primarily expressions of the writer's personal religion. The ambiguity appears especially in those numerous psalms in which the pronouns "I, me, my" are used. Is the speaker an individual or is the community (cf. Ps. 129:1) speaking as a single person (as often in the Old Testament; cf. S. R. Driver, *Notes on the Hebrew Text of the Books of Samuel.* 2nd ed., Oxford, 1913; *ad* I Sam. 5:10)?

The collective interpretation of the "I" in the psalms, which occurs sporadically in the LXX, the ancient Jewish versions and commentaries, and the Church Fathers, was defended by R. Smend (ZAW 8 [1888] 49 ff.). He contended that in general the psalms are congregational songs of which only a few isolated ones were originally individual in character. This extreme viewpoint provoked a vigorous reaction.[13] E. Balla, for instance, defends the thesis that "the 'I'-psalms in the Psalter and in the other books of the Old Testament are all to be understood individually," except when, owing to explicit statements in the text, another understanding of the "I" is required. He concludes that only in Ps. 129 is Israel personified, speaking as an individual.

On the whole, Balla's interpretation has much in its favor. It is also the most natural. To the present day, congregations regularly sing hymns giving expression to personal rather than collective religion. Moreover, since the time of Jeremiah and Ezekiel, and particularly in the period when the psalms were written, Judaism was becoming increasingly a way of salvation for the individual. In spite of the psalms dealing with religion in its national aspects, the Psalter is on the whole the Hebrew handbook of personal religion. But in the last analysis the situation is not entirely clear for many psalms; and their interpretation as utterances of the nation, church, or individual writers is open to discussion. Thus, for instance, the numerous denunciations of "enemies" may be understood as attacks against foreign hostile nations or ungodly Jews; but also against private foes who, like the friends of Job, accused an unfortunate victim of secret wickedness.

Since many of the problems confronting the student of the Psalter cannot be solved finally, owing to the paucity of data, and since so many psalms give expression to a variety of thoughts and emotions, the psalms cannot be definitely classified according to either form (hymns, prayers,

[13] G. Beer, *Individual- und Gemeindepsalmen* (Marburg, 1894). F. Coblenz, *Über das betende Ich in den Psalmen* (Frankfurt a.M., 1897). H. Roy, *Die Volksgemeinde und die Gemeinde der Frommen im Psalter* (Gnadau, 1897). E. Balla, *Das Ich der Psalmen* (Göttingen, 1912). In contrast with the preceding authors, Th. Engert (*Der betende Gerechte der Psalmen*, Würzburg, 1902) defends the thesis of Smend.

meditations, etc.) or content. The most elaborate and minute analysis of the Psalter is that of H. Gunkel (*Einleitung in die Psalmen*). His psalm types (*Gattungen*) include hymns, songs for Jehovah's enthronement, lamentations of the nation, royal psalms, lamentations and songs of gratitude of the individual. Some less common types (blessings and curses, pilgrim songs, odes of victory, Israel's songs of gratitude, legends, the Law) and other classes (prophetic and eschatological psalms, wisdom psalms, mixed types, antiphonal psalms, and liturgies) complete his categories.

No scheme of classification can do full justice to the wealth of literary forms and religious contents of the Psalter. Many of the psalms fit badly in any type of arrangement that has been devised. Nevertheless, we shall try to present a bird's-eye view of this great book. Thus it may be convenient to divide the Psalms into two main groups: those that describe primarily the character and activity of the deity and those that present the religious emotions of the congregation or the individual. There is, of course, no line of demarcation between the two groups. The Psalm of Moses (90), for instance, begins with a contrast between God and man, showing God's immeasurable elevation above the human realm, but ends with a prayer for divine guidance and favor.

The greatness of God appears first of all in the beauty and immensity of the physical world that he has created. "The heavens declare the glory of God" (19:1-6 [H. 19:1-7]). Nature and life are his work (104, based on the hymn of Ikhnaton [Amenophis IV]; cf. 24:1 f.; 95; 136), raging storms his manifestation (18 [= II Sam. 22]; 29; cf. 97; 135). He has defeated Rahab and other mythological monsters of chaos (74; 89; 104) and rules over the raging sea (89:6-12 [H. 89:7-13; cf. 93]). He clothes the earth with vegetation (65:7-13 [H. 65:8-14]; 147).

The contemplation of the heavens, the work of God's hands, raises the question, "What is man?" (8). "His days are as grass" (103; cf. 39; 90); he is a weak and ephemeral being (49; 78; 89; 94; 144; 146). God has created man (33; cf. 94) and controls his life and death (139); God provides for the needs of animals and men (104; 145; cf. 65; 146; 147). God is the universal ruler, "the king over all the earth," as we have noted above in the so-called psalms for the enthronement of Jehovah (47; 93; 96-99; cf. 95; 145); he is in the heavens and does what he pleases (115; 135); he is the greatest of all the gods (82;[14] 86; 89; 95; 96; 97; 135; cf. the tirades against idols in 115 and 135). His power is unlimited (77; 78; 93; 135; 147), his wisdom beyond measure (139; 147; cf. 94; 104). Nothing can escape his knowledge and his presence (139).

One of the most important functions of God as ruler of mankind is the judgment of human actions (67; 96; 98; cf. 7; 9; 58; 97). The justice of

[14] For the mythological background of Ps. 82 see J. Morgenstern in HUCA 14 (1939) 29-126.

God sitting in judgment (36; 92, etc.) is often coupled with his mercy (36; 92; 103; 107; 111; 113; 117; 118; 136; 145). According to the Jewish dogma, God in his justice rewards the righteous with earthly blessings and punishes the wicked with various misfortunes (1; 11; 34; 75; 77; 91; 92; 112; 127; 128). But the bitter experiences of the Pious (lamented in 42; 74; 88; 89) and the spectacle of the prosperity enjoyed by the wicked, led some psalmists to doubt the validity of the dogma of earthly retribution— at least in its more rigid and materialistic forms—without, however, reaching the passionate and heretical outbursts of Job. Thus in 34; 37; 49; 73 faith triumphs over doubt, and in the last one faith is its own reward and no longer requires the confirmation of external blessings.

This bewilderment of certain psalmists over the apparent inconsistencies in God's just rule marks the transition to the second great group of psalms in which the religious emotions find their expression. In its national or congregational aspects, from the fifth to the second centuries, Judaism had its center of gravity in the Temple and the Scriptures (the Law after 400, the Prophets after 200).

Some psalms reflect the significance of the Temple in the life and thought of the Jews, both in Palestine and in the Dispersion. It is true that, under the influence of prophetic teaching, there were psalmists who seriously questioned the religious value of Temple rituals and particularly animal sacrifices. They advocated a more spiritual and moral type of worship (40:1-12 [H. 40:1-13]; 50, a summary of the prophetic ideals in their Deuteronomic formulation; 51; 69; 141; cf. 15; 24:1-6; contrast the ritualistic viewpoint of the glossator in 51:18 f. [H. 51:20 f.]). The Temple is the earthly abode of Jehovah (cf. 9; 48; 80; 99; 135; cf. 87) and from there he listens to prayer (cf. 3; 14; 28; 128; 134, etc.), although his true abode is in the heavens (cf. 2; 7; 11; 18; 29; 33; 57; 68; 76; 92; 93; 96; 102; 103; 115; 123; 136; 144; 150).

Certain psalms seem to have been composed for Temple singing during the processional entrance of the ark into the Holy of Holies in pre-exilic times (24:7-10) or during the annual festivals (61; 66; 67; 81; 100; 118). Others seem to express the longing of the Jews of the Dispersion to attend ceremonial worship in the Temple, either while staying in their distant homes (84; 87; 120) or while on the journey to Zion (121; 123; 125; 128; 129; 132). Their joyful arrival, and their jubilant contemplation of the Temple and its sacred ceremonies perhaps inspired the composition of 48; 122; 133; 134.[15]

Together with the Temple, the Law came to occupy an increasingly important place in the religious life of the Jews (19:7-14 [H. 19:8-15];

---

[15] Psalms comprising the "Egyptian Hallel" (113-118), recited during the paschal meal, and those of the "great Hallel" (136 or 120-136) may have been used in the Temple services.

119; cf. 1; 37; 40; 78; 89; 94; 105). The Pious read, besides the Pentateuch, the historical books to gain information on the past vicissitudes of their nation and especially Jehovah's glorious deeds in its behalf. The numerous historical allusions in the Psalter have been classified by E. Day (in AJSL 37 [1921] 263-299). A few psalms summarize the course of national history from the Exodus to the building of the Temple (78, in which, in the vein of the Chronicler, the rejection of Ephraim and the election of Judah are used in the polemic against the Samaritans), from Abraham to the entrance into Canaan (105, a review of God's guidance and help), or from the Exodus to the Exile (106 and 107, confessions of national apostasy and praises of Jehovah's forgiving grace). Other psalms also draw inspiration for the present from the nation's past experiences (77; 81; 95:7-11; 99; 114; 135; 136). Psalm 137 was not the work of an Exile sitting "by the rivers of Babylon," but of a considerably later writer residing in Jerusalem.

Those of the "royal psalms," as we have seen, not composed in honor of a pre-exilic ruler (45, an ancient song for a royal wedding), Hasmonean princes (2; 110), or Persian monarchs, can also be classed with these historical reminiscences (18; 20; 21; 72; 101; 132; 144:1-10; cf. parts of 89). Some of these were interpreted in a Messianic sense, notably 2; 21; 72; 110; 132, although such an interpretation is not required for any of them. Psalm 22 is sometimes said to be a prophecy of the Messiah's sufferings, but like the poems of the "Servant of the Lord" in Second Isaiah it may well have been a pathetic picture of the sufferings of Israel for the salvation of all the nations of mankind. If such is the case, this psalm would be related to the public lamentations over the sad plight of the Jewish community.

It seems clear that a number of such lamentations were composed during the persecution of the Jewish religion by Antiochus Epiphanes in 168-165 B.C., just before the Maccabean rebellion (44; 74 [74:8 refers to the burning of the synagogues]; 79; 83; also, perhaps, 12; 28; 36; 60 [= 108]; 80; 85; 108; 123; 102 is in part the lament of a sick man [vv. 1-11, 23-24a; H. 1-12, 24-25a] and, for the rest, a lamentation for Zion that lies in ruins). The military successes of Judas Maccabeus against the Syrians may have inspired Pss. 118 and 149; other congregational songs of thanksgiving and praise to God (46-48; 66-68; 76; 87; 113; 124-126; 129; 144) may likewise reflect the revival of nationalism and religion during the Maccabean struggles.

Personal religion finds classical expression in the Psalter. After the downfall of the state in 586, beginning with Jeremiah, religion ceased to be for the Jews a natural concomitant of nationality and gradually became an ideal of righteousness to be attained through unremitting personal effort and the help of the merciful God who has made known his will in his Law and listens to the prayers of his faithful. This new conception of religion as a personal life impregnated with the thought of God and his requirements divided the Jews into two mutually hostile camps: the Pious, or righteous, zealous in their single-minded observance of the Law and frequently poor in worldly goods; and the ungodly, or wicked, more concerned with success in the affairs of this world than with the attainment of righteousness and divine approval, which to them bore no relation to earthly prosperity. Pious and wicked were sharply divided on the question of divine retribution for human deeds, and the wicked stoutly denied that piety inevitably brought tangible rewards. The Psalter is the book of the Pious; the wicked, whose voice is heard in parts of Job, Proverbs, and Ecclesiastes, are denounced and cursed therein with passionate zeal.

The inwardness of Jewish piety reaches its noblest expression in the words, "My flesh and my heart faileth: but God is the strength of my heart, and my portion forever" (73:26). The pious man longs for the presence of God, his soul thirsts for him "as the hart panteth after the water brooks" (42-43 [a single psalm]; 63; 84). The sense of God's nearness banishes fear: the pious man puts his trust in his God unreservedly and commits his spirit into his hand (31); for he knows that his God will deliver him from all evil (3; 11; 13; 16; 23; 27; 32; 62; 91; 107; 116; 121; 127; 130; 131). Therefore the Psalmists raise their voice to God in songs of praise and thanksgiving (4; 9-10 [a single psalm]; 30; 40; 115; 116; 138; 148; 150; cf. 95; 96; 103; 111; 146).

To men of such childlike faith it was most shocking to experience serious trouble—particularly grave illness—notably because their "enemies" (the wicked) saw in their misfortune proof of the futility of their faith and mocked them, saying (42:10 [H. 42:11]), "Where is thy God?" (cf. 13; 22; 31; 35; 38; 39; 41; 69; 71; 86; 109). According to the Pious, this attitude of the ungodly amounted to rank atheism (14 = 53). In many of the psalms in which pious individuals lament the wretchedness of their situation, as in similar Babylonian "Penitential Psalms,"[16] the unhappy speaker is seriously ill (6; 13; 22; 31; 38; 55; 69; 102) and thinks of himself as already dead (6; 22; 42; 69; 88; 143; cf. 16; 28; 31; 86).

In other lamentations there is no reference to illness, only bitter complaints against the "enemies" (4; 5; 7; 11; 17; 27; 37; 52; 54; 56 f.; 59; 62-64; 120; 123; 138; 140; 141; 142; 144) whose ungodliness was probably regarded as hindering the manifestations of God's loving kindness. The intense animosity and savage bitterness voiced against these "enemies" in the imprecatory psalms (35; 55; 69; 83; 109; cf. 5-7; 9-10; 11; 17; 18;

---

[16] Cf. G. Widergren, *The Akkadian and Hebrew Psalms of Lamentation as Religious Documents* (Uppsala, 1936). Also, R. G. Castellino, *Le lamentazioni individuali e gli inni in Babilonia e in Israele* (Torino, 1940).

28; 31; 34; 37; 40; 52; 54; 58; 59; 63; 70; 71; 75; 86; 91; 92; 94; 112; 118;
120; 137; 140; 141; 145; 146; 147) arose from zeal for God's cause
(5:10 f. [H. 5:11 f.]; 10:3 f.) and from the natural feeling of the lower
classes that the rich are their oppressors (73:1-12). There is no need to
assume, with S. Mowinckel (*Psalmenstudien*, Vol. I) that enemies threatening the Pious with sickness, ruin, and death were sorcerers casting over
them spells of black magic. The evidence in the psalms shows that the
ungodly were wealthy Jews of the higher classes (cf. 52), lax in observance of the Law, somewhat skeptical with regard to God's intervention in
human affairs (cf. 94:1 ff.) and, in the Hellenistic period, not averse to
Greek culture (I Macc. 1:11-15; 6:21; 7:5 f., 22, 24, etc.).

Most of the lamentations contain prayers of petition. A long list of
psalms which entreat God to punish the wicked has just been given above.
This obsession with hated enemies, which intrudes even in the Shepherd
Psalm (23:5) and the magnificent Psalm of Creation (104:35), is for
modern readers the most discordant note in the religion of the psalms.
Heman, a legendary Edomite sage, is the only author of a lamentation
for personal woes (strikingly like Job's laments and probably Edomitic
in origin) who has nothing to say about enemies (88). Next to petitions
for the punishment of the wicked and deliverance from foes (imprecatory
psalms), the most common requests are those for recovery from torturing
disease and serious trouble (6; 13; 22; 31; 38; 39; 61; 69; 86; 88; 102; 143;
144). Other psalms contain prayers for forgiveness of sin (25; 51), justification (26), and guidance (141). The favorite psalm of St. Augustine,
Ps. 32, depicts the joy following confession.

This cursory examination of the contents of the Psalter cannot do justice
to the importance and religious significance of this great anthology. But
for the psalms our picture of postexilic Judaism would be awry. Amidst
the legalism of Leviticus and Chronicles we would hardly suspect the
vitality of prophetic counsel about the futility of ritual worship and importance of morality, as also the flowering of an inner piety coupled with
a profound sense of sin and longing for intimate communion with God,
originating with Jeremiah. It is this noble spiritual strain that has made
the Psalter, in spite of its traces of a lower religious level in the nationalistic, imprecatory, legalistic psalms, the song and prayer book of the
Christian Church, in which pious souls throughout the ages have found
comfort and inspiration.

Its literary significance is eclipsed by its religious import. Aside from
isolated pre-exilic (24:7-10; 45) and sixth century (probably 19:1-6 [H.
19:1-7]; 104) psalms, the poems contained in the Psalter were composed
after 500 B.C., in the silver age of Hebrew literature, following the last
masterpieces of the classical period (Job, the ode of Nahum, and Second
Isaiah). The old vigor, terseness, and superb brilliance of ancient Hebrew

poetry, which still echoes in the four psalms mentioned above, give way to high-sounding, ornate, consciously artistic imitations of the old master-pieces, or to such unpretentious, simple, prosaic pieces as the First Psalm (which, contrary to the general opinion, is not in verse but in plain prose) and Pss. 128, 129, 131. The most dreadful example of uninspired Old Testament versification is Ps. 119.

With rare exceptions the Psalmists excelled in religious fervor rather than literary genius. The literary level of the psalms is so uniform that it is difficult to select fifty outstanding poems in the collection. The following list attempts to give fifty representative psalms chosen not only for literary quality but also for originality of thought, popularity, and religious value. At the same time, this selection aims to illustrate the principal literary types found in the Psalter.

Of the hymns in praise of God (*Te Deum*) the most beautiful are those depicting the marvelous works of the Creator of the world (19:1-6; 104), his greatness in contrast to human weakness (8), his majesty and dominion (95:1-7; 96), his infinite mercy (103), his blessings at harvest time (65; 67), his victory over Israel's foes (124; 149).

Among the songs accompanying acts of worship in the Temple, 24:7-10 ("Lift up your heads, O ye gates!"), sung antiphonally perhaps when Solomon brought the ark into the Holy of Holies, is the most ancient and most beautiful in its simplicity. As ritual songs we may class the Processional Psalm 100 ("Enter into his gates with thanksgiving," v. 4) and the songs of Zion sung by the pilgrims (46; 48; 84; 122), the first one of which inspired the great hymn of the Reformation, Luther's "A mighty fortress is our God!" Related to these songs are the congregational prayers and confessions of faith: 121 ("I will lift up mine eyes unto the hills"; an antiphonal pilgrim song); 123 (in which, as in the religion of the Hittites, the worshiper's attitude is that of a slave to his master); 125; 126. Among congregational lamentations and petitions, we may select 79 as a typical example of a Maccabean complaint (168-165 B.C.) and 85 as one of doubtful, although probably similar date. Among the royal psalms, 45 is a purely secular pre-exilic epithalamium; 2, dedicated to Alexander Janneus and his wife presumably on their wedding day; and 72, a prayer for the king, which was interpreted in a Messianic sense, like the other royal psalms. Most virulent of the imprecatory psalms, and the best example of vituperation inspired by holy anger in the Psalter, is 109, a personal expression of indignation later adapted to congregational use.

Best known of personal confessions of faith expressing entire trust in God's abiding protection from dangers and death is 23 ("The Lord is my shepherd; I shall not want"), but no other psalm surpasses 91 (appropriately quoted by Satan in his temptation of Jesus) in voicing the believer's assurance that his God would save him in any crisis. Three other poems, 16 ("Preserve me, O God: for in thee do I put my trust"), 27 ("The Lord is my light and my salvation"), and 34 ("I will bless the Lord at all times") are likewise excellent examples of this type. Allied to this group are psalms of thanksgiving like 116 ("I love the Lord because he has heard my voice") and those expressing a longing for the presence of God, like 42-43, which was originally one psalm ("As the hart panteth after the water brooks, so panteth my soul after thee, O God").

In another group we may class the private lamentations and petitions. The most agonizing complaint and desperate appeal comes from the author of 22 ("My God, my God, why hast thou forsaken me?"). Psalm 130 ("Out of the depths have I cried unto thee, O Lord"; *De profundis*) refers to the nation and is deeply moving in its simplicity. Psalm 102 is the typical prayer of a man afflicted with a serious illness. The Pious regarded sin as the cause of his misfortunes and believed that restoration of his fortunes depended on divine forgiveness. Psalm 51 ("Have mercy upon me, O God") is the classical confession of a contrite heart, whereas 32 ("Blessed is he whose transgression is forgiven") is the cry of joy from a soul whose iniquity has been forgiven. Several psalmists, however, had a clear conscience and requested that God justify them (26, "Judge me, O Lord; for I have walked in mine integrity") or reward them with his help in time of trouble (40, "I waited patiently for the Lord").

Our last category consists of reflective psalms, meditations on some particular or general phase of religion. The greatness of God is the subject of 90 ("Lord, thou hast been our dwelling place in all generations"), in which his eternity is contrasted with the brief span of human life, and 139 ("O Lord, thou hast searched me, and known me"), dealing with God's omniscience and ubiquity. Events in the nation's history are recalled in 114 ("When Israel went out of Egypt"; *In exitu Israel de Aegypto*) and 137 ("By the rivers of Babylon").

Some psalms discover the essence of true religion in the fulfillment of the moral law, according to the teaching of the prophets and Deuteronomy (15, "Lord, who shall abide in thy tabernacle?" and 50, "Offer unto God thanksgiving," v. 14), others in the study and fulfillment of the Law of Moses. By this standard, Jews are divided into pious and wicked and rewarded accordingly by God (1; 128; 129). But the facts of reality did not always fit into this doctrine of earthly retribution; some psalmists, acutely conscious of the injustices patent in the destiny of man and unable to solve the problem of theodicy in a rational manner, sought refuge in mystical communion with God (73).

In the Hebrew Bible, all psalms, with the exception of thirty-four called "orphans" in Jewish writings, have some kind of title. These superscriptions give the name of the traditional author, the occasion on which

David composed the psalm, the literary type, the melody and other musical instructions, and the liturgical use in the Temple service.

1. Authors mentioned in these titles: Moses (90). David (3-9; 11-32; 34-41; 51-65; 68-70; 86; 101; 103; 108-110; 122; 124; 131; 133; 138-145); 73 psalms in all; cf. 72:20. In the LXX, David is mentioned also in 33; 42 (Codex A); 43; 67; 71; 91; 93-99; 104; 137 (but in 122; 124; 131; 133 the attribution to David is omitted). Solomon (72; 127; only 72 in the LXX). The Sons of Korah (42; 44-49; 84; 85; 87; 88). Asaph (50; 73-83). Heman (88, with the Sons of Korah). Ethan (89). Jeduthun or Jedithun, more probably a musical term (39 and 62, with David; 77 with Asaph; in 62 and 77 "upon" Jeduthun). Other authors are mentioned in the LXX: the sons of Jonadab and the first captives (71), Zechariah (138 and, in Codex A, 139), Haggai and Zechariah (146-148), Jeremiah (137; in Codex B, other manuscripts, and in the Vulgate).

2. The occasions in David's life when he composed a given psalm. This historical information, derived from the Books of Samuel, is found in 3 (II Sam. 15); 7 (obscure); [18 = II Sam. 22]; 34 (I Sam. 21:13); 51 (II Sam. 12); 52 (I Sam. 22:9); 54 (I Sam. 23:19); 56 (I Sam. 21:10 or 27:2 f., 7-12); 57 (I Sam. 22:1; 24:3 ff.); 59 (I Sam. 19:11); 60 (II Sam. 8:3, 13); 63 (I Sam. 23:14 ff.; 24:1; 26:2); 142 (I Sam. 22:1; 24:3 ff.).

3. Literary types. *Mizmôr* (psalm) occurs fifty-seven times in the titles (3-6; 8; 9; 12; 13, etc.). *Shîr* (song) occurs with the preceding term (30; 48; 65-68; 75; 76; 83; 87; 88; 92; 108) and with *maskîl* (as *shîr yedhîdhôth*, love song, in 45, which is a wedding song), as well as alone (46; cf. 18) or followed by a genitive (30 [song for the dedication of the Temple]; 45 [see above]; 120-134 [songs of degrees, i.e., pilgrimage songs]). *Tehillâh* (praise, i.e., psalm of praise) occurs only once (145) although it was used in the masculine plural (*tehillîm*) as the Hebrew title of the Psalter. *Tephillâh* (prayer) occurs oftener (17; 86; 90; 102; 142; cf. 72:20; 102 is correctly entitled "A prayer of the afflicted when he is overwhelmed and pours out his complaint before the Lord"). The meaning of the following terms is obscure: *maskîl* (meditation?) (32; 42; 44; 45 [cf. above]; 52-55; 74; 78; 88; 89; 142; cf. 47:8), *mikhtām* (16; 56-60), *shiggayôn* (7; cf. Hab. 3:1).

4. Technical musical instructions. The term *lamenaṣṣeach*, translated "to the chief musician," occurs fifty-five times (4-6; 8; 9; 11-14; 18-22, etc.) and once outside the Psalter (Hab. 3 at the end); its meaning is uncertain.[17] Another common technical term, *selâh*, occurs often, not in the title but in the body of the psalm. It appears seventy-one times in thirty-

---

[17] The LXX translates the word "unto the end" (of time) and the Targum "for praising" (liturgically). Both may mean the perpetual use of these Psalms in the liturgy. Aquila, Symmachus, Theodotion, and Jerome render "for the victor" or "for victory," presumably in a Messianic sense. The English rendering "for the chief musician" (i.e., the director of the orchestra and choir) is based on I Chron. 15:21.

nine psalms (3; 4; 7; 9; 20; 21; 24, etc.), and three times in Hab. 3. It also
occurs in the Psalms of Solomon and early Jewish liturgies. It has been
suggested with some plausibility, on the basis of the LXX, which translates "interlude," that *selâh* indicates a pause in the singing during a short
orchestral intermezzo. A similar meaning would fit the obscure word
higgayôn (9:17, together with *selâh*); in 92:3 (H. 92:4) it seems to mean
the music of stringed instruments. Other terms appear to have a musical
meaning but are incomprehensible to us; they may indicate the musical
mode or tonality, or else the instrumentation: upon *gittîth*[18] (8; 81; 84),
upon *mahalath* (53; 88), unto (an error for "upon") *hannehîlôth* (5),
upon *'alamôth* (46; cf. I Chron. 15:20), upon *hashshemînîth* (6; 12; I
Chron. 15:21), upon *yedhûthun* (62) or *yedhîthun* (77); cf. of Jeduthun
(39). Only "with *negînôth*" (4; 6; 54; 55; 67; 76; cf. 61: upon *n.*), meaning
with stringed instruments, is clear. In other cases, the melody is apparently
indicated by referring to the beginning or title of some well-known song:
upon (i.e., according to) "The hind of dawn" (22); upon "Dove of distant
terebinths" or "Deaf dove in the distance" (56); upon "Death for the son
[?]" (9; cf. upon "death" [48, end]);[19] upon "Lilies" (45; 69), unto "Lilies,
testimony" (80), or upon "A lily, testimony" (60); (upon) "Do not
destroy" or, with a slight correction, "upon 'Destroy'" (57; 58; 59; 75).

5. Liturgical instructions. The title of Ps. 30, "The song for the dedication of the Temple," testifies to the use of this psalm during the festival
of Hanukkah or Rededication, commemorating the rededication of the
Temple by Judas Maccabeus in 165 (I Macc. 4:59; II Macc. 10:6-8; John
10:22); "for the Sabbath day" in 92 and "for the thank offering"
(*lethôdhâh*) (100) are also clear. But there is some question as to the
meaning of *lehazkîr* (38; 70), a word generally explained with reference
to the ritual burning of the *azkarâh* ("memorial"), a portion of the cereal
oblation (Lev. 2:2, 9, 16, etc.); for another interpretation see ZAW 17
(1897) 52, 63 ff. Even more doubtful is the meaning of *lelammēdh* (to
teach) (60) and *le 'annôth* (to sing or to lament?) (88). The LXX and
the other ancient versions are of no assistance whatsoever in determining
the meaning of liturgical and musical terms: strangely enough, when
these versions were made, the meaning had been completely forgotten
among the Jews. Under the circumstances, all modern attempts to discover the original import of these technical terms are doomed to failure.[20]

This musical, historical, and liturgical material attached to the psalms
comes from the pen of editors. It was still in a fluid state when the ancient

[18] Most of the ancient versions render "for the vine presses" (i.e., on the tune of a
vintage song); the Targum understands it to mean "the harp which David brought
from *Gath*."

[19] In both Pss. 9 and 48 "*'al mûth*" (upon death) may be a corruption of "*'al
'alamôth*" (see above, Ps. 46).

[20] S. Mowinckel, *Psalmenstudien*, Vol. II.

versions were made, and varied considerably in the Hebrew manuscripts. It is clear, for instance, that the original LXX lacked the historical titles of Pss. 51; 52; 54; 57; 63; 142. On the other hand, we have seen that the LXX contained liturgical and historical data not found in the standard Hebrew text. The Syriac version has entirely different titles, which reflect the exegetical studies of the School of Antioch.

In addition to the titles, the Psalter contains other secondary material. Exclamatory liturgical sentences have been added at the end of many psalms. This may be demonstrated in the case of alphabetical acrostic poems when the addition stands outside the acrostic scheme (as in 25:22; 34:22 [H. 34:23]),[21] but is extremely probable in the case of brief doxologies or prayers not logically connected with the preceding poem. According to K. J. Grimm (*Euphemistic Liturgical Appendixes in the Old Testament*. Leipzig, 1901), such additions were made particularly to psalms ending originally in a threat, as 2; 3; 7; 13; 14; 19, etc. In some cases, these liturgical additions adapted a psalm purely personal in character to congregational use (e.g., 22:22-31 [H. 22:23-32]; 27:14; 51: 18-19 [H. 51:20-21]; cf. 7:6-11 [H. 7:7-12] in the body of the psalm).

Sometimes collective psalms were attached to individual psalms, as 66:1-12 before 66:13-20 or 102:13-28 (H. 102:14-29) after 102:1-12 (H. 102:1-13); likewise 69:32-36 (H. 69:33-37), 90:13-17 at the end, and 81:1-3 (H. 81:1-4), 95:1-7a at the beginning. In 89, an ancient nature psalm (vv. 5-18 [H. 6-19], in part) was converted into a Maccabean lamentation. Psalm 108, made up of portions of 57 and 60, is an illustration of editorial combinations (cf. 70, which is merely the last part of 40), such as we undoubtedly have in 19; 24; 27; 144. Marginal annotations of readers (e.g., 9:19-20 [H. 9:20-21]; 19:3, 11 [H. 19:4, 12]; 24:4b, 6) are more numerous than is generally recognized.

[21] Other alphabetic psalms (9-10; 37; 119; 145; cf. Nah. 1) exhibit much or little textual corruption; Pss. 111-112 are structurally intact.

CHAPTER II

THE BOOK OF PROVERBS

~~~~~~

The Book of Proverbs has the longest title of any in the Old Testament. The first six verses, a single incomplete sentence, are, in reality, nothing more than the title affixed to the book by its last compiler. This title was already known to Ben Sira (Ecclus. 47:17 refers to I Kings 4:32 [H. 5:12] and to Prov. 1:6) about 180 B.C., and the last edition of the book must therefore be earlier. Ordinarily, however, the first two words of the book (*mishlê shelōmôh,* The Proverbs of Solomon, or only Proverbs) constitute the title by which the book is referred to. This brief title is purely conventional, and does not characterize the contents.

In the first place, the book states that Solomon is not the author of all the sections (and had actually no more to do with the writing of this book than David with the composition of Psalms). In the second place, even the Hebrew *māshāl,* which has a much wider meaning than the English "proverb," does not in the least fit several important parts. The book contains the teachings of wise men and not "proverbs" in the sense of popular bywords or folk maxims.

Like the Psalter, Proverbs is a "collection of collections." Most of the separate collections are provided with subtitles, found in 10:1; 22:17; 24:23; 25:1; 30:1; 31:1; other parts, like the acrostic poem 31:10-31, the general title 1:1-6, and 1:7-9:18, are obvious. It should be noted, however, that the individual units bearing subtitles, except for the shortest ones, consist of two parts about equal in length but different in character. We shall indicate the separate collections of Proverbs by letters of the alphabet, using raised numerals for their subdivisions.

A. 1-9 (A¹: 1:1-6; A²: 1:7-9:18).

B. 10:1-22:16, "The Proverbs of Solomon" (B¹: 10-15; B²: 16:1-22:16).

C. 22:17-24:22, "Words of the Wise" (C¹: 22:17-23:14; C²: 23:15-24:22).

D. 24:23-34, "These also belong to the Wise."

E. 25-29, "These are also the Proverbs of Solomon, which the men of Hezekiah king of Judah collected" (E¹: 25-27; E²: 28-29).

F. 30, "The Words of Agur the son of Jakeh" (F¹: 30:1-10; F²: 30:11-33).

645

G. 31:1-9, "The Words of Lemuel king of Massa, which his mother taught him."

H. 31:10-31, alphabetic acrostic poem on the "virtuous woman" (i.e., the efficient housewife).

The order of the separate collections in the LXX version differs in some important respects from that in the Hebrew (and English); F1 comes before D and E after G, as follows: ABCF1DF2GEH. It would seem, therefore, that after the general preamble (A) come four main collections, two of Solomon (B and E) and two of the "wise" (C and D), inserted between the Solomonic collections. Three of these main collections (C, D, and E) were supplied with miscellaneous supplements (F1 after C, F2G after D, and H after E). In the LXX, the four main collections were followed by their respective supplements (B; C-F1; D-F2G; E-H), whereas in the Hebrew edition extant the supplements were separated from the four main collections (BCDE) and placed at the end of the book (FGH). In the LXX, the title of B ("The Proverbs of Solomon") is omitted, presumably because it was considered superfluous after 1:1; for it is difficult to believe that A and B originally formed a single work, or that the title of B in the Hebrew was subsequently added.

On the whole, however, the order of the LXX seems more original than that of the Hebrew. The latter affords no plausible explanation for the division of F into two collections (the second of which has no title) or the order in the LXX. Aside from the general arrangement, the LXX presents important textual variations from the Hebrew. It omits sentences and entire verses (1:16; 4:7; 7:25b; 8:29a, 33; 10:13a, etc.) and conversely offers new material which, after discarding double translations (1:14, 27, etc.), Biblical quotations (1:7; 3:16, etc.), and glosses (1:18; 4:27), seems to be derived from a Hebrew original (as, for instance, the maxims about the king at the end of C [24:22], and 7:1; 8:28; 9:12, 18, etc.).

Paul de Lagarde, in his classic *Anmerkungen zur griechischen Übersetzung der Proverbien* (Leipzig, 1863), has dealt fully and brilliantly with the relation between the Hebrew and Greek texts of Proverbs; the differences between the Hebrew text and the ancient versions, are listed by A. J. Baumgartner (*Etude critique sur l'état du texte du Livre des Proverbes.* Leipzig, 1890).

A. The several collections present characteristic differences. Following the general title (A1), from which we infer that the purpose of the book is to teach wisdom, comes a lengthy discourse (A2) addressed by the "father" (i.e., teacher) to his "son" (the pupil). This is divided, according to the scheme of the address of Moses in Deuteronomy into three parts (1:7-33; 2-7; 8-9). The theme of the discourse, stated at the beginning (1:7) and near the end (9:10), is that religion ("the fear of the

Lord") is the essence of wisdom. The structural unity of the speech is strengthened by presenting in the first and last parts the appeal made by personified Wisdom to the ignorant (1:20-33; and 8:1-9:6, followed by Madam Folly's address in 9:13-18; 9:7-12 should probably be read after 9:18). The main part of the speech (2-7) presents in ch. 2 (one long single sentence) the topics to be elaborated in 3-7: the blessings of wisdom (2:1-11, 20-22; cf. 3:1-26), a warning against the ways of wicked, dishonest, and criminal men (2:12-15; cf. 3:27-4:27 and 6:1-19), and one against the adulterous woman (2:16-19; cf. 5:1-19 and 6:20-7:27).

B. The first collection of "Proverbs of Solomon" (10:1-22:16) contains exclusively brief maxims comprising only a single line of Hebrew poetry divided into two equal parts (with four accents each). Thus each maxim or Biblical verse is a distich, except 19:7 which consists of three instead of two hemistichs and either lacks a fourth or has one interpolated. Counting 19:7 as one, the B collection contains 375 distichs. The two clauses of the verse, as first noted by R. Lowth (who in 1753 coined the familiar term *parallelismus membrorum*), are somehow parallel: synonymous when the two clauses are analogous in thought (as 19:2, 11, 29); antithetic when the two clauses are opposite in thought (as 11:1-6); synthetic when the second clause completes the thought of the first (as 11:22; 15:17, 24). The majority of distichs in B^1 (10-15), i.e., 169 out of a total of 184, are antithetic; and one-third of the total formulate variously the doctrine of earthly retribution. Conversely, in B^2 (16:1-22:16) only 31 out of 191 distichs are antithetical. Although no logical arrangement may be detected in the B collection, sometimes a few proverbs dealing with the same topic are found together (16:10, 12-15, on the king); some groups of distichs have a word in common (10:6 f., 14 f., 16 f., 18 f., etc.) or contain verses beginning with the same letter (11:9-12 with *b*; 20:4 f., 7-9, 24-26 with *m*, etc.). It is characteristic of the "Proverbs of Solomon" (the B and E collections) that the teaching is presented in purely objective form. Other parts of the book (omitting H, a poem), notably ACDG, contain instead exhortations and warnings addressed by a teacher to a pupil. Not a few proverbs are repeated in full or in part within the B collection (14:12 = 16:25; cf. the list in C. Steuernagel, *Einleitung in das Alte Testament*, p. 679).

C. In this collection of "Words of the Wise" (22:17-24:22), single distichs are rare (22:28; 23:9; 24:7-10) and longer sections predominate. After the introduction at the beginning (22:17-21), thirty distichs or distinct parts comprise the C collection, and this number is mentioned in 22:20, "Have I not written for you *thirty* [i.e., sayings] [so, with the change of a consonant in the Hebrew word] with counsels and knowledge?" The Hebrew compiler of C made free use in C^1 (22:17-23:14) of an Egyptian book, *The Wisdom of Amen-em-ope* (or Amen-em-Apt), which is variously dated in the period 1000-600 B.C.[1]

Of the twelve sayings in C[1], ten are clearly adaptations from the maxims of Amen-em-ope, and the last one (23:12-14) is taken, for the most part, from the *Sayings of Ahikar* (lines 81-82 of the fragments discovered among the papyri from Elephantine). *The Wisdom of Amen-em-ope* has exactly *thirty* chapters ("houses" in Egyptian) and near the end contains the words, "Examine these *thirty* chapters for thyself: they gladden, they instruct, they are the first of all books, they make the ignorant learned" (cf. 22:20 above).

Like its Egyptian prototype, C[1] is a mixture of practical advice for young men seeking success in their career as public officials (including correct etiquette in the dining room, 23:1-3), as well as sound moral and religious counsel. Besides the usual generalities about the value of wisdom addressed to "my son," C[2] warns against adultery and drunkenness, as well as against more subtle sins such as envy, and malicious joy at the misfortune of an enemy (23:17; 24:1, 17-20), even urging deliverance of those condemned to death (24:11 f.) since God perceives hidden thoughts (24:12, 18).

D. The second collection of "words of the wise" (24:23-34) is partly objective and partly hortatory. It contains distichs (24:26) as well as longer sections, such as the witty and vivid picture of the sluggard's field (24:30-34).

E. The two parts of the second collection of "proverbs of Solomon" (25-29) show even more marked differences than those of the first Solomonic collection (B). For while E[2] (28-29) comprises distichs (often antithetic) of the same general character as those of B[1] and B[2], with a strong ethical and religious emphasis (cf. 28:5, 13 f.; 29:13, 18, 25 f.) and constant harping on the doctrine of earthly retribution, E[1] (25-27) is the most secular, and presumably therefore one of the oldest, of the longer sections of the book. Several of the secular proverbs occurring sporadically in B are taken from E[1] (so 10:13b; 17:13a; 18:8; 19:13b, 24; 20:16; 21:9; 22:3, 13), whereas the proverbs which E[2] and B have in common are nearly all the ethico-religious type (12:11; 15:18a; 19:1; 22:2). As with the Book of Ecclesiastes, the injection of pious thoughts in E[1] is secondary: 25:21 f. (or only 25:22b) is a gloss, and 25:5, 26 have been

---

[1] The reader may be referred to G. A. Barton, *Archaeology and the Bible;* to W. O. E. Oesterley, *The Wisdom of Egypt and the Old Testament* (1927), and to the article of Griffith and Simpson in the *Jour. of Egypt. Archaeology* 12 (1926) 191 ff., 232 ff. The most important literature on Amen-em-ope is listed by Johannes Fichtner, *Die altorientalische Weisheit in ihrer israelitisch-jüdischen Ausprägung*, p. 3, n. 4, and p. 4, ns. 3 and 4. The attempt of R. O. Kevin (*Jour. of the Soc. of Orient. Research* [1930] 115 ff.) to prove that *The Wisdom of Amen-em-ope* is dependent on the Hebrew Book of Proverbs and other parts of the Old Testament can hardly be called successful.

tampered with; 26:4, which flatly contradicts the following verse, may be a Jewish correction (cf. 9:7 f.; 23:9; 29:9); 27:11 ("my son") is suspect. For the rest, there is no trace in E¹ of those typical tenets of postexilic Judaism (such as the doctrine of the two ways and earthly retribution) dominating the thought of B and E². The chief topic in 25 is good manners in social intercourse; 26 deals mainly with the fool, the sluggard, and the evil and deceitful tongue; 27 contains a miscellany of secular proverbs. Picturesque comparisons (with or without the particles of comparison, *as . . . so . . . .*) are very frequent in E¹ but occur only twice in B (10:26; 11:22) and twice in E² (28:3, 15, both moralizing in tone). The only really secular proverbs in E² are 28:19; 29:3b, 21.

F. "The words of Agur the son of Jakeh" (F¹, 30:1-10) are the confession of a skeptic unable to understand God and his creation (30:1-4), which reminds us of certain statements of Job, followed by the inevitable Jewish confession of faith, inserted to correct this heresy (30:5 f.), by a prayer (30:7-9) and a distich (30:10). F² (30:11-33) contains eight sayings; all but two (30:17, 32 f.) are "numerical" proverbs (the only other examples are in 6:16-19 and Sirach's Ecclus. 25:1-2; cf. 30:7-9), each one of which lists *four* items having something in common: types of rascals, things that never say "Enough," incomprehensible phenomena, insufferable occurrences, creatures little but exceeding wise, and living things proud in their bearing. The contents of F (except for 30:5-9)² are secular.

G. "The words of Lemuel king of Massa [a tribe living between Edom and Arabia, cf. Gen. 25:14, to which Agur also belonged according to 30:1], which his mother taught him" warn the ruler against sensuality and intoxication, and exhort him to champion the just cause of the needy (31:1-9).

H. The superb poem about the efficient housewife (31:10-31) is by far the best acrostic alphabetic poem in the Old Testament. It describes numerous profitable activities of the ideal wife. According to Oriental customs, she relieves her husband of all tedious work. A religious note has been injected into this secular piece by changing "an intelligent woman" (so the LXX) into "a woman that fears the Lord" in 31:30.

This brief characterization of maxim collections making up the Book of Proverbs has brought out not only a great variety of topics treated but also radical differences in the viewpoint, even more far-reaching than in the Psalter. Irreconcilable notions on the aims of human life and means to their attainment, on the norms of human conduct and motivation of human actions, are presented by wise men, presumably during the course of several centuries, for the instruction of the young. Certain teachers took a realistic view of life. By acute observation of the human scene,

---

² 30:5 is taken from Ps. 18:30 [H. 18:31] = II Sam. 22:31; 30:6 is based on Deut. 4:2; 12:32 [H. 13:1].

witty or sarcastic remarks, vivid characterizations and descriptions, clear reasoning and deflation of humbug, and following the dictates of common sense, they inculcated the homely lesson that success is attained through diligence in work, knowledge, intelligence, and decent living. Other teachers, instead, were ardent and orthodox advocates of the tenets of normative Judaism in its less ritualistic aspects. They did not minimize personal happiness and professional success as goals of human endeavor, nor did they ever present virtue as an end in itself and communion with God (without earthly blessings) as the ultimate bliss. But they firmly believed that a long peaceful life, prosperity, a good name, abundant offspring, and a blessed memory were the rewards held in store by God for the righteous who fulfilled his commandments.

These two schools of thought, so incongruously joined in the Book of Proverbs, persisted after publication in its final form. The author of Ecclesiastes is the most extreme representative of the first, and in his Ecclesiasticus Ben Sirach has left us the outstanding monument of the second. Centuries before the publication of Proverbs, the author of the Book of Job, the greatest ancient Hebrew thinker, presented both views in his magnificent poem, without leaving any doubt as to his personal preference.

We know positively that among the Israelites the secular school flourished before the pious. This is also true of the wisdom literature of Egypt—the oldest of all—which, through the intermediary of the Edomite sages (cf. Jer. 49:7; Obad. 8), exercised a decisive influence on Old Testament writers (cf. I Kings 4:30 [H. 5:10]). Thus, for instance, Ptahhotep recommends fair treatment of inferiors because they are useful, whereas Merikere, a few centuries later, believed in it even when no selfish advantage was thereby to be gained. The wisdom books of Ptahhotep and Kagemni (from the Old Kingdom) and those of Amenemhet and Duauf (from the Middle Kingdom) are purely secular. The first Egyptian wisdom book urging fulfillment of religious ritual duties, because "God knows the man that does something for him," and even stating that virtue is more welcome to God than the oxen of the wicked, is that of Merikere (from the transition period between the Old and Middle Kingdoms). Piety is emphasized in the later books of Ani and Amen-em-ope.

The oldest popular Hebrew proverbs known to us are secular in character: see I Sam. 10:12; 24:13 (H. 24:14); Jer. 23:28; 31:29 = Ez. 18:2; 16:44; I Kings 20:11 (Prov. 10:11 may be a pious elaboration of I Sam. 24:13). In the earliest parts of the Old Testament, "wisdom" merely means native intelligence, shrewdness (Judg. 5:29; II Sam. 13:3; 14:2, 20; 20:16-22), and the term retained the connotation of professional skill even in late times (in the P Code: Ex. 28:3; 31:3, 6; 35:26, 31, etc.). In Dan.

2:12-27, etc., as already in Gen. 41:8 and Ex. 7:11, the wise are the magicians.

Wisdom acquires a metaphysical sense in writings embodying non-Israelitic thought. It is the divine plan of creation, hidden from human knowledge (Job 28, omitting the Jewish gloss 28:28), or an attribute of God (Job 12:13; Ps. 104:24; Prov. 3:19-20; 30:2-3), although there is also human wisdom that comes (or should come) to men of experience and many years (Job 12:12; cf. 32:7). Judaism accepted, with some modifications, the notion of God's wisdom manifested in his creation (Is. 40:14, 28; Jer. 10:12 = 51:15) and even personified the mysterious wisdom of Job 28, after giving it ethical rather than metaphysical characteristics (Prov. 4:5-9; 7:4; 8:1-9:6). But in general the Jews identified wisdom with morality (Prov. 2:6-20; 4:11; 5:1 ff.; 8:33; 29:3, 11, etc.), with revealed normative Judaism (Prov. 1:7, 29 [LXX]; 2:5; 9:10; 15:33; Ps. 111:10, and the gloss in Job 28:28), and even with the Law of Moses (Deut. 4:6; Ezra 7:25; cf. G. F. Moore, *Judaism*, Vol. I, pp. 263 ff.).

That wisdom originally had nothing to do with religion and could even be regarded as antagonistic to piety is also shown by the prophetic denunciations against the wise (Is. 5:21; 10:13; 28:9; 29:14; 31:2; Jer. 4:22; 8:8 f.; 9:23; 18:18). The early idea of wisdom as technical skill is still found in Proverbs side by side with the new religious idea of wisdom (6:6; 21:22; 24:3-6; 30:24-28, etc.), and such human wisdom is contrasted with religion and morals (3:7; cf. particularly Ps. 119:97-104).

Another proof of the gradual identification of secular wisdom with religion and morals is furnished by the growing legend of the wisdom of Solomon, traditional author of two large sections of Proverbs. In the earliest stage (I Kings 5:12; cf. 5:7 [H. 5:26, 21]) Solomon's wisdom consisted of diplomatic skill in making a commercial agreement with Hiram king of Tyre. In a second stage, he was identified with the anonymous king of an Oriental folk tale, in which his wisdom became that of a shrewd judge (I Kings 3:16-28). In the third stage, presented in the postexilic story of his dream at Gibeon (I Kings 3:4-15), his wisdom contrasts with riches and power and acquires a religious aspect by being divinely bestowed. In his interviews with the Queen of Sheba (10:4-8), Solomon's wisdom was typically Oriental: the ability to propound and solve riddles. Finally, Solomon's wisdom was identified with scholarship (4:29-34 [H. 5:9-14]) and he was said to be the author of 3,000 proverbs, 1,005 songs, and disquisitions on botanical and zoological subjects—a scholarly production far in excess of the extant books attributed to him in later ages (Prov., Eccl., Song of Songs, Pss. 72 and 127, the Wisdom of Solomon, the Psalms of Solomon, and the Odes of Solomon).

The increasingly religious conception of wisdom inspired the rewriting of secular proverbs in a pious form. Thus, owing to the popularity of antithetic distichs illustrating the doctrine of the two ways (cf. B[1] and E[2]) some proverbs were restated: 25:5 (which appears in a more moralizing form in 29:14) and 29:22 become antithetic distichs in 16:12 and 15:18, respectively. Purely secular proverbs, such as 26:3, 27; 27:21, reappear in a more Jewish form in 10:13 (cf. 19:29); 28:10, and 17:3, respectively; compare also 29:3 with the priggish rewritings in 10:1; 15:20. The blunt statements about using the rod in bringing up children which we read in 22:15 and, with a touch of humor and sobriety in 23:13 f. (taken from the Wisdom of Ahikar), are rewritten in antithetic form in 13:24 and 29:15; in later restatements the unrefined "rod" is eliminated entirely (19:18; 22:6; 29:17). The pious numerical proverb in 6:16-19 seems to be an imitation of the secular one in 30:11-14.

Apparently in the B collection, the editors inserted acceptable rewritings of proverbs in the proximity of their less devout original prototypes. The uncouth comparison in 11:22 is replaced by one less vivid but more refined in 12:4 (cf. 11:16, LXX). The common-sense view that wealth is the reward of industry (10:4 f.) and "a strong city" for its possessor (10:15) Jewish dogma positively denied in the same chapter (10:2 f., 16, 22; cf. 11:4, 28). A similar correction of 18:11 is found in the preceding verse, and 19:1 (where we must read "rich" instead of "fool," according to the LXX) is likewise an amendment of 18:23; 19:4-7. Other instances of the same sort are found in 12:24; 13:4, 8 (corrected in 13:22 f., 25), and in 15:17; 17:1 (corrected in 15:16; 16:8).

According to 14:28, the power of a king is proportionate to the number of his subjects, but 14:34 conveys the idea of national power as commensurate with national righteousness. Opposite verdicts on the legitimacy and usefulness of bribes are furnished in 17:8, 23. It seems unnecessary to illustrate further this tendency to inject religion into observations and reflections of a profane nature—a tendency also noticeable in E[2] (contrast 29:4 with 28:12, 28 and 29:2, 8, 16).

This same purpose was accomplished by a different method in A[2], where longer sections prevail. The compiler used excellent pieces written in a rather worldly vein, but provided them with devout introductions and conclusions. The graphic sketch of the youth succumbing to the coquetry of a young married woman, who observed her religious vows more faithfully than her marriage vows (7:6-23), is better literature than the compiler of A[2] could produce, far better, in fact, than the parallel passage in the Egyptian Maxims of Ani (2:13-16). Like Horace (*Satires* I: 4, 105-115), the author teaches a moral lesson by example rather than exhortation. Before this piece was inserted into A, its introduction (5: 15-20, 8-14, in this order) and conclusion (6:25-35) were done with vigor and common sense, whether written by the author of the sketch or not. The pious compiler of A[2] felt impelled to remove the introduction and conclusion from the story and substitute his own duller and more wordy exhortations to "my son" at the beginning (7:1-5) and end (7: 24-27)—in the vein of other utterances on the subject in 2:16-19; 5:1-7, 21-23. He quoted 3:19-20 from a work presenting the theological views of the Book of Job and 6:1-15; 9:1-6, 13-18 from other sources, but made no attempt to give these sections a suitable setting in his book. Their style and objectivity contrast with the solemn tone and Deuteronomic teaching of the compiler's own writing (cf. S. R. Driver, *Introduction to the Old Testament*, p. 396).

Although secular and sacred wisdom are mixed in varying degrees and fashion in the A^2 and B collections, these parts of the book are to be regarded, like C^{2}E^2 as compilations of counsels in the Deuteronomic vein. Conversely, the C^{1}DE^{1}FGH collections, in their original form, deal with men's affairs from a purely humanistic point of view, without reference to the tenets of Judaism. These secular writings were "Judaized" in a slight measure, through occasional glosses. In C^1, only 22:19, 23; 23:11 have a distinctly religious flavor, much more pronounced in the Wisdom of Amen-em-ope from which most of this collection is taken. D is entirely secular. E^1 is the most important and oldest anthology of secular proverbs in the book, with only a few pious annotations already noted; the same is true of F^1. In F^2, 30:11-14, 17, 20 may be secondary; in H, only a minor change has been made in 31:30 (cf. LXX).

A systematic comparison of the two types of wisdom represented in Proverbs is precluded here by the exigencies of space; a thorough investigation of this whole matter would be highly rewarding. The following sketch will indicate some of the most significant differences between these two schools of thought.

The theology of secular proverbs is akin to that of Job, Ps. 104, and Ecclesiastes. God is the Creator of the world (3:19 f.) and, in contemplating the cosmic scope of divine activity, man realizes his inability to gain any true "knowledge of the Holy One" (30:2-4). As a universal power, God is the originator of all phenomena, and even directs the steps (16:9; 20:24), the words (16:1), and the mind (21:1) of human beings. He determines the outcome of battles (21:31), of plans (19:21), and of the casting of lots (16:33). Truly, man can do nothing against God (21:30). Such a recognition of the universality of divine sway is not necessarily a confession of faith, for it is self-evident even to a skeptic like Ecclesiastes. As for man, he must attain his aims through his own efforts. Of the good things in life, wealth is considered one of the most precious (10:15; 13:8a; 15:15; 17:8; 19:4, 6; 21:14; 22:7a, etc.). Wealth is acquired through intelligence (24:3 f.) and persistent work (10:4 f., 26; 11:6cd [LXX]; 12:11; 13:4; 14:23; 15:19; 18:9), notably in looking after the flocks (27:23-27), cultivation of the soil (12:11 = 28:19; 24:27

[LXX]; cf. 10:5; 13:23a; 14:4), and fidelity in carrying out commissions (25:13, a saying which has its opposite in 10:26, cf. 26:6; 13:17 is a Jewish restatement). The skilled official will stand before kings (22:29ab; cf. 14:35).

Of course, in a world in which every event is determined by God, riches may vanish overnight (23:4 f.; cf. 27:24a). But even though he cannot provide against such an eventuality, the wise man will do his utmost to retain his property by abstaining from practices that inevitably dissipate wealth, such as laziness (6:6-11; 24:30-34; cf. 26:13-15), commerce with harlots (5:9 f.; 6:26; 23:27 f.; 29:3b), habitual drunkenness (23:20 f.; on excessive drinking see 20:1; 23:29-35; 31:4-7), and becoming surety for a debtor (6:1-5; cf. 22:7, 26 f.; 27:13 = 20:16; the Jewish maxims in 11:15; 17:18 are more sententious and insipid).

In moderation, however, the pleasures of life are not to be shunned: oil and perfume (27:9), wine that makes a man forget his woes (31:6 f.), honey (25:16, 27), social intercourse (25:17), marriage and family (5:15-20; 11:16; 12:4; 14:1; 24:27; 31:10-31; cf. the religious proverbs in 18:22; 19:14) contribute to the attraction of life even though they cause trouble under certain circumstances. A nagging wife, for instance, is one of the greatest woes (17:1; 21:9, 19; 25:24; 27:15; cf. 19:13). While true friendship is precious (17:17 [?]; 18:24; 27:10; cf. 12:25) and worthy of cultivation (17:9; 27:6, 10), frequently friendship is but a sham (16:27-30; 19:4, 6 f.; 20:6; 26:18 f.). Companionship with fools (13:20b), irascible or contentious men (15:17 f.; 17:14, 19; 18:1; 19:19; 20:3; 26:21; 29:22), and flatterers or gossipers (20:19; 26:20-28) is fraught with danger.

There is nothing heroic in the teaching of these secular sages. Wisdom for them is either professional skill (6:6; 20:18; 21:22; 24:3-6; 30:24-28) or middle-class, utilitarian morality, by means of which desirable objectives are attained (14:3; 20:15; 21:20; 24:4 f., 14, etc.). Their denunciations of adultery (6:25-35; 7:22 f.), theft (6:30 f.; 29:24a), wealth acquired through deceit (21:6), usury (28:8), fraud (20:17), and undue haste (13:11; 20:21; 28:22; contrast the moralizing tone in 28:20) are not inspired by morality and religion. Such practices are frowned upon merely because they are attended by serious financial and personal risks.

Even impartiality in judgment is presented as a matter of self-interest for the judge in 24:23-25 (in 31:5, 9 it is urged upon a king as an elementary duty), whereas elsewhere, according to the teaching of the prophets, it is a distinctly religious obligation (17:26; 18:5; 21:15; 28:21; 29:7). Some rather cynical proverbs approve of bribery if it produces results (17:8; 19:6; 21:14), despite the denunciation of Pentateuchal laws and prophets (cf. the religious proverbs 15:27; 17:23).

This ancient lay wisdom is restated in terms of postexilic Judaism by the other school of thought represented in Proverbs. To identify Judaism during the Persian and Greek periods with the teaching of the Priestly Code would be an error. Not a few writings of these periods (Ruth, Jonah, most of Ps. and Prov.) reflect a much more spiritual faith than one would suppose from Leviticus or Chronicles to have even existed. In Proverbs, only 3:9 f. lays emphasis on ritualism and the externalities of Temple worship. For the rest, pious sages either point out like the prophets the insignificance of ritual acts in comparison with right living (15:8, 29; 21:3, 27; 28:9; 30:12 contrasts ritual with moral purity) or advocate the religious, ethical, and philanthropic ideals of Deuteronomy. We have seen that the A² collection is, to some extent, Deuteronomic in structure and thought.

In certain cases, the influence of Deuteronomy seems obvious: compare 11:1; 16:11; 20:10, 23 (cf. Deut. 25:13-16); 3:3; 7:3 (cf. Deut. 6:8 and 11:18); 28:8 (cf. Deut. 23:19 [H. 23:20]); 18:5 (cf. Deut. 16:19); 28:27 (cf. Deut. 15:7 ff.); 22:28 (cf. Deut. 19:14). Prophecy and law are mentioned together in 29:18 (in 28:4, 7, 9 "Torah" may mean the law of Moses). The inwardness and spirituality of religion in 16:2 (= 21:2); 16:6; 20:9, 27; 28:13 (cf. 10:12; 24:29), appeals for kindness toward widow and orphan in 15:25b; 23:10 f., and the poor in general in 14:21, 31; 17:5; 19:17; 21:13; 22:2, 9, 16, 22; 28:3, 8, 27; 29:7, 14; 30:14; 31:9, as well as exhortations to feed an enemy in need (25:21 f.) and not rejoice in his fall (24:17 f.) are all truly in the spirit of the prophets and Deuteronomy, even though in most cases no direct literary dependence need be postulated. The intimate connection of religion and ethics (3:7, 22; 11:20; 14:2; 15:9; 16:6; 28:5; 29:27) points in the same direction. The teachings of the prophets and Deuteronomy, rejected by most Judeans before the Exile notwithstanding the reforms of 621, have become commonplaces in Proverbs.

In the proverbs of the secular school the deity, exalted in power and humanly incomprehensible, was separated by a gulf from man; the wisdom by which God created the world was inaccessible to mortals. Instead, that wisdom is now personified and brought down to earth. At the time of Creation, Wisdom was an infant sporting before God (8:30 f.); the word *amôn* in v. 30 should probably read *amûn* (nursling, ward; cf. Authorized Version), as Aquila did, although many interpreters, following Wisd. of Sol. 7:22, prefer the traditional reading "artificer, craftsman." Later, Wisdom stands at the crossroads urging the children of men to follow her footsteps in the right path of life (1:20-33; 8:1-9:6).

Wisdom is now identified with morals (8:13) or religion (1:7, 29 [LXX]; 2:5; 9:10; 15:33; cf. 13:14 with 14:27), and with both of these (2:1 ff.), according to the prophetic teaching where ethics and religion are inseparable. Secular wisdom achieved through one's own efforts has nothing to do with this ethical and religious wisdom (3:7), a gift of God (2:6-7) against whom human sagacity is of no avail (21:30). Therefore the wise are identified with the pious (9:9; 10:31; 23:24) and contrasted with scoffers (9:8, 12; 13:1; 14:6; 15:12; 21:11; 29:8; cf. the contrast between wisdom and wickedness in 10:23): "The mouth of the righteous brings forth wisdom" (10:31), whereas the intelligence ("heart") of the wicked amounts to little (10:20). Wisdom embraces all that is pious and noble in human life, all that makes life attractive and successful: it is the *summum bonum*, the highest ideal (3:13-18; 8:6-21; 16:16; 25:12) through which long life (6:23; 8:35; 9:11; 13:14, etc.), security (1:33; 4:5 f.; 14:3), honor (3:16; 4:8 f.; 8:18), wealth (3:16; 8:18, 21; 21:20), hope (24:14), divine favor (8:35), one's own happiness (3:13) and that of one's parents (10:1 = 15:20) are obtained.

God is no longer the unapproachable ruler of the world as in 3:19 f.; 30:2-4. He is both the Creator and the judge of mankind (16:4, where the LXX emphasizes the righteousness of God). He sees the hidden thoughts of men (5:21; 15:3; 20:27) as well as the depths of the underworld (15:11), and weighs human hearts (an Egyptian expression, found in 16:2; 21:2; 24:12; cf. 5:21; 17:3) in order to "render to every man according to his work" (24:12). [However, God's mercy is extended to the sinner who confesses and renounces his sins (only 28:13).] This doctrine of the strict divine retribution on earth for each person's actions is no less pervasive in Proverbs than national retribution in Deuteronomy. Throughout the various collections of maxims (with the exception of D, E[1] [in which 25:22 is a gloss], F, G, and H) this dogma is reiterated with untiring persistence: in A (3:6, 8, 10; 8:35), in B (10:29; 11:31; 12:2; 14:27; 15:25; 16:5; 18:10; 19:17; 20:22; 22:4), in C[1] (22:23, lacking in Amen-em-ope), in C[2] (24:12), and in E[2] (28:25; 29:25).

This topic alone suffices to separate the secular from Deuteronomistic collections. In F[2] (30:22b) a fact is even adduced to contradict this doctrine. Such insistence shows that "scoffers" or secular sages (of whom the greatest was the author of the Book of Job) were vigorously attacking this Jewish dogma. These unorthodox teachers recognized in nature and human society the law of cause and effect (25:23; 26:20; 30:33), but they could see no logic in the assertion that greed brings death (1:19) or that contributions to the Temple would fill barns and vats (3:9 f.).

Devout moralists, on the contrary, firmly believed that wealth is a reward for piety, righteousness, and wisdom (3:16; 8:18, 21; cf. 13:18), since Jehovah's blessing, rather than toil and ingenuity, made men rich (10:22; cf. 10:21; 11:28). Wealth obtained hastily or dishonestly has no permanence (13:11; 28:22) and brings punishment (28:20) rather than blessing (20:21). Dishonest shifting of boundary stones (22:28; cf. Deut. 19:14) and the use of false weights (11:1; 20:10, 23; cf. Deut. 25:13-16) are denounced in the Deuteronomic law, which is actually paraphrased here. The giving of bribes, countenanced as we have seen by secular sages, is condemned as a serious offense (15:27; 17:23). Similarly, commerce with harlots (23:28), adultery (2:16-19; 5:1-7, 20-23), and drunkenness (28:7) become moral and religious sins (cf. also 6:16-19) rather than practices to be avoided because of the possibility of unpleasant results.

In their attitude toward wealth, the religious sages stand halfway between their secular colleagues, who praised it unrestrictedly, and the Psalmists, who tended to regard it as something inherently ungodly (e.g., Pss. 49:6, 10, 16 f.; 52:7; 62:10; 73:12 [H. 49:7, 11, 17 f.; 52:9; 62:11]). The Psalms are in general the voice of the lower classes, of the humble and poor, whose only treasure is piety and faith. The Proverbs, instead, reflect the ideals of the prosperous middle classes in town and country. In teaching the children of the rich, the pious moralists strove to give wealth a spiritual meaning, either by eliminating the difference between poor and rich (22:2; 29:13) or by pointing out the perils of both wealth and poverty (30:8 f.); they emphasized the pious (3:9 f.) and philanthropic (11:24-26; 19:17; 22:9; 28:8b, 27, etc.) uses of wealth. They believed that many things in this life were more precious than riches: wisdom (3:14 f.; 8:11, 19; 16:16), religion (cf. 15:16), righteousness (16:8), a good name (22:1), innocence (19:1). They found comfort in the illusion that the poor become rich through oppression and the rich become poor by receiving gifts (22:16). Only once (11:28) did they dare follow the psalmists in identifying the rich with the wicked and the poor with the righteous.

Correlative with the doctrine of retribution is the doctrine of the two ways, which is also of Deuteronomic origin and pervades the religious proverbs. In formulating the standards of religion and morals, the Deuteronomic Code gave the nation a choice of two alternatives: "Behold, I set before you this day a blessing and a curse" (Deut. 11:26; cf. 11:27 f.; 30:15-20 and chapters 8 and 28), or, in the words of Jeremiah (21:8): "Behold, I set before you the way of life and the way of death." The authors of Proverbs added wisdom to the Deuteronomic ideals and applied the doctrine of the two ways to the individual (as Jesus did in Matt. 7:13 f.).[3]

In Proverbs this doctrine is so familiar that the expression "the two ways" (28:6, 18) is perfectly clear, and "the way" comes to mean right conduct in life (15:10; 23:19). The two opposite ways are called respectively paths of uprightness—ways of darkness (2:13), way of life—way of death (5:5 f.; cf. the corrected text of 12:28), even way—way

---

[3] On the doctrine of the two ways in later Judaism, see G. F. Moore, *Judaism* Vol. I, pp. 454 ff.; Strack and Billerbeck, *Kommentar zum Neuen Testament*, Vol. I, pp. 461 ff. On the polemic of Ecclesiastes against this doctrine, cf. JBL 53 (1934) 105 f.

with thorns (15:19), a safe way—a dangerous one (10:9; cf. 11:5 f.; 28:18). Their characteristics are integrity—perverseness (28:6; cf. 19:1), uprightness—injustice (29:27; cf. 28:4), religion—ungodliness (14:2), light—darkness (4:18 f.), divine favor—divine abomination (11:20; 15:9). Numerous other passages refer to one or the other way using similar expressions. Although the figure of the right way is occasionally used in Egypt and Babylonia, in no ancient book of wisdom is this theme developed as fully as in Proverbs. In other Old Testament and Jewish wisdom books, there are allusions to this figure: Job 13:15; 17:9; 23:10; 31:4; Ps. 1; Sirach 2:12; Wisd. of Sol. 1:12; Tob. 4:5; IV Macc. 15:11; *Sayings of the Fathers* (*Pirkê Abôth*) 2:1a.

On the principle that there are only two ways, men are divided into two groups, good and bad. The righteous and wicked, the wise and fools, are repeatedly contrasted in antithetic distichs in B1 (48 times), more rarely in A2 (twice), B2 (six times), C2 (twice), E2 (nine times), never in the secular collections in which the doctrine of the two ways, like that of retribution, is completely missing.

To conclude, the secular proverbs are realistic, practical, and sometimes skeptical and cynical; the religious ones are idealistic, replete with wishful thinking, pious hopes, and blind faith. On the basis of this differentiation, the collections constituting the Book of Proverbs may be classified as follows:

1. Secular collections with a few moralizing and religious interpolations: *a.* distichs: E1; *b.* distichs and longer sections: D; *c.* attributed to non-Israelitic authors: F1 and G; *d.* numerical proverbs: F2; *e.* an alphabetic acrostic poem: H.

2. A collection originally joining secular and religious maxims: C1, whose Egyptian prototype combined practical and religious advice.

3. Collections essentially ethical and religious but reproducing from E1 and other sources secular maxims and descriptions: *a.* collections of distichs: B1 (chiefly antithetic), B2, E2; *b.* exhortations addressed to "my son": A2 and C2.

4. The title of the book as a whole, describing briefly its religious, ethical, and secular contents: A1.

This classification made purely on the basis of the contents gives us at the same time the probable chronological order of the collections. No clues are available for an absolute dating, any more than in the case of Psalms. The book as a whole, in its extant form in Hebrew or Greek, cannot be later than 200 B.C., since it is known to Sirach (Ecclus. 47:17), who attributes to Solomon "songs and proverbs" (with reference to I Kings 4:32 [H. 5:12]) and "riddles and maxims" (with reference to Prov. 1:6).

The book as a whole cannot be earlier than about 400 B.C.: the references to the Law in 28:4, 9 and Law and Prophecy (vision) in 29:18 (even though Law need not necessarily mean the Pentateuch), the advanced and noble religious conceptions of many passages (e.g., 14:31; 16:4, 6; 20:27; 22:2; 24:17 f., 29; 25:21 f.; 28:13), the sharp division of the Jewish congregation into Pious and ungodly, or scoffers (*leṣîm,* a word found only in Ps., Prov., and Is. 29:20: note the contrast between scoffers and humble in 3:34), and many other parallels with the Psalms and other late writings (notably Ecclus. of Sirach), the character of the language and style of certain parts (notably 1-9), the personification of cosmic Wisdom in 8, and other characteristics of the book positively exclude a date before Nehemiah and even reduce the likelihood of one before 300.

Assuming, then, that the latest parts of the book, A¹ and A², are to be dated in the third century, we may surmise that BC²E² belong to the fourth, C¹ to the fifth, and the purely secular collections (E¹, F¹, G, H, D, F², possibly in this order) to an earlier period. Even the earliest collection (E¹) can hardly have been contemporaneous with Isaiah, when for the first time we hear of professional wise men in Judah (cf. also 25:1). Individual sayings of a timeless character, such as abound in the book, could conceivably be earlier, but it is improbable that any collections of maxims were made before 600 B.C. It seems hardly necessary to point out the fallacy of regarding proverbs about the king as *ipso facto* pre-exilic (after the manner of the "royal" psalms). Some have no connection with Israel's history: 22:29 refers to the Pharaoh (being freely translated from Amen-em-ope's book) and 31:1-9 to an Arabian tribal chieftain. As for the rest, it is sufficient to point to "royal proverbs" in later wisdom books such as Ecclesiasticus (7:4-6; 8:1-3; 38:2; cf. 39:4) and Ecclesiastes.

Finally, we must regretfully note that in Proverbs, as elsewhere in the Old Testament, literary excellence is frequently in inverse ratio to religious fervor. The finest writing in Proverbs is to be found in the earliest sections (E¹, 7:6-23, and H in particular), which reflect actual human life without attempting to idealize it or to direct it in accordance with noble principles and the tenets of a great religious faith.

CHAPTER III

THE BOOK OF JOB

~~~~~~

The Book of Job consists of the prose folk tale about Job, whose piety withstood every test (1:1-2:10) and was rewarded by God (42:10b-17); of a discussion between Job and three of his friends on the justice of God in rewarding human conduct (3-27, in verse; with a prose introduction, 2:11-13, and epilogue, 42:7-10a); of a poem on divine wisdom (28); of monologues of Job (29-31); of the speeches of Elihu (32-37, in verse except for 32:1-6a); of the speeches of Jehovah (38:1-40:2, 6-41:34 [H. 41:26]) and Job's replies (40:3-5; 42:1-6). We may summarize the contents of these several parts of the book as follows:

I. *The folk tale in prose* (1:1-2:10; 42:10b-17). Job, renowned for his piety and uprightness, lived prosperously (1:1-5) until the prosecuting angel ("Satan") made a wager with Jehovah that Job's piety would not withstand the loss of property and children (1:6-12). But Job, after his losses, still blessed the name of Jehovah (1:13-22). Satan then proposed a more drastic test (2:1-6) and smote Job with boils (2:7 f.); but in his misery Job still refused to "curse [*sic*] God and die," in accordance with his wife's advice (2:9 f.). After friends and relatives had comforted and helped Job (42:11), Jehovah gave him twice as much as he had before (42:10b) and he lived happily ever after (42:12-17).

II. *The dialogue* (2:11-13; 3-27; 42:7-10a). *Introduction* (2:11-13). Job's three friends (Eliphaz, Bildad, and Zophar) come to comfort him, but are appalled by his misery (2:11-13).

1. Job's lament (3). He curses the day of his birth (3:1-10), wishes he had been born dead (3:11-19), and wonders why life is given to such unfortunates as himself, who long for death (3:20-26).

2. The first cycle of speeches (4-14). *a.* The first speech of Eliphaz (4-5): he gently chides Job, who had formerly comforted the unfortunate, for his outburst (4:1-6), reminds him of God's just retribution of human deeds (4:7-11), and of the sinfulness of all men, revealed to him in a vision (4:12-5:7), and exhorts him to turn to God, who controls nature and mankind (5:8-16); for after he has corrected Job (5:17 f.) he will deliver him from trouble (5:19-23) and make him happy (5:24-27).

b. Job's reply to Eliphaz (6-7). His lament is justified by the intensity of the pain which God has inflicted upon him (6:1-7), causing him to long for death (6:8-13). His friends have deceived him like a dry brook in the desert (6:14-23) and have failed to prove that he deserves his fate (6:24-30). In reality all human life is drudgery (7:1 f.) at its best, or, in his case, unendurable agony (7:3-5) ending only in the underworld (7:6-10). Turning to God, he begs to be left alone (7:11-21).

  c. The first speech of Bildad (8). God is just (8:1-4) and would bless Job if he deserved it (8:5-7). The teaching of former generations (8:8-10) attests that the godless are rooted out (8:11-19). God is equitable (8:20) and if Job deserves joy he will receive it (8:21 f.).

  d. Job's reply to Bildad (9-10). He admits, with Eliphaz (4:17) that a human being cannot be just before God (9:1-3), for in his unlimited might God is not restrained by moral standards (9:4-13). Job therefore cannot contend with God although he is blameless (9:14-21), for God destroys the innocent with the wicked (9:22) and allows the latter to prevail (9:23 f.). His miserable life is fleeting (9:25 f.); innocent or guilty, he can expect neither justice nor mercy from God (9:27-31), a supreme inflexible ruler (9:32 f.) before whom Job is afraid to speak (9:34 f.). All hope being lost, Job will address the deity (10:1 f.): why does God inexplicably oppress him (10:3-7)—since every man is the work of God's hands (10:8-12)—and pursue him incessantly like a hunted beast (10:13-17)? Why has God given him life (10:18 f.; cf. 3:11-19)? Why does God not allow him to end his brief life in peace (10:20-22; cf. 7:16-21)?

  e. The first speech of Zophar (11). Job's boasts of his innocence (11:1-4) may have impressed his hearers, but God could reveal to Job the unconscious sin for which he is punished. Divine wisdom and power are beyond man's understanding (11:5-12). Let Job therefore reform and appeal to God; then he will be safe (11:13-20).

  f. Job's answer to Zophar (12-14). Mocking the wisdom of his friends (12:1 f.), Job asserts that he knows as much as they (12:3; 12:4-6 is a parenthetical reflection on his misery and the prosperity of the wicked), inasmuch as all men (12:3b), animals (12:7), and the earth itself (12:8) know that the Creator, endowed with wisdom and might (12:9-13), rules over nature and mankind (12:14-25). Job is not inferior to them (13:1 f.); they have proved themselves unworthy advocates of God (13:3-12). Job is willing to present his case before God (13:13-19), provided he will not crush him (13:20-22). He invites God to indict him (13:23): why should God otherwise regard him as an enemy (13:24-28)? Being a man, Job does not deserve God's attention. For "man that is born of woman is few of days and full of trouble" (14:1). God should allow man to live his briefly allotted span in peace (14:2-6), for a tree may revive after it is cut down, but there is no hope for a man when he dies (14:7-12). If only

God would hide Job in the underworld and revive him after the divine anger has ceased (14:13-15)! But death is the end for man (14:16-22).

3. The second cycle of speeches (15-21). *a.* The second speech of Eliphaz (15). Job's words are unprofitable and godless (15:1-5): they condemn him (15:6). Is Job that first man ever created, who tried to steal the divine wisdom (15:7 f.)? Is he more informed than his more aged friends (15:9 f.)? Why should he be angry with God (15:11-13)? No man is innocent before God (15:14-16; cf. 4:17-19). According to the teaching transmitted from the ancients (15:17-19; cf. 8:8-10), "the wicked man travaileth with pain all his days" (15:20-35).

b. Job's answer to Eliphaz (16-17). Job has heard all this before (16:1 f.), longs for an end of such "windy words" (16:3), and wishes that the roles were changed so that he could comfort similarly his friends (16:4 f.). Turning to God, he laments bitterly the suffering with which God has afflicted him (16:6-16), though innocent (16:17). He has, however, a witness in heaven (God himself) and appeals to him (16:18-21). His end is near (16:22-17:1), his friends have failed him (17:2-5), he is generally despised (17:6), he wastes away (17:7) to the astonishment of the righteous (17:8 f.), but not of his friends (17:10). In his unceasing agony (17:11 f.) his only hope is the dark silence of the underworld (17:13-16).

c. The second speech of Bildad (18). He refuses to be considered as foolish as a beast (18:1-4; cf. 12:7), and, like Eliphaz (15:20-35), he paints a lurid picture of the fate of the godless (18:5-21).

d. Job's reply to Bildad (19). Reproaching again his friends (19:1-5), Job asserts that God has unjustly afflicted him (19:6-12), alienated from him family and friends (19:13 f.), and even servants (19:15 f.) and wife (19:17); urchins despise him (19:18), friends abhor him (19:19), his body is decaying (19:20). Why should his three friends persecute him (19:21 f.)? In spite of all this, Job expects a future vindication by posterity, for which his words should be written in a book (19:23 f.), and by God himself after his own death (19:25-27): let his friends beware (19:28 f.)!

e. The second speech of Zophar (20). In great agitation (20:1-3) he declares that the triumph of the wicked lasts but a moment (20:4 f.). No matter how exalted they be for a time (20:6), suddenly they disappear like a dream (20:7-11); destroyed by the poison of their wickedness (20:12-16), they suffer manifold calamities (20:17-29).

f. Job's reply to Zophar (21). He requests attention to his words (21:1-3), apologizing for his impatience and horror (21:4-6). He disproves the friends' doctrine about the misfortune of the wicked by pointing out that some scoundrels have prospered all their life (21:7-16) and, conversely, only a few others are overtaken by calamity (21:17 f.); if

their children should suffer after their death they do not know it (21:
19-21). Why attempt to instruct God (21:22)? Death strikes rich and poor
without discrimination, without relation to a just judgment of the wicked
(21:23-26). If his friends should remind him of individual instances of
misfortune overtaking a rascal (21:27 f.), Job refers them to those who
have traveled afar (21:29) who know that the wicked are spared on the
day of calamity (21:30), give no reckoning for their deeds (21:31), and
when they die are buried with pomp and ceremony (21:32 f.). The arguments of the three friends are therefore groundless (21:34).

4. The third cycle of speeches (22-27). *a.* The third speech of Eliphaz
(22). Human virtue is profitable for man, but not for God (22:1-3). Conversely human sin must be punished (22:4). Applying this theory to
Job, Eliphaz concludes that his iniquities are innumerable (22:5) and
gives a list of his misdeeds (22:6-9), which have caused his ruin (22:
10 f.). Job's theory that God is indifferent to human deeds inevitably
brings disaster (22:12-20), but a prompt conversion will restore his
fortunes (22:21-30).

b. Job's reply to Eliphaz (23-24). Job would like to appear in court
before God himself (23:1-7), but is unable to find him (23:8 f.). Aware
of Job's innocence (23:10-12), God does whatever he wishes (23:13 f.)
and terrifies Job (23:15-17). Why has God hidden his purposes even from
the pious? (24:1, omitting "not" in 24:1a with the LXX; cf. Eccl. 3:11 and
JBL 53 [1934] 107). His regulation of human affairs is incomprehensible:
dishonesty and violence are rampant and triumphant, their victims in
country (24:2-11) or city (24:12-17) obtain no redress. Who could deny
these facts (24:25)? (24:18-24 are textually corrupt and seem to defend
the theory of the friends, as also 27:7-10, 13-23.) To remedy the obvious
disorder in chs. 24-27, we shall tentatively rearrange the material as follows: Bildad: 25:1; 27:7-10, 16-23; Job: 26:1-4; 27:11 f.; 25:2-6; 26:5-14;
Zophar: 27:13; 24:21-24, 18-20; 27:14 f.; Job: 27:1-6; 29-31.

c. The third speech of Bildad (25:1; 27:7-10, 16-23). "Let mine enemy
be like the wicked!" (27:7) For although the godless may acquire wealth,
it will not save them from divine punishment (27:8-10, 16-23).

d. Job's reply to Bildad (26:1-4; 27:11 f.; 25:2-6; 26:5-14). Job sarcastically congratulates Bildad for his sound knowledge (26:1-4) and,
addressing all three friends, proposes to teach them the true nature of
God (27:11 f.). He is mighty (25:2a), majestically exalted above heavenly
beings (25:2b-3), above man—that miserable worm (25:4-6)—and the
shades of the underworld (26:5 f.). He is the creator and upholder of
the world (26:7-10). His voice makes the pillars of heaven tremble
(26:11), his power stirs up the sea (26:12a), his breath clears the sky
(26:13a), his hand pierces the primeval monsters of chaos (26:12b, 13b):
these are but "the outskirts of his ways!" (26:14)

e. The third speech of Zophar (27:13; 24:21-24; 24:18-20; 27:14 f.). He merely describes "the portion of the wicked man" (27:13) as a brief span of iniquity (24:21), divinely punished (24:22-24) with death (24:18 f.), oblivion (24:20), and the ruin of his children (27:14 f.).

f. Job's reply to Zophar (27:1-6; 29-31). In spite of the affliction that God has sent to him (27:1 f.), Job still maintains his innocence (27:3-6); he develops this theme more fully in his final monologues (29-31), to which these words are an introduction.

Epilogue (42:7-10a). After his speeches in chs. 38-41, Jehovah reproved Eliphaz and the two other friends of Job for not speaking of himself as rightly as Job (42:7), but accepted their burnt offering and Job's intercession for them (42:8 f.) and restored Job's fortunes (42:10a).

III. *The divine wisdom* (28). After omitting the gloss in 28:28 and rearranging the verses which are out of place, the original poem on man's inability to discover "wisdom" (in the sense of God's plan in creating the world) may be reconstructed conjecturally as follows. The piece had five stanzas, each consisting of the refrain in 28:12, 20 followed by five verses. 1. Mineral treasures lie buried in the earth (28:12, 13, 5 f., 1 f.). 2. Miners in their shafts are able to reach these minerals (28:12, 3 f., 9-11). 3. But wisdom is not to be found in the four parts of the world, the air, the earth, the abyss, and the underworld (28:20 f., 7 f., 14, 22). 4. Nor can wisdom be purchased (28:12, 15-19). 5. God, however, discovered wisdom and according to it he created the world (28:20, 23-27). The two initial verses (28:12 f.) present the theme of the poem. This composition has no logical place in the Book of Job, unless it be the conclusion of Job's confession in 42:1-6, but since its teaching corresponds to that of the author of the book it may have been written by him. The philosophical implications of this chapter were obnoxious to Judaism (cf. ZAW N.F. 11 [1934] 100): in the gloss at the end (28:28) and elsewhere (Deut. 4:6; 30:11-14; Prov. 8, etc.) an attempt was made to reconcile its teaching with the Jewish doctrine of divine revelation.

IV. *Job's monologues* (29-31, the sequel of 27:1-6).

1. Job's former happiness (29, in which 29:21-25 belong after 29:10). Under God's protection (29:1-3) Job was blessed with a happy (29:4 f.) and prosperous family (29:6). In the community he was respected by young and old, and was influential in the council of the elders (29:7-10, 21-25). He was generally praised (29:11) for his benefactions to the needy (29:12-16) and for his championship of justice (29:17). He naturally expected a long life of happiness and glory (29:18-20).

2. Job's present misery (30). Even the children of those miserable wretches who were the object of Job's benefactions in the past now hold him in derision (30:1-8) and spit in his face (30:9 f.), because God has forsaken him (30:11); these vagabonds even persecute him (30:12-15).

In contrast with his former health, a horrible disease now afflicts him (30:16-18); in contrast with the former kindly attitude, God now assails him and turns a deaf ear to his appeals (30:19-23). And yet his former sympathy for the unfortunate (30:24 f.) had led him to expect happiness: on the contrary, dire calamity has been his lot (30:26-31).

3. Job's ethical standards (31, reading 31:35-37 after 31:40a). Job has overcome the lure of sensuality (31:1-4), has avoided falsehood and deceit (31:5 f.), has not yielded to the seduction of ill-gotten wealth (31:7 f.), and has never committed adultery (31:9-12). He has treated his servants fairly (31:13-15); he has helped the poor, the widow (31:16), the fatherless (31:17 f.), and the beggar (31:19 f.). He has not brought an unjust suit against the "upright" (31:21-23, reading *'alê tām* for *'al jāthôm*); he has neither placed his confidence in his wealth (21:24 f.) nor worshiped the sun and moon (31:26-28). The ruin of his enemy did not fill him with joy (31:29 f.). His household never wished that he would provide sufficient food (31:31, omitting both *lô'*); on the contrary, even passers-by were offered generous hospitality (31:32). Finally he has not hypocritically hidden his transgressions in fear of public opinion (31:33 f.) and has not abused his land and its tillers (31:38-40a). Thus he rests his case; wishing that it may be heard by God (31:35-37 [40b]). And God answered him out of the whirlwind (38:1 ff).

V. *The speeches of Elihu* (32-37, an interpolation).

1. Prose introduction (32:1-5). Irritated because Job's friends had been silenced, Elihu, a younger man, now intervenes.

2. Elihu's first speech (32). *a.* In a rhetorical exordium addressed to the three friends (32:6-22) Elihu apologizes for his intervention. Being young, he has waited for older men to finish speaking (32:6 f.), but realizes that divine inspiration rather than old age gives wisdom (32:8-10). The three friends have been unable to convince Job (32:11 f.) and have been silenced by him (32:13-16). He cannot keep silent longer: he is full of ideas (32:17-20) and will speak without regard to persons (32:21 f.). *b.* In a second exordium he invites Job to reply to him without fear, for he is a man and not God (33:1-3, 5 f., 4, 7). *c.* Summary of Job's arguments: Job is innocent (33:8 f.), God persecutes him (33:10 f.) and will not answer his words (33:12 f.). *d.* Elihu begins by answering the third point. God speaks to men (33:14) through dreams (33:15 f.), warning them against pride (33:17 f.), and through illness (33:19-22). When an angel vouches for a man's uprightness (33:23 f.) and he repents of his sins, his health is restored (33:25-28), for the purpose of God's work is to save man (33:29 f.). *e.* Conclusion: Job should continue to listen unless he has an answer (33:31-33).

3. Elihu's second speech (34). *a.* Exordium (34:1-4). *b.* Job's assertion that God has dealt unjustly with him (34:5 f.) is blasphemous (34:7 f.)

and amounts to saying that piety profits nothing (34:9). *c.* On the contrary, God, the supreme ruler, is absolutely just as well as mighty (34:10-20) and rewards each man according to his deserts (34:21-30). *d.* In denying God's justice Job has both erred and revolted against God (34:31-37).

4. Elihu's third speech (35). *a.* Job had asserted that his sin and piety brought no disadvantage or profit either to himself or to God (35:1-3). *b.* Elihu argues that God is too exalted to be affected by human deeds (35:4-7), but the doer bears the consequences (35:8). *c.* The objection that the oppressed cry to God in vain is answered by pointing out their lack of true faith (35:9-13); for this reason God has been deaf to Job's appeals (35:14-16).

5. Elihu's fourth speech (36-37). *a.* Exordium: he will defend God's justice (36:1-4). *b.* God deals justly with men (36:5 f.), as seen in his punishment of proud [Judean?] kings (36:7-10). If the sinner repents he will prosper (36:11), if not he will perish (36:12); for the man who does not even cry unto God in his misfortune (because he is an atheist?) death is the only punishment (36:13 f.). *c.* God uses affliction to strengthen men's faith (36:15), notably so in the case of Job (36:16-21). *d.* "God is great" (36:26); "Great things doeth he, which we cannot comprehend" (37:5b). God is supreme (36:22 f.), man can only sing the praises of his works, which he beholds from far off (36:24 f.). God is above time (36:26). He produces rain (36:27 f.), storms (36:29-33), thunder and lightning (37:1-5a), snow (37:6); he sends tempests and icy winds either in punishment or in mercy (37:7-13). Can Job understand how God makes lightning, balances the clouds, gives heat to the south wind, spreads out the mirrorlike firmament (37:14-20)? As a storm breaks from the north, Elihu concludes that God is mighty and just (37:21-24).

VI. *The speeches of Jehovah* (38-41; Job's replies: 40:3-5; 42:1-6).

1. The wonders of the physical world (38:1-38). Out of the whirlwind (38:1), Jehovah by a series of questions makes Job realize that he does not understand the secrets of nature (38:2 f.), particularly the founding of the earth (38:4-7), the restraint of the sea within its limits (38:8-11), the daily rise of the dawn (38:12-15), the depths of the abyss and the gates of the underworld (38:16-18), the abodes of light and darkness (38:19-21), the storerooms of snow and hail (38:22 f.), the mysteries of wind, lightning, thunder, rain, and ice (38:24-30), the movements and influence of the constellations (38:31-33), the control of rainfall and lightning (38:34 f.), the intelligence of the ibis and the cock [?] (38:36; cf. P. Dhorme, *Le livre de Job*, Etudes Bibliques. Paris, 1926; *ad loc.*), the number of the clouds, and rainstorms pouring out of the bottles of heaven (38:37 f.).

2. The wonders of the animal world (38:39-39:30). By a similar series of questions Jehovah proves that Job is ignorant of the phenomena of biology and has no control over wild animals, the following of which are mentioned: lions (38:39 f.) and ravens (38:41) living off prey; mountain goats and hinds, calving at their appointed times (39:1-4); the untamable wild ass (39:5-8) and wild ox (39:9-12); the swift but thoughtless ostrich (39:13-18, interpolated); the bold battle steed (39:19-25); the hawk, migrating southward in the fall (39:26); the high-soaring, sharp-eyed vulture (39:27-30).

3. Jehovah's challenge and Job's answer (40:1-14). Jehovah invites Job to answer his questions (40:1 f.) and Job admits that he cannot say a word (40:3-5). Then Jehovah concludes his speeches by ironically asking Job to prove himself the equal of God in majesty and power before he dares to judge God; then Jehovah will admit that Job can save himself (40:6-14).

4. Behemoth and Leviathan (40:15-41:34 [H. 40:15-41:26], interpolated). Two additional animals are described by Jehovah. Behemoth (the hippopotamus), endowed with fabulous strength, is at home both on land and in the water (40:15-24). Leviathan (the crocodile) is unconquerable (41:1-8 [H. 40:25-32]), terrifying (41:10, 9, 11 [H. 41:2, 1, 3); incredibly strong (41:12 [H. 41:4], revised text), he has mighty teeth (41:13 f. [H. 41:5 f.]) and is covered with tight-fitting scales (41: 15-17 [H. 41:7-9]); fire and smoke pour from its mouth and nostrils (41:18-21 [H. 41:10-13]); solidly built inside and out, he defies all weapons (41:22-29 [H. 41:14-21]); he leaves a trail on the ground and makes the water boil (41:30-32 [H. 41:22-24]); he has no rival and is the king of all the beasts (41:33 f. [H. 41:25 f.]).

5. Job's second reply to Jehovah (42:1-6). Recognizing God's almighty power (42:1 f.), Job admits that he spoke without understanding (42:3 f.; the beginning of 42:3 and 42:4 are to be omitted, being copied from 38:2, 3b; 40:7b). Having now seen God (42:5), he repents in dust and ashes (42:6).

[For 42:7-10a, see after II, 4, *f*, above; for 42:10b-17, see I, above.]

1. The Critical Problems

The literary problems which have particularly engaged the attention of the critics are those concerning the integrity, the date, and the authorship of the Book of Job.

A. Integrity

The preceding outline of the book indicates that its structure and plan are not always logical and that some of the parts are mutually discrepant.

To remedy these inconsistencies critics have proposed rearrangements and omissions.

The folk tale of the pious Job (1-2; 42:7-17) first aroused the suspicion of scholars (see, for a history of the various theories, K. Kautzsch, *Das sogenannte Volksbuch von Hiob.* Leipzig, 1900). R. Simon (1685) regarded the prologue (1-2) as an historical addition, like the historical introductions to some Psalms. A. Schultens (1737) regarded both the prologue (1-2) and the epilogue (42:7-17) as redactional additions—a view accepted by a number of later critics (e.g. K. Kautzsch and the present writer in a dissertation [*Le problème du livre de Job.* Geneva, 1915]). Some (like G. Studer, *Jahrb. f. Protest. Theol.* [1875] 706 ff.; and E. König, *Hiob.* Gütersloh, 1929) reject only the prologue; others (K. Fullerton, in ZAW 42 [1924] 116-136; L. Finkelstein, *The Pharisees,* Vol. I, p. 235) only the epilogue. Within the prologue, the Satan passages (1:6-12; 2:1-7a) have been questioned by E. König (*Einleitung in das Alte Testament,* p. 415. Bonn, 1893), L. Finkelstein (*loc. cit.*), and earlier critics (cf. König, *loc. cit.*).

On the contrary, other critics regard the prologue and epilogue as a separate book, a *Volksbuch* or folk book, written before the time of the poet.[1] In general it is now thought that the poet himself used this old book as a frame for his own work (e.g., L. Gautier, *Introduction à l'Ancien Testament.* Vol. II, pp. 98 f. 2nd ed., Paris, 1914; P. Volz, in Schriften des Alten Testaments, Vol. III, Pt. 2, 2nd ed., 1921).

Finally some critics (e.g., P. Dhorme, *Job,* pp. lxvii. G. Hölscher, *Hiob.* HAT, 1937) have come to the conclusion that the poet himself wrote the prose folk story at the beginning and end of his poem.

It is thus clear that the critics have suggested every possibility: the prologue, the epilogue, or both (in part or *in toto*) were written by the author of the book, or before him, or after him. As in the case of other problems raised by parts of the Old Testament, the evidence available is not conclusive. It is impossible to prove convincingly that the poet either wrote or did not write the folk tale. The prevailing opinion seems to be that the poet could not have begun his book abruptly at 3:1 or 3:2 or even at 2:11 (e.g., C. Steuernagel, *Einleitung in das Alte Testament,* p. 694) because some information about the hero was necessary before his outburst in ch. 3. In reality all that the reader needs to know about Job is found in chs. 29-31 (G. Studer [*Hiob.* Bremen, 1881] actually regarded chs. 29-30 as the original introduction to the poem) and more-

---

[1] J. Wellhausen, in *Jahrb. f. deutsche Theol.* 1871, 555. K. Budde, *Beiträge zur Kritik des Buches Hiob.* Bonn, 1876; pp. xiii f. HKAT, *Hiob* (2nd ed., 1913). M. Vernes, in RHR 1880, 232. T. K. Cheyne, *Job and Solomon,* pp. 66 f. London, 1887; *Encycl. Bibl.* II, 2467 f. G. Hoffmann, *Hiob,* pp. 22 f. 1891. G. Bickell, *Job,* 1894. B. Duhm, *Hiob,* KHC, pp. vii f. Freiburg, 1897. D. B. Macdonald, in JBL 14 (1895) 63 ff.; and AJSL 14 (1898) 137 ff.

over ancient authors often plunged *in medias res*, as for instance the J document: "Now Jehovah said to Abram, 'Get thee out of thy country . . .'" (Gen. 12:1). The passing reference to Job in Ezekiel 14:14, 20 shows that Job was a famous character of legend, like Abraham, and that the author's readers did not need to be informed about his misfortunes. It may be argued that the poet could begin his book with the words "And Job cursed the day of his birth," on the analogy of Mark's Gospel, "John baptized in the wilderness," and that just as Luke later found it expedient to begin with the birth of John the Baptist, so the story of Job (in chs. 1-2) was prefaced by a later hand.

The question whether the poet wrote the prose story is academic and unimportant. If, as all indicates, we have here a folk tale or legend told orally long before it was fixed in writing, then it is idle to investigate its authorship. It was the merit of J. Wellhausen, whose literary discrimination and sensibility were amazing, to recognize the true character of this story: "not only the material, but also the form were borrowed by the poet from the folk saga."[2] In some form this tale was familiar to Ezekiel and to his hearers (Ez. 14:14, 20) and was therefore circulating among the Judeans in the sixth century and probably long before. Like the stories collected in the S document of Genesis, the story of Job, as shown by its geographical background, originated among the Edomites. Like the story of the Garden of Eden, for instance, it contains impressive statements in verse (Job. 1:21; 2:9 f.), but even its prose at times has a stately rhythm (e.g., 1:1) although E. Sievers (*Metrische Studien I.* Abhandl. d. phil.-hist. Classe d. Königl. Sächsischen Gesellsch. d. Wissensch. XXI, 1901) and others are not justified in regarding chs. 1-2 as poetry.

It may be surmised that in its original form the tale lacked the Satan episodes (1:6-12; 2:1-7a). The visit of the three friends (2:11-13; 42:7-10a) was probably introduced into the tale when it was used as a framework for the poem. By means of God's praise of Job's words and his censure of the friends (42:7), an attempt was made to harmonize the work of the poet, in which Job is no longer the pious and patient sufferer, with the popular tale, in which at the end his fortunes were restored (a proof that God approved of him). Similarly in 1:22; 2:10 the reader seems to be warned of the following impatient and near-blasphemous utterances of Job.

It is clear from this that the folk tale as we have it has been adapted, by means of slight retouches, to the poem, although on the whole it still

[2] See note 1, above. Cf. also J. F. Wood, "Folktales in Old Testament Narratives" (JBL 28 [1909] 34 ff.), and the introductions in the commentaries of B. Duhm, K. Budde, S. R. Driver and G. B. Gray (ICC), P. Dhorme, etc. A. Alt (ZAW N.F. 14 [1937] 265-268) distinguishes an earlier (1; 42:11-17) and a later (1:1-2:13 . . . 42:7-10) form of the folk tale.

preserves the freshness and charm, the vividness and simplicity, of an oft-told story.

The extant version of the tale is Israelitic, as proved by the mention of Jehovah, inconsistent in the mouth of the Edomitic hero (1:21), and perhaps by the role played by Satan (cf. Zech. 3:1 f., where the word has still the article as in Job, and I Chron. 21:1, where "Satan" has become a proper noun). If the poet was, as the present writer believes, an Edomite, he could hardly have written the folk tale as we have it; more probably it was added to his book by a Jewish redactor who reproduced fairly accurately the tale as he heard it from storytellers in Judea (presumably with the Satan episodes) and adapted it slightly to the poem (adding in particular 2:11-13; 42:7-10a). This hypothesis would explain the puzzling discrepancy between the apparent antiquity of the story (reflecting a type of religion which is pre-Deuteronomic and preprophetic, and introducing the Chaldeans in 1:17 as desert nomads and not yet the masters of the world when Nebuchadnezzar was ruling) and some late characteristics of language (cf. K. Kautzsch, *Das Sogenannte Volksbuch von Hiob*, p. 39) and thought (Satan).

The original Edomitic tale of the innocent sufferer is an example of ancient Oriental folklore. The theme of a man suffering undeserved indignities or torments, whether through human (as in the story of Ahikar)[3] or through divine agencies (as in the Indian story of King Harrischandra[4] and in the Babylonian poem "I will praise the lord of wisdom")[5] is common in Oriental folklore, which to some extent is international.

The folk tale should not be regarded as an expression of the poet's views on the problem of the suffering of an innocent man, even if he used it as a framework for his poem. The story, like that of the Garden of Eden, may be the vehicle for a popular pessimistic philosophy: man in general (Adam) and Job in particular suffer by divine decree more than they deserve. But the poet investigated theological and philosophical problems entirely beyond the scope of the tale or of folk philosophy, and used the story much as Plato illustrated by means of myths some of his deepest thoughts.

In the speeches of Job and of his friends (chs. 3-31), apart from brief glosses, the only portions which have been questioned by critics are chs. 24-27, and the poem on wisdom (28).

The third cycle of speeches begins normally with the address of Eliphaz (22) and the first part of Job's answer (23:1-24:17, 25) but con-

[3] English translation and bibliography in R. H. Charles, *The Apocrypha and Pseudepigrapha of the Old Testament*, Vol. II, pp. 715-784. Oxford, 1913.

[4] A. Lods, *Les prophètes d'Israël*, p. 13, n. 4.

[5] M. Jastrow, in JBL 25 (1906) 135-191. R. W. Rogers, *Cuneiform Parallels to the Old Testament*, pp. 164-169. H. Gressmann (Editor), *Altorientalische Texte zum Alten Testament*, pp. 273-281.

tinues and ends in considerable confusion. In 24:18-24, in spite of the obscurity of the text due to serious corruption, Job seems to defend the point of view of the friends; Bildad's speech is not only very brief (25:1-6) but seems to have its sequel in Job's reply (26:5-14); Zophar says nothing, but Job speaks three times (26; 27; 29-31); the statement that Job spoke again (27:1) seems, however, to indicate that he replied to a speech of Zophar; finally in 27:7-10, 13-23 Job, in describing the misfortunes of the wicked, gives support to the doctrine of his friends.

Three remedies, used singly or jointly, have been proposed by critics to bring order in chs. 24-27: rearrangement of sections, ascription to other speakers of some parts, and excision of some portions as secondary. Only a few scholars, for example, K. Budde (*Hiob*, pp. 132 f.), accept the given text, with no substantial changes, as genuine.

The following examples illustrate reconstructions of the text based chiefly on rearrangement and ascription to other speakers (indicated by these abbreviations: J = Job; B = Bildad; Z = Zophar).

B. Kennicott (*Vetus Testamentum Hebraicum*, Vol. II, Oxford, 1780): B 25; J 26:1-27:12; Z 27:13-23; J 28-31. M. H. Stuhlmann (*Hiob.* Hamburg, 1804): B 25, 28; J 26:1-27:10; Z 27:11-23; J 29-31. E. Reuss (*Hiob.* 1888): B 25, 26:5-14; J 26:1-4; 27:1-12; Z 27:13-23 (?); J. 29:31 (interpolated: 28). G. Hoffmann (*Hiob*): B 25, 24:13-25; J 26:1-27:6; Z 27:7-28:28; J 29-31. G. Bickell (*Job*): B 25:1-3; 26:12 f., 14c; 25:4-6; J 26:1-4; 27:2-6; 11 f.; 28; Z 27:7-10, 14-23; J 29-31. B. Duhm (*Hiob.* 1897): B 25:1; 26:1-4; 25:2-6; 26:5-14; J 26:1; 27:2-6, 12; Z 27:7-11, 13-23; J 29-31 (interpolated: 24:1-24; 28; 30:1-8). C. Siegfried (*Job*, in Sacred Books of the Old Testament, edited by P. Haupt. Baltimore, 1893): B 25; 26:5-14; J 26:1-4; 27:2-6; 29-31 (interpolated: 27:7-28:28). L. Laue (*Die Komposition des Buches Hiob.* 1895): B 27:13-23; J 26:1-3; 9:2-24; Z 28; J 12 (27:1-6 is genuine, but its place is not clear). G. A. Barton (JBL 30 [1911] 66 ff.): J 24:1-4, 9-16, 23, 25; B 25:1-6; 24:17 f., 5-8; 30:4-8; 24:21 f., 19 f., 24; J 26; Z 27:7-11, 13-23; J 27:1-6, 12; 29:2-25; 30:1 f., 9-31; 31 (interpolated: 28). P. Dhorme (*Job*): J 23; 24:1-17, 25; B 25:1-6; 26:5-14; J 26:1-4; 27:2-12; Z 27:13, 24:18-24; 27:14-23; J (28), 29-31. M. Buttenwieser (*Job.* 1922) and H. Torczyner (*Hiob.* 1920) have moved more brief sections of Job to new contexts than any other critics. In the summary of the book at the beginning of this chapter, the following rearrangement has been suggested: J 23; 24:1-17, 25; B 25:1, 27:7-10, 16-23; J 26: 1-4; 27:11 f.; 25:2-6; 26:5-14; Z 27:13; 24:21-24, 18-20; 27:14 f.; J. 27:1-6; 29-31. Chapter 28 is out of place and, though perhaps written by the author of Job, is probably no original part of the book.

Other critics have had recourse to excision of considerable portions of chs. 24-27, if not of everything in them. L. Laue (*Die Komposition des Buches Hiob*) omits ch. 25; J. Grill (*Zur Kritik der Komposition des*

Buches Hiob, 1890), 26:2-27:1 and 29-30; G. Studer (*Hiob*) and A. Kuenen, 27:7-28:28; B. Duhm (*Hiob*) 24:1-24; 28; 30:1-8. Reaching more radical conclusions, T. K. Cheyne (*Encycl. Bibl.* 2, 2476) regards chs. 29-30 as the sequel of ch. 19, omitting as secondary the intervening chapters; F. Baumgärtel (*Der Hiobdialog.* BWANT 61, 1933) can discover nothing genuine after ch. 13 except 16:6, 9, 12-21; 19:2-29; 23:2-7, 10-17; 31:35, 37; E. G. Kraeling (*The Book of the Ways of God*) recognizes only a few remnants of the third cycle of speeches in 23:2-7, 10-17; 30:16-31; 31:35, 37, thus accepting substantially the conclusions of Baumgärtel.

The tendency of recent criticism is to regard the superb poem on divine wisdom (ch. 28, omitting 28:28; cf. the restoration proposed above in the summary of the book) as interpolated. The admission that wisdom (the plan of the universe discovered, but not created, by God before he brought the world into existence) is beyond human reach, has no logical justification in the mouth of Job before the speeches of Jehovah (38-40), where the limitations of human knowledge and power are brilliantly demonstrated. Nor can this calm admission in ch. 28 that man cannot pierce the mystery of the universe, implying a resigned acceptance on the part of Job of God's incomprehensible dealing with him, be reconciled with Job's passionate *apologia* (29-31) which follows immediately. The poem on wisdom is truly "intercalated" between the dialogue and Job's monologues, as P. Dhorme (*Job*, p. lxxvi) admits, even though he regards the chapter as authentic. But K. Budde and E. König (in their commentaries) argue for its logical connection with the surrounding sections. Most recent critics, however, have concluded that this piece is "an independent poem, which formed no part of the original work" (S. R. Driver and G. B. Gray, *Job* [ICC], Vol. I, p. xxxviii. 1921; similarly B. Duhm, *Hiob*, p. 134. KHC, 1897; C. Steuernagel, *Einleitung*, p. 698; O. Eissfeldt, *Einleitung*, p. 508; etc.). Although no final conclusion can be reached as to the authorship of ch. 28, the present writer is still inclined, after a quarter of a century, to adhere to his view that the chapter "is an independent composition of the author, which is not an integral part of the poem [of Job]" (*Le problème du livre de Job*, p. 14).

Critics have come to regard the speeches of Elihu (32-37) as a supplement to the original poem. Already Gregory the Great (d. 604) regarded them as of little value. Their authenticity was questioned in the early part of the last century in the commentary of M. H. Stuhlmann (1804), in W. M. L. De Wette's *Introduction* (1817), in the fourth edition of J. G. Eichhorn's *Introduction* (1823-1824), and by the majority of critics since then. Their authenticity was defended in the commentaries of E. F. K. Rosenmüller (2nd ed., 1824), F. W. C. Umbreit (1832), J. G. Stickel (1842), and other works preceding K. Budde's thorough monograph (*Beiträge zur Kritik des Buches Hiob*), after which only a few critics have adopted this position.[6]

The arguments advanced against the genuineness of chs. 32-37 are their lack of any connection with the rest of the book (where Elihu is completely ignored), their language and style (cf., e.g., S. R. Driver and G. B. Gray, *Job* [ICC], Vol. I, pp. xli-xlviii), and their teaching, which in so far as it does not reproduce thoughts and even expressions of the rest of the poem, fails either to contribute to the solution of the problem or to give the author's own conclusions. These arguments did not seem convincing to the present writer in 1915 (*Le problème du livre de Job*, pp. 13 f.); other reasons, however, led him later (cf. ZAW N.F. 3 [1926] 23 f.) to regard the speeches of Elihu as a polemical interpolation condemning much of the teaching of the book and defending Jewish orthodoxy. The author of the Book of Job had presented the opposite theological tenets of Job and his friends and, lifting the discussion to a higher plane in the speeches of Jehovah, had concluded that the ways of God are incomprehensible to man (cf. ch. 28) and therefore, in spite of appearances, should not be said to conflict with what humans regard as right. The author of the speeches of Elihu was so shocked, after reading the Book of Job in its original form, that he felt the urge to write a refutation which he placed in the mouth of a character which he invented, Elihu. It is significant that Elihu's polemic is addressed not only against Job, whose position was decidedly heretical, but also against the friends and even, in a more subtle manner, against the speeches of Jehovah. With the arrogant tactlessness and impertinent self-assurance characteristic of some champions of traditional orthodoxy, he claims possession of the true knowledge through divine inspiration (32:8-10; cf. 33:14-16) and plays the role of final arbiter in the discussion as a spurious *maestro di color che sanno*. He denounces the friends for having been unable to silence Job (32:11-16), he takes issue with the attitude and particular statements of Job (33:8-11; cf. 13:24, 27; 34:5-9; cf. 27:4 f.; 35:3; cf. 7:20), and finally, as one "perfect in knowledge" (36:4), he dares, in 36-37, to present his own improvements to the speeches of Jehovah. Lest there be a misunderstanding, the author has explained in his prose introduction (32:1-5) the purpose of the speeches of Elihu.

Only few critics have questioned the authenticity of the speeches of

---

[6] C. H. Cornill, *Einleitung in das Alte Testament*. Tübingen, 1891 (7th ed., 1913; English translation, 1907). G. Wildeboer, *Die Litteratur des Alten Testaments*. Göttingen, 1895 (2nd ed., 1905; in the Dutch original, 1893; 2nd ed., 1903). K. Budde, *Hiob*. W. Posselt, *Der Verfasser der Elihureden*, Bibl. Stud., Vol. XIV, Pt. 2, 1909. M. Thilo, *Das Buch Hiob*. 1925. An analysis of the speeches of Elihu into parts written by several authors has been presented by Helen H. Nichols in AJSL 1911, 97 ff. (cf. G. A. Barton, JBL 30 [1911] 68).

Jehovah (38-41) *in toto*.[7] The rejection of chs. 38-39, one of the most superb masterpieces in the book, is primarily the result of the critical theory, appearing first in Studer's commentary and fully developed by Baumgärtel and Kraeling, according to which the original poem was confined to a discussion about Job's misfortunes, and grew to its present size through successive editions. According to this gratuitous assumption, the original poet was not concerned with universal problems of human life and with the character of the deity, but merely with the experience of a pious sufferer certain of his innocence in spite of the insinuations of his well-intentioned friends. This theory implies the excision of the parts of the dialogue dealing with the unhappy condition of mortals in general, and with God's indifference or hostility to them. Accordingly, supplementers of the original book must have written some of the most profound and beautiful parts of the book. We should not impose the strait jacket of our Aristotelian logic and consistency on an ancient Oriental poet of great imagination and insight, and expect that his work should fit within one of our categories as purely lyric, epic, dramatic, or didactic. The Book of Job which left the hands of the original author is not necessarily in harmony with the literary standards demanded of it by modern critics.

The prevailing view is still that the speeches of Jehovah, in whole or in part, were written by the author of the Book of Job. But the descriptions of the ostrich (39:13-18), of the hippopotamus (40:15-24), and of the crocodile (41:1-34 [H. 40:25-41:26]) have been suspected of being interpolated. The description of the ostrich is missing in the LXX and does not consist of a series of questions, like the other parts of ch. 39; therefore some critics (G. Bickell, A. Dillmann, B. Duhm, T. K. Cheyne, G. Hölscher [1937], E. G. Kraeling [1939], etc.) reject it as spurious (Kraeling rejects also 39:9-12). This section seems, indeed, to be the work of an imitator, and even more so those on the hippopotamus and the crocodile (40:15-41:34 [H. 40:15-41:26]), which abound in fantastic details contributing nothing to the argument, and should in any case come after ch. 39. Numerous critics, beginning with W. M. L. De Wette (1817) and J. G. Eichhorn (1823-24), reject the whole passage, or at least, following M. H. Stuhlmann (1804), 41:12-34 [H. 41:4-26].[8] P. Dhorme (*Job*,

---

[7] M. Vernes, in RHR 1880, p. 232. G. Studer, *Das Buch Hiob* u.s.w. Bremen, 1881. T. K. Cheyne, *Job and Solomon;* in *Encycl. Bibl.* 2 (1901) 2480 f. P. Volz, in *Die Schriften des Alten Testaments*, Vol. III, Pt. 2 (2nd ed., 1921). W. Knieschke, *Kultur- und Geisteswelt des Buches Hiob*, p. 98 (ZSF 15, 9-12). Berlin-Lichterfelde, 1925. P. Bertie, *Le poème de Job*, 1929. J. Hempel, *Die althebräische Litteratur* (Handbuch der Literaturwiss.). Potsdam, 1930-1934 (the original book ended with ch. 31). F. Baumgärtel, *Der Hiobdialog*. L. Finkelstein, *The Pharisees*, Vol. I, p. 234. E. G. Kraeling, *The Book of the Ways of God*. New York, 1939.

[8] For a history of the criticism and exegesis of these doubtful passages, see the commentaries of E. König and P. Dhorme.

pp. lxxii-lxxvi) is one of the rare contemporary critics who defend the authenticity of 40:15-41:34 (H. 40:15-41:26). A. Merx (*Das Gedicht von Hiob*. Jena, 1871) regarded this section as the work of the author, added to his book from his notes after his death. Unquestionably the section 38:1-42:6 *in its present form* could hardly have received the author's finishing touches. It is strange that Jehovah speakes twice "out of the whirlwind" (38:1; 40:6), challenges Job twice (40:1 f.; 40:6-14), and is answered twice by a much-chastened Job (40:3-5; 42:1-6). To remedy these inconsistencies it is not necessary to excise drastically 40:6-14; 42:1-6 (C. Siegfried, *Job* in *The Sacred Books of the Old Testament*); for 40:6-14 seems to be the indispensable conclusion of Jehovah's speeches. Even less acceptable is the omission of the speeches of Jehovah and Job's confessions *in toto*, as some critics suggest (cf. above, note 7). K. Fullerton (ZAW 42 [1924] 116-136) limits the original poem to chs. 1-19; 38-39; 40: 3-5, and H. Schmidt (*Hiob*, 1927) confines the divine address and Job's humble confession to 40:1-4, O. Eissfeldt (*Einleitung*, p. 514) to 40:6-14 and 42:1-6. Far simpler and more plausible is the suggestion that the insertion of the hippopotamus and crocodile poems (40:15-41:34 [H. 40:15-41:26]) has caused some damage to the surrounding edges, and produced the double address of Jehovah and the double answer of Job. In the original version the speeches of Jehovah were probably contained in 38-39; 40:2, 8-14 and Job's answer in 40:3-5; 42:2-5.[9] We may surmise that the redactor who inserted the hippopotamus and crocodile poems in 40:15 ff. moved the immediately preceding answer of Job (40:3-5) to its present position in order better to fuse the addition with Jehovah's own words in 40:8-14.

B. Date

The chief chronological problem concerning the Book of Job is the determination of the period in which its original author lived; the secondary parts of the book were added before 200 B.C., the approximate date of the final edition of the work. The folk story of Job in its oral version goes back to unknown antiquity, but the prologue and epilogue of the book in which it has been transmitted to us can hardly be earlier than the sixth century.

Nothing is known of the author except what may be inferred from his poem. Unfortunately he makes no allusions to known historical events or persons, and consequently the chronological clues are indirect, vague, and subject to various interpretations. Critical research has yielded conflicting

[9] This theory has been presented by the following critics: G. Bickell (WZKM 6 [1892]; 7 [1893]; *Das Buch Hiob*, 1894). B. Duhm (*Hiob*) C. Steuernagel (*Einleitung*, p. 700). K. Budde (*Hiob*) G. F. Moore (*The Literature of the Old Testament*). J. A. Bewer (*The Literature of the Old Testament*. New York, 1922). E. Sellin (*Einleitung in das Alte Testament*. 6th ed., 1933; English translation, 1923).

results and the only conclusion which may be regarded as generally accepted is that the poet lived between 700 and 200 B.C. Psalms and Proverbs are the only other parts of the Old Testament the possible dating of which extends over a similar period.

A date later than 200 B.C. has never been suggested by scholars, but in the past, dates earlier than 700 B.C.—now generally regarded as absurd—were proposed. The Babylonian Talmud (*Baba Bathra* 14b, 15a) declared apodictically that "Moses wrote his own book, and the passages about Balaam, and Job"; but in the following discussion (cf. the translation in H. E. Ryle, *The Canon of the Old Testament*, pp. 273 ff.; 2nd ed., New York, 1895) the rabbis dated the lifetime of Job or of the author of his book at various periods extending from the time of Isaac and Joseph to the time of Cyrus and Ahasuerus. The Mosaic authorship (*ca.* 1200 B.C.) was defended by J. D. Michaelis (*Einleitung* u.s.w., Vol. I, §12. Hamburg, 1787) and others; in our own day by G. W. Hazelton (BS 71 [1914] 573 ff.) and F. A. Lambert (*Das Buch Hiob* u.s.w., pp. 22 ff. Berlin, 1919). The apocryphal addition at the end of Job in the LXX identifies the hero with Jobab king of Edom (Gen. 36:33), who is said there to have been a grandson of Esau and consequently much earlier than Moses. This identification and genealogy are, of course, absurd. Such a pre-Mosaic date for the lifetime of the hero of the book is also advocated by Eusebius (*Praep. evang.* 9:25), J. G. Carpzov (*Introductio ad libros canonicos*, etc. Leipzig, 1714-1721; 3rd ed. 1741), J. G. Eichhorn (*Einleitung in das Alte Testament*. 4th ed., Göttingen, 1823-1824), and recently by C. van Gelderen (*De Hoofdpunten der Zielsgechiedenis van Job*, 1903).

The time of Solomon was regarded as the date of our book by Gregory Nazianzen (d. *ca.* 390), H. A. C. Hävernick (*Handbuch der historisch-kritischen Einleitung in Alte Testament*, Vol. III. Erlangen, 1849), C. F. Keil (*Lehrbuch der histor.-krit. Einleitung in die kanon. Schriften des Alten Testament*. Frankfurt, 1853), K. Schlottmann (*Das Buch Hiob*. Berlin, 1851), Franz Delitzsch (*Hiob*. 2nd ed., Leipzig, 1876), and others.

These early dates for the Book of Job need no refutation, nor a period in the eighth century preceding Amos and Isaiah (E. W. Hengstenberg, *Das Buch Hiob*, Vol. I, p. 62. Berlin, 1870). With the seventh century, however, we reach the period in which our poet could conceivably have lived. Job has been dated at the beginning of the seventh century by H. Ewald (*Die Dichter des Alten Bundes*, Vol. III. Göttingen, 1854) and E. Riehm (*Einleitung in das Alte Testament*. Halle, 1889-1890), in its first half by J. J. Stähelin (*Spezielle Einleitung* u.s.w. Elberfeld, 1862), Th. Nöldeke (*Die Alttestamentliche Literatur*. Leipzig, 1868), A. Dillmann (*Hiob*), and E. Reuss (*Geschichte der heiligen Schriften Alten Testaments*. Brauschweig, 1881), or in unspecified periods within the century by W. M. L. De Wette (*Lehrbuch der hist.-krit. Einleitung in die . . . Bücher des Alten Testaments.* Berlin. 6th ed., 1844; 7th ed., 1852), A. Merx (*Das Gedicht von Hiob*), F. Bleek *Einleitung in das Alte Testament,* 4th ed. [likewise in earlier and later editions]), and in the commentaries of L. Hirzel (1839), J. G. Stickel (1842), F. Hitzig (1874), W. Volck (1889), and in other publications.

The date which seems the most probable to the present writer (cf. *Le problème du livre de Job,* pp. 8 f.), the time of Jeremiah (or more exactly the period 608-580), has been advocated by P. Kleinert (in TSK 59 [1886] 273), H. Preiss (*Zum Buche Hiob,* p. 38. 1889), E. König (*Einleitung in das Alte Testament,* p. 417; *Hiob,* p. 495), W. W. von Baudissin (*Einleitung in die Bücher des Alten Testament,* p. 768), N. Schlögl (*Das Buch Hiob* u.s.w., *Die Heiligen Schriften* u.s.w. Vienna and Leipzig, 1916; commenting on 3:10 he regards Jeremiah as the author of the book), H. Beveridge (in *Journ. of the Royal Asiat. Soc.* for April 1919), L. H. K. Bleeker (*Job.* Groningen, 1926), and H. Gunkel (in *Religion in Geschichte und Gegenwart,* Col. 1930).

In general, however, recent critics favor a later date. The so-called Exilic Period (586-538 B.C.) is regarded as the time of composition of our book by T. K. Cheyne (*Job and Solomon,* p. 74; cf. *The Prophecies of Isaiah.* 3rd ed., 1884. Vol. II, Essay IX) and A. Dillmann (*Hiob.* 2nd ed. [4th ed. of Hirzel's commentary]. Leipzig, 1891).

While these critics believe, as also the present writer (JBL 45 [1926] 202-206), that the book preceded the Second Isaiah (about 540 B.C.) and while others have found an influence of Job on the notion of the suffering Servant of the Lord in Is. 53 (L. Seinecke, *Der Grundgedanke des Buches Hiob.* Clausthal, 1863; and Hoekstra, "Job de knecht van Jehovah" [TT. 1871]), a number of scholars conversely follow A. Kuenen ("Job en de lijdende knecht van Jahveh" [TT 1873, 492-542]) in regarding the Second Isaiah as earlier.[10] Some of them date Job in the latter part of the sixth century (R. Kittel, *Religion des Volkes Israel,* p. 143 [after 539 B.C.]) or about 500 (G. Hoffmann, *Hiob,* p. 34). J. P. Naish (*Expositor* 9th Ser., 3 [1925] 39-49, 94-104) regards our poet as a pupil of the Second Isaiah and dates his book in 477 B.C. or a little earlier.

A few recent critics regard Job as a work of the fifth century (G. F. Moore, *The Literature of the Old Testament,* p. 240: "or perhaps the fourth"; S. R. Driver and G. B. Gray *Job,* Vol. I, p. lxx), or specifically

[10] A. Kuenen (Historisch-critisch Onderzoek . . . III 1, 102. 6) and A. B. Davidson (*Job,* pp. lxvi [Cambridge Bible for Schools and Colleges]. Cambridge, 1884) argue that the theology of Job is based on that of the Second Isaiah; the opposite view has been presented by the present writer in JBL 45 (1926) 193-202. Kuenen dates Job about 400 B.C. (*ibid.,* 102. 7), Davidson during the Exile (*ibid.,* p. lxvii). P. Dhorme (*Le livre de Job,* pp. cxxii-cxxv) also concludes the author of Job was familiar with the Second Isaiah.

of its first half (B. Duhm, *Hiob,* p. ix; M. Buttenwieser, *The Book of Job,* pp. 75 ff. P. Dhorme, *Job,* p. cxxxv). Others, following A. Kuenen, come down to its end (*ca.* 400 B.C.): A. S. Peake (*Job,* p. 40. New Century Bible, 1906), K. Budde (*Hiob,* p. liii. 1913), and J. A. Bewer (*The Literature of the Old Testament,* p. 317).

The book of Job was written in the fourth century according to O. Eissfeldt (*Einleitung in das Alte Testament,* p. 521) and L. Finkelstein (*The Pharisees,* Vol. I, p. 231); about its middle according to T. K. Cheyne (*Encycl. Bibl.* 2, 2489), in its second half according to C. Steuer-nagel (*Einleitung in das Alte Testament,* p. 710) and J. Meinhold (*Ein-führung in das Alte Testament,* p. 308. 2nd ed., Giessen, 1926: "in the years of the late Persian rule"), or at its close (*ca.* 300 B.C.) according to P. Volz (in Die Schriften des Alten Testaments, Vol. III, Pt. 2, pp. 26 f. 2nd ed., Göttingen, 1921).

The latest dates suggested are in the third century. C. H. Cornill (*Ein-leitung in das Alte Testament,* §43.6. Freiburg, 1891) dated it about 250 B.C., as also O. Holtzmann (in B. Stade, *Geschichte des Volkes Israel,* Vol. II, pp. 351 f.: "in the Ptolemaic period"). In the last edition of his book (7th ed., Tübingen, 1913) Cornill is more vague ("in the latest period of Hebrew literature").

Finally, some critics refrain from giving a definite date. E. Sellin (*Ein-leitung in das Alte Testament,* p. 145. 4th ed., Leipzig, 1925) dates it in the period 600-450 B.C.; W. Staerk (*Die Entstehung des Alten Testament,* p. 125. 2nd ed. Berlin and Leipzig, 1912) in the Persian period (538-332); A. Lods (*Les prophètes d'Israël*) "long after the time of Ezekiel." E. G. Kraeling (*The Book of the Ways of God,* pp. 197-219) presents a rather complicated theory according to which the introductory story (1:1-2:10) dates from the eighth century and after many vicissitudes our book took its final shape in 350-300.

C. The Nationality of the Author

The vast majority of critics tacitly assume that our author was a Judean or a Jew. In reality, however, except for the mention of the name of the God of Israel, Yahweh, in the prologue and epilogue (27 times in 1:1-2:7; 42:7-12), in the superscriptions of Jehovah's speeches (38:1; 40:1, 6) and of Job's answers (40:3; 42:1), and once in a corrupt text (12:9, where some manuscripts read Eloah; in the gloss 28:28 "Yahweh" is written *Adonay,* Lord), and except for the mention of the Jordan in 40:23, which is in a questionable passage and presumably rests on a textual error, the book contains no reference whatsoever to Israel, to its land, history, cul-ture, and religion. It may be asserted positively that the poet never used the divine name "Yahweh" in his poem; he even avoided "Elohim" (a term for "deity" which is not specifically Israelitic; cf. JBL 47 [1928]

184 f.), which occurs, outside of the prologue and the speeches of Elihu, only in 5:8; 20:29; 28:23 (in 38:7, in the expression "sons of God," the term is used adjectivally; cf. W. R. Arnold, *Ephod and Ark*, pp. 29 ff.). The divine names used by the poet are "El" (36 times; also 19 times in Elihu's speeches), "Eloah" (35 times; 6 times in Elihu), and "Shaddai" (25 times; 6 times in Elihu), all of which mean simply "God," and are used interchangeably "to vary the style and avoid the repetition of the same name" (P. Dhorme, *Le livre de Job*, p. liv).

No characteristic Israelitic or Jewish institutions are even remotely referred to in the poet's work, although he often alludes to civil and moral prescriptions. All such references have an international character and represent practices in force among all ancient civilized nations. It is not necessary to see in them, as S. R. Driver (*Introduction to the Old Testament*, p. 32) does, allusions to Pentateuchal laws. This is obvious for the illegal removal of landmarks (24:2; cf. Deut. 19:14; 27:17; Prov. 23:10) and for the three basic crimes punished in every organized human society: murder, adultery, and theft (24:14-16; cf. the 6th, 7th, and 8th Commandments). Even if 22:6 (cf. 24:3, 9) be interpreted to refer to the return before sunset of a garment taken in pledge (according to the law in Ex. 22:26 [H. 22:25]; cf. Deut. 24:12 f.; Am. 2:8; Ez. 18:12) there is no reason to doubt that the retention of the garment (used also as a bed-cover) would have shocked the sensibilities of ancient non-Israelites possessing a modicum of human feelings. The author of our book, as appears from the moral standards, unsurpassed in nobility in the Old Testament, set forth in ch. 31, was obviously far in advance of his contemporaries, whether he was a Judean or not, and could, for instance, have regarded the worship of the heavenly bodies (31:26 f.) as a base superstition without ever having read Jer. 8:1 f. and Deut. 4:19, exactly as Ikhnaton long before had been repelled by the traditional religion of Egypt.

Even if it could be demonstrated that our author was familiar with a number of writings in the Old Testament, as some critics assert (cf. especially P. Dhorme, *Le livre de Job*, pp. cxxi-cxxxiv), it would not follow that he was a Jew. Do not some writers of the Old Testament disclose a surprising knowledge of some Egyptian and Babylonian writings? The author of the Book of Job was not only a sage, and consequently familiar with the "wisdom" of other nations (particularly of Egypt; cf. P. Humbert, *Recherches sur les sources égyptiennes de la littérature sapientiale d'Israël.* Neuchâtel, 1929; and my article in ZAW N.F. 11 [1934] 93-101), but, unless he wrote after Plato, he was the most learned man, up to his time, known to us. If he lived in a country near Palestine, and accordingly spoke a language only dialectically different from Hebrew, he could easily have read Israelitic writings such as Jer. 20:14-18, which may have inspired Job 3.

In reality, however, with the possible exception of Job 3 and Jer. 20 just noted, it is extremely doubtful that the author of Job plagiarized any other writings of the Old Testament. When actual parallels exist between Job and other books (cf. the lists in Dhorme, *loc. cit.* and S. R. Driver and G. B. Gray, *Job* [ICC], Vol. I, p. lxviii) critical opinion is usually divided on whether Job deserves the priority or not. We have noted (cf. above, note 10) that T. K. Cheyne, A. Dillmann, and others consider Job the source of the Second Isaiah, while A. Kuenen, A. B. Davidson, P. Dhorme, and others defend the opposite view. Similarly, while F. Seyring (*Die Abhängingheit der Sprüche Salomonis Cap. 1-9 von Hiob.* 1889), H. L. Strack ("*Die Priorität des B. Hiob gegenüber zu den Sprüchen,*" TSK [1896] 609 ff.), and others (H. Ewald, Franz Delitzsch, A. Dillmann, E. König, etc.) regard Job as earlier than Prov. 1-9, others (F. Hitzig, A. Merx, A. Kuenen, T. K. Cheyne, G. Bickell, K. Budde, P. Dhorme, J. Ley, "Die Abfassungszeit des Buches Hiob" in TSK 71 [1898] 34 ff., etc.) date Prov. 1-9 earlier than Job. The present writer has summarized his conclusions on the decisive influence exercised by the Book of Job on the Second Isaiah, Proverbs, Psalms (and we may add the glosses in Am. 4:13; 5:8 f.; 9:5 f.; Jer. 10:12 f.) in ZAW N.F. 11 (1934) 99-101.

Whoever reads the genuine parts of Job without preconceived ideas and without being aware of their place within the Hebrew Scriptures, will conclude with E. Renan (*Le livre de Job*, p. xvii. 5th ed., Paris, 1894) that "the essence of the ideas of the Book of Job contains nothing particularly Hebraic [i.e., Israelitic]." On the contrary, the reader who regards the Jewish origin of the poem as an axiomatic truth will reach the verdict of P. Dhorme (*Le livre de Job*, pp. cxxi f.), "The Book of Job is an Israelitic work in all points, in spite of its Arabian or Edomitic cloak." In any case, if the author was a Jew he succeeded so well in disguising himself under an "Arabian or Edomitic cloak" and in removing all traces of his Judean origin, that the illusion is complete. His work if so thoroughly Edomitic that it is either what it appears to be or a most successful literary counterfeit. Only two conclusions as to the nationality of the author are possible. Either he was a Jew, living in Jerusalem (L. Finkelstein, *The Pharisees*, Vol. I, p. 231), in southern Judah, on the border of Edom near the desert,[11] or in Egypt,[12] or he was an Edomite.[13]

[11] J. G. Stickel, *Hiob*, 1842. A. Dillmann, *Hiob*. 3rd ed. of L. Hirzel's commentary, 1869 (p. xxix). F. Bleek, *Einleitung*, 4th ed. by J. Wellhausen. Berlin, 1878. (p. 544) W. W. von Baudissin, *Einleitung*, 1901 (pp. 768-70).

[12] F. Hitzig, *Der Prophet Jesaja*. Heidelberg, 1833 (p. 285). L. Hirzel, *Hiob*, 1839. C. J. Bunsen (*Bibelwerk*) regards Baruch as the author.

[13] J. G. von Herder, *Vom Geist der Ebräischen Poesie*, Vol. I, pp. 125 ff. Dessau, 1782-1783. K. D. Ilgen, *Jobi antiquissimi carminis Hebraici natura atque virtutes.* Leipzig, 1789. R. H. Pfeiffer (ZAW N.F. 3 [1926] 13-25; criticized by E. König, *Hiob*, pp. 39 f.). F. H. Foster ("Is the Book of Job a Translation from an Arabic

The present writer prefers the second alternative in view of the lack of proof that the author was a Jew and the abundant evidence pointing to his Edomitic nationality.

The Judean nationality of the author of the Book of Job is regarded by critics as a self-evident truth, so that in general it is no more a matter of discussion than the nationality of Isaiah or Jeremiah. If, however, we inquire into the evidence supporting this assumption we find it to be decidedly dubious. The supposed familiarity of the author with Old Testament writings has been shown to be entirely irrelevant in deciding his nationality, even if the parallels alleged proved the indebtedness of the author to Hebrew writers. Another proof adduced is the allusion to the Exile of the Northern Israelites in 722 B.C. or of the Judeans in 597 or 586, which has been discovered by many critics in 12:17-25 (cf. 9:24). But, aside from the fact that these passages are sufficiently vague to be interpreted as allusions to the conquests of Alexander (so C. Steuernagel, *Einleitung,* p. 710), it should not be forgotten that Assyrian kings, beginning with Tiglath-pileser III (745-727), deported many nations besides the Israelites. Or shall we admit with P. Dhorme (*Le livre de Job,* p. 160; cf. p. cxxxiii) that the mention of priests in 12:19 "shows that Job formulates ideas common in Israel" (as if other nations had no priests), and with B. Duhm (*Hiob,* p. 69) that, since it is probable that the poet referred to the national catastrophe of Judah in 586, the 'êthānîm ("permanent" and powerful families) in 12:19 are "primarily the descendants of David" (as if no other royal families had ever been overthrown)? The argument obviously turns in a circle: since the author was an Israelite his vague references must be interpreted through the history of Israel. And yet the words were addressed by an Edomite, Job, to his three Edomitic friends: even if spoken immediately after the fall of Jerusalem in 586, the friends would not necessarily have understood the words as P. Dhorme and B. Duhm do.

A third argument is derived from the theme of the discussion between Job and his friends, the question whether God rewards the pious and punishes the wicked during their lifetime, or not. It is believed that the author must have derived both the doctrine of individual retribution and the criticism thereof from Old Testament writings. There the divine retribution was originally national in scope (in the early prophets and in Deut. 28) and was applied to the single individual for the first time by Ezekiel (18; 33:7-20), although the personal religion presupposed by Ezekiel appeared already in Jeremiah. It is not certain, however, that Jeremiah also defended the doctrine of individual responsibility (Jer. 31:29 f. may be spurious). The doctrine of just individual retribution was

Original?" AJSL 49 [1932-33] 21-45) regards the author as an Arab; cf. F. M. A. Voltaire's article on Job in his *Dictionnaire Philosophique.*

recognized as contradicting two facts of common occurrence: the righteous often suffers undeserved torments (Jer. 15:10, 15-18) while, on the contrary, the wicked enjoy happiness and prosperity (Jer. 12:1-3; Hab. 1:12-16; Mal. 2:17; 3:13-15).

In spite of superficial resemblances between these passages and Job, it is by no means certain that an organic relation exists between them.[14] The Book of Job belongs to the wisdom literature which not only had no connection with the prophetic teaching before the writing of late Psalms and Proverbs, but was repudiated in no uncertain terms by the prophets (Is. 5:21; 10:13; 29:14; Jer. 8:9; 9:23 [H. 9:22]). When Job was written, prophecy and wisdom were still antagonistic, representing respectively what Paul calls "the wisdom of God" and "the wisdom of this world" (I Cor. 1:20, 24). Of the prophetic doctrine of divine inspiration, of the prophets' call to national conversion and proclamation of doom, there is no sign in our book. Job's religion is entirely individualistic not because he was influenced by Jeremiah and Ezekiel, but because the sages addressed individuals since time immemorial. They presented to their pupils rules of conduct intended to lead to happiness and success, and they recommended reverence for the deity as a good policy for averting the outbreak of God's anger. The real sources of Job's thought are the stories of the S document (particularly those of the Garden of Eden and the Tower of Babel) and ancient Oriental wisdom, particularly Egyptian.[15]

Finally, the presence of the Book of Job in the collection of Hebrew Scriptures does not prove its Jewish origin. Non-Israelitic writers, such as Agur (Prov. 30), the mother of Lemuel king of Massa (Prov. 31:1-9), Heman (Ps. 88), and Ethan (Ps. 89)—the latter two mentioned as famous non-Israelitic sages in I Kings 4:31 (H. 5:11)—are represented in the Bible, and paraphrases of Egyptian writings (Ps. 104 and Prov. 22:17-23:14) are found in it.

While the Book of Job lacks all indications of a Judean or Jewish origin, its thought and language are characteristically Edomitic. The folk tale, which furnished the plot, the geographical, social, and natural background, the philosophy, and the language of the book are characteristically Edomitic (see ZAW 44 [1926] 13-25). P. Dhorme concedes that

---

[14] The theology and religion of Job differ so radically from that of the prophets (cf. JBL 46 [1927] 193-200) that the present writer is puzzled by the assertions of E. G. Kraeling (The Book of the Ways of God, p. 15), who finds that the religious development presupposed in Job could not have repeated itself outside of Israel, and that the uncompromising quest for human righteousness and the torture of soul arising from a sense of innocence and apparent disfavor on the part of God cannot be conceived outside of Israel. In reality, the deepest thoughts and emotions of Job have no parallels in the Old Testament except in Psalms of later date, but have their presuppositions in Egyptian wisdom literature.

[15] For the doctrine of earthly retribution and the criticism thereof in ancient non-Hebrew literature see especially J. Fichtner, Die Altorientalische Weisheit in ihrer israelitisch-jüdischen Ausprägung, pp. 62-64, 72-73, 105-106.

the divine name Eloah indicates the God who comes from Teman in Edom (Hab. 3:3) and is used by Agur (Prov. 30:5), whose language seems to be Edomitic (*Le livre de Job,* p. lxxxix, n. 7), and recognizes that the Hebrew of Job, which is quite unusual, is strongly influenced by Arabic and Aramaic (*ibid.,* pp. cxl-cxliii). To explain these facts, the simplest hypothesis is that the author of the book was an Edomite.

2. Literary Art

The Book of Job has been called by Tennyson "the greatest poem of ancient or modern times," and by Carlyle "one of the grandest things ever written with the pen. . . . There is nothing written, I think, in the Bible or out of it of equal literary merit." Although such enthusiastic tributes are patently exaggerated, it cannot be gainsaid that Job is the greatest poetical work in the Bible and that it has a place among the masterpieces of the world's literature. As the J document may be classed with the *Iliad,* so Job may be classed with Greek tragedies, Lucretius' *On Nature,* Dante's *Divine Comedy,* Milton's *Paradise Lost,* and Goethe's *Faust*; Plato's dialogues may be added if prose works are included. Job is so unique a literary work that its resemblances to these masterpieces are only superficial; what they have in common is chiefly grandiose conceptions, superb style, intense emotion, profound thought, feeling for nature, and noble ideals.

Some scholars have, however, searched for closer literary relationships. The influence of Job on the *Divine Comedy* (cf. Gustav Baur in TSK 29 [1856] 583 ff.), on *Paradise Lost* (cf. T. K. Cheyne, *Job and Solomon,* p. 112), on Klopstock's *Messias,* on *Faust* (O. Vilmar, *Zum Verständnis Goethes,* p. 33), and other works is of course undeniable. But the dependence of our poem on Greek works is improbable.[16] The influence of ancient Oriental literature, particularly the Egyptian wisdom books, the S document, and to a lesser extent the Babylonian writings, is confined to the thought, being entirely negligible with reference to the literary art of our author.

If our poet ranks with the greatest writers of mankind, as can hardly be doubted, his creative genius did not of necessity rely on earlier models

---

[16] R. Lowth (*Praelectiones de sacra poesi Hebraeorum.* Oxford, 1753) compared Job with Sophocles's Oedipus at Colonus (cf. T. M. Barbaliscia, *Giobbe e Sofocle.* Naples, 1917). H. M. Kallen (*The Book of Job as a Greek Tragedy Restored.* With an introduction of G. F. Moore. New York, 1918) tried to prove that in its original form Job was an imitation of a tragedy of Euripides (for a criticism of this theory, cf. C. G. Montefiore in HTR 12 [1919] 219-224). K. Fries (*Das philosophische Gespräch von Hiob bis Plato.* Tübingen, 1904), less questionably, compares it to Plato's dialogues, but the differences overshadow the superficial similarity in structure. O. Holtzmann (in B. Stade, *Geschichte des Volkes Israel,* Vol. II, p. 331) is hardly right, therefore, when he sees in Job an imitation of Plato's philosophical dialogues. Job has even been compared with the Homeric poems (J. Neyrand, in *Etudes* 59 [1922/24] 129-151)

for the general structure of his work and for the working out of its details. Admitting at the outset that there is no close parallel to his poem, in form and substance, we may regard it as one of the most original works in the poetry of mankind. So original in fact that it does not fit into any of the standard categories devised by literary criticism. All general classifications fail to do justice to the overflowing abundance of its forms, moods, and thoughts: it is not exclusively lyric (W. W. Baudissin, P. Volz), nor epic (J. F. Genung, *The Epic of the Inner Life*. Boston, 1891), nor dramatic (B. Szold, *Das Buch Hiob*, p. xvii. Baltimore, 1886; J. Ley, *Neue Jahrb. f. Philos. und Pädagogik*, Vol. 154, pp. 126 f.), nor didactic or reflective (most of the critics), unless the poem is cut down to fit a particular category (as F. Baumgärtel and E. G. Kraeling are inclined to do). Even the more comprehensive characterizations, such as that of Friedr. Delitzsch (*Das Buch Hiob*, p. 15. Leipzig, 1902), "a poem with dramatic movement and essentially didactic tendency," or better still that of J. G. von Herder (*Vom Geist der Ebräischen Poesie*, Vol. I, p. 148), "an epopee of mankind, a theodicy of God," fail to do justice to the scope of the work. According to E. G. Kraeling (*The Book of the Ways of God*, p. 238), the book is a combination of character dialogue (predominating in chs. 1-20) and philosophical dialogue (predominating in chs. 21-42).

A literary appreciation of Job (as well as an understanding of its teaching) depends on the determination of the contents of the original poem. Admitting that every reconstruction is of necessity conjectural, the conclusions of the present writer are set forth here as a basis for the study of form and contents of the book. The work of the poet (who was an Edomite sage writing about 600 B.C.) consisted of a brief framework in prose (2:11-13; 42:7-10a, possibly only partially preserved), of Job's complaint (3), of a discussion between Job and his three friends, in three cycles (4-14; 15-21; 22-27; 29-31; cf. the preceding summary of the book), of the speeches of God (38-39; 40:2, 8-14), and of Job's answer to God (40:3-5; 42:2-5) which may have contained the admission that the divine wisdom is inaccessible to mortals (28:1-27, with some rearrangements; cf. the summary of the book). Numerous short glosses embodied in the several parts of this poem do not affect its general characteristics.

The general structure of the poem, if it was approximately as tentatively reconstructed, is fairly simple and clear. It was a dialogue between Job and his friends, introduced by a bitter lamentation of Job, and concluded by the addresses of God and Job's recantation. O. Eissfeldt (*Einleitung*, p. 520) suggests that the series of speeches in Job has been inspired by the disputations of the sages in the schools or at court and (following L. Köhler, *Die hebräische Rechtsgemeinde*, pp. 11-13. Zurich, 1931) by the opposite pleas in a lawsuit. This may be possible, but the surviving dialogues in Egyptian and Babylonian literatures (and the series of addresses in the Complaint of the Eloquent Peasant, in Egyptian) furnish only a doubtful parallel to the structure of Job, which is an original contribution of the author.

Within the general form of a debate by means of long addresses, the poem contains poetic pieces that may be read as independent compositions. Some of them are doxologies describing through a series of participial clauses, after the manner of Ikhnaton's Hymn to Aton and other Egyptian hymns (cf. the previous discussion of the style of the Second Isaiah), the attributes and works of the deity (5:9-16; 9:4-10; 12:13-25). There are hymns praising the power of the Almighty, in which the participial clauses are used only sporadically (25:2-6 and 26:5-14, a single poem), or not at all, as in 12:7-10 and in the magnificent speeches of God (38-39), couched in a series of sarcastic questions. Another type of lyric poetry represented is the elegiac, occurring in the laments of Job over his fate (3:11-19; 7:2-8, 12-21; 9:25-31; 16:6-17; 17:2, 6-8, 11-16; 19:7-20; 29-30) and in complaints over the misery of the human lot in general (3:20-26; 7:1, 9 f., 17 f.; 14:1-12, 18-22).

As in some Psalms and in the Babylonian penitential psalms, such laments are often joined to ardent appeals to God for deliverance from disease or other misfortunes; such desperate petitions to God occur in 10:1-22; 13:20-28; 14:13-17.

The descriptions of the happiness and success of the righteous (5:17-26; 22:21-30) and of the ruin of the wicked (8:11-19; 15:17-35; 18:5-21; 20:4-29; 24:21-24 + 18-20) are characteristic of the wisdom literature, as also an occasional proverbial saying which has been added to the dialogue by later editors.

> Whoever denies loyalty to his friend
> Forsakes the Fear of God.
> (6:14, revised according to the Syriac,
> the Vulgate, and the Targum)

> (A man) announces a division (of his property) to friends
> while the eyes of his own children fail.
> (17:5)

> And the righteous clings to his way
> And he who has clean hands becomes ever stronger.
> (17:9)

The bright pictures of the joys of the wicked painted by Job (21:7-21, 31-33) may possibly be regarded as sarcastic parodies of the opposite teaching of the sages. We may also class as wisdom literature the dismal portrayal of social chaos in 24:2-17 (cf. 30:3-8)—a time when violence was unrestricted and the lowest classes in country and city were subjected to extreme privations. The pessimistic Egyptian literature of the Middle Kingdom (*ca.* 2100-1788), reflecting the political anarchy and social upheavals of Dynasties Seven-Ten (2270-2100), following the downfall of the Old Kingdom, depicts a similar breakdown of the social order (see A. Erman, *The Literature of the Ancient Egyptians,* pp. 85 ff.). A theme characteristic of Edomitic rather than Egyptian wisdom is the agnostic recognition that the sages investigating the mystery of the world can never discover God's secret wisdom (11:7-12; 28:1-27; cf. Agur in Prov. 30:1-4 and the speeches of Jehovah in Job 38-39).

In addition to this lyric and didactic poetry the Book of Job contains compositions belonging to other types of literature. Job's malediction of his birth (3:3-10) can only be classed with magical formulae. The indictment of Job (22:5-11) and his self-defense, by means of an oath of clearance (31), belong to forensic literature; Job more than once expresses the wish to present his case before God's court of law.

Such more or less incidental pieces belonging to a variety of poetic genres are evidence of the author's inexhaustibly rich poetic vein. With the exception of the poem on wisdom (28), they have a place within the general scheme of the book. To remove even some of them (as F. Baumgärtel and E. G. Kraeling do) would greatly reduce the value of the original poem and imply that the poetic genius of the supplementers was equal if not superior to that of the original poet. For the finest literary masterpieces are to be found among these incidental pieces and in digressions, rather than in the argumentative scaffolding of the book. Like other great poets, the author illogically devotes the best of his art to what may seem unimportant in the general plan of the work, dealing with details as if they had an independent significance. The following vignettes, for instance, are brilliantly drawn: the underworld (3:13-19; 10:21 f.; 17:16), a vision by night (4:12-20), the dried-up brooks in the desert (6:15-20), the tree which blossoms after being cut down (14:7-12), the starving outcasts in the wilderness (24:5-8; 30:2-7), mining operations, presumably in the Sinai peninsula (28:1-11).

The language of the book has characteristics unknown elsewhere in the Old Testament. The vocabulary includes more words of unique occurrence than any other book (cf. the list in Friedr. Delitzsch, *Das Buch Hiob,* pp. 125 ff.). Many of the unusual words are to be explained through Akkadian, the Arabic, and the Aramaic roots (cf. P. Dhorme, *Le livre de Job,* pp. cxl ff.). F. H. Foster (AJSL 49 [1932] 21-25) believed that Job was translated into Hebrew from the Arabic. In general, diction and syntax are greatly influenced by the Aramaic (cf. E. Kautzsch, *Die Aramaismen im Alten Testament.* Halle, 1902). As in Homer, this dialectic variety is to be explained in part as a literary device, to vary the terminology and for poetic effect. In 3:25, for instance, first the Aramaic, then the Hebrew verb "to come" is used; in 16:19 the Hebrew word for "witness" is followed by the Aramaic; cf. also 39:5. In any case, the diction of Job, far from indicating a postexilic origin of the book, as J. Meinhold

(*Einführung in das Alte Testament,* p. 39) claims, equating it absurdly to that of Ezra-Nehemiah, has a "vigor, wealth, conciseness, and classical elegance" without parallel after the Second Isaiah (A. Dillmann, 4th ed. of Hirzel's commentary, p. xxxv). The Aramaic elements in the Hebrew of Job are no clue for the dating of the book, as many critics believe. The mutual influence of the two languages reaches back to early times: Aramaisms occur in the earliest parts of the Old Testament and the inscription of Zakir king of Hamath (*ca.* 800 B.C.) is written in a mixture of Hebrew and Aramaic.

Like Lucretius, Dante, and Goethe, the author of Job possessed at the same time great poetic genius and incredible erudition. His command of language and powers of expression are unmatched at his time; he used the greatest vocabulary of any Hebrew writer (being in this sense the Shakespeare of the Old Testament).[17] He knew all there was to be known in his time, being a consummate scholar of encyclopedic knowledge, and was endowed with the power of introspection to the highest degree. He reflected profoundly and originally on the ultimate problems of theology and religion, attaining results that have hardly been surpassed. Immanuel Kant devoted a considerable portion of his monograph *On the Failure of all Philosophical Attempts in Theodicy* to an exposition of the Book of Job—and reached similar conclusions.

The style of our poet is no less original than his language and thought. Only his meter is the standard one. Much has been written on the subject of his verse and stanzas (cf. the discussion in P. Dhorme, *Le livre de Job,* pp. cxliv ff.), and a rather simple matter has been complicated beyond reasonable bounds by extremely technical analysis. In reality stanzas seem to be seldom used, perhaps only in chs. 31; 38; 39, where the subject demanded brief subdivisions of the chapters, and possibly in chs. 3 and, in a revised text, 28. The verse is the ordinary one: a line divided into two hemistichs each having four stress accents (4:4 meter; cf. part II, chapter VIII, on the poetry in the Pentateuch). The following verse may serve as illustration in English:

There the wicked cease from troubling
And there the weary are at rest
(3:17)

The present writer is at a loss to understand why many critics assert that the prevailing meter in Job is 3:3, when ordinarily a hemistich (as in the verse quoted) contains four words, each of which has an accent; even when a hemistich has three words (e.g., 3:19b, 20b) or even two (3:21b), the rhythm gains by giving two accents to words which are long or con-

[17] In 4:10 f., to quote only one instance, five different words for "lion" are used.

tain a doubled consonant (*wayyáḥprúhû*, 3:21; *weḥáyyím*, 3:20). With G. Bickell and B. Duhm, we should regard the so-called tristichs (e.g., 3:4, 5, 6, 9), in which an additional hemistich ruins the rhythm, as the result of textual corruption or interpolation.

The style of the Book of Job is highly personal. A considerable portion of the poem was written under the spell of intense emotions. The poet seems to have placed in the mouth of Job his own feelings, doubts, and hopes (B. Duhm, *Hiob*, p. ix), thus transforming the pious and patient character of legend into a titanic challenger of the deity, passing from moods of abject despondency and hopeless pessimism to flaming indignation bordering occasionally on hysterical frenzy. With desperate tenacity Job, conscious of his innocence, clings to the remnants of his faith, which brutal reality and the cold doctrine of retribution implacably applied to his case by his friends have miserably wrecked. Occasionally a fleeting glimpse discloses to his tormented soul a vindicator in the heavens, a God of justice who will clear him of false charges (16:18-22; cf. 13:15 f.; 14:13-15). In the famous passage, "I know that my redeemer liveth" (19:25-27), Job seems to be certain that God will avenge him and that he will witness (even though dead) his own vindication (cf. E. G. Kraeling, *The Book of the Ways of God*, pp. 86-92), but the Hebrew text is so badly transmitted that no reliable translation and interpretation can be given (cf. J. Speer in ZAW 25 [1905] 47-140).

These varying moods are reflected in a style rich in contrasts. Nevertheless, there are some general characteristics that may be noted in the literary art of our poet. The basic quality may be defined as the immediate actuality conveyed by his words. His vivid imagination pictures reality in its manifold variety, with little distortion or exaggeration. Only in those glimpses of the vindicator in heaven, just mentioned, does the poet set sail for alluring regions of fancy, otherwise avoiding that imaginary world of blissful illusions in which the Second Isaiah and later apocalyptic writers loved to reside. This sense of reality expresses itself, on the one hand, in admiration for the magnificence and harmony of the natural world and, on the other, in bitter disillusion with regard to the human world.

No poet in the Old Testament has a keener appreciation of nature nor a more scientific understanding of its functioning. The earliest passages in the Old Testament describing God's creation of the world (which is not the subject of Gen. 2:5-3:24) are Ps. 104, based on Ikhnaton's Hymn to Aton, and Job 9:8 f.; 12:7-10; 26:7-10; 28:25 f.; 38. God's rule of all that exists (5:10; 9:4-7; 26:11-13; 39) and his animation of living beings (10:12; 12:10) are similarly stressed. Characteristic of our author and significant for his literary art is his interest in the habits of animals, particularly the untamed birds and beasts of the wilderness. He delights

in painting vignettes of a lion's den (4:10 f.; 38:39 f.), of the ravens
(38:41), of the mountain goats and hinds (39:1-4), of the wild asses
(6:5; 39:5-8), of the wild ox (39:9-12), of the battle steed (39:19-25),
of the hawk (39:26), and of the vulture (39:27-30).

The author is a master in the use of simile and metaphor. Usually he
draws his comparisons from flora, fauna, and natural phenomena, but
also from human activities. The figures employed to illustrate the miserable lot of humans on earth, their brief span of life, the frailty of their
bodies, and the sufferings inflicted by fellow mortals or allegedly resulting from iniquity, may exemplify our author's manifold wealth of imagery.
From the flora he derives the figures of the felled tree (14:7-12), grass
and flowers (8:11 f.; 14:1 f.), leaves, stubble, and chaff driven by the
wind (13:25; 21:18), and an uprooted vine (8:16-18). From the fauna
he chooses the eagle (9:26), the worm (25:6), the moth (4:19), a
spider's web (8:14), wild asses (24:5), dogs (30:1), ostriches (30:29),
and jackals (30:29) for his comparisons or illustrations. From inanimate
nature he draws the following figures: a deceitful dry brook (6:15-20),
rocks worn away by the water (14:19) or precipitating from mountains
(14:18), seas and streams drying up (14:11), clay and dust (4:19; 10:9),
and fleeting shadows (8:9; 14:2; 17:7). Human activities or their products
furnish the following illustrations: military service (7:1; 14:14), a courier
(9:25), a hireling (7:1 f.), a slave longing for the shade (7:2), a physician (13:4), a weaver's shuttle (7:6), a reed boat on the Nile (9:26),
adobe houses (4:19), tent cords (4:21), decayed wineskins and moth-
eaten garments (13:28), and dreams (20:8). In forming the embryo in
the womb, God poured it out like milk and curdled it like cheese, fash-
ioning it like clay (10:8-11).

It is clear that the author's wonder before the magnificence of nature,
which conveys but a faint idea of the power and wisdom of the Creator,
contrasts with his contempt for miserable human beings, in whom God
is no more interested than in wild animals. His vivid imagination personifies natural objects and phenomena, whose beauty enraptures him.
With classic diction he speaks of "the eyelids of the dawn" (3:9), and
of the time when "the stars of the morning sang together" (38:7). Job
appeals to the earth, "O earth, cover not my blood!" (16:18); he calls
the grave his father and the worms his mother and sister (17:14). The
stars of the Little Bear (Ursa Minor) are the children of the Great Bear
(Ursa Major; 38:32). Fields and furrows cry out in protest when they
suffer injury (31:38). The pestilence, "the first-born of death" (18:13),
and the ruler of the underworld, "the king of terrors" (18:14) seem to
be divine beings, as in Babylonia.

In closing this examination of the literary qualities of the Book of Job, we shall examine the seven chapters in which the brilliance of the poet's style appears at its best.

Chapter 3: the lament of a man longing for death. It is possible, as many believe, that this poem was inspired by Jeremiah's anguished curse of his own birth (Jer. 20:14-18), but Job's complaint discloses far greater literary art. Particular attention is given to the structure and subdivisions. The original poem—omitting four verses, 3:8, 15, 16, 23, and the added hemistichs in four "tristichs" (the second hemistich in 3:4, 9 and the first in 3:5, 6)—had exactly twenty verses, and was divided into three parts of corresponding length (3:3-7, 9 f.; 3:11-14, 17-19; 3:20-22, 24-26). In the first part, after stating the theme (3:3) Job curses the day of his birth (3:4-6) and the night in which he was conceived (3:7, 9 f.); in 3:3b we should read with W. R. Arnold "and the night *in which* [*asher* instead of *āmar*] a man child was conceived." The received text of this verse, implying that the night had made a public announcement of the conception of a boy, is patently absurd. In the second part, which consists likewise of seven verses, Job asks why he did not die at birth (3:11 f.), for then he would have been at rest with ancient kings whose palaces lay in ruins (3:13 f.), and would have enjoyed the justice and equality prevailing in the underworld (3:17-19). The third part, having six verses, begins like the second with "Why?" Here Job wonders why life should be given to the unfortunate who long for death (3:20-22), as he longs for it, being subjected to unendurable torments (3:24-26).

Chapter 28: Where is wisdom? This poem, as reconstructed above in the outline of this book, shows likewise the poet's concern with the symmetrical structure of the whole and fine workmanship in each of the parts. Like ch. 3 and other Hebrew poems which are consciously artistic, the number of its verses is a multiple of ten: it consists of five stanzas of six verses, totaling 30 verses. Like the second and third part of ch. 3, each stanza begins with a question, i.e., the refrain "But whence cometh wisdom, and where is the place of understanding?" (28:12, 20). The poet's answer is that wisdom is not to be found in any part of the world known to man: the precious minerals concealed below the surface of the earth (28:13, 5 f., 1 f.) can be excavated by miners (28:3 f., 9-11), but wisdom has not been discovered in any of the four parts of the physical world (28:21, 7 f., 14, 22) nor can it be bought (28:15-19), for God alone has access to it after discovering it before the creation of the world (28:23-27).

Chapter 29: "There is no greater sorrow than remembering happy days in distress" (Francesca, in Dante's *Inferno*). After the omission of secondary material (29:12 f. and the third hemistich in 29:25, following K. Budde, and 29:23 f., following G. Bickell), this poem consists of twenty lines, like ch. 3. It is divided into three parts: Job's former happy and prosperous private life under God's protection (29:2-6); his un-challenged leadership (29:7-10, 21 f., 25) and integrity (29:11, 14-17) in public life; and his vain expectation of a continuation of these fortunate circumstances to the day of his death in a ripe old age (29:18-20).

Chapter 30: Job's present calamities. The serious textual corruption of this chapter has marred its literary quality. Omitting 30:27 (with K. Budde) and added hemistichs in 30:1, 3, 12, 15, we obtain a poem of thirty verses divided into two equal parts: in contrast with his former authority and happiness (ch. 29), Job is now generally despised (30:1-15) and wretchedly ill through a divine visitation (30:16, 30, 17-26, 28 f., 31).

Chapter 31: The code of a gentleman. The ethical standards presup-posed by Job's oath of clearance in this chapter are nobler than those of the Ten Commandments and the other codes in the Pentateuch, nay more spiritual even than the teachings of the prophets. It is therefore not sur-prising that Jewish scribes have annotated this poem more abundantly than other parts of the book. We should omit as glosses 31:3 f., 11 f., 14, 18, 23, 28, 37, 39, some surplus hemistichs (the second in 31:7, 35 and the third in 31:34), and the colophon at the end, obtaining thus a poem of fifteen stanzas of two verses each (thirty lines in all, like chs. 28 and 30). Aside from the introductory (31:1 f.) and concluding (31:35 f., dis-placed) stanzas, each stanza usually consists of an oath that Job has or has not committed certain actions or a malediction upon himself if he has acted in violation of the dictates of his conscience. In 31:1 ("I made a covenant with my eyes") and nowhere else in the Old Testament, there is a notion approaching the Greek (and modern) conception of a moral conscience.

Chapter 38 [vv. 2-38]: heaven and earth in all their glory. This poem, following an exordium (38:2 f.) introducing the speeches of Jehovah in 38-39, comprised originally two parts of sixteen verses each (omitting, with B. Duhm [*Hiob*] 38:13b, 14b, 15, 28). Through a series of sarcastic questions, God convinces Job of his ignorance and incompetence with regard to the functioning of the physical world. The first part deals with the origin and immensity of the four parts of the world: the earth (38:4-7), the sea (38:8-11), the light, conceived as a localized element (38:12-13a, 14a, 19 f.), and the underworld (38:16-18, 21). The second part concerns the phenomena of the heavens: first the treasuries containing snow and hail (38:22 f.), fog, wind, rain, and thunder (38:24-27), ice and hoarfrost (38:29 f.); then the functioning of "the ordinances of the heavens" manifested in the movement of the constellations (38:31 f.) and in the outbreak of storms accompanied by rain, lightning, and thunder (38:33-38). Aside from the exordium, the poem had 32 lines instead of 30 because the poet, in dealing with the four parts of the world, operated with the number four: his scheme is 4 x 4 verses, twice repeated; or, according to B. Duhm, "four times four tetrastichs." It is one of the most grandiose nature poems ever written, and combines the best scientific knowledge of the time with superb literary art.

Chapter 39 [38:39-39:30]: the wonders of the animal world. Owing to the subject matter, this poem lacks the structural unity of the preceding ones and consists of a series of vignettes depicting the characteristics of the following animals, whose life depends from God: lions (38:39 f.), ravens (38:41; according to G. H. B. Wright [*Job*, 1883], B. Duhm and others, we should read *'ereb* [evening] instead of *'oreb* [raven] and refer the verse to the lions), mountain goats (39:1-4), wild asses (39:5-8), wild oxen (39:9-12), ostriches (39:13-18, spurious), cavalry horses (39:19-25), the hawk (39:26), and the vulture (39:27-30). The poet seems to continue to base his structural scheme on the number 4. Omitting the ostrich, eight animals are described, four of them in stanzas of four verses each. The horse has seven and a half verses (presumably eight, originally), the lion has two, the raven one and a half (presumably one, originally), and the hawk one; or probably twelve verses for these four animals. Thus the poem had perhaps originally 4 x 7, or 28 verses; the two poems in 38-39, which form a unit, have therefore a total of 60 verses, if we do not count the exordium in 38:2 f. In dealing with the mystery of animal life, the poet is no less scientific and brilliant than in the preceding composition.

3. The Philosophy of the Book of Job

The chief point at issue in the discussion between Job and his friends, as the author of the Speeches of Elihu (32-37) well knew, was the justice of God in his dealings with human beings. The broader subject is the nature of the deity, so that "The Book of the Ways of God," the title of E. G. Kraeling's recent book, is a suitable characterization of this great poem. Since the author dealt with theological problems broadly, with reference to the whole field of human knowledge, we may, without impropriety, speak of his "philosophy," although technically the word has different connotations in Greece, where it originated.

It should be noted, however, that a number of scholars have denied that the book deals with theological or metaphysical problems. It has been said that the poem is merely a lyrical lament of a man in agony, or a dramatic presentation of psychological experiences, or an edifying exhortation showing how the pious will behave when sorely afflicted, or an inquiry into the beneficial purpose of human suffering and the unselfish character of true piety, or the like. Since the present writer has discussed these various theories elsewhere (*Le problème du livre de Job*), he may be allowed to state merely his own conclusions which, to some extent, agree with those of other critics.

Before attempting a systematic analysis of the author's philosophy, it may be well to summarize the issues debated by Job and his friends. General philosophical ideas are expressed in the course of a discussion that arose out of the conflicting explanations of Job's misfortunes: concrete instance furnishes the occasion for inferences of a philosophical character.

Eliphaz opens the debate and presents with great tact the point of view of the friends (4-5). Surprised at the desperate outburst of Job in ch. 3, because Job had previously comforted persons in trouble, Eliphaz reminds Job that no innocent man ever perished through affliction; on the contrary, only the wicked are consumed by God's anger. Since all men are sinful, Job's affliction may be explained either as a punishment for his natural imperfection or as a chastisement intended to improve his conduct. In any case God is just and merciful, and will deliver Job from misfortune if he commits unto him his cause. As the debate proceeds, the friends become more and more outspoken and vehement in accusing Job of the most glaring iniquity, but contribute nothing of importance to the initial arguments of Eliphaz.

In his rebuttal, Job agrees with two of his friends' assertions: he admits the universality of sinfulness and the almighty power of God. But he denies both the general thesis of the friends—human conduct is justly rewarded or punished on this earth by a just and merciful God—and its application to his own case. Restricting our examination to the second point, Job's specific case, and leaving the philosophical problems for later consideration, we note that Job contends that his own misfortune is entirely undeserved. Admitting that being a mortal he is not sinless (7:21; 19:4) and has committed iniquities in his youth (13:26), he nevertheless asserts that he is both spotless in character (*integer vitae*) (6:10b; 9:21a; 16:17; 23:11 f.; 27:2-6; 29:12-17; 30:25) and innocent of crimes (*scelerisque purus*), nay even of wicked thoughts (31). His arguments to prove his relative nobility of character and innocence are: his good conscience (27:5 f.); his eagerness to stand in judgment before God (13:3, 15b, 18b, 23b; 23:3-7; 31:35-37; contrasting with an evildoer's fear of judgment, 13:16), for God is his judge (16:21), his witness (10:7; 16:19), his vindicator (19:25), his guarantor (17:3); he appeals to the earth to testify for his undeserved death (16:18); until his sickness he was honored and respected by all (29:7-11, 21-25) and anticipated a happy life as a reward for his integrity (29:18-20; 30:26). But, on the contrary, Job had been afflicted beyond endurance through disease (7:3-5; 13:28; 19:17, 20; 30:16-18, 27, 30), nightmares (7:14), despair of recovery (7:6 f.; 17:1, 11-16; 19:10; 30:23), premature death of his sons (8:4), estrangement from his household (19:13-18; cf. 6:15-17) and friends (19:21 f.), general contempt (17:6; 19:18; 30:1-15), and excruciating agonies (3:24 f.; 6:2-4;

7:11, 15 f.; 16:6-16; 17:7; 23:2). He consequently wishes that he had never been born (3:3-23; 7:15; 10:18 f.). In his dealings with Job, God has therefore been unjust and heartless: unjust, because he proves him, perverse (9:20b), torments him without reason (9:17) unceasingly (7:19-21), subverts Job's cause (19:6 f.), and is determined to prove that Job is in the wrong (10:6 f.); heartless, because God created him to torment him (10:3, 8-15), deliberately makes him impure (9:30 f.), is determined to destroy him (6:4; 10:16 f.; 16:11-14), gives him a life of torment while nonexistence would have been preferable (3:20-23; 10:18 f.), and persecutes him relentlessly (7:12-21; 19:8-13, 21 f.).

In this manner, Job's case gives rise to philosophical questions concerning the character of the deity and the validity of the theory of earthly retribution.

The philosophical problem under discussion in the book is what theologians call the problem of theodicy, or the recognition that the presence of evil in the world is not consonant with the existence of a deity which is both omnipotent and just. In the words of Immanuel Kant, theodicy is "the defense of the most exalted wisdom of the Creator of the world against the accusations presented against it by reason, on account of the anomalies in the world."[18] In Job the problem may be stated in these words: since God is responsible for all that exists, he is responsible for evil; unless evil can be shown to have either a rational purpose or a rational explanation in human actions, God cannot be regarded as benevolent and just.

In the human world Job recognizes three kinds of evil, which appear to conflict with the notion of a wise and compassionate creator endowed with almighty power: physical, moral, and mental evil.

Physical pain, illness, penury, and death beset human beings. If the sufferer is directly responsible for his misery, physical pain does not constitute a philosophical problem. Such is the view of Job's friends who argue that human suffering in general and Job's in particular are a just punishment for sins, either conscious or unconscious. Job, who presents the author's convictions, refutes this theory as applied both to himself and to mankind in general. Apparently he can detect no relation whatsoever between man's conduct and man's fate—a theory presented even more explicitly by Ecclesiastes.

With the exception of the myths of Eden and of the Tower of Babel (Gen. 3 and 11, S), the theory of Job's friends, according to which human conduct is *justly* rewarded on this earth, had never been seriously challenged before the publication of our book—whether we date it in 600

---

[18] I. Kant, "Ueber das Misslingen aller philosophischen Versuche in der Theodicee," *Berlinische Monatschrift von J. E. Biester*, p. 194. Berlin, September 1791. In this essay, Kant presents an acute analysis of the philosophy of Job.

or in 400 B.C.—at least not in extant Biblical records. From time immemorial, sudden physical suffering and untimely death have been explained
either as the violation of a taboo or as the work of malevolent demons
(or enraged gods). The first explanation, which regards pain as a punishment, developed into the theory of a just retribution for human conduct
defended by Job's friends; the second, according to which there is no
exact correlation between conduct and fate, is brilliantly presented by
Job. In the myths of Gen. 3 and 11 (cf. the explanation of Uzzah's death
in II Sam. 6:6 f.), as in the *Iliad,* the two explanations are found in combination: the anger of the deity, aroused by human impertinence or defiance, breaks forth blindly and wreaks dreadful havoc out of all proportion to the offense. Obviously the eating of the forbidden fruit in Eden,
the attempt to build a tower reaching heaven, and the disrespect shown
by Agamemnon to Apollo's priest (*Iliad* 1:7-52), do not justify the curses
on Adam, Eve, and their descendants, nor the unending woes resulting
from the division of mankind into mutually hostile nations, nor yet the
pestilence which Apollo's arrows disseminated among the Achaeans besieging Troy (cf. I Sam. 6:19).

Before Amos, Jehovah, like the other ancient deities, was moody and
capricious, subject to violent outbursts of anger. He was the God of Israel,
concerned with the welfare of his people, but occasionally he was subject
to inexplicable fits of wrath and acted like a pernicious wilderness demon
(Ex. 4:24; cf. Gen. 32:24 f. [H. 32:25 f.]). Without apparent reason he
caused famine (Gen. 41:25-32), allowed enemies to despoil (Judg. 6:13)
and defeat (I Sam. 4:3; II Kings 10:32) Israel, incited Shimei to curse
David (II Sam. 16:10), and afflicted Uzziah with leprosy (II Kings 15:5).
Who can say to Jehovah, "Wherefore hast thou done so?" (II Sam. 16:10).

It was Amos who asked himself this question and found an answer. At
first, puzzled by the calamities with which Jehovah threatened Israel, he
interceded for the nation and was granted his request (Am. 7:1-6). Later
he recognized that the calamities which befell the nation were inflicted
by Jehovah as a warning or as a punishment for Israel's wickedness (Am.
2:6 ff.; 4:1-11, etc.). What was startlingly new in the teaching of Amos
was not the conviction that Jehovah inflicts penalties for sin—a very
ancient notion (Gen. 19:13; 49:5-7; II Sam. 12:14, etc.)—but that Jehovah
was absolutely just in his dealings with man. He was never partial nor
indulgent with his own people (Am. 3:2), never incapable of restraining
his consuming vehement wrath, never moody and capricious. Demonic
and nationalistic traits disappear from Jehovah's nature, for Amos conceived him as the embodiment of what is right (cf. Am. 5:4 with 5:14).
This new theology of Amos and of the reforming prophets who followed
him eventually precipitated the problem debated in the Book of Job.

The corollary of the dogma that God is absolutely just in dealing with

Israel is that God inevitably rewards and punishes his nation according to its deserts. The prophets merely announced the coming ruin of the people as a divine punishment of its sins, but did not promise that it would prosper by fulfilling God's will. Going one step further, the Deuteronomic Code of 621 B.C. proclaimed that Jehovah has made a covenant with Israel, by the terms of which the nation would be divinely blessed if it fulfilled the will of God but atrociously cursed if it violated the covenant (Deut. 5:2 f.; 8; 28).

This doctrine of national retribution on earth, first expounded in its completeness by the authors of the Deuteronomic Code (and later in Lev. 26) was applied to the single periods of Israel's history by the Deuteronomistic editors of 600 (Kings) and of 550 B.C. (Joshua and Judges). This collective retribution was soon made individual. In reality it may be surmised that the average Israelite had always been more concerned with his own personal troubles than with the fate of the nation, which was paramount to him only in time of war. Before the Exile few Israelites probably accepted the prophetic teaching about the absolute justice of Jehovah's visitations and the Deuteronomic teaching about the exact retribution of the nation's conduct. Nor were sudden misfortunes befalling an individual always regarded as a well-deserved punishment of his sins: they were at times explained as the result of black magic, or of the malice of demons.[19] They even believed that a man could suffer for the sins of others and quoted the proverb, "The fathers have eaten sour grapes, and the children's teeth are set on edge" (Jer. 31:29; Ez. 18:2).

Jeremiah and Ezekiel took issue with these popular notions. Through his own experiences, Jeremiah discovered that religion was not merely a national institution, but an inner life and a personal relationship with God. Ezekiel, after the downfall of the nation, stressed the notion of personal responsibility. Thus these two prophets laid the foundation for the doctrine of individual retribution, which Ezekiel expounded casuistically (Ez. 18). Jehovah judges every individual according to his ways (Ez. 18:30) and rewards him accordingly.

Some of the difficulties inherent in personal retribution on earth, a natural corollary of God's justice, were perceived by Jeremiah when this doctrine was taking shape. His own personal agonies of spirit, resulting from his devotion to God's cause (Jer. 20:7-18), and the prosperity of the wicked (12:1-3; cf. Hab. 1:13 f.), seemed to refute conclusively the belief that the God of justice, who knew the innermost thoughts of everyone (20:12), requited every man according to his conduct.

[19] On sorcery among the Israelites see, for instance, L. Blau, *Das altjüdische Zauberwesen*. 2nd ed., Berlin, 1914. A. Jirku, *Materialen zur Volksreligion Israels* Leipzig, 1914. A. Lods, *Israël*, pp. 241-249. On demons, see H. Duhm, *Die bösen Geister im Alten Testament*. Tübingen, 1904. A. Jirku, *Die Dämonen und ihre Abwehr im Alten Testament*. Leipzig, 1912.

The facts of daily experience did not, however, invalidate for Jeremiah and for orthodox Jews later the dogma that God's justice *must* reward every individual according to his ways. But the spectacle of the wicked enjoying to the full the goods of this life was a constant shock to the pious (Mal. 3:15; Ps. 10:3-11; 37:1, 7, 35; 73:3; 92:7 [H. 92:8]; 94:3-7, etc.). The righteous, usually afflicted with poverty and disease, sometimes wondered whether they served God in vain, without receiving any profit from their zeal in fulfilling the Law (Mal. 3:14). In a frantic search for an answer to such tormenting doubts, the believers tried to convince themselves that the prosperity of the wicked was but a prelude to their inevitable downfall and that the triumph of the righteous was imminent (Pss. 1; 7; 9; 32; 37; 68; 119; 145; 146; 147; Prov. 2:21 f.; 3:33; 10:24-30; 11:5-8; 21:12; 29:16). In this manner, the chimerical dreams of apocalypse, applied to individual Jews rather than to the nation, served to strengthen the faith of the doubters. Some nobler spirits attained inner peace in the midst of trials through the gratification of a clear conscience (Pss. 7:9-11; 17:3-5) and, like Jeremiah, through blissful communion with God, the "stronghold in time of trouble" (Ps. 37:39 f.), the soul's rock and portion forever, even when recovery from disease was beyond hope (73:26). "The nearness of God is my good" (73:28).

In spite of these doubts and misgivings, in spite of the testimony of daily experience, the doctrine of individual earthly retribution triumphed in postexilic Judaism, and it was even inferred, as in the case of Job, that a man suffering misfortune was guilty of conscious or unconscious sins for which he was receiving proper punishment.[20] The needy (expressing themselves in the Psalms), the middle class (whose views are reflected in Proverbs), and the clergy (represented by the Chronicler) clung to this dogma with the tenacity of theologians reasoning from axiomatic premises, with a supercilious disregard for actual reality. Eventually, when their position became untenable, they withdrew to lines of defense beyond the reach of facts. Physical evil was attributed to Satan (Wisd. of Sol. 2:24; cf. I Chron. 21:1; Job 1-2; Zech. 3:1) and the final just retribution for human deeds was postponed to the time when God would raise the dead from their graves to receive their rewards and punishments (Dan. 12:2; cf. Is. 26:19).[21]

Job's three friends, like the orthodox Jews whose views have been summarized, explained physical evil (disease, poverty, sudden death, etc.)

---

[20] Thus the Chronicler regards the misfortunes of Saul, Jehoram, Uzziah, Josiah, and Zedekiah as divine punishments (I Chron. 10:13 f.; II Chron. 21:10 ff.; 26:16 ff.; 35:20 ff.; 36:12 ff.).

[21] For fuller expositions of the problem of evil in the Old Testament, see the monographs listed in HTR 27 (1934) 286; and A. C. Knudson, *The Religious Teaching of the Old Testament*, pp. 266-289.

as a divine punishment for sin.[22] On the contrary, Job, presenting the convictions of the author of the book, proves not only that a single cause cannot explain suffering, but that this theory is entirely erroneous.

Human suffering of course is frequently the direct result of human actions, either individual or collective. The pain inflicted by evildoers could only be regarded as a divine punishment of the victims by making God responsible for criminal actions; in strict logic, God would then force a man to sin and then punish him for evil acts for which his own will was not responsible. This curious determinism appears sporadically in the Old Testament (Ex. 4:21; 9:12, etc.; Deut. 2:30; Josh. 11:20; Is. 6:10) but seems to be alien to Job. Our author does not accuse God of being responsible for human iniquity.

Individual criminals bring financial ruin to a man through theft, heartless creditors despoil the poor, dishonest farmers move landmarks, robbers drive away flocks (20:19; 22:6, 7, 9; 24:2 f., 9 f.). Under the protection of the night, murderer, thief, and adulterer commit their crimes (24:14-16).

Human societies through hereditary inequalities in rank and property inflict privation and humiliations on the lowest classes. "From out of the populous city men groan" (24:12); out in the steppe "the poor of the earth hide themselves together" living like wild asses in the wilderness, naked and without shelter (24:4-8; cf. 30:3-8); and on the farms the hired laborers go hungry and thirsty (24:10 f.).

Besides these afflictions caused by criminals and social inequalities in normal times, revolutions and wars add considerably to the sum of human misery. Wretched outcasts are driven from the midst of men and are pursued like thieves (30:5). After a disastrous war, kings are led away captive, nations are destroyed or deported (12:17-25). The weapons of war slay many (19:29; 20:24-26).

Nature is no less cruel than man. "In sober truth, nearly all things which men are hanged or imprisoned for doing to one another, are nature's everyday performances. . . . Nature impales men. . . . All this nature does with the most supercilious disregard both of mercy and of justice" (John Stuart Mill, *Essay on Nature*). In the land of the author wild beasts still threatened human life (5:22), particularly lions (10:16) and poisonous snakes (20:14, 16). Thistles grew instead of wheat (31:40), caravans finding the watering places dry perished of thirst (6:15-20; 24:19), and natural conflagrations took their toll in human life (15:34; 18:15; 20:26).

[22] The friends' theme, with many variations of detail, is that the consequence of sin is calamity (4:7-9; 5:2-6; 8:3 f., 11-19; 11:20; 15:20-35; 18:5-21; 20:5-29; cf. 27:7-23) and that virtue and piety are amply rewarded on earth (4:6 f.; 5:8-27; 8:20-22; 11:13-19; 22:21-30). They definitely regard Job's misfortunes as evidence of his wickedness and assure him repeatedly that timely conversion to God will restore his fortunes.

In summing up the woes which afflict mankind, Eliphaz lists famine, death, war, the scourge of the tongue, destruction, and the beasts of the field (5:20-22) without even approaching completeness. The author adds to the ills caused by men and nature already mentioned, pestilence (27:15), illness (7:5; 18:13, etc.), nightmares (7:13 f.), childlessness and the loss of children (27:14), utter loneliness when ostracized by friends (19:13-19) and abhorred by neighbors (30:1 ff.), and finally the arrival of death, "the king of terrors" (18:14)—and ultimate oblivion (18:17).

The Israelites were of course sadly familiar with all these calamities, but they never lost their delight in life, which was to them the most precious of all things. The four Israelites who committed suicide were either mortally wounded (Judg. 9:54; I Sam. 31:4) or expected to be executed (II Sam. 17:23; I Kings 16:18). Even Jeremiah who, overcome by mental agony, cursed the day of his birth (Jer. 20:14-18), conquered this mood and even looked forward optimistically to a glorious future for his people.

The gloomy pessimism pervading the Book of Job is alien to the writers of Israel, even to Ecclesiastes. It finds a parallel in some of the Egyptian poems and wisdom books, and in the S document, particularly the story of Eden (Gen. 3). In Job human life is regarded as incurably evil, unbearably sad, atrociously tragic. This attitude of the author arose less from the occasional calamities enumerated above than from a sense of the futility and misery of existence, of man's imperfect adaptation to his natural environment, of the contrast between conduct and fate, between ideals and reality. Including only the human world, this pessimism does not embrace the cosmos. The author admires the greatness, order, and wisdom of the physical and animal world, but with regard to man he could have endorsed Homer's dictum, "there is nothing more wretched than man of all things that breathe and move about upon this earth" (*Iliad* 17:446 f.).

"Man that is born of woman is few of days and full of trouble" (14:1). He is nothing but a worm, a maggot (25:6); his days are a military service, like those of a hireling (7:1). Ephemeral like a cut blossom, like a fleeting shadow (14:2), he dwells in a body of clay whose foundations are in the dust (4:19; cf. Gen. 2:7). His life is like a breath (7:7), his days are swifter than a weaver's shuttle (7:6), swifter than a runner, than fast ships, than a swooping vulture (9:25 f.), and flee away without hope (7:6), without good (9:25). Life's brief span (10:20) is inexorably fixed by God (14:5; 21:21). After his allotted "months of vanity" and "wearisome nights" (7:3-4), during which man discovers that his confidence is "gossamer" and his trust "a spider's web" (8:14) and becomes a burden to himself (7:20), the human being whose soul is weary of life

(10:1) finally lies in the dust and is covered with worms (21:26; cf. 24:20). There is hope for a tree when it is cut down if some of its fibers remain intact, but when man dies, till heavens be no more he shall not awake again (14:7-12, 14).

And yet, the misery of human existence may become so acutely unbearable that men like Job long for the release offered by death and envy those who died in the womb without seeing the light of day (3; 10:18 f.; 14:1-22; cf. Eccl. 4:1-3; 9:1-10). "Not to be born is the most to be desired; but having seen the light, the next best is to go whence one came as soon as may be" (Sophocles, *Oedipus Coloneus* 1225 f.).

It is thus clear that the author did not regard physical evil as exceptional in human life, but as inherent in human nature and existence, and therefore ultimately of divine origin. Similarly, in contrast with the prevailing view among the Israelites, moral evil is not confined to occasional transgressions, but is a taint of human nature. No human being is free from sin (4:17-21; 15:14-16; 25:4-6).

Job's protestations of innocence (see particularly ch. 31) against the veiled or explicit accusations of his friends, understood literally, would contradict this doctrine of the universality of sin. But in reality Job, if pressed, would never have denied being tainted with the moral imperfection inherent in all human beings. This taint appears with the first man created, who attempted to steal the divine wisdom (15:7 f.; cf. Gen. 3; Ez. 28:1-19; the myths of Prometheus and of Adapa are apparently variants of the same myth) and is even characteristic also of divine beings (4:18; 15:15; 25:5; cf. Gen. 6:1-4; Is. 14:12-15; Ez. 28:14 f., 17; Greek and Babylonian myths likewise know of conflicts between the higher and the lower gods).

The author's conviction that all men are sinful arose from the observation of human conduct, which dismally violates the tenets of his moral code, the noblest in the Old Testament. The author's moral standards rise far above the civil and criminal codes of his day, in which the three basic crimes (murder, theft, and adultery; cf. 24:14 f.) and dishonest practices (moving of landmarks; cf. 24:2) were condemned. The author's enlightened conscience condemns actions disregarded in the official codifications. Some of them are inspired by greed, *auri sacra fames* (Vergil, *Aeneid* 3:57): deceit (31:5), fraud (31:7), heartless foreclosure of mortgages and retention of pledges (22:6; 24:2 f., 9), unfair exploitation of the fields and of the hired husbandmen (31:38-40). Other actions disclose utter callousness for the needs of the unfortunate or sadistic oppression of helpless people: brutal display of one's power against the fatherless (31:21) or the servants (31:13); unfeeling indifference for the desperate plight of the widow and the orphan (22:9; 31:16 f.), the starving (22:7), the naked (31:19), and the homeless wanderer (31:31 f.).

Finally, ascending to a level otherwise unattained in the Old Testament, the author condemns purely mental offences, wicked thoughts which do not produce any concrete harm to others: lustful glances at a virgin (31:1; cf. Matt. 5:28), pride and joy in one's wealth (31:24 f.), gratification for an enemy's misfortune (31:29 f.), covetousness (31:7b; cf. the Tenth Commandment), secret adoration of the heavenly bodies (31:26 f.), and hypocrisy (31:33 f.). Such a spiritualization of sinfulness, reaching the most secret thoughts, is unknown before our author. For even Jeremiah's notion of the obduracy of the heart, as the ultimate root of iniquity, manifests itself in words and actions and does not take into account mere fleeting evil impulses arising from subconscious depths. For Job, moral evil is neither a violation of a divine law nor stubborn selfishness, but an inevitably pervasive concomitant of human nature, reaching even to the higher sphere of divine beings. "Who can bring a clean thing out of an unclean?" (14:4).

It is thus clear that our author deals with the problem of evil from a philosophical point of view unknown elsewhere in the Old Testament outside of the S document, where an editor illustrates his pessimistic views through ancient myths. Our author regards pain and sin, which mar human life, as concomitants of human nature—as natural laws, we would say—rather than as occasional accidents. Characteristically, he connects human sinfulness with man's ephemeral body of clay, while admitting, however, that even spiritual beings are not morally perfect (4:17-21). Outside of our book, the recognition of universal sinfulness in Israel (Jer. 5:1-5; 8:6; Ez. 16:20) or in mankind in general (I Kings 8:46; Ps. 14; Prov. 20:9; Eccles. 7:20) have religious rather than philosophical premises. Job's doctrine of man's miserable status in nature was considered a heresy in Judaism and was refuted in Ps. 8.

Job's conclusion that sin and pain far from being related as cause and effect are merely parallel aspects of man's lowly earthly nature, for which the universal Creator is necessarily responsible, is a source of mental torment—the third evil besetting mortals. Whatever be the divine wisdom manifested in nature, the miserable condition of man is without remedy. There is no justice in man's fate, and God, in his dealings with man, must be a despot for whom the human standards of fairness and benevolence have no meaning. The realization that the universal God is neither benevolent nor just when he torments him without reason, and that, as for man in general, only death (the gate to the eternal darkness and silence of the underworld) could bring him relief, was more distressing to Job than physical pain. Clinging with desperate frenzy to the wreckage of his shattered faith to save his distracted mind from the whirlpool of insanity, Job in moments of illumination, closing his eyes to the dismal reality, contemplated an alluring world of fancy in which

injustice has no place. There, a witness in heaven vindicates Job's innocence against the cruelty of the Creator, whose power crushes him like a
moth. Although this Utopic hope may be realized only after Job's death,
nevertheless he will be conscious of his own vindication (13:15 f., 22;
14:13-17; 16:19-22; 17:2 f.; 19:25-27).

These significant glimpses of a god of justice arising to defend Job
against the god of power may well reflect inner experiences of the author.
But in any case such daring intuitions, contradicting the logical conclusions of his rational thought, have no place in his philosophy. It is only
when the religious emotions of the author recoiled with horror from the
ultimate conclusions of his argument that he ceases to be rational and
becomes a dreamer. Ecclesiastes, on the contrary, when his observations
and arguments led to skepticism, contemplated the total ruin of his
religious convictions with perfect equanimity and utter indifference, feeling no emotional need for a faith which gave substance to things hoped
for, but was rationally impossible.

The author's notions about the functions and character of the deity
contrast sharply with his religious aspirations and chimerical hopes. The
basic principle of his theology is the soleness of God. His monotheism is
never stated explicitly (as in Is. 40-55), but is axiomatic. It is only in
moments of blissful fancy that Job appeals to the god of justice against
the god of power, but his reason tells him that the almighty Creator of
the world is the sole God in existence. The justice of God in dealing with
mortals would not have been questioned if misfortunes could have been
attributed to unfriendly deities and deliverance could be expected from
a friendly god. Subordinate divine beings, such as the spirits controlling
the astral bodies (25:5; 38:7), play no role in the discussion, being entirely subjected to God (25:2) and unworthy of human worship (31:
26 f.).

Monotheism has been attained either by endowing a national god with
international and cosmic jurisdiction or by postulating behind all phenomena a single ultimate cause. The first process is characteristic of
Judaism: Amos, by identifying Jehovah with the right, extended his
power over all nations; and the Second Isaiah, under the influence of Job,
attributed to Jehovah (the ruler of history) the creation of the physical
world, concluding that no other god could exist by the side of Jehovah,
whose control embraced both mankind and nature. The second process
is characteristic of Greek philosophy, which first recognized the unity of
the cosmos and then the soleness of the divine being or universal intelligence responsible for regulating the course of the world. In the first
process a personal god becomes a cosmic force; in the second, universal
intelligence and power may either be endowed with personal traits or
be identified with the abstract absolute.

Job's theology is more akin to the Greek than to the Israelitic notion of the deity. Nothing indicates that Job's universal deity was previously a national god like Jehovah. The author never refers to God by a personal name: the name Jehovah occurs only in the prologue, in the redactional titles of chs. 38-42, in a gloss (28:28), and in a corrupt verse (12:9). The author uses only general terms meaning the deity (*elōhîm*, three times; *ēl*, 55 times; *elōah*, 41 times) and *shadday* (31 times), a word whose meaning and etymology are utterly obscure (the LXX translates it with *pantokrátōr*, almighty [cf. Is. 13:6; Joel 1:15], deriving it from the root *shadad*, to act violently, to destroy). More significantly, the functions and attributes of the deity in Job indicate that the author conceived his God primarily as a cosmic force, not as the patron god of a nation, primarily concerned with human affairs. This anonymous deity is not connected with any nation nor is it the object of worship. Although God appears as a person in addressing Job out of the whirlwind (38-41), the personality of this God is a postulate of religion and a poetic device required by the drama, rather than a philosophic conclusion. In essence God is a universal force and as such can hardly have the characteristic of human personality. The only human traits of God are that he hears Job and answers him in intelligible Hebrew poetry, as was required by the dramatic structure of the book. For the rest, the gap between God and man is impassable. God is not an idealized man of immense power and knowledge, but a being so infinitely superior to man that the latter is insignificant before God. The difference of degree is such that it is equivalent to a difference in nature. Accordingly, the personality of God, if by personality we understand something characteristic of human beings, is philosophically questionable. "He is not a man, as I am, that I should answer him, and we should come together in judgment" (9:32). "Hast thou eyes of flesh? Or seest thou as man seeth? Are thy days as the days of man?" (10:4-6). What can the deity, whose power is beyond comprehension, whose wisdom is forever hidden from man, whose works are "past finding out (9:10), who is eternal, spiritual, invisible (9:11), have in common with a creature as ephemeral, insignificant, and miserable as man? Even man's noblest ideals of justice and right are meaningless for God (9:14-20). Needless to say, the anthropomorphic expressions by which the poet ascribes to a transcendent God human organs such as eyes (11:4), a face (13:20, 24; 23:15), lips (11:5; 23:12), arms (40:9), hands (10:3, 7 f.; 11:9, and often elsewhere), a heart (10:13), and even teeth (16:9), are merely poetic metaphors. Modern theologians may claim that God is at the same time a person—having perceptions, thoughts, emotions, consciousness, and volitions—and the *movens non motus*, the ultimate cause of all that exists. But our author (in contrast with the Second Isaiah) was unable to discover in the universal Creator the characteristics of human personality. He could see nothing in common between the eternal and the ephemeral, the Almighty and the worm, the Creator and the creature, the dweller in the heavens and the dweller in the clay, the Omniscient and the ignorant, the ruler of fate and the victim of fate, the cosmic despot throning above all laws and man struggling to fulfill the ideals of justice and mercy.

In our book the deity is not, like Jehovah before the Second Isaiah, either a national god or a god of justice and love, concerned primarily with a nation or with mankind; he is an inscrutable and irresistible cosmic force. This appears clearly in the functions and attributes which the author ascribes to the deity.

The divine activity is manifested in the creation of the world, in its upholding, and in the animation of living creatures, including man. God created the world out of chaos, after he discovered "wisdom." Creation is not *ex nihilo.* Chaos and wisdom—contrasting entities—had always existed: the cosmos emerged when God victoriously joined chaos and wisdom into a synthesis. Chaos seems to have been a seething amorphous mixture of air, water, and fire (the elements named in 28:25 f.), a boiling fluid in a state of eternal anarchy such as John Milton (*Paradise Lost,* Book II) describes it:

> The womb of nature and perhaps her grave
> Of neither sea, nor shore, nor air, nor fire,
> But all these in their pregnant causes mix'd
> Confus'dly, and which thus must ever fight,
> Unless th' almighty Maker them ordain
> His dark materials to create more worlds.

When the world was in this chaotic state, God discovered wisdom which had hitherto been hidden: he "perceived the way to it and found its place" (28:23). "In the beginning was the Logos [reason]." Having seen it for the first time, God studied it, set it up as a model for his work, and tested it in creating the world (28:27). For the rationality of wisdom revealed, by contrast, the turbulent anarchy of the elements and by imposing on the confused agitation of chaos the norms of wisdom (28:25-27) God brought the ordered world into existence.

This preliminary organization of chaos is only the beginning of God's creative work. The control of the chaotic storms allowed the solid earth to emerge, and God provided it with a solid foundation (the pillars of the earth, 9:6), laying the cornerstone thereof while the morning stars sang together (38:4-7). God established the earth firmly over empty space (26:7). But the surface of the earth was at once in danger of being flooded by the primeval ocean bursting forth from the womb of chaos (38:8). After swaddling the new-born abyss with thick clouds (38:9), God prevented the inundation of the earth first by confining the waters behind bars and doors (38:10), but later by merely saying *"Non plus ultra!"* (38:11). Deep below the surface of earth God formed the springs of the deep (38:16), and yet deeper the underworld (26:5), with its gates and gatekeepers (38:17). At the extreme limits of the earth's surface, which had been carefully measured (38:5), God placed the houses of light and darkness (38:19 f.). The pillars of heaven (26:11) supporting the firmament, which God stretched out like a tent (9:8), were likewise placed on the circumference of the ocean surrounding the earth. The ends of the earth enclosing what is under heaven (28:24) are therefore called the "circle of the heavens" (22:14) or the "circle on the face of the waters" (26:10, *sic;* cf. Prov. 8:27). Over this heavenly vault (the divine throne, 26:9), God placed the treasuries of snow and hail (38:22 f.), the chambers of the winds (cf. 38:24), and the storehouses of rain and thunderbolts (cf. 38:25 f.), of dew, ice, and hoarfrost (cf. 38:28-30). High above the earth, the constellations were attached to the heavenly vault (9:9; 38:31 f.); their courses are regulated by laws whose influence is felt upon the earth (38:33). Controlled by God, the clouds fly below the stars pouring out water on the earth (38:34-38), and lightning bolts dash at the divine command (38:35).

The first man was brought forth "before the hills" and was a mythical being sitting in the councils of God (15:7 f.). Moreover, every man is a new creation of God (31:15): he fashions the embryo like clay, pours him out like milk, clothes him with skin and flesh, and knits him together with bones and sinews (10:9-12). Presumably every animal is likewise a special creation of God.

Besides creating all that exists (see also 4:17; 5:9; 12:7-9), except wisdom and the elements of chaos, God is responsible for the course of nature and the animation of all living beings. He removes mountains, shakes the earth, and prevents the sun from rising (9:5-7); he binds the waters in his clouds and spreads clouds over the sky (26:8 f.). Morning and dawn, whose coming dispels criminals (38:13-15) operating under the cover of darkness (24:13-17), obey God's voice (38:12). He gives rain upon the earth (5:10) and life to every living thing (10:12; 12:10). He endows wild animals with boldness and strength, and provides for their needs (38:39-39:30, omitting 39:13-18). Human fate, in good fortune or bad, is determined by God: he wounds and heals (5:18), his arrows bring disease (6:4), he sends nightmares (7:14), and exalts or destroys nations and their leaders (12:17-25).

Although God's essential nature and purposes cannot be scrutinized by man (11:7), some of his attributes can be inferred from his activity, at least from that part of it which is known (26:14), for *in toto* God's works are past finding out (5:9; 9:10). In their immensity of scope and co-ordination of details, God's works in creating and controlling heaven and earth disclose to our author an energy and knowledge at least sufficient for the execution of this prodigious task. The two obvious attributes of God are unlimited power and wisdom: "He is wise in heart and mighty in strength" (9:4); "With him is wisdom and might" (12:13; cf. 12:16).

Nature gives evidence of God's immense power, which nothing in existence can equal. God's sway over the four parts of the world (the heavens, the earth, the sea, and the underworld; cf. ch. 26) is absolute. Nothing can challenge his dominion over all that exists. He has crushed every attempted rebellion against him. He conquered chaos at the beginning and broke the power of the mythical monsters of the primeval chaotic mass: the swift serpent (26:13), Rahab with her allies (26:12; 9:13), Leviathan (cf. 3:8). God set a watch over the dragon (7:12) and imprisoned the primeval giants under the waters (26:5). God restrained the ocean bursting forth from the womb of chaos by means of bars and doors (38:8-10; cf. 7:12), and stayed its proud waves with his word (38:11). Since these victories at the time of creation, God has ruled supreme in the world. Although his heavenly hosts are innumerable (25:3) and untrustworthy (4:18; 15:15; 21:22), God keeps peace in his high places because dominion and fear are with him (25:2 f.). His power is equal to every task: "What his soul desires, even that he does" (23:13).

Vast as God's power is his wisdom, reaching to the ends of the earth (11:6, 8 f.). The physical world (38:37) and the realm of living beings (39:26) exhibit the unfathomable scope of the divine wisdom which, after a vain attempt of the first man to steal it unto himself (15:7 f.), has remained forever hidden from men and beasts because it is not in any part of the physical world (ch. 28). One would nearly surmise that, like Plato's ideas, this metaphysical wisdom is outside of space.

In wisdom and power God towers loftily above the sphere of man and the rest of creation. If the greatest of his works are but the outskirts of his ways (26:14), how exalted in majesty, how mysteriously transcendent and inviolably pure must not be his innermost nature! The very heavens (15:15) and the stars (25:5) are not pure in his sight, and the moon has no brightness in comparison with him (25:5). God is higher than heaven, deeper than the underworld, longer than the earth, broader than the sea (11:8 f.); thus God's nature extends beyond the limits of the four parts of the world. P. Dhorme (*Le livre de Job*, p. 191) has even said that it is outside of the four dimensions and therefore inaccessible. The holiness of God in Job has therefore a metaphysical rather than an ethical connotation: it expresses his transcendence, his majestic inviolability, his shining purity—in a word, it signifies the qualities by which God is exalted above man and differs entirely from him.

Conversely, man's noblest ethical ideals, justice and mercy, which in their perfection became attributes of Jehovah after Amos and Hosea (cf. Ex. 34:6 f.), for the very fact that they are human could not be characteristic of a deity so exalted and transcendent as the God of Job.

This a priori inference is confirmed a posteriori: God's activity indicates that he is not bound by the standards of human justice and mercy. On the contrary, "God does not withdraw his anger" (9:13), but like a lion tears men in his wrath (16:9) and pours upon mortals the fury of his anger (20:23; cf. 10:17; 21:20). Job denies that such outbursts, utterly merciless, are dictated by justice, for both the righteous and the wicked are the victims of divine ire. In God's dealing with men Job can find no justice: "As for power—he is strong; but as for justice, who will summon him?" (9:19, slightly revised.) Therefore Job expects no fair treatment from God: were he innocent, God's own mouth would condemn him, the deity would prove him perverse (9:20, reading *pîw* for *pî*, according to Olshausen, Merx, Siegfried, and others). "Innocent or guilty—he annihilates!" (9:22) He even laughs at the plight of innocent sufferers (9:23). Confronted by the problem of evil, by man's generally sad fate on this earth, by the success and happiness of rascals and the calamities afflicting the noblest of men, the author of Job could only have cleared God of responsibility for evil by admitting (as J. Stuart Mill did in his *Essay on Nature*) that God was good but not sufficiently powerful to eliminate evil. Such a notion, if he ever entertained it, was discarded as absurd, and never appears in the book. Upon the premise that God is the Creator and Controller of the world, he could only choose the other alternative: God is almighty, but not good—at least according to the human standards of right and mercy. When, for instance, a country suffers injustice at the hand of a wicked despot, if God is not responsible, who then? (9:24). Philosophically the dilemma—almighty or good—is still "the squaring of the circle in the field of religious consciousness" (W. Windelband, *Präludien*, p. 435. 3rd ed., Tübingen, 1907): one should not seek the origin of evil in God, but where then if God is the sole cause of all phenomena? It does not appear that modern philosophers have advanced toward a solution beyond Job, who denied the ethical perfection of God, and Plato (*Timaeus* 46 C, E; 48 A; 56 C, etc.), who on the contrary limited the omnipotence of a deity ethically perfect.

Our author fully realizes that, in view of God's inscrutable transcendence and man's limited understanding, a solution of the problem of theodicy is impossible. He therefore recognizes that the only rational solution acceptable to him—God is almighty but not just—cannot be final. God's nature and wisdom can only be imperfectly known from "the outskirts of his ways," but in their full reality are a mystery. Who knows? Man is an insignificant being in the magnificently glorious world around him, a world which manifests so clearly God's power and wisdom. His own miseries may have an incomprehensible purpose in the scheme of things or, if such is not the case, they are so infinitesimal in the cosmos that they can hardly mar the perfection of God's creation and the character of the Creator. Such was perhaps the final conclusion of our author.

CHAPTER IV

THE SONG OF SONGS

~~~~~~

According to the title, "The Song of Songs which is Solomon's" (1:1), this book of verse is the most beautiful of the 1,005 songs which legend tells us Solomon composed (I Kings 4:32 [H. 5:12]). In Hebrew the expression "song of songs," like "vanity of vanities," "holy of holies," is used to indicate the superlative. Need we state that the attribution of this book to Solomon's pen is no less fictitious than that of Proverbs, Ecclesiastes, Wisdom, Psalms and Odes of Solomon to this ancient and opulent monarch? The repeated mention of Solomon in the course of the book (1:5; 3:7, 9, 11; 8:11 f.), which in ch. 3 definitely identifies the bridegroom with King Solomon, may have prompted the editor responsible for the title to ascribe the book to him.

Song of Songs is a short anthology of love poems of various length, sung by the bride, the bridegroom, and their friends. The individual poems, whose beginning and end are not always well marked, may be the work of a number of authors and are arranged without any definite plan. Some verses occur twice (2:16, 6:3; 2:17a, 4:6a; 2:17b, 8:14; 2:6 f., 8:3 f.), and the same topics tend to recur (cf. 3:1-5 with 5:2-7). For convenience, however, we may group the songs as follows:

1. Songs of the bride (1:2-8). The maiden yearns for her beloved, "the King" (1:2-4); she apologizes to the ladies of the harem ("the daughters of Jerusalem") for her dark complexion (1:5 f.); out in the fields she arranges a rendezvous with the shepherd she loves (1:7 f.).

2. A duet between bride and groom (1:9-2:7). The bridegroom sings the maiden's praises (1:9-11) and she responds appropriately (1:12-14); their dialogue becomes animated (youth, 1:15; maiden, 1:16 f.; maiden, 2:1; youth, 2:2; maiden, 2:3); the maiden requests her lover to take her to a tavern—an allegory of the joys of love (2:4-6); the section ends with a playful adjuration to the daughters of Jerusalem (2:7), occurring also in 3:5; 8:4.

3. Reminiscences of the bride (2:8-3:5). One night the youth sang of love and springtime to the maiden, who invited him to return in the morning (2:8-17; 2:15, about the little foxes despoiling the vineyards, and 2:16 [cf. 6:3] interrupt the context). The maiden dreams that one night

708

she missed her beloved, searched for him in the city and, after finding him, took him to her mother's house (3:1-5).

4. The palanquin of Solomon (3:6-11). The rustic wedding processions of bridegroom and bride are described with extravagant imagery.

5. Songs of the youth (4:1-5:1). A highly imaginative description of the bride's lovely features from her head to her breasts (4:1-7; 4:6 seems intrusive) is followed by passionate expressions of love for the maiden (4:8; 4:9-11), who is compared to an enclosed fragrant garden (4:12-5:1a; 4:16 is the reply of the bride; 5:1b is a joyful cry of the friends of the young couple).

6. The search for the lost bridegroom (5:2-6:3). One night, after the maiden has retired, her beloved knocks at the door, but vanishes when she goes out to him; searching in the city she is treated roughly by the guards (5:2-7); like the bride's recollection of a similar experience (3:1-5), this is probably a dream (cf. 5:2). Adjuring the daughters of Jerusalem to bring a message to her beloved, upon their request she gives an imaginative description of his comeliness (5:8-16); when they inquire where he is to be found, she replies that he is in his garden (6:1-3).

7. The charming beauty of the bride (6:4-7:9 [H. 7:10]). As in a previous poem (4:1-7, in part identical with 6:5-7), the details of the bride's lovely head are described by the youth (6:4-9; 6:10); 6:11-12 are incongruous here and seemingly belong to a song of the maiden (6:12 is textually corrupt). As the bride performs the Mahanaim dance (probably the war or sword dance), the wedding guests sing of her beauty beginning with the feet and moving upward to the head, as was natural in the case of a dancing maiden (6:13-7:5 [H. 7:1-6]); in consequence this description is less restrained than that confining itself to the upper part of a maiden's figure in repose (4:1-7; 6:4-10). The youth expresses his love with more passion than elsewhere (4:9-5:1), comparing the maiden to a palm tree (7:6-9 [H. 7:7-10]).

8. Songs of the bride (7:10 [H. 7:11]-8:4). The maiden longs to walk in the fields in springtime with her beloved (7:10-13 [H. 7:11-14]) and wishes that he were her brother so she could kiss him in public (8:1-4).

9. Miscellaneous songs and fragments (8:5-14). After two disconnected fragments (8:5a, 5b) comes the climax of the book, the maiden's eloquent description of love as the most irresistible, most precious, and strongest of all things (8:6 f.)—one of the classics in the erotic poetry of mankind. When the bride was a child, her brothers intended taking measures to preserve her virginity but, as she says, her very charms protected her (8:8-10). Happy in the possession of his little vineyard (i.e., his bride), the lover does not envy even Solomon's immense estates

(8:11 f.). Asked to sing, the maiden responds (8:13 f.) with a verse of a previous poem (2:17; cf. 4:6a).

These subdivisions are to some extent indicated by the text itself: adjuration to the daughters of Jerusalem in 2:7; 3:5; 8:4 marks the end of parts 2, 3, and 8; part 4, which differs radically from the rest of the book, is obviously a separate unit, and part 9 is a miscellaneous appendix. One could, however, regard parts 1-2 and 5-7 as two divisions instead of five.

If we disregard their capricious order, the individual songs in the book may be classified as follows:

I. The palanquin of Solomon (preparations for a rural wedding): 3:6-11.

II. Songs of the maiden.

1. Reminiscenes: 2:4-7; 2:8-14, 16 f.; 3:1-5; 5:2-7.

2. Description (called *wasf* in Arabic) of the youth's comely features, with a dramatic framework: 5:8-6:3 (5:8 f. and 6:1-3 constitute the framework).

3. Effusions of love for the beloved: 1:2-4; 7:10-13 (H. 7:11-14); 8:1 f., 6 f.; 8:3 repeats 2:6.

4. Miscellaneous nonerotic reflections: 1:5 f.; 8:8-10 and perhaps 6:12; 8:5b.

III. Songs of the youth.

1. Description (*wasf*) of the attractive features of the maiden: 4:1-7 (4:6 is added from 2:17); 6:4-7 (6:4-5a introductory, the rest is taken from 4:1-3). Cf. 6:13-7:5 (H. 7:1-6) (a *wasf* of the dancing maiden sung by the spectators).

2. Effusions of love for the maiden: 4:9-11; 7:6-9 (H. 7:7-10).

3. Miscellaneous reflections: 6:8 f.; 8:11 f.

IV. Duets of the lovers: 1:7 f., 9-11, 12-17; 2:1-3; 4:12-5:1a.

V. Miscellaneous fragments.

1. Rural scenes: 2:15; 6:11.

2. Questions and exclamations spoken by wedding guests: 6:10; 8:5a; 8:13 (supplemented with 8:14, cf. 2:9, 17); cf. the framework of 6:13-7:5 (H. 7:1-6) (see above under III, 1).

3. Probable glosses and editorial additions in the book: 1:1; "beside the shepherds' tents" (1:8); 2:9a; "and the voice of the turtle is heard in our land" (2:12); "(with) the tender grape" (2:13; the Hebrew word [*semādar*] is taken from 2:15, cf. 7:12 [H. 7:13]); "upon the mountains of Bether" (2:17); 3:4b (cf. 8:2); "from the daughters of Jerusalem" (3:10, reading "ebony" for "love"); 4:6 (cf. 2:17); 4:8; "(my) spouse" (ungrammatical in Hebrew) is a gloss explaining "my sister" in 4:9, 10, 12; 5:1 and is secondary in 4:11 (it occurs elsewhere only in 4:8, which is interpolated); "spikenard and" "myrrh and aloes" (4:14); 5:1b; "my beloved"

(5:4); "my soul failed when he spake" (5:6); "from me" "the keepers of the walls" (5:7); "by the rivers of waters" (5:12); "terrible as an army with banners" (6:4, inserted from 6:10); 7:12b (H. 7:13b); 8:3 f. (taken from 2:6 f.).

If this analysis of Song of Songs is justified, it is clear from the variety of subjects and situations, the repetitions and parallels and the lack of logical order that the book is an anthology of love lyrics and related poems rather than a collection of songs for a specific purpose, or a single lyrical or dramatic poem. Some poems are identified with a given occasion: 3:6-11 could have been sung at weddings when the bridegroom was crowned as king by his mother (3:11) and was seated on a rough threshing board erected as a throne on the threshing floor; 6:13-7:5 (H. 7:1-6) could be sung in honor of the bride dancing before the wedding guests. But nothing else in the book has definite reference to wedding festivities, although the descriptions of the bride (4:1-5, 7; 6:4-7) and bridegroom (5:8-6:3, without the framework) could have been used as wedding songs. No poem in our book, however, resembles the genuine Hebrew epithalamium, sung on the occasion of royal nuptials and preserved for us as Ps. 45. For the most part, the book consists of simple and charming love idylls in springtime, without reference to marriage, sung by either or both of the lovers.

The pastoral atmosphere pervading the book does not signify that the poems are genuine examples of ancient Israelitic folk poetry—they are far too sophisticated and elaborate. But the author or authors who composed these lyrics unquestionably drew inspiration from the rustic songs of shepherds and peasants at their wedding celebrations—songs probably similar to those of modern Syrian and Palestinian peasants and Arabian Bedouins collected by G. Dalman (*Palästinischer Diwan*, Leipzig, 1901), E. Littmann (*Neuarabische Volkspoesie*, 1902), A. Musil (*Arabia Petraea*, Vol. III. Vienna, 1908), and St. H. Stephan ("Modern Palestinian Parallels to the Song of Songs," JPOS 2 [1922] 199-278). These lyrics, like the love poetry of ancient Egypt (cf. A. Erman, *The Literature of the Ancient Egyptians*, pp. 243-251), Assyria (for which we have a catalogue of love songs listing the first lines, see T. J. Meek, JBL 43 [1924] 245-252), and pre-Islamic Arabia (cf. the poem on pp. 105 f. of R. A. Nicholson, *A Literary History of the Arabs*. New York, 1907) are to be classed as belles-lettres rather than as folk songs. To be sure, they are less artificial and rhetorical than some of the pastoral love poetry of Theocritus and later poets.

The influence of Egyptian love poetry is apparent in the use of "my sister" in addressing the bride (4:9, 10, 12; 5:1, 2). This expression was so unfamiliar to Hebrew ears that it was glossed with "bride" in each occurrence except the last (where other terms explained its meaning). Egyptian in feeling likewise is the rapturous admiration of flowers, trees, vineyards, doves, gazelles, and of the charms of nature in springtime (for which our book has no parallel in the Old Testament); and also such details as the comparison of the bride with a garden: "I am thy first sister. I am unto thee like a garden, which I have planted with flowers and with all manner of sweet smelling herbs" (A. Erman, *The Literature of the Ancient Egyptians,* pp. 248 f.); cf. "A garden enclosed is my sister, etc." (4:12-5:1a; cf. 6:2). A feeling for nature's magnificent beauties in their grander aspects is characteristic of Ps. 104, inspired likewise by an Egyptian poem, the Hymn to Aton of Ikhnaton, and of Job, a work in which Egyptian influence is less direct but nevertheless decisive. Otherwise the marvel at nature's ever-changing charms is rare among the Israelites.

The delightful descriptions of nature's awakening (the best example is 2:10-13; cf. 4:1-5; 5:10-13; 6:11; 7:11-13 [H. 7:12-14]), reveal an aesthetic appreciation of the beauty of natural scenery and a literary art in depicting them for their own sake without ulterior motives (as in Ps. 104 and Job) known only in the literatures of Egypt and Greece, before the beginning of our era. In *The Messages of the Poets* (New York, 1911), N. Schmidt compares our book to the erotic epigrams of Meleager and Philodemus, who were born at Gadara in Palestine and spent their youth in Transjordania. Even though there are general resemblances in the connection of nature's beauty with the ardor of love, depicted with sensuous abandon although in elegant form, these Greek poets living in the first century B.C. are considerably later in date than our book. However, if their poetry was inspired by the songs of their native land, there must have existed in Palestine during the last centuries before our era a considerable amount of erotic poetry, of which our book alone survives by accident.

Since Song of Songs is an anthology rather than a single poem, the authorship and date cannot be determined with any finality. The description of Solomon's palanquin (3:6-11) stands apart, and may come from the pen of a poet not otherwise represented in the book: only here is there a definite reference to the wedding festivities and to the "daughters of Zion." Another poem with characters of its own and possibly distinct authorship is the song for the maiden's dance (6:13-7:5 [H. 7:1-6]) in which alone the maiden is called "the Shulammite," or the maid from Shulem (i.e., Shunem near Jezreel), an allusion to the beautiful Abishag the Shunammite who ministered to David at the end of his life (I Kings 1:3, 15; 2:17, 21 f.).[1]

---

[1] According to another interpretation, "the Shulammite" is the feminine of "Solomon" (*Shelomith,* "Solomoness"); see E. J. Goodspeed in AJSL 50 (1933-1934) 102-104 and H. H. Rowley in AJSL 56 (1939) 84-91.

For the rest, omitting miscellaneous fragments and short pieces, the book exhibits not only uniformity of style but numerous recurring refrains and repetitions that indicate, if not unity of authorship, at least thorough editorial rewriting by a professional poet. It is possible that some of the briefer poems in ch. 8 (8:1 f., 5b, 8-10, 11 f.) were genuine folk songs, at any rate in their original form. On the whole, however, the idyllic background so unlike the sordid reality; the free relations between youth and maiden, unknown in the ancient Orient even in the country districts; the artificial décor, now royal now pastoral; the elusive geographical background, now Judean (Jerusalem, Engedi) now Northern Israelitic (Tirzah, Carmel, Shunem, Sharon, Hermon, Amana, Senir, Lebanon), now Transjordanic (Gilead, Heshbon); the undisguised sensuous passion joined to tender emotions; the sense of the beauty of fields, orchards, and vineyards; the elaborate imagery and consummate literary skill—all these features point unmistakably to vivid imagination and expert poetic art rather than to actual situations in life sung naïvely by simple folk in the countryside.

The language serves as the only clue for dating the book. Although the Hebrew is vivid and colorful, Aramaic forms and words are frequent and the language resembles most that of the latest books in the Old Testament, Ecclesiastes and Esther. Names of spices and other foreign products (in 1:13 f.; 3:6, 10; 4:13 f.; 5:14 in particular), the Persian word for "garden" (*pardes,* "paradise"), in 4:13, the Greek word for "palanquin" (H. *appiriôn,* Gr. *phoreion*) in 3:9, and other terms could hardly have been in use before Alexander. Unless they be regarded as editorial, these indicate that our book was probably written as we have it in the first half of the third century B.C. Since Aramaic was then the vernacular of the Jews in Palestine, folk songs at weddings must have been in Aramaic rather than Hebrew. If our book contains such songs, they must date back to a time when Hebrew was still spoken, or else have been translated from the Aramaic, of which there is no indication.

In conclusion, Song of Songs is an anthology of erotic poems, probably composed by more than one poet; they depict with brilliant imagination and consummate art the thrills, delights, torments, and dreams of love between man and woman—love in the bud and in full bloom—against the background of the charming Palestinian countryside in the springtime. Our book dates from about 250 or shortly before, and although some individual poems may be based on older ones, none of them in their extant form is earlier than the time of Alexander.

Note on the History of the Interpretation of Canticles

"Know, my brother," wrote Saadia Gaon (d. 942), at the beginning of his commentary on Song of Songs, "that you will find a great diversity of opinion as regards the interpretation of this Song of Songs." Since then the scope of interpretations has grown until it has surpassed by far differences of opinion about any other part of Scripture.[2] The several interpretations may be classified into two main groups, allegorical and literal, both of which reach back to the end of the first century A.D.

At that time, Rabbi Akiba (d. 132) supported the canonicity of Song of Songs with unrestrained praise: "The entire age from the beginning until now is not worth as much as the day on which the Song of Songs was given to Israel" (Mishna *Yadaim* 3:5). He obviously understood it allegorically (so, ostensibly, IV Ezra 5:24-26, dated about 90 A.D.) and therefore fulminated against a literal interpretation of the book by irreverent young men who were singing parts of it as erotic ditties in the wine houses (*Tosefta Sanhedrin* xii).

The *allegorical interpretation,* by discovering a deeper meaning under the plain love poetry, made possible the canonization of the book. The allegory of married love for relations between Jehovah and his people was first used by Hosea (1-2) and is not infrequent thereafter (Jer. 2:2; 3:1-13; Is. 50:1; 54:5; 62:4 f.; Ez. 16, 23; etc.). In the Talmud (completed about 500 A.D.), the bridegroom of Canticles is taken to be God, and the bride the Congregation of Israel. The Targum (*ca.* 550), a paraphrase of the book in Aramaic, and the homiletic midrash *Hazita* (*ca.* 800) see in it an allegory of Israel's history from the Exodus to the coming of the Messiah, as also Saadia Gaon, other Jewish and a few Christian interpreters (C. F. Keil, 1849). Martin Luther sees in the bride "the happy state under the dominion of Solomon."

But most Christian interpreters discovered in the book an allegory of the love of Christ for his Church (Hippolytus, d. 234; Origen, d. 254; Jerome, d. 420; Augustine, d. 430, etc.; the last one is E. W. Hengstenberg in 1853; see in particular the running chapter headings of the Authorized Version) or else an allegory of the mystical union of a believing soul with God or Christ (Origen; Gregory of Nyssa, d. *ca.* 396; Theodoret, d. *ca.* 457; St. Bernard, d. 1153; Madame J. M. Guyon, d. 1717; M. Stuart [1845]). The Islamic Sufis likewise express the mystical ecstasy in erotic poetry (cf. R. A. Nicholson, *The Mystics of Islam,* pp. 102 ff. London, 1914.) The Jewish and Christian allegories are combined by Nicholas de Lyra (d. 1340), followed by Th. Brightmann, 1600. The eccentric

[2] An excellent conspectus of Jewish and Christian interpretations of Canticles up to 1856 is given by C. D. Ginsburg, *The Song of Songs,* pp. 20-102. London, 1857. See also: S. Salfeld, *Das Hohelied Solomons bei den jüdischen Erklären des Mittelalters,* 1879. W. Riedel, *Die Auslegung des Hohenliedes in der jüdischen Gemeinde und der griechischen Kirche,* 1898. Paul Vulliaud, *Le Cantique des Cantiques d'après la tradition juive.* Paris, 1925. For recent interpretations see A. Vaccari, "Il Cantico dei Cantici nelle recenti publicazioni," *Biblica* 9 (1928) 443-457; H. H. Rowley, "The Interpretation of the Song of Songs," JTS 38 (1937) 337-363; K. Kuhl, "Das Hohelied und seine Deutung," *Theol. Rundschau* 9 (1937) 137-167.

allegorical interpretation of E. F. K. Rosenmüller (*Scholia*, Vol. 9, 1829-1830) follows Abrabanel and Leon Hebraeus in seeing "wisdom" in the bride (cf. Wisd. of Sol. 8:2, 9, 16); J. L. Hug (1813), G. P. C. Kaiser (1825), and H. A. Hahn (1852) also adopt such interpretations.

In our day, the allegorical interpretation has been revived in a pagan guise: according to N. de Jassy (*Le Cantique des Cantiques et le mythe d'Osiris-Hetep*. Paris, 1914) our book is in part a translation of Egyptian litanies used in the Osiris cult. W. Erbt (*Die Hebräer*, pp. 196-201. 1906), T. J. Meek (AJSL 39 [1922] 1-14; and in *The Song of Songs. A Symposium*, pp. 48-79. Philadelphia, 1924; cf. JBL 43 [1924] 245-252), W. L. Schoff (in *The Song of Songs. A Symposium*, pp. 80-120), E. Ebeling (ZDMG 78 [1924] lxviii f.), W. Wittekindt (*Das Hohe Lied und seine Beziehungen zum Istarkult*. 1926), and to some extent, L. Waterman (JBL 44 [1925] 171-187) have discovered in our book a liturgy used in the Tammuz (Adonis) cult (a view criticized by N. Schmidt in JAOS 46 [1926] 154-164).

Although declared heretical by the Church when proposed by Theodore of Mopsuestia (d. *ca.* 428) and S. Castellio (d. 1563), the *literal interpretation of Canticles* has finally prevailed, but in two radically different forms, dramatic and lyrical. Among the critics who, following G. Wachter (1722) and J. F. Jacobi (1771), consider our book a drama, a few find in it two main characters only, whereas the majority (like Jacobi) add to Solomon and the Shulammite, her rustic husband or lover to whom she remains faithful in spite of the king's blandishments. In his *Introduction to the Old Testament*, S. R. Driver summarizes both dramatic schemes, according to Franz Delitzsch (1851, 1875) and H. Ewald (1826, 1867), respectively.

Song of Songs has been dramatized by the following: K. F. Stäudlin (1792), Ammon (1795), F. W. C. Umbreit (1820), F. Böttcher (1850), F. Hitzig (1855), C. D. Ginsburg (1857), E. Renan (1860), W. Robertson Smith (1876), J. G. Stickel (1888), S. Oettli (1889), Ch. Bruston (1891), S. R. Driver (1891), E. König (1893), W. F. Adeney (1895), A. Harper (1902), J. W. Rothstein (1911), L. Cicognani (*Il Cantico dei Cantici*. Turin, 1911), S. Minocchi (1924), G. Pouget and J. Guitton (*Le Cantique des Cantiques*, Paris, 1934), A. Hazan (*Le Cantique des Cantiques enfin expliqué*. Paris, 1936).

An intermediate position between the dramatic and lyric conceptions of our book is taken by followers of Origen, who called it "a nuptial poem composed in dramatic form," and regarded it as a dramatic epithalamium celebrating Solomon's marriage with Pharaoh's daughter. This view is echoed by H. Grotius (1644), Bishop J. B. Bossuet (1693), J. Lightfoot (d. 1675), Bishop R. Lowth (1753), and Bishop T. Percy (1764), who, however, added to the literal meaning a secondary allegorical sense to preserve the religious value and canonical status of the book (attacked by W. Whiston in 1723); the allegorical meaning was given up entirely by J. D. Michaelis (1758). F. Dornseiff (ZDMG 90 [1936] 589-601) sees in it an erotic poem with a certain dramatic structure.

Two tendencies are noticeable among those who regard Song of Songs as a collection of detached erotic lyrics. Some view them as folk songs recited during the week of the nuptial festivities; others ignore or deny such a purpose in the poems in their present form. J. G. Wetzstein, Prussian consul in Damascus, published a description of the nuptial ceremonies and festivities among the Syrian peasants (Bastian's *Zeitschr. f. Ethnologie* 5 [1873].270-302, particularly 287-294; cf. von Kremer, *Mittelsyrien und Damascus,* p. 123. 1853). On the day of the wedding, there are processions: during the sword dance of the bride the guests sing a description of her charms (*wasf*) composed for the occasion (cf. 6:13-7:5 [H. 7:1-6]). During the following "royal week," the married couple are honored as king and queen and sit on a "throne" consisting of rustic seats placed over the threshing board resting on the threshing floor (cf. 3:6-11).

Since then many have considered our book a collection of nuptial songs composed for similar festivities in antiquity: J. G. Wetzstein (in the commentary of Franz Delitzsch, 1875, pp. 162-177), B. Stade (*Geschichte des Volkes Israel,* Vol. II, pp. 197 f.), K. Budde (*New World,* March 1894, 56 ff.), E. Riehm (1889-91), C. H. Cornill (1891), E. Kautzsch (1896), C. Siegfried (1898), T. K. Cheyne (1899, 1909), M. Jastrow, Jr. (1921), J. A. Bewer (1922), U. Cassuto (GSAI N.S. 1 [1925] 23-52), E. J. Goodspeed (AJSL 50 [1933-34] 102-104), and others.

Other critics regard the book as a collection of love lyrics, some of which at least have no direct connection with wedding festivities. This view has been adopted by the present writer in the preceding pages. Although first presented by Richard Simon (1678), it received its classical presentation in an epoch-making study of J. G. von Herder (1778) and has been defended in various forms by J. G. Eichhorn (1780-83), J. F. Kleuker (1780), Goethe (*Noten zum Diwan*), J. C. C. Döpke (1829), L. Zunz (1832), E. J. Magnus (1842), G. R. Noyes (1846), E. Meier (1854), H. Graetz (1871), E. Reuss (1879), D. Castelli (1892), W. W. Baudissin (1901), G. Jakob (1902), P. Haupt (1902, 1907), W. Staerk (1911), R. Dussaud (1919), A. Lods (1920), O. Eissfeldt (1936), and others.

CHAPTER V

THE BOOK OF RUTH

The Book of Ruth is one of the most charming short stories in Hebrew literature: Goethe assigned it a pre-eminent position among epics and idylls. The plot of the story is well known. In the days of the judges during a famine, Elimelech with his wife Naomi and his two sons Mahlon and Chilion migrated from Bethlehem in Judah to the land of Moab. After Elimelech's death, Mahlon and Chilion married Moabitic women, Orpah and Ruth, respectively. But the two husbands soon died (1:1-5). Upon hearing that the famine had ended, Naomi took leave of her two daughters-in-law, having resolved to go back to Bethlehem. Orpah returned to her father's house but Ruth said to Naomi, "Intreat me not to leave thee, . . . for whither thou goest I will go; . . . thy people shall be my people, and thy God my God: where thou diest, will I die, and there will I be buried. . . ."

Thus these two arrived in Bethlehem at the beginning of the barley harvest (1:6-22). Ruth went out into the fields to glean after the reapers, as it happened on the land of Boaz, a wealthy kinsman of her father-in-law Elimelech (2:1-3). Noticing Ruth, and learning that she was the daughter-in-law of Naomi, Boaz treated her with great deference (2:4-17), much to Naomi's gratification (2:18-23).

As the end of the barley harvest drew near, Ruth followed the shrewd advice of Naomi and placed herself at the feet of Boaz, who spent the night in the field, and induced him to ask for her hand (3:1-18). After a nearer kinsman had renounced his right and duty to purchase Naomi's field and marry Ruth, ratifying his refusal by the archaic symbolical act of removing his shoes (cf. Deut. 25:5-10), Boaz married Ruth. She bore him a son, Obed, who became the grandfather of David (4:1-17). The book ends with a genealogy of David, reaching up to Perez, son of Judah and Tamar (4:18-22; cf. I Chron. 2:9-16, where the father of Boaz is called Salmah instead of Salmon as in Ruth).

The date of this book is controversial, even though its traditional attribution to Samuel (Talmud [*Baba Bathra* 14b] and Christian writers) is no longer regarded as tenable. To join Ruth with Judges (and Lam. to Jer.), as Josephus does (*Against Apion* 1:8), counting 22, instead of 24, books in the Old Testament, means to disregard (according to the LXX)

717

the canonization of Ruth and Lamentations among the Hagiographa rather than among the Prophets. The most significant evidence is to be found in 4:7, where a custom, still current at the time Deut. 25:5-10 was written, became so obsolete that it had to be elucidated; as also in 4:18-22, a genealogy, which like its counterpart in I Chron. 2:9-16, is clearly postexilic (e.g., the Hebrew word for "begat" is that used in the genealogies of the Priestly Code but not in the earlier writings).

But if these two passages are regarded as glosses—and 4:18-22 is now generally considered spurious (being either an amplification of 4:17 or a gloss to 4:12)—the pre-exilic date for the book defended by S. R. Driver (*Introduction to the Old Testament*, pp. 454-456) and others is by no means impossible. The general character of the Hebrew vocabulary and syntax, the use of ancient idiomatic expressions current in the best prose of the Old Testament (J and the old source of Sam.), and the classical purity of style could be adduced in favor of an early date. On the other hand, the literary excellence of the book and the occurrence of a number of archaic verbal terminations may well be the manifestations of a gifted author's good taste and wide reading.

On the whole, a postexilic date (*ca.* 400) seems preferable. By placing his story "in the days of the judging of the judges" (1:1), the author discloses familiarity with the Deuteronomic edition of Judges (*ca.* 550 B.C.) rather than with the rude and barbaric period which he so gracefully idealizes in his charming romance. For it is plain that the book is fiction (like Jon., Esther, Jth., and Tob.) rather than history: the significant names of some of the characters (Mahlon, "sickness"; Chilion, "wasting"; Orpah, "stiff-necked"; Naomi, "my sweetness" [cf. 1:20]; according to the Syriac version, Ruth is a contraction of *re'uth*, i.e., "the companion"); the exemplary conduct and noble character of Ruth, Naomi, and Boaz; the picturesque details of ancient life from which all unpleasant traits have been eliminated; the simple and strong religious faith devoid of ceremonies and doctrine (cf. 1:6, 8 f., 13, 16 f., 20 f.; 2:12, 20; 4:11-14), not unlike that of Abraham in the J stories; the accidents producing the plot and leading to a happy ending—all this savors more of good fiction than actual life.

For his purposes, the author did not even hesitate to give a fanciful and unwarranted interpretation of the law of the levirate marriage (Deut. 25:5-10)[1] and the custom of removing the shoe in 4:3-10, and to disregard completely the categorical law forbidding Moabites' becoming members of the "congregation of Jehovah" or marrying members thereof (Deut. 23:3 [H. 23:4]). He allowed his heroine to violate flagrantly both prescriptions with public approval. Although clearly a liberal, to use a modern expression, with obviously no sympathy for the prohibition of

[1] Cf. M. Burrows in JBL 59 (1940) 445-454.

mixed marriages enforced by Nehemiah (Neh. 13:1-3, 23-27; cf. Ezra 10), the author's book should not be regarded as a protest against Nehemiah's measures.

Nor did the author write primarily to supplement the Books of Samuel by relating something about David's ancestors (according to I Sam. 22:3 f., he may actually have had Moabitic connections), or to enforce the duty of the levirate marriage or, like Jonah, to advocate benevolence toward the heathen and missionary zeal for their conversion. Questions debated about 400 B.C. may have unconsciously influenced the author as he was writing this story, but he had no ulterior motive—least of all did he compose a midrash on the alleged cult-myth of a Bethlehem fertility cult, as W. E. Staples (AJSL 53 [1937] 147-157) imagines. No, he simply set out to tell an interesting tale of long ago, and he carried out his purpose with notable success.

CHAPTER VI

THE BOOK OF LAMENTATIONS

~~~~~~

Originally this small collection of five elegies bore no title. In Hebrew editions, both manuscript and printed, the first word of three of the poems (1:1; 2:1; 4:1), *êkhah,* "Ah how!" serves as a superscription. But in the Talmud and in the *Prologus Galeatus* of Jerome (*"cinoth"*), the book is named after its contents *qînôth* (dirges), and this term in translation served as title in the versions: *thrēnoi* in the LXX and *threni* or *lamentationes* in the Latin versions (usually with the addition "of Jeremiah").

The five poems constituting the book, each of which corresponds to one of the five chapters, lament the destruction of Jerusalem in 586 B.C. and its dire aftermath. The first four are alphabetic acrostics. In 1, 2, and 3, each stanza, beginning with the appropriate letter of the alphabet, has three verses, in 4 only two; in 3, each of the three verses of the stanza begins with the same letter, an elaboration of the acrostic device found only in Ps. 119 (where each stanza has eight verses beginning with the same letter).

The first poem presents the usual order of letters in the alphabet (*'ain* before *pe*), whereas in 2-4 the *pe* precedes the *'ain.* The fifth poem is a prayer rather than an elegy and, although having twenty-two verses corresponding to the number of letters in the alphabet, it lacks the acrostic alphabetic arrangement and has the usual poetic meter (each of the two halves of the verse has four stress accents) rather than the "elegiac (*qînâh*) meter" of the others. In the elegiac meter, the two parts of the verse are of unequal length: the first has four accents, the second three; more accurately, a rest replaces the last foot of the verse. The oldest and best example of this *qînâh* meter is found in Am. 5:2:

> Fallen no more to rise—Virgin of Israel
> Hurled upon her soil—None to raise her!

Besides Lam. 1-4, other poems in the Old Testament exhibit this elegiac meter: usually they are elegies (Is. 14:4b-21; 15; 22:1-5; 47; Jer. 9:9b-10, 18, 20 f.; 15:5-9; Ez. 19; 26:17 f.), but often poems that do not bemoan the death of an individual or a nation (Is. 1:2 f., 10 f.; 2:6-8; 13:2 ff.; 37:22-29; 52:7-12; 57:1-12; Jer. 22:6 f., 21-23; Pss. 19:7-14 [H. 19:8-15];

65:4-7 [H. 65:5-8]). The elegies of David (II Sam. 1:17-27; 3:33 f.), earliest of all, are not in the elegiac but in ordinary meter.

Only 1, 2, and 4, as their first word already indicates, are essentially dirges in the strict sense of the word—mournful songs for the dead, in this case for the tragic end of Jerusalem. The third poem is the lament of an individual (becoming collective in vv. 40-47), and the fifth a lament and prayer of the congregation. But even in 1, 2, and 4 the style of the dirge is not consistently carried through: in 1:9c, 11c-16, 18-22, the deceased city is personified and bemoans her fate; in 2:11-19, the poet expresses his grief and addresses the daughter of Zion who then (2:20-22) lifts up her voice in prayer to the Lord; in 4:17-20, the men who attempted to flee from the doomed city with their king Zedekiah (cf. II Kings 25:4 f.) relate their harrowing experience, and in 4:21 f. the poet addresses Edom and Zion.

CONTENTS

In 1, Jerusalem weeps bitterly like a lonely widow over her own desolation and exiled inhabitants, recalling past glories and confessing her sinfulness. The invocation to God at the end asks for a similar fate for Judah's enemies.

In 2, the poet bemoans the ruin that Jehovah has wrought in his anger: desolation of the land, demolition of the strongholds of Zion, exile of the king and princes, cessation of worship, and horrors of the famine during the siege (v. 11c-12). Then he addresses Zion, blaming the prophets for the plight that evoked only scorn from her foes, and exhorting her to weep and cry unto Jehovah for mercy (vv. 13-22).

In 3, "the man that has seen affliction by the rod of his wrath" (v. 1)— the personified nation according to R. Smend, the poet according to most critics—bitterly bewails God's unsparing onslaught against him, but finds comfort and hope in the assurance of God's mercies for those who seek him (vv. 1-39). Therefore, "let us search and try our ways, and turn again to the Lord" (vv. 40-47). After weeping and calling on God, the poet is certain that God will take vengeance on his foes (vv. 48-66).

In 4, the poet vividly describes the horrors of the siege, notably the pathos and anguish of starving children, the desperate hunger of the rich and of the mothers driven to eat their own infants (vv. 1-10). Priests and prophets were the chief culprits; now their defilement makes them unclean even in the sight of the heathen (vv. 11-16). Hope of help from Egypt proved vain (v. 17). Finally, when Zedekiah, "the breath of our nostrils, the anointed of the Lord," fled from the city that was about to fall into the hands of Nebuchadnezzar, he was swiftly overtaken (vv. 18-20). Edom's triumph will not last long, for Zion's iniquity has been expiated (vv. 21-22).

In 5, half a century after the calamity of 586, the congregation begs God to take note of their misery (v. 1)—their lands and homes in the hands of aliens, members enslaved or in want, women ravished, the sanctuary on Zion a pile of ruins and inhabited by jackals (vv. 2-18)— and prays for restoration (vv. 19-22).

According to ancient tradition, Jeremiah was the author of the Book of Lamentations. Thus clearly in the LXX, where the book begins with these words, "And it came to pass, after Israel was led into captivity and Jerusalem laid waste, that Jeremiah sat weeping and lamented with this lamentation over Jerusalem, and said, . . ." This statement seems to have been translated from the Hebrew and could conceivably have stood, with the Book of Lamentations, after II Chron. 36:21. The Chronicler seems to allude to our book in II Chron. 35:25, regarding Lam. 4 as the elegy that Jeremiah composed for Josiah (cf. 4:20 which, according to the Targum, refers to Josiah)—an elegy written with others "in the lamentations" (*ibid.*).[1] The other ancient versions (Vulgate, Targum, etc.), as well as the Talmud and the Church Fathers in general, also attribute our book to Jeremiah. This tradition, far more plausible than ascribing some books to the pen of Solomon, is now usually discredited. It was natural to attribute these lamentations over the destruction of Jerusalem in 586 to the only great prophet and writer known to us who witnessed that calamity (with the exception, perhaps, of Ezekiel).

The detailed analysis of the diction of the book made by M. Löhr (ZAW 14 [1894] 31-50; cf. 51-59, 24 [1904] I-16, and 25 [1905] 173-198) has uncovered parallels with Jeremiah's phraseology, but also with that of Ezekiel, Second Isaiah, and particularly the Psalms. The style and ideas of Lamentations are often very different from those of the prophet. Jeremiah regarded the Babylonians as instruments of God's punishment, and he could hardly have written Lam. 1:21 and 3:59-66; nor would he during his lifetime have spoken of the cessation of prophetic oracles (2:9c) or have blamed the prophets in general (2:14; 4:13) for the calamity; Jeremiah neither expected help from Egypt (4:17) nor safety under the "shadow" of Zedekiah (4:20). Our book was never part of the Book of Jeremiah: it stands in the third, not in the second, part of the Hebrew canon. Obviously the literal translation of Lamentations in the LXX was not made by the same men who produced the free translation of Jeremiah.

It is far from certain, if not extremely improbable, that the five

---

[1] Josephus (*Antiquities* 10:5, 1) says that the dirge of Jeremiah over Josiah was extant in his time, and he presumably regarded Lam. 4 as the elegy in question; cf. also Jerome's comments on Zech. 12:11. All that we can infer from the passage in II Chronicles is that our Book of Lamentations, ascribed at least in part to Jeremiah, was sung liturgically by professional singers about 250 B.C.

Lamentations were composed by the same author. Even the discrepancy in the arrangement of letters of the alphabet between 1, which follows the standard order, and 2-4, and the differences in form and meter of 5 militate against common authorship. From the literary viewpoint Lam. 2 and 4 are the best and clearly the earliest. Their dramatic descriptions of the horrors of the siege could have been written by eyewitnesses of those dreadful events; both lament the plight of the rulers (2:6, 9; 4:19 f.) and small children (2:11 f.; 4:2-4; cf. 2:20; 4:10). Both could be the work of one poet; in any case, the authors (or author) seem to be acquainted with Ezekiel's oracles and, since they witnessed the fall of Jerusalem, and were presumably exiled in 586, they wrote in Babylonia probably before 560. Conversely 5, which feelingly describes the sad state of Judeans in the homeland, seems to have been written in Jerusalem at least one generation after the catastrophe of 586 (v. 7, "Our fathers have sinned and are no more") but sometime before the rebuilding of the Temple in 520-516 (v. 18), i.e., about 530.

The other two poems, 1 and 3, are clearly later. In 1:10, the law of Deut. 23:3 [H. 23:4] forbidding the admittance of an Ammonite or Moabite into the "congregation" of Jehovah is already interpreted to mean the exclusion of heathen in general from the Temple in Jerusalem, after the prescription of Ez. 44:9. There is no longer any mention of a king but only "priests and elders" (1:19) and "princes" (1:6) as the highest authorities (contrast the hostility against the priests in 4:13, 16). The first Lamentation is not from the pen of an eyewitness but a writer familiar with Lam. 2 and 4, and probably with the Second and Third Isaiah; if we may draw an inference from 1:3 f., the author lived in Jerusalem after the rebuilding of the Temple (520-516) but before the wretched community of Jerusalem awakened to new life through Nehemiah's reforms (444).

The third Lamentation is the most artificial of all, both in acrostic structure and in style, and we can rightly date it later than the other four. The author may have intentionally composed it as a personal lament of Jeremiah. Literary reminiscences abound, as in some late psalms. The author lacks originality of thought and expression and deserves more praise for his piety and good intentions than for his literary ability. The imagery of woe in vv. 2-17 is forced and unnatural; reflections on the abounding mercies of the Lord in vv. 18-39 are commonplaces in the Psalter. Judging from vv. 55-60, the situation in the community in Jerusalem seems much improved over that in Lam. 3: the Lord has heard its appeal and redeemed its life. The author lived after the time of Nehemiah: it is difficult to choose between the fourth and third centuries as the date for this individual lament, although its low literary level, theological meditations, and similarity to Ps. 119 tend to tip the scales in favor of the third century.

CHAPTER VII

THE BOOK OF ECCLESIASTES

The unknown author of this book, according to 1:12, assumed the enigmatic pseudonym of *qōhéleth* (Greek *ekklēsiastḗs*, from which, through the Latin, we get the English title), and is regularly called so in the book (1:1 f.; 7:27; 12:8-10). The Hebrew word comes from *qāhāl* (congregation, Greek *ekklēsía*) and is a feminine participle, although construed as a neuter used in a masculine sense and meaning "one who addresses an assembly or congregation," or, with the Authorized Version and Luther, a "preacher" (Jerome: *concionator*). The author states that he has been king in Jerusalem (1:12) and the superscription of the book (1:1) unmistakably identifies him with Solomon (cf. 2:4-11); in all probability, the name *qōhéleth* for Solomon was suggested by I Kings 8:1.

That Solomon was not the author of the book is perfectly obvious from the thought and language, as well as from such statements as 4:15; 10:4 f. One of the editors of the book knew that the author was not a king but a wise teacher who composed and collected many proverbs (12:9 f.) of great value (12:11); another editor, far from believing Solomon the author, warned the reader against the teaching of this book in the name of the good old Jewish religion (12:12 f.).

On the whole, Ecclesiastes is written in prose except 1:2-8, 15, 18; 2:14a; 3:2-8; 4:5 f.; 5:3 (H. 5:2); 6:7; 7:1-11; 8:1, 5; 9:7 f., 17 f.; 10:1-3, 6-20; 11:1, 3a, 4, 6a, 7, 9 f.; 12:1-8. Sometimes prose and poetry can hardly be distinguished. The author collects his reflections on a variety of subjects, without striving for either consistency of thought or logical order, particularly after he has stated his chief conclusions in the first three or four chapters, which seem more coherent than any other part.

He presents at the beginning his thesis that all is vanity and that human life in particular is futile (1:2 f.): the course of nature and the succession of generations are but aimless and monotonous circuits which lead back inexorably to the beginning (1:4-11). The author has found through personal experience that wisdom (1:12-18) and the mad round of pleasures (2:1-11) are all inane. Looking at his fellow men, he sees that the advantage of wisdom over folly is as ephemeral (2:12-17) as the accumulation of riches (2:18-23); hence, there is nothing better for a man than to enjoy

himself during his brief life (2:24-26). There is an appointed time for
every activity (3:1-8), but God has concealed from man the order of
future events just to vex him (3:9-11): therefore let him enjoy the
present (3:12-15).

Miscarriage of justice in its administration (3:16) cannot be redressed
in a future life (3:17), for at death the same fate overtakes both man
and beast (3:18-21)—another reason for making the best of the present
(3:22). The tears of the oppressed convinced Ecclesiastes that death is
preferable to life (4:1-3). Jealousy is the incentive for hard work (4:4)
and folly for idleness (4:5-6); a miser without family and friends toils to
no purpose for useless riches (4:7-12); a clever youth just out of prison
through a *coup d'état* dethrones a senile king only to suffer eventually the
same fate (4:13-16)—nothing but utter futility and striving after the
wind.

Pausing for a word of advice, the author recommends caution in the
performance of religious ceremonies (5:1 [H. 4:17]), utterance of vows,
that are to be kept under all circumstances (5:2-7 [H. 5:1-6]), and criticism of venal government officials (5:8 f. [H. 5:7 f.]). Reflecting again on
the futility of riches, which God may grant for a season only to snatch
away, and the frustration of a long joyless life, he concludes that idle
desires should be curbed and man be satisfied with his lot (5:10-6:9 [H.
5:9-6:9]), for he is indeed helpless before fate (6:10-12). A miscellany
of maxims follows, in which sobriety is said to be preferable to levity
(7:1-6) and resignation to indignation (7:7-14); moderation in both
wisdom and folly is earnestly recommended (7:15-22).

Resuming his confessions, the author admits that he failed in his search
for wisdom (7:23 f.). With a twinkle in his eye, he adds that his researches
led him to the conclusion that woman is "more bitter than death" (7:25-
29). After several maxims on wisdom (8:1) and obedience to kings
(8:2-4), he discusses the invincible power of fate (8:5-9) bringing luck
to the wicked and misery to the pious (8:10-14), and concludes that,
since God's acts are incomprehensible and the same fate—death—ultimately overtakes the righteous and the wicked, it is best "to eat, and to
drink, and to be merry" (8:15-9:9) and to work intensely, before all
activity comes to an end in the underworld (9:10). "The race is not to
the swift, nor the battle to the strong"; men are the victims of chance
(9:11 f.). He recalls that a poor wise man who delivered his city from
a siege was promptly forgotten (9:13-16).

After an initial commendation of wisdom (9:17-10:3), the second series
of miscellaneous maxims is pessimistic in character: the shocking anomalies of human society (10:4-7), occupational hazards (10:8-11), silliness
in fools (10:12-15), and the despotism of governments (10:16-20) are but
a few of the evils noticed. In a happier mood, the author recommends

benevolence (11:1-3), strenuous work, even though its result depends on God (11:4-6), and the enjoyment of one's days on earth (11:7 f.). The last theme is developed in 11:9-12:8, beginning with the words, "Rejoice, O young man, in thy youth." The infirmities of old age, described imaginatively in a famous allegory (12:1-8), deprive life of all attractiveness and are but the anteroom of death, when "shall the dust return to the earth as it was: and the spirit return unto God who gave it."

The book closes with the two editorial appendices, the first of which commends the teaching of Ecclesiastes (12:9-11), while the second, deprecating the writing of many books (such as this one) and much investigation, prefers the practice of the Jewish religion, since all human actions will eventually be judged by God (12:12 f.).

Ecclesiastes is one of the most original thinkers in the Old Testament —as well as the most radical. Brought up in the teachings of orthodox Judaism (as we find them expounded in Ecclus.), his personal experiences and his observations of the physical world and human society led him to the conclusion that traditional religion on the whole is nothing but wishful thinking. Convinced, like Bertrand Russell, "that it is undesirable to believe a proposition when there is no ground whatever for supposing it true," he became skeptical of all beliefs unsupported by facts as he saw and understood them (cf. JBL 53 [1934] 100-109).

The phenomena of nature and of life proved the existence of a cosmic force producing them, namely, God. But his God, who produces all events (3:11; 8:17; 11:5), determining their order (3:15) and fixing their time (3:1-8) inexorably (3:14; 7:13), is not the God of Israel (the name Jehovah never occurs in the book), nor a just and merciful ruler of mankind, but rather a blind and fickle fate. The Creator is in heaven, far from man (5:2 [H. 5:1]); his activity incomprehensible, partly because of the limitations of human intelligence (3:10 f.; cf. 8:17; 11:5)—for men are but beasts (3:18)—partly because God produces contrasting events so capriciously that the future is unpredictable (7:14). Therefore man stands in dread before God (3:14b) and should fulfill the obligations of external worship merely to escape, by conforming to traditional practices, the undesirable attention of the deity (5:1-7 [H. 4:17-5:6]; cf. 7:18; 8:2).

God gives life to men (man's spirit comes from God, 12:7) and fixes the length of their days on earth (5:18 [H. 5:17]; 8:15; 9:19), allotting to each vexations (1:13; 3:10) and also pleasures (2:24, 26; 3:13; 5:19 f. [H. 5:18 f.]) which may suddenly be snatched from him (6:2)—without regard to his worth. The success of human undertakings is governed by chance (9:11 f.), not justice; for the same fate overtakes the righteous and the wicked (9:1 f.) and there is no reward in this life (6:8; 8:10b, 14a) or after death (5:15 f. [H. 5:14 f.]; 6:6; 9:5 f., 10; 11:8; 12:7) for piety or wisdom, no punishment for wickedness or folly. For there is no life after death (3:19 f.; 12:7).

Just as no plan of God is to be discovered in human life, so likewise in nature God's work seems futile. With inexpressible weariness and monotony, sun, wind, and rivers run their appointed circuits without ever producing anything new (1:5-11). The same is true of the generations of men (1:3 f.). In human society, many evils have been caused by God himself (3:10-15), others by wicked rulers (3:16). The poor are oppressed without a comforter (5:8 [H. 5:7]; cf. 4:1; 8:9; 10:5-7). Mobs are ready to follow worthless demagogues (4:13-16) but readily forget the savior of their city (9:14 f.).

Since the future is unknowable (3:11, 22; 6:12; 7:14, 24; 8:7, 17; 10:14) and from all appearances merely a repetition of the past (1:9 f.; 3:14 f.; 6:10), apocalyptic hopes of a Messianic millennium are chimeric dreams, "things that increase vanity" (6:11), like the expectation of a blessed resurrection of the pious dead proclaimed by Dan. 12:2 (9:4-6, 10): "a living dog is better than a dead lion." Since there is no redress for human injustice in this world or in the next, and the Jewish doctrine of the exact divine retribution for human deeds is a *pium desiderium* without basis in reality, the notion of the two ways of conduct has no validity.

After testing the way of wisdom and that of folly successively (1:17a; 2:12a; 7:25), the author discovers that they are equally futile. Search for wisdom leads to sorrow (1:18) rather than an understanding of God's work (8:16 f.; cf. 3:11; 7:14 f.; 8:10, 14; 9:1; 11:5): "I said, I will be wise; but it was far from me" (7:23 f.). And the way of folly proves equally disappointing, for pleasures are vain (2:1 f.) and wealth and luxury a mere striving after the wind (2:4-11). Wealth never suffices to still the craving for it (4:8; cf. 6:7), robs its owner of sleep (5:12 [H. 5:11]), and is impermanent: it may be lost through an accident (5:13 f. [H. 5:12 f.]) and at death (5:15 [H. 5:14]) must be left to someone who has not labored for it (2:18-23; cf. 2:25; 4:7 f.).

As for the ways of piety and ungodliness, far from affecting human fate (9:1-3a), they may even lead to conditions diametrically opposed to expectations (8:14; cf. 7:15; 8:10). In any case, the author discovered no sharp distinction between opposite ways, for in his folly some wisdom remained in him (2:3) and pure righteousness is an illusion, since wickedness is universal (7:20; 9:3b). Moreover, both ways ultimately lead to the same end—death (2:14b; cf. 2:15) and oblivion (2:16): "What advantage has the wise over the fool?" (6:8).

Besides his experiences and observations, a vague philosophical notion of time led Ecclesiastes to his skeptical attitude toward the tenets of Judaism. Reality is the ceaseless flux of phenomena in a purely arbitrary order fixed by God: man has a notion of the flow of events in time but is completely ignorant of their order which, though predetermined by the deity, appears accidental to the human mind. "(God) made everything appropriately in its season, and he also placed in their mind (the notion of) eternity lest mankind should discover the work which God accomplishes from beginning to end" (3:11). This notion of abstract time, which is the ultimate reach of the human mind in the investigation of reality, leaves man entirely in the dark with regard to a future succession of phenomena, and thus cannot even lift the edge of the veil with which God has covered his mysterious purposes in a world perpetuated by his incessant work.

In such a world of uncertain future where the only abiding realities known to man are the deity determining the capricious flow of events and the earth on which they take place (1:4), human beings are powerless to change their fate and should obviously drift with the current. The search for knowledge, happiness, and virtue is doomed in advance to failure: "What profit has a man of all his labor which he takes under the sun?" (1:3). Such ideals, which Ecclesiastes apparently considered human inventions (7:29) merely increasing futility (6:11), can of course be chosen as life's goal by the children of men, for their will is free (1:13, 17; 2:1-10; 7:15-17; 8:10-15; 9:2 f.). But the attainment of these goals and others, in the midst of events controlled by an unfriendly deity, is "in the hand of God" (9:1) and therefore accidental (9:11 f.). The final verdict can only be "Vanity of vanities, all is vanity" (1:2; 12:8, at the beginning and end of the book).

In theory, death, or nonexistence, is preferable to life (4:2 f.; cf. 2:17; 6:3-5); in practice Ecclesiastes recommends, like the pessimists in ancient Egypt and Babylonia, the full enjoyment of whatever joys the present may offer, without zeal for wisdom and piety, or stupid eagerness for their opposites (7:16 f.). One should work with zest (9:10) and serenely enjoy the pleasures of life (2:24 f.; 3:12 f., 22; 5:18-20 [H. 5:17-19]; 8:15; 9:7-9; 11:9 f.) before the infirmities of old age (12:1-6) and death (12:7) forever remove the capacity for enjoyment.

Contemporary Judaism produced no orthodox philosopher capable of attacking the theoretical premises of the skepticism and eudaemonism of Ecclesiastes. The annotators of his book (as those of the Book of Job) took issue primarily with the denial of the divine retribution on earth, and vigorously asserted that wisdom (7:11 f., 19; 12:11) and righteousness (2:26; 7:18b, 26b; 8:12 f.), the two highest ideals of the time which had already been identified in the Book of Proverbs (cf. Eccl. 7:25b; 8:5, both of which are glosses) bring a terrestrial reward, because God judges human conduct and compensates men according to their deserts (3:17; 8:11; 11:9b; 12:13 f.).

If Ben Sira knew our book (as Th. Nöldeke believed; cf. ZAW 20

[1900] 91 ff.), he may have had its author in mind when he denounced "the sinner that goes two ways" (Ecclus. 2:12), objecting primarily to the arguments against the doctrine of the two ways adduced in the book. The author of the Wisdom of Solomon (1:16-2:9) likewise directed the darts of his bitter sarcasm against the practical conclusions of Ecclesiastes (his denial of a future life and his advice to enjoy the pleasures of the present [cf. I Cor. 15:32]), which he presents as wicked hedonism, rather than against this sage's metaphysics. In spite of such objections, the book received canonical status because of its popularity, its fictitious attribution to Solomon and, last but not least, because of the above-mentioned pious annotations.

Several critics have attempted to identify the contributions of a number of editors. C. Siegfried has presented in his commentary (1898) the most elaborate theory: the original book of Koheleth was annotated by a Sadducee with Epicurean tendencies, by a member of the guild of the wisemen, by an orthodox pious Jew, and by a collector of maxims; a first redactor edited the book as a whole (adding 1:1 at the beginning and 12:8 at the end, besides a few concluding clauses within the book), and a second attached the appendixes at the end (12:9-14). L. Laue (1900) recognized only one editor, the pious Jew and the two redactors of Siegfried in one person; A. H. McNeile (1904), two editors, one concerned with wisdom and the other with piety; similarly G. A. Barton (1908) and E. Podechard (1912).

Since the author pretended to be Solomon, his confessions are to some extent fictitious; for instance, 2:4-11 is a picture of Solomon's legendary wealth and glory rather than a recital of the author's actual experiences. Nevertheless, it seems likely that Ecclesiastes had the means for travel and for the comforts as well as the luxuries of life. He seems to have been annoyed by the possibility that a fool would inherit his patrimony (2:18-23; cf. 4:7 f.). He lived in Jerusalem (5:1 [H. 4:17]; 8:10), but he may have visited Alexandria in Egypt (11:1); the expression "eternal home" for "grave" (12:5) is Egyptian, although it also occurs in Punic and Palmyrene inscriptions. A visit to Alexandria, where a Greek-speaking Jewish colony flourished, might well explain his contact with Hellenism, although his indirect and vague knowledge of Greek culture could have been acquired in Jerusalem. Some of his expressions sound like translations from the Greek: "to do good" (3:12) in the sense of living comfortably and pleasantly; "chance, accident" (Greek, *tychē*) (2:14; 3:19; 9:2 f.); "good which is beautiful" (Gr. *kalòs kàgathós*) (5:18 [H. 5:17]); "a good day" (Gr. *euēmería*) (7:14); "*tûr*" in the sense of "to speculate [philosophically]," like Gr. *sképtesthai* (1:13; 7:25).

Many close parallels between Ecclesiastes and Greek authors have been pointed out; see especially H. Ranston, *Ecclesiastes and the Early*

Greek Wisdom Literature (London, 1925),[1] where much evidence is collected to show that Theognis, in particular, influenced the Biblical author. It is by no means certain that Ecclesiastes could read Greek works in the original, but he must have come more or less indirectly into contact with Greek thought in the market places and possibly in the schools of Alexandria or Jerusalem. Otherwise it is hard to understand his skeptical attitude toward the tenets and practices of Judaism, his eudaemonism, his notions of time and the cosmic flow—in fact, his attempt to understand the world as a whole. Only a Jew having some slight acquaintance with Hellenism would have been inclined to glance behind the scenes, behind the comfortable, accepted views of the community, in order to test the validity of his people's faith, thereby reaching philosophical conclusions that were both novel and revolutionary. Conversely, Ben Sira, who betrays no knowledge whatsoever of Greek thought, remains firm in the orthodox Judaism of his day.

Neither the influence of Egyptian[2] nor Babylonian wisdom would have led Ecclesiastes to criticize orthodox Judaism. Like Ecclesiastes, the Egyptian "Song of the Harpist" (A. Erman, *The Literature of the Ancient Egyptians*, pp. 132-134), and the Babylonian "Gilgamesh Epic" urge the enjoyment of the present in view of the inevitable approach of death. But Judaism likewise tolerated a similar attitude of mind (cf. Ecclus. 14:11-19, where the same thought is presented in a religious form). If, then, Ecclesiastes heard echoes of Greek thought and was deeply stirred thereby, as seems certain, we may say that in a sense his book is the first attempt to make a synthesis of Judaism and Hellenism, and that the Wisdom of Solomon and Philo, although conforming far more to orthodox Judaism and far better acquainted with Greek philosophy, in that respect followed in his steps.

The author's mental background places him chronologically. We have no external clues for dating of the book, since the parallels between Ecclesiastes and Ben Sira (who wrote about 180 B.C.) fail to prove that the second author knew the first; on the other hand, the allusions to definite historical events (4:13-16; 9:14 f.) are too indistinct to be identified with historical occurrences. Nevertheless, the thought and language of the book exclude a date before Alexander (proposed by Franz

---

[1] Cf. Ranston's later book, *The Old Testament Wisdom Books and their Teaching* (1930). Allgeier (in his commentary on Ecclesiastes in *Die Heilige Schrift des Alten Testamentes*, edited by Feldmann and Herkenne. Bonn, 1925) finds some connections between our book and the cynic-stoic diatribe.

[2] The Egyptian influence on Ecclesiastes is stressed perhaps to excess by P. Humbert (*Recherches sur les sources égyptiennes de la littérature sapientale d'Israël*); cf. A. Causse, "Sagesse égyptienne et sagesse juive," RHPR [1929] 149 ff.; K. Galling, "Koheleth-Studien," ZAW 50 (1932) 276-299.

Delitzsch, T. K. Cheyne, and others). The influence of Hellenism on thought and expression seems unmistakable.

In general, as shown in detail by Franz Delitzsch (1875) and C. H. H. Wright (1883), the language contains numerous words and constructions occurring nowhere else in the Old Testament but common in Aramaic or in the Mishna (cf. S. R. Driver, *Introduction to the Old Testament*, pp. 474 f.). The character of the language alone would relegate our book among the latest in the Old Testament; the Hebrew of Ben Sira is far more classical. Since it can hardly be later than the Wisdom of Solomon (*ca.* 100-50 B.C.), we may confidently assert that it was written between 250 and 150 B.C. Although most critics would date it about 200, shortly before Ecclesiasticus (180), the period 170-160 cannot be excluded and indeed seems most in harmony with the characteristics of thought and language. However, later dates as proposed by E. Renan (*ca.* 125), Leimdörfer and König (*ca.* 100), and Graetz (the time of Herod the Great, d. 4 B.C.) are hardly probable. In Palestine at least, the animosity against Hellenism and the ardent zeal for the Law of Moses were so prevalent after the Maccabean rebellion, that even if a Jew could have written such a book in which Judaism was criticized from the viewpoint of Hellenism, it would never have at once acquired sufficient popularity to be given a place in the canon of Scriptures.

CHAPTER VIII

THE BOOK OF ESTHER

~~~~~~

The Book of Esther is a brief historical novel relating the vicissitudes of Esther at the court of Persia and the origin of the Jewish festival of Purim. In the Hebrew Bible the book is included in the third canon, the Writings or Hagiographa, and is one of the "five scrolls," generally the fifth, preceding Daniel. In the Greek Bible it usually stands after the historical books (or after the poetical books), before the prophetic books: in the English Bible it is found between the historical and the poetical books. Its contents may be summarized as follows.

1. *Ahasuerus's repudiation of Queen Vashti* (1:1-22). Ahasuerus (Xerxes I [485-465 B.C.], not Artaxerxes I [465-424] according to Josephus, *Antiquities* 11:6 [§§186-296], following the LXX which has "Artaxerxes" [I, II, or III]) invited all the dignitaries of the Persian Empire to a great festival celebrated at Susa in Elam (his spring residence) during 180 days (1:1-4). Following this he entertained magnificently the residents of Susa during one week (1:5-8), while Queen Vashti had invited the ladies (1:9). On the last day the king ordered the queen to show herself to his guests (1:10 f.), but she refused (1:12). After consultation with his astrologers who were expert jurists (1:13-15) and following the advice of Memucan, who recommended the deposition of Vashti for her defiance and for her bad example of wifely insubordination (1:16-20), the king sent letters to all provinces and announced the publication of an irrevocable decree deposing Vashti and enforcing the submission of wives to their husbands (1:21 f.).

2. *Esther's elevation to the rank of queen* (2:1-18). Ahasuerus in a calmer mood regretted his rejection of Vashti (2:1) and his chamberlains suggested that the most beautiful maidens of the realm should be brought to Susa for royal inspection, leading to the selection of a new queen (2:2-4a; cf. I Kings 1:1-4). The king acted accordingly (2:4b). Esther (or Hadassah) had been raised in Susa by her cousin Mordecai, a Benjamite descendant of Kish (Saul's father, I Sam. 9:1). Mordecai had been deported by Nebuchadnezzar in 597—124 years before, according to exact chronology (2:5-7). With other maidens Esther was placed in the harem in charge of Hegai, who showed her special favor (2:8 f.). In contrast with Daniel (Dan. 1:8), Esther concealed her Jewish religion

and nationality, although Mordecai inquired daily after her welfare (2:10 f.). After a year devoted to beauty treatments, the maidens were brought to the king, one each day, and became his concubines (2:12-14). In the tenth month of Ahasuerus's seventh year (four years after Vashti's rejection) Esther's turn came and she was crowned queen (2:15-17); a great banquet and a "release" commemorated the occasion (2:18).

3. *Mordecai's discovery of a conspiracy* (2:19-23). Sitting in the king's gate, Mordecai discovered that two chamberlains were plotting the assassination of the king, and through Esther communicated the information to Ahasuerus (2:19-22; 2:19, which is puzzling [or 2:19 f.], may be a gloss). The traitors were hanged and the event was recorded in the royal chronicles (2:23).

4. *Haman's plot against the Jews* (3:1-15). Between the seventh and the twelfth year of Ahasuerus, Haman, a descendant of Agag, the Amalekite king defeated by Saul (I Sam. 15:8 ff.), became the grand vizier (3:1). Proud of being a Jew, Mordecai refused to bow down before Haman (3:2-4). The pompous vizier in his rage decided to have all the Jews in Persia executed (3:5 f.). By casting a lot (*pûr*) he determined the thirteenth of Adar (February-March) as the auspicious day for the pogrom (3:7, supplementing with the LXX "and the lot fell on the fourteenth day [*sic*, for 13th] day [of the twelfth month, which is the month Adar]"). Haman then reported to the king that "a certain people" scattered throughout the empire observed its own laws rather than those of the realm (3:8) and promised to pay into the royal treasury 10,000 silver talents (the equivalent of 18 million dollars; nearly two-thirds of the revenues of the empire, cf. Herodotus 3:95) if they be destroyed (3:9). The king placed his signet ring on Haman's hand, telling him to proceed and keep the money (3:10 f.). Eleven months before the thirteenth of Adar (the day of the proposed pogrom) the sanguinary decree was drafted and sent to every part of the empire (3:12-15).

5. *Esther's resolve to save the Jews* (4:1-17). In their consternation, Mordecai and the Jews mourned bitterly (4:1-3). Unaware of the decree, Esther sent a robe to Mordecai so that he might come to her in the palace (cf. 4:2), but he refused and through Hathach sent her a copy of the decree, urging her intervention before the king in behalf of the Jews (4:4-9). Esther replied that she could not enter the inner court to appear before the king unless summoned by him, under penalty of death (4:10-12). Mordecai, somewhat illogically, argued that if the decree was enforced she would perish, and if the Jews were saved without her intervention the same fate would await her (4:13 f.; the last clause is obscure). Esther finally decided to go to the king unannounced at the risk of her life (4:15-17).

6. *Esther versus Haman* (5:1-14). Three days later, wearing queenly

apparel, Esther entered the forbidden inner court and was graciously received by the king (5:1 f.). Requested to state her wish, Esther merely invited the king and Haman to a dinner (5:3-5). When wine was served at the end of the meal, instead of presenting to the king her petition she invited her guests to another banquet on the morrow (5:6-8). Haman's high spirits in leaving the banquet were turned into vexation at the sight of the unobsequious Mordecai (5:9). But controlling his anger, he assembled his friends and advisers to boast of his good fortune and of the particular honor by which the queen had signalized him (5:10-12), complaining however that Mordecai's mere presence at the king's gate poisoned his whole life (5:13). On the advice of his wife and friends, Haman erected gallows over 83 feet high on which to hang Mordecai on the morrow (5:14).

7. *Mordecai's royal reward* (6:1-14). Unable to sleep, Ahasuerus ordered the royal chronicles to be read to him, but strangely this soporific failed (6:1). When the story of Mordecai's disclosure of a conspiracy (see 2:21-23) was reached (6:2), the king was told that nothing had been done to reward Mordecai (6:3). Haman, who had come to court early to obtain permission to hang Mordecai, was summoned. Asked how a faithful subject should be honored, Haman recommended that the man should be led through the streets on horseback, attired in a royal garment, and preceded by a crier proclaiming the meaning of the honor (cf. Gen. 41:38-44), for Haman arrogantly believed that none but himself could be signalized for high distinction (6:4-9). Upon hearing that none other than Mordecai, the man for whom he had prepared the gibbet, was to be honored, the crestfallen Haman in person carried out his own recommendation unflinchingly (6:10 f.). Filled with ominous misgivings, Haman hastened to pour out his grief before his wife and wise counselors, but they, recalling perhaps the predictions of Amalek's doom (Ex. 17:16; Num. 24:20; Deut. 25:17-19; I Sam. 15), could only anticipate the downfall of the "Agagite" Haman (cf. 3:1) before the "Jew" Mordecai (6:12 f.). At that moment Haman was summoned to the queen's banquet (6:14).

8. *Haman's end* (7:1-10). At the end of the meal, the king for the third time (cf. 5:3, 6) requested Esther to state her petition (7:1 f.) and she finally implored that she and her people should not be annihilated (7:3 f.; 7:4bβ is textually corrupt and unintelligible). Amazed, the king asked who had concocted this murderous plan (7:5) and was told that Haman was the man (7:6). In great agitation the king went out into the garden (7:7) and returning after a moment found Haman prostrated on the couch at the feet of the queen; absurdly suspecting that Haman was assaulting Esther, Ahasuerus ordered his execution (7:8) on the gallows that he had prepared for Mordecai (7:9 f.).

9. *The triumph of the Jews* (8:1-17). Mordecai was installed as grand vizier in place of Haman (8:1 f.) and Esther, with patriotic disregard of personal risk (cf. 4:11), implored the king to reverse the bloody edict of Haman (8:3-6). Unable to revoke it (cf. 1:19), the king authorized Mordecai to issue a royal edict making the former one harmless for the Jews (8:7 f.). On the twenty-third of Sivan (May-June), seventy days after Haman's edict was proclaimed (cf. 3:12), Mordecai dispatched by swift couriers, to all the 127 provinces, a royal edict allowing the Jews to massacre and despoil whoever attacked them on the fateful thirteenth of Adar (8:9-14). Greeted by an ovation, Mordecai went forth from the palace in royal attire (8:15). Throughout the empire the Jews rejoiced and many heathen, in their panic, became Jewish proselytes (8:16 f.).

10. *The feast of Purim celebrating the revenge of the Jews* (9:1-32). When the two opposite decrees went into effect on the thirteenth of Adar, the Jews gathered themselves for the fray while their foes were terrified (9:1 f.). The provincial authorities, fully aware of Mordecai's sway, sided with the Jews (9:3 f.), abetting the massacre of the heathen (9:5). In Susa the Jews slew 500 men (9:6), in addition to the ten sons of Haman, but without availing themselves of the permission (cf. 8:11) to take plunder (9:7-10; the names of Haman's sons in the Masoretic text are written in a perpendicular column because they were hanged [cf. 9:13 f.], according to legend, one over the other). On the following day the king, indifferent to the slaughter of his subjects, granted Esther's request to continue the butchery another day and to hang the sons of Haman; so on the fourteenth of Adar the Jews slew 300 more men of Susa, without taking spoil (9:11-15). In the provinces the Jews had slain 75,000 (15,000 in the LXX) of their enemies on the thirteenth of Adar and celebrated a joyous festival on the fourteenth (9:16 f.). In Susa, after two days of slaughter, the Jews celebrated on the fifteenth (9:18). This explains why rural Jews celebrate Purim on the fourteenth and the urban Jews on the fifteenth (9:19; cf. the supplement in some manuscripts of the LXX, and 9:21). Mordecai (9:20-28) and Esther (9:29-32, omitting "and Mordecai the Jew" in 9:29), however, wrote letters instructing the Jews to celebrate Purim both on the fourteenth and on the fifteenth by "feasting and gladness, sending portions [of food] one to another, and gifts to the poor" (9:22; cf. 9:17, 19); according to 9:31, the fast mentioned in 4:3 (cf. 4:16 f.) is also to be observed annually.

11. *Epilogue* (10:1-3). Ahasuerus imposed a tribute on his subjects (10:1). After the manner of the Book of Kings, the reader is referred for a full account of the reign of Ahasuerus and for Mordecai's greatness to the Chronicles of the Kings of Media and Persia (10:2; cf. 2:23; 6:1). Notwithstanding his exalted position, Mordecai furthered the welfare of the Jews and was greatly beloved by them (10:3).

As in the case of Daniel, the Greek version (LXX) of Esther contains additions to the Hebrew text. While the Masoretic text comprises but 163 verses, the Greek has 270. These supplements were not in the Hebrew during the first half of the third century A.D., according to Origen (*ad Afric.* 3), but were in the LXX in the first century A.D., when Josephus (*Antiquities* 11:6) paraphrased them (with the exception of A and F, see below). Nevertheless, even though they were soon added to the orginal Greek version made late in the second or in the first century B.C., nothing indicates that they ever belonged to the Hebrew book. It is now generally admitted that they were not translated from the Hebrew or Aramaic. The longer sections, which Jerome relegated to the end of the book outside of their context (chapters 11-16 in the Vulgate), are to be found in the Apocrypha; the shorter additions are given in English translation by L. B. Paton (*Esther* [ICC], 1908), as also additions found in the two Aramaic translations (Targums); these expansions are omitted, perhaps deliberately, in the text of the first Targum printed in the Antwerp polyglot (1569), reproduced in the Paris polyglot (1645).

The longer additions in the LXX are the following, according to the versification of the Vulgate:

A. The Dream of Mordecai (11:2-12:6; before 1:1 in the LXX). B. Edict of Artaxerxes against the Jews (13:1-7; after 3:13 in the LXX). C. Prayer of Mordecai (13:8-14:19, after 4:17 in the LXX). D. Prayer of Esther (15:4-19, after C in the LXX). E. Edict of Artaxerxes in favor of the Jews (16:1-24, after 8:12 in the LXX). F. Interpretation of Mordecai's dream explaining the feast of Purim (10:4-11:1, at the end of the book in the LXX). The last verse of F is a colophon stating that a (Greek) translation of Esther ("the above Letter of Purim"), prepared by Lysimachus, son of Ptolemy, was brought to Egypt by Dositheus, a priest and Levite, and his son Ptolemy, in the fourth year of Ptolemy and Cleopatra. The following Ptolemies had wives named Cleopatra: Ptolemy V (203-181), VI (181-145), VII (145-116), VIII (116-108, 88-80), but only Ptolemy VIII was married to a Cleopatra in his fourth year. If he is meant, the Greek translation is dated in 113 B.C. (cf. B. Jakob, in ZAW 10 [1890] 274 ff.). H. Willrich (*Judaica*, pp. 1-28. 1900), however, identifies these rulers with Ptolemy XII and Cleopatra VII who ruled jointly from 51 to 47 B.C. Unfortunately, the credibility of this colophon is by no means above suspicion.

The critical problems raised by the Book of Esther concern its integrity, historicity, date, and purpose.

1. Integrity

On the whole the Hebrew text of Esther is fairly well preserved, although Jerome, who assures us that he translated verbatim from the

Hebrew into Latin, seems to have had occasionally a text differing in minor points from our Masoretic text. Only two passages have become seriously corrupted in transmission (the last clauses of 1:22; 7:4). The only section which has been regarded as interpolated (besides 2:19 or 2:19 f.) is the end of the book (9:20-10:3). The peculiarities of this section were first noticed by J. D. Michaelis in 1783. The language and some of the details in the recapitulation (9:20-32) differ from the rest of the book. The ordinance of fasting and lamentation on Purim (9:31) contrasts with the previous prescriptions of a joyful celebration (9:17, 19; cf. 9:22), which has remained in practice to the present day, and the difference between the dates of the festival in city and hamlet (9:19, adding with the LXX: "but those who dwell in cities keep also the fifteenth of Adar as a joyous and good day by sending portions to their neighbors") is disregarded in 9:20-22, 27 f., 31. The summary in 9:24 f. disregards the role of Esther in saving the Jews and assumes (contrary to 7:9 f.; 9:13 f.) that Haman and his sons were killed on the same day. It is therefore possible that 9:20-32 and perhaps also 10:1-3 are early interpolations; they occur, however (except for 9:30), in the LXX translation, which was made within a century after the publication of the book. The supposition that these sections were quoted from another book, a collection of Jewish legends (cf. 10:2), is entirely groundless.

2. Historicity

The Book of Esther, like Ruth, Jonah, Daniel and other Hebrew or Aramaic works of fiction, purports to be the recital of actual events, and was regarded as historical by orthodox Jews and Christians of ancient and modern times. The only support for this view is to be found in the fairly accurate knowledge which the author possessed about Persian royal palaces (cf. M. Dieulafoy, *L'Acropole de la Suse* [1890]; and BS 66 [1889] 626-653; see also H. Gunkel, in TLZ 44 [1919] 2-4) and about Persian manners and customs (cf. 1:6-8, 14; 3:2, 7, 13; 4:2; 5:14; 6:8; 8:10; in L. B. Paton, *Esther* [ICC], 1908, will be found references to classical historians containing parallels to these passages). But the correct reproduction of local color and the lack of glaring inconsistencies and supernatural happenings, do not necessarily prove that the incidents related actually occurred.

The majority of critics have come to the conclusion that the story of Esther is not history, but fiction. The only historical character in the book known from other sources is King Ahasuerus—no matter with what Persian king he be identified. Although every king of Media and Persia, from Cyaxares to Artaxerxes III Ochus (625-338 B.C.) has been suggested as the prototype of this monarch, it is now generally recognized, on the basis of philology and history, that Ahasuerus is Xerxes I (485-465 B.C.).

If such is the case, the book presents some serious historical difficulties. The queen of Xerxes was neither Vashti nor Esther, but Amestris (Herodotus 7:114; 9:112) who, despite the apparent similarity of the names, cannot be identified with Esther. She was not a Jewess, but the daughter of a Persian general, and married Xerxes not only (as Esther) before his seventh year (2:16), but even before his third (1:3), according to Herodotus 7:6; Ctesias 38b. It is true that the character of Xerxes resembles that given in other sources, and that the incidents related do not contradict the history of his reign. So, for instance, the gap of four years between the deposition of Vashti and the coronation of Esther corresponds approximately to the period in which Xerxes was engaged in his unsuccessful expedition against the Greeks (483-480).

But numerous details of the story are highly improbable, if not actually incredible. Our author (1:1; 8:9) adds seven provinces to Daniel's 120 "satrapies" (Dan. 6:1 [H. 6:2]), drawing like Josephus, who reckons 360 provinces for Darius the Mede (*Antiquities* 10:11, 4 [§249]), on his imagination. The author, likewise, derives apparently from Daniel (Dan. 6:8, 12, 15 [H. 6:9, 13, 16]) the statement about the irrevocability of Medo-Persian laws (1:19; 8:8)—a practice otherwise unconfirmed (except for Diodorus Siculus 17:30) and presumably fictitious; the same applies to the death penalty allegedly imposed on whoever came to the king unannounced (4:11). It is hardly consistent with Persian customs for a king to appoint an "Agagite" (Amalekite) or a Jew as grand vizier (3:1; 8:1 f; 10:3) and to make a non-Persian woman his queen (2:17; contrast Herodotus 3:84). Like the author of Daniel, our author had no conception of the actual length of the Persian period. He obviously assumed that Xerxes followed shortly after Nebuchadnezzar, for he was obviously unaware of the chronological difficulty involved in Mordecai's career. He tells us that Mordecai was deported from Jerusalem in 597 B.C. (2:6) and became grand vizier in the twelfth year of Xerxes (8:2; cf. 3:7), or 473 B.C., when he would have been more than 124 years old; and yet he had a cousin (not niece, according to Jerome *ad* 2:7), Esther, about a hundred years younger than he was.

Aside from these historical difficulties, the book has the characteristics of fiction. A number of its inconsistencies are required by the plot. It must remain secret until the denouement that Esther was a Jewess (2:10, 20; 7:3 f.), and yet her cousin Mordecai, who had brought her up (2:7) and visited her daily (2:11), was not only known to be a Jew (2:5, etc.), but admitted it freely to Haman's associates (3:4) and refused to bow to Haman, in defiance to a royal order, because he was a Jew (3:2). Haman obtained a decree ordering the extermination of the Jews, "the people of Mordecai" (3:6), to avenge himself on this irritating Jew, and yet his intimate friends and advisers, nay his own wife, seem to be in doubt concerning the nationality of Mordecai (6:13). After Xerxes authorized the pogrom (3:11), he signally honored Mordecai the Jew (6:10 f.) and was later amazed in hearing of the extermination plotted by Haman (7:3-6). The second massacre of Gentiles in Susa (9:15) serves to explain the celebration of Purim on two successive days 9:18 f., 20).

Another characteristic of fiction, notably of popular storytelling, is the tendency to exaggerate. The royal feast, which all civil and military authorities of the Persian Empire attended (1:3), lasted six months (1:4). A multitude of maidens (2:3, 8) received a beauty treatment lasting one year (2:12 f.). Haman promised to pay into the treasury 10,000 talents of silver (about $18,000,000) if allowed to exterminate the Jews or, as the Targums noticed, one mina for each of the 600,000 Israelite males of Num. 26:51. Haman's gallows were fifty cubits (83 feet) high (5:14). All nations trembled before the Jews (9:2) who, with impunity and without a casualty, slew 75,510 Gentiles in a single day (9:6-9, 16).

A third characteristic is the artificial symmetry of the story. The actors in the drama are neatly arranged into two corresponding groups, with an irresponsible and impressionable monarch playing the role of umpire. Since the author was an ardent Jew writing for the glorification of his race—not of his religion, as Daniel—the outcome of the conflict between Jews and Gentiles was inevitably predetermined. The Gentiles held sway at first, the Jews triumphed in the end. Vashti was rejected, Esther became queen; Haman was hanged, Mordecai became grand vizier. The anti-Semitic edict was nullified through a pro-Jewish one, so that the proposed pogrom was turned into a slaughter of the Gentiles. The highest positions next to the throne open to a woman and to a man must be taken from Gentiles and given to Esther and Mordecai. This scheme, popular in Jewish tales of the second century, was carried out more mechanically in Esther than in Daniel, Judith, Tobit, and the Ahikar romance, all of which are earlier than our book. In all of them the enemies of the Jews met their doom at the moment of their greatest triumph. Moreover, our author was fascinated by poetic justice, as classically stated in Prov. 26:27: "Whoso diggeth a pit shall fall therein." In Daniel the men who cast the three Jews into the fiery furnace were consumed by its flames (Dan. 3:22) and the accusers of Daniel were devoured by the very lions intended for him (6:24 [H. 6:25]). Similarly Haman was forced to confer on Mordecai the honors which he had suggested for himself (6:7-11) and was hanged on the gallows which he had prepared for Mordecai (7:10).

In conclusion, we must regard the Book of Esther as a work of fiction and all characters in the book, with the exception of Xerxes, as purely imaginary. It is true that the author refrained from including impossible or supernatural events in his tale and that, aside from some improbable details, the incidents narrated could have happened. But in view of the anachronisms, the extraordinary coincidences, the artificiality of the plot, and the transparent purpose, we are not justified in crossing the gap between verisimilitude and reality. It is idle to speculate on the possibility that some incidents may be based on fact, for such guesses lack all confirmation. The accuracy of some of the local color proves only that the author knew nearly as much about Persian culture as modern archaeologists. All recent defenses of the historicity of our book,[1] no matter how learned and ingenious, remain unconvincing because they fail to do justice to the real nature of the book. Thus J. Hoschander, who has presented the fullest argument for its historicity, admits that the incidents narrated can hardly be fitted into the reign of Xerxes, but overcomes this difficulty by accepting the LXX reading "Artaxerxes" for "Ahasuerus." He identifies the monarch with Artaxerxes II Mnemon (404-358) and discovers parallels to our book in Plutarch's life of Artaxerxes II. The proposed massacre of the Jews (according to Dr. Hoschander) resulted from their opposition to the worship of the goddess Anahita, and their deliverance was actually the occasion for the institution of Purim. But besides increasing the age of Mordecai when he became grand vizier to more than two hundred years, this theory contradicts our book in suggesting that the proposed pogrom was a religious persecution.

3. Date

The date of the Book of Esther can only be determined through internal evidence. None of the characters of the book (except Xerxes) nor the festival of Purim is mentioned before our book had attained wide circulation among the Jews. The first reference of this sort is in II Macc. 15:36, according to which the "Day of Nicanor" on the thirteenth of Adar (celebrating the victory of Judas Maccabeus over Nicanor in 161) came "a day before the Day of Mordecai" (i.e., Purim on the 14th and 15th of Adar). We cannot infer that Purim was known to Judas Maccabeus (for I Macc. 7:49, dating from about 100 B.C., mentions the day of Nicanor without referring to Purim) and we can only conclude that the book and the festival were known in Palestine about the middle of the first century, when II Maccabees was written. If the ambiguous and questionable colophon at the end of the LXX (cf. above) really proved that the Greek translation of Esther was taken to Egypt in 113 B.C., we would have a valuable datum for fixing the time when the book was written; but

---

[1] M. Wolff, in TT 50 (1916) 75-120. J. Hoschander, "The Book of Esther in the Light of History," JQR 9-12 (1918-1922); in book form, Philadelphia, 1923 (cf. J. P. Naish, *Expositor* 25 [1923] 56-66). A. T. Olmstead, *History of Palestine and Syria to the Macedonian Conquest.* New York, 1931.

neither its interpretation nor its veracity is certain. Before 113, if some value is to be attributed to the colophon, the silence about Esther is absolute. Particularly significant is the failure of Ben Sira (*ca.* 180 B.C.) to remember Mordecai and Esther among the Jewish heroes in his "Hymn of the Fathers" (44-49). It is clear that Esther, like Daniel, was not yet written at the time. An early date in the Persian or Greek period (fifth or fourth century) as proposed by H. Gunkel (*Esther.* Religionsge-schichtliche Volksbücher II, 19-20. Tübingen, 1916) for the book or for its alleged briefer prototype, can hardly be considered seriously. The Persian Empire had long since disappeared and was but a dim memory (1:1, 13 f.; 4:11; 8:8); the Persian period, which lasted two centuries, had been curtailed to one or two generations (2:6), as in Daniel and Tobit. The language of the book, though patterned on the ancient Hebrew classics, is that of the Hellenistic period and presents affinities with Chronicles, Daniel, and Ecclesiastes.[2] The diction indicates that the author's ver-nacular was Aramaic, and that Hebrew was for him only a literary medium. Some of the Persian words relating to government affairs which occur in Daniel (particularly in the Aramaic parts) appear also in our book.

Veiled allusions to conditions in the time of the author, rather than in the time of Xerxes, may fix the date of composition more exactly. It is difficult to conceive the bitter hatred of the Jews for the Gentiles before the persecutions of Antiochus Epiphanes (168-165 B.C.). The author does not contemplate, like Ezekiel, Joel, and other apocalyptic writers, a divine extermination of the heathen hosts which have attacked Jerusalem, but a massacre of defenseless Gentiles on a given day, within a great peaceful empire, with the connivance of the central government. Thus indeed were the pious Jews butchered by the troops of Antiochus on a Sabbath, without offering resistance (I Macc. 2:29-38). Haman looks like a caricature of Antiochus: he objects to the Jews on the ground that "their laws differ from those of every people and the king's laws they do not observe" (3:8), exactly as Antiochus, eager to make all peoples sub-ject to him one in culture, ordered that peculiar national customs be discontinued (I Macc. 1:41 f.). Haman's edict (3:13) is a travesty of that of Antiochus (I Macc. 1:44-50) but removes from it all reference to religious institutions, which have no place in Esther. Antiochus him-self, like Haman, was determined to root out the Jews and obliterate their memory, settling others in their districts and distributing their land by lot (I Macc. 3:34-36). The background of Esther is not, as in Daniel, the period of persecution (168-165 B.C.) when the pious martyrs had

[2] H. Striedl (ZAW N.F. 14 [1937] 73-108) has carefully analyzed the syntax and the style of the book and quotes the most important studies on its linguistic charac-teristics.

received but "a little help" (Dan. 11:34) through the heroic deeds of
Judas Maccabeus, but that of subsequent Jewish triumphs over the
heathen. While Daniel was concerned with the restoration of the Jewish
worship in the Temple and with the observance of the Law, when they
were proscribed by Antiochus, and, despairing of human means, looked
forward to a divine overthrow of the heathen power, in Esther the
Jews had taken matters into their own hands with great success. In contrast with the resigned pacifism of Daniel, Esther is belligerently militant.
The Jews have taken the offensive, they are not even attacked as in
Judith: reversing the policy of Antiochus, they force the heathen to
become proselytes under penalty of death (8:17). An increasing seculari-
zation is noticeable: when Daniel was written (168-165) the Jews rose
in arms to defend their faith; when this objective was attained they
continued to fight for political independence (attained in 141)—a struggle reflected in Judith written about 150, before Daniel's religious fervor
had died out; after 141 the Jews continued their wars, no longer for the
religious ideals of Daniel nor for the patriotic objective of Judith, but
merely to subjugate the heathen, to take vengeance for past wrongs, and
to increase Jewish power and territory. The Book of Esther reflects the
third, and spiritually lowest, of these stages and particularly the reign
of John Hyrcanus (135-104), who drastically forced the conquered
Idumeans to adopt Judaism by compulsory circumcision. Such forcible
conversions to Judaism, alluded to in 8:17 (the LXX and Josephus add
that these proselytes were circumcized), are unknown before Hyrcanus;
for there was no Judaism in the days of the Gibeonites (Josh. 9). We
may conclude that Esther was written during his reign, about 125 B.C.,
at the height of the worldly power of the Hasmonean dynasty and before
its decline beginning soon after his death.

4. Purpose

The book's purpose, which the author took no pains to disguise, fits
admirably with this date. The author's ideal was Hyrcanus who, like
Mordecai, undaunted by adverse circumstances at the beginning of his
reign, when Antiochus VII Sidetes (139-127) forced the capitulation of
Jerusalem, set out to restore the kingdom of David when he heard that
Sidetes had thrown himself from a cliff to escape being captured by the
Parthians. He began his conquests in Transjordania, continued them in
Sichem and Idumea, and crowned his career with the total destruction
of Samaria. The whole nation, including the formerly pacifistic Pious
(Hasidim), was inflamed with patriotism and with hatred for the
Gentiles, and his reign was remembered, in the troubled times which fol-
lowed, as one of the peaks of Israel's worldly glory. It may be surmised
that Hyrcanus, who was at the same time king and high priest, fulfilled

his religious duties punctiliously but in the rather cynical spirit of Ecclesiastes (Eccl. 5:1-7 [H. 4:17-5:5]; 7:16-18); he relied on military force and political intrigue, rather than on divine help, to achieve the triumph of the Jews over the Gentiles.

The author of our book was likewise more ardent in his patriotism than in his religious zeal. He presumably conformed outwardly to the religious practices and, to judge from his emphasis on fasting, sackcloth, and ashes (4:1-3, 16; cf. 9:31), regarded mere forms and rites as the sum total of religion. For the rest, however, like some of the Sadducees later, he appears to have made no demands on God and to have expected that God would make none of him. God and Judaism have no place in his book, the only one in the Bible where God is not even mentioned. It is clear that the book is deliberately nonreligious, for the author scrupulously avoids all references to Jewish piety even when the context seems to demand them. When Mordecai says that help for the Jews will arise "from another place" (4:14) he ostentatiously avoids saying "from God" (cf. Lucian's LXX, Josephus, and the Targums), and it is most unlikely that he used "place" as a metonymy for God (cf. G. F. Moore, *Judaism*, Vol. III, n. 113a). In the crisis the Jews fast, but do not pray (4:1-3, 16), in their triumph and in its annual commemoration they feast and rejoice without praising their God (9:17-19, 22). The author even seems to go out of his way to offend the susceptibilities of the stricter Jews. Mordecai's boorish impertinence (3:1-4) puzzled the rabbis (cf. the LXX) but delighted the author. He likewise approved the admission of a Jewish maiden to a heathen harem (2:8)—a violation of the Priestly law which shocked later generations (cf. the LXX and L. Ginzberg, *The Legends of the Jews,* Vol. IV, p. 388)—her disregard of the Mosaic dietary laws in concealing her nationality (2:10; contrast Dan. and Jth.), not to speak of the barbaric massacre of defenseless Gentiles. He goes so far as to name the leading Jewish characters of his book, Esther and Mordecai, after the names of two Babylonian deities, Ishtar and Marduk (Merodach in the Bible), who were likewise cousins.[3] It would seem that for the author the Jewish religion was only a garment to be discarded whenever it hindered the pursuit of worldly aims.

This religious indifference, with a touch of sarcasm for Jewish sacred institutions, is in sharp contrast with the author's passionate, sanguinary patriotism. His chauvinistic loyalty to his race, as in the case of some modern patriots, has no relation to religion. Likewise his bitter hatred

[3] The use of these Babylonian divine names and other features of the book have given rise to a mythological interpretation of the book or of the festival of Purim (see, for summaries of some of these views, L. B. Paton, *Esther* [ICC], pp. 87-94. 1908). Even if the author utilized mythical elements, which is most questionable, he intended his story to be taken literally, as an historical narrative dealing with the vicissitudes of human beings.

for the heathen, probably unparalleled in ferocity, is dictated by political rather than religious motives. This intense patriotism and this fury against the Gentiles are a reaction against the faith and piety of the Hasidim, reflected in Daniel. This invincible faith, humanly speaking, had only sent the strictest Jews to their martyrdom. On the contrary, the military and diplomatic successes of the Maccabees and of the Hasmonean dynasty had brought deliverance and vengeance to the Jews, by transforming the sheep of the flock (the Pious) into fiery battle steeds (cf. Zech. 10:3). The pride in the achievements of the Jews and the contempt for the helplessness of the heathen reflected in Esther 9 (cf. 6:13) could only have arisen when the Hasmoneans were at the height of their power in the reign of Hyrcanus, when piety was submerged by a wave of patriotic enthusiasm: shortly before, as we see in Judith (*ca.* 150), patriotism and piety were balanced; shortly after, under Alexander Janneus (103-76), the pious Jews led by the Pharisees asserted themselves vigorously against the secular chauvinism of the Hasmoneans; eventually the pacifism of the Pharisees prevailed among the Jews.

Like other books of the Old Testament whose influence was outstanding (Deut., the Second Is., the Priestly Code, Dan.), Esther appeared at the psychological moment, both expressing and molding the fleeting mood of the day. The author's purpose was to intensify the patriotic fervor of his people, in the moment of its triumph over the Gentiles, not only by means of a dramatic tale of long ago, but also by means of an institution (Purim) destined to kindle yearly the people's pride for all time to come.

5. Purim

The ingenuity of the critics has been sorely taxed in their endeavor to explain the origin of the Purim festival and the etymology of its name. Our author tells us that Haman's lot, by which he determined the auspicious day for that extermination of the Jews, was called *pûr* (3:7; 9:24) and that the celebration of the Jewish deliverance was called accordingly *pûrîm*, in the plural (9:26, 28 f., 31 f.). But no word *pûr*, meaning lot, is known in Persian or in any other language. Nevertheless, numerous attempts have been made to explain the word; to the etymologies listed in the Hebrew dictionaries (particularly the latest editions of Gesenius-Buhl), most of which are discussed, for instance, in L. B. Paton's commentary, we may now add a new theory worked out by J. Lewy (HUCA XIV [1939] 127-151; *Revue Hittite et Asianique*, Fascic. 36 [July 1939] 117-124). He identifies Purim with the Persian festival called *Farvardîgân*, celebrated in honor of the dead (an identification first suggested by J. von Hammer in *Wiener Jahrb. f. Litteratur* 38 [1872] 49; and accepted by Paul de Lagarde, *Purim*, 1887). The Jews (according to Lewy) explained this Persian word through two folk etymologies, deriving it from Akkadian *purruru* (to destroy) and *pūrum* (lot).

In regard to the festival, similarly, nothing is known about its origin except what we read in Esther 9; all our actual information on the celebration of Purim in antiquity is summarized in three pages by G. F. Moore (*Judaism*, Vol. II, pp. 51-54). It should be unnecessary to say that all theories which attempt to pierce the total darkness lying outside the radius of our book (and before the reign of Hyrcanus) rest on problematical combinations and must remain hypothetical. With equal plausibility it has been asserted that the festival originated among the Jews in Persia, of Ptolemaic Egypt (H. Willrich), in Jerusalem, in the Judean countryside (L. Finkelstein, *The Pharisees*, Vol. II, p. 679); and that it was either of purely Jewish origin or an adaptation of Greek, Persian, or Babylonian festivals.

The present writer has come to the conclusion that the eminent critics who have investigated these problems and have presented learned solutions have, through their wealth of erudition, failed to see the woods for the trees. The explanation suggested here, like Columbus's egg, seems to be too obvious to have occurred to anyone.

The facts of the case are these: the word "purim" has no sensible etymology, the festival of Purim was never celebrated by Jews before the publication of our book and never was connected with anything but the triumph of Mordecai over Haman; the story of Esther is fiction pure and simple; the purpose of the book is to introduce the celebration of Purim —a patriotic festival of a purely secular character against which religious authorities at first raised objections until eventually the rabbis of the Mishna and Talmud incorporated it into the sacred calendar.

The most natural inference from these facts is simply that the author of the book invented *in toto* the festival of Purim and also its name, as well as the story of Esther which explained its origin. The success of this brilliant hoax is due to the fact that the story and the festival expressed so exactly the popular feelings in the reign of Hyrcanus: Hurrah for the Jews! Death to the heathen! Moreover, the masses never object to joyous banquets, riotous merrymaking, and Mardi Gras revelry.

Nor was such a successful deception unprecedented among the Jews. From the modern point of view, three of the most influential writings in the Old Testament—the Deuteronomic Code, the Priestly Code, and Daniel—were technically fraudulent—although their authors were sincere men, free from guile, and inspired by noble religious ideals. The author of Esther, no matter how cynical in religious matters, was no less sincere than they in his rabid patriotism. With the support of public authorities the D Code introduced in Jerusalem a nearly forgotten festival, the Passover, and abolished the provincial shrines; and the P Code introduced not only new rites in old festivals, but new festivals as well. In P and in Daniel, not to speak of Chronicles, fiction is presented—and accepted— as genuine history.

If the author, as everything indicates, coined the word "*pûr*" (plural "*pûrîm*") arbitrarily, as the word "Kodak" was coined in our own time, he had a precursor, in this philological legerdemain, in the Priestly author, who fabricated the word "Thummim" on the basis of "Urim" (cf. W. R. Arnold, *Ephod and Ark*, pp. 134-136). In fact it is possible that "Purim" was coined on the words "Urim and Thummim." These words in the P Code refer to some purely fictitious objects belonging to the high priestly vestments, but, as W. R. Arnold has shown, had some connection with the ancient practice of divination; and "Pur" was the "lot" by means of which Haman divined (3:7).

It is not without significance, as J. D. Michaelis (*Orientalische und Exegetische Bibliothek* II [1772]) observed long ago, that the day on which the Jews slew the Gentiles, the 13th of Adar, is identical with the day in which Judas Maccabeus defeated Nicanor and his Syrian army, presumably with considerable slaughter (I Macc. 7:39-50; II Macc. 15:20-36). This victory was celebrated annually on the 13th of Adar (I Macc. 7:49), "a day before the Day of Mordecai [i.e., Purim]" (II Macc. 15:36). Our author, after inventing the festival of Purim, dated it exactly on the two days following the Nicanor Day—the only purely secular and patriotic festival observed by the Jews when our author published his book.

Thus he not only stirred the patriotism of the masses and their hatred for the Gentiles, but he also contributed to the glory of the Hasmonean dynasty. It is probable that upon the publication of the book the masses were delighted to prolong the celebration of the Day of Nicanor during two more days and that John Hyrcanus not only allowed the celebration of Purim, but, for obvious reasons, encouraged it despite the reserved attitude of the more devout Jews. In any case, it was popular enthusiasm that forced the Synagogue to canonize the Book of Esther and to give official sanction to the celebration of Purim, which eventually completely absorbed and obliterated the "Day of Nicanor." The two feasts are, however, still distinguished in the "Fasting Scroll" (*Megillath Ta'anith* 12:30-31), a sacred calendar written in Aramaic before 200 A.D.

It is clear then that the author wrote the book for publication in Jerusalem, not in Susa or some other Oriental Jewish center. The author reflects the chauvinism of the Jews in Palestine during the reign of Hyrcanus and must have resided in Jerusalem a considerable time. His acquaintance with Persian manners and customs and Persian architecture, which should not be overrated, could have been acquired through travel or even in Jerusalem through contact with Oriental Jews. If he was an

Oriental Jew, he probably settled in Jerusalem for some years; for it is difficult to imagine that he wrote the book in Persia without a firsthand knowledge of the spirit prevailing in Jerusalem under Hyrcanus.

6. *Moral and Literary Appreciation*

An objective appreciation of the Book of Esther will avoid extreme praise or extreme abuse. Maimonides (d. 1204) ranked it with the Law of Moses in declaring that, although the other Scriptures should pass away when the Messiah came, yet the Law and Esther would remain. Conversely Martin Luther (d. 1546) said, "I am so hostile to the book and to Esther that I wish they did not exist at all; for they Judaize too much and have much heathen perverseness" (*Tischreden;* in the Weimar edition: XXII, 2080). Since religion is deliberately excluded from the book even when it had a natural place in it, any verdict based on religious values is manifestly out of place, whether it be favorable or unfavorable.

From the moral point of view the book has little to commend it to civilized persons enjoying the benefits of peace and freedom, whatever their race. For the book was written in the heat of battle, in the exaltation of victory, to inflame the spirit of the fighters to a war to the finish, ending with a brutal slaughter of helpless foes. Nationalistic to the core, it extols utter devotion for one's kindred, even at the cost of one's life (4:16), and implacable undying hatred for the enemy. The book is morally neither better nor worse than the violent "hymns of hatred" penned, down to our own day, in the feverish excitement and brutal frenzy of war. It is unfair to regard the book as evidence of the Jewish *odium generis humani* (hatred for the human race), for its ferocity is that of the battlefield, and it mirrors primarily the Jewish state of mind in the reign of Hyrcanus. Christians have written far too much in this viciously bellicose vein, to be the first to "cast a stone" at Esther.

Although, from a literary point of view, the Book of Esther is not a masterpiece and belongs to the last period of ancient Hebrew letters, it is a good example of what we call a short story. Well constructed, with good characterizations and dialogues, it holds the attention of the reader with its dramatic suspense until the denouement brings—from the Jewish point of view—a happy ending. Although such a secular book hardly deserves a place in the canon of Sacred Scriptures, even when provided with the pious additions of the LXX and the Targums, its canonization may be condoned, since it saved from oblivion this interesting and historically significant work of fiction.

CHAPTER IX

THE BOOK OF DANIEL

The Book of Daniel is written in two languages: Hebrew and, in 2:4b-7:28, Aramaic; a marginal rubric, at the beginning of this section ("in Aramaic," 2:4) calls attention to the sudden change of language. Outside of this book, Aramaic texts are found in Ezra 4:8-6:18; 7:12-26; Jer. 10:11, and in the words "Jegar-sahadutha" (the heap of witness) in Gen. 31:47. The book is divided into two parts of analogous size (1-6, 7-12) which do not, however, correspond to the two languages. The contents may be summarized as follows:

I. *Stories: Daniel and his friends remain true to their religion in spite of persecution* (1-6).

1. Introduction (1). Taken captive to Babylon by Nebuchadnezzar in the third year of Jehoiakim or 606 B.C. (1:1 f.; as we know from Kings and Jeremiah, there was no deportation in that year; the author's source is II Chron. 36:6 f.), Daniel and his three friends (Hananiah, Mishael, and Azariah) were educated at court for the royal service (1:3-6). Their names were changed to Belteshazzar, Shadrach, Meshach, and Abednego (1:7). They steadfastly refused to violate the Jewish dietary laws by partaking of the king's food (1:8-17). At the end of three years they were found to be outstanding in wisdom (1:18-21).

2. Nebuchadnezzar's dream (2). In his second year (603 B.C.) Nebuchadnezzar was troubled by a dream (2:1) and asked his wise men to tell it to him as evidence of their ability to interpret it (2:2-11). When they failed in this, the king ordered the execution of all the wise men of Babylon (2:12), including Daniel and his companions (2:13). Daniel requested the opportunity to fulfill the king's wish (2:14-16). Daniel and his companions prayed to God (2:17 f.), the secret was revealed to him (2:19), and he sang a psalm of thanksgiving (2:20-23). Brought before Nebuchadnezzar (2:24-30), Daniel reported that in his dream the king had seen a colossal statue with head of gold, chest and arms of silver, abdomen of brass, legs of iron, and feet of iron and potsherds mixed, and that this image had been shattered by a stone which smote the feet and became a great mountain (2:31-36). According to Daniel's interpretation, the golden head is Nebuchadnezzar's Babylonian kingdom (2:37 f.; 605-561 B.C.), the silver chest is a second kingdom, the Median

(625-550), the brass chest is a third one, the Persian (2:39; 550-331), the iron legs a fourth one, Alexander's (2:40; 336-323). The mixture of iron and clay in the feet indicates the division of Alexander's kingdom and the rise of the rival kingdoms of the Ptolemies in Egypt (323-30) and the Seleucids in Babylonia and Syria (312-64). In 2:41-43 we should omit "and the toes" (2:41), 2:42 entire, and the beginning of 2:43 (which repeats the end of 2:41). The stone represents God's eternal kingdom, i.e., the Messianic empire of the Jews (2:44 f.). Nebuchadnezzar worshiped Daniel (2:46), recognized the greatness of his God (2:47), made him governor of Babylon and chief of the magicians (2:48), and appointed his three friends to be his assistants (2:49).

3. The golden image and the fiery furnace (3). Nebuchadnezzar erected a colossal golden idol and at the time of its solemn dedication in the presence of all high public officials ordered that at the playing of the orchestra all should fall down and worship it (3:1-6). All did so (3:7) with the exception of Shadrach, Meshach, and Abed-nego, whose defiance was reported to the king (3:8-12). When questioned by Nebuchadnezzar, they declared that, whether their God delivered them from a martyr's death or not, they would never worship idols (3:13-18). They were at once bound and cast into the fiery furnace, which had been heated to an unusual degree (3:19-23). To his astonishment the king beheld them walking unhurt in the midst of the fire, in the company of a divine personage (3:24 f.), and, summoning the three confessors, whose garments and bodies exhibited no ill effects from the fire, he acknowledged their God and promoted them to a higher rank in the administration (3:26-30).

4. Nebuchadnezzar's decree, reporting his dream, his insanity, and his restoration following his conversion (4:1-37 [H. 3:31-4:34]). The following sections are metrical: 4:3, 10b-12, 14-17 and, in part, 4:34-37 (H. 3:33; 4:7b-9, 11-14 and, in part, 4:31-34). After the salutation (4:1-3 [H. 3:31-33]), Nebuchadnezzar reports that in a dream he saw a colossal tree hewn down so that only its stump was left (4:4-18 [H. 4:1-15]; in 4:15 [H. 4:12] read, "let them feed him with the grass of the field" and omit "in the grass of the earth" [C. C. Torrey]). According to Daniel's interpretation, the dream meant that for seven years Nebuchadnezzar would be insane and live like a beast (4:19-27 [H. 4:16-24]). While the king was boasting of Babylon's greatness, he became demented according to Daniel's prediction (4:28-33 [H. 4:25-30]). Eventually Nebuchadnezzar, again in his right senses, sang a psalm of praise, and was restored to his throne (4:34-37 [H. 4:31-34]).

5. Belshazzar's banquet (5:1-31 [H. 5:1-6:1]). While Belshazzar and a thousand of his lords drank wine out of the sacred vessels taken from the Temple in Jerusalem (5:1-4), a mysterious hand wrote on the wall a

secret message (5:5) which the wise men of Babylon could not interpret (5:6-9). On the suggestion of the queen (5:10-12), Daniel was consulted (5:13-16) and, after rebuking the king (5:17-24), read the writing as "mene mene tekel upharsin" (5:25) or rather "mene tekel peres" (cf. 5:26-28), meaning "numbered weighed divided" or, less probably, "mina shekel half-mina" (5:26-28). Daniel was honored (5:29), but that same night Belshazzar was slain (5:30) and Darius the Mede (i.e., Darius I the Persian) received the kingdom (5:31 [H. 6:1]).

6. Daniel in the lions' den (6:1-28 [H. 6:2-29]). Darius appointed 120 satraps and over them three presidents of whom Daniel was one (6:1 f. [H. 6:2 f.]). Jealous of Daniel, whom the king thought of appointing over the whole realm (6:3 [H. 6:4]), the presidents and satraps induced the king to issue an irrevocable decree forbidding for a month all petitions to any god or man, except the king (6:4-9 [H. 6:5-10]). Daniel, however, continued to pray to Jehovah three times a day facing toward Jerusalem (6:10 [H. 6:11]) and the king, in obedience to the law, reluctantly ordered Daniel to be cast into the lions' den (6:11-18 [H. 6:12-19]). On the morrow, happy in finding Daniel safe (6:19-23 [H. 6:20-24]), Darius consigned his accusers to the lions (6:24 [H. 6:25]) and ordered his subjects to reverence Daniel's God (6:25-28 [H. 6:26-29]; 6:26b-27 [H. 6:27b-28] are in verse).

II. *Daniel's four visions: the end of the heathen empires and the advent of the Kingdom of God* (7-12).

1. The first vision (dated in the first year of Belshazzar): the four beasts and the one like unto a son of man (7). The following verses are metrical: 7:9 f., 13 f., 23-27. Four beasts emerged from the sea: a lion with eagle's wings, a bear with three ribs in its mouth, a leopard with four wings and four heads, and a terrible beast with ten horns, three of which were rooted out by a little horn "speaking big things" (7:1-8). Sitting on a throne in the heavenly assize, God ("an ancient of days") judged the beasts: the fourth one was slain and burned (7:9-11), the others lost their dominion but lived on for a time (7:12). Then "one like unto a son of man" (i.e., a being having a human figure) arrived with the clouds of heaven and received everlasting dominion (7:13 f.). An angel explained to Daniel that the four beasts were (heathen) kingdoms, i.e., the Babylonian, Medic, Persian, and Hellenistic (Seleucid) empires (7:15-17); the human figure represents the Jews, "the people of the saints of the Most High" (7:18). As for the fourth beast (7:19-22), its ten horns were ten kings, presumably either Alexander and nine Seleucids or ten Seleucid kings and pretenders (7:23-24a); the little horn was Antiochus IV Epiphanes (175-164 B.C.) and the three horns that he rooted out were either Seleucus IV, Heliodorus, and Demetrius Soter or Heliodorus, Demetrius, and Ptolemy VI; Antiochus Epiphanes persecuted the Jews

for "a time, times, and half a time," i.e., three years and a half, from 168 to 165 (7:24b-25). Then the kingdom would pass to the Jews (7:26-28).

2. The second vision (dated at Susa in the third year of Belshazzar): the ram and the buck (ch. 8, with which Hebrew is again used instead of Aramaic). The verses 8:23-26 are metrical. A ram with two horns of different lengths was butting to the west, the north, and the south; and no beast could resist it (8:1-4) until a buck with a notable horn broke the ram's horns and smote him; but the buck's horn was eventually broken and four horns came up in its stead (8:5-8). Out of one of them came a little horn which grew exceedingly southward and eastward (8:9, omitting the last two words); it even exalted itself against the heavenly hosts and against Jehovah, desecrating his sanctuary and interrupting its daily sacrifice for 2,300 evenings and mornings, or three years and two months (8:10-14). Gabriel interpreted the vision to Daniel as follows (8:15-18): the ram represents the Medo-Persian kings (8:19 f.), the buck is the Greek Kingdom, the buck's horn is Alexander the Great (8:21), and the other four horns the kingdoms of the Diadochi, i.e., Cassander in Macedonia, Lysimachus in Thrace, Seleucus I in Syria, and Ptolemy I in Egypt (8:22). The little horn is Antiochus IV Epiphanes, who proscribed the Jewish worship from 168 to 165 (8:23-27).

3. The third vision (dated in the first year of Darius): the meaning of the seventy years of Jerusalem's desolation predicted in Jer. 25:11; 29:10 (9; 9:24-27 are more or less metrical). After meditating on this prophecy of Jeremiah (9:1 f.), Daniel prayed to Jehovah, confessing the national sinfulness (9:3-15) and imploring God to bring to an end the desolation of his Temple (9:16-19). Gabriel then explained that Jeremiah's seventy years are really seventy weeks of years (or 490) after which the iniquity of the Jews would be atoned for (9:20-24). This period is divided as follows: seven weeks (49 years) from Zedekiah in 586 to the high priest Joshua in 538 (9:25a); sixty-two weeks (434 years) from Joshua to the slaying of the high priest Onias III in 171 (9:25b); one week from the death of Onias to the inauguration of the Kingdom of God (171-164). During the first half of this last week (171-168), Antiochus Epiphanes showed favor to renegade Jews, during the second half he not only proscribed the Jewish religion but placed in the Temple an altar dedicated to the Olympian Zeus, called in Hebrew *ba'al shamayim* [Lord of Heaven]. This expression was satirically distorted to *shiqqus shōmem* [cf. 11:31; 12:11] or "the Abomination of Desolation" (9:26 f.; cf. I Macc. 1).

4. The fourth vision (dated in the third year of Cyrus): a revelation of the final period preceding the Messianic age, from Cyrus in 538 to the death of Antiochus Epiphanes in 164 (10-12). After Daniel had fasted for three weeks (10:1-3), while standing by the Euphrates (10:4, omit-

ting the misleading gloss "which is the Tigris") he saw an angel (10:5-8). Until Michael intervened, this divine being had been prevented by the guardian angel of Persia from coming to the prophet (10:9-14). Daniel was overcome by the vision, but the angel encouraged him (10:15-19) and promised that before returning to fight the angel of Persia he would reveal unto him the truth (10:20-11:2a, containing glosses and doublets). After Cyrus will come three more kings of Persia, presumably the three others named in the Bible, i.e., Xerxes, Artaxerxes I, and Darius III (11:2b). Alexander's empire will be divided up among rulers not belonging to his kin (11:3 f.; cf. 8:7 f.). Seleucus I after helping Ptolemy I defeat Antigonus at Gaza in 312 will become the master of Mesopotamia and Syria (11:5). Antiochus II (262-246) will divorce his wife Laodice in order to marry Berenice, the daughter of Ptolemy II with whom he "will make an alliance": but eventually Laodice will succeed in having Antiochus, Berenice, and her son assassinated (11:6). To avenge his sister Berenice, Ptolemy III will defeat Seleucus II (246-226), son of Laodice, and return to Egypt with heavy booty (11:7-8a). But Seleucus II will make a counterattack and a truce will be signed (11:8b-9). Two sons will follow Seleucus II on the throne, Seleucus III (227-223) and Antiochus III the Great (223-187), the second of whom will be successful in war (11:10). After being defeated by the Egyptians at Raphia in 217 (11:11 f.), Antiochus will recapture Palestine through his victories over the Egyptians at Gaza in 201 (11:13-15) and Banias in 199 (11:16). He then will make an alliance with Egypt giving his daughter Cleopatra in marriage to Ptolemy V (11:17). But when "he will set his face unto the isles" and try to conquer Pergamon and Greece, a Roman "captain," Lucius Cornelius Scipio, will utterly defeat him at Magnesia in 190 (11:18) and he will suddenly die in 187 looting the temple of Bel in Elymais (11:19). Seleucus IV (187-175) will send forth "an exactor," Heliodorus, to replenish the treasury depleted by the indemnity paid to Rome after Magnesia, and will be assassinated by the same (11:20; cf. II Macc. 3). "A contemptible person," Antiochus IV Epiphanes (175-164), a son of Antiochus III, will then come to the throne illegally (11:21). He will slay the "prince of the covenant," the high priest Onias III, in 171 (11:22; cf. 9:26; II Macc. 4:34), and, acting deceitfully, he will loot some of his provinces and lavish public works on others (11:23 f.). In his first campaign against Egypt (170 or 169), Antiochus will return with much booty and will begin to plan the abolition of Judaism (11:25-28). When his second Egyptian campaign in 168 will be cut short by Roman intervention ("the ships of Kittim") in the person of Gaius Popilius Laenas (11:29-30a; cf. Polybius 29:27; Livy 45:12), he will vent his "indignation" (cf. II Macc. 5:11) against the Jews, favoring apostates (11:30b; cf. I Macc. 1:11) and desecrating the Temple by abolishing the daily sacrifice and setting up the "abomination of desolation" (11:31; cf. above on 9:26 f.). While hypocrites will renounce Judaism, the Hasidim, or Pious, "will instruct many," suffer cruel persecution (I Macc. 1:60-64; 2:29-38), and receive only "a little help" (in 168-165) through the heroism of Judas Maccabeus (11:32-35, cf. I Macc. 3-4). Antiochus, who will magnify himself by calling himself "god manifest" (Epiphanes), will substitute Zeus for Apollo—the patron of the dynasty, suppress the Adonis cult ("the desire of women"), and generally show his disrespect for the gods by robbing their temples (11:36-39). At the end of time Antiochus will conquer Egypt, Libya, and Ethiopia, but will meet his doom in the Holy Land (11:40-45; Antiochus really died in Persia; here the prophecy ceases to be historical and becomes apocalyptic). Then shall Michael, the angel of Israel, stand up; in a time of great distress the Jews whose names are inscribed in "the book" will be delivered; many of the dead shall be raised, some to "everlasting life" others to "reproach and everlasting contempt"; the "wise" (the Hasidim) shall shine like stars (12:1-3; 12:3 is poetry). Daniel is ordered to "seal the book" (12:4). An angel then asks of Gabriel how long the persecution of Antiochus will last and he replies that it will last three years and a half (12:5-7; cf. 7:25). Daniel himself anxiously inquires about the final outcome and is assured that after his death he will rise again (12:8-10, 13). Two early glosses, suggested by the failure of the fulfillment of the prophecy at the time named, predict the advent of the Messianic age 1,290 (12:11) or 1,335 (12:12) days after Antiochus desecrated the Temple (i.e., later than stated in 7:25; 8:14; 9:27; 12:7).

In both extant Greek translations of Daniel, the original LXX (extant only in the Chigi Manuscript [Holmes and Parsons 88], and in the Syriac translation called "Syro-Hexaplaric") and Theodotion's version (found in the other manuscripts of the LXX), there are long passages lacking in the Hebrew (cf. the Greek Esther) and relegated to the Apocrypha. These additions include: the Story of Susanna (which the LXX places at the end and Theodotion at the beginning of the book); the Stories of Bel and of the Dragon (which follow Susanna in the LXX and 12:13 in Theodotion); and the digression which follows 3:23 and comprises the Prayer of Azarias (3:24-45, LXX), some details about the heating of the furnace and the preservation of the three confessors (3:46-51, LXX), and the song of the three men in the midst of the furnace (3:52-90, LXX). This last addition was translated from the Hebrew, but the original language of the other two is uncertain. The date of these supplements cannot be determined exactly.

1. Critical Problems

Although some of the apocalyptic sections of the Book of Daniel are written in deliberately obscure language and some verses defy interpretation, the literary problems raised by the book as a whole are comparatively simple. On fundamental points, except on the singleness of authorship, critical opinion has reached less divergent conclusions than for a considerable number of Old Testament writings. The chief problems concern the historicity of the seer Daniel and the historical background of the book, the sources used by the author, the unity and date of the book.

A. The Historical Background

The book is a collection of stories about Daniel and his comrades (1-6) and of visions and revelations which came to him (7-12). The obvious implication is not only that Daniel was a historical character, but that he wrote the book, or at least the first vision (7:1) and the final revelation in chs. 10-12 (12:4). The name "Daniel" (meaning "El [a god] has judged") occurs in Akkadian and other Semitic languages and, outside of this book, was borne by legendary heroes in a poem from Ras Shamra[1] and in Ez. 14:14, 20; 28:3 (in the first two passages he is mentioned between Noah and Job as a famous saint, in the third as a famous sage), and by ordinary individuals in Semitic inscriptions and in the Old Testament (a son of David [I Chron. 3:1, erroneously], a priest [Ezra 8:2; Neh. 10:6 = H. 10:7]). In Enoch 6:7; 69:2 Daniel is one of the fallen angels. The names of Daniel's companions, Hananiah, Mishael, and Azariah appear likewise in the lists of Ezra-Nehemiah (Ezra 10:28 and Neh. 10:23 [H. 10:24]; Neh. 8:4; Ezra 7:1, 3 and Neh. 10:2 [H. 10:3]; etc.). The Daniel of Ezekiel could conceivably be identical with that of Ras Shamra, but hardly with the hero of our book who, being at least ten years younger than Ezekiel, could hardly be classed with Noah; moreover, in 591 and 586 when Ezekiel was writing those passages, our Daniel had barely begun his career, which extended from 606 to 535 according to the explicit statements of our book (1:1; 10:1).[2] Nor could our hero be identified with a contemporary of Ezra and Nehemiah, since he must have died long before—assuming for the moment that he was a historical character.

There is therefore no evidence outside of the book that could be used in solving the dilemma: was Daniel a historical character, the author of autobiographical records like Jeremiah or Nehemiah, or was he a legendary character like Job, or Jonah in the belly of the fish?

Although according to the Talmud (*Baba Bathra,* 15a) the "Men of the Great Synagogue" in the time of Ezra and Nehemiah "wrote" (i.e.,

---

[1] Ch. Virolleaud, *La légende phénicienne de Daniel.* Paris, 1936. Cf. W. F. Albright in BASOR No. 63 (October 1936), pp. 23-27.

[2] C. C. Torrey (*Pseudo-Ezekiel,* pp. 98 f.) by dating Dan. 1-6 in 246-240 and Ezekiel in 230 reaches the conclusion that Ezekiel referred to chs. 1-6 of our book when he mentioned Daniel, and that in 31:5 f., 10, 12b, 13 he was dependent on Dan. 4:10-17 (H. 4:7-14).

edited) Daniel, the traditional view in Judaism and Christianity was that Daniel wrote his book in the sixth century. This theory is still stoutly defended, by means of arguments drawn from archaeology, by some conservative scholars.[3] S. R. Driver (*Introduction to the Old Testament*, pp. 510 f.) does not hesitate to say that "Daniel, it cannot be doubted, was a historical person, one of the Jewish exiles in Babylon . . . who . . . foretold, as a seer, something of the future fate of the Chaldaean and Persian empires."

This traditional theory, by accepting the book at its face value, necessarily presupposes the reality of the supernatural and the divine origin of the revelations it contains. Such miracles as the revelation to Daniel of the details of Nebuchadnezzar's dream and their meaning (2:19, 30, 31 ff.), the divine deliverance of the three confessors from the fiery furnace (3:24-28) and of Daniel from the lions (6:22-24 [H. 6:23-25]), and a hand without a body writing a message on a wall (5:5) lie outside the realm of historical facts. Similarly the correct prediction in the sixth century of the course of history down to the second century (2:31-43; cf. the outline above) belongs to the realm of the supernatural. Historical research can deal only with authenticated facts which are within the sphere of natural possibilities and must refrain from vouching for the truth of supernatural events. The historicity of the Book of Daniel is an article of faith, not an objective scientific truth—no offense being intended for its learned and able advocates. In a historical study of the Bible, convictions based on faith must be deemed irrelevant, as belonging to subjective rather than objective knowledge.

The historical background of Daniel, as was discovered immediately after its publication, is not that of the sixth but of the second century. In the Sibylline Oracles (3:381-400, a passage written about 140 B.C.) the "ten horns" of 7:7, 20, 24 are already recognized to be ten kings preceding Antiochus Epiphanes (175-164) on the throne. In the first century of our era Josephus correctly identified the little horn in 7:20-27 with Antiochus Epiphanes, although he erroneously regarded the fourth kingdom as Rome (*Antiquities* 10:11, 7). In the second century the

---

[3] J. M. Fuller, "The Book of Daniel in the Light of Recent Discoveries" (*Expositor*, March and June 1885); cf. his commentary (Speaker's Commentary), 1876. J. E. H. Thompson, *Daniel* (Pulpit Commentary), 1897. C. H. H. Wright, *Daniel and His Critics*, 1906; *Daniel and His Prophecies*, 1906. R. D. Wilson, *Studies in the Book of Daniel*, New York, 1917; see also his series of articles in PTR 13-22 (1915-1924). A. C. Welch, *Visions of the End*, London, 1922. C. Boutflower, *In and Around the Book of Daniel*, London, 1923; *Dadda-'Idri*, 1931. Roman Catholic scholars generally defend the traditional theory: see the commentaries of J. F. d'Envieu (4 vols., Paris, 1888-91), J. Knabenbauer (in *Cursus Scripturae Sacrae*, Paris, 1891), J. Göttsberger (in *Die Heilige Schrift des Alten Testamentes*, edited by Feldmann and Herkenne), and others.

Seder Olam Rabbah recognized that Daniel describes prophetically the times of Alexander the Great. But the real discoverer of the historical allusions in Daniel was the Neo-Platonic philosopher Porphyry (d. *ca.* 304 A.D.), who devoted the twelfth volume of his *Arguments* [*lógoi*] *against the Christians* to the subject. The extant portions of this work have been preserved by Jerome (d. 420) in his commentary, which is the most important of all studies on Daniel. Porphyry assailed the historicity of Daniel by proving in detail that ch. 11 presents a history (not a prophecy) of the Seleucids and Ptolemies culminating in the persecution of the Jews by Antiochus Epiphanes. Jerome honestly accepted the views of this foe of Christianity, although in 11:21-45 he identified the tyrant with the Antichrist (cf. II Thess. 2:3-12) and not with Antiochus Epiphanes.

The Book of Daniel contains five historical recapitulations, in obscure oracular language, extending from the sixth to the third or second century (chs. 2; 7; 8; 9; 11). In three of them the historical events are presented symbolically under the figure of a statue (2) or of beasts (7; 8), in the last two without allegory either through a chronological calculation (9) or through enigmatic prediction (11). It will be noticed at once that the amount of historical information gradually improves as we move from the days of Nebuchadnezzar to those of Antiochus Epiphanes.

The information for the periods preceding Alexander is sketchy and erroneous. The first historical reference (1:1 f.) is incorrect. We know from reliable sources (Kings and Jer.) that Nebuchadnezzar did not take Jerusalem in the third year of Jehoiakim (606), nor carry this king captive to Babylonia (in 1:2 we should omit "to the house of his god," following the original LXX). Jehoiakim ruled in Jerusalem for eleven years (609-598), and died there, not in exile (II Kings 24:6). Nebuchadnezzar was not yet "king of Babylon" in Jehoiakim's third year, for he succeeded Nabopolassar in 605, after the victory at Carchemish (cf. II Kings 24:7; Jer. 46:2), following which Jehoiakim remained an obedient vassal of Nebuchadnezzar for three years (II Kings 24:1). The writer has confused the statement of II Kings 24:1 with II Chron. 36:6 f., (cf. I Esd. [III Ezra] 1:38 f.), and quotes Chronicles. By combining these two passages he invents a new deportation. To change Jehoiakim to Jehoiachin does not free the passage from contradiction with the facts. Josephus (*Antiquities* 10:10, 1) bluntly dates Daniel's exile in 586, twenty-one years later.

Another anachronism in relation to Nebuchadnezzar's reign is the use of "Chaldeans" not in its original sense (an Aramaic tribe in Southern Babylonia from which Nebuchadnezzar's dynasty had sprung) but, as in Greek and Roman authors, in the sense of "astrologers" or "diviners"

(1:4; 2:2, etc.). The use of Persian and Greek (3:5, 15, etc.) words is likewise puzzling in the Neo-Babylonian period.

The series of four successive monarchies (chs. 2 and 7), of which the first is indubitably the Neo-Babylonian or Chaldean (625-538) and the fourth certainly the Hellenistic empire of Alexander (and the kingdoms of his successors) requires the anachronistic displacement of the Medic kingdom (the second in the series) between the Neo-Babylonian and the Persian (550-330). As a matter of fact the Medic kingdom (625-550) was conquered by Cyrus before the Neo-Babylonian.

This misconception in regard to the chronological position of the Medic Empire follows the erroneous precedent of Is. 13:17; 21:2; Jer. 51:11, 28, according to which the Medes (who took Nineveh in 612) conquered Babylon in 538. Accordingly we read that "Darius the Mede" (5:31 [H. 6:1]), and not Cyrus or his general Gubaru (Gobryas), conquered Babylon. To add to the confusion this imaginary Darius living before Cyrus (cf. 6:26 [H. 6:29]; 10:1) is said to be "the son of Ahasuerus [Xerxes, 485-465], of the secd of the Medes" (9:1). In the author's muddled mind the conquests of Babylon by Cyrus (538) and by Darius I (521) were identified and Darius, after being turned into a Mede, was placed before Cyrus; unless of course "Darius" is merely a title of Gobryas (W. F. Albright, JBL 40 [1921] 112 f.). He was then made the son of Ahasuerus because according to Ezra 4:6-24—where the order of the kings of Persia is erroneously Cyrus (550-530), Xerxes I (485-465), Artaxerxes I (465-424), Darius I (521-485)—Darius lived later than Xerxes. On the basis of this passage the author concluded that the kings of Persia from Cyrus to Alexander were only four (11:2; cf. 7:6), whereas they were eleven. According to 11:2, it would seem that in the fourth king the author confused Darius I, his last king, with Xerxes, who waged war against Greece, and with Darius III, deposed by Alexander; but the text is obscure and probably corrupt (cf. J. A. Montgomery in his com· mentary [ICC] *ad loc.*)

It seems clear that our author's misconceptions about the Persian period are derived to a great extent from late parts of the Old Testament and possibly from other sources of questionable trustworthiness. In particular, his compression of the period from the fall of Jerusalem in 586 to the conquests of Alexander in 334-331 is characteristic of Jewish writings. Just as he knows only four kings of Persia, so he passes from Nebuchadnezzar (605-561) to Belshazzar in 538, regarding the latter as the former's son (5:2, 11, 18; cf. Bar. 1:11), although one of the three intervening kings, Evil-merodach, is mentioned in II Kings 25:27 and Jer. 52:31. Herodotus (1:188) likewise knows only one successor of Nebuchadnezzar; the full dynastic list is given by Berossos (quoted by Josephus, *Against Apion* 1:20). Belshazzar (*Bel-šar-uṣur*) was in reality the son of the last king of the dynasty, Nabonidus (555-538), and co-ruler with him.[4] Our author confused Nebuchadnezzar with Nabonidus not only by making him the father of Belshazzar, but probably also in the story of Nebuchadnezzar's madness (ch. 4). This unhistorical tale seems to be a confused reminiscence of the years which Nabonidus spent at Teima in Arabia, while Belshazzar was acting as regent. Such a protracted and unexplained residence in the deserts of Arabia, far from the luxury of Babylon, must have puzzled his contemporaries and given occasion for gossip. Eusebius (*Praep. evang.* 9:41; 6; *Chronicle*, ed. Schoene 1:42; cf. J. A. Montgomery, *Daniel* [ICC], p. 22) has preserved from Abydenus (second century B.C.) a story of Megasthenes (*ca.* 300 B.C.) which may well represent an earlier recension of the legend of Dan. 4. For Nebuchadnezzar and Nabonidus are still distinguished: the first one, in a prophetic rapture, predicted the Persian conquest of Babylon and cursed the "son of the Medes" (Nabonidus, whose mother was Medic) wishing that he might be driven through the desert, where wild beasts pasture, to wander among rocks and ravines.

A similar abridgment of the periods in question occurs in Esther, where, according to 2:5, Mordecai was deported to Babylonia in 597 and was appointed grand vizier (3:7; 8:2) in the twelfth year of Xerxes (473) or 124 years later, according to exact chronology, but much less according to the author's. Even more fantastic in its chronology is the Book of Judith, according to which (4:3) the Jews had returned from the Exile and had rededicated the Temple during the reign of Nebuchadnezzar. The first treatise on Jewish historical chronology, the *Seder Olam Rabbah* (second century A.D.), reckons 52 years for the Medic and Persian periods, and 34 years from the rebuilding of the Temple (516) to Alexander's conquest of the Persian Empire (331).

The chronology of Daniel is sufficiently elastic to allow the author to superimpose on the course of history a mechanical scheme based on the interpretation of Jeremiah's seventy years as seventy weeks of years, or 490 years (9:24-27). He divides the seventy weeks into three periods: seven weeks from 586 to 538 (with close approximation, 48 instead of 49 years), sixty-two weeks from 538 to 171 (actually 367 instead of 434 years), and, correctly, one week from 171 to 164.

In conclusion, the author's information on the period preceding Alexander is extremely vague, being partly drawn from his imagination and partly from unreliable sources. Only two details of his stories are genuinely historical and, being ignored by Hebrew and Greek historians, would seem to be an echo of Babylonian writings. We shall presumably

---

[4] All the data on these two rulers are collected by R. P. Dougherty in his monograph entitled *Nabonidus and Belshazzar* (Yale Oriental Series XV), New Haven, 1929.

never know how our author learned that the new Babylon was the creation of Nebuchadnezzar (4:30 [H. 4:27]), as the excavations have proved
(see R. Koldewey, *Excavations at Babylon,* 1915), and that Belshazzar,
mentioned only in Babylonian records, in Daniel, and in Bar. 1:11, which
is based on Daniel, was functioning as king when Cyrus took Babylon in
538 (ch. 5).

While the author knows very little about the history of his first three
world empires, his information about the fourth, particularly in its later
phases, is exact and detailed. Founded through Alexander's conquests,
which are definitely mentioned in the Bible only in our book (2:33a, 40;
8:6-8a, 21; 10:20; 11:3 f.), the Greek Empire was divided into four kingdoms after his death in 323 (8:8, 22; 11:4). Two of these, Egypt under
the Ptolemies and particularly Syria under the Seleucids, interest our
author. He knows that their two dynasties, usually hostile, attempted in
vain to cement a union by means of royal marriages (2:41-43), and describes their relations and particularly the history of the Seleucids with
considerable detail (11:5-20). He ends his history with a full account
of the reign of Antiochus IV Epiphanes (175-164) and of his persecution
of the Jews (11:21-39; cf. 7:8, 20 f., 24 f.; 8:9-12, 23-25; 9:26 f.).

The last historical event predicted in the book is the rededication of
the Temple by Judas Maccabeus on the twenty-fifth of Kislev (approximately December) 165 (8:14; cf. I Macc. 4:36-61; II Macc. 10:1-9).
Exactly three years before a little altar dedicated to the Olympian Zeus
(II Macc. 6:2) had been erected over the altar for burnt offerings in
the court of the Temple (I Macc. 1:54, where we should read "25th"
instead of "15th" of Kislev; cf. *ibid.,* 1:59; 5:52-54): this is the "abomination of desolation" or more literally the "appalling abomination" (9:27;
11:31; 12:11; cf. I Macc. 1:54; Mark 13:14; Matt. 24:15) a vituperative
distortion of "heavenly Baal," the Hebrew equivalent of Zeus (E. Nestle
in ZAW 4 [1884] 248). The author reckons that the *tāmîd* (regular morning and evening sacrifice in the Temple), which was stopped by Antiochus shortly before the erection of this heathen altar (I Macc. 1:45),
lapsed for 1,150 days (8:14) or three years and a half (9:27; cf. 7:25;
12:7); early glossators extended the period to 1,290 (12:11) or to 1,335
(12:12) days.

What lies beyond December 165 is not historical reality but apocalyptic
dream. Although Antiochus died only a few months after that date, during a campaign against the Parthians at Elymais (I Macc. 6:1-16; Josephus, *Antiquities* 12:9, 1; Elymais is the land of Elam rather than a
city, cf. Tob. 2:10) or at Tabae [Gabae?] in Persia (Polybius 31:11; cf.
II Macc. 9), our author gives an imaginary picture of his end. After a
successful conquest of Egypt, Libya, and Ethiopia, Antiochus shall meet
his end in his camp between Jerusalem and the Mediterranean (11:40-45).

"broken without hand" by a supernatural agency (8:25). This unfulfilled prediction follows the pattern set by earlier apocalypses, which had forecast a final conflict betwen heathen and Jews in the vicinity of Jerusalem (Joel 3:9-21 [H. 4:9-21]; Zech. 12:2-9; 14:2 f.; Ez. 38-39, etc.). The destruction of Antiochus and of his kingdom was decreed in the last judgment (7:9-11, 26). Then comes the resurrection (12:2, 13), the glorification of the pious Jews (12:3), and the establishment of God's Kingdom on earth (a Jewish empire) by supernatural means (2:34 f., 44 f.; 7:13 f., 27 f.).

B. Unity of the Book

The preceding observations on the historical background of the Book of Daniel furnish the main evidence for a solution of the literary problems which it raises.

The fact that there is no clear allusion to Antiochus Epiphanes in the narrative part of the book (chs. 1-6) and that the apocalyptic part (chs. 7-12), on the contrary, refers to his proscription of Judaism in each of the four visions (7:8, 25; 8:11-14, 24-26; 9:26 f.; 11:31-36), and the use of two languages (Hebrew in 1:1-2:4a and 8-12, Aramaic in the intervening section) have been adduced against the unity of authorship. Baruch Spinoza (d. 1677) and Sir Isaac Newton (d. 1727) attributed to the pen of Daniel only chs. 8-12 or 7-12, respectively. J. G. Eichhorn (*Einleitung in das Alte Testament,* §615) separated chs. 1; 7-12 from chs. 2-6; his view was substantially accepted by J. Meinhold (in his dissertation [1884], in his *Beiträge zur Erklärung des Buches Daniel* [1888], and in his commentary in the Strack and Zöckler series [1889]): he dated 2:4b-6:29 (to which ch. 7 was added later) about 300 and 1:1-2:4a; 8-12 in 168-165. E. Sellin (*Einleitung in das Alte Testament;* 6th Edit. 1933; English translation, 1923) dates the "biography of Daniel" (chs. 1-7) in the third century, and 8-12 (as well as the interpolations in 2:33, 43, 45; 7:8, 20 f., 24 f.) in the time of Antiochus Epiphanes. G. Hölscher (TSK 92 [1919] 113-138) dated chs. 1-6, and 7 (which he considered later), in the third century, and 8-12 in 168-164; 1:1-2:4a were translated from Aramaic into Hebrew; the glosses in chs. 2 and 7, referring to Antiochus, are later than chs. 8-12, and 9:4-20; 12:11 f. later still. M. Haller (TSK 93 [1920-21] 83-87) follows Hölscher but dates ch. 7 in the time of Alexander. M. Noth (TSK 98-99 [1926] 143-63) dates not only ch. 7, but also ch. 2, except for glosses, in the later part of the fourth century. This division of the book into a collection of legends of the third century (1-6 or 1-7) and a collection of visions of the time of Antiochus (7-12 or 8-12) has likewise been advocated by C. C. Torrey (Transactions of the Connecticut Academy of Arts and Sciences XV [1909] 241-282; cf. *Pseudo-Ezekiel,* p. 98 f.), W. F. Albright (JBL 40 [1921] 116 f.), W.

Baumgartner (*Das Buch Daniel*, 1926), J. A. Montgomery (*Daniel* [ICC], 1927), R. B. Y. Scott (AJSL 47 [1930-31] 289-296), O Eissfeldt (*Einleitung in das Alte Testament*), A. Bentzen (*Daniel*, HAT, 1937), and E. Bickermann (*Der Gott der Makkabäer*, 1937).

Other theories, attributing the book to several authors and redactors, have been advanced by J. D. Michaelis (*Oriental. und exeget. Bibliothek* 1 [1771] 190), L. Bertholdt (*Daniel*, Erlangen, two parts, 1806 and 1808), and G. A. Barton (JBL 17 [1898] 62-86), but have been justly ignored in recent criticism.

Conversely the literary unity of the book, championed not only by conservative scholars but also by numerous higher critics in the past, still has defenders. After F. Bleek (*Theolog. Zeitschr.*, Heft 3 [Berlin, 1822], 171-294), A. von Gall (*Die Einheitlichkeit des Buches Daniel.* Giessen, 1895) argued for the unity of the book (except for the prayer in 9:4-20, which he considered interpolated) and for its publication as a whole and not, as E. Reuss (*La Bible*, Vol. 7, 1879) believed, in separate sections issued and circulated separately. The unity of the book has not only been maintained by eminent critics of the past generation (J. Wellhausen, K. Marti, G. F. Moore, C. H. Cornill, S. R. Driver, W. W. Baudissin, C. Steuernagel, etc.), but recently by J. A. Bewer (*The Literature of the Old Testament*, 1922), R. H. Charles (*Commentary on Daniel*, 1929), and H. H. Rowley (*Darius the Mede and the Four World Empires in the Book of Daniel*, 1935).

The arguments advanced for the attribution of our book to two distinct authors separated by nearly a century do not seem compelling to the present author, who not only sees no valid reason for questioning the unity of the book but, like many others, finds in both its parts the same aim and the same historical background.

Neither the alternation of languages of the book nor the lack of direct allusions to Antiochus Epiphanes in chs. 1-6 gives support to the division of Daniel into two books. It is obvious to all that the Aramaic section (2:4b-7:28) could never have constituted a separate work without the Hebrew section preceding it, or at least without 2:1-4a. Moreover, ch. 7 belongs to the first part according to the language but to the second according to its contents: if it is attached to the first part it would date all of it in the time of Antiochus, unless we accept the drastic curtailments of E. Sellin, G. Hölscher, M. Haller, and M. Noth; if it is attached to the second, with C. C. Torrey, J. A. Montgomery, and others, then the argument from the alternation of languages becomes invalid. In any case, ch. 7 is closely parallel to ch. 2 and at the same time inseparable from ch. 8 (cf. 8:1) so that it constitutes a serious obstacle to a clear-cut separation of Daniel into two books.

The problem of the two languages of the book has not been solved, although the inception of the Aramaic in 2:4b with the words of "Chaldeans," or diviners, may well have been intentional (Nebuchadnezzar, however, had addressed them in Hebrew, 2:3). A sensible motive for the existing distribution of the languages cannot be discovered. All the contradictory conjectures offered by critics (cf. J. A. Montgomery, *Daniel* [ICC], pp. 90-92) presuppose that parts of the book are now preserved in translation, but they have not brought the puzzle nearer to a solution. Scholars defending the separate authorship of the two parts of the book are inclined to assume that 1:1-2:4a was translated from the Aramaic into Hebrew, and that ch. 7 was translated from Hebrew into Aramaic (G. Dalman, *Worte Jesu*, 1898, p. 11; C. C. Torrey, Transact. Conn. Acad. XV [1909] 249; H. Preiswerk, *Der Sprachwechsel im Buche Daniel* [Dissertation]. Berne, 1902; J. A. Montgomery, *loc. cit.*). Others seek to explain why ch. 7 was written originally in Aramaic, and regard only 1:1-2:4a as a translation (G. Hölscher, TSK 92 [1919] 113-138; H. H. Rowley, *Darius the Mede*, etc.; O. Eissfeldt, *Einleitung*, p. 581).

The chief argument for the division of the book into two separate works is the difference between 1-6 and 7-12. Divergences are emphasized by the advocates of this theory, while similarities (as between chs. 2 and 7) are explained as imitation of the first book on the part of the author of the second. Without thus begging the question, dual authorship can be established only by proving that in style and ideas the two parts are incompatible, and that the first part was written before the lifetime of the man who wrote chs. 7-12 in 168-165. In reality, the differences between 1-6 and 7-12, aside from those inevitably distinguishing stories from prophecies, are elusive. They have so much in common that O. Eissfeldt (*Einleitung*, p. 580) admits that "the author of chs. 7-12 needed to make hardly any changes in chs. 1-6." Long before, L. Bertholdt (*Daniel*, 1806-1808) recognized that the authors of the later sections knew and supplemented the early parts. The inclusion of narratives and visions in the same book is no evidence of dual authorship, for the prophets from Amos to Zechariah included visions and autobiographical accounts (often in the third person, as in Dan. 1-6; 7:1 f.; 10:1; cf. Am. 7:10-14; Hos. 1), as well as prophetic oracles, in their books.

Aside from the lack of direct allusions to the attempted suppression of Judaism on the part of Antiochus, to be considered below, the most conspicuous difference between the two parts noted by J. A. Montgomery (*Daniel*, p. 90) is that chs. 1-6 "are of Babylonian *provenance*"; their "sumptuous barbaric scenery" contrasts with the "arid scenery" of chs. 7-12. But the variation of the locale does not necessarily imply disparate authorship. The Babylonian background of the first part is the creation of the author's imagination (nourished by his sources of information) rather than an eyewitness description, and is scarcely more accurate than the picture of Nineveh in the Book of Jonah, penned long after the city had ceased to exist, and certainly less accurate than the Persian background of the Book of Esther. "The fact that almost all the Akkadian and Persian words appear in chs. 1-6" (*ibid.*) is irrelevant in view of the fact that these chapters are in Aramaic, except 1:1-2:4a which may be a translation into Hebrew. Aramaic is closer to Akkadian than Hebrew and more hospitable to Persian, and even Greek (cf. 3:4 f., etc.) words. The change of locality from Babylonia to Palestine is apparently intended. As Montgomery suggests (*ibid.*) the author apparently implied that Daniel returned to Jerusalem when Cyrus released the Jews in 538; the names of Daniel and of his companions occur in the Chronicler's lists of returned exiles (Neh. 10:6, 23, 2 [H. 10:7, 24, 3]; 8:4, etc.) and may well have been chosen from among them by the author, whose chronology is so vague that he included them among the (imaginary) exiles of 606 B.C.

The chronological argument for the division of the book is equally inconclusive. The chief clue for dating chs. 1-6 is 2:43, a probable allusion to the ill-fated marriage of Antiochus II with Berenice, the daughter of Ptolemy II, in 247 B.C., as Polychronius, bishop of Apamea (d. *ca.* 430) recognized long ago. We may infer from this that ch. 2 and, presumably, the rest of chs. 1-6, could not have been written *before* 247, but hardly that they could not have been written in 168-165, for ch. 11 contains an allusion to the same event (11:6). Why chs. 1-6 should necessarily have been written "very soon after 246 and presumably before 240" (C. C. Torrey, art. "Daniel" in *Encycl. Brit.*, 14th ed.) is not apparent. Even if it could be proved that chs. 1-6 ignore Antiochus Epiphanes entirely, the inference that the author lived before his reign is a questionable argument from silence. In reality, however, it is by no means certain that Nebuchadnezzar and Darius were *not* "types of the infamous Antiochus" (J. A. Montgomery, *Daniel*, pp. 89 f.). On the contrary, the fictitious religious measures attributed to Nebuchadnezzar in ch. 3 and to Darius in ch. 6 could only have been suggested by the two phases of Antiochus' policy. Negatively Antiochus proscribed the practice of Jewish ordinances (I Macc. 1:44-49) under penalty of death (*ibid.*, 1:50), positively he placed an altar dedicated to the Olympian Zeus in the Temple at Jerusalem and other pagan altars elsewhere (*ibid.*, 1:54 f.). Darius forbade by an edict the worship of any god except himself during a whole month under penalty of death (Dan. 6); Antiochus, by assuming the title "Epiphanes" (god manifest) and by using the title *"theós"* (god) on his coins, likewise deified himself (cf. 11:36: the author of ch. 11 attributes this self-apotheosis *only* to Antiochus IV, although it was not unknown before). And the image which Nebuchadnezzar ordered all nations to worship (3) is manifestly a reflection of the Olympian Zeus substituted by Antiochus for Apollo as the dynastic and national deity (cf. 11:37 f.).

The features of Zeus were increasingly adopted for the king's portraits on coins.

That the author of chs. 3 and 6 had in mind Antiochus is shown by two further considerations. In those stories Daniel and his companions act exactly like the Hasidim, or strict Jews, at the time of Antiochus's persecution: they prefer a martyr's death to a violation of the Law of their God (3:16 f.; 6:10; cf. I Macc. 1:62 f.). More convincing still is the fact that before the edicts of Antiochus in 168 no nation had ever been forced by law to forsake its god and adopt another one. In no other apocalypse of the Old Testament is there the vaguest allusion to a religious persecution of the Jews. It is inconceivable that a Jew writing before 168 should have even imagined that a king could proscribe Judaism and much less should have written two stories which could have suggested the plan to a tyrannical ruler. The destruction of the temple of Jehovah in Elephantine (ca. 410 B.C.) was not sanctioned by the king. The "anti-Semitism" alleged by J. A. Montgomery (Daniel, p. 89) to explain these stories was confined to written or spoken words, to polemic pamphlets current in Alexandria, but did not become a legalized pogrom before 168. Even Belshazzar's sacrilegious use of the sacred vessels (6) may have been suggested by Antiochus's plunder of the Temple (I Macc. 1:21-24), and the mania of Nebuchadnezzar (4) may allude to the sarcastic distortion of Antiochus's title "Epiphanes" (god manifest) to "Epimanes" (madman).

In conclusion, there is no compelling reason to ascribe the two parts of the book to different authors. On the contrary, all its parts, either through the example of strict observance of Jewish Law in times of persecution or through the alluring promise of the imminent advent of the Kingdom of God superseding the four successive pagan empires (2:34 f., 44 f.; 7:9-14, 26 f.), have the purpose of encouraging the faithful to remain steadfast during the tribulations of the years 168-165, and to trust in the invincible power of their God.

C. Date of the Book

In dating an apocalypse such as Daniel, the period in which the seer is said to have received the revelations is entirely irrelevant. Beginning with Daniel, it became the practice to attribute the apocalyptic revelations to ancient notables, belonging either to the earliest periods (Adam, Seth, Enoch, Abraham, Moses) or to the Exile and the Restoration (Daniel, Jeremiah, Baruch, Ezra). After the canonization of the prophetic oracles and their publication in four volumes (Is., Jer., Ez., and the Twelve [Minor Prophets]) about 200 B.C., it was thought that prophetic inspiration had come to an end (Ps. 74:9; I Macc. 4:46; 9:27; 14:41) and it therefore was no longer possible for authors to obtain credence for prophecies issued in their own name, or even (as formerly in the case

of the Second Isaiah; Is. 24-27; Zech. 9-11; 12-14, etc.) anonymously.
It is significant that Ezra was the latest man of note to whom such visions
of the unfolding of later history were ascribed, for it became a dogma
that prophetic inspiration ceased with the time of Ezra (Josephus,
Against Apion 1:8). The *Seder Olam Rabbah* (second century A.D.)
states, in connection with the time of Alexander described prophetically
in Daniel, that "the prophets have predicted through the Holy Spirit
until this time; from then on only the sages were active" (cf. H. Graetz,
in MGWJ [1886] 281 ff.).

Disregarding therefore the imaginary lifetime of Daniel, the date of
the book is to be determined, as in the case of all apocalypses, by the
last historical event occurring before the advent of the Messianic age.
The author refers repeatedly to the extirpation of Judaism decreed by
Antiochus Epiphanes in 168-165 (7:8, 20 f., 24 f.; 8:9-12, 23-25; 9:26 f.;
11:21-39), but in predicting the circumstances of the tyrant's death
(11:40-45) he betrays utter ignorance of the fact that he died in Persia
in the winter of 164. The lower limit depends on the interpretation of
8:14: after 1,150 days "the Sanctuary shall be vindicated." Is this a
prophecy of the rededication of the Temple in December 165 written
before the event or is it a reference to the fact after it took place? Many
scholars (K. Marti, *Daniel* [KHC], p. 60; G. F. Moore, *Judaism,* Vol. II,
p. 281; J. A. Montgomery, *Daniel,* pp. 98 f.; the last-named gives other
pertinent references) adopt the first alternative and deny that the author
wrote after December 165; others, on the contrary, see in 8:14 a prophecy
post eventum: C. H. Cornill ("Die Siebzig Jahreswochen Daniels," in
Theol. Stud. und Skizzen aus Ostpreussen 2, 1 ff.); W. W. Baudissin (*Einleitung in die Bücher des Alten Testaments,* p. 628); G. Behrmann
(*Daniel,* HKAT, 1894, *ad* 8:14); E. Meyer (*Ursprung und Anfänge des
Christentums,* Vol. II, p. 186. 1925). This question cannot be settled,
but it is not important.

The book (or at least chs. 7-12) is generally dated in 168-165. But this
date is questioned by conservative critics, who regard Daniel as a historical character and as the author of the book (cf. n. 3, above; W. Erbt,
in OLZ 21 [1919] 6-17, 33-41, has allegedly discovered five editions of
the book published from 562 to 486), and by a few critics who date it in
Roman times: E. Havet (*Le christianisme et ses origines* III [1878], p.
304 ff.) dates chs. 7-12 in the reign of Herod (37-4 B.C.); P. de Lagarde
(*Götting. gelehrt. Anzeige* 1891, 497-520) dates chs. 7, 9-12 in 69 A.D.;
E. Hertlein (*Der Daniel der Römerzeit,* 1908) maintains a Roman date
for chs. 2-7. Daniel's fourth kingdom is interpreted as the Roman Empire
in II [IV] Esd. 12:11-30 and in Josephus, *Antiquities* 10:11, 7.

The second century date for the book as a whole is supported not
only by its historical allusions and general characteristics of thought and

language, but also by the inexplicable omission of Dan. 1-6, if it was written about 240, from the comprehensive collection of prophetic writings published in four volumes about 200 B.C. (called "the books" in 9:2) and by Ben Sira's neglect to name Daniel in his "hymn of the fathers" (Ecclus. 44:1-50:24) listing the great men of Israel from Enoch to the high priest Simon, including Ezekiel (49:8), the "Twelve [Minor] Prophets" (49:10), Zerubbabel (49:11), Joshua (49:12), and Nehemiah (49:13). In the Hebrew Bible Daniel is not included among the Prophets, but among the Writings.

D. Sources of the Book

The author of the Book of Daniel was obviously a very learned man. Like the imaginary hero of his book, the author was not only a seer, but also a sage. His range of reading was wide and his knowledge of popular tales, circulating orally, quite extensive. Nevertheless, we can only surmise the amount of earlier material which he utilized because he mentions only one of his sources (Jer. 25:11 f.; 29:10; see Dan. 9:2), and because most of them are now lost. The investigation of the possible sources utilized has been carried on in three fields, the form of the book, the stories, and the visions.

The literary form of Daniel has no real antecedents in Hebrew literature, although a vague similarity with the Blessings of Jacob (Gen. 49) and Moses (Deut. 33), and the oracles of Balaam (Num. 22-24) may suggest itself. The book is technically an *apócryphon*, literally a book allegedly written by an ancient man of God and *hidden* until the moment decreed by God for its publication (12:4; cf. II [IV] Esd. 12:37; 14:45 f.). Such esoteric and pseudonymous revelations of the future became very popular among the Jews after Daniel (until the rabbis of the second century A.D. began to proscribe them), and among the early Christians, who preserved in translation some of the Jewish apocalypses and composed others, such as the Revelation of St. John which was eventually canonized.

It has been plausibly suggested (cf. J. A. Montgomery, *Daniel*, pp. 77 f.) that the type of literature represented by Daniel may have been derived from Babylonian and especially Egyptian models. For the latter see a monograph of C. C. McCown (in HTR 18 [1925] 357-411); for Babylonian influence cf. G. H. Dix in JTS 26 [1925] 241-265. In particular, the veiled predictions in Dan. 11 have a parallel in the Egyptian "Demotic Chronicle" written in the third century B.C. containing a series of oracles, which are individually interpreted, sketching the periods of Persian and Greek domination to be followed by a political and religious restoration of Egypt.

To what extent the author of Dan. 1-6 utilized folk tales and legends cannot be determined exactly. The previously noticed mention of Daniel in Ez. 14:14, 20; 28:3 and, with his three companions, in the Ezra-Nehemiah lists, offers two possible sources from which the author could have derived the name of his hero—but nothing else. Although Daniel in Ezekiel, as in our book, is both pious and wise, he could not have lived in the period reaching from Nebuchadnezzar to Cyrus, nor could he have been the object of religious persecution. The transparent allusions to the tribulations of the Jews in the reign of Antiochus Epiphanes in chs. 1-6 prove that in the main the plots of the stories were created by our author, although he used unquestionably traditional material for some of the details. The individual stories are mutually independent (in ch. 3 Daniel is not even mentioned) and are not molded together into a dramatic unity (although there are allusions to chs. 2 and 4 in 5:11, 20 f.). Our author could not "have found them already in a collection" (C. Steuernagel, *Einleitung*, p. 654), since he manifestly contributed the Maccabean background and the chronological scheme which are inherent to the stories. At most he rewrote some individual tales circulating orally among the Jews of his time, but he did not reproduce chs. 1-7 substantially intact and chs. 8-12 with considerable changes from existing writings, as H. Preiswerk (*Der Sprachwechsel im Buche Daniel*) contends. He probably had earlier prototypes for his stories of Nebuchadnezzar's madness (4) and Belshazzar's banquet (5). We have noted, in connection with the discussion of the historical background, that these two chapters contain the only genuinely historical data for the period before Alexander; this information could have been derived only from earlier sources. Moreover, the story about Nebuchadnezzar, preserved by Eusebius (*Praep. ev.* 9:41, 6), as we have seen, may well be an antecedent for the fictitious tale of Nebuchadnezzar's madness (4); and both Herodotus (1:191) and Xenophon (*Cyropaedia* 7:5, 15) relate that Babylon was taken after a night of revelry (cf. Dan. 5) on the occasion of a festival (cf. J. A. Montgomery, *Daniel*, pp. 68 f.), although the name of Belshazzar was unknown to them.

For the rest we no longer have any literary parallels to the stories of Daniel, although a number of details have been compared with those in ancient Oriental writings (cf. the articles listed in HTR 27 [1934] 324). The genuine Persian background of some of the stories (cf. O. Eissfeldt, *Einleitung*, pp. 577 f.) may indicate that the author utilized earlier materials: C. C. Torrey (*Ezra Studies*, p. 48) plausibly suggests that the "127 [so with the original LXX] satraps" (cf. Esth. 1:1) and the "three presidents" of 6:1 f. (H. 6:2 f.) are derived from the Story of the Three Youths (I [III] Esd. 3:1, 9), which, incidentally, may have suggested vaguely to our author the story of ch. 3.

We are even more in the dark with reference to the sources which the author may have employed in chs. 7-12. A Babylonian mythological background has been discovered in ch. 7 by H. Gunkel (*Schöpfung und Chaos*, pp. 323-335. 1895) and others (cf. J. A. Montgomery, *Daniel*, pp. 321-324). Recently E. G. Kraeling has detected "Some Babylonian and Iranian Mythology in the Seventh Chapter of Daniel" (*Oriental Studies in Honor of D. S. C. E. Pavry*, pp. 228-231. Oxford, 1934). F. Cumont (*Klio* 9 [1909] 263-273) explains the use of the ram and the buck (8) for the Medo-Persian and Greek kings, respectively, as a reflection of the ancient theory that each country was subject to one of the signs of the Zodiac. O. Eissfeldt (*Baal Zaphon*, pp. 25-27. 1932; *Einleitung*, p. 578) explains the monsters of ch. 7 through North Syrian mythology, pointing to the occurrences of the expression "king father of years" (cf. 7:9) in a mythological poem from Ras Shamra. Without denying that Jewish apocalypse, particularly after Daniel, used for its fantastic symbolism elements drawn from the mythology of ancient Oriental nations, the utmost caution is to be recommended in postulating mythological sources for our book, which was written by a man far more repelled by heathenism in all its forms than even Ezekiel. If our author was influenced by alien myths, it was only indirectly and unconsciously, and in his finished work these have been sterilized and disguised with great thoroughness. E. G. Kraeling (*op. cit.*, p. 229) can discover only one instance, the puzzling plural "thrones" in 7:9, in which the author "forgot to obliterate this last trace of the pagan origin of his material"; but other explanations of the plural are conceivable.

While no written sources need be assumed for the vague mythological notions that may be embodied in the visions of Daniel, for they were not beyond the ken of the average man, the exact and detailed information about the relations between Ptolemies and Seleucids from 312 to 175 B.C. (11:5-20) seems to be based on written sources, though not necessarily non-Jewish as G. A. Barton (JBL 17 [1898] 76) believes.

In conclusion, the author of the Book of Daniel used oral or written sources chiefly for matters of detail, occasionally drawing from them the idea for one of the stories, but in the general conception and plan of the book, in the definite teaching and exhortation presented in it, and in many of the details (as for instance the guessing of a dream in ch. 2 [cf. B. Heller in ZAW 43 (1925) 243-246]) the author gives evidence of great originality. When his book appeared at the beginning of the Maccabean rebellion it must have electrified the readers, as may be surmised from its immediate influence on Jewish literature. It is quoted in Enoch, *Sibylline Oracles* 3:388-400; I Macc. 1:54; 2:59 f., the Testaments of the Twelve Patriarchs, etc., as well as in Josephus and the New Testament; and it became the model of later apocalypses. Such spontaneous literary success, perhaps even greater than that of the Second Isaiah and of the

Book of Job, would be inexplicable if the first half of the book had been known for over seventy years, if chs. 8-12 were merely a rewriting of an exilic document (H. Junker, *Untersuchungen über literarische und exegetische Probleme des Buches Daniel,* 1932), or if chs. 1-7 originated in the Persian period (B. D. Eerdmans, *Godsdienst van Israël,* Vol. II, pp. 49-55. 1930; M. A. Beek, *Das Danielbuch,* 1935). A patchwork of well-known material could not have kindled the spirits in 168-165 nor have contributed to Judaism's triumph over a vicious attack, as the Book of Daniel unquestionably did.

2. Literary Characteristics

At the beginning of the Maccabean period, when our author was writing, Aramaic was the vernacular of the Jews in Palestine, and Hebrew, after the manner of Latin in the Middle Ages, was the language of scholars and churchmen. It is therefore not surprising that the author of Daniel knew Aramaic better than Hebrew and that the Aramaic portions of the book (2:4b-7:28) are better literature than the Hebrew parts. One has the impression that at times while writing Hebrew he is thinking in Aramaic, even though the actual Aramaic terms in his Hebrew are not abundant. In any case his Hebrew is decidedly postclassic, inferior to that of Nehemiah in the fifth century and even to that of the Chronicler in the third. It may be compared to that of Ecclesiastes and Esther, written shortly after Daniel in the second century, but it is often less idiomatic and forceful than that of Ben Sira shortly before.

The "Biblical Aramaic" used in Daniel and Ezra (with no important differences) represents a stage in the development of Western Aramaic which is later than that of the papyri from Assuan and Elephantine dating from 471 to 408 B.C. (cf. C. C. Torrey, *Ezra Studies,* pp. 161-166; J. A. Montgomery, *Daniel,* pp. 15-20), though patently earlier than Syriac, and the Aramaic of the Targums. During the Persian and early Greek periods there must have been a vast body of popular Aramaic fiction, often written with a moralizing purpose and interspersed with wise sayings, which, though pagan in origin, exercised a deep influence on Jewish writers. Unfortunately only one incomplete specimen has come down to us in the original language, the story of Ahikar, Aramaic fragments of which were discovered among the papyri of Elephantine of the fifth century (A. Cowley, *Aramaic Papyri of the Fifth Century,* pp. 204-248. Oxford, 1923; cf. for the other versions: R. H. Charles (Editor), The *Apocrypha and Pseudepigrapha of the Old Testament.* 2 vols. Oxford, 1913; Vol. II, pp. 715 ff.). The Jewish author of Tobit was acquainted with this tale (cf. Tob. 1:21 f.; 11:17; 14:10). The Greek text of the Story of the Three Youths in I [III] Esd. 3-4 (omitting the Jewish interpolations in 4:13 [Zerubbabel] and 4:43-63), as C. C. Torrey has shown (*Ezra Studies,* pp. 18-30, 37-61), is a translation from a pagan Aramaic original, dating from the beginning of the third century. Aramaic stories such as these must have been known to the author of Dan. 1-6, but how much he derived from them can no longer be determined owing to the total disappearance of this literature except for the two tales just mentioned.

The author of Daniel is far more notable for his religious zeal than for his literary art. Even the best parts of his book (chs. 2-7), which he wrote in Aramaic, are not to be classed with earlier (Ruth, Jon., Tob.) and later (Jth., Esth., Sus.) Hebrew short stories. In comparison with these, Daniel's style is crude, the plots are elementary, and the happy endings are produced less subtly and more artificially by an abrupt intervention of the *deus ex machina*. The six Aramaic chapters are arranged somewhat mechanically in pairs within pairs, like three concentric Chinese spheres: 2 and 7, 3 and 6, 4 and 5, dealing respectively with the passing of the four pagan empires and the advent of the Jewish one, with the miraculous deliverance of the martyrs, and with the divine humiliation of arrogant tyrants. In spite of the notable variation of the details, the recurrence of the same themes produces a certain monotony which would have been avoided by a writer of greater talent and imagination. The individual stories are separate, self-contained entities, without mutual connections. This abruptness, to a lesser degree, may be noted occasionally within the single episodes and gives to the collection an anecdotic character, depriving it of that organic unity, that dramatic concatenation of events which is one of the outstanding literary qualities of the Joseph stories in J and E—a masterpiece which our author emulated without remotely equaling.

Like the author of the Priestly Code and the Chronicler, our writer is a theorist rather than a brilliant storyteller. All three use narrative material merely to substantiate dogma and to provide legal precedents. Being uninterested in the tales per se, they fail to visualize scenes and persons, and lack the skill needed to create the illusion of reality: their characters are shadowy types, their scenery is mere stage setting. In Daniel, for instance, it is impossible to imagine the form of the fiery furnace (3:19-26) and of the den of lions (6:16 f., 23 f. [H. 6:17 f., 24 f.]), or to conceive even vaguely the appearance of the fourth beast (7:7 f.).

This sense of unreality is increased by implausible exaggerations which are not charmingly naïve, like those of fairy tales, but conventional and stilted, like those of P and the Chronicler, being dictated by dogma and, in Daniel, also by symbolism. Mathematical ratios applied to such imponderables as Daniel's wisdom (ten times better than that of the Babylonian magicians, 1:20) and the heat of the furnace (seven times greater than usual, 3:19) are meaningless. The dimensions of the stone which became a mountain filling the whole earth (2:35), of the idol

(3:1), and of the tree (4:10-12, 20 f. [H. 4:7-9, 17 f.]) are fantastic. Miracles are of course commonplace events in the stories, and range from the dramatic deliverance of apparently doomed martyrs to the astonishingly beneficial effects on four Jewish youths of a ten-day diet of pulse and water (1:15).

The author's mind was fascinated by the colossal, and appropriately he had, like the little horn, "a mouth speaking great things" (7:8). There is something baroque in his style, particularly in the speeches, which are usually pompously grandiloquent. Hyperbolically, the greatness of pagan kings is said to reach unto heaven and their dominion to the ends of the earth (4:22 [H. 4:19]); they are accordingly addressed, even by Jews, with obsequious pomp and ceremony (2:37 f.; 4:19 [H. 4:16]; 5:18 f.), except for the impertinent words of the three bold confessors (3:16). Likewise the kings express themselves with ostentatious dignity and majesty (3:4-6, 14 f., 28 f.; 4:1-3 [H. 3:31-33]; 4:9, 30, 36 [H. 4:6, 27, 33]; 5:13-16). This ceremonious formality reaches its apex in the doxologies extolling the almighty power and eternal dominion of God (2:20-23, 28, 47; 3:28; 4:2 f., 17, 25, 32, 34 f., 37 [H. 3:32 f.; 4:14, 22, 29, 31 f., 34]; 6:26 f. [H. 6:27 f.]).

It has often been observed that Daniel's prayer in 9:4-19 differs in style and in thought from the rest of the book and following A. von Gall (*Die Einheitlichkeit des Buches Daniel*) some critics have regarded 9:4-20 as an interpolation; similarly, in the LXX, a prayer of Azariah in the fiery furnace is added after 3:23. There are striking similarities between the prayer of Daniel (imitated in Bar. 1:15-2:19) and that of Azariah: they are liturgical in character, Deuteronomistic in style, and patterned after I Kings 8; Jer. 26; 32; 44; Ezra 9; Neh. 1; 9. In contrast with the rest of the book they stress the justice and mercy of God and the wickedness of Israel: they are confessions of national sin and appeals, *de profundis,* for divine help. The arguments against the authenticity of 9:4-20 have some force but are not decisive (cf. E. Bayer, *Danielstudien* I [AA iii, 5]. 1912).

Except for the prolix and resounding speeches and royal decrees in the book, the style is generally concise and abrupt, often factual and un-adorned like that of the Priestly Code. In contrast with the great prophets of earlier times, the writer seldom uses similes. His comparisons are obvious and usually derived from other writings: for example, the chaff (2:35; cf. Hos. 13:3; Ps. 1:4), the oxen (4:25, 32 f. [H. 4:22, 29 f.]; 5:21; cf. Is. 11:7; Job 40:15), the firmament and the stars (12:3; cf. Ez. 8:2. Enoch 39:7; 43:4; 104:2; Wisd. of Sol. 3:7; Matt. 13:43 contain later references to the brilliance of the elect). In 10:6, the beryl, the lightning, the torches of fire, the polished brass, and the sound of a multitude are reminiscent of Ez. 1:7, 13, 16, 24. At times, with extreme conciseness, the author uses the *comparatio compendiaria* in which a part is likened to a whole, as "his heart was made like [the heart of] the beasts" (5:21): see 1:10; 4:16, 33 (H. 4:13, 30).

The author retells some of his episodes more or less verbatim, after the manner of popular storytellers (2:31-36, cf. 2:38-42; 3:4 f., cf. 3:7, 10 f., 15; 4:10-17, cf. 4:20-26 [H. 4:7-14, 17-23], 5:20 f.; 6:7 f., cf. 6:12 [H. 6:8 f., 13]; 7:7 f., cf. 7:19 f.). Another peculiarity of his style, which is characteristic of the Priestly Code, is the tedious use of catalogues. He lists punctiliously the public officials (3:2, 3), the various magicians (two to four classes: 1:20; 2:2, 10, 27; 4:7 [H. 4:3]; 5:7, 11, 15), the musical instruments (3:5, 7, 10, 15), the garments (3:21), and "peoples, tribes, and languages" (3:4, 7, 29; 4:1 [H. 3:31]; 5:19; 6:25 [H. 6:26]; 7:14); see also 5:2, 3, 23; 5:4, 23; 1:4, 17 and 5:12; etc. Such fixed formulations and their reiteration do not deprive the style of vitality and charm, as they do in the Priestly Code.

The style of the Hebrew part of the book, particularly chs. 8-12, is deliberately mysterious, befitting the revelation of secrets as in chs. 2; 4; 5; 7, but (aside from ch. 8) less fantastically picturesque, more prosaic and abstract.

Despite its stylistic blemishes, the Book of Daniel is a great literary monument, the first real apocalypse and the classic example of this literary genre. The numerous Jewish and Christian imitations are evidence of the importance of our book in the history of literature. The stress on the colossal, the grotesque, the imaginary, as well as the mechanical structure, pomposity, and aridity of the style may not be pleasing to our modern literary taste. Nevertheless, the author achieved occasionally dramatic power (3:17 f.; 4:29-31 [H. 4:26-28]; 5:29 f.) and epic grandeur (7). The present writer would consider the vision of the four beasts and of the heavenly assizes (ch. 7) as the outstanding creation of our author: the contrast between the horrible chaotic monsters and the luminous heavenly scene dominated by the dignified "ancient of days" and the "one like unto a son of man" arriving on the clouds of heaven, is depicted magnificently, with admirable restraint and noble simplicity. The abysmal chasm separating mankind's "storm and stress" on this earth and its Utopic dreams of "peace on earth, good will toward men" has hardly ever been visualized more dramatically.

3. Religious Thought

Daniel and Ecclesiastes represent the latest phase of religious thought in the Old Testament: Daniel the prevalent orthodoxy destined to triumph in Judaism, Ecclesiastes a philosophical heresy and an attack (which Judaism did not take seriously) on Daniel's doctrine of the resurrection.

The author of our book belonged to that group of intensely religious Jews who called themselves "Hasidim" (Pious) to distinguish themselves from the more worldly-minded. It seems probable that the party of the Pharisees developed later out of this movement. The Book of Daniel may be regarded as the manifesto of the Hasidim, issued to encourage the pious Jews persecuted by Antiochus Epiphanes (168-165), although the book was privately written and did not acquire its official standing until after publication.

When Antiochus proscribed the observance of the Law of Moses and ordered the Jews to sacrifice to pagan gods in 168 (I Macc. 1:41-61), some Jews, choosing to save their life at the cost of their religion, became apostates (I Macc. 1:43, 52). The Hasidim, on the contrary, preferred martyrdom to idolatry, and even to the violation of the least of the commandments (cf. I Macc. 1:62 f.). Their motto is well expressed by Daniel's friends, "If our God whom we serve is able to deliver us, he will deliver us from . . . thy hand, O king; but if not, be it known to thee, O king, that we will not serve thy gods . . ." (3:17 f.). At the beginning of the persecution a group of Jews, obviously Hasidim although not specifically called so, fled to the wilderness and preferred to be slaughtered with their families rather than to violate the Law and the "tradition of the elders" by defending themselves on the Sabbath (I Macc. 2:29-38). Thus many died for their faith (11:32b-33, 35; I Macc. 1:60-64).

When Judas Maccabeus, inspired by his father's boldness (I Macc. 2:15-28), raised the standard of rebellion, the Hasidim were at first reluctant to join forces with him. For they placed their trust in God's power to deliver them (Dan. 3:17 f.) and mistrusted the "little help" (11:34a) which Judas could offer through human agencies, particularly since not a few questionable characters (11:34b; cf. I Macc. 6:21-27) had joined the movement. Eventually, however, the Hasidim made common cause with the Maccabees (I Macc. 2:42-44; cf. 7:12 f.; II Macc. 14:6 even regards Judas as the leader of the Hasidim) and actually consented to fight on the Sabbath in self-defense (I Macc. 2:40 f.). Only the gravity of the crisis could induce the Hasidim, who were pacifists on principle and looked forward to a supernatural deliverance, to become warriors. This temporary change of attitude, which is not yet apparent in Daniel, is pictured in Enoch 90:6-9 under the symbol of the horns that grew on the little lambs. Nevertheless, even in the darkest hours, when all hope of divine assistance seemed lost, the Hasidim cried unto God vehemently, begging him to arise and plead his own cause (Ps. 74, which was probably written during the persecution of Antiochus; cf. Pss. 44; 79; 83, which may be slightly later in date) and believed with the author of Daniel that the triumphant intervention of Jehovah, who needed no human assistance (2:34, 45; 8:25), was imminent.

This assurance of supernatural deliverance pervading the Book of Daniel rests on the doctrine that Jehovah is the only God and that his power is irresistible. Pagan gods are merely idols of wood, stone, or metal (5:4), devoid of sensation or knowledge (5:23). "The living God" (6:20, 26 [H. 6:21, 27]), on the contrary, is "the God of gods and the lord of kings" (2:47; cf. 11:36; Deut. 10:17) and "the King of heaven" (4:37 [H. 4:34]; cf. 5:23). He is everlasting (6:20 [H. 6:21]), endowed with wisdom and might (2:20-22; cf. Job 12:13), and just in his judgment (4:37 [H. 4:34]; in 9:4-19 he is righteous, compassionate, and forgiving). He dwells in the heavens (2:28) but controls the course of human history (2:21) and the angelic hosts (4:35 [H. 4:32]; cf. Is. 24:21) irresistibly, so that none can stay his hand and say, "What doest thou?" (4:35 [H. 4:32]; cf. Job 9:12; Is. 45:9; Eccl. 8:4). His kingdom and his dominion are eternal (4:3, 34; 6:26 [H. 3:33; 4:31; 6:27]): he rules over the kingdom of men, giving it to whomsoever he pleases (4:17, 25, 32 [H. 4:14, 22, 29]; cf. 2:21). He works signs and wonders in heaven and earth (6:27 [H. 6:28]; cf. 4:2 f. [H. 3:32 f.]), giving of his wisdom and might to men like Daniel (2:21, 23; cf. 5:11, 14), and rescuing the faithful (6:27 [H. 6:28]).

It will be observed that, with the exception of the liturgical Deuteronomistic prayer in 9:4-19, the authenticity of which has been questioned, the theology of the book lays stress on the wisdom and power, rather than on the justice and love, of God. This emphasis is not peculiar to our author. His thought was influenced by the Book of Job where the same divine qualities entirely overshadow the moral attributes. The author's theology seems to be that of the Hasidim during the period of persecution, as we may surmise from their psalms composed at the time (Ps. 74) or a few years later (Pss. 44; 79; 83). In these four psalms the Jews, suffering intolerable indignities at the hand of the heathen (who in Ps. 74:19 as in Dan. 7 are conceived as wild beasts), urge God to avenge them through his great power manifested in nature and in history; as in Daniel (aside from 9:4-19), these Psalmists, in contrast with the prophets and the Deuteronomists, deny that Israel is suffering for its sins and do not beseech God to forgive their transgressions (except in Ps. 79:8 f.).

This theology is easily explained by the historical situation. Crushed by the empires of the heathen, persecuted by Antiochus, the Hasidim could see no possibility of human help. If, however, their God were to deliver them, he would have to be primarily a God of sufficient power to crush world empires: his might in that crisis was more essential than his justice and compassion. Having fulfilled their obligations in observing the Law, they naturally expected God to intervene miraculously in their behalf and establish his Kingdom on earth.

Thus the doctrine of the omnipotence of God in Daniel is not, as in Job, a corollary of the wonders of the physical world, but a postulate of faith (as already in the Second Isaiah, whose thought for the rest differs radically from that of Daniel). The almighty power of God was conceived not metaphysically but historically by the Hasidim and the author of Daniel: it meant for them that their God was supreme in the world and would inexorably carry out his purposes among men—nothing can withstand or thwart his decision. Such a stress on the absolute sway of God's power logically leads to determinism, as in Calvinism and Islam. Future events are not only determined, but inscribed in God's "Book of Truth" (10:21) and Nebuchadnezzar's downfall was decreed in advance by the angels (4:17 [H. 4:14]). It was generally held at the time, moreover, that Israel's future had been predicted by the ancient prophets and that by a correct interpretation of predictions in the prophetic canon (Is., Jer., Ez., and the Twelve) it was possible to discover the date of Israel's triumph (9:2).

The author's faith prevented him from drawing from such deterministic premises the ultimate conclusions, as Ecclesiastes did (cf. JBL 53 [1934] 100-109). Far from becoming intellectually a skeptic and emotionally a resigned eudaemonist, our author, with the bold inconsistency of religious enthusiasm, believed that God revealed the future, permitted men to take free decisions, and conformed their fate to their conduct. Nebuchadnezzar was allowed a period of a year to "break off" his sins through "righteousness" (meaning probably almsgiving) and mercy for the unfortunate (4:27 [H. 4:24]) and, after the blow had fallen, was restored to his throne following his repentance (4:34-37 [H. 4:31-34]). Ecclesiastes, on the contrary, taking issue with the teaching of Daniel, or at least of the Hasidim, denied that man, through his conduct, could change his fate, which God has determined once for all (Eccles. 3:14; 6:10; 7:13; 9:1) without regard to his deserts (Eccles. 6:8; 7:15; 8:10, 14; 9:2, 11 f., etc.).

The fundamental difference between Daniel and Ecclesiastes is that, according to Daniel, God operates in accordance with a universal plan which he has partly revealed to the prophets, but according to Ecclesiastes, as far as men can tell, purely arbitrarily and unpredictably. Just as Job had recognized that God created the world according to a plan, "wisdom" (Job 28), so Daniel discovered a divine plan in the history of mankind—a plan revealed to the prophets, not hidden like Job's "wisdom." Daniel's philosophy of history is not confined to Israel as is that of the Deuteronomists (cf. Judg. 2:6-23), but embraces all mankind, like that of S and of P in Gen. 1-11. Similar to S, Daniel pessimistically regards the course of human history as a progressive deterioration passing through four stages corresponding to Hesiod's gold, silver, bronze, and iron ages (Dan. 2, cf. 7; see J. A. Montgomery, *Daniel*, pp. 188 f.). But in contrast with S, Daniel envisages at the end of time, after the four pagan empires, a golden age for Israel and perhaps for mankind, God's kingdom on earth which will last eternally (2:34 f., 44 f.; 7:13 f., 27 f.). The Priestly Code's plan, in spite of some superficial resemblances, is radically different: the four revelations to Adam, Noah, Abraham, and Moses, respectively, divide history into four eras of progressive conformity to God's will. The fourth era marks the establishment of the theocratic community, God's holy Kingdom, organized in accordance with the Law revealed to Moses. In contrast with Daniel's future Kingdom of God superseding the four pagan empires, P's theocracy was established in the time of Moses and is both ancient and ultimate, being perfect and eternal in every detail. This contrast between P and Daniel marks one of the basic differences between Judaism and early Christianity. P has remained the charter of Judaism to the present day, whereas Daniel's visions of a future Kingdom of God inspired the hopes of the early Christians.

Daniel visualizes the future Kingdom of God under two figures: the stone shattering the statue representing the four pagan empires (2:34 f., 44 f.) and the "one like unto a son of man" to whom, after God had pronounced the sentence against the four beasts, was given eternal and universal dominion (7:13 f., 27 f.). Critics differ in interpreting these two symbols (cf. J. A. Montgomery, *Daniel*, pp. 190-192, 317-324), but it seems fairly certain that the author used both as types of the true Israel, "the people of the saints of the Most High" (7:27; cf. 7:18, 21 f., 25). The expression "son of man" occurs first in the Code of Hammurabi in the sense of "gentleman" and "minor." It is a common Semitic idiom meaning literally "human being" in general (Num. 23:19; Job. 16:21; 25:6; 35:8; Is. 51:12; Ps. 8:4 [H. 8:5], always in parallelism with "man"; in the plural: Dan. 2:38; 5:21; 10:16, and elsewhere in the Old Testament) or a particular individual (8:17 for Daniel, and about a hundred times in Ezekiel [Ez. 2:1, etc.] for Ezekiel). It is used figuratively for "Israel" not only in Dan. 7 but also in Ps. 80:17 (H. 80:18), where it is also contrasted with the boar and the wild beast representing the heathen (80:13 [H. 80:14]; cf. 74:19). Although in Daniel there is no trace of a personal Messiah descended from David, the "son of man" (*bar 'enash*) of Dan. 7 was soon understood to be the Messianic king. This arbitrary interpretation appears in Enoch 46:1-6; 48:2-10, etc. (paraphrasing Dan. 7:9, 13; the date of these passages is probably 100-60 B.C.), Sibylline Oracles 5:414 ("a blessed man" coming from heaven); cf. 3:46-50 ("the immortal king," "the holy ruler"), II [IV] Esd. 13:3 ("a form like a man" [*tamquam similitudinem hominis*] arose from the heart of the stormy seas and "this man flew with the clouds of heaven"); 13:6 ("he cut out for himself a great mountain and flew upon it," cf. Dan. 2:34 f., 45; II Esd. 13 is dated about 90 A.D.), and in the New Testament (Mark 14:61 f.; Matt. 26:63 f.

[cf. Luke 22:69], where Dan. 7:13 is combined with Ps. 110:1; Mark 13:26; Matt. 24:30; Acts 7:56; Rev. 1:13 [in 14:14 the manlike being is apparently an angel; cf. 14:15]). The Messianic interpretations of the "Servant of the Lord" in the Second Isaiah and of the "Son of Man" in Daniel, despite their antiquity and persistence through the centuries, are misleading and inject into the books in question notions entirely alien to their authors.

After the manner of the earlier apocalypses, Daniel conceives history as a drama in two acts: the triumph of the heathen and the triumph of the Jews. In the first act the Babylonian, Medic, Persian, and Greek empires follow one another on the scene, each surpassing the previous one in wickedness and brutality (chs. 2 and 7). Depravity reaches its apex in the Greek period, particularly at its end during the reign of Antiochus Epiphanes. The author is acutely conscious of the difference between the Greeks and the Orientals who preceded them in the hegemony of the world. The fourth beast was "diverse from them all, exceeding terrible" (7:19; cf. 7:7, 23) and alone of the four was slain and cremated (7:11 f.). In reality only in the Greek period was Judaism seriously threatened: first by the subtle lure of the wide-spreading brilliant Hellenistic culture, then by Antiochus' attempt to suppress Judaism and Hellenize the Jews. Under the other empires the Jews had only lost their political independence, and the Priestly Code had provided a substitute with its holy commonwealth that could flourish within an alien empire, but under the Greek rulers the Jews were in danger of losing their very soul and faith. The author and the other Hasidim were unable to conceive a fusion of Greek and Jewish ideals and customs. They regarded the Jews whose rejection of Hellenism was not uncompromising, as renegades worthy of death. Since no agreement between the two cultures was possible without a surrender of Jewish principles and since, particularly after Antiochus decided to Hellenize all his subjects, the two cultures became mutually exclusive, at least for the Hasidim, one or the other was bound to be wiped off the face of the earth. A final conflict between God and the pagan world became inevitable: God himself had been insulted and defied by Antiochus (7:25; 8:11, 25; 11:36).

The inevitable outcome of this conflict is the subject of the second act of the great drama. The two phases of the denouement are negatively the elimination of paganism and positively the triumph of the Jews. Since God is almighty and disdains any human collaboration, there is no battle as in some of the older apocalypses: he gains his victory "in a moment, in the twinkling of an eye," as Paul said (I Cor. 15:52). The day has been fixed by God at the end of the "seventy weeks" (9:27b), three years and a half after Antiochus Epiphanes proscribed Judaism (7:25; 9:27;

12:7), interrupting the morning and evening offering in the Temple for
1,150 days (8:14; according to the glosses 12:11, 12 after 1,290 or 1,335
days). Then suddenly a stone "cut out without hands" will strike the
feet (i.e., the Ptolemaic and Seleucid kingdoms) of the statue, instantly
crumbling it into dust which the wind will blow away (2:34 f., 45). On
that day God will sit in judgment (7:9 f.) and the fourth beast with its
little horn (Antiochus) will immediately be slain and burned with fire
(7:11). Or, in plain language, the tyrant Antiochus "will be broken
without hand" (8:25), supernaturally coming to his end in the tents of
his camp between Jerusalem and the Mediterranean (11:45).

No sooner is the pagan power swept into oblivion than the world
hegemony will be given in perpetuity to the pious Jews (the Hasidim),
"the people of the saints of the Most High," represented either as "one
like unto a son of man" (7:13 f.) or as the stone which "became a great
mountain and filled the whole earth" (2:35; cf. 2:44 f.).

According to another prophecy, however, the new era will not be
ushered in without birth pangs. Israel's patron angel, Michael (cf.
10:13, 20 f.; on national angels cf. Deut. 32:8 f. [LXX]; Jubilees 15:31 f.),
will arise to defend the Jews and, after a period of distress without
parallel in history (cf. Joel 2:2; Mark 13:19 = Matt. 24:21), the pious
Jews whose names have been inscribed in "the book" (cf. 7:10; Ex.
32:32 f.; Is. 4:3; Ps. 69:28 [H. 69:29]) shall be saved (12:1). "And many
[not all!] of them who sleep in the dusty ground shall awake, some to
everlasting life and some to . . . everlasting abhorrence" (12:2). The
"wise," the students and teachers of the Law, the Hasidim, whose
martyrdom during the persecution had justified many (11:35; cf. Is.
53:11), will shine with celestial brilliance (12:3).

These visions of the end in Daniel exercised a profound influence on
later apocalypses. Individual angels—Gabriel and Michael, the angel of
revelation (8:16; 9:21; cf. Luke 1:19 f., 26) and the champion of Israel
(10:13-21; cf. Jude 9), respectively—are first named in Daniel (in the
Hebrew Bible), and in Tobit, where Raphael, the angel of healing, plays
an important role (Tob. 5:4, etc.; according to 12:15 he is one of the
seven interceding angels). Four (Michael, Uriel, Raphael, and Gabriel:
see Enoch 9:1; elsewhere in Enoch, Phanuel takes the place of Uriel) or
seven (Enoch 20; cf. Rev. 8:2) archangels appear later. The transcendent
elevation of the deity above the world tended to increase the functions
of subordinate divine beings, to whom were ascribed revelation, the
control of natural phenomena, and the championship of nations and individuals. A hierarchy of these ministers of God, classed in numerous
orders, was finally introduced.

The doctrine of resurrection is first stated as a dogma in Dan. 12:2. A
poetic reference to a resurrection of the Jews occurs earlier in Is. 26:19

(possibly inspired by Ez. 37:12-14; Is. 66:7-9). But in these earlier passages the authors were concerned with a national rebirth and not, as in Daniel, with individual retribution after death of the Jewish martyrs, who had died for their faith by order of Antiochus Epiphanes, and of the apostate Jews, who had saved their life by renouncing their God (for the fate of the latter, cf. Is. 66:24). Unless God be guilty of injustice, he must justify his saints after their death. The Maccabean crisis transformed Job's dream of a vindication of his innocence after his death (Job 16:19-21 and perhaps 19:25-27; cf. 13:15 f., 22; 14:13-15; 17:13) into a dogma. The Pharisees, who were presumably the successors of the Hasidim, developed the doctrine of the resurrection and generalized it (Ps. of Sol. 3:11-16; 13:9-11; Josephus, *Antiquities* 18:1, 3 [§14]; *War of the Jews* 2:8, 14 [§163]). On the contrary, the Sadducees, finding no trace of it in the Pentateuch, denied it categorically (Acts 23:6-8; Mark 12:18 = Matt. 22:23 = Luke 20:27; Josephus, *ibid.*). Shortly before Daniel, Ben Sira had no notion whatsoever of rewards and punishments after death (Ecclus. 10:11; 38:16-23; 40:1, 11; 41:1-4) and shortly after Daniel, Ecclesiastes seems to have attacked the new doctrine of resurrection as unscriptural and absurd (Eccl. 3:18-21; 12:7, where the author alludes to Gen. 2:7; 3:19). Nevertheless, the dogma of the resurrection became basic in Judaism. According to the Second Book of Maccabees (7:9, 11, 14, 29, 36; 14:46; cf. 12:42-45) the hope of a miraculous restoration of their bodies inspired the Jewish martyrs in the time of Antiochus; later the vital question of some zealous Jews became, "What shall I do that I may inherit eternal life?" (Mark 10:17 = Matt. 19:16 = Luke 18:18). In the apocalypses the resurrection becomes one of the chief features of the future glorification of Israel (Enoch 51:1-5; 61:5; 63:13-16; 91:10; 92:3-5; 102-103, etc.; Bar. 30:1-3; 42:7; 50:2; Testament of the Twelve Patriarchs: Judah 25, Benjamin 10, Simeon 6, Zebulon 10; II [IV] Esd. 5:45; 7:32; 14:35, etc.).

This Pharisaic doctrine of the resurrection of the flesh was eventually confused in Christianity with the totally different Platonic notion of the immortality of the spirit. The latter doctrine made no impression on Palestinian Judaism, but was entertained by some philosophically trained Hellenistic Jews in Alexandria during the half centuries preceding and following the beginning of our era; we find it expounded in the Wisdom of Solomon (3:1-6; 4:14-19; 5:15; 6:19; cf. 9:15), in IV Maccabees (7:19; 9:8; 16:25; 17:5; 18:3), and in the writings of Philo (*De Abrahamo* 258 [M II, 37]; cf. *Leg. alleg.* I, 105 [M I, 64]; etc.). Josephus, in describing the doctrine of the Pharisees for Greek and Roman readers, uses terms more suitable to the immortality of the spirit: "all souls are imperishable" (*War* 2:8, 14 [§163]); "their belief is that the souls have a deathless vigor" (*Antiquities* 18:1, 3 [§14]).

The following teachings of Daniel became current in later apocalypse: the transcendent power of the deity and its absolute control of nature and history either directly or through angelic agents; the gradual deterioration of the pagan kingdoms culminating in an orgy of evil and suffering; their sudden supernatural annihilation and the triumph of the pious Jews, either living or raised from the grave; and the revelation of these divinely preordained events together with their exact future date to an ancient seer, who is to guard the secret until after their consummation.

The personal piety of the Jews, as reflected in the Book of Daniel, is probably as characteristic of the Hasidim as the theology. Particular emphasis is placed, among the prescriptions of the Law, on the dietary prohibitions. Daniel and his friends refused to partake of the food from Nebuchadnezzar's table (1:8) and thrived wonderfully on a diet of pulse and water (1:9-16). They followed the principle stated in Jubilees 22:16, "Separate thyself from the nations [or the heathen] and eat not with them." Similarly some Jews in Rome mentioned by Josephus (*Life*, §3) ate only figs and nuts, and Judith when she went to Holophernes brought her own viands and drinks (Jth. 10:5; 12:1-4, 19; cf. Tob. 1:10 f.; II Macc. 5:27). Even more serious than Gentile victuals were the foods specifically forbidden in the Law, which the Hasidim during the persecution avoided even at the cost of their life (I Macc. 1:62 f.).

Prayer occupies a prominent place in the religion of Daniel (2:17-23, etc.). Fasting was regarded as a potent concomitant of prayer since ancient times (II Sam. 12:15-23; cf. Ps. 35:13; Ezra 8:21-23; Matt. 17:21). Daniel prayed "with fasting, sackcloth, and ashes" (9:3; cf. II Macc. 13:12) and beheld his final vision after three weeks of fasting (10:2 f.). Daniel 6:10 (H. 6:11) is of historical interest for the details about private prayer: Daniel prayed in his upper chamber (cf. Acts. 1:13 f.; 9:37, 39 f.; 20:8) three times a day, in the evening and at the time of the morning and afternoon *tāmîd* Temple sacrifices (cf. Ps. 55:17 [H. 55:18]); he knelt (cf. Ezra 9:5) before an open window looking toward Jerusalem (cf. JBL 47 [1928] 186 f.). The banks of rivers were also chosen for private devotions and revelations were received there (8:2; 10:4; 12:5; cf. Ez. 1:1).

The religious life of the devout Hasidim living outside of Judea, in addition to scrupulous observance of the Law, fasting, and prayer, included also almsgiving and good works, which atoned for sin (4:27 [H. 4:24]; cf. Ecclus. 3:30; 7:10; 12:3; Tob. 12:9; 14:11). Repentance is only mentioned in connection with Nebuchadnezzar, but its effectiveness in the case of a heathen monarch illustrates its importance for the Jews (4:27, 34 [H. 4:24, 31]; 5:21). It should be noted, however, that neither Nebuchadnezzar nor Darius, who extolled the greatness of

Jehovah (2:47; 3:28-4:3 [H. 3:28-33]; 4:34-37 [H. 4:31-34]; 6:26-28), be-came proselytes in the technical sense: they were neither circumcised nor baptized, nor did they fulfill the prescriptions of the Law. They are types of those Gentiles in the Hellenistic world who were attracted by Jewish monotheism and morality, and even attended the synagogue services, but were still Gentiles in the eyes of strict Jews, like the devout and God-fearing centurion Cornelius (Acts 10:1 f., 22) in the eyes of Peter (10:28; cf. Luke 7:5 f.). Although a missionary zeal appears in Judaism before it arose in any other religion of the Mediterranean world (cf. Is. 56:6-8), it is totally absent in Daniel, written at a time of a life-and-death struggle between Judaism and paganism which, according to the revelations, was to end in a decisive triumph of the Jews. In that crisis the task of our author was to encourage the persecuted Hasidim to remain steadfast in their faith but not to save the heathen from the wrath to come. The Second Isaiah's ideal of mankind's conversion to Jehovah's religion (cf. Is. 2:2-4; Zech. 14:9; Tob. 13:11; 14:6) reappears, however, after Daniel (cf. Enoch 50:2 f.) and presumably animated the missionary activity of the Pharisees (Matt. 23:15), which was inherited by the Christian Church but gradually subsided in the Synagogue.

Despite its limitations, imposed to a great extent by the historical situation from which it arose, the Book of Daniel is a noble book, inspired by the faith that the God of Israel is the king of the universe, and that he will soon vindicate his people and usher in the new age when the Kingdom of Heaven will belong to the poor, and the meek will inherit the earth.

CHAPTER X

THE BOOKS OF CHRONICLES

~~~~~~

The Hebrew title of Chronicles, which like Samuel and Kings was originally a single volume, means literally "things of the days," i.e., "events of [past] time," "history." The Greek title, also adopted in the Latin Bible, is *Paraleipomena* (omitted things [concerning the kings of Judah]) and characterizes the book as a supplement to Samuel and Kings. Chronicles is a history of Judaism from Adam to Cyrus (538 B.C.), running parallel to Genesis-Kings and concluded in Ezra-Nehemiah. Jerome (in his *Prologus galeatus*) suggested the title "chronicle of the whole of sacred history" and thus he unwittingly inspired the title of the book in English and other modern languages.

The contents of Chronicles may be summarized as follows:

I. From Adam to David (I 1-9; genealogical lists). *a.* From Adam to Jacob (1:1-34; cf. Gen. 5:3-32; 10; 11:10-26; 25:12-16a, 1-4, 19-26); the sons of Esau and kings of Edom (1:35-54; cf. Gen. 36:4-5a, 10-14, 20-28, 31-43). *b.* The sons of Jacob (2:1 f.; cf. Gen. 35:22b-26; Ex. 1:1-6). *c.* The descendants of Judah (2:3-4:23): 1. The five sons of Judah (2:3-8; cf. Gen. 38:2-7, 29 f.; 46:12a; Num. 26:19 f.; Gen. 46:12b; Num. 26:21; Ruth 4:18; Josh. 7:1; I Kings 4:31 [H. 5:11]). 2. The descendants of Hezron: the ancestors of David (2:9-17; cf. Ruth 4:19-22; I Sam. 16:6-9; II Sam. 2:18; 17:25); Caleb (2:18-24); Jerahmeel (2:25-41); Caleb (2:42-45, 47, 49, 50aα belong with 2:18-24; 2:46, 48, 50aβ-55 are secondary); the descendants of David: his children (3:1-9; cf. II Sam. 3:2-5; 5:5, 14-16), the kings of Judah (3:10-16; cf. I and II Kings), thirteen generations descended from Jehoiachin (3:17-24). 3. The descendants of Judah's five sons (4:1-23). *d.* Simeon (4:24-43; cf. 4:24 with Gen. 46:10; Ex. 6:15; Num. 26:12 f.; and 4:28-33 with Josh. 19:2-8). *e.* Reuben (5:1-10; cf. 5:3 with Gen. 46:9; Num. 26:5 f.). *f.* Gad (5:11-17); war with the Hagrites (5:18-22). *g.* East Manasseh: (5:23-26). *h.* Levi (6:1-81 [H. 5:27-6:66]): 1. The Sons of Levi (6:1-3 [H. 5:27-29]; cf. Ex. 6:16-20; Num. 3:17-19). 2. The high priests from Eleazar, son of Aaron, to 586 B.C. (6:4-15 [H. 5:30-41]). 3. The descendants of Levi's sons, Gershom, Kohath, and Merari (6:16-30 [H. 6:1-15]; cf. Ex. 6:16-24; I Sam. 1:1; 8:2) and the three guilds of Levitical singers, Heman, Asaph, and Ethan (6:31-47 [H. 6:16-32]); the distinction between Levites and priests (6:48 f. [H.

6:33 f.]). 4. The high priests from Aaron to Ahimaaz, in the time of Solomon (6:50-53 [H. 6:35-38]). 5. The cities of the priests, the sons of Aaron (6:54-60 [H. 6:39-45]) and of the Levites (6:61-81 [H. 6:46-66]), for which cf. Josh. 21:10-19, 5-9, 20-39. *i*. Issachar (7:1-5). *j*. Benjamin, or rather Zebulun (7:6-11; 7:6 should be revised according to Gen. 46:14). *k*. Dan. (7:12, to be read, "The sons of Dan, Hushim, his son, one" according to Gen. 46:23; cf. Num. 26:42). *l*. Naphtali (7:13; cf. Gen. 46:24 f.; Num. 26:48 f.). *m*. West Manasseh (7:14-19), Ephraim (7:20-27), and their territory (7:28 f.). *n*. Asher (7:30-40). *o*. Benjamin (8): 1. The sons of Benjamin (8:1-5; cf. Gen. 46:21). 2. The descendants of Ehud, the judge of Judg. 3:12-30 (8:6-28). 3. King Saul's genealogy (8:29-38 = 9:35-44; 8:39 f.; on 8:33 f.; cf. I Sam. 14:49, 51; II Sam. 2:8; 4:4; 9:12). 4. The citizens of Jerusalem (9:1-34; on 9:2-17, 22a; cf. Neh. 11:3-19). 5. King Saul's genealogy (9:35-44=8:29-38).

II. David (I 10-29). A. His reign (10-20). *a*. Saul's death (10; cf. I Sam. 31:1-13). *b*. David anointed king of Israel (11:1-3; cf. II Sam. 5:1-3; II Sam. 1-4, significantly, are disregarded). *c*. David captures Jerusalem (11:4-9; cf. II Sam. 5:6-10). *d*. David's heroes and soldiers; their military exploits (11:10-12:40 [H. 11:10-12:41]; 11:10-47 is taken from II Sam. 23:8-39, but 23:9b-11a have been accidentally omitted): 1. The three heroes (11:10-14). 2. The exploit of the three at Bethlehem (11:15-19). 3. Abishai and Benaiah (11:20-25). 4. The valiant heroes (11:26-47; Zabad in 11:41 and the fifteen in 11:42-47 are added to the list in II Sam. 23:24-39a). 5. David's soldiers at Ziklag before he became king (12:1-22 [H. 12:1-23]). 6. The number of men who made David king at Hebron (12:23-40 [H. 12:24-41]), amounting to 339,600, excluding Issachar. *e*. The ark brought from Kirjath-jearim to the house of Obed-edom (13:1-14; cf. II Sam. 6:1-11). *f*. David's temporal affairs in Jerusalem (14; cf. II Sam. 5:11-25) are for the Chronicler (in contrast to II Sam. 5:11-6:11) a mere incident in the transportation of the ark to Jerusalem and are disposed of during the three months in which the ark was in the house of Obed-edom. *g*. The ark brought to Jerusalem (15-16; cf. II Sam. 6:12-23). 1. Preparations for the ceremony (15:1-15). 2. Musical arrangements (15:16-24). 3. The ark brought up from the house of Obed-edom (15:25-16:3; cf. II Sam. 6:12b-19). 4. Appointment of Levites to minister before the ark (16:4-6). 5. A psalm of thanksgiving (16:7-36, compiled from Ps. 105:1-15 [16:8-22], 96 [16:23-33], 106 [16:34-36]). 6. Appointment of Levites (16:37-43, continuing 16:4-6). *h*. Nathan's oracle to David (17; cf. II Sam. 7). *i*. David's conquests (18:1-13; cf. II Sam. 8:1-14) and leading officials (18:14-17; cf. II Sam. 8:15-18). *j*. David's war with the Ammonites and Arameans (19:1-20:3, based on II Sam. 10:1-19; 11:1; 12:26, 30 f.; David's adultery with Bathsheba and its aftermath are omitted). *k.* The slaying of Philistine champions (20:4-8; cf. II Sam. 21:18-22; II Sam. 13-20 is disregarded).

B. David's provisions for the building of the Temple and its administration (I 21-29). *a.* The site of the Temple is revealed to David after Satan induces him to take a census (21:1-22:1; cf. II Sam. 24). *b.* David provides the materials and workers for building the Temple, and appoints Solomon (cf. 23:1) in charge (22:2-19). *c.* Organization of the clergy: 1. The Levites: their divisions and duties (23). 2. The twenty-four courses of priests (24:1-19). 3. Another list of the divisions of Levites (24:20-31; cf. 23:7-23; probably interpolated). 4. The twenty-four courses of Temple singers (25; the last nine names in 25:4, beginning with Hananiah, can be read as a petition to God). 5. The gatekeepers (26:1-19). 6. The keepers of the Temple treasures (26:20-28). 7. Administrators of secular affairs (26:29-32). *d.* Organization of government: 1. The army under twelve generals (27:1-15). 2. The chiefs of the twelve tribes (27:16-24). 3. The twelve overseers of the king's property (27:25-31). 4. David's counselors (27:32-34). *e.* David's last assembly (28-29): 1. God has selected Solomon as David's successor (28:1-8). 2. Solomon is to build the Temple (28:9 f.) and all the divinely revealed building plans are transferred to him (28:11-19); he is assured of the collaboration of clergy and army (28:20 f.). 3. David (29:1-5) and the chiefs of Israel (29:6-9) contribute fabulous sums to the building of the Temple. 4. David closes the assembly with a prayer (29:10-19), a blessing (29:20), sacrifices (29:21), and a sacred feast (29:22a). 5. Solomon is anointed king (29:22b-25; cf. I Kings 2:12a). *f.* Concluding remarks on the reign of David (29:26-30; 29:27 is based on I Kings 2:11, less accurate than II Sam. 5:5).

III. Solomon (II 1-9). *a.* Introduction: Jehovah's revelation to Solomon at Gibeon (II 1:1-13; cf. I Kings 3:4-13, 15b; 4:1); Solomon's riches (1:14-17; cf. I Kings 9:25-28; 10:26-29). *b.* The building of the Temple (2:1-7:22 [H. 1:18-7:22]): 1. Preparatory steps, negotiations with Hiram (2:1-18 [H. 1:18-2:17]; cf. I Kings 5:1-18 [H. 5:15-32]). 2. Description of the Temple (3:1-13; cf. I Kings 6:2 f., 15-18, 29 f. [3:3-7], 16-20 [3:8 f.], 23-28 [3:10-13]). 3. The furnishings of the Temple (3:14-5:1; cf. I Kings 7:15-22 [3:15-17], 23-26 [4:2-6], (49) [4:7 f.], 39b-47 [4:10-18], 48-50 [4:19-22], 51 [5:1]). 4. The dedication of the Temple (5:2-7:10; cf. I Kings 8). 5. God's answer to Solomon's prayer (7:11-22; cf. I Kings 9:1-9). *c.* Miscellaneous activities of Solomon (8:1-9:28; cf. I Kings 9:10-28; 10:1-29): 1. Hiram gives twenty cities to Solomon (8:1 f.; vice versa in I Kings 9:10-14). 2. Various buildings of Solomon (8:3-11). 3. Inauguration of the regular Temple worship (8:12 f.) and appointment of the officiating clergy (8:14-16). 4. Commerce, wisdom, and wealth of Solomon (8:17-9:28). *d.* Concluding remarks (9:29-31; cf. I Kings 11:41-43).

IV. From Rehoboam to Cyrus (II 10-36). *a.* Rehoboam and the division of the kingdom (10-12): 1. The secession of North Israel (10:1-11:4; cf. I Kings 12:1-24, omitting 12:20). 2. The prosperity of Rehoboam (11:5-23). 3. Rehoboam's sin is punished through the invasion of Shishak (12:1-12; cf. I Kings 14:25-28 with II Chron. 12:2a, 9-11). 4. Concluding remarks (12:13-16; cf. I Kings 14:29-31). *b.* Abijah (13:1-22; 14:1 [H. 13:1-23]; cf. I Kings 15:1 f., 7 f.). With 400,000 men he defeats Jeroboam's 800,000 men, killing 500,000 (13:3-20). *c.* Asa (14:2-16:14 [H. 14:1-16:14]; cf. 14:2 f. [H. 14:1 f.]; 15:16-19; 16:1-6, 11-14 with I Kings 15:11-24). His victory over Zerah at the head of an army of a million Ethiopians (14:9-15 [H. 14:8-14]). *d.* Jehoshaphat (17-20, of which 17:1b-19; 19:1-20:30 have no parallels in I Kings 15:24b; 22:1-35a, 41-5C [H. 22:41-51]). Judicial reorganization (17:7-9; 19:4-11) and victory over the Moabites and Ammonites (20:1-30). *e.* Jehoram (21; cf. 21:5-10, 20 with II Kings 8:16-24). Crimes (21:2-4), threatening letter from Elijah (21:12-15), and punishment (21:16-20). *f.* Ahaziah (22:1-9; cf. II Kings 8:25-29; 9:16-28; 10:12-14). *g.* Athaliah (22:10-23:21; cf. II Kings 11:1-20). *h.* Joash (24; cf. 24:1-14, 23-27 with II Kings 11:21-12:21 [H. 12:1-22]). Idolatry of Joash after the death of the high priest, Jehoiada (24:15-22). *i.* Amaziah (25; cf. 25:1-4, 11, 17-28 with II Kings 14:1-14, 17-20). *j.* Uzziah (26; cf. 26:1-4, 21-23 with II Kings 14:21 f.; 15:2-7). His prosperity (26:6-15) leads to sacrilegious pride (26:16-20). *k.* Jotham (27; cf. 27:1-3, 7-9 with II Kings 15:33-36, 38). *l.* Ahaz, the most detestable of the kings of Judah according to Chronicles (28; cf. 28:1-4, 26 f. with II Kings 16:2-4, 19 f.). *m.* Hezekiah (29-32; cf. 29:1 f. and 32:1-26 with II Kings 18:2 f. and 18:13-19:37 [omitting 18:14-16]; 20, respectively). Purification of the Temple (29:3-36), celebration of the Passover (30), and provisions for the support of the Temple and its clergy (31). *n.* Manasseh (33:1-20; cf. 33:1-10 with II Kings 21:1-10). His captivity and repentance (33:11-17). *o.* Amon (33:21-25; cf. II Kings 21:19-24). *p.* Josiah (34-35; cf. 34:1 f., 8-32; 35:1, 18-24, 26 f. with II Kings 22; 23:1-3, 21-23, 28-30). His religious reforms in Judah did not follow (as in Kings) but preceded the discovery of the Book of the Law (34:1-8, 14-19); the removal of abominations in North Israel follows (34:33). *q.* Jehoahaz (36:1-4; cf. II Kings 23:31-34). *r.* Jehoiakim (36:5-8; cf. II Kings 23:36 f.; 24:1, 5 f.). *s.* Jehoiachin (36:9 f.; cf. II Kings 24:8 f., 13, 17). *t.* Zedekiah (36:11-21; cf. II Kings 24:18 f., 20b; 25:8-11). *u.* Cyrus (36:22 f., repeated in Ezra 1:1-3a; Ezr.-Neh. conclude Chron., being written by the same author).

1. The Religion of the Chronicler

Chronicles is both a sequel and supplement to the Priestly Code—a sequel because it takes up the history where P leaves off and carries it on to Nehemiah; and a supplement because, having developed in the course of two centuries, the sacred institutions of Judaism in the middle of the fifth century described by P needed to be restated in order to conform to the practice in the time of the Chronicler.

Like most epigonous imitators, the Chronicler does not rank with the author of P as a creative thinker. The Priestly Code is the grandiose plan of the Jewish religious system, conceived with such clearness and logic, such precision of detail and architectural symmetry, that it became the charter of normative Judaism. The Chronicler is not the great architect of the edifice but a humble restorer and decorator who reverently adds to its usefulness for a subsequent age.

As an historian the Chronicler is a disciple of the Priestly author. Like him, he uses the deductive rather than the inductive method. P conceived the ideal of the Kingdom of God on earth and proceeded to picture concretely its divine sovereign, subjects, laws, and territory, and to trace punctiliously its origin and vicissitudes. Being the description and history of a Utopia, P's picture of ancient times has no real concern with the actual facts. It is a theoretical history harmonizing with certain fundamental premises. The main characters in P, Adam, Noah, Abraham, Moses, Aaron, and Joshua, even when as unquestionably historical as Moses, become abstractions devoid of human traits. They are not even characters of myth and legend, but mere symbols of a particular phase in the establishment of God's Kingdom on earth.

For the historical period covered, the author of P arbitrarily selected written information that suited his purpose, ignoring the rest, and from these fragments he drew a picture inspired equally by his imagination and the practices of his own day. In accordance with the basic principle of this history, the Creator of heaven and earth becomes sovereign of the Jews, and in his omnipotence directs the course of events to the fulfillment of his will, disclosed in the Law which he has revealed to Moses.

On a less grandiose scale is the history in Chronicles—a history of God's Jewish kingdom in a later period. The Chronicler not only adopted the methods and principles of P but deliberately wrote a sequel to it. P spanned the period from Adam to Joshua. The history from Joshua to the Exile in Joshua-Kings was not written according to P but according to the Deuteronomic Code. The Chronicler therefore supplied a history in the spirit of P from Joshua to Nehemiah, beginning, like P, with Adam and covering the period from Adam to David with genealogies and brief summaries.

The period from Joshua to David was not treated in detail by the Chronicler for two reasons: first of all, Judah's role was then insignificant and unknown; secondly, the time of the Judges had already been branded by the Deuteronomists as a time of recurring apostasy and

wickedness, and a time of wars irreconcilable with the complete conquest and distribution of Canaan made by Joshua. As for Saul, he had
long before been dismissed, by postexilic Jews, as a Godforsaken,
illegitimate ruler (cf. I Chron. 10:13 f.).

The Judges are mentioned in the book only in a quotation from II Sam.
7 (I 17:6, 10) and Joshua not at all. However, the connection with P is
obvious: the tabernacle built by Moses, the only sanctuary in P, is still
the only one in the time of David (I 9:19-23; 16:39 f.; 21:29 f.) and
Solomon (II 1:5), until the Temple took its place (I 23:25 f.; II 5:5).
Similarly, in all ritual matters the Chronicler emphasizes the unbroken
continuity between the institutions and clergy of P and those of the
period beginning with David.

The resemblance between the historical method of the Chronicler
and that of the Priestly Code is manifest in form and subject matter. Of
course Chronicles lacks the rigid and logical structure of P as a whole:
first, because, being a supplement to that work, it can take the constitution of God's Kingdom for granted; secondly, because the Chronicler is
not a philosopher like the Priestly author. And yet, even the general plan
of Chronicles-Ezra-Nehemiah seems to be patterned after P. Both works
consist of a main part with four divisions. In P the four periods begin
with Adam, Noah, Abraham, and Moses; in Chronicles with Adam, David,
Solomon, and Rehoboam (to Zedekiah). Both works end with an appendix
—Joshua and Ezra-Nehemiah, respectively—dealing with the organization (or reorganization) of the Kingdom in the Chosen Land. Joshua's
two functions, the new proclamation of the Law and the territorial organization, seemingly correspond to those of Ezra, who promulgated the
law, and Nehemiah, who reorganized the Jewish community ethnically
and territorially. Moreover, according to the Chronicler, just as the
Israelites invaded Canaan under Joshua so the true Israel came from
Babylonia under Zerubbabel and Ezra to take possession of the Holy
Land and drive out apostates and heathen. Thus in each work, the
climax—occupation of the land—is the same, and the central, supreme
event is the building of the shrine—Tabernacle of Moses and Temple of
Solomon—and the organization of its clergy according to divinely revealed specifications.

This similarity extends to matters of detail. Every political event in
both histories is a corollary of the principle that the omnipotent Creator
is the ruler of the Jews. The great historical figures, whether in Israel
or among the Gentiles, are but puppets in God's hand. The Lord hardens
the heart of Pharaoh in order to crush Egypt and miraculously bring
out the Israelites (Ex. 7:1-5, P); he punishes Moses and Aaron for
neglecting to ascribe to the Lord the glory due him for his marvelous

deeds (Num. 20:12, 24, P). It is likewise the Lord who turned Nebuchadnezzar against Jerusalem (II 36:17); he "slew" Saul (I 10:14, although Saul had committed suicide, cf. 10:4) in order to give his kingdom to David. The human agency in history is thus reduced to the vanishing point. Men are either Jehovah's tools or, if stubbornly rebellious to his will, they are swept away by his anger—a generalization based on the superb verses of Isaiah (Is. 10:5-7, 13-15abα). In accomplishing his ends, God can and does dispense entirely with human agencies, particularly in war.

Both authors lived during periods of relative peace, when probably no Jewish soldiers participated in military engagements, and neither had the slightest conception of a real army or battle. Therefore in their histories the heroism and martial spirit of the old sources is replaced with an ecclesiastical distaste for armed conflicts (cf. I 22:8; 28:3). Joshua does not fight to conquer Canaan, the Lord gives the land to him ready to be distributed to the tribes (Josh. 14:1; cf. II 20:6 f.). Because the narrative of Samuel and Kings was incapable of being suppressed, armies and wars appear in Chronicles, but the outcome of all battles is settled by the Lord in advance. Without the slightest notion of real warfare the Chronicler writes glibly of colossal military forces: 400,000 and 800,000 men, with 500,000 of the latter killed in battle (II 13:3, 17); one million Ethiopians wiped out to the last man before the 580,000 men of Asa (II 14:8-13 [H 14:7-12]); Jehoshaphat's 1,160,000 men in Jerusalem, besides those in outlying fortifications (II 17:14-19); Uzziah's 307,500 men and his catapults (II 26:13-15).

But aside from embellishing the stories, these fantastic armies really serve no purpose whatsoever. When the Moabites, Ammonites, and Meunim march against Judah, Jehoshaphat forgets that he has an army of more than a million under arms, and cries out, "We have no might against this great multitude . . ." (II 20:12). Then, encouraged by an inspired Levite, he goes to meet them with the church choir—and the attacking foes butcher one another (II 20:14-30). When Jeroboam marches against Abijah, and the men of Judah are surrounded, "the priests sounded with the trumpets. Then the men of Judah gave a shout and . . . God smote Jeroboam and all Israel . . ." (II 13:14 f.)—just so were the walls of Jericho leveled to the ground! Similarly, the Lord helps Uzziah (II 26:7), smites the Ethiopians before Asa (II 14:12 [H. 14:11]), and through an angel destroys the Assyrian host (II 32:21).

These miraculous victories were rewards for faith in God.[1] On the other hand, the Lord sends an enemy to humble his people when king or nation forsake him. So in the case of Saul (I 10), Rehoboam (II 12:2),

[1] On faith in Chronicles see I 29:11-19; II 14:11 [H. 14:10]; 16:7-9; 20:12.

Jehoram (21:10, 16 f.), Joash (24:23 f.), Amaziah (25:20), Ahaz (28:5, 19), Manasseh (33:10 f.), Josiah (35:20-27), and Zedekiah (36:14-17). For relying on Benhadad of Damascus rather than on the Lord, Asa is afflicted with a painful attack of gout (16:7) but, still unregenerate, he calls in physicians instead of turning contritely to his God (16:12). We even read that the Lord anoints Jehu—a ruler of the rebellious and apostate Northern Kingdom—to wipe out the descendants of Ahab in Israel and Judah, and that he brings about the downfall of Ahaziah for fighting against Jehu (II 22:7)! Conversely, the fleet of Jehoshaphat sank ignominiously because he had allied himself with Ahab's son (20:35-37).

It is perfectly obvious that the Chronicler, exactly like the Priestly author, manufactured these stories, or parts of them, to illustrate the manner of God's control over the course of history, and draws the details lacking in Samuel and Kings from the storehouse of his vivid imagination. But he goes one step further than P. He teaches theology by a more direct manner, in numerous sermons, oracles, and prayers scattered throughout the book.[2] One wonders if in his day sermons were preached in the synagogue and inspired this feature of his book, for which the P Code did not furnish a precedent; or whether the Chronicler merely imitated the Deuteronomistic sermons and prayers in Joshua-Kings, which were ultimately inspired by the actual preaching of the great prophets.

The Chronicler made no important contributions to theological thought, but presented the notions about God found in the Pentateuch and later in the Psalms. He was not in the least troubled by the inconsistency in regarding the sole universal deity as being the King of the Jews. The Priestly author and Second Isaiah were acutely aware of this contradiction, but solved it in two diametrically opposite ways—Israel the chosen nation, and Israel the Servant sacrificed for the benefit of mankind.

Of course the Chronicler followed the Priestly Code, blissfully unaware of the contradiction between a God exalted above everything (I 29:11), who ruled over all kingdoms (II 20:6) and owned everything in the world (I 29:11 f.), and a God of Israel, father (I 29:10) and King of the Jews only (I 17:14; 28:4 f.; 29:23; II 13:8), who "is not with [North]

---

[2] Such edifying utterances are attributed to: David (I 22:6-19; 28:2-10, 20 f.; 29:1-5, 10-19), Solomon (II 6; cf. I Kings 8; II 7:12-22), Abijah (II 13:4-12), Asa (14:11 [H. 14:10]), Azariah, son of Oded (15:1-7), Hanani the seer (16:7-9), Jehu, son of Hanani (19:2 f.), Jehoshaphat (19:6 f., 9-11; 20:5-12, 20), Jahaziel, son of Zechariah, the Levite (20:14-17), Eliezer, son of Dodavahu (Dodijjahu?) (20:37), Elijah's epistle (21:12-15), Zechariah, son of Jehoiada the priest (24:20), a man of God (25:7-9), a prophet (25:15 f.), Oded (28:9-11), Hezekiah (29:5-11; 30:6-9, 18 f.; 32:7 f), Josiah (35:3-6), Necho king of Egypt (35:21).

Israel, even with all the children of Ephraim" (II 25:7). This sole uni-versal deity, whose eyes "run to and fro throughout the whole earth" (II 16:9) searching all hearts (I 28:9; cf. 29:17) and to whom belong the greatness, the power, and the glory (I 29:11 f.; II 20:6), is so identi-fied with the Jews ("the Lord's people" II 23:16), that whoever fights against them fights against God (II 13:12). The Lord will, however, defeat Judah if there are North Israelites in its army (II 25:7 f.). Such is his "fierce anger" against the Northern Kingdom (II 28:13; 30:8) that he denounces Jehoshaphat's alliance with Ahab in these words, "Should you help the wicked and love them that hate the Lord?" (II 19:2).

Although the Chronicler seems to identify the kingdom of God with the Judean kingdom under the Davidic dynasty (I 28:4-7; II 13:5), actually the holy commonwealth is not a political state. It is not even a nation in the usual sense, but, as in the Priestly Code, a church. Although racial purity plays an important role in qualifying for membership (as the genealogies in I 1-9 and elsewhere show), it is neither sufficient nor necessary. Only those who worship the Lord to the exclusion of other gods and fulfill his will as revealed in the Law of Moses are true subjects of the divine King. Consequently, Judeans may be excluded and Ephraimites admitted—in fact, the Northern Israelites in II 30:6-9 are invited to join the Jewish Church, and some are allowed to participate in the celebration of the Passover in Jerusalem (30:10-21; cf. 11:16).[3] As for the native Jews, unless they obey God's will, they are not within the fold: "the Lord is with you while you are with him; and if you seek him he will be found by you; but if you forsake him, he will forsake you" (II 15:2; cf. 16:9).

Although individual Jews may be apostates and rejected by God, the Chronicler in general regards Judah as the holy congregation: "Also in Judah was the hand of God to give them one heart to do the command-ment which the king and the princes had given according to the word of the Lord" (II 30:12). Despite certain lapses under wicked kings, Judah rejoices in keeping the Law and participating in the ritual worship (I 13:4; 15:28; 29:6-9, 20-22; II 1:3; 7:3, 8-10; 13:18; 15:9-15; 20:26 f.; 24:9 f.; 29:36; 30; 31:1, 5-8; 34:32 f.; 35:18). The Chronicler is more lenient than the Deuteronomists (in Kings) in excusing worship at the "high places," inasmuch as it was offered to the Lord (II 33:17). As for apostates, although in principle the Chronicler follows the Priestly Code in condemning them to death (II 15:13), he is actually more inclined to emphasize divine leniency for those who humble themselves, seek the Lord, and turn from their evil ways (II 7:14; 30:9), and he illustrates

---

[3] According to the Priestly Code (Lev. 22:25) and the Deuteronomistic prayer of Solomon (I Kings 8:41-43, reproduced in II Chron. 6:32 f. and in Josephus, *Antiqui-ties* 8: 4, 3) even a heathen could offer sacrifice in the Temple.

this lesson by the example of wicked kings whose sins were forgiven: Rehoboam (II 12:6 f.), Manasseh (33:10-13); cf. Jehoshaphat (19:1-3).

In the Priestly Code, which pictures dogmatically the days of Moses and Joshua, all Israel was the true church. In Chronicles, after the Northern tribes forsook the Lord and adopted the worship of "pseudo-gods" under Jeroboam I (II 13:9), only Judah is left, together with "the congregation that came out of Israel and the strangers [proselytes] that came out of the land of Israel and that dwelt in Judah" (II 30:25). Judah alone is in possession of the legitimate sanctuary, clergy, and rites of the Lord (II 13:4-12).

The sovereign of the Jewish congregation is the Lord, the sole God; the subjects are Judah and its proselytes; its Law is now the Pentateuch, particularly the Priestly Code which it contains. It is only in quotations or reminiscences from Kings that the Deuteronomic Code is "the law" (II 25:4 copied from II Kings 14:6, which quotes Deut. 24:16; II 34:24 is an expansion of II Kings 22:16 and refers to Deut. 28:15-68). The Chronicler even believes the book found in the Temple in 621 (II Kings 22), which was unquestionably the first edition of Deuteronomy, to be the completed Pentateuch, and accordingly changes the text of Kings. He omits "and he read it" in II Kings 22:8 (II 34:14 f.) and changes "and Shaphan read it before the king" (II Kings 22:10) into "read therein" (II 34:18), for Shaphan could hardly have read the whole Pentateuch twice in one day.

To the best of our knowledge, the Chronicler is the first writer attributing the whole Pentateuch to the inspired pen of Moses. He speaks explicitly of a book written by Moses (II 23:18; 30:16; 35:12) and makes it clear elsewhere that this book contained the Priestly Code, for whenever he refers to the commandment of Moses he describes ritual practices ordained only in the Priestly Code: I 6:48 f. (H. 6:33 f.) (cf. Num. 3:7; Ex. 27:1-8; 30:1-7; Num. 4:16; Lev. 16:34); 15:15 (cf. Num. 1:50; 4:15; 7:9); II 5:10 (cf. the late passages Deut. 10:5; I Kings 8:9, 21); 8:13 (a revision of I Kings 9:25 in accordance with Lev. 23); 24:6, 9 (cf. Ex. 30:11-16; 38:25 f.).

Disregarding the general and noncommittal references in I 22:13 and II 33:8, we find only one instance in which Chronicles appeals to the Law of Moses for a rite at variance with P and the whole Pentateuch: in II 35:6, 12 the Levites instead of the laymen (according to Ex. 12:3-8) slay the paschal lambs, although they were not required to do so by the people's ritual uncleanness (as in II 30:16 f.). Such may have been the practice of certain pilgrims coming to Jerusalem for the Passover celebration until, with the destruction of the Temple in 70 A.D., the domestic celebration prevailed. Unless, of course, the practice was merely imaginary and advocated by the Chronicler to increase the prestige of the Levites.[4]

It is significant that, even in this single instance, the Chronicler was certain that the practice agreed with the Law of Moses. In general, he believed that the Law was fulfilled punctiliously in the Temple rituals: see also I 16:40 (cf. Ex. 29:38; Num. 28:3, P^s); I 23:30 f.; II 2:3; 31:3 (cf. Num. 28-29, P^s). Thus, with a supercilious contempt for any facts contradicting his dogma (and this also characterizes P and other theologians) the Chronicler glibly asserts that the Law (including P and P^s) goes back to Moses and was observed, with occasional lapses, since his day—although he knew as well as Josiah that "our fathers have not *heard* [so with II Kings 22:13, LXX, and Syriac] the word of the Lord to do according to all that is written in this book" (II 34:21).

2. *Prerogatives of the Clergy*

It is only in two matters pertaining to the clergy, the temporal authority of the high priest and the status of the Levites, that the Chronicler discloses the developments during the two centuries following the writing of the Priestly Code, thus supplementing the prescriptions of the Pentateuch. Both developments, however, had their germs in the Priestly Code and do not run counter to its general tendency.

Early in the Persian period, the high priest began to regard his authority as at least equal to that of the governor of Judea under the Persian king (Zech. 6:9-15, where the original text has been willfully corrupted). When later the governor's residence was removed from Jerusalem to Samaria, the high priest became the leading citizen of Jerusalem and acquired municipal authority. The Priestly Code not only ascribes to the high priests the insignia of royalty (anointing, the purple, and the crown, Ex. 29:5-7), but places the high priest Eleazar before Joshua in allotting the land of Canaan (Josh. 14:1).

In Chronicles, the temporal authority of the high priest seems well established. According to Ezekiel's dream (Ez. 45:16 f.), the kings are concerned primarily with the performance of the sacred rites in the Temple, but are not allowed arrogantly to usurp, as Uzziah attempted to do with disastrous effect (II 26:16-21), the proper functions of the priests. Uzziah violated the ordinances of the Priestly Code (Ex. 30:1-10; Num. 16:40; 18:1-7) and was not only rebuked but driven out of the Temple by the high priest, Azariah. Even greater is the authority of Jehoiada. As head of the royal guard and the Levites, he crowned Joash, had Athaliah slain, and

---

[4] E. Schürer (*Geschichte des Jüdischen Volkes*, Vol. II, p. 293, n. 49) suggests that according to II 29:34; 35:11 the Levites joined the priests in sacrificing when the multitude of worshipers required it.

remained the real ruler under Joash (even choosing his two wives) until he was buried "in the city of David among the kings" (II 23-24).

Most significant, however, is the description of the judicial reorganization partly begun by David (I 23:4; 26:29-32), and completed by Jehoshaphat (II 19:5-11), who was chosen for this work by the Chronicler primarily because his name means "Jehovah is judge" (cf. 19:6 f.). Priests, Levites, and heads of the fathers' houses were to sit in Jerusalem, as a supreme court of appeal from the provincial courts. For sacred matters their chairman was the high priest Amariah; for secular affairs, Zebadiah, ruler of the house of Judah, presided.

With great plausibility, J. Wellhausen, W. Robertson Smith, and others see reflected in this reference to a supreme court in Jerusalem an institution operating in the time of the Chronicler. If such is the case, this is the earliest reference to the Sanhedrin under the presidency of the high priest. The high priests are listed in I 6:1-15 (H. 5:27-41), from Aaron to the Exile, and in 6:50-53 (H. 6:35-38), from Aaron to the building of the Temple. The first and longer list is supplemented in Neh. 12:10 f. with the high priests from the end of the Exile to Jaddua, who lived in the reign of Darius III Codomannus (336-331) and, according to Josephus (*Antiquities* 11:8), was a contemporary of Alexander the Great (333-323).

For the priests and Levites the Chronicler also knew ordinances which could not be attributed to Moses since they are still unknown in the Priestly Code and its supplements. The Chronicler is aware of the fact that the division of the priests into twenty-four courses, officiating in succession for stated periods, was not ordained by Moses. He attributes this to David, "according to the ordinance . . . of Aaron" (I 24:19). However, he discloses earlier stages of this organization. Only four clans of priests returned with Zerubbabel (Ezra 2:36-39 = Neh. 7:39-42, 4,289 priests) and were known in the time of Ezra eighty years later (Ezra 10:18-22), although elsewhere we hear of twenty-two courses in the time of Zerubbabel and Joshua (Neh. 12:1-7) as also in the time of Joshua's successor, Joiakim (Neh. 12:12-21), and of two additional clans, Gershom and Daniel, who came with Ezra to join the four clans in Jerusalem (Ezra 8:2). In the time of Nehemiah, twenty-one courses are listed (Neh. 10:2-8 [H. 10:3-9]), of which only fourteen correspond to those listed in Neh. 12:1-7, 12-21.

The historical value of some or all of these lists is probably nil. But the division of the priesthood into twenty-four courses, according to I 24:1-19, indubitably corresponds to the actual organization at the time the list was compiled and remained standard until the destruction of the Temple in 70 A.D. The number twenty-four is attested by the Mishna (*Jer. Taanith* IV:68a; *Tosefta Taanith* II) and some of the courses are named in the Talmud, in I Macc. 2:1; 14:29 (Jehoiarib), and in Luke 1:5 (Abijah). This list in I 24 contains only a third of the names occurring in the list of twenty-two courses in Neh. 12:1-7, 12-21 and begins with Jehoiarib (the 17th or 16th in Neh. 12) presumably because he was regarded as the ancestor of the Hasmoneans (I Macc. 2:1; 14:29). For these reasons, the list in I 24 may be later than the Chronicler,[5] although not necessarily. A subsequent editor could have placed Jehoiarib at the beginning, and the Chronicler himself is by no means consistent.

The Chronicler is, however, much more interested in the Levites than in the priests and their chief. The distinction between priests and Levites is still unknown in the Deuteronomic Code, where the legitimate clergy (at Jerusalem) is called "the priests the Levites" (i.e., Levitical priests). But as a result of Josiah's reforms in 621, the provincial priests allowed by the Deuteronomic law to officiate at Jerusalem (Deut. 18:6-8a) were prevented from doing so for practical reasons (II Kings 23:9; cf. the later passage I Sam. 2:36). Thus originated the distinction between priests (the descendants of Zadok officiating in the Temple at Jerusalem) and Levites (descendants of the provincial priests). First formulated by Ezekiel (Ez. 44:9-16) as a new regulation, it was taken for granted by the Priestly Code (Num. 18, P), and regarded as an everlasting divine ordinance dating from the time of Moses, although the P[s] stratum of the story of Korah's rebellion (Num. 16-17) makes it clear that the Levites did not accept their degradation without protest.

It was conceivably under pressure of such overt discontent that the Priestly authors liberalized the provisions of Ezekiel, according to which only the sons of Zadok could officiate as priests, and allowed a goodly number of "Levites" into the ranks of the priests by tracing back their ancestry far beyond Zadok to Aaron. Thus to the Zadokites, descended from Eleazar, son of Aaron, were added the priests descended from Ithamar, the other son of Aaron. The two other sons of Aaron, Nadab and Abihu (Ex. 6:23), perished on account of their sin (Lev. 10:1 f.).

There were, however, several isolated and ineffective protests against the inclusion of Ithamar's line in the priesthood: according to Num. 25:12 f. (later than P), the Lord granted "the covenant of an everlasting priesthood" only to Phinehas and his seed (i.e., the Zadokites) and even Ben Sira (Ecclus. 45:23 f. and, in the Hebrew text, 50:24 and 51:12.i) seems to regard the sons of Zadok as the only divinely appointed priests. It is characteristic of the Chronicler's championship of the cause of the Levites that he fully approves the Priestly Code's legalization of Ithamar's line (I 24; Ezra 8:2) which, in Ezekiel's program, had no legitimate claim to the priesthood and was implicitly classed with the Levitical Temple servants.

[5] Cf. E. Schürer, *Geschichte des jüdischen Volkes*, Vol. II, p. 290, n. 45.

The Chronicler's open advocacy of the lower clergy and Temple at-tendants blurs his picture of the position and functions of the Levites. The contrast between the real and the ideal status of the Levites, which he as one of them deems their divinely given right, has raised serious difficulties. Most of the students blame these contradictions on the dif-ferences between the written sources utilized and the Chronicler's aspira-tions. But C. C. Torrey (*Ezra Studies*, pp. 227-231, Chicago, 1910) has convincingly shown that these sources are imaginary.

Here, as elsewhere, the Chronicler's writings are best understood as apologetic and polemical utterances. He takes an active part in the struggle between the "sons of Aaron," eager to keep the other Levites in a servile status, and the Levites, no less ambitious to attain higher rank. A few of the priests' campaign pamphlets found their way into the Pentateuch as supplements to the Priestly Code, which in its original form attempted to be impartial and bring the strife to an end. On the one hand, these pamphlets exalted the sons of Aaron and particularly the line of Eleazar as the only real priests (Num. 25:6-15); on the other hand, they degraded the Levites to the status of mere property (a "wave-offering," 8:11-22) delivered by Israel to the Lord as a ransom for the first-born (Num. 3:11-13, 40-51), or to Aaron and his sons to be their servants (3:5-10). They were not to see or touch the holy objects in the Tabernacle lest they die (4:15-20),[6] and any attempt on their part to usurp priestly functions, as in the case of the Levite Korah and his followers, would instantly bring about their undoing (Num. 16:8-11; 17:1-5). Conversely, in the Pentateuch only the fantastic assignment to the Levites of forty-eight cities and their surrounding pasturages (Num. 35:1-8; cf. Josh. 21 where 13 cities are assigned to the priests and 35 to the Levites) seems to have been written by a champion of the Levites. In I 6:54-81 (H. 6:39-66) the Chronicler reproduces the list of priestly and Levitical cities given in Josh. 21:10-19, 5-9, 20-39 (Ps). The same tendency may perhaps be de-tected in two other passages, Deut. 33:8-11 and Mal. 2:4-8, in which the priestly functions are ascribed to the Levites in general, and not ex-clusively to the sons of Aaron.

The Chronicler champions the cause of the "hewers of wood and drawers of water" in the Temple no less aggressively than does the leader of a modern labor union. He goes so far as to threaten, vaguely and indirectly, a strike of Temple menials. This seems implied, for the present writer, in the reluctance of the Levites in Babylonia to come to Judea. Whatever historical basis there may be for this hesitancy—in any case less than some historians assume—it is clear that the Chronicler's report contains an ominous note. Only 74 Levites, 128 singers, 139 porters,

---

[6] In the Priestly Code (Num. 18:1-7) the line of demarcation between priests and Levites is drawn sharply but in a less brutal manner.

and 392 Temple servants, as against 4,289 priests, returned from Babylonia with Zerubbabel in 538 (Ezra 2:36-58), and no Levite appeared
among the 1,500 men ready to return to Judea with Ezra in 458, until
Ezra's expostulations persuaded 38 Levites and 220 Temple servants to
join the returning Exiles (Ezra 8:15-20). The implication is that such a
walkout of the Levites could be repeated, and that they consented to join
Zerubbabel and Ezra only after some of their demands had been met.

That these figures are tendentious rather than historical is confirmed
by the Chronicler's large number of Levites in comparison with the
priests (cf. II 29:34)—as must have been the case in the Second Temple.
Even if R. Kittel (*Geschichte des Volkes Israel*, Vol. III, Pt. 2, pp. 407 ff.)
is right in supposing that the majority of Levites was not taken into
captivity by Nebuchadnezzar, the figures in Ezra are still significant.
According to the Chronicler, only the Exiles were the true Israel, and he
would scarcely have admitted, with R. Kittel, that the majority of Levites
officiating in the Temple in his time were descended from those never in
exile. For the Chronicler, theory is more important than fact and, even
if he faithfully reproduced ancient sources, he had an ulterior motive in
recording the fact that the number of returned Levites was surprisingly
small.

In general, however, the Chronicler pleads the cause of the Levites not
by such veiled threats but by alluring pictures of their outstanding role
in the ancient history of the holy congregation.[7] Their importance is by
no means confined to the Temple worship. Whenever possible, he gives
greater prominence to the Levites than to the priests, as when David
brought the ark to Jerusalem (I 15:2-27). Later, David divided the 38,000
Levites, aged thirty or more, into four groups: 24,000 overseers of "the
work (i.e., the administration, not the erection) of the house of the Lord,"
6,000 officers and judges, 4,000 doorkeepers, and 4,000 singers (I 23:3-5;
cf. 26).

The ritual duties of the Levites are specified in I 23:28-32 (cf.
9:26b-32); characteristically, they are in charge of holy objects the mere
sight of which, as we have seen (Num. 4:15-20; cf. 18:3b), should have
annihilated them. When the kingdom was divided, the Levites left their
lands in North Israel and came to Rehoboam (II 11:13-17; cf. 13:9 f.).
Jehoshaphat appointed Levites as teachers of the Law (II 17:7-9) and
judges (19:8-11). They played a decisive part (not mentioned in Kings)
in the coronation of Joash and in the overthrow of Athaliah (II 23:2-20).
They defied the order of Joash to collect money for the repair of the
Temple (24:4-7), but co-operated wholeheartedly with Hezekiah in
cleansing the Temple (29:4-19), in celebrating the Passover (30:13-27),

---

[7] The contrast with Samuel and Kings, where the Levites are only mentioned in
three late glosses (I Sam. 6:15; II Sam. 15:24; I Kings 8:4), is particularly striking.

and in administering the offerings and tithes brought to the Temple (31:11-19). They did the same under Josiah (34:9-13; 35:3-18).

The Chronicler enhances the prestige of the Levites not only with these freely invented stories, but also with catalogues of names of Levites (I 15:16-24; 16:4 f.; 23:6-23; 24:20-30; II 17:8; 23:1; 29:12-14; 31:12 f.; 34:12; 35:8 f.). Moreover, he daringly imputes to individual Levites the important functions of the scribes (I 24:6; II 34:13) and even of the prophets (II 20:14-17). In one instance, he rashly states that "the Levites were more earnestly concerned with sanctifying themselves than the priests" (II 29:34)!

The Chronicler's endeavor to raise the rank and prestige of the Levites to those of the priests is particularly evident when he endows them with functions belonging to the priests according to the P Code. In I 23:29, 31, where the language is slyly ambiguous, and more clearly in I 9:32; II 29:34 (contrast 29:22, 24), the Levites usurp the priests' sac· rificial functions; in II 17:8 f.; 35:3 they teach the *Torah*; in II 23:6; 35:3 they are called "holy." The contrast with the Priestly Code is striking. It is hardly an accident that the Chronicler describes twice in some detail the celebration of the Passover (II 30:13-22; 35:1-19), in which the Levites played an outstanding role, but mentions the Temple sacrifices and the other festivals only *en passant*.

Among the Levites, the Chronicler regards the Temple singers (particularly the guild of Asaph to which he may have belonged) as the most important. Significantly he lists the Levites' functions in this order: "to sing praises, and to minister before the priests, as the duty of every day required" (II 8:14).

The Chronicler discloses an exact and detailed knowledge of the musical, and particularly the vocal, parts of the Temple services (cf. I 15:19-21). The sacrificial rites interest him far less. He is certain that, since David, no important undertaking (including war) was carried out without the singing of hymns (I 15-16; II 5:12 f.; 20:19, 21 f., 28; 23:13, 18; 29:25-30; 35:15). The orchestra accompanying the hymns included psalteries, harps, and cymbals (I 13:8; 15:16, 19-21; 16:5; II 9:11; 5:12; 20:28; 29:25; Neh. 12:27). The striking together of the two brass cymbals was a signal for the song to begin.

According to Josephus (*Antiquities* 7:12, 3), the psaltery had twelve strings and the harp ten; the harp was played with a plectrum (although in ancient times with the hand, I Sam. 16:23; 18:10; 19:9) and the psaltery with the hand (*ibid.*). According to the Mishna (*Arachin* II:3, 5), the Temple orchestra included from two to six psalteries and nine or more harps, showing that the latter probably carried the melody and the former the accompaniment. The trumpets were blown by the priests

(I 15:24, 28; 16:6; II 5:12; 13:12, 14; 29:26-28) and, notwithstanding I 13:8; 16:42; II 5:13; 20:28, were no part of the orchestra.

As intimated above, the Chronicler's interest lies primarily in vocal music, and occasionally he even gives the text of the hymns (I 16:8-36, a psalm compiled from parts of Pss. 105, 96, 106) and doxologies (II 5:13; 20:21) that were sung. However, there are not sufficient grounds for attributing the references to orchestral music (I 15:19-24a, 28; II 5:11b-13a, etc.) to a later glossator.

Sacred songs were sung to the accompaniment of psalteries in the ancient Israelitic sanctuaries, at least as early as the middle of the eighth century (Am. 5:23), but, if we believe Amos, this music was crude and noisy. Ezekiel and the Pentateuch ignore the Temple music completely, and we may date its flowering into an art and its execution by professional guilds somewhere in the period 400-250, between the canonization of the Pentateuch and the writing of Chronicles.

Since the organization of the musical parts of the service could not be attributed to Moses, the alleged author of the Pentateuch, the Chronicler selected David, known to be a poet and musician, as the organizer of the singers' and musicians' guilds and composer of hymns (I 15:16-24; 25:1-31; II 7:6; 8:14; 23:18; 29:25-30; 35:15). We read that David, who was himself a "man of God" (II 8:14), divinely inspired, chose as his counselors in the organization of the Temple ritual Samuel (I 9:22)—who died before David came to the throne—Gad, and Nathan (II 29:25); and that both David and Solomon put these regulations into writing (II 35:4).

In addition to priests, Levites, and singers, the Chronicler mentions the gatekeepers, and the two classes of Temple servants, *nethinim* and the sons of Solomon's servants. The gatekeepers daily set twenty-four watches, under their respective chiefs, at the four points of the compass around the Temple (I 26:12-18; cf. 9:17-27). The nethinim and the sons of Solomon's servants were the humblest Temple attendants, and their work purely menial. We cannot determine what distinguished the two groups, but apparently the less important "Solomon's servants" (mentioned only in Ezra 2:55, 58; Neh. 7:57, 60; 11:3) were eventually absorbed into the larger group of the nethinim: in quoting Neh. 11:3, I 9:2 omits the servants of Solomon after the nethinim.

The word "nethinim," which often occurs in Ezra–Nehemiah but elsewhere only in I 9:2, means "given" (in the plural masculine). Exactly as the Lord gave the Levites to Aaron and his sons to serve them (Num. 3:9; 8:19; 18:6; L. W. Batten [*The Books of Ezra and Nehemiah*, pp. 87 f. ICC. New York, 1913] has discovered the word "nethinim" in these passages), so David gave the nethinim unto the Levites (Ezra 8:20). They were probably the "hewers of wood and drawers of water" (Josh. 9:27) for the

Temple. In the time of Nehemiah, when they appear for the first time in our sources, they dwelt appropriately on Ophel, by the "Water Gate" (Neh. 3:26; cf. 11:21; 3:31 refers to another house of theirs). Like the Levites, they also lived in various Judean villages when not engaged in their work.

As late as the time of Ezekiel (Ez. 44:6-8), the Temple servants were uncircumcised alien slaves, but, following his protest, the nethinim that took their place in the fifth century were neither uncircumcised aliens nor slaves. The Chronicler traced their appointment back to the time of David (Ezra 8:20) and listed them as part of the true congregation returning from Babylonia with Zerubbabel (Ezra 2:43-54, 58, 70 = Neh. 7:46-56, 60, 73) and Ezra (Ezra 7:7; 8:20 [in 8:17 "nethinim" is a gloss]); they swore wholehearted allegiance to the Law of Moses (Neh. 10:29). A decree (from the Chronicler's pen) exempts these humble Temple servants from taxation of any kind, even as the priests, Levites, singers, and gatekeepers (Ezra 7:24). So sacrosanct is the lowliest person connected with the Temple in the eyes of the Chronicler!

Finally, the Chronicler proves the unimpeachable validity of the ecclesiastical orders of priests and Levites by tracing their unbroken "apostolic succession" not only to Moses and Aaron, but to Levi the son of Jacob (I 6:1-53 [H. 5:27-6:38]; 9:10-34; cf. Neh. 11:10-19; 15:1-24, 23-26; Ezra 2:1-69 = Neh. 7:6-71; Neh. 12:1-26). As imagined by the Chronicler, the tribe of Levi is a purely artificial concept, a word of professional significance with no genealogical or ethnological reality. Levites are all those concerned with the Temple services, from high priest down to gatekeepers, but excluding the nethinim and the sons of Solomon's servants for whom no Levitical genealogy is given.

The dogma that the entire Old Testament clergy, both high and low, is genealogically related seems to be at least as early as the Priestly Code, but has no historical basis. Whenever we can test the Chronicler's genealogies with authentic ancient documents we discover that in correcting them, he willfully sacrificed historical facts on the altar of doctrinal and ecclesiastical presuppositions. This is true of all his work. It is only in David's lineage (I 2:13-17; 3:10-16, and perhaps 3:17-24) and Saul's (I 8:29-38 = 9:35-44) that he gives authentic genealogies. On the contrary, although the Levitical genealogies may include some historical characters, they are concocted on the basis of the artificial genealogies in the Priestly Code for two purposes: to provide a mutual blood relationship for the various classes of Temple functionaries, and secondly, to prove that the ecclesiastical organizations of the middle third century can trace their origin to David if not to Moses himself, and are therefore valid.

In agreement with his dogma that all ecclesiastics are descendants of Levi, the Chronicler transforms the Ephraimite (I Sam. 1:1) Samuel

(I 6:22-28, 33-38 [H. 6:7-13, 18-23]) and the Gittite (I 13:13; II Sam 6:10 f.) Obed-edom (I 16:38; 26:1-8; cf. 15:18, 21, 24; 16:5) into genuine Levites, serenely unaware of the contradiction between I 13:13; 15:25 and I 15:18, 21, 24. The Chronicler had precursors in this dog-matic sleight of hand, through which any Israelite or non-Israelite could be instantly changed into a Levite. By a stroke of the pen, the glossator in I Sam. 2:27-36 (cf. 14:3a) made all the priests named in Samuel sons of Aaron and, with the exception of Zadok, descendants of Eli. Zadok, ancestor of the priests of Jerusalem, was presumably a Gibeonite (W. R. Arnold, *Ephod and Ark*, pp. 61 f.) but the glosses and accidental textual corruptions in II Sam. 8:17 (contrast 20:25) furnished the Chronicler (I 6:8 [H. 6:34]; 18:16) with a welcome, but otherwise unexisting, family tree for Zadok, "high priest" in the time of David and Solomon.

Internal evidence also proves the Levitical genealogies to be fictitious. Obed-edom is at the same time a Philistine captain of David hailing from Gath (I 13:13), a gatekeeper (I 15:18, 24), the eponym of a guild of gatekeepers (26:4-8, 15), a member of a guild of harp players (15:21; cf. 16:5), and, in the same verse (16:38, patently annotated), both musician and gatekeeper. His father, Jeduthun (16:38), is a shadowy figure: originally a musical tonality or mode (in the title of Pss. 39 [sic, in the Hebrew]; 62; 77), he was transformed into a person and became identified with Ethan (cf. I 15:17, 19), as the eponym of one of the three guilds of singers (I 16:41; 25:1-6; II 5:12; 29:13-15; 35:15). Like his son, Obed-edom, in the annotated verse I 16:38, so Jeduthun in the similarly glossed verse 16:42, is both a singer and a gatekeeper.

The case of Ethan (= Jeduthun) is even more bewildering. A famous sage belonging to the Edomitic clan of Ezrah or Zerah (I Kings 4:31 [H. 5:11]; on Zerah, cf. Gen. 36:13, 17, 33; I Chron. 1:37) and the supposed author of Ps. 89, he was first given Judean citizenship when the Zerah clan became Judean (Gen. 38:30; Num. 26:20; Josh. 7:1, 18, 24; I Chron. 2:4, 6; 9;6; Neh. 11:24); but he eventually became a full-fledged Levite through both Gershom, son of Levi (I 6:42 [H. 6:27]), and, according to the standard view, through Merari, son of Levi (I 6:44 [H. 6:29]; 15:17). Zerah also became a Levitical link in the lineage of Gershom (I 6:21, 41 [H. 6:6, 26]). The vicissitudes of Heman resemble those of his colleague Ethan. The metamorphosis of Korah is likewise illuminating (see above, in the chapter on the Psalms).

Finally, the unreality of the Chronicler's genealogical concoctions ap-pears from another bit of internal evidence. In his lineage of the high priests from Levi to the fall of Jerusalem in 586 (I 6:1-15 [H. 5:27-41]) he lists twenty-six generations; in the lineage of a singers' guild (6:33-38 [H. 6:18-23]) he reckons twenty-two generations from Levi to Heman, contemporary of David, leaving only four generations for the four centuries from David to the destruction of Jerusalem (for which he has 12 generations of high priests). His fourteen generations of high priests from Levi to David correspond to twenty-two contemporary generations of singers. Moreover, the twenty-two generations from Levi to Heman (I 6:33-38 [H. 6:18-23]) correspond to only fifteen generations to Asaph (I 6:39-43 [H. 6:24-28]).

While it is thus clear that the Chronicler emphatically affirmed the Levitical origin of the Temple singers and gatekeepers, it is by no means certain that this view was generally accepted in his day. The majority of scholars contend that their Levitical status was not recognized in the time of Ezra and Nehemiah, and of course earlier in the time of Zerubbabel. This view presupposes, in the first place, that the passages in question (Ezra 2:40-58 = Neh. 7:43-60; Ezra 2:70; 7:7, 24; 10:23 f.; Neh. 7:1, 73; 10:28, 39 [H. 10:29, 40]; 12:44-47; 13:5, 10) must clearly affirm the non-Levitical status of the singers and gatekeepers and, in the second place, that sixth and fifth century sources substantiate these statements from the pen of the Chronicler. As C. C. Torrey contends (*The Composition and Historical Value of Ezra-Nehemiah*, pp. 22 f. Beih. ZAW 2. Giessen, 1896), the special mention of singers and gatekeepers so close to the Levites shows that their guilds "were restored complete when the exiles returned"—not that these third century guilds were not yet classed with the Levites at that time. Moreover, as we shall see, the Chronicler had apparently no contemporary sources—except for II Kings, Haggai, Zechariah, and the genuine memoirs of Nehemiah, all of which are irrelevant in this connection—for his description of the lower clergy in the sixth and fifth centuries. The Priestly Code was his sole authority.

The real problem is whether the picture presented by the Chronicler corresponds to the actual conditions in his time or whether here, as elsewhere, he idealizes facts in order to enhance the position of the lower clergy. Although no final solution is possible, since all our evidence is in Chronicles-Ezra-Nehemiah, it is not at all unlikely that the guilds of singers and gatekeepers, organized sometime between 400 and 250 B.C., were still struggling for recognition and higher rank in the Chronicler's time, and that he championed their cause by attributing to them, as early as the time of David, a higher status than they actually enjoyed. At least the singers eventually succeeded in realizing some of their aspirations. Not long before 70 A.D., Agrippa II, with the consent of the Sanhedrin, granted them the right to wear linen garments like the priests (Josephus, *Antiquities* 20:9, 6).

3. The Sources of the Chronicler

Another controversial problem is that of the sources used by the Chronicler. The matter is of course clear with regard to the canonical books, Genesis-Kings (omitting Judg.) and Ruth, from which he drew information suitable to his purpose. These historical sources, often quoted verbatim, have been cited above in the summary of our book, and the author's indebtedness to the Priestly Code and its supplements has already been shown. In writing his ecclesiastical history, the Chronicler never hesitated to modify the narratives of Samuel and Kings whenever it suited his purpose, which was to show how the theocracy founded by Moses according to the Priestly Code continued without a break from David to Nehemiah. But the canonical authority of Samuel-Kings compelled the Chronicler to present, with glaring inconsistency, both the data of his sources and his own view of the matter. Thus, for instance, he says that David wore a linen ephod (according to II Sam. 6:14) and at the same time a robe of fine linen (I 15:27).

In general, the Chronicler modified the canonical sources through suppression, addition, expansion, and change, to make his story conform with the Priestly Code and the sacred institutions of his day (e.g., I 13-16, 22-29), to glorify Judah (I 22:14; 29:3-8; II 7:4, etc.), and cast aspersion on North Israel (II 13:3-20; etc.)—i.e., the hated Samaritan community of his time—and to remove from the story whatever was inconsistent with his religious views (I 21:1; cf. II Sam. 24:1, etc.) or his fanciful notion of historical facts (I 20:5; cf. II Sam. 21:19, etc.).

Whenever possible, however, the Chronicler reproduced his sources intact: I 10:1-11:47 (= I Sam. 31; II Sam. 23:8-39); 17:1-20:8 (= II Sam. 7, 8, 10); II 6:1-39 (= I Kings 8:12-50); 9:1-11:4 (= I Kings 10:1-48; 11:41-43; 12:1-24); 18:3-34 (= I Kings 22:4-35); 33:1-9 (= II Kings 21:1-9); 34:15-31 (= II Kings 22:8-23:3), etc. In most cases the variations between Chronicles and the extant wording of Samuel and Kings is due to the fact that the Chronicler's text for these books differs in minor details from ours, and frequently presents an earlier and better version. The additions which the Chronicler makes in these passages (e.g., I 10:13 f.; 11:41b-47; II 9:26) illustrate his pseudo-historical method.

In other instances (e.g., I 15:25-28; 21:1-30; II 22:10-23:21; 24:4-14; 34), the Chronicler finds it necessary to rewrite the narratives of Samuel and Kings entirely, retaining little of the original wording, in order to make the stories conform with his views. When extensive stories in the earlier books could be neither reproduced in full nor entirely omitted, he summarized them briefly with considerable differences in detail (II 22:7-9, cf. II Kings 9:1-28; 10:11-14; 32:1-23; cf. II Kings 18:13-19:37; 34:4-7; cf. II Kings 23:4-20). Occasionally the Chronicler expanded a brief notice in the earlier books into a detailed story, as in the case of Josiah's death (II 35:20-26; cf. II Kings 23:29 f.).

His editorial method in reproducing canonical sources accessible to us is thus manifest. In accordance with his premises, he deals with Samuel and Kings arbitrarily, rewriting whatever suits his purpose with complete freedom and no scruples about historical accuracy or verisimilitude. About one-half the material in Chronicles is inspired by canonical books. In the other half, which shows no dependence whatsoever on extant earlier literature, the Chronicler is unhampered by the earlier histories. Here he discloses his greatest originality and gives the clearest expression to his purposes and religious convictions. Did he have at his command, for this part of his book which lacks parallels in Samuel and Kings, one or more sources no longer in existence? Or did he compose freely? Critical opinion is sharply divided on this matter.

After the manner of the first Deuteronomist in Kings, the Chronicler refers the reader to other books which present similar or additional material, although he never suggests that he himself quoted from them or used them as his sources.

One group of documents mentioned by the Chronicler consists of histories of the kings of Judah and Israel which cannot be identified with the canonical Books of Samuel and Kings. The latter, conversely, are often excerpted but never mentioned. These books are: 1. The Book of the Kings of Israel and Judah (I 9:1 [so with the ancient versions]; II 27:7; 35:27; 36:8). 2. The Book of the Kings of Judah and Israel (II 25:26; 28:26; 32:32 [cf. No. 15, below]) or The Kings' Book of Judah and Israel (II 16:11). 3. The Book of the Kings of Israel (II 20:34 [cf. No. 13, below]; on I 9:1, cf. 1, above). 4. The Acts of the Kings of Israel (II 33:18). 5. The Midrash [interpretation or teaching] of the Book of Kings (II 24:27).

A second group includes works attributed to prophets and seers: 6. The Acts of Samuel the Seer (i.e., clairvoyant) (I 29:29). 7. The Acts of Nathan the Prophet (I 29:29; II 9:29). 8. The Acts of Gad the Seer (i.e., prognosticator) (I 29:29). 9. The Prophecy of Ahijah the Shilonite (II 9:29). 10. The Visions (i.e., prognostications) of Iddo (written Je'di or Je'do) the Seer (i.e., prognosticator) concerning Jeroboam, son of Nebat (II 9:29). 11. The Acts of Shemaiah the Prophet and Iddo the Seer (i.e., prognosticator) (II 12:15). 12. The Midrash [cf. 5, above] of the Prophet Iddo (II 13:22). 13. The Acts of Jehu, son of Hanani, "which are inserted in the Book of the Kings of Israel" (II 20:34). 14. A book containing the history of Uzziah, written by Isaiah, son of Amoz, the prophet, for which the title is not given (II 26:22). 15. The Vision (prognostication) of Isaiah, son of Amoz [= Is. 1:1], the prophet (II 32:32, reading with the versions "*and* in the Book of the Kings of Judah and Israel"). 16. Acts of (the) Seers (prognosticators) (II 33:19), according to the Greek versions; the Hebrew and the Vulgate read "Acts of Hozai"; the Syriac, "Acts of Hanan the Prophet."

Finally there are passing references in Chronicles to: 17. A genealogical

register of Gad made in the days of Jotham and Jeroboam II (I 5:17).
18. The Chronicles of King David (I 27:24). 19. A Writing from the hand
of the Lord (I 28:19) containing the architectural plan of the Temple.
20. The Writing of David King of Israel and the Writing of Solomon his
Son (II 35:4) outlining the organization of the Levites. 21. The Lamentations (II 35:25) for Josiah by Jeremiah and others (presumably our Book
of Lamentations; cf. Josephus, *Antiquities* 10:5, 1).

These sources are mentioned in connection with all the kings of Judah
except Jehoram, Ahaziah, Queen Athaliah, Amon, Jehoahaz, Jehoiachin,
and Zedekiah. The royal histories (Nos. 1-5, above) include genealogies
(I 9:1) and biographies of the kings of Judah from Asa to Jehoiakim.
The prophetic books of Samuel, Nathan, and Gad (Nos. 6-8) deal with
David; those of Nathan, Ahijah, and Iddo (Nos. 7, 9, 10) with Solomon
and, in the case of the last one, with Jeroboam I. The others concern the
following kings: Rehoboam (No. 11), Abijah (No. 12), Jehoshaphat
(No. 13), Uzziah (No. 14), Hezekiah (No. 15), and Manasseh (No. 16;
cf. No. 4).

It is clear that the royal histories (Nos. 1-5) are a single book quoted
under different titles. Moreover, it is admitted that this book, which
critics usually call the Midrash of the Book of Kings (cf. II 24:27),
included the prophetic books (Nos. 6-16) with the possible exception of
the last, quoted as a separate work (II 33:18, 19). But the prayer of
Manasseh was included in both No. 4 and No. 16. In one instance (II
20:34 and perhaps in 32:32), we are specifically told that a prophetic
book was part of the royal history and, with the possible exception of
II 32:32 and 33:18 f., the sources of information given for each king are
either the royal history *or* a prophetic book, never both.

It is clear that the Chronicler attributed the Books of Samuel and Kings
to the pen of various prophets and that, before the adoption of chapters
and verses, specific sections were quoted by name, as when Paul refers
to I Kings 19:10, 14 with the words, "Do you not know what the scripture
says 'in Elias'?" (Rom. 11:2 f.). Under fifteen or sixteen different titles,
referring to the work as a whole (Nos. 1-5) or to special pericopes within
it (Nos. 6-15 or 6-16), the Chronicler accordingly calls the reader's attention to a Midrash of the Book of Kings. This work cannot possibly be
identical with our canonical Samuel and Kings, for it contains material
missing in them (I 9:1; II 20:34; 27:7; 33:18; 36:8). Conceivably in II
32:32 the Chronicler refers separately to the identical stories about Isaiah
and Hezekiah found in II Kings 18:13, 17-20:19 and Is. 36-39. It is not
certain that in II 33:18 f. he actually has in mind two different books,
for in 33:18 he says that the "Acts (or words) of the Seers" are part of
the "Acts of the Kings of Israel," and the contents of the two works seem
to be identical. But for the rest, we cannot separate the prophetic writings

from the Midrash of the Book of Kings, and J. Wellhausen is probably right in concluding with earlier critics (Carpzov, Movers, Bertheau, and others) that all sixteen different titles quoted by the Chronicler always refer to one and the same book (*Prolegomena,* p. 221. 6th ed., Berlin, 1905).

Had the Chronicler actually seen this Midrash of the Book of Kings? Most scholars, German in particular, have assumed its existence. Ewald, followed by Wellhausen, even believed that this midrash contained the Prayer of Manasseh (cf. II 33:18 f.), one of the Apocrypha of the Old Testament preserved in some Greek manuscripts of the Bible, although this Prayer may originally have been composed in Greek some time after the Chronicler. If the midrash was in circulation when the Chronicler wrote his book, he either made no use of it whatsoever (in which event it is irrelevant for the study of Chronicles) or else he derived from it all of the material which does not belong to Samuel and Kings. But for excerpts from Samuel and Kings, the diction, style, and thought of Chronicles are so consistently uniform and so persistently characteristic in their peculiarities that a separation of two authors (the Chronicler and the author of the midrash) is out of the question.

Even Wellhausen (*Prolegomena,* p. 223) admits that it is more or less equivalent whether we say Chronicles or Midrash of the Book of Kings; they are offspring of the same parent and cannot be distinguished in spirit and language. To suppose with S. R. Driver (*Introduction to the Old Testament,* p. 525, note) that two distinct authors, the compiler of the midrash and the Chronicler, may have used similar "style and diction," is to discard one of the fundamental canons of literary criticism. Since this "midrash" did not include the history of Zerubbabel, Ezra, and Nehemiah, Driver's incredible conjecture remains the only possible explanation of the similarity between considerable portions of Ezra-Nehemiah, written by the Chronicler, and the parts of Chronicles not taken from Samuel and Kings—unless, of course, they are also entirely from the pen of the Chronicler. To say, in conclusion, that the Chronicler made extensive use of this phantom midrash, identical in thought and style with his own writings, is like solving the Homeric question after the fashion of the undergraduate who wrote, "The Iliad was not written by Homer, but by another man of the same name" (cf. G. F. Moore, *The Literature of the Old Testament,* p. 125). Whether such a "midrash" existed in reality or only in the imagination of the Chronicler, the material in Chronicles not derived from Samuel and Kings "was all freely composed by the Chronicler himself, in pursuit of his apologetic aim" (C. C. Torrey, *Ezra Studies,* p. 231). When the midrashic ghost source of the Chronicler has been relegated to the limbo of illusions where it rightly belongs, critics will cease to regard the Chronicler as a mere compiler or redactor and recognize, with Professor Torrey, that he is a writer of great originality, vivid imagination, and granitic convictions (cf. C. C. Torrey, *Ezra Studies,* pp. 208-251).

4. *The First Apology of Judaism*

It is an error to consider the Chronicler as a writer of history. It is futile to inquire seriously into the reality of any story or incident not taken bodily from Samuel or Kings. His own contributions should be classed, with the Books of Jonah, Esther, Tobit, Judith, and the like, as historical fiction. It is true that his conception of Judah's history prevailed until recently in Jewish and Christian orthodox circles and that eminent historians, including E. Meyer, still find a factual basis in some of his fiction—no mean tribute to his power as a writer and to the earnestness of his convictions. Nevertheless, the Chronicler is utterly devoid of historical sense and even of a genuine curiosity about the actual events and the culture of Judah when not yet a church but still a kingdom. The picture mirrors not the days of David and his successors on the throne of Judah, but the Jewish congregation of his own day and particularly the sacred institutions connected with the Temple. Anachronisms may be detected on every page of his book; imaginary characters appear on the scene and historical ones are unrecognizable in their new roles, miracles abound, and, were it not for the devout, earnest purpose of the author and for his ecclesiastical pedantry, the fantasy and picturesque detail of his tales would make him an eligible contributor to the Arabian Nights.

It is unfair to judge the Chronicler as an historian and to dismiss him with a shrug of the shoulders as a distorter of facts. When his book was accepted as genuine history among orthodox believers, his real significance could not be appreciated. We must visualize the small Jewish community in Jerusalem in the middle third century B.C.—its poverty and insignificance among the empires that arose after the death of Alexander —to realize the daring boldness of our author in writing the first apology of Judaism. Against the claims of the Samaritans, who possessed the Law of Moses and a rival temple on Mt. Gerizim, against the pretensions of the Gentiles of Europe and Asia, the Chronicler set out to prove that the religion of that infinitesimal community was the only true one and that the Temple was the religious center of mankind, the sole earthly abode of the only God in existence.

Of course, the validity of such grandiose pretensions could never have been established by means of a sober assembling of the facts of past or contemporary history. No rational proof of the truth of such a faith can ever be given. Of necessity and through his natural inclination, the Chronicler was led to fabricate wonderful evidence to prove his case. Like all later apologists, he gave two arguments for the validity of his religion:

its extraordinary antiquity and marvelous achievements. By the side of such historical apologetics, we find in Prov. 1-9 the beginning of a philosophical defense of Judaism. Just as the Chronicler is a forerunner of Josephus, so Prov. 1-9 is the germ of the Wisdom of Solomon and, to a lesser degree, of Philo.

As we have seen, the Chronicler traces the sacred institutions of Judaism back to Moses and Aaron or, when that was impossible, to David. According to him, the Sanhedrin was organized by Jehoshaphat. With the antiquity of the church, he describes its glorious, unbroken history through the centuries. The Chronicler is less single-minded than Ezekiel or the authors of the Priestly Code, who conceived the Jews merely as a church, a holy congregation, without much concern about political and national activities. For him the Jews are both a holy church (according to P) and a mighty nation of pure racial stock (as Nehemiah believed) —and this confusion between two quite distinct notions of Jewry has persisted from the time of the Chronicler to the present day. Thus, in glorifying the history of the Jews, the Chronicler, on the one hand, depicts the marvels of Temple ritual and the magnificent organization of the clergy, in the spirit of P, while, on the other hand, he emphasizes the purity of blood and the national might of the Jews.

Both viewpoints are well illustrated in the Chronicler's account of David's reign. David not only organized the work of the sacred functionaries and prepared for the building of the Temple (I 22-29), but he was a king of fabulous power and wealth; "and the fame of David spread into all countries, and the Lord brought the fear of him upon all nations [or 'all heathen']" (I 14:17; similarly in the time of Jehoshaphat, II 17:10; 20:29). To give us some slight idea of David's wealth and power, the Chronicler calmly states (contradicting II Sam. 2:8-11) that about 350,000 men, representing all of the twelve tribes, came to David to crown him at Hebron (I 12:23-40 [H. 12:24-41]), that when he resided in Jerusalem he commanded an army of more than one million and a half, exclusive of Levi and Benjamin (I 21:5 f.; cf. II Sam. 24:9), and that he set aside for the building of the Temple the equivalent of more than three billion gold dollars (I 22:14; 29:3 f., 7 f.).

In thus glorifying the kingdom of David and exaggerating its wealth and power beyond the reach of his own imagination, the Chronicler tacitly omits from his extravagant picture whatever in the ancient sources casts discredit on David—and similarly on Solomon—with the exception of one sin, the taking of the census (I 21:1-22:1; cf. II Sam. 24). This one misdeed could not be forgotten because it resulted in the revelation of the site on which the Temple was to be built. Nevertheless, in Chronicles it was not Jehovah (II Sam. 24:1) but Satan (I 21:1), in his hostility to Israel, who instigated David to count the people. For the rest, David and Solomon become models of piety and spotless character. The intrigues by which both kings attained the throne, David's treasonable willingness to fight in the ranks of the Philistines against Saul, his affair with Bathsheba and the astute murder of her husband, Absalom's rebellion, Solomon's marriages with foreign wives (except for Pharaoh's daughter, II 8:11) and his despotic enslavement of the Israelites, as also other scandalous incidents, are all consigned to oblivion.

Later, when North Israel seceded from Rehoboam, Judah alone was the Kingdom of God. Priests and Levites came from Israel to strengthen Judah (II 11:13-17). For the Chronicler it is inconceivable that, according to I Kings 12:26-31; 14:22-24, Judah could at that time have violated the divine Law and offended the Lord no less flagrantly than Israel: there was a momentary lapse in the fourth year of Rehoboam (II 12:1), but the immediate punishment through the invasion of Shishak brought king and people to their senses (II 12:1-16 omits entirely the account of the religious apostasy in I Kings 14:22-24).

In contradiction to Kings, the Chronicler asserts that all pious monarchs before Josiah removed the "high places," and he brands the wicked kings of Judah, like all of North Israel's sovereigns, as rank heathen, persecutors of the Lord's religion. Ahaz, for instance, introduced the paganism of Damascus and closed up the Temple (II 28:23 f.). Such black pagan interludes, far from marking the slow religious process of Judah under the teaching of the prophets, are regarded by the Chronicler as temporary interruptions of the true worship which originated with Moses, was reorganized by David, and remained thereafter identical in all its details.

5. The Polemic against Non-Jews

This apology of Judaism tacitly implies a polemic against the heathen and, in particular, against the Samaritans. The assurance of the Jews that their religion was the only true one, and its two inevitable corollaries, the falsity of all other religions and the eventual conversion of all men to the true faith, seem to have originated with the Second Isaiah (Is. 40-55). No other religion in the ancient Mediterranean world ever made such claims.

As we have noticed, the Chronicler never doubted that Judaism was the sole true religion, but in contrast with the Second Isaiah (Is. 40:18-22; 41:5-7; 44:9-17; 45:20; 46:6 f.; 48:5) and numerous other Jews after him (cf. JBL 43 [1924] 229-240), he refrains from pouring sarcasm on the religion of the Gentiles. He freely invents stories about the idolatry of wicked kings of Judah (II 24:18; 25:14; 28:2; 33:15) but for two reasons he abstains from ridiculing the idolatry of the heathen. In the first place, after the legitimate Jewish worship had been codified in the Priestly Code, heathen idolatry ceased to be a living issue for the holy congregation: all idolatrous Jews were automatically cut off, excommunicated (cf. Ez. 14:7 f.), occasionally executed. Only violent animosity against Gentiles, of which there is no sign in Chronicles, could inspire the virulent and ironical polemic against the worship of images. In the second place, far from detesting the Gentiles, the Chronicler was eager for their conversion.

This missionary zeal, ultimately inspired by the Second Isaiah, had already borne fruit before the time of the Chronicler (cf. Is. 56:6-8, the best description of converts to Judaism in the Old Testament). The Chronicler dates this missionary work back to the days of Hezekiah (II 30:1-12, 25; cf. I 13:2), although he speaks of proselytes in the time of Asa (II 15:9). This story about Hezekiah is of course an anachronism, but in it we may detect an allusion to the complete failure of the missionary work among the Samaritans (i.e., Ephraim, II 30:10) and the beginning of the conversion of Galilee to Judaism (Asher, Manasseh, and Zebulun, 30:11) in the days of the Chronicler. Similarly, in Ps. 68:28 only Benjamin, Judah, and the Galilean tribes (Zebulun and Naphtali) are represented in a religious procession. Less than a century later, in 164 B.C., the Jews were, however, still a minority in the midst of the pagans in Galilee (I Macc. 5:14-17, 20-23); it was probably Aristobulus I (104-103 B.C.) who forced them to embrace Judaism (cf. Josephus, *Antiquities* 13:11, 3).

In the days of the Chronicler the Samaritan community was to Judaism a more serious adversary than heathenism. The Chronicler (Neh. 13:28) ostensibly traces the origin of the Samaritan sect to the banishment of one of the grandsons of the high priest, during Nehemiah's second visit to Jerusalem (432 B.C.). Nehemiah begs God to punish the young priest who defiled the holy orders by marrying a daughter of Sanballat, governor of Samaria (Neh. 13:28-29). Even if this incident is historical, it does not mark the origin of the Samaritan schism, which must have occurred about a century later. The Pentateuch, which is the Samaritan Bible, was canonized about 400, certainly not much earlier. Moreover, the Jews of Elephantine (at the southern border of Egypt), who wrote in 408 B.C. to the authorities in Jerusalem complaining of Egyptian persecution, would scarcely have mentioned a similar appeal to the sons of Sanballat in Samaria had they known of the schism (A. Cowley, *Aramaic Papyri of the Fifth Century B.C.*, pp. 108-122, particularly p. 110). Josephus (*Antiquities* 11:7, 2; 8, 2-7), probably quoting from an Alexandrian Jewish book glorifying Judaism (cf. *ibid.* 13:3, 4), gives a purely fictitious account of the founding of the Samaritan church—similar in essence to Neh. 13:28—but dates the event shortly before the coming of Alexander in 332. Elsewhere (*ibid.*, 13:9, 1) he dates the founding of the Samaritan temple on Mt. Gerizim 200 years before its destruction in 128, or 328, which seems approximately correct.

Whatever the antecedents of the schism, the break became incurable not through rivalry between the Jews of Shechem and those of Jerusalem, nor even through the building of the temple on Gerizim, but only when the Samaritans claimed that this temple, and not the one in Jerusalem, was "the place which Jehovah . . . shall choose out of all your tribes to put his name there, even . . . his habitation" (Deut. 12:5, etc.). They substantiated their claim by referring to Deut. 27:4 (cf. 11:29; 27:11-26; Josh. 8:33 f.), where the original text read "Gerizim."

These claims of the Samaritans were extremely embarrassing to the Jews. They went so far as to change "Gerizim" into "Ebal" in the crucial text, Deut. 27:4, and also in Josh. 8:30. Early Jewish interpreters, like Rabbi Eliezer son of Hyrcanus (about 90 A.D.) even said the Mt. Gerizim in Deut. 11:29; 27:12 was not the "blessed mountain" of the Samaritans but another hill of the same name; the Samaritans countered by adding in their Pentateuch at the end of Deut. 11:30 the words "in front of Shechem," and were therefore accused, by the Jews of the second century A.D.,[8] of falsifying the Torah. It seems clear, however, that the present text of Deut. 11:30, according to which Ebal and Gerizim are not at Shechem but in the Jordan valley, by Gilgal, has been deliberately corrupted by the Jews (E. Meyer, *Die Israeliten,* pp. 544 f.; C. C. Torrey, *Ezra Studies,* p. 322, n. 48).

In the time of the Chronicler, the geographical location of the unique place where Jehovah should be worshiped (cf. John 4:20) was the only issue on which Jews and Samaritans could never agree. This irreconcilable dilemma—Zion or Gerizim—created the final schism which seems to have been mentioned for the first time in Zech. 11:14, where the cutting asunder of the staff called "Binders" indicates the break of "the brotherhood between Judah and Israel." But for the rest, the Samaritans worshiped Jehovah with the same ritual as the Jews, according to the same Law, the Pentateuch. That this was undeniable to the Chronicler appears in the fact that the consecration of the priests of Jeroboam I (i.e., the Samaritan priests) punctiliously follows the prescriptions of the Priestly Code (II 13:9; cf. Ex. 29:1), even though the legitimacy of this clergy is not granted in the least.

Although the defense of the legitimacy of the Jerusalem Temple and its ritual against Samaritan claims was one of the primary purposes of the Chronicler, he could not inveigh against these schismatics with the outspoken bluntness of Ben Sira (Ecclus. 50:25 f.). Since he was pretending to write about ancient history, his polemic must needs be subtle and dis-

---

[8] On the attitude of the Jews toward the Samaritans after the beginning of the Christian Era, see H. L. Strack and P. Billerbeck, *Kommentar zum Neuen Testament aus Talmud und Midrash,* Vol. I, pp. 538-560; cf. L. Ginzberg, *The Legends of the Jews* (index, *sub voce* Samaritan).

guised. Following the pattern of earlier polemists (II Kings 17:24-41), he regarded the Samaritans ethnically as alien rabble (Ezra 4:1-3, 7-11; 5:3, 6; 6:6), and religiously as semiheathen (II 13:4-12), Godforsaken (II 25:7-10) mobs, over whom the divine wrath rests because of their abominations (II 28:9-15).

Elsewhere the Chronicler largely ignores the Northern Kingdom, not only because it is outside the pale of the holy congregation (confined to Judah) and therefore irrelevant to its glorification, but also because the Samaritans took pride in the achievements of the ancient Northern Israelites, whom they naturally regarded as their ancestors—to the dismay and horror of the Jews. In the sermon of Abijah (II 13:4-12), the Chronicler sums up the contrast between the Lord's own church in Judah and the heretical practices of the Samaritans. So firm is his conviction in the matter, that he seems rather naïvely to believe that the best Northern Israelites (or Samaritans) would have agreed with him (II 11:16; 15:9; 19:2; 28:12-15).

To conclude, just as the Chronicler under the guise of the kingdom of Judah depicts the idealized Jewish community of his time, so, behind the mask of the ancient kingdom of Israel, he portrayed the detested Samaritan community, which Ben Sira less than a century later contemptuously called "the foolish nation that dwells in Shechem"—nay "no nation" at all (Ecclus. 50:25 f.).

6. Date and Style of the Book

It is generally recognized that the Chronicler wrote between 350 and 250 B.C., or more exactly in the second half of this period. With considerable ingenuity, W. F. Albright (JBL 40 [1921] 104-124) has argued that he was no other than Ezra (400-350), who reorganized Judaism in 398 after Nehemiah's activity. We may agree with him that no final conclusions may be drawn from the list of the Davidic descendants of Jeconiah (I 3:17-24). The corruption of the text does not allow us to determine whether five or eleven generations are listed after Zerubbabel (about 520 B.C.) and hence whether the last generation belongs to the period shortly before 400, or about 270 B.C. Similarly, it is impossible to determine whether the last high priest mentioned, Jaddua in the time of "Darius the Persian" (Neh. 12:22), lived during the reign of Darius III (336-331), according to Josephus (*Antiquities* 11:7, 2; 8, 5, 7), or under Darius II (424-405), according to E. Meyer (*Der Papyrusfund von Elephantine*, p. 72, n. 1. 1912), and Albright (JBL 40 [1921] 112 f.).

Definite clues are lacking to fix the date of the Chronicler between Nehemiah in 444 and Ben Sira (Ecclus. 47:8-10 is obviously dependent on I 23-29) in 180, or between 400 and 200. But Albright's date for the Chronicler (400-350 B.C.) is revolutionary in its implications. Such a date implies (*ibid.*, p. 124) that the Pentateuch was completed in Babylonia before 520 B.C., and that the latest additions to Samuel and Kings (such as II Sam. 7; I Kings 7:48; 8:3 ff.) must be earlier than 400. In other words, only scholars who reject the Wellhausen theory *in toto* could accept Albright's dating.

Nothing precludes our dating of the Chronicler about 250 B.C. or a few years before; in fact, the language and spirit of his work favors such a dating. The organization of the priests and Levites, of singers' and porters' guilds, the office of high priest, the currency of vocal and orchestral music in the worship, the notion that David organized Temple music and composed psalms, the flaming animosity against the Samaritans, the missionary activity, the type of scriptural interpretation called *midrash*, the mention of *darics* in the time of David (I 29:7), the title "King of Persia" (II 36:22 f.; cf. Neh. 12:22, etc.)—in the Persian period the title was "the King" (cf. the Elephantine papyri and Neh. 2:7)—these and other specific or general matters indicate that the Chronicler wrote a considerable period after Nehemiah and the canonization of the Pentateuch. Evidence of this sort cannot fix an exact date, but merely tends to limit the period of the Chronicler to the first half of the third century.

If the Chronicler wrote in the first part of the third century, as seems clear, his vernacular was no longer Hebrew but Aramaic. Hebrew was for him a learned language, and his diction is therefore artificial and decadent, abounding with Aramaic expressions and new Hebrew constructions and words. A list of 136 words, expressions, and syntactical uses more or less peculiar to the Chronicler is given by E. L. Curtis (*Chronicles* [ICC] pp. 28-36. 1910).

In spite of its slovenliness and artificiality, the Chronicler's style is less stilted and standardized than that of the Priestly Code, his model. The Chronicler takes delight in giving a touch of reality to his imaginary tales by adding vivid details taken from life (I 12:39; 28:2; II 16:14; 20:5, 16; 26:14, 19, etc.) and picturesque comparisons (I 11:23; 12:8, etc.). Such realistic touches flow from his pen even when he is copying stories from Samuel and Kings (I 11:23, cf. II Sam. 23:21; II 35:20, cf. II Kings 23:29, etc.). These imaginative contributions, however, fail to lift his work to the level of great literature, and to infuse it with the historical reality so unmistakable in the genuine Memoirs of Nehemiah.

CHAPTER XI

THE BOOKS OF EZRA AND NEHEMIAH

In the Hebrew Bible the Books of Ezra and Nehemiah were regarded as one volume until 1448, when, following the Vulgate, the division was introduced in a Hebrew manuscript. The ancient lists of Biblical books (Josephus, *Against Apion* 1:8; *Baba Bathra* 15a; Melito of Sardes), the testimony of Jerome, and the final Masora leave no doubt on the matter. Even in the original LXX, according to the uncial manuscripts, the two books were still joined together and called "II Esdras." But Origen already knows of their separation in the Greek; in the time of Jerome Ezra and Nehemiah were distinct volumes in both Greek and Latin Bibles: in the Vulgate I Esdras is Ezra and II Esdras is Nehemiah. In the most important manuscripts of the LXX, "I Esdras" is the "Greek Ezra" (II Esdras in the Lucianic recension of the LXX; III Esdras in the Latin Bible), printed as I Esdras in the Apocrypha, where "II Esdras" is the title of the Ezra apocalypse (IV Esdras in the Latin Bible), often called "IV Ezra."

The book of Ezra-Nehemiah is the sequel of Chronicles and was written by the Chronicler (II Chron. 36:22 f. is repeated verbatim in Ezra 1:1-3a). It relates the history of the Jews during the century which elapsed from the edict of Cyrus allowing the Exiles to return (538 B.C.) to Nehemiah's second visit to Jerusalem (432 B.C.; Neh. 13:6 f.; cf. 5:14), and may be summarized as follows:[1]

1. *The return of the Exiles and the rebuilding of the Temple* (Ezra 1-6; 538-516 B.C.). *a.* The decree of Cyrus (538 B.C.) allowing the Jewish Exiles to return from Babylonia to Jerusalem (Ezra 1:1-4; cf. II Chron. 36:22 f.; Ezra 5:13-15; 6:3-5) and their return under the leadership of Sheshbazzar (1:5-11; cf. 5:13-16). *b.* List of the Exiles who returned with Sheshbazzar and Joshua (2:1-67; cf. Neh. 7) and report of their contributions to the Temple treasury (2:68 f., 70). *c.* The rebuilding of the altar on Zion (3:1-3) and the celebration of the Feast of Tabernacles (3:4-6). *d.* Inception of the building of the Temple (3:7-8bα, 10a) in the

---

[1] The sections Ezra 4:8-6:18; 7:12-26 are written in Aramaic (cf. the marginal note, "In Aramaic" at the end of 4:7; similarly Dan. 2:4a). The other parts of the Old Testament written in this language are: Dan. 2:4b-7:28; Jer. 10:11, and the words "the heap of witness" in Gen. 31:47.

second year (in reality, not in 536 but in the second year of Darius I, or 520; cf. 5:1 f.; Hag. 1:14 f.; 2:18; Zech. 1:7, 16; 8:9) and the appointment of the Levites (3:8bβ-9); the celebration at the laying of the cornerstone (3:10b-13). The confused text of 3:7-10a should be revised, reading 3:10a before the last clause in 3:8, in accordance with I Esd. 5:54-58. *e.* Opposition of the Samaritans to the rebuilding of the Temple after their co-operation had been rejected (4:1-5); interruption of the work (4:24) from the reign of Cyrus (538) to the second year of Darius I (520). *f.* Accusations against the inhabitants of Jerusalem in the time of Xerxes I (485-465) or Ahasuerus (4:6), and of Artaxerxes I (465-424) on the part of Bishlam and others (4:7), and of Rehum and Shimshai (4:8-16); in his reply to Rehum and Shimshai (4:17-23), Artaxerxes forbids the fortification of Jerusalem. The passage 4:6-23, dealing with the rebuilding of the walls of Jerusalem (4:12 f., 16) long after the Temple was completed, belongs *after* 6:18. In I Esdras a parallel to this passage, erroneously referring to the building of both the Temple and the walls, is likewise displaced (I Esd. 2:16-30); in any case 4:1-5 is immediately followed by 4:24 in I Esd. 5:66-73. *g.* The rebuilding of the Temple in the reign of Darius I (521-485), from 520 to 516 (5:1-6:18). Zerubbabel and Joshua, supported by Haggai and Zechariah, began to rebuild the Temple in 520 (5:1 f.) but Tattenai the satrap of Syria reported the matter to Darius (5:3-17) who, upon discovery at Ecbatana of the decree of Cyrus (6:1-5; cf. 1:1-4), ordered that the Temple be rebuilt (6:5-8) and sacrifices therein be provided at public expense (6:9 f.); violations of this decree shall be severely punished (6:11 f.). So the Temple was completed (6:13-15) and dedicated (6:16-18) in 516. *h.* The celebration of the Passover (6:19-22). Although no year is mentioned, this event seems to have taken place before 516 and the passage may belong after ch. 3.

2. *The activity of Ezra* (7-10, concluded in Neh. 7:73b-10:39 [H. 10:40]). *a.* Ezra's ancestry (7:1-5) and journey from Babylonia to Jerusalem in 458 (7:6-10). *b.* A letter of Artaxerxes I (465-424) authorizing Ezra to draw on the treasury of Syria to defray the Temple's expenses and to appoint judges (7:11-26); Ezra's doxology (7:27 f.). *c.* List of the Exiles who returned with Ezra (8:1-14); at the river Ahava some Levites were persuaded to join Ezra (8:15-20). *d.* Without a royal guard, but under divine protection (8:21-23), after placing the precious things in the charge of the Levites (8:24-30), the caravan set forth and reached Jerusalem safely (8:31-36). *e.* Shocked by the toleration of mixed marriages in Jerusalem (9:1-5), Ezra confessed the national sins in a prayer (9:6-15) which stirred the congregation to repentance (10:1-5). He then called together a national assembly (10:6-8). In spite of some opposition, the mixed marriages were ordered dissolved (10:9-17); 113 men of the

clergy and of the laity had married foreign women (10:18-44). The text breaks off abruptly without telling us whether they divorced their wives.

3. *Nehemiah's administration of Judea as Persian governor, in 444 and 432 B.C.* (Neh. 1-12). *a.* Nehemiah, a cupbearer of Artaxerxes I, informed at Susa of the plight of Jerusalem (Neh. 1:1-3), fasted and prayed (1:4-11). *b.* When Artaxerxes noticed Nehemiah's sadness (2:1 f.) and was informed of its reason (2:3), he allowed his cupbearer to go to Jerusalem (2:4-8). So he came to Jerusalem (2:9 f.). *c.* Nehemiah's secret inspection of the ruined walls of Jerusalem (2:11-16). The decision to rebuild the walls (2:17 f.) evoked the scorn of Sanballat and Tobiah (2:19 f.; cf. 2:10). *d.* List of the wall builders (3:1-32). *e.* Neither the scorn (4:1-6 [H. 3:33-38]) nor the war threats (4:7-14 [H. 4:1-8]) of Sanballat and his friends interrupted the work, which was carried on under military protection (4:15-23 [H. 4:9-17]). *f.* Economic hardship, resulting in scarcity of food for children, mortgaging of land, and slavery for debt (5:1-5), was promptly remedied by Nehemiah (5:6-13), who served twelve years as governor of Judea (444-432; cf. 5:14) without compensation and contributed from his own purse for worthy causes (5:14-19). *g.* Plots of Sanballat, Tobiah, and Geshem (cf. *e*, above) against Nehemiah: treacherous invitations to a conference (6:1-4), slanderous political accusations (6:5-9), and inducement to sacrilege through the prophet Shemaiah (6:10-14). The completion of the walls in September 444, after 52 days of work (6:15), resulted in consternation of the enemies (6:16) and further plots in Jerusalem (6:17-19). *h.* Guards were stationed at the city gates (7:1-3). *i.* Alarmed by the small population in Jerusalem, Nehemiah called a general assembly (7:4-5a; continued in ch. 11). *j.* Register of the Exiles who returned with Zerubbabel (7:5b, 6-73a), reproducing with slight changes in the order the list in Ezra 2. *k.* Ezra's reading of the Law of Moses before the congregation (7:73b-8:12) and, on the following day, celebration of the Feast of Tabernacles (8:13-18). Nehemiah 7:73b-9:37 (and perhaps also 9:38-10:39 [H. 10:1-40]) belong after Ezra 10. *l.* On the 24th of Tishri the congregation observed a day of penance (9:1-3) and solemnly confessed its sins in a long prayer (9:4-37). *m.* Nehemiah and the leaders of the congregation subscribed a covenant ratifying the Law (9:38-10:29 [H. 10:1-30]). In particular they promised to avoid mixed marriages, to observe the Sabbath and the Sabbatical year, to pay individually the annual Temple tax (cf. Ex. 30:11-16), to supply the wood for the sacred service, to provide offerings for the support of the clergy, and generally to be concerned with the Temple (10:30-39 [H. 10:31-40]). *n.* To increase the population of Jerusalem, one out of ten Jews, chosen by lot, dwelt in the capital (11:1-2, the sequel of 7:4-5a). Lists of Judeans (11:3-6), Benjamites (11:7-9), priests (11:10-14), Levites (11:15-18), and gatekeepers (11:19)

dwelling in Jerusalem (the lists in 11:4-19a are identical with those in I Chron. 9:3-17a); lists of the inhabitants of other Judean cities, including the nethinim (11:20 f.), of the chiefs of the Levites (11:22 f.), and of civil authorities (11:24) in Jerusalem; and lists of Judean (11:25-30) and Benjamite (11:31-36) villages. *o.* Lists: the priests and Levites who returned with Zerubbabel in 538 (12:1-9); the high priests from Joshua [Jeshua] to Jaddua, i.e., 538-331 B.C. (12:10 f., a sequel to I Chron. 6:3-15); the heads of priestly families in the time of the high priest Joiakim son of Joshua, early in the fifth century (12:12-21); the Levites in the time of Nehemiah (12:22-26). *p.* The dedication of the walls of Jerusalem (12:27-30) and the list of civil and religious authorities that took part in the celebration (12:31-43, the sequel of 7:3). *q.* Appointment of the collectors of the offerings due to the clergy, on the day in which the walls were dedicated (12:44-47).

4. *Nehemiah's second visit to Jerusalem in 432 B.C.* (13). *a.* Introduction: in accordance with the law of Deut. 23:3-7, Ammonites, Moabites, and other heathen were excluded from Israel (13:1-3). *b.* Tobiah (the Ammonite servant named in 2:10, 19 and in chs. 4 and 6) had received a chamber in the Temple from the high priest Eliashib; upon his return, Nehemiah drove him out (13:4-9). *c.* Nehemiah enforced the payment of the portions due to the Levites (13:10-14). *d.* Nehemiah stopped preparation and delivery of farm produce on the Sabbath (13:15-22). *e.* Nehemiah took measures to stop mixed marriages (13:23-27) and drove out a grandson of the high priest who had married a daughter of Sanballat (cf. 2:10; 4:1 [H. 3:33], etc.), the enemy of Nehemiah (13:28 f.). *f.* Conclusion: summary of Nehemiah's enforcement of the Law (13:30 f.).

1. Historical Problems

All genuine information on the history of the Jews during the Persian period (538-331 B.C.), except for purely religious ideas and institutions, is contained in the prophecies of Haggai and Zechariah 1-8 (for the three years 520-518) and in Ezra-Nehemiah (in Hebrew as well as in the Greek I [III] Esdras).[2] Since our book is the only history of the Jews from 538 to 432 B.C. (Josephus contributes nothing but legends), a critical evaluation of the historical sources contained therein is of obvious importance. The individual sources in the book may be listed as follows:

1. The edict of Cyrus (Ezra 1:1-4; II Chron. 36:22 f.; Esd. 2:1-7; cf. Ezra 6:3-5; Esd. 6:24-26; Josephus, *Antiquities* 11:1) and the return of

---

[2] The references to I [III] Esdras (abbreviated Esd.) are given according to the versification of the Authorized Version of the Apocrypha; some editions of the LXX in common use differ in the versification as follows: English 2:6-30; 5:41-73; 6:11-34; 8:43-96 correspond to Greek 2:6-25; 5:41-70; 6:11-33; 8:43-92, respectively. In R. H. Charles's English edition of the Apocrypha and Pseudepigrapha, the texts of Chronicles-Ezra-Nehemiah and of Esdras are printed conveniently in parallel columns.

the Exiles in 538 under Sheshbazzar, bringing gifts and the Temple vessels (Ezra 1:5-11; Esd. 2:8-15; cf. Ezra 5:13-16; Esd. 6:17-20); list of these Exiles (Ezra 2:1-67; Neh. 7:6-69; Esd. 5:7-43; summarized in Josephus, *Antiquities* 11:3, 10);[3] their contributions to the Temple and settlement in their cities (Ezra 2:68-70; Neh. 7:70-73a; Esd. 5:44-46).

2. The beginning of the building of the Temple in 536, and its interruption until 520. An altar was erected by Joshua [Jeshua] and Zerubbabel "in the seventh month" presumably of the year of the return (538)— although in Neh. 7:73b (Esd. 9:37), belonging to the same context, a much later year is implied—and the Feast of Tabernacles was observed (Ezra 3:1-6; Esd. 5:47-53; Josephus, *Ant.* 11:4, 1). In the second month of the second year of the return (536) the cornerstone of the Temple was laid and the Levites were appointed (Ezra 3:7-13; Esd. 5:54-65; Josephus, *Ant.* 11:4, 2). But the "adversaries" of Judah prevented the Jews from carrying on the work of rebuilding the Temple until the year 520 (Ezra 4:1-5, 24; Esd. 5:66-73; Josephus, *Ant.* 11:4, 3-4); contrast Ezra 5:13-16; Esd. 6:17-20.

3. The building of the Temple in 520-516. The beginning of the work (Ezra 5:1-5; Esd. 6:1-6; Josephus, *Ant.* 11:4, 4-5). Report of Tattenai (Sisinnes in the Greek texts) to Darius, and the latter's order to provide funds for the building of the Temple and for its sacrifices (Ezra 5:6-6:12; Esd. 6:7-34; Josephus, *Ant.* 11:4, 6-7). The completion of the Temple, its dedication, and the celebration of the Passover (Ezra 6:13-22; Esd. 7; Josephus, *Ant.* 11:4, 7-9).

4. The work of Ezra (Ezra 7-10 and Neh. 7:73b-10:39 [H. 10:40]). Esdras 8:1-9:55 corresponds to Ezra 7-10 and Neh. 7:73-8:12, and breaks off abruptly with the words "and they were assembled" in Neh. 8:13. Josephus relates the story of Ezra in *Antiquities* 11:5, 1-5. The events in Ezra 7-10 are dated in the seventh, those of Neh. 8-10 in the twentieth year of Artaxerxes. If Artaxerxes I Longimanus (465-424) is meant, the years in question would be 458 and 445; if Artaxerxes II Mnemon (404-358), the dates would be 397 and 384. Josephus reads "Xerxes" (485-465) instead of "Artaxerxes." These stories about Ezra include an Aramaic edict of Artaxerxes, defining Ezra's authority (Ezra 7:[11], 12-26); the memoirs of Ezra composed in the first person (Ezra 7:27-9:15, including a prayer in 9:6-15; cf. Neh. 10 where the first person plural is used); and an account in the third person of Ezra's journey (7:1-10) and of his attempted dissolution of mixed marriages (Ezra 10, including a list of the offenders in 10:18-44); an account in the third person of Ezra's reading of the Law (Neh. 7:53b-8:18) and of the national confession of sin which followed (Neh. 9:1-37); the account of the ratification of the Law (Neh.

[3] The number of returned Exiles, 42,360 exclusive of slaves and singers, is increased by Josephus to 4,628,000 (B. Niese's critical edition of the Greek text).

9:38-10:39 [H. 10:40]), in the first person plural, names Nehemiah but not Ezra.

5. "The Words of Nehemiah the son of Hecaliah" (Neh. 1:1), written in the first person (1:1-7:73a; 13:4-31), including a list of returned Exiles quoted from "the Book of Genealogy" (7:6-73a, reproduced in Ezra 2). According to 5:14, Nehemiah was the governor of Judea from the twentieth to the thirty-second year of Artaxerxes (Xerxes in Josephus); if, as seems certain, Artaxerxes I is meant, the dates would be 445-433 or 444-432 B.C. Inconsistently, in 13:4-31 we have Nehemiah's own account of his reforms during a second visit to Jerusalem in 433 or 432 B.C. Josephus gives the story of Nehemiah in *Antiquities* 11:5, 6-8.

6. Aramaic public documents relating to opposition against the rebuilding of Jerusalem and its walls: accusation against the Jews in the time of Xerxes I (Ezra 4:6, in Hebrew; the text of the documents is omitted); documents from the time of Artaxerxes, presumably Artaxerxes I (4:[7], 8-23; Esd. 2:16-30; Josephus, *Ant.* 11:2, 1-2).

7. Supplements to the memoirs of Nehemiah (Neh. 11:1-13:3). Narratives: 11:1-2, supplementing 7:4-5a; 12:27-43, supplementing 7:1-3; 12:44-47, the sequel of 12:43; 13:1-3, an introduction to 13:4-9. Nehemiah speaks in the first person in 12:31, 38, 40. Lists: 11:3-12:26 (12:32-35, 41 f.).

A cursory glance at this classification of the several documents included in Ezra-Nehemiah brings out some obvious facts. In the first place, the material is not arranged in chronological order; in the second place, no attempt is made to give an uninterrupted history of the Jews; in the third place, except for passing allusion to other kings, the sources refer to the reigns of Cyrus, Darius, and especially Artaxerxes; and finally, except for some lists, the return of the Jews from Babylonia in various caravans, and the activity of Nehemiah, the documents are concerned with the Temple and its clergy. Under the circumstances it is not surprising that the interpretation and evaluation of these sources presents very serious difficulties and that in solving the historical and literary problems scholars have reached the most diverse conclusions.

From the historical point of view the two main problems are the identity of "Artaxerxes" (I, or II, or both in different parts of the book) and the date of the several documents.

Artaxerxes is named in our book in connection with Ezra (Ezra 7:1, 7, 11 f., 21; 8:1) and Nehemiah (Neh. 2:1; 5:14; 13:6); moreover, reference is made to a letter written to this king (Ezra 4:7), and the Aramaic text of a letter of Rehum to Artaxerxes and of the king's reply is given verbatim (4:8-23). Although the book offers no clue for the identification of Artaxerxes, it is certain that its author (the Chronicler), whatever may have been the meaning of his sources, obviously considered "Artaxerxes" as the same king throughout. The Chronicler and later Jews (like the author of Daniel) had only vague and confused notions about the chronology of the Persian period and the order of the Persian kings. Only in Ezra 6:14 (Cyrus, Darius, Artaxerxes) is there a memory of the actual sequence, although the reference to Artaxerxes in connection with the building of the Temple (finished in 516) is anachronistic. Elsewhere Darius I precedes Cyrus, and in Ezra 4 Darius I (under whom the Temple was built) is confused with Darius II (424-404); "Darius the Persian" in Neh. 12:22 is Darius III (336-330).

Although decisive evidence is lacking, the majority of the critics assume that the Artaxerxes under whom Nehemiah built the walls of Jerusalem (and therefore also the king in Ezra 4:7-23) is Artaxerxes I Longimanus (465-424). This view is supported by the mention of Sanballat, assuming that he be the enemy of Nehemiah, in a papyrus from Elephantine (Sachau 1:29) dated in 408 (cf. A. Cowley, *Aramaic Papyri of the Fifth Century,* pp. 108-110). Some critics, however, regard Artaxerxes II Mnemon (404-358) as the patron of Nehemiah (J. Marquart, *Fundamente israelitischer und jüdischer Geschichte,* 1897, p. 31; H. P. Smith, *Old Testament History,* pp. 382 ff. New York, 1906). The views of C. C. Torrey have changed through the years: in 1896 (*The Composition and Historical Value of Ezra-Nehemiah,* p. 65) he left the question in doubt; in 1910 (*Ezra Studies,* pp. 140, 335) he was inclined to identify the king with Artaxerxes I; later he has argued for the identification with Artaxerxes II (*The Second Isaiah,* pp. 456 ff. New York, 1928; JBL 47 [1928] 380-389). Unfortunately the chief evidence favoring Artaxerxes II (and two district governors of Samaria named Sanballat) is drawn from Josephus, whose chronology of the Persian period is no less confused than that of the Chronicler and whose story of the Samaritan Schism in the time of Alexander (*Antiquities* 11:7, 2; 8, 2-7) "is not embellished legend but pure fiction" (G. F. Moore, *Judaism,* Vol. I, p. 24). Since there are no compelling reasons for dating Nehemiah in the time of Artaxerxes II, it seems preferable to accept the current view and to assume that he lived under Artaxerxes I.

With regard to Ezra, the evidence for identifying the Artaxerxes who gave him a firman is even more elusive. His "Memoirs" lack the genuine historicity of those of Nehemiah and his life is far more legendary. If we regard the account of his activity as substantially historical, it is difficult to reconcile it with Nehemiah's Memoirs. The Chronicler, unaware of the contradictions, apparently regards Ezra and Nehemiah as contemporaries (Neh. 8:9; 12:36). In reality, if Artaxerxes I had dispatched Ezra to Jerusalem with full powers in 458, he could hardly have sent Nehemiah with similar authority in 445-444, when Ezra was still active; nor could one leader have put an end to mixed marriages in Jerusalem without being aware of a similar reform enforced a few years before by the other.[4] Some critics believe that by dating Nehemiah under Artaxerxes I and Ezra under Artaxerxes II the glaring inconsistencies of our book are eliminated: De Saulcy (*Etude chronologique des livres d'Esdras et de Néhémie*. Paris, 1868); A. van Hoonacker (Néhémie et Esdras, Muséon 9, 1890; *Néhémie en l'an 20 d'Artaxerxes I, Esdras en l'an 7 d'Artaxerxes II.* Ghent, 1892; RB 32 [1923] 491-494; 33 [1924] 33-64); W. H. Kosters (*Het herstel van Israel,* 1894; German translation by Basedow: *Die Wiederherstellung Israels,* 1895); L. W. Batten (*Ezra and Nehemiah* [ICC]), J. Touzard (RB 24 [1915] 59-133); S. Mowinckel (*Statholderen Nehemia.* Kristiania, 1916); W. F. Albright (JBL 40 [1921] 104-124), A. Lods (*Les Prophètes,* p. 342), and others. F. X. Kugler (*Von Moses bis Paulus,* pp. 215-233. Münster, 1922.) has defended the traditional dates for Ezra (458, 445) by ingeniously showing that, if the revised dating is adopted, Ezra, according to our texts, would have violated the Sabbath law. We are forced to admit that the serious difficulties in our book cannot be solved by merely changing the dates of Ezra and Nehemiah's missions. The date and credibility of considerable portions of the book are in question and the identity of Artaxerxes is irrelevant for the evaluation of these documents.

With the exception of Haggai and Zechariah, we lack reliable confirmation for any of the events related in our book. A determination of the value of our sources must rely entirely, except for the rebuilding of the Temple, on internal evidence and historical criticism. The credibility of each of the seven sources listed above must be tested separately.

1. The edict of Cyrus (538 B.C.) has been transmitted in Hebrew (Ezra 1:1-4 and partially in II Chron. 36:22 f.) and in Aramaic (Ezra 6:3-5; cf. 5:13-15). A comparison of the two versions discloses very great differences. According to the Hebrew version, Cyrus "King of Persia,"[5] after declaring that "Jehovah, the God of heaven" had given him "all the kingdoms of the earth" (cf. Is. 45:11 ff.) and had charged him with building the Temple at Jerusalem (cf. Is. 44:28), ordered the Jews in Babylonia to go to Jerusalem to rebuild the Temple; moreover, the

---

[4] These and other contradictions between the work of Ezra and that of Nehemiah, assuming that Ezra preceded Nehemiah, are discussed by L. W. Batten, *The Books of Ezra and Nehemiah,* pp. 28-30.

[5] The frequent use of this title in the actual edict (II Chron. 36:23; Ezra 1:2, but not in Ezra 6:3) and elsewhere (II Chron. 36:22; cf. 36:20; Ezra 1:1, 8; 3:7; 4:3, 5; Dan. 10:1; cf., for other Kings, Ezra 4:7, 24; 7:1) is suspicious. Outside of the Old Testament and Greek histories, it occurs for Cyrus only in a Babylonian chronicle, with reference to events ten years before the conquest of Babylon (*Cambridge Ancient History,* Vol. IV, pp. 8 f.). Persia there does not mean, as in the Bible, the Persian Empire, but a province of Iran. Before his conquests, Cyrus was "King of Anshan" (or Anzan). Neither Cyrus nor his successors used the title "King of Persia," which became current for them only in the Hellenistic period.

Babylonians among whom the "remnant" of the Jews was residing, must contribute heavily to the costs of the new edifice. According to the Aramaic version, Cyrus ordered the building of the Temple (giving exact specifications concerning its dimensions and walls) at the cost of "the house of the King"; at the same time he decreed that the golden and silver vessels removed by Nebuchadnezzar from the Temple be restored to their place.

It is clear that, in view of the differences, both decrees cannot be authentic. The second cannot be the latter part of the first,[6] for it purports to be complete, nor a summary of the first. Most critics[7] recognize that the wording of the first is so characteristically Jewish that it cannot be attributed to Cyrus: for this king to have ordered his Babylonian subjects to contribute substantially to the worship of an alien God, Jehovah, is unthinkable. However, the authenticity of the second decree, in Aramaic, is generally maintained.

Cyrus, whose liberal policy toward the religions of his subjects is well known, would not have forbidden the rebuilding of the Temple, if the Jewish community in Jerusalem had expressed a desire to undertake the work. Cyrus, under the suggestion of Jewish leaders in Babylonia, could even have issued a decree ordering the rebuilding of the Temple at his own expense—and ordered the return of the Jewish Exiles. But the gap between historical possibility (and even plausibility) and historical fact should never be lightly overlooked. In reality, we know positively that, if Cyrus actually issued one or two edicts ordering the Exiles to return to Jerusalem and to build the Temple, these edicts remained a dead letter—they were simply cast into the wastepaper basket (J. Wellhausen and G. Hölscher). The unimpeachable testimony of Haggai and Zechariah shows that in 520 nothing was known of any decree of Cyrus issued in 538. More significant still, these prophets had never heard of a considerable number of returned Exiles dwelling in Jerusalem nor of any previous plans for rebuilding the Temple (cf. S. A. Cook, in the *Apocrypha and Pseudepigrapha of the Old Testament* edited by R. H. Charles, Vol. I, pp. 6-8). We must therefore choose between two horns of the dilemma: either Cyrus issued his decree and mysteriously no one took notice of it (so R. Kittel, *Geschichte des Volkes Israel*, Vol. III, 313), or the decree is a Jewish forgery (so particularly W. H. Kosters and C. C. Torrey). The second alternative seems more plausible. The dreams of the Second Isaiah and of Ezekiel about the glorious return of all the Exiles and about the new Temple were transformed by the Chronicler

[6] C. C. Torrey (*Ezra Studies*, p. 144, n. 12) says, on the contrary, that if Ezra 6:3aβ followed immediately after 1:2-4, so that the complete edict included 1:2-4; 6:3aβ-5, "the whole document would be perfectly harmonious and homogeneous."

[7] Even E. Meyer (*Die Entstehung des Judenthums*, p. 49. Halle, 1896), who regards the letters and edicts as genuine, rejects Ezra 1:2-4.

into alleged historical realities. The account of Sheshbazzar's journey to Jerusalem bearing the 5,400 (2,499 is the actual total) gold and silver Temple vessels (5,469 according to Esdras), given by the Chronicler in Ezra 1:5-11, needs no refutation;[8] with the exception of the name of the Persian treasurer, Mithredath (1:8; cf. 4:7), and the fanciful list of vessels, the information is derived from 5:13-15.

The itemized list in Ezra 2 purports to be a census of the Exiles who returned in 538, but is in reality a copy of Neh. 7:6-73a—a register of the inhabitants of the province of Judah (the holy "Congregation" [Ezra 2:64]) compiled conceivably in the fifth century, before Nehemiah's mission, if we believe that Nehemiah found it in "the book of genealogy" (Neh. 7:5). C. C. Torrey may possibly have gone too far in considering the list a concoction of the Chronicler (although the present writer tends to agree with him). It is barely possible that the list rests on an actual census taken in the time of Nehemiah, as W. H. Kosters, J. Wellhausen, G. Hölscher, and others believe. With suitable retouches the Chronicler, whose notions of the chronology of the Persian period are woefully incorrect, utilized it twice: in Ezra 2 for the caravan of the Exiles who (if we believe him) returned in 538, and in Neh. 7 for the inhabitants of Judea in the time of Nehemiah. He was blissfully unaware of the intervening century.

If we recall that according to the most reliable statistics (Jer. 52:28-30) Nebuchadnezzar in three deportations (in 597, 586, 581) exiled a total of 4,600 men, we shall find it difficult to believe that fifty years later 42,360 men descended from them (Ezra 2:64) returned to Jerusalem with Sheshbazzar, leaving many of their compatriots in Babylonia. In reality, "many of them stayed in Babylonia, being unwilling to leave their possessions" (Josephus, *Antiquities* 11:1, 3). In speaking of the Jewish community in Jerusalem at his time, Nehemiah is unaware of any returned Exiles in its midst (Neh. 1:2 f.).

2. It seems clear that for the events from the return of the Exiles in 538 to the inception of the building of the Temple in 520 the Chronicler lacked written sources and drew entirely on his imagination (Ezra 3:1-4:5, 24). His characteristic style, his zeal for ritualistic Judaism, and his hatred for the Samaritans are conspicuously manifest. With his usual disregard for facts and dates, he assumes that regular morning and evening burnt offering was already presented *before* the Temple was rebuilt (3:3, 5; 3:4 f. is a summary of the festal calendar in Num. 28 f. [Ps]). He states that the Levites were at least twenty years old when they began their

---

[8] H. H. Schaeder (*Ezra der Schreiber,* 1930; and Iranische Beiträge, I, 1930) and K. Galling (ZDPV [1937] 177-183) regard the list (1:7-11) as an official document. Galling regards 1:9-11 as a translation of the Aramaic catalogue attached to the firman granted to Sheshbazzar.

service in 536 (3:8)—nay even in the time of Hezekiah (II Chron. 31:17) and of David (I Chron. 23:24). Such was patently the practice in his own time, but the Pentateuchal law specified that the Levites should not serve before their thirtieth or twenty-fifth year (Num. 4:3; 8:24 [Ps]). He dates the Samaritan Schism in 536, nearly a century before Nehemiah, when he attributes the interruption of the reconstruction of the Temple to Samaritan opposition (4:1-5, 24), utilizing as his evidence a letter of later date to Artaxerxes opposing the rebuilding of Jerusalem's walls (4:6-23). In view of these absurdities none of the information about the events of 538-536 is trustworthy.

3. The account of the rebuilding of the Temple in 520-516 (Ezra 5:1-6:22) is based on actual facts, in contrast with the preceding fictitious story of the laying of the cornerstone in 536. This section consists of the Chronicler's story written in Aramaic (5:1 f., the sequel of 4:24, and 6:15-18; C. C. Torrey omits 4:24; 5:1 f. and adds 6:9 f.) and in Hebrew (6:19-22); and of state documents enclosed within a narrative (5:3-6:14, in Aramaic).

For the inception of the reconstruction of the Temple (5:1 f.) the Chronicler could give genuine historical information derived from Haggai and Zechariah; but for its completion (6:15-22), lacking written sources, he relied as usual on his imagination. With a glaring inconsistency the Chronicler admits that, according to Haggai's unimpeachable statement, the building of the Temple began in the second year of Darius (4:24; 5:1 f.) whereas elsewhere (3:8-13; 5:16) it is said to have begun under Cyrus. If, as C. C. Torrey (*Ezra Studies*, p. 60) believes, "Darius" according to the Chronicler was not Darius I (521-485) but Darius II (424-404), the confusion becomes utter chaos.

The problems raised by the Aramaic documents (5:3-6:14) are more complex. We should obviously distinguish the text of the official papers (a letter to Darius, 5:[6-7a], 7b-17; and the king's reply thereto, consisting of the decree of Cyrus, 6:3-5, and of an incomplete letter, 6:5-12) from the narrative surrounding them (5:3-5; 6:1 f., 13 f.). For if the official pieces are genuine and were written by Persians, they are necessarily earlier than the Jewish stories explaining their origin and results. The authenticity of the Aramaic letters has been defended with the greatest energy by E. Meyer (*Die Entstehung des Judenthums*, pp. 8-71) and has been attacked no less vigorously by C. C. Torrey (*Ezra Studies*, pp. 140-207). Critics are still sharply divided on this question, but have contributed little to the arguments of Meyer and Torrey.

The presence of the decree of Cyrus (6:3-5) in the imperfectly preserved letter of Darius does not favor the authenticity of the documents, unless we suppose that Cyrus's decree was never proclaimed publicly, but

forgotten in the archives of Ecbatana—contrary to the categorical statements of the other document (5:13-17). Since it is certain that in 520 the
Jews in Jerusalem were still saying, "The time for the house of Jehovah to
be built has not yet arrived at present" (Hag. 1:2) and since we know
that before the cornerstone was laid in that year no stone had been laid
on stone in the Temple (Hag. 2:15), the assertion on the part of the
Jewish elders that the work had been progressing without interruption
for sixteen years (Ezra 5:13-17) is manifestly false. This invalidates the
genuineness of the document. For we can hardly believe that these responsible elders would have lied so brazenly to the Persian authorities
(who could verify the untruth at once) and that a mythical decree of
Cyrus (of which Haggai and Zechariah knew nothing) would be conveniently discovered at Ecbatana to prove that their lie was the truth.
In other words, these documents can only be considered historical if the
Jews succeeded in placing a faked decree of Cyrus—a forgery so perfect
that it deceived Darius and his ministers—in the royal archives of Ecbatana. It was clearly much simpler for a later Jewish writer to forge
Persian documents in his book, and thus deceive not only his readers but
also eminent modern historians like E. Meyer.

Moreover, is it likely that Darius would have allowed the Jews to draw
from the Syrian satrapy's treasury unlimited funds to pay for the building of their Temple (6:8)? Not to speak of provision out of public funds
for all the expenses of the worship (6:9 f.)? If such had been the case,
would the new Temple have looked pitifully "as nothing" (Hag. 2:3) in
comparison with Solomon's Temple, which some of the onlookers still
remembered?

In view of the disagreement of these documents with historical facts,
as well as in view of their obvious Jewish character and linguistic characteristics, the most plausible conclusion is that "all the Persian documents
in Ezra are no less spurious than those in Josephus, *Antiquities* 11: 4, 9
[§118 f.]" (J. Wellhausen, *Israel. und jüd. Geschichte*, p. 155, n. 1. 1914).
They were written by the author of the narratives in which they are contained, one or two centuries after the time of Darius I—if not later.

4. The problems raised by the Ezra stories are the most difficult in the
book. What is in question is not only the date of Ezra's activity (before
or after Nehemiah; cf. above), the authorship and extent of the "Ezra
Memoirs," and their credibility, but even the historical reality of Ezra
himself. The evidence on the latter point is so ambiguous that opposite
conclusions have been reached. Thus C. C. Torrey (*The Composition and
Historical Value of Ezra-Nehemiah*, pp. 57, 60; cf. *Ezra Studies*, pp. 238-
248) could declare that "the story of Ezra is the Chronicler's masterpiece"
and "has no basis of fact" (G. Hölscher reaches the same verdict); while

W. F. Albright (JBL 40 [1921] 104-124), admitting with Torrey that the Chronicler wrote this story, concludes that Ezra is not only a historical character but that he is the Chronicler in person!

The complicated literary problems concerning the authorship of the Ezra stories may be reserved for a later section of this chapter. Here we are concerned with the credibility of Ezra's story, with the historical reality of the events narrated. Though closely interrelated, the date of a document and its conformity to actual facts are obviously different matters.

The introduction (Ezra 7:1-10) gives Ezra's genealogy and summarizes his character and activity. That this genealogy going back to Aaron (7:1-5) is a worthless concoction of the Chronicler needs no demonstration. It is a reproduction of the line of the high priests from Seraiah, the alleged father of Ezra, through Hilkiah and Zadok, back to Aaron (I Chron. 6:3-14 [H. 5:29-40]; cf. 6:50-53 [H. 6:35-38]) which is demonstrably false in making Zadok a son of Ahitub (cf. W. R. Arnold, *Ephod and Ark,* pp. 14 f.).[9]

The only datum in this introduction the validity of which deserves discussion is the date of Ezra's mission (the seventh year of Artaxerxes, 7:7 f.). Unfortunately this unique chronological datum for Ezra is ambiguous, depending, as we have seen, on the identification of Artaxerxes, and not easily reconciled with Nehemiah's residence in Jerusalem as governor in 444 and 432 (Neh. 5:14). If the date is taken seriously and correctly transmitted, it can only be either 458 (Artaxerxes I) or 397 (Artaxerxes II). The Chronicler, of course, regards the activity of Ezra as contemporaneous with that of Nehemiah (Neh. 8:9; 12:36). In reality Ezra's reforms, particularly his planned abolition of mixed marriages, are incongruous either before or after the governorship of Nehemiah, and, in view of Nehemiah's silence, could hardly belong to his time.

The introduction is followed by an Aramaic firman granted by Artaxerxes to Ezra, allegedly (7:11) reported verbatim (7:12-26). By royal decree, "Ezra, the priest, the scribe of the Law of the God of heaven" (7:12) was sent to Jerusalem: to investigate conditions in accordance with the Law of his God which he brought with him (7:14); to bring a large sum contributed by the king (7:15), the silver and gold found in Babylonia (7:16), and the gifts of the Exiles (7:16) for the support of the Temple worship; to deliver sacred vessels (7:19); to draw for additional Temple expenses on the royal treasury (7:20) and on the treasury of all Syria (7:21 f.); to prevent the taxation of the clergy (7:24); to

[9] Moreover, if Ezra was the son of Seraiah he was born not more than a year after 586, when Seraiah was put to death (II Kings 25:18-21) and would have been at least 127 years old when he went to Jerusalem in 458 (the earliest possible date for his mission).

appoint judges in all Syria (7:25) in order that all violations of the Jewish law be strictly punished (7:26).

Although it is generally recognized that the terminology of this decree is typically Jewish (notably in 7:15-17, 24-26; on the identification of the Law with wisdom [7:25] see G. F. Moore, *Judaism*, Vol. I, pp. 263-265), its authenticity is stoutly maintained by many scholars. The Jewish style is explained either as the result of a revision (so S. R. Driver, *Introduction to the Old Testament*, p. 550), or (*mirabile dictu!*) by assuming that Ezra himself or other Jews actually had a hand in the redaction of the decree (R. Kittel, *Geschichte des Volkes Israel*, Vol. III, p. 583), or at least that the decree simply reproduced the wording of Ezra's petition (E. Meyer, *Die Entstehung des Judenthums*, pp. 64 ff.).[10] But, aside from the form, no amount of critical curtailment and revision can produce a decree that is historically plausible unless it is rewritten *in toto*. The powers given to Ezra are incredible, within the Persian administration, in a man who was not a public official of any sort. They surpass by far those of Nehemiah, who was governor of Judea. Ezra is to enforce the Jewish law in all Syria and, after making its contents known to all, appoint judges to punish violations of it: not a word is said of the restriction of these provisions to the Jews. On the contrary, Ezra is to raise large sums of money for the Temple among the Gentiles in Babylonia. The enormous sums brought by Ezra and to be obtained from the royal treasurers in Syria contrast sharply with what we know of Jerusalem in the time of Nehemiah, where no trace of this wealth can be detected. One thing is certain: as in the case of the decree of Cyrus, the provisions of this firman dealing with Ezra's measures in Judea remained forever a dead letter. If, as everything indicates, this decree, like the other Aramaic documents, is a Jewish forgery, it casts serious suspicion on "Ezra's Memoirs" in the first person, of which, according to 7:27 f., it was an integral part.

Ezra's Memoirs in the first person are limited to 7:27-9:15 (in which 8:35 f. are in the third person). This account of Ezra's journey (8)—including lists of the Exiles who returned with him (8:1-14), of the Levites who were persuaded to join him (8:18-20), and of the precious things brought to Jerusalem (8:26 f.)—and of Ezra's shock at being informed of the mixed marriages in Jerusalem (9:1-5, followed by a prayer, 9:6-15), is obviously incomplete. But it continues without a break with a story told in the third person (10): the congregation was stirred

---

[10] H. H. Schaeder (*Ezra der Schreiber*, pp. 42-55, Beiträge zur historischen Theologie 5. Tübingen, 1930) takes the final step. The title "scribe of the Law of the God of heaven" (7:12) means for him "Secretary [or: Minister] of the Law of the God of heaven." Ezra was therefore the Persian official in charge of Jewish affairs and his office was the antecedent of that of the Exilarch in later times (pp. 48 f.). The edict was written in the imperial chancellery by Ezra, in this capacity (p. 55). Unfortunately these conjectures are supported by no evidence.

(10:1-5) and in a meeting of the popular assembly (10:6-8) Ezra suggested that a census of mixed married couples be taken (10:9-17); 113 Jews were found to have foreign wives (10:18-44; the end is textually corrupt and incomplete).

Opening magnificently with a glorious firman of Artaxerxes, granting to Ezra full authority to enforce the Jewish law, the story breaks off abruptly before Ezra has accomplished anything, except to lead a caravan of Exiles to Jerusalem and deliver the treasures in his charge. *Parturiunt montes.* . . . Did Ezra's attempt to cleanse the Jewish blood from foreign pollution end in a dismal failure? If so, Ezra could not have been a royal plenipotentiary armed with Artaxerxes' firman (which, according to 8:36, was duly presented to the Persian authorities in Syria and produced their full collaboration). But if Ezra accomplished his mission triumphantly, how could the climactic end of his Memoirs have been lost? These intrinsic difficulties of a historical character, in addition to the fact that these memoirs are written in the style of the Chronicler, with scant regard for historical plausibility, raise serious doubts about the genuineness and historicity of Ezra's Memoirs.

It should not be forgotten that Ezra is said to have been a "scribe," in fact, the first member of this profession. Since the scribes are the interpreters of the Law, the profession could not have existed before the canonization of the Pentateuch. Ezra, however, was a scribe before he read the Law to the congregation and had it ratified.

These difficulties are not solved by merely disregarding the date of Ezra's mission (458, Ezra 7:7 f.) and moving Ezra's activity after that of Nehemiah, as has been argued from the mention of Jehohanan the son of Eliashib (Ezra 10:6; cf. Neh. 12:10 f., 22 f.) who lived after Nehemiah. According to the Elephantine papyri (Sachau 1: 18; 2: 17), Jehohanan was the high priest in 408. Once this unique chronological reference for Ezra (Ezra 7:7) is abandoned, it becomes impossible to discover when Ezra lived, and his activity becomes even more hypothetical.

The general attribution of Neh. 8-10 (or parts thereof) to Ezra's Memoirs does not help us in piercing the mist surrounding Ezra's personality and work. The facts of the case are puzzling. Ezra is said to have read the Law (Neh. 7:73b-8:18), but is not mentioned in the text of the story of the national confession of sins (9:1-37; the LXX reads, however, "And Ezra said" before 9:6) and of the ratification of the Law (9:38-10:39 [H. 10]). Nehemiah is the first to sign the ratification (10:1 [H. 10:2]), but Ezra who had read the Law is not among the signers; the mention of Nehemiah in connection with the reading of the Law (8:9) is generally regarded as spurious. The events of Neh. 8-10 are not dated: the assumption that the Law was read in 444 rests on mere conjecture.

The historicity of any part of Neh. 8-10, when critically examined, must remain as doubtful as the chronology.

It is most regrettable that no historical information may be obtained from Neh. 8, the story of the reading of the Law of Moses. In spite of innumerable attempts to utilize the story for the critical study of the Pentateuch, it yields no helps whatsoever. For we do not know the date of this event nor the identity of the Law which was read. In fact the whole ceremony may be merely an imaginary repetition of Josiah's promulgation of the Deuteronomic Code in 621. If Ezra came from Babylonia in 458 with the Law of God in his hand, it is incredible that he would wait till 444 to promulgate it. Ezra could have brought from Babylonia no extant code of law unknown to the priests in Jerusalem, except the Holiness Code or Ezekiel's plan of restoration, both of which had been written in Babylonia a century before. But the Law which was read by Ezra contained much more than the Holiness Code. As for the Priestly Code, promulgated about 450, it could not have been brought by Ezra from Babylonia because it was written in Jerusalem, as proved by the fact that it embodies the ritual of the Second Temple in the fifth century. It would seem that the author of the story believed that Ezra's Law was the whole Pentateuch, but it could hardly have existed in Nehemiah's time. The reading of the Law according to the story in Neh. 8 cannot be demonstrated to be historical by dating it before or after 444. If we date the reading of the Law in 458 (with H. H. Schaeder, *Ezra der Schreiber*, p. 12) we cannot explain Nehemiah's failure to enforce until 432 (according to Neh. 13:4-31). If we date it in 432, we are puzzled by the ratification of the Law before that date (according to Neh. 10). A date after 400 would of course automatically rule out the historicity of Neh. 10 and 13, which seem to presuppose the publication of the Law in the time of Nehemiah.

In conclusion the "Ezra Memoirs" as we now have them (Ezra 7-10, concluded perhaps in Neh. 8-10) fail to give a consistent historical report of actual events. Rearrangements of the various stories and changes in the chronology have been suggested by critics in a bewildering variety, covering nearly every possibility. But since no proposed scheme removes the historical inconsistencies, none of these conjectures has gained the support of a considerable number of scholars. It would therefore seem that, even though Ezra may have been a historical character, the information about him is on a par with that offered by the Chronicler on David when he is not quoting from ancient sources. G. Hölscher (*Geschichte der israelitischen und jüdischen Religion,* p. 140) could even regard Ezra as a purely legendary figure, still unknown to Ben Sira (Ecclus. 49:11-13) in 180.

5. In contrast with the confused and legendary "Memoirs of Ezra,"

the autobiography of Nehemiah contained in Neh. 1:1-7:73a is admittedly genuine beyond the shadow of a doubt (except for later additions to be determined in a later discussion). Written by Nehemiah himself after 432 (5:14) and recounting his activities during the twelve preceding years, these Memoirs report frankly and vividly, as one would do in a personal diary not intended for publication, the actual events and the emotions which they aroused in the writer. Being the only unimpeachable source for Jewish history between Haggai and Zechariah in 520-516 and I Maccabees for the period 175-135, they are invaluable. They are not only one of the most accurate historical sources in the Old Testament, but they pierce for a moment the darkness enveloping the political history of the Jews during the Persian period.

The conclusion of Nehemiah's Memoirs in 13:4-31, dealing with his enforcement of Pentateuchal laws, is less obviously authentic than the first part. The verdict of critics is not unanimous: although most of them recognize the genuineness of this report on Nehemiah's second visit to Jerusalem in 432 (contradicting 5:14, according to which Nehemiah was governor from 444 to 432), C. C. Torrey (*Ezra Studies,* pp. 248 f.) regards ch. 13 as one of the Chronicler's stories, written without using a reliable source.

6. The report (Ezra 4:6-24, in Aramaic except 4:6 f.) on abortive attempts to rebuild the walls of Jerusalem under Xerxes I (485-465) and under Artaxerxes I (465-424), before Nehemiah's mission, is obviously displaced. The Chronicler in 4:24 erroneously confuses the opposition to the building of the city walls (the subject of 4:7-23, and apparently of 4:6) with the opposition to the rebuilding of the Temple at a much earlier date. This misinterpretation of Rehum's letter to Artaxerxes (4: 7-16) and of the king's answer (4:17-22, 23) does not per se impair the genuineness of these documents. Even the textual corruptions and the possible retouches of the Chronicler in 4:9b, 10a (and his notes in 4:6 f., 24) do not militate against it. On the contrary, the fact that the Chronicler misunderstood these texts and placed them in the wrong context proves that he could hardly have been their author, as W. H. Kosters (*Die Wiederherstellung Israels,* pp. 61 ff., 116. 1895) believed.

An examination of the documents fails to show conclusively whether they were genuine, or composed by a Jew some years before the Chronicler wrote. On the one hand, the fact that these are the only Aramaic documents in which the enemies of the Jews triumph and the Persian king opposes Jewish aspirations, could be adduced in favor of their authenticity. But, on the other hand, their historicity is not above suspicion. For Nehemiah knows of no earlier attempts to repair the walls; and the enemies of the Jews could have stopped the work without royal edict, as shown by the powerful opposition to Nehemiah despite his authority as governor. Moreover, the exaltation of the power of David and Solomon, whose kingdom is said to have included Syria (4:20), seems to be inspired by Jewish patriotism and can hardly have been recorded in the archives of Artaxerxes (even the Assyrian and Babylonian records know nothing of Omri's predecessors). In general it seems unlikely that two obscure Persian officials in Palestine would write to the king directly and receive a personal answer from him; they should have brought the matter to the attention of the satrap of Syria. These records, while not such obvious forgeries as some of the others, are suspect and presumably concocted by a Jew.

7. The supplements to the Memoirs of Nehemiah (Neh. 11:1-13:3) consist of miscellaneous narratives and lists. C. C. Torrey ascribes them *in toto* to the pen of the Chronicler, while other critics regard them as extracts from "the book of chronicles" (Neh. 12:23) which is supposed to have been one of the Chronicler's sources. There is nothing in these chapters that may be used confidently for the history of Nehemiah's time, but it is not to be excluded that some information may be gleaned here for the history of the Chronicler's time, about the middle of the third century.

2. Literary Problems

The literary analysis of the Books of Ezra and Nehemiah has shown beyond the shadow of a doubt that their author is the Chronicler and that he utilized written sources. But a wide difference of opinion prevails among critics in assigning the material to the Chronicler and to his sources. Nehemiah's autobiography is the only source whose genuineness and independent existence before the Chronicler's time have never been questioned. In general, however, the Memoirs of Ezra and the Aramaic collection of official letters are considered to be also independent sources of the greatest historical value.

The extent of the Ezra Memoirs is uncertain. It is only in Ezra 7:27-9:6 that Ezra speaks in the first person. To this torso we must add the letter of Artaxerxes (7:11-26) at the beginning, and Ezra's prayer (9:6-15) at the end; but the story still remains incomplete. Many critics assume that the rest of Ezra's Memoirs, or a considerable portion thereof, is extant in a later rewriting; but opinions vary in the determination of the original extent and order of these edited portions.

A few examples may illustrate the variety of results attained by scholars in reconstructing the contents of the Ezra Memoirs. They have been identified with the following sections: Ezra 7-10 and Neh. 7:73b to ch. 10 (F. Bleek, *Einleitung in das Alte Testament*, 4th ed., 1878). Ezra 7:12-9:15 and perhaps Neh. 7:73b to ch. 10 (S. R. Driver, *Introduction to the Old Testament*. 7th ed., 1898). Ezra 7:37-8:34; 9 and, in rewritten form,

Ezra 10 (W. H. Kosters, *Encycl. Bibl.* 2 [1901], 1479; Kosters is unable to decide whether Neh. 7:6 to ch. 10 belonged to the Memoirs of Ezra or of Nehemiah). Ezra 7:27-9:15 and, in rewritten form, Ezra 7:1-10; 10; Neh. 7:73b to ch. 10 (C. Siegfried, *Ezra, Nehemiah, und Esther*, in KHAT, 1901). Ezra 7:27-9:15 and Ezra 10; Neh. 7:73b to ch. 10 (W. W. Baudissin, *Einleitung in das Alte Testament.* 1901). Ezra 7:27-8:34; 9:1-15 and, in rewritten form, Ezra 10; Neh. 7:73b to ch. 9 (A. Bertholet, *Ezra und Nehemia*, in KHC, 1902). Ezra 7:1-10, 27 f.; 8; Neh. 7:70-8:18; Ezra 9-10; Neh. 9-10 (C. C. Torrey, *Ezra Studies*, 1910; all of this, according to Torrey, was written by the Chronicler). Ezra 7:12-9:15 (E. Sellin, *Einleitung in das Alte Testament.* 1910). Ezra 7:12-9:15; Neh. 9:38-10:39 [H. 10:1 (2-28), 29-40] and, in rewritten form, Ezra 7:1a, 6, 11; 10; Neh. 7:73b-9:37 (C. Steuernagel, *Einleitung in das Alte Testament.* 1912). Ezra 7:12-9:15; Neh. 9:6 to ch. 10 and, in rewritten form, Neh. 7:73-9:5 (C. C. Cornill, *Einleitung in das Alte Testament.* 7th ed., 1913). Ezra 7:27 f.; 8:15-19, 21-25, 28 f., 31 f. [36]; 9:1-11a, 13-15 and perhaps, in rewritten form, Ezra 10; Neh. 8, but not Neh. 10 (L. W. Batten, *Ezra and Nehemiah* [ICC], 1913). Ezra 7-8; Neh. 8; Ezra 9-10 (J. A. Bewer, *The Literature of the Old Testament.* 1922). Ezra 7:27-8:36; Neh. 8; Ezra 9-10 (R. Kittel, *Geschichte des Volkes Israel*, Vol. III, pp. 567 f. 1929). Ezra 7-8; Neh. 7:6-9:37; Ezra 9-10 (H. H. Schaeder, *Ezra der Schreiber*, 1930). Ezra 7:11-8:36 (Neh. 8-9); Ezra 9:1-5 [6-15]; [10] (O. Eissfeldt, *Einleitung in das Alte Testament.* 1934). Ezra 7-10 and Neh. 8-9, in an expanded form (A. Lods, *Les Prophètes*, 1935).

All attempts to determine the original contents of the Ezra Memoirs must forever remain conjectural; nay, the very assumption that Ezra wrote a diary, parts of which are preserved in the Chronicler's writings, cannot be convincingly demonstrated. Serious objections have been raised against the hypothesis, still generally held, according to which Ezra 7-10; Neh. 7:73b to ch. 10, *in toto* or in part, verbatim or in an expanded form, were written by Ezra. Equally questionable is the view of S. Mowinckel (*Ezra der Skriftlaerde.* Kristiania, 1916), who asserts that Ezra 7-10 and Neh. 8 were written by a devout eyewitness of the events. In reality the Ezra stories, whether in the first or the third person, are written from beginning to end in the Chronicler's style and with his preoccupations, as C. C. Torrey has proved beyond cavil. If we remove from the stories all references to the Law, the Levites, the singers, the ritual practices of the Second Temple, and all else in which the Chronicler, writing *after* the Pentateuch was canonized (about 400 B.C.), was interested, hardly anything remains. The story, however, obviously presupposes that Ezra was active *before* the canonization of the Pentateuch.

Once it is recognized that the Ezra stories yield no historical information for the years immediately before or after Nehemiah's residence in

Jerusalem, the literary problems about the authorship, extent, and date of these narratives cease to be important. The only alternative is whether the Chronicler wrote the Ezra stories (so C. C. Torrey and G. Hölscher) or whether he edited an historical romance composed in the fourth century.[11] Unfortunately the Chronicler was so skillful that no clue remains for solving this dilemma. On the one hand, the passages in the third person (Ezra 7:1-11; 8:35 f.) added to the autobiographical accounts seem to indicate that the Chronicler has annotated an independent source; but elsewhere (as in Neh. 8-9) we gain the impression that the Chronicler himself is writing freely or at least restating in his own words the contents of a source. While we cannot exclude the possibility that the Chronicler utilized a book on Ezra, we are unable to gain the faintest notion of its contents and character.[12]

If such a story of Ezra existed, it could well have contained not only the firman of Artaxerxes in favor of Ezra (Ezra 7:12-26), but the other Aramaic documents as well (4:8-6:18). These official papers are no less unhistorical than the Ezra Memoirs and, in their present form, considerably later than the days of the Persian kings to whom they are attributed, as shown by the pervasive Jewish coloring, the characteristics of the Aramaic,[13] and their contents in general. From the point of view of literary history it is worth noting that for the first time, in extant writings, an official dossier (it does not matter that it be forged) is included verbatim in an historical work. This literary device reappears in Daniel, Esther, I Maccabees, Josephus, and later writings; but it is unknown before the Book of Ezra.

The Jewish origin of the records in Ezra 4:8-6:18 is easily recognized. But more precise inferences as to the authorship and date are precarious. It is not to be excluded a priori that the Chronicler himself wrote all this, but the current theory, according to which he incorporated in his work an Aramaic source, is more probable. Two conflicting theories on the date of this Aramaic source have been proposed. A. Klostermann

---

[11] A third possibility has been proposed by W. W. Baudissin, R. Kittel, and others: the Chronicler did not use the actual memoirs of Ezra, but a revised and amplified edition thereof. The redactor responsible for this work added the firman of Artaxerxes in Ezra 7:12-26, wrote an introduction in 7:1-11, and is chiefly responsible for Ezra 10. This view seems to complicate matters without necessity; moreover, this supposed link between original sources and the Chronicler, like the midrash which is said to have been used in I-II Chronicles, is both elusive and imaginary.

[12] It may be noted, as a minor clue to the late date of Ezra's Memoirs, that Nehemiah still uses the names of months (Neh. 1:1; 2:1) whereas Ezra, like the Chronicler, indicates them by an ordinal number (Ezra 8:31; 10:9; cf. Neh. 7:73b).

[13] The Aramaic of Ezra is obviously later than that of the Elephantine Papyri (495-400 B.C.). The linguistic evidence shows that the Aramaic portions of Ezra were written at most as early as ca. 300 B.C. (W. Baumgartner, ZAW N.F. 4 [1927] 123; cf. C. C. Torrey, G. Hölscher, Bauer and Leander, quoted ibid., n. 1) rather than in the period 400-350 (W. F. Albright, JBL 40 [1921] 119).

(*Geschichte des Volkes Israel,* pp. 212-217. 1896), followed by R. Kittel (*Geschichte des Volkes Israel,* Vol. III, pp. 602 f. [1929]) and H. H. Schaeder (*Ezra der Schreiber,* p. vi. 1930), read Ezra 4:7: "And in the days of Artaxerxes, in agreement with Mithredath, Tabeel and the rest of his companions wrote to Artaxerxes. . . ." Accordingly he regarded Ezra 4:8-6:18 as a defense of the Jews presented by Tabeel (a Jew, not an enemy of the Jews) to Artaxerxes I shortly before 446. C. C. Torrey, on the other hand, reaching radically different conclusions, dated the Aramaic source in the last years of the fourth century. He confined the Chronicler's additions to Ezra 6:9 f., 15-18 (*Ezra Studies,* p. 158. 1910), although he had previously (*Composition and Historical Value of Ezra-Nehemiah,* pp. 7-9. 1896) attributed to the Chronicler also Ezra 4:9 f., 24. The present writer is inclined to regard Professor Torrey's theory as the more plausible of the two, and believes that, in spite of his changed view, the Chronicler is responsible for the displacement of 4:7-23 before 5:1-6:15 and for the harmonistic note in 4:24.

In view of the ambiguous nature of the evidence, we cannot arrive at a definite conclusion in regard to the sources utilized by the Chronicler in writing Ezra-Nehemiah, except in regard to the manifest genuineness of Nehemiah's Memoirs. His two other alleged sources, Ezra's Memoirs and the Aramaic official papers, could well have been composed by him without using any written materials. It seems likely, however, that he transcribed at least some of the Aramaic documents from a collection circulating in his day (7:12-26, however, seems to be his own composition), rearranging the contents to suit his purposes. Moreover, although the Chronicler seems to be the author of the Ezra Memoirs, Ezra need not be a purely fictitious character. He may well have been a devout Jew living in Jerusalem in the days of Nehemiah, whose name was remembered in later generations. The Chronicler, according to his usual method (illustrated conspicuously in his fantastic portrait of King David), apparently selected Ezra for the role of founder of the guild of the scribes and concocted his fictitious biography. The scribes, or students of the Law, arose after the canonization of the Pentateuch (*ca.* 400 B.C.), not before the middle of the fourth century. Just as the Chronicler traced the Temple singers back to the time of David, so, with a slightly less glaring anachronism, he dated the beginning of general instruction back in the time when Jehoshaphat (875-851 B.C.), if we believe him, sent out a commission of princes, priests, and Levites to teach the people the "Law of the Lord" (II Chron. 17:7-9). Similarly he traced the profession of the scribes (H. *sôphēr;* New Testament: *grammateús* or *nomikós*) to Ezra, who, being both a priest and a scribe (Ezra 7:11), "had set his mind to study the Law of the Lord [the Pentateuch], and to do it, and to teach Israel statutes and ordinances" (Ezra 7:10). The scholarly and educational pursuits of the scribes, first described in some detail by Ben Sira in 180 B.C. (Ecclus. 38:24-39:11), could not be summarized better! Unfortunately, however, there could have been no such scribes in the fifth century. Ben Sira is the first to mention an organized Jewish school (*beth ha-midrash*), in the Hebrew text of Ecclus. 51:23. In conclusion, whether Ezra is a historical or an imaginary person, he could not have been a scribe and could not have written his memoirs in the form in which they have come down to us within the Chronicler's book.

Before leaving Ezra's Memoirs, the two prayers in Ezra 9:6-15 and Neh. 9:6-37 should receive special notice. J. Geissler (*Die literarischen Beziehungen der Ezramemorien insbes. zur Chronik and den hexateuch. Quellenschriften*, p. 12. Chemnitz, 1899) has noted that their diction discloses far less relation to that of the Chronicler than the narrative parts of Ezra's Memoirs. But C. C. Torrey (*Ezra Studies*, p. 246, n. 49) rightly observes that the prayers which the Chronicler intersperses in his history "consist chiefly of a tissue of quotations from Deut., which was the favorite devotional book . . . until it was finally supplanted by the Psalms." A. C. Welch (ZAW N.F. 6 [1929] 130-137; *Post-Exilic Judaism*, 1935), however, has argued that the prayer in Neh. 9 (omitting the editorial additions in vv. 1, 4 f., and perhaps 7 f.) is actually "a litany written for the worship of Northern Israel on the occasion of a day of fasting, confession and prayer," like Ps. 80, and would date it in North Israel soon after 722 B.C. He also believed that Neh. 10 was written before Cyrus's edict (538 B.C.), being the reports of a compact between the Judeans left in the homeland in 586 and the Northern Israelites who had not lost their religious and national fervor in the midst of alien settlers. The purpose of this compact was to preserve the national identity by means of religious observances and avoidance of intermarriage with foreigners (ZAW N.F. 7 [1930] 175-187). Unfortunately this identification of invaluable sources, illuminating two of the most obscure periods of the history of Israel, must remain conjectural.

The genuineness of the Memoirs of Nehemiah has never been questioned, but their extent is disputed. They are the only authentic record which the Chronicler unquestionably transcribed in Ezra-Nehemiah. Most scholars ascribe to this document Neh. 1-7; 12:27-43; 13:4-31; some omit 12:27-30, 33-36 or add 11:1 f.; 13:1-4. C. Steuernagel (*Einleitung in das Alte Testament*, p. 426. 1912) regards Neh. 1:1-7:73a; 11:1 f.; 12:31 f., 37-40; 13:4-31 and the kernel of 11:3-24 as Nehemiah's Memoirs; O. Eissfeldt (*Einleitung in das Alte Testament*, p. 589. 1934) identifies this work with Neh. 1:1-7:5; 11:1 f.; 12:27-43; 13:4-31; but L. W. Batten (*Ezra-Nehemiah* [ICC], p. 15, 1913) limits Nehemiah's contribution to Neh. 1:1-4; 1:11b-2:7; 3:33-7:5a; 13:6-31, and C. C. Torrey (*The Composition and Historical Value of Ezra-Nehemiah,* p. 50. 1896) to 1:1-2:6, 9b-20; 3:33, 34aβ-5:13a; 5:13bβ-6:19 (dating this writing tentatively in 372 B.C.).

Such differences of opinion among critics indicate that "The words of Nehemiah the son of Hecaliah" (1:1) have not been preserved intact. In their extant form they have suffered through revisions, supplements, and excisions primarily at the hand of the Chronicler when he incorporated them into his work. The recovery of the original text is inevitably tentative.

The account of Nehemiah's first visit to Jerusalem in 444 and his successful restoration of the city walls and gates is given in Neh. 1:1-7:73a; 11-12; his second visit in 432, to enforce the Law, is found in Neh. 13. We are, however, faced at once with a chronological difficulty: according to 5:14, Nehemiah was governor of Judea from 444 to 432; according to 13:6, Nehemiah received permission to visit Jerusalem a second time in 432 when, according to 5:14, he was still in Jerusalem. Obviously both these statements cannot be true, and critics are forced either to question the validity of 5:14 or to regard Nehemiah's second visit (ch. 13) as unhistorical. The first alternative seems preferable to the present writer: first of all, because Artaxerxes obviously granted Nehemiah a short leave in 444 (2:6) and nothing is said of its subsequent extension to twelve years; and secondly, because Nehemiah completed his task, the restoration of the walls, in all haste, during fifty-two days (6:15) of feverish activity. It seems likely that the original text of 5:14 was revised in accordance with 13:6, by changing "from the twentieth to the twenty-second [or twenty-first] year" into "from the twentieth to the thirty-second year." In any case the events reported during Nehemiah's first visit occupy less than one year.

Some parts of Neh. 1:1-7:73a; 11-12 seem to be contributions of the Chronicler or otherwise interpolated. Nehemiah's prayer in 1:5-11 seems to have been revised and amplified by the Chronicler. It resembles the petitions of Ezra (Ezra 9:6-15) and of Daniel (Dan. 9:4-19), which are likewise, on the whole, national confessions of sin made up of standard phrases taken generally from Deuteronomy (including its latest parts). Only the last clause in 1:6 and especially 1:11 ring true and fit the occasion.

The text of 2:6 is not intact and traces of editorial revision appear in 2:7-9a. Although the enumeration of the gates and of the portions of city walls restored (3:1-32) is an invaluable source for the topography of ancient Jerusalem (cf. H. G. Mitchell in JBL 22 [1903] 85-163), its authorship is questionable: C. C. Torrey attributes it to the Chronicler; G. Hölscher (in the Kautzsch Bible, 4th ed., 1922) regards it as an official record; L. W. Batten (*Ezra-Nehemiah* [ICC], p. 207) and M. Burrows (AASOR XIV [1934] 115-140; cf. JBL 54 [1935] 29-39; BASOR No. 64 [1936] 11-21) attribute 3:1-15 and 3:16-32 to different authors, other than

Nehemiah and the Chronicler. In any case, 3:1-32 does not seem to be an original portion of the Memoirs.

The mentions of "Samaria" in 3:34aα and of "the Congregation" in 5:13bα are characteristic retouches of the Chronicler (C. C. Torrey), whose hand is apparent in 7:1-3.

The lists of men in Ezra-Nehemiah present special problems. As we have seen, even the list of the wall builders (Neh. 3:1-32)—the least suspect of all—was probably added to Nehemiah's words. It seems likely that all the other lists were compiled by the Chronicler (cf. C. C. Torrey, *Ezra Studies*, pp. 249 f.), but whether he used official census reports or drew entirely on his imagination must remain uncertain. In any case, they cannot be used as historical sources for the Persian period. The long list of the Exiles who returned from Babylonia with Zerubbabel (Neh. 7:6-73a) reproduces with slight variations the register in Ezra 2. With a glaring inconsistency, the list, according to the introductory remarks to it (Neh. 7:4-6) is said to have been the genealogical register (discovered in the archives by Nehemiah) listing either those "who came up first" (ungrammatical gloss in 7:5b) with Zerubbabel in 538 (7:6), or the "sons of the province" (7:6), i.e., the inhabitants of Judea in the time of Nehemiah. Some critics assume that the list represents a census taken by Nehemiah, erroneously regarded by the Chronicler as a list of Exiles who had returned with Zerubbabel more than a century before. The Chronicler regarded only the returned Exiles as the true Israel and would inevitably identify the "sons of the province" in the days of Nehemiah with them or their descendants. In reality, however, the list itself is ambiguous: it is partly genealogical and partly (7:25-37) topographical (mentioning localities quite different from those in 3:1-32 and 11:25-36). The genealogical listing is suitable for a caravan of returning Exiles, as also the mention of beasts of burden (7:68 f.). On the other hand, the listing by localities, the suspension of priests from the Temple service (7:65, incongruous with reference to the time of the first return of the Exiles, for the Temple was finished in 516), the reference to the "Congregation" (7:66) rather than a caravan, all indicate a national census of Judea. Although a final verdict on this list cannot be pronounced, we may regard the Chronicler responsible for the confusion between a list of Exiles and a census of Judea, for the inappropriate insertion of the list here (in 7:4-5a Nehemiah calls an assembly for taking a census, and the story continues in ch. 11), if not for the compilation itself. Without misgivings we may attribute to him the lists contained in the Ezra Memoirs (Ezr. 8:1-14, 16, 18-20; 10:18-44), in Neh. 8:4, 7; 9:4 f.; 10:1-27 (H. 10:2-28), and within the supplements to Nehemiah's Memoirs (11:3; 11:4-19a = I Chron. 9:3-17a; 11:19b-12:26, for 11:1 f. [the sequel of 7:4-5a] should be followed by 12:27-30 [the sequel of 7:3]; 12:31-43).

We may therefore conclude that, within Neh. 1-12, "The Words of Nehemiah" are confined to 1-2; 3:33-6:19 (with some revisions in 1:5-11; 2:7-9; 3:34a; 5:13b) and possibly to a much-revised substratum in 7:1-5a; 11:1 f.; 12:31, 37-40. The rest was penned by the Chronicler who, if he had any sources besides Nehemiah's own book, has rewritten them beyond recognition.

The story of Nehemiah's second visit to Jerusalem (Neh. 13, omitting the Chronicler's introduction in 13:1-3) raises serious difficulties. It cannot be gainsaid that the style and ideas of the Chronicler appear here and there: notably in vv. 5 ("and there aforetime they used to place . . ." [to the end]), 10-14, 18, 22a, 26, 29b, 30b-31a. But, on the other hand, the vividness and concreteness of the narrative, particularly in vv. 15-27, as well as the characteristic concluding invocations to God (13:14, 22, 29, 31; cf. 5:19; 6:14) and the animosity against Sanballat and Tobiah, are entirely in the manner of Nehemiah. The present writer is therefore inclined to regard the kernel of 13:4-31 as part of Nehemiah's Memoirs (though retouched by the Chronicler) and cannot subscribe to C. C. Torrey's dictum, "the Nehemiah of 12:27-13:31 is simply Ezra (i.e., the Chronicler) under another name" (*Ezra Studies*, p. 248). For Ezra, as we know him, did not possess Nehemiah's irascible temperament, physical strength, and political authority; he could not have threatened to lay his hand upon the merchants (13:21), and actually have smitten some Jews tolerating mixed marriages and plucked out their hair (13:25)—as Nehemiah did.

Nehemiah was essentially a man of action. Deeply concerned over the plight of the pitiful Jewish community in Jerusalem, through his indomitable energy, self-denial, and shrewd unmasking of hostile plots, he brought new life to it. He enforced the stern measures required for strengthening it physically, through the restoration of the walls, socially, by improving the lot of the economically distressed classes, and nationally, by preventing its assimilation with foreigners through mixed marriages and disregard of Jewish ordinances. His passionate zeal and his rabid intolerance, his despotic methods and overbearing tactlessness, may seem objectionable, as also his concern about having his good works credited to him by God (5:19; 13:14, 22, 31). But these minor blemishes are insignificant in comparison with the magnitude of his accomplishments: he revived the dying Jewish community in Palestine and endowed it with deathless vigor.

From the literary point of view, the Memoirs of Nehemiah are something new. They are the earliest autobiography extant written by a man who was not a king, with the exception of the grave inscriptions of Egyptian nomarchs in the Middle Kingdom (translated by J. H. Breasted in his *Ancient Records of Egypt*, Vol. I, 3rd impression, Chicago, 1927).

Stylistically, as S. Mowinckel has shown (*Eucharisterion*, Vol. I, pp. 278-322. FRLANT 19, 1), Nehemiah's words are, however, more akin to the royal inscriptions of Babylonia, Assyria, Elam, North Syria, Moab (Mesha inscription), and Persia (Behistun inscription of Darius I), than with the Egyptian autobiographies. Another close parallel, we may add, is the "Apology" of Hattushil III, king of the Hittites (*ca.* 1281-1260 B.C.), edited and translated by E. H. Sturtevant and G. Bechtel (*A Hittite Chrestomathy*, pp. 42-99. Philadelphia, 1935). Nothing in the Old Testament, not even the spurious Memoirs of Ezra patterned after Nehemiah's, can be compared to Nehemiah's *apologia pro domo sua*. Like Hattushil and other ancient rulers of Western Asia, Nehemiah reports his good deeds and justifies his action before the deity, in the hope of receiving his reward. This purpose alone, apart from other basic differences, precludes a comparison with Jeremiah's confessions—mystical outpourings of a soul seeking peace in the communion with God.

When Nehemiah wrote, the Hebrew language was gradually dying out as the vernacular of the Jews (cf. Neh. 13:23 f.) and was soon to be replaced by Aramaic. His book is therefore the last Hebrew work written while this language was still living. Although he used at least three Aramaic expressions (in 2:6; 5:7, 15), his diction and grammar are notably more classical than those of the rest of Ezra-Nehemiah, where the characteristics of the Chronicler's artificial and strenuously labored Hebrew-Aramaic diction are apparent. Most appropriately, therefore, Ben Sira (180 B.C.) ended the summary of the Old Testament in his "Praise of the Fathers of Old" (Ecclus. 44:1-49:13) with Nehemiah, "who raised up our ruins and healed our breaches"; he ignored entirely the legendary figure of Ezra. Indeed, with Nehemiah an epoch came to its end—the heroic and tragic Hebrew period of the Old Testament—and a new one began: the Holy Congregation of Normative Judaism.

ABBREVIATIONS

ABBREVIATIONS

A. OLD TESTAMENT

Am.	Amos	Josh.	Joshua
Cant.	Canticles (Song of Sol.)	Judg.	Judges
Chron.	Chronicles	Kings	Kings
Dan.	Daniel	Lam.	Lamentations
Deut.	Deuteronomy	Lev.	Leviticus
Eccl.	Ecclesiastes	Mal.	Malachi
Esth.	Esther	Mic.	Micah
Ex.	Exodus	Nah.	Nahum
Ez.	Ezekiel	Neh.	Nehemiah
Ezra	Ezra	Num.	Numbers
Gen.	Genesis	Obad.	Obadiah
Hab.	Habakkuk	Pr.	Proverbs
Hag.	Haggai	Ps.	Psalms
Hos.	Hosea	Ruth	Ruth
Is.	Isaiah	Sam.	Samuel
Jer.	Jeremiah	Song	Song of Songs (Cant.)
Job	Job	Zech.	Zechariah
Joel	Joel	Zeph.	Zephaniah
Jonah	Jonah		

B. NEW TESTAMENT

Acts	Acts of the Apostles	Mark	Mark
Col.	Colossians	Matt.	Matthew
Cor.	Corinthians	Pet.	Peter
Eph.	Ephesians	Phil.	Philippians
Gal.	Galatians	Philem.	Philemon
Hebr.	Hebrews	Rev.	Revelation
Jam.	James	Rom.	Romans
John	John	Thess.	Thessalonians
Jude	Jude	Tim.	Timothy
Luke	Luke	Tit.	Titus

C. APOCRYPHA

Bar.	Baruch	Macc.	Maccabees
Bel	Bel and the Dragon	Sus.	Susanna
Ecclus.	Ecclesiasticus	Tob.	Tobit
Esd.	Esdras	Wisd.	Wisdom of Solomon
Jth.	Judith	of Sol.	

D. Pseudepigrapha

Arist.	Letter of Aristeas	Mart. Is.	Martyrdom of Isaiah
Asc. Mos.	Ascension of Moses	Ps. of Sol.	Psalms of Solomon
Enoch	Ethiopic Enoch	Sibyl.	Sibylline Oracles
Gr. Bar.	Greek Baruch	Slav. En.	Slavic Enoch
Jub.	Jubilees	Syr. Bar.	Syriac Baruch
Macc.	Maccabees	Test. XII	Testament of the XII Patriarchs

E. Miscellaneous

		ff.	following verses or pages
ad loc.	on the passage	Gr.	Greek
A.V.	Authorized Version	H.	Hebrew Bible
Beih.	Beiheft	*ibid.*	same place
Beitr.	Beitrag, Beiträge	Jud.	Judean
ca.	about	*op. cit.*	work quoted
cf.	compare	LXX	the Septuagint
ch.	chapter	Ms., Mss.	manuscript, manuscripts
cod.	codex	n.	footnote
d.	date of death	N.F., N.S.	Neue Folge, New Series
ed.	edition, editor	R.V.	Revised Version
Engl.	English	u.s.w.	etc.
Ephr.	Ephraimitic (North Israelitic)	v.	verse
		Zeit.	Zeitung
f.	following verse or page	Zeitschr.	Zeitschrift

F. Publications

AA	Alttestamentliche Abhandlungen (edited by J. Nikel). Münster i. W.		die Alttestamentliche Wissenschaft
		Bibl.	Biblica. Rome
AASOR	Annual of the American Schools of Oriental Research	BS	Bibliotheca Sacra
		BW	Biblical World
		BWANT	Beiträge zur Wissenschaft vom Alten und Neuen Testament
AFO	Archiv für Orientforschung		
AJSL	American Journal of Semitic Languages and Literatures	BWAT	Beiträge zur Wissenschaft vom Alten Testament
AJT	American Journal of Theology	BZ	Biblische Zeitschrift
		BZAW	Beih. ZAW
AO	Der Alte Orient	BZF	Biblische Zeitfragen
ARW	Archiv für Religionswissenschaft	EB	Etudes Bibliques
		EH	Exegetisches Handbuch zum Alten Testament. Münster i. W.
ATR	Anglican Theological Review		
Beih. ZAW	Beihefte zur Zeitschrift für	ET	Expository Times

Exp.	The Expositor		zum Alten Testament. Tübingen
FRLANT	Forschungen zur Religion und Literatur des Alten und Neuen Testament. Göttingen	M	Th. Mangei, *Philonis Judaei Opera Omnia*, 2 vols. Paris, 1742.
GSAI	Giornale della Società Asiatica Italiana	MGWJ	Monatschrift für Geschichte und Wissenschaft des Judentums
GTT	Gereformeerd Theologisch Tijdschrift	MVAG	Mitteilungen der Vorderasiatischen Gesellschaft
HAT	Handbuch zum Alten Testament. Tübingen	NKZ	Neue Kirchliche Zeitschrift
HKAT	Handkommentar zum Alten Testament. Göttingen	NTS	Nieuwe Theologische Studiën
HTR	Harvard Theological Review	NTT	Nieuw Theologisch Tijdschrift
HUCA	Hebrew Union College Annual, Cincinnati	OLZ	Orientalistische Literaturzeitung
ICC	International Critical Commentary. Edinburgh and New York	PEF QS	Palestine Exploration Fund, Quarterly Statement
JA	Journal Asiatique	PJ	Palästina Jahrbuch
JAOS	Journal of the American Oriental Society	PSBA	Proceedings of the Society of Biblical Archaeology
JBL	Journal of Biblical Literature and Exegesis	PTR	Princeton Theological Review
JBR	Journal of Bible and Religion	RB	Revue Biblique
		REJ	Revue des Etudes Juives
JEA	The Journal of Egyptian Archaeology	RHPR	Revue d'Histoire et de Philosophie Religieuses
JJGL	Jahrbuch für Jüdische Geschichte und Literatur	RHR	Revue de l'Histoire des Religions
		RR	Ricerche Religiose
JPOS	Journal of the Palestinian Oriental Society	RS	Revue Sémitique
		RSR	Recherches de Science Religieuse
JPT	Jahrbücher für Protestantische Theologie	RTP	Revue de Théologie et de Philosophie
JQR	Jewish Quarterly Review	STZ	Schweitzerische Theologische Zeitschrift
JR	Journal of Religion		
JRAS	Journal of the Royal Asiatic Society	Theol.	Theology
		Theol. Rundschau	Theologische Rundschau
JSOR	Journal of the Society of Oriental Research	TLZ	Theologische Literaturzeitung
JTS	Journal of Theological Studies	TQ	Theologische Quartalschrift
KAT	Kommentar zum Alten Testament. Leipzig	TSK	Theologische Studien und Kritiken
KHC	Kurzer Hand-Commentar		

TT	Theologisch Tijdschrift		Morgenländischen Gesellschaft
WC	Westminster Commentaries. London	ZDPV	Zeitschrift des Deutschen Palästina-Vereins
WZKM	Wiener Zeitschrift für die Kunde des Morgenlandes	ZNW	Zeitschrift für die Neutestamentliche Wissenschaft
ZA	Zeitschrift für Assyriologie	ZS	Zeitschrift für Semitistik
ZAW	Zeitschrift für die Alttestamentliche Wissenschaft	ZST	Zeitschrift für Systematische Theologie
ZDMG	Zeitschrift der Deutschen		

NOTE ON THE CITATION OF BIBLICAL PASSAGES

The following examples (from pp. 188 f.) illustrate the mode of citation. The English Bible is cited (except on pp. 82-4), the Hebrew verses (H.) being added when different.

a. 25:12 means "Genesis, chapter 25, verse 12." The name of the book (Gen.) is understood after a preceding mention and is regularly omitted when it is obvious; thus "Is." is omitted before references to passages in Isaiah on pp. 416-81.

b. 7:6, 11, 13 means "Genesis, chapter 7, verses 6, 11, *and* 13"; 6:9–22 means "Genesis, chapter 6, verses from 9 to 22, *inclusive*"; 10:22 f. means "Gen., ch. 10, vv. 22 and 23."

c. 27:46–28:9 means "Gen. from ch. 27, v. 46 to ch. 28, v. 9, *inclusive*."

d. 2:4a means, "Gen., the first half of v. 4 of ch. 2"; 4b would be the second half of the verse. In Hebrew the *atnach* marks the demarcation between the two halves. When a verse contains two lines of poetry, the four hemistichs are indicated by a, b, c, d. Gen. 31:18aβb means v. 18 omitting the first part (18aα) of the first half of the verse. A semicolon (;) separates different chapters or books.

e. Brackets (as in: Gen. 48:3–6, [7]) indicate secondary material.

CHAPTER AND VERSE DIFFERENCES
BETWEEN THE HEBREW AND ENGLISH
BIBLES

English	*Hebrew*	*English*	*Hebrew*
Genesis			
31:55–32:32	32:1–33		
		Deuteronomy	
Exodus		5:17–20	5:17
8:1–32	7:26–8:28	5:21–33	5:18–30
22:1–31	21:37–22:30	12:32–13:18	13:1–19
		22:30–23:25	23:1–26
Leviticus		29:1–29	28:69–29:28
6:1–30	5:20–6:23		
Numbers		**Joshua**	
16:36–17:13	17:1–28		
26:1a	25:19	21:36–37	omitted
29:40–30:16	30:1–17	21:38–45	21:36–43

English	Hebrew	English	Hebrew
I Samuel		Jonah	
19:2a	19:1b	1:17–2:10	2:1–11
20:42–21:15	21:1–16	Micah	
23:29–24:22	24:1–23	5:1–15	4:14–5:14
II Samuel		Nahum	
18:33–19:43	19:1–44	1:15–2:13	2:1–14
I Kings		Zechariah	
4:21–5:18	5:1–32	1:18–2:13	2:1–17
18:33b	18:34a	Malachi	
20:2b	20:3a	4:1–6	3:19–24
22:22a	22:21b	Psalms[1]	
22:43	22:43–44	Job	
22:44–53	22:45–54	41:1–34	40:25–41:26
II Kings		Song of Songs	
11:21–12:21	12:1–22	6:13–7:13	7:1–14
Isaiah		Ecclesiastes	
9:1–21	8:23–9:20	5:1–20	4:17–5:19
64:1–12	63:19–64:11	Daniel	
Jeremiah		4:1–37	3:31–4:34
9:1–26	8:23–9:25	5:31–6:28	6:1–29
Ezekiel		Nehemiah	
20:45–21:32	21:1–37	4:1–23	3:33–4:17
Hosea		9:38–10:39	10:1–40
1:10–2:23	2:1–25	I Chronicles	
11:12–12:14	12:1–15	6:1–81	5:27–6:66
13:16–14:9	14:1–10	II Chronicles	
Joel		2:1–18	1:18–2:17
2:28–32	3:1–5	14:1–15	13:23–14:14
3:1–21	4:1–21		

[1] In the English Bible the superscriptions of the Psalms are not counted as verses, whereas in the Hebrew they are all or part of v. 1. As a result, in the following Psalms v. 1 in the English corresponds to v. 2 of the Hebrew, and so forth (add one to the English verse to obtain the Hebrew verse): 3–9, 12, 13, 18–22, 30, 31, 34, 36, 38–42, 44–49, 53, 55–59, 61–65, 67–70, 75–77, 80, 81, 83–85, 88, 89, 92, 102, 108, 140, 142. In the following Psalms the superscription is only part of v. 1 in Hebrew, which includes also v. 1 of the English, and consequently there is no difference in the verse number: 11, 14–17, 23, 24, 29, 32, 50, 66, 73, 74, 78, 79, 82, 86, 87, 90, 98, 100, 101, 109, 110, 120–134, 139, 141, 143, 145. In Ps. 13, included in the first list, vv. 5–6 correspond to v. 6 in the Hebrew. Finally in the following Psalms the title occupies vv. 1–2 of the Hebrew and two must be added to the English verses to obtain the corresponding Hebrew ones: 51, 52, 54, 60.

SELECTED BIBLIOGRAPHY

SELECTED BIBLIOGRAPHY

~~~~~~

PART I: THE OLD TESTAMENT AS A WHOLE

A. GENERAL WORKS

1. Bibliographies

a. Comprehensive: W. M. Smith, *A List of Bibliographies of Theological and Biblical Literature published in Great Britain and America, 1595–1931.* Coatesville, Pa., 1931.

b. For publications earlier than 1905: H. L. Strack, *Einleitung in das Alte Testament.* 6th ed., Munich, 1906.

c. For publications after 1905: the current bibliographies published in Bibl., BZ, ZAW, and in the *Bibliographisches Beiblatt* of the TLZ (vol. I, the literature of 1921. Leipzig, 1922; and later volumes). J. A. Maynard, *Seven years of Old Testament Study.* A Critical Bibliograph of Old Testament Research from 1917–1924 (Reprinted from JSOR). London, 1927. E. D. Coleman, *The Bible in English Drama.* The New York Public Library, 1931. R. H. Pfeiffer, "The History, Religion, and Literature of Israel. Research in the Old Testament, 1914–1925" (HTR 27 [1934] 241–325). Beatrice L. Goff, in JBR 6 (1938) 140–143, 171 (standard books in English).

2. Encyclopedias and Bible Dictionaries

The Encyclopaedia Britannica, 11th ed., Cambridge, 1910–1911 (14th ed., New York, 1929).

THEOLOGICAL ENCYCLOPAEDIAS

a. Protestant: F. Litchtenberger, *Encyclopédie des Sciences Religieuses* (13 vols., Paris 1877–1882). J. J. Herzog, *Realenzyklopädie für Protestantische Theologie und Kirche*, 3rd ed. by A. Hauck (24 vols, Leipzig, 1896–1913). *The New Schaff-Herzog Encyclopedia of Religious Knowledge* (12 vols., New York, 1908–1912), based on the preceding work. J. Hastings, *Encyclopaedia of Religion and Ethics* (13 vols., Edinburgh and New York, 1908–1926). H. Gunkel and L. Zscharnack, *Die Religion in Geschichte und Gegenwart*, 2nd ed. (6 vols., Tübingen, 1927–1932).

b. Roman Catholic: The Catholic Encyclopaedia (16 vols., New York, 1907–1914; Suppl. I, 1922). M. Buchberger, *Lexikon für Theologie und Kirche*, 2nd ed. (10 vols. Freiburg i. B., 1930–1938).

c. Jewish: The Jewish Encyclopedia (12 vols., New York, 1901–1906). *Encyclopaedia Judaica* (10 vols., reaching from *A* to *Lyra*, Berlin, 1928–1934). *The Universal Jewish Encyclopedia.* New York, 1939 ff.

BIBLE DICTIONARIES

T. K. Cheyne and J. S. Black, *Encyclopaedia Biblica* (4 vols., London, 1899–1903). J. Hastings, *A Dictionary of the Bible* (5 vols., Edinburgh, 1898–1904; one-vol. ed., New York, 1909). F. Vigoroux, *Dictionnaire de la Bible* (5 vols., Paris, 1895–1912); 3 suppl. vols. (*A-Herméneutique*) by L. Pirot (Paris, 1928–1938; Roman Catholic). A. Westphal, *Dictionnaire encyclopédique de la Bible* (2 vols., Paris, 1932, and Valence–sur-Rhône, 1935). M. W. Jacobus, E. E. Nourse, and A. C. Zenos, *A New Standard Bible Dictionary*, 3rd ed. (New York, 1936). K. Galling, *Biblisches Reallexikon* (in HAT; Tübingen, 1935–1937). J. D. Davis, *The Westminster Dictionary of the Bible*, revised and rewritten by H. S. Gehman. Philadelphia, 1944.

MISCELLANEOUS

M. Ebert, *Reallexikon der Vorgeschichte*. 15 vols. in 16. Berlin, 1924–1932. Pauly-Wissowa, *Realenzyklopädie der klassischen Altertumswissenschaft*. New ed. by W. Kroll and K. Mittelhaus. Stuttgart, 1893 ff. W. H. Roscher, *Ausführliches Lexikon der griechischen und römische Mythologie*. Leipzig, 1884 ff.

3. Collections of Miscellaneous Monographs and "Festschriften"

Old Testament and Semitic Studies in Memory of William Rainey Harper, edited by R. F. Harper, F. Brown, and G. F. Moore. 2 vols. Chicago, 1908. *Studies in the History of Religions presented to Crawford Howell Toy*, edited by D. G. Lyon and G. F. Moore. New York, 1912. *Studien zur semitischen Philologie und Religionsgeschichte Julius Wellhausen . . . gewidmet . . .* , edited by K. Marti (Beih. ZAW 27). Giessen, 1914. *Festschrift Eduard Sachau . . . gewidmet . . .* , edited by G. Weil, Berlin, 1915. *Edouard Montet: Etudes orientales et religieuses*. Mélanges publiés à l'occasion de sa 30ᵐᵉ année de professorat. Geneva and Paris, 1917. *Festschrift Adolf Schwarz . . . gewidmet*. Berlin, 1917. *Orientalische Studien Fritz Hommel . . . gewidmet*. 2 vols. (MVAG 21 and 22). Leipzig, 1917 and 1918. *Abhandlungen zur semitischen Religionsgeschichte und Sprachwissenschaft, Wolf Wilhelm Grafen von Baudissin . . . überreicht . . .* , edited by W. Frankenberg and F. Küchler. (Beih. ZAW 33). Giessen, 1918. *Studia semitica et orientalia*, presented to Dr. James Robertson. Glasgow, 1920. F. X. Kugler, *Von Moses bis Paulus*. Münster, 1922. *Beiträge zur alttestamentliche Wissenschaft, Karl Budde . . . gewidmet . . .* ,edited by K. Marti (Beih. ZAW 34). Giessen, 1920; *Karl Budde's Schrifttum*. . . . Eine Festgabe dargebracht von der Stadt Essen . . . (Beih. ZAW 54). Giessen, 1930. *Festgabe von Fachgenossen und Freuden Adolf von Harnack . . . dargebracht*. Tübingen, 1921. *Teologiska Studier tillägnade Erik Stave*. Uppsala, 1922. *Aus Schrift und Geschichte*. Theologische Abhandlungen Adolf Schlatter . . . dargebracht. . . . Stuttgart, 1922. *Eucharisterion*. Studien zur Religion und Literatur des Alten und Neuen Testaments, Herrmann Gunkel . . . dargebracht (FRLANT XIX, 1). Göttingen, 1923. The second volume deals with the New Testament. A. S. Peake (Editor), *The People and the Book*. Oxford, 1925. *Vom Alten Testament, Karl Marti . . . gewidment . . .* , edited by K. Budde (Beih, ZAW 41). Giessen, 1925. *Studier tilegenede Frants Buhl . . .* , edited by J. Jacobsen. Kopenhagen, 1925. Societas Orientalis Fennica. *Studia Orientalia*, vol. I (dedicated to Knut Tallqvist). Helsingfors, 1925. *Hebrew Union College Jubilee Volume* (1875–1925), edited by D. Philipson and others. Cincinnati, 1925. *Oriental Studies published in Commemoration of the fortieth Anniversary (1883–1923) of Paul Haupt as Director of the Oriental Seminary of the Johns Hopkins University*, edited by C. Adler and

A. Ember. Baltimore, 1926. *Old Testament Essays*, edited by D. C. Simpson. London, 1927. *Beiträge zur Religionsgeschichte und Archäologie Palästinas, Ernst Sellin . . . dargebracht*, edited by A. Jirku. Leipzig, 1927. *Jewish Studies in Memory of Israel Abrahams*, by . . . the Jewish Institute of Religion. New York, 1927. R. H. Kennett, *Old Testament Essays*. Cambridge, 1928. *Zum Sechzigjährigen Bestehen der Hochschule für die Wissenschaft des Judentums in Berlin* (Bericht 49). Berlin, 1931. *Aus Fünfzig Jahren deutscher Wissenschaft . . . , Friedrich Schmidt-Ott . . . überreicht*, edited by G. Abb. Berlin, 1930. *The Macdonald Presentation Volume*. Studies in Biblical Criticism, Ancient History, and Religion form a Volume of Tribute to Dr. Duncan Black Macdonald. Princeton University Press, 1933. *Festschrift Otto Procksch . . . überreicht*. Leipzig, 1934. *Miscellanea Biblica edita a Pontificio Instituto Biblico ad celebrandum annum XXV ex quo conditum est Institutum (1909–1934)*. Vol. I: Biblica 15, 1934; vols II and III, Rome, 1934. *Annuaire de l'Institut de Philologie et d'Histoire Orientales et Slaves IV: Mélanges Franz Cumont*. Paris, 1936. *Werden und Wesen des Alten Testaments*. Vorträge . . . zu Göttingen vom 4.–10. September, 1935, edited by J. Hempel and others (Beih. ZAW 66). Berlin, 1936. *Quantulacumque*. Studies presented to Kirsopp Lake . . . , edited by R. P. Casey, Silva Lake, and Agnes K. Lake. London, 1937. *Record and Revelation*. Essays on the Old Testament . . . , edited by H. Wheeler Robinson. Oxford, 1938. *The Old Testament*. Papers read at the Summer School of Catholic Studies held at Cambridge. . . . London, 1939. *The Study of the Bible Today and Tomorrow*, edited by H. R. Willoughby. The University of Chicago Press, 1947.

4. History of Biblical Interpretation and Criticism

W. Bacher, *Die Bibelexegese der Jüdischen Religionsphilosophen des Mittelalters vor Maimuni*. Strassburg, 1892. T. K. Cheyne, *Founders of O. T. Criticism*. London, 1893. A. Duff, *History of Old Testament Cricitism*. New York, Putnam's, 1910. E. McQ. Gray, *Old Testament Criticism: Its Rise and Progress*. New York, 1923. C. C. Torrey, *The Jewish Foundations of Islam*. London and New York, 1933. S. Rosenblatt, *The Interpretation of the Bible in the Mishna*. Johns Hopkins University Publications, 1935. A. Vis, *An Inquiry into the Rise of Christianity out of Judaism*. Amsterdam, 1936. Beryl Smalley, *The Study of the Bible in the Middle Ages*. Oxford, 1941. J. Coppens, *Histoire critique des livres de l'Ancien Testament*, 3rd edition. Bruges, Desclée and de Brouwer, 1942. (English translation: *The Old Testament and Its Critics*. Paterson, N. J., 1942). Sh. E. Johnson, "The Biblical Quotations in Matthew" (HTR 36 [1943] 135–153). C. W. Dugmore (editor), *The Interpretation of the Bible*. London, 1944. J. Guillet, "Les exégèses d'Alexandrie et d'Antioche: conflit ou malentendu?" (RSR 34 [1947] 257–302). R. M. Grant, "The Bible of Theophilus of Antioch" (JBL 66 [1947] 173–196). H. A. Wolfson, *Philo*. 2 vols. Harvard University Press, 1947.

B. BIBLE EDITIONS

British Museum, *Catalogue of Printed Books: Bible*. Three parts and appendix. London, 1892–99. T. H. Darlow and H. F. Moule, *Historical Catalogue of Printed Editions of the Holy Scriptures in the Library of the British and Foreign Bible Society*. Two vols. London, 1903 ff.

1. Hebrew Texts

R. Kittel, *Biblia Hebraica*, Leipzig, 1906; 3rd ed. (giving Ben Asher's text edited by P. Kahle) edited by A. Alt and O. Eissfeldt. Stuttgart, 1929–1937. C. D. Ginsburg, *The Old Testament diligently revised according to the Massorah and the Early Editions, with the Various Readings from Manuscripts and the Ancient Versions.* 4 vols. London, 1926. S. Baer and Franz Delitzsch have edited the individual Biblical books (except Ex.-Deut.) according to the Masoretic text. Leipzig, 1869–1895. P. Haupt (Editor), *The Sacred Books of the Old Testament. A critical Edition of the Hebrew Text printed in colors, with notes.* Leipzig, 1893 ff. Gen. (C. J. Ball, 1896), Lev. (S. R. Driver and H. A. White, 1894), Num. (J. A. Paterson, 1895), Josh. (W. H. Bennett, 1895), Judg. (G. F. Moore, 1900), Sam. (K. Budde, 1894), Kings (B. Stade, 1904), Is. (T. K. Cheyne, 1899), Jer. (C. H. Cornill, 1895), Ez. (C. H. Toy, 1899), Ps. (J. Wellhausen, 1895), Prov. (A. Müller and E. Kautzsch, 1901), Job (C. Siegfried, 1893), Dan. (A. Kamphausen, 1896), Ezra-Neh. (H. Guthe and L. W. Batten, 1901), Chron. (R. Kittel, 1895).

2. Modern Critical Versions

P. Haupt (Editor), *The Sacred Books of the Old Testament. A New English Translation.* New York, 1898 ff. The translators are identical with the editors of the Hebrew text in the preceding work. Lev. (1898), Josh. (1899), Judg. (1898), Is. (1898), Ez. (1899), Ps. (1898). Revisions of the Authorized (or "King James") Version of 1611: English Revised (Oxford, 1885; revised Apocrypha, 1895); American Revised (New York, 1900–1901); *The Holy Scriptures: A New Translation* (Philadelphia, The Jewish Publication Society of America, 1917). *The Holy Bible, edited with Various Renderings and Readings from the best Authorities,* by T. K. Cheyne, S. R. Driver, R. I. Clarke, A. Goodwin, W. Sanday. 3rd ed., London, 1891 (known as the "Variorum Bible"). The "Variorum Apocrypha" were edited by C. J. Ball (London, 1892). H. E. Monser published a similar edition, with "variorum readings and renderings," of the American Revised Bible (*The Cross Reference Bible,* Champaign, Ill., 1910). James Moffatt, *The Old Testament: A New Translation.* New York, 1922. *The Old Testament: An American Translation,* edited by J. M. P. Smith. Chicago, 1927. *The Apocrypha: An American Translation,* by E. J. Goodspeed. Chicago, 1938. E. Kautzsch (Editor), *Die Heilige Schrift des Alten Testaments.* 2 vols. 3rd ed., Tübingen, 1909; 4th ed. edited by A. Bertholet, 1923. *La Sainte Bible, traduction nouvelle* (Bible du Centenaire). Paris, 1916 ff.

C. COMMENTARIES

1. In English

The *International Critical Commentary* (ICC) began to appear at Edinburgh and New York in 1895 and still lacks Ex., Lev., Josh., Kings (the latter has been prepared in manuscript by J. A. Montgomery), Is. 28–66, Jer., and Ruth-Canticles-Lam. It is the most thorough and technical in English. Volumes available: Gen. (J. Skinner, 1910; 2nd ed., 1930), Num. (G. B. Gray, 1903; 2nd ed., 1912), Deut. (S. R. Driver, 1895; 3rd ed., 1902), Judg. (G. F. Moore, 1895), Sam. (H. P. Smith, 1899), Is. 1–27 (G. B. Gray, 1912), Ez. (G. A. Cooke, 2 vols., 1937), Am. and Hos. (W. R. Harper, 1905), Mic.-Joel (J. M. P. Smith, W. H. Ward, and J. A. Bewer, 1911), Hag.-Mal. and Jonah (H. G. Mitchell, J. M. P. Smith, and J. A. Bewer, 1912), Ps. (C. A. Briggs, 2 vols., 1906–1907), Prov. (C. H. Toy, 1899), Job (S. R. Driver and G. B. Gray, 2 vols., 1921), Eccl. (G. A. Barton, 1905), Esth. (L. B. Paton, 1908), Dan. (J. A. Montgomery, 1927), Ezra-Neh. (L. W. Batten, 1913), Chron. (E. L. Curtis, 1910). The following volumes of the *Westminster Commentaries* (WC), edited by W. Lock and D. C. Simpson (London, Methuen) have appeared: Gen. (S. R. Driver, 2nd ed., 1904), Ex. (A. H. McNeile, 1908), Num. (L. E Binns, 1927), Is. (G. W. Wade;

1912), Jer. (L. E. Binns, 1919), Ez. (H. A. Redpath, 1907), Hos. (S. L. Brown, 1932), Am. (G. A. Cooke, 1914), Mic., Obad., Joel, Jonah (G. W. Wade, 2 vols., 1906, 1925), Zeph., Nah., Hab. (G. G. V. S. Stonehouse and G. W. Wade, 1929), Ps. (W. E. Barnes, 2 vols., 1931), Prov. (W. O. E. Oesterley, 1929), Job (E. C. S. Gibson, 1899), II (IV) Esdr. (W. O. E. Oesterley, 1933). The following commentaries (all complete) are briefer and more popular: *The Expositor's Bible,* edited by W. R. Nicoll (London, Hodder and Stoughton, 1887 ff.). *The Cambridge Bible for Schools and Colleges,* edited by A. F. Kitrkpatrick (Cambridge University Press, 1880 ff.). *The New Century Bible,* edited by W. F. Adeney (Edinburgh and New York, 1904 ff.). In one volume: *The Abingdon Bible Commentary* (Edited by F. C. Eiselen and others). New York, 1929.

2. In German and Dutch

Kurzgefasstes exegetisches Handbuch zum Alten Testament, 17 vols. (Leipzig, 1838 ff.): Gen. (A. Knobel; 6th ed. by A. Dillmann, 1892), Ex.-Lev. (Knobel; 2nd ed. by Dillmann, 1880; 3rd ed. by V. Ryssel, 1897), Num., Deut., Josh. (Knobel; 2nd ed. by Dillmann, 1886), Judg., Ruth (E. Bertheau, 2nd ed., 1883), Sam. (O. Thenius; 3rd ed. by M. Löhr, 1898), Kings (Thenius, 2nd ed., 1873), Is. (Knobel; 5th ed. by Dillmann, 1890; 6th ed. by R. Kittel, 1898), Jer. (F. Hitzig, 2nd ed., 1866), Ez. (Hitzig; 2nd ed. by R. Smend, 1880), XII Prophets (Hitzig; 4th ed. by H. Steiner, 1881), Ps. (J. Olshausen, 1853), Job (L. Hirzel; 4th ed. by Dillmann, 1891), Prov. (Bertheau) and Eccles. (Hitzig; 2nd ed. of both by W. Nowack, 1883), Cant. (Hitzig) and Lam. (Thenius, 1855), Dan. (Hitzig, 1850), Ezra-Neh. and Esth. (Bertheau, 1862; 2nd ed. by Ryssel, 1887), Chron. (Bertheau, 2nd ed., 1874). *Biblischer Commentar über das Alte Testament,* by C. F. Keil (Gen.-Judg., Ruth, Sam., Kings, Jer., Lam., Ez., XII Prophets, Esth., Ezra-Neh., Chron.) and Franz Delitsch (the rest). Leipzig, 1861–1893. *Kurzgefasster Kommentar zu den heiligen Schriften des Alten (und Neuen) Testamentes, sowie zu den Apokryphen,* edited by H. L. Strack and O. Zöckler, Munich, 1886 ff. Gen.-Num. (Strack, 1894), Deut.-Judg. (S. Öttli, 1893), Sam. and Kings (A. Klostermann, 1887), Is. and Jer. (C. von Orelli, 3rd ed., 1904 and 1905), Ez. and XII Prophets (von Orelli, 2nd ed., 1896), Ps. (H. Kessler, 1899), Prov. (Strack, 2nd ed., 1899), Job and Eccles. (W. Volck, 1889), Cant. and Lam. (Öttli, 1889), Esth, and Ezra-Chron. (Öttli, 1889), Dan. (J. Meinhold, 1889), Apocrypha (Zöckler, 1891). *Handkommentar zum Alten Testament* (HKAT), edited by W. Nowack. Göttingen, 1892 ff. Gen. (H. Gunkel, 3rd ed., 1910; 4th ed., 1917; 5th ed., 1922; English translation of the introduction: *The Legends of Genesis,* 1901), Ex.-Num. (B. Baentsch, 1903), Deut. and Josh. (C. Steuernagel, 2nd ed., 1923), Judg. and Ruth (Nowack, 1900), Sam. (Nowack, 1902), Kings (R. Kittel, 1900), Is. (B. Duhm, 4th ed., 1923), Jer. (F. Giesebrecht, 2nd ed., 1907), Ez. (R. Kraetzschmar, 1900), XII Prophets (Nowack, 3rd ed., 1922), Ps. (F. Bäthgen, 3rd ed., 1904; 4th ed., H. Gunkel, 1926), Prov. (W. Frankenberg, 1898), Job (K. Budde, 2nd ed., 1913), Eccles. and Cant. (C. Siegfried, 1898), Lam. (M. Löhr, 2nd ed., 1907), Dan. (G. Behrmann, 1894), Ezra-Neh. and Esth. (Siegfried, 1901), Chron. (R. Kittel, 1902). *Kurzer Hand-Commentar zum Alten Testament* (KHC), edited by K. Marti. Freiburg and, later, Tübingen, 1897–1903. Gen.-Num. (H. Holzinger, 1898–1903), Lev. and Deut. (A. Bertholet, 1901 and 1899), Josh. (Holzinger, 1901), Judg. and Sam. (K. Budde, 1897 and 1902), Kings (I. Benzinger, 1899), Is. and XII Prophets (Marti, 1900 and 1904), Jer. (B. Duhm, 1901), Ez. (Bertholet, 1897), Ps. and Job (Duhm, 2nd ed. of Ps., 1922; Job, 1897), Prov. (G. Wildeboer, 1897), Cant.-Esth. (Budde, Bertholet, and Wildeboer, 1898), Dan. (Marti, 1901), Ezra.-Neh. (Bertholet, 1902), Chron. (Benzinger, 1901). *Kommentar zum Alten Testament* (KAT), edited by E. Sellin, Leipzig, 1913 ff. Gen. (O. Procksch, 2nd and 3rd ed., 1923), Deut. (E. König, 1917), Sam.

(W. Caspari, 1925), Is. 1–39 (Procksch, 1930), Is. 40–66 (P. Volz, 1932), Jer. (Volz. 2nd ed., 1928), Ez. (J. Herrmann, 1924), XII Prophets (Sellin, 2nd and 3rd ed., 2 vols., 1929 and 1930), Ps. (R. Kittel, 5th and 6th ed., 1929), Ruth and Lam. (W. Rudolph, 2 vols., 1939), Eccles. (H. W. Hertzberg, 1932), I Chron. (J. W. Rothstein and J. Hänel, 2 vols., 1927). *Handbuch zum Alten Testament* (HAT), edited by O Eissfeldt. Tübingen, 1935 ff. Ex. (G. Beer, 1939), Josh. (M. Roth, 1937), Jer. (W. Rudolph, 1947), Ez. (A. Bertholet and K. Galling, 1937), Hos.-Mic. (T. H. Robinson, 1936), Nah.-Mal. (F. Horst, 1938), Ps. (H. Schmidt, 1934), Prov. (B. Gemser, 1937), Job (G. Hölscher, 1937), the Five Scrolls (Ruth, Cant., Lam., Esth. by M. Haller; Eccl. by K. Galling), Dan. (A. Bentzen, 1937), Wisdom of Solomon (J. Fichtner, 1938). *Die Schriften des Alten Testaments in Auswahl*, by H. Gunkel, W. Staerk, P. Volz, H. Gressmann, and M. Haller. 7 vols. Latest ed., Göttingen, 1921–25. *Text en Vitleg*, edited by F. M. T. Böhl and van Veldhuisen. Groningen, den Haag, 1928 ff. Roman Catholic commentaries: *Exegetisches Handbuch zum Alten Testament* (EH), edited by J. Nikel and A. Schulz. Münster, 1911 ff. Judg. (V. Zapletal, 1923), Sam. (A. Schulz, 2 vols., 1919 and 1920), Kings (A. Šanda, 2 vols., 1911 and 1912), Is. (F. Feldmann, 2 vols., 1925 and 1926), Job (N. Peters, 1928), Tobit (Schumpp, 1933), Ecclus. of Sirach (Peters, 1913), Wisd. of Sol. (P. Heinisch, 1912). *Die Heilige Schrift des Alten Testaments* (HS), edited by F. Feldmann and H. Herkenne Bonn, 1923 ff. Gen. and Ex. (P. Heinisch, 1930 and 1934), Deut. (H. Junker, 1933), Josh. (A. Schulz, 1924), Judg. and Ruth (Schulz., 1926), Sam. (K. L. Leimbach, 1936), Kings (S. Landersdorfer, 1927), Is. (J. Fischer, 2 vols., 1937 and 1939), Jer. (F. Nötscher, 1934), Ez. (P. Heinisch, 1923), XII Prophets (vol. I: J. Lippl and J. Theis, 1937; vol. II: H. Junker, 1938), Prov. (H. Wiesman, 1923), Job (P. Szczygiel, 1931), Cant. (A. Miller, 1927), Eccles. (A. Allgeier, 1925), Dan. (J. Göttsberger, 1928), Chron. (J. Göttsberger, 1939), I and II Macc. (H. Bévenot, 1931), Ecclus. of Sirach (A. Eberharter, 1925), Wisd. of Sol. (F. Feldmann, 1926), Baruch and Epistle of Jer. (E. Kalt, 1932).

3. In French (Roman Catholic)

Etudes Bibliques (EB). Paris, 1903 ff. Judg. (M. J. Lagrange, 1903), Sam. (P. Dhorme, 1910), Is. (A. Condamin, 1905), Jer. (Condamin, 3rd ed., 1936), the XII Prophets (A. van Hoonacker, 1908), Job (Dhorme, 1926), Cant. (G. Pouget and J. Guitton, 1934), Eccles. (E. Podechard, 1912). The series includes books on the archaeology and geography of Palestine; ethnographic studies (A. Jaussen, *Coutumes des Arabes au pays de Moab*, 1908); studies on ancient religions (Lagrange, *Etudes sur les religions sémitiques*, 2nd ed., 1905; *Le Messianisme chez les Juifs*, 1909; *Le Judaïsme avant Jésus Christ*, 1931); etc.

4. In Latin (Roman Catholic)

R. Cornely, J. Knabenbauer, F. de Hummelauer (Editors), *Cursus Scripturae Sacrae*. Latest ed., Paris, 1908–1938.

D. History of the Text and of the Canon

F. Buhl, *Kanon und Text des Alten Testaments*. Leipzig, 1891. English translation: *Canon and Text of the Old Testament*. Edinburgh, 1892. W. F. Lofthouse, *The Making of the Old Testament*. London, 1915.

1. Text and Versions

A. Loisy, *Histoire critique du texte et des versions de la Bible*. 2 vols. Paris, 1892 and 1895. C. D. Ginsburg, *Introduction to the Massoretico-Critical Edition of the Hebrew Bible*. London, 1897. E. Nestle, "Urtext und Übersetzungen der Bibel" (in *Realenzyklopädie für Protestantische Theologie und Kirche*, vol. III, pp. 1–179, 1897). A. S. Geden, *Outlines of Introduction to the Hebrew Bible*. Edinburgh, 1909. T. A. Fernández, *Breve introducción a la critica textual de Antiguo Testamento*. Rome, 1917. A. F. Truyols, *Estudios de critica textual y leteraria*. Rome, 1917. H. B. Swete, *An Introduction to the Old Testament in Greek*. Cambridge, 1900; 2nd ed., 1902; revised by R. R. Oettley, 1914. J. Vandervorst, *Introduction aux textes hébreu et grec de l'Ancien Testament*. Malines, 1935. H. Wheeler Robinson (editor), *The Bible in its Ancient and English Versions*. Oxford University Press, 1940. F. Kenyon, *Our Bible and the Ancient Manuscripts*. New York 1940.

2. History of the Cannon

J. Fürst, *Der Kanon des Alten Testaments*. Leipzig, 1868. G. Wildeboer, *The Origin of the Canon of the Old Testament* (translated by B. W. Bacon). London, 1895. H. E. Ryle, *The Canon of the Old Testament*. London and New York, 1892; 2nd ed., 1895. *Philo and Holy Scripture*. London, 1895. W. Robertson Smith, *The Old Testament in the Jewish Church*. Edinburgh and London, 1881; 2nd ed., 1892; 3rd ed., 1926. K. Budde, "Canon: Old Testament" (in *Encyclopaedia Biblica* I [1899] 647–674). G. F. Moore, "The Definition of the Jewish Canon and the Repudiation of Christian Scriptures" (in *Essays in Modern Theology and Related Subjects: A Testimonial to C. A. Briggs*, pp. 99–125. New York, 1911). M. L. Margolis, *The Hebrew Scriptures in the Making*. Philadelphia, 1922. W. R. Arnold, "Observations on the Origins of Holy Scripture" (in JBL 42 [1923] 1–21). S. Zeitlin, *A Historical Study of the Canonization of the Hebrew Scriptures* (in *Proceedings* of the American Academy for Jewish Research 3 [1932] 121–158).

E. INTRODUCTIONS TO THE OLD TESTAMENT

1. Detailed

A. IN ENGLISH

S. Davidson, *An Introduction to the Old Testament*. 3 vols. London, 1862–1863. S. R. Driver, *An Introduction to the Literature of the Old Testament*. Edinburgh, 1891; 7th ed., 1898 (later reprints). German translation by J. W. Rothstein (Berlin, 1896). C. A. Briggs, *General Introduction to the Study of Holy Scripture*. London, 1899. C. H. Cornill, *Introduction to the Canonical Books of the Old Testament* (translated from the 5th German ed. by G. H. Box). New York, 1907. H. Creelman, *An Introduction to the Old Testament chronologically arranged*. New York, 1917. L. W. Batten, *The Old Testament*. Sewanee, 1917. F. C. Eiselen, *Biblical Introduction Series: The Pentateuch*, New York, 1916; *The Prophetic Books*, 2 vols., 1923; *The Psalms and other Sacred Writings*, 1918. W. O. E. Oesterley and T. H. Robinson, *An Introduction to the Books of the Old Testament*. London, 1934. J. E. Steinmueller, *A Companion to Scripture Studies*. 3 vols. New York, 1941–43 (Roman Catholic).

B. IN GERMAN AND OTHER LANGUAGES

A. Kuenen, *Historisch-critisch Onderzoek naar het onstaan en de verzameling van den Bocken des Ouden Verbonds*. 3 vols. Leiden, 1861–1865; 2nd ed., 1885–1893. German translation of Weber and Müller: *Historisch-kritische Einleitung*, u.s.w. Leipzig, 1887–1894.   F. Bleek, *Einleitung in das Alte Testament*. 4th ed. by J. Wellhausen (who wrote the parts on Judg.-Kings, Canon and Text, and the history of Old Testament research). Berlin, 1878.   C. H. Cornill, *Einleitung in die Kanonischen Bücher des Alten Testaments*. Tübingen, 1891; 7th ed., 1913. English translation (cf. above). E. König, *Einleitung in das Alte Testament mit Einschluss der Apokryphen und der Pseudepigraphen Alten Testaments*. Bonn, 1893.   F. Vigoroux, *Manuel Bibilique . . . à l'usage des Seminaires*. 2 vols. Paris, 10th ed., 1897; 14th ed. (by M. Bacuez and A. Bressac), 1917–1920 (Roman Catholic).   F. Kaulen, *Einleitung in die Heilige Schrift des Alten und Neuen Testamentes*. Freiburg, 1876–1881; 5th ed. by G. Hoberg, 1911 (Roman Catholic). W. W. Baudissin, *Einleitung in die Bücher des Alten Testamentes*. Leipzig, 1901.   C. Steuernagel, *Lehrbuch der Einleitung in das Alte Testament, mit einem Anhang über die Apokryphen und Pseudepigraphen*. Tübingen, 1912.   L. Gautier, *Introduction à l'Ancien Testament*. Lausanne, 1906; 3rd ed., 1939. H. Höpfl, *Introductionis in sacros utriusque Testamenti libros Compendium*. 2 vols. Rome, 1922; Subiaco, 1921; 5th ed., Rome, 1931–46. (Roman Catholic).   J. Nikel, *Grundriss der Einleitung in das Alte Testament*. Münster. 1924 (Roman Catholic).   J. Göttsberger, *Einleitung in das Alte Testament* (Herder's Theologische Grundrisse). Freiburg i.B., 1928 (Roman Catholic).   R. Cornely, *Introductionis in S. Scripturae libros Compendium*. 2 vols. 10th ed. by A. Merk, Paris, 1930; 12th ed., 1940.   In French (translated from the 9th ed.), 2nd ed.; Paris, 1930 (Roman Catholic).   O. Eissfeldt, *Einleitung in das Alte Testament, unter Einschluss der Apokryphen und Pseudepigraphen*. Tübingen, 1934.   W. Möller, *Einleitung in das Alte Testament*. Zwickau, 1934.   O. Weber, *Bibelkunde des Alten Testaments*. 2 vols. Berlin, 1935; new ed., 1936.   M. Thilo, *Alttestamentliche Bibelkunde*. Stuttgart, 1935.

2. Concise

A. IN ENGLISH

J. E. McFadyen, *Introduction to the Old Testament*. London, 1905; 2nd ed., London, 1932 (New York, 1933).   G. F. Moore, *The Literature of the Old Testament* (Home University Library). London and New York, 1913. Italian translation by A. Pincherle (Bari, 1924).   G. B. Gray, *A Critical Introduction to the Old Testament*. London and New York, 1913; 2nd ed., 1919.   E. B. Redlich, *An Introduction to Old Testament Study*. London, 1920.   E. Sellin, *Introduction to the Old Testament*. Translated from the German by W. Montgomery. London, 1923.   G. H. Box, *A Short Introduction to the Literature of the Old Testament*. 4th ed., London, 1924.   H. R. Purinton, *Literature of the Old Testament*. New York, 1924.   I. G. Matthews, *Old Testament Life and Literature*. New ed., New York, 1934.   S. A. Cook, *The Old Testament: A Reinterpretation*. London and New York, 1936.   H. Wheeler Robinson, *The Old Testament: Its Making and its Meaning*. Nashville, 1937.   Mary Ellen Chase, *The Bible and the Common Reader*. New York, 1944.   S. A. A. Cartledge, *A Conservative Introduction to the Old Testament*. Second edition. University of Georgia Press, 1944.   L. B. Longacre, *The Old Testament: Its Forms and Purpose*. New York and Nashville, 1945.

B. IN GERMAN AND OTHER LANGUAGES

H. L. Strack, *Einleitung in das Alte Testament, einschlisslich Apokryphen und Pseudepigraphen*. Munich, 1883; 6th ed., 1906.   E. Sellin, *Einleitung in das Alte Testament*. Leipzig, 1910; 7th ed., 1935. English translation (cf. above).   M. Löhr, *Einführung in das Alte Testament* (Wissenschaft und Bildung, 102). Leipzig, 1912.   W. Staerk, *Die Entstehung des Alten Testamentes* (Sammlung Göschen). Berlin and Leipzig, 1912; 2nd ed., 1918.   P. Thomsen, *Das Alte Testament. Seine Entstehung und seine Geschichte*

(Aus Natur und Geisterwelt, 669). Leipzig and Berlin, 1918. J. Meinhold, *Einführung in das Alte Testament: Geschichte, Literatur und Religion Israels*. Giessen, 1919; 3rd ed., 1932. E. Montet, *Histoire de la Bible* (Collection Payot). Paris, 1924. G. Beer, *Kurze Übersicht über den Inhalt der Alttestamentlichen Schriften*. Tübingen, 1926; 2nd ed., 1932. A Hudal, *Kurze Einleitung in die Heiligen Bücher des Alten Testamentes*. 4th and 5th ed. by J. Ziegler. Graz, 1936 (Roman Catholic). A. Weiser, *Einleitung in das Alte Testament*. Stuttgart, 1939.

3. Recent Bibliographies (including literary histories of the Old Testament and books on special topics)

W. Baumgartner, "Wellhausen und der heutige Stand der alttestamentlichen Wissenschaft" (*Theol. Rundschau* N.F. 2 [1930] 287–307); "Alttestamentliche Einleitung under Literaturgeschichte" (*ibid.* 8 [1936] 179–222). E. Klostermann, "Alttestamentliche Literatur," Part I (*Theol. Rundschau* N.F. 9 [1937] 313–328). O. Eissfeldt, "Die literarkritische Arbeit am Alten Testament in den letzen 12 Jahren" (*Theol. Rundschau* N.F. 10 [1938] 255–328); in English: H. Wheeler Robinson (editor), *Record and Revelation*, pp. 74–109. Oxford, 1938. H. H. Rowley, "Introduction to the Old Testament" (in T. T. Manson [editor], *A Companion to the Bible*, pp. 31–77. Edinburgh, 1939).

F. Literary Histories of the Old Testament

1. In English

E. Kautzsch, *An Outline of the History of the Literature of the Old Testament* (translated from the German by J. Taylor). New York and London, 1899. H. T. Fowler, *A History of the Literature of Ancient Israel*. New York, 1912. J. A. Bewer, *The Literature of the Old Testament in its Historical Development* (Records of Civilization: Sources and Studies). New York, 1922; 2nd ed., 1933. H. M. Chadwick and N. K. Chadwick, *The Growth of Literature*. Vol. 2, pp. 629–777. Cambridge, 1936.

2. In German and Other Languages

T. Nöldeke, *Die Alttestamentliche Literatur in einer Reihe von Aufsätzen dargestellt*. Leipzig, 1867. French translation: Paris, 1873. G. Wildeboer, *De letterkunde des Ouden Verbonds*, etc. Groningen, 1893; 3rd ed., 1905. German translation by Risch: *Die Litteratur des Alten Testaments*. Göttingen, 1895; 2nd ed., 1905. H. Gunkel, "Die Israelitische Literatur," in *Die Orientalischen Literaturen* (Kultur der Gegenwart, I, 7). Berlin and Leipzig, 1906; 2nd ed., 1925. K. Budde, *Geschichte der althebräischen Litteratur; Apokryphen und Pseudepigraphen*, von A. Bertholet (Die Litteraturen des Ostens in Einzelndarstellungen). Leipzig, 1906; 2nd ed., 1909. S. Bernfeld, *Die Jüdische Literatur*. Part I: Bibel, Apokryphen und jüdisch-hellenistisches Schriftum. Berlin, 1921. Also in Hebrew: 2 vols., 1923. J. Hempel, *Die Althebräische Literatur und ihr hellenistisch-jüdisches Nachleben* (Handbuch der Literaturwissenschaft). Wildpark-Potsdam, 1930–1934.

G. History of Israel

1. In English

H. Ewald, *History of Israel* (translation of *Geschichte des Volkes Israel*, 8 vols., 3rd ed. 1864–1868). London, 1869–1883. J. Wellhausen, "Israel" in *Eycyclopaedia Britannica*,

9th ed., 1875–1889; published with his *Prolegomena* as a separate volume: *Prolegomena to the History of Israel*. Edinburgh, 1885. E. Renan, *History of Israel*, 5 vols., 1888–1895 (translation of *Histoire du peuple d'Israel*, 5 vols., Paris, 1887–1893). R. Kittel, *History of the Hebrews* (from the German). 2 vols. 1895. C. F. Kent, *History of the Hebrew People* (2 vols.) and *History of the Jewish People* (2 vols., the second by J. S. Riggs). New York, 1896–1900. G. W. Wade, *Old Testament History*. New York, 1901; 5th ed., 1908. H. P. Smith, *Old Testament History*. New York, 1903. I. J. Peritz, *Old Testament History*. New York, 1915. C. Noyes, *The Genius of Israel*. Boston, 1924. S. A. Cook, in the *Cambridge Ancient History*. Cambridge, 1923 ff. Vol. II (1924); vol. III (1925); vol. VI (1927). A. T. Olmstead, *History of Palestine and Syria to the Macedonian Conquest*. New York, 1931. K. Galling, "Geschichte Israels" (*Theol. Rundschau* N.F. 2 [1930] 94–128). Bibliography. W. O. E. Oesterley and T. H. Robinson, *A History of Israel*, 2 vols. Oxford, 1932. A Lods, *Israel from its Beginning to the Middle of the Eighth Century*. London, 1932; *The Prophets and the Rise of Judaism*. New York, 1937. Titles of the French original volumes (in the series, "Evolution de l'Humanité"): *Israël des origines au milieu du VIIIᵉ siècle*. Paris, 1930; *Les Prophètes et le débuts du Judaïsme*. Paris, 1935. W. L. Wardle, *The History and Religion of Israel* (The Clarendon Bible, vol. I). Oxford, 1936. E. W. K. Mould, *Essentials of Bible History*. New York, 1939.

2. In German and Other Languages

B. Stade, *Geschichte des Volkes Israel*. 2 vols. Berlin, 1887–1888. Part of vol. II by O. Holzmann. J. Wellhausen, *Israelitische und jüdische Geschichte*. Berlin, 1894; 7th ed., 1914. E. Meyer, *Geschichte des Altertums*. 5 vols. Stuttgart, 1884–1902. 2nd and 3rd ed. of vols. I–III (in 5 vols.), 1910–1937. H. Guthe, *Geschichte des Volkes Israel*. Tübingen, 1899; 3rd ed., 1914. R. Kittel, *Geschichte des Volkes Israel*. 2 vols. Gotha, 1888, 1892; 7th ed., Stuttgart, 1932, 1925. Vol. III, 1927, 1929. L. Desnoyers, *Histoire du peuple Hébreu des Juges à la captivité*. 3 vols. Paris, 1922–1930. A Jirku, *Geschichte des Volkes Israel*. Leipzig, 1931. G. Ricciotti, *Storia d'Israele*. 2 vols. Turin, 1932 and 1934. French translation: vol. 1, Paris, 1939. English translation projected.

H. ARCHAEOLOGICAL DISCOVERIES AND THE OLD TESTAMENT

1. Bibliographies

P. Thomsen, *Die Palästina-Literatur*. Leipzig, 1908 ff. Vol. I (for 1895–1904), 1908; vol. II (for 1905–1909), 1911; vol. III (for 1910–1914), 1916; vol. IV (for 1915–1924), 1927; vol. V (for 1925–1934), 1938. E. F. Weidner, *Die Assyriologie, 1914–1922*. Leipzig, 1922. Ida A. Pratt, *Assyria and Babylonia: A list of references in the New New York Public Library*. New York, 1918; *List of Works in the New York Public Library relating to Persia*. New York, 1915; *Ancient Egypt: Sources of Information in the New York Public Library*. New York Public Library, 1925; *Ancient Egypt, 1925–1941* (A Supplement to *Ancient Egypt*, 1925). New York Public Library, 1942. B. Schwarz, *The Hittites: A List of References in the New York Public Library*. New York, 1939. J. P. Hyatt, in JBR 6 (1938) 144–145, 172–174.

On Ras Shamra (Ugarit): C. F. A. Schaeffer, *Ugaritica*. Paris, 1939. W. Baumgartner, "Ras Schamra und das Alte Testament, I" (*Theol. Rundschau* N.F. 12 [1940] 163–188; 13 [1941] 1–20, 85–102, 157–183). J. P. Hyatt, "The Ras Shamra Discoveries and the Interpretation of the Old Testament" (JBR 10 [1942] 67–75). H. L. Ginsberg, *The Legend of King Keret*, pp. 9–12. BASOR, Supplementary Studies, Nos. 2–3. New Haven, Conn., 1946; see also "Ugaritic Studies and the Bible" (*Biblical Archaeologist* 8 [1945] 41–58). R. De Langhe, *Les Textes de Ras Shamra-Ugarit et leurs Rapports avec le Milieu Biblique de l'Ancien Testament.* 2 vols. Gembloux and Paris, 1945.

2. Books in English

S. R. Driver, *Modern Research as Illustrating the Bible.* London, 1909. A. Jeremias, *The Old Testament in the Light of the Ancient East.* 2 vols. London, 1911 (from the German). S. A. B. Mercer, *Extra-Biblical Sources for Hebrew and Jewish History.* New York, 1913. M. Jastrow, Jr., *Hebrew and Babylonian Traditions.* London, 1914. L. W. King, *Legends of Babylonia and Egypt in Relation to Hebrew Tradition* (Schweich Lectures, 1916). London, 1918. W. L. Wardle, *Israel and Babylon.* 2nd ed., London, 1925. R. A. S. Macalister, *A Century of Excavation in Palestine.* New York, 1925. R. W. Rogers, *Cuneiform Parallels to the Old Testament.* 2nd ed., New York, 1926. W. F. Albright, "The excavation of Tell Beit Mirsim" AASOR 12 (1932), 13 (1933), 17 (1938), 21–22 (1943). E. A. Speiser, *Mesopotamian Origins.* Philadelphia, 1930; AASOR 13 (1933) 13–54. W. F. Albright, *The Archaeology of Palestine and the Bible.* 3rd ed., New York, 1935. C. R. North, "Archaeology and Criticism" (*London Quarterly* and *Holborn Review,* 1936, 52–63). G. A. Barton, *Archaeology and the Bible.* 7th ed., Philadelphia, 1937. M. Burrows, *The Basis of Israelite Marriage.* New Haven, 1938. E. Grant (Editor), *The Haverford Symposium on Archaeology and the Bible.* The American Schools of Oriental Research (New Haven, Conn.), 1938. H. Torczyner, L. Harding, A. Lewis, and J. Starkey, *The Lachish Letters* (Lachish [Tell ed-Duweir], vol. I). London, 1938; cf. W. F. Albright in *BASOR* No. 82, pp. 18–24; 1941. J. W. and Grace M. Crowfoot, *Early Ivories from Samaria.* London, 1938. N. Glueck, *The Other Side of the Jordan.* New Haven, 1940; *The River Jordan.* New Haven, 1946. C. H. Gordon, *The Living Past.* New York, 1941. M. Burrows, *What Mean These Stones?* New Haven, 1941. J. W. Crowfoot, Kathleen M. Kenyon, and E. L. Sukenik, *The Buildings at Samaria.* London, 1942. A. Heidel, *The Babylonian Genesis.* The University of Chicago Press, 1942; *The Gilgamesh Epic and the Old Testament Parallels.* 1946. C. C. McCown, *The Ladder of Progress in Palestine.* New York, 1943. S. N. Kramer, *Sumerian Mythology* (American Philosophical Society, Memoirs, Vol. 21). Philadelphia, 1944. J. Finegan, *Light from the Ancient Past: The Archaeological Background of the Hebrew-Christian Tradition.* The Princeton University Press, 1946. H. and H. A. Frankfort, J. A. Wilson, Th. Jacobsen, and W. A. Irwin, *The Intellectual Adventure of Ancient Man.* The University of Chicago Press, 1946. C. C. McCown, J. C. Wampler, and others, *Tell en-Naṣbeh.* 2 vols. New Haven, 1947. H. Frankfort, *Kingship and the Gods: A Study of Ancient Near Eastern Religion as the Integration of Society and Nature.* The University of Chicago Press, 1948.

Ras Shamra-Ugarit (a few selected publications in addition to the bibliographies mentioned above). Z. S. Harris, "Ras Shamra" (in *Smithsonian Report for 1937*, pp. 479–502. Washington, 1938). C. H. Gordon, *The Loves and Wars of Baal and Anat.* Princeton University Press, 1943; "The Poetic Literature of Ugarit" (*Orientalia* 12 [1943] 31–75). J. H. Patton, *Canaanite Parallels in the Book of Psalms.* The John Hopkins Press, 1944. C. I. K. Story, "The Book of Proverbs in Northwest Semitic Literature" (*JBL* 64 [1945] 319–337). T. H. Gaster, "A Canaanite Ritual Drama" (*JAOS* 66 [1946] 49–76); "A King without a Castle" (*BASOR* No. 101, pp. 21–30. 1946). J. Obermann, "How Daniel was blessed with a Son" (Amer. Orient. Soc., Offprint No. 20. Supplement to *JAOS* April-June 1946. New Haven 1946); *Ugaritic Mythology.* Yale University Press, 1948.

3. In German and Other Languages

E. Schrader, *Die Keilinschriften und das Alte Testament.* 3rd ed. by H. Zimmern and H. Winckler. Berlin, 1903. H. Vincent, *Canaan d'après l'exploration récente.* Paris, 1907;

2nd ed., 1914. P. Thomsen, *Palästina und seine Kultur in fünf Jahrtausenden* (Der Alte Orient, 30). Leipzig, 1909; 3rd ed., 1931. F. M. T. Böhl, *Kananäer und Hebräer* (BWAT 9). Stuttgart, 1911. A. Jirku, *Altorientalischer Kommentar zum Alten Testament.* Leipzig, 1923. H. Gressmann (Editor), *Altorientalische Texte und Bilder zum Alten Testament.* 2 vols. 2nd ed., Berlin, 1926 and 1927. C. Contenau, *Manuel d'archéologie orientale.* 4 vols. Paris, 1927-1947. A. Jeremias, *Das Alte Testament im Lichte des Alten Orients.* 4th ed., Leipzig, 1930. C. Watzinger, *Denkmäler Palästinas.* 2 vols. Leipzig, 1933–1935. D. Diringer, *Le iscrizioni antico-ebraiche palestinesi.* Florence, 1934. L. Hennequin, "Fouilles et champs de fouilles en Palestine et en Phénicie" in *Supplément au Dictionnaire de la Bible* of F. Vigoroux, vol. 3, cols. 318–524. Paris, 1936. A. G. Barrois, *Précis d'archéologie biblique.* Paris, 1935; *Manuel d'archéologie biblique,* vol. I. Paris, 1939. M. Noth, *Die Welt des Alten Testaments.* Berlin, 1940. A. Parrot, *Archéologie mésopotamienne.* Paris, 1946. W. Baumgartner, "Ugaritische Probleme und ihre Tragweite für das Alte Testament" (*Theologische Zeitschrift* 3 [1947] 81–100).

I. Civilization of Palestine and of Israel

Historical Geography

G. A. Smith, *Historical Geography of the Holy Land.* 25th ed., New York, 1932 (and later reprints). F. Buhl, *Geographie des alten Palästina.* Freiburg, 1896. F. M. Abel, *Géographie de la Palestine.* 2 vols. Paris, 1933 and 1938. Ellen C. Semple, *The Geography of the Mediterranean Region: Its Relation to Ancient History.* New York, 1931. G. E. Wright, F. V. Filson, and W. F. Albright, *The Westminster Historical Atlas to the Bible.* Philadelphia, 1945.

1. In English

L. Wallis, *Sociological Study of the Bible.* Chicago, 1911; *God and the Social Progress.* Chicago, 1935. T. G. Soares, *The Social Institutions and Ideals of the Bible.* New York, 1915. E. R. Goodenough, "Kingship in Early Israel" (JBL 48 [1929] 169–205). H. J. Cadbury, *National Ideals in the Old Testament.* New York, 1920. R. A. S. Macalister, *A History of Civilization in Palestine.* 2nd ed., Cambridge, 1921. A. Bertholet, *A History of Hebrew Civilization.* London, 1926. Translated from *Kulturgeschichte Israels.* Göttingen, 1919. French translation: Paris, 1929. H. Schaeffer, *The Social Legislation of the Primitive Semites.* New Haven, 1915; *Hebrew Tribal Economy and the Jubilee as illustrated in Semitic and Indo-European Village Communities.* Leipzig, 1923. J. Pedersen, *Israel: Its Life and Culture.* London, 1926 (from the Danish: Copenhagen, 1920); *Israel,* vols. 3 and 4: *Hellighed og Guddomlighed* (on the religion of Israel). Copenhagen, 1934. J. M. P. Smith, *The Origin and History of Hebrew Law.* Chicago, 1931. J. Garstang, *The Heritage of Solomon.* London, 1934. S. W. Baron, *A Social and Religious History of the Jews.* 3 vols. New York, 1937. D. Davidson, *The Social Background of the Old Testament.* Hebrew Union College Press, 1942. Madeleine S. and J. L. Miller, *Encyclopedia of Bible Life.* New York, 1944.

2. In German and Other Languages

W. Nowack, *Lehrbuch der hebräischen Archäologie.* 2 vols. Freiburg, 1894. H. Gunkel, *Schöpfung und Chaos in Uhrzeit und Endzeit.* Göttingen, 1895. A. Bertholet, *Die Stellung der Israeliten und der Juden zu den Fremden.* Freiburg, 1896. F. X. Kortleiner, *Archaeologia*

Biblica. New ed., Innsbruck, 1917 (Roman Catholic). P. Volz, *Die Biblischen Alter-tümer.* Calw and Stuttgart, 1914; 2nd ed., 1925. A Causse, *Les "Pauvres" d'Israël.* Strassburg and Paris, 1922; *Du groupe ethnique à la communauté religieuse.* Paris, 1937; *Les dispersés d'Israël.* Paris, 1929. I. Benzinger, *Hebräische Archäologie.* 3rd ed., Leipzig, 1927. M. Löhr, *Das Asylwesen im Alten Testament* (Königsberger Gelehrten Gesell-schaft, Geisteswissenschaftliche Klasse; Jahr 7, Heft 3). Halle, 1930. A. Jepsen, *Nabi.* Munich, 1934.

J. RELIGION OF ISRAEL

H. F. Hahn, *Religions of the Ancient Near East* (to 323 B. C.): A Bibliography, 1920–1939. The Review of Religion, Columbia University, no date (ca. 1941).

1. General Histories of Religion

G. F. Moore, *History of Religions* (International Theological Library). Vol. II: *Judaism, Christianity, Mohammedanism.* New York, 1919. P. Hinneberg (Editor), *Kultur der Gegenwart: Die Religionen des Orients.* 2nd ed., Leipzig, 1913; *Die Christliche Religion (Religion of Israel,* by J. Wellhausen). 1905. P. D. Chantepie de la Saussaye, *Lehrbuch der Religionsgeschichte.* 2 vols. 4th ed. by A. Bertholet and E. Lehmann. Tübingen, 1925. A. Bertholet (Editor), *Religionsgeschichtliches Lesebuch.* 17 vols. 2nd ed., Tübingen. 1926–1932. Vol. 17: A. Bertholet, *Die Religion des Alten Testaments,* 1932. P. Tacchi Venturi (editor), *Storia delle Religioni.* 2 vols. Turin, 1939. G. Ricciotti, "La Religione d'Israele," is in Vol. II, pp. 361–450 (Roman Catholic).

2. Comparative Studies, Utilizing Non-Biblical Sources

W. W. Baudissin, *Studien zur Semitischen Religionsgeschichte.* 2 vols. Leipzig, 1876 and 1878. F. Baethgen, *Beiträge zur semitischen Religionsgeschichte.* Berlin, 1888. J. Wellhausen, *Reste arabischen Heidentums.* Berlin, 1887; 2nd ed., 1897. W. Robertson Smith, *Lectures on the Religion of the Semites.* London, 1889; 3rd ed. by S. A. Cook, 1927. C. G. Montefiore, *Lectures on the Origin and Growth of Religion as Illustrated by the Religion of the Ancient Hebrews.* London, 1892. S. I. Curtiss, *Primitive Semitic Religion To-day.* London, 1902. B. Baentsch, *Altorientalischer und israelitscher Monotheismus.* Tübingen, 1906. J. Hehn, *Sünde und Erlösung nach biblischer und babylonischer Anschauung.* Leipzig, 1903; *Die biblische und die Babylonische Gottesidee.* Leipzig, 1913. W. W. Baudissin, *Adonis und Esmun.* Leipzig, 1911. W. C. Wood, "The Religion of Canaan" (JBL 35 [1916] 1–133, 164–279). J. R. Frazer, *The Golden Bough: A Study in Magic and Religion.* 12 vols. 3rd ed., London and New York, 1911–1920; *Folk-lore in the Old Testament.* 3 vols. London, 1918 (a one-volume abridgment is also available). S. Mowinckel, *Psalmenstudien.* 5 vols. Oslo, 1921–1924. D. S. Margoliouth, *Relations between Arabs and Israelites prior to the rise of Islam* (Schweich Lectures for 1921). London, 1923. W. Wundt, *Völkerpsychologie* (10 vols.). Vols. 4–6: *Mythus und Religion.* 3rd ed., Leipzig, 1923. R. Kittel, *Die hellenistische Mysterienreligion und das Alte Testament* (BWAT N.F. 7). Stuttgart, 1924. Cf. J. A. Bewer in JBL 45 (1926) 1–13. J. Schefte-lowitz, *Alt-Palästinensischer Bauernglaube in religionsvergleichender Beleuchtung.* Hanover, 1925. K. Galling, *Der Altar in den Kulturen des alten Orients.* Berlin, 1925. C. C. McCown, "Hebrew and Egyptian Apocalyptic Literature" (HTR 18 [1925] 357–411). H. Gressmann, *Die hellenistische Gestirnreligion* (Beih. Alte Orient 5). Leipzig, 1925; *The Tower of Babel.* New York, 1928. S. A. Cook, *The Religion of Ancient Palestine in the Light of Archaeology* (Schweich Lectures for 1925). London, 1930.

S. Langdon, *Semitic Mythology* (*The Mythology of All Races*, vol. 5). Boston, 1931. S. H. Hooke (Editor), *Myth and Ritual*. London, 1933; *The Labyrinth*. London, 1935. J. A. Montgomery, *Arabia and the Bible*. Philadelphia, 1934. G. A. Barton, *Semitic and Hamitic Origins*. Philadelphia, 1934. A Titius, *Die Anfänge der Religion bei den Ariern und Israeliten*. Göttingen, 1934. C. W. Harris, *The Hebrew Heritage*. New York, 1935. T. J. Meek, *Hebrew Origins*. New York, 1936. E. A. Leslie, *Old Testament Religion in the Light of its Canaanite Background*. New York, 1936. W. C. Graham and H. G. May, *Culture and Conscience*. Chicago, 1936. S. H. Hooke, *The Origins of Early Semitic Ritual* (Schweich Lectures). London, 1938. W. F. Albright, *From the Stone Age to Christianity*. The Johns Hopkins Press, 1940; *Archaeology and the Religion of Israel*. The Johns Hopkins Press, 1942. E. Engnell, *Studies in Divine Kingship in the Ancient Near East*. Uppsala, 1943. J. B. Pritchard, *Palestinian Figurines*. Amer. Orient. Series 24. New Haven, 1943.

3. *Israel's Religious History According to the Old Testament*

A. Kuenen, *De Godsdienst van Israel tot den Ondergang van den Joodschen Staat*. 2 vols. Haarlem, 1869–1870. English translation, 3 vols. London, 1874–1875; *National Religions and Universal Religion* (Hibbert Lectures). London, 1882. R. Smend, *Lehrbuch der alttestamentlichen Religionsgeschichte*. Freiburg, 1893; 2nd ed., 1899. K. Budde, *Religion of Israel to the Exile*. New York, 1899 (in German: Giessen, 1900; 2nd ed., 1905). T. K. Cheyne, *Jewish Religious Life after the Exile*. New York, 1898 (German translation: Giessen, 1899). E. Kautzsch, "Religion of Israel" in Hastings' *Dictionary of the Bible*, extra vol., pp. 612–734. New York, 1904. In German: Tübingen, 1911. B. Stade, *Biblische Theologie des Alten Testaments*. Vol. I: *Die Religion Israels und die Entstehung des Judentums*. Tübingen, 1905. Vol. II: A. Bertholet, *Die jüdische Religion von der Zeit Ezra bis zum Zeitalter Christi*. Tübingen, 1911. M. Löhr, *Alttestamentliche Religionsgeschichte* (Sammlung Göschen). Leipzig, 1906; 2nd ed., 1919. English translation: *A History of the Religion of the Old Testament*. New York, 1936. A Loisy, *La religion d'Israël*. 2nd ed., Paris, 1908; 3rd ed., 1933. English translation: *The Religion of Israel*. New York, 1910. Italian translation: Piacenza, 1910. K. Marti, *The Religion of the Old Testament*. London, 1910 (translated from the 5th German ed., Strassburg, 1907). F. Giesebrecht, *Die Grundzüge der israelitischen Religionsgeschichte* (Aus Natur and Geisteswelt 52). 2nd ed., Leipzig, 1908; 3rd ed. by A. Bertholet, 1919. J. P. Peters, *The Religion of the Hebrews*. Boston, 1914. H. P. Smith, *The Religion of Israel*. Edinburgh, 1914. E. König, *Geschichte der alttestamentliche Religion kritisch dargestellt*. Gütersloh, 1915; 3rd and 4th ed., 1924. H. T. Fowler, *The Origin and Growth of the Hebrew Religion*. Chicago, 1917. G. A. Barton, *The Religion of Israel*. New York, 1919; 2nd ed., Philadelphia, 1928. R. Kittel, *Die Religion des Volkes Israel*. Leipzig, 1921; 2nd ed., 1929. English translation: *The Religion of the People Israel*. London, 1925. G. Hölscher, *Geschichte der israelitischen und jüdischen Religion* (Sammlung Töpelmann). Giessen, 1922. R. Kreglinger, *La religion d'Israël*. Brussels, 1922; 2nd ed., 1926. L. Gautier, *Etudes sur la religion d'Israël*. Lausanne, 1927. G. Beer, *Welches war die älteste Religion Israels?* Giessen, 1927. W. Baumgartner, "Alttestamentliche Religion" (ARW 26 [1928] 52–114). Bibliography for 1917–1927. W. O. E. Oesterley and T. H. Robinson, *Hebrew Religion: Its Origin and Development*. New York, 1930; 2nd ed., 1937. C. Toussaint, *Les origines de la religion d'Israël*. Vol. I: *L'ancien Jahvisme*. Paris, 1931. J. Hänel, *Die Religion der Heiligkeit*. Gütersloh, 1931. E. Sellin, *Alttestamentliche Theologie auf religionsgeschichtlicher Grundlage*. Vol. I: *Israelitisch–jüdische Religionsgeschichte*. Leipzig, 1933. Vol. II: *Theologie des Alten Testaments*, 1933. E. Dhorme, *L'évolution religieuse d'Israël*. Vol. I: *La religion des Hébreux nomades*. Brussels, 1937. L. Finkelstein, *The Pharisees*. 2 vols. Philadelphia,

1938. A. Lods, *La religion d'Israël*. Paris, 1939. I. G. Matthews, *The Religious Pilgrimage of Israël*. New York, 1947.

K. THEOLOGY OF THE OLD TESTAMENT

H. Schultz, *Alttestamentliche Theologie*. Braunschweig, 1869; 5th ed., 1896. English translation: Edinburgh, 1892. W. L. Alexander, *System of Biblical Theology*. Edinburgh, 1888. A. Dillmann, *Handbuch der alttestamentlichen Theologie*. Edited by R. Kittel. Leipzig, 1895. W. H. Bennett, *The Theology of the Old Testament*. London, 1896. A. B. Davidson, *The Theology of the Old Testament*. Edited by S. D. F. Salmond. Edinburgh, 1904. H. Metzenauer, *Theologia Biblica*. Vol. I: *Old Testament*. Feiburg i.B., 1908 (Roman Catholic). H. Wheeler Robinson, *The Religious Ideas of the Old Testament*. New York, 1913. A. C. Knudson, *The Religious Teaching of the Old Testament*. New York, 1918. E. König, *Theologie des Alten Testaments kritisch und vergleichend dargestellt*. 3rd and 4th ed., Stuttgart, 1923. L. Köhler, *Theologie des Alten Testaments*. Tübingen,1936. W. Eichrodt, *Theologie des Alten Testaments*. Vol. I: Gott und Volk. Leipzig, 1933. Vol. II: *Gott und Welt*, 1935. Vol. III: *Gott und Mensch*, 1939. L. Köhler, "Alttestamentliche Theologie" (*Theol. Rundschau* N.F. 7 [1935] 255–318; 8 [1936] 55–59 and 247–284). Bibliography. H. E. Fosdick, *A Guide to Understanding the Bible*. New York, 1938. P. Heinisch, *Theologie des Alten Testamentes* (in HS). Bonn, 1940 (Roman Catholic). C. T. Craig, "Biblical Theology and the Rise of Historicism" (JBL 42 [1943] 281–294). J. D. Smart, "The Death and Rebirth of Old Testament Theology" (Journ. of Religion 23 [1943] 1–11, 125–136). G. E. Wright, *The Challenge of Israel's Faith*. The University of Chicago Press, 1944. W. Eichrodt, *Das Menschenverstandnis des Alten Testaments*. Basel. 1944. W. A. Irwin, "The Reviving Theology of the Old Testament" (Journ. of Religion 25 [1945] 235–246). H. H. Rowley, *The Re-discovery of the Old Testament*. London, 1945; and Philadelphia, 1946. M. Burrows, *An Outline of Biblical Theology*. Philadelphia, 1946. J. C. Rylaarsdam, *Revelation in Jewish Wisdom Literature*. The University of Chicago Press, 1946. N. H. Snaith, *The Distinctive Ideas of the Old Testament*. Philadelphia, 1946.

L. SPECIAL TOPICS IN THE RELIGION OF ISRAEL

1. Particular Historical Periods

E. R. Bevan, *Jerusalem under the High Priests*. London, 1904. M. Haller, *Religion, Recht and Sitte in den Genesissagen*. Bern, 1905. J. A. Montgomery, *The Samaritans*. Philadelphia, 1907. H. Gressmann, *Mose und seine Zeit*. Göttingen, 1913. W. F. Badé, *The Old Testament in the Light of To-day*. New York, 1915. L. E. Browne, *Early Judaism*. Cambridge, 1920. J. M. P. Smith, *The Religion of the Psalms*. Chicago, 1922. A. Wiser, *Die Religion and Sittlichkeit der Genesis*, u.s.w. Heidelberg, 1928. A. Vincent, *La religion des Judéo-Araméens d'Eléphantine*. Paris, 1937.

2. The Prophets

C. H. Cornill, *The Prophets of Israel*. Chicago, 1897. In German: *Der israelitischer Prophetismus*. 11th–12th ed., Strassburg, 1916; *Der jüdische Prophetismus*. 13th ed. Berlin, 1920. Italian translation: Bari, 1923. W. Robertson Smith, *The Prophets of Israel*. New ed., London, 1907. E. Sellin, *Der alttestamentliche Prophetismus*. Leipzig, 1912. G. Hölscher, *Die Propheten*. Leipzig, 1914. J. M. P. Smith, *The Prophet and his Problems*. New York, 1914. M. Buttenwieser, *The Prophets of Israel from the Eighth to the*

Fifth Century. New York, 1914.   A. C. Knudson, *Beacon Lights of Prophecy.* New York, 1914.   W. Gossmann, *Die Entwicklung des Gerichtsgedankens bei den alttestamentlichen Propheten* (Beih. ZAW 29).   Giessen, 1915.   B. Duhm, *Israels Propheten.* Tübingen, 1916; 2nd ed., 1922.   A. R. Gordon, *The Prophets of the Old Testament.* New York, 1916.   H. Gunkel, *Die Propheten.* Göttingen, 1917.   E. Tobac. *Les Prophètes d'Israël.* Vol. I, Lierre, 1919; vols. II and III, Malines, 1921; new ed. by J. Coppens, Malines, 1932.   T. H. Robinson, *Prophecy and the Prophets in Ancient Israel.* London, 1923.   J. Hänel, *Das Erkennen Gottes bie den Schriftpropheten.* Berlin, 1923.   J. Lindblom, *Die literarische Gattung der prophetischen Literatur.* Uppsala, 1924.   J. M. P. Smith, *The Prophets and their Times.* Chicago, 1925; 2nd ed. by W. A. Irwin, 1941. T. H. Robinson, "Neuere Propheten-Forschung" (*Theol. Rundschau* N.F. 3 [1931] 75–103). Bibliography.   Louise P. Smith, "The Prophetic Targum as a Guide and Defense for the Higher Critic" (JBL 52 [1933] 121–130).   J. Lindblom, "Die Gesichte der Propheten" (*Studia Theologica* 1, pp. 7–28. Riga, 1935).   W. C. Graham, *The Prophets and Israel's Culture.* Chicago, 1935.   C. M. Prugh, *Der Patriotismus der Propheten Israels* (Heidelberg Dissertation). Heidelberg, 1935.   A. Guillaume, *Prophecy and Divination among the Hebrews and other Semites.* New York, 1938.   E. A. Leslie, *The Prophets Tell their Own Story.* New York, 1939.   E. F. Siegman, *The False Prophets of the Old Testament* (Catholic Univesity of America Dissertation). Washington, D. C., 1939. B. D. Cohon, *The Prophets.* New York, 1939.   A. R. Johnson, *The Cultic Prophet in Ancient Israel.* Cardiff, 1944.   R. B. Y. Scott. *The Relevance of the Prophets.* New York, 1944.   H. H. Rowley, "The Nature of Prophecy in the Light of Recent Study" (HTR 38 [1945] 1–38).   A. Haldar, *Associations of Cult Prophets among the Ancient Semites.* Uppsala, 1945.   S. Mowinckel, *Prophecy and Tradition* (Norske Videnskaps-Akademi i Oslo, Hist.-Filos. Kl. 1946, No. 3). Oslo, 1946.   J. Ph. Hyatt, *Prophetic Religion.* New York and Nashville, 1947.   R. Calkins, *The Modern Message of the Minor Prophets.* New York, 1947.   J. Paterson, *The Goodly Fellowship of the Prophets.* New York, 1948.

3. The Conception of God

A. Von Gall, *Die Herrlichkeit Gottes.* Giessen, 1900.   P. Volz, *Der Geist Gottes, u.s.w.* Tübingen, 1910.   E. Pace, *Ideas of God in Israel: Their Content and Development.* London, 1924.   P. Volz, *Das Dämonische in Jahwe.* Tübingen, 1924.   J. Hempel, "Jahwegleichnisse der israelitischen Propheten" (ZAW N.F. 1 [1924] 74–104). H. Schmökel, *Jahwe und die Fremdvölker* (Breslauer Studien zur Theologie I). Breslau, 1934.   F. Stier, *Gott und seine Engel Alten Testament.* (Tübingen Dissertation, Roman Catholic). Tübingen, 1934.

4. Morals and Piety

J. Köberle, *Natur und Geist nach der Auffassung des Alten Testaments.* Munich, 1901; *Sünde und Gnade im religiösen Leben des Volkes Israel bis auf Christum.* Munich, 1905. M. Kegel, *Das Gebet in Alten Testament.* Gütersloh, 1908.   F. Heiler, *Das Gebet.* 3rd ed., Munich, 1920; 4th ed., 1921.   J. Hempel, *Gebet und Frömmigkeit im Alten Testament.* Göttingen, 1922.   A. S. Peake, *Brotherhood in the Old Testament* (John Clifford Lectures). London, 1923.   J. M. P. Smith, *The Moral Life of the Hebrews.* Chicago, 1923. H. Duhm, *Der Verkehr Gottes mit den Menschen in Alten Testament.* Tübingen, 1926. N. Glueck, *Das Wort ḥesed im alttestamentlichen Sprachgebrauche, u.s.w.* (Beih. ZAW 47). Giessen, 1927.   K. Galling, *Die Erwählungstraditionen Israels* (Beih. ZAW 48). Giessen, 1928.   H. Schmidt, *Das Gebet des Angeklagten im Alten Testament* (Beih. ZAW 49).

Giessen, 1928. F. Baumgärtel, *Die Eigenart der alttestamentlichen Frömmigkeit*. Schwerin, 1932. A. Wendel, *Das freie Laiengebet im Vorexilischen Israel*. Leipzig, 1932. A. S. Sommer, *Der Begriff der Versuchung im Alten Testament und Judentum* (part of a Breslau Dissertation). Breslau, 1935. S. H. Blank, "Studies in Post-Exilic Universalism" (HUCA 11 [1936] 159–191). J. Hempel, *Gott und Mensch in Alten Testament*. (BWANT III, 2). 2nd ed., Stuttgart, 1936; *Das Ethos des Alten Testaments*. Berlin, 1938. J. J. Stamm, *Erlösen und Vergeben im Alten Testament*. Bern, 1940.

5. Sacrifices and Offerings

G. F. Moore, "Sacrifice" in Cheyne's *Encyclopaedia Biblica*, vol. 4, cols. 4183–4233. London, 1903. O. Eissfeldt, *Erstlinge und Zehnten im Alten Testament*. Leipzig, 1917. A. Loisy, *Essai historique sur le sacrifice*. Paris, 1920. R. Dussaud, *Les origines cananéennes du sacrifice israélite*. Paris, 1921. G. B. Gray, *Sacrifice in the Old Testament*. Oxford, 1924. I. Elbogen, *Der jüdische Gottesdienst in seiner geschichtlichen Entwickelung*. 2nd ed., Frankfurt, 1924. M. Löhr, *Räucheropfer im Alten Testament*. Halle, 1927. A. Wendel, *Das Opfer in der alttestamentlichen Religion*. Leipzig, 1927. A. Lods, "Israelitische Opfervorstellungen und -bräuche" (*Theol. Rundschau* N.F. 3 [1931] 347–366). Bibliography. D. Schötz, *Schuld- und Sündopfer im Alten Testament* (Breslauer Studien zur historischen Theologie 18). Breslau, 1934. W. O. E. Oesterley, *Sacrifices in Ancient Israel*. New York, 1937.

6. Priests and Sanctuaries

W. W. Baudissin, *Die Geschichte des alttestamentlichen Priestertums*. Leipzig, 1889. A. von Gall, *Altisraelitische Kultstätte* (Beih. ZAW 3). Giessen, 1898. G. Westphal, *Jahwes Wohnstätte* (Beih. ZAW 15). Giessen, 1908. W. R. Arnold, *Ephod and Ark* (Harvard Theological Studies 3). Cambridge, Mass., 1917. K. Möhlenbrink, *Der Tempel Salomos*. Stuttgart, 1932. A. C. Welch, *Prophet and Priest in Old Israel*. London, 1936. J. Hoschander, *The Priests and the Prophets*. New York, 1938. G. E. Wright "Solomon's Temple Reconstructed" (*Biblical Archaeologist* 4 [1941] 17–32).

7. National Hopes

H. Gressmann, *Der Ursprung der israelitisch-jüdischen Eschatologie* (FRLANT 6). Göttingen, 1905; *Der Messias*. Göttingen, 1929. B. Duhm, *Der kommende Reich Gottes*. Tübingen, 1910. M. Messel, *Die Einheitlichkeit der jüdischen Eschatalogie* (Beih. ZAW 30). Giessen, 1915. N. Schmidt, "The Origin of Jewish Eschatology" (JBL 41 [1922] 102–114). G. Hölscher, *Die Ursprünge der jüdischen Eschatologie* (Theologische Konferenz zu Giessen 41) Giessen 1925. E. L. Dietrich, "*Schub sch'but.*' *Die endzeitliche Wiederherstellung bei den Propheten* (Beih. ZAW 40). Giessen, 1925. H. Schmidt, *Der Mythos vom wiederkehrenden König im Alten Testament* (Schriften der hessischen Hochschulen, Universität Giessen 1). Giessen, 1925. E. König *Die Messianische Weissagungen des Alten Testaments vergleichend, geschichtlich und exegetisch behandelt*. 2nd and 3rd ed., Stuttgart, 1925. L. Dürr, *Ursprung und Aufbau der israelitisch üdischen Heilandserwartung*. Berlin, 1925. W. Staerk, *Soter*. *Die Biblische Erlösererwartung als religionsgeschichtlicher Problem*, Part I, Gütersloh, 1933 G. Dahl, "The Messianic Expectation in the Psalter" (JBL 57 [1938] 1–12). H. H. Rowley, *The Relevance of Apocalyptic*. London, 1944.

8. Life after Death

R. H. Charles, *A Critical History of the Doctrine of a Future Life*. London, 1899. A Lods, *La croyance à la vie future et le culte des morts dans l'antiquité israélite*. 2 vols. Paris, 1906. P. Torge, *Seelenglaube und Unsterblichkeitshoffnung im Alten Testament*. Leipzig, 1909. L. B. Paton, "The Hebrew Idea of the Future Life" (*Biblical World* 1910, pp. 8–20, 80–92, 159–171); *Spiritism and the Cult of the Dead in Antiquity*. New York, 1921. A Bertholet, *Die israelitische Vorstellungen vom Zustand nach dem Tode*. 2nd ed., Tübingen, 1914. W. O. E. Oesterley, *Immortality and the Unseen World*. London, 1921. G. Quell, *Die Auffassung des Todes in Israel*. Leipzig, 1925. F. Noetscher, *Altorientalischer und alttestamentlicher Auferstehungsglauben*. Würzburg, 1926.

PART II: THE PENTATEUCH

A. THE PENTATEUCH AS A WHOLE

1. General Works

E. C. Bissell, *The Pentateuch*. New York, 1885 (includes a bibliography of 2,000 titles). A. Westphal, *Les sources du Pentateuque*. 2 vols. Paris, 1888 and 1892. J. Wellhausen, *Die Composition des Hexateuchs und der historischen Bücher des Alten Testaments*. Berlin, 1889; 3rd ed., Berlin, 1899. First published in *Jahrbücher für Deutsche Theologie*, vols. 21–22, 1876–1877. H. Holzinger, *Einleitung in den Hexateuch*. Freiburg, 1893. J. E. Carpenter and G. Harford-Battersby, *The Hexateuch according to the Revised Version*. 2 vols. London and New York, 1900; J. E. Carpenter and G. Harford, *The Composition of the Hexateuch*. London and New York, 1902. R. Smend, *Die Erzählung des Hexateuchs*. Berlin, 1912. E. S. Brightman, *The Sources of the Hexateuch*. New York, 1918. O. Eissfeldt, *Hexateuch Synopse*. Leipzig, 1922. A. Bea, *De Pentateucho*. Rome, 1928; 2nd ed., 1933 (Roman Catholic). A. S. Yahuda, *Die Sprache des Pentateuch in ihren Beziehungen zum Ägyptischen*. Berlin, 1929; *The Language of the Pentateuch in its Relation to Egyptian*, vol. I. Oxford, 1933; *The Accuracy of the Bible*. The Stories of Joseph, the Exodus and Genesis confirmed and illustrated by Egyptian Monuments and Language. London, 1934. G. von Rad, *Das Formgeschichtliche Problem des Hexateuchs* (BWANT IV, 26). Stuttgart, 1938. O. T. Allis, *The Five Books of Moses*. Philadelphia, 1943.

2. The Individual Sources

a. J. and S: E. Meyer (and B. Luther), *Die Israeliten und ihre Nachbarstämme*. Halle, 1906. J. Morgenstern, "The Sources of the Paradise Story" (*Journal of Jewish Lore and Philosophy* 1 [1919] 105–123, 225–240). Beatrice L. Goff, *The J Document in the Hexateuch* (unpublished dissertation). Boston University, 1933. H. Hellbarth, *Der Jahwist und die Biblische Urgeschichte* (Dissertation). 1935.

b. E: O. Proksch, *Das nordhebräische Sagenbuch; die Elohimquelle*. Leipzig, 1906.

c. D: J. Hempel, *Die Schichten des Deuteronomiums*. Leipzig, 1914. J. A. Bewer, L. B. Paton, and G. Dahl, "*The Problem of Duteronomy. A Symposium*" (JBL 47 [1928] 305–379). L. Köhler, "Der Dekalog" (*Theol. Rundschau* N.F. [1929] 161–184). Bibliography. W. Baumgartner, "Der Kampf um das Deuteronomium" (*Theol. Rundschau*

N.F. 1 [1929] 7–25). Bibliography. G. von Rad, *Das Gottesvolk im Deuteronomium* (BWANT III, 11). Stuttgart, 1929; *Deuteronomium-Studien* (FRLANT N.F. 40). Göttingen, 1947. A. R. Siebens, *L'origine du code deutéronomique.* Paris, 1929. F. Horst, *Das Privatrecht Jakwes* (FRLANT N.F. 28). Göttingen, 1930. H. H. Krause, *Das Deuteronomium in der wissenschaftlichen Bearbeitung des 19. und 20. Jahrhundert,* nebst zwei Anhänge: Der Bericht 2 Könige 22–23 und die Stilgattung des Deuteronomiums (Breslau Dissertation). Breslau, 1931. H. Breit, *Die Predigt der Deuteronomisten.* Munich, 1933.

d. P: W. Eichrodt, *Die Quellen der Genesis von neuem untersucht* (Beih. ZAW 38). Giessen, 1916. J. Morgenstern, "The Sources of the Creation Story" (AJSL 36 [1920] 169–212) M. Löhr, *Untersuchungen zum Hexateuchproblem.* I: *Der Priestercodex der Genesis* (Beih. ZAW 38). Giessen, 1924. G. von Rad, *Die Priesterschrift im Hexateuch* (BWANT IV, 13). Stuttgart, 1934.

B. THE INDIVIDUAL BOOKS

G. F. Moore, "Genesis," "Exodus," "Leviticus," "Numbers," 'Deuteronomy," in Cheyne's *Encyclopaedia Biblica,* vols. 1–3, 1899–1902. E. König, *Die Genesis eingeleitet, übersetzt und erklärt.* 2nd and 3rd ed., Gütersloh, 1925. U. Cassuto, *La questione della Genesi.* Florence, 1934. P. Humbert, "Die neuere Genesis-Forschung" (*Theol. Rundschau* N.F. 6 [1934] 147–160, 207–228). Bibliography.

J. H. Greenstone, *Numbers with Commentary* (The Holy Scriptures). The Jewish Publication Society of America, 1939; J. Reider, *Deuteronomy* (*ibid.*), 1937.

PART III: THE FORMER PROPHETS

1. Historical Writing in the Old Testament

G. F. Moore, "Historical Literature," in Cheyne's *Encyclopaedia Biblica,* vol. 2, 1901; "Joshua" and "Judges" (*ibid.*). J. Wellhausen, *Prolegomena zur Geschichte Israels.* 6th ed., Berlin, 1905. English translation: Edinburgh, 1885. H. Duhm, "Zur Geschichte der alttestamentlichen Geschichtsschreibung," in the *Festschrift für Plüss,* pp. 118–163. Basel, 1905. H. Schmidt, *Die Epochen der alttestamentlichen Geschichts-schreibung* (Religionsgeschichtliche Volksbücher II, 16). Tübingen, 1911. R. Smend, "JE in den geschichtlichen Büchern des Alten Testaments" (ZAW 39 [1921] 181–217). Edited by H. Holzinger. A. Bruno, *Das Hebräische Epos.* 2 vols. Uppsala, 1935.

2. Joshua

J. Garstang, *Foundations of Bible History: Joshua and Judges.* London, 1931.

3. Judges

C. F. Burney, *The Book of Judges with Introduction and Notes.* 2nd ed., London, 1920. O. Eissfeldt, *Die Quellen dis Richterbuches.* Leipzig, 1925.

4. Samuel

S. R. Driver, *Notes on the Hebrew Text and the Topography of the Books of Samuel*. Oxford, 1890; 2nd ed., 1913. M. H. Segal, "Studies in the Books of Samuel" (JQR N.S. 5–10, 1914–1920). H. Titkin, *Kritische Untersuchungen zu den Büchern Samuelis* (FRLANT N.F. 16). Göttingen, 1922. L. Rost, *Die Überlieferung von der Thronnachfolge Davids* (BWANT III, 6). Stuttgart, 1926. O. Eissfeldt, *Die Komposition der Samuelisbücher*. Leipzig, 1931. I. Hylander, *Der literarische Samuel-Saul-Komplex (1. Sam. 1-15) traditionsgeschichtlich untersucht* (Uppsala Dissertation). Uppsala, 1932. R. Press, "Der Prophet Samuel. Eine traditionsgeschichtliche Untersuchung" (ZAW N.F. 15 [1938] 177–225).

5. Kings

C. F. Burney, *Notes on the Hebrew Text of the Books of Kings*. Oxford, 1903. I. Benzinger, *Jahwist und Elohist in den Königsbüchern* (BWAT N.F. 2). Stuttgart, 1921. G. Hölscher, "Der Buch ser Könige, seine Quellen und seine Redaktion" in *Eucharisterion für H. Gunkel* (FRLANT 19, 1), vol. I, pp. 158–213. Göttingen, 1923. J. Begrich, *Die Chronologie der Könige von Israel und Juda und die Quellen des Rahmens der Königsbücher*, Tübingen, 1929. S. Mowinckel, "Die Chronologie der israelitischen und jüdischen Könige" (*Acta Orientalia* 10 [1932] 161–277). E. R. Thiele, "The Chronology of the Kings of Judah and Israel" (*Journ. of Near Eastern Studies* 3 [1944] 137–186).

PART IV: THE LATTER PROPHETS

1. Isaiah

A. Neubauer, and S. R. Driver, *The Fifty-third Chapter of Isaiah according to the Jewish Interpreters*. 2 vols. Oxford, 1876–77; cf. H. A. Fischel in HUCA 18 (1944) 53–76. T. K. Cheyne, *The Prophecies of Isaiah: A New Translation with Commentary* Appendices. New York, 1880; 4th ed., 1886; 5th ed., 1889; *Introduction to the Book of Isaiah*. London, 1895. S. R. Driver, *Isaiah: His Life and Times* (Men of the Bible). New York, 1888; 2nd ed., 1893. H. G. Mitchell, *Isaiah: A Study of Chapters 1–11*. New York, 1897. W. O. E. Oesterley, *Studies in Isaiah 40–66*. London, 1916. Louise P. Smith, "The Messianic Ideal of Isaiah" (JBL 36 [1917] 158–212). E. König, *Das Buch Jesaja eingeleitet, übersetzt und erklärt*. Gütersloh, 1926. C. Boutflower, *The Book of Isaiah in the Light of Assyrian Monuments*. London, 1930. J. Begrich, "Das Priesterliche Heilsorakel" (ZAW N.F. 11 [1934] 81–92). J. Lindblom, *Die Jesaia-Apokalypse: Jes. 24-27*. Lund, 1938. Sh. H. Blank, "Studies in Deutero-Isaiah" (HUCA 15 [1940] 1–46); cf. J. Morgenstern, "Deutero-Isaiah's Terminology for 'Universal God' " (JBL 62 [1943] 269–280). E. J. Kissane, *The Book of Isaiah*. Dublin, 1943 (Roman Catholic).

2. Jeremiah

T. K. Cheyne, *Jeremiah: His Life and Times* (Men of the Bible). New York, 1888. S. Mowinckel, *Zur Komposition des Buches Jeremia*. Kristiania, 1914. J. Skinner, *Prophecy and Religion: Studies in the Life of Jeremiah*. Cambridge, 1922. W. F. Lofthouse, *Jeremiah and the New Covenant*. London, 1925. G. A. Smith, *Jeremiah* (The Baird Lecture for 1922). London, 1923; 4th ed., 1929. A. C. Welch, *Jeremiah: His*

Time and His Work. Oxford, 1928. E. Podechard, "Le livre de Jérémie: Structure et formation" (RB 37 [1928] 181–197). R. Calkins, *Jeremiah the Prophet: A Study in Personal Religion.* New York, 1930. P. Volz, *Der Prophet Jeremia.* 3rd. ed., Tübingen, 1930. T. C. Gordon, *The Rebel Prophet.* New York, 1932. H. Bardke, "Jeremia der Fremdvölkerprophet" (ZAW N.F. 12 [1935] 209–239; 13 [1936] 240–262). J. Kroeker, *Jeremia.* Giessen, 1937. V. Herntrich, *Jeremia der Prophet.* Gütersloh, 1938. H. G. May, "Toward an Objective Approach to the Book of Jeremiah: The Biographer" (JBL 61 [1942] 139–155). J. Ph. Hyatt, "Jeremiah and Duteronomy" (*Journ. of Near Eastern Studies* 1 [1942] 156–163).

3. Ezekiel

C. H. Cornill, *Das Buch des Propheten Ezechiel.* Leipzig, 1886. C. Kuhl, *Die Literarische Einheit des Buches Ezechiel* (Dissertation). Tübingen, 1917. W. F. Lofthouse, *The Prophet of Reconstruction: A Patriot's Ideal for a New Age.* London, 1920. L. Dürr, *Die Stellung des Propheten Ezechiel in der israelitisch-jüdischen Apokalyptik* (AA IX, 1). Münster, 1923. J. Phol, *Die Messiaserwartung beim Propheten Ezechiel.* Bonn, 1929. C. C. Torrey, *Pseudo-Ezekiel and the Original Prophecy.* New Haven, 1930; cf. S. Spiegel, "Ezekiel or Pseudo-Ezekiel?" (HTR 24 [1931] 245–321). M. Buttenwieser, "The Date and Character of Ezekiel's Prophecies" (HUCA VII). Cincinnati, 1930. W. Gronkowski, *Le Messianisme d'Ezéchiel.* Strassburg, 1930. C. Kuhl, "Zur Geschichte der Hesekiel-Forschung" (*Theol. Rundschau* N.F. 5 [1933] 92–118). Bibliography. I. G. Matthews, *Ezekiel* (An American Commentary to the Old Testament). Philadelphia, 1939. W. A. Irwin, *The Problem of Ezekiel.* Chicago, 1943.

4. Hosea

P. Cruveilhier, "De l'interpretation historique des événements de la vie familiale du prophète Osée (I–III)" (RB 25 [1916] 342–362). P. Humbert, "Les trois premiers chapitres d'Osée (RHR 1918, pp. 1–15); "Osée le prophète Bedouin" (RHPR 1 [1921] 97–118). A. Heermann, "Ehe und Kinder des Propheten Hosea" (ZAW 40 [1922] 287–312). H. Schmidt, "Die Ehe des Hosea" (ZAW 42 [1924] 245–272). N. Peters, *Osee und die Geschichte.* Paderborn, 1924. K. Budde, "Der Abschnitt Hosea 1–3" (TSK 96–97 [1925] 1–89); cf. JBL 45 (1926) 280–297, 53 (1934) 118–133. E. Sellin, "Die geschichtliche Orientierung der Prophetie des Hoseas" (NKZ 36 [1925] 607–658). L. W. Batten, "Hosea's Message and Marriage" (JBL 48 [1929] 257–273). T. H. Robinson, "Die Ehe des Hosea" (TSK 106 [1935] 301–313). H. S. Nyberg, *Studien zum Hoseabuche.* Uppsala, 1935. R. E. Wolfe, *Meet Amos and Hosea.* New York, 1945.

5. Joel

W. Baumgartner, "Joel 1 und 2" in *Beiträge zur alttestamentlichen Wissenschaft Karl Budde . . . gewidmet* (Beih. ZAW 34), pp. 10–19. Giessen, 1920. L. Dennefeld, "Les problèmes du livre de Joël" (*Recherches des Sciences Religieuses* 15 [1925] 35–57, 591–608). (Roman Catholic). A. Jepsen, "Kleine Beiträge zum Zwölfprophetenbuch" (ZAW N.F. 15 [1938] 85–96).

6. Amos

M. Löhr, *Untersuchungen zum Buch Amos* (Beih. ZAW 4). Giessen, 1901; E. Baumann, *Der Aufbau der Amosreden* (*ibid.* 7), 1903. L. Köhler, *Amos.* Zürich, 1917;

Amos, der älteste Schriftprophet. Zürich, 1920. L. Desnoyers, "Le prophète Amos" (RB 26 [1917] 218–246). H. Schmidt, *Der Prophet Amos.* Tübingen, 1917. R. M. Gwynn, *The Book of Amos.* Cambridge, 1927. R. S. Cripps, *A Critical and Exegetical Commentary on the Book of Amos.* London and New York, 1929. A. Weiser, *Die Prophetie des Amos* (Beih. ZAW 53). Giessen, 1929. L. Köhler, "Amos Forschung von 1917 bis 1932" (*Theol. Rundschau* N.F. 4 [1932] 105–212). Bibliography. J. Morgenstern, "Amos Studies" (HUCA XI [1936] 19–140; XII–XIII [1937–1938] 1–53; XV [1940] 59–304; to be continued). Cincinnati, 1936–1940.

7. Obadiah

G. A. Peckham, *An Introduction to the Study of Obadiah* (Dissertation). Chicago, 1910. T. H. Robinson, "The Structure of the Book of Obadiah" (JTS 17 [1916] 402–408). W. W. Cannon, "Israel and Edom" (*Theol.* 1927, pp. 129–140; 191–200). W. Rudolph, "Obadja" (ZAW N.F. 8 [1931] 222–231).

8. Jonah

H. Schmidt, *Jona, eine Untersuchung zur vergleichenden Religionsgeschichte* (FRLANT 9). Göttingen, 1907.

9. Micah

K. Budde, "Das Rätsel von Micha 1" (ZAW 37 [1917–1918] 77–108); "Micha 2 und 3" (ZAW 38 [1919–1920] 2–22); "Verfasser und Stelle von Micha 4:1–4 (Is. 2:2–4)" (ZDMG 81 [1927] 152–158). H. Gunkel, "Der Micha Schluss" (ZS 2 [1923] 145–178). J. Lindblom, "Micha, literarisch untersucht" (*Acta Academiae. Aboensis. Humaniora* VI, 2). Helsingfors, 1929.

10. Nahum

W. R. Arnold, "The Composition of Nahum 1:2–2:3" (ZAW 21 [1901] 225–265). P. Humbert, "Essai d'analyse de Nahoum 1:2–2:3" (ZAW 44 [1926] 266–280); "La vision de Nahoum 2:4–11" (AFO 5 [1928] 14–19); "Le problème du livre de Nahoum" (RHPR 12 [1932] 1–15). A. Haldar, *Studies in the Book of Nahum.* Uppsala, 1947.

11. Habakkuk

H. Bévenot, "Le cantique d'Habacuc" (RB 42 [1933] 499–525). H. H. Walker and N. W. Lund, "The Literary Structure of the Book of Habakkuk" (JBL 53 [1934] 355–370). C. C. Torrey, "The Prophecy of Habakkuk" (in *Jewish Studies in Memory of G. A. Kohut*, pp. 565–582. New York, 1935). W. A. Irwin, "The Psalm of Habakkuk" (*Journ. of Near Eastern Studies* 1 [1942] 10–40).

12. Zephaniah

F. Schwally, "Das Buch Sephanjâ" (ZAW 10 [1890] 165–240).   C. H. Cornill, "Die Prophetie Zephanjas" (TSK 89 [1916] 297–332).   H. Weiss, *Zephanja Kap. 1 und seine Bedeutung als religionsgeschichtliche Quelle* (Dissertation). Königsberg, 1922. C. V. Pilcher, *Three Hebrew Prophets and the Passing of Empires;* being a study of Nahum, Habakkuk and Zephaniah. London, 1931.

13. Haggai and Zechariah

J. W. Rothstein, *Die Nachtgesichte des Sacharja* (BWAT 8). Stuttgart, 1910.   K. Marti, "Die Zweifel an der prophetischen Sendung Sacharjas" in *Studien zur semitischen Philologie und Religionsgeschichte Julius Wellhausen . . . gewidmet* (Beih. ZAW 27). Giessen, 1914.   P. F. Bloomhardt, "The Poems of Haggai" (HUCA 5 [1928] 153–195).   E. G. Kraeling, "The historical situation in Zechariah 9:1–10" (AJSL 41 [1924–1925] 24–33).   B. Heller, "Die letzten Kapitel des Buches Sacharja im Lichte des späteren Judentums" (ZAW N.F. 4 [1927] 151–155).   W. W. Cannon, "Some Notes on Zechariah c. 11" (AFO 4 [1927] 139–146).   J. Kremer, *Die Hirtenallegorie im Buche Zacharias auf ihre Messianität hin untersucht* (AA XI, 2). Münster, 1930.   A. Bentzen, "Quelques remarques sur le mouvement messianique parmi les Juifs aux environs de l'an 520 avant Jésus Christ" (RHPR 10 [1930] 493–503).

14. Malachi

A. von Bulmerincq, *Der Prophet Maleachi.* Vol. I: *Einleitung in das Buch des Propheten Maleachi* (*Acta et Commentationes Universitatis Dorpatensis*). Dorpat, 1926: Vol. II: *Kommentar zum Buche des Propheten Maleachi.* Dorpat, 1932.   O. Holzmann, "Der Prophet Maleachi und der Ursprung des Pharisäertums" (ARW 29 [1931] 1–21).

PART V: THE WRITINGS

1. Psalms

H. Gunkel, *Ausgewählte Psalmen.* Göttingen, 1905; 4th ed., 1917.   K. Budde, *Die schönsten Psalmen.* Leipzig, 1915.   M. Löhr, *Psalmenstudien* (BWAT N.F. 3). Stuttgart, 1922.   F. Stummer, *Sumerisch-akkadischen Parallelen zum Aufbau, alttestamentlichen Psalmen* (Studien zur Geschichte und Kultur des Altertums XI, 1–2). Paderborn, 1922.   J. P. Peters, *The Psalms as Liturgies.* New York, 1922.   F. Wutz, *Die Psalmen textkritisch untersucht.* Munich, 1925.   G. Quell, *Das kultische Problem der Psalmen* (BWAT 36). Stuttgart, 1926.   D. C. Simpson (Editor), *The Psalmists.* Oxford, 1926. A. C. Welch, *The Psalter in Life, Worship and History.* London, 1926.   E. König, *Die Psalmen eingeleitet, übersetzt und erklärt.* Gütersloh, 1927.   H. Gunkel and J. Begrich, *Einleitung in die Psalmen* (HKAT). 2 vols. Göttingen, 1928 and 1933.   G. Marshall, *Die Gottlosen des ersten Psalmbuches.* Münster, 1929.   M. Haller, "Ein Jahrzehnt Psalmenforschung" (*Theol. Rundschau* N.F. 1 [1929] 377–402). Bibliography.   J. A. Montgomery, "Recent Developments in the Study of the Psalter" (ATR 16 [1934] 185–198).   C. G. Cummings, *Assyrian and Hebrew Hymns of Praise.* New York, 1934. A. Weiser, *Die Psalmen ausgewählt, übersetzt und erklärt.* Göttingen, 1935; 2nd ed. 1939. H. L. Jansen, *Die Spätjüdische Psalmendichtung: ihr Entstehungskreis und ihr "Sitz im*

Leben," u.s.w. (Norske Videnskaps Akademie, Hist.-filos. Kl. 1937, 3). Oslo, 1937.
W. O. E. Oesterley, *A Fresh Approach to the Psalms*. New York, 1937; *The Psalms, Translated with Textcritical and Exegetical Notes*. London, 1939. M. Buttenwieser, *The Psalms, chronologically treated with a New Translation*. Chicago, 1938. F. James, *Thirty Psalmists* (Bohlen Lectures for 1936). New York, 1938.

2. Proverbs (and Old Testament wisdom literature in general)

T. K. Cheyne, *Job and Solomon or the Wisdom of the Old Testament*. London, 1887. H. (i.e., J.) Meinhold, *Die Weisheit Israels in Spruch, Sage und Dichtung*. Leipzig, 1908. O. Eissfeldt, *Der Maschal im Alten Testament* (Beih. ZAW 24). Giessen, 1913. A. Hudal, *Die religiösen und sittlichen Ideen des Spruchbuches*. Rome. 1914. H. J. Cadbury, "Egyptian influences on the Book of Proverbs" (JR 9 [1929] 99–108). C. H. Gordon, "Rabbinic Exegesis in the Vulgate of Proverbs" (JBL 49 [1930] 384–416). H. Ranstom, *The Old Testament Wisdom Books and their Teaching*. London, 1930. F. James, "Some Aspects of the Religion of Proverbs" (JBL 51 [1932] 31–39). J. Fichtner, *Die altorientalische Weisheit in ihrer israelitisch-jüdischen Ausprägung* (Beih. ZAW 62). Giessen, 1933. W. Baumgartner, *Israelitische und altorientalische Weisheit* (Sammlung gemeinverständlicher Vorträge und Schriften, u.s.w. 166). Tübingen, 1933; "Die Israelitische Weisheit literatur" (*Theol. Rundschau* N.F. 5 [1933] 259–288). Bibliography. W. Zimmerli, "Zur Struktur der alttestamentilichen Weisheit" (ZAW N.F. 10 [1933] 177–204). G. Boström, *Proverbiastudien. Die Weisheit und das fremde Weib in Sprüche 1–9*. Lund, 1935. J. Schmidt, *Studien zur Stilistik der alttestamentlichen Spruchliteratur* (AA XIII, 1). Münster, 1936. D. B. Macdonald, *The Hebrew Philosophical Genius: A Vindication*. Princeton, 1936. O. S. Rankin, *Israel's Wisdom Literature: Its Bearing on Theology and the History of Religion* (Kerr Lectures). London, 1936. H. Ringgren, *Word and Wisdom: Studies in the Hypostatization of Divine Qualities and Functions in the Ancient Near East*. Lund, 1947.

3. Job

Bibliography: E. G. Kraeling, *The Book of the Ways of God*, pp. 265–270. New York, 1939; A. Lods, "Recherches récentes [1920–1934] sur le livre de Job" (RHPR 14 [1934] 501–533). B. D. Eerdmans, *Studies in Job*. Leiden, 1939 (1. The Conception of God; 2. Leviathan). E. D. Kissane, *The Book of Job*. New York, 1946 (Roman Catholic).

4. Songs of Songs

Bibliography: P. A. Vaccari, "Il Cantico dei Cantici nelle recenti pubblicazioni" (*Bibl.* 9 [1928] 443–457). H. H. Rowley, "The Interpretation of the Song of Songs" (JTS 38 [1937] 337–363); "The Song of Songs: An Examination of Recent Theory" (JRAS 1937, 251 ff.). C. Kuhl, "Das Hohelied und seine Deutung" (*Theol. Rundschau* N.F. 9 [1937] 137–167).

5. Ruth

H. Gunkel, *Reden und Aufsätzen*, pp. 65–92. Göttingen, 1913. L. Köhler, "Ruth" (STZ 37 [1920] 3–14). W. W. Cannon, "The Book of Ruth" (*Theol.* 16 [1928] 310–319).

6. Lamentations

Hedwig Jahnow, *Das hebräische Leichenlied im Rahmen der Völkerdichtung* (Beih. ZAW 36). Giessen, 1923. H. Wiesemann, "Zur Characteristic der Klagelieder des Jeremias" (*Bonner Zeitschrift für Theologie und Seelsorge* 5 [1928] 97–118); "Die literarische Art der Klagelieder des Jeremias" (TQ 110 [1929] 381–428); "Der geschichtlicher Hintergrund des Büchleins der Klagelieder" (BZ 22 [1934] 20–43); "Der Verfasser des Büchleins der Klagelieder ein Augenzeuge der behandelten Ereignisse?" (*Bibl.* 17 [1936] 71–84).

7. Ecclesiastes

G. Kuhn, *Erklärung des Buches Koheleth* (Beih. ZAW 43). Giessen, 1926. H. Odeberg, *Qohaelaeth, a Commentary on the Book of Ecclesiastes*. Uppsala, 1929. J. Pedersen, "Scepticisme israélite" (RHPR 10 [1930] 317–370); republished in Cahiers RHPR, 1931. A. Lamorte, *Le Livre de Qoheleth*. Paris, 1932. K. Galling, "Kohelet-Studien" (ZAW N.F. 9 [1932] 276–299); "Stand und Aufgabe der Kohelet-Forschung" (*Theol. Rundschau* N.F. 6 [1934] 355–373). Bibliography. F. Dornseiff, "Das Buch Prediger" (ZDMG 89 [1935] 243–249). W. Zimmerli, *Die Weisheit des Predigers Salomo* (Aus der Welt der Religion, Biblische Reihe 11). Berlin, 1936. R. Gordis, *The Wisdom of Ecclesiastes*. New York, 1945.

8. Esther

P. Haupt, *Purim* (Beiträge zur Assyriologie VI, 2). Leipzig, 1906. S. Jampel, *Das Buch Ester auf seine Geschichtlichkeit untersucht*. Breslau, 1907 (reprinted from MGWJ 1905–1906). A. E. Morris, "The Purpose of the Book of Esther" (ET 42 [1930–1931] 124–128). H. Striedl, "Untersuchung zur Syntax und Stilistik des hebräischen Buches Esther" (ZAW N.F. 14 [1937] 73–108).

9. Daniel

Bibliography: J. A. Montgomery, *A Critical and Exegetical Commentary of the Book of Daniel* (ICC), pp. xv–xxvi. New York, 1927; W. Baumgartner, in *Theol. Rundschau* N.F. 11 (1939) 59–83, 125–144, 201–228. R. H. Charles, *Critical and Exegetical Commentary on the Book of Daniel*. Oxford, 1929.

10. Chronicles, Ezra, and Nehemiah

C. C. Torrey, *The Composition and Historical Value of Ezra-Nehemiah* (Beih. ZAW 2). Giessen, 1896; *Ezra Studies*. Chicago, 1910. E. Podechard, "Les references du Chroniqueur" (RB 24 [1915] 236–247). M. Kegel, *Die Kultusreformation des Ezra*. Gütersloh, 1921. W. F. Albright, "The Date and Personality of the Chronicler" (JBL 40 [1921] 104–124). G. von Rad, *Das Geschichtsbild des chronistischen Werkes* (BWANT IV, 3). Stuttgart, 1930; "Die levitische Predigt in den Büchern der Chronik" in *Festschrift Otto Procksch*, pp. 113–124. Leipzig, 1934. J. Hänel, "Das Recht des Opferschlachtens in der chronistischen Literatur" (ZAW N.F. 14 [1937] 46–67). A. C. Welch, *The Work of the Chronicler: Its Purpose and its Date* (Schweich Lectures). London, 1939. A. Bea, "Neuere Arbeiten zum Problem der Chronikbücher" (*Bibl.* 22 [1941] 46–58) (Roman Catholic).

PART VI: THE APOCRYPHA AND PSEUDEPIGRAPHA

GENERAL WORKS

1. Bibliography

Ralph Marcus has published a comprehensive bibliography (for the years 1920-1945) on the Jews in the Hellenistic and Roman periods in the *Proceedings of the American Academy for Jewish Research, Vol. XVI (1947)*; cf. A. T. Olmstead, "Intertestamental Studies" (JAOS 56 [1936] 242–257). For earlier publications see the works of E. Schürer and J. Juster listed below (No. 6). There are useful lists of books in: H. Frick (editor), *Einführung in das Studium der Evangelischen Theologie*. Giessen, 1947.

2. Text (in Greek, Latin, and Syriac)

P. de Lagarde, *Libri Veteris Testamenti apocryphi syriace*. Leipzig, 1861. O. F. Fritsche, *Libri apocryphi Veteris Testamenti graece*. Leipzig, 1871; *Libri Veteris Testamenti pseudepigraphi selecti*. Leipzig, 1871 (Psalms of solomon, IV and V Esdras. Apocalypse of Baruch, Assumption of Moses). Editions of the LXX (for the Apocrypha).

3. Translations

E. Kautzsch (Editor), *Die Apokryphen und Pseudepigraphen des Alten Testaments*, 2 vols. Freiburg i. B. and Leipzig, 1900; reprinted in 1921. R. H. Charles (Editor), *The Apocrypha and Pseudepigrapha in English*, with Introductions and Critical and Explanatory Notes to the Several Books. 2 vols. Oxford, 1913. W. O. E. Oesterley and G. H. Box, *Translations of Early Documents*. London, 1916 ff. A series of translations of individual books. M. R. James, *The Lost Apocrypha of the Old Testament*. London, 1920.

4. Commentaries

O. F. Fritzsche and C. L. W. Grimm, *Kurzgefasstes exegetisches Handbuch zu den Apokryphen des Alten Testamentes*. 6 vols. Leipzig, 1851–1860 (still unsurpassed). O. Zöckler, *Die Apokryphen nebst einem Anhang über die Pseudepigraphenlitteratur* (in Strack, and Zöckler's *Kurzgefasster Kommentar*). Munich, 1891. H. Wace (Editor), *The Holy Bible . . .* ("Speaker's Commentary"): *Apocrypha*. 2 vols. London, 1888.

5. Critical Introductions

E. Schürer, *Geschichte des Jüdischen Volkes im Zeitalter Jesu Christi*. Vol. III; 4th ed., Leipzig, 1909 (with full bibliography). The English translation (*A History of the Jewish People in the Time of Jesus Christ*. 5 vols. Edinburgh, 1886–1890) is antiquated, but the latest edition in German is still indispensable. W. Christ, *Geschichte der griechischen Literatur bis auf die Zeit Justinians*. 6th ed. edited by O. Stählin and W. Schmidt. Pt. II, vol 1, pp. 535–658 (by Stählin). *Handbuch der Altertumswissenschaft* (edited by W. Otto), Abt. VII. Munich, 1921. C. C. Torrey, *The Apocryphal Literature: A Brief Introduction*. New Haven, 1945.

The following authors deal with the Apocrypha and Pseudepigrapha in their Introductions to the Old Testament (which are listed above, Part I, E): König, Strack, Cornill (only 3rd and 4th ed.), Sellin, Steuernagel, Eissfeldt; also A. Bertholet in K. Budde's *Geschichte der althebräische Literatur*. Roman catholic Introductions deal with the Apocrypha. See also the articles in Bible Dictionaries and Encyclopaedias, particularly E. Schürer (in Herzog-Hauck, Realenzyklopädie, vol. 1, pp. 622 ff.; on the Apocrypha) and G. Beer (*ibid.*, vol. 16, pp. 229 ff.; on the Pseudepigrapha). On the Apocrypha see: L. E. T. André, *Les apocryphes de l'Ancien Testament*. Florence, 1903. W. O. E. Oesterley, *The Books of the Apocrypha: Their Origin, Teaching, and Contents*. London, 1914; *An Introduction to the Books of the Apocrypha*. New York, 1935. R. Marcus, *Law in the Apocrypha* (Columbia University Oriental Studies, 26). New York, 1927. H. T. Herford, *Talmud and Apocrypha*. London, 1933. E. J. Goodspeed, *The Aprocrypha: An American Translation*. University of Chicago Press, 1938; *The Story of the Apocrypha*, 1939.

6. Political and Cultural Histories of the Hellenistic and Roman Periods

J. G. Droysen, *Geschichte des Hellenismus*. 2 vols. Hamburg, 1836, 1843; 2nd edit., Gotha, 1877. B. Stade, *Geschichte des Volkes Israel*, vol. II, pp. 271–674 (by O. Holzmann). Berlin, 1888. B. Niese, *Geschichte der Griechischen und Makedonischen Staten seit der Schlacht bei Chaeronea*. 3 vols. Gotha, 1893–1903. E. Schürer, *Geschichte des Jüdischen Volkes im Zeitalter im Zeitalter Jesu Christi*. 4 vols., 3rd and 4th edit. Leipzig, 1901–1911. E. R. Bevan, *The House of Seleucus*. London, 1902; *A History of Egypt under the Ptolemaic Dynasty*, 1927. A. Bouché-Leclercq, *Historie des Lagides*. 4 vols. Paris, 1903–1907; *Histoire des Seleucides*, 1913. P. Wendland, *Die Hellenistisch-Römische Kultur* (Handbuch zum Neuen Testament I, 2). Tübingen, 1907; 3rd edit., 1912. J. Juster, *Les Juifs dans l'empire romain*. 2 vols. Paris, 1914. E. Meyer, *Ursprung und Anfänge des Christentums*, vol. II. Stuttgart, 1922. K. J. Beloch, *Griechische Geschichte*, vol. IV, part I. 2nd edit. Berlin and Leipzig, 1925. P. Jouguet, *L'impérialisme macédonien et l'hellénization de l'Orient*. Paris, 1926; English translation: *Macedonian Imperialism*. London, 1928. J. Kaerst, *Geschichte des Hellenismus*, 2nd edit., 2 vols. Leipzig and Berlin, 1917 and 1926. *The Cambridge Ancient History*, vols. VI–XIII. Cambridge, 1927–1939. W. W. Tarn, *Hellenistic Civilization*. 2nd edit. London, 1930. A. H. M. Jones, *The Herods of Judaea*. Oxford University Press, 1938. M. Rostovtzeff, *The Social and Economic History of the Hellenistic World*. 3 vols. Oxford, 1941.

7. Histories of Judaism from 200 B.C. to A.D. 200

P. Volz, *Jüdische Eschatologie von Daniel bis Akiba*. Tübingen, 1903. O. Holzmann, *Neutestamentliche Zeitgeschichte*. 2nd edit. Tübingen, 1906. L. Couard, *Die religiösen und sittlichen Anschauungen alttestamentlichen Apokryphen und Pseudepigraphen*. Gütersloh, 1907. H. M. Hughes, *The Ethics of Jewish Apocryphal Literature*. London, 1909. A. Bertholet, *Die Jüdische Religion von der Zeit Esras bis zum Zeitalter Christi* (Vol. II of B. Stade's *Biblische Theologie des Alten Testaments*). Tübingen, 1911. R. H. Charles, *Religious Development between the Old and New Testaments* (Home University Library). London and New York, 1914. F. C. Burkitt, *Jewish and Christian Apocalypses*. London, 1914. H. J. Wicks, *The Doctrine of God in the Jewish Apocryphal and Apocalyptic Literature*. London, 1915. L. Ginzberg, "Some Observations on the Attitude of the Synagogue towards the Apocalyptic-Eschatological Writings" (JBL 41 [1922] 115–136). W. Bousset, *Die Religion des Judentums in späthellenistischen Zeitalter*. 3rd ed. by H. Gressmann. Tübingen, 1926. G. F. Moore, *Judaism in the First Centuries of the Christian Era: The Age of the Tannaim*. 3 vols. Harvard University Press, 1927 and 1930. R. T. Herford, *Judaism in the New Testament Period*. London, 1928. M. J. Lagrange, *Le Judaïsme avant Jésus Christ* (EB). Paris, 1931. G. H. Box,

Judaism in the Greek Period. Oxford, 1932.   S. Zeitlin, *The History of the Second Jewish Commonwealth: Prolegomena*. Philadelphia, 1933; *Who Crucified Jesus?* New York, 1942; 2nd edit., 1947.   P. Volz, *Die Eschatologie der jüdischen Gemeinde im neutestamentlichen Zeitalter*. Tübingen, 1934.   E. Bickermann, *Die Makkabäer*. Berlin, 1935; *Der Gott der Makkabäer*. Berlin, 1937.   J. Bonsirven, *Le Judaïsme palestinien au temps de Jésus-Christ*. 2 vols. Paris, 1935.   C. Guignebert, *Le monde juif vers le temps de Jésus*. Paris, 1935; English translation: *The Jewish World in the Time of Jesus*. London, 1939.   W. O. E. Oesterley, *Judaism and Christianity*. 3 vols. London, 1937–38; *The Jews and Judaism During the Greek Period*. New York, 1941.

INDEX OF AUTHORS

INDEX OF PASSAGES

I. OLD TESTAMENT[1]

Genesis

1-50..130 f.; cf. 142-144, 160, 168-170, 188 f., 250, 272-277
1 192-196
1:1 76
1:27 f. 273
2:16 76
2:23 272
3:14-19 272
4-9 .... 204 f.
4:11 272
4:23 f. 274
8:22 272
9:1-16 273
9:25-27 .... 274 f.
12:1-3 273
14:19 272
15:6 7
15-18b 273
16:11 f. 273
17:1 f., 4 f. 273
17:5 7
24:60 273
25:23 273
26:24 273
27:19 91
27:27-29, 39 f. 273
27:33, 40 92
28:13 f. 273
29:31-30:24 .... 276 f.
35:10 405
48:15 f., 20 273
49:2-27 275-7
49:10 271

Exodus

1-40..131; cf. 144-146, 170, 189, 250 f., 253
3:14 95
3:15 92
9:8 92
15:1-18 281

15:1-19, 21 274
15:3 271
15:21 272
16:8 405
17:14, 16 274
18:13-27 211
20:2-17 228-32
20:22-23:33 211-26
23:29 f. 298
31:13-14a 241
32:18 273
34:10-26 221-6
34:28 51
34:29 124
35-40 110

Leviticus

1-27.....131 f.; cf. 189, 239-241, 251, 253-255
11-15 241
11:6 .... 105n.
17-26 239-50
19:20 212

Numbers

1-36..132 f.; cf. 146, 170 f., 189 f., 251-253, 255 f.
5-6 241
6:24-26 280
10:354 274
12:1 78
12:6-8 279
15:37-41 241
21:14 f., 17 f. 274
21:27-30 274
23:7-10, 18-24 279
24:3-9, 15-24 .... 277 f.
28-29 822

Deuteronomy

1-34..133; cf. 187, 227-234
*5:6-21 .... 72, 228-32
6:4 f. 72, 235

6:5 3
7:22 f. 298
10:20 77
12 381
12-26 232-8
14:7 .... 105n.
15:12-18 212-7
16 .... 222 f.
19:16-20 ..... 213, 215
21:15-21 214
21:23 75
22:13-29 212-7
24:1-4, 7 214
25:1-12 ... 214-6, 215 f.
25:4 5
25:5-12 214
27:15-26 226-8
31:16-30 280
32:1-44 280
32:36 406
33 .... 278 f.
33:2-5, 26-29 281
33:16b 276

Joshua

1-24..293 f.; cf. 146, 190, 302 f., 308 f.
1 .... 304 f.
3-11 .... 302 f.
5-7 295
8:30 227
8:30-35 304-6
10:28-39 .... 309n.
13:13 298
13:14-33 308
13:15-33 312
14:6-14 302
15-17 298
15-19 .... 309 f.
19:47 .... 298-300, 316
19:49 f. 302
22:7-34 309
22:25 .... 113n.
23 304
24 ...302 f., 303 f., 312

[1] Only a small selection of the thousands of Old Testament references could be listed here. An asterisk (*) precedes the passages in which the Hebrew differs in chapter and verse from the English, which is used here (see pp. 844 f.).

VII. RABBINICAL WRITINGS

INDEX OF SUBJECTS

f., 318, 352 f., 358, 360, 377, 624, 631, 636, 640

Armenian Version, 118

Arpad, 508

Artaxerxes I, 817 f., 819 f., 825, 829

Artaxerxes II Mnemon, 740

Artaxerxes III Ochus, 447 629

Arts and crafts, 162, 164

Asa, religious reforms of, 224

Asaph, 621, 623 f., 627-629, 797

Ashdod, 343, 426 f., 433, 578

Ashêrâh, 181, 402, 546

Ashurbanipal, 178, 180, 487-489

Ashur-uballit, 488

Assault and battery, 212, 234, 238

Assumption of Moses, 66

Assyria, history, 178, 382, 423-434, 487-489; religion, 178, 181; law, 211, 214, 219; in Kings, 400 f.; in the prophetic books, 430, 435 f., 438, 440, 445, 534, 566, 570, 573, 591, 595 f., 599

Astarte, 87, 304, 360

Astral deities, 233, 482; cf. Assyria; Babylonia

Asylum, law of, 54, 220, 233, 235

Atheism, 638

Aton, 21, 36, 468, 631

Atonement, 254, 263 f., 267, 269 f., 524; cf. Day of Atonement

Authority of Scriptures, 3 ff.

Authorship and date of Old Testament books (traditional views), 41-43, 50-70

Azariah, 334, 422 f., 425, 792

Azarias, 753

Baal, 87 f., 329, 404 f., 546, 569, 572, 600, 759

Baasha, oracle against, 411

Babel, Tower of, 161 f., 164

Babylonia, history, 427, 488, 491 f., 498; literature, 36, 88 ff., 95 f., 161, 194, 199, 204 f., 211, 394 f., 427, 638, 766, 768; Jewish Exiles, 470 f.; influence on Ez., 519 f., 529 f., 533-535, 539 f., 544, 553; in. Is. 40-66, 462 f., 466, 469, 480; in Dan., 748, 759, 762 f.; oracles against, 443 f., 446, 450, 486, 507

Bagoas, 446

Balaam, 33, 41 f., 147, 171, 174, 277-279

Ban, 306, 361

Banquet songs, 24

Bar-Cocheba, 75

Baruch, 485, 496 f., 500-502, 504 f.

Bathsheba, 353, 356, 358 f.

Battle song, 25

Bedouins, 25, 30 f., 148; Bedouin Code, 218-221

Beer-lahai-roi, 152 f.

Beersheba, 152 f., 155, 168, 284, 578

Bel-ibni, 401

Belshazzar, 444, 749 f., 757, 759, 764

Ben-hadad, 397, 409, 789

Benjamin, 144, 169 f., 307, 316, 323, 355

Bethel, 144, 152-156, 168 f., 172 f., 181, 297, 316, 323, 328, 381, 402, 577-579, 582

Bethlehem, 123, 152, 323, 590

Bethshean, 327, 350

Bethshemesh, 309

Bible, origin of word, 71

Biblical criticism, history of, 41-49, 135-141

Biography, 358 f., 383 ff., 403 ff., 831 ff.

Blasphemy, 84-86, 218 f.,

240, 249, 251, 360, 515

Blessings, 147, 182, 184, 207, 273-280

Blood-revenge, 30, 219 f.

Bohairic, 116, 118

Book of the Dead, 71

Books, ancient, making of, 71 ff.

Bosheth (shame), 87

Bribes, 228, 238, 245, 590, 652, 654, 657

Buildings of Solomon, 385 ff.

Butchery, 235, 248 f.

Byblos, 32, 71

Caesarea, 109, 123

Cain, 30, 161-166, 204, 277

Caleb, 251, 297, 316, 350, 622

Cambyses, 507

Canaan, promised to Israel, 202 f., 252, 295 f.; conquered by Israel, 145 ff., 293-308, 316 f., 323-328, 335, 358; allotted to Israel, 306-310; influence on Israel, 150-154, 181, 572, 624, 633; alphabet, 73; legislation, 215, 221-226; miscellaneous, 21, 142-148, 162, 170-172, 233, 236, 251 f., 274 f., 325, 327, 357

Canaanitic Civil Code, 213-218, 221 ff., 237 f., 247

Canon, history of, 50-70

Cantica (odes), 114

Canticles, 12, 708-716

Carchemish, 486, 488, 490, 506, 598

Carmel, 348, 403, 406 f.

Carthage, 69, 115

Catholic doctrine and exegesis, 45, 47, 69, 122, 382

Census, 251 f., 353, 807, 822, 836

Centralization of worship at Jerusalem, 55, 181, 232 ff.; cf. Josiah

Mourning rites, 233, 239 f., 245, 248, 513

Murder, laws on, 212, 217-220, 238, 240, 244, 250, 253, 259

Music, in worship, 621, 623 f., 631-633, 636, 640, 655, 797-799, 801

Mystics, 498

Nabal, 348

Nabatean kingdom, 584, 614

Nabonidus, 444, 488

Nabopolassar, 488, 596, 598

Naboth, 405

Nahum, Book of, 272, 594-597

Napata, 427

Narratives, 27-29

Nash Papyrus, 72 f., 184

Nathan, 41, 356, 359

Nationalism, in Deborah, 326 ff.; in Judg., 320 f.; in Gen. 49, 276; in J, 148 f.; in Sam., 358, 366; in E, 174; in Balaam, 277; in Deut. 33, 278; in the prophets, 60, 443; in Am., 581; in Is., 425, 435 f.; in Mic. 594; in D, 180; in Jer., 484, 489 f., 491, 493, 496, 503, 510, 516 f.; in Nah., 595 f.; in Obad., 586; in Second Is., 471-474; in Hag., 586; in Zech., 607; in Jonah, 589; in Deut. 32, 280 f.; in Ex. 15, 281; in Joel, 574, 576; in P, 259; in Chron., 787 ff., 807 f.; in Dan., 773 ff.; in Esth., 743-746

Nations, table of, 206

Nature, in Jer., 512; in Job, 661-667, 686, 688-692, 698, 705 f.; in Ps., 635; in Cant., 712; in Eccl., 726 f.

Nazarenes, 75, 135

Nazarite, 255, 263, 267, 269, 319

Nebuchadnezzar, in Hab., 598; in Jer., 483-486,

488-494, 498 f., 507 f.; in Ez., 520, 532 f., 537 f., 553, 561; in Lam., 721; in Second Is., 470; in Chron., 788, 822; in Dan., 748 f., 755-765; in Esth., 732

Necho, 486, 488-491, 508, 532, 598

Necromancy, 218 f., 239, 248, 349 f.

Negeb, 350, 584 f.

Nehemiah, 57, 94, 256 f., 813 ff., 828 f., 834-838

New Covenant, sect of, 65

New Moon, 524

New Testament, 3-8, 81, 107 f., 134, 415 f., 460 f., 625

New Year festival, 240, 243

Nicanor, 740, 746

Nineveh, 180, 428 f., 488; in Zeph., 601; in Nah., 594-597; in Jonah, 587-589

Nisibis, School of, 44 f.

Noah, 161, 197, 200, 204, 207, 210, 274 f.

Nob, 348, 351, 368-370

Nomads, 30 f., 218-221, 274 f.

Non-Israelitic writings, 21, 192 f., 444, 682

North Israel, 103, 151, 160, 166, 213, 278 f., 297, 355, 403, 410-412, 422 f., 426, 432 f., 482, 484, 790 f., 802

Numbers, Book of, 82, 84, 145 ff., 170 f., 189 f., 251-253, 255 f., 272, 274, 277-280

Nuzi, 275

Obadiah, Book of, 486, 584 ff.

Obed-edom, 623, 800

Oblation, in Ez., 556; oblations in P, 255

Offerings, in Am., 582; in Mic., 591; in ritual Decalogue, 221; in D, 233; in H, 240, 244; in Ez., 243, 524, 558; in Mal., 614; in P, 253-

255, 262, 264-270; in Joel, 576; in Ezra, 822; in Job, 664

Og, 171, 306, 308

Old Latin version, 84, 87, 103, 115, 122-125

Omens, 32, 50

Omri, 380-382, 406, 593

Onias III, 72, 446, 751 f.

Onkelos, 78, 98, 120

Ophir, 385

Optimism in P, 196

Oracles, 24, 32 f., 50 f.; poetic oracles, 272-281

Oral traditions, 150 ff., 171, 311, 319 f., 329

Ordeal, 255, 267 f.

Original sin, 166

Othniel, 297, 333

P and Pˢ, see Priestly Code

Paganism, condemned in Hos., 567, 569-572; in Jer., 482, 485, 490; in D, 182, 186, 217, 232-236; in Zeph., 600 f.; in Ez., 519-521, 559; in H, 239, 245, 248; in Judg., 329, 331; in Second Is., 447; traces in S, 165

Palestine, P's topography of, 309 f.

Palestinian Targums, 77 f., 90

Panegyrics, 26 f.

Papyrus, 71 f.

Parables, 38 f.

Parents, laws on, 218, 228, 239, 244

Paris Polyglot, 99, 117, 121, 736

"Participial Code," 31, 227 f., 238, 246 f., 249

Pāsēq, 82 f.

Passover, 52, 62, 182, 223 f., 234, 240, 243, 250 f., 257, 268, 307, 524, 558, 620, 625, 797, 814, 817

Patriarchs, 143, 150, 151-154, 175 f., 197 f., 200 f., 204

Patriotism, see Nationalism

Paul, St., 4-7, 9, 12, 166
Peace, 593 f.
Pekah, 425 f., 426, 429
Pekahiah, 425, 566
Pentateuch, 129-289; canonization, 56 f.; Greek version (LXX), 104 ff.
Pentecost, 62, 240, 625
Penuel, 152, 155, 317
Pericopes, 81 f.
Persecution of Jews, 637, 756, 759, 764, 773, 809
Persia, 257 ff., 533 f., 602, 737 f., 763, 767
Personal religion, 696 f.; in Job, 682; in Jer., 515 f.; in Ez., 550 f.; in Ps., 619 f., 634, 637-641; in Dan., 780
Personification, 18 f.
Peshitta, 117 f., 120 ff.
Pessimism, 35; in S, 163 f.; in Job, 670, 698-700; in Jer., 497 f., 512 f.; in Ez., 541, 545; in Third Is., 481; in Lam., 720-723; in Dan., 775; in Eccl., 724-728
Phanuel, 778
Pharaoh, 144 f., 149 f., 169 f.
Pharisees, 779
Philistia, in prophetic oracles: Am., 579; Is., 433 f.; Jer., 486, 508; Zech., 608, 610 f.; Joel, 574
Philistines, 319 f., 341-350, 352, 357-362, 365 f.
Philosophy, 35 f.; in Job, 687, 692 ff.; in Eccl., 727-730
Philosophy of history, in S, 161, 163-166; in Sam., 362 ff.; in Deut., 186 f.; in Josh., 300 f., 305-307; in Judg., 332-336; in Kings, 380-383; in Chron., 786-790; in Dan., 775
Phinehas, son of Eleazar, 252, 304, 412; son of Eli, 342, 360, 363, 369
Phoenicia, 71-73, 101,

154, 193, 428, 435, 608, 611; cf. 275
Piety in Ps., 638 f.
Pilgrims, Pss. of, 620 f., 628 f., 636, 640
Pillars of brass, in Solomon's Temple, 388
Pillars and posts, 233, 236
Pious, in Job, 663; in Mal., 615; in Prov., 650-652, 656, 659; in Ps., 620, 636-639, 641
Plagues, 343, 400 f., 574, 608 f.; of Egypt, 145, 170, 174
Poetry, 12 f., 21-27; cf. 271 ff.; anthologies, 272, 274; secular, in Ps., 619
Pollution, 217, 236, 239, 243, 245, 249, 254 f., 256, 262, 265 f., 267, 406, 546, 550, 555 f., 602
Polyglot Bibles, 98 f., 117
Porters, 621
Potiphar, 154, 169, 175, 284
Prayers, 33 f.
Prayer of Manasseh, 805
Precedents in case law, 211
Predictions, 59 f.
Priesthood, early history, 32, 50 f., 173, 175, 322, 348, 356, 368-373, 570; in D, 181, 235; in H, 239 f., 244 f., 249; in Ez., 524, 547, 555-557; in Mal., 612, 614; in P, 251-255, 263-265; in Joel, 575; in Chron., 621 f., 792-801, 815 f., 825; in New Testament, 7
Priestly cities, 308 f., 313
Priestly Code (P), in the Pentateuch, 188-209, 250-270, 273 f., cf. 153, 159-161, 239-250; in Josh., 306-310, 312 f.; influence on other writings, 412, 650, 785-791; influence of Ez., 554, 557
Primogeniture, 233

Prince, in Ez., 553, 556, 558
Procedure, law of, 213, 215, 238
Profanation, in Ez., 557
Property, law of, 217, 238, 240
Prophecy, history of, 32 f., 42, 50 f.; in historical books, 329, 360, 374 f., 397 ff., 403-408, 410 f.; in prophetic books, 483, 574, 589, 608-610, 775; in D, 236; end of, 764 f.; in Christianity, 5-9; influence on later books, 51-55, 173 f., 179 f., 192, 230-233, 241-246, 260 f., 280 f., 374, 475 f., 636, 639, 641, 655, 659, 721 f., 803; psychology of, 345, 347, 361, 366, 423 f., 446, 463, 493-498 passim, 503, 513 f., 516, 518-522, 535-542, 579, 604 ff.; cf. Symbolical actions, Symbolism, Visions
Prosperity, 422 f., 425, 470, 578 ff., 590, 606, 639 f.
Prostitution, sacred, 555, 567 f., 570, 582
Proverbs, Book of, 645-659; influenced by Job, 680
Proverbs, folk, 37 f., 650 f.
Psalms, 12, 42 f., 90, 114, 145; outside Psalter, 280 f., 367, 483, 589, 594, 598, 748; cf. Cantica; influenced by Jer., 510 f., 514 f., and Job, 680
Psalter, 46, 83, 619-644; Latin, 122 f.; in New Testament, 5 f.
Psamtik I, 445, 488, 494; II, 445, 491
Pseudo-Aristeas, 104-106
Pseudo-Jonathan, Targum, 78
Ptah-hotep, 71, 650
Ptolemies, 104 f., 442,